# ASPLOS XVI

## Sixteenth International Conference on Architectural Support for Programming Languages and Operating Systems



**March 5–11, 2011**
**Newport Beach, CA, USA**

**Sponsored by:**

**SIGARCH**
**SIGPLAN**
**SIGOPS**

Association for Computing Machinery

**With Support from:**

**NSF, Google, VMware, Intel, Hewlett-Packard, Qualcomm, Sun Oracle, AMD, Microsoft Research, and IBM**

Association for
Computing Machinery

*Advancing Computing as a Science & Profession*

**The Association for Computing Machinery**
**2 Penn Plaza, Suite 701**
**New York, New York 10121-0701**



**ISBN:** 978-1-4503-0266-1

Additional copies may be ordered prepaid from:

**ACM Order Department**
PO Box 30777
New York, NY 10087-0777, USA

Phone: 1-800-342-6626 (USA and Canada)
+1-212-626-0500 (Global)
Fax: +1-212-944-1318
E-mail: acmhelp@acm.org
Hours of Operation: 8:30 am – 4:30 pm ET

**ACM Order Number** 415115

Printed in the USA

# Message from the Chairs

It is our great pleasure to welcome you to the sixteenth edition of ASPLOS and to introduce what we feel will be an outstanding and thought-provoking technical program. This year's conference continues and reinforces the ASPLOS tradition of publishing innovative multidisciplinary research spanning the boundaries of hardware, computer architecture, compilers, languages, operating systems, networking, and applications.

We received 152 full paper submissions by the July 28th deadline, which was fewer than last year's record-setting year, but above average over the past three years. (127, 113 and 181 full papers were submitted in 2008, 2009, and 2010, respectively.) 22 submissions had PC members as co-authors. The dominant technical theme this year was parallelism (once again), with more than half of the submissions explicitly indicating a technical keyword specific to parallel processing. There was a nice mixture of submissions spanning the disciplines of operating systems (36%), compilers and programming languages (34%), and architecture (60%), with 38% of submissions spanning multiple of these areas.

Regarding the paper reviewing process, we continued with two changes that had been adopted the previous year: we had two rounds of reviews, and we used an External Review Committee that was preselected by the Program Chair. Each paper was initially reviewed by one PC member and two ERC members. The rationale for having two ERC reviews during the first round (as opposed to one, as was the case last year) was that it gave us the most flexibility to match a paper with the experts who were most qualified to review that specific topic. Based upon these reviews (as well as follow-up discussions for any borderline cases), 103 papers were selected for a second round of reviews, where they received two more reviews from PC members. In general, any paper that received at least one vote for acceptance during the first round was selected for second round reviews. Through this two-round mechanism, we were able to limit the reviewing load per PC member to no more than 14 papers, and more importantly we allowed them to spend the bulk of their time on papers with a significant chance of being accepted. We would especially like to thank the ERC members for their hard work and dedication to the reviewing process; the typical ERC member reviewed 5 papers this year.

One change that we made to the reviewing form this year was that in addition to evaluation categories that had been used in previous years (e.g., the degree of novelty, whether the paper was convincing, etc.), we added a new category where we asked reviewers to rate the extent to which a paper would be thought-provoking. Our goal was to make sure that we paid special attention to submissions that might inspire people to change the way that they think about how they approach their own technical research problems. We are pleased that this emphasis appears to have translated well into a highly thought-provoking technical program.

We are also pleased to report that all reviews had been submitted in time for the authors to respond to them during the author rebuttal period. After the rebuttal period, the PC members and ERC members took the rebuttal comments into account as they discussed the papers online and potentially updated their scores accordingly.

The PC met in person on the Carnegie Mellon University campus for a one-day meeting on October 21st, 2010. 81 papers were discussed at the meeting. PC-authored papers were handled roughly halfway through the meeting, using the hotseat approach. Jim Larus, Margaret Martonosi, and David Patterson managed the discussion of papers where the PC Chair had a conflict. The PC chose 32 papers to be presented at the conference, for an overall acceptance rate of 21.1%. 7 of the 32 papers have PC members as co-authors. Continuing with another change that was made last year, all papers were assigned a shepherd to ensure that the final papers adequately addressed the concerns of the reviewers.

We would like to extend a special thanks to the PC Chair's administrative assistant Diana Hyde for all of her help throughout the process (and especially during the day of the PC meeting), to Michelle Goodstein (a CMU PhD student) for being the PC webmaster, and to Rich Gerber (at SoftConf) for being extremely responsive to questions and short-notice requests regarding the paper web site.

The extensive logistics behind organizing this conference have been handled by the tireless effort of a team of volunteers: Iulian Neamtiu (UCR), Ras Bodik (UC Berkeley), Evelyn Duesterwald (IBM Research), Soner Onder (MTU), Jun Yang (Pitt), Youtao Zhang (Pitt), Chris Gniady (U. Arizona), Brian Demsky (UCI), Philip Brisk (UCR), and Min Feng (UCR). Each member of this team played an important role in making ASPLOS XVI a success. In addition, the ASPLOS Steering Committee gave us timely and valuable guidance over the last year. We want to thank all members of the organizing committee and the steering committee for the time and attention they have invested in this conference. As always, the support and guidance of the ACM staff was very valuable.

ACM SIGARCH, SIGPLAN and SIGOPS are the sponsors of ASPLOS XVI. We want to thank them for their continued support of this unique and important venue that weaves together the interests of multiple SIGs. VMware, Google, Intel, Hewlett Packard, Qualcomm, AMD, Oracle, IBM, Microsoft Research, and IBM have provided generous financial support to this conference. We thank them for their generous contribution and for their vote of confidence in this premier conference. We also want to thank the National Science Foundation (NSF) for generously supporting our effort to provide travel grants to graduate and undergraduate students and to junior faculty members from underrepresented minorities and non-research universities. Additional funding for student travel grants was also provided by the sponsoring SIGs.

Finally, we want to thank all of you for attending ASPLOS in Newport Beach. We are privileged to have had the opportunity to put together this year's conference. We hope you will find inspiration from the technical program and from interactions with your colleagues from around the world. On behalf of the organizers, we also hope you have an enjoyable visit.

**Rajiv Gupta**
*ASPLOS 2011 General Chair*
*University of California, Riverside*

**Todd C. Mowry**
*ASPLOS 2011 Program Chair*
*Carnegie Mellon University*

# Table of Contents

## Session 5: Enhancing Device Driver Reliability

Session Chair: Yuanyuan Zhou *(University of California, San Diego)*



## Session 6: Ideas and Perspectives Session

Session Chair: Ras Bodik *(University of California, Berkeley)*

## Session 7: Novel Computing Platforms

Session Chair: Luis Ceze *(University of Washington)*



## Session 8: Saving Power and Energy

Session Chair: Jim Larus *(Microsoft Research)*



## Session 9: Recognizing Software and Concurrency Bugs

Session Chair: Emery Berger *(University of Massachusetts, Amherst)*

## Session 10: Rethinking and Protecting Operating Systems

Session Chair: Orran Krieger *(VMware)*



## Session 11: Learning from the Past: Drawing Conclusions from Extensive Measurement Studies

Session Chair: Orran Krieger *(VMware)*



## Session 12: New Compiler Optimizations

Session Chair: Scott Mahlke *(University of Michigan)*



## Session 13: Exploiting Parallelism on GPUs

Session Chair: Kunle Olukuton *(Stanford University)*



## Session 14: Novel Performance Improvements

Session Chair: Kunle Olukuton *(Stanford University)*

# ASPLOS 2011 Organization

**General Chair:** Rajiv Gupta, *University of California, Riverside*

**Program Chair:** Todd C. Mowry, *Carnegie Mellon University*

**Poster Session Chair:** Iulian Neamtiu, *University of California, Riverside*

**Ideas and Perspectives Session Chair:** Ras Bodik, *University of California, Berkeley*

**Workshops/Tutorials Chair:** Evelyn Duesterwald, *IBM Research*

**Publicity Chair:** Soner Onder, *Michigan Technological University*

**Publications Chair:** Youtao Zhang, *University of Pittsburgh*

**Registration Chair:** Chris Gniady, *University of Arizona*

**Finance Chair:** Jun Yang, *University of Pittsburgh*

**Student Volunteer Chair:** Brian Demsky, *University of California, Irvine*

**Web Chair:** Min Feng, *University of California, Riverside*

**Student Travel Grant Chair:** Philip Brisk, *University of California, Riverside*

**PC Webmaster:** Michelle Goodstein, *Carnegie Mellon University*

**Steering Committee:**
Vikram Adve, *University of Illinois at Urbana-Champaign*
Frank Bellosa, *University of Karlsruhe (SIGOPS Representative)*
Doug Burger, *Microsoft Research, Redmond (SIGARCH Representative)*
Susan Eggers, *University of Washington*
James C. Hoe, *Carnegie Mellon University*
Mary Jane Irwin, *Penn State University*
Norm Jouppi, *HP Laboratories (SIGARCH Representative)*
Jim Larus, *Microsoft Research*
Chandra Krintz, *UC Santa Barbara (SIGPLAN Representative)*
Todd C. Mowry, *Carnegie Mellon University*
Mary Lou Soffa, *University of Virginia*

**Program Committee:**

Sarita Adve, *University of Illinois at Urbana-Champaign*
Saman Amarasinghe, *Massachusetts Institute of Technology*
David August, *Princeton University*
Emery Berger, *University of Massachusetts, Amherst*
Doug Burger, *Microsoft Research*
Luis Ceze, *University of Washington*
Shimin Chen, *Intel Labs*
Sandhya Dwarkadas, *University of Rochester*
Antonio Gonzalez, *Intel Labs and UPC*
Mary Hall, *University of Utah*
Frans Kaashoek, *Massachusetts Institute of Technology*
Orran Krieger, *VMware*
James Larus, *Microsoft Research*
James Laudon, *Google*
David Lie, *University of Toronto*
Scott Mahlke, *University of Michigan*
Milo Martin, *University of Pennsylvania*
Margaret Martonosi, *Princeton University*
Todd C. Mowry (Chair), *Carnegie Mellon University*
Onur Mutlu, *Carnegie Mellon University*
Kunle Olukotun, *Stanford University*
David Patterson, *University of California, Berkeley*
Mendel Rosenblum, *Stanford University*
Margo Seltzer, *Harvard University*
Michael Swift, *University of Wisconsin-Madison*
Thomas F. Wenisch, *University of Michigan*
Yuanyuan Zhou, *University of California, San Diego*

**External Review Committee:**

Tor Aamodt, *UBC*
Ali-Reza Adl-Tabatabai, *Intel*
Anant Agarwal, *MIT*
Todd Austin, *Michigan*
Luiz Barroso, *Google*
Ricardo Bianchini, *Rutgers*
Pradip Bose, *IBM*
Eric Brewer, *UC Berkeley*
David Brooks, *Harvard*
Angela Brown, *Toronto*
Mihai Budiu, *Microsoft*
Brad Calder, *Microsoft*
Trishul Chilimbi, *Microsoft*
Alan Cox, *Rice*
Pradeep Dubey, *Intel*
Dawson Engler, *Stanford*
Mattan Erez, *UT Austin*
Babak Falsafi, *EPFL*
Jason Flinn, *Michigan*
Phillip Gibbons, *Intel*
Steve Gribble, *Washington*
David Grove, *IBM*
Tim Harris, *Microsoft*
Kim Hazelwood, *Virginia*
Laurie Hendren, *McGill*
Maurice Herlihy, *Brown*
Urs Holzle, *Google*
Robert Hundt, *Google*
Natalie Enright Jerger, *Toronto*
Norm Jouppi, *HP*
Michael A. Kozuch, *Intel*
John Kubiatowicz, *UC Berkeley*
Alvin Lebeck, *Duke*
Calvin Lin, *UT Austin*

**External Review Committee: (continued)**

Geoff Lowney, *Intel*
Chuck Moore, *AMD*
Andreas Moshovos, *Toronto*
Eliot Moss, U Mass, *Amherst*
Satish Narayanasamy, *Michigan*
Ed Nightingale, *Microsoft*
John Ousterhout, *Stanford*
Yale Patt, *UT Austin*
Keshav Pingali, *UT Austin*
Rodric Rabbah, *IBM*
Ravi Rajwar, *Intel*
Eric Rotenberg, *N.C. State*
Amir Roth, *Penn*
Norm Rubin, *AMD*
Karu Sankaralingam, *Wisconsin*
Vivek Sarkar, *Rice*
Steve Scott, *Cray*
Tim Sherwood, *UCSB*
Jaswinder Pal Singh, *Princeton*
Mary Lou Soffa, *Virginia*
Dan Sorin, *Duke*
Greg Steffan, *Toronto*
Per Stenstrom, *Chalmers*
Karin Strauss, *Microsoft*
Edward Suh, *Cornell*
David Tarditi, *Microsoft*
Josep Torellas, *UIUC*
T.N. Vijaykumar, *Purdue*
Emmett Witchell, *Texas*
David Wood, *Wisconsin*
Kathy Yelick, *UC Berkeley*
Cliff Young, *D.E. Shaw*
Antonia Zhai, *Minnesota*

# ASPLOS 2011 Sponsors & Supporters

**Sponsors:**

**Supporters:**

# The Cloud Will Change Everything

James R. Larus
eXtreme Computing Group
Microsoft Research
Redmond, WA, USA
larus@microsoft.com

## Abstract

"Cloud computing" is fast on its way to becoming a meaningless, oversold marketing slogan. In the midst of this hype, it is easy to overlook the fundamental change that is occurring. Computation, which used to be confined to the machine beside your desk, is increasingly centralized in vast shared facilities and at the same time liberated by battery-powered, wireless devices. Performance, security, and reliability are no longer problems that can be considered in isolation – the wires and software connecting pieces offer more challenges and opportunities than components themselves. The eXtreme Computing Group (XCG) in Microsoft Research is taking a holistic approach to research in this area, by bring together researchers and developers with expertise in data center design, computer architecture, operating systems, computer security, programming language, mobile computation, and user interfaces to tackle the challenges of cloud computing.

***Categories and Subject Descriptor*** C.5.5 [Computer Systems Organization]: Computer System Implimentation—Servers

***General Terms*** Design, Languages, Performance, Reliability

***Keywords*** cloud computing

## Bio

James Larus is a Director of the eXtreme Computing Group (XCG) in Microsoft Research. Larus has been an active contributor to the programming languages, compiler, and computer architecture communities. Larus became an ACM Fellow in 2006. Larus joined Microsoft Research as a Senior Researcher in 1998 to start and, for five years, led the Software Productivity Tools (SPT) group, which developed and applied a variety of innovative techniques in static program analysis and constructed tools that found defects (bugs) in software. This group's research has both had considerable impact on the research community, as well as being shipped in Microsoft products such as the Static Driver Verifier and FX/Cop and other, widely-used internal software development tools. Larus then became the Research Area Manager for programming languages and tools and started the Singularity research project, which demonstrated that modern programming languages and software engineering techniques could fundamentally improve software architectures. Subsequently, he helped start XCG, which is developing the hardware and software to support cloud computing.

Before joining Microsoft, Larus was an Assistant and Associate Professor of Computer Science at the University of Wisconsin-Madison, where he published approximately 60 research papers and co-led the Wisconsin Wind Tunnel (WWT) research project with Professors Mark Hill and David Wood. WWT was a DARPA and NSF-funded project investigated new approaches to simulating, building, and programming parallel shared-memory computers. Larus's research spanned many areas: including new and efficient techniques for measuring and recording executing programs' behavior, tools for analyzing and manipulating compiled and linked programs, programming languages for parallel computing, tools for verifying program correctness, and techniques for compiler analysis and optimization.

Larus received his MS and PhD in Computer Science from the University of California, Berkeley in 1989, and an AB in Applied Mathematics from Harvard in 1980.


*ASPLOS'11* March 5–11, 2011, Newport Beach, California, USA.
ACM 978-1-4503-0266-1/11/03.

# Improving Software Diagnosability via Log Enhancement

Ding Yuan‡† Jing Zheng† Soyeon Park† Yuanyuan Zhou† Stefan Savage†
†University of California, San Diego, ‡University of Illinois at Urbana-Champaign
{diyuan,j3zheng,soyeon,yyzhou,savage}@cs.ucsd.edu

## Abstract

Diagnosing software failures in the field is notoriously difficult, in part due to the fundamental complexity of trouble-shooting *any* complex software system, but further exacerbated by the paucity of information that is typically available in the production setting. Indeed, for reasons of both overhead and privacy, it is common that only the run-time log generated by a system (e.g., syslog) can be shared with the developers. Unfortunately, the ad-hoc nature of such reports are frequently insufficient for detailed failure diagnosis. This paper seeks to improve this situation within the rubric of existing practice. We describe a tool, *LogEnhancer* that automatically "enhances" existing logging code to aid in future post-failure debugging. We evaluate *LogEnhancer* on eight large, real-world applications and demonstrate that it can dramatically reduce the set of potential root failure causes that must be considered during diagnosis while imposing negligible overheads.

***Categories and Subject Descriptors*** D.2.5 [*Testing and Debugging*]: Diagnostics

***General Terms*** Reliability

***Keywords*** Log, Software Diagnosability, Static Analysis

## 1. Introduction

Complex software systems inevitably have complex failure modes: errors only triggered by some combination of latent software bugs, environmental conditions and/or administrative errors. While considerable effort is spent trying to eliminate such problems before deployment or at run-time [9, 14, 38, 48], the size and complexity of modern systems combined with real time and budgetary constraints on developers have made it increasingly difficult to deliver "bullet-proof" software to end-users. Consequently, many software failures still occur in fielded systems providing production services.

### 1.1 Production Failure Reporting

Production failures are problematic at two different levels. First, they demand tremendous urgency; a production failure can have direct impact on the customer's business, and system vendors must make the diagnosis and remediation their highest priority. Unfortunately, this goal conflicts with a second problem — the substantial difficulty in analyzing such failures. Indeed, diagnosing rare failures can be challenging even in a controlled setting, but production deployments are particularly daunting since often support engineers are given insufficient information to identify the root cause, let alone reproduce the problem in the lab.

To address this problem, a range of research efforts have focused on techniques for capturing external and non-deterministic inputs, thereby allowing post-mortem deterministic replay [13, 20, 28, 33, 40, 44, 49, 50, 52, 55]. However, these approaches have been slow to gain traction in the commercial world for several reasons, including high overhead, environmental complexity (e.g., interactions between multiple licensed software and hardware from different vendors), and substantive privacy concerns.

A more established vehicle for diagnosis is the "core dump", which captures memory context and execution state in a file. However, core dumps have their own drawbacks. They are typically collected only *at the time* of the crash failure. They only capture program state but no execution history information (which is frequently critical for diagnosis), and the comprehensive capture of process state can once again preclude sharing such files due to privacy concerns [1].

Consequently, the *sine qua non* of production failure debugging remains the log file. Virtually all software systems, whether commercial or open source, log important events such as error or warning messages, as well as some *historic* intermediate progress/bookkeeping information generated during normal execution. It is a common industry practice for support engineers to request such logs of their customers upon failure, or even for customers to allow their systems to transmit such logs automatically (i.e., "call home" [18]). Since these logs focus on the system's own status and "health", they are usually considered to be less sensitive than other data. Moreover, since they are typically human-readable, customers can inspect them first (either after a failure or during initial contract negotiations). Consequently, most modern systems today from EMC, NetApp, Cisco, Dell are able to collect logs from at least 50% of their customers, and many of them even have enabled the capability to automatically send logs to the vendor [1, 2, 18, 47].

### 1.2 Diagnosing via Log Messages

Thus in many cases, log messages are the sole data source available for vendors to diagnose reported failures. Support engineers then attempt to map log message content to source code statements and work backwards to infer what possible conditions might have led to the failure. While a range of research projects have shown that statistical machine learning techniques can be used to detect anomalies or catch recurring failures that match known issues [3, 8,

[1] Some systems, such as Windows Error Reporting [26] and Mozilla's Quality Feedback Agent [41] attempt to mitigate the privacy issues through data minimization (typically limiting the scope of captured state to the execution context and stack trace) but at the cost of yet reduced debugging effectiveness. Indeed, these systems succeed because they aggregate large numbers of failures with common causes, rather than due to their ability to substantively aid in the debugging of any singular failure instance.


*ASPLOS'11* March 5–11, 2011, Newport Beach, California, USA.

**Bug Report in Lighttpd:**
"Log remote IP for message 'request timed out after writing..." will be very useful!"

**Patch in Lighttpd, server.c**

```
if (...) {
- log_error_write(srv, "sbsosds",
+ log_error_write(srv, "ssbsosds",
+   inet_ntop_cache_get_ip(srv, &(con->dst_addr)),
    "NOTE: a request for",
```

**Bug Report in Apache HTTPD:**
When mod_ssl logs OpenSSL errors it doesn't include the associated error string.. **Omitting the error string renders the error output almost useless.**

**Patch in ssl_engine_loc.c**

```
if (at)
  ap_log_error(file, line, level, 0, s,
-  "SSL Library Error: %lu %s %s", e, err, at);
+  "SSL Library Error: %lu %s %s %s",e, err, data, at);
```

**Bug Report in Apache Ant:**
Improve error message on "[war] error while reading original manifest: error opening zip file" Adds filename to output error message!

**Patch in Jar.java**

```
} catch (Throwable t) {
  log("error while reading original manifest: " +
-       t.getMessage(),
+       t.getMessage() + zipFile.toString(),);
```

**Figure 1.** Example of real-world patches just for the purpose of enhancing log messages.

16, 29, 56], the detective work of mapping log messages to source statements and then sifting through potential causes of individual crashes remains a heavily manual activity.

Recent work on the SherLog system [57] addresses the first part of this problem by automating this manual inference process. SherLog is a post-mortem diagnosis tool that uses failure log messages as starting points to automatically infer what source code paths may have been executed during a failed execution. Although SherLog can conduct deeper inference than manual efforts, it is still limited by the amount of information available in log messages. Just like manual inference by the programmers, if a log message does not contain enough information, automatic log inference engines have limited starting information to disambiguate between different potential causal paths that led to a failure. It is precisely this limitation that motivates the work in this paper. In Section 4.2 we will show three real world cases to demonstrate how automatic log inference engines like SherLog can perform better after log messages are enhanced with more causally-related information that is automatically collected by *LogEnhancer.*

At its essence, the key problem is that existing log messages contain too little information. Despite their widespread use in failure diagnosis, it is still rare that log messages are systematically designed to support this function. In many cases, logging statements are inserted into a piece of software in an ad hoc fashion to address a singular problem. For example, in many cases, an error log message may simply contain "system failed" without providing any further context for diagnosis. While there are a number of "rules of thumb" for designing better logging messages (e.g., such as logging the error symptoms [51] and the thread ID with each message [57]), these still do not capture the specific information (e.g., state variable values) that are frequently necessary to infer a problem's root cause. Instead, developers update log messages to add more information as they discover they need it. For example, there are more than 900 different error log messages in apache httpd, capturing various failure types, and over its five year history, we have identified 5,409 "enhancements" in the form of patches to these messages to improve their fidelity. Figure 1 shows three such enhancements, each of which expanded the log messages to capture distinct pieces of diagnostic state. In our work we propose to systematically and automatically add such enhancements to log messages, and thereby improve the diagnostic power of logging in general.

### 1.3 Our Contributions

In the remainder of this paper, we present a tool called *LogEnhancer*, that modifies *each* log message in a given piece of software to collect additional *causally-related* information to ease diagnosis in case of failures [2]. To be clear: *LogEnhancer* does not detect bugs nor failures itself. Rather it is a tool for reducing the burden of failure diagnosis by enhancing the information that programmers should have captured when writing log messages. Such additional log information can significantly narrow down the number of possible code paths and execution states for engineers to examine to pinpoint a failure's root cause.

In brief, we enhance log content in a very specific fashion, using program analysis to identify *which* state should be captured at each log point (a logging statement in source code) to minimize causal ambiguity. In particular, we say that the "uncertainty" around a log message reflects the control-flow paths or data values that are causally-related but cannot be inferred from the original log message itself. Using a constraint solver we identify which candidate variable values, if known, would resolve this ambiguity. Note we do not try to disambiguate the entire execution path leading to the log message. For example, a branch whose directions have no effect for the execution to reach the log message will not be resolved since it is not causally-related.

We explore two different policies for collecting these variable values: **delayed collection**, which captures only those causally-related key values that are "live" at the log point or can be *inferred* directly from live data, and **in-time collection**, which, in addition to those recorded in delayed collection, also records *historical* causally-related key values before they are overwritten prior to the log point. The latter approach imposes additional overhead (2-8% in our experiments) in exchange for a richer set of diagnostic context, while delayed collection offers the reverse trade-off, annotating log messages with only variable values "live" at log points, while imposing minimal overhead (only at the time an existing message is logged).

We also develop a variant of the delayed collection method that derives equivalent information from a core dump. Thus we can perform a similar analysis with unmodified binaries when core files are available.

Finally, we evaluate *LogEnhancer* with 8 large, real-world applications (5 servers and 3 client applications). We find that *LogEnhancer automatically* identifies 95% of the same variable values that developers have added to their log messages over time. Moreover, it identifies an additional set of key variable values (10-22) which, when logged, dramatically reduce the number of potential causal paths that must be considered by a factor of 35. We also selected 15 representative, *real-world* failures (with 13 caused by bugs and 2 caused by mis-configurations) from the above applications to demonstrate how the enhanced log messages can help diagnosis. In all these cases, the enhanced log messages would quickly reduce the number of possible partial execution paths and run-time states, helping both manual diagnosis and automatic log inference engines like SherLog to narrow down and identify the root causes. Finally, we show that both log size and run-time overhead are small, and almost negligible with delayed collection.

To the best of our knowledge, our work is the first attempt to *systematically* and *automatically* enhance log messages to collect *causally-related* information for diagnosis in case of failures. It can be used to enhance *every* existing log message in the target software prior to release, oblivious to what failure might occur in production.

[2] We target for production failure diagnosis even though our work can also be useful for in-house testing and debugging.

```
1  int remove_entry (char *filename, struct dirent *dp){
2  # ifndef __GLIBC__
3    struct stat sbuf;
4    if (dp)
5      is_dir = (dp->d_type == DT_DIR) ? T_YES : T_NO;
6    else {
7      if (lstat (filename, &sbuf))
8        ...
9      is_dir = S_ISDIR (sbuf.st_mode) ? T_YES : T_NO;
10   }
11
12   if (is_dir == T_NO) {
13     if (unlink(filename) == 0)
14         return RM_OK;
15
16     error (0, errno, "cannot remove %s", filename);
17     return RM_ERROR;                          Log Point 1
18   }
19 #endif
20   return RM_NONEMPTY_DIR;
21 }
22
23 int remove_cwd_entries (...) {
24     if ((dp = readdir (dirp)) == NULL) { return; }
25     tmp_status = remove_entry (f, dp);
26 }
27
30 int rm_1 (...) {
31   status = remove_entry (filename, dp);
32 }
```

```
1  int remove_entry (char *filename, struct dirent *dp){
2  # ifndef __GLIBC__
3    struct stat sbuf;
4    if (dp)
5      is_dir = (dp->d_type == DT_DIR) ? T_YES : T_NO;
6    else {
7      if (lstat (filename, &sbuf))
8        ...
9      is_dir = S_ISDIR (sbuf.st_mode) ? T_YES : T_NO;
10   }
11
12  if (is_dir == T_NO) {
13     if (unlink(filename) == 0)
14         return RM_OK;                          dp: 0x100120
15
16 error (0, errno,"cannot remove %s, %x", filename,dp);
17     return RM_ERROR;                          Log Point 1
18   }
19 #endif
20   return RM_NONEMPTY_DIR;
21 }
22
23 int remove_cwd_entries (...) {
24     if ((dp = readdir (dirp)) == NULL) { return; }
25     tmp_status = remove_entry (f, dp);
26 }
27
30 int rm_1 (...) {
31   status = remove_entry (filename, dp);
32 }
```

May-Execute | Must-Execute | Must-Not-Execute

(A) Original code. (B) Remaining Uncertainty if dp was printed at line 16.

**Figure 2. Highly simplified code for `rm` in coreutils-4.5.4.** Different colors highlight which information can be inferred given the log message was printed on line 16. For example, "Must-Execute" reflects code paths that can be completely inferred based on the given log message. Variable values that cannot be inferred are also highlighted.

## 2. Overview

To explain how *LogEnhancer* works, we first examine how diagnosis is performed manually today. Figure 2(A) shows a simplified version of a real world failure case in the `rm` program from the GNU core utilities. This is a particularly hard-to-diagnose failure case since it has complex environmental requirements and only manifests on FreeBSD systems using NFS that do not have GLIBC installed. In particular, when executing `rm -r dir1` for an NFS directory `dir1` in such an environment, `rm` fails with the following error message:

`rm: cannot remove 'dir1/dir2':Is a directory`

### 2.1 Manual Diagnosis

Upon receiving such a failure report, a support engineer's job is to find the "log point" in the source code and then, working backwards, to identify the *causally-related* control flow and data flow that together could explain why the message was logged. Pure control flow dependencies are relatively easy to reason about, and upon inspection one can infer that the error message (printed at line 16) can only be logged if the conditional at line 12 (`is_dir == T_NO`) is taken and the conditional at line 13 (`unlink(filename == 0)`) is not taken. This suggests that `rm` treated `filename` (`dir1/dir2` in this case) as a *non-directory* and subsequently failed to "unlink" it. Indeed, purely based on control flow, one can infer that lines 14–15, and 20–22 could not have been executed (highlighted in Figure 2(A) as "Must-Not-Execute"), while lines 1–4, 11-13, and 16–19 must have been executed (similarly labeled in the figure as "Must-Execute"). Already, the amount of ambiguity in the program is reduced and the only remaining areas of uncertainty within the function are on lines 5–10, and lines 23-32 (also highlighted in Figure 2(A) as "May-Execute").

However, further inference of why `is_dir` equals `T_NO` is considerably more complicated. There are two possibilities for the branch at line 4, depending on the value of `dp`, and both paths may set `is_dir` to be `T_NO`. Further, since `dp` is a parameter, we must find the caller of `remove_entry`. Unfortunately, there are two callers and we are not sure which one leads to the failure. In other words, given only the log message, there remain several *uncertainties* that prevent us from diagnosing the failure. Note that this challenge is not a limitation of manual diagnosis, but of how much information is communicated in a log message. In Section 4.2 we will show that automatic log inference engines such as SherLog can do no better than manual inference in this case.

In addition to control flow, backward inference to understand a failure also requires analyzing data flow dependencies, which can be considerably more subtle. We know from our control flow analysis that the conditional at line 12 is satisfied and therefore `is_dir` must equal `T_NO`. However, *why* `is_dir` holds this value depends on data flow. The value of `is_dir` was previously assigned at either line 5 or 9, and has data dependencies on either the value of `dp->d_type` or `sbuf.st_mode`, respectively. Determining which data dependency matters goes back to control flow: which branch did the program follow at line 4?

Unfortunately, the error message at line 16 simply does not provide enough information to answer this question conclusively. The conditional at line 4 is **uncertain** — either path (line 5, or line 7 to 10) could have been taken (indicated as "may-execute" in Figure 2(A)). Similarly, the values of `dp->d_type` and `sbuf.st_mode` are also uncertain, as is the context in which `remove_entry()` was called. While the ambiguity is modest in this small example, it is easy to see how the number of options that must be considered can quickly explode when diagnosing a system of any complexity.

However, a complete execution trace is not necessary to resolve this uncertainty. Indeed, if the program had simply included the single value of `dp` in the logging statement at line 16, the situation would have been far clearer (we illustrate how this piece of new information would help in Figure 2(B)). In this case `dp` is non-zero, and thus the code at line 5 is now in a "must-execute" path, while lines 6–10 "must not" have executed. In turn, it removes the need to consider the value of `sbuf.st_mode` since `is_dir` now only depends on `dp->d_type`.

The remaining uncertainties then include: (1) which function (`remove_cmd_entries` or `rm_1`) called `remove_entry`? (2) What was the value of `dp->d_type` at line 5? Resolving these would require logging some additional information such as the call stack frames, and `dp->d_type` (or, some *equivalent value* that can be used to infer `dp->d_type`'s value at line 5; we will discuss how to find an equivalent value in Section 3.2).

The goal of *LogEnhancer* is to automate exactly the kind of analysis we described above — identifying *causally-related* variable values for each "log point" and enhancing the log messages to incorporate these values. Moreover, because it is automatic, *LogEnhancer* can be applied comprehensively through out the entire program, thereby capturing the information needed to diagnose unanticipated failures that may occur in the future.

### 2.2 Usage

*LogEnhancer* is a source-based enhancement tool that operates on a program's source code and produces a new version with enhanced data logging. It can be used to enhance *every existing* log printing statement in the target software's source code or to enhance any *newly inserted* log printing statement. The only real configuration requirement is for the developer to identify log points (i.e., typically just the name of the logging functions in use). For example, the `cvs` revision control system uses GLIBC's standard logging library `error()`, so simply issuing

```
LogEnhancer --logfunc="error" CVS/src
```

is sufficient for *LogEnhancer* to do its work.

Once invoked, *LogEnhancer* leverages the standard `make` process to compile all program source code into the CIL intermediate language [45], then identifies log points (e.g., statements in cvs that call `error()`), uses program analysis to identify key *causally-related variables*, instruments the source code statically to collect the values of these variables at the log points and then re-compiles the modified source to generate a new binary.

During production-runs, when an log message is printed, the additional log enhancement information (variable values and call stack) will be printed into a *separate* log file. *LogEnhancer* can also be optionally configured to record additional log enhancement information only when *error* messages are printed.

In the `rm` example, at the log point at line 16, the following information will be added: *(1)* `dp`: helps determining the control flow in line 4; *(2) The call stack:* helps knowing which call path leads to the problem; *(3)* `dp->d_type` or `sbuf.st_mode` depending on the value of `dp` helps determining why `is_dir` was assigned to `T_NO`; *(4)* `filename`: since it's used in `unlink` system call, whose return value determines the control flow to log point at line 16; *(5)* `dirp` in function `remove_cwd_entries` *if* this function appears on the call stack.

During diagnosis, *LogEnhancer*'s enhanced log from production run can be manually examined by developers at each log message, or can be fed to automatic inference engines such as SherLog, which automatically infer execution paths and variable values. Section 4.2 shows three such examples.

### 2.3 Architecture Overview

The complexity in our system is largely in the analysis, which consists of three main tasks:

**(1) Uncertainty Identification**: This analysis identifies "uncertain" control-flow and variable values that are causally-related and whose state could not be resolved using only the original log message. Starting from each log point and working backwards, we identify the conditions that *must* have happened to allow the program execute to each log point (e.g., `is_dir == T_NO` and `unlink(filename)` are such conditions in `rm`). Using these conditions as clues, we continue to work backwards to infer *why* these conditions occurred through data-flow analysis (e.g., `dp`, `dp->d_type` and `sbuf.st_mode` are identified through data-flow analysis starting from `is_dir`). This process is repeated recursively for each potential caller (e.g., the data dependency on `dirp` from `remove_cwd_entries` is identified in this step). To prune out infeasible paths, *LogEnhancer* uses a SAT solver to eliminate those combinations with contradictory constraints.

**(2) Value Selection**: This analysis is to identify key values that would "solve" the uncertain code paths or values constrained by the previous analysis. It consists the following sub-steps: (i) Identify values that are certain from the constraint (i.e., the conditions for the log message to be printed), and prune them out using a SAT solver; (ii) Parse the uncertain values into a *conditional value* format, e.g., `[dp]:dp->d_type`, indicating the value `dp->d_type` is only meaningful under condition `dp!=NULL`; (iii) Identify the values that would be overwritten before the target log point; (iv) Find equivalent values that can be used to infer those overwritten key values; (v) From the uncertain value set, find the minimum set by eliminating redundant values that can be inferred by remaining uncertain values. Finally, *LogEnhancer* builds an *Uncertain Value Table* to identify the selected variable values to be recorded for each log point.

**(3) Instrumentation**: Before each log point, *LogEnhancer* inserts a procedure `LE_KeyValues(LogID)` to record the variable values in the Uncertain Value Table corresponding to the `LogID`, where `LogID` is a unique identifier for each log point. At run-time, `LE_KeyValues()` collects these variable values from the stack and heap *only at the log point*(delayed collection). For in-time collection, *LogEnhancer* further instruments source code to keep a "shadow copy" of any key values that will be overwritten before the log point and cannot be inferred via equivalent values live at the log point.

### 2.4 LogEnhancer's Assumptions

No tool is perfect, and *LogEnhancer* is no exception. There is an inevitable trade-off between the completeness and scalability. We make certain simplifying assumptions to make implementation practical and to scale to large real world programs, at the cost of a few incomplete (missing certain variable values) and/or unsound (logging non-causally-related variable values) results. However, *LogEnhancer* does not impact the validity of diagnosis since all values recorded by *LogEnhancer* are obtained right from the failed execution. We briefly outline the issues surrounding our assumptions and their impact below.

*(1) How far and deep can LogEnhancer go in analysis?* To avoid path explosion, *LogEnhancer* places a number of limits on how far its analysis is applied within a program. Given the problem of inferring causally-related information, our design focuses on analyzing only the functions that *must* have a causal relationship with the log point (i.e., functions that are on the call-stack or whose return values are causally-related to a log point), while ignoring the side-effects of other functions. Moreover, we do not perform program analysis more than one level deep into functions that are not on the call stack at the log point. Each function is analyzed only once, ignoring the side-effects caused by recursive calls.

Although we limit our analysis in this fashion, we still identify an average of 108 causally-related branches for each log point (with a max of 22,070 such branches for a single log point in PostgreSQL). Moreover, our experience is that the variables with most diagnostic value are commonly on the execution path to a log point and such variables are naturally collected using *LogEnhancer*'s style of analysis.

*(2) What and how many values are logged per message?* The core of our analysis is to first identify causally-related branches to each log point and then infer a compact set of values that resolve those branch choices. In our evaluation, 108 causally-related branches are identified for each log point on average, that can be resolved by 16.0 variable values (this includes the effects of removing redundant values).

*(3) What about privacy concerns?* Just as with existing log messages, the information we record focuses narrowly on the system's own "health". Because we are only recording a small number of variable values per message, it is much easier, compared with core dumps, for users to to check that no private information is revealed. It is also easier to combine our system with automatic privacy information filtering techniques (e.g., [12] that can filter data that can potentially leak private user information). In addition, collected logs can be analyzed at customers' sites by sending an automatic log analysis engine like SherLog [57] to collect back the inferred and less-sensitive information (e.g. the execution path during the occurred failure).

*(4) How do we handle inter-thread or inter-process data dependencies?* Due to the limitations of static analysis, we do not analyze data dependencies across threads or processes. Any values that are causally-related to the log point through these dependencies thus would be missed. In most cases, such dependencies do not interfere with our analysis since most shared data do not make a big impact on control flows and are not causally-related to a log message. However, in some rare cases, we may not log enough information to figure out why certain shared key variables have particular values. The sub-steps (iii)-(v) in our value selection might also be inaccurate on shared data since the inter-thread data-flow is not analyzed. Therefore, for applications with very intensive inter-thread data dependencies on *control* variables, we might disable these sub-steps and conservatively treat any shared data as overwritten ones at the log point.

Note this limitation does not mean that we cannot handle concurrent programs. For concurrent programs, we still analyze the intra-thread/process data flow to identify key variables to log. Such variables are useful for diagnosing failures in programs (sequential and concurrent). Five of our evaluated applications are concurrent, including Apache, CVS, Squid, PostgreSQL and lighttpd. Section 4 shows our evaluation results on these applications. Note that a majority of failures in real world are caused by semantic bugs and mis-configurations, not by concurrency bugs [36].

Also, our objective is to collect more diagnostic information, not to to pinpoint the exact root cause (although it would be extremely nice, it is too ideal to be realistic). So even for concurrency bugs, the causally-related key variable values from intra-thread/process analysis is still useful to reduce the diagnostic space.

Additionally, unlike static analysis for bug detection, inaccurate data flow analysis does *not* introduce false bug reports since all the recorded values are from the production-run execution. The only consequence is that some logged variable values may be less useful for diagnosis or that we are still missing some causally-related variable values. However, the recorded variable values are still valid, just as if programmers manually added those variables into logging statements.

Addressing these issues would require more complicated thread-aware code analysis. For each variable that is causally-related to the log message, in addition to analyzing the intra-thread or intra-process data flow, we would also need to analyze any inter-thread or inter-process modifications. Although theoretically we can still use the same Uncertainty Identification algorithm to recursively follow intra-thread/process *and* inter-thread/process data-flow, we imagine practical scalability and precision issues might arise. Given an uncertain variable value `V` in function `F`, any modifications to `V` that might be executed concurrently with `F` need to be considered. Without precise information about which functions might be executed concurrently and with the complications caused by pointer aliasing, we might end up analyzing many data-flows that are not causally related to the log point at all. This might add significant overhead to our analysis, and more importantly, end up recording a huge number of irrelevant variables. Annotations can be used in expressing which functions are concurrent [19, 24], while techniques presented in RacerX can help to automatically infer this information [23]. Previous work [42, 43] also show that for memory safe languages like Java where pointer usages are are limited, it is possible to analyze the concurrency behavior of a program much more precisely. Leveraging these techniques to handle inter-thread/process data-flows remains as our future work.

*(5) What if there is no log message?* In this work, we are trying to improve the world as it is. As mentioned in our introduction, most commercial and open source software already contains significant number of logging statements as logging has become a standard practice. Hence we focus on enhancing existing log messages, and *assume* that such log messages exist. If a software program generates no log message at all, *LogEnhancer* offers no value. Fortunately, this is usually not the case in most commercial and open source software.

## 3. Design and Implementation

*LogEnhancer*'s source code analysis is implemented using the Saturn static analysis framework [5]. Saturn models C programs precisely and allows user to express the analysis algorithm in a logic programming language. It is summary-based, meaning it conducts its analysis for each function separately and then generates a summary for each function. At the calling sites of a function, the summary is used instead of going deep into the function. Saturn also provides a SAT solver.

In this section we will not repeat the all the details of Saturn. Except for the Data-flow analysis described in Section 3.1, all the analysis processes, design and implementation issues are unique to *LogEnhancer* and solved by us.

### 3.1 Uncertainty Identification

For each log message in the target software, the goal of Uncertainty Identification is to identify uncertain control or data flows that are causally-related to this log point but cannot be determined assuming the log point is executed. Our analysis starts from those variable values that are directly included in the conditions for the log point to be executed. It then analyzes the data-flow of these variable values to understand *why* these conditions hold.

Within each function $f$, *LogEnhancer* starts from the beginning and goes through each instruction once. At any program point $P$ within $f$, *LogEnhancer* simultaneously performs two kinds of analysis: (1) *data-flow analysis* that represents *every* memory location $f$ accesses in the form of a *constrained expression* (CE); (2) *control-flow analysis* that computes the control-flow constraint to reach $P$. If the current $P$ is a log point $LP$, *LogEnhancer* takes the control-flow constraint $C$, and converts each memory location involved in $C$ to its CE. Thus both the control and data flow branch conditions related to the log point can be captured together in one constraint formula, and it is stored as the summary of $f$ to reach $LP$. The same process is recursively repeated into the caller of $f$. At the end of the analysis, for every function $f'$ along a possible call-chain to a log point $LP$, a summary of $f'$ is generated which captures the causally-related constraint within $f'$ to eventually reach $LP$.

**Data-flow analysis and memory model:** *LogEnhancer* directly uses Saturn's memory model for data-flow analysis. Saturn models every memory location accessed by function $f$ at every program point $P$ in the form of a constrained expression (CE). A CE is represented in the format of `V=E:C`, indicating the value of `V` equals the expression `E` under condition `C`. At the beginning of each function $f$, Saturn first statically enumerates all the memory locations (heap and stack) accessed by $f$, and initializes each location `V` as `V=V:True`, indicating the value of `V` is unknown (symbolic). This is possible because we model the loops as tail-recursive functions, thus each function body is loop-free (see Handling Loops later this section). At an assignment instruction $P$, `V=exp;`, the value of `V` is updated to `exp:C`, where `C` is the control-flow constraint to reach $P$. At any merge point on the control-flow graph (CFG), all the conditions of `V` from every incoming edge are merged. This will prune all non-causally-related conditions to reach $P$. Figure 3 shows the CE of `is_dir` in `rm` at log point 1.

$$is\_dir = \begin{cases} \texttt{T\_YES:} & C_{yes} = \texttt{dp\&\&dp->d\_type==DT\_DIR} \\ & \texttt{||!dp\&\&S\_ISDIR(sbuf.st\_mode)} \\ \texttt{T\_NO:} & C_{no} = \texttt{dp\&\&dp->d\_type!=DT\_DIR} \\ & \texttt{||!dp\&\&!S\_ISDIR(sbuf.st\_mode)} \end{cases}$$

**Figure 3.** The constrained expression for `is_dir` at line 16. $C_{yes}$ and $C_{no}$ are constraints for `is_dir` to hold value `T_YES` and `T_NO` respectively.

Each variable involved in the CE is a *live-in* variable to the function $f$, i.e. variable whose value is first read before written in $f$ [4]. Thus we can represent all memory locations accessed by $f$ with a concise set of variable values (i.e. live-ins) to reduce the number of redundant values to record. For example, `is_dir` is not a live-in variable, and its value can be represented by a small set of live-in values such as `dp`, `T_YES`, etc., as shown in Figure 3.

**Control-flow analysis:** At each program point $P$, *LogEnhancer* also computes the constraint for the control-flow to reach $P$. At a log point $LP$, every variable value involved in the control-flow constraint would be replaced by its constrained expression. Then this constraint is solved by a SAT solver to test its satisfiability. An unsatisfiable constraint indicates no feasible path can reach $LP$, therefore, we can prune out such a constraint. The satisfiable constraint thus contains all the causally-related control and data-flow conditions to reach $LP$. This constraint $C$ will be stored as a part of this function's summary, along with the location of $LP$. It records that function $f$ would reach $LP$ under constraint $C$. Non-standard control flows such as `exit`, `abort`, `_exit` and their wrappers are identified and adjusted on the CFG. `longjmps` are correlated with `setjmps` through function summaries in a manner similar to that described in [57].

In the `rm` example, the control-flow constraint within `remove_entry` to reach log point 1 would be `is_dir==T_NO && unlink(filename)!=0`. Then `is_dir` is replaced by its CE as shown in Figure 3. The SAT solver determines `T_YES` cannot satisfy this control-flow constraint, thus `T_YES` and its constraint are pruned. The remaining result is a simplified, feasible constraint $C_r$, which is stored as the summary of `remove_entry` to reach log point 1:

$$C_r = \texttt{(dp \&\& dp->d\_type!=DT\_DIR || !dp \&\& !S\_ISDIR(sbuf.st\_mode)) \&\& unlink(filename)}$$

**Inter-Procedural analysis:** The above process is then recursively repeated in the caller by traversing the call-graph in bottom-up order. In `rm`, after analyzing `remove_entry`, *LogEnhancer* next analyzes its caller `remove_cwd_entries` in the same manner: a linear scan to compute the CE for each memory location and control-flow constraint for each program point. At line 25, it finds a call-site to a function with a summary (`remove_entry`), indicating that reaching this point might eventually lead to log point 1, so it takes the control-flow constraint ($C_c$ = `(readdir(dirp)!=NULL)`), and replaces every variable with its CE (in this case the CE for `dirp`).

Besides $C_c$, for context sensitivity, *LogEnhancer* also takes the $C_r$ from `remove_entry` and substitutes it to produce the following:

$$C'_r = \texttt{(readdir(dirp) \&\& readdir(dirp)->d\_type!=DT\_DIR || !readdir(dirp)) \&\& f==Sym}$$

Here, `readdir(dirp)` is the substitution for `dp` in $C_r$; `S_ISDIR (sbuf.st_mode)` is pruned since it is not visible in the caller's context; `f==Sym` is the substitution for `unlink (filename)`. `Sym` is a symbolic value and `f` is the substitution of `filename` in caller. `f==Sym` indicates we should plug-in the CE of `f` to track the inter-procedural data-flow, while not enforcing any constraint on `f`'s value. Finally, $C'_r \wedge C_c$ is stored as the summary for `remove_cwd_entries` to reach log point 1.

Such bottom-up analysis traverses upward along each call chain from the log point. It ignores functions that are not in the call chains for the log point—we refer them as "sibling functions". Sibling functions may also be causally-related to the log point. Therefore, if a sibling function's return value appears in the constraint for the log point, *LogEnhancer* also analyzes the function and identifies the control- and data flow dependencies for its return value. This analysis is implemented as a separate analysis pass after the bottom-up analysis. Currently we limit the analysis to descend only one level into such functions due to scalability concerns. If a causally-related sibling function is a library call with no source code (e.g. `unlink()` in the `rm` example), we simply plug in its parameter into our constraint so we may choose to record the parameter.

**Handling Loops** Loops are modeled as tail-recursive functions so that each function is cycle-free, which is a key requirement allowing us to statically enumerate all the paths and memory locations accessed by each function. Each loop is handled similarly to ordinary functions except that it is traversed *twice*, to explore both loop entering and exiting directions. A variable `V` modified within the loop body is propagated to its caller as `V==Sym` to relax the value constraint, since we are not following the multiple iterations as in run-time. In this way, constraint from the loop body can be conservatively captured.

**Efficiency and Scalability** Uncertainty Identification scans the program linearly, a key to our scalability to large applications. We further use *pre-selection* and *lazy SAT solving* for optimization. The former pre-selects only those functions that on the call-stack of any log point to analyze, and the latter queries the SAT solver lazily only at the time when function summaries are generated.

**Pointer Aliasing:** Intra-procedural pointer aliasing is precisely modeled by Saturn's constrained expression model [5]. Inter-procedural pointer aliasing analysis is only performed on function pointers to ensure that *LogEnhancer* can traverse deep along the call-chain. The other types of pointers are assumed to be non-aliased, which might cause us to miss some causally-related variable values. Note that for Value Selection we enable inter-procedural alias analysis for all types of pointers for *conservative* liveness checking.

## 3.2 Value Selection

Value Selection selects, from all constraints identified by the previous step, what key variable values to record at each log point. In this section, we refer an expression without any Boolean operator (i.e., `&&`, `||`, `!`) as a *uni-condition*. For example, "`dp!=NULL`" is a uni-condition (note `!=` is not one of the three Boolean operators). A constraint is thus a formula of uni-conditions combined together using Boolean operators.

*(1) Pruning Determinable Values:* Some variable values can be inferred knowing that a given log point is executed. We call them *determinable values*. For example, in constraint `a==0 && b!=0`, it

can be determined that "a" must equal zero, while b's value is still uncertain. A determinable value V is identified if: (i) V is involved in a *necessary* uni-condition $uc$ of constraint $C$, i.e., $\neg uc \wedge C$ is unsatisfiable; (ii) $uc$ is in the form of V==CONSTANT. A determinable value can be pruned out since it need not be recorded.

*(2) Identifying the condition for a value to be meaningful:* After the above step, all remaining values are uncertain. However, not every value is meaningful under all circumstances. In rm, dp->d_type is meaningful only if dp!=NULL. Recording a non-meaningful value could result in an invalid pointer dereference or reading a bogus value. Therefore, for each un-pruned value, we also identify under what condition this value would be meaningful, writing this as [C]:V, indicating value V is meaningful under condition C. Our runtime recording will first check C before recording V.

*(3) Liveness Checking and Equivalent Value Identification (EVI):* A value can also be *dead* (overwritten or gone altogether along with its stack frame) prior to a given log point and we cannot delay the recording until the log point. To identify such dead values, we perform *conservative* liveness analysis, i.e., if a variable value *might* be modified before the log point, we conservatively mark it as "dead". To be conservative, we run Saturn's global pointer alias analysis [30] before the liveness checking. Any pointers passed into a library call where source code is unavailable are conservatively treated as "dead" after the call (we manually exclude some common C libraries such as strlen). Any extern values not defined inside the program are also conservatively treated as dead.

However, we do not give up on recording dead values so easily. For each dead value, we try to find some equivalent variable values which live until the log point and can be used to infer the dead value. More specifically, a value EV is *equivalent* to another value V if and only if: (i) it is defined as EV=V op UV, where UV are other live values, and (ii) both have the same control flow constraint. Therefore, if a dead value V has an equivalent EV, we simply record EV and UV.

### 3.3 Run-time Value Collection

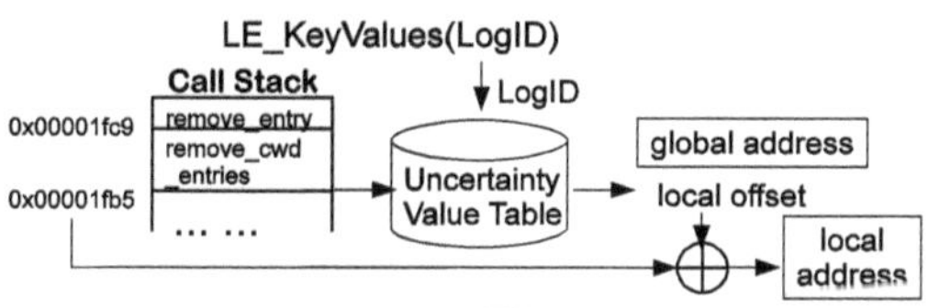


**Figure 4.** Run-time recording for Delayed Collection.

**Delayed Collection:** We instrument the source code of the target application right before each log point by adding a function call LE_KeyValues() to record the values of identified live variables. The addresses of these variables are obtained from the compiled binary by parsing the DWARF debugging information [22]. Local variables' addresses are the offsets from the stack frame base pointer. Heap values' addresses are represented the same way as they are in the original code. Each live value is represented by its address and the condition for it to be meaningful is stored into an Uncertain Value Table (UVT) that corresponds to the log point. At the end of our analysis, each UVT is output to a separate file. These files are released together with the target application.

Figure 4 shows the run-time process of LE_KeyValues(). It is triggered only at the log point, i.e., when a log message is being printed. When triggered, it first uses the LogID of the log point to load the corresponding UVT into memory. It then obtains the current call stack, using it to index into the UVT to find what values to record. For each value, the condition for it to be meaningful is first tested. A local variable's dynamic address is computed by reading the offset from UVT and then adding this offset to the dynamic stack frame base pointer obtained by walking the stack. Note that the UVT is only loaded into memory during the execution of LE_KeyValues(), so the delayed recording does not add any overhead during normal execution, i.e., when no log message being printed. We also record the dynamic call stack.

By default, *LogEnhancer* records only basic type values. For example, for a pointer value, we only record the address stored in this pointer. To further provide meaningful diagnostic information, we add two extensions. First, if the variable is of type char* and is not NULL, then we record the string with a maximum of 50 characters (of course, if the string is shorter than 50, we record only the string). Second, if the variable is a field within a structure, in addition to that field, we also record the values of other fields. This is because structures are often used to represent multiple properties of a single entity, such as a request in apache httpd.

Although we are already very cautious in our design to record only meaningful and valid values to ensure memory safety, due to the limitation of static analysis, we might still access an invalid memory location (e.g., caused by multi-threading). To be conservative, we further ensure memory safety by intercepting SIGSEGV signals without crashing the running application. For applications such as apache which also intercept SIGSEGV signals, we add a wrapper to filter out those caused by our log recording. In our experiments, we have never encountered such a signal.

**In-time Collection:** In addition to instrumentation at log points, the in-time collection method further saves a shadow copy of every dead value X that has no equivalent value by instrumenting the code in the following way:

```
- if (X)
+ if (LE_InTime(&X, Lint32) && X)
```

LE_InTime() always returns 1. It simply copies Lint32 number of bytes starting from &X. Note that LE_InTime() can record X directly without checking any condition since it is within the same context as the use of X.

All recorded values from LE_KeyValues() and LE_InTime() are first stored into buffers in memory (both currently 40 KB) respectively. At *error* messages, both buffers are flushed to disk. LE_KeyValues()'s buffer is also flushed when it becomes full, whereas LE_InTime() simply recycles the shadow buffer from the beginning. Each thread has its own private buffer.

We also implement a variation of the delayed method as a core dump analyzer (referred as a **Core Dump Digger**) that automatically identifies the key values (or equivalent values) from a core dump at a log point (if there is such core dump). When a core dump is generated, our Core Dump Digger derives equivalent information to delayed collection from the core dump. Note that not every log point has a core dump, especially those for book-keeping or warning messages.

## 4. Evaluation

We use *LogEnhancer* to enhance *all 9,125* log messages in 8 different real-world applications as shown in Table 1. Five of them are server applications, including 2 web servers (apache httpd, lighttpd), a database server (postgresql), a concurrent version control server (cvs), and a web cache (squid). For server applications where there are multiple log files, we enhance all messages printing into the error log file. Currently we do not enhance other types of log files such as access logs. In the default verbosity mode, all applications only print error messages (some of them also prints warning messages). Therefore, during normal execution with the default verbosity mode, there are few log message printed besides a few messages indicating system start/stop.

For any diagnostic tools like *LogEnhancer*, the most effective evaluation method is of course user study: having it used by real programmers for a period of time who then report their experi-

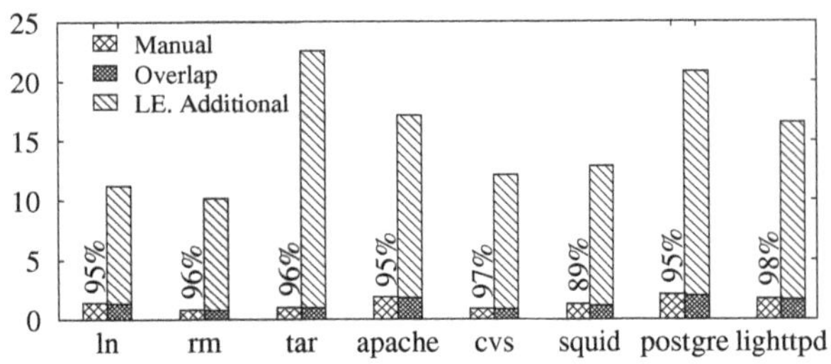


(A) Variables Recording at each log point

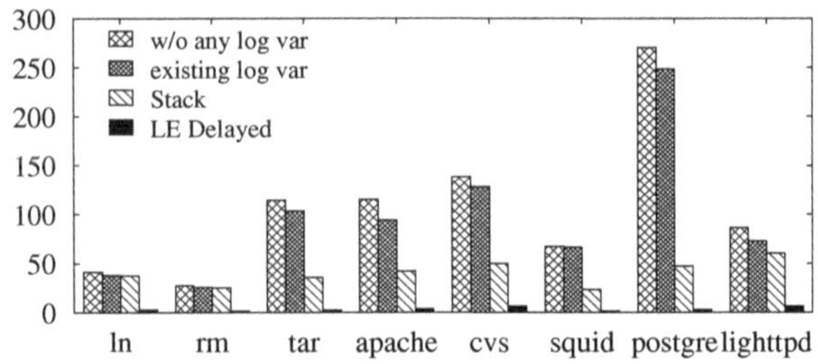


(B) Number of Uncertain Branches

**Figure 5. Overall Result of *LogEnhancer*.** In (A), we compare the number of variables per message logged manually by developers with the ones inferred automatically by *LogEnhancer*. "Overlap" shows the number of variable values that are selected by both programmers and *LogEnhancer*. The percentages of overlap are marked beside each bar. "LE-additional" shows the additional variable values only identified by *LogEnhancer*. In (B), we compare the amount of uncertain branches that are causally related to each log point given different types of information recorded: without any variables (the original uncertainty space); existing variables included by developers; call stack in addition to existing variables; variables inferred by *LogEnhancer* and call stack using the delayed collection method.

| Application | Version | LOC | Log Points | |
|---|---|---|---|---|
| | | | All | Default |
| ln | 4.5.1 | 20K | 26 | 14 (ERR) |
| rm | 4.5.4 | 18K | 28 | 25 (ERR) |
| tar | 1.22 | 86K | 210 | 176 (ERR) |
| apache | 2.2.2 | 317K | 1,654 | 1,093 (WARN) |
| cvs | 1.11.23 | 148K | 1,088 | 762 (ERR) |
| squid | 2.3.S4 | 69K | 1,116 | 402 (ERR) |
| postgresql | 8.4.1 | 1,029K | 4,876 | 4,403 (WARN) |
| lighttpd | 1.4.26 | 56K | 127 | 127 (ERR) |

**Table 1.** Evaluated applications. LOC is lines of code of the entire application. "All" shows the total number of log points for the most verbose level. "Default" shows the default verbose-level of log message printed (in bracket) and the number of log points at this level.

ences. Unfortunately, this would be a time-consuming process and it is hard to select samples to be representative. Given these constraints, we try to evaluate *LogEnhancer* both quantitatively and qualitatively using three sets of experiments, all conducted on a Linux machine with eight 2.33GHz Xeon processors and 16GB of memory. Since the analysis is done off-line, *LogEnhancer* currently runs as single process, single thread (even though the analysis can potentially be parallelized to reduce the analysis time).

*(1) Value selection.* First, we investigate how well our algorithm captures the variable whose values are useful for failure diagnosis by comparing against manual selection ( variable values that have already been recorded in existing logging statements by programmers). Then, we also evaluate how many new variables are selected for logging *in addition* to those manually added by programmers over time (i.e., how many new variable values would be logged by *LogEnhancer*) and how effective these additional logged values can help reducing the number of code paths to be considered in postmortem diagnosis.

*(2) Diagnostic effectiveness.* In the second set of experiments we select 15 real world failure cases caused by 13 bugs and 2 misconfigurations to show the usefulness of the information collected by *LogEnhancer* in failure diagnosis. In particular, we also show how automatic log inference tools like SherLog can be improved given the information added by *LogEnhancer* into log messages.

*(3) Logging overhead.* The third set of experiments evaluate the overhead introduced by *LogEnhancer*'s run-time logging for both in-time and delayed collection methods.

### 4.1 Effectiveness in Variable Recording

Figure 5 (A) shows *LogEnhancer*'s comparison with existing log variables included manually by programmers into log messages over the years. On average, 95.1% (with minimum 89% and maximum 98%) of these log variables are selected *automatically* by *LogEnhancer*. In all the applications except `squid`, *LogEnhancer* achieves a coverage over 95%[3]. This high coverage is an evidence that our design matches with the intuition of programmers in recording key values to help diagnosis. It implies that *LogEnhancer* can do at least as well as manual effort.

The small fraction (4.9% on average) of existing log variables that are not automatically selected by *LogEnhancer* are mainly book-keeping information that is not very useful for inferring the execution path to the log point. For example, when CVS detects an invalid configuration entry, it outputs the line number of that entry in the configuration file. Since this line number is not used in any branches to determine the control flow, it is thus missed by *LogEnhancer*. Note that the invalid configuration entry string itself is identified by *LogEnhancer*. So even without the line number, recording the configuration entry string itself is enough for users/developers to locate the error in the configuration file.

There are four main categories of manually-identified variables that are missed by *LogEnhancer*, together contributing to 97% of the few missed cases. *(1) Book-keeping values logged immediately after initialization (37%).* For example, immediately after receiving a request, the length of the request is logged before it is actually used. All these log messages are verbose mode messages that do not indicate any error. *(2) The line number of invalid entry in configuration file (28%). (3) General configuration (host-names, PID, program names, etc.) (24%)* that are not causally-related to the log point. Note causally-related configuration information would be identified *LogEnhancer*. *(4) Redundant multi-variables (8%)* that are always updated together while only one used in branch. *LogEnhancer* only identifies the one used in branch and the missed values can be inferred from the identified one.

In addition to automatically selecting most of existing log variables manually included by programmers, *LogEnhancer* also selects an average of 14.6 additional *new* variable values for each log message. Recording these values (including the call stack) can eliminate an average of 108 uncertain branches for each log point as shown in Figure 5 (B). From the 108 original uncertain branches per log point, existing log variables can reduce it to 97, whereas *LogEnhancer*'s delayed recording scheme can reduce this number to 3, meaning that, on average for each log point, there are only 3 unresolved branches for programmers to consider to fully understand why the log point was reached. The remaining uncertain branches are caused by uncertain values that are dead at log points,

[3] Many variable values are converted to human readable strings when printing to log message. For example "inet_ntoa" converts an IP address into string. We count the value as covered by *LogEnhancer* only if by recording the non-text value we can *deterministically* infer the text string.

| | uncert. br. (avg/med/max/min) | | # of Var | | |
|---|---|---|---|---|---|
| Apps. | w/o any var | L.E. (delay) | all | live | logged |
| ln | 41/43/78/7 | 2.9/1/8/0 | 11.3 | 9.8 | 10.1 |
| rm | 28/27/57/6 | 1.4/1/9/0 | 10.2 | 9.3 | 9.5 |
| tar | 114/35/1419/2 | 2.2/1/20/0 | 22.6 | 19.5 | 21.6 |
| apache | 115/78/626/1 | 3.5/2/35/0 | 17.2 | 14.7 | 15.9 |
| cvs | 139/62/3836/1 | 6.5/3/38/0 | 12.2 | 8.7 | 10.6 |
| squid | 67/19/4409/1 | 1.3/0/17/0 | 13.0 | 11.6 | 12.5 |
| postgre | 270/61/22070/1 | 1.2/0/48/0 | 20.9 | 14.7 | 18.1 |
| lighttpd | 86/88/222/5 | 6.4/6/40/0 | 20.7 | 15.2 | 18.8 |

**Table 2.** Detailed result showing the number of uncertain branches and uncertain variable values per log point. The large difference between average and median in "w/o any var" is caused by small number of log points inside some library functions, that have a large number of uncertain branches accumulated from many possible call stacks. Once we differentiate call stacks in "Stack" approach, this difference between average and median significantly reduces.

which can be recorded by our in-time collection if overhead is not a concern. If we record only the stack frames in addition to the original log messages, the number of uncertain branches is reduced from 97 to 40 on average. Table 2 shows the detailed number of uncertain branches.

Table 2 also shows the number of variable values identified by *LogEnhancer* at different analysis stages. On average, 16.0 uncertain values are identified for each log point ("all"). 14.6 of these can be recorded at log points ("logged") without introducing normal-run overhead. Among these 14.6 variables, 12.9 are not overwritten before log point (i.e., they are "live"), and the remaining 1.7 are recovered from Equivalent Value Identification (EVI). On average 49% of the dead values can be recovered by EVI. The remaining 51% of dead values can be collected only via in-time collection, at the cost of some overhead to normal execution.

**Analysis Time** Table 3 shows the analysis time of *LogEnhancer* on each application. For all applications except postgresql, *LogEnhancer* finishes the entire analysis within 2 minutes to 4 hours. For postgresql, it takes 11 hours since there are 4,876 logging points in 1M lines of code. Since we expect *LogEnhancer* to be used off-line prior to software release, the analysis time is less critical. Additionally, the summary-based design allows it to be parallel or incrementally applied [5]. The memory usage in all cases is below 2.3GB.

| Analysis Time and Memory Usage | | | | | | | | |
|---|---|---|---|---|---|---|---|---|
| ln | 3m | 579MB | rm | 2m | 172MB | tar | 1.5h | 263MB |
| apache | 2.1h | 1.3GB | cvs | 3.0h | 1.7GB | squid | 3.8h | 2.3GB |
| postgre | 10.7h | 1.5GB | lighttpd | 19.5m | 532M | | | |

**Table 3. Analysis performance.**

## 4.2 Real World Failures

We evaluated *LogEnhancer* by analyzing 15 real-world failures, including 13 software bugs and 2 configuration errors, to see how our enhanced log messages would help failure diagnosis. In all these cases, the original log messages were insufficient to diagnose the failure due to many remaining uncertainties, while with *LogEnhancer*'s log enhancement these uncertainties were significantly reduced and almost entirely eliminated. Due to space limitations, in this section we will show 3 cases in detail to demonstrate the effectiveness of *LogEnhancer*. The other 12 cases are summarized in Table 4.

We also compared the inference results of SherLog [57] before and after *LogEnhancer*'s enhancement.

| Fail. | Description |
|---|---|
| rm | reports a directory cycle by mistake for a healthy FS. |
| cp | fails to replace hardlinks given "–preserve=links". |
| ln | ln –target-directory failed by missing a condition check. |
| apache1 | denies connection after unsuccessful login attemp. |
| apache2 | OS checking procedure failed causing server to fail. |
| apache3 | Server mistakenly refuses SSL connections. |
| apache4 | A structure field wasn't initialized properly causing unpredictable failure symptoms. |
| squid | wrong checking function caused access control failed. |
| cvs | login with OS account failed due to misconfiguration. |
| tar 1 | failed since archive_stat.st_mode improperly set. |
| tar 2 | tar failed to update non-existing tar-ball. |
| lighttpd | Proxy fails when connecting to multiple backends. |

**Table 4.** Real-world failures evaluated.

**Case 1: rm.** For the `rm` failure described in Figure 2, *LogEnhancer* recorded the call stack being:

```
...remove_cwd_entries:25 -> remove_entry.
```

In addition, *LogEnhancer* records the following variable values at log point 1: `dp=0x100120, filename="dir1/dir2", dp->d_type = DT_UNKNOWN`. Programmers can infer that the failed execution took the path at line 5 and came from caller `remove_cwd_entries`. They can also tell that `readdir` returns a non-NULL value `dp`, but `dp->d_type`'s value is `DT_UNKNOWN` in the failed execution, which is exactly the root cause: the programmers did not expect such a type for `dp->d_type`. In this case, just as if `dp` is NULL, the program should use `lstat` to determine the directory type. So the fix is straightforward as shown below:

```
4: - if (dp)
4: + if (dp && dp->d_type!=DT_UNKNOWN)
```

Without *LogEnhancer*'s enhancement, SherLog inferred a total of 13 possible call paths (not even complete execution paths, only function call sequences) that might have been taken to print the error message. Developers need to further manually determine among these which one actually lead to the failure. SherLog also failed to infer the value of `dp` and `dp->d_type`, leaving no clues for developers to infer branch direction at line 4. With *LogEnhancer*'s result, SherLog can pinpoint the only possible call path, and developers can easily examine the value of `dp` and `dp->d_type`.

**Case 2: Apache bug.**

Figure 6 shows a bug report in apache. With only the error log message at line 2, the developer could not diagnose the failure, so he asked the user for all kinds of run-time information in a total of 95 message exchanges. Actually only two pieces of information are key to identifying the root cause: One is the value of `keepalives` and the other is the request type, `proxyreq`, both of which are unfortunately buried deep in large and mostly irrelevant data structures.

*LogEnhancer* automatically identifies `c -> keepalive` and `r-> proxyreq` to be collected for this log message. `keepalive` is identified since it is used at line 12 as the constraint for the execution to reach the log point. `proxyreq` is identified in similar manner. So if the developers had used *LogEnhancer* to enhance their log messages automatically, *LogEnhancer* would have helped them by saving a lot of time in discussions back and forth with the user. Interestingly, after such painful experience, the programmers added a patch whose sole purpose was to log the value of `keepalives` in this function.

Without *LogEnhancer*'s enhancement, SherLog inferred 63 possible call paths and not be able to infer the value of `keepalive` or `proxyreq`. With *LogEnhancer*'s enhancement, SherLog can narrow down to only one possible call path, and infer the value of `keepalive` and `proxyreq`.

**Bug Report for Apache**

U: Apache httpd configured with mod_proxy and virtual hosting. Client browsers got error messages and status code 502. The problem occurs only under load tests, no problem if single client.

D: Ask for back trace.

D: Ask for debug level log.

D: Ask partial heap image.

D: Work around posted.

U: Problem still occurs.

D: Configuration file posted.

D: Patch issued.

Total 95 discussion messages before correct diagnosis!!!

**Patched Code**

```
proxy_process_response(..){
 1 if (ap_getline(...)<=0) {
 2  ap_log_rerror(
 3  "error reading status line from"
 3  "remote server");
 4+ if (c->keepalives &&
 5+   r->proxyreq==PROXY_REVERSE) {
 6+  return OK;
 7+ }
 8  return aperror(HTTP_BAD_GATEWAY,
 9    "Error reading remote server");
10 }

11 determine_connection(..) {
12   if (c->keepalives ..)   constraint for
13     err = ...             return value
14   if (err!=SUCCESS) return ERROR;
15 }

16 proxy_http_handler (...) {
17  if(determine_connection(..)!=OK)
18      goto cleanup;         control-
19  ...                       dependent
20 if(proxy_process_response(.)!=OK)
21      goto cleanup;
21 }
```

**Figure 6.** Apache bug example. "U" stands for apache user while "D" for developer. Patched code is highlighted.

```
1 ap_mpm_run (...) {
2   if (rv = mutex_method(nmutex, mech))
3       return rv;
4   rv = nmutex->meth->create(...);
5   if (rv != APR_SUCCESS)
6     ap_log_error (
7      "Couldn't create cross-process lock");
8 }

9  mutex_method(nmutex, mech) {
10   switch (mech) {
11   case APR_LOCK_DEFAULT:
12     nmutex->meth =
13     &apr_mutex_unix_sysv_methods;
14   }
15 }
```

Error Log:
[emerg] No space left on device: Couldn't create cross-process lock

**Figure 7.** Apache configuration error. The dependencies to identify variable `mech` are marked as arrows.

**Case 3: Apache configuration error.**

A misconfiguration failure in Apache occurs with the log message shown in Figure 7. It warns of no space on disk, while users' file system and disk are perfectly healthy with plenty of free space available. From the source code, it is certain that the message was printed at line 6, as a result of an unsuccessful call to `create()` at line 4. However, developers had no other clues why this call failed.

*LogEnhancer* identifies `mech` as a key value to collect at line 6, since it is used at line 10 in function `mutex_method`, whose `nmutex` is causally related to the log point at line 6. If apache had been enhanced by *LogEnhancer*, the log message would record the value of `mech` being `APR_LOCK_DEFAULT` and the value of `nmutex->meth` being `apr_mutex_unix_sysv_methods`. This indicates that apache was using the default lock setting which caused the failure. In a multi-threaded mode, apache should use fnctl-based locking instead. To fix this, users should explicitly add "AcceptMutex fcntl" into the configuration file.

Note that, without *LogEnhancer*'s enhancement, SherLog cannot infer the value of `mech` from the original log message and would not be able to narrow down to the lock setting configuration as the root cause.

## 4.3 Overhead

**Execution Time:** Table 5 shows the *LogEnhancer*'s recording overhead during applications' normal execution under the default verbosity mode. Few log messages are printed in the default verbosity mode during normal execution. Thus there is no overhead for *LogEnhancer* with the delayed collection method. The in-time collection incurs small (1.5-8.2%) overhead due to shadow copying. This number can be reduced by eliminating those shadow recording in frequently invoked code paths (e.g., inside a loop). For example in postgresql, by disabling two instrumentations in the `hash_seq_search` library function, the slow-down can be reduced to 1%.

| Applications and Slow-down | | |
|---|---|---|
| tar 0.0%, 1.5% | apache 0.0%, 3.9% | postgre 0.0%, 7.6% |
| cvs 0.0%, 1.7% | squid 0.0%, 8.2% | lighttpd 0.0%, 3.4% |

**Table 5. Overhead of *LogEnhancer* in normal execution (default verbosity mode).** The first number is the overhead for the delayed collection, and the second is for the in-time collection. `rm` and `ln`'s results are not reported since the execution times are too short. `Tar` is measured in response time, while the servers are measured in throughput degradation when fully loaded.

Figure 8 shows *LogEnhancer*'s performance during normal execution with other verbosity modes. Turning on debug level logging degrades the throughput by 13% even *without LogEnhancer*. With *LogEnhancer*, there is an additional 3-7% overhead (measured in throughput degradation) on top of the original.

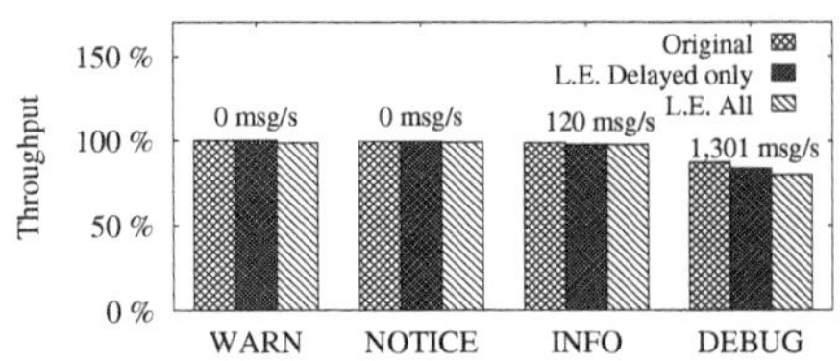


**Figure 8.** Normal execution throughput on fully loaded Apache for different verbosity modes. All numbers are normalized over the throughput of unmodified apache under default verbosity level (WARN).

**Memory Overhead:** As mentioned in Section 3.3, delayed collection does not introduce any memory overhead during normal execution (i.e., no log message printed). For in-time collection, the only memory overhead is the size of the buffer, which is set to 40KB in our experiment. If a log point is executed at run-time, `LE_KeyValues()` introduces additional memory overhead by loading the UVT into the memory. In all the 8 applications, the median and average sizes of UVT are 395 bytes and 354 KB respectively.

**Comparison with Core Dump** Table 6 compares *LogEnhancer*'s recording time and data size with core dump at a failure. On average, *LogEnhancer* only needs 0.43 millisecond. The recorded data has only 66 bytes on average. In comparison, core dumps require 1000 times recording time, and 55MB in size. The large overhead of core dumps makes it impractical to collect the entire memory image with each log message.

Table 6 shows *LogEnhancer*'s average log size is 66 bytes per message, which is in the same magnitude as original log message.

| Failure | Time and Size (B) | | | |
|---|---|---|---|---|
| | *LogEnhancer* | | Core dump | |
| ln | 0.45ms | 41 (original 45) | 630ms | 55M |
| rm | 0.45ms | 113 (original 51) | 610ms | 55M |
| tar 2 | 0.39ms | 39 (original 96) | 630ms | 55M |
| cvs | 0.44ms | 54 (original 52) | 60ms | 772K |
| apache 1 | 0.41ms | 82 (original 196) | 670ms | 3.2M |

**Table 6.** Comparison between *LogEnhancer* and core dump. We reproduced 5 failures in table 4 and forced a core dump to be generated at each log point using `gcore` [25] library call. The log size of *LogEnhancer* does not include the size of the original log. The size of original log (without *LogEnhancer*) is shown in the parenthesis.

A large portion of this log is the call stack encode in clear text. We can further compress this portion since calling contexts are likely to remain the same for a log point. Other variable values in our log are encoded in binary format and are converted to human readable form post-mortemly.

## 5. Related Work

**Log analysis for failure diagnosis** Existing log analysis work focuses on post-mortem diagnosis using logs, learning statistical signatures [3, 8, 16, 29, 56] or inferring partial execution paths and run-time states [57]. Xu et al. [56] use statistical techniques to efficiently learn a decision tree based signature from large number of console logs. This signature can be used to effectively detect and diagnose anomalies.

In particular, the closest related work, SherLog [57], uses static analysis to infer the partial execution paths that can connect the run-time log messages. It infers both control and data value information post-mortemly, providing a similar user-experience as an interactive debugger without dynamically re-executing the program.

*LogEnhancer* is different from but complementary to log analysis work like SherLog [57] in several aspects:

*(1) LogEnhancer* has a completely different focus: it aims to improve software's diagnose-ability by adding more causally related information in log messages to make failure diagnosis easier. Such information benefits not only manual diagnosis but also automatic log analysis engines like SherLog.

*(2) LogEnhancer* logs only those variables that *cannot* be inferred (manually or automatically with SherLog) from what is already available in log messages.

*(3)* Although *LogEnhancer* leverages summary-based static analysis similar to SherLog, the different objectives lead to several major new design and implementation issues. For example, *LogEnhancer* needs to perform uncertain control/data identification, value selection, liveness analysis, equivalent variable identification, and finally instrument the source code to log those selected variables at run-time. None of this would be needed in a log inference engine like SherLog.

*(4)* As the real world case studies in Section 4.2 have shown, automatic log inference engines like SherLog can significantly benefit from *LogEnhancer*'s log enhancement information. For example, in our second case study, the additional information added by *LogEnhancer* can help SherLog pinpoint the execution path from a total of 63 possibilities before the enhancement.

**Logging design** Existing guidelines for logging design are purely empirical [32, 51]. Kernighan and Pike [32] argued the importance of well-designed log messages in failure diagnosis. Schmidt summarized some empirical logging practices [51]. To the best of our knowledge, *LogEnhancer* is one of the first to automatically enhance log messages.

**Use of core dump for failure diagnosis** Several systems collect partial memory image [6, 26, 27, 46] when a system crashes. Windows Error Reporting [26] monitors the system for crashes or hangs, and records a "mini-dump". Crash Reporter [6], NetApp Savecore [46] and Google Breakpad [27] also collect compressed memory dumps.

Some core dump analyzers infer diagnostic information from the core dump. Their techniques are applicable on *LogEnhancer*'s recording result as well. PSE [39] and ESD [58] perform offline diagnosis of program crashes from core dump. Weeratunge, et al. [54] diagnose Heisenbugs by diff-ing the core dumps from a failing run and passing run.

As discussed early in Introduction, our work is complementary to core dumps. *LogEnhancer* can collect historic, intermediate information prior to failures and also provide diagnostic information when no core dump is available. It also significantly reduces overhead and data size by recording only causally-related information.

**Profiling for diagnosis** Many of diagnostic tools collect run-time profiling such as low-level performance counters [10, 16] or execution traces [7, 13, 15, 29, 37, 52, 60]. Liblit et al. [37] sample profiling information from many users to offload the monitoring overhead, and isolate the most correlated information using statistical techniques. Chen et al. [13] propose hardware solution to accelerate instruction-level monitoring. Rather than collecting tailored, causally-related information for each log message as *LogEnhancer*, these profiling tools collect general information. Our work is complementary to these work in that we collect causally-related information specific to *each* log messages.

DCop [59] records the acquisition of each lock involved in a deadlock to speed up the debugging process of deadlock failures. Our work is also complementary to DCop in that we can help the diagnosis of other kinds of failures that print log messages.

**Logging for deterministic replay** Other work [20, 34, 35, 40, 44, 49, 53, 55] attempts to deterministically replay failed execution, which generally requires high run-time logging overhead especially for multiprocessor systems. To reduce the overhead, recently SMP-Revirt [21] made clever use of page protection. Our work is complementary and mainly targets to the cases when failure reproduction is difficult due to privacy concerns, unavailability of execution environments, etc.

**Other Static Analysis Work** Compiler techniques similar to *LogEnhancer* are also used to address some other software reliability problems [11, 17, 31, 58]. KLEE [11] and ESD [58] use full symbolic execution engine to expose bugs in testing or infer paths from core dump. Carburizer [31] uses data-flow analysis to locate dependencies on data read from hardware. Although *LogEnhancer* also uses symbolic execution, due to the very different objectives, it starts from each log message and walks backward along the call chain to conduct "inference", instead of walking forward to explore every execution path. In addition, our work also has to use many other techniques and analysis such as control/data flow analysis, variable liveness analysis, equivalent variable analysis, run-time value collection, etc.

## 6. Conclusions

In this paper we presented a tool, *LogEnhancer*, perhaps as the first work to systematically enhance every log message in software to collect causally-related diagnostic information. We applied *LogEnhancer* uniformly on 9,125 different log messages in 8 applications including 5 server applications. Interestingly, we found 95% of the variables included in the log messages by developers over time can be automatically identified by *LogEnhancer*. More importantly, *LogEnhancer* adds on average 14.6 additional values per log message, which can reduce the amount of uncertainty (number of uncertain branches) from 108 to 3 with negligible overhead. This information not only benefits manual diagnosis but also automatic log inference engines.

## Acknowledgments

We thank the anonymous reviewers and our paper shepherd Todd C. Mowry for their insightful feedback, the UCSD Opera research group and Michael Vrable for useful discussions and paper proofreading. This research is supported by NSF CNS-0720743 grant, NSF CCF-0325603 grant, NSF CNS-0615372 grant, NSF CNS-0347854 (career award), NSF CSR Small 1017784 grant and NetApp Gift grant.

## References


[1] Cisco system log management.

[2] EMC seen collecting and managing log as key driver for 94 percent of customers.

[3] M. K. Aguilera, J. C. Mogul, J. L. Wiener, P. Reynolds, and A. Muthitacharoen. Performance debugging for distributed systems of black boxes. In *SOSP'03*.

[4] A. V. Aho, M. S. Lam, R. Sethi, and J. D. Ullman. *Compilers: Principles, Techniques, and Tools (2nd Edition), Page 528.*

[5] A. Aiken, S. Bugrara, I. Dillig, T. Dillig, P. Hawkins, and B. Hackett. An overview of the Saturn project. In *PASTE'07*.

[6] Apple Inc., CrashReport. Technical Report TN2123, 2004.

[7] A. Ayers, R. Schooler, C. Metcalf, A. Agarwal, J. Rhee, and E. Witchel. Traceback: First fault diagnosis by reconstruction of distributed control flow. In *PLDI'05*.

[8] P. Barham, A. Donnelly, R. Isaacs, and R. Mortier. Using magpie for request extraction and workload modelling. In *OSDI'04*.

[9] E. D. Berger and B. G. Zorn. Diehard: probabilistic memory safety for unsafe languages. In *PLDI'06*.

[10] S. Bhatia, A. Kumar, M. Fiuczynski, and L. Peterson. Lightweight, high-resolution monitoring for troubleshooting production systems. In *OSDI'08*.

[11] C. Cadar, D. Dunbar, and D. R. Engler. Klee: Unassisted and automatic generation of high-coverage tests for complex systems programs. In *OSDI'08*.

[12] M. Castro, M. Costa, and J.-P. Martin. Better bug reporting with better privacy. In *ASPLOS'08*.

[13] S. Chen, M. Kozuch, T. Strigkos, B. Falsafi, P. B. Gibbons, T. C. Mowry, V. Ramachandran, O. Ruwase, M. Ryan, and E. Vlachos. Flexible hardware acceleration for instruction-grain program monitoring. In *ISCA'08*.

[14] L. Chew and D. Lie. Kivati: fast detection and prevention of atomicity violations. In *EuroSys'10*.

[15] T. M. Chilimbi, B. Liblit, K. Mehra, A. V. Nori, and K. Vaswani. HOLMES: Effective statistical debugging via efficient path profiling. In *ICSE'09*.

[16] I. Cohen, S. Zhang, M. Goldszmidt, J. Symons, T. Kelly, and A. Fox. Capturing, indexing, clustering, and retrieving system history. In *SOSP'05*.

[17] M. Costa, M. Castro, L. Zhou, L. Zhang, and M. Peinado. Bouncer: securing software by blocking bad input. In *SOSP'07*.

[18] Dell. Streamlined Troubleshooting with the Dell system E-Support tool. *Dell Power Solutions*, 2008.

[19] D. L. Detlefs, K. R. M. Leino, K. Rustan, M. Leino, G. Nelson, and J. B. Saxe. Extended static checking. In *TR SRC-159, COMPAQ SRC*, 1998.

[20] J. Devietti, B. Lucia, M. Oskin, and L. Ceze. Dmp: Deterministic shared-memory multiprocessing. In *ASPLOS'09*.

[21] G. Dunlap, D. Lucchetti, M. Fetterman, and P. Chen. Execution replay of multiprocessor virtual machines. In *VEE*, 2008.

[22] The DWARF Debugging Format. `http://dwarfstd.org`.

[23] D. Engler and K. Ashcraft. Racerx: effective, static detection of race conditions and deadlocks. In *SOSP'03*.

[24] C. Flanagan, K. R. M. Leino, M. Lillibridge, G. Nelson, J. B. Saxe, and R. Stata. Extended static checking for java. In *PLDI'02*.

[25] Man page for gcore (Linux section 1).

[26] K. Glerum, K. Kinshumann, S. Greenberg, G. Aul, V. Orgovan, G. Nichols, D. Grant, G. Loihle, and G. Hunt. Debugging in the (very) large: ten years of implementation and experience. In *SOSP '09*.

[27] Google Inc., Breakpad.

[28] Z. Guo, X. Wang, J. Tang, X. Liu, Z. Xu, M. Wu, M. F. Kaashoek, and Z. Zhang. R2: An application-level kernel for record and replay. In *OSDI'08*.

[29] J. Ha, C. J. Rossbach, J. V. Davis, I. Roy, H. E. Ramadan, D. E. Porter, D. L. Chen, and E. Witchel. Improved error reporting for software that uses black-box components. In *PLDI'07*.

[30] B. Hackett and A. Aiken. How is aliasing used in systems software? In *FSE'06*.

[31] A. Kadav, M. J. Renzelmann, and M. M. Swift. Tolerating hardware device failures in software. In *SOSP'09*.

[32] B. W. Kernighan and R. Pike. *The Practice of Programming*. Addison-Wesley, 1999.

[33] S. T. King, G. W. Dunlap, and P. M. Chen. Debugging operating systems with time-traveling virtual machines. In *USENIX ATC'05*.

[34] T. J. LeBlanc and J. M. Mellor-Crummey. Debugging parallel programs with instant replay. *IEEE Trans. Comput.*, 36(4), 1987.

[35] D. Lee, B. Wester, K. Veeraraghavan, S. Narayanasamy, P. M. Chen, and J. Flinn. Respec: efficient online multiprocessor replay via speculation and external determinism. In *ASPLOS'10*.

[36] Z. Li, L. Tan, X. Wang, S. Lu, Y. Zhou, and C. Zhai. Have things changed now? An empirical study of bug characteristics in modern open source software. In *ASID '06: Proceedings of the 1st workshop on Architectural and system support for improving software dependability*, October 2006.

[37] B. Liblit, A. Aiken, A. X. Zheng, and M. I. Jordan. Bug isolation via remote program sampling. In *PLDI'03*.

[38] B. Lucia, L. Ceze, and K. Strauss. Colorsafe: architectural support for debugging and dynamically avoiding multi-variable atomicity violations. In *ISCA'10*.

[39] R. Manevich, M. Sridharan, S. Adams, M. Das, and Z. Yang. PSE: Explaining program failures via postmortem static analysis. *SIGSOFT Softw. Eng. Notes*, 29(6):63–72, 2004.

[40] P. Montesinos, L. Ceze, and J. Torrellas. Delorean: Recording and deterministically replaying shared-memory multiprocessor execution efficiently. In *ISCA'08*.

[41] Mozilla Quality Feedback Agent. `http://support.mozilla.com/en-US/kb/quality+feedback+agent`.

[42] M. Naik and A. Aiken. Conditional must not aliasing for static race detection. In *POPL'07*.

[43] M. Naik, A. Aiken, and J. Whaley. Effective static race detection for java. In *PLDI'06*.

[44] S. Narayanasamy, G. Pokam, and B. Calder. Bugnet: Continuously recording program execution for deterministic replay debugging. In *ISCA'05*.

[45] G. C. Necula, S. McPeak, S. P. Rahul, and W. Weimer. Cil: Intermediate language and tools for analysis and transformation of c programs. In *CC'02*.

[46] NetApp Inc., Savecore. ONTAP 7.3 Manual Page Reference, Volume 1, Pages 471-472.

[47] NetApp. Proactive health management with auto-support. *NetApp White Paper*, 2007.

[48] G. Novark, E. D. Berger, and B. G. Zorn. Exterminator: automatically correcting memory errors with high probability. In *PLDI'07*.

[49] M. Olszewski, J. Ansel, and S. Amarasinghe. Kendo: Efficient Deterministic Multithreading in software. In *ASPLOS'09*.

[50] S. Park, W. Xiong, Z. Yin, R. Kaushik, K. H.Lee, S. Lu, and Y. Zhou. Pres:probabilistic replay with execution sketching on multiprocessors. In *SOSP*, 2009.

[51] S. Schmidt. 7 more good tips on logging. `http://codemonkeyism.com/7-more-good-tips-on-logging/`.

[52] E. Vlachos, M. L. Goodstein, M. A. Kozuch, S. Chen, B. Falsafi, P. B. Gibbons, and T. C. Mowry. Paralog: enabling and accelerating online parallel monitoring of multithreaded applications. In *ASPLOS'10*.

[53] VMware. Using the integrated virtual debugger for visual studio. http://www.vmware.com/pdf/ws65_manual.pdf.

[54] D. Weeratunge, X. Zhang, and S. Jagannathan. Analyzing multicore dumps to facilitate concurrency bug reproduction. *SIGARCH Comput. Archit. News*, 38(1):155–166, 2010.

[55] M. Xu, R. Bodik, and M. Hill. A "flight data recorder" for enabling full-system multiprocessor deterministic replay. In *ISCA'03*.

[56] W. Xu, L. Huang, M. Jordan, D. Patterson, and A. Fox. Mining console logs for large-scale system problem detection. In *SOSP'09*.

[57] D. Yuan, H. Mai, W. Xiong, L. Tan, Y. Zhou, and S. Pasupathy. SherLog: Error diagnosis by connecting clues from run-time logs. In *ASPLOS'10*.

[58] C. Zamfir and G. Candea. Execution synthesis: a technique for automated software debugging. In *EuroSys'10*.

[59] C. Zamfir and G. Candea. Low-overhead bug fingerprinting for fast debugging. In *Runtime Verification*, volume 6418 of *Lecture Notes in Computer Science*, pages 460–468. 2010.

[60] Q. Zhao, R. Rabbah, S. Amarasinghe, L. Rudolph, and W.-F. Wong. How to do a million watchpoints: efficient debugging using dynamic instrumentation. In *CC'08*.

# DoublePlay: Parallelizing Sequential Logging and Replay

Kaushik Veeraraghavan Dongyoon Lee Benjamin Wester Jessica Ouyang
Peter M. Chen Jason Flinn Satish Narayanasamy
University of Michigan
{kaushikv,dongyoon,bwester,jouyang,pmchen,jflinn,nsatish}@umich.edu

## Abstract

*Deterministic replay systems record and reproduce the execution of a hardware or software system. In contrast to replaying execution on uniprocessors, deterministic replay on multiprocessors is very challenging to implement efficiently because of the need to reproduce the order or values read by shared memory operations performed by multiple threads. In this paper, we present DoublePlay, a new way to efficiently guarantee replay on commodity multiprocessors. Our key insight is that one can use the simpler and faster mechanisms of single-processor record and replay, yet still achieve the scalability offered by multiple cores, by using an additional execution to parallelize the record and replay of an application. DoublePlay timeslices multiple threads on a single processor, then runs multiple time intervals (*epochs*) of the program concurrently on separate processors. This strategy, which we call* uniparallelism, *makes logging much easier because each epoch runs on a single processor (so threads in an epoch never simultaneously access the same memory) and different epochs operate on different copies of the memory. Thus, rather than logging the order of shared-memory accesses, we need only log the order in which threads in an epoch are timesliced on the processor. DoublePlay runs an additional execution of the program on multiple processors to generate checkpoints so that epochs run in parallel. We evaluate DoublePlay on a variety of client, server, and scientific parallel benchmarks; with spare cores, DoublePlay reduces logging overhead to an average of 15% with two worker threads and 28% with four threads.*

***Categories and Subject Descriptors*** D.4.7 [*Operating Systems*]: Organization and Design; D.4.8 [*Operating Systems*]: Performance

***General Terms*** Design, Performance, Reliability

***Keywords*** Deterministic Replay, Uniparallelism

## 1. Introduction

Deterministic replay systems record and reproduce the execution of a hardware or software system. The ability to faithfully reproduce an execution has proven useful in many areas, including debugging [15, 36, 40], fault tolerance [5], computer forensics [9], dynamic analysis [7, 26], and workload capture [22, 46].


*ASPLOS'11,* March 5–11, 2011, Newport Beach, California, USA.


Deterministic replay systems work by logging all nondeterministic events during a recording phase, then reproducing these events during a replay phase. On uniprocessors, nondeterministic events (e.g., interrupts and data from input devices) occur relatively infrequently, so logging and replaying them adds little overhead [46]. If there are multiple threads running on the uniprocessor, these can be replayed at low overhead by logging and reproducing the thread schedule [33]. On multiprocessors, however, shared-memory accesses add a high-frequency source of nondeterminism, and logging and replaying these accesses can drastically reduce performance.

Many ideas have been proposed to reduce the overhead of logging and replaying shared-memory, multithreaded programs on multiprocessors, but all fall short in some way. Some approaches require custom hardware [12, 20, 21, 45]. Other approaches cannot replay programs with data races [32] or are prohibitively slow for applications with a high degree of sharing [10]. Some recent approaches provide the ability to replay only while the recording is in progress [18] or sacrifice the guarantee of being able to replay the recorded execution without the possibility of a prohibitively long search [1, 30, 43, 47].

In this paper, we describe a new way to guarantee deterministic replay on commodity multiprocessors. Our method combines the simplicity and low recording overhead of logging a multithreaded program on a uniprocessor with the speed and scalability of executing that program on a multiprocessor.

Our key insight is that one can use the simpler and faster mechanisms of single-processor record and replay, yet still achieve the scalability offered by multiple cores, by using an additional execution to parallelize the record and replay of an application. Our goal is for the single-processor execution to be as fast as a traditional parallel execution, but to retain the ease-of-logging of single-processor multithreaded execution.

To accomplish this goal, we observe that there are (at least) two ways to run a multithreaded program on multiple processors, which we call *thread parallelism* and *epoch parallelism*. With thread parallelism, the threads of a multithreaded program run on multiple processors. While this traditional method of parallelization can achieve good scalability, it is expensive to log the shared-memory accesses from multiple threads running simultaneously. With epoch parallelism, multiple time intervals (*epochs*) of the program run concurrently. This style of parallelism has also been called Master/Slave Speculative Parallelism by Zilles [48] and Predictor/Executor by Süßkraut [39].

*Uniparallel execution* runs a thread-parallel and an epoch-parallel execution of a program concurrently. It further constrains the epoch-parallel execution so that all threads for a given epoch execute on a single processor. This strategy makes logging much easier because multiple threads in an epoch never simultaneously access the same memory, and because different epochs operate on different copies of the memory. Thus, rather than logging the order of shared-memory accesses, we need only log the order in which threads in an epoch are timesliced on the processor.

To run epochs in parallel, we must generate checkpoints from which to start each of the epochs, and we must generate these checkpoints early enough to start future epochs before the earlier ones finish. Uniparallel execution generates these checkpoints speculatively by combining thread parallelism and online replay [18]. A thread-parallel execution runs ahead of the epoch-parallel execution and generates checkpoints from which to start future epochs. If these checkpoints diverge from the state produced by the epoch-parallel execution, we abort all epochs that started after the divergence, roll back, and restart from the last matching state. We reduce the chance of divergence by logging a subset of the non-deterministic events in the thread-parallel execution (e.g., the order of synchronization operations) and using this log to guide the execution of the epoch-parallel execution down a similar path.

This approach supports deterministic replay on commodity multiprocessors without needing to log shared-memory accesses. Replaying multithreaded programs on multiprocessors becomes as easy as replaying multithreaded programs on uniprocessors, while still preserving the speed and scalability of parallel execution. The main overhead of this approach is the use of more cores to run two instances of the program during logging. We believe the advent of many-core processors makes this a worthwhile tradeoff: the number of cores per computer is expected to grow exponentially, and scaling applications to use these extra cores is notoriously difficult.

To demonstrate these ideas, we implement a system called *DoublePlay* that can take advantage of spare cores to log multithreaded programs on multiprocessors at low overhead and guarantee being able to replay them deterministically. We evaluate the performance of DoublePlay on a variety of client, server, and scientific parallel benchmarks. We find that, with spare cores, DoublePlay increases run time by an average of 15% with two worker threads and 28% with four worker threads, and that DoublePlay can replay the run later without much additional overhead. On computers without spare cores, DoublePlay adds approximately 100% overhead for CPU-bound applications that can scale to 8 cores; this compares favorably with other software solutions that provide guaranteed deterministic replay.

Our paper is organized as follows. Section 2 describes other approaches to replaying multithreaded programs on multiprocessors. Section 3 discusses the principle of uniparallelism. Sections 4 and 5 describe the design and implementation of DoublePlay. Section 6 reports on how DoublePlay performs for a range of benchmarks, and Section 7 concludes.

## 2. Related work

Because of its wide array of uses, deterministic replay has been the subject of intense research by the hardware and software systems communities.

Many of the early replay systems focused on uniprocessor replay; e.g., IGOR [11], Hypervisor [5], Mach 3.0 Replay [33], DejaVu [6], ReVirt [9], and Flashback [36]. The designers of these systems observed that when executing a multithreaded program on a uniprocessor, there are many fewer thread switch events than accesses to shared memory. DoublePlay leverages this observation by logging and replaying epochs that each run the multithreaded program on a single processor, while taking advantage of multiple processors by starting multiple epochs in parallel.

Multiprocessor replay has been a particular area of focus in recent years because of the growing prevalence of multi-core processors. The main difficulty in replaying multithreaded programs on multiprocessors is logging and replaying shared memory accesses efficiently. One approach is to log the order of shared accesses [16], but this incurs high overhead. SMP-ReVirt [10] uses page protections to log only the order of conflicting accesses to memory pages, but this still incurs high overhead for some applications because of the cost of memory protection faults and false sharing. Another approach is to log and replay the values returned by load instructions [4, 23], but this also incurs high overhead.

One way to reduce the overhead of logging multiprocessors is to add hardware support. The most common strategy is to modify the cache coherence mechanism to log the information needed to infer the order of shared memory accesses [2, 12, 20, 21, 24, 42]. While these approaches are promising, we would like to support deterministic replay on commodity multiprocessors.

Another response to the high overhead of logging multiprocessors is to reduce the scope of programs that can be replayed. RecPlay [32] logs only explicit synchronization operations and so is unable to replay programs with unsynchronized accesses to shared memory (data races). DoublePlay also logs synchronization operations, but it uses these only as hints to guide the execution of the epoch-parallel run; DoublePlay guarantees deterministic replay for programs with and without data races by logging all non-determinism in the epoch-parallel run.

Researchers have also tried to reduce logging overhead by relaxing the definition of deterministic replay. Instead of requiring that all instructions return the same data returned in the original run, these approaches provide slightly weaker guarantees, which still support the proposed uses of replay. PRES [30] and ODR [1] guarantee that all failures in the original run are also visible during replay, where failures are usually defined as the output of the program and program errors (e.g., assertions). Respec [18] guarantees that both the output and the ending state of the replayed execution match the logged execution. DoublePlay requires the same criteria as Respec for deterministic replay when evaluating whether the epoch-parallel execution matches the thread-parallel execution, since this guarantees that each checkpoint that starts a future epoch matches the ending state of the prior epoch.

Respec also distinguishes between online and offline replay [18]. Online replay refers to the ability to replay while the recording is in progress; offline replay refers to the ability to replay after the recording is complete. Respec provides only online replay. DoublePlay uses online replay, but only for the purpose of guiding the epoch-parallel execution. DoublePlay supports offline replay by logging and replaying the epoch-parallel execution.

Another way to reduce logging overhead is to shift work from the recording phase to the offline replay phase. To achieve this, recent research has investigated an alternate approach to deterministic replay based on *search* [1, 17, 30, 43, 47]. Rather than logging enough data to quickly replay an execution, these systems record a subset of information (e.g., synchronization operations or core dumps), then use that information to guide the search for an equivalent execution. The search space includes all possible orders of shared-memory accesses that are allowed by the logged information, so it grows exponentially with the number of racing accesses. With good heuristics, search-based replay can often find equivalent executions quickly, especially for programs with few racing accesses. However, because of the exponential search space, they may not be able to find an equivalent execution within a reasonable time frame. In addition, even if the search succeeds within a few tries, the execution of the program during search can be slowed by several orders of magnitude due to the need to log the detailed order of shared-memory accesses [30]. DoublePlay logs similar information as some of these systems (e.g., the SYS configuration in PRES [30]), so its recording should add a similar amount of overhead to the original application. One can view DoublePlay as using extra cores to search for an equivalent replay *during the original run*. However, while other systems risk not being able to later find an equivalent run quickly (or at all), DoublePlay verifies during recording that the epoch-parallel execution matches the thread-parallel execution. While DoublePlay must execute intervals that contain races sequentially, this is unlikely to slow the program significantly because these intervals are likely to be a small fraction of the overall execution time.

Deterministic replay helps reproduce non-deterministic multiprocessor executions. An alternative approach is to ensure that all inter-thread communication is deterministic for a given input [3, 8, 13, 28]. This approach eliminates the need to log the order of shared-memory accesses. However, current solutions for deterministic execution only support programs that are free of data races [28], require language [13] or hardware [8] support, or only support programs with fork-join parallelism.

Finally, DoublePlay applies ideas from research on using speculation to run applications in parallel, such as thread-level speculation [29, 35, 37]. In particular, Master/Slave Speculative Parallelization [48], Speck [26], and Fast Track [14] also use a fast execution to start multiple slow executions in parallel. DoublePlay applies this idea in a new way by using a fast, thread-parallel execution on multiple processors to start multiple uniprocessor executions that execute threads sequentially on one processor. As both the thread-parallel and uniprocessor executions run the same program, DoublePlay could leverage the speculative control and data flow prediction scheme introduced in SlipStream [38] so the leading thread-parallel execution communicates values and branch outcomes to the trailing epoch-parallel execution, further reducing logging overhead.

In summary, DoublePlay distinguishes itself from prior software-only multiprocessor deterministic replay systems by adding little overhead to application execution time during recording while also guaranteeing that the recorded execution will be able to be replayed in the future in a reasonable amount of time. The cost of this guarantee is that DoublePlay must use additional cores to run two executions of the program during recording.

## 3. Uniparallelism

Many properties are difficult or slow to achieve on a multiprocessor but easy to achieve on a uniprocessor. For example, one can guarantee deterministic replay on a uniprocessor by recording external inputs and scheduling events such as interrupts, but on a multiprocessor, one must also record or infer the order or value of shared memory operations. Other properties that are easier to guarantee on a uniprocessor include sequential consistency and detecting or avoiding certain types of races. Importantly, the cost to provide these properties on a multiprocessor may be much higher than 2x for many benchmarks; techniques that work well on a uniprocessor may become infeasible when two threads execute concurrently on different cores.

Uniparallelism is a technique for achieving the benefits of executing on a uniprocessor, while still allowing application performance to scale with increasing processors. A uniparallel execution consists of both a thread-parallel and epoch-parallel execution of the same program. The epoch-parallel execution runs all threads of a given epoch on a single processor at a time; this enables the use of techniques that run only on a uniprocessor. Unlike a traditional thread-parallel execution that scales with the number of cores by running different threads on different cores, an epoch-parallel execution achieves scalability in a different way, namely by concurrently running different epochs (time slices) of the execution on multiple cores. Epoch-parallel execution thus requires the ability to predict future program states; such predictions are generated by running the second, thread-parallel execution concurrently. Consequently, for CPU-bound workloads, uniparallel execution requires twice the number of cores as a traditional execution, leading to an approximately 100% increase in CPU utilization and energy usage (assuming energy-proportional hardware).

Uniparallelism improves performance in two cases. First, if a workload is not CPU-bound or an application cannot scale to effectively use all cores of a multicore computer, the cost of uniparallelism can be much less than 100% (typically less than 20% in our experiments). Second, when the property being provided is more than twice as expensive on a multiprocessor as on a uniprocessor (as is often the case for deterministic replay), it is more efficient in terms of both time and energy to run the application twice with uniparallelism than to provide the property directly on the multiprocessor version of the application. For instance, even without spare cores, DoublePlay's energy and performance overhead is lower than that of all prior systems which guarantee deterministic replay on commodity multiprocessors.

## 4. Design overview

The goal of DoublePlay is to efficiently record the execution of a process or group of processes running on a multiprocessor such that the execution can later be deterministically replayed as many times as needed. DoublePlay is implemented inside the Linux operating system, and its boundary of record and replay is the process abstraction. The operating system itself is outside the boundary of record and replay, so DoublePlay records the results and order of system calls executed by the process and returns this data to the application during replay.

Figure 1 shows an overview of how DoublePlay records process execution. DoublePlay simultaneously runs two executions of the program being recorded. Each execution uses multiple cores. The execution on the left, which we refer to as the *thread-parallel execution*, runs multiple threads concurrently on the cores allocated to it. DoublePlay partitions the thread-parallel execution into time slices called *epochs*. At the beginning of each epoch, DoublePlay creates a copy-on-write checkpoint of the state of the thread-parallel execution.

The execution on the right, which we refer to as the *epoch-parallel execution*, runs each epoch on one of the cores allocated to it. All threads of a given epoch run on the same core, which simplifies the task of deterministically replaying the resulting execution. DoublePlay achieves good performance by running *different* epochs of the same process *concurrently*. As shown in Figure 1, both the thread-parallel execution and the epoch-parallel execution start running the first epoch simultaneously. However, the thread-parallel execution runs the epoch much faster because it uses more cores. When the thread-parallel execution reaches the start of the second epoch, DoublePlay checkpoints the process state and uses that state to start running the second epoch in the epoch-parallel execution. By the time the thread-parallel execution is running the fourth epoch, the epoch-parallel execution is able to fully utilize the four cores allocated to it. From this point on, the epoch-parallel execution can achieve speedup from parallelization roughly equivalent to that achieved by the thread-parallel execution.

During recording, DoublePlay saves three items that are sufficient to guarantee that the process execution can be replayed deterministically in the future. First, DoublePlay records the initial state of the process at the start of recording. Second, DoublePlay records the order and results of system calls, signals, and low-level synchronization operations in GNU `libc`. Finally, DoublePlay records the schedule of thread execution (i.e., when context switches between threads occur) of the epoch-parallel execution. Note that since each epoch is executed on a single core in the epoch-parallel execution, DoublePlay does not need to record the ordering or results of any shared memory operations performed by multiple threads; the three items above are sufficient to exactly recreate identical operations during replay.

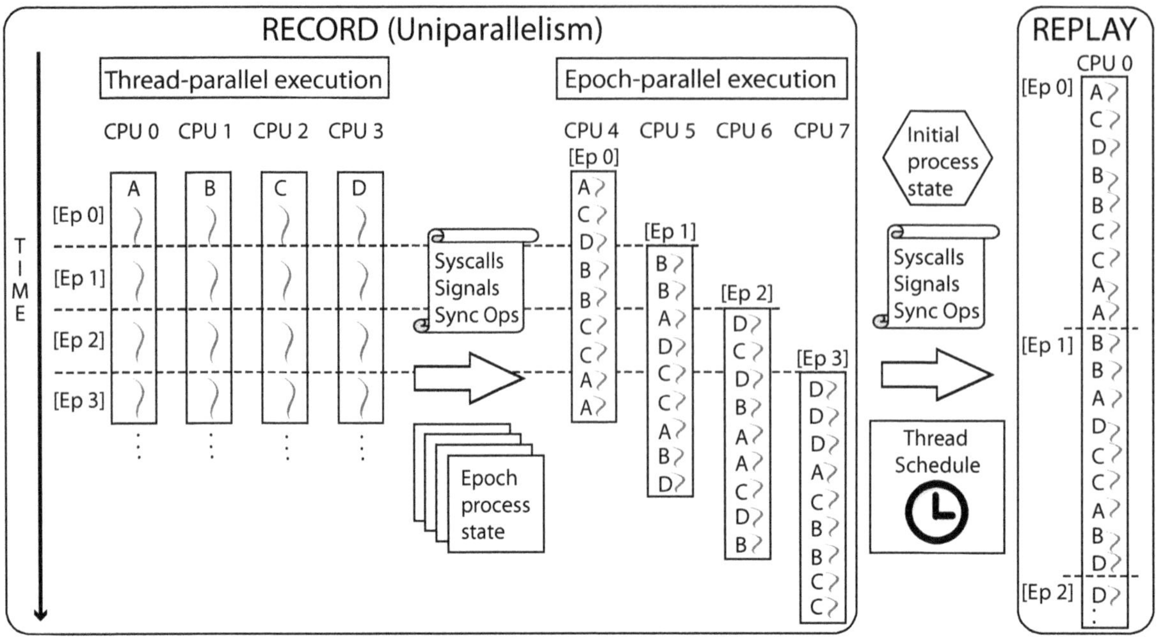


**Figure 1.** Overview of DoublePlay record and replay

The two executions can be viewed as follows. The epoch-parallel execution is the actual execution of the program that is being recorded. Because each epoch of the epoch-parallel execution runs on a single core, DoublePlay can use the simple and efficient mechanisms for uniprocessor deterministic replay to record and replay its execution. The thread-parallel execution allows the epoch-parallel execution to achieve good performance and scale with the number of cores. The thread-parallel execution provides a *hint* as to what the future state of the process execution will be at each epoch transition. As long as this hint is correct, the state of the process at the beginning of each epoch in the epoch-parallel execution will match the state of the process at the end of the previous epoch. This means that the epochs can be pieced together to form a single, natural execution of the process. This process is akin to splicing movie segments together to form a single coherent video.

But, what if the hint is incorrect? In such an instance, two epochs cannot be pieced together to form a single natural run; the logged run will contain unnatural transitions in program values at epoch boundaries akin to artifacts in a bad video splice. To detect such events, DoublePlay compares the process state (memory values and registers) of the thread-parallel and the epoch-parallel runs at each epoch transition. If the state of the epoch-parallel execution has diverged from the state of the thread-parallel execution, DoublePlay squashes the execution of all subsequent epochs for both executions. It restores the state of the thread-parallel execution to the checkpoint at the beginning of the epoch and restarts both executions from this point.

In Section 5.2.4, we discuss two different implementations for rolling back execution state. The first is a simpler design that rolls both executions back to the start of the epoch that diverged and restarts execution. The second is more complicated, but guarantees forward progress; it rolls both executions back to the state of the epoch-parallel execution at the divergence and restarts both executions from that state.

DoublePlay prevents the process from externalizing any output that depends on the execution of an epoch that may subsequently be rolled back. This means that output cannot be externalized until all prior epochs have been found to be free of divergence. Under the simpler design that rolls back to the start of the epoch, the current epoch must also be checked for divergence. Under the second design, output can be released as soon as the system call that generates that output is called by the epoch-parallel execution.

A divergence between the thread-parallel and epoch-parallel executions can slow performance substantially because it may lead to DoublePlay squashing the execution of several subsequent epochs. DoublePlay uses *online replay* [18] to reduce the frequency of such divergences and their resulting slowdown. During the thread-parallel execution, DoublePlay logs the ordering and results of all system calls and low-level synchronization operations in `libc`. When the epoch-parallel execution executes a system call or synchronization operation, DoublePlay returns the logged result instead of executing the operation. It also delays the thread execution to match the order of operations in the log. Further, DoublePlay logs signals and delivers them only on kernel entry or exit, making their effects deterministic. These actions are sufficient to ensure that the thread-parallel and epoch-parallel executions are identical (and, hence, do not diverge) for any epochs that are free of data races. The only situation in which the thread-parallel and epoch-parallel executions might diverge is when the program contains a data race and two threads execute unsynchronized, conflicting operations on a shared memory address.

At any subsequent time, DoublePlay can replay a recorded execution by (1) restoring the initial state of the recorded process, (2) replaying it on a single core using the logged system calls, signals, and synchronization operations, and (3) using the same schedule of thread execution that was used during the epoch-parallel execution.

Our current implementation only uses a single core during replay. However, DoublePlay could also use uniparallelism to speed up replay. In other words, DoublePlay could execute multiple threads of a replayed process on multiple cores and use the results to spawn concurrent replays of multiple epochs, each on a single core. As during recording, the executions could diverge, in which case, DoublePlay would squash future (incorrect) epochs and start again from the epoch that caused the divergence. This technique would be useful, for example, to skip ahead to the next break point during debugging.

## 5. Implementation

The implementation of DoublePlay leverages our prior Respec [18] work to provide deterministic online replay. Respec ensures that two concurrent executions of the same process are *externally deterministic*, which we define to mean that the two executions execute the same system calls in the same order, and that the program state (values in the address space and registers) of the two processes are identical at the end of each epoch of execution.

Respec only ensures external determinism while two processes execute at the same time. It does not address deterministic replay of a process after the original execution completes; therefore, it cannot be used for offline debugging, intrusion analysis, and other activities that must take place after an execution finishes. DoublePlay builds on top of Respec to provide this capability.

We first provide background information about the design and implementation of Respec. We then describe how DoublePlay extends Respec to support offline deterministic replay.

### 5.1 Respec background

Respec is a system in the Linux kernel that runs two executions of a multithreaded process (or set of processes) concurrently. When Respec is invoked by a process, Respec duplicates the process's state via a *multi-threaded fork* that clones both its address space and the execution state of all concurrently executing threads. Respec then executes the cloned copy concurrently with the original execution.

The original and cloned executions have a producer-consumer relationship. When the original execution performs a system call, Respec writes the arguments and results of the call to a circular buffer. Respec logs the total order of system call entry and exit across all threads. During the cloned execution, Respec enforces the same total order by blocking threads when they enter or exit a system call until all prior entries in the circular buffer have been consumed. For most system calls, Respec does not re-execute the actual system call during the cloned execution; instead, it simply provides the results obtained by the original execution. Respec does re-execute system calls such as `clone` and `mmap` that change the process's address space to support subsequent loads and stores; it serializes these operations in both executions to ensure that they are performed deterministically. Respec also logs the value and timing of signals in this log, and delivers signals at the same point in both executions. To reduce log size, we modified Respec to assume that the underlying file system is copy-on-write [31, 34], so that it can delay logging large file reads until such files are actually modified. File system interfaces exist that let systems such as Respec create custom file versioning policies [41].

At user-level, Respec also writes to a circular buffer the low-level synchronization operations in `libc` performed by the original execution, such as lock acquisition, waits, and wakeups. In contrast to the system calls, Respec only records a happens-before partial order of synchronization operations and enforces this partial order during the cloned execution. Enforcing the recorded partial order for synchronization operations ensures that all shared memory accesses are ordered, provided the program is race free.

Combined, these mechanisms are sufficient to ensure that the original and cloned executions execute identically in the absence of data races. However, a benign or malign data race may cause the two executions to diverge. Respec divides the executions into semi-regular intervals called epochs. During each epoch, it compares the arguments passed to all system calls, and, at the end of each epoch, it verifies that the memory and register state of the original and cloned executions match. To reduce the cost of such comparisons, Respec only compares memory pages modified during the execution of the prior epoch.

Respec uses Speculator [25] to checkpoint the original execution at the beginning of each epoch. Each checkpoint is a copy-on-write fork of the process address space, so that only pages modified in an epoch are duplicated. Read-shared pages thus do not increase memory or cache overhead. If the divergence check succeeds, Respec commits the checkpoint. If the check fails, it rolls back the state of both executions to the checkpoint and tries the execution again. During an epoch, the recording process is prevented from committing any external output (e.g., writing to the console or network). Instead, its outputs are buffered in the kernel. Outputs buffered during an epoch are only externalized after both processes have finished executing the epoch and the divergence check succeeds. They are discarded on a rollback. Thus, epochs that are later rolled back are not visible to any external observer.

To summarize, the guarantees provided by Respec are: (1) the original and cloned executions produce the same external outputs (more precisely, the same system calls) in the same order, and (2) the memory and register state of the two executions are identical at epoch boundaries.

### 5.2 Supporting offline replay

DoublePlay uses Respec during recording to coordinate the thread-parallel and epoch-parallel executions. From the point of view of Respec, the thread-parallel execution is the original execution and the epoch-parallel execution is the cloned execution. DoublePlay makes several enhancements to the basic Respec infrastructure in order to support offline replay, which we describe in the following sections.

#### 5.2.1 Enabling concurrent epoch execution

DoublePlay needs to run multiple epochs concurrently, while Respec runs only a single epoch at a time. DoublePlay therefore makes multiple copies of the thread-parallel execution by calling the multi-threaded fork primitive before starting the execution of each individual epoch. This primitive creates a new process whose state is identical to that of the thread-parallel execution at that point in its execution. Each time a new process is created, DoublePlay does not let it begin execution, but instead places it in an *epoch queue* ordered by process creation time.

The DoublePlay scheduler is responsible for deciding when and where each process will run. Currently, the scheduler uses a simple policy that reserves half of the available cores for the thread-parallel execution and half for the epoch-parallel execution. It uses the Linux *sched_setaffinity* system call to constrain process execution to specific cores. As long as cores remain available, the scheduler pulls the next process from the epoch queue, allocates a core to it, constrains it to execute on only that core, and wakes up the process. When the process completes executing the epoch, it informs the scheduler that the core is now free, and the scheduler allocates the core to the next process in the epoch queue.

Even though DoublePlay starts execution of the epochs in the epoch-parallel execution in sequential order, there is no guarantee that epoch execution will *finish* in order, since some epochs are much shorter than others. DoublePlay uses an adaptive algorithm to vary epoch lengths. It sets the epoch length to 50 ms after a rollback. Each epoch without a rollback increases the epoch length by 50 ms up to a maximum of one second. Further, by leveraging output-triggered commits [27], DoublePlay ends an epoch immediately if a system call requires synchronous external output and no later than 50 ms after asynchronous external output. Network applications have much external output, so they have many short epochs even with few rollbacks.

Even though epochs may finish out of order, DoublePlay ensures that they commit or roll back in sequential order. When a epoch completes execution, DoublePlay performs a divergence check by comparing its memory and register state to that of the checkpoint associated with the next epoch. Once this check passes, DoublePlay allows the process to exit and allocates its processor to another epoch. If all prior epochs have been committed, DoublePlay also commits the epoch and discards the checkpoint for that epoch. Otherwise, it simply marks the epoch as completed. After all prior epochs commit, DoublePlay will commit that epoch.

In its strictest form of verification, DoublePlay considers a divergence check to fail if (1) a thread in the epoch-parallel execution calls a different system call from the one called by the corresponding thread in the thread-parallel execution, (2) the two threads call different `libc` synchronization operations, (3) the two threads call the same system call or synchronization operation, but with different arguments, or (4) the registers or memory state of the two executions differ at the end of the epoch. In Section 5.2.5, we describe how we loosen these restrictions slightly to reduce unnecessary rollbacks.

When a divergence check fails, DoublePlay terminates all threads executing the current epoch and any future epochs in the epoch-parallel execution, as well as all threads of the thread-parallel execution, by sending them kill signals. However, epochs started prior to the one that failed the divergence check may still be executing for the epoch-parallel execution. DoublePlay allows these epochs to finish and complete their divergence checks. If these checks succeed, DoublePlay restarts the thread-parallel execution from the failed epoch. If a check for one of the prior epochs fails, it restarts execution from the earliest epoch that failed.

### 5.2.2 Replaying thread schedules

DoublePlay guarantees deterministic offline replay by executing each epoch on a single core using the same thread schedule that was used during recording by the epoch-parallel execution. There are two basic strategies for providing this property. One strategy is to use the same *deterministic scheduler* during epoch-parallel execution and offline replay. The second strategy is to *log the scheduling decisions* made during epoch-parallel execution and replay those decisions deterministically during offline replay.

To implement these strategies, we added a custom scheduler layer that chooses exactly one thread at a time to be run by the Linux scheduler and blocks all other threads on a wait queue. When the DoublePlay scheduler decides to execute a new thread, it blocks the previously-executing thread on the wait queue and unblocks only the thread that it chooses to run. It would also have been possible to implement these strategies by modifying the Linux scheduler, but this would have required instrumenting all scheduling decisions made in Linux.

To implement the first strategy (the deterministic scheduler), DoublePlay assigns a strict priority to each thread based on the order in which the threads are created. DoublePlay always chooses to run the highest-priority thread eligible to run that would preserve the total ordering of system calls and the partial ordering of synchronization operations.

To preserve system call ordering, the thread-parallel execution assigns a sequence number to every system call entry or exit when it is added to the circular buffer. A thread in the epoch-parallel execution only consumes an entry if it has a sequence number one greater than the entry last consumed. Thus, a high-priority thread whose next entry is several sequence numbers in the future must block until low-priority threads consume the intervening entries. Similarly, DoublePlay uses multiple sequence numbers to represent the partial order of user-level synchronization operations. Specifically, the address of each lock or futex accessed in a synchronization operation is hashed to one of 512 separate counters, each of which represents a separate sequence number. Note that once a low-priority thread consumes an entry in either buffer, a higher-priority thread may become eligible to run. In this instance, DoublePlay immediately blocks the low-priority thread and unblocks the high-priority thread. For any given set of system calls and synchronization operations, this algorithm produces a deterministic schedule. That is, context switches always occur at the same point in each thread's execution.

This first strategy is relatively easy to implement and requires no additional logging. However, it is difficult to allow preemptions in this strategy, because doing so would require inserting preemptions deterministically [28]. Allowing preemptions has two benefits: it allows uniparallel to reproduce any bug that manifests on sequentially-consistent hardware, and it maintains liveness in the presence of spin locks.

To allow preemptions, we implemented a second strategy for replaying thread schedules deterministically, which is to log the preemptions that occur during epoch-parallel execution and replay those decisions deterministically during offline replay. In order to deterministically reproduce preemptions, we record the instruction pointer and branch count of a thread when it is preempted during epoch-parallel execution. The branch count is necessary because the instruction could be inside a loop, and we must replay the preemption on the correct iteration [19]. These branch counts are maintained per thread and obtained using hardware performance monitoring counters configured to count branches executed in user-space [5]. We compensate for return from interrupt (`iret`) branches, which would otherwise cause interrupts to perturb the branch count non-deterministically. After recording the instruction pointer and branch count, we unblock the next thread. In offline replay, we preempt a thread when it reaches the recorded instruction pointer and branch count and allow the next thread to run.

As with all deterministic replay systems, DoublePlay perturbs the execution that it is logging. When using deterministic replay for debugging, such perturbations may change the likelihood of encountering particular bugs. Epoch parallelism avoids the perturbation due to instrumenting shared memory accesses, but adds perturbation due to timeslicing a multithreaded program onto a uniprocessor. The degree to which timeslicing changes the likelihood that a particular bug will manifest depends on the particular scheduling algorithm being used (e.g., certain race conditions may occur infrequently with coarse-grained timeslicing).

### 5.2.3 Offline replay

To support offline replay, DoublePlay records the system calls and synchronization operations executed during an epoch in a set of log files (for simplicity, DoublePlay uses a separate log for each thread). After committing each epoch, DoublePlay marks the entries belonging to that epoch as eligible to be written to disk. It then writes the marked records out asynchronously while other epochs are executing. Note that DoublePlay only has to record the results of synchronization operations and system calls, since the arguments to those calls will be deterministically reproduced by any offline replay process. This reduces log size considerably for system calls such as `write`. Signals are logged with the system calls after which they are delivered.

If a rollback occurs, DoublePlay deallocates any records in the circular buffer that occurred after the point in the thread-parallel execution to which it is rolling back (these records cannot have been written to disk since the epoch has not yet committed). It also ensures that all entries that precede the rollback point are written to disk before restoring the checkpoint. The checkpoint includes the sequence numbers at the point in execution where the checkpoint was taken, so subsequent entries will have the correct sequence number. Thus, there is no indication of the divergence or the rollback in the logs on disk.

DoublePlay saves the initial state of the process when recording began. To perform an offline replay, it starts from this initial copy. DoublePlay currently runs the offline replay on a single processor and uses the scheduling algorithm described in Section 5.2.2 to constrain the order of thread execution for the offline replay process. When an offline replay thread executes a system call or synchronization operation, DoublePlay returns the results recorded in its log file. The only system calls that DoublePlay actually executes are ones that modify the process address space, such as `mmap` and `clone`. DoublePlay delivers recorded signals at the same point in process execution that they were delivered during recording.

As mentioned in Section 4, DoublePlay could potentially use uniparallel execution to accelerate replay in the same manner that it accelerates recording. With this optimization, we would expect offline replay execution time to be no worse than recording time.

### 5.2.4 Forward recovery

We implemented two different rollback strategies in DoublePlay. Initially, we decided to roll both executions back to the checkpoint at the beginning of the epoch that failed the divergence check. Both executions would restart from this point. If the divergence check again failed, we would roll back and try again. However, we saw some executions in which a given epoch would roll back several times in a row before the divergence check succeeded, presumably because it contained one or more frequently-diverging data races. Frequent rollbacks imposed a substantial performance overhead for some applications; in the worst case, a program with many frequent races could fail to make forward progress.

After consideration, we realized that this strategy reflected the incorrect view that the thread-parallel execution was the run being recorded. In fact, the epoch-parallel execution is the "real" execution being recorded — it is after all the one that is being executed on a single core with a known thread schedule. The epoch-parallel execution is also a perfectly legal execution that could have occurred on the thread-parallel execution with a particular set of relative speeds among the processors (since we verify the ending state of the prior epoch matches the starting state of the next epoch). The thread-parallel execution exists merely as a means for generating hints about future process state so that multiple epochs can be executed in parallel.

Once we viewed the epoch-parallel execution as the one being recorded, it was clear that the state of its execution at the time the divergence check fails is a valid execution state that can be deterministically reproduced offline. Therefore, DoublePlay can use the epoch-parallel process state at the time the divergence check fails as a checkpoint from which to restart execution. We call this process *forward recovery*.

A complication arises because the kernel state is associated only with the thread-parallel execution (because it is the process that actually executes all system calls), while the correct process state is associated with the epoch-parallel execution. DoublePlay detects when the thread-parallel and epoch-parallel executions diverge by comparing the order and arguments of system calls, and the memory and registers after each epoch. At the point of divergence, the (logical) kernel states of the two executions are guaranteed to be identical because the executions have issued the same sequence of system calls up to that point. Because the logical kernel states are identical, it is correct to merge the kernel state of the thread-parallel execution with the memory and register state of the epoch-parallel execution.

DoublePlay logs an undo operation for each system call that modifies kernel state, so that forward (and regular) recovery can roll back kernel state by applying the undo operations. It can thus roll back the thread-parallel execution's kernel state to the system call at which a divergence was detected. It then makes the contents of the address space of the thread-parallel execution equal to the contents of the address space of the epoch-parallel execution at the point where the divergence check failed.

For instance, consider a process with a data race that causes the memory states of the two executions to differ at the end of an epoch. DoublePlay's divergence check already compares the address space of the epoch-parallel execution with a checkpoint of the thread-parallel execution. If any bytes differ, DoublePlay simply copies the corresponding bytes from the epoch-parallel address space to the checkpoint's. DoublePlay then restores the checkpoint to restart the thread-parallel execution; new epoch-parallel executions will be spawned as it proceeds.

Forward recovery guarantees that DoublePlay makes forward progress, even when a divergence check fails. All work done by the epoch-parallel execution up until the divergence check, including at least one data race (the one that triggered the divergence), will be preserved. In the worst case, every epoch may contain frequent data races, and divergence checks might always fail. However, even in this case, DoublePlay should be able to approach the speed of uniprocessor replay since a single core can always make progress. In the expected scenario where data races are relatively infrequent, DoublePlay runs much faster.

### 5.2.5 Looser divergence checks

In our initial design for DoublePlay, we made the divergence check very strict because we wanted to detect a divergence as soon as possible in order to minimize the amount of work thrown away on a rollback. However, once we implemented forward recovery, we decided that strict divergence checks might no longer be best. As long as the epoch-parallel execution can continue its execution, any work that it completes will be preserved after a rollback.

Even with forward recovery, it is still necessary to check memory and register state at each epoch boundary. If the process state at the end of an epoch of the epoch-parallel execution does not match the state from which the next epoch execution starts, the epoch-parallel executions of all subsequent epochs are invalid and must be squashed. However, strict divergence checks are not necessarily required *within* an epoch.

As long as the external output of the epoch-parallel execution continues to match the external output of the thread-parallel execution, then the system calls and synchronization operations performed by the two executions can be allowed to diverge slightly. On the other hand, if one of these operations can affect state external to the process, then the state changes cannot be made visible to an external entity and all subsequent results from system calls and synchronization operations must be consistent with the divergence.

Based on this observation, we modified DoublePlay to support three slightly looser forms of divergence checks within an epoch. First, if a thread's circular buffer contains a system call with no effect outside that thread, but the epoch-parallel execution omits that system call, we allow it to skip over the extra record in the buffer. Examples of such system calls are `getpid` and `nanosleep`.

Second, if a thread executes a system call that produces output for an external device such as the screen or network, the epoch-parallel execution is allowed to execute the same system call with different output. Because DoublePlay buffers such output in the kernel until after both executions have completed the system call, no external entity observes this output prior to the execution of the call by the epoch-parallel execution. Because that execution is logically the "real" execution, we simply release its output, rather than the output from the thread-parallel execution, to external observers. The observers therefore see the same output during recording and offline replay. The output produced by the thread-parallel execution can be viewed as an incorrect hint that is later corrected.

Third, if a thread executes a set of self-canceling synchronization operations or system calls during the thread-parallel execution, but omits them in the epoch-parallel execution, then all members of the set can be skipped. By self-canceling, we mean two or more operations that when executed together have no effect on state external to the thread. For example, lock and unlock operations for the same low-level lock are a self-canceling pair. If the thread-parallel execution performed both operations, then the epoch-parallel execution can achieve the same effect by performing neither.

Looser divergence checks have two benefits. First, the epoch parallel execution can run longer before a rollback is needed. Second, a rollback can sometimes be avoided all together when the divergence in process state is transitory. For example, one application we tested (pbzip2) has a benign race in which one thread spins waiting for another to set a value. Since the thread calls `nanosleep` periodically, the spin loop executes different numbers of iterations in different executions. With strict divergence checks, such behavior leads to rollbacks. However, with looser divergence checks, the epoch-parallel execution continues past this loop. While different calls to `nanosleep` leave temporary differences on the thread's stack, these differences are soon overwritten by subsequent system calls. Thus, unless the epoch boundary happens immediately after the spin loop, the divergence in program state heals and no rollback is needed.

#### 5.2.6 Reverse scheduling

We implemented one final feature as an option to the deterministic scheduling algorithm, which we refer to as reverse scheduling. The idea behind reverse scheduling is to try to avoid rollbacks when a divergence check fails by finding a different schedule whose execution causes the check to pass. Thus, when a check fails, DoublePlay runs another epoch-parallel execution of the failed epoch on the processor allocated for that epoch, but it uses the opposite scheduling priorities from the ones it used in the failed execution. That is, the last thread created has the highest, not the lowest, priority. The idea is that if there is a single data race in the epoch, then either the normal or reverse schedule is very likely to reproduce the same program state produced by the thread-parallel execution. If the second execution passes the divergence check, the epoch is committed and no rollback occurs. The reverse thread schedule is recorded in the DoublePlay log so that it is also used during replay.

Our results with reverse scheduling were mixed. We found that this feature did in fact eliminate many rollbacks. However, for the applications we tested, fewer rollbacks did not lead to improved performance. One reason is that the forward recovery and loose replay optimizations already eliminated many rollbacks entirely and reduced the performance impact of the remaining ones. Another reason is that reverse scheduling may use CPU time for the second execution yet not eliminate the need for rollback. Thus, while reverse scheduling may prove useful for applications we have not yet tested, DoublePlay currently does not use this feature.

## 6. Evaluation

Our evaluation answers the following questions:

- What is the overhead of DoublePlay record and replay for common applications and benchmarks?
- How often do applications roll back, and what is the effect of rollback on replay time?
- Do our optimizations, namely forward recovery and loose replay, reduce overhead for applications with data races?

### 6.1 Methodology

We used two different 8-core computers to parallelize our evaluation. The first has a 2 GHz 8-core Xeon processor with 3 GB of RAM, while the second has a 2.66 GHz 8-core Xeon with 4 GB of RAM. Both computers run CentOS Linux version 5.3. The kernel is a stock Linux 2.6.26 kernel, modified to include DoublePlay. We also modified the GNU glibc library version 2.5.1 to support DoublePlay. We use our first strategy for replaying thread schedules, i.e. the deterministic scheduler that runs threads according to a strict priority.

We evaluated DoublePlay with 9 benchmarks: five parallel applications (pfscan, pbzip2, aget, the Apache web server, and the mysql database server) and 4 SPLASH-2 [44] benchmarks (fft, radix, ocean, and water). We report three values for each experiment: the original execution time of the application running on a stock system, the execution time during DoublePlay recording, and the execution time for DoublePlay offline replay. The record time measures the time for both the thread-parallel and epoch-parallel executions to finish.

DoublePlay periodically writes the kernel and user-level replay logs to disk so they can be used for offline replay. We report the size of the log and include the time taken to write the log in the recording cost.

We evaluate pbzip2 compressing a 311 MB log file in parallel. We use pfscan to search in parallel for a string in a directory with 952 MB of log files. We extended the benchmark to perform 100 iterations of the search so that we could measure the overhead of deterministic replay over a longer run while ensuring that data is in the file cache (otherwise, our benchmark would be disk-bound). Aget is a bandwidth-stealing application that takes advantage of I/O parallelism by opening multiple connections to a remote server. We used aget to retrieve a 21 MB file over a local network from a server configured to limit each connection to a maximum download bit rate of 1MB/sec. We tested Apache using ab (Apache Bench) to simultaneously send 100 requests from eight concurrent clients over a local network. We evaluate mysql using sysbench version 0.4.12. This benchmark generates 3000 total database queries on a 9 GB myISAM database; 2000 queries are read-only, 600 are updates, and 400 are other types such as table lock and unlock. Since mysql uses a separate worker thread to handle each client, we vary the number of concurrent clients depending on the number of worker threads we are evaluating in each trial.

For each benchmark, we vary the number of worker threads from one to eight for the original execution. DoublePlay uses two cores per worker thread, so we measure its performance with up to four worker threads. Many benchmarks have additional control threads which do little work during the execution; we do not count these in the number of threads. Pbzip2 uses two additional threads: one to read file data and one to write the output; these threads are also not counted in the number of threads shown. Unless otherwise mentioned, all results are the mean of five trials.

### 6.2 Record and replay performance

Table 1 shows the overall performance results for DoublePlay. The first three columns show the application or benchmark executed, the number of worker threads used, and the execution time of the application without DoublePlay. The next seven columns give statistics about DoublePlay execution: the number of user-level synchronization operations logged, system calls logged, epochs executed, memory pages compared, size of the DoublePlay logs written to disk, the average number of rollbacks that occurred per execution, and the time to record an execution. The next column shows the overhead added by DoublePlay during recording, compared to two configurations of the original application. The first overhead is relative to the original application with the same number of appli-

| app | worker threads | original time (s) & stdev. | synch. ops. | system calls | epochs | pages compared | log size (MB) | average rollbacks per run | record time (s) & stdev. | recording overhead | offline time (s) & stdev. |
|---|---|---|---|---|---|---|---|---|---|---|---|
| pfscan | 1 | 193.93 (0.11) | | | | | | | | | |
| | 2 | 100.99 (0.89) | 23302 | 7528 | 101 | 1325 | 1.60 | 0 | 108.38 (0.87) | 7% / 105% | 193.73 (0.26) |
| | 3 | 69.01 (0.26) | 22250 | 7531 | 60 | 868 | 1.55 | 0 | 78.91 (1.01) | 14% / 112% | 190.23 (2.88) |
| | 4 | 52.97 (0.18) | 21575 | 7534 | 50 | 760 | 1.52 | 0 | 59.20 (0.92) | 12% / 102% | 188.19 (1.16) |
| | 6 | 37.18 (0.04) | | | | | | | | | |
| | 8 | 29.26 (0.03) | | | | | | | | | |
| pbzip2 | 1 | 91.65 (0.06) | | | | | | | | | |
| | 2 | 46.08 (0.03) | 26182 | 5481 | 46 | 573243 | 1.30 | 0 | 50.42 (0.41) | 9% / 111% | 92.88 (0.11) |
| | 3 | 31.45 (0.77) | 26025 | 5207 | 31 | 574131 | 1.28 | 0 | 35.92 (0.09) | 14% / 119% | 92.94 (0.29) |
| | 4 | 23.94 (0.38) | 26393 | 5066 | 23 | 562705 | 1.29 | 0 | 29.38 (0.43) | 23% / 128% | 92.85 (0.10) |
| | 6 | 16.38 (0.07) | | | | | | | | | |
| | 8 | 12.90 (0.03) | | | | | | | | | |
| aget | 1 | 21.19 (0.04) | | | | | | | | | |
| | 2 | 10.73 (0.02) | 25243 | 33495 | 22 | 267 | 27.41 | 0.4 | 10.80 (0.06) | 1% / 99% | 0.28 (0.01) |
| | 3 | 7.22 (0.01) | 21564 | 29022 | 20 | 263 | 26.54 | 0.2 | 7.31 (0.08) | 1% / 102% | 0.26 (0.01) |
| | 4 | 5.42 (0.01) | 19618 | 27372 | 20 | 277 | 26.13 | 0.2 | 5.54 (0.15) | 2% / 104% | 0.25 (0.02) |
| | 6 | 3.62 (0.01) | | | | | | | | | |
| | 8 | 2.71 (0.00) | | | | | | | | | |
| apache | 1 | 44.36 (0.13) | | | | | | | | | |
| | 2 | 43.59 (0.27) | 3756 | 3944 | 393 | 5264 | 0.14 | 0.1 | 43.95 (0.33) | 1% / 10% | 0.04 (0.00) |
| | 3 | 41.67 (0.35) | 3682 | 3923 | 386 | 5285 | 0.14 | 1.0 | 42.74 (0.59) | 3% / 11% | 0.04 (0.00) |
| | 4 | 40.13 (0.27) | 3636 | 3904 | 389 | 5383 | 0.14 | 1.7 | 40.75 (0.65) | 2% / 9% | 0.04 (0.00) |
| | 6 | 38.39 (0.41) | | | | | | | | | |
| | 8 | 37.35 (0.61) | | | | | | | | | |
| mysql | 1 | 29.97 (0.08) | | | | | | | | | |
| | 2 | 29.25 (0.09) | 195903 | 46691 | 3035 | 195903 | 13.86 | 0 | 34.89 (0.23) | 19% / 19% | 0.53 (0.00) |
| | 3 | 29.28 (0.08) | 199952 | 46792 | 3052 | 199952 | 14.07 | 0 | 34.98 (0.21) | 19% / 19% | 0.54 (0.00) |
| | 4 | 29.20 (0.08) | 200598 | 46951 | 3069 | 200598 | 14.10 | 0.2 | 34.25 (1.39) | 17% / 17% | 0.55 (0.00) |
| | 6 | 29.33 (0.12) | | | | | | | | | |
| | 8 | 29.35 (0.14) | | | | | | | | | |
| fft | 1 | 117.88 (0.19) | | | | | | | | | |
| | 2 | 58.12 (0.06) | 15689 | 3011 | 67 | 547619 | 0.90 | 0 | 68.72 (0.25) | 18% / 106% | 115.65 (0.11) |
| | 4 | 33.33 (1.08) | 32242 | 3041 | 41 | 333837 | 1.77 | 0 | 43.47 (0.17) | 30% / 131% | 106.61 (0.15) |
| | 8 | 18.79 (0.15) | | | | | | | | | |
| radix | 1 | 177.84 (0.96) | | | | | | | | | |
| | 2 | 89.10 (0.39) | 4571 | 471 | 41 | 1295817 | 0.22 | 0 | 96.88 (0.15) | 9% / 114% | 177.58 (0.23) |
| | 4 | 45.28 (0.28) | 11140 | 607 | 41 | 1313664 | 0.53 | 0 | 53.43 (0.23) | 18% / 127% | 177.73 (0.24) |
| | 8 | 23.50 (0.03) | | | | | | | | | |
| ocean | 1 | 56.67 (0.03) | | | | | | | | | |
| | 2 | 28.19 (0.67) | 108808 | 149 | 32 | 914104 | 4.88 | 0 | 46.09 (0.06) | 63% / 222% | 56.45 (0.03) |
| | 4 | 14.31 (1.35) | 218788 | 222 | 27 | 745697 | 10.44 | 0 | 31.75 (0.26) | 121% / 278% | 53.24 (0.25) |
| | 8 | 8.39 (0.09) | | | | | | | | | |
| water | 1 | 154.57 (1.97) | | | | | | | | | |
| | 2 | 81.70 (1.95) | 5376008 | 21404 | 88 | 275484 | 207.33 | 0 | 89.00 (3.78) | 9% / 106% | 160.57 (3.63) |
| | 3 | 57.78 (1.25) | 6756393 | 21741 | 65 | 279701 | 260.64 | 0 | 63.10 (1.45) | 9% / 89% | 160.60 (2.13) |
| | 4 | 43.15 (0.03) | 8131526 | 21537 | 54 | 334339 | 313.81 | 0 | 56.32 (1.96) | 31% / 92% | 162.99 (1.05) |
| | 6 | 33.39 (0.52) | | | | | | | | | |
| | 8 | 29.33 (0.22) | | | | | | | | | |

Results are the mean of five trials. Values in parentheses show standard deviations. Note that DoublePlay uses more cores than the original execution during recording since it executes two copies of the application. The overhead column shows the overhead of DoublePlay with respect to two configurations of the original application. The first overhead is relative to the original application with the same number of application threads; this shows the overhead of DoublePlay when it can take advantage of unused cores. The second overhead is relative to the original application with twice as many application threads; this shows the overhead of DoublePlay relative to an application configured to use the same number of cores as DoublePlay.

**Table 1.** DoublePlay performance

cation threads; this shows the overhead of DoublePlay when it can take advantage of unused cores. The second overhead is relative to the original application with twice as many application threads; this shows the overhead of DoublePlay relative to an application configured to use the same number of cores as DoublePlay. The last column shows the offline replay execution time.

| app | threads | rollbacks w/o opt. | rollbacks with opt. | execution time(s) & stdev. w/o opt. | execution time(s) & stdev. with opt. | relative reduction in exec. time |
|---|---|---|---|---|---|---|
| pbzip2 | 2 | 2.2 | 0 | 53.32 (2.61) | 50.42 (0.41) | 6% |
| | 3 | 1.2 | 0 | 38.54 (3.77) | 35.92 (0.09) | 8% |
| | 4 | 0.8 | 0 | 32.59 (3.04) | 29.38 (0.43) | 13% |
| aget | 2 | 0.4 | 0.4 | 10.80 (0.06) | 10.84 (0.12) | 0% |
| | 3 | 0.2 | 0.2 | 7.31 (0.08) | 7.30 (0.02) | 0% |
| | 4 | 0.2 | 0.2 | 5.54 (0.15) | 5.57 (0.03) | 0% |
| apache | 2 | 0.1 | 0.1 | 43.95 (0.33) | 43.81 (0.31) | 0% |
| | 3 | 1.0 | 1.0 | 42.74 (0.59) | 41.78 (0.48) | 2% |
| | 4 | 1.7 | 1.7 | 40.75 (0.65) | 41.09 (1.28) | -1% |
| mysql | 4 | 0.2 | 0.2 | 34.25 (1.39) | 34.25 (1.39) | 0% |

**Table 2.** Benefit of forward recovery and loose replay.

The availability of unused cores significantly impacts the overhead added by DoublePlay during recording. If there are sufficient unused cores, DoublePlay adds little overhead to the recorded application execution time. On average, 2 worker threads add about 15% overhead to the application run time. The overhead gradually increases to 28% with 4 threads. For the five real applications, the maximum overhead of any benchmark is 23% (for pbzip2 with 4 worker threads) — the average overhead is only 7% with 2 worker threads and 11% with 4 worker threads. Apache and aget are limited by the speed of our local network; mysql is limited by disk I/O, and the remaining benchmarks are CPU bound. DoublePlay shows more overhead for the SPLASH-2 benchmarks, generally because they perform many more synchronization operations per second and dirty memory pages more rapidly, which increases the number of pages compared. As shown in the Respec paper [18], Ocean is a challenging benchmark as most of its overhead derives from sharing the limited memory bandwidth and processor caches between the thread-parallel and epoch-parallel executions. As expected, Ocean incurs approximately the same overhead with DoublePlay as it incurs with Respec.

If all cores can be productively used by the application, then DoublePlay incurs much higher overhead because it executes the application twice during recording, and this uses cores that could have been used by the application. When compared to an application configured to use the same number of cores as DoublePlay, DoublePlay adds approximately 100% overhead to CPU-bound applications that can scale to eight cores (this does not affect Apache, which is network bound, or mysql, which is disk bound). For comparison, iDNA adds an average of 1100% overhead [4], and SMP-ReVirt adds 10-600% overhead [10]. SMP-ReVirt does not incur DoublePlay's overhead of executing the application twice, but SMP-ReVirt does incur high overhead for applications that share data frequently (including false sharing due to tracking ownership at page granularity) because of the cost of memory protection faults. DoublePlay also scales well up to 8 cores (e.g., its average overhead across all benchmarks without spare cores is 99% with 2 threads and 110% with 4 threads), while SMP-ReVirt does not scale well for some applications even up to 4 cores.

Thus, DoublePlay is well suited for three settings that require deterministic replay (e.g., for forensic or auditing purposes): (1) applications which cannot scale effectively to use all cores on the machine, (2) sites that are willing to dedicate extra cores to provide deterministic replay, and (3) applications that share data frequently between cores (for which DoublePlay is the lowest overhead solution). In particular, we believe that many machines will have unused cores that DoublePlay can take advantage of because the number of cores per computer is expected to grow exponentially, and scaling applications to use these extra cores is notoriously difficult. In such settings with spare cores, DoublePlay incurs only modest overhead.

For CPU-bound benchmarks, DoublePlay's offline replay takes approximately the same amount of time as a single-threaded execution of the application. This is due to our current implementation, which limits offline replay to executing on one core. If we used two executions to accelerate replay in the same way we accelerate recording, the offline replay time should be approximately the same as the record time for these benchmarks. Aget runs much faster during offline replay than during recording because it obtains its data from sequential disk reads rather than from network receives. Apache runs even faster because it uses Linux's zero-copy `sendfile`: thus, no data is copied into or out of its address space on replay. Mysql also benefits from sequential disk I/O.

DoublePlay's offline replay performance is a substantial improvement over system such as PRES and ODR that log partial information during recording, then search during replay for an execution that matches the original execution. In its low-recording overhead mode (SI-DRI), ODR's replay time is reported as ranging from 300 to over 39000 times the original application time, with some replays not completing at all. During the first replay of an execution, PRES records the global order of accesses to shared variables from different threads (called the RW scheme) to guide its search for an execution that matches the recorded run. This is reported to have an overhead from 28% (for network applications to several hundred times (for CPU-bound applications and benchmarks) the original execution time. This additional work is necessary to guarantee that the produced replay can be reproduced at will. Further, PRES may try several executions before finding a matching one. When PRES records synchronization operations and system calls (similar to DoublePlay), it takes 1-28 tries to replay most runs, and is unable to replay one run within 1000 tries. Once a valid replay is found, subsequent PRES replays do not incur this searching overhead. Thus, DoublePlay's contribution compared to these prior systems is (1) to guarantee that a replay can be produced in a bounded amount of time, and (2) to substantially lower relative replay time. The main cost of these contributions is that DoublePlay uses twice as many cores during recording to run two executions of CPU-bound applications.

### 6.3 Forward recovery and loose replay

Of the nine benchmarks we used in our evaluation, four (pbzip, aget, Apache, and mysql) experience application-level benign data races. For instance, pbzip2 has a benign data race in which an output thread spins waiting for a worker thread to set a value. Aget has a benign race where a thread reads and displays a progress counter without grabbing a lock. Apache has a benign race in which worker threads increment an idle counter in a spin loop with an atomic compare-and-swap implemented using low-level locks. If two worker threads contend, one may experience an additional iteration of the spin loop, which leads to an additional paired lock-unlock sequence.

As shown in Table 2, DoublePlay's loose replay optimization reduces the frequency of rollbacks for pbzip2 — in fact, all rollbacks were eliminated during our evaluation. Eliminating rollbacks improves execution time from 6% of the original execution time with two threads to 13% with four threads. In all runs during our evaluation, the loose replay optimization was able to continue the execution of the epoch-parallel execution past the spin loop. While extra system calls create a transient difference in stack values, the process states soon converge when the thread overwrites those values during subsequent function calls.

For aget and Apache, no rollbacks were avoided. Although loose replay allows epoch-parallel execution to proceed when aget outputs a different progress value to the console, the output values usually remain in a buffer in `libc` at the end of the epoch, which is detected as a divergence. The data races in Apache lead to complicated divergences in synchronization operations and system calls for which loose replay cannot be used. Further, for these two applications, forward recovery does not have a measurable performance impact. For aget, the reason is that DoublePlay saves a copy of data received over the network until the epoch that received the data is committed (otherwise, the received data would be lost). On a rollback, the subsequent execution reads the copied data from memory rather than the network, so those system calls are much faster. Apache also benefits from this behavior, but it also takes frequent epochs because it sends external output over the network quite often. Consequently, the amount of work preserved by a forward recovery is very small. Since divergence check failures are relatively infrequent, the effect of forward recovery on the execution time of the two applications is negligible. We observed only one rollback during the mysql benchmarks; as with Apache, this rollback could not be avoided due to a complicated divergence, but the performance impact was negligible due to frequent epochs. Thus, while forward recovery and loose replay are often successful in reducing rollbacks and preserving work done during a failed epoch, they appear to be most beneficial for CPU-bound applications with longer epoch durations.

## 7. Conclusion

Providing efficient deterministic replay for multithreaded programs running on multiprocessors is challenging. While many prior solutions have been proposed, all fall short in some way. For instance, they may require custom hardware support, be prohibitively slow for many applications, or not guarantee that a replayed execution can be produced in a reasonable amount of time. Compared to these prior systems, DoublePlay's contribution is to provide guaranteed software-only record and replay with a minimal overhead to execution time, at the cost of using more cores. The key insight in DoublePlay is that one can use the simpler and faster mechanisms of single-processor record and replay, yet still achieve the scalability offered by multiple cores, by using an additional execution to parallelize the record and replay of an application. On machines with spare cores, this insight allows DoublePlay to record application execution with only an average of 15% overhead with 2 threads and 28% with 4 threads.

## Acknowledgments

We thank the anonymous reviewers for comments that improved this paper. The work is supported by the National Science Foundation under awards CNS-0905149 and CCF-0916770. The views and conclusions contained in this document are those of the authors and should not be interpreted as representing the official policies, either expressed or implied, of NSF, the University of Michigan, the U.S. government, or industrial sponsors.

## References

[1] ALTEKAR, G., AND STOICA, I. ODR: Output-deterministic replay for multicore debugging. In *Proceedings of the 22nd ACM Symposium on Operating Systems Principles* (October 2009), pp. 193–206.

[2] BACON, D. F., AND GOLDSTEIN, S. C. Hardware assisted replay of multiprocessor programs. In *Proceedings of the 1991 ACM/ONR Workshop on Parallel and Distributed Debugging* (1991), ACM Press, pp. 194–206.

[3] BERGER, E. D., YANG, T., LIU, T., AND NOVARK, G. Grace: safe multithreaded programming for c/c++. In *Proceeding of the 24th ACM SIGPLAN conference on Object oriented programming systems languages and applications* (Orlando, Florida, USA, 2009), pp. 81–96.

[4] BHANSALI, S., CHEN, W., DE JONG, S., EDWARDS, A., AND DRINIC, M. Framework for instruction-level tracing and analysis of programs. In *Second International Conference on Virtual Execution Environments* (June 2006), pp. 154–163.

[5] BRESSOUD, T. C., AND SCHNEIDER, F. B. Hypervisor-based fault tolerance. *ACM Transactions on Computer Systems 14*, 1 (February 1996), 80–107.

[6] CHOI, J. D., ALPERN, B., NGO, T., AND SRIDHARAN, M. A perturbation free replay platform for cross-optimized multithreaded applications. In *Proceedings of the 15th International Parallel and Distributed Processing Symposium* (April 2001).

[7] CHOW, J., GARFINKEL, T., AND CHEN, P. M. Decoupling dynamic program analysis from execution in virtual environments. In *Proceedings of the 2008 USENIX Technical Conference* (June 2008), pp. 1–14.

[8] DEVIETTI, J., LUCIA, B., CEZE, L., AND OSKIN, M. DMP: Deterministic shared memory multiprocessing. In *Proceedings of the 2009 International Conference on Architectural Support for Programming Languages and Operating Systems (ASPLOS)* (March 2009), pp. 85–96.

[9] DUNLAP, G. W., KING, S. T., CINAR, S., BASRAI, M. A., AND CHEN, P. M. ReVirt: Enabling intrusion analysis through virtual-machine logging and replay. In *Proceedings of the 5th Symposium on Operating Systems Design and Implementation* (Boston, MA, December 2002), pp. 211–224.

[10] DUNLAP, G. W., LUCCHETTI, D. G., FETTERMAN, M., AND CHEN, P. M. Execution replay on multiprocessor virtual machines. In *Proceedings of the 2008 ACM SIGPLAN/SIGOPS International Conference on Virtual Execution Environments (VEE)* (March 2008), pp. 121–130.

[11] FELDMAN, S. I., AND BROWN, C. B. IGOR: A system for program debugging via reversible execution. In *PADD '88: Proceedings of the 1988 ACM SIGPLAN and SIGOPS Workshop on Parallel and Distributed Debugging* (1988), pp. 112–123.

[12] HOWER, D. R., AND HILL, M. D. Rerun: Exploiting episodes for lightweight memory race recording. In *Proceedings of the 2008 International Symposium on Computer Architecture* (June 2008), pp. 265–276.

[13] JR., R. L. B., ADVE, V. S., DIG, D., ADVE, S. V., HEUMANN, S., KOMURAVELLI, R., OVERBEY, J., SIMMONS, P., SUNG, H., AND VAKILIAN, M. A type and effect system for deterministic parallel java. In *OOPSLA* (2009), pp. 97–116.

[14] KELSEY, K., BAI, T., DING, C., AND ZHANG, C. Fast Track: A software system for speculative program optimization. In *Proceedings of the 2009 International Symposium on Code Generation and Optimization (CGO)* (March 2009), pp. 157–168.

[15] KING, S. T., DUNLAP, G. W., AND CHEN, P. M. Debugging operating systems with time-traveling virtual machines. In *Proceedings of the 2005 USENIX Technical Conference* (April 2005), pp. 1–15.

[16] LEBLANC, T. J., AND MELLOR-CRUMMEY, J. M. Debugging parallel programs with instant replay. *IEEE Transaction on Computers 36*, 4 (1987), 471–482.

[17] LEE, D., SAID, M., NARAYANASAMY, S., YANG, Z. J., AND PEREIRA, C. Offline symbolic analysis for multi-processor execution replay. In *International Symposium on Microarchitecture (MICRO)* (2009).

[18] LEE, D., WESTER, B., VEERARAGHAVAN, K., CHEN, P. M., FLINN, J., AND NARAYANASAMY, S. Respec: Efficient online multiprocessor replay via speculation and external determinism. In *Proceedings of the 15th International Conference on Architectural Support for Programming Languages and Operating Systems* (Pittsburgh, PA, March 2010), pp. 77–89.

[19] MELLOR-CRUMMEY, J. M., AND LEBLANC, T. J. A Software Instruction Counter. In *Proceedings of the 1989 International Conference on Architectural Support for Programming Languages and Operating Systems* (April 1989), pp. 78–86.

[20] MONTESINOS, P., CEZE, L., AND TORRELLAS, J. DeLorean: Recording and deterministically replaying shared-memory multiprocessor execution efficiently. In *Proceedings of the 2008 International Symposium on Computer Architecture* (June 2008), pp. 289–300.

[21] NARAYANASAMY, S., PEREIRA, C., AND CALDER, B. Recording shared memory dependencies using Strata. In *ASPLOS-XII: Proceedings of the 12th International Conference on Architectural Support for Programming Languages and Operating Systems* (2006), pp. 229–240.

[22] NARAYANASAMY, S., PEREIRA, C., PATIL, H., COHN, R., AND CALDER, B. Automatic logging of operating system effects to guide application-level architecture simulation. In *International Conference on Measurements and Modeling of Computer Systems (SIGMETRICS)* (June 2006), pp. 216–227.

[23] NARAYANASAMY, S., POKAM, G., AND CALDER, B. BugNet: Continuously recording program execution for deterministic replay debugging. In *Proceedings of the 32nd Annual International Symposium on Computer Architecture (ISCA)* (June 2005), pp. 284–295.

[24] NETZER, R. H. B. Optimal tracing and replay for debugging shared-memory parallel programs. In *Proceedings of the ACM/ONR Workshop on Parallel and Distributed Debugging* (1993), pp. 1–11.

[25] NIGHTINGALE, E. B., CHEN, P. M., AND FLINN, J. Speculative execution in a distributed file system. In *Proceedings of the 20th ACM Symposium on Operating Systems Principles* (Brighton, United Kingdom, October 2005), pp. 191–205.

[26] NIGHTINGALE, E. B., PEEK, D., CHEN, P. M., AND FLINN, J. Parallelizing security checks on commodity hardware. In *Proceedings of the 13th International Conference on Architectural Support for Programming Languages and Operating Systems* (Seattle, WA, March 2008), pp. 308–318.

[27] NIGHTINGALE, E. B., VEERARAGHAVAN, K., CHEN, P. M., AND FLINN, J. Rethink the sync. In *Proceedings of the 7th Symposium on Operating Systems Design and Implementation* (Seattle, WA, October 2006), pp. 1–14.

[28] OLSZEWSKI, M., ANSEL, J., AND AMARASINGHE, S. Kendo: efficient deterministic multithreading in software. In *Proceedings of the 2009 International Conference on Architectural Support for Programming Languages and Operating Systems (ASPLOS)* (March 2009), pp. 97–108.

[29] OPLINGER, J., AND LAM, M. S. Enhancing software reliability using speculative threads. In *Proceedings of the 2002 International Conference on Architectural Support for Programming Languages and Operating Systems (ASPLOS)* (October 2002), pp. 184–196.

[30] PARK, S., ZHOU, Y., XIONG, W., YIN, Z., KAUSHIK, R., LEE, K. H., AND LU, S. PRES: Probabilistic replay with execution sketching on multiprocessors. In *Proceedings of the 22nd ACM Symposium on Operating Systems Principles* (October 2009), pp. 177–191.

[31] PETERSON, Z. N. J., AND BURNS, R. Ext3cow: A time-shifting file system for regulatory compliance. *ACM Transacations on Storage 1*, 2 (2005), 190–212.

[32] RONSSE, M., AND BOSSCHERE, K. D. RecPlay: A full integrated practical record/replay system. *ACM Transactions on Computer Systems 17*, 2 (May 1999), 133–152.

[33] RUSSINOVICH, M., AND COGSWELL, B. Replay for concurrent non-deterministic shared-memory applications. In *Proceedings of the ACM SIGPLAN 1996 Conference on Programming Language Design and Implementation* (1996), pp. 258–266.

[34] SANTRY, D. S., FEELEY, M. J., HUTCHINSON, N. C., VEITCH, A. C., CARTON, R. W., AND OFIR, J. Deciding when to forget in the Elephant file system. *SIGOPS Operating Systems Review 33*, 5 (1999), 110–123.

[35] SOHI, G. S., BREACH, S. E., AND VIJAYKUMAR, T. N. Multiscalar processors. In *Proceedings of the 1995 International Symposium on Computer Architecture* (June 1995), pp. 414–425.

[36] SRINIVASAN, S., ANDREWS, C., KANDULA, S., AND ZHOU, Y. Flashback: A light-weight extension for rollback and deterministic replay for software debugging. In *Proceedings of the 2004 USENIX Technical Conference* (Boston, MA, June 2004), pp. 29–44.

[37] STEFFAN, J. G., AND MOWRY, T. C. The potential for using thread-level data speculation to facilitate automatic parallelization. In *Proceedings of the 1998 Symposium on High Performance Computer Architecture* (February 1998), pp. 2–13.

[38] SUNDARAMOORTHY, K., PURSER, Z., AND ROTENBERG, E. Slipstream processors: improving both performance and fault tolerance. In *Proceedings of the 9th International Conference on Architectural Support for Programming Languages and Operating Systems* (November 2000), pp. 257–268.

[39] SÜSSKRAUT, M., KNAUTH, T., WEIGERT, S., SCHIFFEL, U., MEINHOLD, M., FETZER, C., BAI, T., DING, C., AND ZHANG, C. Prospect: A compiler framework for speculative parallelization. In *Proceedings of the 2010 International Symposium on Code Generation and Optimization (CGO)* (April 2010), pp. 131–140.

[40] TUCEK, J., LU, S., HUANG, C., XANTHOS, S., AND ZHOU, Y. Triage: Diagnosing production run failures at the user's site. In *Proceedings of the 21st ACM Symposium on Operating Systems Principles* (October 2007), pp. 131–144.

[41] VEERARAGHAVAN, K., FLINN, J., NIGHTINGALE, E. B., AND NOBLE, B. quFiles: The right file at the right time. In *Proceedings of the 8th USENIX Conference on File and Storage Technologies* (San Jose, CA, February 2010), pp. 1–14.

[42] VLACHOS, E., GOODSTEIN, M. L., KOZUCH, M. A., CHEN, S., FALSAFI, B., GIBBONS, P. B., AND MOWRY, T. C. ParaLog: Enabling and accelerating online parallel monitoring of multithreaded applications. In *Proceedings of the 15th International Conference on Architectural Support for Programming Languages and Operating Systems* (Pittsburgh, PA, March 2010), pp. 271–284.

[43] WEERATUNGE, D., ZHANG, X., AND JAGANNATHAN, S. Analyzing multicore dumps to facilitate concurrency bug reproduction. In *Proceedings of the 2010 International Conference on Architectural Support for Programming Languages and Operating Systems (ASPLOS)* (March 2010), pp. 155–166.

[44] WOO, S. C., OHARA, M., TORRIE, E., SINGH, J. P., AND GUPTA, A. The SPLASH-2 programs: Characterization and methodological considerations. In *Proceedings of the 22nd International Symposium on Computer Architecture* (June 1995), pp. 24–36.

[45] XU, M., BODIK, R., AND HILL, M. D. A "flight data recorder" for enabling full-system multiprocessor deterministic replay. In *Proceedings of the 2003 International Symposium on Computer Architecture* (June 2003), pp. 122–135.

[46] XU, M., MALYUGIN, V., SHELDON, J., VENKITACHALAM, G., AND WEISSMAN, B. ReTrace: Collecting execution trace with virtual machine deterministic replay. In *Proceedings of the 2007 Workshop on Modeling, Benchmarking and Simulation (MoBS)* (June 2007).

[47] ZAMFIR, C., AND CANDEA, G. Execution synthesis: A technique for automated software debugging. In *Proceedings of the 2010 European Conference on Computer Systems (EuroSys)* (April 2010), pp. 321–334.

[48] ZILLES, C., AND SOHI, G. Master/slave speculative parallelization. In *Proceedings of the 35th Annual ACM/IEEE International Symposium on Microarchitecture (MICRO)* (2002), pp. 85–96.

# Hardware Acceleration of Transactional Memory on Commodity Systems

Jared Casper Tayo Oguntebi Sungpack Hong
Nathan G. Bronson Christos Kozyrakis Kunle Olukotun
Pervasive Parallelism Laboratory
Stanford University
{jaredc, tayo, hongsup, nbronson, kozyraki, kunle}@stanford.edu

## Abstract

The adoption of transactional memory is hindered by the high overhead of software transactional memory and the intrusive design changes required by previously proposed TM hardware. We propose that hardware to accelerate software transactional memory (STM) can reside outside an unmodified commodity processor core, thereby substantially reducing implementation costs. This paper introduces Transactional Memory Acceleration using Commodity Cores (TMACC), a hardware-accelerated TM system that does not modify the processor, caches, or coherence protocol.

We present a complete hardware implementation of TMACC using a rapid prototyping platform. Using this hardware, we implement two unique conflict detection schemes which are accelerated using Bloom filters on an FPGA. These schemes employ novel techniques for tolerating the latency of fine-grained asynchronous communication with an out-of-core accelerator. We then conduct experiments to explore the feasibility of accelerating TM without modifying existing system hardware. We show that, for all but short transactions, it is not necessary to modify the processor to obtain substantial improvement in TM performance. In these cases, TMACC outperforms an STM by an average of 69% in applications using moderate-length transactions, showing maximum speedup within 8% of an upper bound on TM acceleration. Overall, we demonstrate that hardware can substantially accelerate the performance of an STM on unmodified commodity processors.

***Categories and Subject Descriptors*** C.1.4 [*Processor Architectures*]: Parallel—Distributed Architectures

***General Terms*** Algorithms, Design, Performance

***Keywords*** Transactional Memory, FPGA, Hardware Acceleration

## 1. Introduction

Transactional memory (TM) [19, 23] is a potential way to simplify parallel programming. Ideally, TM would allow programmers to make frequent use of large transactions and have them perform as well as highly optimized fine-grain locks. However, this ideal cannot be realized until there are real systems capable of executing large transactions with low overhead. Our aim in this paper is to describe a TM system that strikes a reasonable balance between performance, cost and system implementation complexity.

Researchers have proposed a wide variety of TM systems. There are systems implemented completely in hardware (HTMs), completely in software (STMs), and more recently, systems with both hardware and software components (*hybrid* TMs). To put our contributions in context, we now briefly review the strengths and weaknesses of the various TM design alternatives.

### 1.1 TM Design Alternatives and Related Work

#### STM

Software transactional memory (STM) systems [15, 18, 25, 31, 32, 36] replace the normal loads and stores of a program with short functions ("barriers") that provide versioning and conflict detection. These transactional read and write barriers must themselves be implemented using the low-level synchronization operations provided by commodity processors. The barriers can be inserted automatically by a transaction-aware compiler [1, 2, 39] or managed runtime [31], added by a dynamic instrumentation system [28], or invoked manually by the programmer. STMs increase the number of executed instructions, perform extra loads and stores, and require metadata that takes up cache space and needs to be synchronized. The resulting inherent performance penalty means that despite providing good scalability, most STMs fall far short of the performance offered by hardware-based approaches to TM. There have been proposals that reduce the overhead required [39], but they do so by giving up on the promise of TM–they require small transactions that are used rarely. Hence, using these STMs is as difficult as using fine-grain locks. As a result of these limitations, STMs have been largely constrained to the domain of research [9].

#### HTM

At the opposite end of the spectrum from STM is hardware transactional memory (HTM) [4, 5, 11, 17, 24, 29]. HTM systems eliminate the need for software barriers by extending the processor or memory system to natively perform version management and conflict detection entirely in hardware, allowing them to demonstrate impressive performance. Version management in an HTM is performed by either buffering speculative state (typically in the cache or store buffer) or by maintaining an undo log. Metadata that allows conflict detection is typically stored in Bloom filters (signatures) or in bits added to each line of the cache. The close synergy of the hardware with the processor core and cache allow these systems to provide very high levels of performance; however this tight relationship causes the system to be inflexible and more costly. Recent advances in HTM design address both of these problems



*ASPLOS'11,* March 5–11, 2011, Newport Beach, California, USA.

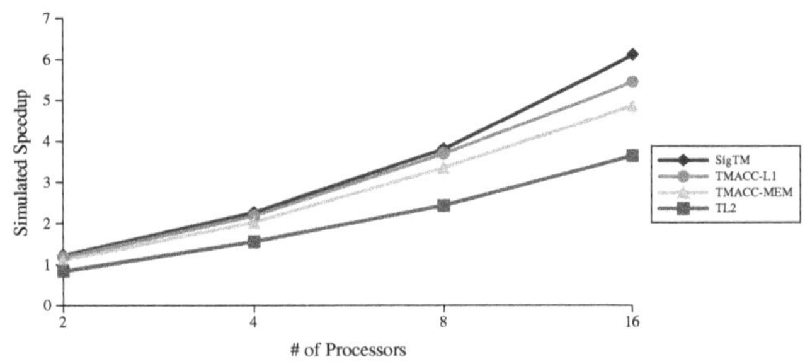


**Figure 1.** Average (mean) performance on the STAMP suite of two simulated TMACC systems, one two cycles away from the core (L1) and one two hundred cycles away (MEM). These are compared to TL2, a pure STM, and an in-core hybrid TM system much like SigTM.

by minimizing the coupling between the TM and the processor core [33, 40], but even decoupled HTM designs introduce non-trivial design complexity and disturb the delicate control and data paths in the processor core. The first-level cache has the effect of hiding loads and stores from the outside world, making it impossible to construct an out-of-core pure HTM system. Previous studies have not explored the possibility of adding transactional acceleration hardware without modifying a commodity processor core.

#### HybridTM

One way of limiting the complexity required by an HTM is to provide a limited best-effort HTM that falls back to an STM if it is unable to proceed [12, 14, 20, 22, 38]. These systems are particularly well-suited for supporting lock-elision and small transactions. However, applications that use large transactions (or cannot tune their transactions to avoid capacity and associativity overflows) will find that they derive no benefit. This approach is especially problematic as the research community explores transactional memory as a programming model, since it prescribes a limit on how transactions may be used efficiently.

#### Hardware Accelerated STM

Hardware accelerated STMs are a type of hybrid TM that use dedicated hardware to improve the performance of an STM. This hardware typically consists of bits in the cache or signatures that accelerate read set tracking and conflict detection. Existing proposals extend the instruction set to control new data paths to the TM hardware. Explicit read and write barriers then use the TM hardware to accelerate conflict detection and version management [7, 30, 34].

### 1.2 TMACC Motivation

We observe that hardware acceleration of an STM's barriers only requires that the runtime be able to communicate with the hardware; the TM hardware need not be part of the core or connected to the processor with a dedicated data path. Commodity processors are already equipped with a network that provides high bandwidth, low latency, and dedicated instructions for communication: the coherence fabric. This leads to the unexplored design space of hardware accelerated TM systems that do not modify the core, or Transactional Memory Acceleration using Commodity Cores (TMACC). Early simulation results, presented in Figure 1, show the promising potential of TMACC systems to perform within five to ten percent of an in-core hybrid TM system. These results also suggest that much of that performance can be realized despite a relatively large latency between the processing cores and the TMACC hardware.

Keeping the hardware outside of the core maintains modularity, allowing architects to design and verify the TM hardware and processor core independently. This significantly reduces the cost and risk of implementing TM hardware and allows designers to migrate a core design from one generation to the next while continuing to provide transactional memory acceleration.

There is therefore great benefit in exploring TM systems that can be feasibly constructed using commodity processors. Such systems will allow researchers to:

1. better understand and fine-tune TM semantics using real hardware and large applications
2. explore the extent of speedup and hardware acceleration possible without modifying the processor core
3. better understand the issues associated with tolerating the latency of out-of-core hardware support for TM

To derive these benefits in this paper, we describe the design and implementation of a hardware accelerated TM system, implemented with commodity processor cores. Like the accelerators presented in systems like FlexTM [33], BulkSC [10], LogTM-SE [40], and SigTM [7], we use Bloom filters as signatures of a transaction's read and write sets. Unlike these previous proposals, our Bloom filters are located outside of the processor and require no modifications to the core, caches, or coherence protocol. In this paper we also address the non-trivial challenges encountered when the acceleration hardware is moved out of the core.

The major contributions of this paper are:

- We present a system (both software and hardware) for Transactional Memory Acceleration using Commodity Cores (TMACC). We detail two novel algorithms for transactional conflict detection, both of which employ general purpose out-of-core Bloom filters. (Section 3).
- We describe two techniques for tolerating the latency of fine-grained asynchronous communication with an out-of-core accelerator (Section 2).
- We construct a complete hardware implementation of TMACC using FARM [27], a rapid prototyping platform. We also shed light on practical intuition gained regarding issues one must consider when adding TM acceleration hardware (Section 2.3).
- We demonstrate the potential of TMACC by evaluating our implementation using a custom microbenchmark and the STAMP benchmark suite. We show that, for all but short transactions, it is not necessary to modify the processor to obtain substantial improvement in TM performance. TMACC outperforms an STM by an average of 69%, showing maximum speedup within 8% of an upper bound on TM acceleration (Section 4).

The rest of the paper is structured as follows: Section 2 introduces our overall approach, details our hardware platform and TM acceleration modules on the FPGA, and describes techniques to mitigate the high communication latencies between the cores and the out-of-core hardware. Section 3 describes the TM schemes we propose and explains how the hardware is utilized in these schemes. Section 4 presents the results of experiments using our microbenchmark and the STAMP suite and projects the performance of an ASIC TMACC implementation. Finally, Section 5 concludes.

## 2. Accelerating TM

In this section we present our system for Transactional Memory Acceleration using Commodity Cores, or TMACC. We first give a high level overview of our design decisions and describe our general use of Bloom filters. We then briefly introduce our experimentation vehicle, the FARM prototyping platform. We follow with a more detailed description of our Bloom filter hardware, which is general and flexible enough to be placed anywhere in the system. We describe how we implement this hardware using FARM. Finally we present techniques to tolerate the command reordering encountered while communicating with off-chip acceleration hardware.

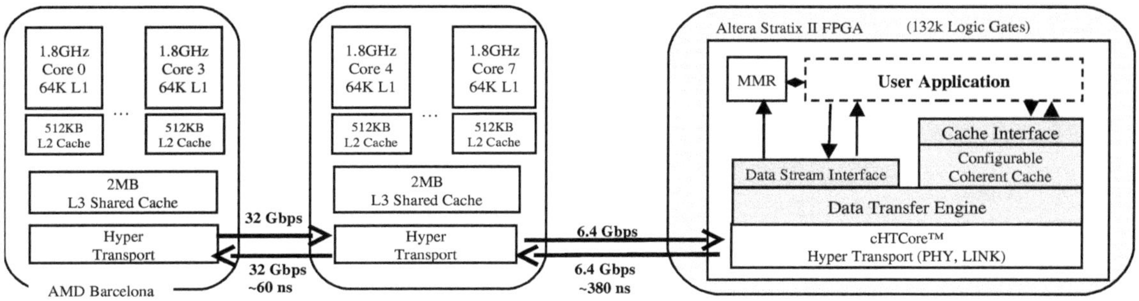


**Figure 2.** Diagram of system topology on the FARM platform.

In any TM system, the processor must have very low latency access to transactionally written data while hiding that data from other executing threads. Performing this version management in hardware and being able to promptly return speculatively written data would almost certainly require modification of the L1 data cache or the data path to that cache. Previously proposed HTM systems use buffers next to the L1, or the L1 itself, to store this speculative data until the transaction commits. Imposing out-of-core latencies on these accesses would significantly degrade performance. We therefore conclude that performing hardware-based or hardware-assisted version management in a TMACC system is impractical.

To address this issue of version management, our software runtime uses a heavily optimized chaining hash table as a write buffer. A transactional write simply adds an address/data pair to this hash table. Each transactional read must first check for inclusion of the address in the write buffer. If it is present the associated data is used; otherwise, a normal load is performed. The hash table is optimized to return quickly in the common case where the key (the address) is not in the table. Once the transaction has been validated and ordered (i.e. given permission to commit), the write buffer is walked and each entry applied directly to memory. The details of our implementation are out of the scope of this paper as write buffer data structures are more thoroughly explored elsewhere [13, 15, 25, 31].

Application of the write buffer could potentially be performed by the TMACC hardware, freeing the processor up to continue on to the next transaction. However, initial experiments showed that any benefit is outweighed by the impact of reloading the data into processor's cache after application of the write buffer. This is an area of potential future work.

Like version management, checkpointing the architectural state at the beginning of a transaction and restoring that state upon rollback would require significant modification to the processor core in order to be effectively and efficiently handled in hardware. We thus perform this entirely within the software runtime using the standard `sigsetjmp()` and `longjmp()` routines.

This leaves conflict detection as the best target for out-of-core hardware acceleration. After all, the speculative nature of an optimistic TM system means that the latency of the actual detection of conflicts is not on the critical path. Conflict detection is a primary contributor to execution overhead in STM systems, and many STM proposals have attempted to improve it.

In this work, we present two novel methods for performing conflict detection, both of which use Bloom filters as signatures of a transaction's read and write set. Bloom filters [3] have been shown to be an effective data structure for holding sets of keys with very low overhead and have been used for multiple applications, including the acceleration of transactional memory [7, 10, 36, 40]. Like several other TM proposals, TMACC uses Bloom filters to encode the read and write sets of running transactions. When a transaction commits, each address that is written can be quickly checked against the read and write sets of other concurrent transactions in order to discover conflicts. Details of the TM algorithm can be found in Section 3. The TMACC system presented in this work assumes a lazy optimistic STM. There are no fundamental reasons, however, why TMACC could not be used to accelerate an eager pessimistic system. We have a working draft of such a scheme, but do not present it in this paper.

### 2.1 FARM Prototyping Platform

In order to fully qualify a TMACC design, we needed a platform which would allow for easy experimentation with real applications. Due to its performance and flexibility, the FARM system [27] represents such a platform. FARM features an FPGA coherently connected to two commodity CPUs and physically interconnected through a backplane via HyperTransport. Figure 2 shows a diagram of its topology. As shown in the figure, FARM provides two logical interfaces for communication with the CPU: a) a *coherent interface* which uses cache lines managed by the coherence protocol and b) a *data stream interface* which provides streaming (or "fire-and-forget") non-coherent communication. For brevity, we omit the implementation and performance details of the system and refer the reader to the paper on FARM [27] for this information.

### 2.2 Bloom filters

Figure 3 presents a block diagram of a collection of Bloom filters. Note that while logic symbols are used, Figure 3 does not represent a physical implementation, but a logical diagram of the functionality provided. In addition to the normal add, clear, and query operations, each individual Bloom filter provides functionality to copy bits in from another filter or broadcast out its bits to other filters. Each Bloom filter also has a tag associated with it, which can be used, for example, to associate a Bloom filter with a particular thread of execution. Programmability of the module is achieved in the control block, which can be programmed to translate high level application-specific operations to the low level operations (add, query, clear, copy in, and copy out) sent to each individual Bloom filter. These operations can potentially be predicated by the $tag\_hit$ and $tag\_gt$ signals.

On FARM, the Bloom filters are placed in the placeholder marked "User Application" in Figure 2. We use four randomly selected hash functions from the $H_3$ class [8]. We considered using PBX hashing [41], which is optimized for space efficiency, but we were not constrained by logic resources on the FPGA. We perform copying by stepping through the block ram word by word. In order to reduce the number of cycles needed to copy, filters requiring copy support use additional RAM blocks to widen the

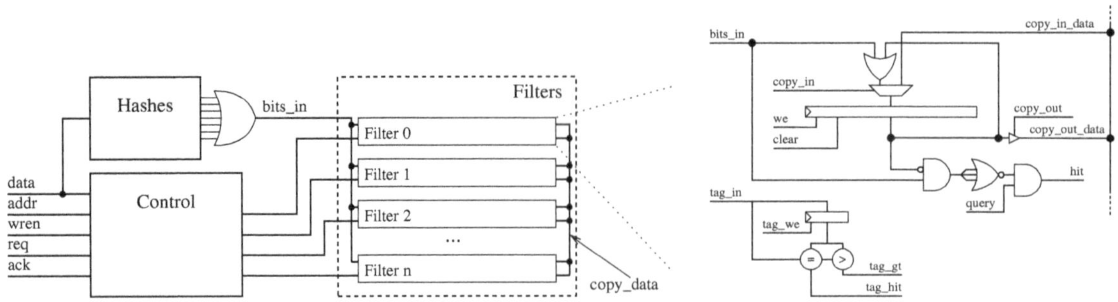


**Figure 3.** Logical block diagram of Bloom filters.

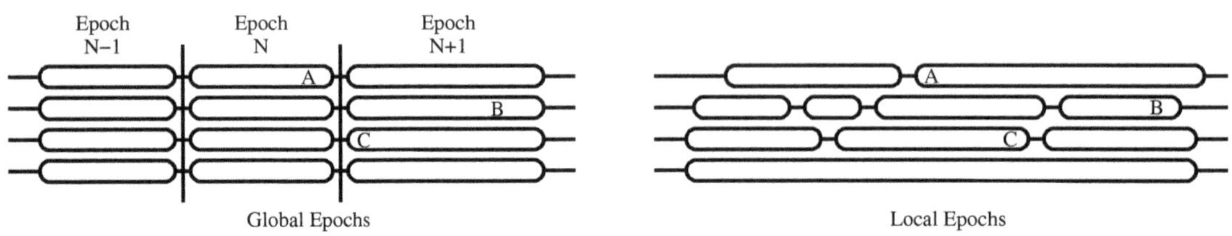


**Figure 4.** To determine the ordering of events, time is divided into epochs, either globally or locally. In the global epochs example, it is known that A comes before B and C, but not the relative ordering of B and C. In the local case, it is known that C comes before B, but not the ordering of A and B or A and C because their epochs overlap.

interface, resulting in more logic cells for the datapaths. All filters are logically 4 Kbits in size.

Software communicates with the Bloom filters using the memory subsystem, which is the fastest (both highest bandwidth and lowest latency) I/O path to and from a commodity processor core. Uncached "fire-and-forget" stores can be used to send asynchronous commands to the filters, such as a request to add an address to a transaction's read set. FARM's data stream interface provides similar functionality; however, its Barcelona processors are not able to perform true fire-and-forget stores. Instead, "write-combining" memory is used to provide a way to stream data to the FPGA with minimal impact on the running processor [27]. The Bloom filter hardware performs commands serially in the order they are received by the FPGA. The implementation is pipelined, allowing the filters to easily process all incoming commands even when the link is fully saturated.

For asynchronous responses, such as a filter match notification indicating a conflict between transactions, the filters use FARM's coherent interface to store a message in a previously agreed upon memory location, or *mailbox*[26]. The application receives notification of Bloom filter matches (i.e. conflicts) by periodically reading this mailbox. In the common case of no conflicts, this check is very cheap as it consists of a read that hits the processor's L1 cache.

Using out-of-core Bloom filters that communicate using the memory system allows us to easily perform virtualization. The software runtime maintains the pool of Bloom filters, explicitly managing the binding between software threads and hardware filters. Issues such as interrupt handling, context switching, and thread migration are thus transparent to the acceleration hardware. If the hardware were added to the processor core, these issues would become much more complex and expensive, as the core would be physically tied to a specific Bloom filter.

### 2.3 Tolerating command reordering

For many applications, like TM, that require fine-grained (frequent) communication between the processor and an accelerator, asynchronous communication is essential for performance. When using fully asynchronous communication to out-of-core devices, however, it is incorrect to assume that commands are received by the accelerator in the same order they were dispatched from the processors. Consider the following example: One processor sends a command to add an address to a transaction's read set; this command stalls in the processor's write-combining buffer. Later, a committing transaction on another processor sends notification that it is writing to that same address. This notification arrives immediately (before the preceding add to read set by the first processor) and thus the conflict is missed because the FPGA sees the commit notification and the add to the read set command in reverse order. To avoid the performance penalty of a more synchronous communication scheme (e.g. an mfence after each command), accelerators such as those in TMACC must therefore reason about possible command reorderings.

To address this serious issue, we present epoch-based reasoning and apply the technique to our Bloom filter accelerators. In this scheme, we split time into variable sized epochs, either locally determined (local epochs) or globally agreed upon (global epochs). Global epochs can be implemented using a single shared counter variable that is atomically incremented when a thread wants to move the system into a new epoch. To inform the accelerator of the epoch in which a command is executed, the epoch counter, which will usually be in the L1 cache, is read and included in the command. The accelerator then compares the epochs of commands to determine a coarse ordering, with the atomic increment providing the necessary happens-before relationship between threads. The accelerator cannot determine the ordering of commands with the same epoch number, since it may only assume the commands were fired at some point during the epoch (see Figure 4). Thus, the granularity of epoch changes determines the granularity at which the accelerator is able to determine ordering.

The potentially high overhead of maintaining a single global counter can be eliminated by using epochs local to each thread. When a thread wants to move into a new local epoch, it sends a command to the accelerator to inform it of an epoch change and performs a memory fence to ensure any command tagged with the new epoch number happens after the accelerator sees the epoch change. The epoch change command can often be included in an

| Function | Description |
|---|---|
| `HW_AddToReadSet(tid, reference, epoch)` | Asynchronously adds `reference` to `tid`'s read set and enables notification for any write that could possibly make this read inconsistent. Queries each write set that has an epoch number less than or equal to `epoch` for `reference`, triggering a conflict in `tid` if a match is found or if `epoch` is less than the epoch of the oldest write set. |
| `HW_WriteNotification(tid, reference, epoch)` | Asynchronously queries all reads sets, except `tid`'s, and triggers a conflict in any transaction whose read set includes `reference`. Adds `reference` to the write set for epoch `epoch`, clearing and replacing an old epoch's write set if necessary. |
| `HW_AskToCommit(tid)` | Synchronously processes all outstanding commands and returns the conflict status of `tid`. |

**Table 1.** TMACC hardware functions used by TMACC-GE.

**Algorithm 1** Pseudocode for the TMACC-GE runtime.

```
procedure WRITEBARRIER(tid, ptr, val)
    AddToWritebuffer(tid.wb, val)
procedure READBARRIER(tid, ptr)
    HW_AddToReadSet(tid, ptr, global_epoch)
    if WritebufferContains(tid.wb, ptr) then
        return WritebufferLookup(tid.wb, ptr)
    WaitForFreeLock(ptr)
    Return *ptr
procedure COMMIT(wb)
    AcquireLocksForWB(wb)
    epoch = global_epoch
    if (violation_mailbox[wb.tid] == true) then return failure
    for entry in wb do
        HW_WriteNotification(wb.tid, entry.address, epoch)
    violated = HW_AskToCommit(wb.tid)                ▷ Synchronous
    if violated then ReleaseLocks(); return failure
    for entry in wb do *(entry.address) = entry.specData
    AtomicIncrement(global_epoch)
    ReleaseLocks()
    return success
```

existing synchronous command with low cost. While this scheme has less overhead, it leaves the accelerator with less information about the ordering of events. Like the global scheme, the accelerator may only assume the command was fired at some point during the epoch; therefore the relative ordering of commands from different threads can only be determined if their epochs do not overlap, as illustrated in Figure 4.

## 3. Algorithm Details

We propose two different transactional memory algorithms in this paper: one using global epochs (TMACC-GE) and one using local epochs (TMACC-LE). In both of these schemes, a filter match represents a conflict that requires a transaction to abort, and a pre-set mailbox is used to notify the STM runtime. Both schemes provide privatization safety. Publication safety could be provided by constraining the commit order as in an STM; we don't expect TMACC to make this either easier or harder.

When using Bloom filters to perform conflict detection, an important decision is what logical keys are put into the Bloom filter to designate a shared variable. This decision determines the granularity at which conflicts are detected. In our systems, we simply use the virtual address of the shared variable as the key (later referred to as a reference). For structures and arrays, each unique word is a separate shared variable. An object identifier or something similar could be also be used as a reference.

### 3.1 Global Epochs

In the global epoch scheme, the Bloom filters are split into two banks. One bank maintains the read set for each active transaction in the system. Each read set holds the references read during the execution of the associated transaction. The other bank contains filters which hold the write set for a given epoch; the write set is composed of writes that were performed by any transaction during that epoch. The Bloom filter tags are used to determine which Bloom filter in this bank corresponds to what epoch. When the filters receive a *HW_AddToReadSet*, the reference is added to the transaction's read set and checked against the write set for the given and all previous epochs. A conflict is signalled on any match, thus ensuring a match against any write that could have occurred prior to the read. When the filters receive a *HW_WriteNotification*, the reference is added to the given epoch's write set and checked against each transaction's read set, ensuring that any read that could possibly come after, or has come after, the associated write will signal a conflict. In the case that there is not a filter currently associated with the epoch of a *HW_WriteNotification*, and the epoch is greater than the oldest epoch for which a filter exists (i.e. this is a new epoch), the write set filter of the oldest epoch is cleared and replaced with a new write set containing the address to be added (and tagged with the new epoch number). If no filter exists for the epoch in either a *HW_WriteNotification* or a *HW_AddToReadSet*, and the epoch is older than the oldest epoch for which a write set exists, then the command comes from an epoch that is too old to have a filter and conservatively triggers a conflict. Since the ordering of reads and writes within the same epoch cannot be determined, this scheme has the effect of logically moving all reads to the end of the epoch in which they are performed and all writes to the beginning. These operations are summarized in Table 1.

Algorithm 1 gives high level pseudo-code for the algorithm used by the TMACC-GE software runtime. Each read is instrumented to inform the Bloom filters of the reference being read. Since the command is asynchronous, the only per read barrier cost of doing conflict detection is the cost of firing off the command to the FPGA. To commit the transaction, the runtime first acquires locks for each address in its write buffer, using a similar low-overhead striped locking technique as TL2 [15]. To ensure that all of its writes are assigned to the same epoch, a local copy of the global epoch counter is stored and used to inform the hardware of all the references that are about to be committed. Locks are necessary to ensure that any readers of partially committed state perform the read in the same epoch as the commit. Without them, the epoch could be incremented and a read of a partial commit performed in the following epoch. This read would (incorrectly) not be flagged as a conflict. Once all of the locks are obtained, the running transaction must synchronize with the filters to ensure that it has not been violated up until the point the filters perform the *HW_AskToCommit* operation. If the transaction read a value that had been committed in the current or any previous epoch, either the *HW_WriteNotification* would have matched on the read set and triggered a conflict, or the *HW_AddToReadSet* would have matched against one of the epoch's write sets. Therefore, when the *HW_AskToCommit* is performed on the FPGA, the transaction's

| Function | Description |
|---|---|
| `HW_AddToReadSet(tid, reference)` | Asynchronously adds `reference` to `tid`'s read set, and enables notification for any write that could possibly make this read inconsistent. Queries `tid`'s missed set and the write set for every other transaction for `reference`, triggering a conflict in `tid` on a match. |
| `HW_WriteNotification(tid, reference, epoch)` | Asynchronously queries all reads sets except `tid`'s, triggering a conflict in transactions whose read set includes `reference`. Adds `reference` to `tid`'s read set and to `epoch`'s write set. |
| `HW_ClearMissedSet(tid)` | Asynchronously clears `tid`'s missed set, moving this transaction to a new local epoch. |
| `HW_ClearWriteSet(tid)` | Asynchronously copies the content of `tid`'s write set into every other transaction's missed set, then clears the write set. |
| `HW_AskToCommit(tid)` | Synchronously processes all outstanding commands and returns the conflict status of `tid`. Clears `tid`'s read and missed set in preparation for a new transaction. |

**Table 2.** TMACC hardware functions used by TMACC-LE.

**Algorithm 2** Pseudocode for the TMACC-LE runtime.

```
procedure WRITEBARRIER(tid, ptr, val)
    AddToWritebuffer(tid.wb, val)
procedure READBARRIER(tid, ptr)
    HW_AddToReadSet(tid, ptr)
    if WritebufferContains(tid.wb, ptr) then
        return WritebufferLookup(tid.wb, ptr)
    if TimeForNewLocalEpoch() then
        HW_ClearMissedSet(tid); mfence
    Return *ptr
procedure COMMIT(wb)
    for entry in wb do
        HW_WriteNotification(wb.tid, entry.address)
    violated = HW_AskToCommit(wb.tid)                ▷ Synchronous
    if violated then return failure
    for entry in wb do *(entry.address) = entry.specData
    HW_ClearWriteSet(wb.tid)
    return success
```

read set is coherent and consistent if no conflict has been seen by the FPGA. The transaction is then placed in the global ordering of transactions on the system and allowed to apply its write buffer to memory. Once the write buffer has been applied, the transaction atomically increments the global epoch counter so that any thread that reads the newly committed value will read it in the new epoch and not be violated. It then releases the locks and returns.

It is important to note that the locks used in TMACC-GE are simple mutex locks only used to ensure the atomicity of a commit, not the versioned locks used for conflict detection in TL2. TMACC-GE can thus use coarser grain locking than TL2. We found that $2^{16}$ locks is idle for TMACC-GE, while TL2 performs best with $2^{20}$.

### 3.2 Local Epochs

To perform conflict detection using local epochs, each transaction is assigned three filters: a read set, a write set, and a missed set. As before, the read set maintains the references read during the transaction. The write set holds references that are currently being committed by a transaction, and the missed set holds references committed by any other transaction during the local epoch. When a filter receives a *HW_AddToReadSet*, the reference is checked against all other transactions' write sets and the reading transaction's missed set, ensuring that any write that could have occurred before the associated read (i.e. in the current local epoch) will trigger a conflict. A *HW_WriteNotification* causes the reference to be added to the transaction's write set and checked against all other transactions' read sets, ensuring a conflict will be triggered for any read that could have potentially seen the result of the corresponding write. The written reference is also added to the transaction's read set, preventing write-write conflicts which cause a race during write buffer application. Finally, *HW_ClearWriteSet* first copies (merges) the write set into all other missed sets and then clears the write set. This allows each transaction to independently decide when it no longer needs to consider missed writes as potentially conflicting. The transaction does this with *HW_ClearMissedSet* which clears its own missed set, effectively moving it into a new local epoch. *HW_WriteNotification* could add references directly to the other transaction's missed sets, but having the intermediate step of using the local write set allows the transaction to abort a commit without polluting the other missed sets.

Algorithm 2 gives high level pseudo-code for the algorithm used by the TMACC-LE software runtime. The main difference in this software runtime, as compared to TMACC-GE, is the absence of locks during commit. Locks are not needed when using local epochs because the missed sets cause all of the writes performed during a commit to be logically moved to the beginning of an epoch defined locally for each transaction, not globally. Therefore, each transaction individually ensures that any of its own reads of a partial commit will signal a conflict, an effort which won't be frustrated by the update of a global epoch outside of the transaction's control.

In the local epoch scheme, an epoch is implicitly defined by what writes are contained in the transaction's missed set filter; thus no explicit local epoch counter is needed. In addition to firing a *HW_AddToReadSet* and locating the correct version of the datum, read barriers may choose to begin a new local epoch by sending a *HW_ClearMissedSet* command. A memory fence is then used to ensure that any subsequent read (and its corresponding *HW_AddToReadSet*) must wait until the *HW_ClearMissedSet* is complete and a new missed set has begun to collect writes performed in the new epoch. This eliminates the possibility that a conflicting read is performed during a local epoch update and the conflict lost. Periodically incrementing the local epoch is not necessary for correct operation but reduces the number of false conflicts and is especially important in applications using long-running transactions.

## 4. TMACC Performance Evaluation

In this section, we present the performance and analysis of the TMACC-GE and -LE architectures implemented on FARM. We present the performance results in two parts. First, we present results from a microbenchmark that is used to explore the full range of TM application parameters. Second, we present results of full applications from the STAMP benchmark suite [6]. We show where the STAMP applications fit into the design space as characterized by the microbenchmark parameters and how these parameters explain the performance results. Finally, we project the performance of an ASIC TMACC implementation.

**Algorithm 3** Pseudocode for microbenchmark.

```
static int gArray1[A1];
static int gArray2[A2];
procedure UBENCH(A1, A2, R, W, T, C, N, tid)
    prob_rd = R/(R+W);
    for t = 1 to T do
        TM_BEGIN();
        for j = 1 to (R + W) do
            do_read = random(0,1) ≤ prob_rd ? true : false;
            addr1 = random(0,A1/N) + tid*A1/N;
                                    ▷ addr1 does not conflict with others
            if do_read then
                TM_READ(gArray1[addr1]);
            else
                TM_WRITE(gArray1[addr1]);
            if C == true then
                addr2 = random(0,A2);
                                    ▷ addr2 possibly conflicts with others
                if do_read then
                    TM_READ(gArray2[addr2]);
                else
                    TM_WRITE(gArray2[addr2]);
        TM_END();
```

### 4.1 Microbenchmark Analysis

In order to characterize the performance of TMACC-LE and TMACC-GE, we used an early version of EigenBench [21] which is a simple synthetic microbenchmark specially devised for TM system evaluation. This microbenchmark has two major advantages over a benchmark suite composed of complex applications. First, transactional memory is a complex system whose performance is affected by several application parameters. The microbenchmark makes it simple to isolate the impact of each parameter, independently from the others. Second, a microbenchmark allows us to get a theoretical upper bound on the best possible performance given a set of parameters. We arrive at this bound by simply executing a multi-threaded trial run without the protection of transactional memory or locking. Doing this with a real application would almost certainly produce incorrect results. We call this unattainably good performance the "unprotected" version.

Algorithm 3 shows the pseudocode for the microbenchmark. The algorithm, at the core, is nothing more than multiple threads executing a random set of array accesses. Several parameters are necessary: $A1$ and $A2$ are the sizes of two arrays, the first a partitioned array for non-conflicting accesses, the second a smaller shared array for conflicting accesses; $R$ and $W$ are, respectively, the average number of reads and writes, per transaction; $T$ is the number of transactions executed per thread; $N$ is the number of threads; and $C$ is a flag determining whether or not conflicting accesses should be performed. Note that if $C$ is unset, there should be no violations since every thread only accesses its partition of the array. If $C$ is set, then the shared $A2$ array is accessed in addition to the normal accesses to $A1$, decoupling the working set size and the read/write ratio from the probability of violation.

We now use the microbenchmark to evaluate the performance of our two TMACC systems across several different variables. Table 3 shows the parameter sets used in the study, and the performance results are displayed in Figure 5. All graphs in this section show both speedup relative to sequential execution with no locking or transactional overhead (solid lines) and the percentage of started transactions that were violated (dotted lines). In all graphs except for (e), speedup is shown for 8 threads.

Throughout our analysis, the baseline STM for comparison is TL2 [15], which is generally regarded as a high-performing, modern STM implementation that is largely immune to performance pathologies. We use the basic GV4 versioned locks in TL2, the default in the STAMP distribution [37]. We use TL2 because its algorithms for version management and conflict detection are the closest match to the TMACC algorithms, allowing for the best indication of the speedup achieved using the hardware. SwissTM [16] is the highest performing STM of which the authors are aware and provides 1.1 to 1.3 times the performance of TL2 on the STAMP applications presented here. We also present the best possible performance using the aforementioned "unprotected" method as an upper bound. Note that this is truly an upper bound and usually unattainable because it will produce incorrect results in the face of any conflicts. Throughout the analyses of results, TMACC-GE and TMACC-LE represent the schemes described in Section 3.

Graph (a) shows the impact of working set size on TM systems. The prominent knee in the performance of each system corresponds to the working set size outgrowing the on-chip cache. Below the knee, where all user data and TM metadata fit on-chip, TL2 is spared from off-chip accesses and outperforms the TMACC systems which must still pay the costly round trip communication with the FPGA. This effect would be heavily mitigated with faster (or closer) hardware, and it is certainly rare for the working set of real parallel workloads to fit in the on-chip cache.

Above the knee, we observe that both TMACC-GE and TMACC-LE significantly outperform TL2, around 1.35x and 1.75x respectively, approaching the upper bound of 1.95x. In this region, TL2's performance suffers because its extra metadata causes significant cache pressure. Specifically, TL2 relies on its metadata for conflict detection, so its metadata grows proportionally to a transaction's read set. TMACC-GE, on the other hand, uses metadata only for commit, so its metadata grows with a transaction's write set, which is almost always smaller than its read set.

Graph (b) explores the impact of transaction size on speedup and violation rate. In this graph, we see a well-defined difference in speedup among the systems. In the flat region in the middle, the speedup of each system is nearly identical to the speedup of large working sets in graph (a). For small transactions, TMACC-GE's speedup diminishes because the relative cost of the FPGA round trip latency and global epoch management grows as transaction size decreases. We will take a closer look at short transactions in graph (e). For large transactions, the performance of TMACC-LE drops because the lack of ordering information in local epochs causes the missed sets to become polluted and emit more false positives. This is one case where global epochs are preferred over local epochs.

Graph (c) depicts the impact of varying the probability of violations by turning on $C$ and varying the size of $A2$ in our microbenchmark. Note that the graph uses semi-log axes. With a small $A2$, there are many violations and transactional retries dominate performance, making the conflict detection overhead less important. As $A2$ grows, contention decreases and the conflict detection overhead becomes more important, explaining the expanding performance gap between TMACC-LE, with its low-overhead conflict detection, and the others.

Graph (d) explores the impact of write set size, and again it is not surprising that the false positive rate of TMACC-LE becomes non-trivial due to the inherent pessimism in the local epoch scheme. However, these false positives are not enough to outweigh the performance advantage of low-overhead conflict detection.

Interestingly, TMACC-GE also shows diminishing speedup as write-set size increases. On closer inspection, we found that this degradation is due to the cache line migration of locks between the two CPU sockets during commit. As explained in Section 3.1, TL2 uses more locks than TMACC-GE so it is not as sensitive to this issue. Increasing the number of locks used by TMACC-GE diminishes the effect, but reduces overall performance. Having the FPGA participate in the coherence fabric significantly increases the

| | parameter set label | A1*sizeof(int) | A2 | R | W | C | N |
|---|---|---|---|---|---|---|---|
| (a) | working-set size | 0.5 $\sim$ 64 (MB) | - | 80 | 4 | $false$ | 8 |
| (b) | transaction size | 64 (MB) | - | 10 $\sim$ 400 | $max(1, R * 0.05)$ | $false$ | 8 |
| (c) | true conflicts | 64 (MB) | 256 $\sim$ 16,384 | 40 | 2 | $true$ | 8 |
| (d) | write-set sizes | 64 (MB) | - | 80 | 1 $\sim$ 128 | $false$ | 8 |
| (e) | # of threads (med-sized TX) | 64 (MB) | - | 80 | 4 | $false$ | 1 $\sim$ 8 |
| | # of threads (small-sized TX) | 64 (MB) | - | 4 | 1 | $false$ | 1 $\sim$ 8 |

**Table 3.** Parameter sets used in the microbenchmark evaluation. The labels here match those used in Figure 5.

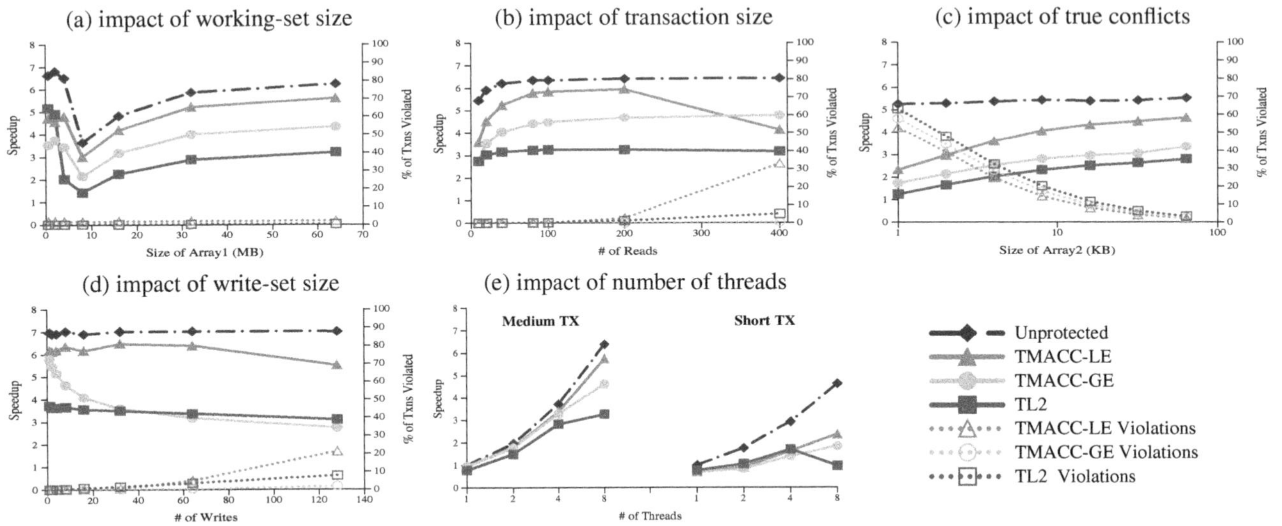


**Figure 5.** Microbenchmark performance for various parameter sets. Speedup is shown for 8 threads (except in (e))

last level cache miss penalty for all processors. This is a prominent factor in the TMACC-GE results, and experiments in Section 4.3 show that moving to an ASIC implementation would largely eliminate the performance degradation of TMACC-GE seen here.

Graph (e) examines the impact of number of threads using both medium-sized transactions and small-sized transactions. Overall, the systems show worse performance for small-sized transactions because they all pay a constant overhead per transaction, which is not easily amortized by short transactions. With the long communication delay to the FPGA, TMACC-GE and TMACC-LE are unable to achieve better performance than TL2 for short transactions running on 2 or 4 threads. While the FARM system limits us to 8 threads, scalability to many more threads can be achieved using multiple FPGAs. This scheme would require communication between the FPGAs and is left for future work.

The dramatic drop in TL2 performance for short transactions at 8 threads is the result of moving from a single chip to two chips and the large miss penalty described above. Taking the FPGA out of the system eliminates this drop in performance as shown in Section 4.3. We note that this poor TL2 performance on FARM is only present when transactions are very short.

To summarize, we see that TMACC provides significant acceleration of transactional memory except when transactions are too short to amortize the extra overhead imposed by communicating with the Bloom filters. We also find that in the case of TM acceleration, global epochs only perform better than local epochs when a large number of shared reads and writes are performed in a relatively short running transaction. In this case, the lack of ordering information is a larger factor in system performance.

### 4.2 Performance Evaluation using STAMP

In this section, we evaluate the performance of TMACC on FARM using STAMP[6], a transactional memory benchmark suite composed of several applications which vary in data set size, memory access patterns, and size of transactions. Intruder, bayes, and yada from the STAMP suite did not execute correctly in the 64-bit environment of FARM (even using TL2) due to bugs in the STAMP code and have been omitted from the study. Bayes's and yada's long transactions with a high violation rate are similar to those in labyrinth, and intruder's short transactions are similar to those in kmeans-high. Thus, the absence of these apps does not significantly reduce the coverage of the suite. Table 4 summarizes the input parameters and the key characteristics of each application. Cycles per transaction were measured during single-threaded execution with no read and write barriers. We can roughly group the applications into two sets by transaction size: vacation, genome, and labyrinth have larger transactions while ssca2 and kmeans use smaller transactions. Kmeans has large amounts of spatial locality in its data access and thus uses fewer cycles per transaction despite having more shared reads and writes.

For this analysis, we include RingSTM [36]. This STM system uses a similar approach to accelerating transactional barriers as TMACC, but the Bloom filters are implemented in software rather than hardware. Like TMACC but unlike TL2, RingSTM provides privatization safety. Our RingSTM implementation is based on the latest open-source version [35] and uses the single-writer algorithm. To provide a better comparison to TL2 and our TMACC variants, this implementation uses the write buffer implementation from TL2 instead of the hash table typically used in RingSTM. In our experiments, the ring is configured to have 1024 entries, where each entry is a 1024-bit filter.

| Name | Input parameters | RD/tx | WR/tx | CPU cycles/tx | Memory usage (MB) | Conflicts |
|---|---|---|---|---|---|---|
| vacation-low | n2 q90 u98 r1048576 t4194304 | 220.9 | 5.5 | 37740 | 573 | very low |
| vacation-high | n4 q60 u90 r1048576 t4194304 | 302.14 | 8.5 | 37642 | 573 | low |
| genome | g16384 s64 n16777216 | 55.8 | 1.9 | 48836 | 1932 | low |
| kmeans-low | m256 n256 65536-d32-c16.txt | 25 | 25 | 690 | 16 | high |
| kmeans-high | m40 n40 65536-d32-c16.txt | 25 | 25 | 680 | 16 | low |
| ssca2 | s20 i1.0 u1.0 l3 p3 | 1 | 2 | 2360 | 1320 | very low |
| labyrinth | x512-y512-z7-n512.txt | 180 | 177 | $6.1 * 10^9$ | 32 | high |

**Table 4.** STAMP benchmark input parameters and application characteristics.

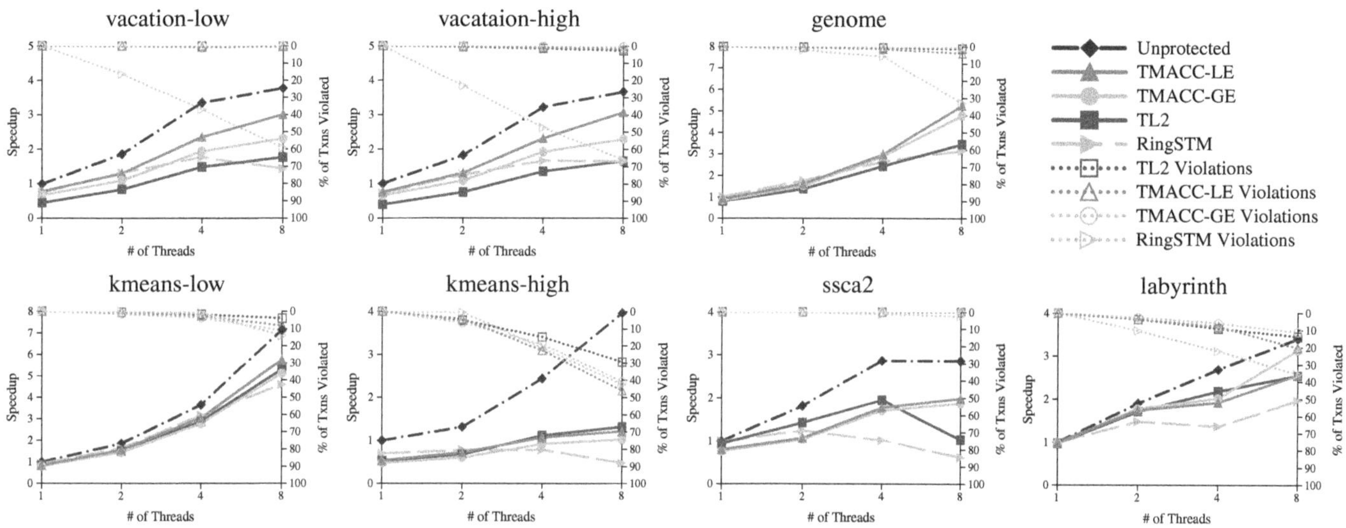


**Figure 6.** STAMP performance on the FARM prototype.

Figure 6 shows performance results from executing the STAMP applications on the FARM prototype. In this graph, we present speedups of 1, 2, 4 and 8 cores and the percentage of started transactions that were violated. At first glance, we see that the general trends we saw in the microbenchmark are present in the STAMP applications; TMACC performs well with large transactions but is unable to provide acceleration to small transactions. We also provide the unprotected execution time, using the same method we used in Section 4.1. As before, the result of such execution is incorrect and serves as a strict upper bound. As expected, not all applications were able to run unprotected; some would crash or fall into infinite loops.

For vacation-high, vacation-low, and genome, the common characteristics are a relatively large number of reads per transaction, small number of writes per transaction, and small number of conflicts. See Table 4 for exact values. Commit overhead is low due to the small write set and minimal time wasted retrying transactions because of the small number of conflicts. Also, constant overheads such as register checkpointing are amortized over the long running length. Thus, in these large-transaction applications, the numerous reads make the barrier overhead the dominant factor influencing performance of the TM system. We saw this effect in Figure 5.(b). This graph uses a microbenchmark parameter set which corresponds to the characteristics of these applications, and we see a very similar spread in performance results for the large-transaction STAMP applications. Performance gain with respect to TL2 for these applications averages 1.36x for TMACC-GE and 1.69x for TMACC-LE. Unprotected execution provides an average speedup of 2.18x. Note that for vacation-high running on TMACC-LE, while the number of reads is about 300, the drop shown in Figure 5.(b) does not happen because vacation-high does not have as many writes as the microbenchmark used in that graph.

The TMACC systems perform similar to RingSTM for low thread counts but do not suffer from the drop in performance at higher thread counts like RingSTM. The drop in performance at higher thread counts seen in RingSTM arises because it is unable to quickly check individual reads against write set filters like TMACC is able to do. It instead checks read set filters against write set filters, and this filter to filter comparison has a much higher probability of false positives, leading to very high false conflict rates and significantly degrading performance.

Kmeans-low features a relatively small number of reads, large number of writes, and small number of conflicts. From Figure 5.(b), we can expect that a small number of reads will diminish the performance gap between TL2 and TMACC. We also see in Figure 5.(d) that the large number of writes will further diminish TMACC-GE's performance. The combined effect explains what we see for kmeans-low in Figure 6 where for 8 threads TMACC-LE shows a 9% acceleration over TL2 but TMACC-GE is 5% slower.

Even though kmeans-high has very similar characteristics to kmeans-low except for the number of conflicts, the large number of violations in kmeans-high overshadows any other effects and limits the speedup of all three systems to a mere 1.3x with 8 threads. This situation is captured in Figure 5.(c) where the performance of the three systems converges as the rate of violation increases. As in kmeans-low, the small transactions make it difficult to amortize the communication overheads of TMACC and it is not able to achieve any speedup over TL2. Both TMACC systems were addi-

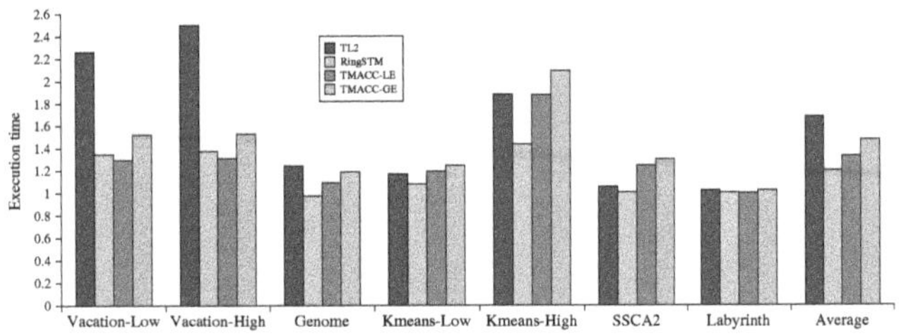


**Figure 7.** Single threaded execution time relative to sequential execution.

| WR \ RD | 2 | 4 | 6 | 8 | 10 | 12 | 14 |
|---|---|---|---|---|---|---|---|
| 14 | 3 | 3 | 3 | 3 | 3 | 3 | 3 |
| 12 | 3 | 3 | 3 | 3 | 3 | 3 | 3 |
| 10 | 3 | 3 | 3 | 3 | 3 | 3 | 3 |
| 8 | 2 | 2 | 3 | 3 | 3 | 3 | 3 |
| 6 | 1 | 2 | 2 | 3 | 3 | 3 | 3 |
| 4 | 1 | 1 | 2 | 2 | 2 | 2 | 3 |
| 2 | 1 | 1 | 1 | 1 | 2 | 3 | 3 |

1 TL2 performs better by more than 3%
2 Two schemes show similar performance
3 TMACC-GE performs better by more than 3%

**Figure 8.** Performance comparison of TMACC-GE (ASIC) and TL2 for short transactions.

tionally undermined by an even larger number of violations than TL2, which is interesting because Figure 5.(c) shows the TMACC systems having fewer violations in the face of true conflicts. We suspect this is a result of TL2's versioned locks giving more importance to the lower bits of the address in performing conflict detection. This causes TL2 to have fewer false positives when addresses are close together, as they are in kmeans-high. The single-writer variant of RingSTM we use is not able to scale because of the large number of writes in both kmeans-low and kmeans-high, even though its violation rate is comparable to the other systems.

Like kmeans-low and kmeans-high, TMACC performance on ssca2 is bound by communication latency. The characteristics of ssca2 are well captured by the microbenchmark parameter set used to produce the short transactions graph in Figure 5.(e) which mirrors the ssca2 speedup graph in Figure 6. Refer to the discussion of graph (e) in Section 4.1 for an explanation of the results. RingSTM violates 2.5% of transactions when running 8 threads while the others violate less than 0.01%. ssca2 has such a large number of transactions that even a 2.5% violation rate adds significant overhead.

Labyrinth is a special case. As seen in Table 4, this application has a very large number of computational cycles inside each transaction. The execution time is therefore decided by nondeterministic execution paths and the number of violated transactions rather than TM overhead. In Figure 5.(c) we saw that, in general, TMACC-GE has fewer false positives than the other systems. So in labyrinth with 8 threads, the TMACC-GE system minimized the number of violations and performed well. For labyrinth's long-running transactions, the periodic intra-transaction increment of the TMACC-LE local epoch was especially important.

Finally, Figure 7 highlights the single thread overhead of the systems using the single threaded execution time relative to sequential execution time. We see that TMACC and RingSTM have less overhead than TL2 running vacation because of the frequent barriers. As transactions get smaller in applications like kmeans and ssca2, commit time becomes more important and the TMACC systems suffer, while RingSTM continues to do well. Note that TMACC-GE consistently has more overhead than TMACC-LE because of the extra time required to (unnecessarily) obtain the locks during commit. With few barriers and very long transactions, labyrinth has almost no overhead in any of the systems.

### 4.3 Performance Projection for TMACC ASIC

In the previous sections, we have observed a few artificial effects caused by the large cache miss penalty in the FARM system. Since both TMACC and TL2 witness performance degradation due to these issues, an interesting question is whether the conclusions drawn thus far would still be valid in a system absent of these latency anomalies, such as an off-chip ASIC or part of the *uncore* on a chip. The acceleration hardware as presented does not require a high clock frequency and would occupy a small silicon footprint in modern processes. Thus in this section, we modify our system to project the performance of TMACC onto the design point of an off-chip ASIC. This could be either a stand-alone chip, or part of the system's north bridge or memory controller, for example. The performance of an on-chip TM accelerator would be even better, since it has a shorter round-trip latency.

To simulate the performance of an ASIC TMACC implementation, we first detach the FPGA from the system, eliminating the FPGA-induced snoop latency witnessed by all coherent nodes on every cache miss. Then, we replace FPGA-communication software routines with idle loops in which we control the number of iterations to simulate different desired communication latencies. In addition, we change the conflict detection to report a conflict randomly with a given probability. We keep all the STM overheads but simulate hardware latency. This modified system is a performance simulator; like the unprotected version it does not provide serializable execution, but can serve as good indicator of real performance.

For the projection study, we repeated the microbenchmark experiments performed in Section 4.1 using these techniques. We used the measured off-chip cache miss latency as the communication latency in our simulation, the rationale being that the ASIC is about as "far" away from the processor as DRAM. In general, we found the trends and conclusions are the same as those presented in Section 4.1 expect where we explicitly mentioned otherwise in the discussions of graphs (d) and (e) of Figure 5. We omit graphs of the results due to space constraints.

A common trend seen in all the experiments is that the performance of TMACC-GE now comes closer to the unprotected, since the ASIC design point significantly reduces the cache migration latency, and thus the overhead of global epoch management. As noted in the discussion of graph (d) in Section 4.1, the dramatic performance degradation of TMACC-GE as the write set grows disappears with the reduced cache miss penalty of an ASIC implementation. Also, the performance of TL2 with small transactions no longer drops dramatically when moving to a dual socket configuration. Both TMACC systems also performed better than before for short transactions; TMACC-LE outperforms TL2 on 8 threads by 9% now, but TMACC-GE still falls 5% short of TL2 performance.

To determine the point where TMACC-GE begins to outperform TL2, we repeated the short transaction experiment from Figure 5.(e), sweeping the number of reads and writes from 2 to 14, the result is presented as a schmoo plot in Figure 8. When there are more than 8 reads or writes, TMACC-GE is able to match the performance of TL2. When there are more than 12, there are enough accelerated barriers to compensate for the extra cost of communication, and TMACC-GE outperforms TL2. TMACC-LE outperformed TL2 for all of these points. The inability of TMACC to accelerate very small transactions suggests that TMACC would compliment a system that targets small transactions, such as a best-effort HTM that uses a processor's write buffer to store speculative data and falls back to using TMACC for larger transactions.

### 4.4 Comparison with Simulation

We now briefly contrast our experiences and results with hardware to our early exploratory work done using software simulation. Considerable effort went in to making our simulations "cycle accurate", and our performance predictions for SigTM and TL2, presented in Figure 1, roughly matched the results presented in the corresponding papers. Initial results from the actual hardware, however, were quite different from those the simulator had predicted. One main reason for the discrepancy was the difference between the simulated and actual CPUs. The simplistic CPU model used in simulation (in-order with one non-memory instruction per cycle) drastically overstated the importance of reducing the instruction count in the transactional read and write barriers. Modern processors, such as those in FARM, are much more tolerant of extra instructions in barriers, reducing the benefit of eliminating those instructions.

Another primary source of inaccuracy arose from the fact that our simulated interconnect did not model variable latency and command reordering. The presence of these in a real system led us to develop the global and local epoch schemes presented in this paper and thus significantly impacted the performance of the system. In addition, our simulator assumed the processors were capable of performing true "fire-and-forget" stores with weak consistency without affecting the execution of the core. We therefore did not model the write combining buffer and its effect on system performance. In addition, smaller data sets used to run simulation in a reasonable time frame affected the system performance very differently than a real workload, in terms of bandwidth consumption, caching effects and TLB pressure.

Even though we could have performed a more accurate simulation and we eventually approached our desired performance using a modified design, we believe our experiences provide a strong example of the importance of building actual hardware prototypes. Although developing and verifying hardware requires increased time and effort when compared with using a simulator, hardware is essential to accurately gauge the performance of proposed architectural improvements and to bring out the many issues one might encounter in actually implementing the idea. Having a hardware implementation is also a strong evidence of the correctness and validity of a system.

## 5. Conclusion

In conclusion, we have presented an architecture, TMACC, for accelerating STM without modifying the processor cores. We constructed a complete hardware implementation of TMACC using a commodity SMP system and FPGA logic. In addition, two novel algorithms which use the TMACC hardware for conflict detection were presented and analyzed. Using the STAMP benchmark suite and a microbenchmark to quantify and analyze the performance of a TMACC accelerated STM, we showed that TMACC provides significant performance benefits. TMACC outperforms a plain STM (TL2) by an average of 69% in applications using moderate-length transactions, showing maximum speedup within 8% of an upper bound on TM acceleration. TMACC provides this performance improvement even in the face of the high communication latency between TMACC and the CPU cores. Overall, this paper demonstrates that it is possible to accelerate TM with an out-of-core accelerator and mitigate the impact of fine-grained communication with careful design.

## Acknowledgments

This work was funded by DOE contract, Sandia order 942017; Army contract AHPCRC W911NF-07-2-0027-1; DARPA contract, Oracle order 630003198; and the Stanford PPL affiliates program, Pervasive Parallelism Lab: NVIDIA, Oracle/Sun, AMD, and NEC.

We also thank A&D Technology Inc. for their help with the Procyon system and Michael Spear for providing a custom RingSTM implementation for our use.

## References

[1] A.-R. Adl-Tabatabai, B. Lewis, V. Menon, B. R. Murphy, B. Saha, and T. Shpeisman. Compiler and runtime support for efficient software transactional memory. In *PLDI '06: ACM SIGPLAN Conference on Programming Language Design and Implementation*, 2006.

[2] W. Baek, C. Cao Minh, M. Trautmann, C. Kozyrakis, and K. Olukotun. The OpenTM transactional application programming interface. In *PACT '07: 16th Internation Conference on Parallel Architecture and Compilation Techniques*, 2007.

[3] B. Bloom. Space/time trade-offs in hash coding with allowable errors. *Communications of ACM*, 1970.

[4] C. Blundell, J. Devietti, E. C. Lewis, and M. M. K. Martin. Making the fast case common and the uncommon case simple in unbounded transactional memory. In *ISCA '07: 34th International Symposium on Computer Architecture*, 2007.

[5] J. Bobba, N. Goyal, M. Hill, M. Swift, and D. Wood. Tokentm: Efficient execution of large transactions with hardware transactional memory. In *ISCA '08: 35th International Symposium on Computer Architecture*, 2008.

[6] C. Cao Minh, J. Chung, C. Kozyrakis, and K. Olukotun. STAMP: Stanford transactional applications for multi-processing. In *IISWC '08: Proc. The IEEE International Symposium on Workload Characterization*, 2008.

[7] C. Cao Minh, M. Trautmann, J. Chung, A. McDonald, N. Bronson, J. Casper, C. Kozyrakis, and K. Olukotun. An effective hybrid transactional memory system with strong isolation guarantees. In *ISCA '07: 34th International Symposium on Computer Architecture*, 2007.

[8] J. L. Carter and M. N. Wegman. Universal classes of hash functions. *Journal of Computer and System Sciences*, 18(2), 1979.

[9] C. Cascaval, C. Blundell, M. Michael, H. W. Cain, P. Wu, S. Chiras, and S. Chatterjee. Software transactional memory: Why is it only a research toy? *Queue*, 6(5), 2008.

[10] L. Ceze, J. Tuck, P. Montesinos, and J. Torrellas. BulkSC: bulk enforcement of sequential consistency. In *ISCA '07: 34th International Symposium on Computer architecture*, 2007.

[11] H. Chafi, J. Casper, B. D. Carlstrom, A. McDonald, C. Cao Minh, W. Baek, C. Kozyrakis, and K. Olukotun. A scalable, non-blocking approach to transactional memory. In *HPCA '07: 13th International Symposium on High Performance Computer Architecture*, 2007.

[12] S. Chaudhry, R. Cypher, M. Ekman, M. Karlsson, A. Landin, S. Yip, H. Zeffer, and M. Tremblay. Simultaneous speculative threading: a novel pipeline architecture implemented in sun's rock processor. In *ISCA '09: 36th Intl. Symposium on Computer Architecture*, 2009.

[13] L. Dalessandro, M. F. Spear, and M. L. Scott. NOrec: streamlining STM by abolishing ownership records. In *PPoPP '10: 15th ACM SIGPLAN Symposium on Principles and Practice of Parallel Programming*, PPoPP '10, 2010.

[14] P. Damron, A. Fedorova, Y. Lev, V. Luchangco, M. Moir, and D. Nussbaum. Hybrid transactional memory. In *ASPLOS '06: 12th Internation Conference on Architectural Support for Programming Languages and Operating Systems*, October 2006.

[15] D. Dice, O. Shalev, and N. Shavit. Transactional locking II. In *DISC '06: 20th Internation Symposium on Distributed Computing*, 2006.

[16] A. Dragojević, R. Guerraoui, and M. Kapalka. Stretching transactional memory. In *PLDI '09: ACM SIGPLAN Conference on Programming Language Design and Implementation*, 2009.

[17] L. Hammond, V. Wong, M. Chen, B. D. Carlstrom, J. D. Davis, B. Hertzberg, M. K. Prabhu, H. Wijaya, C. Kozyrakis, and K. Olukotun. Transactional memory coherence and consistency. In *ISCA '04: 31st International Symposium on Computer Architecture*, 2004.

[18] T. Harris and K. Fraser. Language support for lightweight transactions. In *OOPSLA '03: 18th ACM SIGPLAN Conference on Object-oriented Programing, Systems, Languages, and Applications*, 2003.

[19] M. Herlihy and J. E. B. Moss. Transactional memory: Architectural support for lock-free data structures. In *ISCA '93: 20th International Symposium on Computer Architecture*, 1993.

[20] O. S. Hofmann, C. J. Rossbach, and E. Witchel. Maximum benefit from a minimal HTM. In *ASPLOS '09: 14th International Conference on Architectural Support for Programming Languages and Operating Systems*, 2009.

[21] S. Hong, T. Oguntebi, J. Casper, N. Bronson, C. Kozyrakis, and K. Olukotun. Eigenbench: A simple exploration tool for orthogonal tm characteristics. In *IISWC '10: International Symposium on Workload Characterization*, 2010.

[22] S. Kumar, M. Chu, C. J. Hughes, P. Kundu, and A. Nguyen. Hybrid transactional memory. In *PPoPP '06: 11th ACM SIGPLAN Symposium on Principles and Practice of Parallel Programming*, 2006.

[23] J. Larus and R. Rajwar. *Transactional Memory*. Morgan Claypool Synthesis Series, 2006.

[24] M. Lupon, G. Magklis, and A. González. FASTM: A log-based hardware transactional memory with fast abort recovery. In *PACT '09: 18th International Conference on Parallel Architecture and Compilation Techniques*, 2009.

[25] V. J. Marathe, W. N. Scherer III, and M. L. Scott. Adaptive Software Transactional Memory. In *DISC '05: 19th International Symposium on Distributed Computing*, 2005.

[26] S. S. Mukherjee, B. Falsafi, M. D. Hill, and D. A. Wood. Coherent network interfaces for fine-grain communication. In *ISCA '96: 23rd International Symposium on Computer Architecture*, 1996.

[27] T. Oguntebi, S. Hong, J. Casper, N. Bronson, C. Kozyrakis, and K. Olukotun. FARM: A prototyping environment for tightly-coupled, heterogeneous architectures. In *FCCM '10: 18th Symposium on Field-Programmable Custom Computing Machines*, 2010.

[28] M. Olszewski, J. Cutler, and J. G. Steffan. JudoSTM: A dynamic binary-rewriting approach to software transactional memory. In *PACT '07: 16th International Conference on Parallel Architecture and Compilation Techniques*.

[29] H. E. Ramadan, C. J. Rossbach, D. E. Porter, O. S. Hofmann, A. Bhandari, and E. Witchel. Metatm/txlinux: transactional memory for an operating system. *SIGARCH Computer Architecture News*, 35(2), 2007.

[30] B. Saha, A. Adl-Tabatabai, and Q. Jacobson. Architectural support for software transactional memory. In *MICRO '06: International Symposium on Microarchitecture*, 2006.

[31] B. Saha, A.-R. Adl-Tabatabai, R. L. Hudson, C. Cao Minh, and B. Hertzberg. McRT–STM: A high performance software transactional memory system for a multi-core runtime. In *PPoPP '06: 11th ACM SIGPLAN Symposium on Principles and Practice of Parallel Programming*, 2006.

[32] T. Shpeisman, V. Menon, A.-R. Adl-Tabatabai, S. Balensiefer, D. Grossman, R. L. Hudson, K. Moore, and B. Saha. Enforcing isolation and ordering in stm. In *PLDI '07: Conference on Programming Language Design and Implementation*, 2007.

[33] A. Shriraman, S. Dwarkadas, and M. L. Scott. Flexible decoupled transactional memory support. In *ISCA '08: 35th International Symposium on Computer Architecture*, 2008.

[34] A. Shriraman, M. F. Spear, H. Hossain, V. J. Marathe, S. Dwarkadas, and M. L. Scott. An integrated hardware-software approach to flexible transactional memory. *SIGARCH Computer Architecture News*, 35, June 2007.

[35] M. F. Spear. Lightweight, robust adaptivity for software transactional memory. In *SPAA '10: 22nd ACM Symposium on Parallelism in Algorithms and Architectures*, 2010.

[36] M. F. Spear, M. M. Michael, and C. von Praun. RingSTM: scalable transactions with a single atomic instruction. In *SPAA '08: 20th Symposium on Parallelism in Algorithms and Architectures*, 2008.

[37] STAMP: Stanford transactional applications for multi-processing. `http://stamp.stanford.edu`.

[38] F. Tabba, M. Moir, J. R. Goodman, A. Hay, and C. Wang. NZTM: Nonblocking zero-indirection transactional memory. In *SPAA '09: 21st Symposium on Parallelism in Algorithms and Architectures*, 2009.

[39] C. Wang, W.-Y. Chen, Y. Wu, B. Saha, and A.-R. Adl-Tabatabai. Code generation and optimization for transactional memory constructs in an unmanaged language. In *CGO '07: International Symposium on Code Generation and Optimization*, 2007.

[40] L. Yen, J. Bobba, M. R. Marty, K. E. Moore, H. Volos, M. D. Hill, M. M. Swift, and D. A. Wood. LogTM-SE: Decoupling Hardware Transactional Memory from Caches. In *HPCA '07: 13th International Symposium on High Performance Computer Architecture*, 2007.

[41] L. Yen, S. Draper, and M. Hill. Notary: Hardware techniques to enhance signatures. In *MICRO '08: 41st International Symposium on Microarchitecture*, 2008.

# Hybrid NOrec: A Case Study in the Effectiveness of Best Effort Hardware Transactional Memory *

Luke Dalessandro[1] François Carouge[2] Sean White[2]
Yossi Lev[3] Mark Moir[3] Michael L. Scott[1] Michael F. Spear[2]

[1]University of Rochester
{luked, scott}@cs.rochester.edu

[2]Lehigh University
{frc309, saw207, spear}@cse.lehigh.edu

[3]Oracle Labs
{yossi.lev, mark.moir}@oracle.com

## Abstract

Transactional memory (TM) is a promising synchronization mechanism for the next generation of multicore processors. Best-effort Hardware Transactional Memory (HTM) designs, such as Sun's prototype Rock processor and AMD's proposed Advanced Synchronization Facility (ASF), can efficiently execute many transactions, but abort in some cases due to various limitations. *Hybrid TM* systems can use a compatible software TM (STM) in such cases.

We introduce a family of hybrid TMs built using the recent NOrec STM algorithm that, unlike existing hybrid approaches, provide *both* low overhead on hardware transactions *and* concurrent execution of hardware and software transactions. We evaluate implementations for Rock and ASF, exploring how the differing HTM designs affect optimization choices. Our investigation yields valuable input for designers of future best-effort HTMs.

***Categories and Subject Descriptors*** C.1.4 [*Computer System Organization*]: Parallel Architectures; D.1.3 [*Software*]: Concurrent Programming

***General Terms*** Algorithms, Design

***Keywords*** Transactional Memory

## 1. Introduction

As the industry shifts to pervasive multicore computing, considerable effort is being invested in exploring hardware support for concurrency and parallelism. Transactional Memory (TM) [25] is a leading example of such support. It allows the programmer to mark regions of code that should be executed atomically, without requiring them to specify *how* that atomicity is achieved. Typical implementations are based on speculation. While proposals exist for unbounded and fully virtualized hardware TM (HTM) [24], concrete industry proposals are currently focused on *best-effort* HTM that imposes limits on hardware transactions. Sun's prototype multicore SPARC™ processor code named Rock [8], and AMD's proposed Advanced Synchronization Facility (ASF) extension to the x86 architecture [3] are two prominent examples. The limitations of such systems can be hidden from programmers using a *hybrid* approach, in which logical transactions can be executed using HTM, but resort to a software TM (STM) alternative when necessary.

Early hybrid TM algorithms [11, 30] support *concurrent* execution of hardware and software transactions, achieved by instrumenting a hardware transaction's memory operations with accesses to STM metadata, allowing it to detect conflicts with software transactions. This approach enables logical transactions to switch to software on a per-transaction basis but imposes significant overhead on hardware transactions and constrains the STM implementation. This results in systems with both high overheads and limited scalability.

Lev et al.'s PhTM hybrid significantly reduces the impact on hardware transactions by establishing global *phases* of execution [29]. As a result hardware transactions need instrumentation only at the boundaries of transactions, to detect global phase changes. PhTM performs significantly better than prior options when hardware transactions are mostly successful, and allows more flexibility for the STM implementation, which is no longer constrained by the potential for concurrent hardware transactions. However, PhTM's phase changes amount to application-wide synchronization barriers that result in poor performance for workloads in which switching becomes frequent. In addition, tuning of PhTM's phase change protocol is complicated and prone to overfitting.

Our goal is to develop a family of novel hybrid TM algorithms that combine the best features of both HyTM and PhTM: support for concurrent hardware and software transactions without the overhead of per-access instrumentation for hardware transactions. We achieve this by using Dalessandro et al.'s NOrec STM [10] as the software component. Section 2 presents more detailed background about best-effort HTM and previous hybrid TM algorithms. Section 3 expands a two-paragraph hybrid TM sketch appearing in Dalessandro et al. [10] into a simple but full-fledged hybrid design and then discusses a variety of novel, hardware-independent refinements that address its obvious weaknesses. Sections 4 and 5 develop platform-specific implementations, optimizations, and evaluations for Rock and ASF respectively.

While direct performance comparisons between Rock hardware and the ASF simulator are not meaningful, differences between their HTM implementations result in different optimization choices. Section 6 elaborates on these differences, and highlights some of the advantages and disadvantages of each platform in supporting a NOrec-based hybrid system—a contribution that we believe provides useful guidance to designers of future HTM. Section 7 gives an overview of related work and Section 8 concludes.

## 2. Background

Comprehensive coverage of TM proposals and implementations is available in a recent book by Harris et al. [24]. Here we focus on issues of particular relevance to our work.

* At the University of Rochester, this work was supported by NSF grants CNS-0615139, CCF-0702505, CSR-0720796, and CCR-0963759. At Lehigh University, this work was supported by NSF grant CNS-1016828.



*ASPLOS'11,* March 5–11, 2011, Newport Beach, California, USA.

## 2.1 Hardware TM

Herlihy and Moss [25] proposed TM as a hardware mechanism to support the development of non-blocking data structures. In this proposal, and in many others that followed it, the atomicity of transactions is enforced by using the cache coherence protocol.

To avoid revealing speculative state to other processors, transactional stores are typically buffered locally until the transaction completes. Herlihy and Moss use a special transactional cache, which bounds the size of transactions, for this purpose.

To ensure that successful transactions appear to occur atomically, a processor attempts to acquire exclusive ownership of all cache lines modified by its transaction. If successful, it can then decide locally to commit the transaction, at which point requests for any cache lines modified by the transaction will receive the data written by the transaction; partial effects are never visible.

HTM implementations must also ensure that reads are consistent and current at commit time. Again, many proposals use cache coherence to achieve this: if the processor retains (at least shared) ownership of every cache line read by the transaction up to the point of its commit, then each of the locations read is unchanged and the transaction is consistent at the commit. Typically the transaction is aborted if such a cache line is invalidated or evicted.

A key issue is how a processor responds to a request for a cache line it holds transactionally. The *requestor-wins* policy provides the requested line and aborts the local transaction. While simple, this policy can lead to poor performance and livelock: competing transactions may abort each other repeatedly. Backoff is effective in avoiding this effect, but can be difficult to tune. More sophisticated conflict resolution mechanisms are appealing but entail more implementation complexity.

Some HTM implementations, such as the $\beta$-TVP proposal of Tabba et al. [40], can reacquire ownership of a lost cache line, check that any values read from it previously are current, and thus avoid aborting the transaction. Similar *value based validation* is found in some STM systems, including the NOrec algorithm.

As described, HTM implementations cannot commit transactions that exceed the size or geometry of the hardware structures used to track the cache lines accessed by a transaction and to buffer speculative stores. Proposals for *unbounded* HTM [4, 5, 21, 33, 35] overcome such limitations, but introduce significant complexity; commercial systems built or proposed to date do not attempt to implement unbounded transactions.

Without unbounded transactions, an STM alternative is needed to support transactions that exceed hardware limits. Given this, it is reasonable for hardware transactions to fail occasionally for other reasons, such as interrupts, traps, etc. The option of an occasional spurious failure simplifies hardware design, because difficult corner cases can be resolved simply by aborting the transaction.

This design strategy is known as *best-effort* HTM: the hardware attempts to support as many transactions as possible given the constraints of the implementation, but can abort any transaction for any reason. It is important for software to receive good feedback about the reason for a particular abort, to enable sensible decisions about whether and when to retry a hardware transaction.

Sun's prototype Rock processor and AMD's ASF proposal are concrete examples of best-effort HTMs. While their designs are similar in some ways, they have different interfaces, capabilities, and reasons for aborting transactions. For example, Rock uses a core's store buffer to hold transactional stores, imposing a limit of 32 stores per transaction. The ASF specification simply states that conforming implementations will support (potentially repeated or redundant) stores to at least 4 elements. We examine the design decisions of Rock and ASF in more detail as we develop hybrid TM implementations for them in Sections 4 and 5 respectively.

```
padded orec orecs []

HW_READ(address)
  value = *address
  if (orecs[hash(address)].mode != WRITE)
    return value
  abort

HW_WRITE(address, value)
  if (orecs[hash(address)].mode != UNOWNED)
    abort
  *address = value
```

**Figure 1.** Pseudocode illustrating HyTM instrumentation for hardware, from Damron et al. [11]. This code assumes the STM counterpart uses visible (or semivisible) readers. We use **padded** to indicate variables that are padded to avoid false sharing.

## 2.2 Hybrid TM

We use the term *hybrid TM* for systems that can execute a logical transaction in hardware, or use a compatible STM implementation when this is not successful. Hybrid systems [11, 30] do not require that the hardware be able to commit any particular transaction. Some other hybrid-like systems [10, 26] depend on the HTM to be able to commit at least some small transactions. Next we briefly describe two hybrid TM systems most closely related to this paper.

HyTM[1] [11] generates two code paths for each source-level transaction—a software path targeting an ownership record (*orec*)-based STM, and a hardware path in which memory accesses are instrumented to perform appropriate checks of the STM metadata.

A software transaction modifies the mode of each orec covering a location it accesses, and hardware transactions access this information on each memory access in order to detect conflicts with software transactions. The instrumentation for hardware-path accesses is shown in Figure 1. The instrumentation ensures that a hardware transaction detects a conflict with a software one, either by observing that the mode of an orec indicates a conflict, or by aborting when a software transaction modifies the mode after the hardware transaction has read it. The overhead imposed on hardware transactions by this per-access instrumentation is considerable, including both additional instructions and the use of scarce, best-effort HTM resources to track per-location metadata (i.e., orecs).

PhTM [29] introduces global phases of execution, typically hardware-only and software-only. It employs simple instrumentation at transaction start and finish to enforce the phase discipline, and eliminates the costly per-access instrumentation of other hybrid systems. Because hardware and software transactions do not run concurrently, PhTM also allows more flexibility in implementing the STM used in software phases. However, if transactions must frequently be executed in software, phase changes incur system-wide synchronization barriers that severely impact performance and scalability. In addition, the algorithms used to trigger phase changes are difficult to tune and susceptible to overfitting. For workloads in which most transactions can succeed in hardware, the software-only phase may be implemented as a single, serial transaction running with minimal software instrumentation [29]. This design has been shown to lower the cost of phase synchronization barriers, at the cost of significantly less concurrency [9].

The emergence of STMs that do not employ per-location metadata (e.g., the NOrec STM [10] described in Section 3) provides an opportunity to reevaluate HyTM's defining characteristic—the con-

[1] We use *HyTM* to both refer to Damron et al. [11], and to describe algorithms in which hardware and software transactions execute concurrently.

```
1  padded unsigned seqlock

3  thread local unsigned snapshot
4  thread local ReadSet reads
5  thread local WriteSet writes

6  SW_VALIDATE
7    snapshot = seqlock
8    if (snapshot & 1)
9      goto 7
10   foreach (addr, val) in reads
11     if (*addr != val)
12       SW_ABORT
13   if (snapshot != seqlock)
14     goto 7

15 SW_BEGIN
16   snapshot = seqlock
17   if (snapshot & 1)
18     goto 16

19 SW_COMMIT
20   if (writes.empty())
21     return
22   while (!CAS(&seqlock, snapshot,
           snapshot + 1))
23     SW_VALIDATE
24   foreach (addr, val) in writes
25     *addr = val
26   seqlock = seqlock + 1
27   reads.reset(), writes.reset()

28 SW_READ(addr)
29   if (addr in writes)
30     return writes.find(addr)
31   val = *addr
32   if (snapshot != seqlock)
33     SW_VALIDATE
34     goto 31
35   reads.append(addr, val)
36   return val

38 SW_WRITE(addr, val)
39   writes.append(addr, val)

41 SW_ABORT
42   reads.reset(), writes.reset()
43   /* restart transaction */
```

**Figure 2.** The basic NOrec algorithm. The CAS on line 22 represents atomic compare-and-swap. Read and write sets are implemented at byte granularity and thus compatible with the draft C++ TM specification [1].

current execution of hardware and software transactions—without per-access instrumentation overhead on hardware transactions. That is the goal of the work described herein.

## 3. NOrec Hybrid Design

Our family of hybrid TM algorithms begins with Dalessandro et al. NOrec STM (Figure 2) [10]. NOrec does not require fine-grained, shared metadata, merely a single global sequence lock [27] (seqlock) for concurrency control. Transactions buffer transactional writes and log read address/value pairs in thread local structures. Committing writers increment the seqlock before writeback. Active transactions poll the global seqlock for changes indicating concurrent writer commits. A new value is evidence of possible inconsistency and triggers validation, done in a value-based style by comparing the logged address/value pairs to the actual values in main memory [17, 22, 34, 40].

An odd seqlock value indicates that a transaction is performing writeback; it effectively locks the entire shared heap. A consequence of this protocol is that only a single writer can commit and perform writeback at a time. This sequential bottleneck is minimized by validation *prior* to acquiring the seqlock for commit (Figure 2, Line 22). Successfully incrementing seqlock transitions a writer to a committed state in which it immediately performs its writeback and then releases the lock. A read-only transaction need only confirm that its reads were consistent and can commit without modifying seqlock.

NOrec scales well when its single-writer commit serialization does not represent the overall application bottleneck, i.e., writeback does not dominate the run time, and has been shown to have low latency. NOrec supports the *privatization* idiom [24] as required for compatibility with the C++ draft TM standard [1] and provides strong *publication* guarantees [32].

For the purposes of initial development, we assume that the best-effort HTM is strongly atomic [6], and that we can issue *nontransactional loads* within the context of a transaction—i.e., that we can load a location without adding it to our transactional read set. This second capability is not fundamental, but is useful for some optimizations and is supported by both Rock and ASF. In Sections 4 and 5 we discuss the implementation of variants of these algorithms on Rock and ASF, respectively.

In a NOrec-based hybrid TM, hardware transactions must respect the integrity of NOrec's single-writer commit protocol. Accordingly, hardware transactions that modify program data cannot commit during software writeback, and must signal their commit so as to trigger validation by concurrent software transactions. These

```
transaction {          transaction {
  x = 1                  if (x != y)
  y = 1                    STATEMENT
}                      }
```

(a) Static transactions.

Initially: x == y == 0

```
1 SW_WRITEBACK         HW_POST_BEGIN
2   x = 1
3                        r1 = x
4                        r2 = y
5                        if (r1 != r2)
6                          STATEMENT
7   y = 1
```

(b) Dynamic execution trace.

**Figure 3.** Execution of two transactions resulting in a hardware transaction observing inconsistent state.

two constraints neither impose requirements on hardware transactions in the absence of active software transactions, nor restrict the behavior of read-only transactions, however one further detail must be addressed in the hybrid TM design; hardware transactions may become *logically inconsistent* due to a concurrent software transaction's non-atomic writeback.

Consider the execution in Figure 3. The logical transaction in the left column executes and commits as a software transaction, while the logical transaction on the right executes in hardware. The dynamic trace shows one possible interleaving of operations from the software transaction's writeback with the hardware transaction's execution.

The hardware transaction performs an inconsistent read at Line 4—its read of x on Line 3 returns the value written by the software transaction, while the read of y returns the value written *before* the software transaction occurred. The strongly atomic hardware transaction will ultimately detect this inconsistency when the software transaction performs its update of y on Line 7, but can perform arbitrary actions in the meantime.

The danger here is that the inconsistent transaction may perform an action that has visible effects (e.g., a nontransactional store) that is not consistent with the semantics of the program. This situation is nearly identical to that of *zombie* transactions in STM [14, 38, 41], where inconsistent software transactions may perform most of the same dangerous operations that an inconsistent hardware transaction could. The difference is that a zombie transaction cannot com-

```
1  padded unsigned seqlock

5  HW_POST_BEGIN
6    if (seqlock & 1)
7      while (true) // await abort

9  HW_PRE_COMMIT
10   seqlock = seqlock + 2
```

(a) Our naive algorithm

```
1  padded unsigned seqlock
2  padded unsigned counter

5  HW_POST_BEGIN
6    if (seqlock & 1)
7      while (true) // await abort

9  HW_PRE_COMMIT
10   counter = counter + 1
```

(b) 2-Location

```
1  padded unsigned seqlock
2  padded unsigned counter[]
3  thread local unsigned id

5  HW_POST_BEGIN
6    if (seqlock & 1)
7      while (true) // await abort

9  HW_PRE_COMMIT
10   counter[id] = counter[id] + 1
```

(c) P-Counter

**Figure 4.** Instrumentation of hardware transactions in our basic hybrid NOrec algorithms. Line 7 spins until the committing software transaction completes writeback and releases the seqlock *at which point the hardware transaction aborts and restarts.* 2-Location adds a counter location that only hardware transactions modify, P-Counter distributes this counter to reduce cache contention. The HW_* instrumentation occurs *within* the scope of a hardware transaction, and all accesses are transactional.

mit from an inconsistent state, while a hardware transaction could if not prevented. We use the term zombie to refer to inconsistent logical transactions with the understanding that they are slightly different in hardware and in software.

In STM one of two solutions is used to avoid incorrect behavior due to inconsistent execution. An implementation may eliminate zombies by ensuring that each operation performed by a transaction is done from a consistent state, a property known as *opacity* and detailed by Guerraoui and Kapalka [20]. Alternatively, an implementation may admit the possibility of zombie execution and include appropriate preventative and recovery code, a process known as *sandboxing* and employed by Harris et al. [23] and Saha et al. [37]. Each of these approaches is possible in hybrid TM designs. Our initial algorithms are opaque (satisfy opacity); we discuss sandboxing hardware transactions in Section 3.2.

### 3.1 Basic Algorithms

The code in Figure 4a represents a naive integration of NOrec and a strongly atomic HTM. We instrument hardware transactions with a HW_POST_BEGIN barrier in which they read NOrec's shared seqlock. This includes seqlock in their read sets, effectively *subscribing* hardware transactions to software commit notifications: an abort is triggered when a software transaction acquires the lock to commit. If a hardware transaction starts and detects that a software transaction already owns the seqlock it spins until the software transaction completes writeback and releases the lock. Hardware transactions update seqlock in a HW_PRE_COMMIT barrier, *signaling* their commits to software transactions.

This implementation trivially satisfies the two constraints mentioned above. The HW_POST_BEGIN seqlock read and corresponding branch ensure both that no hardware transaction can commit during software writeback, and that the overall implementation is opaque: no transactional load can occur while the seqlock is held by software for writeback, thus logical zombies are impossible. The increment and write of the seqlock in HW_PRE_COMMIT notifies active software transactions of the need to validate their consistency.

Unfortunately, each hardware transaction conflicts with every software transaction (due to the early read of seqlock in HW_POST_BEGIN), and will abort when any software transaction commits, regardless of actual data conflicts. Similarly, each hardware transaction conflicts with every other hardware transaction (due to the early read of seqlock and the write of seqlock in HW_PRE_COMMIT), and will abort when any hardware transaction commits. These conflicts exist for each transaction's full duration, eliminating concurrency.

***2-Location*** Figure 4a uses the NOrec global seqlock for bidirectional communication: hardware transactions read it to subscribe to software commit notification and increment it to signal their commits to software transactions. Dalessandro et al. observe that a simple modification can address this shortcoming: a second shared location, counter, decouples subscribing from signaling.

As shown in Figure 4b,[2] hardware transactions still subscribe to software commits by reading seqlock in HW_POST_BEGIN, but they use counter to signal their own commits. This reduces the window of vulnerability to metadata conflicts between hardware transactions from the entire hardware transaction to the time that it takes to execute the increment in HW_PRE_COMMIT and commit.

Where software transactions previously polled only seqlock (Figure 2, Line 32) they must now maintain snapshots for, and poll, both seqlock and counter. NOrec's SW_COMMIT must also now perform additional validation after acquiring seqlock, in order to detect any hardware commit(s) that occurred before the CAS (Figure 2, Line 22). This validation consists of reading the hardware counter, and performing value-based validation if it has changed. This extra validation adds serial overhead to software transactions.

***P-Counter*** In 2-Location, hardware transactions use the counter to signal their commits to software transactions, but *not* to coordinate with other hardware transactions. Thus, hardware-hardware conflicts during counter increments are artificial and can be reduced or eliminated by distributing counter. Figure 4c assigns each processor core its own hardware counter. Hardware transactions modify different counter variables in HW_PRE_COMMIT and thus no longer conflict with each other. Any number of counters and any mapping of threads to counters can be used; we explore some variants in Section 4.

Where the 2-Location modification required software transactions to poll two locations, P-Counter requires them to poll $n + 1$, where $n$ is the number of counters. Thus, there is a tradeoff: using more counters reduces conflicts between hardware transactions, but increases overhead on software transactions—including the serial overhead in their SW_COMMIT barriers due to validation as described above. In practice, it makes sense to dynamically determine the number of counters and the thread-to-counter mapping based on current system conditions; this is future work. 2-Location can be seen as the degenerate case in which all threads share a single counter.

[2] This algorithm is slightly different than that presented in Dalessandro et al.. Their version requires progress guarantees for 2-location transactions, which we do not assume here.

```
HW_POST_BEGIN
  return

HW_PRE_COMMIT
  if (seqlock & 1) while (true);
  ...

HW_VALIDATE
  while (non_tx_load(seqlock) & 1)
    ; // spin

HW_READ(address)
  value = *address;
  HW_VALIDATE;
  return value;
```

**Figure 5.** Code to ensure opacity in a system with lazy subscription. Uses a nontransactional read in HW_VALIDATE. All other accesses are transactional.

```
padded unsigned sw_exists

SW_BEGIN
  atomic_add(sw_exists,1)
  ...

SW_COMMIT, SW_ABORT
  atomic_add(sw_exists,−1)
  ...

HW_PRE_COMMIT
  if ( sw_exists == 0) return
  ...
```

(a) SW-Exists

```
thread local bool readonly

HW_POST_BEGIN
  non_tx_store(readonly, true)
  ...

HW_POST_WRITE
  non_tx_store(readonly, false
    )

HW_PRE_COMMIT
  if (non_tx_load(readonly))
    return
  ...
```

(b) Read-Only

**Figure 6.** Filters that allow hardware transactions to avoid accesses to seqlock and counter in HW_PRE_COMMIT. The pseudo-code augments the underlying algorithm's metadata and instrumentation. HW_* instrumentation occurs within the scope of a hardware transaction.

### 3.2 Lazy Subscription and Sandboxing

In the HW_POST_BEGIN barriers of the hybrid algorithms described so far, a transactional read of the NOrec seqlock subscribes hardware transactions to software commit notification, and the corresponding branch stalls hardware transactions while software transactions write back. This both establishes opacity and prevents hardware writers from committing during software writeback.

The early read of the seqlock is conservative as it forces all hardware transactions to abort whenever any software transaction commits, regardless of true data conflicts. We can be more optimistic—and admit more concurrency—by delaying the transactional read of seqlock until commit time, as shown in Figure 5. In this manner, hardware transactions subscribe to software commit notification immediately prior to committing, increasing hardware-software concurrency by reducing the number of false aborts received by hardware transactions.

Delaying the read of seqlock sacrifices opacity, as nothing prevents a hardware transaction from reading inconsistent data during software writeback. The listing in Figure 5 re-establishes opacity by adding a HW_READ barrier that polls the seqlock nontransactionally and pauses if it is locked. This requires instrumentation on the hardware path. While per-access instrumentation in HyTM was shown to be a significant obstacle, this instrumentation neither performs writes nor uses scarce best-effort HTM resources, and is thus worth exploring.

As observed previously, sandboxing exists as an alternative to opacity. Rather than instrumenting all loads for consistency, we instrument only instructions whose effects may expose a transaction's inconsistency. Fortunately, sandboxing best-effort hardware transactions appears simpler than sandboxing STM [2, 23, 34, 37], as many of the behaviors that must be avoided (divide by zero, bus error, an infinitely looping thread reaching a context switch) cause hardware transactions in most best-effort HTM systems to abort without software intervention. Others can be avoided with software assistance by inserting a HW_VALIDATE call in front of any instruction that may be dangerous to perform from an inconsistent state (nontransactional store, indirect branch, etc.). The number of such instructions is likely to be significantly smaller than the number of reads.

### 3.3 Communication Filters

Recall that our constraints for the serializability of hardware and software transactions apply to writer transactions only in the presence of active software transactions. Our algorithms so far are thus overly conservative. We can "filter out" a significant number of cache misses and false aborts by avoiding competition for shared counters in the absence of software transactions.

The SW-Exists filter introduces a shared location, sw_exists, for use as an early exit test in the HW_PRE_COMMIT barrier. Software transactions make their presence visible by setting this location; hardware transactions may elide counter updates if sw_exists is not set. Figure 6a shows a simple atomic counter implementation of SW-Exists; a more scalable mechanism such as Ellen et al.'s [18] scalable non-zero indicator (SNZI) may be desirable depending on best-effort HTM characteristics. The atomic counter implementation causes a hardware transaction that has read it to abort on every change, and induces cache contention among the software transactions seeking to modify it; SNZI limits aborts to the important cases—the transitions between the zero and non-zero states—while reducing software contention.

Some transactions can be statically shown by the compiler to be read-only and in this case HW_PRE_COMMIT can be omitted in its entirety. Alternatively, a transaction may dynamically track its read-only status using a HW_WRITE barrier. Figure 6b presents instrumentation to update a thread-local flag after writing, and then test it at commit time. Note that the combined use of lazy subscription with sandboxing and the Read-Only filter requires at least a HW_VALIDATE barrier before committing because without it, the readonly flag may be based on inconsistent execution.

## 4. Rock

Sun's prototype multicore processor code named Rock uses aggressive checkpointing and speculative execution to improve single-threaded performance [8], and uses the same mechanisms to provide HTM via new *checkpoint* and *commit* instructions. Rock's checkpointing mechanism restores all registers when a transaction aborts. Memory accesses within a transaction are transactional unless explicitly marked nontransactional.

Rock augments L1 cache lines to track speculative reads, and holds speculative writes in the store buffer until commit or abort. Thus transactions can read as many lines as fit in the L1 data cache (limited by associativity), and can write as many locations as fit in the store buffer (32 in the configuration we used). Nontransactional stores are held in the store buffer as well; they cannot be used to circumvent its limited capacity. Some instructions cause aborts deterministically, as do some TLB misses and all page faults. Furthermore, any misspeculation (e.g., due to branch misprediction) during a transaction's execution will trigger an abort. The programmer should assume that every transaction may need to fall back to software mode even in the absence of contention or capacity overflow [12, 13].

### 4.1 Algorithms

We initially built both a Rock-compatible implementation of the NOrec-hybrid sketched in Dalessandro et al. [10] along with a straightforward implementation of P-Counter. We had to modify the former algorithm slightly to eliminate its dependence on small hardware transactions in the software commit protocol, because Rock does not guarantee such transactions will commit. We found that results using this algorithm were indistinguishable from P-Counter using a single counter, so we do not consider it further. The distributed counter in P-Counter uses a fixed number of counters, and threads are mapped to them by thread id.

***Lazy Subscription*** Rock's HTM lends itself well to the sandboxing implementation of lazy subscription (Section 3.2). Memory accesses are transactional by default and therefore have no effect if the transaction aborts. Most potential side effects of executing with inconsistent data, such as exceptions, simply cause the transaction to abort and therefore do not have a visible effect. We believe manual sandboxing instrumentation is needed only for commit instructions, nontransactional stores, and indirect branches that potentially lead to one of these (including unintentionally branching into executable data that may contain them). Referring to Figure 5, HW_PRE_COMMIT serves to sandbox commit instructions, so to fully sandbox Rock transactions, we must simply insert calls to HW_VALIDATE before nontransactional stores and indirect branches.

We find that lazy subscription and sandboxing consistently outperforms both eager HW_POST_BEGIN subscription and lazy subscription with read instrumentation. Admittedly, our benchmarks use neither nontransactional stores nor indirect branches. Rock's limitation on the total number of stores in a transaction implies that the use of nontransactional stores will be limited. Thus we do not anticipate significant overhead related to instrumenting them. Indirect branches are more common: they are used to implement function call returns, virtual function calls, and computed gotos. We *do* expect that sandboxing will show overheads for transactions that use these operations. Hardware validation requires a load (commonly a cache hit) and an easily predicted branch. As an indirect branch is already a relatively high overhead operation, indirect branch instrumentation should be proportionally less expensive than that of a load or store.

***SW-Exists*** We have found that it is always beneficial to use the SW-Exists filter, implemented using the SNZI algorithm variant from Lev et al. [28]. The simple implementation in Figure 6a, by contrast, suffers frequent cache misses and aborts as the counter changes among non-zero values.

***Read-Only*** We considered the Read-Only optimization but dismissed it for two reasons. First, it consumes precious locations in the store buffer, as multiple writes to the same location, even if thread local and nontransactional, are not necessarily coalesced. We can overcome this cost with a write barrier that checks the value of the flag and only updates it if it is not yet set, but we have seen in HyTM that branching in a barrier has severe negative consequences. Second, as discussed above, using this optimization in a sandboxed algorithm requires validating in HW_PRE_COMMIT, which we had initially hoped to avoid. We do believe that statically identifying read-only transactions and using HW_VALIDATE as the HW_PRE_COMMIT barrier for such cases is likely to be profitable.

### 4.2 Test Results

We used the same Rock processor used by Dice et al. [12, 13], and the Deque, Hashtable, and Red-Black Tree microbenchmarks [13]. The STAMP benchmarks, used in Section 5, were not an option on Rock due to hardware limitations—specifically, the fact that function calls within a transaction usually cause an abort. All microbenchmarks use the draft transactional C++ API [1], compiled with an internal development version of Oracle's transactional C++ compiler. STM compilation targets the open-source SkySTM library [28] interface; our hybrid and STM implementations implement this interface.

We report results for four TM systems. CGL is a pessimistic software implementation that simply acquires a global lock in SW_BEGIN and releases it in SW_COMMIT. This admits no concurrency, but is useful when comparing single-thread overheads. NOrec is the software implementation given in Figure 2. PhTM-NOrec is Lev et al.'s [29] PhTM algorithm as implemented by Dice et al. [12] and configured to use NOrec rather than TL2 [14] in the STM phase. (Separate experiments confirm that PhTM-NOrec consistently outperforms the equivalent PhTM-TL2 on our system.)

HyTM-NOrec is the P-Counter algorithm with lazy subscription, sandboxing, and the SNZI SW-Exists optimization. This combination consistently performed best. Algorithm suffixes indicate the number of counters used.

For all experiments in this paper, we take five data points, drop the high and low ones, and average the remaining ones. Variance was generally low, except as discussed or indicated.

***Deque benchmark*** In this benchmark, threads are divided evenly between the two ends of a deque, where they each perform 100, 000 operations chosen at random. Accesses to opposite ends of the deque usually do not conflict, so some parallelism is available, but contention among operations on each end means we cannot expect more than a $2\times$ speedup regardless of the number of threads. Results are shown in Figure 7a. For completeness, we also compare to McKenney's state-of-the-art lock-based, two-queue deque implementation [31]—a simple but clever concurrent algorithm that eluded noted concurrency experts for several years [12]. It is interesting that HyTM-NOrec largely closes the performance gap between the simple CGL and McKenney's algorithm without impacting programming complexity.

While CGL performs best with one thread, every transactional method outperforms it in all multithreaded cases, and every hybrid method outperforms NOrec. PhTM-NOrec either matches or slightly improves on the performance of the HyTM-NOrec variants with one and two threads, but then degrades to the point that it is worse than single-threaded throughput at sixteen threads. This is consistent with prior results [12], and suggests that added contention forces PhTM-NOrec into system-wide software mode frequently.

HyTM-NOrec allows a transaction to switch to software mode without causing all other transactions to do so, and thus avoids the cascade effect that PhTM-NOrec suffers. With 16 threads (8 for each end of the deque), only about 3% of operations caused PhTM-NOrec to switch to a software phase, but almost 24% of them *committed* using STM. In contrast, with HyTM-NOrec-1C, 0.6% of transactions switched to software without causing others to switch, allowing for a much higher success rate for hardware transactions, and better throughput and scalability as a result.

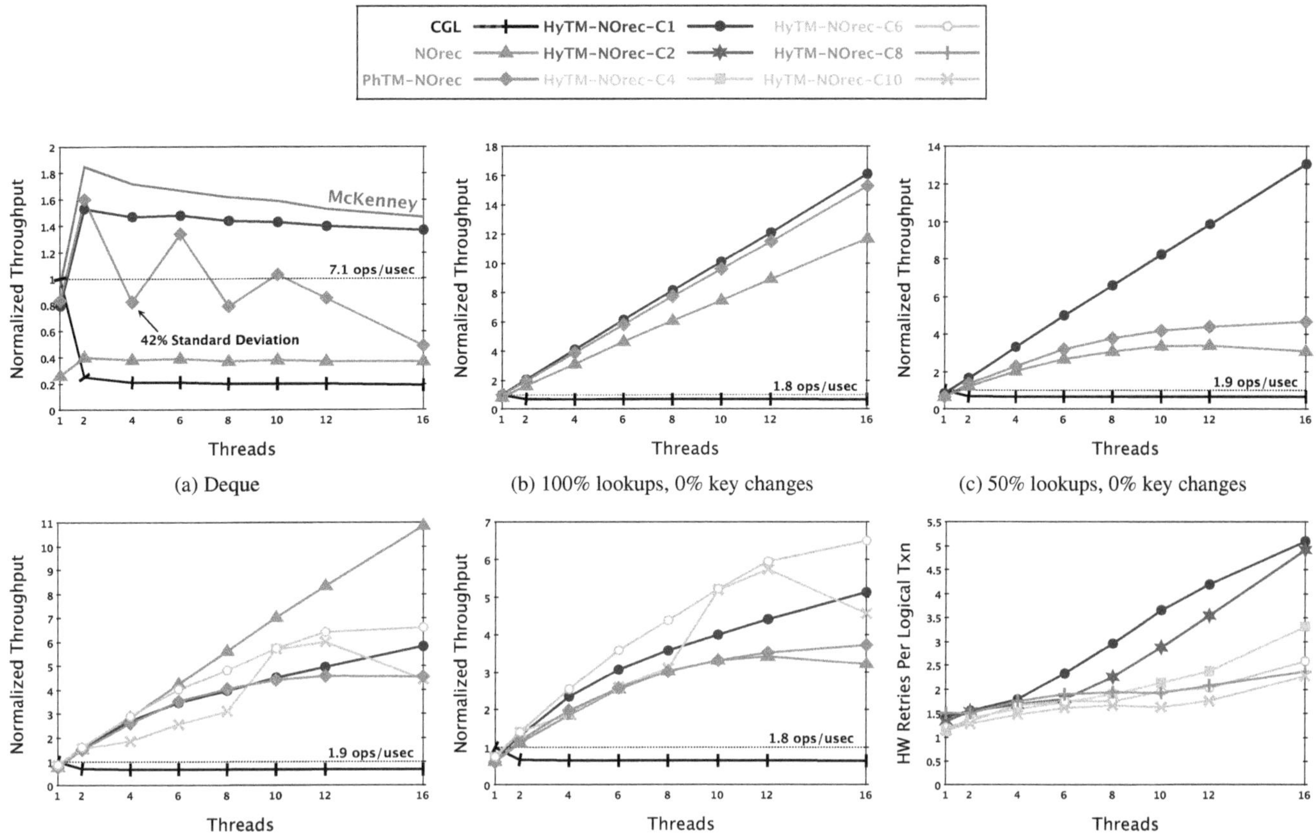


(a) Deque

(b) 100% lookups, 0% key changes

(c) 50% lookups, 0% key changes

(d) 95% lookups, 5% key changes

(e) 50% lookups, 5% key changes

(f) 50% lookups, 5% key changes

**Figure 7.** Selected Hashtable and Deque Results. Hashtable results are all for 128K key sets. -NC suffix indicates N hardware counters. Throughput is normalized to the single-threaded CGL results, which are explicitly given. In graphs 7a, 7b, and 7c we show only HyTM-NOrec-1C results as they are indistinguishable from other options. In 7d and 7e we add 6C and 10C results to illustrate their differences.

***Hashtable benchmark*** This benchmark consists of lookup, insert, and delete operations on a large hashtable ($2^{17}$ buckets), parameterized by the number of keys to access. Large key ranges result in access to the entire table, a working set that exceeds Rock's L1 cache capacity, while small key ranges fit comfortably in cache. In either case, conflicts between transactions are rare, and transactions are small and should be able to succeed in hardware. Prior hardware-assisted methods have been able to achieve fast, scalable performance with this workload. This predictable behavior provides us the opportunity to test hybrid TM performance as a function of the number of transactions failing to software in a controlled manner. To do so, we introduce a fourth type of operation, *key change*, which contains an instruction that is not supported in Rock transactions, and thus *must* complete in software.

We have conducted experiments with this benchmark for both small and large key ranges, and with a variety of operation mixes. Although all algorithms are faster when using a small key range such that the hashtable fits in the L1 cache, the results achieved for small and large key ranges are qualitatively similar. A representative sample, all using the large key range (128K), is shown in Figures 7b through 7e.

The HyTM-NOrec family outperforms PhTM-NOrec in almost all cases, often by significant margins. In the 100% lookup case (Figure 7b), almost all transactions succeed in hardware with all HTM-assisted algorithms, and their performance is similar. However, if we introduce a small number of key change operations (Figure 7d), all of the hardware-assisted algorithms perform worse, but PhTM-NOrec is affected worse than most of the HyTM-NOrec variants. This again illustrates the advantage that HyTM-NOrec has over PhTM-NOrec: one transaction switching to software does not cause a cascade of other transactions to do so too.

Although HyTM-NOrec outperforms PhTM-NOrec, it turns out that NOrec significantly outperforms all hardware-assisted methods in some cases; Figure 7d shows one example. There are several reasons for this. First, the workload is heavily dominated by read-only transactions, and NOrec overhead is low for such transactions: its serialized writeback phase is executed infrequently and therefore does not become a bottleneck.

Second, all of our hybrid TM implementations first try to use a hardware transaction, repeatedly in some cases, before switching to software if they do not succeed. The time spent on such transactions is largely wasted when they ultimately resort to software, as at least the key change operations must in this case. There are several possible ways to improve this situation. If the HTM gave clearer feedback about which transactions are unlikely to succeed, we might be able to switch to software more quickly. Relatedly, an HTM that does not fail transactions due to transient conditions such as cache misses and branch prediction may require less retrying in order to achieve good performance for some cases, thus allowing transactions that are going to switch to software to do so sooner. Finally, if compiler analysis or profiling could identify transactions that are unlikely to succeed using HTM, the system could run them in software from the outset.

Third, a transaction switching to software not only makes that operation slower, but can also degrade the performance of ongoing hardware transactions. For example, software transactions cause changes to the SW-Exists mode which causes hardware aborts due to branch misprediction. Moreover, software transactions require hardware transactions to increment counters that are often not present in their caches, adding substantial overhead to otherwise fast transactions. Therefore, hardware transactions are much more likely to fail when executed while software transactions are running. To avoid a cascade effect, the HyTM-NOrec logic sets a much higher threshold for failing to software if it observes, after a hardware transaction fails, that a SW transaction is already running.

As the number of non-read-only operations increases, NOrec's serialized writeback phase becomes a bottleneck, resulting in negative scalability at high thread counts. The HyTM-NOrec algorithms continue to increase throughput with larger numbers of threads, while the PhTM-NOrec performance is limited by that of its STM component. This can be seen clearly in Figure 7c. Even as we force some transactions to software (Figure 7e), the HyTM-NOrec variants outperform NOrec.

Within the HyTM-NOrec family, we observe that larger numbers of counters reduce hardware-hardware contention. This is due to reduced contention on the counters, and thus fewer conflicts between hardware transactions. For example, Figure 7f shows how adding counters reduces the abort rate. However, it is not always the case that such reduced contention increases overall throughput. Observe, for example, that performance becomes worse in Figure 7e going from 12 to 16 threads when using 10 counters. This is not surprising. More counters means validation of software transactions takes longer. Especially at higher threading levels, this in turn means there is more chance of a concurrent hardware transaction committing, forcing the software transaction to revalidate. Additionally, the SW_COMMIT barrier requires that software transactions read all of the hardware counters—likely missing in cache for some of them—after acquiring seqlock at commit, thus increasing NOrec's serial bottleneck. Similarly, in workloads in which there is application-level contention, slower validation makes it more likely that an actual conflict occurs, forcing the software transaction to retry. Thus, different numbers of counters are preferable for different workloads and threading levels.

We have not experimented with adaptive policies, such as varying the number of counters used, nor with static analysis to identify which transactions should attempt to use hardware transactions, and which should resort to software more quickly, or even immediately. We did experiment with various more sophisticated synchronization mechanisms between hardware and software transactions, but as in previous work [13], code used to implement more complex decisions about whether and when to retry a failed hardware transaction can affect cache, branch predictor, and TLB state, often reducing the chances for a subsequent attempt to succeed. Therefore, a more robust best-effort HTM may be needed to effectively implement such policies.

***Red-black tree benchmark*** We have also performed experiments with red-black trees (not shown), similar to those reported in Dice et al. [13]. In experiments with 100% lookups on small trees (key ranges of 128 and 512), HyTM-NOrec-1C performs best or close to best in all multithreaded tests. However, as we increase the key range and/or the fraction of operations that modify the tree, transactions acquire larger read sets and unpredictable branches, and have more trouble succeeding, for reasons similar to those reported by Dice et al. [13]. Again, a best-effort HTM that is less prone to failure due to misspeculation may be needed to improve our results for these kinds of workloads.

***Discussion*** We also tested a variant of PhTM whose software phase executes a single, uninstrumented transaction at a time (SEQUENTIAL-NOABORT mode in Lev et al. [29]), as tested by Christie et al. [9]. While it outperformed other algorithms in some of our tests, we do not consider this a viable solution. It cannot support explicit user-level abort due to its lack of instrumentation. It cannot execute multiple transactions concurrently, even if they are read-only. In contrast, NOrec allows read-only transactions to run concurrently without interference, and serializes only the writeback phase of non-read-only transactions, not the entire transaction. A simple variant of the SEQUENTIAL-NOABORT PhTM mode could allow read-only transactions to execute concurrently by using a reader-writer lock. However, this mode can be used only by transactions that are known in advance to be read-only. NOrec overcomes all of these problems.

It is tempting focus on performance comparisons between our new hybrid algorithms and previous systems. However, in our experience, performance of these systems can be highly dependent on idiosyncrasies of Rock, and minor changes in tuning parameters, optimizations, retry policies, etc. can have significant impact on performance. Thus, conclusions we would draw from such comparisons may be invalid for more robust HTM implementations. It is more important to identify specific implementation-related challenges to performance and scalability, and how these challenges differ between our system and previous work.

We have observed that tuning of PhTM—for example when to switch to and from STM phase or which STM to use in that phase—is sensitive to a number of factors, including specific characteristics of workloads. An unnecessary phase switch in PhTM can be expensive, and if this occurs frequently, it can have disastrous consequences for performance. In contrast, HyTM systems make these decisions on a per-transaction basis, and thus overall performance is much less sensitive to occasional wrong decisions.

On the other hand, we have seen that NOrec-based hybrid solutions on Rock do not isolate hardware and software performance as much as expected, as the software transactions influence the performance of concurrent hardware transactions more strongly than the basic algorithm implies on its surface.

## 5. ASF

AMD's ASF proposal [3, 15] extends the x86_64 architecture with explicit transactional constructs. ASF guarantees that transactions accessing four or fewer locations will never abort due to limited capacity. This bound admits an implementation that tracks the cache lines accessed by a transaction in a 4-way set-associative cache, while leaving open the possibility of using a separate hardware "Locked Line Buffer" (LLB) instead [9]. ASF hardware is not currently available; we used PTLsim, a cycle-accurate out-of-order x86 simulator [43], running Linux 2.6.20.

Within transactions, loads and stores must be prefixed with the x86 LOCK prefix to be considered transactional; unlabeled accesses are nontransactional. The exact memory model for the resulting mix of transactional and nontransactional access is not clearly defined [3], but the implication (and the behavior of the current simulator) is that ordinary accesses propagate immediately, and become globally visible, without preserving program order with respect to transactional stores. ASF checkpoints only the program counter and stack pointer at the beginning of a transaction; any rollback of general registers on abort must be achieved by software (e.g., using compiler support or setjmp). A transaction that suffers a page fault is restarted automatically after completion of the usual kernel page-in operation. Diestelhorst et al. [16] discuss the challenges that out-of-order execution presents to progress guarantees.

ASF transactions that encounter traps, exceptions, infinite loops, etc., abort without visible side effects, such as segmentation violations (Section 4.1). Because nontransactional stores do not consume transactional resources on ASF, programmers and compilers may choose to use them more than they would on Rock. Such use may increase the cost of sandboxing, because each nontransactional store may need to be instrumented with HW_VALIDATE.

### 5.1 Algorithms

As in Section 4, we implement 2-Location as a baseline hybrid TM system. Given ASF's guarantees for small transactions, we use HTM to emulate a double-location compare-and-swap (DCAS), as proposed by Dalessandro et al. [10]. We keep both counters on the same virtual page, so SW_COMMIT will never fail due to capacity or pathological page allocation. However, by using a hardware transaction to perform the DCAS, software transactions lose the livelock-free guarantee of the original NOrec algorithm.

We find that the Read-Only filter (Figure 6b) is always beneficial on ASF as the nontransactional write to readonly does not consume HTM resources. Every hybrid algorithm described in this section includes the Read-Only filter.

We refer to our ASF variant of 2-Location with the Read-Only filter as 2-Location-ASF, or 2LA.

***Lazy subscription*** In addition to 2LA, we tested lazy subscription algorithms based on the naive algorithm in Figure 4a, with the read and branch on seqlock delayed from HW_POST_BEGIN to HW_PRE_COMMIT for hardware transactions. We tested both the Opaque and Sandbox methods described in Section 3 for avoiding incorrect behavior due to inconsistent execution.

Opaque uses post-read validation barriers as detailed in Figure 5. The use of nontransactional loads in HW_VALIDATE avoids conflicts and allows a transaction to survive concurrent software writer commits, but it does not let the transaction make progress during those commits. This algorithm requires one line of transactional capacity for metadata in writing transactions, as we read seqlock transactionally in HW_PRE_COMMIT. Sandbox relies on sandboxing for correctness, rather than calling HW_VALIDATE after every read.

***SW-Exists*** Opaque and Sandbox update seqlock in non-read-only transactions, regardless of the presence of software transactions. In Opaque-SWExists and Sandbox-SWExists, we add the SW-Exists filter (Figure 6a) to avoid this. As spurious updates of seqlock do not affect correctness, we leverage nontransactional loads to avoid some artificial conflicts, while using a transactional load to prevent races due to a software transaction arriving, executing, and committing concurrently with a hardware transaction committing. The pseudocode below demonstrates how we handle this circumstance by subscribing to the sw_exists field when attempting to commit without modifying seqlock. (Variants that do not use the SW-Exists filter do not include lines 5, 6, 10 and 11.)

```
1  HW_PRE_COMMIT:
2    if (non_tx_load(readonly))
3      HW_VALIDATE // not needed in Opaque
4      return
5    if (non_tx_load( sw_exists ) != 0)
6      HW_VALIDATE
7      reg = tx_load(seqlock)
8      if (reg & 1) asf_abort
9      tx_store(seqlock, reg+2)
10   else
11     if (tx_load( sw_exists ) != 0) asf_abort
```

Calling HW_VALIDATE before loading seqlock transactionally helps to avoid subscribing to seqlock during a software transaction writeback, which forces the hardware transaction to abort.

We used a simple counter for sw_exists, not a SNZI. Similarly, we did not experiment with separate counter(s) for hardware transactions to signal their commits. The Read-Only and SW-Exists optimizations are effective in reducing contention from hardware transactions on seqlock, and our use of ample hardware resources (see Section 5.2) further avoids the need to resort to software frequently. Furthermore, even when transactions do resort to software, if transaction commits are infrequent enough that contention on sw_exists or seqlock is unlikely, using SNZI and separate counters is unnecessary. Nonetheless, for different workloads and/or system configurations, it may be necessary to revisit the use of SNZI and/or separate counters to aid scalability.

### 5.2 Test Results

We evaluated our hybrid NOrec algorithms using the STAMP benchmark suite [7] on the PTLsim ASF simulator [43]. We did not employ a transactifying compiler for ASF, instead putting all hybrid instrumentation in libraries. This enabled us to easily add per-access instrumentation to hardware transactions. Furthermore, as STAMP is manually instrumented, this decision avoided unnecessary instrumentation due to imprecise compiler analysis, which could produce unnecessary best-effort HTM capacity overflows. We did not add any sandboxing instructions to STAMP for our experiments, and thus our results provide a best-case estimate of performance. This decision appears safe based on a review of STAMP's code, and because STAMP provides limited post-operation sandboxing, based on programmer knowledge, with an explicit abort-and-restart macro.

We used PTLsim's ASF out-of-order core module (asfooo) with a locked-line buffer (LLB) of 256 entries. We modified the simulator to support up to 16 cores, but report results here for only 8: performance at 16 was uniformly poor, and noisy as well, suggesting an inherent lack of scalability in the simulated machine. Code was compiled with gcc 4.3.2, using –O3 optimizations. Results were generated using the default "simulator" input parameters for STAMP. Due to space constraints, we present only a subset of these results; the trends and observations we report extend to the entire suite. We tested basic CGL and NOrec implementations as well as the five hybrid NOrec variants described above. In addition, we tested PhTM-Serial, a version of PhTM in which software-mode consists of a single serial transaction that executes with lightweight instrumentation so as to support user-level aborts. Blundell et al.'s [5] use of such serial execution in unbounded HTM suggests that this may be a viable alternative if hardware aborts are rare. Our hybrid infrastructure is configured to retry hardware transactions repeatedly with exponential backoff unless a transaction exceeds the capacity of the 256-entry LLB, in which case it falls back to software.

With a 256-entry LLB, few STAMP transactions exceed the capacity of the LLB and therefore need to run in software; see Table 1. Furthermore, comparing the behavior of algorithms that do not allow conflicts on metadata between hardware transactions (such as PhTM-Serial) and those that do, we find that the abort rates are very similar for most workloads, suggesting that there are few such conflicts and therefore that the use of SNZI and multiple counters would probably not provide significant benefit for these workloads at the threading levels we tested.

***The Benefit of Lazy Subscription*** Our results support the intuition that PhTM-Serial is inappropriate for general purpose use. In Bayes (not shown) and Labyrinth (Figure 8a) it does not scale at all. For most of the STAMP benchmarks, 2LA scales well to 8 threads, and offers better performance than the NOrec algorithm on which it is based. Lazy subscription reduces the time a hardware transaction is vulnerable to aborts by software commits, and as a result the lazy subscription algorithms often outperform 2LA. However,

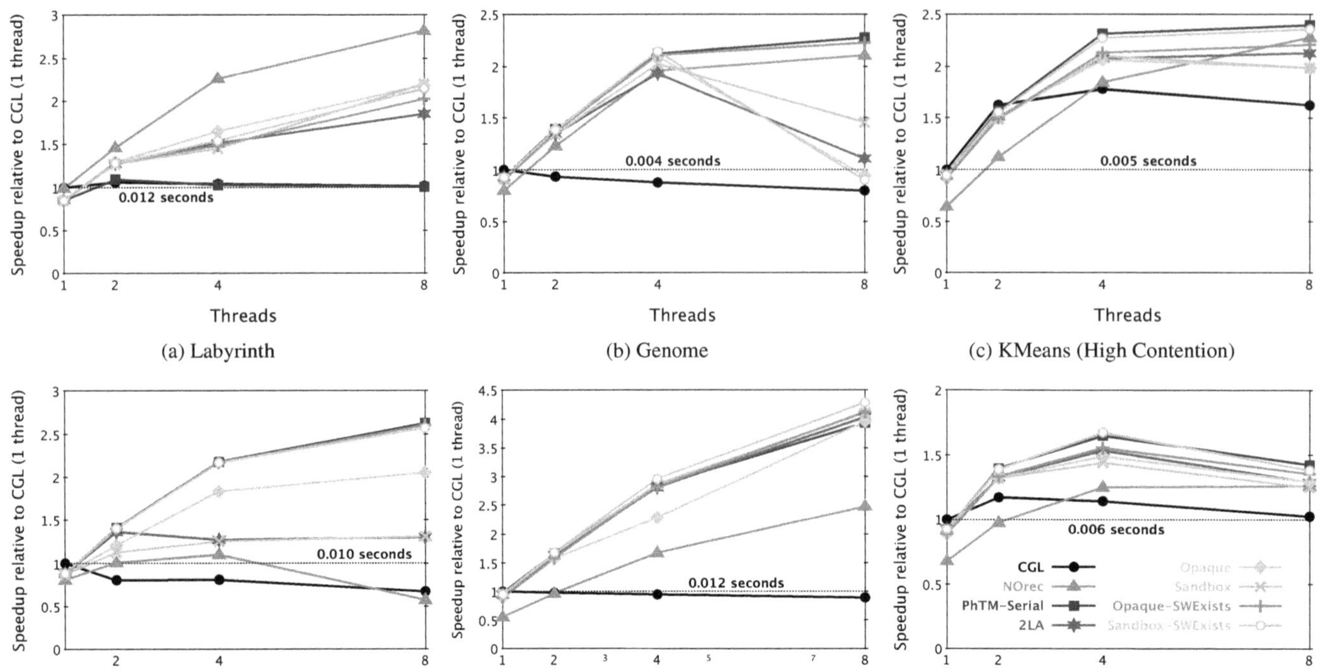


(a) Labyrinth (b) Genome (c) KMeans (High Contention)

(d) SSCA2 (e) Vacation (High Contention) (f) Intruder

**Figure 8.** STAMP benchmarks, run on a simulated 8-core ASF x86_64 system. Results are shown as speedups over the CGL single-threaded execution time, which is also explicitly given.

| Benchmark | Total Transactions | Percent Hardware |
|---|---|---|
| Labyrinth | 194 | 94.3% |
| Genome | 5912 | 99.4% |
| KMeans | 8193 | 99.9% |
| SSCA2 | 47257 | 99.9% |
| Vacation | 4096 | 97.7% |
| Intruder | 11209 | 99.5% |

**Table 1.** Dynamic transaction count and percentage that fit in the ASF LLB, allowing them to complete in hardware (single-threaded execution).

they suffer the same metadata conflicts between hardware transactions, which can eliminate the benefit of lazy subscription if those conflicts occur frequently. For example, in the SSCA2 benchmark, Sandbox performs just as poorly as 2LA. The SW-Exists filter can avoid these conflicts, as discussed below, allowing the lazy subscription algorithms to outperform all others. Thus, while lazy subscription is not always sufficient in its own right, it is a key enabler for the best algorithms.

***The SW-Exists Filter*** By comparing Sandbox-SWExists to Sandbox and Opaque to Opaque-SWExists, we can assess the benefit of avoiding metadata modifications when committing writer transactions. For this evaluation, we used SSCA2 (Figure 8d) which executes roughly 47K transactions, all of which modify shared state, and perform at most six memory operations (and therefore never need to fall back to STM).

NOrec cannot scale on this workload, as its single counter becomes a bottleneck. Among hybrid algorithms, PhTM-Serial is best, as there are no software transactions, and PhTM-Serial does not require metadata updates for hardware transactions. Furthermore, the low abort rate for PhTM-Serial indicates that conflicts on program data are rare.

The algorithms that use the SW-Exists filter perform almost as well as PhTM-Serial. The -SWExists implementations avoid any modification of metadata when all transactions run in hardware mode, and thus the slight slowdown relative to PhTM-Serial, which is not coupled with a noticeable increase in abort rate, indicates that Opaque-SWExists and Sandbox-SWExists are paying a small amount in unnecessary instrumentation, but are not wasting work by aborting due to metadata conflicts.

In contrast, the algorithms that do not use the SW-Exists filter (2LA, Sandbox, and Opaque) experience an increase in aborts as the thread count increases, resulting in significantly worse performance. For example, Sandbox reaches 1.1 aborts per commit at 8 threads, whereas PhTM-Serial has only 0.002 aborts per commit at the same thread count. As Sandbox and Sandbox-SWExists differ only in their use of the SW-Exists filter (and likewise Opaque and Opaque-SWExists), we conclude that the aborts in Sandbox and Opaque are a consequence of conflicting updates to metadata, which the SW-Exists filter avoids.

***Opacity vs. Sandboxing*** Although neither of these approaches is a clear winner, we observe Sandbox-SWExists outperforming Opaque-SWExists in most cases, due to its lower instrumentation costs. In some cases, however, the opposite is true. Recall that both opaque and sandboxing algorithms access seqlock transactionally whenever a writing transaction commits. When this variable is not cached at commit time, the commit operation may take longer, increasing vulnerability to unnecessary aborts due to conflicts with in-flight transactions. For the opaque algorithms, HW_VALIDATE is called on every read, and thus seqlock is likely to remain in cache. For the sandboxing algorithms, compiler-inserted calls to

HW_VALIDATE can have the same prefetching effect. However, as our instrumentation omitted these calls, the sandboxing algorithms were more likely to experience a cache miss on seqlock at commit time.

***When Software TM is Better*** While only 5% of transactions exceed the hardware's transactional capacity in Labyrinth, the cost of running these transactions almost to completion in hardware before aborting and retrying in software resulted in worse performance than NOrec even at 1 thread. In Labyrinth, transactions first perform thousands of nontransactional loads and stores, then up to several hundred transactional loads and stores. Thus, a hardware transaction that overflows the LLB capacity does so after performing a lengthy prefix, magnifying the cost of the overflow.

Across all workloads, the relative benefit of hybrid TM seems to diminish at higher thread counts. This is not surprising because NOrec is livelock-free, its transactions do not abort due to false sharing, and it is effective at preventing aborts, whereas hybrid TM with requester-wins conflict detection is prone to livelock and can experience high abort rates, even in workloads with few conflicts. Labyrinth at 8 threads provides an extreme example: across all threads, NOrec aborted 8 times when committing 208 transactions; every hybrid algorithm aborted at least 600 times.

More generally, when the fraction of execution time that all software transactions spend in the commit operation is small, the instrumentation and shared metadata inherent in STM algorithms can become less of a bottleneck, and the wasted work due to excessive hybrid TM aborts can outweigh its lower instrumentation overhead. This can be particularly true as read-write conflicts are not deferred until commit time by hybrid TM: seemingly benign conditions such as a software transaction validating, or sharing between a committing reader and in-progress writer, can cause hardware transactions to abort.

## 6. Discussion

A concern with NOrec has been the lack of scalability of its serialized writeback mechanism: a workload that performs many write-dominated transactions will perform poorly. STAMP's SSCA2 benchmark is an example; Figure 8d clearly illustrates NOrec's weakness. Our results show that NOrec-based hybrids can avoid this problem. If an application completes a large fraction of its logical transactions in hardware, then its scalability is determined more by the hardware than by the STM algorithm. Our tests show NOrec-based hybrid scalability to be good for such workloads, including for SSCA2. Admittedly, some applications may include frequent transactions that are ill suited for execution using either HTM or NOrec, in which case it may be desirable to include modes that use more scalable STM algorithms.

In addition to achieving some encouraging results, we have made observations about the impact that aspects of best-effort HTM design have on its effectiveness in NOrec-based, hybrid systems. Neither PhTM-NOrec nor the HyTM-NOrec variants are competitive with NOrec when transactions commonly require software execution, because logical transactions that ultimately succeed in software do so only after failed attempts as hardware transactions. HyTM implementations have a potential advantage over PhTM in dealing with this problem: static analysis, profiling, and programmer guidance may allow transactions that are unlikely to succeed using HTM to aggressively switch to software, without forcing the entire system to undergo a mode change. We would like to construct more adaptive retry policies. However, limitations of best-effort HTM make it difficult without sacrificing performance in other cases. Below we discuss the impact of Rock's and ASF's HTM designs on our hybrid systems, and make some suggestions for designers of future HTM features to consider.

***Branch prediction*** Rock's sensitivity to branch misprediction in transactions negatively impacts adaptive policies, which often branch between alternatives based on the contents of a shared variable. By nature, shared variables are not necessarily cached, and the branches associated with such adaptation can be unpredictable. Rock provides *speculation barriers* [13] that can avoid the need to predict a branch accurately, but their high overhead prevents their ubiquitous use. We strongly urge HTM implementors to avoid dependence on branch prediction for transactional success.

***Contention management*** ASF's guarantees for small transactions are attractive but apply only in the absence of conflicts. In practice, backoff is necessary to avoid livelock. This is inherent to the requestor-wins conflict resolution policy used by both ASF and Rock. Backing off just long enough to avoid conflicts is difficult. Thus, STM sometimes outperforms HTM because it can actively resolve conflicts, rather than merely avoid them using backoff.

Requestor-wins has a subtle effect in our HyTM-NOrec implementations. A software transaction reads data, including program data as well as metadata such as counters, in order to detect potential conflicts. If a concurrent hardware transaction has speculatively written such data, requestor-wins will cause the hardware transaction to abort, without guaranteeing that the software transaction will succeed. This increases the potential for poor performance and livelock, even in workloads where true conflicts are infrequent.

***Unlabeled Accesses*** Rock and ASF both provide the capability to execute transactional and nontransactional accesses within a transaction. Both Rock and ASF require one type to be explicitly labeled, and treat unlabeled accesses as the other type. However, they make opposite choices: Unlabeled ASF accesses are nontransactional whereas Rock considers them to be transactional. Rock's approach allows the same code to be used both transactionally and nontransactionally and supports the use of libraries inside transactions, Transactional Lock Elision (TLE) [13] with a single code path, and straightforward compilation of transactional code. ASF's choice carries the implicit assumption that transactional accesses have large incremental costs and require careful use. This is true in a minimally conforming ASF implementation and a good assumption even in PTLsim's default 256 LLB implementation. However it complicates code generation and library reuse.

Rock's prohibition on CAS inside transactions limits some of the benefits of treating unlabeled accesses as transactional. Consider memory allocation, where a hardware transaction calls a thread-safe malloc implemented with a CAS-based lock. On Rock, the transaction will fail due to the restriction on CAS. On ASF, it *can* succeed, but a worse problem arises if a transaction aborts while executing malloc, because it will fail to release the lock, preventing all subsequent memory allocation. An ideal implementation would allow ordinary code to be executed within hardware transactions, and have its effects negated upon abort, but provide for unfettered use of nontransactional operations too.

Sandboxing for lazy subscription requires validation barriers on nontransactional accesses. If nontransactional accesses are more common on ASF than on Rock, then sandboxing may be more expensive on ASF.

***Nontransactional accesses*** ASF and Rock both support nontransactional accesses within transactions, but with different memory-model semantics. Rock's nontransactional accesses are required to preserve TSO regardless of the surrounding transaction's success or failure. The specification for ASF's nontransactional accesses is currently incomplete, but the implication (and PTLsim's implementation) is that they can become globally visible without respecting the program order of interleaved transactional accesses.

Several of our key optimizations depend on support for nontransactional loads from shared locations, for which ASF's and

Rock's differing semantics are both effective. Riegel et al. [36] find that it is beneficial to be able to access shared data with a nontransactional CAS instruction inside a transaction (Section 7), provided the CAS becomes visible before the transaction is committed.

We do not currently have a use for nontransactional stores to shared locations, but we do find nontransactional stores to thread private locations useful. For these, strong ordering with respect to stores of other threads is not needed. PTLsim effectively supports such accesses and the corresponding optimizations. However, Rock's requirement that nontransactional stores respect TSO leads them to occupy a store buffer slot, inhibiting their use significantly. For example, on Rock, dynamically tracking whether a transaction performs a store (for the Read-Only optimization) requires us to avoid writing the flag on every store, complicating the write barrier code and introducing a branch we would prefer to avoid.

We recommend that designers carefully consider how they can support flexible use of nontransactional accesses, as well as the interaction of those accesses with the memory consistency model. White and Spear [42] suggest that it may be useful to distinguish between nontransactional stores that become visible before the transaction commits and those that respect (say) TSO order.

***Visibility into transactional execution*** Information about the behavior of a transaction that is executing can be useful for a variety of reasons. For example, a cheap way to determine how many loads and stores a transaction has performed would provide a convenient solution to the problem of determining whether a Read-Only optimization can be applied in a given transaction, or could inform a decision about whether and when to retry. It is also useful for code to be able to determine whether it is executing in a transaction (for example to allow a TLE implementation to decide between committing a transaction and releasing a lock). Numerous other kinds of information are potentially useful, such as addresses accessed, addresses that cause conflicts, etc. In addition, transaction-aware performance counters and sampling mechanisms may be useful.

***Scalability with contention*** With requestor-wins conflict resolution, it is not surprising that the naive HyTM-NOrec algorithm that requires every hardware transaction to increment a shared counter at the end performs poorly. It may be tempting for designers to consider this "a software problem," especially in light of our success in distributing the counters in the SW-Exists algorithm. However, the techniques we used not only complicate our algorithms but entail performance tradeoffs, such as requiring software transactions to read more counters. By aiming to avoid pathological performance under contention in such cases, designers can allow us to avoid these mechanisms, or at least to use fewer counters. Possible approaches include more sophisticated conflict resolution policies, (perhaps limited) support for nesting, and support for nontransactional CAS within transactions.

## 7. Related Work

In related concurrent work, Felber et al. [19] and Riegel et al. [36] evaluate hybrid TM systems on the ASF simulator. Like ours, one of their hybrids starts with the sketch from Dalessandro et al. [10], leading to some overlap with the basic algorithm that we have presented. This includes lazy subscription via read instrumentation, though not with sandboxing, and the Read-Only filter. Riegel et al. observed that ASF's nontransactional CAS capability allows hardware transactions to modify the `seqlock/counter` nontransactionally within a transaction in order to avoid unnecessary conflicts between hardware transactions. While this capability is not clearly supported by the ASF documentation, it works using the current simulator implementation, and is shown to be effective at preventing counter contention from causing unnecessary aborts.

Interestingly, the nontransactional CAS optimization is both orthogonal and complementary to the most effective of our ASF optimizations, Read-Only and SW-Exists. Our limited testing suggests that integrating the three techniques often slightly outperforms Read-Only with SW-Exists for the STAMP applications. This avenue deserves more attention as the ASF specification matures.

## 8. Conclusion And Future Work

We have explored the use of best-effort HTM to implement several hybrid versions of the low-overhead NOrec. These NOrec-based HyTM algorithms support the concurrent execution of hardware and software transactions, as previous hybrid TMs do, but with the low overhead on hardware transactions previously achieved only in phased TMs.

Our results show the significant potential for this approach, but also reveal a number of challenges in realizing that potential. We expect to continue to improve our results using the Rock and (simulated) ASF best-effort HTM as currently designed. However, it appears that overcoming some of the challenges will require better best-effort HTM support than the existing implementations and proposals provide. An important contribution of our work is to identify and discuss such issues, in order to guide designers of future best-effort HTMs.

Perhaps the greatest opportunities lie in adaptation. The P-Counter algorithm, for example, would benefit from a dynamic choice of an appropriate number of counters. We also need better ways to identify transactions that should start in software mode. The decision might be made using compile-time static analysis or profiling feedback, or using runtime lightweight statistics gathering and dynamic adaptation [39]. Even with good initial choices, we need faster ways to determine when a given dynamic transaction should resort to software, rather than retrying in hardware.

## Acknowledgments

Our thanks to Dave Dice for his implementation of NOrec STM, to Dan Nussbaum for his initial integration of NOrec into Oracle's SkySTM hybrid infrastructure, to Stephan Diestelhorst for updated PTLsim source code and advice on extending it to larger numbers of threads, and to our shepherd Milo Martin for his patience and helpful advice.

## References

[1] A.-R. Adl-Tabatabai and T. Shpeisman (Eds.). Draft Specification of Transactional Language Constructs for C++. `research.sun.com/scalable/pubs/C++-transactional-constructs-1.0.pdf`, Aug. 2009. Version 1.0.

[2] A.-R. Adl-Tabatabai, B. T. Lewis, V. Menon, B. R. Murphy, B. Saha, and T. Shpeisman. Compiler and Runtime Support for Efficient Software Transactional Memory. In *ACM SIGPLAN Conf. on Programming Language Design and Implementation*, Jun. 2006.

[3] Advanced Micro Devices. Advanced Synchronization Facility: Proposed Architectural Specification. Publication #45432, rev. 2.1, `developer.amd.com/assets/45432-ASF_Spec_2.1.pdf`, Mar. 2009.

[4] C. S. Ananian, K. Asanovic, B. C. Kuszmaul, C. E. Leiserson, and S. Lie. Unbounded Transactional Memory. In *11th Intl. Symp. on High-Performance Computer Architecture*, Feb. 2005.

[5] C. Blundell, J. Devietti, E. C. Lewis, and M. M. K. Martin. Making the fast case common and the uncommon case simple in unbounded transactional memory. *SIGARCH Comput. Archit. News*, 35:24–34, June 2007.

[6] C. Blundell, E. C. Lewis, and M. M. K. Martin. Subtleties of Transactional Memory Atomicity Semantics. *Computer Architecture Letters*, 5(2), Nov. 2006.

[7] C. Cao Minh, J. Chung, C. Kozyrakis, and K. Olukotun. STAMP: Stanford Transactional Applications for Multi-processing. In *IEEE Intl. Symp. on Workload Characterization*, Sep. 2008.

[8] S. Chaudhry, R. Cypher, M. Ekman, M. Karlsson, A. Landin, and S. Yip. Rock: A High-Performance SPARC™ CMT Processor. *IEEE Micro*, 29(2):6–16, Mar.-Apr. 2009.

[9] D. Christie, J.-W. Chung, S. Diestelhorst, M. Hohmuth, M. Pohlack, C. Fetzer, M. Nowack, T. Riegel, P. Felber, P. Marlier, and E. Riviere. Evaluation of AMD's Advanced Synchronization Facility within a Complete Transactional Memory Stack. In *EuroSys Conf.*, Apr. 2010.

[10] L. Dalessandro, M. F. Spear, and M. L. Scott. NOrec: Streamlining STM by Abolishing Ownership Records. In *15th ACM Symp. on Principles and Practice of Parallel Programming*, Jan. 2010.

[11] P. Damron, A. Fedorova, Y. Lev, V. Luchangco, M. Moir, and D. Nussbaum. Hybrid Transactional Memory. In *12th Intl. Conf. on Architectural Support for Programming Languages and Operating Systems*, Oct. 2006.

[12] D. Dice, Y. Lev, V. J. Marathe, M. Moir, D. Nussbaum, and M. Oleszewski. Simplifying Concurrent Algorithms by Exploiting Hardware Transactional Memory. In *22nd ACM Symp. on Parallelism in Algorithms and Architectures*, 2010.

[13] D. Dice, Y. Lev, M. Moir, D. Nussbaum, and M. Olszewski. Early Experience with a Commercial Hardware Transactional Memory Implementation. SMLI TR-2009-180, Sun Microsystems Laboratories, Oct. 2009.

[14] D. Dice, O. Shalev, and N. Shavit. Transactional Locking II. In *20th Intl. Symp. on Distributed Computing*, Sep. 2006.

[15] S. Diestelhorst and M. Hohmuth. Hardware Acceleration for Lock-Free Data Structures and Software-Transactional Memory. In *Wkshp. on Exploiting Parallelism with Transactional Memory and other Hardware Assisted Methods*, Apr. 2008.

[16] S. Diestelhorst, M. Pohlack, M. Hohmuth, D. Christie, J.-W. Chung, and L. Yen. Implementing AMD's Advanced Synchronization Facility in an Out-of-Order x86 Core. In *5th ACM SIGPLAN Wkshp. on Transactional Computing*, Apr. 2010.

[17] C. Ding, X. Shen, K. Kelsey, C. Tice, R. Huang, and C. Zhang. Software Behavior Oriented Parallelization. In *ACM SIGPLAN Conf. on Programming Language Design and Implementation*, Jun. 2007.

[18] F. Ellen, Y. Lev, V. Luchangco, and M. Moir. SNZI: Scalable NonZero Indicators. In *26th ACM Symp. on Principles of Distributed Computing*, Aug. 2007.

[19] P. Felber, C. Fetzer, P. Marlier, M. Nowack, and T. Riegel. Brief announcement: Hybrid time-based transactional memory. In N. Lynch and A. Shvartsman, editors, *Distributed Computing*, Lecture Notes in Computer Science. Springer Berlin/Heidelberg, 2010.

[20] R. Guerraoui and M. Kapalka. On the Correctness of Transactional Memory. In *13th ACM Symp. on Principles and Practice of Parallel Programming*, 2008.

[21] L. Hammond, V. Wong, M. Chen, B. D. Carlstrom, J. D. Davis, B. Hertzberg, M. K. Prabju, H. Wijaya, C. Kozyrakis, and K. Olukotun. Transactional Memory Coherence and Consistency. In *31st Intl. Symp. on Computer Architecture*, Jun. 2004.

[22] T. Harris and K. Fraser. Revocable Locks for Non-Blocking Programming. In *10th ACM Symp. on Principles and Practice of Parallel Programming*, Jun. 2005.

[23] T. Harris, M. Plesko, A. Shinar, and D. Tarditi. Optimizing Memory Transactions. In *ACM SIGPLAN Conf. on Programming Language Design and Implementation*, Jun. 2006.

[24] T. Harris, J. Larus, and R. Rajwar. *Transactional Memory*. Synthesis Lectures on Computer Architecture. Morgan Claypool, 2nd edition, 2010.

[25] M. Herlihy and J. E. Moss. Transactional Memory: Architectural Support for Lock-Free Data Structures. In *20th Intl. Symp. on Computer Architecture*, May. 1993.

[26] S. Kumar, M. Chu, C. J. Hughes, P. Kundu, and A. Nguyen. Hybrid Transactional Memory. In *11th ACM Symp. on Principles and Practice of Parallel Programming*, Mar. 2006.

[27] C. Lameter. Effective Synchronization on Linux/NUMA Systems. In *May 2005 Gelato Federation Meeting*, May. 2005.

[28] Y. Lev, V. Luchangco, V. J. Marathe, M. Moir, D. Nussbaum, and M. Olszewski. Anatomy of a Scalable Software Transactional Memory. In *4th ACM SIGPLAN Wkshp. on Transactional Computing*, 2009. `http://research.sun.com/scalable/pubs/TRANSACT2009-ScalableSTMAnatomy.pdf`.

[29] Y. Lev, M. Moir, and D. Nussbaum. PhTM: Phased Transactional Memory. In *2nd ACM SIGPLAN Wkshp. on Transactional Computing*, Aug. 2007.

[30] S. Lie. Hardware Support for Unbounded Transactional Memory. Master's thesis, Massachusetts Institute of Technology Department of Electrical Engineering and Computer Science, May 2004.

[31] P. E. McKenney. Is Parallel Programming Hard, And, If So, What Can You Do About It? `http://www.rdrop.com/users/paulmck/perfbook/perfbook.2010.01.23a.pdf`, 2010. [Viewed Jan. 24, 2010].

[32] V. Menon, S. Balensiefer, T. Shpeisman, A.-R. Adl-Tabatabai, R. L. Hudson, B. Saha, and A. Welc. Practical Weak-Atomicity Semantics for Java STM. In *20th ACM Symp. on Parallelism in Algorithms and Architectures*, June 2008.

[33] K. E. Moore, J. Bobba, M. J. Moravan, M. D. Hill, and D. A. Wood. LogTM: Log-based Transactional Memory. In *12th Intl. Symp. on High-Performance Computer Architecture*, Feb. 2006.

[34] M. Olszewski, J. Cutler, and J. G. Steffan. JudoSTM: A Dynamic Binary-Rewriting Approach to Software Transactional Memory. In *16th Intl. Conf. on Parallel Architectures and Compilation Techniques*, Sep. 2007.

[35] R. Rajwar, M. Herlihy, and K. Lai. Virtualizing Transactional Memory. In *32nd Intl. Symp. on Computer Architecture*, Jun. 2005.

[36] T. Riegel, P. Marlier, M. Nowack, P. Felber, and C. Fetzer. Optimizing Hybrid Transactional Memory: The Importance of Nonspeculative Operations. TUD-FI10-06-Nov.2010, Technische Universitaet Dresden, Nov. 2010.

[37] B. Saha, A.-R. Adl-Tabatabai, R. L. Hudson, C. C. Minh, and B. Hertzberg. McRT-STM: A High Performance Software Transactional Memory System For A Multi-Core Runtime. In *11th ACM SIGPLAN Symp. on Principles and Practice of Parallel Programming*, Mar. 2006.

[38] M. Spear, V. Marathe, W. Scherer, and M. Scott. Conflict detection and validation strategies for software transactional memory. In S. Dolev, editor, *Distributed Computing*, Lecture Notes in Computer Science. Springer Berlin/Heidelberg, 2006.

[39] M. F. Spear. Lightweight, Robust Adaptivity for Software Transactional Memory. In *22nd ACM Symp. on Parallelism in Algorithms and Architectures*, June 2010.

[40] F. Tabba, A. W. Hay, and J. R. Goodman. Transactional Value Prediction. In *4th ACM SIGPLAN Wkshp. on Transactional Computing*, Feb. 2009.

[41] C. Wang, W.-Y. Chen, Y. Wu, B. Saha, and A.-R. Adl-Tabatabai. Code Generation and Optimization for Transactional Memory Constructs in an Unmanaged Language. In *Intl. Symp. on Code Generation and Optimization*, Mar. 2007.

[42] S. White and M. Spear. On Reconciling Hardware Atomicity, Memory Models, and __tm_waiver. In *2nd Workshop on the Theory of Transactional Memory (WTTM)*, Sep. 2010.

[43] M. Yourst. PTLsim: A Cycle Accurate Full System x86-64 Microarchitectural Simulator. In *2007 IEEE Intl. Symp. on Performance Analysis of Systems and Software*, Apr. 2007.

# Efficient Processor Support for DRFx, a Memory Model with Exceptions

Abhayendra Singh* Daniel Marino† Satish Narayanasamy* Todd Millstein† Madanlal Musuvathi‡

*University of Michigan, Ann Arbor †University of California, Los Angeles ‡Microsoft Research, Redmond

## Abstract

A longstanding challenge of shared-memory concurrency is to provide a memory model that allows for efficient implementation while providing strong and simple guarantees to programmers. The C++0x and Java memory models admit a wide variety of compiler and hardware optimizations and provide sequentially consistent (SC) semantics for data-race-free programs. However, they either do not provide any semantics (C++0x) or provide a hard-to-understand semantics (Java) for racy programs, compromising the safety and debuggability of such programs.

In earlier work we proposed the DRF$x$ memory model, which addresses this problem by dynamically detecting potential violations of SC due to the interaction of compiler or hardware optimizations with data races and halting execution upon detection. In this paper, we present a detailed micro-architecture design for supporting the DRF$x$ memory model, formalize the design and prove its correctness, and evaluate the design using a hardware simulator. We describe a set of DRF$x$-compliant complexity-effective optimizations which allow us to attain performance close to that of TSO (Total Store Model) and DRF0 while providing strong guarantees for all programs.

***Categories and Subject Descriptors*** C.0 [*Computer Systems Organization*]: Hardware/software interfaces

***General Terms*** Design, Performance

***Keywords*** memory models, data-races, memory model exception, soft fences

## 1. Introduction

A memory consistency model (or simply a *memory model*) forms the foundation of shared-memory multi-threaded programming. It defines the order in which memory operations performed by one thread become visible to other threads. A programmer needs to understand the memory model in order to determine the behavior of a concurrent program. Every layer in the compute stack has to ensure that any transformations it performs retain the semantics of the source program with respect to the memory model.

Sequential consistency (SC) [27] is the most intuitive memory model for programmers. SC guarantees that all the memory operations executed across different threads appear in one total order that is consistent with the per-thread program order. Many compiler and hardware optimizations that are valid for sequential programs (such as register promotion, common subexpression elimination, out-of-order execution, store buffers, etc.) can break the SC semantics of concurrent programs. The resulting performance limitation has forced modern hardware architectures and mainstream programming languages to support weaker memory models.

In particular, recently proposed memory models for C++0x [9] and Java [30] are based on the data-race-free-0 (DRF0) memory model [1]. These models require that a programmer explicitly classify shared-memory variables into *synchronization* and *data*.[1] The intention is that programmers use synchronization variables for *all* inter-thread communication and that there are no data races on data variables. In other words, two threads in the program are not allowed to concurrently access the same data variable unless both accesses are reads. For such data-race-free programs, DRF0 guarantees SC. To provide this guarantee, DRF0 requires the language runtime to execute synchronization accesses in SC order with few optimizations. On the other hand, the runtime is allowed to perform most *sequentially valid* (i.e., correct on a single thread in isolation) optimizations in synchronization-free regions of the program. In this way DRF0 can be efficient and at the same time provide strong guarantees for data-race-free programs.

However, DRF0-based memory models provide weak or no guarantees for programs with data races. For instance, C++0x gives no semantics to racy programs. As a result, compiler and hardware optimizations can introduce arbitrary behavior for a racy program, potentially compromising the program's correctness and security properties. As this situation is unacceptable for type-safe languages, the Java memory model (JMM) provides a weak semantics for racy programs that precludes a class of adversarial behaviors. This semantics is subtle and complex and therefore makes understanding and debugging multithreaded program executions extremely difficult. It also makes it difficult to develop compiler and hardware optimizations that properly respect the JMM [13, 38].

Motivated by this difficulty, prior work [8, 16, 17, 19, 29, 32] has proposed a *fail-stop* semantics for racy programs. The basic idea is to treat data races as program errors and dynamically terminate racy executions with a *memory-model (MM) exception.* Doing so ensures that programmers are not exposed to the obscure effects of weak memory models by guaranteeing that executions not terminated with an MM exception are SC.

We recently developed a memory model based on this approach called DRF$x$ [32]. Our key observation is that full data-race detection is unnecessary for the purpose of providing strong memory-model guarantees to programmers. For example, it is acceptable to allow a racy program to execute without raising an MM exception, as long as the execution is guaranteed to be SC. Accordingly, the

[1] Synchronization variables are annotated with type qualifiers such as `volatile` (in Java) or `atomic` (in C++). Unannotated variables are data variables.



*ASPLOS'11,* March 5–11, 2011, Newport Beach, California, USA.

DRF$x$ memory model provides two simple and strong properties to programmers. First, a program execution that is not terminated with an MM exception is SC. Second, a program execution that is terminated with an MM exception has a data race. We presented a design for a compiler and runtime system that ensures these properties. The compiler partitions the program into *regions* and communicates region boundaries to the hardware via memory fences. The compiler and hardware may perform most sequentially valid optimizations within a region but may not optimize across region boundaries. Therefore, the DRF$x$ properties can be ensured by dynamically detecting conflicting memory accesses between concurrently executing regions [29, 32]. If no such conflicts arise, then the execution is *region-serializable* which implies SC; otherwise the detected conflict indicates the presence of a data race in the program.

In this paper, we propose a detailed micro-architecture design for supporting the DRF$x$ memory model. Our approach builds on a hardware design sketched in our prior work [32] but extends it with several important optimizations. Further, we have carefully formalized the approach, including these optimizations, at the micro-architectural level and have proven that it ensures the DRF$x$ properties. Finally, we have built a simulator for our proposed hardware which, in conjunction with a DRF$x$-compliant compiler [32], allows us to perform an end-to-end performance comparison with the DRF0 memory model.

We have made a set of design choices in order to keep the hardware support for DRF$x$ simple while still allowing optimizations for efficiency, both of which are critically important for future acceptance by processor vendors. First, we propose a *lazy* conflict detection scheme for DRF$x$ that does not change the cache architecture or the coherence mechanism of the baseline DRF0 hardware. Unlike transactional memory (TM) support [23], DRF$x$ cannot tolerate false conflicts arising either from regions accessing different words in the same cache line or from accesses occurring in mispredicted branches. Rather than modifying the cache coherence mechanism to track a region's access information at word granularity [29], we instead store the addresses accessed by a region in a dedicated *region buffer*. To commit a region, a processor sends the accessed addresses to other cores for a conflict check. While lazy conflict detection can delay an MM exception beyond the first instruction that results in a non-SC state, our implementation ensures that this state is not observable to the rest of the system by throwing the exception before any subsequent system call.

Second, performing conflict detection over unbounded-size regions would tremendously increase the complexity of the hardware support needed, due to the possibility of overflowing the region buffer. Indeed, this issue has been one of the main impediments to TM support in hardware. We observe that, unlike a TM system, the DRF$x$ compiler has the flexibility to choose region boundaries and can therefore bound the number of memory accesses in each region in order to allow the hardware to perform conflict detection with finite resources. We employ a simple and conservative static analysis for this purpose.

While bounded regions simplify conflict detection, they can also lead to significant performance loss by limiting the instruction and memory parallelism available to the processor. To solve this problem, the DRF$x$ compiler generates two kinds of fences to demarcate regions. *Hard* fences behave like traditional memory fences and are introduced at synchronization operations in order to preserve the programmer-intended ordering semantics. In contrast, *soft* fences indicate region boundaries introduced solely to bound the number of memory accesses per region. We propose and validate the following optimizations involving soft fences. First, a processor can execute, and even commit, soft-fenced regions out-of-order while still properly detecting conflicts as required by DRF$x$. Second, contiguous soft-fenced regions executed in a processor can be coalesced at runtime to form larger regions if space is available in the region buffer, which reduces the frequency of conflict checks. Finally, the conflict checks for regions in different processors can proceed in parallel, and a processor can continue to execute instructions while concurrently servicing conflict check requests from remote processors.

We have built a DRF$x$-compliant hardware simulator using the Simics-based FeS2 simulator [34]. In conjunction with a DRF$x$-compliant C compiler [32] built on top of LLVM [28], we compared the performance of DRF$x$ to that of DRF0 compiler and hardware. For additional reference, we also evaluated the performance of executing a program compiled by the baseline LLVM compiler on an x86-like total-store-order (TSO) hardware. On a set of applications from the PARSEC benchmark suite [5], we find that the overhead of DRF$x$ is 6.49% on average when compared to DRF0.

## 2. Background

This section provides the motivation for the DRF$x$ memory model and reviews its guarantees and requirements.

### 2.1 DRF0-based Memory Models

Mainstream programming languages have recently converged on DRF0-based [1] memory models [9, 30]. These models assume that program variables are properly labeled as *synchronization* variables (using annotations such as `volatiles` or `atomic`) and *data* variables. A *data race* occurs when two threads simultaneously access a data variable and at least one of them is a write. A program is said to contain a data race if there exists a sequentially consistent execution in which a data race occurs. A program is *data-race free* otherwise. Programs containing one or more data races are simply referred to as *racy* programs.

DRF0-based memory models guarantee sequential consistency for data-race-free programs while permitting the compiler and the hardware to perform a large class of optimizations on data variables. A programmer still has the flexibility of writing lock-free code and using shared memory for synchronization, provided that appropriate variables are labeled as synchronization in order to satisfy the data-race-free requirement.

### 2.2 Need for a Fail-stop Semantics for Racy Programs

While DRF0-based memory models provide strong (SC) guarantees for data-race-free programs, they only provide weak guarantees for racy programs. For instance, the C++ memory model treats data races as program errors and provides no semantics for a racy program (akin to programs with buffer-overflow errors). The compiler and the hardware are therefore allowed to introduce arbitrary effects into a racy program, which can compromise the program's correctness and safety. Indeed, it is possible for reasonable compiler optimizations to introduce security vulnerabilities in the presence of data races [9].

Further, while data races are usually considered program errors, they are easy for programmers to inadvertently introduce and difficult to detect. Therefore, when debugging a large C++ system, the programmer has to assume the possibility of a data-race in some component of the system and therefore reason about the interplay of optimizations with races to understand the program's behavior. Type-safe languages like Java mitigate these problems by providing strong-enough guarantees for racy programs to ensure important memory-safety properties [30]. However, this weak semantics is subtle and complex for programmers to reason about, and it has been challenging to ensure that compiler and hardware optimizations in fact respect this semantics [13, 38].

One possible solution to this problem is to design languages and static analyses that simply prevent programmers from introducing data races, and this is an active area of research (e.g., [7, 10, 11]). However, current approaches typically only account for lock-based synchronization, are overly conservative due to imprecise information about pointer aliasing, and require programmer annotations. A promising alternative is to instead provide a fail-stop semantics for racy programs [8, 16, 17, 19, 29, 32]. In this style, the runtime system dynamically detects data races and terminates execution of the program before the non-SC behavior becomes observable to the rest of the system. Therefore, all program executions are guaranteed to behave in an SC manner, despite the possibility of data races.

### 2.3 Fail-Stop Semantics Requires a Compiler-Hardware Co-design

We argue that efficiently providing fail-stop semantics for racy programs requires an end-to-end solution that involves a co-design of both the compiler and the hardware. Note that such a fail-stop mechanism has stringent requirements on correctness and performance. First, it is unacceptable to halt a data-race-free program. This means that any data-race detection mechanism cannot have false error reports. Second, the overhead of any fail-stop mechanism has to be smaller than the performance obtained from compiler and hardware optimizations. Otherwise, one is better off simply preventing all non-SC transformations in the compiler and the hardware.

The performance requirement clearly rules out existing software-based data-race detection algorithms that add a runtime overhead of 8x or more [18]. More fundamentally, any software-based approach must take care not to introduce data races as part of the detection mechanism itself, since that would expose the mechanism to the weaker guarantees provided by the lower layers of the runtime platform, making it difficult to ensure correctness. All existing data-race detection algorithms maintain some metadata per variable and update the metadata on an access to the variable. When performed without synchronization, these updates can introduce data races in an otherwise data-race-free program.[2] However, as these updates happen at every memory access, adding synchronization for these updates would prevent most optimizations and thereby add significant overhead.

On the other hand, a fail-stop mechanism cannot be implemented in the hardware without any support from the compiler. The weak semantics provided by the Java and C++ memory models makes it impossible to precisely detect source-level data races in the binary. For example, a compiler optimization could introduce data races, causing the hardware to detect a false race. Further, a compiler optimization could *remove* a data race, causing the hardware to fail to detect an actual race. Both the Java and C++ memory models allow the compiler to perform transformations that have these effects [37].

### 2.4 DRFx Memory Model

Our fail-stop semantics for racy programs is made precise by the DRF$x$ memory model [32], which introduces the notion of a dynamic *memory model (MM) exception* that halts a program's execution. The model ensures the following properties for any program P:

- **DRF:** If P is data-race free then every execution of P is sequentially consistent and does not raise an MM exception.
- **Soundness:** If an execution is not terminated with an MM exception, then that execution is SC.
- **Safety:** If an execution of P invokes a system call, then the observable program state at that point is reachable through an SC execution of P.

These properties provide a simple and strong guarantee to programmers. Any program execution that does not raise an MM exception is guaranteed to be SC. Therefore, a program execution can always be analyzed and debugged under an assumption of SC behavior, without requiring the programmer to know whether the program has a race. Further, if an execution of P raises an MM exception, then the programmer knows that the program definitely has a data race.

Despite the strong guarantees in the model, the properties are designed to allow flexibility in an implementation. First, a racy program execution need not be halted unless the execution violates SC. This means that one does not require a full-blown data-race detector. On the other hand, the implementation still has the choice to halt a racy execution even if it does not violate SC. This means that one does not require a precise SC-violation detector either. Finally, the Soundness property only ensures that an SC violation will *eventually* be caught, thereby allowing for a lazy detection scheme in the hardware. However, the Safety property requires that violations are at least caught before the next system call, thereby prohibiting undefined program behavior from becoming externally visible.

### 2.5 The Compiler-Hardware Contract

Our earlier work on DRF$x$ describes a set of requirements for a compiler and hardware implementation that provably ensure the DRF$x$ properties defined above [32]. The key idea is for the compiler to partition a program into single-entry, multiple-exit portions called *regions*. All compiler optimizations are restricted to instructions within a region. In addition, DRF$x$ imposes two restrictions on the compiler. First, any transformation should be *sequentially valid*, meaning that executing the region in isolation from an arbitrary program state should take the program to the same state before and after the transformation. This restriction allows many common optimizations disallowed by the SC memory model, such as common subexpression elimination and register promotion. Second, optimizations are not allowed to introduce reads and writes that are not present in the original program, as they can introduce a data race.[3] However, an optimization is allowed to eliminate reads and writes provided it satisfies the first condition above.

Each synchronization operation must be placed in its own region, thereby preventing reorderings across such accesses. To ensure the DRF$x$ model's Safety property, each system call must also be placed in its own region. Otherwise, region boundaries are unconstrained. The compiler inserts a fence instruction at the entry of each region in order to communicate these boundaries to the hardware.

The hardware must also respect region boundaries (as enforced by memory fences), and it additionally detects conflicting accesses to the same memory location (i.e., accesses where at least one is a write) from concurrently executing regions. If such a region conflict is detected, the hardware throws a memory-model exception and the detected conflict is a witness to a data race in the source program. On the other hand, if there are no region conflicts, then the execution is *region-serializable* — equivalent to an execution in which each region is executed atomically in some global sequential order consistent with the per-thread order of regions — and hence SC.

The following example makes the compiler-hardware contract concrete. Consider the C++ program in Figure 1(a), in which thread

[2] Two threads in a data-race-free program can simultaneously read the same variable. The corresponding metadata updates result in a data race.

[3] DRF0 already precludes a compiler from introducing writes in the program.

```
X* x = null;
bool init = false;

  // Thread t        // Thread u
A: x = new X();    C: if(init)
B: init = true;    D:    x->f++;
```

(a)

```
// Thread t            // Thread u
B: init = true;
                      C: if(init)
                      D:    x->f++;
A: x = new X();
```

(b)

```
// Thread t            // Thread u
B: init = true;
A: x = new X();
                      C: if(init)
                      D:    x->f++;
```

(c)

**Figure 1.** (a) Program with a data race. (b) Interleaving that exposes the effect of a compiler or hardware reordering. (c) Interleaving that does not. [32]

`t` uses a boolean flag `init` to communicate to thread `u` that variable `x` has been properly initialized. In the absence of an annotation to declare `init` a synchronization variable (e.g., `volatile` in Java [30] or `atomic` in C++0x [9]), this program is racy. Suppose the compiler puts A and B in a single region, and similarly for C and D. Because A and B are in the same region, they can be potentially reordered, as shown in Figure 1(b). The execution depicted in that figure has a concurrent region conflict and so will be halted with an MM exception. Indeed, if not halted this execution will result in a null pointer dereference, which cannot happen on any SC execution of the original program. On the other hand, the execution shown in Figure 1(c) has no concurrent region conflict and so will not be halted. This execution exhibits SC behavior despite the instruction reordering.

### 2.6 Realizing the DRFx Compiler and Hardware Design

In this paper we present a complete realization and evaluation of a DRF$x$-compliant platform, including both a conforming compiler adapted from our earlier DRF$x$ work and a hardware simulator. Our approach is based on two high-level ideas [32]. First, conflict detection for a region is performed *lazily*, once the region has completed execution. This design supports conflict detection without requiring modifications to the processor's cache architecture or coherence mechanism, which would otherwise be necessary to avoid detecting false conflicts. Second, the compiler bounds the size of each region to ensure that conflict detection can be performed using finite hardware resources. While smaller regions limit the scope of optimizations, a notion of *soft fences* allows the hardware to safely optimize across most region boundaries.

Compared to a traditional memory model based on DRF0 [2], DRF$x$ has two main sources of inefficiency that must be assessed. First, there is a loss of performance due to the restriction to only optimize within a region. Second, there is additional overhead due to the region conflict detection mechanism. We previously built a DRF$x$-compliant compiler and used it to evaluate the first cost above [32], but the hardware design was not realized. In this paper, we propose a concrete DRF$x$ compliant hardware design, formalize the design along with several important optimizations and prove the design's correctness, implement the design in a hardware simulator, and conduct an end-to-end performance evaluation versus the traditional DRF0 model as well as TSO hardware.

## 3. DRFx Processor Design

In this section, we discuss our proposed DRF$x$ processor architecture. We describe lazy conflict detection using bloom filter signatures, and several optimizations that allow efficient execution in spite of the small, bounded regions created by the DRF$x$ compiler. This section discusses the intuition behind the correctness of these optimizations while a more formal presentation will be given in Section 4.

### 3.1 Overview

To satisfy DRF$x$ properties, the runtime has to detect a conflict when region-serializability may be violated due to a data-race and raise a memory model exception (Section 2.5). Figure 3 presents an overview of our DRF$x$ hardware design which supports this conflict detection. Additions to the baseline DRF0 hardware are shaded in gray. The state of several hardware structures at some instant of time during an execution of a sample program is also shown.

Unlike many hardware transactional memory designs, data-race detection requires the hardware to perform conflict detection at byte granularity. Performing precise byte-level eager conflict detection complicates the coherence protocol and cache architecture [29]. For instance, such a scheme would require us to maintain byte-level access state for every cache block, maintain the access state even after a cache block migrates from one processor to another, and clear the access state in remote processors when a region commits.

Instead, we employ lazy conflict detection [21]. Each processor core has a *region buffer* which stores the physical addresses of memory accesses executed in a region. An entry is created in the region buffer when a region executes a memory access. A memory access in a region *completes* its execution when it is *committed* from the reorder buffer and, in the case of stores, *retired* from the store buffer. When all the memory accesses in a region have completed their execution, the processor broadcasts the address set for the region to other processors for conflict checks. Once the requesting processor has received acknowledgments from all other processors indicating lack of conflicts, it commits the region and reclaims the region buffer entries. We reduce the communication and conflict check overhead by using bloom filter signatures to represent sets of addresses [14]. A *signature buffer* is used to store the read and write signatures for all the in-flight regions in a processor core.

The region buffer has to be at least as large as the maximum number of instructions allowed to be executed in a soft-fenced region created by our DRF$x$ compiler. The static analysis used by our DRF$x$ compiler to guarantee this bound is necessarily conservative and may create regions that are much smaller than the desired bound. Frequent soft-fences leads to frequent conflict checks. We reduce this cost by coalescing the soft-fenced regions at runtime. We can support this optimization by using a region buffer slightly larger than the maximum possible region-size guaranteed by the compiler.

To execute a hard fence, a processor has to stall the execution of all future memory accesses until the operations before the hard fence have completed. Forcing the frequent soft-fences introduced by a conservative compiler analysis to adhere to such strict memory ordering requirements results in prohibitive performance overhead due to the hardware being unable to exploit instruction and memory level parallelism across small, soft-fenced regions.

We show that treating a soft fence as a hard fence is unnecessary and indeed leads to significant performance loss. We make several observations that enable the hardware to optimize across soft fences. We show that we can allow memory accesses from a region to execute even if earlier regions that are separated by soft fences have not committed. In addition, we demonstrate that regions separated by a soft fence can be committed out of order. The formal proofs outlined in Section 4 take these optimizations into account and establish that the DRF$x$ runtime requirements are still satisfied.

### 3.2 Signature-based Lazy Conflict Detection

Let us assume that a processor treats soft fences similar to hard fences, an assumption that we will relax later in the discussion. DRF$x$ hardware employs lazy conflict detection to detect when region-serializability could have been violated due to a data-race.

Each processor core has a *region buffer*. A region buffer entry stores the physical address of a memory access in a region. The DRF$x$ compiler bounds the size of a soft-fenced region to defined bound B, which determines the minimum size that a processor needs to provision for a region buffer.

Similar to DRF0 hardware, the memory accesses within a region can execute out-of-order, and in the case of stores, retire from a store buffer out-of-order. An entry in the region buffer is created for a memory access when it is in the decode stage of the pipeline. Its effective address is eventually written to the region buffer once it is resolved, but before issuing the memory access.

Once all the memory accesses of a region have committed from the re-order buffer (ROB), and stores are retired from the store buffer, the corresponding processor broadcasts the address set to the other processors to perform conflict checks. On receiving a conflict check request, a processor detects a conflict if the addresses in its region buffer intersect with the address set received. If the intersection is empty, an acknowledgment is sent to the requester. On receiving acknowledgments from all the other processors, a processor commits a region by deleting its address entries from the region buffer.

Broadcasting addresses accessed by every region and checking their membership in every processor's region buffer is clearly expensive. To reduce this cost, we propose using bloom filter signatures [14]. Memory addresses accessed by a region are represented using a read and a write signature. Signatures for the in-flight regions are stored in the *signature buffer* (more than one region could be in-flight due to our out-of-order execution optimizations discussed later in Section 3.5). To perform conflict checks for a region, a processor first broadcasts only its signatures. Each processor performs AND operations over the incoming signatures with the contents in its signature buffer. On detecting a potential conflict, a NACK is sent to the requester. On receiving a NACK, a processor sends the full address set for the region so that precise conflict detection can be performed.

The size of signatures needs to be large enough so that false conflicts are rare, avoiding frequent transmission of full address sets. On the other hand, large signatures could incur significant communication overhead. We observed that the average dynamic region size is relatively small (36 in our experiments). But, since we allow many regions to be in-flight in a processor at once, the signature may be compared with many remote regions, increasing the probability of getting a false conflict. To address this problem, we use large signatures (1024 bits) to avoid false conflicts, but compress the signatures before transmission to reduce communication overhead. Because many regions have small access sets, their signatures are effectively compressed using a simple, efficient run-length encoding scheme (RLE). Using this strategy, we observed very high compression ratios which significantly reduced communication overhead.

Note that our conflict detection architecture does not require additional state to be maintained in the cache, nor does it require changes to the coherence protocol as the DRF$x$ conflict check messages are independent of coherence messages.

### 3.3 Concurrent Region Conflict Check and Region Execution

We observe that when a processor P receives a conflict check request for R$'$, it need not stall the execution of its current region R while it performs the conflict check. A conflict check can be performed in parallel with the execution of a local region. The intuition here is that any memory address that gets resolved for R during the conflict check can be shown to have executed after the memory accesses in R$'$. Thus, we can order R$'$ before R in the region serialization of the execution.

However, care must be taken to not raise a false conflict over a speculative memory access. The region buffer entry and signature buffer is updated once the address for a memory access is resolved. It is possible that a branch before the memory access is mispredicted, and therefore there is a risk that the memory access could get aborted in future. To avoid raising false exceptions, once a processor detects a conflict, it delays the exception until the conflicting memory access is committed from the ROB. If the memory access gets aborted due to misprediction, then an acknowledgment is sent if there were no other conflicts for the check. In our experiments, we observed that only very rarely we detect a conflict with a memory access in the wrong path. Therefore, the cost of delaying a response to a conflict check due to such conflicts is negligible.

The signature for a region is updated when one of its memory access' address is resolved. When a memory access is aborted due to a branch misprediction we do not update the signatures corresponding to its region. This could result in additional false positives, but we expect the performance impact to be negligible.

### 3.4 Coalescing Soft-Fence-Bounded Regions

The DRF$x$ compiler uses a conservative static analysis to estimate the maximum number of instructions executed in a region. This could result in frequent soft fences. We observe that dynamically a processor can ignore a soft fence if the preceding soft-fenced region executed fewer memory accesses than a pre-determined threshold T. Combining two contiguous soft-fenced regions at runtime does not violate DRF$x$ guarantees, because any conflict detected over the newly constructed larger region is possible only if there is a race, and ensuring serializability of the larger, coalesced soft-fenced regions is sufficient to guarantee SC for the original unoptimized program.

However, the processor needs to ensure that the newly constructed region does not exceed the size of its region buffer. Our design guarantees this by using a region buffer that is of size T + B, where B is the compiler specified bound for a soft-fenced region, and T is the threshold used by a processor to determine when to ignore a soft fence. Too high a value for the threshold T would result in large regions at runtime, which might negatively impact performance, because the probability of aliases in signatures increase. Also, it could undermine out-of-order commit optimization.

### 3.5 Out-of-Order Execution and Commit of Regions

In the discussion so far, we have assumed that a soft fence behaves like a hard fence. However, we observe that two important restrictions that need to be obeyed for hard fences can be relaxed for soft fences, which allows us to attain performance close to DRF0.

First, we allow out-of-order execution of soft-fenced regions. In the case of a hard fence, before a processor can execute memory accesses from a region, it has to wait for all the memory accesses in the preceding regions to complete. We refer to this restriction as *in-order execution of regions*. This is clearly a requirement for hard fences, since we may detect false conflicts if memory accesses are allowed to be reordered across hard fences that demarcate synchronization operations. However, we observe that this memory ordering can be relaxed for soft fences. For the example in Figure 2, $I_7$ can be allowed to execute even if regions $R_0$ and $R_1$ have pending memory accesses in the ROB or the store buffer. If there is a pending store ($I_1$) in previous regions, its value can be forwarded to a load in a later region ($I_7$).

The correctness of the above optimization can be intuitively understood by observing that executing memory accesses out-of-order only results in more in-flight accesses that needs to be conflict checked. Therefore, it does not mask any conflicts that would have been detected before. Also, aggressive reordering of soft-fenced regions does not reorder accesses across synchronization operations, so any conflicts detected guarantees presence of data races.

Second, we observe that once a region's memory accesses are completed, a processor can initiate conflict checks and commit the region from the region buffer if the check succeeds. Since the ROB commits instructions in-order, it is guaranteed that when a region is ready to commit, all the memory accesses from preceding regions would have also committed from the ROB. There could, however, be stores in the store buffer pending for the earlier regions. As a result, those earlier regions would not yet be ready to commit. Under this scenario, we claim that it is correct to conflict check and commit a later region as long as all its accesses have committed from the ROB and retired from the store buffer.

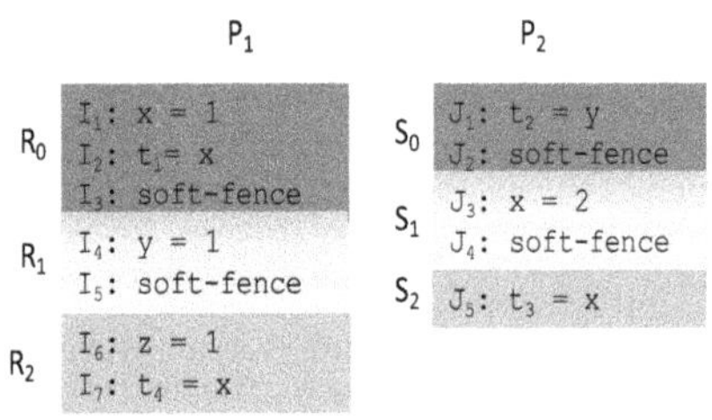


**Figure 2.** An Example Binary Compiled Using DRF*x* Compiler.

For example, in Figure 2, say region $R_0$ is waiting for its store $I_1$ to be retired from the store buffer. In the meantime, $I_4$ has completed and has retired from the store buffer. Now $R_1$ is ready to commit. We claim that a processor can perform conflict checking for $R_1$ and commit by deleting its corresponding entries from the region and signature buffers. This optimization can be intuitively understood by observing that even if $R_1$ commits, as long as $R_0$ does not raise a conflict, there would be a global serial order for all the soft-fenced regions.

These relaxations on concurrent conflict detection and region execution obviate the need for the arbiter used in other lazy conflict detection schemes [14, 21]. The formalism presented in Section 4 accounts for out-of-order region execution and commit.

### 3.6 Handling Context Switches

A thread can incur a context switch at runtime for a variety of reasons. When possible, we require that the context switch be delayed until the subsequent soft fence instruction. As our regions are bounded in the number of memory instructions, most well-behaved programs will eventually execute a soft fence after a finite amount of time. To account for adversarial programs that can perform unbounded computation (while still performing a bounded number of memory accesses), we require that the DRF*x* compiler insert additional soft fences in regions that could potentially execute unbounded number of instructions. By doing so, we make it possible for scheduler-induced thread context switches be delayed without affecting the fairness of the operating system scheduler. For such delayed context switches, the hardware waits until all prior regions are committed and performs the context switch when the region buffer is empty.

Certain context switches, such as those induced by page faults and device interrupts, are critical and cannot be delayed. We observe that DRF*x*-style conflict detection should be disabled for low-level system operations such as the page-fault handler. It is unclear if halting such critical functionality with a memory-model exception is a good design choice. Instead, we propose that such low-level code be (either manually or statically) verified to be data-race free. This observation leads to a simple solution that does not require virtualizing the region buffer.

When critical context switches occur, the processor retains the region buffer entries for the switched out thread. When the processor is executing the page-fault or the interrupt handler, it continues to perform conflict detection on behalf of the switched-out thread. Since conflict detection is disabled for the handler, no new entries are added to the region buffer. When the handler has finished, we require that the operating system schedule the switched-out thread on the same processor core. At this point, the thread continues using the region buffer, which contains the same entries it had at the time it was switched out.

While a page fault is being serviced for a thread, a processor can execute other threads instead of waiting for the data to be fetched from the disk. We can allow `N` context switches while handling a page-fault by provisioning a region buffer with a size that is `N` times that of the maximum bound specified by the compiler. For example, if the compiler bounds the region size to 64 locations and region buffer size is 512, we can allow 8 context switches.

### 3.7 Debugging Support

When a program is terminated with an MM exception, the processor provides the addresses of the starting and ending fence instructions of each conflicting region to assist in debugging. Exact addresses of the conflicting instructions could be provided with additional storage overhead by extending each region buffer entry to track the program counter (PC) of each memory instruction.

A processor may encounter non-MM exceptions such as a null-pointer dereference, division by zero, etc., while the current region is yet to complete. In this scenario, the processor stalls the execution of the current region and performs conflict detection for the partially executed region. If the conflict check succeeds, indicating no data race, it raises the non-MM exception. But if a conflict is detected, the processor throws an MM exception instead.

An MM exception in our design is imprecise in the sense that the state of the program when an exception is raised may not be SC. Because, the compiler or hardware could have already performed SC-violating optimizations in regions that contain racing accesses. Even an eager conflict detection scheme can only guarantee that the program state at the time of an exception is SC with respect to the compiled, binary program [29]. The state could still be non-SC with respect to the source program due to compiler optimizations.

### 3.8 System Calls and Safety

The DRF*x* compiler places each system call in its own region, separated from other regions by hard fences. Furthermore, the compiler generates code to ensure that system calls only access thread-local storage. Any user data potentially read by a system call is copied to thread-local storage before executing the preceding hard fence, and any user data written by the system call is copied out of thread-local storage after the succeeding hard fence.

An adversarial program may not obey the DRF*x* compiler requirement that every region's size be bounded to a predefined limit. When a program executes a region that exceeds the bound, the

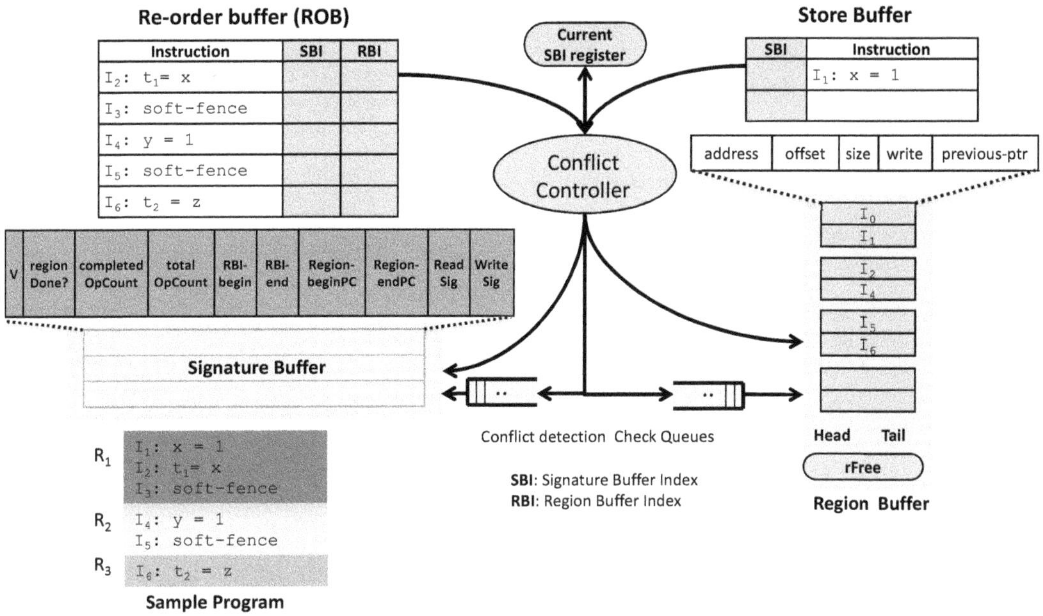


**Figure 3.** Architecture Support for DRF$x$ (shown in gray).

DRF$x$ hardware can trivially detect that condition and raise an MM exception to ensure safety.

### 3.9 DRF$x$ Hardware Design Details

Region and signature buffers for each processor core are the main extensions to the baseline hardware structures. We assume a snoop-based architecture which we extend with additional messages to support conflict checking. Conflict check messages are independent of coherence messages. Figure 3 shows our DRF$x$ hardware extensions to a baseline out-of-order processor with store buffer. We now describe these extensions in detail.

When a hard fence is decoded, a new region is created by first finding a free entry in the signature buffer (one with its `valid` bit unset), initializing the entry's fields, and storing its index in the current Signature Buffer Index (SBI) register. The `SBI` register keeps track of the signature buffer entry corresponding to the region that is currently being fetched and decoded. When a soft fence is decoded, we create a new region only if the current region size (stored in the `totalOpCount` field of the region's signature buffer entry) exceeds a pre-determined threshold `T` (32 in our experiments). If a soft fence does not start a new region, it is turned into a `nop` in the decode stage. If a hard or soft fence starts a new region, its instruction address is stored in the `Region-beginPC` field of the new region's signature buffer entry. This information is used while reporting an MM exception.

When a memory instruction is decoded, a region buffer entry is allocated for it. The register `rFree` keeps track of the total number of free entries in the region buffer. If no free region entry is available, the memory access is stalled in the decode stage of the pipeline. Since regions can commit out-of-order, we maintain a linked-list to track the free region buffer entries. The `head` and `tail` registers point to the first and last entries in the free list respectively. Free entries, and also those allocated to a region are linked through the `ptr` fields. The `ptr` for the first memory access of a region is set to null. The `ptr` for any later memory access of a region points to its immediately preceding memory access's region buffer entry. The head and tail of a region is stored in the `RBI-begin` and `RBI-end` fields in the signature buffer entry of that region (RBI stands for Region Buffer Index).

Instead of allocating one region buffer entry for each memory access in a region, we could potentially coalesce accesses to the same memory location into one entry. We opted not to do this in order to simplify the design, such as the logic required for deleting region buffer entries when memory accesses get aborted due to a branch misprediction.

The number of memory accesses decoded as part of the current region is maintained by incrementing the `totalOpCount` field in the current region's signature buffer entry (specified by the `SBI` register). Completion of memory accesses of a region is maintained by incrementing the `completedOpCount` field when a load commits from the ROB or a store retires from the store buffer. These counts are used to determine when a region is ready to commit.

When a memory operation's address is resolved, completed or aborted, corresponding entries in the signature and region buffer need to be updated. To determine these entries, each ROB entry contains two pointers: the Region Buffer Index (RBI) that points to the memory access' region buffer entry, and the SBI of the region that the memory access corresponds to.

When a memory access is aborted due to a branch misprediction, its region buffer entry is deallocated and its region's `totalOpCount` is decremented. Note that a store in the store buffer does not need the RBI pointer as it is non-speculative. It does however need the SBI pointer to update the `completedOpCount` in the signature buffer when it retires.

When a hard or a soft fence commits from the ROB, its region's `regionDone` bit is set in the signature buffer. Also, its region's `Region-endPC` is updated with its instruction address. A region is ready to commit, if its `regionDone` bit is set and `completedOpCount` is equal to `totalOpCount`. Before committing a region, its addresses need to be conflict checked with all the in-flight regions in remote processor cores. During this process, the region's SBI is used as its identifier in the conflict check messages.

If the conflict check succeeds, the region is committed by deallocating its entries in the signature and region buffers. The signature buffer entry is identified using the region's SBI used during its conflict check. The start and end of a region's entries in the region buffer are determined using the `RBI-begin` and `RBI-end` fields stored in that region's signature buffer entry. Committed region's region buffer entries are added to the free list.

### 3.9.1 Region Buffer and Signature Buffer Sizes

The number of entries in the region buffer needs to be at least as large as the bound assumed by the DRF$x$ compiler for a soft-fenced region (512 entries for our study). But a larger buffer allows us to coalesce regions. Also, a larger region buffer could expose additional opportunities for out-of-order execution across regions. We assume a 544-entry region buffer in our evaluation (512 is the compiler bound, additional 32 entries support coalescing).

DRF$x$ requires byte-level, precise conflict detection, but storing an entry for each byte accessed would be inefficient. To minimize region buffer space, we optimize for the common case, which is word-level access. Thus, a region buffer entry includes the word address, byte offset, and the number of bytes accessed. This requires 81 bits per region buffer entry: 8 bytes for double word aligned address, 3 bits for byte offset, 3 bits for access size, a read/write bit, and 10 bits for `ptr`. Thus, the size of a region buffer in each core is 5.38KB.

The region buffer is designed as a banked content addressable memory (CAM). This allows us to perform fast membership tests using word addresses when performing precise conflict checking for a remote region. Only when a potential word-level conflict is detected do we perform a precise byte-level address comparison. We expect that the CAM would be accessed relatively infrequently, only when a signature-based conflict check finds a potential conflict.

Each core has a signature buffer with 17 entries, as there can only be a maximum of 17 in-flight regions in our design with 544-entry region buffer and a coalescing threshold (T) of 32. Each entry has a read and a write signature of size 1024 bits to capture the addresses accessed in a region. In addition, each entry contains a valid bit, a `regionDone` bit, `RBI-begin`, `RBI-end`, `completedOpCount`, `totalOpCount` (10 bits each since there are 544 region buffer entries which is also the maximum number of memory operations in a coalesced region), and starting and ending program counter values of a region (64 bits each). Thus, a signature buffer with 17 entries is of size 4.60KB.

## 4. Correctness of Design

In this section we describe the formal arguments we use to show that our optimized hardware design satisfies the two key requirements for a DRF$x$-compliant execution environment: exception-free executions are region serializable and only compiled programs that contain a data race can raise an MM exception. Full proofs of the lemmas and theorems are omitted, but can be found in the accompanying technical report [40].

In showing the correctness of the design, we must model certain orderings that hold between various events in the system. Keep in mind that none of the orderings we describe are violated by the optimizations described in Section 3. In particular we make no assumptions about the order in which memory accesses from adjacent soft-fenced regions complete or the order in which those regions commit. We consider three events in a (memory access) instruction's execution: address resolution, commit from the reorder buffer, and (for store instructions) retirement from the store buffer. For any particular instruction, a processor performs each of these events in this order. Any events that can be shown to have a causal relationship within a processor give rise to a partial order on events that is consistent with physical time. We will refer to this partial order as the processor happens before order (PHB). So, for an instruction $M$, we have $M$ `resolved` $<_{\text{PHB}}$ $M$ `committed` $<_{\text{PHB}}$ $M$ `retired`. In an attempt to treat loads and stores more uniformly in the formalism, we will also refer to an instruction being *completed.* We consider a store completed when it has retired from the store buffer ($M$ a store and $M$ `retired` $\Rightarrow$ $M$ `completed`). Loads and all other instructions will be considered completed as soon as they have been committed from the reorder buffer ($M$ not a store and $M$ `committed` $\Rightarrow$ $M$ `completed`).

| | |
|---|---|
| $\langle R\rangle$ | Send the conflict detection msg for region $R$ |
| $\langle P \leftarrow R\rangle$ | Receive a conflict detection msg for region $R$ at processor $P$ |
| $\langle P\checkmark R\rangle$ | Send an ack msg for $R$ from $P$ back to originating processor |
| $R$ `committed` | Commit region $R$, clearing all its entries in region buffer |

**Table 1.** Events in Conflict Detection

We also include in PHB the causal order between instruction execution events and the events performed as part of conflict detection, which are shown in Table 1. A processor waits for all instructions in a region to be completed (all instructions committed and all stores flushed from store buffers) before sending a conflict detection message. So, for all instructions $M$ in region $R$ we have $M$ `completed` $<_{\text{PHB}}$ $\langle R\rangle$. Furthermore, although regions may be committed out of order, because instructions are committed from the reorder buffer in-order, we know that for all instructions $M$ in regions program-ordered before region $R$, we have $M$ `committed` $<_{\text{PHB}}$ $\langle R\rangle$. We also know that a processor must receive a request for conflict detection before it performs detection and eventually sends an acknowledgment. We also use PHB to capture this: $\langle P \leftarrow R\rangle <_{\text{PHB}} \langle P\checkmark R\rangle$.

The fact that the conflict detection mechanism does not find a conflict can also indicate events that are ordered by PHB. It is clear that if a processor $P$ is performing conflict detection in response to a request from processor $P'$ for a region $R'$ and there is an address-resolved, conflicting entry in the region buffer for the entirety of the conflict detection process, then an exception will be raised. Furthermore, conflict detection for $R'$ occurs strictly between the time that the request is received and the acknowledgment is sent. This reasoning makes no assumptions about the order of execution of instructions in different regions, the number of regions in flight, the order of region commit, or whether or not conflict detection for multiple requests (or a coalesced request) is proceeding in parallel.

So, the following proposition captures what orderings we can infer if a conflict is *not* detected in our fully optimized design.

**Proposition 1.** *If $M$ and $M'$ are conflicting memory accesses contained respectively in region $R$ executing on processor $P$ and region $R'$ executing on processor $P'$ where $P \neq P'$, and if the execution does not raise an MM exception, then either:*

1. *$R$ `committed` $<_{\text{PHB}}$ $\langle P\checkmark R'\rangle$*
   *or*
2. *$\langle P \leftarrow R'\rangle <_{\text{PHB}}$ $M$ `resolved`.*

We model the fact that a message must be sent by one processor before it is received by another processor by a partial order called message happens before (MHB). So we have $\langle R\rangle <_{\text{MHB}} \langle P \leftarrow R\rangle$, and also $\langle P\checkmark R\rangle <_{\text{MHB}}$ $R$ `committed` since the originating processor must receive acknowledgments from all other processors before it commits the region. (We've left the reception of the acknowledgment as an implicit event since it won't be needed in the proofs). Since both PHB and MHB are partial orders that arise from causal relationships and are consistent with physical time, we know that their union is acyclic. We will call this partial order the system happens before relation: SHB $=$ PHB $\cup$ MHB.

Notice that Proposition 1 is symmetric in $M$ and $M'$. But, it cannot be the case that both $R$ `committed` $<_{\text{PHB}}$ $\langle P\checkmark R'\rangle$ and $R'$ `committed` $<_{\text{PHB}}$ $\langle P'\checkmark R\rangle$. Otherwise we would have a cycle in SHB : $R$ `committed` $<_{\text{PHB}}$ $\langle P\checkmark R'\rangle <_{\text{MHB}}$ $R'$ `committed` $<_{\text{PHB}}$ $\langle P'\checkmark R\rangle$ $<_{\text{MHB}}$ $R$ `committed`. Neither can it be the case that both $\langle P \leftarrow R' \rangle <_{\text{PHB}} M$ **resolved** and $\langle P' \leftarrow R \rangle <_{\text{PHB}} M'$ **resolved**. Again, this would contradict the acyclicity of SHB since $\langle P \leftarrow R' \rangle <_{\text{PHB}} M$ **resolved** $<_{\text{PHB}} \langle R \rangle <_{\text{MHB}} \langle P' \leftarrow R \rangle <_{\text{PHB}} M'$ **resolved** $<_{\text{PHB}} \langle R' \rangle <_{\text{MHB}} \langle P \leftarrow R' \rangle$. So we incorporate this information to state a stronger version of the proposition.

**Proposition 2.** *If $M$ and $M'$ are conflicting memory accesses contained respectively in region $R$ executing on processor $P$ and region $R'$ executing on processor $P'$ where $P \neq P'$, and if the execution does not raise an MM exception, then either:*

1. $R$ `committed` $<_{\text{PHB}} \langle P \checkmark R' \rangle$ *and* $\langle P' \leftarrow R \rangle <_{\text{PHB}} M'$ `resolved`
   *or*
2. $\langle P \leftarrow R' \rangle <_{\text{PHB}} M$ `resolved` *and* $R'$ `committed` $<_{\text{PHB}} \langle P' \checkmark R \rangle$.

We now describe some orderings on memory operations. Our cache coherence protocol guarantees us a total order on writes to the same memory location. We will call this order CO. This can be extended to a partial order EO on loads and stores to the same memory location by ordering a load after the store that it reads and before the store that follows that store in CO. In order to define region serializability, we consider the lifting of EO to regions, denoted by $\text{EO}^R$. We define $R_1 <_{\text{EO}^R} R_2$ to hold if there exist conflicting memory operations $M_1 \in R_1$ and $M_2 \in R_2$ such that $M_1 <_{\text{EO}} M_2$. We can now state the definition of region serializability in terms of $\text{EO}^R$ and the program order of regions within a thread, which we will call TO.

**Definition 1.** *Let the region ordering relation* RO *be defined as* $\text{RO} = \text{EO}^R \cup \text{TO}$. *An execution is* region serializable *if* RO *is a partial order.*

In order to prove that an exception-free execution is region serializable, we first establish the following two lemmas.

**Lemma 1.** *If a memory access $M$ in region $R$ executing on processor $P$ conflicts with a memory access $M'$ in region $R'$ executing on $P'$ where $P \neq P'$, and if $\langle P' \leftarrow R \rangle <_{\text{PHB}} M'$ `resolved` and the execution is MM-exception-free, then $M <_{\text{EO}} M'$.*

**Lemma 2.** *If $M$ and $M'$ are conflicting memory accesses contained respectively in region $R$ executing on processor $P$ and region $R'$ executing on processor $P'$ where $P \neq P'$, and if the execution does not raise an MM exception, and if $M <_{\text{EO}} M'$, then $R$ `committed` $<_{\text{PHB}} \langle P \checkmark R' \rangle$ and $\langle P' \leftarrow R \rangle <_{\text{PHB}} M'$ `resolved`.*

We use these lemmas to establish the following theorem.

**Theorem 1.** *An execution on our optimized hardware that does not raise an MM exception is region serializable.*

We further demonstrate that if two conflicting memory accesses are ordered by synchronization operations ($M <_{\text{TO}} S <_{\text{EO}} S' <_{\text{TO}} M'$), then they cannot cause a memory model exception to be raised. This is the result of the stringent ordering constraints that the hardware places on the hard fences surrounding synchronization operations.

**Theorem 2.** *If a compiled program is free of data races, then our optimized hardware will not raise an MM exception during its execution.*

Full proofs for these theorems and lemmas can be found in [40]. Theorems 1 and 2 can be combined with the results shown for a DRF$x$-compliant compiler in [31] in order to establish the end-to-end DRF$x$ guarantees.

## 5. Results

This section discusses results analyzing the cost of supporting DRF$x$, which includes the cost of optimizations lost due to compiler constructed soft-fences and runtime conflict detection.

### 5.1 Simulation Methodology

We implemented three compiler versions using LLVM[28] to study the performance of TSO, DRF0 and DRF$x$. The TSO compiler is the baseline LLVM compiler at `-O3` optimization level. The DRF0 compiler inserts a hard fence using the `llvm.memory.barrier` intrinsic before and after every synchronization call and access to a volatile variable. Also, we disabled speculative optimizations. [4] For the DRF$x$ compiler, we inserted soft fences before performing any compiler optimization to bound region sizes to 512 memory accesses. The size is estimated using a conservative static analysis over the control-flow-graph. In addition, our compiler conservatively adds a soft fence at every back-edge of a loop.

We modeled three hardware architectures, TSO, DRF0 and DRF$x$ using a cycle-accurate, execution driven, Simics based x86_64 simulator called FeS2 [34]. Our processor configuration is shown in Table 2. The model includes a MOESI coherence protocol and a store buffer to hold pending stores that have been committed from the ROB. For TSO, the store buffer is organized as a FIFO queue to enforce in-order retirement of stores. For DRF0 and DRF$x$, the store buffer can retire stores between two hard fences out-of-order. We also allow two stores to the same cache block to be coalesced into one entry in the store buffer for the DRF0 and DRF$x$ models.

We modeled a hierarchical switch network with a fan-out degree of 4, 512-bit link width, 1-cycle link latency. We assume a virtual channel (VC) for each message type: address, control, broadcasting signatures in DRFx, and unicast messages in DRFx (request full address set, reply full address set, acknowledgments). We also modeled 2-cycle latency for issuing a message into the interconnect. Limited message buffer capacity at each switch was not modeled.

Our model includes speculative load execution support for TSO [20]. It allows a load to be speculatively reordered before another load. A misspeculation is detected when a processor receives an invalidation request for a cache block that was read speculatively by a load before that load commits from the ROB. In the event of a misspeculated load, the load and its subsequent instructions are squashed and re-executed. This optimization is not necessary for DRF0 and DRF$x$ as they can re-order loads and stores between two hard fences.

For all the models, memory accesses are not allowed to execute until preceding hard fence has committed. A hard fence is committed only after all the preceding memory accesses have retired from the store buffer.

For DRF$x$ we modeled a region buffer of size 512 (compiler bound) + 32 (to support region coalescing). This buffer is divided into 8 banks and each bank is a CAM. We assume 2 cycle latency for associative accesses to this structure, which we estimated using CACTI [12]. For signature based designs, we use a 1024 bit signature and use the hash used in Bulk [14]. We used a signature buffer of size 17, which allows a maximum of 17 regions to be in-flight in a processor core.

We evaluated the performance of various designs over PARSEC [5] and SPLASH-2 [43] benchmarks. Table 3 lists the IPC for the baseline DRF0 model. All of these benchmarks are run to the completion. For PARSEC benchmarks, we used the `sim-medium`

[4] Specifically, we modified `llvm::isSafeToLoadUnconditionally`, `Instruction::isSafeToSpeculativelyExecute` and `MachineInstr::isSafeToMove` to return false if instruction is a load

input set (except for streamcluster, for which we used the `sim-small` input). For SPLASH-2 applications we use the default inputs.

| | |
|---|---|
| Processor | 4-core CMP. Each core operating at 2Ghz. |
| Fetch/Exec/Commit width | 4 instructions (maximum 2 loads or 1 store) per cycle in each core. |
| Store Buffer | TSO: 64 entry FIFO buffer with 8 byte granularity. DRF0, DRF$x$: 8 entry unordered coalescing buffer with 64 byte granularity. |
| L1 Cache | 64 KB per-core (private), 4-way set associative, 64B block size, 1-cycle hit latency, write-back. |
| L2 Cache | 1MB private, 4-way set associative, 64B block size, 10-cycle hit latency. |
| Coherence | MOESI snoop protocol |
| Interconnection | Hierarchical switch, fan-out degree 4 512-bit link width, 1-cycle link latency. |
| Memory | 80-cycle DRAM lookup latency. |
| RegionBuffer | 544 entry, 8 banks, 2-cycle CAM access. |
| Bloom filter | 1024 bits. 2 banks indexed by 9 bit field after address permutation[14]. 2-cycle access latency. |

**Table 2.** Processor Configuration

| Application | Avg. IPC (DRF0) | Application | Avg. IPC (DRF0) |
|---|---|---|---|
| blackscholes | 1.97 | bodytrack | 1.75 |
| canneal | 0.27 | facesim | 0.53 |
| streamcluster | 1.61 | barnes | 1.59 |
| fft | 1.41 | radix | 0.99 |
| raytrace | 0.59 | | |

**Table 3.** Average IPC for DRF0

### 5.2 DRFx Memory Model Performance Comparison

Figure 4 compares the performance of TSO, DRF0 and DRF$x$. The results are normalized to the execution time of DRF0. For DRF$x$, we show two results. The first result labeled as `DRF0 + soft-fence` represents the compiler cost of DRF$x$ and is the maximum performance our DRF$x$ hardware can hope to achieve. To obtain this result, we executed a program compiled using DRF$x$ compiler on DRF0 hardware, treating every soft-fence as a no-op. The second result for DRF$x$ is for a processor configuration that employs all the optimizations we discussed in this paper. It represents the compiler and hardware conflict detection cost to support DRF$x$.

We find that the average performance overhead to support DRF$x$ is about 6.49% when compared to DRF0. `barnes` has the highest overhead of 24%. DRF$x$ conflict detection adds only about 2.3% higher overhead to `DRF0 + soft-fence`. As demonstrated in the next section, our optimizations are crucial for achieving close to the best possible hardware performance.

The remaining cost in DRF$x$ is due to restricting compiler optimizations to soft-fence bounded regions. For example, DRF$x$ model for `bodytrack` is about 12.84% slower than DRF0, but almost all of this overhead is due to the DRF$x$ compiler. Our current compiler bounding analysis is very conservative, especially regarding loops, and so we believe that this cost could be significantly improved.

We found that soft fences constitute 6% of total committed instructions. Average dynamic size of compiler constructed soft-fenced regions is about 10 memory operations. However, our runtime coalescing optimization increases this to 36 memory operations. We could improve this further by increasing the region buffer size. Small regions result in frequent conflict checks, but compressing signatures avoids excessive communication overhead for these checks. We find that run-length encoding of signatures compresses signatures by 4.34x on average, significantly reducing network bandwidth requirement. The amount of data communicated processor cores increased by 84% due to conflict messages in DRF$x$ when compared to DRF0. More aggressive coalescing could potentially reduce this overhead further.

TSO represents the performance gotten by compiling a program using a stock compiler and executing it on stock hardware. We found that TSO is nearly as fast as DRF0 on our benchmarks.

### 5.3 Effectiveness of Out-of-Order Optimizations

Figure 5 compares the effectiveness of three of our optimizations: out-of-order region execution, out-of-order region commit, and coalescing contiguous regions. All of the configurations assume signature-based conflict detection. The performance results are normalized to the DRF0 execution time.

If we had not distinguished between hard and soft fences, none of the above three optimizations would have been feasible. This configuration is represented as `io-exec, io-commit`. We find that the performance overhead without the three optimizations would be on average 121% slower than DRF0. Allowing regions to execute out-of-order brings the overhead down to about 27%. Allowing regions to commit out-of-order further reduces the overhead down to about 7.7% on average. Finally, coalescing regions at runtime reduces the overhead to about 6.49%. This optimization is especially effective for programs for which our conservative compiler bounding analysis constructs very small regions. For instance, on `streamcluster` the overhead is reduced from 36% to about 15%.

Conflict detection in our design can negatively impact performance by stalling the execution of a processor core only under two circumstances. One, a region buffer entry is not available for a memory operation to issue. Two, even after all the memory accesses in the regions preceding a hard fence have completed, the processor must stall to allow conflict detection to complete. We measured the proportion of the processor cycles that are stalled due to these two reasons for a configuration with in-order commit and one allowing out-of-order commit. The results are shown in Figure 6. We observe that out-of-order commit significantly reduces both kinds of stalls for most benchmarks.

### 5.4 Effectiveness of Signature-Based Conflict Detection

Figure 7 compares the performance of DRF$x$ with and without signature based conflict check optimization. We observe that, on average, the signature based scheme improves performance by 7%. The average false positive rate for bloom filter checks was 1.39% and the maximum was 12% on `bodytrack`.

### 5.5 Scalability

Figure 8 shows the performance of DRF$x$ when compared to the baseline DRF0 as the number of cores scale. We find the network bandwidth is adequate to provide scalable performance up to 16-cores. For `blackscholes` there is a noticeable performance difference as we go from 4 to 8 cores. This is due to an increased number of false conflicts when signatures are compared to a larger number of regions on more cores. On detecting a potential conflict, we have to perform expensive, precise conflict check over the complete set of addresses. For `blackscholes`, precise conflict detection was performed for about 13% of regions in the 8-core configuration as opposed to only 5% in the 4-core configuration.

### 5.6 Exceptions

We detected conflicts due to a few benign data races in the applications we studied. One source of benign races was programmer constructed barrier synchronizations and semaphores. These synchronization variables were not typed as `volatile` in the program which caused the conflicts. Also, we detected two conflicts due to benign data races in `glibc` – one in `__drand48_iterate()` and another in `__cfree` and `malloc_consolidate` functions. To ensure correctness even under DRF0, a programmer needs to correctly flag the racy variables in these functions as `volatile`.

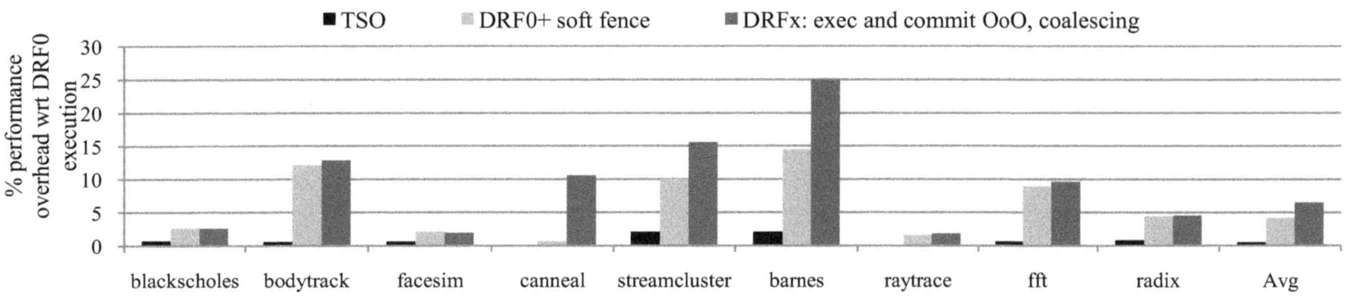


**Figure 4.** Performance of the three memory models we evaluated. `DRF0 + soft-fence` represents only the compiler cost of DRF$x$

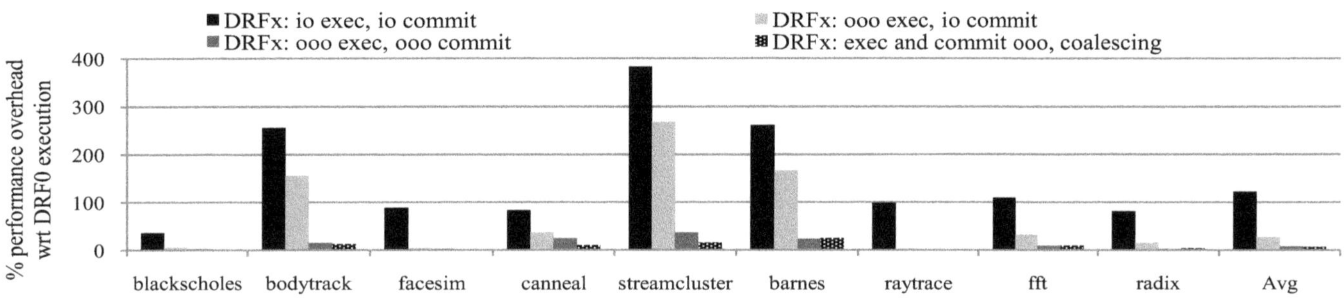


**Figure 5.** Effectiveness of Region Coalescing, and Out-Of-Order Region Execution and Commit Optimizations.

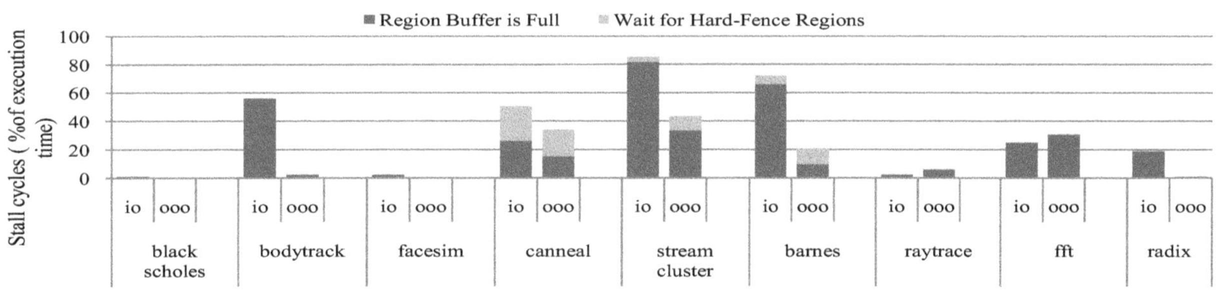


**Figure 6.** Processor Stall Cycles Due to Conflict Detection

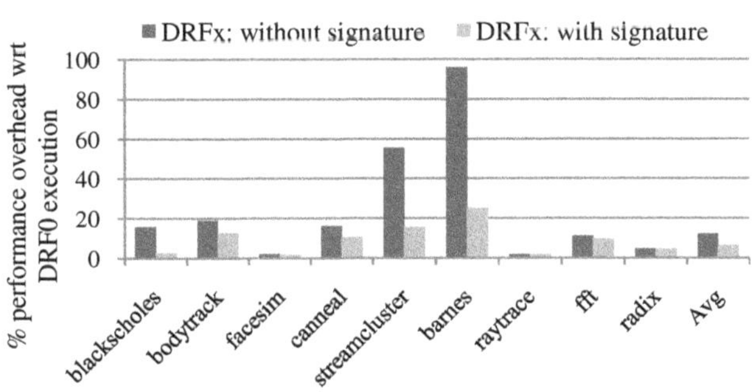


**Figure 7.** Effectiveness of Signature Based Conflict Detection

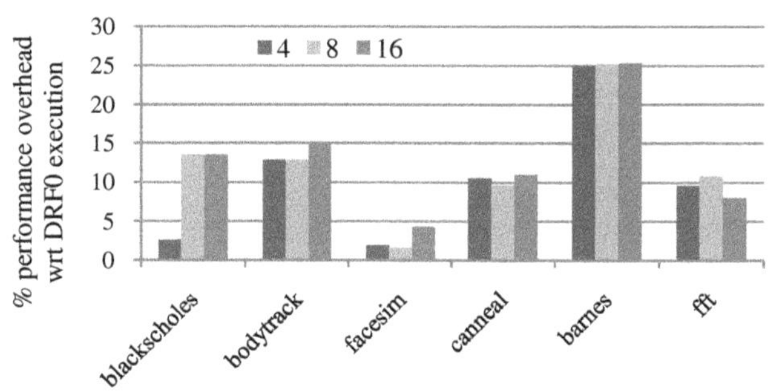


**Figure 8.** Performance overhead of DRF$x$ for 4, 8 and 16 cores with respect to the DRF0 performance for the same number of cores.

## 6. Related Work

This section discusses the most closely related work.

### 6.1 Memory Models With Exceptions

The C++ memory model [9] and the Java memory model [30] are based on DRF0 [1] and share its limitations for racy programs which we discussed in Section 1.

Concurrently with our earlier work on DRF$x$, Lucia *et al.* defined *conflict exceptions* [29], which also use a notion of regions to detect language-level SC violations in hardware. Their approach can be viewed as a realization of DRF$x$-compliant hardware, but it differs in important ways from our design. First, in their approach a conflict exception is reported *precisely*, just before the second of the conflicting operations is to be executed. Precise conflict detection is arguably complex in hardware as one has to track access state for each cache word and continue to track it even when a cache block migrates to a different processor core. Further, when a region commits, its access state needs to be cleared in remote processors. Finally, while this approach delivers a precise exception with respect to the binary, the exception is not guaranteed to be precise with respect to the original source program. Second, in their approach region boundaries are placed only around synchronization operations, thereby ensuring serializability of *maximal synchronization-free regions*, which is a stronger guarantee than SC. While this property could be useful for programmers, it can result in unbounded-size regions and thereby considerably complicates the hardware detection scheme and system software.

Adve et al. [3] proposed to detect data races at runtime using hardware support. Elmas et al. [17] augment the Java virtual machine to dynamically detect bytecode-level data races and raise a `DataRaceException`. Boehm [8] provided an informal argument for integrating an efficient always-on data-race detector to extend the DRF0 model by throwing an exception on a data race. However, detecting data races either incurs 8x or more performance overhead in software [18] or incurs significant hardware complexity [33, 35]. A full data-race detector is inherently complex as it has to dynamically build the *happens-before* graph [26] to determine racy memory accesses. It is further complicated by the fact that racy accesses could be executed arbitrarily "far" away from each other in time, which implies the need for performing conflict detection across events like cache evictions, context switches, etc. In contrast, DRF$x$ hardware is inherently simpler as it requires that we track memory access state and perform conflict detection over only the uncommitted, bounded regions.

Gharachorloo and Gibbons [19] observed that it suffices to detect SC violations directly rather than data races. Their goal was to detect potential violations of SC due to a data-race and report that to the programmer. However, their detection was with respect to the compiled version of a program. DRF$x$ incorporates the notion of compiler-constructed regions and allows the compiler and hardware to optimize within regions while still allowing us to dynamically detect potential SC violations at the language level.

### 6.2 Efficiently Supporting Sequential Consistency

If the hardware and the compiler can guarantee SC, it is clearly preferable to weaker memory models. There have been several attempts to reduce the cost of supporting SC.

Bulk compiler [4] together with the BulkSC hardware [15] provide support for guaranteeing SC at the language level. The bulk compiler constructs chunks similar to regions, but a chunk could span across synchronization accesses and could be unbounded. The BulkSC hardware employs speculation and recovery to ensure serializable execution of chunks. Conflicts are detected using a signature-based scheme and they are resolved through rollback and re-execution of chunks. Forward progress may not be possible in the presence of repeated rollbacks. The Bulk system addresses this issue and the unbounded chunk problem using several heuristics. When the heuristics fail, it resorts to serializing chunks and executing safer unoptimized code.

DRF$x$ hardware could be simpler than Bulk hardware as it avoids the need for speculation (especially across I/O) and unbounded region sizes which have been the two main issues in realizing a practical transactional memory system. However, DRF$x$ requires precise conflict detection, whereas Bulk can afford false conflicts. Our observations that certain regions can execute and commit out-of-order, and that conflict checks and region execution in different processors can all proceed in parallel is unique. It may help improve the efficiency and complexity of Bulk system as well.

SC can be guaranteed at the language level even on hardware that supports a weaker consistency model using static analysis to insert fences [24, 39, 41]. However, computing a minimal set of fences for a program is NP-complete [25]. One approach to reduce the number of fences is to statically determine potentially racy memory accesses [24, 41] and insert fences only for those accesses. These techniques are based on pointer alias analysis, sharing inference, and thread escape analysis. In spite of recent advances [10, 11], a scalable and practically feasible technique for implementing a sound static data race detector also remains an unsolved problem, as all the techniques require complex, whole-program analysis.

There has been much work on designing an efficient, sequentially consistent processor. But this only guarantees SC at the hardware level for the compiled program [6, 15, 36, 42].

### 6.3 Transactional Memory

Hardware transactional memory (HTM) systems [23] also employ conflict detection between concurrent regions. However, unlike TM systems, regions in DRF$x$ are constructed by the compiler and hence can be bounded. Also, on detecting a conflict, a region need not be rolled back. This avoids the complexity of a speculation mechanism. Thus, a DRF$x$ system does not suffer from the two issues that have been most problematic for practical adoption of TM.

Hammond et al. [22] proposed transactional coherency and consistency (TCC) memory model based on a transactional programming model [23]. The programmer and the compiler ensure that every instruction is part of some transaction. The runtime guarantees serializability of transactions, which in turn guarantees SC at the language level. Unlike this approach, DRF$x$ is useful for any multi-threaded program written using common synchronization operations like locks, and it does not require additional programmer effort to construct regions. TCC also requires unbounded region and speculation support. TCC suggests that hardware could break large regions into smaller regions, but that could violate SC at the language level.

Our lazy conflict detection algorithm is similar to the one proposed by Hammond et al. [22] but without the need for speculation and conflict detection over unbounded regions. Also, we employ signatures to reduce the cost of conflict checks. Unlike TM, DRF$x$ cannot afford false conflicts, which our design takes care to eliminate. But lazy conflict detectors like TCC assume some form of a commit arbiter to regulate concurrent commit requests for regions in different processors. As we discussed, we can allow all regions to be conflict checked in parallel with the execution of current regions, which could be simpler. Also, soft-fenced regions can be executed and committed out-of-order.

## 7. Conclusion

The DRF$x$ memory model provides strong and easy-to-understand guarantees for both data-race-free and racy programs while safely supporting most sequentially valid compiler and hardware optimizations. A significant challenge in bringing DRF$x$ to practice is the cost of runtime conflict detection. Processor support can reduce this cost, but it can be realized in practice only if it is both efficient and simple.

This paper addresses this challenge through careful design choices and optimizations of a DRF$x$-compliant micro-architecture. We employ a lazy conflict detection design in order to avoid modifying the existing cache architecture and coherence mechanism. We leverage interaction with the compiler to partition a program into bounded-size regions, thereby avoiding the need to handle overflow of hardware resources during conflict detection. Further, the cost of bounded-size regions is significantly reduced by several novel optimizations that we have formalized and proven correct.

We used a DRF$x$-compliant compiler and a hardware simulator to evaluate our design. We find that the average performance overhead is about 6.5% when compared to DRF0 memory model.

## Acknowledgments

We thank our shepherd Kunle Olukotun for comments that helped us improve this paper. This work is supported by the National Science Foundation under awards CNS-0725354, CNS-0905149, and CCF-0916770 as well as by the Defense Advanced Research Projects Agency under award HR0011-09-1-0037.

## References

[1] S. Adve and K. Gharachorloo. Shared memory consistency models: a tutorial. *Computer*, 29(12):66–76, 1996.

[2] S. V. Adve and M. D. Hill. Weak ordering—a new definition. In *ISCA '90*, pages 2–14. ACM, 1990.

[3] S. V. Adve, M. D. Hill, B. P. Miller, and R. H. B. Netzer. Detecting data races on weak memory systems. In *ISCA '91*, 1991.

[4] W. Ahn, S. Qi, J.-W. Lee, M. Nicolaides, X. Fang, J. Torrellas, D. Wong, and S. Midkiff. BulkCompiler: High-performance sequential consistency through cooperative compiler and hardware support. In *42nd International Symposium on Microarchitecture*, 2009.

[5] C. Bienia, S. Kumar, J. P. Singh, and K. Li. The PARSEC benchmark suite: Characterization and architectural implications. In *Proceedings of PACT*, October 2008.

[6] C. Blundell, M. Martin, and T. Wenisch. InvisiFence: performance-transparent memory ordering in conventional multiprocessors. In *ISCA '09*, pages 233–244, 2009.

[7] R. Bocchino, V. Adve, D. Dig, S. Adve, S. Heumann, R. Komuravelli, J. Overbey, P. Simmons, H. Sung, and M. Vakilian. A type and effect system for Deterministic Parallel Java. In *OOPSLA*, 2009.

[8] H. J. Boehm. Simple thread semantics require race detection. In *FIT session at PLDI*, 2009.

[9] H. J. Boehm and S. Adve. Foundations of the C++ concurrency memory model. In *PLDI '08*, pages 68–78. ACM, 2008.

[10] C. Boyapati and M. Rinard. A parameterized type system for race-free Java programs. In *OOPSLA '01*, pages 56–69, 2001.

[11] C. Boyapati, R. Lee, and M. Rinard. Ownership types for safe programming: Preventing data races and deadlocks. In *OOPSLA '02*, pages 211–230, 2002.

[12] Cacti. Hp labs. cacti 4.2. URL `http://quid.hpl.hp.com:9081/cacti`.

[13] P. Cenciarelli, A. Knapp, and E. Sibilio. The Java memory model: Operationally, denotationally, axiomatically. In *ESOP '07*, 2007.

[14] L. Ceze, J. Tuck, J. Torrellas, and C. Cascaval. Bulk disambiguation of speculative threads in multiprocessors. In *ISCA '06*, 2006.

[15] L. Ceze, J. Tuck, P. Montesinos, and J. Torrellas. BulkSC: bulk enforcement of sequential consistency. In *ISCA '07*, pages 278–289, 2007.

[16] L. Ceze, J. Devietti, B. Lucia, and S. Qadeer. The case for system support for concurrency exceptions. In *USENIX HotPar*, 2009.

[17] T. Elmas, S. Qadeer, and S. Tasiran. Goldilocks: a race and transaction-aware Java runtime. In *PLDI '07*, pages 149–158, 2007.

[18] C. Flanagan and S. Freund. FastTrack: efficient and precise dynamic race detection. In *PLDI '09*, pages 121–133, 2009.

[19] K. Gharachorloo and P. Gibbons. Detecting violations of sequential consistency. In *SPAA '91*, pages 316–326, 1991.

[20] K. Gharachorloo, A. Gupta, and J. Hennessy. Two techniques to enhance the performance of memory consistency models. In *Proceedings of ICPP*, volume 1, pages 355–364, 1991.

[21] L. Hammond, B. D. Carlstrom, V. Wong, B. Hertzberg, M. Chen, C. Kozyrakis, and K. Olukotun. Programming with transactional coherence and consistency (TCC). In *ASPLOS-XI*, pages 1–13, 2004.

[22] L. Hammond, V. Wong, M. K. Chen, B. D. Carlstrom, J. D. Davis, B. Hertzberg, M. K. Prabhu, H. Wijaya, C. Kozyrakis, and K. Olukotun. Transactional memory coherence and consistency. In *ISCA*, pages 102–113, 2004.

[23] M. Herlihy and J. E. B. Moss. Transactional memory: architectural support for lock-free data structures. In *ISCA '93*, pages 289–300. ACM, 1993.

[24] A. Kamil, J. Su, and K. Yelick. Making sequential consistency practical in Titanium. In *Proceedings of the 2005 ACM/IEEE conference on Supercomputing*, page 15. IEEE Computer Society, 2005.

[25] A. Krishnamurthy and K. Yelick. Analyses and optimizations for shared address space programs. *Journal of Parallel and Distributed Computing*, 38(2):130–144, 1996.

[26] L. Lamport. Time, clocks, and the ordering of events in a distributed system. *Communications of the ACM*, 21(7):558–565, 1978.

[27] L. Lamport. How to make a multiprocessor computer that correctly executes multiprocess programs. *IEEE transactions on computers*, 100(28):690–691, 1979.

[28] C. Lattner and V. Adve. LLVM: A compilation framework for lifelong program analysis & transformation. In *Proceedings of CGO*. IEEE Computer Society, 2004.

[29] B. Lucia, L. Ceze, K. Strauss, S. Qadeer, and H. Boehm. Conflict exceptions: Providing simple parallel language semantics with precise hardware exceptions. In *ISCA '10*, pages 210–221, 2010.

[30] J. Manson, W. Pugh, and S. Adve. The Java memory model. In *POPL '05*, pages 378–391. ACM, 2005.

[31] D. Marino, A. Singh, T. Millstein, M. Musuvathi, and S. Narayanasamy. DRFx: A simple and efficient memory model for concurrent programming languages. Technical Report 090021, UCLA Computer Science Department, Nov. 2009. URL `http://fmdb.cs.ucla.edu/Treports/090021.pdf`.

[32] D. Marino, A. Singh, T. Millstein, M. Musuvathi, and S. Narayanasamy. DRFx: A simple and efficient memory model for concurrent programming languages. In *PLDI '10*, 2010.

[33] A. Muzahid, D. Suarez, S. Qi, and J. Torrellas. SigRace: signature-based data race detection. In *ISCA '09*, pages 337–348, 2009.

[34] N. Neelakantam, C. Blundell, J. Devietti, M. M. K. Martin, and C. Zilles. FeS2: A full-system execution-driven simulator for x86. In *Poster session at ASPLOS '08*, 2008. URL `http://fes2.cs.uiuc.edu/acknowledgements.html`.

[35] M. Prvulovic and J. Torrelas. Reenact: Using thread-level speculation mechanisms to debug data races in multithreaded codes. In *Proceedings of ISCA*, San Diego, CA, June 2003.

[36] P. Ranganathan, V. Pai, and S. Adve. Using speculative retirement and larger instruction windows to narrow the performance gap between memory consistency models. In *SPAA '97*, pages 199–210, 1997.

[37] J. Sevcík. Private communication.

[38] J. Sevcík and D. Aspinall. On validity of program transformations in the Java memory model. In *ECOOP '08*, pages 27–51, 2008.

[39] D. Shasha and M. Snir. Efficient and correct execution of parallel programs that share memory. *ACM Transactions on Programming Languages and Systems (TOPLAS)*, 10(2):282–312, 1988.

[40] A. Singh, D. Marino, S. Narayanasamy, T. Millstein, and M. Musuvathi. Efficient processor support for DRFx: Technical report. Technical Report 110002, UCLA Computer Science Department, Mar. 2011.

[41] Z. Sura, X. Fang, C. Wong, S. Midkiff, J. Lee, and D. Padua. Compiler techniques for high performance sequentially consistent java programs. In *Proceedings of PPoPP*, pages 2–13, 2005.

[42] T. Wenisch, A. Ailamaki, B. Falsafi, and A. Moshovos. Mechanisms for store-wait-free multiprocessors. In *ISCA'07*, 2007.

[43] S. C. Woo, M. Ohara, E. Torrie, J. P. Singh, and A. Gupta. The splash-2 programs: Characterization and methodological considerations. In *ISCA'95*, pages 24–36, 1995.

# RCDC: A Relaxed Consistency Deterministic Computer

Joseph Devietti Jacob Nelson Tom Bergan Luis Ceze Dan Grossman
University of Washington, Department of Computer Science & Engineering
{devietti,nelson,tbergan,luisceze,djg}@cs.washington.edu
http://sampa.cs.washington.edu

## Abstract

*Providing deterministic execution significantly simplifies the debugging, testing, replication, and deployment of multithreaded programs. Recent work has developed deterministic multiprocessor architectures as well as compiler and runtime systems that enforce determinism in current hardware. Such work has incidentally imposed strong memory-ordering properties. Historically, memory ordering has been relaxed in favor of higher performance in shared memory multiprocessors and, interestingly, determinism exacerbates the cost of strong memory ordering. Consequently, we argue that relaxed memory ordering is vital to achieving faster deterministic execution.*

*This paper introduces RCDC, a deterministic multiprocessor architecture that takes advantage of relaxed memory orderings to provide high-performance deterministic execution with low hardware complexity. RCDC has two key innovations: a hybrid HW/SW approach to enforcing determinism; and a new deterministic execution strategy that leverages data-race-free-based memory models (e.g., the models for Java and C++) to improve performance and scalability without sacrificing determinism, even in the presence of races. In our hybrid HW/SW approach, the only hardware mechanisms required are software-controlled store buffering and support for precise instruction counting; we do not require speculation. A runtime system uses these mechanisms to enforce determinism for arbitrary programs.*

*We evaluate RCDC using PARSEC benchmarks and show that relaxing memory ordering leads to performance and scalability close to nondeterministic execution without requiring any form of speculation. We also compare our new execution strategy to one based on TSO (total-store-ordering) and show that some applications benefit significantly from the extra relaxation. We also evaluate a software-only implementation of our new deterministic execution strategy.*

***Categories and Subject Descriptors*** D.1.3 [*Programming Languages*]: Concurrent Programming—Parallel Programming; C.1.4 [*Processor Architectures*]: Parallel Architectures; D.3.4 [*Programming Languages*]: Processors—Run-time environments

***General Terms*** Reliability, Design, Performance



*ASPLOS'11,* March 5–11, 2011, Newport Beach, California, USA.


## 1. Introduction

Even if given the same exact input, a multithreaded program may not produce the same output. Nondeterminism in current multiprocessor systems severely complicates debugging, testing, replication, and deployment of multithreaded programs. Once a bug is found, it is hard to reproduce its behavior during debugging. When a multithreaded program is tested, there are no guarantees that it will behave the same way after deployment. Moreover, nondeterminism complicates fault-tolerant systems, since multithreaded replicas may have divergent behavior.

Deterministic multiprocessing promises to eliminate nondeterminism in the execution of multithreaded programs, effectively eliminating the problems described above. As such, determinism provides a large step toward improved programmability of multicore systems.

Recent research has begun to explore ways to execute multithreaded programs deterministically. Kendo [26] is a software-only approach that provides determinism for race-free programs, but offers no guarantee for programs with data races. The essential idea is to allow a thread to complete a synchronization operation only when all other threads have completed more total instructions. DMP [14] proposed two alternate strategies using novel hardware: the first uses data-ownership tracking and periodic barriers to guarantee that all data movement between threads happens deterministically; the second uses support for transactional memory (TM) to speculate that regions of execution do not have any inter-thread communication, rolling-back and re-executing if inter-thread communication does happen. Neither strategy assumes race freedom, thus they both provide determinism for arbitrary programs. However, both strategies produce only sequentially consistent executions. This property likely affects performance and scalability of the first strategy, and while the TM-based strategy has high performance, it entails always-on speculation with resultant complexity and energy costs. Subsequently, CoreDet [4] argued that this TM-based approach is a poor fit for software TM, and thus needs hardware support. CoreDet improved scalability by proposing a deterministic execution strategy and a software-only implementation that uses deterministic store buffers to weaken the memory consistency model from sequential consistency to total-store-order (TSO) and consequently improves scalability without using speculation. While CoreDet demonstrated reasonable scalability, the high cost of software-based store buffers led to significant overheads.

Relaxing memory ordering has proven instrumental in improving performance and scalability in conventional nondeterministic shared memory multiprocessor architectures [1, 17]. While speculation alleviates some of the costs of strong ordering [11, 18, 32, 34] in complex architectures, we still relax memory ordering to allow compiler optimizations and to simplify hardware. Interestingly, strong memory ordering has a much higher cost in deterministic multiprocessing than in nondeterministic multiprocessing. Therefore we argue that, in deterministic multiprocessors, it is even more important to give up strong memory ordering in favor of higher performance and lower complexity.

This paper proposes RCDC, a relaxed consistency deterministic multiprocessor computer system. RCDC improves prior work in two ways:

- RCDC implements a *new deterministic execution algorithm*, called DMP-HB (for "happens-before"), which relaxes memory consistency even further than TSO while still supporting data-race-free-based memory models (*e.g.*, those of Java and C++). This improves performance and scalability by requiring fewer costly fences, which leads to less serialization. DMP-HB does not employ speculation and does not sacrifice determinism in the presence of races.
- RCDC uses a *lower complexity hybrid hardware/software implementation* in which the hardware provides only two simple mechanisms, software-controlled store buffering and instruction counting, leaving the rest of the implementation to software. Implementing store buffering in hardware has the pleasant side effect of reducing the effects of false sharing. RCDC can be implemented on a commodity multiprocessor architecture and does not interfere with software (*e.g.*, the OS) that does not choose to use it.

The rest of this paper is organized as follows. We first discuss prior deterministic execution algorithms and how they relate to memory ordering, and also explain our new algorithm for deterministic execution (Section 2). We then provide an overview of how RCDC works, highlighting the responsibilities of hardware and software (Section 3). We follow with implementation details of RCDC's hardware components, protocols, and software runtime system (Section 4). We then discuss system issues such as page swapping and context switches (Section 5). We evaluate RCDC in comparison with prior approaches and also include an evaluation of a software-only implementation of DMP-HB (Section 6). We end with related work and closing remarks (Sections 7 and 8).

## 2. Relaxed-Consistency Deterministic Execution

This section presents our new deterministic execution algorithm, DMP-HB. For expository purposes, we first describe two related deterministic execution algorithms from prior work (DMP-SERIAL [14] and DMP-TSO [4][1]).

### 2.1 DMP-SERIAL

The simplest way to run a multithreaded program deterministically is to serialize its execution in a deterministic way. For example, we can schedule threads in a round-robin fashion so that execution is serial. Each thread is scheduled for one finite *logical* time slice, or *quantum*; a *round* consists of all threads executing one quantum each. To ensure determinism it suffices to ensure that the length of each quantum and the scheduling order are both deterministic.

### 2.2 DMP-TSO: Store Buffering

One way to recover parallelism is to isolate threads using store buffers. In this approach, each round is divided into three modes, a *parallel mode*, a *commit mode*, and a *serial mode*. During parallel mode, all stores are buffered in a thread-local store buffer, giving each thread a private view of shared memory. After parallel mode, all threads enter a commit mode in which the local store buffers are published to the global memory space. This commit happens deterministically. The effect is a serial commit order, but the implementation uses parallelism to avoid a sequential bottleneck. After commit mode is a short serial mode in which threads execute in a deterministic serial order and operate on shared memory directly. Serial mode is used to execute atomic synchronization operations, as described below.

Figure 1a illustrates one round of execution in DMP-TSO. Each thread executes one quantum per round, where, as in DMP-SERIAL, a quantum is some deterministic number of instructions. DMP-TSO is deterministic due to four properties: (1) quantum lengths are deterministic; (2) threads are isolated in parallel mode, preventing nondeterministic interference from other threads; (3) commit mode ensures that writes to shared memory happen in a deterministic order; and (4) serial mode ensures that atomic synchronization happens in a deterministic order. Note that the deterministic guarantee offered by DMP-TSO does not depend on a race-free assumption — data races are resolved deterministically as a result of the isolation provided by parallel mode, combined with the deterministic order on writes provided by commit mode.

Notice that execution under DMP-TSO is not sequentially consistent; stores are not globally visible until commit mode, effectively reordering them after loads in the same quantum. This reveals the need for serial mode — without serial mode, synchronization would not happen atomically. Further, it reveals the need to define the semantics of a memory fence. In DMP-TSO, thread $T$ ends its parallel mode when it reaches a memory fence. This flushes $T$'s local store buffer, implementing the semantics of a full memory fence. Because DMP-TSO does not distinguish between different types of memory fences, it implements the total-store-order (TSO) memory model.

DMP-TSO achieves high performance when serial mode is empty and parallel mode is *balanced*, meaning that all quanta in a round execute in the same amount of real time. Serial mode is empty when synchronization is rare; prior work [4] has shown how to use instruction counting to achieve balanced parallel modes when serial mode is empty. When synchronization does happen, it forces DMP-TSO into serial mode, whereby every synchronization operation causes global coordination. Synchronization not only causes serialization but also *imbalance* in parallel mode, which results in additional lost parallelism due to excess waiting. When synchronization is frequent, the effects of serialization and imbalance dominate and performance suffers.

### 2.3 DMP-HB: Leveraging Data-Race-Free Memory Models

DMP-HB addresses the major weakness of DMP-TSO: synchronization. Like DMP-TSO, DMP-HB uses deterministic store buffers and divides execution into quantum rounds with parallel modes and commit modes. However, DMP-HB introduces a new approach to deterministic synchronization that improves on DMP-TSO in two respects. First, DMP-HB implements a data-race-free [1] (DRF) relaxed memory model based on the *happens-before* relation between threads (hence "DMP-HB"). This model requires fewer memory fences than TSO, which makes parallel mode less likely to end early, thus increasing parallelism. However, weakening consistency alone does not remove all impediments to scalability, as DMP-TSO requires that synchronization execute in a globally serialized fashion. To remove this further bottleneck, DMP-HB eliminates the need for an explicit serial mode by using the Kendo algorithm [26] to execute synchronization directly in parallel mode, while still providing determinism even for programs with races. Overall, these optimizations let DMP-HB execute with less serialization and less imbalance than DMP-TSO, leading to improved parallelism as illustrated in Figure 1b.

The key observation of DMP-HB is that language-level memory models have weaker consistency guarantees than TSO. Specif-

[1] In [4], DMP-TSO was named DMP-B; this paper uses the name DMP-TSO for improved contrast with DMP-HB.

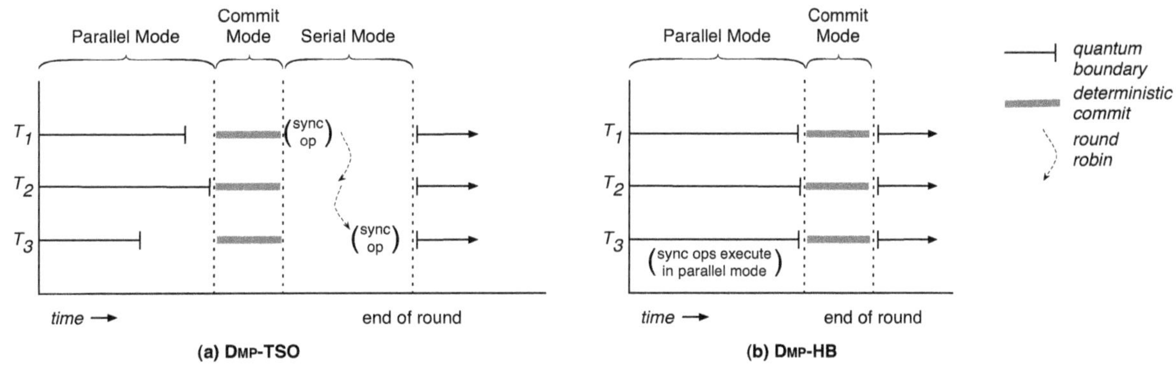


**Figure 1.** Timeline of a quantum round in DMP-TSO and DMP-HB, showing the division of each round into parallel, serial, and commit modes. DMP-HB improves DMP-TSO by allowing synchronization to happen in parallel mode, eliminating the need for serial mode.

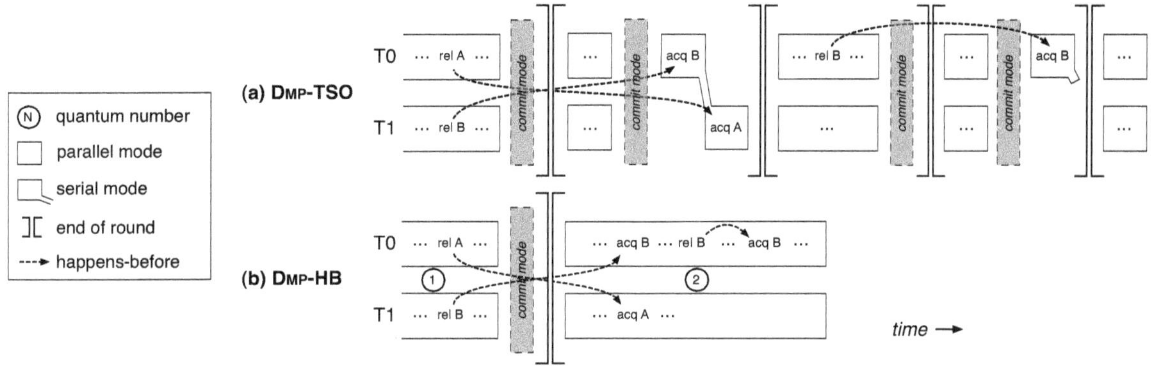


**Figure 2.** A comparison of execution under DMP-HB with execution under DMP-TSO, showing how DMP-HB extracts more parallelism from programs with frequent synchronization.

ically, Java [22] and C++ [10] define consistency models based on the data-race-free model [1]. From the programmer's perspective, it does not matter that the execution layer (*e.g.*, the hardware) provides TSO when other layers of the system (*e.g.*, the compiler) guarantee only DRF. Further, the need to precisely control memory visibility causes nondeterministic processor-local fences to become global operations in deterministic systems like DMP-TSO, which suggests that strong memory ordering has a much higher cost in deterministic systems than in nondeterministic systems. Both these observations imply that deterministic systems should relax consistency as much as possible. As DRF-based models are specified by high-level languages, they represent the limit to which memory ordering can be relaxed.

### 2.3.1 Synchronization in DMP-HB

As DMP-TSO is a deterministic version of a TSO consistency model, DMP-HB is a deterministic version of a DRF consistency model. DMP-HB differs from DMP-TSO in its approach to synchronization. The rest of this section presents the basic ideas of DMP-HB. We describe details of the DMP-HB synchronization algorithm along with our synchronization library in Section 4.4.

Consider mutex locks in a language with a DRF-like model, such as Java or C++. In these languages, the visibility of stores is guaranteed only along happens-before edges, which can arise from program order between consecutive operations in a thread or from synchronization operations across threads. When thread $T$ acquires lock $L$, this creates a happens-before edge $E$ from the previous releaser of $L$ to $T$. The DRF model guarantees that from this point forward, $T$ will see stores that transitively happen-before its acquire of $L$. Other stores need not be visible. Therefore, in DRF models, $T$ needs a memory fence after acquiring lock $L$ *only* when happens-before edge $E$ is not redundant. When $E$ is redundant, the fence can be elided.

DMP-HB exploits two happens-before redundancies: (1) thread-local edges, and (2) cross-quantum edges. First consider thread-local redundancies: if $T$ was the previous releaser of $L$, then lock $L$ has not been handed off to another thread, and we say that happens-before edge $E$ is *local* to thread $T$. A fence is not needed in this case because edge $E$ is redundant with program order. Prior work has had this same insight but in the context of nondeterministic systems, and furthermore has shown that lock locality is very common in Java programs [30, 33].

Cross-quantum redundancies are more interesting. They follow from the observation that all quanta in round $N$ are connected to all quanta in round $N+1$ by implicit happens-before edges. These implicit edges arise from the bulk-synchronous style of execution used by DMP-HB, illustrated in Figure 1b. The important result is that an explicit fence is not necessary when synchronization is separated by a quantum boundary. Thus, by matching quantum length with the frequency of synchronization, DMP-HB can eliminate many unnecessary fences, increasing performance and scalability.

Figure 2b demonstrates both the above redundancies. An example of a redundant cross-quantum edge is shown when thread $T0$ acquires lock $B$ in quantum 2: this creates a happens-before edge with the release of lock $B$ by thread $T1$ in quantum 1. Because this edge crosses a quantum boundary (*i.e.*, it crosses a *commit mode*), $T0$ does not need to execute an explicit fence when acquiring lock $B$. In contrast, note that under DMP-TSO, $T0$ must execute a fence, *i.e.*, end its quantum, before acquiring lock $B$.

An example of a thread-local redundancy is also shown in quantum 2, where $T0$ reacquires lock $B$. As $T0$'s updates are automatically visible to itself, there is no need for a fence. The extra serialization necessary to enforce the stronger TSO memory model is illustrated in Figure 2a.

Further, Figure 2b shows that DMP-HB does not require a serial mode, in contrast to DMP-TSO, which executes all lock acquires in serial mode. Even with the weaker DRF memory model, serializing all synchronization eliminates the ability to exploit thread-local redundant fences. Recall that DMP-TSO uses a serial mode to guarantee both atomicity and a deterministic order of synchronization. For correctness and determinism, DMP-HB must make these same two guarantees. Our solution is to use the Kendo algorithm [26] to impose a deterministic total order on all synchronization within a single quantum round. This algorithm allows synchronization to operate directly on the global memory space, bypassing the store buffer so the operation happens atomically. We describe this algorithm along with our synchronization library in Section 4.4.

### 2.3.2 Language Memory Models

Even though DRF does not specify the semantics of races, DMP-HB's deterministic guarantees hold even for programs with data races. DMP-HB's DRF memory model naturally matches the C++ memory model; however, the Java memory model specifies some behavior for data races, *e.g.*, to prevent "out-of-thin-air" values. DMP-HB does not itself introduce any potential "out-of-thin-air" values because it does not employ any form of speculation. A Java compiler must (still) ensure that its optimizations do not violate the Java memory model and also must ensure that proper synchronization and fences are inserted. Therefore, compiling Java code for DMP-HB's memory model is no more complex than compiling for a weak ordering system.

## 3. RCDC System Overview

RCDC provides an efficient implementation of DMP-HB through a combination of hardware and software mechanisms, as summarized in Figure 3. The four main components of RCDC are (1) a precise instruction-count mechanism to divide each thread's instruction stream into balanced quanta efficiently, (2) a store-buffer mechanism that allows threads to execute in isolation from other threads, (3) a deterministic commit mechanism that concludes each quantum round, and (4) a custom synchronization library that implements a pthreads interface while enforcing DMP-HB's memory-consistency model. These components are implemented as a combination of hardware and software designed for maximal flexibility and minimal hardware complexity.

**Quantum formation** is an ideal use case for hardware, as counting instructions involves nearly zero overhead in hardware but causes substantial slowdown in software. The hardware instruction-counting mechanism simply counts instructions as they retire, triggering a user-level `QuantumReached` trap when a pre-defined total is reached. This trap is responsible for actually starting the commit process that makes buffered data visible.

Our synchronization library requires the ability to disable and enable instruction counting for the local processor, and also to read the current instruction counts of remote processors. For this purpose the instruction-count mechanism can be controlled and queried via the `StopInsnCount`, `StartInsnCount`, and `ReadInsnCount` instructions.

Deterministic quantum formation beyond simply counting instructions is also possible. Section 4.1 describes a more advanced strategy that uses opcodes and store buffer hit/miss information to construct quanta with better balance.

The **store buffer** mechanism is also a natural fit for hardware, where processor-private caches can isolate an executing thread from other threads in the system (like in hardware transactional memory, but without an abort mechanism) with additional bits of cache line state. We rely on simple compiler modifications or binary rewriting to replace existing store instructions with our new `BufferedStore` instruction. With more sophisticated analysis, ordinary non-buffered store instructions can, without any loss of determinism, replace buffered stores to locations that are provably thread-private. This increases the effective capacity of the store buffer without additional hardware resources.

The **deterministic commit** mechanism is triggered by software, via a new `Commit` instruction. The actual commit process is implemented in hardware, as described in Section 4.3. The commit process is invoked by software in response to `QuantumReached` and `BufferFull` traps, as well as to enforce the memory consistency requirements of DMP-HB. Hardware triggers a `BufferFull` trap immediately when a store buffer overflows. Note that our cache replacement policy, described in Section 4.2, is designed to ensure that store buffer overflows happen deterministically.

Finally, our custom **synchronization library** acts as a drop-in replacement for pthreads. It uses the instructions described above to enforce DMP-HB's consistency model. Because the decision of *when* to commit is left to software, our synchronization library can easily be modified to implement other consistency models, *e.g.*, DMP-TSO.

## 4. Implementation

We now discuss implementation details for the major hardware and software components described in Section 3.

### 4.1 Quantum Formation

For quantum formation, the **hardware** does instruction counting and sets a trap after a software-defined quantum budget is exhausted. This mechanism is initialized by system **software** when a process is created. This code registers a user-level trap that is invoked whenever the quantum size is reached, establishes the size of quanta, and executes the `StartInsnCount` instruction.

Thus far, we have discussed quantum formation in terms of counting instructions. However, it is possible to provide better quantum balance by giving instructions non-uniform weights, *e.g.*, based on opcode. One useful optimization leverages the deterministic contents of the store buffer. Memory accesses deterministically either hit in the store buffer (*i.e.*, hit to a written cache line) or miss the store buffer (which means either hitting to a non-written cache line or missing to the next-level cache or beyond). Knowing whether the memory operation is a load or a store lets us, in many cases, accurately assess the latency of that operation deterministically. Loads that miss the store buffer are often hits to a clean line, so we assign them a low weight. But stores that miss in the store buffer tend to be cache misses, and thus have high latency. Assigning higher weights to such stores results in better quantum balance since the weight assigned to each instruction better approximates its actual latency. Finally, we add to the sum of instruction weights as instructions retire, allowing access to hit/miss information, and also avoiding any issues with wrong-path instructions.

### 4.2 Buffering

RCDC's **hardware** provides support for buffering data, while **software** (*i.e.*, the compiler) controls what data is buffered via the `BufferedStore` instruction. This section details how buffering support is implemented as an extension to the cache hardware.

Cache-based data buffering imposes a few system requirements: (1) buffered lines cannot be provided to remote requests; (2) the commit protocol, which makes buffered data available to all processors, needs to be deterministic; and (3) the system needs to support context switches. RCDC provides this functionality on top of a conventional directory-based MOESI cache coherence protocol and implements buffering in private caches, while still naturally

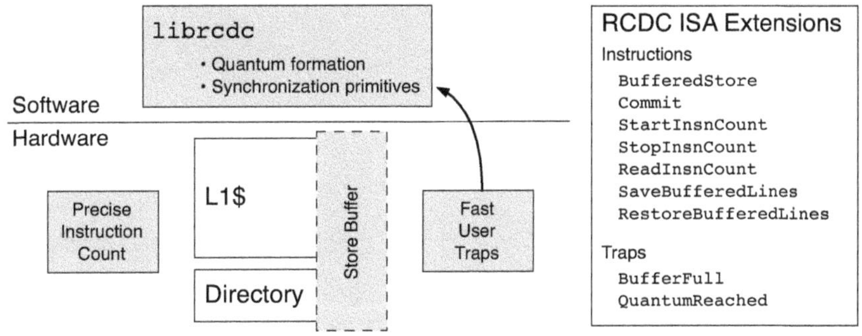


**Figure 3.** RCDC system overview, showing the division of responsibility between hardware and software. The shaded boxes show RCDC's additions.

supporting higher-level shared caches. For simplicity of explanation, we consider only a single private L1 cache per processor in the discussion below.

***Cache Extensions for Store Buffering*** Each L1 cache line is extended with a *write-mask*, which has as many bits as bytes in the cache line. When a `BufferedStore` is executed, the corresponding write-mask bits are set. Consequently, lines with non-null write-masks contain buffered data.

To ensure that store buffer capacity is exhausted deterministically, we modify the cache eviction policy to always preferentially evict unwritten cache lines from a set. This ensures determinism while maximizing the amount of progress a processor can make before running out of store buffer capacity. When all lines of a cache set are buffered and an eviction needs to happen, RCDC triggers a `BufferFull` trap and the runtime system ends the quantum.

Non-buffered stores to cache lines in the non-buffered state proceed normally, following the conventional MOESI protocol. Non-buffered stores to cache lines in the buffered state are treated like `BufferedStores`. Note that buffering data from a non-buffered store is valid with respect to the instruction semantics as it is always correct to buffer private data — it just will not bring any benefit. If a non-buffered store necessarily cannot be buffered because of program semantics, then software needs to guarantee that this does not happen (*e.g.*, using careful memory layout).

***Coherence Operations*** We augment the transitions in a conventional MOESI protocol to handle our new `BufferedStore` instruction. This requires three changes to a conventional MOESI protocol. First, if an L1 cache receives a request for a line whose write-mask is non-null, the request is *nacked*. The requester then goes to a shared higher-level cache (or memory) to fulfill its request. This is necessary to guarantee that buffered data is never provided to remote requests. Second, a line must be in the Shared state before it can be written by a `BufferedStore` instruction. Finally, our commit protocol (Section 4.3) moves lines to the Owned state after they have been published. As a consequence of these last two changes, moving a line to the Shared state to satisfy a `BufferedStore` may require a write-back operation (*e.g.*, because that line may have been buffered in the previous round).

Interestingly, isolating each thread's updates into separate store buffers also yields a solution to false sharing, by allowing threads to perform updates to the same cache line within a quantum round without any serialization via the coherence protocol. The line becomes temporarily incoherent, but the updates are merged deterministically at the end of the round. If threads' updates are in conflict (*i.e.*, two threads update the same bytes), there is a data race in the user program — data-race free programs can never observe this relaxation of coherence.

***Context Switches*** The kernel can context switch away from and back to a thread at any time, even during parallel mode, as long as it invokes the `SaveBufferedLines` and `RestoreBufferedLines` instructions to save and restore a thread's current store buffer.

These instructions make use of a per-thread, in-memory data structure called the Buffered Data Table (BDT), which contains the saved store buffer contents for a given thread. A BDT has a row for each cache line in a processor's store buffer, with one column for the line's data, another for the line's write-mask, and a third for a "next" pointer whose use is described below. A row in the BDT is considered valid if its write-mask is non-null. The `SaveBufferedLines` instruction simply flushes all buffered lines from the cache to the BDT. As it does so, it clears the write-masks of all buffered lines in the L1 cache and transitions them to the Invalid state, making them available for the next thread to be switched in. The `RestoreBufferedLines` instruction iterates over all buffered lines in a given BDT, restoring them into the L1 cache. After a line is restored from the BDT to the L1 cache, its write-mask is cleared in the BDT to signify that the line is no longer saved in-memory.

These two instructions additionally maintain a separate, per-process table called the Buffered Address Map (BAM). The BAM is a table of pointers mapping each line address to a linked list of BDT entries storing the in-memory versions of that line. The pointer in each BDT entry points to the next thread's BDT entry in the list. Each BDT entry represents the saved state of one buffered version of the given cache line. By walking the list, the BAM table can be used to enumerate all in-memory versions of a buffered line. BAMs are used during the commit process as described in the following section.

We highlight that these instructions can be expensive, not only on their own, but also because of the extra work they impose on the commit process. In Section 5 we describe a few kernel scheduling optimizations that make these instructions infrequent.

### 4.3 Committing Buffered Data

In DMP-HB, the transition to commit mode is controlled by **software**, which uses the `Commit` instruction to initiate the actual commit process in **hardware**. The RCDC software runtime executes the following pseudocode for each thread when it reaches its quantum boundary, *e.g.*, when its quantum budget has been exhausted:

```
end_quantum() {
  global_barrier()
  Commit
  global_barrier()
}
```

The first barrier represents the transition from parallel mode to commit mode; the `Commit` instruction represents commit mode; and the second barrier represents the transition back to parallel mode to start the next quantum (see Figure 1b). The first barrier ensures that all threads are ready to commit, while the second

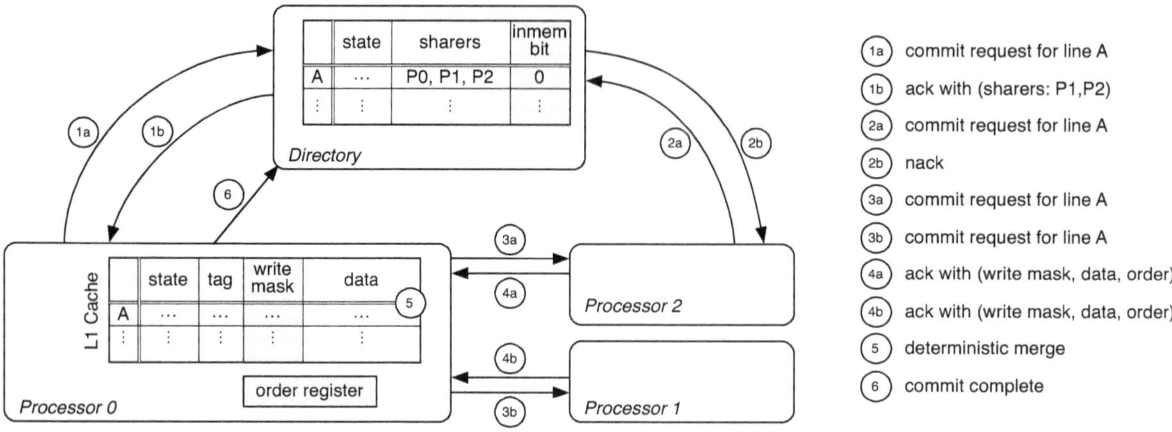


**Figure 4.** RCDC commit process when all application threads are scheduled. Shaded areas are RCDC additions.

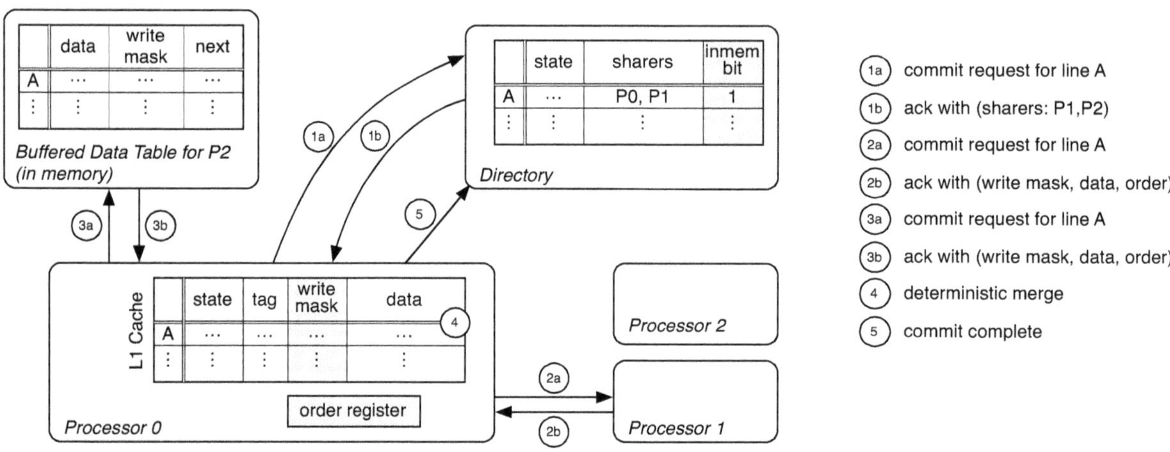


**Figure 5.** RCDC commit process when an application thread is switched out.

barrier ensures that all threads have finished publishing the contents of their store buffers.

The goal of the commit process is to merge buffered data deterministically and publish it globally. If a line has no buffered data in any cache, commit has no effect on that line. When a line has buffered data in one or more caches, the commit process deterministically merges all buffered data and then publishes this data to the rest of the system by moving the merged line to the Owned state.

A processor executes the commit instruction by iterating over all lines in its cache that have buffered data, *i.e.*, those lines with non-null write-masks. For each of those lines, the processor executes the commit protocol. The commit protocol coordinates with the directory and with other processors, collects all buffered versions of a line, and then deterministically merges them. Once the commit protocol has been executed for all of the processor's buffered lines, the `Commit` instruction retires. At this point, the processor's entire store buffer has been globally published.

The commit protocol needs to handle two cases: committing when all buffered versions of a line are in-cache; and committing when at least one buffered version of a line is out-of-cache (*i.e.*, because the thread was context-switched out). We describe both cases in detail below.

***In-cache Commit (all threads running)*** The processor issues a commit message for the given line to the directory; the directory replies with an acknowledgment for commit and a list of sharers for that line. The processor sends a commit message to each sharer. Upon receipt of a commit message, each sharer returns a reply indicating if it has the line, and if so, it includes the write-mask and the data for the requested line, as well as its deterministic *order id*; it then clears its write-mask and moves the line to Invalid state. When the committing processor receives a reply, it merges the other processor's data into its own line. Once the processor has collected replies from all sharers, it clears the line's write-mask and moves the line to the Owned state, making the line visible to all processors.

The merge algorithm takes lines from two processors, *P0* and *P1*, and computes the result of *P0*'s writes happening before *P1*, where *P0* has the smaller order id. This algorithm is straightforward and has been described by prior work [4].

Note that if the directory nacks the request for commit of a given line, this implies that some other processor has already started the commit for that line; the requester then waits until it receives a commit request for the line from another processor. Also note that while the commit process can actually happen in any order, the final state is guaranteed to be deterministic because the merge process is deterministic. Moreover, when the sharers list includes only the committing processor, no merge is necessary; the processor simply clears the line's write-mask and moves the line to the Owned state.

*Example.* Figure 4 illustrates how RCDC deals with multiple caches trying to commit to the same line *A*. Processors *P0*, *P1*, and *P2* all have buffered copies of line *A*. First, *P0* and *P2* send concurrent commit requests for line *A* to the directory (1a, 2a). *P0*'s message arrives first, and the directory responds to *P0* with an acknowledgment message (1b), including the list of sharers, allowing *P0* to proceed with committing line *A*. Since commit has

```
1  sync_acquire(o: SyncObject) {
2    if (o.quantum < curr_quantum ||
3        o.releaser == self) {
4      return // fence not necessary
5    }
6    end_quantum()
7  }
8
9  deterministic_lock(l: Lock) {
10   StopInsnCount
11   while (true) {
12     wait_for_turn()
13     if (CAS(l.locked, 0, 1))) {
14       sync_acquire(l)
15       StartInsnCount
16       return
17     }
18     end_quantum()
19   }
20 }

21 sync_release(o: SyncObject) {
22   o.quantum = curr_quantum
23   o.releaser = self
24 }
25
26
27
28
29 deterministic_unlock(l: Lock) {
30   StopInsnCount
31   wait_for_turn()
32   sync_release(l)
33   l.locked = 0
34   StartInsnCount
35 }
```

**Figure 6.** Deterministic Locking for DMP-HB

started for line *A*, the directory responds to *P2* with a negative acknowledgment (2b) and *P2* waits for a commit request (which it is bound to get since it is guaranteed that another processor is committing *A*). *P0* continues by sending commit messages to all sharers of *A* (3a, 3b). *P1* and *P2* respond with a message containing their data, write mask, and deterministic order (4a, 4b) and then invalidate their copy of the line. Upon receiving the acks, *P0* deterministically merges the data with its own (5) and notifies the directory that line *A* has been committed (6).

***Out-of-cache Commit (at least one thread is switched out)*** We now describe the more general case where at least one sharer has been switched out. RCDC supports this case with a simple extension to the directory: each directory entry, in addition to the sharers, also includes a single bit called the *in-memory bit*, which indicates if the line has data in an in-memory Buffered Data Table. This in-memory bit is set by the `SaveBufferedLines` instruction.

When a committing processor issues a commit message for a line to the directory, the directory replies with an acknowledgment and a list of sharers as before, and the processor communicates with the sharers as before. However, the directory also replies with the state of the in-memory bit. If the in-memory bit is set, the committing processor walks rows in Buffered Data Tables via the Buffered Address Map table to enumerate all in-memory versions of the line being committed. The processor merges these versions into its own line using the same algorithm as before, and then sends a commit-complete message to the directory. At this point the directory can clear the in-memory bit.

Note that commit still proceeds correctly even if the only thread that has a given line buffered is switched out, since that thread will invoke the `Commit` instruction when it is eventually switched in. (The barrier on line 4 of `end_quantum` ensures this.) Also, note that the directory serves as a serialization point for the cache line operations performed by the `Commit`, `SaveBufferedLines`, and `RestoreBufferedLines` instructions; this prevents races between the commit process and context switches, making it safe for the kernel to switch out a thread at any time without sacrificing determinism (note especially that a thread can be safely switched out between lines 2 and 3 of `end_quantum`).

*Example.* Figure 5 illustrates how RCDC commits line *A* when a thread that has buffered line *A* has been switched out. *P0*, *P1*, and *P2* all had buffered copies of line *A*. The thread on *P2* is ready for commit but was switched out just before the commit process starts. The buffered data is saved in *P2*'s Buffered Data Table in memory, and the in-memory bit set in the directory. *P0* sends a commit message (1a) to the directory for line *A*. The directory replies with an acknowledgment (1b), including the list of sharers and the in-memory bit. *P0* then sends a commit message for line *A* to *P1* (2a), which replies with an acknowledgment (2b) before invalidating the copy of the line. At the same time, *P0* accesses the Buffered Address Map to enumerate the list of in-memory lines, and notices that *P2*'s BDT contains a copy of line *A* (3a). *P2*'s saved line is found and returned to *P0* (3b), and then removed from the Buffered Data Table. Next, *P0* merges both received versions of line *A* with its own version (4) and clears the write mask. Finally, *P0* notifies the directory that the commit for line *A* is complete (5), and the directory resets line *A*'s in-memory bit.

### 4.4 Synchronization Library

Our synchronization library is implemented using two basic building blocks: *conditional memory fences* and *deterministic serialization.* Conditional memory fences enforce DMP-HB's memory model. A mechanism for deterministic serialization based on the Kendo algorithm [26] is used to execute synchronization during parallel mode of DMP-HB.

Figure 6 shows our implementation of deterministic mutex locks. The `sync_acquire` and `sync_release` functions represent conditional memory fences, while `wait_for_turn` represents deterministic serialization. Other synchronization objects such as barriers, condition variables, and even lock-free data structures can be built from these same building blocks. For brevity we describe only a lock implementation in this paper.

***Conditional Memory Fences*** We use the functions `sync_acquire` and `sync_release` to implement deterministic `lock` and `unlock` just as traditional nondeterministic implementations of `lock` and `unlock` use acquire and release fences [17]. The key difference is the conditional on lines 2-3 of `sync_acquire`: when this conditional is true, the release-to-acquire happens-before edge is redundant and a fence can be elided. When this conditional is false, a fence is necessary: `end_quantum` is invoked, which executes the `Commit` instruction. This conditional implements the observation noted earlier in Section 2.3.1: a fence is not necessary when the happens-before edge is local to a thread (line 3) or crosses a quantum boundary (line 2). Note also that when lines 2-5 are removed, `sync_acquire` is a full fence, and so the remaining algorithm implements a consistency model equivalent to TSO.

***Deterministic Serialization*** We use the Kendo algorithm [26] to serialize synchronization deterministically. The basic idea is as follows: before performing synchronization, thread $T$ must wait for its *turn*, meaning it must wait until it has the global minimum instruction count (where ties are broken by thread ID). While waiting for its turn, $T$ must disable instruction counting by invoking `StopInsnCount`; this ensures deterministic instruction counting since $T$ may have to wait a nondeterministic amount of time before its turn arrives. After synchronization is complete, $T$ invokes `StartInsnCount`. The `wait_for_turn` function can be implemented by polling other threads' instruction counts via the `ReadInsnCount` instruction.[2]

Note that lines 13-14 and lines 32-33 execute atomically: `wait_for_turn` designates the beginning of an atomic region that is ended by `StartInsnCount`.[3] It is within these regions that the lock object is updated. For these updates to appear atomically, they must apply directly to the global memory space; *i.e.*, all reads and updates of lock objects must bypass the store buffer. To ensure that lock objects are never buffered, lock objects can never exist on the same cache line as ordinary data; this introduces a *partition* of shared memory into lock objects and ordinary data.

## 5. System Issues

***Support for nondeterministic execution*** The use of store buffers is a software choice. Therefore, programs can choose to execute nondeterministically. Kernel code, for example, would not need to be executed deterministically.

One caveat is that our eviction policy risks monopolizing the cache. Recall that buffered lines are pinned in the cache; if a cache set fills with buffered lines, it cannot be reused until the store buffer has committed. This can accidentally prevent important systems code (*e.g.*, context switch code) from running. We have two solutions. The first is to reserve a small victim buffer for non-buffered cache lines; and the second is to reserve just $N - 1$ lines of a set for buffered data, where the cache uses $N$-way sets.

***Processes*** In RCDC, each process is by default its own determinism domain; in other words, threads within a process behave deterministically with respect to each other. Deterministic processes can run alongside nondeterministic processes. Moreover, if multiple processes share memory pages, the processes can be aggregated into a single determinism domain, much like the deterministic process group abstraction in dOS [5]. As long as different determinism domains do not share memory pages, the boundary of determinism domains can be defined completely by software without any extra hardware support.

***Context Switches*** To maintain determinism, RCDC requires that a thread's current instruction count and the contents of its store buffer be saved and restored across context switches. To reduce the amount of state that must be saved and restored, the OS kernel can be modified in two ways, described below.

First, the kernel can be modified to context switch away from a deterministic thread only at a quantum boundary, *i.e.*, just after line 4 of `end_quantum` (Section 4.3). This eliminates the need to save and restore the contents of store buffers, since store buffers are always empty at a quantum boundary.

Additionally, if there are $N$ CPUs but more than $N$ threads in a given determinism domain, the kernel can schedule threads in groups of $N$ per quanta, much like gang scheduling [27]. This considerably reduces the need to save and restore the contents of store buffers. It also can improve quantum balance, by eliminating the underutilization that occurs when $N+1$ threads must be scheduled per round, yet there are only $N$ processors available.

***Paging*** It is important to make sure that none of the pages that have buffered data are paged out. The simplest way to provide this guarantee is to restrict paging so it happens only at the end of commit mode. In addition, the runtime system can provide the kernel with a list of pages that are provably unshared; these can be paged out at any time.

***Memory Errors*** As discussed in Section 4.4, `librcdc`'s lock objects must be partitioned from ordinary data. If this partition is broken by some memory operation, *e.g.*, due to a memory error in a type unsafe language like C++, then that memory operation is a potential source of nondeterminism. For example, an errant read that happens to address a lock object will return a nondeterministic value, since that read can race with some other thread performing a lock acquire.

***Store Buffer Parameters and Determinism*** The parameters of the store buffer (*i.e.*, the cache geometry) can affect quantum boundaries because buffer overflows cause a quantum to end. Thus, RCDC cannot guarantee the same deterministic execution will arise on two machines with different cache/store buffer configurations. One can address this potential issue by restricting store buffer usage such that its effective size is the same across different machines. The number of threads a program uses, and the parameters used to build quanta (*e.g.*, size) are also implicit inputs that must be replicated to ensure repeatability.

## 6. Results

The goals of our evaluation are to understand the effects of memory ordering relaxation on deterministic execution and to understand how RCDC's mechanisms behave dynamically. To these ends, we evaluate RCDC in two basic ways: (1) a hardware simulator of the actual mechanisms described in the paper; and (2) a software-only implementation of DMP-HB using a compiler and runtime system.

We built a hardware simulation infrastructure using the Intel Pin [21] binary instrumentation tool. The model focuses on the first order effects and includes RCDC's major components, including store buffering in private caches, quantum formation, committing, and consistency models for both DMP-TSO and DMP-HB. For the memory system, private 8-way 32KB L1 and private 8-way 256KB L2 caches for each core, with a 16-way 8MB shared L3. All caches have 64B lines. Instructions take 1 cycle to execute, and it takes an additional 1, 10, 35 and 120 cycles to access the L1, L2, L3 and main memory, respectively. We modeled 2, 4, 8 and 16 processor systems. With the exception of Figure 10, all workloads are run with a target quantum size of 50,000 instructions, except for ferret (25k), fluidanimate (1k) and streamcluster (1k). We determined these parameters by finding the best performance of our workloads, at 16 processors, for each quantum size in the range shown in Figure 10. Quantum commit costs 100 cycles. Error bars indicate the 95% confidence interval for the mean of 10 runs.

Our hardware simulations use version 2.1 of the PARSEC [7] benchmark suite. We used the simsmall input set for each workload. Due to excessive memory usage, we were not able to run the freqmine, raytrace and facesim workloads. Due to a lack of support for reader-writer locks and lock-free synchronization in our run-

[2] Alternatively, we could implement `wait_for_turn` via interprocessor interrupts rather than polling.

[3] Atomicity for the lock release is necessary to guarantee that concurrent releases of the same lock (*e.g.*, due to programmer error) still result in a deterministic outcome.

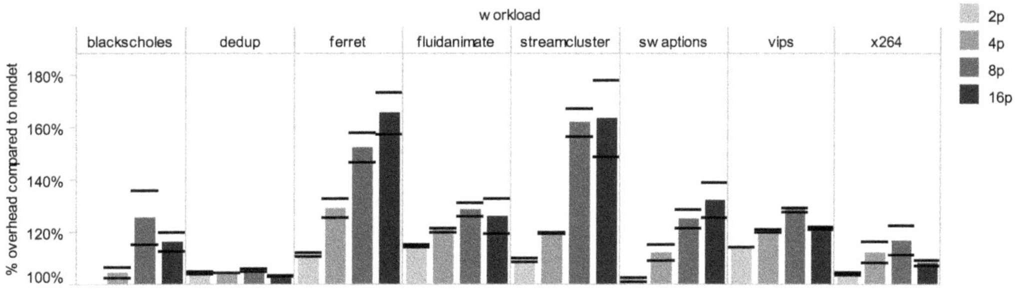


**Figure 7.** Performance of RCDC normalized to NONDET for 2, 4, 8 and 16 processors.

time system, we were not able to run the bodytrack and canneal workloads, respectively.

Our software-only implementation was built on top of the publicly-available CoreDet [4] compiler and runtime system infrastructure. The source code for our simulator, modifications to CoreDet, and experimental data are available from `http://sampa.cs.washington.edu`.

### 6.1 Performance and Scalability

We start with a performance comparison of RCDC and the nondeterministic baseline (NONDET), as measured using our hardware simulator. Figure 7 plots performance of DMP-HB for 2, 4, 8, and 16 processors normalized to NONDET with the same number of processors. Most applications suffer little performance degradation, but the overheads are still just over 60% in the worst case with 16 threads. Broadly, the performance costs in RCDC come from imbalance (periodic barriers at the end of parallel mode), extra stalls due to costly fences in synchronization operations, and the cost of committing buffered data. We characterize these costs more precisely below. Overall, RCDC provides fully deterministic execution for a modest runtime cost for many of our workloads.

From Figure 7 we can also see how RCDC's performance scales with additional cores. In a minority of cases (*e.g.*, ferret), RCDC does not scale as well as NONDET. Most of the time, however, RCDC scales just as well as NONDET does, as evidenced by a consistent slowdown despite increasing core counts. Sometimes (*e.g.*, vips) RCDC even closes the performance gap at higher core counts because the underlying benchmark does not scale well even with NONDET. Some of RCDC's overheads, like reduced cache capacity due to store buffering, can take advantage of additional parallel resources even when the underlying application cannot.

We also implemented a version of DMP-TSO on top of RCDC to assess the benefit of the extra memory reordering relaxation offered by DMP-HB. Figure 8 compares the performance of RCDC-DMP-HB and RCDC-DMP-TSO, normalized to NONDET with the same number of processors. We include only the benchmarks ferret, fluidanimate, and vips; other benchmarks have less frequent synchronization, so the performance of DMP-HB and DMP-TSO is essentially identical. For these three benchmarks, DMP-HB yields markedly better performance compared to DMP-TSO, which comes from the fact that DMP-HB is able to elide many costly fences (*i.e.*, quantum boundaries) that DMP-TSO cannot elide. Figure 9 further justifies these results.

### 6.2 Characterization

To better understand RCDC's behavior, Figure 9 breaks down the reasons for quantum boundaries. The three reasons a quantum can end are: *instruction count*, which is simply when a quantum has reached its maximum size; *store buffer overflows*, when the store buffer overflows and the thread cannot continue until its buffered data is committed; and *fences*, when a synchronization operation needs a memory fence to ensure the consistency model is upheld.

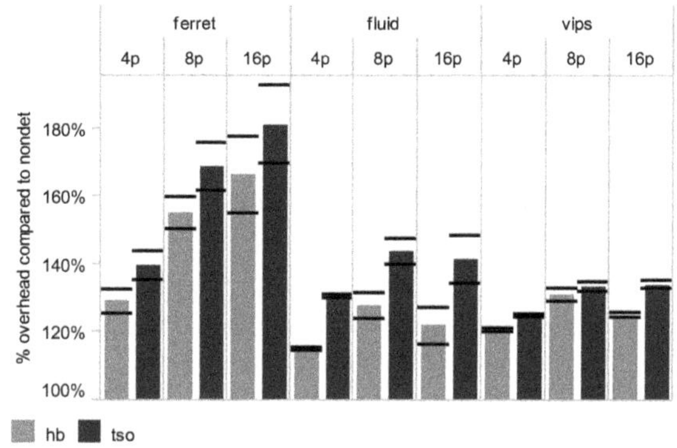


**Figure 8.** Performance of RCDC-DMP-HB and RCDC-DMP-TSO normalized to NONDET for 4, 8 and 16 processors.

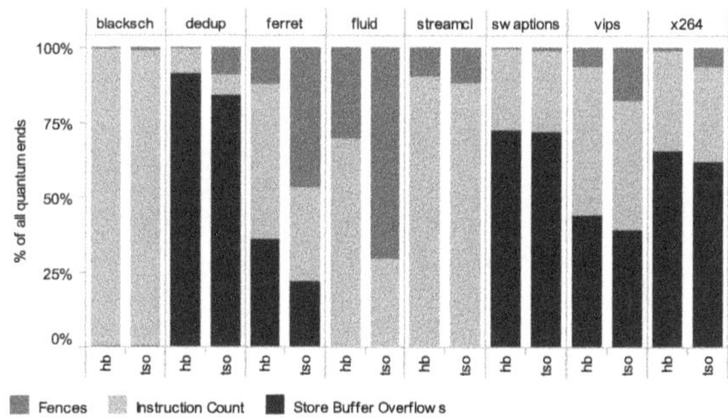


**Figure 9.** Reasons why quanta end for DMP-HB and DMP-TSO implemented in RCDC, for 16 processors.

Note that DMP-HB has many fewer commits due to fences (the top segment of each bar) than DMP-TSO. This quantifies the effect discussed in Section 2.3 (Figure 2), which is the essence of why DMP-HB offers significantly better performance than DMP-TSO.

Store buffer overflows are a frequent source of quantum imbalance for several workloads. While DMP-HB is effective at reducing the number of fences, some of the premature quantum ends that would have been a fence with DMP-TSO are then replaced with store buffer overflows, which still result in quantum imbalance.

### 6.3 Sensitivity to Quantum Size

We end our RCDC evaluation with a characterization of how maximum quantum size affects performance. Figure 10 shows performance of ferret on a 16-processor RCDC system. The relationship between performance and quantum size can be highly non-linear: for ferret, larger quanta help smooth the effects of frequent quantum rounds, but beyond 25k instructions the extra imbalance of large quanta hurts performance. This effect was noticeable with both DMP-HB and DMP-TSO.

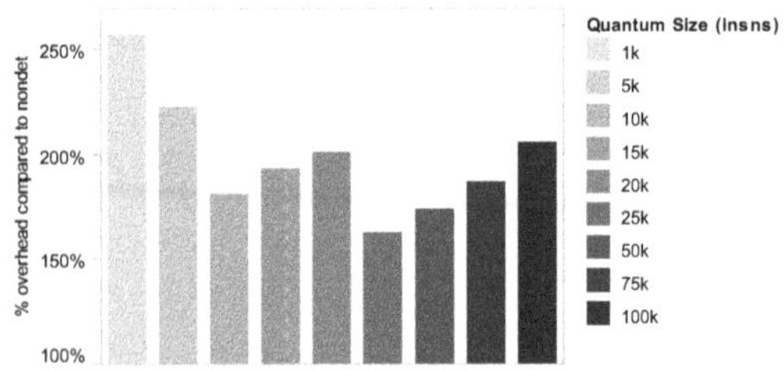


**Figure 10.** Performance of ferret with 16 processors using different quantum sizes.

### 6.4 Compiler-Runtime Implementation

In addition to the above hardware simulation, we implemented DMP-HB in CoreDet [4]. This implementation required changes only to CoreDet's synchronization library, not to the compiler nor other parts of the runtime. We evaluated our CoreDet implementation using the PARSEC and SPLASH2 benchmark suites, and include a comparison of the performance of DMP-HB with the performance of DMP-TSO. For this evaluation, we enabled all of CoreDet's compiler optimizations.

Figure 11 summarizes this evaluation. The performance of DMP-HB is largely the same as that of DMP-TSO, with two exceptions: fluidanimate and fmm. Both these benchmarks have a relatively high frequency of synchronization. DMP-HB's improved handling of synchronization allows it to increase performance by about 20%: from 5x to 4x overhead for fluidanimate and from 4.5x to 3.5x overhead for fmm. This shows that the benefits of relaxed consistency determinism are not limited to hardware.

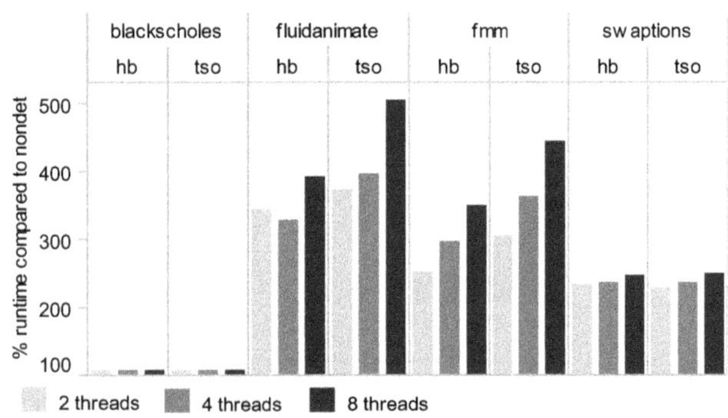


**Figure 11.** Performance of CoreDet implementations of DMP-HB and DMP-TSO normalized to NONDET for 2, 4, and 8 threads.

## 7. Related Work

We discussed the most related recent work on deterministic execution [4, 14, 26] in Section 1. DMP [14] is a mostly-hardware approach that yields only sequentially consistent executions. CoreDet [4] follows with a software-only implementation that leverages relaxed memory ordering in a TSO fashion. Calvin [19], done concurrently with our work, is a pure-hardware implementation of DMP-TSO. The dOS [5] operating system provides deterministic execution for unmodified binaries by tracking memory ownership via page tables. Kendo [26] is a synchronization library that provides deterministic guarantees for data-race-free programs written using pthreads. Note that while RCDC also leverages data-race-free models for performance, it does *not* sacrifice determinism in the presence of races, which we believe is instrumental in reaping the full benefits of deterministic execution. Grace [6] is a runtime system that provides deterministic execution for C/C++ fork-join parallel programs, executing each thread in a fork region atomically and committing them deterministically. Grace's implementation uses page-based software transactional memory techniques.

There is a significant body of work on deterministic parallel programming languages. Stream-based programming languages, such as StreamIt [31], offer deterministic behavior because communication happens only via explicitly defined channels (streams). Similarly, SHIM [16] is a parallel language that supports explicit communication only via deterministic message passing. NESL [8] and Data Parallel Haskell [12] are examples of data-parallel functional languages that expose sequential semantics to programmers and yield deterministic programs. Another notable class of deterministic languages are implicitly parallel languages, such as Jade [29]. In this model, programmers write programs in a sequential, imperative language and then augment the code with information about how data is accessed. The system then extracts parallelism without violating the original sequential program semantics. More recently, Bocchinno et al., developed Deterministic Parallel Java (DPJ) [9], which is a set of extensions to Java that enable programmers to write deterministic programs via a type and effect system. Determinator [3] proposes a deterministic consistency model that is defined only for programs that are written according to a specialized programming model. Determinator's implementation is a microkernel that provides deterministic execution using page-based isolation. While deterministic languages are a long-term solution to the problem, the existing options are typically domain-specific and are not widely used: the vast majority of parallel and concurrent programs written today still use mainstream languages like C, C++, and Java.

A widely explored approach to dealing with nondeterminism is recording and replaying interprocessor interaction via shared memory. A notable example is FDR [35, 36], which records shared accesses that lead to communication between processors and performs transitive reduction [25] to reduce log size. More recent work [20, 23, 24] exploited coarse regions of execution to achieve shorter log sizes; other recent work also explored recording partial information during execution and performing search during replay [2, 28]. Tern [13] extends this idea by memoizing partial schedules during testing and steering execution toward these tested paths on future, untested inputs. In contrast to record and replay systems, deterministic execution provides repeatable behavior by default without having to log the shared-memory interactions between processors.

Relaxing memory ordering is a recurring theme in research on shared memory multiprocessors (*e.g.*, weak-ordering [1] and release-consistency [17]). The key motivation for relaxing memory ordering is to allow the system (*i.e.*, the hardware and compiler) to reorder memory operations and consequently enable important performance optimizations. To allow the programmer to control when ordering is required for correctness, relaxed memory models provide fence operations which are typically high-latency operations. For that reason, prior work has explored ways to reduce the cost of fences. A notable example is conditional memory ordering (CMO) [33]. CMO delays the effect of fences until a synchronization operation actually leads to a happens-before relationship between processors. This is an effective optimization because locks typically exhibit locality. CMO's implementation uses conditional memory fences that are equivalent to RCDC's `sync_acquire` and `sync_release`.

One of the indirect benefits of RCDC is decreasing the cost of false sharing; when multiple quanta within a round write to the same cache line, they do not need to repeatedly re-acquire exclusive ownership of the line since writes are buffered. Delayed consistency [15] leads to a similar effect but does not provide any deterministic guarantees.

## 8. Conclusions

We have presented RCDC, a new deterministic multiprocessing architecture that leverages memory ordering relaxation to improve performance. We propose a new deterministic execution algorithm that combines deterministic synchronization with weak memory ordering to improve performance by reducing unnecessary stalls when enforcing determinism for arbitrary multithreaded programs. We also propose a hybrid hardware/software design that requires the hardware to provide only software-controlled store buffering and precise instruction counting, thereby reducing hardware complexity. Our results show that RCDC is competitive with non-deterministic multiprocessors, in terms of both absolute performance and scalability, without employing speculation. Moreover, our HW/SW approach allows precise control of when determinism should be enforced, providing flexibility to system software.

We believe this work is an important step toward realistic systems for the deterministic execution of arbitrary programs. Relaxed memory ordering aids performance by avoiding global barriers for synchronization operations while our HW/SW approach provides simplicity and flexibility.

## 9. Acknowledgments

We would like to thank the anonymous reviewers for their valuable comments. We also thank the members of the Sampa group for their feedback on the manuscript. This work was supported in part by NSF CAREER grant CCF-0846004 and a Microsoft Research New Faculty Fellowship.

## References

[1] S. Adve and M. Hill. Weak Ordering – A New Definition. In *ISCA*, 1990.

[2] G. Altekar and I. Stoica. ODR: Output-Deterministic Replay for Multicore Debugging. In *SOSP*, 2009.

[3] A. Aviram, S.-C. Weng, S. Hu, and B. Ford. Efficient System-Enforced Deterministic Parallelism. In *OSDI*, 2010.

[4] T. Bergan, O. Anderson, J. Devietti, L. Ceze, and D. Grossman. CoreDet: a Compiler and Runtime System for Deterministic Multithreaded Execution. In *ASPLOS*, 2010.

[5] T. Bergan, N. Hunt, L. Ceze, and S. Gribble. Deterministic Process Groups in dOS. In *OSDI*, 2010.

[6] E. Berger, T. Yang, T. Liu, , and G. Novark. Grace: Safe and Efficient Concurrent Programming. In *OOPSLA*, 2009.

[7] C. Bienia, S. Kumar, J. P. Singh, and K. Li. The PARSEC Benchmark Suite: Characterization and Architectural Implications. In *PACT*, 2008.

[8] G. Blelloch. NESL: A Nested Data-Parallel Language (Version 3.1). Technical report, Carnegie Mellon University, Pittsburgh, PA, 2007.

[9] R. Bocchino, V. Adve, D. Dig, S. Adve, S. Heumann, R. Komuravelli, J. Overbey, P. Simmons, H. Sung, and M. Vakilian. A Type and Effect System for Deterministic Parallel Java. In *OOPSLA*, 2009.

[10] H.-J. Boehm and S. Adve. Foundations of the C++ Concurrency Memory Model. In *PLDI*, 2008.

[11] L. Ceze, J. Tuck, P. Montesinos, and J. Torrellas. BulkSC: Bulk Enforcement of Sequential Consistency. In *ISCA*, 2007.

[12] M. M. T. Chakravarty, R. Leshchinskiy, S. P. Jones, G. Keller, and S. Marlow. Data Parallel Haskell: A Status Report. In *Workshop on Declarative Aspects of Multicore Programming (DAMP)*, 2007.

[13] H. Cui, J. Wu, C. che Tsai, and J. Yang. Stable Deterministic Multithreading through Schedule Memoization. In *OSDI*, 2010.

[14] J. Devietti, B. Lucia, L. Ceze, and M. Oskin. DMP: Deterministic Shared Memory Multiprocessing. In *ASPLOS*, 2009.

[15] M. Dubois, J. Wang, L. Barroso, K. Lee, and Y. Chen. Delayed Consistency and Its Effects on the Miss Rate of Parallel Programs. In *Supercomputing*, 1991.

[16] S. A. Edwards and O. Tardieu. SHIM: A Deterministic Model for Heterogeneous Embedded Systems. In *EMSOFT*, 2005.

[17] K. Gharachorloo, D. Lenoski, J. Laudon, P. Gibbons, A. Gupta, and J. Hennessy. Memory Consistency and Event Ordering in Scalable Shared-Memory Multiprocessors. In *ISCA*, 1990.

[18] C. Gniady, B. Falsafi, and T. N. Vijaykumar. Is SC + ILP = RC? In *ISCA*, 1999.

[19] D. Hower, P. Dudnik, D. Wood, and M. Hill. Calvin: Deterministic or Not? Free Will to Choose. In *HPCA*, 2011.

[20] D. Hower and M. Hill. ReRun: Exploiting Episodes for Lightweight Memory Race Recording. In *ISCA*, 2008.

[21] C. K. Luk, R. Cohn, R. Muth, H. Patil, A. Klauser, G. Lowney, S. Wallace, V. J. Reddi, and K. Hazelwood. PIN: Building Customized Program Analysis Tools with Dynamic Instrumentation. In *PLDI*, 2005.

[22] J. Manson, W. Pugh, and S. Adve. The Java Memory Model. In *POPL*, 2005.

[23] P. Montesinos, L. Ceze, and J. Torrellas. DeLorean: Recording and Deterministically Replaying Shared-Memory Multiprocessor Execution Efficiently. In *ISCA*, 2008.

[24] S. Narayanasamy, C. Pereira, and B. Calder. Recording Shared Memory Dependencies Using Strata. In *ASPLOS*, 2006.

[25] R. H. B. Netzer. Optimal Tracing and Replay for Debugging Shared-Memory Parallel Programs. In *PADD*, 1993.

[26] M. Olszewski, J. Ansel, and S. Amarasinghe. Kendo: Efficient Deterministic Multithreading in Software. In *ASPLOS*, 2009.

[27] J. Ousterhout. Scheduling Techniques for Concurrent Systems. In *ICDCS*, 1982.

[28] S. Parka, W. Xiong, Z. Yin, R. Kaushik, K. Lee, S. Lu, and Y. Zhou. Do You Have to Reproduce the Bug at the First Replay Attempt? – PRES: Probabilistic Replay with Execution Sketching on Multiprocessors. In *SOSP*, 2009.

[29] M. Rinard and M. Lam. The Design, Implementation, and Evaluation of Jade. *ACM TOPLAS*, 20(3), 1988.

[30] K. Russell and D. Detlefs. Eliminating synchronization-related atomic operations with biased locking and bulk rebiasing. In *OOPSLA*, 2006.

[31] W. Thies, M. Karczmarek, and S. Amarasinghe. StreamIt: A Language for Streaming Applications. In *CC*, 2002.

[32] E. Vallejo, M. Galluzzi, A. Cristal, F. Vallejo, R. Beivide, P. Stenstrom, J. E. Smith, and M. Valero. Implementing Kilo-Instruction Multiprocessors. In *ICPS*, July 2005.

[33] C. von Praun, H. Cain, J. Choi, and K. Ryu. Conditional Memory Ordering. In *ISCA*, 2006.

[34] T. F. Wenisch, A. Ailamaki, B. Falsafi, and A. Moshovos. Mechanisms for Store-wait-free Multiprocessors. In *ISCA*, 2007.

[35] M. Xu, R. Bodik, and M. Hill. A "Flight Data Recorder" for Enabling Full-System Multiprocessor Deterministic Replay. In *ISCA*, 2003.

[36] M. Xu, M. Hill, and R. Bodik. A Regulated Transitive Reduction for Longer Memory Race Recording. In *ASPLOS*, 2006.

# Specifying and Checking Semantic Atomicity for Multithreaded Programs

Jacob Burnim George Necula Koushik Sen
University of California, Berkeley
{jburnim,necula,ksen}@cs.berkeley.edu

## Abstract

In practice, it is quite difficult to write correct multithreaded programs due to the potential for unintended and nondeterministic interference between parallel threads. A fundamental correctness property for such programs is *atomicity*—a block of code in a program is *atomic* if, for any parallel execution of the program, there is an execution with the same overall program behavior in which the block is executed serially.

We propose *semantic atomicity*, a generalization of atomicity with respect to a programmer-defined notion of equivalent behavior. We propose an assertion framework in which a programmer can use *bridge predicates* to specify noninterference properties at the level of abstraction of their application. Further, we propose a novel algorithm for systematically testing atomicity specifications on parallel executions with a bounded number of *interruptions*—i.e. atomic blocks whose execution is interleaved with that of other threads. We further propose a set of sound heuristics and optional user annotations that increase the efficiency of checking atomicity specifications in the common case where the specifications hold.

We have implemented our assertion framework for specifying and checking semantic atomicity for parallel Java programs, and we have written semantic atomicity specifications for a number of benchmarks. We found that using bridge predicates allowed us to specify the natural and intended atomic behavior of a wider range of programs than did previous approaches. Further, in checking our specifications, we found several previously unknown bugs, including in the widely-used `java.util.concurrent` library.

***Categories and Subject Descriptors*** D.2.4 [*Software Engineering*]: Software/Program Verification; D.2.5 [*Software Engineering*]: Testing and Debugging; F.3.1 [*Logics and Meanings of Programs*]: Specifying and Verifying and Reasoning about Programs

***General Terms*** Algorithms, Reliability, Verification

## 1. Introduction

With the growing prevalence of multicore processors, it is increasingly necessary for programmers to write parallel software. Yet parallel programming remains notoriously difficult. A key reason for this difficulty is that the parallel threads of a multithreaded program may nondeterministically interfere with one another.


*ASPLOS'11,* March 5–11, 2011, Newport Beach, California, USA.


Thus, a fundamental parallel correctness property for multithreaded programs is *atomicity* [9]. A block of code is *atomic* if it appears to execute all at once, indivisibly and without interruption from any other program thread. The behavior of an *atomic* code block can be understood and reasoned about *sequentially*, as no parallel operations can interfere with its execution.

Many researchers have proposed using *transactional memory* hardware, libraries, and/or language constructs to implement such atomic blocks. But in much existing multithreaded code, desired atomicity is implemented using a variety of synchronization techniques, including coarse or fine-grained locking and non-blocking synchronization with primitives such as atomic compare-and-swap. Correctly implementing atomicity using these techniques can be difficult and error-prone. Thus, as we discuss in Section 6, there has been great interest in techniques enabling programmers to specify what fragments of their concurrent programs behave as if atomic, and in techniques for testing or verifying that such programs conform to their atomicity specifications.

Traditional notions of atomicity are often too strict in practice, however, because they require the existence of serial executions that result in an state identical to that of the interleaved execution. We propose an assertion framework that allows programmers to specify that their code is *semantically* atomic—that any parallel, interleaved execution of an atomic block will have an effect *semantically equivalent* to that of executing the block serially. Programmers specify this semantic equivalence using *bridge predicates* [3]—predicates relating pairs of program states from the interleaved and the equivalent serial execution. Such predicates allow the equivalence of executions to be defined at the level of abstraction of an application.

We further propose an approach to check our semantic atomicity specifications by testing whether or not specified programs are *semantically linearizable*. We choose to check linearizability because (1) this stronger notion is significantly easier to check since the restriction on allowed serial executions significantly reduces the space of serial executions that we must search, and (2) the notion of linearizability is often used to describe the parallel correctness of various concurrent data structures. Essentially, to test linearizability for a particular interleaving we need to consider only permutations of atomic blocks that overlapped in the interleaved execution.

The key to the efficiency of our approach is based on two observations. First, linearizability can be checked efficiently for a parallel execution in which only a small number of atomic blocks overlap, since we need to examine only a small number of similar sequential executions. Second, our experience shows that most atomicity bugs can be reproduced with a small number of overlapping atomic blocks. Thus, we test linearizability of a program by generating parallel executions with only a small number of interrupted atomic blocks. Our experiments show that we can effectively find serious atomicity errors in our benchmarks by testing such *interruption-bounded* executions.

To further reduce the search space for the linearized execution, we propose a set of sound heuristics and optional user annotations. We show in our experiments that in the presence of such annotations we can often find the linearized execution in the first attempt.

We have implemented our assertion framework for Java and used it to specify the intended atomicity of a number of benchmarks. We found that the ability to specify atomicity at the *semantic* level, using bridge predicates, is crucial for capturing the intended atomic behavior of many of our of the benchmarks. Such benchmarks contain sections of code that, while semantically atomic, are not atomic under more strict, traditional notions of atomicity.

In summary, we describe the following contributions:

- We propose using *bridge predicates* to specify that regions of parallel programs are intended to be *semantically atomic*. Our notion of *semantic atomicity* is more general than traditional strict notions of atomicity and is applicable to a wider range of parallel programs.
- We propose an approach to test efficiently and effectively a program's semantic atomicity specification by checking the *linearizability* of program executions with a bounded number of interrupted atomic sections. We further propose program annotations and corresponding heuristics to reduce significantly the search space that must be explored during testing, without sacrificing any ability to find atomicity errors.
- We implement an assertion framework for Java for specifying and testing semantic atomicity specifications and evaluate our approach on a number of Java benchmarks. We find that bridge predicates are required in a majority of the examples. We show that the heuristics we propose make the testing approach both reasonably efficient and effective at finding bugs.
- We find a number of previously unknown atomicity errors, including several in Java's built-in data structure libraries.

```
Queue q = new ConcurrentLinkedQueue();
q.add(1);  q.add(1);

thread1:                       thread2:
 @assert_atomic {               @assert_atomic {
     q.remove(1);                   q.remove(1);
 }                              }
              bridge predicate:
                  q.equals(q')
```

**Figure 1.** Example program with highly-concurrent queue. The queue initially contains two copies of the value 1, and two parallel threads each try to remove a 1 from the queue. These remove operations are specified to execute as if atomic. The program is not strictly atomic, but is *semantically* atomic with respect to the given *bridge predicate*.

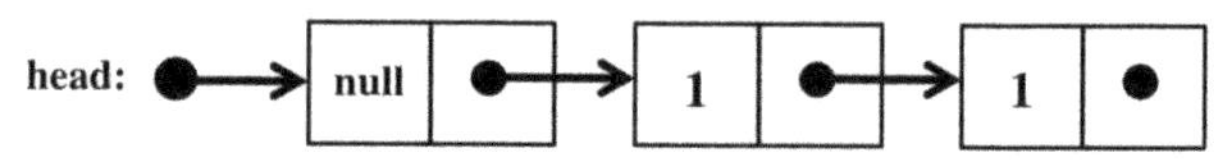


**Figure 2.** Initial internal structure of queue q.

**Figure 3.** Internal structure of queue q after *any* serial execution of the example program.

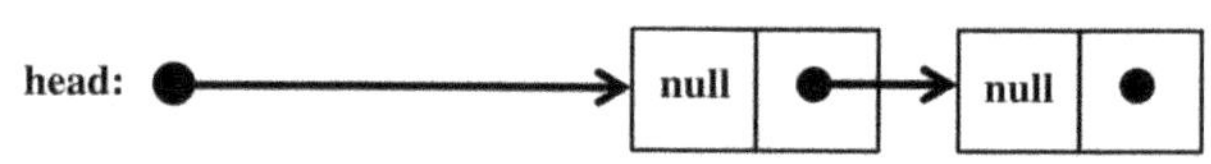


**Figure 4.** Possible structure of q after a parallel, interleaved execution of the example program.

## 2. Specifying Semantic Atomicity

In this section, we informally describe atomicity and motivate our proposal for semantic atomicity specifications. We first describe a real-world motivating example. We then expand on semantic atomicity specifications using two simpler examples. In Section 2.1, we discuss the effort involved in programmers writing such atomicity specifications.

We consider parallel programs in which certain regions of code are annotated as *atomic blocks*. This annotation specifies the programmers *belief* or *intention* that each atomic block is written so that, however the block is actually executed, the effect is *as if* the block's execution occurred all-at-once, with no interference or interruption from other parallel threads. For simplicity, we consider each indivisible program instruction that is not in a user-annotated atomic block to be in its own implicit, single-instruction block.

***Example 1: Concurrent Queue*** Consider the example program in Figure 1 using Java's `ConcurrentLinkedQueue` data structure, an implementation of Michael and Scott's non-blocking queue [23]. `ConcurrentLinkedQueue`, from the `java.util.concurrent` package, is implemented in a lock-free, non-blocking manner, updating its internal structure using compare-and-swap operations. If two parallel queue operations conflict, one of the operations will detect the conflict and retry.

The implementation of `ConcurrentLinkedQueue` is designed to ensure that, when multiple queue operations occur concurrently, their result is the same as if all queue operations had been executed atomically. We specify this intended atomicity in Figure 1 by enclosing each parallel call to `remove(1)` in a specified *atomic block*, which we write as `@assert_atomic {...}`.

If our specification was a strict atomicity specification, it would assert: for any parallel execution of the program, in which the calls to `remove(1)` can interleave, there there must exist a *serial* execution, in which each call to `remove(1)` occurred atomically, producing an *identical* final state. But this strict atomicity specification does not hold.

Internally, a `ConcurrentLinkedQueue` is a linked list. Nodes in the list can be lazily deleted—i.e. a remove operation can set the data field of a node to `null`, indicating that the corresponding data element is no longer in the queue, but leave removing the node to some future operation.

Before the parallel threads execute `remove`, the internal list structure is as shown in Figure 2. In any serial execution of the two calls to `remove`, the second call will lazily delete the node `null`'ed by the first call, yielding the final internal queue structure shown in Figure 3. But in a parallel execution in which the two calls to `remove` are interleaved, it is possible for neither call to clean up after the other, yielding the final internal state of the queue shown in Figure 4.

Thus, under a traditional, strict definition of atomicity, the `remove` method is *not* atomic, as a non-serial, interleaved execution can yield a program state not reachable by any serial execution. But in either case the abstract, semantic state of queue q is the same—the queue is empty! That is, the code is atomic, but only at the *semantic* level of the contents of the queue.

```
int balance = 0;

void deposit1(int a) {
  @assert_atomic {
    int t = balance;
    t += a;
    balance = t;
  }
}
```

```
int balance = 0;

void deposit2(int a) {
  @assert_atomic {
    int t = balance;
    while (!CAS(&balance, t, t + a)) {
      t = balance;
    }
  }
}
```

```
int conflicts = 0;
int balance = 0;

void deposit3(int a) {
  @assert_atomic {
    int t = balance;
    while (!CAS(&balance, t, t + a)) {
      conflicts += 1;
      t = balance;
    }
  }
}
    bridge predicate:
      balance == balance'
```

**Figure 5.** Three different implementations of a function to make a deposit into a bank account. Implementation `deposit1` is not atomic, while `deposit2` *is* atomic. Implementation `deposit3` is not strictly atomic, but it is *semantically* atomic with respect to the bridge predicate `balance==balance'`.

To capture this kind of parallel correctness property, we propose *semantic atomicity*. Blocks of code are semantically atomic when, however their execution is interleaved with that of other code, their effect is *semantically equivalent* to their effect when executed serially. The desired semantic equivalence is specified by a programmer using a *bridge predicate*. For this program, semantic equivalence is given by the bridge predicate $\Phi(\sigma, \sigma')$:

$$\texttt{q.equals}(\texttt{q}')$$

This bridge predicate compares two program states, $\sigma$ and $\sigma'$, the first from an interleaved, parallel execution of our example program and the second from a serial execution. The unprimed `q` refers to the queue in state $\sigma$ and the primed $\texttt{q}'$ refers to the queue in state $\sigma'$. This bridge predicate specifies states $\sigma$ and $\sigma'$ are semantically equivalent when the `equals` method of `ConcurrentLinkedQueue` returns *true* on the queues from the two states—that is, when the two queues contain the same elements, independent of their internal structure.

This semantic atomicity specification *does hold* for our example program. For any parallel execution of the program, there exists a serial execution that produces an equivalent final queue `q`.

***Example 2: Bank Account*** Consider the code in Figure 5 for function `deposit1` for making a deposit into a bank account whose balance is stored in variable `balance`. The atomic specification in `deposit1` *does not hold* because there is an interleaved execution for which there is no equivalent serial execution. Suppose two threads call `deposit1`(100) in parallel, with `balance` initially 0. Under certain interleavings, both calls to `deposit1` can read a `balance` of 0 and then both can write 100 to `balance`, producing a wrong final result: `balance=100`. In contrast, any serial execution of the two threads, in which the body of `deposit1` cannot be interleaved with any other code, must produce the final result `balance=200`.

Note that atomicity violations can occur even in code that is free of data races. For example, if `deposit1` held a shared lock while reading and writing to `balance`, but released the lock in between when executing "`t += a`", then the procedure would be free of data races but would still not be atomic.

Consider instead the implementation `deposit2` in Figure 5, which uses an atomic compare-and-swap (`CAS`) operation to modify variable `balance`. In this implementation, the atomicity specification *does hold*. Each call to `deposit` reads `balance` into a temporary `t` and then attempts to atomically update `balance` to $\texttt{t} + \texttt{a}$, succeeding if `balance` still equals `t`. If some other thread interferes, changing `balance` between the read of `balance` and the `CAS`, then the atomic update fails and `deposit` re-reads `balance` and tries again.

Finally, consider the implementation `deposit3` in Figure 5. This code is identical to `deposit2`, except that a count is kept, in shared variable `conflicts`, of the approximate[1] number of failed compare-and-swap operations during runs of `deposit3`.

Due to the introduction of shared counter `conflicts`, the atomic specification no longer holds. In a parallel execution with two calls to `deposit3(100)`, if the execution of the methods interleave, it is possible for `conflicts` to be incremented to 1. But in any execution in which the methods are executed serially, the value of `conflicts` will be 0.

However, the `deposit3` implementation is semantically atomic with respect to the bridge predicate:

$$\texttt{balance} == \texttt{balance}'$$

That is, if some interleaved execution produces a final `balance`, there will exist a serial execution producing a final $\texttt{balance}'$ such that `balance` and $\texttt{balance}'$ are equal.

***Example 3: Multiset Stored as a List*** Consider the example program in Figure 6, in which two threads accumulate integers into a shared `list`. If the programmer cares about the exact order of the final elements in `list`, then this code is *not* atomic. Although method `add` of `Vector` is synchronized, an interleaved execution of this example program can yield a final list of `[1,3,2,4]`, while a serial execution of the two atomic blocks could yield only `[1,2,3,4]` or `[3,4,1,2]`.

```
List list = new Vector();

thread1:                 thread2:
@assert_atomic {         @assert_atomic {
    ...                      ...
    list.add(1);             list.add(3);
    ...                      ...
    list.add(2);             list.add(4);
}                        }

    bridge predicate:
      equalMultisets(list, list')
```

**Figure 6.** Example program in which two atomic blocks insert elements into a synchronized list.

[1] Such performance counters are often not synchronized, as developers reason that the cost of synchronization is too great and approximate counts are often suitable for performance debugging.

But this code can be thought of as atomic if the programmer cares only about the *multiset* of elements in the final `list`. That is, the example program in Figure 6 is semantically atomic with respect to some bridge predicate like `equalMultisets(list,list')`, where `equalMultisets` is a function that compares two collections to see if they have equal multisets of elements.

### 2.1 Writing Semantic Atomicity Specs

Our above examples demonstrate that we can reap the benefits of atomicity as a specification and reasoning tool in many more contexts if we consider the more relaxed form of semantic atomicity with respect to an application-specific bridge predicate. But how much effort is involved in writing such a specification for a parallel program?

To write a semantic atomicity specification for a program, a programmer must: (1) Indicate with `@assert_atomic` which static blocks of code are intended to execute as if atomic, and (2) Write a bridge predicate to define when two final states of the program are semantically equivalent. We believe neither task should be difficult for the author of a parallel program.

We believe that, when writing multithreaded software, programmers must already be thinking about the possible interference between parallel tasks and how to prevent harmful interference using, for example, thread-safe data structures, locks, or atomic primitives such as compare-and-swaps. That is, programmers are already thinking about how to ensure that program tasks are atomic at some semantic level. Thus, it should not be difficult to specify which blocks of code are intended to behave equivalently whether or not other program tasks are run concurrently—for example, a modification to concurrent queue data structure or a deposit to a bank account. Further, in our experimental evaluation (Section 5), we found it to be quite simple to identify the intended atomic blocks in our benchmark programs. We specified between one and eight atomic blocks for each such benchmark.

We similarly believe that it is straightforward to specify when two program results are semantically equivalent using a bridge predicate. This specification task does not require reasoning about possible program interleavings, but simply identifying which variables or objects hold the final result of a program and considering when two such final results are semantically the same—for example, that two queues are equivalent if they contain the same elements in the same order, independent of the structure of their internal linked lists. Further, in our experimental evaluation (Section 5), we found that writing such bridge predicates required only a few lines of specification for each benchmark.

## 3. Semantic Atomicity and Linearizability

In this section we elaborate on several possible interpretations of atomicity specifications. We first describe these notions at a high level, and compare them to other notions of parallel correctness and non-interference. Later in this section we give the precise formal foundations on which we developed the checking algorithm described in the rest of this paper.

### 3.1 Overview

At a high-level, we think of a parallel program annotated with atomic blocks as having two different execution semantics: (1) In the *interleaved* or *non-serial* semantics, the atomic annotations have no effect—the parallel operations of different threads can be freely interleaved. (2) In the *serial* or *non-interleaved* semantics, when one program thread enters an atomic block, no other thread may execute until the first thread exits that atomic block. (Because we treat every instruction as being in an implicit single-instruction atomic block, we can think of the *serial* semantics as having a global re-entrant lock that each thread must acquire to enter any atomic block and that is released on exiting a block.)

Traditional parallel correctness properties such as *atomicity*, *serializability*, or *linearizability* hold for a program when, for any interleaved execution of the program, there exists a *similar* serial execution that produces an identical final program state. The differences between these correctness properties are in their definitions of *similar* executions:

- *Atomicity* [9] requires only that, for each interleaved execution, there exists a serial execution yielding the same final program state. The interleaved and serial executions need not be similar in any other way.
- *Serializability* [28] requires that, for each interleaved execution, there exists a serial execution which both yields the same final program state and in which all the same atomic blocks are executed.

  *Conflict-serializability* [28] further requires that all corresponding atomic blocks perform the same conflicting read and write operations in the interleaved and parallel execution, and that all pairs of conflicting operations occur in the same relative order. Conflict-serializability, though very strict, can be checked efficiently, and is thus used in many atomicity testing and verification tools, (e.g., [8–10, 12, 37]).
- *Linearizability* [17], like serializability, requires that, for each interleaved execution, there exists a serial execution which both yields the same final program state and in which the same atomic blocks are executed. Further, it requires that any pair of atomic blocks whose execution does not overlap in the interleaved execution must occur in the same order in the serial execution.

  Note that this definition of linearizability is somewhat different than that of [17] and later generalization [24], which formalize atomic blocks as having distinguished *responses* or *return values* and compare program states via observational equivalence—i.e. whether sequences of atomic blocks would return the same values. Our definition is appropriate for general atomic blocks without distinguished return values, while capturing the key requirement that a serial execution is equivalent only if it preserves the ordering of non-overlapping atomic blocks.

All three properties defined above require that, for each interleaved execution, there exists some serial execution producing an *identical* final state. As discussed in Section 2, such strict state equality is too restrictive to capture critical noninterference properties for many programs. For such programs, we propose employing a user-specified *bridge predicate* [3]—a predicate relating a pair of program states from an interleaved and a serial execution—to define a *semantic* equivalence between final program states.

That is, we can define *semantic atomicity*, *semantic serializability*, and *semantic linearizability*, all with respect to a user-specified bridge predicate $\Phi$, by allowing in the above definitions that, for any interleaved execution with final state $\sigma$, the equivalent serial execution can have any final state $\sigma'$ such that $\Phi(\sigma, \sigma')$.

The checking algorithm described in Section 4 tests semantic linearizability, primarily because linearizability is significantly easier to check, as it constrains the search space of similar serial executions to those that preserve the ordering of non-overlapping atomic blocks. But before describing out testing algorithm, we will briefly formalize in Section 3.2 these three parallel correctness properties.

### 3.2 Formal Definitions

In this section, we briefly formalize the above definitions of *semantic atomicity*, *serializability*, and *linearizability*.

Let *Thread* denote the set of program threads, $\Sigma$ denote the set of program states including the thread-local states, *Atomic* denote the set of static program block *annotated* as atomic, and *Op* denote the set $\{\texttt{begin}(a) : a \in \mathit{Atomic}\} \cup \{\texttt{end}, \epsilon\}$ of atomic block operations. Intuitively, the operations are used to label the state transitions as follows. `begin(a)` marks the beginning of a dynamic instance of the static atomic block $a$, `end` marks the end of the last open atomic block, and $\epsilon$ is used for all other state transitions. We assume that atomic blocks are properly nested, and all instructions are inside one atomic block. If an instruction is not inside a programmer-annotated atomic block, then we assume that there is an implicit atomic block containing just that instruction.

**Definition 1.** *A program $P$ consists of an initial program state $\sigma_0$ and a transition relation $\rightarrow$:*

$$\rightarrow \;\subseteq\; \Sigma \times \mathit{Thread} \times \mathit{Op} \times \Sigma$$

We write $\sigma \xrightarrow{t:\texttt{op}} \sigma'$ when the program can transition from state $\sigma$ to $\sigma'$ by executing the atomic block operation `op` by thread $t$.

**Definition 2.** *An **execution** of program $P = (\rightarrow, \sigma_0)$ is a sequence of transitions in the operational semantics $\rightarrow$:*

$$\sigma_0 \xrightarrow{t_1:op_1} \sigma_1 \xrightarrow{t_2:op_2} \cdots \xrightarrow{t_n:op_n} \sigma_n$$

*An execution is **complete** if all `begin(a)` have a matching `end` operation in the same thread.*

**Definition 3.** *An execution $E$ is **serial** iff, for each matched $t$ : `begin`$(a)$ and $t$ : `end` transition in $E$, there are no transitions between the two by any other thread $s \neq t$.*

**Definition 4.** *A transition $t : op$ in an execution $E$ is a **top-level** transition if it does not occur between any matched $t$ : `begin`$(a)$ and $t$ : `end` by the same thread.*

Note that all top-level transitions are a `begin` or `end` since we assume that all instructions are part of atomic blocks.

**Definition 5.** *A complete execution $E = \sigma_0 \xrightarrow{\cdots} \sigma_n$ of program $P$ is **semantically linearizable with respect to** $\Phi$ iff there exists a serial execution $E' = \sigma_0 \xrightarrow{\cdots} \sigma'_{n'}$ of $P$ such that:*

*(1) $\Phi(\sigma_n, \sigma'_{n'})$,*
*(2) for every thread $t \in$ Thread, the sequence of top-level operations performed by $t$ is the same in $E$ and $E'$.*
*(3) non-overlapping top-level atomic blocks in $E$ appear in the same order $E'$.*

*A program $P$ is **semantically linearizable with respect to** $\Phi$ iff every execution of $P$ is semantically linearizable.*

Note that if we remove conditions (2) and (3) above we obtain the notion of *semantic atomicity*. Similarly, if we remove only the condition (3) above we obtain the notion of *semantic serializability*. And when the bridge predicate $\Phi(\sigma, \sigma')$ is strict state equality $\sigma = \sigma'$, we obtain traditional linearizability, atomicity (removing conditions 2 and 3), and serializability (removing condition 3). We prefer to work with the stronger notion of linearizability because it is significantly easier to check.

Note that, for the purpose of checking similarity between the parallel and the serial executions, we identify the dynamic instances of atomic blocks by the combination of the thread that runs them, the static label of the atomic block, and the index of the dynamic occurrence in the execution.

## 4. Testing Semantic Linearizability

Now that we have defined semantic linearizability for programs with atomic block specifications, we can address the problem of checking the linearizability of such atomicity specifications.

Suppose $P$ is a program with atomic blocks specified to be semantically linearizable with respect to bridge predicate $\Phi$. Checking the linearizability of $P$ consists of two problems:

(1) Given an interleaved execution $E$ of a program $P$, is $E$ semantically linearizable with respect to $\Phi$?

(2) Is program $P$ semantically linearizable with respect to bridge predicate $\Phi$? That is, is every interleaved execution of $P$ semantically linearizable?

Given a solution to the first problem, we can in theory solve the second by enumerating all interleaved executions of $P$ and checking if each is linearizable. In practice, however, it is typically not feasible to enumerate all executions of a parallel program.

Instead, we resort to checking the linearizability of only a subset of the interleaved executions of $P$. Such a checking procedure will be *sound*—if we discover any executions of $P$ that are not linearizable, then $P$ cannot be linearizable—but *incomplete*—even if all checked executions are linearizable, we cannot know for certain that $P$ itself is linearizable.

There are a number of existing techniques and tools that can be applied to generate a subset of the parallel, interleaved executions of a program for testing and verification—for example, a preemption-bounded model checker [25] such as CHESS [26] or an active testing [29, 30] tool such as CalFuzzer [18]. We describe in Section 5.1 the details of our technique for generating the interleaved executions to test.

The key to the effectiveness of our approach, however, is to consider only those interleaved executions in which only a small number of atomic blocks either have their execution *interrupted* by the operations of other threads or themselves interrupt the atomic blocks of other threads.

We show in the Sections 4.1 and 4.2 that we can efficiently check the linearizability of such *interruption-bounded* executions. And in Section 4.3 we will describe a technique, leveraging optional programmer-supplied hints to further increase the efficiency of such testing. Our experimental results demonstrate that testing a program for linearizability only on *interruption-bounded* interleaved executions is sufficient to find real atomicity errors.

### 4.1 Interruption-Bounded Executions

Let $E$ be an interleaved execution of some program $P$:

$$E \;=\; \sigma_0 \xrightarrow{t_1:op_1} \sigma_1 \xrightarrow{t_2:op_2} \cdots \xrightarrow{t_n:op_n} \sigma_n$$

We say a top-level atomic block $t : \texttt{begin}(a_i), \ldots, t : \texttt{end}$ in thread $t$ in $E$ is *interrupted* if any operations by other threads occur between $t : \texttt{begin}(a_i)$ and $t : \texttt{end}$ in $E$. The interrupting operations in the other threads are part of atomic blocks that *interrupt* the atomic block $t : \texttt{begin}(a_i), \ldots, t : \texttt{end}$.

Suppose an execution $E$ has $R$ interrupt*ed* atomic blocks and $K$ interrupt*ing* atomic blocks. (Note that a single block may be both interrupted and interrupting). We ask the question, how many possible linear orderings are there of the top-level atomic blocks of $E$ that preserve the order of non-overlapping atomic blocks in $E$?

We show below in Theorem 6 that such an execution $E$ has no more than $(K + 1)^R$ possible linear orderings of its top-level atomic blocks that preserve the order of non-overlapping atomic blocks. As we discuss in the next section, to check that an execution $E$ is semantically linearizable, we will examine linear orderings of the top-level atomic blocks of $E$ that preserve the ordering of non-overlapping blocks in $E$. Thus, if execution $E$ is *interruption-*

*bounded*—i.e. has no more than $R$ interrupted atomic blocks and no more than $K$ interrupting blocks—then there will be no more than $(K+1)^R$ serial schedules that need to be examined.

**Theorem 6.** *Suppose an execution $E$ has $R$ top-level interrupt*ed *atomic blocks and $K$ top-level interrupt*ing *atomic blocks. There are no more than $(K+1)^R$ possible linear orderings of the top-level atomic blocks of $E$ that preserve the order of non-overlapping atomic blocks.*

*Proof.* The proof is by induction on $R$. For the base case $R = 1$, the bound is $K+1$, because the $K$ interrupting blocks are themselves non-overlapping and thus their linear order is fixed. The interrupted block can be placed in $K+1$ positions in the order.

Suppose $E$ has $R$ interrupted atomic blocks and $K$ interrupting atomic blocks. There exists some set $S$ of $c \geq 1$ blocks in $E$ such that: (1) every block in $S$ is interrupted, and (2) no block in $S$ interrupts any block not in $S$.

Suppose that such an $S$ exists with $c = |S| = 1$. Then, there are no more than $(K+1)^{R-1}$ linear orderings of the remaining blocks, with the single block in $S$ removed. And there are no more than $K+1$ ways to add back the single block into any such order, yielding the desired bound.

Suppose instead that an $S$ exists only with $c = |S| > 1$. Then every block in $S$ is both interrupt*ed* and interrupt*ing*. (If any block were not interrupting, then it would be an $S$ with $c = 1$.) Thus, there are no more than $(K+1-c)^{R-c}$ linear orderings of the remaining atomic blocks, of which $R-c$ are interrupted and no more than $K-c$ are interrupting. Consider the number of distinct ways in which the $c$ blocks of $S$ could appear in such an ordering of the remaining blocks. There are $c!$ linear orderings of the $c$ blocks of $S$. And, relative to the remaining $K-c$ interrupting blocks, there are no more than $K-c+1$ possible positions for each of the $c$ blocks in $S$. Thus, the number of ways to add one linear ordering of the $c$ blocks of $S$ to one linear ordering of the remaining blocks is no more than $K!/c!(K-c)!$, which is the the number of ways to partition a sequence of length $c$ into $K-c+1$ segments, allowing empty segments. The desired bound holds, as:

$$(K+1-c)^{R-c} \cdot c! \cdot \frac{K!}{c!(K-c)!} \;\leq\; (K+1)^R \qquad \square$$

## 4.2 Testing Linearizability of Interruption-Bounded Executions

Algorithm 1 lists *CheckLinearizable*$(P, \Phi, E)$, our algorithm for testing the semantic linearizability, with respect to $\Phi$, of an execution $E$ of a program $P$.

We say that a *schedule* is a sequence $(t_1, a_1), \ldots, (t_n, a_n)$ of pairs of thread identifiers $t_i$ and atomic block labels $a_i$. We assume that all sources of nondeterminism in a program $P$, besides the scheduling of parallel threads, have been eliminated. For example, the input to $P$ and the environment in which $P$ runs must be fixed. Thus, the behavior of the serial executions of $P$, in which no atomic block interrupts the execution of any other block, are uniquely identified by the *schedule* in which the top-level atomic blocks occur.

Then, let *Linearizations*$(E)$ be a procedure computing the set of all schedules of the top-level atomic blocks in $E$ that preserve the order of non-overlapping atomic blocks in $E$. A serial execution can be a witness to the linearizability of $E$ only if it corresponds to one of the schedules in *Linearizations*$(E)$. By Theorem 6, the number of such schedules, and thus the number of such serial executions, is bounded by the number of interruptions in $E$.

We need only a mechanism for controlling the execution of a program $P$ to force it along a schedule $s$. Let *Execute*$(P, s)$ denote such a procedure. At a high level, for a program $P$ and a schedule $s = (t_1, a_1), \ldots, (t_n, a_n)$, procedure *Execute*$(P, s)$ will, for each $i$ from 1 to $n$:

- If thread $t_i$ is not active or the next top-level atomic block to be started by $t_i$ is not labeled $a_i$, then *Execute*$(P, s)$ fails.
- Otherwise, we let thread $t_i$ execute `begin`$(a_i)$ and let it continue to run until it executes a matching `end`. If thread $t_i$ blocks, *Execute*$(P, s)$ fails.

  Similarly, *Execute*$(P, s)$ fails if $t_i$ runs forever without ever reaching a matching `end`. As the termination of $t_i$ is undecidable, the best we can do is for *Execute*$(P, s)$ to fail after $t_i$ does not reach a matching `end` in a specified amount of time or number of instructions.

**Algorithm 1** *CheckLinearizable*$(P, \Phi, E)$

$\sigma \leftarrow$ final state of execution $E$
**for** $s \in$ *Linearizations*$(E)$ **do**
  **if** *Execute*$(P, s)$ succeeds, yielding $\sigma'$ **then**
    **if** $\Phi(\sigma, \sigma')$ **then**
      **return** true
    **end if**
  **end if**
**end for**
**return** false

## 4.3 Hints for More Efficient Testing

In testing the semantic linearizability of the atomic blocks in a program $P$, we expect to have to test the linearizability of many interleaved executions of $P$. We expect that the great majority of these tested interleavings will be linearizable—concurrency errors such as atomicity violations tend to occur only on a small fraction of executions, especially in well-tested and widely-used software. (Our experimental results match this expectation.)

If an interleaved execution $E$ is *not* linearizable, then we will have to look at all serial ways to schedule the top-level atomic blocks of $E$ that are consistent with the ordering of non-overlapping blocks in $E$. But if an interleaved execution $E$ *is* linearizable, we can determine this fact by finding a single equivalent serial execution. This raises the possibility that, for executions that turn out to be linearizable, we could make the testing procedure described in Section 4.2 more efficient by prioritizing the order in which we examine the possible linearizations of $E$.

Thus, we propose two kinds of optional hints that a programmer can add to their multithreaded code, along with their semantic atomicity specification. For an interleaved execution $E$, the hints will suggest which serial orderings of the overlapping atomic blocks should give equivalent results. Before falling back to a complete search of all linearizations of $E$, we will first try the linearizations consistent with these hints from the programmer.

Our optional hints take two forms: (1) linearization points, and (2) distinguished reads and writes:

***Linearization Points*** First, a user can specify *linearization points* (also called *commit points*) for atomic blocks. Any dynamic execution of an atomic block should reach at most one annotated linearization point.

This hint indicates that, if two atomic blocks overlap and both execute a linearization point, then the block that executed its linearization point first should be ordered first in any serial execution.

Manually-annotated linearization points are often used in efforts to prove or verify the correctness of concurrent data structures [5, 7, 35, 38]. However, it has been observed [2, 5, 35] that it may be very difficult to identify or annotate all linearization points for some programs.

***Distinguished Reads and Writes*** Second, a user can annotate certain reads and writes of shared variables as *distinguished* reads and writes. When linearization points cannot be identified statically, one could often identify some distinguished shared memory accesses (i.e. reads and writes) whose ordering determines the ordering between the atomic blocks. For example, if an atomic block inserts (i.e. writes) an item to a list and another overlapping atomic block gets (i.e. reads) the same item from the list, then the ordering between the write and read accesses determines the ordering between the atomic blocks. If a CAS operation succeeds, then a shared memory write performed by the CAS is considered distinguished. On the other hand, if a CAS operation fails, then the shared memory read performed by the CAS operation can be ignored (i.e. not considered distinguished). In several of our benchmarks, we have found that even if we cannot identify the linearization points of all atomic blocks, we can identify distinguished reads and writes and use them to determine the ordering among overlapping atomic blocks. We next describe how we use distinguished operations to order atomic blocks.

Given *distinguished* operations $op_1$ and $op_2$ on the same shared variable, we say that $op_1$ is *ordered before* $op_2$ if at least one of the two operations is a write and if $op_1$ is executed first.

Suppose atomic blocks $B_1$ and $B_2$ overlap. These hints indicate that $B_1$ should be ordered before $B_2$ in any serial execution if, for any variable $v$, some distinguished write to $v$ in $B_1$ or the last distinguished read to $v$ in $B_1$ is ordered before a distinguished write to $v$ in $B_2$ or the last distinguished read of $v$ in $B_2$.

These hints may indicate that $B_1$ should come before $B_2$ and that $B_2$ should come before $B_1$, in which case we ignore the distinguished reads/writes for ordering $B_1$ and $B_2$ with respect to each other.

***Using Hints in Testing Linearizability*** Given an interleaved execution $E$, we use a depth-first search to find a serial ordering consistent with the annotated hints in $E$. And if no execution is consistent including both the *linearization points* and the *distinguished reads and writes*, we find an ordering consistent with just the *linearization points*. We test this single serial ordering to see if it is a witness to the semantic linearizability of $E$, and, if not, we fall back to the exhaustive search in Section 4.2.

Our experimental results demonstrate that these hints can improve our linearizability testing to the point where the first serial execution to be examined is found to satisfy the bridge predicate. Furthermore, using these optimizations is *sound* because the testing procedure falls back to searching all other possible serial linearizations when a programmer's hints do not guide us to a witness to linearizability.

## 5. Evaluation

In this section, we describe our efforts to experimentally evaluate our approach to specifying and checking semantic atomicity for multithreaded programs. Specifically, we seek to demonstrate that:

1. We can find real atomicity errors in multithreaded programs by testing the semantic linearizability of random interleaved executions with a small number of interrupted and overlapping atomic blocks.
2. In the common case where a tested interleaving *is* linearizable, we can soundly increase the efficiency of our testing using optional programmer annotations.

### 5.1 Implementation

In order to evaluate our claims, we implemented our approach for Java programs. Our implementation consists of several components: (1) an annotation and assertion library for specifying which blocks of code in a Java program are intended to be semantically atomic, as well as for specifying the bridge predicate with respect to which the blocks are intended to be atomic; (2) a component to generate random, interruption-bounded interleaved executions of a multithreaded test program; (3) a component to test the semantic linearizability of a given interleaved execution by generating and examining all serial executions that are linearizations of the interleaved execution.

```
class Atomic {

  static void open()

  static void close()

  static void assert(Object o, Predicate p)

  interface Predicate {
      boolean apply(Object a, Object b)
  }
}
```

**Figure 7.** Core atomicity specification API.

***Atomicity Assertion Library*** Figure 7 shows the core API of our atomic assertion library. A programmer calls `Atomic.open()` and `Atomic.close()` to indicate the beginning and end of semantic atomic blocks in their code. Each call to `open` is uniquely identified by its location in the program source (accessible by, e.g., examining a call stack trace).

The bridge predicate giving the desired semantic equivalence between interleaved and serial executions is specified via `Atomic.assert`. In an interleaved execution, a sequence of calls to `Atomic.assert(obj,pred)` indicates that there must exist some serial execution—a linearization of the interleaved execution—in which each corresponding call `Atomic.assert(obj',pred)` is such that `pred.apply(obj,obj')` returns true.

That is, suppose the $n^{\text{th}}$ call to `Atomic.assert(obj,pred)` in an interleaved execution records the serialized value of object `obj`. (We require that all objects passed to `Atomic.assert` implement the `Serializable` interface so that this recording is possible. Most common objects in the Java standard library can be serialized in this way.) Then, in a serial execution, while testing the linearizability of this interleaved execution, the $n^{\text{th}}$ call to `Atomic.assert(obj',pred)` reads the previously serialized object `obj` and checks if `pred.apply(obj,obj')` holds. The serial execution is reported to be equivalent to the interleaved execution iff the same number of `Atomic.assert` calls are made and `pred.apply(obj,obj')` returns true for each one.

***Sampling Interleaved Executions*** Our tool for randomly generating interleaved executions of a multithreaded test program is built on top of the publicly-available and open-source CalFuzzer [18] framework for testing concurrent Java programs. CalFuzzer uses Soot [33] to instrument Java bytecode, adding calls to a user's analysis/testing code on every read, write, lock, unlock, etc.—we use these calls to take control of the parallel scheduling of a Java program and replace it with our own scheduler.

Our thread scheduler is parameterized by a maximum number $R$ of atomic blocks to *interrupt*, a number $K$ of other atomic blocks to execute while the atomic block is interrupted, and a bound $C$ on the number of times to interrupt at each distinct program statement. After any statement executes in the test program, the scheduler picks the next thread to execute a statement as follows:

| Benchmark | Approx. LoC (Benchmark + Library) | # Static Atomic Blocks | Interruption-Bounded Interleavings | | | Avg. # of Serial Executions | | | Conflicts |
|---|---|---|---|---|---|---|---|---|---|
| | | | total | non-linear. | errors | linear. | linear. (heuristics) | non-linear. | |
| ConcurrentLinkedQueue | 200 | 6 | 241 | 7 | 2 | 2.96 | 1.20 | 4.29 | 4 |
| ConcurrentSkipListMap | 1400 | 6 | 487 | 6 | 2* | 2.54 | - | 4.83 | 4 |
| ConcurrentSkipListSet | 100 | 6 | 463 | 5 | 2* | 2.57 | - | 4.6 | 4 |
| CopyOnWriteArrayList | 600 | 6 | 222 | 0 | 0 | 6.23 | 1.0 | - | 0 |
| CopyOnWriteArraySet | 60 | 6 | 221 | 0 | 0 | 4.39 | 1.0 | - | 0 |
| LockFreeList | 100 | 6 | 319 | 57 | 1 | 2.08 | - | 3.46 | 2 |
| LazyList | 100 | 8 | 231 | 0 | 0 | 2.46 | 1.02 | - | 2 |
| PJ pi | 150 + 15,000 | 1 | 20 | 5 | 1 | 1.0 | - | 4.8 | 1 |
| PJ keysearch | 200 + 15,000 | 1 | 904 | 0 | 0 | 1.0 | - | - | 0 |
| PJ mandelbrot | 250 + 15,000 | 1 | 73 | 0 | 0 | 1.0 | - | - | 0 |
| PJ phyl | 4400 + 15,000 | 2 | 605 | 27 | 1 | 1.0 | - | 125.56 | 2 |

**Table 1.** Experimental results.

- If the last statement was a top-level `Atomic.close` and no thread has an open atomic block, then pick the next thread randomly from among all active threads.
- If the last statement was by thread $t$ and thread $t$ has an open atomic block, then subject to certain constraints, we *interrupt* the atomic block thread $t$ is executing, selecting a random different active thread to run next.

  The constraints are: (1) We perform no more than $R$ interruptions during an execution. (2) For each statement in each possible calling context, we interrupt at that statement only if it is in the first $C$ occurrences in the current execution of the statement and calling context, and only if we have not interrupted at that statement, calling context, and occurrence combination in any other run.
- If the last statement was a top-level `Atomic.close` and other threads have open, interrupted blocks:

  If we have executed $K$ complete atomic blocks since interrupting the longest-open atomic block, we select, if possible, a random active thread *in an interrupted atomic block* to run next.

  Otherwise, randomly select to execute next any active thread *not* in an interrupted atomic block.

Overall, generated interleaved executions will have roughly $K^R$ expected possible linearizations. In our experiments, we use parameters $R = 1$, $K = 4$, and $C = 4$.

***Checking if an Interleaving is Linearizable*** Recall from the previous section that we can use CalFuzzer [18] to control the scheduling of a parallel Java application. We use this ability to implement procedure *Execute*$(P, s)$, described in Section 4.2, for executing a program $P$ along a serial schedule $s = (t_1, a_1), \ldots, (t_n, a_n)$.

We then implement Algorithm 1, given this `Execute`$(P, s)$ procedure and using the atomic assertion library described above to check the specified bridge predicate.

### 5.2 Benchmarks

We evaluated our approach on a number of Java benchmarks. The name, size, and number of static blocks specified as atomic is given for each of these benchmarks in Table 1.

The first group of benchmarks are concurrent data structures from the Java standard library `java.util.concurrent` and elsewhere. `ConcurrentLinkedQueue`, `ConcurrentSkipListMap`, `ConcurrentSkipListSet`, and `CopyOnWriteArrayList` are from the Oracle Java SDK 6 (update 20). `LockFreeList` is a concurrent, lock-free list from [16], used as a benchmark by [4]. Benchmark `LazyList` is a concurrent set, implemented as a linked list with lazy deletion, from [35].

As our technique is designed to be applied to whole, closed programs, we must create a test harness for each data structure benchmark. Each harness creates one instance `obj` of the data structure and then calls four to eight methods on the instance in parallel, recording the return values. Each method call is specified to be semantically atomic with respect to a bridge predicate requiring both that `obj.equals(obj')` and that all method return values be the same. For additional details, please see our benchmarks and test harnesses, which can be downloaded from: `http://www.cs.berkeley.edu/~jburnim`.

The other group of benchmarks are from the Parallel Java (PJ) Library [19]. The PJ benchmarks include an app for computing a Monte Carlo approximation of $\pi$ (`pi`), a parallel cryptographic key cracking app (`keysearch3`), an app for parallel rendering of Mandelbrot Set images (`mandelbrot`), and a parallel branch-and-bound search for optimal phylogenetic trees (`phylogenetic`). Each of these benchmarks relies on roughly 15,000 lines of PJ library code for threading, synchronization, etc.

### 5.3 Experimental Setup and Results

For each benchmark, we execute our systematic random scheduler, described in Section 5.1 to generate a number of interleaved, *interruption-bounded* executions. We test each generated execution to see if it is semantically linearizable.

The number of *interruption-bounded* executions generated for each benchmark is listed in Column 4. Column 5 lists the number of executions found to *not* be semantically linearizable. We found non-linearizable executions for four of the data structure benchmarks and two of the PJ application benchmarks. In Column 6, we report the number of distinct bugs exposed by these atomicity-violating executions. We discuss some of these errors in detail in the next section. Note that every violation of the linearizability of our semantic atomic blocks indicated a true error.

For the linearizable executions of each benchmark, Columns 7 and 8 report the average number of serial executions that had to be examined to find a witness to the linearizability, without and with heuristically using any hints from programmer annotations[2]. Our annotations greatly reduce the number of serial executions that must be examined for several of the data structure benchmarks.

[2] Note that, for the PJ benchmarks, because the different atomic blocks are largely independent, it is usually the case that the first serial execution we examine witnesses the linearizability.

Column 9 reports the number of serial executions examined for non-linearizable interleavings. For most benchmarks, this number is small, as expected, because we are testing the linearizability of *interruption-bounded* executions. [3]

Finally, Column 10 reports the number of atomic blocks in each data structure that are not conflict-serializable. We discuss these numbers in the next section.

### 5.4 Atomicity Errors Found

We now discuss several atomicity errors found by our testing.

***ConcurrentLinkedQueue*** Our automated testing of our semantic atomicity specification for Java's `ConcurrentLinkedQueue` found two errors. As far as we can determine, these errors have not previously been reported.

The code in Figure 8 gives a simple test harness that exposes one of the two errors. Initially, queue `q` contains elements 1 and 2. We expect that, because methods `add`, `remove`, and `size` should all be atomic, in any parallel, interleaved execution the call to `q.size()` must return that the queue contains one element (after `q.remove(1)` but before `q.add(3)`) or two elements (before the `remove` or after the `add`). However, it is possible for `q.size()` to incorrectly report that the queue `q` contains **three** elements!

This source of this error is that computing the number of elements in a `ConcurrentLinkedQueue` requires traversing its internal linked list structure and counting the number of elements. Suppose `thread2`'s call to `q.size()` begins its traversal, finding and counting elements 1 and 2. But, before the call sees that it is at the tail of the list, it is interrupted by `thread1`. The calls by `thread1` to `q.remove(1)` and then `q.add(3)` eliminate element 1 from the head of the list and insert element 3 at the tail of the list. Then, when `thread2`'s call to `q.size()` continues, it finds and counts element 3 and returns that queue contains three items.

Our testing found a similar error for the `toArray` method of `ConcurrentLinkedQueue`. Further, while our test harness only exercised the `add`, `remove`, `size`, and `toArray` methods of `ConcurrentLinkedQueue`, manual inspection of its source code revealed that methods `equals` and `writeObject` can similarly return non-atomic results due to iterating over the elements of the queue without checking for concurrent modifications.

We note that although `ConcurrentLinkedQueue`'s documentation[4] specifies that iteration through such a queue is only "weakly consistent", no such warning is given for methods `size`, `toArray`, `equals`, or `writeObject`. In fact, the documentation for the `size` method states:

> "Beware that, unlike in most collections, this method is NOT a constant-time operation. Because of the asynchronous nature of these queues, determining the current number of elements requires an O(n) traversal."

which seems to specify that `size`, although it requires $O(n)$ time, will return a consistent value (i.e., be linearizable). We thus judge that the unexpected behaviors of these methods are errors.

***ConcurrentSkipListMap and Set*** Our testing of benchmarks `ConcurrentSkipListMap` and `ConcurrentSkipListSet` found two violations of our semantic atomicity specifications for each benchmark. In particular, our test harnesses for these benchmarks each concurrently performs two insertions, two deletions, a call to `size()`, and a call to `toArray()` (or `keySet().toArray()` for `ConcurrentSkipListMap`). Our specification asserts that all six method calls execute semantically as if atomic, and our testing finds that neither method `size` nor method `toArray` is semantically atomic.

Note that the documentation[5] for `ConcurrentSkipListMap` and `ConcurrentSkipListSet` do warn for method `size`:

> "Additionally, it is possible for the size to change during execution of this method, in which case the returned result will be inaccurate. Thus, this method is typically not very useful in concurrent applications."

Thus, our specification is too strict in this case, as method `size` is not expected to be semantically atomic. Further, the documentation makes it clear that some bulk methods such as `equals`, `putAll`, etc., are not intended to be atomic. It is not clear from this documentation whether or not `toArray` is intended to be atomic.

```
Queue q = new ConcurrentLinkedQueue();
q.add(1);  q.add(2);
int sz = 0;

thread1:                      thread2:
 @assert_atomic {
    q.remove(1);               @assert_atomic {
 }                                sz = q.size();
 @assert_atomic {              }
    q.add(3);
 }
          bridge predicate:
             q.equals(q') && (sz == sz')
```

**Figure 8.** Simple harness for `ConcurrentLinkedQueue` that reveals an atomicity error involving `add`, `remove`, and `size`. The annotated blocks are *not* semantically linearizable with respect to the bridge predicate.

***Lock-Free List*** Our automated testing of our semantic atomicity specification for the lock-free list from [16] found one previously known error. In this lock-free list, two concurrent calls to `remove` can incorrectly both report that they have successfully deleted the same single element from a list. The online errata to [16] corrects this error.

***PJ phyl Branch-and-Bound Search*** We also found a previously-unknown atomicity error in Parallel Java benchmark `phyl`. Figure 9 presents a very simplified, high-level version of the benchmark that illustrates the nature of the error.

Benchmark `phyl` is a parallel branch-and-bound search to find a minimum-cost phylogenetic tree for a given collection of DNA sequences. The search is nondeterministic—there may exist multiple minimum-cost trees and the search could return different minimum-cost trees on different runs, depending on the thread schedule and the resulting order in which the candidate trees are evaluated.

The benchmark can be thought of as parallel `for`-loop over possible phylogenetic trees. For each tree `t`, the cost is computed and the global minimum cost `min_cost` is updated. This update is safe, as proper synchronization is used to protect updates to the minimum cost. Thus, the final value of `min_cost` will always be correct.

Updates to `min_tree`, however, are not properly synchronized. Suppose one parallel loop iteration finds a new minimum-cost tree, updates `min_cost`, and enters the body of the `if`-statement with

[3] Difficulties controlling the Java scheduler benchmark `phyl`, however, lead to extra, unwanted interruptions and thus a larger number of serial executions that must be examined.

[4] `http://download.oracle.com/javase/6/docs/api/java/util/concurrent/ConcurrentLinkedQueue.html`

[5] `http://download.oracle.com/javase/6/docs/api/java/util/concurrent/ConcurrentSkipListMap.html` and `Set.html`

```
parallel-for (t in trees) {
   @assert_atomic {
      cost = compute_cost(t)
      synchronized (min_cost) {
         min_cost = min(min_cost, cost)
      }
      if (cost == min_cost) {
         min_tree = t
      }
   }
}
      bridge predicate:
         min_tree.equals(min_tree')
            && (min_cost == min_cost')
```

**Figure 9.** Simplified version of PJ `phyl` benchmark highlighting the nature of the atomicity error found by our technique.

condition `cost == min_cost`, but is then interrupted by some other parallel loop iteration. The other iteration could further decrease `min_cost` and write to `min_tree`. But then when the first loop iteration continued, it would incorrectly overwrite `min_tree` with a tree no longer of minimal cost. Such an inconsistent value for `min_tree` cannot occur in a serial execution in which the body of iteration of the parallel `for`-loop occurs atomically.[6]

### 5.5 Discussion

***Comparison to Conflict-Serializability*** Most existing tools for detecting atomicity violations check whether executions of a test program are conflict-serializable. As discussed in Section 3.1, conflict-serializability is a strict notion of atomicity, requiring that, for each interleaved execution, there exist a serial run in which every atomic block executes the same set of conflicting read and write operations, all in the same relative order.

Column 10 of Table 1 shows that several of the data structure benchmarks had atomic blocks that were not conflict-serializable, despite being semantically linearizable. Note that this column reports the number of *static* atomic blocks found to not be conflict-serializable in at least one dynamic, parallel execution. When run on all of the interruption-bounded interleavings in our experiments, a traditional atomicity analysis based on conflict-serializability would report 100+ dynamic atomicity violations for most of these benchmark. These would all be false positives (except for the few also violating semantic atomicity) that a user would have to examine. Burckhardt et al. [2] have also found that traditional atomicity analyses produce hundreds of false warnings for similar concurrent data structures.

Every atomicity violation reported by our approach, on the other hand, indicated a real atomicity violation, leading to program results not equivalent to those of any serial execution.

***Effectiveness of Interruption-Bounded Testing*** Our experimental results demonstrate that we can find many real semantic atomicity errors by testing linearizability on interleaved executions with a small number of interruptions. There are some errors, however, that require more interruptions to detect. For example, there is a known[7] atomicity violation in the version of Java's `ConcurrentLinkedQueue` we tested (JDK 6, update 20), involving concurrent calls to `poll()` and `remove(o)`. In particular, it is possible for a call to `remove(o)` to return true—indicating that it removed object `o` from the queue—while a parallel call to `poll()` appears to remove and return the same object `o`. But this error can occur only if the call to `remove(o)` locates `o` at the head of the queue, then `poll()` interrupts and starts to (non-atomically) remove `o` from the queue, and then `remove(o)` interrupts `poll()` and finishes its remove.

***Comparison to Determinism*** The error we detect in the Parallel Java (PJ) `phyl` benchmark was missed by our previous work [3], which attempted to verify the semantic deterministic behavior of this and other benchmarks. In [3], we checked a semantic deterministic specification for the benchmark like:

```
deterministic {
   // Phylogenetic branch-and-bound search.
   ...
} assert (min_cost == min_cost');
```

This specification asserts the following. For any pair of executions $E$ and $E'$ of this code pair from initial state $\sigma_0$ to final states $\sigma$ and $\sigma'$, it must be the case that `min_cost` in $\sigma$ equals `min_cost` in $\sigma'$. That is, letting $\Phi_{\text{det}}$ denote bridge predicate `min_cost == min_cost`, it asserts:

$$\forall \sigma_0 \xrightarrow{E} \sigma.\ \forall \sigma_0 \xrightarrow{E'} \sigma'.\ \Phi_{\text{det}}(\sigma, \sigma')$$

To compare, let $\Phi_{\text{atm}}$ denote our bridge predicate `min_tree.equals(min_tree')` $\wedge$ `(min_cost == min_cost')` for semantic linearizability. Then, our semantic atomicity specification is that, for any execution $E$ from $\sigma_0$ to $\sigma$, there exists one serial execution $E'$ from $\sigma_0$ to $\sigma'$ such that $\Phi_{\text{atm}}(\sigma, \sigma')$ and $E'$ is a linearization of $E$. That is:

$$\forall \sigma_0 \xrightarrow{E} \sigma.\ \exists \sigma_0 \xrightarrow{E'} \sigma'.\ \Phi_{\text{atm}}(\sigma, \sigma')\ \wedge\ E' \text{ a linearization of } E$$

*This difference between existential and universal quantification in the specification is the core difference between the complementary notions of atomicity and determinism.* Many parallel programs are intended to be deterministic—that is, to always produce semantically equivalent output for the same input, no matter the thread schedule. Deterministic specifications can exactly capture this intended determinism. But many parallel programs employ algorithms that are inherently nondeterministic and which can correctly return different final results in different runs on the same input. For example, the branch-and-bound search PJ `phyl`, which can correctly return different minimum-cost trees depending on the nondeterministic scheduling of its threads.

For such programs, a semantic atomicity specification can be thought of as specifying the nondeterministic behavior that is acceptable or intended—the results of any serial execution of the program, in which the atomic blocks may execute in a nondeterministic order but their executions cannot be interleaved. At the same time, the specification asserts that no additional nondeterminism—from the nondeterministic interleaving of specified atomic blocks in a parallel execution—should appear in the final results of the program. That is, the result of any interleaved execution must be semantically equivalent to the result of some serial execution.

***Future Work*** Our experimental results provide promising evidence both that it is feasible to write semantic atomicity specifications for parallel applications and data structures, and that we can effectively test such specifications by checking them on interruption-bounded executions. Our parallel application benchmarks are of somewhat limited size, however, and much work remains to validate our approach on a wider range of programs. In particular, we must investigate what challenges larger applications pose to writing semantic atomicity specifications and to the scalability of our testing technique.

[6] The error in the `phyl` source is that each worker thread's call to `globalResults.addAll(results)` is not atomic. This method updates the global list of minimum-cost trees with each worker thread's list of locally-minimum-cost trees.

[7] `http://bugs.sun.com/view_bug.do?bug_id=6785442`

## 6. Related Work

A large body of work has focused on verifying and testing atomicity in multithreaded programs, including static verification via type systems [9, 10], dynamic detection of atomicity violations [1, 6, 8, 12, 36, 37], model checking of atomicity [14], and active testing [18, 30] for atomicity violations. These generally have focused on verifying that such atomic blocks are *conflict serializable* [28].

Some research efforts have focused on verifying and testing notions of atomicity that are less strict than conflict serializability of atomic sections. For example, [7] uses model checking to verify linearizable of atomic sections, but requires all atomic sections to be annotated with a linearization point which specifies the linear order in which the atomic sections must be executed in the matching serial execution. Similarly, [11] generalizes type-based verification of conflict-serializability (via reduction [22]) to account for non-conflict-serializable but side-effect-free operations like a failing compare-and-swap in a busy-waiting loop.

Another such weaker notion is *atomic-set serializability* [34], which groups storage locations into *atomic sets* and requires, for each atomic set, all atomic blocks are conflict-serializable with respect to the locations in the set. Violations of atomic-set serializability are detected dynamically by [13] and found through active testing [18, 30] by [21].

A related area of research is verifying and testing linearizability[17] for concurrent objects. A concurrent object is linearizable if, for any client program which interacts with the object only through its methods and for which all such method calls are specified to be atomic, all executions of the client are linearizable. Several efforts have manually proved linearizability for certain highly-concurrent data structures [5, 31, 32]. Further, [38], [35], Line-Up [2], and CoLT [4] model check linearizability of concurrent objects.

At a high level, our approach to testing semantic linearizability of atomic blocks is similar to the approach of Line-Up [2]. Line-Up generates all serial executions of a test harness using a given concurrent object, and then uses preemption-bounded model checking [25] to enumerate interleaved executions and to test that each such execution is equivalent to one of the pre-generated serial ones. Our approach, however, works on larger programs for which it is neither feasible to pre-generate all serial executions or to perform exhaustive preemption-bounded model checking, even with a small preemption bound. Rather, we randomly sample *interruption-bounded* interleaved executions and, for each such execution, examine only the corresponding serial executions (i.e. those with the same ordering of non-overlapping atomic blocks). Further, our approach is applicable to any program with annotated atomic blocks, not just concurrent objects, and our approach checks *semantic* linearizability.

A large body of work on *transactional memory* has developed hardware and software techniques for *implementing* atomic blocks. While such work provides hardware support, libraries, or language constructs that guarantee that blocks of code intended to be atomic are, in fact, executed atomically. Our work focuses instead on testing that a program correctly implements its intended atomicity. The kind of of semantic atomicity we test is analogous to transactional memory work on open nesting [27], transactional boosting [15], and coarse-grained transactions [20]. These lines of work achieve greater concurrency in running transactions in parallel by ignoring conflicts at the low level of reads and writes and focusing on whether data structure operations abstractly/semantically commute or conflict. For example, two calls to the `add` method of a concurrent list may conflict at both the level of individual reads and writes and when the data structure is viewed as an abstract list. But such calls can be seen to commute if the list is instead viewed as an abstract multiset.

## 7. Conclusion

The traditional notions of atomicity and linearizability require each interleaved execution to correspond to a serial execution that produces an identical final state. Our experiments show that the traditional interpretation of these properties is often too strong. Instead, we propose to allow the programmer to specify a bridge predicate that expresses a more relaxed, application-dependent notion of equivalence between the allowable final states.

The resulting semantic linearizability property is not only widely applicable but also effectively testable. We described and demonstrated experimentally one possible testing strategy, based on the observation that most atomicity bugs can be reproduced in parallel executions with a small number of atomic block interruptions, executions for which the set of candidate linear schedules is also small. This set of candidates can be further reduced by using programmer-annotated commit points in atomic blocks, to the point where in the common case we find the desired serial schedule on the first try. In our experiments all instances when a serial schedule could not be found were atomicity violations.

## Acknowledgments

We would like to thank Tayfun Elmas, Benjamin Lipshitz, our shepherd Margo Seltzer, and our anonymous reviewers for their valuable comments on this paper. This research supported in part by Microsoft (Award #024263) and Intel (Award #024894) funding and by matching funding by U.C. Discovery (Award #DIG07-10227), by NSF Grants CNS-0720906, CCF-1018729, and CCF-1018730, and by a DoD NDSEG Graduate Fellowship. Additional support comes from Par Lab affiliates National Instruments, NEC, Nokia, NVIDIA, Samsung, and Sun Microsystems.

## References

[1] R. Agarwal, A. Sasturkar, L. Wang, and S. D. Stoller. Optimized run-time race detection and atomicity checking using partial discovered types. In *Proceedings of the 20th IEEE/ACM International Conference on Automated Software Engineering (ASE)*, pages 233–242. ACM, 2005.

[2] S. Burckhardt, C. Dern, M. Musuvathi, and R. Tan. Line-Up: A complete and automatic linearizability checker. In *Proceedings of the 2010 ACM SIGPLAN Conference on Programming Language Design and Implementation (PLDI)*, pages 330–340. ACM, 2010.

[3] J. Burnim and K. Sen. Asserting and checking determinism for multithreaded programs. In *Proceedings of the 17th ACM SIGSOFT Symposium on the Foundations of Software Engineering (FSE)*, pages 3–12. ACM, 2009.

[4] P. Černý, A. Radhakrishna, D. Zufferey, S. Chaudhuri, and R. Alur. Model checking of linearizability of concurrent list implementations. In *Proceedings of the 22nd International Conference on Computer Aided Verification (CAV)*, pages 465–479. Springer, 2010.

[5] R. Colvin, L. Groves, V. Luchangco, and M. Moir. Formal verification of a lazy concurrent list-based set algorithm. In *Proceedings of the 18th International Conference on Computer Aided Verification (CAV)*, pages 475–488. Springer, 2006.

[6] A. Farzan and P. Madhusudan. Monitoring atomicity in concurrent programs. In *Proceedings of the 20th International Conference on Computer Aided Verification (CAV)*, pages 52–65. Springer, 2008.

[7] C. Flanagan. Verifying commit-atomicity using model-checking. In *Proceedings of the 11th International SPIN Workshop on Model Checking of Software*, pages 252–266. Springer, 2004.

[8] C. Flanagan and S. N. Freund. Atomizer: a dynamic atomicity checker for multithreaded programs. In *Proceedings of the 31st ACM SIGPLAN-SIGACT Symposium on Principles of Programming Languages (POPL)*, pages 256–267. ACM, 2004.

[9] C. Flanagan and S. Qadeer. A type and effect system for atomicity. In *Proceedings of the 2003 ACM SIGPLAN Conference on Programming*

*Language Design and Implementation (PLDI)*, pages 338–349. ACM, 2003.

[10] C. Flanagan and S. Qadeer. Types for atomicity. In *Proceedings of the 2003 ACM SIGPLAN International Workshop on Types in Languages Design and Implementation (TLDI)*, pages 1–12. ACM, 2003.

[11] C. Flanagan, S. N. Freund, and S. Qadeer. Exploiting purity for atomicity. *IEEE Transactions on Software Engineering*, 31(4):275–291, Apr. 2005.

[12] C. Flanagan, S. N. Freund, and J. Yi. Velodrome: a sound and complete dynamic atomicity checker for multithreaded programs. In *Proceedings of the 2008 ACM SIGPLAN Conference on Programming Language Design and Implementation (PLDI)*, pages 293–303. ACM, 2008.

[13] C. Hammer, J. Dolby, M. Vaziri, and F. Tip. Dynamic detection of atomic-set-serializability violations. In *Proceedings of the 30th ACM/IEEE International Conference on Software Engineering (ICSE)*, pages 231–240. ACM, 2008.

[14] J. Hatcliff, Robby, and M. B. Dwyer. Verifying atomicity specifications for concurrent object-oriented software using model-checking. In *Proceedings of the 5th International Conference on Verification, Model Checking and Abstract Interpretation (VMCAI)*, pages 175–190. Springer, 2004.

[15] M. Herlihy and E. Koskinen. Transactional boosting: a methodology for highly-concurrent transactional objects. In *Proceedings of the 13th ACM SIGPLAN Symposium on Principles and Practice of Parallel Programming (PPoPP)*, pages 207–216. ACM, 2008.

[16] M. Herlihy and N. Shavit. *The Art of Multiprocessor Programming*. Morgan Kaufmann Publishers, Inc., 2008.

[17] M. P. Herlihy and J. M. Wing. Linearizability: a correctness condition for concurrent objects. *ACM Transactions on Programming Languages and Systems (TOPLAS)*, 12(3):463–492, 1990.

[18] P. Joshi, M. Naik, C.-S. Park, and K. Sen. An extensible active testing framework for concurrent programs. In *Proceedings of the 21st International Conference on Computer Aided Verification (CAV)*, pages 675–681. Springer, 2009.

[19] A. Kaminsky. Parallel Java: A unified API for shared memory and cluster parallel programming in 100% Java. In *Proceedings of the 21st IEEE International Parallel and Distributed Processing Symposium (IPDPS)*, page 231. IEEE Computer Society, 2007.

[20] E. Koskinen, M. Parkinson, and M. Herlihy. Coarse-grained transactions. In *Proceedings of the 37th ACM SIGPLAN-SIGACT Symposium on Principles of Programming Languages (POPL)*, pages 19–30. ACM, 2010.

[21] Z. Lai, S. C. Cheung, and W. K. Chan. Detecting atomic-set serializability violations in multithreaded programs through active randomized testing. In *Proceedings of the 32nd ACM/IEEE International Conference on Software Engineering (ICSE)*, pages 235–244. ACM, 2010.

[22] R. J. Lipton. Reduction: A method of proving properties of parallel programs. *Communications of the ACM (CACM)*, 18(12):717–721, Dec. 1975.

[23] M. M. Michael and M. L. Scott. Simple, fast, and practical non-blocking and blocking concurrent queue algorithms. In *Proceedings of the 15th annual ACM Symposium on Principles of Distributed Computing (PDOC)*, pages 267–275. ACM, 1996.

[24] N. Mittal and V. K. Garg. Consistency conditions for multi-object distributed operations. In *Proceedings of the 18th International Conference on Distributed Computing Systems (ICDCS)*, pages 582–. IEEE Computer Society, 1998.

[25] M. Musuvathi and S. Qadeer. Iterative context bounding for systematic testing of multithreaded programs. In *Proceedings of the 2007 ACM SIGPLAN Symposium on Programming Language Design and Implementation (PLDI)*, pages 446–455. ACM, 2007.

[26] M. Musuvathi, S. Qadeer, T. Ball, G. Basler, P. A. Nainar, and I. Neamtiu. Finding and reproducing heisenbugs in concurrent programs. In *Proceedings of the 8th USENIX Symposium on Operating Systems Design and Implementation (OSDI)*, pages 267–280. USENIX Association, 2008.

[27] Y. Ni, V. S. Menon, A.-R. Adl-Tabatabai, A. L. Hosking, R. L. Hudson, J. E. B. Moss, B. Saha, and T. Shpeisman. Open nesting in software transactional memory. In *Proceedings of the 12th ACM SIGPLAN Symposium on Principles and Practice of Parallel Programming (PPoPP)*, pages 68–78. ACM, 2007.

[28] C. H. Papadimitriou. The serializability of concurrent database updates. *Journal of the ACM (JACM)*, 26(4):631–653, Oct. 1979.

[29] C.-S. Park and K. Sen. Randomized active atomicity violation detection in concurrent programs. In *Proceedings of the 16th ACM SIGSOFT International Symposium on Foundations of Software Engineering (FSE)*, pages 135–145. ACM, 2008.

[30] K. Sen. Race directed random testing of concurrent programs. In *Proceedings of the 2008 ACM SIGPLAN Conference on Programming Language Design and Implementation (PLDI)*, pages 11–21. ACM, 2008.

[31] V. Vafeiadis. Shape-value abstraction for verifying linearizability. In *Proceedings of the 10th International Conference on Verification, Model Checking, and Abstract Interpretation (VMCAI)*, pages 335–348. Springer, 2009.

[32] V. Vafeiadis, M. Herlihy, T. Hoare, and M. Shapiro. Proving correctness of highly-concurrent linearisable objects. In *Proceedings of the 11th ACM SIGPLAN Symposium on Principles and Practice of Parallel Programming (PPoPP)*, pages 129–136. ACM, 2006.

[33] R. Vallée-Rai, P. Co, E. Gagnon, L. Hendren, P. Lam, and V. Sundaresan. Soot - a Java bytecode optimization framework. In *Proceedings of the 1999 Conference of the Centre for Advanced Studies on Collaborative Research (CASCON)*, pages 13–. IBM Press, 1999.

[34] M. Vaziri, F. Tip, and J. Dolby. Associating synchronization constraints with data in an object-oriented language. In *Proceedings of the 33rd ACM SIGPLAN-SIGACT Symposium on Principles of Programming Languages (POPL)*, pages 334–345. ACM, 2006.

[35] M. Vechev, E. Yahav, and G. Yorsh. Experience with model checking linearizability. In *Proceedings of the 16th International SPIN Workshop on Model Checking Software*, pages 261–278. Springer, 2009.

[36] L. Wang and S. D. Stoller. Run-time analysis for atomicity. In *Proceedings of the 3rd Workshop on Runtime Verification (RV)*, pages 191–209. Elsevier, 2003.

[37] L. Wang and S. D. Stoller. Accurate and efficient runtime detection of atomicity errors in concurrent programs. In *Proceedings of the 11th ACM SIGPLAN Symposium on Principles and Practice of Parallel Programming (PPoPP)*, pages 137–146. ACM, 2006.

[38] J. M. Wing and C. Gong. Testing and verifying concurrent objects. *Journal of Parallel and Distributed Computing*, 17(1-2):164–182, Jan. 1993.

# Mnemosyne: Lightweight Persistent Memory

A memory is what is left when something happens and does not completely unhappen.
– Edward de Bono

Haris Volos[1], Andres Jaan Tack[2] *, Michael M. Swift[1]

[1] Computer Sciences Department, University of Wisconsin–Madison
[2] Skype Limited
[1] {hvolos, swift}@cs.wisc.edu, [2] andres.jaan.tack@skype.net

## Abstract

New storage-class memory (SCM) technologies, such as phase-change memory, STT-RAM, and memristors, promise user-level access to non-volatile storage through regular memory instructions. These memory devices enable fast user-mode access to persistence, allowing regular in-memory data structures to survive system crashes.

In this paper, we present *Mnemosyne*, a simple interface for programming with persistent memory. Mnemosyne addresses two challenges: how to create and manage such memory, and how to ensure consistency in the presence of failures. Without additional mechanisms, a system failure may leave data structures in SCM in an invalid state, crashing the program the next time it starts.

In Mnemosyne, programmers declare global persistent data with the keyword "pstatic" or allocate it dynamically. Mnemosyne provides primitives for directly modifying persistent variables and supports consistent updates through a lightweight transaction mechanism. Compared to past work on disk-based persistent memory, Mnemosyne reduces latency to storage by writing data directly to memory at the granularity of an update rather than writing memory pages back to disk through the file system. In tests emulating the performance characteristics of forthcoming SCMs, we show that Mnemosyne can persist data as fast as 3 microseconds. Furthermore, it provides a 35 percent performance increase when applied in the OpenLDAP directory server. In microbenchmark studies we find that Mnemosyne can be up to 1400% faster than alternative persistence strategies, such as Berkeley DB or Boost serialization, that are designed for disks.

***Categories and Subject Descriptors*** D.4.2 [*Operating Systems*]: Storage Management; D.4.5 [*Operating Systems*]: Reliability; D.4.8 [*Operating Systems*]: Performance

***General Terms*** Design, Languages, Performance, Reliability

***Keywords*** Persistent memory, storage-class memory, persistence, memory transactions, performance

* Work done while a student at the University of Wisconsin – Madison



*ASPLOS'11,* March 5–11, 2011, Newport Beach, California, USA.


## 1. Introduction

Fast, cheap, and persistent memory has long been a dream for computer designers. Until recently, non-volatile storage was either slow (*e.g.*, disks) or expensive (*e.g.*, NVRAM). However, several new technologies promise cheap and fast storage that survives across system boot. For example, phase-change memory (PCM) provides near-DRAM speeds and is currently available in sizes up to 64 MB, and memristors may enable multiple terabytes of non-volatile memory to be placed on-chip [61]. These devices are termed *storage-class memory* (SCM) because they provide the interface of memory (load and store instructions) but the persistence of disks.

Existing operating systems are designed for a strict bifurcation of devices into *memory*, volatile, fast devices, and random-access devices erased on reboot, and *storage*, persistent, slow block-based devices. Thus, research on SCM tends to follow the same path. For example, recent work investigates use of phase-change memory within file systems [17], or as a low-power volatile DRAM replacement [39, 34]. Neither of these approaches exposes the full power of SCM to programmers.

We propose that operating systems should expose SCM as a *persistent memory* abstraction to provide direct access to the durability of SCM technologies. This abstraction enables programmers to make in-memory data structures persistent without first converting them to a serialized format. Thus, trees, lists, and hashes can survive program and system failures. Furthermore, direct access reduces latency to storage because it bypasses many software layers, including system calls, file systems, and device drivers.

We see persistent memory not as a replacement for files, but as a fast mechanism to store moderate amounts of data. For example, Firefox 3 had a problem with calling `fsync` too frequently [19], bringing the system to a crawl by frequent flushes to disk. Persistent memory could address this problem by providing low-latency storage of moderate amounts of data. Other possible uses are configuration changes, snapshots of in-progress edits, and logs, such as in distributed agreement protocols [12]. Applications should still use files for interchanging data and for compatibility between program versions when internal data-structure layouts change.

We have three goals for our system to expose persistent memory. First, it must be simple for a programmer to declare data as persistent, and persistence must fit naturally into existing programming models for volatile data structures. Second, and more importantly, the system must support *consistent modifications* of data structures. The system must enable programmers to move data structures between consistent states, automatically recovering to such a state after a failure. Finally, we seek a design that is compatible with existing commodity processors: this enables the adoption of SCM without the processor support required by other proposals [17, 16], and avoids the chicken-and-egg problem of which comes first, SCM or processor support.

This paper presents *Mnemosyne*[1], a lightweight system for exposing persistent memory to user-mode programs. It provides a low-level programming interface, similar to C, for accessing persistent memory. Mnemosyne provides three key services that simplify programmer use of persistence. First, Mnemosyne provides *persistent memory regions*, segments of virtual memory stored in SCM rather than volatile memory. Regions can be created automatically to hold variables labeled with the keyword `pstatic` or allocated dynamically. Mnemosyne virtualizes persistent regions by swapping SCM pages to a backing file. Second, Mnemosyne provides *persistence primitives*, low-level operations that support consistently updating data. Finally, Mnemosyne provides a *durable memory transaction* mechanism that enables consistent in-place updates of arbitrary data structures.

Compared to past work on persistent memory and persistent object stores such as ObjectStore, Thor, Texas, LRVM, and QuickStore [36, 40, 56, 58, 64], Mnemosyne provides a low-level interface allowing both simple consistent updates (Section 3.2) as well as high-level transactions (Section 3.3). Upon this base, higher-level services such as garbage collection and safe references, to ensure that persistent data does not point to volatile data, can be provided by language frameworks. Furthermore, SCM enables the implementation to be much simpler as data can be made persistent without writing it out through the file system, and much lower latency by persisting data directly to memory at the granularity of an update rather than a page. The concurrently-developed NV-heaps project [16] also provides user-level transactional updates to persistent data. NV-heaps provide some features not currently found in Mnemosyne, such as type-safe pointers and garbage collection via reference counting. However, NV-heaps force the programmer to use a specific object framework and requires modifications to the processor.

We implement Mnemosyne as a pair of libraries and a small set of modifications to the Linux kernel for allocating and virtualizing SCM pages. We designed Mnemosyne to run on conventional processors, requiring no special support beyond the necessary memory controller for SCM, and implement it using regular x86 instructions with a performance emulator for SCM accesses.

In the evaluation, we show that Mnemosyne provides a simple abstraction for programmers to make data structures persistent. We compare Mnemosyne performance against Berkeley DB running on a RAM disk with the performance of phase-change memory. For small data sizes, Mnemosyne transactions perform 6–14 times better than Berkeley DB. We also convert two applications, OpenLDAP and Tokyo Cabinet, to use persistent memory and find the performance of moving existing in-memory data structures to persistent memory is 35–117 percent faster than Berkeley DB's optimized storage or flushing the whole structure to a file.

The contributions of our work are:

- A complete layered architecture for managing and exposing storage-class memory to programs.
- An exploration of mechanisms for consistent updates to in-memory data, and a library of primitives supporting consistent updates to data storage-class memory.
- A software transactional memory system that provides durability with SCM.
- A novel mechanism for atomic log writes without multiple barriers.

The rest of this paper begins with a short overview of storage-class memory technologies, followed by a high-level description of our design in Section 3. Section 4 describes the implementation of Mnemosyne, and Section 5 describes how we implement transactions in persistent memory. Section 6 demonstrates the performance and programming benefits of Mnemosyne, and we finish with related work and conclusions.

[1] Mnemosyne is the personification of memory in Greek mythology, and is pronounced *nee–moss–see–nee*.

| | Technology | Read | Write | Endurance |
|---|---|---|---|---|
| Present | DRAM | 60 ns | 60 ns | $> 10^{16}$ |
| Present | NAND Flash | 25 $\mu$s | 200–500 $\mu$s | $10^4$ - $10^5$ |
| Present | PCM | 115ns | 120 $\mu$s | $10^6$ |
| Future | PCM | 50 – 85 ns | 150 – 1000 ns | $10^8$–$10^{12}$ |
| Future | STT-RAM | 6 ns | 13 ns | $10^{15}$ |

**Table 1. Access latency and endurance (in number of overwrites) of current and future DRAM, PCM, STT-RAM, and Flash memories. Prospective characteristics are based on demonstrated prototypes. Memristor figures are not available.**

## 2. Storage-Class Memory

We use the term *storage-class memory* to refer to technologies that allow persistent storage to be attached to the memory bus and accessed through load and store instructions [25]. We do not consider flash as storage-class memory because it is only accessible as a block device through a driver.

Three recent technologies are promising implementations of SCM: phase-change memory (PCM) [39], spin-torque-transfer RAM (STT-RAM) [32], and memristors [61]. While the performance and reliability details differ, they all provide byte-granularity access and the ability to store data persistently across reboots without battery backing.

We assume, like others [17], that SCM is placed directly on the memory bus side-by-side with DRAM, allowing access through normal load/store instructions. We believe this is a reasonable design choice given that computer architects have already studied phase-change memory, a form of SCM, as a DRAM replacement in general-purpose systems [39, 53, 67].

While SCM is currently only available in small sizes, scaling projections indicate that within a few years larger sizes (*e.g.*, 1 GB) will become available. Eventually, it may be economically feasible, and perhaps cheaper, to outfit a system completely with SCM and no DRAM [39, 53, 67].

***Phase-Change Memory.*** We prototype Mnemosyne with the characteristics of PCM because it is closest to commercial deployment: Samsung recently announced that it is shipping 512 Mbit PCM chips for use in mobile devices [55]. Furthermore, its scaling properties and low power make it viable as a DRAM replacement. Table 1 shows the performance and reliability properties of PCM and flash for comparison. Compared to DRAM, currently available PCM [49] is approximately 2 times slower for read accesses and 2000 times slower for write accesses. However, access latencies for PCM, as demonstrated by research prototypes [5, 63], are expected to match those of DRAM for reads and be 2-17 times slower for writes. Furthermore, current technologies suffer from wear-out after $10^8$ writes, although many solutions for this problem have been proposed [34, 39]. These solutions change the mapping of physical address to locations in SCM to level writes across more locations. We assume such wear leveling is present and do not address it in Mnemosyne.

While memory systems for SCM are not yet available, we make several assumptions about the features they provide. First, we assume they can support an atomic write of at least 64 bits [17]. Second, we assume that it is possible to stall execution until a write has made it all the way to PCM, similar to the `fsync` call for file systems.

***Failure Models.*** While data stored in SCM is persistent, data stored in a processor cache is not. Thus, after a failure, only data actually resident in SCM survives. A system using SCM could reduce this restriction with low-level software that flushes data from the processor cache on application or OS failure. However, without battery backing, sudden loss of power or hardware faults could still cause data loss. We therefore assume that on a system failure, in-flight memory operations may fail, and that atomic updates either complete or do not modify memory.

## 3. Design

The purpose of Mnemosyne is to reduce the cost of making data persistent. Current program devote large bodies of code to formatting data for persistence, either in a file system or database, managing consistency of persistent data. They also carefully decide when to make data persistent, as writing data out to disk frequently leads to poor performance. In contrast, with Mnemosyne, a program should be able to make any data persistent, at any time, with little extra effort.

Mnemosyne presents an abstraction of persistent memory to programmers. We have three goals for the system:

1. *User-mode access* to persistence avoids the latency of entering the kernel and provides flexibility in how persistence is achieved.
2. *Consistent updates* modify persistent data without jeopardizing correctness in the presence of failures.
3. *Conventional hardware* lowers the barrier to adoption by allowing existing processors to work with new memory technologies.

Mnemosyne is designed as a low-level interface to persistent memory, providing necessary methods for consistency. It leaves the separation of volatile and persistent data and prevention of memory leaks to higher levels of software.

Mnemosyne achieves the first goal with *persistent regions*, a segment of memory that is created and virtualized by the kernel but may be accessed directly from user mode. Mnemosyne provides a two-layer solution to the second goal. The lower layer of Mnemosyne provides *persistence primitives*, which are support routines for programming with persistent memory. The upper layer of Mnemosyne provides *durable memory transactions* supported by a compiler to enable general-purpose code to create and modify persistent data structures. To satisfy the third goal, our consistent update mechanism relies on hardware primitives available in existing architectures. Figure 1 shows how the components are divided between user and kernel modes. While we designed Mnemosyne for a system with both DRAM and SCM, it applies equally well to a system that uses SCM for volatile storage as well.

### 3.1 Persistent Regions

Mnemosyne exposes storage-class memory directly to application programmers through the *persistent region* abstraction: a segment of data that user-mode code can read or write, and that survives application or system crashes. Persistent regions are mapped at fixed virtual addresses to support pointer-based data structures. This abstraction makes persistence explicit: only a portion of a process address space persists across restarts. In addition, programs must take explicit steps to guarantee persistence, such as writing data with special instructions or within a transaction to ensure data makes it all the way to SCM. However, data in a persistent region can be read and cached with regular instructions.

Mnemosyne supports both static and dynamic creation of persistent regions. A programmer can declare a C/C++ variable `pstatic`, which tells the linker to place it in a persistent region.

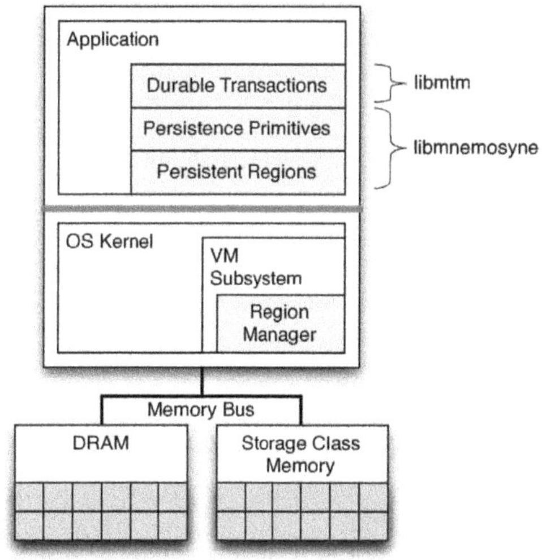


**Figure 1. Mnemosyne architecture. User-mode components layer on top of a kernel region manager.**

Similar to static variables, persistent static variables are initialized once when the program first runs, and then retain their value across invocations. A programmer can also explicitly create a persistent region with the `pmap` function, which provides functionality similar to `mmap`. While dynamic persistent regions offer programmers a generic way to store data of any size and structure, Mnemosyne also provides a persistent heap (Section 3.2.2), which enables dynamically allocated persistent variables.

Mnemosyne virtualizes regions by (i) recording the virtual–physical mapping of persistent regions in SCM, and (ii) swapping SCM pages to *backing files* that it allocates when creating a region. Thus, multiple applications can time-share or space-share access to SCM. As we discuss in Section 3.4, virtualization prevents a memory leak in one program from monopolizing a finite amount of SCM.

Static persistent regions are most appropriate for programs that allow only a single instance of the program to run per user, such as most office productivity applications and some web browsers. For programs that allow multiple simultaneous instances, Mnemosyne provides an environment variable to indicate which backing file contains the data for this instance.

Mnemosyne lets programmers annotate the target of a pointer type as persistent with the `persistent` keyword, which functions similar to the `const` keyword. The annotation has a shallow effect on the target: annotating a target as persistent does not indicate that its members persistent. The annotation also has no control over whether the data is allocated in volatile or persistent memory. It only serves as an indication to the compiler of the persistence type of the target, which can be used to identify potentially dangerous assignments of volatile address to a `persistent` pointer, and vice versa. This ensures that persistent data, which survives restarts, does not refer to volatile data that is lost. However, this cannot detect when the only pointer to persistent data is *stored in* volatile memory; in this case, the persistent data could be leaked if the program crashes.

### 3.2 Consistent Updates

Persistence requires a mechanism for application programmers to update persistent data in without risking corruption after a failure. File systems use a variety of techniques to ensure consistency, such as shadow updates [8, 54, 17], journaling [62], soft updates [42], and post-reboot checking [43]. We seek to give programmers similar flexibility in implementing consistency.

A *consistent update* is a transformation that takes data from one consistent state to another consistent state; an update may contain any number of store and load instructions. For example, in a hash table, a consistent update may be the addition of a new value.

#### 3.2.1 Ensuring consistency

The primary mechanism for ensuring consistency is *ordering writes*, for example to ensure that new data exists before changing a pointer to reference the new data. We identify four common mechanisms for consistently updating data in Table 2 in increasing order of flexibility. The more specific mechanisms can provide higher performance for certain data structures, while the more general mechanisms support a wider range of usage patterns. Mnemosyne supports all four methods.

**Single variable update.** The simplest update is atomically writing to a single variable. This is useful for recording when a program has been initialized or for storing statistics such as counters. These updates are totally ordered with respect to each other.

**Append updates.** An append update is used by logs and writes new data to empty space after the previous update, thus never modifying existing data. The individual stores comprising an append update are unordered, but separate appends must complete in order. After a failure, an incomplete append (there can be only one) is discarded.

**Shadow updates.** Similar to append updates, a shadow update writes all data to a new location. Once new data is persistent, the program atomically modifies the reference to the old data to refer to the new data. While there are no ordering constraints between the stores writing the new data, the reference can only be modified after the new data has completed writing. Shadow updates work best for tree-like structures where data is reachable through a single pointer, and must allocate new memory for every update. After a failure, a program must find and release unreferenced new data.

**In-place updates.** An in-place update can modify any data structure, such as a doubly linked list or a B-tree. It ensures consistency with transactions that undo or complete changes after a failure. As a result, the program must make a copy of either the old data for rolling back, or the new data for rolling forward. Stores updating a data structure must be ordered after stores that create the copy. Unlike the preceding consistency mechanisms, in-place updates can be used to modify any data structure and therefore enable existing volatile structures to be persistent. However, they perform worse than other consistency methods because they copy data for recovery.

#### 3.2.2 Persistence Primitives

Mnemosyne provides a set of *persistence primitives*, which are low-level operations that enable programmers to implement these consistency mechanisms. At the lowest level, Mnemosyne provides hardware primitives for writing data persistently and ordering writes (described next), which is useful for single variable updates. The system also provides a *persistent heap* for allocating small blocks of memory. Allocated memory and the size of allocations persist across program invocations, so memory can be allocated during one invocation and freed during the next. The persistent heap supports shadow updates by providing space for new data. Mnemosyne also provides a *log facility* to support append-only updates. The log provides a simple double-ended buffer, allowing consistent appends to the tail of the log and truncation at the head of the log.

#### 3.2.3 Mapping consistency onto hardware

A key challenge in implementing consistent updates is ensuring that data reaches SCM in the right order. Unlike disks, which are only accessed through software, SCM is attached to the memory bus and is subject to caching by the processor. While the cache can greatly improve read and write performance, it can also reorder updates to SCM: the cache may evict cached data at any time and in any order. Thus, if a program accesses SCM like normal memory, updates may not be consistent. Prior work on SCM addresses this problem with hardware support for programs to express ordering constraints [17]. However, the proposed hardware requires extensive modifications to processor caches, including an additional *epoch* tag per cache line and the ability to globally flush all caches lines in an epoch.

Mnemosyne's consistent updates mechanism exposes explicit commands to write data persistently and consistently. It relies on three hardware primitives found in most processors [33]: (i) *write-through stores*, which write data directly to memory rather than to the cache, (ii) *fences*, which prevent subsequent writes from completing before preceding writes, and (iii) *flushes*, which writes a cache line out to memory. Durable updates to persistent memory are implemented as write-through stores, ensuring that they will not be delayed by caching. If a program wishes to separate durability from writing data, so it may re-read data before it becomes durable, it can use a regular store and then flush the data later. Mnemosyne guarantees ordering constraints by issuing a fence between ordered updates, ensuring that a later update will not become persistent before an earlier update. In addition, a program wishing to stall until data is persistent can also use a fence.

### 3.3 Durable Memory Transactions

Mnemosyne provides *durable memory transactions* to support in-place updates. Leveraging recent advances in transactional memory, Mnemosyne provides a compiler to convert regular C/C++ code into transactions. A programmer places the `atomic` keyword before a block of code that updates a persistent data structure, and the compiler produces code that passes all memory references to a transaction system.

The transaction system ensures that all modifications are *atomic* and *durable*, so updates from committed transactions will survive restarts and uncommitted transactions roll back, and *isolated*, so no transaction can see intermediate states of other transactions. Unlike the checkpoint mechanism used by some previous persistent memory systems [17, 58], transactions thus allow multiple threads to concurrently update different data structures.

### 3.4 Persistent Memory Leaks

Memory leaks of volatile data may cause a program to crash, but can often be repaired by restarting the program. In contrast, leaks of persistent memory may use all the SCM in a system and be fatal to a program. Mnemosyne provides two mechanisms to help prevent leaks. During allocation, Mnemosyne requires that programs provide a persistent pointer to receive the memory, thereby ensuring that memory is not lost if a crash happens. Second, Mnemosyne virtualizes persistent memory by swapping it to files. This ensures that a leak in one program only affects that program and does not reduce the availability of persistent memory to other programs. When leaks do occur, a program can recover by allocating a new persistent region and then copying live data from the existing regions into the new region.

In addition, there are a variety of language-level techniques for preventing leaks, including conservative garbage collection [7], and smart pointers that perform reference counting as demonstrated by other persistent stores [40, 58, 64, 16].

| Method | Ordering constraints within update | | Data structures |
|---|---|---|---|
| | Count | Description | |
| Single variable update | 0 | None | flag, pointer |
| Append update | 0 | None | log, extent |
| Shadow update | 1 | Store modifying reference ordered after stores writing data | tree, bitmap |
| In-place update | N-1 | Stores modifying original data ordered after stores making copy | any |

**Table 2. Methods for consistently updating persistent memory and the number of ordering requirements within an update.**

# 4. Implementation

This section describes the implementation of Mnemosyne for Linux. The system consists of (i) kernel modifications to expose and virtualize storage-class memory, (ii) libraries to implement persistent regions, persistence primitives and the transaction system, and (iii) a compiler/linker that supports persistent variables and transactions. We implement our system for x86-64 Linux version 2.6.33.

The total implementation is comprised of about 450 new lines of kernel code and 10,050 lines of user-mode library code, not including comments. The user-mode code is further broken down into 3,500 lines for implementing persistent regions and persistence primitives, 3,100 lines for implementing the persistent heap, and 3,450 lines for implementing the transaction system.

## 4.1 Hardware Platform

Mnemosyne provides four memory primitives for consistently updating persistent data. As described in Section 3.2, we rely on two fundamental operations, *write through* and *fence*, to order updates and to guarantee that updates have reached memory. In addition, Mnemosyne provides a *store* operation, to update persistent memory in the cache, and *flush* to force cached data out to SCM. These allow data written to the cache immediately so it can be returned by later loads, and asynchronously flushed to SCM.

Given the long latency of PCM operations, a goal for the primitives is high throughput by batching multiple operations. We rely on the x86 *write-combining buffers*, which are provided for high-speed data streaming [2]. Write combining allows data to be stored temporarily in a buffer and merged with other data writes to the cache block before the processor writes them to memory. These buffers allow the processor to write multiple words in a single bus transaction to effectively utilize memory bandwidth. The block size is usually that of the cache line, and is 64 bytes on our platform. Without using these buffers, writes to the same cache line would require separate bus transactions and sacrifice performance.

The write-through operation issues streaming writes to the write-combining buffers with the `movntq` instruction. Fences use the `mfence` instruction, which delays execution until write-combining buffers have been flushed. Thus, any memory access after the fence waits until the data has been written stably to SCM. For regular writes, `store()` just invokes `mov`, and `flush()` issues a `clflush` (flush cache line). These operations are all implemented as macros for performance.

## 4.2 Persistent Regions

The Mnemosyne persistent region abstraction is provided by a combination of kernel support, library support, and compiler support for declaring persistent variables. As shown in Table 3, Mnemosyne provides both static and dynamic persistent regions. Static regions contain persistent global variables that are declared and initialized by a programmer at compilation time. A programmer declares a global variable as persistent by annotating it using the `pstatic` keyword. This keyword inserts a compile-time annotation with the `__attribute__ ((section("persistent")))`. The static linker coalesces all persistent variables into a single `.persistent` ELF section in the executable.

Programmers create dynamic persistent regions at runtime by calling the `pmap` function, similar to memory mapping files with `mmap`. Mnemosyne automatically maps dynamic regions created by the program on previous invocations into the address space when it initializes. To prevent newly created sections from being lost if the application crashes, the `pmap` function takes as an in/out parameter a persistent variable to receive the region's address. A programmer deletes a persistent region by calling the `punmap` function, which takes the starting address and the length of the region.

Mnemosyne lets programmers annotate pointer targets with the `persistent` keyword. This keyword inserts a compile-time annotation with the `__attribute__ ((address_space(1)))`. This annotation is interpreted by the Sparse semantic parser [1], which designates such annotated pointer targets in address space *1* and all other pointer targets in address space *0*. Sparse essentially treats pointers with identical target types but different address spaces as distinct types, and warns about code that mixes pointers to different address spaces. This allows Mnemosyne to identify code that accidentally assigns a pointer to persistent data to volatile data instead (and vice versa).

Persistent regions present two challenges: how to ensure that mappings are persistent, and how to virtualize a finite amount of SCM to support use by many applications. For regular volatile memory, pages are swapped to a shared page file or swap partition and mappings are deleted when a program terminates. However, for persistent regions the mappings of virtual addresses to physical SCM pages must survive system restarts. In addition, data swapped out of SCM must also survive system restarts.

Our implementation follows a two-layered approach. A kernel-mode layer, the *region manager*, exposes SCM to user-mode code as a memory-mapped file. A user-mode layer, *libmnemosyne*, associates each persistent region with a specific file and records the address of each region.

***Region manager.*** The region manager is an extension of the existing Linux virtual memory system. The region manager creates a new zone of memory for SCM, and all allocations for persistent regions come from this zone using the existing Linux page allocator. We add a new flag, `MAP_PERSIST`, to the `mmap` system call implementation to indicate that a file should be mapped to SCM and not DRAM. The region manager records the list of virtual pages currently stored in SCM in the *persistent mapping table*. This table, stored at the base of physical SCM, stores triples of the form $\langle scm_{fn}, i, p_{off} \rangle$, which associate an SCM frame's number $scm_{fn}$ with a page offset $p_{off}$ in the file identified by inode $i$[2].

The region manager reconstructs persistent regions when the OS boots. It scans the persistent mapping table and (i) updates the Linux page descriptor for each mapped SCM page, and (ii) creates a VFS inode for the backing file of every mapping. The manager places SCM frames not in the table on a free list. After boot, the page descriptors and inodes enable the kernel to evict SCM pages to their proper files. When starting a process with persistent regions, all accesses to SCM pages already in memory are treated as soft page faults that update the page table without copying data from

[2] Uniquely identifying a file requires two extra pieces of information: device and inode generation numbers, which we omit for clarity of discussion.

| Class | API | Description | Section |
|---|---|---|---|
| **H/W primitives** | flush(addr) | Writes back and invalidates the cache line that contains the linear address *addr*. | 4.1 |
| | store(addr, val) | Writes value *val*. | 4.1 |
| | wtstore(addr, val) | Writes value *val* to SCM. | 4.1 |
| | fence() | Prevents subsequent writes from completing before preceding writes. | 4.1 |
| **Persistent regions** | `pstatic` var | Allocates the variable *var* in the static region. | 4.2 |
| | pmap(addr, len, prot, flags) | Creates a dynamic region. | 4.2 |
| | punmap(addr, len) | Deletes part or all of a dynamic region. | 4.2 |
| | type `persistent` * ptr | Declares the target of the pointer *ptr* as persistent. | 4.2 |
| **Persistent heap** | pmalloc(sz, ptr) | Sets *ptr* to point to a newly allocated persistent memory chunk of size *sz*. | 4.3 |
| | pfree(ptr) | Deallocates the persistent memory chunk pointed by *ptr* and then nullifies *ptr*. | 4.3 |
| **Log** | log_create(flags, cbf) | Creates a log. | 4.4 |
| | log_append(rec) | Writes record *rec* by appending it at the end of the log. | 4.4 |
| | log_flush() | Blocks until all prior writes to the log reach SCM. | 4.4 |
| | log_truncate() | Drops any records written to the log. | 4.4 |
| **Durable transactions** | atomic {...} | Atomically updates persistent state. | 5 |

**Table 3. Summary of Mnemosyne's programming interface, including low-level operations implemented with processor instructions and high-level APIs for managing persistent regions.**

the backing file. During process execution, the region manager may swap persistent memory pages back to the file system if there is memory pressure.

***libmnemosyne.*** The libmnemosyne library creates and records the persistent regions for a process. Mnemosyne allocates all regions in a one terabyte *reserved range* of virtual address space (easily changed to any power-of-two sized region). This allows a quick determination of whether an address refers to persistent data and prevents persistent regions from conflicting with dynamically allocated address space. The library reserves 16KB in the static persistent region to store a *region table* containing the process's persistent regions. If the region table exceeds 16KB, it can overflow to a dynamically allocated page.

To create a dynamic region, the `pmap` function in libmnemosyne creates an empty backing file and invokes `mmap` to map the file into SCM. In the region table, libmnemosyne records the tuple $\langle r_{addr,len}, b, m \rangle$ that associates the region's starting address *addr* and length *len*, with the backing file *b*, and metadata *m*, which includes protection flags. The region table also serves as an intention log: libmnemosyne writes a flag indicating the successful completion of a `pmap` operation. When an application starts, libmnemosyne recreates previously allocated persistent regions and destroys partially created ones.

For the static regions containing variables labeled `pstatic`, libmnemosyne creates a new backing file the first time the program executes. It populates the new region with the initial values found in the executable. If a program wishes to discard existing contents of a static persistent region and revert to the data in the executable, a program can delete the backing file and restart. Static persistent variables serve as pointers into dynamically allocated persistent regions.

All the region backing files, including the region table's file, are stored by default in the program's current working directory. This location can be changed via the environment configuration variable `MNEMOSYNE_REGION_PATH`, thus allowing multiple concurrent instances of the same program to use separate backing files.

### 4.3 Memory allocation

Mnemosyne provides a persistent heap [3] in libmnemosyne. Table 3 lists the programming interface to this heap. Similar to `pmap`, the `pmalloc` call takes a persistent pointer as an argument to ensure that memory is not leaked if the system fails just after an allocation. The `pfree` call takes a pointer to a persistent pointer as an argument to ensure that the persistent pointer does not continue to point to the deallocated chunk of memory if the system fails just after a deallocation.

We base our implementation on two popular volatile memory allocators, Hoard [6] and dlmalloc [38], which we modify to allocate from a persistent region. While Hoard was originally designed for use in multiprocessor environments, we leverage its superblock-based structure to minimize the persistent state required to track allocations. Hoard splits the heap into superblocks, which are fixed-size regions containing an array of fixed-size blocks (different superblocks may have different block sizes). We modify Hoard to store a *persistent bitmap vector* per superblock to track allocated blocks; allocating memory requires only one write to SCM to set a bit in the superblock's vector. We separate bitmap vectors from allocated data to reduce the risk of corruption [41]. Hoard's indexes, which speed allocation, are in volatile memory and must be regenerated when a program starts. The allocator guarantees atomicity of its operations by logging the write to the bitmap vector and the destination/source pointer.

Mnemosyne uses the modified Hoard allocator for requests smaller than a superblock (8 KB). If the requested block is larger, Mnemosyne falls back to dlmalloc, which we chose for its scalability to large block sizes. Since we expect dlmalloc to be infrequently used, we have not modified it except to add logging to ensure allocations are atomic.

### 4.4 Logging

Mnemosyne relies on a log to make memory allocations and transactions atomic. This log is exposed to programmers by libmnemosyne for implementing append-only data structures. Table 3 lists the log programming interface. A program writes to the log with `log_append`, which writes data but does not guarantee persistence. The `log_flush` call ensures all prior log writes are persistent. Finally, logs are truncated with `log_truncate`. A program can synchronously truncate the log by interspersing truncates with appends in a single thread. Alternatively, the application can asynchronously truncate the log from another thread, which moves the latency of truncating off the critical path. In addition, a program may truncate logs at startup. Mnemosyne's durable transaction mechanism supports all three uses.

We implemented a high-performance *raw word log* (RAWL) and associated manager that logs uninterpreted word-size values. Such a semantic-free log can be the basis for other semantic-rich logs, such as journals. The log is implemented as a fixed size single-consumer/single-producer Lamport circular buffer, which allows simultaneous appends and truncations without locking [37]. The log manager implements functions to access the log and recover log contents after a failure.

The main challenge in implementing a log is maximizing performance while ensuring that appends are atomic. As logs are

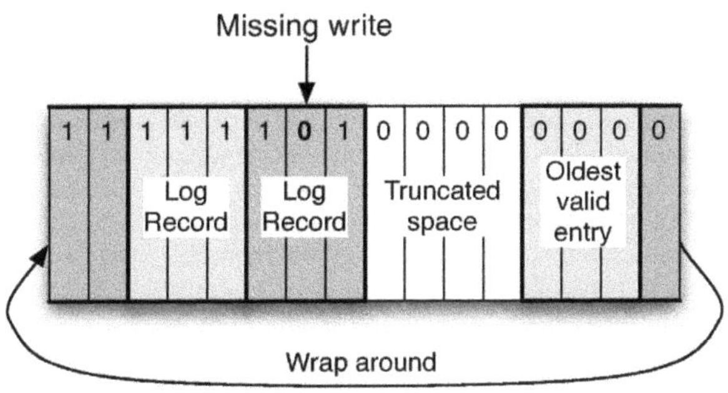


**Figure 2. Example of missing write detection in the RAWL. Entries written on the current pass through the log have a torn bit of '1', while entries written the previous pass have a '0'. A missing write is detected by an incorrect torn bit.**

always written sequentially, Mnemosyne uses the x86 streaming write instruction `movntq` to write log data. To achieve high performance, these instructions do not guarantee that writes are executed in program order. If the system crashes, later writes may have completed while earlier ones did not. When restarting, the log manager must identify whether all the writes that comprise an append operation completed. This problem is similar to the torn-write problem in databases and file systems, where only part of a multi-sector write completes. The common solution in file systems is to use two fences: write the data, wait for the data writes to complete with a fence, then write a commit record, and wait for the commit record to complete with a fence. A second option is to append a checksum of the data [51]. However, both these techniques have high overhead. Commit records require two long-latency fences, and checksumming adds substantial overhead to every write.

Mnemosyne instead implements a novel *tornbit RAWL* that requires only one fence. The tornbit RAWL reserves a single *torn bit* in every 64-bit word. This bit has the same value for all writes in one pass over the log buffer, and reverses sense when the log is overwritten. Thus, completely written log entries will have the same torn bit, while incomplete entries will mix values. Figure 2 demonstrates the use of torn bits. When Mnemosyne creates a log, it initializes the memory to zeroes. The log manager treats the incoming 64-bit words to be written to the log as a stream of bits. It forms and writes out to the log 64-bit words that are composed of 63 bits taken from the head of the stream and the proper torn bit. On a `log_flush` the log manager writes out to the log any bits left in the stream. Upon recovery, Mnemosyne locates the head of the log and scans forward until it reaches the end of the log, where the torn bit reverses, or until it finds a log word with an out-of-sequence torn-bit, indicating a partial write.

### 4.5 Limitations

**Shared Memory.** The recovery mechanisms used for logging and memory allocation execute when a process starts. Furthermore, the allocator caches index information in volatile memory for performance. Therefore, these mechanisms may be unsafe if a persistent region is shared between processes. However, sharing is safe if the processes cooperate to ensure that (i) within each region, only one process writes to a log or allocates from a heap, and (ii) both processes have started and completed recovery before accessing shared data. Thus, producer-consumer style communication, where a single process is responsible for creating and later deleting work items, can be implemented safely.

**Wearout.** Our prototype implementation does not address wearout of storage-class memory. However, virtualization enables remapping heavily used virtual pages to spread writes to different physical PCM frames. Additionally, our system's structures, such as mapping tables and RAWL, may be relocated to spread writes around. For example, RAWL's tornbits may periodically be shifted to avoid writing 0's and 1's continuously to the same bits. Finally, our system could benefit from work on wear-leveling mechanisms that reduce wearout of PCM when that technology is used as DRAM replacement in main-memory systems [34, 52].

```
update_hash(key, value) {
  atomic {
    pmalloc(&bucket, sizeof(*bucket));
    bucket->key = key;
    bucket->value = value;
    insert(bucket);
  }
}
```

**Figure 3. Example of a durable memory transaction.**

## 5. Durable Memory Transactions

Mnemosyne supports in-place updates with *durable memory transactions*. Updates within a transaction execute to completion, at which point the changes persist across failures, or the changes are rolled back upon restart. Figure 3 shows an example use of the `atomic` block language construct to form a transaction (Table 3).

Memory transactions are implemented by three components: a compiler to create transactions from ordinary C or C++ code, a transaction system to store data necessary for recovery, and a transaction log. The *libmtm* library provides the transaction system on top of the persistence primitives in libmnemosyne.

**Compiler.** We use Intel's STM Compiler [48] to automatically generate object code with calls into a transaction system. The compiler emits compiled code that invokes the transaction system when a transaction begins, commits, and on every memory reference within the transaction.

**Transaction system.** Mnemosyne transactions are based on TinySTM [24] a lightweight software transactional memory (STM) implementation. The Mnemosyne transaction system implements *lazy version management* [46] with write-ahead redo logging, and *eager conflict detection* [46] with encounter-time locking.

With write-ahead redo logging, new values written during the transaction and their addresses are added to a log and also buffered in volatile memory. The transaction system performs a quick range check against the reserved persistent address range and logs only writes to persistent memory. At commit, the log is flushed to SCM, and the new values can optionally be written back. During a transaction, memory at a variable's address still contains unmodified values. When called to read data, the transaction system checks whether the data was modified. If so, it returns the new data from the buffer and if not returns the value from memory.

We implement write-ahead redo logging because it reduces the ordering constraints on writes to SCM: the only requirement is that the log is written completely before any data values are updated. In contrast, undo logging, where old values are written to a log and new values are written to memory, would require ordering a log write before every memory update. However, buffering writes has a performance cost: transaction commits are slower because the new values have to be written out to memory, and reads within transactions have to check if new values exist.

For encounter-time locking, we use a global array of volatile locks, with each lock covering a portion of the address space. When accessing a memory location, the transaction first identifies the lock that covers the memory address, and if it does not own the lock it tries to acquire it. If successful, the transaction brings the lock in its lock-set and continues with the access. Otherwise, the transaction aborts by releasing all locks acquired, discarding any buffered updates, and writing to the log a mark to indicate the transaction as aborted. When a program starts, Mnemosyne replays all completed transactions by writing the data at the logged address.

**Transaction log.** We implement the redo log in persistent memory using a RAWL. The transaction log can be truncated after data values are forced to SCM. We implement both *synchronous* and *asynchronous* truncation. Synchronous truncation forces new values to memory during transaction commit. After flushing the log, the transaction system walks the buffer of modified data and calls `flush` on every address written. It then truncates the entire log. Under heavy load, this prevents the transaction log from growing too large. Asynchronous truncation retains the log after transaction commit, so the latency of committing is shorter. A separate log manager thread consumes the log and forces values out to memory before truncating the log. However, if the log manager thread is unable to execute, program threads may stall until there is free log space.

For better multiprocessor scalability, Mnemosyne keeps a per-thread log. This slightly complicates recovery as Mnemosyne must ensure that transactions are redone in the order executed by the program. Mnemosyne relies on TinySTM's existing global timestamp counter, which is incremented at every transaction completion. Mnemosyne captures a total order over transactions by storing this global counter along with each transaction in the log. During recovery, transactions from different threads are replayed in counter order.

**Discussion.** The cost of durable transactions is two writes to SCM for every update: once to store recovery information in the log, and once to write the data itself. Other consistent-update mechanisms may perform better. But, they come at the cost of increased complexity, such as recovery code to replay logs for append-only updates, garbage collection for memory lost during shadow updates, and explicit fences to order updates.

## 6. Evaluation

The goal of Mnemosyne is to abstract storage-class memory at low latency for program use. We evaluate three questions about the system:

1. *Does it work?* Can existing programs benefit from persistent memory, and does Mnemosyne provide persistence across crashes?
2. *How fast is it?* How does Mnemosyne perform, both in latency and throughput, across a range of workloads, and how beneficial are Mnemosyne's mechanisms?
3. *With which technologies can it work?* How does Mnemosyne's performance depend on the latency of the underlying SCM technology?

While programmers may program directly with persistence primitives, they require a sophisticated understanding of recovery protocols similar to databases or file systems [8, 45]. Durable transactions provide a much simpler interface to persistent memory and require few application changes, so we concentrate our evaluation on transaction performance.

### 6.1 Methodology

Because real memory systems based on PCM are not available, we developed a simple performance emulator based on DRAM to evaluate performance of our system. There are a wide variety of projections for PCM's performance, and the specific design of the memory system can have a great impact on performance [39]. So, we limit our emulation to the most important aspect of performance: slow writes.

To account for PCM's slower writes relative to DRAM, we introduce a delay after each write into the hardware access macros. The emulator adds delays on operations that already go to DRAM (not the cache), so the delay is only for the *additional latency* of PCM. For cacheable writes (`store` operations) we insert the delay on the subsequent `flush`, while for non-cacheable ones we insert the delay in-place. We also insert the delay after each memory fence to account waiting for outstanding writes to PCM. For sequential write-through (`wtstore`) we model write bandwidth by inserting a proper delay after the write sequence completes to limit the effective bandwidth.

In all cases we implement the delay with a loop that reads the processor's timestamp counter (TSC) in each iteration. The loop continues until the requested delay has elapsed. In calibration tests, we found that inserted delays are at least equal to the target delay, and that our bandwidth model is accurate to within 4%.

Our emulator does not account for additional latency on loads. However, the primary benefit of SCM is fast, durable updates, and our workloads focus on write rather than read performance. Furthermore, many loads will hit the cache, so only misses will incur a penalty from PCM. Also, our model does not account for the effect of cache evictions or read-after-write bank conflicts, where reads may be queued behind long writes to the same bank, thus increasing read latency.

To compare Mnemosyne against other uses of PCM, we constructed an emulator, *PCM-disk*, for a PCM-based block device. Base on Linux's RAM disk (`brd` device driver), PCM disk introduces delays when writing a block. We model block writes using sequential write-through operations as described above, and mount an ext2 file system.

We performed our experiments on an Intel Core 2 quad-core based machine equipped with 4GB of physical DRAM (accessible via the DDR2-800 interface) running our modified x86-64 Linux version 2.6.33 kernel at 2.5GHz. All tests add 150 ns of extra latency and are limited to 4GB/s of write bandwidth unless otherwise noted. We estimated write bandwidth based on projections provided by Numonyx [21]. For all our experiments we report averages of at least five runs.

### 6.2 Applications use of Persistent Memory

Applications that can immediately benefit from persistent memory are difficult to find: the long latency of writing to disk has taught programmers to avoid frequently committing data. We expect that a common use will be for applications to create a useful in-memory data structure, such as a tree or hash table, and then make it persistent by allocating it from a persistent heap and wrapping updates in transactions. For reliability and to support conversion between program versions, the program should periodically export serialized version of the structure.

We model this use of persistent memory by adapting programs that *already* maintain a fast in-memory data structure for frequent access and a separate version for consistent, durable updates. We converted two programs that take different approaches to persistence for use with Mnemosyne: OpenLDAP and Tokyo Cabinet. One program frequently commits data to disk using a storage manager, and the other periodically snapshots a whole data structure to disk.

**OpenLDAP.** OpenLDAP is an implementation of the Lightweight Directory Access Protocol (LDAP). OpenLDAP supports a number of storage backends; the default is *back-bdb*, which provides transactional storage using Berkeley DB. An alternative, *back-ldbm*, also uses Berkeley DB but without transactions; instead, it periodically asks Berkeley DB to flush dirty data to disk to mini-

| Application | Backend | Workload | Updates/s |
|---|---|---|---|
| OpenLDAP | back-bdb on PCM-disk | SLAMD | 5428 |
| | back-ldbm on PCM-disk | | 6024 |
| | back-mnemosyne | | 7350 |
| Tokyo Cabinet | `msync` on PCM-disk | 64B | 19,382 |
| | | 1024B | 2,044 |
| | Mnemosyne | 64B | 42,057 |
| | | 1024B | 30,361 |

**Table 4. Update throughput for OpenLDAP and Tokyo Cabinet.**

mize the window of vulnerability. To improve query performance, each backend maintains its own cache of data outside Berkeley DB [14]. We believe that such read-mostly caches can benefit from lightweight persistent memory: the backing store can be removed, leaving only a persistent cache.

To test this hypothesis, we modified the back-ldbm backend to remove Berkeley DB and to make the cache persistent with durable transactions. The cache is organized using an AVL tree, which we make persistent by allocating nodes with `pmalloc` and placing `atomic` blocks around updates in four places.

While we do not generally encourage keeping pointers to volatile memory in a persistent region, we found this useful in OpenLDAP. The cache entries of the original back-ldbm and our back-mnemosyne store pointers to a description of each attribute, which is kept by the front end in volatile memory. Instead of modifying the frontend to keep those descriptions in persistent memory, we found it more convenient to keep the descriptions in volatile memory and have the persistent cache entry keep pointers to those volatile descriptions. Because the volatile descriptions become stale after a restart, we augmented each cache entry with a version number that is used to determine whether the persistent pointer is up-to-date.

We use the SLAMD distributed load generation engine to exercise three versions of the server: (1) *back-bdb*, the default unmodified transactional backend with the cache and Berkeley DB, (2) *back-ldbm*, the unmodified back-ldbm backend with the cache and Berkeley DB, and (3) *back-mnemosyne*, our modified backend based on back-ldbm. We set the cache sizes large enough to avoid evictions due to capacity. We used a LDIF template to generate a workload of 100,000 directory entries.

**TokyoCabinet.** Tokyo Cabinet is a high-performance key-value store [31]. It stores data in a B+ tree and periodically calls `msync` on a memory-mapped file to flush modified pages to disk. These syncs can reduce performance by 96 percent [47], so they are rarely invoked. As a result, the application loses unsaved data after a crash.

We modified Tokyo Cabinet to allocate its B+ tree in a persistent region and perform updates in durable transactions. While we re-used the existing update code, in several cases we had to duplicate functions to create separate persistent and volatile versions with different allocators. We completely removed the persistence code that calls `msync`. We also removed the locks used for synchronizing concurrent accesses to the tree and relied on transactions for concurrency control.

**Performance.** Table 4 lists throughput of the OpenLDAP server for a workload that adds new records. OpenLDAP is configured to run with 16 threads (4 threads per core) as advised by its tuning manual. While the three backends perform similarly, back-ldbm offers a lower level of reliability than the other two backends. This close performance arises because PCM is fast enough that the time to write updates is a small fraction of the total time to service a request. These results demonstrate that with Mnemosyne it may not be necessary to create specialized structures optimized for persistence, such as Berkeley DB's tables. Instead, standard in-memory data structures (in this case an AVL tree) provide simpler programming, in addition to durability and consistency, all with similar or better performance than a highly tuned storage engine.

Table 4 also shows the throughput of 64-byte and 1024-byte insert/delete queries with Tokyo Cabinet for single-thread configurations. As a comparison, we ran the standard implementation of Tokyo Cabinet on our PCM-disk emulator and configured it to save data with `msync` after every update. Mnemosyne was about 2 – 15 times faster in these tests, while at the same time providing *stronger* consistency guarantees than the `msync` version, which can suffer from torn writes if the system fails while flushing pages. For multiple-thread runs, we found that the throughput of Tokyo Cabinet Mnemosyne degrades by 9% because of increased contention on the tree, causing transactions to abort. The throughput of Tokyo Cabinet on PCM-disk increases by 10%, but is still far below Mnemosyne.

**Reliability.** We validate that Mnemosyne works correctly by injecting synthetic failures. We intentionally crashed OpenLDAP in the middle of a transaction, and verified that after every restart, the data affected by the transaction were still available. In addition, we wrote a crash stress program, which uses transactions to perform random updates to memory using a known seed. We verified that after a crash, memory contains the correct random values. Finally, we tested the torn-bit feature of the RAWL by injecting bit flips into the log before a crash. In all cases, Mnemosyne correctly recovered after the crash.

### 6.3 Microbenchmark Performance

Programmers wishing to persist in-memory data structures today have a wide variety of choices. We evaluate two common approaches: (i) use a storage manager for data storage and caching, and (ii) serialize the data structure to a file. With a storage manager such as Berkeley DB [59], a program can commit small changes to a data structure, such as adding a record to a hash table. We compare the performance of a simple hash table [15]. using Mnemosyne transactions for persistence against using Berkeley DB's hash table. We store the database files on our PCM-disk emulator. In both cases, data is committed to storage on every update.

Figures 4 and 5 compare write latency and update throughput of Mnemosyne to Berkeley DB for different number of threads and record sizes. Deletes are introduced at the same rate as writes to ensure steady progress. Update throughput is aggregate throughput of writes and deletes. For single threaded runs and transactions that update records smaller than 2048B, Mnemosyne's direct access of memory achieves a write latency that is almost six times better than Berkeley DB. Mnemosyne's performance for small transactions is limited by the cost of (i) transaction instrumentation in the code, which adds a function call to every load and store, (ii) fences to force the log to memory and (iii) flushes to force data to memory. With a microbenchmark, we measured the cost of instrumenting and logging each word written as 190 ns when the transaction's write set size is smaller than 128 cache lines. For larger write sets, this cost increases linearly with the number of distinct cache lines written. The cost of committing a transaction, which consists of a fence and flushing data out to SCM, adds up to 250 ns per distinct cache line flushed. These costs represent the overhead of supporting in-place updates. A hash table insert of 64 bytes requires on average 15 updates to 5 distinct cache lines, for a total cost of 4.3 $\mu$s. With larger data sizes, Berkeley DB's optimizations for disk-like performance, such as large sequential writes and infrequent fences (once per block in PCM-disk), give it better write latency.

With multiple threads, Mnemosyne achieves 10-14x improvement in update throughput compared to Berkeley DB. Mnemosyne improves throughput almost linearly with the number of threads,

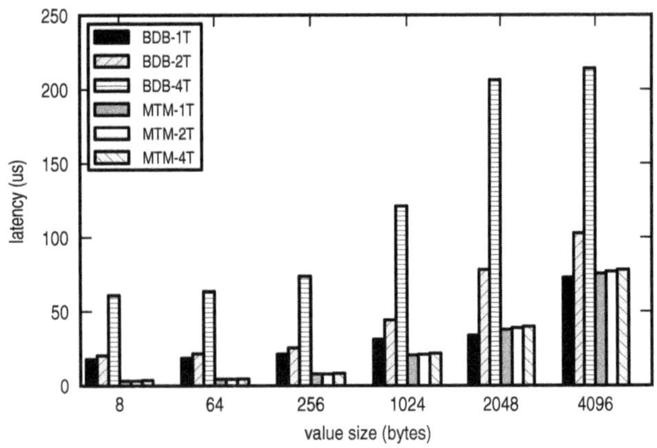


**Figure 4. Write latency for a hashtable with durable transactions compared to Berkeley DB.**

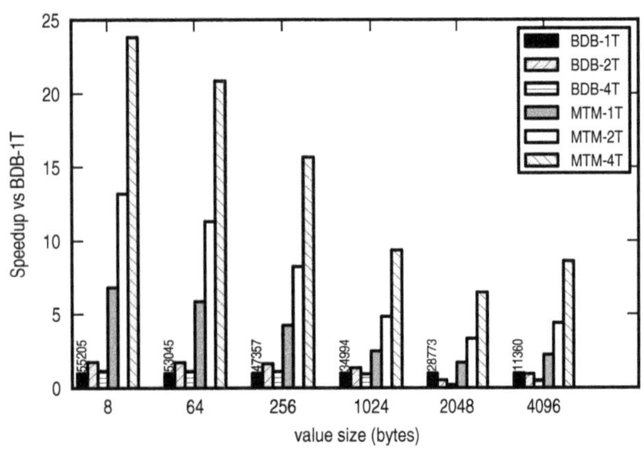


**Figure 5. Update throughput for a hashtable with durable transactions compared to Berkeley DB. Numbers above the bars are the absolute updates per second for the Berkeley DB single-threaded version.**

without hurting write latency. The slight increase in write latency is due to contention on the global timestamp counter in the transaction system, which is relatively more expensive for short transactions. In contrast, Berkeley DB does not scale beyond 2 threads. We found this is due to contention on the centralized log buffer, which becomes the serialization bottleneck as I/O latency becomes shorter. Also, Berkeley DB's throughput improvement with 2 threads comes at the cost of increasing write latency, possibly due to group commit, which is not necessary with Mnemosyne's fine-grain memory transactions. Finally, while Berkeley DB's write latency is lower than Mnemosyne's for for values larger than 2048 bytes, the Mnemosyne's throughput is higher because it is the aggregate of writes and deletes, and delete latency remains almost constant for Mnemosyne as value size increases.

An alternative approach, often used for less structured data, is to serialize the data into a buffer and write it to a file. For example, productivity applications including word processors use this approach for periodic *fast saves*. We compare the cost of maintaining a red-black tree with 128 byte nodes in persistent memory against the cost of keeping it in DRAM and periodically serializing it and storing it in a file. Using small data sizes maximizes the overhead of transactions, because there is not much data to write out between fences.

| Tree Size | Insert Latency | Serialize Latency | Inserts per Serialization |
|---|---|---|---|
| 1 K | 4.7 $\mu$s | 517 $\mu$s | 189 |
| 8 K | 5.1 $\mu$s | 3,413 $\mu$s | 1,345 |
| 64 K | 5.5 $\mu$s | 33,859 $\mu$s | 9,202 |
| 256 K | 5.8 $\mu$s | 143,776 $\mu$s | 24,788 |

**Table 5. Performance of Mnemosyne updates and Boost serialization of red-black trees. The right-most column shows the number of Mnemosyne updates that can be performed in the time for a single Boost serialization of the tree.**

| Record Size (B) | 8 | 64 | 256 | 1024 | 2048 | 4096 |
|---|---|---|---|---|---|---|
| Base (MB/s) | 17 | 128 | 416 | 881 | 1088 | 1244 |
| Tornbit (MB/s) | 34 | 227 | 591 | 929 | 1045 | 1093 |

**Table 6. Throughput of base and tornbit RAWLs..**

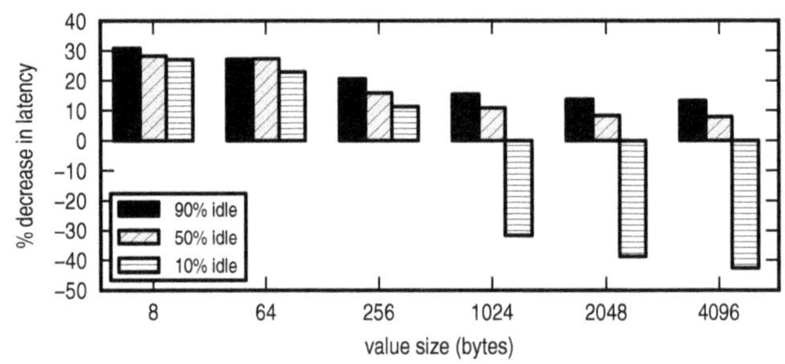


**Figure 6. Decrease in write latency of hashtable with asynchronous over synchronous truncation.**

Table 5 compares the cost of updating the tree with Mnemosyne transactions against the cost of periodically serializing it using Boost [9] and storing it on PCM-disk. Tree updates cost 5-6 $\mu$s with Mnemosyne, and on average 10 percent of the tree can be updated for the cost of serializing and storing the tree just once. Thus, even data structures with high rates of change can more efficiently be made persistent with transactions than by serializing and storing.

### 6.3.1 Optimizations

Mnemosyne implements two optimizations to reduce the cost of transactions: the torn bit in the RAWL, and asynchronous log truncation. Table 6 compares performance of torn bit against an implementation of the RAWL that writes a commit record, with a separate fence. For log records smaller than 2048 bytes, the torn-bit log performs up to 100 percent better. Above 2048 bytes, the torn bit log performs *worse* than a separate commit record. The cost of the fence is fixed, while the cost of bit manipulation to implement torn bits scales with the amount of data. Thus, for large records, the cost of manipulating bits to make space for the torn bit is larger than the cost of a single extra fence. As Mnemosyne targets smaller transactions, the torn bit log is a valuable optimization but should be omitted if large transactions are expected.

Asynchronous log truncation may reduce latency and improve performance under low load because it moves flushing modified data off the critical path. Instead, a separate thread processes the log to flush all modified data to PCM, after which it truncates the log. Figure 6 compares performance when the hash table thread is idle 90, 50, and 10 percent of the time. We find that for 50 and 90 percent idle time, the truncation thread can keep up with the active thread and achieves a reduction of 7-31% in write latency.

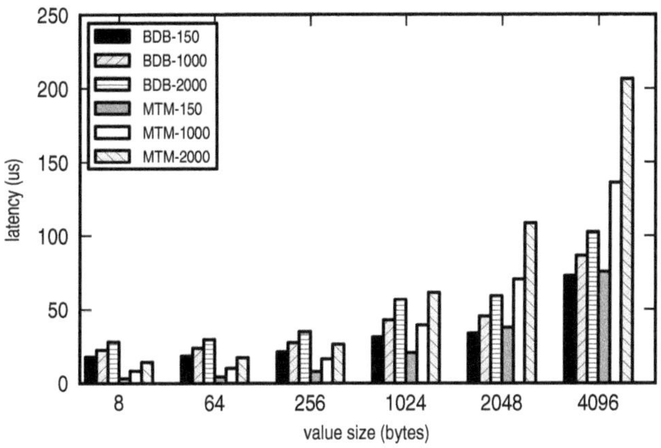


**Figure 7. Mnemosyne's performance relative to Berkeley DB for different memory access latencies.**

However, with only 10 percent idle time, the active thread stalls for extended periods while the truncation thread flushes data, which can increase latency by up to 42% for 4KB writes. Thus, this optimization is most helpful for transactions with a moderate duty cycle.

#### 6.3.2 Reincarnation Cost

There are two reincarnation costs associated with Mnemosyne: (i) the cost to reconstruct persistent regions when the OS boots, and (ii) the cost to remap persistent regions to a process' address space, scavenge the persistent heap, and replay all completed but not flushed transactions when a program starts. For (i), we measured the worst case scenario cost, which is to reconstruct a persistent region for each SCM frame. This takes approximately 734 ms for 1GB of SCM, indicating that reincarnation contributes less than 1s overhead to the OS boot process. For (ii), we found the overall cost in our workloads to be less than 100 ms. Specifically, we measured the cost to remap the persistent regions to be about 1.1 ms, while the cost to scavenge the persistent heap region and reconstruct the heap's volatile indexes was about 89 ms. This high cost is due to the incremental allocation of memory needed by the volatile indexes, which results to a large number of `brk` system calls. We believe this cost could be reduced via bulk allocation or lazy construction of the indexes but have not implemented any of these optimizations. Finally, we found the cost to replay a completed but not flushed transaction ranges between 3 to 76 $\mu$s. In the case of synchronous truncation, the number of completed but not flushed transactions is bounded by the number of threads, which for 4 threads results in a worst case cost of about 300 $\mu$s.

### 6.4 Sensitivity to Memory Performance

Mnemosyne exposes persistent memory directly to programs as memory. If however, SCM latencies are long, then applications may perform better treating SCM like disk, with associated optimizations to overlap I/O and computation and to optimize for sequential access. We evaluate the impact of different memory latencies by comparing the performance of Mnemosyne transactions on a hash table to Berkeley DB, which optimizes for disk-like performance.

Figure 7 shows the relative performance of Mnemosyne over Berkeley DB as a function of data element size for three different latencies: 150 ns, 1000 ns, and 2000 ns. For small data sizes, Mnemosyne is always faster because it needs to write much less data. However, for longer latencies the benefit is much lower: 200 percent better performance for 1000 ns latencies and 100 percent for 2000 ns latencies. Furthermore, the benefit drops off faster with larger data sizes: at 2000 ns, Berkeley DB and Mnemosyne perform the same for 1024 byte inserts.

Thus, Mnemosyne is most useful when SCM latencies are close to those of DRAM, because the benefit of modifying small amounts of data outweighs the latency of access. For larger latencies, SCM may best be treated as a disk and accessed through the file system. Should someone prefer using Mnemosyne though, then our optimizations that remove latency off the critical path become even more evident. For example, under low load (10 percent idle) and 2000 ns latency to SCM, asynchronous truncation would be able to reduce write latency for 1024 and 2048 bytes by 70% and 60% respectively, enabling Mnemosyne to still perform better than the disk-based interface.

## 7. Related Work

NV-heaps [16] is a concurrently developed, project that also seeks to provide transaction updates to data in storage-class memory. However, the focus of the two projects is different: NV-heaps focus on on persisting user-defined *objects*, so they support transactions via an object-based transactional memory system. In contrast, Mnemosyne supports transactions via a word-based transactional memory system, which can be used to transactionally update any data kept in persistent memory. Nevertheless, NV-heaps provide some features not currently found in Mnemosyne, such as type-safe pointers and garbage collection via reference counting. Finally, NV-heaps require processor support, while Mnemosyne can be used with existing commodity processors.

We next discuss past projects on persistent objects/languages, recoverable memory, transactional memory, and transaction processing.

**Persistent memory.** Several projects have investigated the use of a large battery-backed memory for persistent storage [10, 18, 23]. Unlike Mnemosyne, the memory in these systems is accessible only through a driver to prevent corruption, and hence only available through a DBMS or file system. The eNVy system [65] focuses on the architecture of attaching flash to the memory bus as persistent memory, and uses a battery-backed SRAM buffer to hide the block-addressable nature of flash. Mnemosyne instead focuses on the programming model and can be used with eNVy's architecture.

**Persistent objects/languages.** Previous research on persistent object systems attempted to provide language level persistence through the integration of database systems and programming languages [3, 4, 11, 36]. Virtual memory-based persistent object systems, such as Texas [58], QuickStore [64] are most similar. However, these systems rely on a C++ object-oriented programming model, which limits the applicability of the system to programs non-OO programs. Furthermore, Texas provides a checkpoint mechanism for consistency, which is insufficient in the presence of multiple threads. Finally, these systems operate on virtual memory pages, which makes the system heavier weight, as they must read or write more data at a time and rely on optimizations such as page-diffing to reduce the amount of data written. However, the higher-level interface to these systems and others, such as Thor [40], allows them to provide better safety properties, such as only allowing pointers in persistent data structures to reference other persistent data (or, in the case of Thor, to make persistent any volatile structures referenced). Their knowledge of all pointers in a data structure also enable garbage collection to prevent memory leaks. These mechanisms could be layered on top of Mnemosyne's primitives to provide the same guarantees.

**Durable memory transactions.** Mnemosyne is similar to lightweight recoverable virtual memory (RVM) [56] and Rio Vista transactions [41]. Mnemosyne borrows the notion of persistent regions from RVM, but commits data at word granularity rather than at page granularity. Unlike Rio Vista, Mnemosyne transactions operate completely at user level and do not require a battery back-up system. Several IBM systems have provided transactions in memory by marking pages accessed by a transaction in a TLB-like structure [13, 60]. Similar to RVM, this provides coarse-grained transactions at the page granularity, and relies on a disk for durability.

Stasis is a user-mode library that generalizes write-ahead-logging (WAL) to provide transactional storage to applications [57]. Unlike Mnemosyne, Stasis does not provide compiler support for transactions [57], so programmers must explicitly code transactional writes and reads.

**Transactional memory.** Recent work on transactional memory focuses on the concurrency of transactions, through automatic detection of conflicts, rather than on durability [30, 29]. Mnemosyne relies on software transactional memory techniques to automatically annotate program code in a compiler, and to implement efficient commit processing. As a result, our system benefits from recent research in the area [66]. Recent work by FusionIO on atomic updates to flash storage uses a technique similar to the torn-bit RAWL [50], but does not need to use sense reversing.

**Transactional processing.** The use of transactions as the basic unit of atomicity and durability has been the focus of the database and systems research community for almost three decades [27, 28, 45]. Similar to many database systems, Mnemosyne relies on write-ahead logging for recovery. Mnemosyne differs from disk-based transactions in that it cannot control when data is evicted from the cache, and as a result must force log writes early. In addition, the low cost of SCM access raises the cost of sophisticated logging and recovery mechanisms [45]. Similar to Mnemosyne, databases must deal with partial writes, but often solve it with checksums [44]. Main-memory databases [26, 20] store all data in memory rather than caching data, but still rely on a disk for persistently storing a log of committed updates.

**Storage-class memory for files.** Other work focuses on SCM as a replacement/acceleration for flash or magnetic storage media. One approach is to store just metadata or frequently accessed data in SCM [22, 35], treating it as a block device. BPFS instead leverages SCM's byte addressability to reduce the amount of metadata written during an update and achieves consistency through shadow updates [17]. These approaches all improve performance for file access, but do not provide fine-grained persistence to programs.

## 8. Conclusions

Programmers trained in the era of disks have learned that frequently updating persistent state should either be avoided or be handled by a database engine. Storage class memory presents new opportunities for fast data persistence that obsolete these rules. Mnemosyne provides lightweight persistent memory, and common in-memory data structures can be made persistent using durable transactions. Thus, programmers can create a single data structure, optimized for memory, rather than designing separate in-memory and update-optimized persistent representations. Compared to past work on persistent object systems, Mnemosyne provides greater flexibility, by not requiring C++ objects, and lower latency by persisting data directly to memory at the granularity of a a single update rather than a whole page.

## Acknowledgments

This work is supported in part by the National Science Foundation (NSF) grants CNS-083447 and CNS-0720565. We would like to thank Mark Hill and Arkaprava Basu for valuable discussions during the initial stages of the project. We would also like to thank our shepherd, Emery Berger, and the anonymous reviewers for their invaluable feedback. Swift has a significant financial interest in Microsoft.

## References

[1] Sparse - a semantic parser for C. `sparse.wiki.kernel.org`.

[2] AMD, Inc. Software optimization guide for AMD64 processors. `http://support.amd.com/us/Embedded\_TechDocs/25112.PDF`, 2005.

[3] M. P. Atkinson, P. J. Bailey, K. J. Chisholm, P. W. Cockshott, and R. Morrison. An approach to persistent programming. *Computer Journal*, 26(4):360–365, Nov 1983.

[4] M. P. Atkinson, L. Daynès, M. J. Jordan, T. Printezis, and S. Spence. An orthogonally persistent java. *SIGMOD Rec.*, 25(4):68–75, 1996.

[5] F. Bedeschi, C. Resta, O. Khouri, E. Buda, L. Costa, M. Ferraro, F. Pellizzer, F. Ottogalli, A. Pirovano, M. Tosi, R. Bez, R. Gastaldi, and G. Casagrande. An 8Mb demonstrator for high-density 1.8V phase-change memories. In *VLSI Circuits*, pages 442 – 445, June 2004.

[6] E. D. Berger, K. S. McKinley, R. D. Blumofe, and P. R. Wilson. Hoard: a scalable memory allocator for multithreaded applications. In *ASPLOS 9*, Nov. 2000.

[7] H.-J. Boehm and M. Weiser. Garbage collection in an uncooperative environment. *Softw., Pract. Exper.*, 18(9):807–820, 1988.

[8] J. Bonwick, M. Ahrens, V. Henson, M. Maybee, and M. Shellenbaum. The zettabyte file system. Technical report, Sun Microsystems.

[9] Boost C++ Libraries. Serialization overview. `http://www.boost.org/doc/libs/1\_42\_0/libs/serialization/doc/index.html`, Nov. 2004.

[10] T. C. Bressoud, T. Clark, and T. Kan. The design and use of peristent memory on the DNCP hardware fault-tolerant platform. In *DSN*, 2001.

[11] M. J. Carey, D. J. DeWitt, M. J. Franklin, N. E. Hall, M. L. McAuliffe, J. F. Naughton, D. T. Schuh, M. H. Solomon, C. K. Tan, O. G. Tsatalos, S. J. White, and M. J. Zwilling. Shoring up persistent applications. *SIGMOD Rec.*, 23(2):383–394, 1994.

[12] T. D. Chandra, R. Griesemer, and J. Redstone. Paxos made live: an engineering perspective. In *PODC 26*, Aug. 2007.

[13] A. Chang and M. F. Mergen. 801 storage: Architecture and programming. *ACM Transactions on Computer Systems*, 6(1), Feb. 1988.

[14] J. H. Choi, H. Franke, and K. Zeilenga. Enhancing the performance of OpenLDAP directory server with multiple caching. In *International Symposium on Performance Evaluation of Computers and Telecommunications Systems (SPECTS)*, July 2003.

[15] Christopher Clark. C hash table. `http://www.cl.cam.ac.uk/~cwc22/hashtable/hashtable.c`.

[16] J. Coburn, A. M. Caulfield, A. Akel, L. M. Grupp, R. K. Gupta, R. Jhala, and S. Swanson. NV-Heaps: Making persistent objects fast and safe with next-generation, non-volatile memories. In *ASPLOS 16*, Mar. 2011.

[17] J. Condit, E. B. Nightingale, C. Frost, E. Ipek, B. Lee, D. Burger, and D. Coetzee. Better I/O through byte-addressable, persistent memory. In *SOSP 22*, pages 133–146, Oct. 2009.

[18] G. Copeland, T. Keller, R. Krishnamurthy, and M. Smith. The case for safe RAM. In *VLDB 15*, Aug. 1989.

[19] J. Corbet. Fsyncers and curveballs (the firefox 3 fsync() problem). `http://lwn.net/Articles/283745/`, May 2008.

[20] D. J. DeWitt, R. H. Katz, F. Olken, L. D. Shapiro, M. R. Stonebraker, and D. Wood. Implementation techniques for main memory database systems. *SIGMOD Rec.*, 14(2):1–8, 1984.

[21] E. Doller. Phase change memory and its impacts on memory hierarchy. `http://www.pdl.cmu.edu/SDI/2009/slides/Numonyx.pdf`, 2009.

[22] N. Edel, D. Tuteja, E. L. Miller, and S. A. Brandt. MRAMFS: A compressing file system for non-volatile RAM. In *Proceedings of thje IEEE/ACM International Symposium on Modeling, Analysis, and Simulation of Computer and Telecommunication Systems (MASCOTS)*, pages 596–603, Oct. 2004.

[23] F. Eskesen, M. Hack, A. Iyengar, R. P. King, and N. Halim. Software exploitation of a fault-tolerant computer with a large memory. In *FTCS*, 1998.

[24] P. Felber, C. Fetzer, and T. Riegel. Dynamic performance tuning of word-based software transactional memory. In *PPoPP 13*, Feb. 2008.

[25] R. F. Freitas and W. W. Wilcke. Storage-class memory: the next storage system technology. *IBM J. Res. Dev.*, 52(4):439–447, 2008.

[26] H. Garcia-Molina and K. Salem. Main memory database systems: An overview. *IEEE Trans. on Knowl. and Data Eng.*, 4(6):509–516, 1992.

[27] J. Gray. The transaction concept: Virtues and limitations. In *VLDB 7*, Sept. 1981.

[28] J. Gray, P. Mcjones, M. Blasgen, B. Lindsay, R. Lorie, and T. Price. The recovery manager of the System R database manager. *ACM Computing Surveys*, 13:223–242, 1981.

[29] T. Harris, S. Marlow, S. P. Jones, and M. Herlihy. Composable memory transactions. In *PPoPP 10*, June 2005.

[30] M. Herlihy and J. E. B. Moss. Transactional memory: Architectural support for lock-free data structures. In *ISCA 20*, May 1993.

[31] M. Hirabayashi. Tokyo cabinet: a modern implementation of DBM. `http://1978th.net/tokyocabinet/`, 2010.

[32] Y. Huai. Spin-transfer torque MRAM (STT-MRAM): Challenges and prospects. *AAPPS Bulletin*, 18(6):33–40, Dec. 2008.

[33] Intel Corp. Intel 64 and ia-32 architectures software developers manual volume 1: Basic architecture. `http://www.intel.com/assets/pdf/manual/253665.pdf`, Mar. 2010.

[34] E. Ipek, J. Condit, E. B. Nightingale, D. Burger, and T. Moscibroda. Dynamically replicated memory: building reliable systems from nanoscale resistive memories. In *ASPLOS 15*, Mar. 2010.

[35] J. Jung, Y. Won, E. ki Kim, H. Shin, and B. Jeon. Frash: Exploiting storage class memory in hybrid file system for hierarchical storage. *ACM Transactions on Storage*, 6(1), 2010.

[36] C. Lamb, G. Landis, J. Orenstein, and D. Weinreb. The ObjectStore database system. *Commun. ACM*, 34(10):50–63, 1991.

[37] L. Lamport. Proving the correctness of multiprocess programs. *IEEE Transactions on Software Engineering*, 3(2), Mar. 1977.

[38] D. Lea. A memory allocator. `http://gee.cs.oswego.edu/dl/html/malloc.html`.

[39] B. C. Lee, E. Ipek, O. Mutlu, and D. Burger. Architecting phase change memory as a scalable DRAM alternative. In *ISCA 36*, June 2007.

[40] B. Liskov, A. Adya, M. Castro, M. Day, S. Ghemawat, R. Gruber, U. Maheshwari, A. C. Myers, and L. Shrira. Safe and efficient sharing of persistent objects in Thor. In *SIGMOD Conference*, pages 318–329, 1996.

[41] D. E. Lowell and P. M. Chen. Free transactions with Rio Vista. In *SOSP 16*, Oct. 1997.

[42] M. K. McKusick and G. R. Ganger. Soft updates: A technique for eliminating most synchronous writes in the fast filesystem. In *Proceedings of FREENIX*, June 1999.

[43] M. K. McKusick, W. N. Joy, S. J. Leffler, and R. S. Fabry. Fsck - the unix file system check program. Unix System Manager's Manual - 4.3 BSD Virtual VAX-11 Version, Apr. 1986.

[44] Microsoft Corp. SQL server 2008 books online: Memory management architecture: Buffer management. `http://msdn.microsoft.com/en-us/library/aa337525.aspx`.

[45] C. Mohan, D. Haderle, B. Lindsay, H. Pirahesh, and P. Schwarz. ARIES: a transaction recovery method supporting fine-granularity locking and partial rollbacks using write-ahead logging. *ACM Trans. Database Syst.*, 17(1):94–162, 1992.

[46] K. E. Moore, J. Bobba, M. J. Moravan, M. D. Hill, and D. A. Wood. Logtm: Log-based transactional memory. In *HPCA 12*, pages 258–269, Feb. 2006.

[47] MySQL Performance Blog. Tokyo tyrant the extras part i : Is it durable? `http://www.mysqlperformanceblog.com/2009/11/10/tokyo-tyrant-the-extras-part-i-is-it-durable/`, Nov. 2009.

[48] Y. Ni, A. Welc, A.-R. Adl-Tabatabai, M. Bach, S. Berkowits, J. Cownie, R. Geva, S. Kozhukow, R. Narayanaswamy, J. Olivier, S. Preis, B. Saha, A. Tal, and X. Tian. Design and implementation of transactional constructs for C/C++. In *OOPSLA 23*, Oct. 2008.

[49] Numonyx. Omneo P8P PCM 128-Mbit Parallel PCM. `www.numonyx.com/Documents/Datasheets/316144_P8P_DS.pdf`, Aug. 2010.

[50] X. Ouyang, D. Nellans, R. Wipfel, D. Flynn, and D. K. Panda. Beyond block I/O: Rethinking traditional storage primitives. In *HPCA 17*, Feb. 2011.

[51] V. Prabhakaran, L. N. Bairavasundaram, N. Agrawal, H. S. Gunawi, A. C. Arpaci-Dusseau, and R. H. Arpaci-Dusseau. IRON File Systems. In *SOSP 20*, pages 206–220, Brighton, United Kingdom, Oct. 2005.

[52] M. K. Qureshi, J. Karidis, M. Franceschini, V. Srinivasan, L. Lastras, and B. Abali. Enhancing lifetime and security of PCM-based main memory with start-gap wear leveling. In *MICRO 42*, Dec. 2009.

[53] M. K. Qureshi, V. Srinivasan, and J. A. Rivers. Scalable high performance main memory system using phase-change memory technology. In *ISCA 36*, June 2007.

[54] M. Rosenblum and J. K. Ousterhout. The design and implementation of a log-structured file system. *ACM Trans. Comput. Syst.*, 10(1):26–52, Feb. 1992.

[55] Samsung. Samsung ships industry's first multi-chip package with a pram chip for handsets. `http://www.samsung.com/us/business/semiconductor/newsView.do?news\_id=1149`, Apr. 2010.

[56] M. Satyanarayanan, H. H. Mashburn, P. Kumar, D. C. Steere, and J. J. Kistler. Lightweight recoverable virtual memory. In *SOSP 14*, Dec. 1993.

[57] R. Sears and E. Brewer. Stasis: flexible transactional storage. In *OSDI 8*, Dec. 2008.

[58] V. Singhal, S. V. Kakkad, and P. R. Wilson. Texas: good, fast, cheap persistence for c++. *SIGPLAN OOPS Mess.*, 4(2):145–147, 1993.

[59] Sleepycat Software. Sleepycat software: Berkeley DB database. http://www.sleepycat.com

[60] F. G. Soltis. *Inside the AS/400*. Duke Press, second edition, 1997.

[61] D. B. Strukov, G. S. Snider, D. R. Stewart, and R. S. Williams. The missing memristor found. *Nature*, 453:80–83, 2008.

[62] S. C. Tweedie. Journaling the Linux ext2fs File System. In *The Fourth Annual Linux Expo*, Durham, North Carolina, May 1998.

[63] C. Villa, D. Mills, G. Barkley, H. Giduturi, S. Schippers, and D. Vimercati. A 45nm 1Gb 1.8V phase-change memory. In *ISSCC 2010*, pages 270 –271, Feb. 2010.

[64] S. J. White and D. J. DeWitt. Quickstore: A high performance mapped object store. *VLDB Journal*, 4(4):629–673, 1995.

[65] M. Wu and W. Zwaenepoel. eNVy: a non-volatile, main memory storage system. In *ASPLOS 6*, Oct. 1994.

[66] P. Wu, M. M. Michael, C. von Praun, T. Nakaike, R. Bordawekar, H. W. Cain, C. Cascaval, S. Chatterjee, S. Chiras, R. Hou, M. F. Mergen, X. Shen, M. F. Spear, H. Wang, and K. Wang. Compiler and runtime techniques for software transactional memory optimization. *Concurrency and Computation: Practice and Experience*, 21(1):7–23, 2009.

[67] P. Zhou, B. Zhao, J. Yang, and Y. Zhang. A durable and energy efficient main memory using phase change memory technology. In *ISCA 36*, June 2007.

# NV-Heaps: Making Persistent Objects Fast and Safe with Next-Generation, Non-Volatile Memories


Joel Coburn Adrian M. Caulfield Ameen Akel Laura M. Grupp
Rajesh K. Gupta Ranjit Jhala Steven Swanson

Department of Computer Science and Engineering
University of California, San Diego
{jdcoburn, acaulfie, aakel, lgrupp, rgupta, jhala, swanson}@cs.ucsd.edu



## Abstract

Persistent, user-defined objects present an attractive abstraction for working with non-volatile program state. However, the slow speed of persistent storage (i.e., disk) has restricted their design and limited their performance. Fast, byte-addressable, non-volatile technologies, such as phase change memory, will remove this constraint and allow programmers to build high-performance, persistent data structures in non-volatile storage that is almost as fast as DRAM. Creating these data structures requires a system that is lightweight enough to expose the performance of the underlying memories but also ensures safety in the presence of application and system failures by avoiding familiar bugs such as dangling pointers, multiple free()s, and locking errors. In addition, the system must prevent new types of hard-to-find pointer safety bugs that only arise with persistent objects. These bugs are especially dangerous since any corruption they cause will be permanent.

We have implemented a lightweight, high-performance persistent object system called NV-heaps that provides transactional semantics while preventing these errors and providing a model for persistence that is easy to use and reason about. We implement search trees, hash tables, sparse graphs, and arrays using NV-heaps, BerkeleyDB, and Stasis. Our results show that NV-heap performance scales with thread count and that data structures implemented using NV-heaps out-perform BerkeleyDB and Stasis implementations by 32× and 244×, respectively, by avoiding the operating system and minimizing other software overheads. We also quantify the cost of enforcing the safety guarantees that NV-heaps provide and measure the costs of NV-heap primitive operations.



***Categories and Subject Descriptors*** D.4.2 [*Operating Systems*]: Storage Management—Storage hierarchies; D.3.4 [*Programming Languages*]: Processors—Memory management (garbage collection); E.2 [*Data*]: Data Storage Representations

***General Terms*** Design, Performance, Reliability

***Keywords*** Non-volatile Heap, Persistent Objects, Phase-change Memory, Spin-torque Transfer Memory, ACID Transactions, Pointer Safety, Memory Management, Transactional Memory





*ASPLOS'11,* March 5–11, 2011, Newport Beach, California, USA.




## 1. Introduction

The notion of memory-mapped persistent data structures has long been compelling: Instead of reading bytes serially from a file and building data structures in memory, the data structures would appear, ready to use in the program's address space, allowing quick access to even the largest, most complex persistent data structures. Fast, persistent structures would let programmers leverage decades of work in data structure design to implement fast, purpose-built persistent structures. They would also reduce our reliance on the traditional, un-typed file-based IO operations that do not integrate well with most programming languages.

Many systems (e.g., object-oriented databases) have provided persistent data structures and integrated them tightly into programming languages. These systems faced a common challenge that arose from the performance and interface differences between volatile main memory (i.e., DRAM) and persistent mass storage (i.e., disk): They required complex buffer management and de(serialization) mechanisms to move data to and from DRAM. Despite decades of work optimizing this process, slow disks ultimately limit performance, especially if strong consistency and durability guarantees are necessary.

New non-volatile memory technologies, such as phase change and spin-torque transfer memories, are poised to remove the disk-imposed limit on persistent object performance. These technologies are hundreds of times faster than the NAND flash that makes up existing solid state disks (SSDs). While NAND, like disk, is fundamentally block-oriented, these new technologies offer both a DRAM-like byte-addressable interface and DRAM-like performance. This potent combination will allow them to reside on the processor's memory bus and will nearly eliminate the gap in performance between volatile and non-volatile storage.

Neither existing implementations of persistent objects nor the familiar tools we use to build volatile data structures are a good fit for these new memories. Existing persistent object systems are not suitable, because the gap between memory and storage performance drove many design decisions that shaped them. Recent work [13, 14] has shown that software overheads from the operating system, file systems, and database management systems can squander the performance advantages of these memories. Removing these overheads requires significant reengineering of the way both the kernel and application manage access to storage.

Managing non-volatile memory like conventional memory is not a good solution either. To guarantee consistency and durability, non-volatile structures must meet a host of challenges, many of which do not exist for volatile memories. They must avoid dangling pointers, multiple free()s, memory leaks, and locking errors, but they also must avoid several new types of hard-to-find programming errors. For instance, pointers from non-volatile data structures into volatile memory are inherently unsafe, because they are meaningless after the program ends. The system must also perform some kind of logging if non-volatile structures are to be robust in the face of application or system failure. Trusting the average programmer to "get it right" in meeting these challenges is both unreasonable and dangerous for non-volatile data structures: An error in any of these areas will result in permanent corruption that neither restarting the application nor rebooting the system will resolve.

This paper proposes a new implementation of persistent objects called *Non-volatile Memory Heaps* (NV-heaps). NV-heaps aim to provide flexible, robust abstractions for building persistent objects that expose as much of the underlying memory performance as possible. NV-heaps provide programmers with a familiar set of simple primitives (i.e., objects, pointers, memory allocation, and atomic sections) that make it easy to build fast, robust, and flexible persistent objects. NV-heaps avoid OS overheads on all common case access operations and protect programmers from common mistakes: NV-heaps provide automatic garbage collection, pointer safety, and protection from several novel kinds of bugs that non-volatile objects make possible. NV-heaps are completely self-contained, allowing the system to copy, move, or transmit them just like normal files.

In designing NV-heaps, our goals are to provide safe access to persistent objects, to make persistent objects easy to program, and to achieve high performance. To this end, our system has the following of properties:

1. **Pointer safety.** NV-heaps, to the extent possible, prevent programmers from corrupting the data structures they create by misusing pointers or making memory allocation errors.
2. **Flexible ACID transactions.** Multiple threads can modify NV-heaps concurrently. NV-heaps are robust against application and system failure.
3. **Familiar interface.** The programming interface for NV-heaps is similar to the familiar interface for implementing volatile data structures.
4. **High performance.** Access to the data in an NV-heap is as fast as possible relative to the speed of the underlying non-volatile memory.
5. **Scalability.** NV-heaps are designed to scale to very large (many gigabytes to terabytes) data structures.

The paper describes the NV-heaps model and our Linux-based implementation in detail. It highlights the aspects of NV-heaps that minimize software overheads and evaluates its performance using emulated fast memories. We use a set of benchmarks that includes several complex data structures as well as a non-volatile version of SSCA [5], a sparse graph analysis application. We also convert a persistent version of Memcached [16], the popular memory object caching system, to use NV-heaps. We compare NV-heaps to Stasis [53] and BerkeleyDB [46], two other interfaces to non-volatile data that target conventional block devices (e.g., disks). We also evaluate the performance scalability of NV-heaps, and evaluate the impact of the underlying non-volatile storage technology on their overall performance. In particular, we focus on phase-change memory (PCM) and spin-torque transfer memory (STTM) technologies.

Our results show that NV-heaps out-perform BerkeleyDB and Stasis by 32× and 244×, respectively, because NV-heaps eliminate the operating system from common-case operations and minimize other software overheads. We also compare NV-heaps to a Rio Vista-like [38] version of the system that provides no safety guarantees and find that the cost of safety is a 11× drop in performance. Our experience programming with NV-heaps and the unsafe version of the system leads us to conclude that the benefits in terms of ease-of-use more than make up for the performance cost.

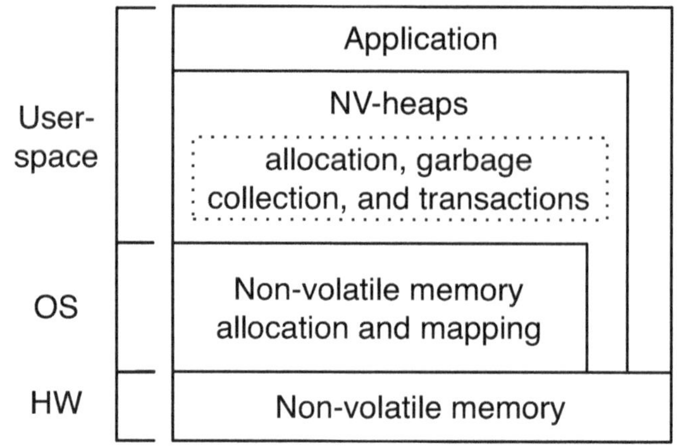


**Figure 1. The NV-heap system stack** This organization allows read and write operations to bypass the operating system entirely.

The remainder of this paper is organized as follows. We present an overview of NV-heaps in Section 2. Section 3 describes our implementation of NV-heaps. Sections 4 and 5 describe our methodology and results. Section 6 concludes.

## 2. NV-heaps

The goal of NV-heaps is to make it easy to build and use robust, persistent data structures that can exploit the performance that emerging non-volatile, solid-state memories offer. To achieve this, NV-heaps provides an easy-to-use application-level interface to a persistent object system tailored to emerging non-volatile memories. The designs of previous persistent object systems [3, 10, 12, 34, 57, 61] focus on hiding disk latency rather than minimizing software overhead, making them a poor fit for these new memory technologies.

NV-heaps provide a small set of simple primitives: persistent objects, specialized pointer types, a memory allocator, and atomic sections to provide concurrency and guard against system or application failure. NV-heaps hide the details of locking, logging, and memory management, so building a data structure in an NV-heap is very similar to building one in a conventional, volatile heap.

To use an NV-heap, the application opens it by passing the NV-heap library a file name. The library maps the NV-heap directly into the application's address space without performing a copy, which is possible because the underlying memory is byte-addressable and appears in the processor's physical address space. Once the mapping is complete, the application can access the NV-heap's contents via a *root pointer* from which all data in the NV-heap is accessible.

Figure 1 shows the relationship between NV-heaps, the operating system, and the underlying storage. A key feature of NV-heaps is that they give the application direct access to non-volatile memory, eliminating operating system overhead in most cases and significantly increasing performance.

Below, we make the case for the strong safety guarantees that NV-heaps provide. Then, we describe the transaction, pointer safety, performance, and usability features that NV-heaps include along with an example of NV-heaps in action. We discuss the differences between NV-heaps and existing persistent object systems throughout. Section 3 describes the implementation in detail.

## 2.1 Preventing programmer errors

Integrating persistent objects into conventional programs presents multiple challenges. Not only must the system (or the programmer) maintain locking and memory allocation invariants, but it must also enforce a new set of invariants on which objects belong to which region of memory. Potential problems arise if one NV-heap contains a pointer into another NV-heap or into the volatile heap. In either case, when a program re-opens the NV-heap, the pointer will be meaningless and potentially dangerous. Furthermore, violating any of these invariants results in errors that are, by definition, persistent. They are akin to inconsistencies in a corrupt filesystem.

We believe that if persistent objects are to be useful to the average programmer, they must be fast *and* make strong safety guarantees. Providing a low-level interface and expecting the programmer to "get it right" has proven to be a recipe for bugs and unreliability in at least two well-known domains: Memory management and locking disciplines. In both of those instances, there is a program-wide invariant (i.e., which code is responsible for `free()`ing an object and which locks protect which data) that the source code does not explicitly describe and that the system does not enforce. A persistent object system must contend with both of these in addition to the constraints on pointer usage in NV-heaps.

To understand how easy it is to create dangerous pointers in NV-heaps, consider a function

```
Insert(Object * a, List<Object> * l) ...
```

that inserts a pointer to a non-volatile object, `a`, into a non-volatile linked list, `l`. The programmer must ensure that `a` and `l` are part of the same non-volatile structure, but there is no mechanism to enforce that constraint since it is not clear whether `a` is volatile or non-volatile or which NV-heap it belongs to. One incorrect call to this function can corrupt `l`: It might, for instance, end up containing a pointer from an NV-heap into volatile memory. In either case, if we move `l` to another system or restart the program, `l` is no longer safe to use: The pointer to object `a` that the list contains has become a "wild" pointer.

There is also real-world evidence that non-volatile data structures are difficult to implement correctly. Microsoft Outlook stores mail and other personal information in a pointer-based Personal Folder File (PFF) file format [43]. The file format is complex enough that implementing it correctly proved difficult. In fact, Microsoft eventually released the "Inbox Repair Tool" [44] which is similar to `fsck`-style tools that check and repair file systems.

Another system, BPFS [17], highlights what it takes to build a robust non-volatile data structure on top of raw non-volatile memory. BPFS implements a transactional file system directly atop the same kind of byte-addressable non-volatile memories that NV-heaps target. BPFS uses carefully designed data structures that exploit the file system's tree structure and limited set of required operations to make transactional semantics easy to implement in most cases. In doing so, however, it enforces stringent invariants on those structures (e.g., each block of data has only a single incoming pointer) and requires careful reasoning about thread safety, atomicity, and memory access ordering. BPFS is an excellent example of what skilled programmers can accomplish with non-volatile memories, but average users will, we expect, be unwilling (or unable) to devise, enforce, and reason about such constraints. NV-heaps remove that burden, and despite additional overheads, they still provide excellent performance (see Section 5).

Existing systems that are similar to NV-heaps, such as Rio Vista [38] and RVM [51], provide direct access to byte addressable, non-volatile memories and let the programmer define arbitrary data structures. But these systems do not offer protection from memory allocation errors, locking errors, or dangerous non-volatile pointers. Concurrent work on a system called Mnemosyne [60] goes further and provides a set of primitives for operating on data in persistent regions. It would be possible to implement the key features of NV-heaps using these primitives. Systems that target disk-based storage have either implemented persistent objects on top of a conventional database (e.g., the Java Persistence API [7]) or in a specialized object-oriented database [3, 10, 12, 34, 57, 61]. In these systems, the underlying storage system enforces the invariants automatically, but they extract a heavy cost in terms of software overhead.

## 2.2 Transactions

To make memory-mapped structures robust in the face of application and system failures, the system must provide useful, well-defined guarantees about how and when changes to a data structure become permanent. NV-heaps use ACID transactions for this purpose because they provide an elegant method for mediating access to shared data as well as robustness in the face of failures. Programmer-managed locks cannot provide that robustness. Recent work on (volatile) transactional memory [8, 22, 24, 26, 27, 50, 56] demonstrates that transactions may also be easier to use than locks in some cases.

Systems that provide persistence, including persistent object stores [34, 37, 57, 61], some persistence systems for Java [7, 41], Rio Vista [38], RVM [51], Mnemosyne [60], Stasis [53], Argus [36], and QuickSilver [25], provide some kind of transactions, as do relational databases. However, the type of transactions vary considerably. For example, Stasis provides page-based transactions using write-ahead logging, a technique inspired by databases [45]. Mnemosyne also uses write-ahead logging, but operates at the word granularity. RVM and Rio Vista provide transactions without isolation, and RVM provides persistence guarantees only at log flushes. Single-level stores have taken other approaches that include checkpoints [55] and explicitly flushing objects to persistent storage [58].

## 2.3 Referential integrity

Referential integrity implies that all references (i.e., pointers) in a program point to valid data. Java and other managed languages have demonstrated the benefits of maintaining referential integrity: It avoids memory leaks, "wild" pointers, and the associated bugs.

In NV-heaps, referential integrity is more important and complex than in a conventional system. Integrity problems can arise in three ways, and each requires a different solution.

**Memory allocation** NV-heaps are subject to the memory leaks and pointer bugs that all programming systems face. Memory leaks, in particular, are more pernicious in a non-volatile setting. Once a region of storage leaks away, reclaiming it is very difficult. Preventing such problems requires some form of automatic garbage collection.

NV-heaps use reference counting, which means that space is reclaimed as soon as it becomes dead and that there is never a need to scan the entire NV-heap. The system avoids memory leaks due to cycles by using a well-known technique: weak pointers that do not affect reference counts. Several other garbage collection schemes [33, 47] for non-volatile storage have been proposed, and integrating a similar system into NV-heaps is a focus of our ongoing work.

Previous systems have taken different approaches to memory management. Non-volatile extensions to Java [4, 41] provide garbage collection, but Rio Vista [38], RVM [51], and Mnemosyne [60] do not. Java's persistence API [7] requires the programmer to specify a memory management policy via flexible (and potentially error-prone) annotations. Object-oriented databases have taken a range of approaches from providing simple garbage collection [10] to allowing applications to specify complex structural invariants on data structures [3].

**Volatile and non-volatile pointers** NV-heaps provide several new avenues for creating unsafe pointers because they partition the address space into a volatile memory area (i.e., the stack and volatile heap) and one or more NV-heaps.

This partitioning gives rise to four new types of pointers: Pointers within a single NV-heap (*intra-heap* NV-to-NV pointers), pointers between two NV-heaps (*inter-heap* NV-to-NV pointers), pointers from volatile memory to an NV-heap (V-to-NV pointers), and pointers from an NV-heap to volatile memory (NV-to-V pointers).

Ensuring referential integrity in NV-heaps requires that the system obey two invariants. The first is that there are no NV-to-V pointers, since they become meaningless once the program ends and would be unsafe the next time the program uses the NV-heap.

The second invariant is that there are no inter-heap NV-to-NV pointers. Inter-heap pointers become unsafe if the NV-heap that contains the object is not available. Inter-heap pointers also complicate garbage collection, since it is impossible to tell if a given location in an NV-heap is actually dead if a pointer in another (potentially unavailable) NV-heap may refer to it.

NV-heaps enforce these invariants via a simple dynamic type system. Each pointer and each object carries an identifier of the heap (NV-heap or volatile heap) that it belongs to. Mismatched assignments are a run-time error. As far as we know, NV-heaps are the first system to explicitly identify and prohibit these types of dangerous pointers. Rio Vista [38] and RVM [51] make no attempts to eliminate any of these pointer types. Also, full-fledged persistent object systems such as ObjectStore do not guard against these dangerous pointers, leaving the system and underlying database vulnerable to corruption [23]. However, other systems effectively eliminate dangerous pointers. JavaCard [2], a subset of Java for the very constrained environment of code running on a smart card, makes almost all objects persistent and collects them in a single heap. In Java's persistence API [7] the underlying database determines which NV-to-NV pointers exist and whether they are well-behaved. It prohibits NV-to-V pointers through constraints on objects that can be mapped to rows in the database.

**Closing NV-heaps** Unmapping an NV-heap can also create unsafe pointers. On closing, any V-to-NV pointers into the NV-heap become invalid (but non-null). Our implementation avoids this possibility by unmapping NV-heaps only at program exit, but other alternatives are possible. For instance, a V-to-NV pointer could use a proxy object to check whether the NV-heap it points into is still open.

### 2.4 Performance and scalability

NV-heaps provide common case performance that is close to that of the underlying memory for data structures that scale up to the terabyte range. All common case operations (e.g., reading or writing data, starting and completing transactions) occur in user space. NV-heaps make system calls to map themselves into the application's address space and to expand the heap as needed. Entering the OS more frequently would severely impact performance since system call overheads are large (e.g., 6 $\mu$s for a 4 KB read on our system) compared to memory access time.

The result is a system that is very lightweight compared to previous persistent object systems that include sophisticated buffer management systems to hide disk latency [11, 30, 34, 57, 61] and/or costly serialization/deserialization mechanisms [7]. Unlike these systems, NV-heaps operate directly on non-volatile data that is accessible through the processor-memory bus, thereby avoiding the operating system. Rio Vista [38] is similar to NV-heaps, since it runs directly on battery-backed DRAM, but it does not provide any of the safety guarantees of NV-heaps. Mnemosyne [60] also provides direct access to fast, non-volatile memories, but providing the level of safety in NV-heaps requires more effort.

We have designed NV-heaps to support multi-terabyte data structures, so we expect that the amount of non-volatile storage available in the system may be much larger than the amount of volatile storage. To allow access to large structures, NV-heaps require a fixed, small amount of volatile storage to access an NV-heap of any size. NV-heaps also ensure that the running time of operations, including recovery, are a function only of the amount of data they access, not the size of the NV-heap.

### 2.5 Ease of use

To be useful, NV-heaps need to be easy to use and interact cleanly with each other and with existing system components. NV-heaps also need to make it clear which portions of a program's data are non-volatile and which NV-heap they belong to.

NV-heaps exist as ordinary files in a file system in a manner similar to previous persistent object store implementations [57, 61]. Using files for NV-heaps is crucial because the file system provides naming, storage management, and access control. These features are necessary for storage, but they are not needed for systems like [48, 49, 62] that simply use non-volatile memories as a replacement for DRAM.

Like any file, it is possible to copy, rename, and transmit an NV-heap. This portability means that NV-heaps must be completely self-contained. The prohibition against NV-to-V and inter-heap NV-to-NV pointers guarantees this isolation. An additional feature, relative pointers (described in Section 3), provides (nearly) zero-cost pointer "swizzling" and makes NV-heaps completely relocatable within an application's address space.

We chose to make NV-heaps self-contained to make them easier to manage with existing file-based tools. However, this choice means that NV-heaps do not natively support transactions that span multiple NV-heaps. Implementing such transactions would require that NV-heaps share some non-volatile state (e.g., the "committed" bit for the transaction). The shared state would have to be available to both NV-heaps at recovery, something that self-contained NV-heaps cannot guarantee. It is possible to move objects between non-volatile data structures, but those structures need to reside in the same NV-heap.

While NV-heaps make it easy to implement non-volatile data structures, they do not provide the "orthogonal persistence" that persistent object stores [34, 57, 61] and some dialects of Java [4, 18, 41] provide. Orthogonal persistence allows programmers to designate an existing pointer as the "root" and have all objects reachable from that pointer become *implicitly* persistent regardless of their type. This is an elegant abstraction, but using reachability to confer persistence leads to several potential problems. For instance, the programmer may inadvertently make more data persistent than intended. In addition, the abstraction breaks down for objects that cannot or should not be made persistent, such as an object representing a network connection, a file descriptor, or a secret key. Finally, it is possible for a single object to be reachable from two roots, leading to the confusing situation of multiple copies of the same object in two different persistent structures.

NV-heaps provide an alternative model for persistence. Each NV-heap has a designated root pointer, and everything reachable from the root is persistent and part of the same NV-heap. The difference is that the program *explicitly* creates a persistent object in the NV-heap and attaches it to another object in the heap with a pointer. This does not prevent all errors (e.g., it is still possible to inappropriately store a file descriptor in an NV-heap), but it requires that the programmer explicitly add the data to the NV-heap. It also prevents a single object from being part of two NV-heaps.

```
class NVList : public NVObject {
  DECLARE_POINTER_TYPES(NVList);
public:
  DECLARE_MEMBER(int, value);
  DECLARE_PTR_MEMBER(NVList::NVPtr, next);
};

void remove(int k)
{
  NVHeap * nv = NVHOpen("foo.nvheap");
  NVList::VPtr a =
           nv->GetRoot<NVList::NVPtr>();
  AtomicBegin {
    while(a->get_next() != NULL) {
      if (a->get_next()->get_value() == k) {
        a->set_next(a->get_next()->get_next());
      }
      a = a->get_next();
    }
  } AtomicEnd;
}
```

**Figure 2. NV-heap example** A simple NV-heap function that atomically removes all links with value k from a non-volatile linked list.

This model for persistence is similar to what is imposed by the Thor [37] persistent object store, but Thor does so through a type-safe database programming language.

### 2.6 Example

The code in Figure 2 provides an example of how a programmer can create a non-volatile data structure using NV-heaps. The code removes the value k from a linked list. Declaring the linked list class as a subclass of `NV_Object` marks it as non-volatile. The `DECLARE_POINTER_TYPES`, `DECLARE_MEMBER`, and `DECLARE_PTR_MEMBER` macros declare the smart pointer types for NV-to-NV and V-to-NV pointers (`NVList::NV_Ptr` and `NVList::V_Ptr`, respectively) and declare two fields. The declarations generate private fields in the class and public accessor functions (e.g., `get_next()` and `set_next()`) that provide access to data and perform logging and locking.

The program uses `NVHOpen()` to open an NV-heap and then retrieves the root object, in this case a list of integers. It stores the pointer to the linked list as a NVList::V_Ptr. `AtomicBegin` starts a transaction. When the atomic section is complete, the NV-heap attempts to commit the changes. If it fails or if the system crashes, it will roll the operations back.

In the next section we describe the implementation of the NV-heap library in detail.

## 3. Implementing NV-heaps

Two considerations drove our implementation of NV-heaps: The need for strong safety guarantees and our goal of maximizing performance on fast, non-volatile memories. We implemented NV-heaps as a C++ library under Linux. The system is fully functional running on top of a RAM disk backed by DRAM. Below, we describe the technologies that NV-heaps target and the support they require from the OS and hardware. Then we describe our implementations of memory management, reference safety, and transactions. Finally, we discuss the storage overheads and how we validated our implementation.

### 3.1 Fast, byte-addressable non-volatile memories

NV-heaps target solid-state memory technologies that present a DRAM-like interface (e.g., via LPDDR [31]) and achieve performance within a small factor of DRAM. To evaluate NV-heaps we consider two advanced non-volatile memories: phase change memory (PCM) and spin-torque transfer memory (STTM).

PCM stores data as the crystalline state of a chalcogenide layer [9] and has the potential to become a viable main memory technology as DRAM's scaling falters [35, 49, 62]. PCM may also eventually surpass flash memory in density according to the ITRS [29]. The analysis in [35] provides a good characterization of PCM's performance and power consumption.

STTM stores bits as a magnetic orientation of one layer of a magnetic tunnel junction [20]. We assume 22nm STTM technology and base our estimates for performance on published papers [32, 59] and discussions with industry.

PCM and, to a lesser extent, STTM, along with most other non-volatile memories require some form of wear management to ensure reasonable device lifetime. Many wear-leveling schemes are available [15, 19, 35, 48, 62] and some can provide excellent wear-leveling at the memory controller level for less than 1% overhead. NV-heaps (like BPFS [17]) assume that the system provides this service to all the applications that use the storage.

### 3.2 System-level support

NV-heaps require a few simple facilities from the system. To the file system, NV-heaps are normal files. To access them efficiently, the file system should be running on top of byte-addressable non-volatile memory that appears in the CPU's physical address space. To open an NV-heap, the system uses `mmap()`. Normally, the kernel copies `mmap()`'d data between a block device and DRAM. In a system in which byte-addressable non-volatile memories appear in the processor's address space, copying is not necessary. Instead, `mmap()` maps the underlying physical memory pages directly into the application's virtual address space. In our kernel (2.6.28), the brd ramdisk driver combined with ext2 provides this capability.

The second requirement is a mechanism to ensure that previous updates to non-volatile storage have reached the storage and are permanent. For memory-mapped files, `msync()` provides this functionality, but the system call overhead is too high for NV-heaps. Instead, NV-heaps rely on architectural support in the form of the atomic 8-byte writes and epoch barriers developed for BPFS [17] to provide atomicity and consistency. Epoch barriers require small changes to the memory hierarchy and a new instruction to specify and enforce an ordering between groups of memory operations. Section 4 describes how we model the overhead for these operations. BPFS also provides durability support by incorporating capacitors onto the memory cards to allow in-progress operations to finish in the event of a power failure. We assume similar hardware support.

### 3.3 Memory management

The NV-heap memory management system implements allocation, automatic garbage collection, reference counting, and pointer assignments as simple, fixed-size ACID transactions. These basic operations form the foundation on which we build full-blown transactions.

**Atomicity and Durability** The allocator uses fixed-size, non-volatile, redo-logs called *operation descriptors* (similar to the statically-sized transactions in [56]) to provide atomicity and durability for memory allocation and reference-counted pointer manipulation. There is one set of operation descriptors per thread and the design ensures that a thread only ever requires one of each type of

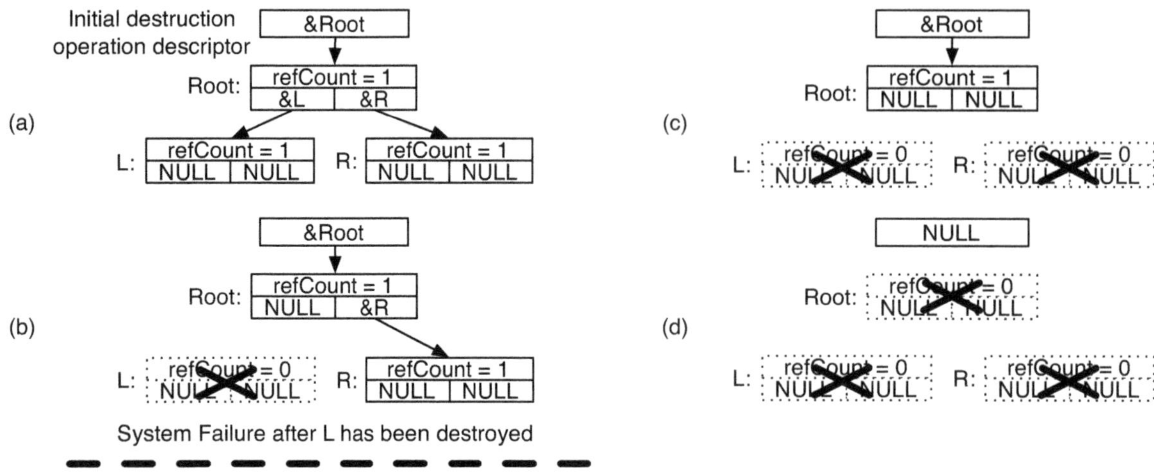


**Figure 3. Restartable object destruction** Durable, atomic reference counting requires being able to restart the recursive destruction of a potentially large numbers of objects. In this example the root node of a tree is destroyed and triggers the deletion of the entire tree. After a system failure, the process resumes and completes during the recovery process.

descriptor for all operations. Epoch barriers ensure that the descriptors are in a consistent state before the operation logically commits.

**Concurrency** To provide support for concurrent accesses to objects, each persistent object contains a lock that protects its reference count. The transaction system protects the other data in the object.

Locks are volatile by nature because they only have meaning during run-time. Therefore, to operate correctly, all locks must be released after a system failure. This could necessitate a scan of the entire storage array, violating our scalability requirement.

We avoid this problem by using *generational locks*: We associate a current *generation number* with each NV-heap, and the system increments the generation number when the NV-heap is reloaded. A generational lock is an integer. If the integer is equal to the current generation number, a thread holds it, otherwise, it is available. Therefore, incrementing the NV-heap's generation instantly releases all of its locks.

**Allocation** The allocator uses per-thread free lists and a shared global free list to reduce contention. If free space is not available, the NV-heap library expands the file that holds the NV-heap and maps that storage into the address space.

Prior work in memory management for multi-core systems played a part in the design of the NV-heap allocator. Memory allocators such as Hoard [6] use a global heap and per-thread heaps to efficiently support parallel applications. McRT-Malloc is a memory allocator designed specifically for a software transactional memory system in a multi-core environment [28].

**Deallocation** When the reference counting system discovers that an object is dead, it deallocates the storage. The deallocation routine atomically calls the destructor, deallocates the memory, and sets the requester's pointer to NULL. Deallcoation is a potentially complex process since the destructor may cause the reference counts on other objects to go to zero, necessitating their destruction as well.

To implement atomic recursive destruction, the NV-heap records the top level object to be destroyed in the *root deletion* operation descriptor and then calls its destructor. When the destructor encounters a pointer to another object, it checks that object's reference count. If the reference count is one (i.e., this is the last pointer to the object), it performs that deallocation using the *non-root deletion* descriptor. If that deletion causes a further recursive deletion, the non-root descriptor is reassigned to that deletion. The combination of the root and non-root descriptors provide a snapshot of the recursive deletion process that 1) requires only two descriptors regardless of recursion depth and 2) allows the process to restart in the case of failure.

On recovery, the NV-heap processes the non-root descriptor first to restore the invariant that all non-null pointers in the structure point to valid objects. It then restarts the root deletion, which will try to perform the same set of recursive destructions. It will encounter NULL pointers up until the point of the system failure and then resume deletion.

Figure 3 shows the algorithm in action. The system has just begun to delete a tree rooted at `Root` since the last pointer to it has just been set to NULL by the application. In (a), the operation descriptor for the starting point for the deletion holds the address of `Root`. The destruction proceeds by destroying the left child, `L`, and setting the left child pointer in `Root` to NULL.

At this point (b), the system fails. During recovery, it finds a valid operation descriptor and restarts the delete. Since the original destruction of `L` was atomic, the pointer structure of the tree is still valid and the destruction operation can destroy `R` (c) and `Root` before invalidating the operation descriptor (d).

The only caveat is that an object's destructor may be called more than once. In most cases, this is not a problem, but some idioms that require the destructor to, for instance, track the number of live instances of an object will be more difficult to implement. In our experience using the system, however, this has not been a significant problem.

**Recovery** To recover from a system failure, the memory allocator performs the following two steps. First, it replays any valid operation descriptors for basic storage allocation and deallocation operations. Then, it replays any reference count updates and reference counting pointer assignments, which may include the recursive destruction process described above. When this is complete, all the reference counts are valid and up-to-date and the recovery process moves on to the transaction system.

### 3.4 Pointers in NV-heaps

The NV-heap library uses operator overloading to implement pointer types for NV-to-NV, V-to-NV, and weak NV-to-NV pointers. Their assignment operators, copy constructors, and cast operators work together with the memory allocator to enforce correct semantics for each pointer type.

The pointers play a key role in preventing the creation of inter-heap NV-to-NV pointers and NV-to-V pointers. NV-to-NV pointers are "wide" and include a pointer to the NV-heap they belong to. Non-volatile objects contain a similar pointer. The assignment operators for the pointer check that the assignment is valid (i.e., that the pointer and the object belong to the same NV-heap).

The smart pointer types also allow NV-heaps to be relocatable. Instead of holding the actual address (which would change from application to application or execution to execution), the pointer holds an offset from the pointer's address to the data it points to.

Below we describe the implementation of each pointer type.

**NV-to-NV pointers** NV-heaps support two types of NV-to-NV pointers. Normal NV-to-NV pointers affect reference counts and are the most common type of pointer in the applications we have written. They reside in the NV-heap and point to data in the same NV-heap.

*Weak* NV-to-NV pointers are similar but they do not affect an object's reference count. Weak pointers are required to implement cyclic data structures (e.g., doubly-linked lists) without introducing memory leaks. Ensuring that non-null weak NV-to-NV pointers point to valid data requires that when the object they refer to becomes dead (i.e., no more non-weak pointers refer to it), all the weak pointers should atomically become NULL. This may lead to an unexpected NULL pointer dereference, but it cannot result in corrupted data.

We use proxy objects to implement this behavior. Weak NV-to-NV pointers refer indirectly to the object via a proxy that contains a pointer to the actual object. When an object dies, its destructor sets the pointer in its proxy to NULL, instantly nullifying all the weak pointers. The system manages proxy objects with reference counting, similar to regular objects, because they must survive as long as there are weak pointers that refer to them.

**V-to-NV pointers** There are three key requirements for V-to-NV references. First, a V-to-NV reference must be sufficient to keep an object alive. Second, when a program exits and all the V-to-NV references are destroyed, the objects' reference counts must be adjusted accordingly. Third, the system must eventually reclaim any objects that become dead when a program exits and destroys all of the V-to-NV pointers.

To address the these issues, we add a second count of V-to-NV references to each object. One attractive solution is to store these counts in volatile memory. This would ensure they were reset correctly on exit, but, in the event of a system or application failure, the V-to-NV reference counts would be lost, making any dead objects now impossible to reclaim.

Our implementation stores the count of volatile references in non-volatile memory and uses the generation number technique we used for non-volatile locks to reset it. To locate orphaned objects, the NV-heap maintains a per-thread list of objects that only have V-to-NV references. On startup, the NV-heap reclaims everything in the list.

### 3.5 Implementing transactions

NV-heaps provide fine-grain consistency through atomic sections that log all updates to the heap in non-volatile memory. Atomic sections for NV-heaps build on previous work developing transactional memory systems for volatile memories [8, 22, 24, 26, 27, 50, 56]. The NV-heap transaction system is software-only (except for epoch barrier support), and it relies heavily on the transactional memory allocator and reference counting system described in Sections 3.3 and 3.4.

**Transactions in NV-heaps** Our implementation of NV-heaps provides ACID semantics for programs that meet two criteria: First, a program must use the accessor functions to access object fields and it must not use unsafe casts to circumvent the C++ type system. Second, transactions should not access shared *volatile* state, since the NV-heap transaction system does not protect it. We have not found this to be a significant problem in our use of NV-heaps, but we plan to extend the system to cover volatile data as well. Failure to adhere to the second condition only impacts isolation between transactions.

NV-heap's log processing is the main difference relative to conventional volatile transactional memory systems. NV-heaps maintain a volatile read log and a non-volatile write log for each transaction. When a transaction wants to modify an object, it must be opened for writing, meaning the system will make a copy of the object so that any changes can be rolled back in case of an abort or system/application failure. When this happens, the running atomic section must take ownership of the object by acquiring a volatile lock in a table of ownership records indexed by the low-order bits of the object's unique ID. If another transaction owns the object, a conflict has occurred, and the atomic section retries. Once the atomic section becomes the owner, the NV-heap copies the object into the log. To open an object for reading, NV-heaps store a pointer to the object and its current version number in the read log.

After the system makes a copy of the object, the application can safely modify the original object. If a system or application failure occurs or the atomic section aborts, the NV-heap rolls back the object to its original state by using the copy stored in the write log.

We choose to copy entire objects to the log rather than individual object fields, and this is a common trade-off in transactional memory systems. In NV-heaps, each log operation requires an epoch barrier which has some performance cost. Copying the entire object helps to amortize this cost, and it pays off most when transactions make multiple updates to an object, which is a common feature of the data structures that we studied.

NV-heaps borrow ideas from DSTM [26], RSTM [40], DracoSTM [21], and McRT-STM [50]. The system logs entire objects as opposed to individual fields, and uses eager conflict detection for writes. It detects read conflicts by validating objects at access time using version numbers. It stores undo logs for outstanding transactions in non-volatile memory for recovery. The contention management scheme [52] backs off and retries in case of conflict. NV-heaps flatten nested transactions into a single transaction.

**Transaction abort and crash recovery** The processes for aborting a transaction and recovering from a system or application failure are very similar: NV-heaps roll back the transaction by restoring the backup copies from the log. In the case of a crash, the system first follows the recovery procedure defined in Section 3.3 to ensure that the memory allocator is in a consistent state and all reference counts are up-to-date.

An additional concern with crash recovery is that recovery must be restartable in the case of multiple failures. NV-heaps recover from failure by only rolling back valid log entries and using an epoch barrier to ensure that an entry's rollback is durably recorded in non-volatile storage before marking the entry invalid.

### 3.6 Storage and memory overheads

The storage overheads of NV-heaps are small. Each NV-heap contains a control region that holds the root pointer, pointers to the free lists, the operation descriptors, version information, and the current generation number. The storage requirement for the control area is 2 KB plus 1.5 KB per thread for operation descriptors. The NV-heap also uses 0.5 KB of volatile memory.

NV-to-NV and V-to-NV pointers are 128-bits which includes a 64-bit relative pointer and dynamic type information to prevent assignments that would create unsafe pointers. Each object includes 80 bytes of metadata including reference counts, a unique ID, ownership information, a generational lock, and other state. For small objects such as primitive data types and pointers, we provide an array object type to amortize the metadata overhead across many elements.

Supporting transactions requires 80 bytes of per-thread transaction state (e.g., pointers to logs) in addition to storage for the write logs.

### 3.7 Validation

To validate our implementation of the NV-heap allocator and transaction system, we created a set of stress tests that create complex objects and perform concurrent transactions on them. These tests exercise the concurrency and safety of the memory allocation operations, pointer assignments, and the user-defined transactions which run on top of them. We run these tests with up to eight threads for long periods (many hours) and observe no deadlock or data corruption.

To test recovery from failures, we run the tests and kill the program with `SIGKILL` at random intervals. During the recovery process we record which logs and operation descriptors the recovery system processes. Then we perform a consistency check. After killing our test programs thousands of times, we have observed numerous successful recoveries involving each descriptor and log type. In all cases, the recoveries were successful and the consistency checks passed.

## 4. Modeling fast non-volatile storage

NV-heaps aim to support systems with many gigabytes of high-performance non-volatile memory, but mature products based on those memories will take several years to appear. In the meantime, we use two emulation systems to run applications for many billions of instructions while simulating the performance impact of using advanced non-volatile memories.

### 4.1 Modeling byte-addressable storage

The first emulation system models the latency for memory-level load and store operations to advanced non-volatile memories on the processor's memory bus. The system uses Pin [39] to perform a detailed simulation of the system's memory hierarchy augmented with non-volatile memory technology and the atomicity support that NV-heaps require. The memory hierarchy simulator accounts for both the increased array read time and the added delay between a write and the operations that follow, allowing it to accurately model the longer read and write times of PCM and STTM memories. For PCM we use the performance model from [35] which gives a PCM read time of 67 ns and a write time of 215 ns. We model STTM performance (29 ns reads and 95 ns writes) based on [59] and discussion with industry. The baseline DRAM latency for our system is 25 ns for reads and 35 ns for writes, according to the datasheet.

We run the simulation on the first 100 million instructions out of each one billion instructions executed. The simulation provides the average latency for last level cache hits and misses and for the epoch barriers. After the simulation phase, we use hardware performance counters to track these events on a per-thread basis, and combine these counts with the average latencies to compute the total application run-time. The model assumes that memory accesses execute serially, which makes our execution time estimates conservative.

To calibrate our system we used a simple program that empirically determines the last-level cache miss latency. We ran the program with the simulated PCM and STTM arrays and its estimates matched our target latencies to within 10%.

### 4.2 Modeling block device based on advanced non-volatile memory

In Section 5, we compare NV-heaps to two systems, Stasis [53] and BerkelelyDB [46], that target a block device (i.e., a disk) instead of a non-volatile main memory. To model a non-volatile memory-based block device, we modified the Linux RAM disk driver to let us insert extra delay on accesses to match the latency of non-volatile memories. Measurements with a simple disk latency benchmark show that the emulation is accurate to within about 2%.

## 5. Results

This section describes our evaluation of NV-heaps. We describe the test system and then present experiments that measure basic operation latency. Next, we evaluate its scalability and performance on a range of benchmarks. We examine the overheads that NV-heaps incur to provide strong safety guarantees. Then, we compare NV-heaps to Stasis [53] and BerkeleyDB [46], transactional storage systems that target conventional block devices. Finally, we evaluate performance at the application level by implementing a version Memcachedb [16], a persistent key-value store for dynamic Web applications, with NV-heaps.

### 5.1 System configuration

We present results collected on two-socket, Core 2 Quad (a total of 8 cores) machines running at 2.5 GHz with 64 GB of physical DRAM and 12 MB L2 caches. These machines are equipped with both a conventional 250 GB hard drive and a 32GB Intel Extreme flash-based SSD. We configure the machines with a 32GB RAM disk. We use 24 GB for emulated non-volatile memory and 8 GB for program execution. For the experiments that use disks and the SSD we report "wall clock" timing measurements.

### 5.2 Basic operation performance

Table 1 summarizes the basic operation latencies for several implementations of NV-heaps that isolate different overheads that NV-heaps incur. BASE, SAFE, TX, and C-TX represent four layers of the system that offer varying levels of safety and performance. The BASE layer provides manual memory management and checkpointing, yielding a system very similar to Rio Vista [38]. The SAFE layer adds automatic memory management and pointer safety. The third layer, TX, extends SAFE with transactions for atomicity and durability in single-threaded programs. Layer C-TX provides support for concurrency through multi-threaded transactions. Finally, the version NoDur is a volatile transactional memory system without support for durability. The table reports latencies for each implementation of NV-heaps running on DRAM. It also reports measurements for the C-TX version running on emulated STTM and PCM.

The value for "new/delete" is the time to allocate and deallocate a very small object. The three "ptr" rows give the time to assign to a pointer and then set it to NULL. The "nop tx" is the time to execute an empty transaction. "Log for read" and "Log for write" give the times to log an object before access.

For C-TX (i.e., full-fledged NV-heaps), the most expensive operation is logging an object for writing. This operation only occurs once per modified object per transaction and requires an allocation, a copy, one pointer manipulation, and several epoch barriers. The cost of an epoch barrier depends on the size of the epoch and whether or not the corresponding cache lines have been written back yet. Our operation descriptors tend to be small, so the cost is often the time to flush a only single cache line.

In contrast, V-to-NV pointer manipulation and read logging are extremely inexpensive, because they do not require durability guarantees or, therefore, epoch barriers. In fact, these operations

| Layer | BASE | SAFE | TX | C-TX | | | NoDur |
|---|---|---|---|---|---|---|---|
| Storage technology | DRAM ($\mu$s) | | | DRAM ($\mu$s) | STTM ($\mu$s) | PCM ($\mu$s) | DRAM ($\mu$s) |
| new/delete | <0.1 | <0.1 | <0.1 | <0.1 | 0.75 | 2.16 | <0.1 |
| V-to-NV ptr | 0.03 | 0.05 | 0.11 | 0.13 | 0.13 | 0.13 | 0.08 |
| NV-to-NV ptr | 0.03 | 0.05 | 0.17 | 0.25 | 0.72 | 1.68 | 0.13 |
| weak NV-to-NV ptr | n/a | 0.05 | 0.20 | 0.25 | 0.78 | 1.84 | 0.15 |
| nop tx | n/a | n/a | 0.05 | 0.05 | 0.05 | 0.05 | 0.05 |
| log for read | n/a | n/a | 0.17 | 0.26 | 0.26 | 0.26 | 0.21 |
| log for write | n/a | n/a | 1.68 | 1.99 | 5.55 | 12.67 | 1.00 |

**Table 1. Basic operation latency for NV-heaps** Support for durability at various levels and the increased latency for PCM and STTM both exact a toll in terms of basic operation latencies. Latencies for "new/delete" are listed as <0.1 because of inconsistencies due to caching effects.

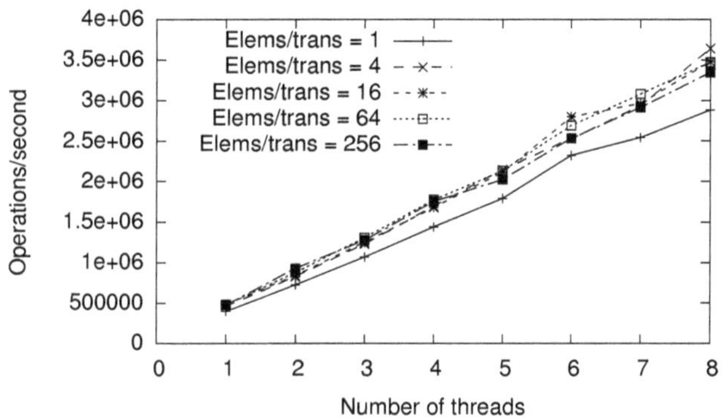


**Figure 4. Throughput vs. transaction size.** We scaled the number of elements a transaction modifies from one to 256 as we scaled the number of threads in order to show the effect of transaction size on throughput.

| Name | Footprint | Description |
|---|---|---|
| SPS | 24 GB | Random swaps between entries in an 8 GB array of integers. |
| SixDegs | 8 GB | Concurrently performs two operations: 1) Search for a path of length no more than six between two vertices in a large, scale-free graph 2) modify the graph by inserting and removing edges. |
| BTree | 4 GB | Searches for an integer in a B-tree. Insert it if it is absent, remove it otherwise. |
| HashTable | 8 GB | Searches for an integer in an open-chain hash table. Insert it if it is absent, remove it otherwise. |
| RBTree | 24 GB | Searches for an integer in a 24 GB red-black tree. Insert it if it is absent, remove it otherwise. |
| SSCA | 3 MB | A transactional implementation of SSCA 2.2 [5]. It performs several analyses of a large, scale-free graph. |

**Table 2. Workloads** We use six workloads of varying complexity to evaluate NV-heaps.

can occur entirely in the CPU's caches, so the impact of longer memory latencies is minimal.

The PCM and STTM data show the impact that slower underlying memory technology will have on basic operation performance. PCM's longer write latency increases the cost of write logging by 6.4× relative to DRAM. STTM shows a smaller increase — just 2.8×.

Figure 4 shows how performance scales with transaction size. It measures throughput for updates to an array of one million elements as we vary the number of updates performed in a single transaction from one to 256. The overhead of beginning and completing a transaction is most pronounced for transactions that access only a single element. Increasing the number of elements to four amortizes most of this cost, and beyond that, the improvement is marginal. Overall, the scaling is good: Eight threads provide 7.5× the throughput of a single thread.

### 5.3 Benchmark performance

Because existing interfaces to non-volatile storage make it difficult to build complex data structures in non-volatile memory, there are no "off the shelf" workloads with which to evaluate our system. Instead, we have written a set of benchmarks from scratch and ported an additional one to use NV-heaps. Table 2 describes them.

Figure 5 shows the performance of the benchmarks. The numbers inside each bar are the operations (inserts/deletes for BTree, RBTree, and HashTable; path searches for SixDegs; updates or swaps for SPS; iterations through the outer loop of the final phase for SSCA) per second. The graph normalizes performance to NoDur with one thread.

The difference between the NoDur and DRAM bar in each group shows that adding durability to the transaction and memory management systems reduces performance by 40% on average. The cost is largest for SixDegs, because it executes complex transactions and requires frequent epoch barriers. The remaining bars show that the impact of increasing latency of the underlying memory technology is roughly proportional to the change in latency.

Differences in program behavior lead to varied scaling behavior. SPS, HashTable, and BTree scale very well (7.6×, 7.3×, and 7×, respectively, with 8 threads), while SixDegs and SSCA scale less well due to long transactions and additional conflicts between atomic sections with increasing thread count. We have found that much of this contention is due to the applications rather than NV-heaps. For instance, reducing the search depth in SixDegs from six to one improves scalability significantly.

### 5.4 The price of safety

To understand the cost of NV-heap's usability features, we have implemented our benchmarks in the layers BASE, SAFE, TX, and C-TX described previously. Figure 6 shows the performance of our benchmarks implemented in each NV-heaps layer. The absolute performance is given in operations per second in the BASE bar

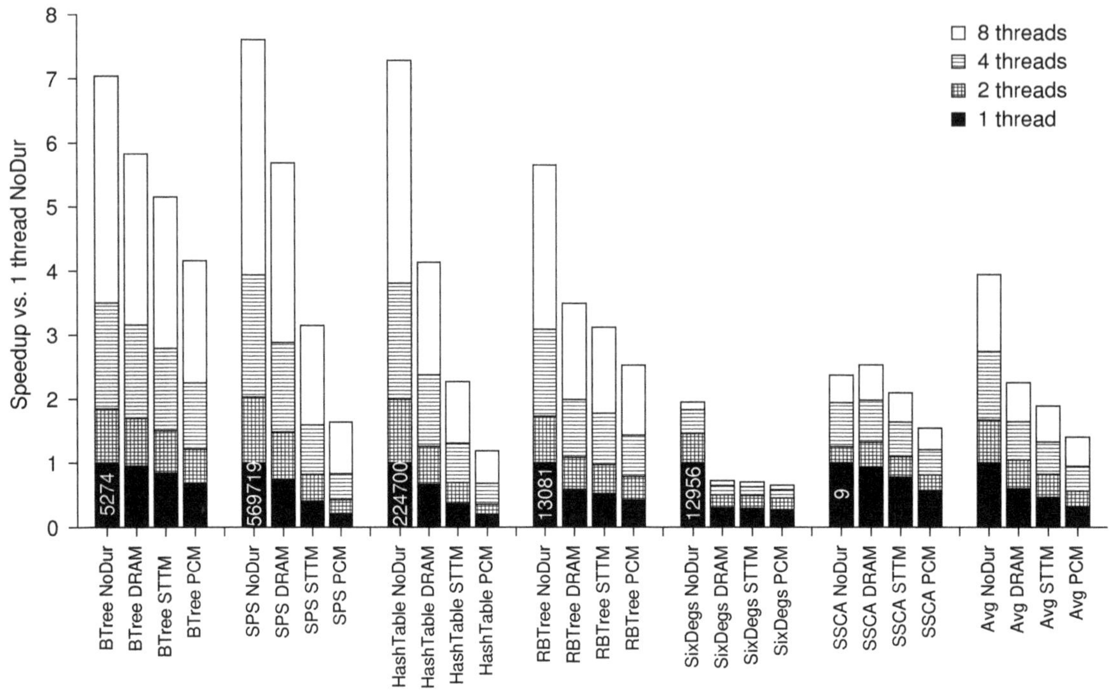


**Figure 5. NV-heap performance** Both adding durability and running on non-volatile memory affect NV-heap performance. Numbers in the bars are the throughput for the single-threaded version.

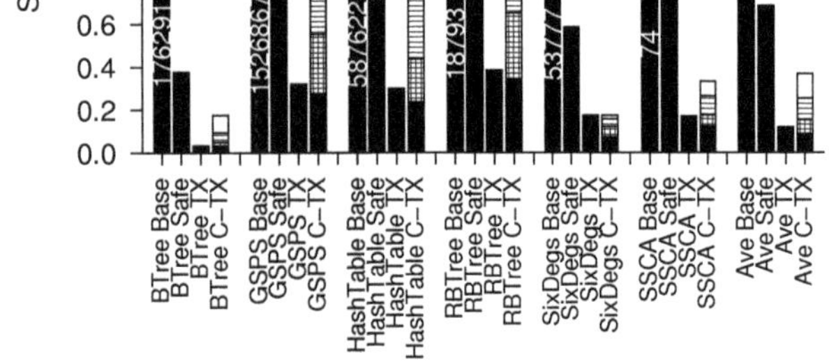


**Figure 6. The price of safety in NV-heaps** Removing safety guarantees improves performance by as much as 11×, but the resulting system is very difficult to use correctly. The different layers highlight the safety and performance trade-off.

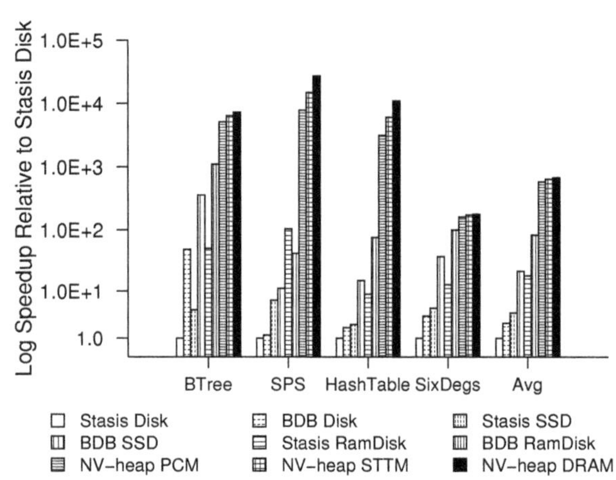


**Figure 7. Comparison to other persistent storage systems** NV-heaps outperform Berkeley DB and Stasis by 33 and 244× on average in large part because NV-heaps do not require system calls to provide durability guarantees.

for each benchmark. For a single thread, BASE provides the highest performance, but SAFE results in only a modest performance hit for most applications. One exception is BTree, which makes extensive use of NV-to-NV and weak NV-to-NV references, resulting in 62% lower performance for SAFE. This suggests that, for many applications, the extra safety that SAFE provides will be worth the performance penalty.

TX exacts a larger toll, reducing performance by 82% on average versus SAFE. The cost of durability is due to the copying required to log objects in non-volatile memory. The price is especially steep for BTree, because writing a node of the tree into the log requires many pointer copies.

Adding support for concurrency and conflict detection in C-TX has a small effect on peformance (30% on average relative to TX), and allows HashTable, RBTree, and SPS to reclaim much of their lost performance.

The gap in performance between BASE and C-TX, 11× on average for single-threaded programs, is the cost of safety in our system. The increase in performance of BASE is significant, but the price in terms of usability is high. The programmer must explicitly manage concurrency, atomicity, and failure recovery while avoiding the accidental creation of unsafe pointers. Whether this extra effort is worth the increased performance depends on the application and the amount of time the programmer is willing to spend testing and debugging the code. We found programming in this style to be tedious and error-prone.

### 5.5 Comparison to other systems

This section compares NV-heaps to two other systems that also provide transactional access to persistent state. We compare NV-heaps to Stasis [53], a persistent object system that targets disk and BerkeleyDB [54], a lightweight database. Both provide ACID transactions.

NV-heaps, Stasis, and BerkeleyDB have a similar high-level goal — to provide an easy-to-use interface to persistent data with strong consistency guarantees. Stasis and BerkeleyDB, however, target conventional spinning disks rather than byte-addressable storage. This means they must use system calls to force updates to disk and provide durability while NV-heaps take advantage of fast epoch barriers to enforce ordering.

Figure 7 compares NV-heap DRAM, NV-heap STTM, and NV-heap PCM to Stasis and BerkeleyDB running on three different hardware configurations: An enterprise hard disk, an Intel Extreme 32 GB SSD, and a RAM-disk. We implemented the data structures in Stasis ourselves. We used BerkeleyDB's built-in BTree and HashTable implementations and implemented SixDegs by hand. The vertical axis is a log scale. The data are for four threads. These results are for smaller, 4 GB data sets to keep initialization times manageable for the disk-based runs.

The first six bars in each group measure BerkeleyDB's and Stasis' performance on disks, SSDs, and the RAM-disk. The data show that while BerkeleyDB and Stasis benefit from running on fast non-volatile memory (e.g., BerkeleyDB on the RAM-disk is 3.2× faster than on the SSD and 24× than running on disk), the benefits are only a fraction of the raw speedup that non-volatile memories provide compared to SSDs and hard disks.

The next three bars in each group show that NV-heaps do a much better job exploiting that raw performance. NV-heap DRAM is between 2 and 643× faster than BerkeleyDB, and the performance difference for Stasis is between 13 and 814×. Two components contribute to this gap. The first is the `fsync()` and/or `msync()` required for durability on a block device. Removing this overhead by disabling these calls (and sacrificing durability) improves performance by between 2 and 10× for BerkeleyDB. The remaining gap in performance is due to other software overheads.

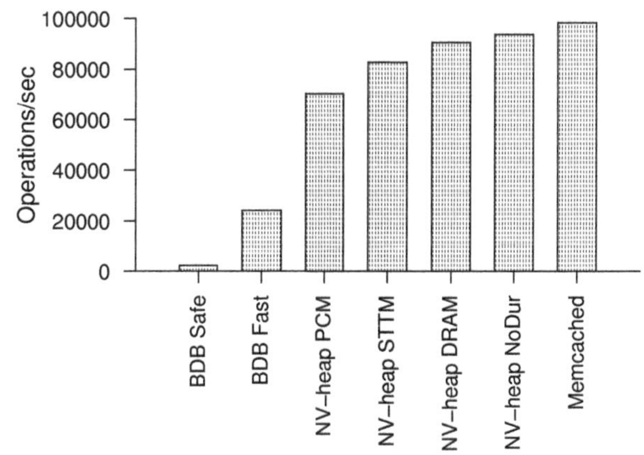


**Figure 8. Memcached performance** Using NV-heaps brings performance to within 8% of the original, non-durable Memcached, and the NV-heaps version achieves 39× higher throughput than Memcachedb (BDB Safe) which provides similar safety guarantees.

Comparing NV-heap performance to BerkeleyDB demonstrates that NV-heaps are both flexible and efficient. The NV-heap PCM BTree is 6.7× faster than BerkeleyDB running on the same technology, despite the fact that the BerkeleyDB version is a highly-optimized, specialized implementation. In contrast, the NV-heap implementation uses just the components that NV-heaps provide. We see similar performance for SPS and HashTable. For SixDegs, BerkeleyDB is nearly as fast as the NV-heaps, but this is, in part, because the BerkeleyDB version does not include reference counting. Removing dead nodes from the graph requires a scan of the entire table that stores them.

It is worth noting that our results for comparing BerkeleyDB and Stasis do not match the results in the original Stasis paper [53]. We suspect this is due to improvements in BerkeleyDB over the past five years and/or inefficiencies in our use of Stasis. However, assuming results similar to those in the original paper would not significantly alter the above conclusions.

### 5.6 Application-level performance

This section measures the impact of NV-heaps at the application level. We focus on Memcachedb [16], a version of Memcached [42] that provides a persistent key-value store. By default, Memcachedb uses BerkeleyDB to store the key-value pairs and provide persistence.

Our version of Memcachedb uses the NV-heap open-chaining hash table implementation we evaluated in Section 5.3 to hold the key-value store. All operations on the key-value store are transactional.

Figure 8 shows the throughput of insert/delete operations for the original Memcached application, the Berkeley DB implementation (Memcachedb), and our NV-heap implementation. All tests use 16 byte keys and 512 byte values. The multi-threaded client test program uses the libMemcached [1] library, and it runs on the same machine as the server to put maximum pressure on the key-value store. We measure performance of the BerekeleyDB-based version of Memcachedb with (BDB Safe) and without (BDB Fast) synchronous writes. Memcachedb uses the BerkeleyDB hash table implementation and runs on a RAM disk.

Compared to the original Memcached running in DRAM, adding persistence with NV-heaps results in only an 8 to 16% performance penalty depending on the storage technology. When we run NV-heaps without durability (NoDur), performance is within just 5% of Memcached, indicating that the overhead for durability can be low in practice.

The data show that our hash table implementation provides much higher throughput than BerkeleyDB and that the overhead for providing transactional reliability is much lower with NV-heaps. NV-heap DRAM outperforms BDB Safe by up to 39× and NV-heap NoDur outperforms BDB Fast by 3.9×. BerkeleyDB provides many features that our hash table lacks, but for this application those features are not necessary. This highlights one of the advantages of NV-heaps — they allow programmers to provide (and pay the performance penalty for) only the features they need for a particular application.

## 6. Conclusion

We have described NV-heaps, a system for creating persistent data structures on top of fast, byte addressable, non-volatile memories. NV-heaps prevent several classes of well-known programming errors as well as several new types of errors that arise only in persistent data structures. As a result, NV-heaps allow programmers to implement very fast persistent structures that are robust in the face of system and application failures. The performance cost of the protections that NV-heaps provide is modest, especially compared to the overall gains that non-volatile memories can offer.

## Acknowledgements

The authors would like to thank Geoff Voelker for his valuable feedback, Michael Swift and Haris Volos for their comments, and Amir Roth for his encouragement. We would also like to thank the reviewers for their feedback and suggestions that have improved this paper significantly.

## References

[1] B. Aker. Libmemcached. http://libmemcached.org/.

[2] P. Allenbach. Java card 3: Classic functionality gets a connectivity boost, March 2009. http://java.sun.com/developer/technicalArticles/javacard/javacard3/.

[3] T. Andrews and C. Harris. Combining language and database advances in an object-oriented development environment. In *OOPSLA '87: Conference proceedings on Object-oriented programming systems, languages and applications*, pages 430–440, New York, NY, USA, 1987. ACM.

[4] M. P. Atkinson, L. Daynès, M. J. Jordan, T. Printezis, and S. Spence. An orthogonally persistent java. *SIGMOD Rec.*, 25(4):68–75, 1996.

[5] D. A. Bader and K. Madduri. Design and implementation of the hpcs graph analysis benchmark on symmetric multiprocessors. In *HiPC 2005: Proc. 12th International Conference on High Performance Computing*, pages 465–476, December 2005.

[6] E. D. Berger, K. S. McKinley, R. D. Blumofe, and P. R. Wilson. Hoard: a scalable memory allocator for multithreaded applications. In *ASPLOS-IX: Proceedings of the ninth international conference on Architectural support for programming languages and operating systems*, pages 117–128, New York, NY, USA, 2000. ACM.

[7] R. Biswas and E. Ort. The java persistence api - a simpler programming model for entity persistence, May 2006. http://java.sun.com/developer/technicalArticles/J2EE/jpa/.

[8] C. Blundell, J. Devietti, E. C. Lewis, and M. M. K. Martin. Making the fast case common and the uncommon case simple in unbounded transactional memory. In *ISCA '07: Proceedings of the 34th annual international symposium on Computer architecture*, pages 24–34, New York, NY, USA, 2007. ACM.

[9] M. J. Breitwisch. Phase change memory. *Interconnect Technology Conference, 2008. IITC 2008. International*, pages 219–221, June 2008.

[10] P. Butterworth, A. Otis, and J. Stein. The gemstone object database management system. *Commun. ACM*, 34(10):64–77, 1991.

[11] M. J. Carey, D. J. DeWitt, G. Graefe, D. M. Haight, J. E. Richardson, D. T. Schuh, E. J. Shekita, and S. L. Vandenberg. The exodus extensible dbms project: an overview. pages 474–499, 1990.

[12] R. G. Cattell. *Object Data Management: Object-Oriented and Extended.* Addison-Wesley Longman Publishing Co., Inc., Boston, MA, USA, 1994.

[13] A. M. Caulfield, J. Coburn, T. I. Mollov, A. De, A. Akel, J. He, A. Jagatheesan, R. K. Gupta, A. Snavely, and S. Swanson. Understanding the impact of emerging non-volatile memories on high-performance, io-intensive computing. In *Proceedings of the 2010 ACM/IEEE International Conference for High Performance Computing, Networking, Storage and Analysis*, SC '10, pages 1–11, Washington, DC, USA, 2010. IEEE Computer Society.

[14] A. M. Caulfield, A. De, J. Coburn, T. I. Mollov, R. K. Gupta, and S. Swanson. Moneta: A high-performance storage array architecture for next-generation, non-volatile memories. In *Proceedings of the 43nd Annual IEEE/ACM International Symposium on Microarchitecture*, MICRO 43, pages 385–395, New York, NY, USA, 2010. ACM.

[15] S. Cho and H. Lee. Flip-n-write: a simple deterministic technique to improve pram write performance, energy and endurance. In *Proceedings of the 42nd Annual IEEE/ACM International Symposium on Microarchitecture*, MICRO 42, pages 347–357, New York, NY, USA, 2009. ACM.

[16] S. Chu. Memcachedb. http://memcachedb.org/.

[17] J. Condit, E. B. Nightingale, C. Frost, E. Ipek, B. Lee, D. Burger, and D. Coetzee. Better i/o through byte-addressable, persistent memory. In *Proceedings of the ACM SIGOPS 22nd symposium on Operating systems principles*, SOSP '09, pages 133–146, New York, NY, USA, 2009. ACM.

[18] A. Dearle, G. N. C. Kirby, and R. Morrison. Orthogonal persistence revisited. In *Proceedings of the Second international conference on Object databases*, ICOODB'09, pages 1–22, Berlin, Heidelberg, 2010. Springer-Verlag.

[19] G. Dhiman, R. Ayoub, and T. Rosing. Pdram: a hybrid pram and dram main memory system. In *DAC '09: Proceedings of the 46th Annual Design Automation Conference*, pages 664–469, New York, NY, USA, 2009. ACM.

[20] B. Dieny, R. Sousa, G. Prenat, and U. Ebels. Spin-dependent phenomena and their implementation in spintronic devices. *VLSI Technology, Systems and Applications, 2008. VLSI-TSA 2008. International Symposium on*, pages 70–71, April 2008.

[21] J. E. Gottschlich and D. A. Connors. Dracostm: a practical c++ approach to software transactional memory. In *LCSD '07: Proceedings of the 2007 Symposium on Library-Centric Software Design*, pages 52–66, New York, NY, USA, 2007. ACM.

[22] L. Hammond, V. Wong, M. Chen, B. D. Carlstrom, J. D. Davis, B. Hertzberg, M. K. Prabhu, H. Wijaya, C. Kozyrakis, and K. Olukotun. Transactional memory coherence and consistency. In *ISCA '04: Proceedings of the 31st annual international symposium on Computer architecture*, page 102, Washington, DC, USA, 2004. IEEE Computer Society.

[23] D. M. Hansen, D. R. Adams, and D. K. Gracio. In the trenches with objectstore. *TAPOS*, 5(4):201–207, 1999.

[24] T. Harris and K. Fraser. Language support for lightweight transactions. In *OOPSLA '03: Proceedings of the 18th annual ACM SIGPLAN conference on Object-oriented programing, systems, languages, and applications*, pages 388–402, New York, NY, USA, 2003. ACM.

[25] R. Haskin, Y. Malachi, W. Sawdon, and G. Chan. Recovery management in quicksilver. In *SOSP '87: Proceedings of the eleventh ACM Symposium on Operating systems principles*, pages 107–108, New York, NY, USA, 1987. ACM.

[26] M. Herlihy, V. Luchangco, M. Moir, and W. N. Scherer, III. Software transactional memory for dynamic-sized data structures. In *PODC '03: Proceedings of the twenty-second annual symposium on Principles of distributed computing*, pages 92–101, New York, NY, USA, 2003. ACM.

[27] M. Herlihy and J. E. B. Moss. Transactional memory: architectural support for lock-free data structures. In *ISCA '93: Proceedings of the 20th annual international symposium on Computer architecture*, pages 289–300, New York, NY, USA, 1993. ACM.

[28] R. L. Hudson, B. Saha, A.-R. Adl-Tabatabai, and B. C. Hertzberg. Mcrt-malloc: a scalable transactional memory allocator. In *ISMM '06:*

*Proceedings of the 5th international symposium on Memory management*, pages 74–83, New York, NY, USA, 2006. ACM.

[29] International technology roadmap for semiconductors: Emerging research devices, 2009.

[30] H. V. Jagadish, D. F. Lieuwen, R. Rastogi, A. Silberschatz, and S. Sudarshan. Dalí: A high performance main memory storage manager. In *VLDB '94: Proceedings of the 20th International Conference on Very Large Data Bases*, pages 48–59, San Francisco, CA, USA, 1994. Morgan Kaufmann Publishers Inc.

[31] Jedec standard: Low power double data rate 2 (lpddr2), March 2009.

[32] T. Kawahara, R. Takemura, K. Miura, J. Hayakawa, S. Ikeda, Y. M. Lee, R. Sasaki, Y. Goto, K. Ito, T. Meguro, F. Matsukura, H. Takahashi, H. Matsuoka, and H. Ohno. 2 mb spram (spin-transfer torque ram) with bit-by-bit bi-directional current write and parallelizing-direction current read. *Solid-State Circuits, IEEE Journal of*, 43(1):109–120, Jan. 2008.

[33] E. K. Kolodner and W. E. Weihl. Atomic incremental garbage collection and recovery for a large stable heap. In *SIGMOD '93: Proceedings of the 1993 ACM SIGMOD international conference on Management of data*, pages 177–186, New York, NY, USA, 1993. ACM.

[34] C. Lamb, G. Landis, J. Orenstein, and D. Weinreb. The objectstore database system. *Commun. ACM*, 34(10):50–63, 1991.

[35] B. C. Lee, E. Ipek, O. Mutlu, and D. Burger. Architecting phase change memory as a scalable dram alternative. In *ISCA '09: Proceedings of the 36th annual international symposium on Computer architecture*, pages 2–13, New York, NY, USA, 2009. ACM.

[36] B. Liskov. Distributed programming in argus. *Commun. ACM*, 31(3):300–312, 1988.

[37] B. Liskov, A. Adya, M. Castro, S. Ghemawat, R. Gruber, U. Maheshwari, A. C. Myers, M. Day, and L. Shrira. Safe and efficient sharing of persistent objects in thor. In *SIGMOD '96: Proceedings of the 1996 ACM SIGMOD international conference on Management of data*, pages 318–329, New York, NY, USA, 1996. ACM.

[38] D. E. Lowell and P. M. Chen. Free transactions with rio vista. In *SOSP '97: Proceedings of the sixteenth ACM symposium on Operating systems principles*, pages 92–101, New York, NY, USA, 1997. ACM.

[39] C.-K. Luk, R. Cohn, R. Muth, H. Patil, A. Klauser, G. Lowney, S. Wallace, V. J. Reddi, and K. Hazelwood. Pin: building customized program analysis tools with dynamic instrumentation. In *PLDI '05: Proceedings of the 2005 ACM SIGPLAN conference on Programming language design and implementation*, pages 190–200, New York, NY, USA, 2005. ACM.

[40] V. J. Marathe, M. F. Spear, C. Heriot, A. Acharya, D. Eisenstat, W. N. Scherer III, and M. L. Scott. Lowering the overhead of software transactional memory. In *ACM SIGPLAN Workshop on Transactional Computing*. Jun 2006. Held in conjunction with PLDI 2006. Expanded version available as TR 893, Department of Computer Science, University of Rochester, March 2006.

[41] A. Marquez, J. N. Zigman, and S. M. Blackburn. Fast portable orthogonally persistent java. *Softw. Pract. Exper.*, 30(4):449–479, 2000.

[42] Memcached. http://memcached.org/.

[43] J. Metz. E-mail and appointment falsification analysis analysis of e-mail and appointment falsification on microsoft outlook/exchange. http://sourceforge.net/projects/libpff/files/.

[44] http://office.microsoft.com/en-us/outlook/ha010563001033.aspx.

[45] C. Mohan, D. Haderle, B. Lindsay, H. Pirahesh, and P. Schwarz. Aries: a transaction recovery method supporting fine-granularity locking and partial rollbacks using write-ahead logging. *ACM Trans. Database Syst.*, 17(1):94–162, 1992.

[46] Berkeley db. http://www.oracle.com/technology/products/berkeley-db/index.html.

[47] J. O'Toole, S. Nettles, and D. Gifford. Concurrent compacting garbage collection of a persistent heap. In *SOSP '93: Proceedings of the fourteenth ACM symposium on Operating systems principles*, pages 161–174, New York, NY, USA, 1993. ACM.

[48] M. K. Qureshi, J. Karidis, M. Franceschini, V. Srinivasan, L. Lastras, and B. Abali. Enhancing lifetime and security of pcm-based main memory with start-gap wear leveling. In *MICRO 42: Proceedings of the 42nd Annual IEEE/ACM International Symposium on Microarchitecture*, pages 14–23, New York, NY, USA, 2009. ACM.

[49] M. K. Qureshi, V. Srinivasan, and J. A. Rivers. Scalable high performance main memory system using phase-change memory technology. In *Proceedings of the 36th annual international symposium on Computer architecture*, ISCA '09, pages 24–33, New York, NY, USA, 2009. ACM.

[50] B. Saha, A.-R. Adl-Tabatabai, R. L. Hudson, C. C. Minh, and B. Hertzberg. Mcrt-stm: a high performance software transactional memory system for a multi-core runtime. In *PPoPP '06: Proceedings of the eleventh ACM SIGPLAN symposium on Principles and practice of parallel programming*, pages 187–197, New York, NY, USA, 2006. ACM.

[51] M. Satyanarayanan, H. H. Mashburn, P. Kumar, D. C. Steere, and J. J. Kistler. Lightweight recoverable virtual memory. In *SOSP '93: Proceedings of the fourteenth ACM symposium on Operating systems principles*, pages 146–160, New York, NY, USA, 1993. ACM.

[52] W. N. Scherer, III and M. L. Scott. Advanced contention management for dynamic software transactional memory. In *PODC '05: Proceedings of the twenty-fourth annual ACM symposium on Principles of distributed computing*, pages 240–248, New York, NY, USA, 2005. ACM.

[53] R. Sears and E. Brewer. Stasis: flexible transactional storage. In *OSDI '06: Proceedings of the 7th symposium on Operating systems design and implementation*, pages 29–44, Berkeley, CA, USA, 2006. USENIX Association.

[54] M. Seltzer and M. Olson. Libtp: Portable, modular transactions for unix. In *Proceedings of the 1992 Winter Usenix*, pages 9–25, 1992.

[55] J. S. Shapiro and J. Adams. Design evolution of the eros single-level store. In *ATEC '02: Proceedings of the General Track of the annual conference on USENIX Annual Technical Conference*, pages 59–72, Berkeley, CA, USA, 2002. USENIX Association.

[56] N. Shavit and D. Touitou. Software transactional memory. In *PODC '95: Proceedings of the fourteenth annual ACM symposium on Principles of distributed computing*, pages 204–213, New York, NY, USA, 1995. ACM.

[57] V. Singhal, S. V. Kakkad, and P. R. Wilson. Texas: An efficient, portable persistent store. In *POS*, pages 11–33, 1992.

[58] F. G. Soltis. *Inside the as/400*. Twenty Ninth Street Press, 1996.

[59] R. Takemura, T. Kawahara, K. Miura, J. Hayakawa, S. Ikeda, Y. Lee, R. Sasaki, Y. Goto, K. Ito, T. Meguro, F. Matsukura, H. Takahashi, H. Matsuoka, and H. Ohno. 2mb spram design: Bi-directional current write and parallelizing-direction current read schemes based on spin-transfer torque switching. *Integrated Circuit Design and Technology, 2007. ICICDT '07. IEEE International Conference on*, pages 1–4, 30 2007-June 1 2007.

[60] H. Volos, A. J. Tack, and M. M. Swift. Mnemosyne: Lightweight persistent memory. In *ASPLOS '11: Proceeding of the 16th international conference on Architectural support for programming languages and operating systems*, New York, NY, USA, 2011. ACM.

[61] S. J. White and D. J. DeWitt. Quickstore: a high performance mapped object store. In *SIGMOD '94: Proceedings of the 1994 ACM SIGMOD international conference on Management of data*, pages 395–406, New York, NY, USA, 1994. ACM.

[62] P. Zhou, B. Zhao, J. Yang, and Y. Zhang. A durable and energy efficient main memory using phase change memory technology. In *ISCA '09: Proceedings of the 36th annual international symposium on Computer architecture*, pages 14–23, New York, NY, USA, 2009. ACM.

# A Declarative Language Approach to Device Configuration

Adrian Schüpbach Andrew Baumann * Timothy Roscoe Simon Peter

Systems Group, Department of Computer Science, ETH Zurich

www.systems.ethz.ch

## Abstract

C remains the language of choice for hardware programming (device drivers, bus configuration, etc.): it is fast, allows low-level access, and is trusted by OS developers. However, the algorithms required to configure and reconfigure hardware devices and interconnects are becoming more complex and diverse, with the added burden of legacy support, "quirks", and hardware bugs to work around. Even programming PCI bridges in a modern PC is a surprisingly complex problem, and is getting worse as new functionality such as hotplug appears. Existing approaches use relatively simple algorithms, hard-coded in C and closely coupled with low-level register access code, generally leading to suboptimal configurations.

We investigate the merits and drawbacks of a new approach: separating hardware configuration *logic* (algorithms to determine configuration parameter values) from *mechanism* (programming device registers). The latter we keep in C, and the former we encode in a declarative programming language with constraint-satisfaction extensions. As a test case, we have implemented full PCI configuration, resource allocation, and interrupt assignment in the Barrelfish research operating system, using a concise expression of efficient algorithms in constraint logic programming. We show that the approach is tractable, and can successfully configure a wide range of PCs with competitive runtime cost. Moreover, it requires about half the code of the C-based approach in Linux while offering considerably more functionality. Additionally it easily accommodates adaptations such as hotplug, fixed regions, and "quirks".

***Categories and Subject Descriptors*** D.1.6 [*Software*]: Programming Techniques—Logic Programming; D.4.9 [*Software*]: Operating Systems—Systems Programs and Utilities

***General Terms*** Algorithms, Design, Languages

***Keywords*** Constraint logic programming, Eclipse CLP, Hardware programming, PCI configuration

## 1. Introduction

Although many attempts have been made to improve on it, C remains the language of choice for writing code to program hardware, including device drivers, bus configuration, and interrupt routing. C is fast, provides low-level access to hardware registers, and is trusted by OS developers.

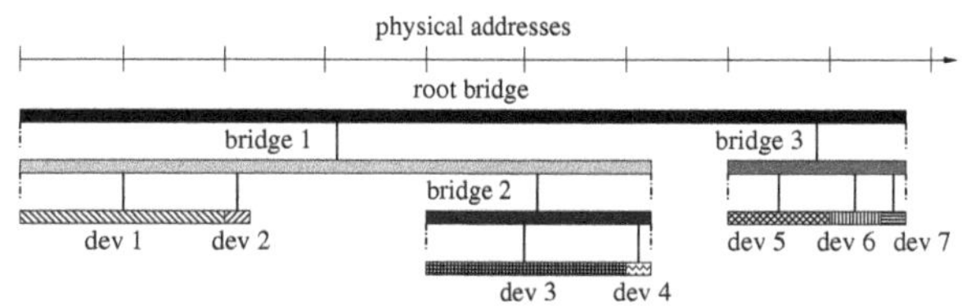


**Figure 1.** Example PCI tree with one root, three bridges, and 7 devices, showing the decoding of addresses from one physical memory space (e.g. non-prefetchable). Bridge base addresses are bounded by the union of the base and limit addresses of their children.

However, trends in hardware are making efficient and correct OS code for hardware access more difficult to write. Hardware platforms and system interconnects are becoming more complex and diverse, while at the same time it is increasingly important for overall performance to derive efficient configurations of devices, interrupts, and memory regions.

Configuring the hardware, I/O bridges and memory regions by interacting with platform firmware, is a surprisingly complex problem in a modern computer. The same is true for allocating and routing interrupts, handling device hotplug, etc., and it is getting worse as new functionality appears. Existing operating systems code uses relatively simple algorithms to achieve these goals. These algorithms are simple by the necessity of being hard-coded: they require low-level access to device registers to achieve their goals, and usually run early at system start-up within the OS kernel.

Figure 1 illustrates a simplified PCI-based device configuration, and the way that it is handled by typical operating systems. The OS code must allocate memory regions to each PCI device, and each PCI bridge in the bus hierarchy, in such a way that every device receives correctly-sized areas of memory in distinct regions (prefetchable, and non-prefetchable) of two different address spaces (I/O and memory). These areas must all be aligned to device-specific boundaries, may not overlap, and should fit into the total amount of physical address space available for such hardware in the system.

We describe the PCI configuration problem in detail in Section 2, but two factors make this allocation problem particularly hard. First, hotplugging means that devices can come and go in the hierarchy, which may entail reconfiguring entire subtrees, which is in turn disruptive to running device drivers. Second, there are numerous restrictions on device allocation: certain devices or bridges must be placed at a fixed address, others incorrectly decode addresses not assigned to them, and platform hardware components such as ACPI sometimes reserve regions of physical address space, which means that the address ranges must be allocated "around" these holes. As computer architectures become more complex, this list of problems is likely to grow, and to vary widely from one sys-

* Now at Microsoft Research.



*ASPLOS'11,* March 5–11, 2011, Newport Beach, California, USA.

tem to another. We fully expect to see analogous issues for future interconnects or platform functions.

Most existing OSes deal with this problem with simple algorithms in C such as sorting devices by address range size, modified with much special-case code. The result is complex and hard to debug, and (as we show in Section 5) can lead to unpredictable and inefficient allocation of space as devices are hotplugged. In some cases such as Linux on Intel platforms, the OS does not even try to solve the allocation problem, instead relying on the platform BIOS to provide an initial allocation, which is difficult to change.

Our aim is to find techniques for this general class of resource allocation that result in cleaner, smaller, more flexible code which still accommodates the various quirks, bugs, and legacy restrictions imposed by real-world hardware. Our goal is to make such OS code easier to write and evolve over time, and more reliable in the face of ever-more-complex hardware.

In this paper we investigate the costs and benefits of a radically different approach: separating configuration *logic*, such as the algorithms to determine which configuration parameter values should be employed, from the configuration *mechanism* (actually reading and writing device registers). The latter we keep in C as part of the kernel, but the former we encode in a logic programming language with constraint-solving extensions in the system knowledge base [26], running as an OS service.

Hardware-related code can be roughly divided into "data path" functionality (interrupt handlers, packet processing, descriptor management, etc.), and configuration management (PCI programming, ACPI initialization and interpretation, memory region and I/O space allocation, etc.). Both are critical to the performance and correct functioning of a system. However, whereas the former must have bounded resource utilization, particularly in terms of its runtime where it is often on the fast-path, the performance of the latter code is instead measured in terms of the correctness and optimality of the resource allocation and configuration it produces, while its speed is less critical. As we have pointed out [26], these two areas of functionality are at present typically implemented in the same code base, inside the OS kernel, as low-level C code.

Our hypothesis is that the balance is tipping in favor of expressing configuration logic, and hardware configuration information, in a rich and high-level language. This enables complex resource allocation and configuration algorithms to be succinctly expressed, while being more amenable to adaptation due to changes in hardware technology, faulty hardware information ("quirks"), varying resource constraints and optimization goals, and device hotplug. Moreover, the same framework gives applications and user-level runtimes greater visibility into the available hardware resources and their current configuration.

We introduce three main contributions. First, in Section 2 we use PCI as an example to demonstrate the complexity of hardware configuration as an emerging issue in system software, and propose the use of declarative language techniques to mitigate its complexity as hardware becomes both more diverse and more complex.

Second, in Section 3 we describe in detail our initial approach to PCI bus configuration using the ECL$^{i}$PS$^{e}$ constraint logic programming (CLP) system [2], a language with constraint-satisfaction extensions, and in Section 4 our solution to the related problem of interrupt allocation. We have implemented full PCI configuration and interrupt assignment for the Barrelfish [8] research operating, using the system knowledge base's (SKB) [26] CLP solver.

Finally, in Section 5 we present a combined evaluation of this work, focusing on its complexity, adaptability, and performance in comparison to the traditional approach, and in Section 6 discuss our experience with the new approach so far. The drawbacks include the need for a complex code base for the language runtime, and increased time to calculate configuration information. In exchange, the benefits include flexibility, efficiency of resulting configurations, conciseness of expression, and easy accommodation of special cases, and the ability to easily integrate extra information to guide resource allocation. We also discuss how trends in hardware and software are likely to affect this tradeoff.

## 2. Background: PCI allocation

Configuring the PCI bridges found in a typical modern computer is emblematic of a wide class of hardware-related systems software challenges: it involves resource discovery followed by allocation of identifiers and ranges from compact spaces of identifiers and addresses. More importantly, a range of hardware bugs and/or ad-hoc constraints on particular devices lead to a plethora of special cases which make it hard to express a correct algorithm in imperative terms. Worse, new hardware (whether system boards or devices) appears all the time, and system software must continue to work, or evolve to handle new cases with a minimum of disruptive engineering effort.

In this section, we describe the PCI programming challenge in detail. We start with the "idealized" problem, which appears relatively straightforward, and progressively introduce the complexities that, combined, are the reason that even modern operating systems only partially solve the full problem.

### 2.1 PCI background

A PCI (or PCI Express) interconnect is logically an n-ary tree whose internal nodes are *bridges* and whose leaves are *devices* [9, 23]. The root of the tree is known as the *root bridge* or *root complex*. Connections in the tree are known as *buses* (in legacy PCI they are electrically buses, whereas in PCI Express the bus is a logical abstraction over point-to-point messaging links). Non-root bridges are said to link *secondary buses* (links to child bridges and devices) to a *primary bus* (the link to the bridge's parent). High-end PCs often have two or four root complexes, and hence multiple PCI trees within a single system. Non-root devices can be attached to any bus in a PCI interconnect. Each device implements one or more distinct *functions*. A PCI function is in fact what we think of an independent "device" which has an own address represented by the bus number, the device number and the function number and which operates independently of other functions.

Driver software on host CPUs accesses PCI functions by issuing memory reads and writes or (in the case of the x86 architecture) I/O instructions. These requests are routed down the tree by the bridges, before being decoded by a single leaf device. Each function decodes a portion of the overall memory and I/O address spaces using a mapping that is configured by the host system through standard PCI-defined registers on each bridge and function.

Each "function" of a non-bridge device may decode up to 6 independent regions of either memory or I/O address space. These regions are defined and configured by *base address registers* (BARs) implemented by each function. The PCI driver queries each BAR to determine its required size, alignment, address space (memory or I/O), and, in the case of a memory-space BAR, whether the memory is *prefetchable* or *non-prefetchable*. Although it goes against strict PCI terminology, in the rest of this paper we will use "device" to denote a PCI function, i.e. a single logical device with up to 6 BARs.

Bridges also decode addresses to route requests between their parent and secondary buses. Unlike other devices, however, bridges use three pairs of base and limit registers instead of BARs, one each for prefetchable memory, non-prefetchable memory, and I/O space. Each bridge therefore decodes 3 independent, contiguous regions of IO or memory address space. The addresses used by every device below a bridge (including bridges on secondary buses) must lie within these three regions.

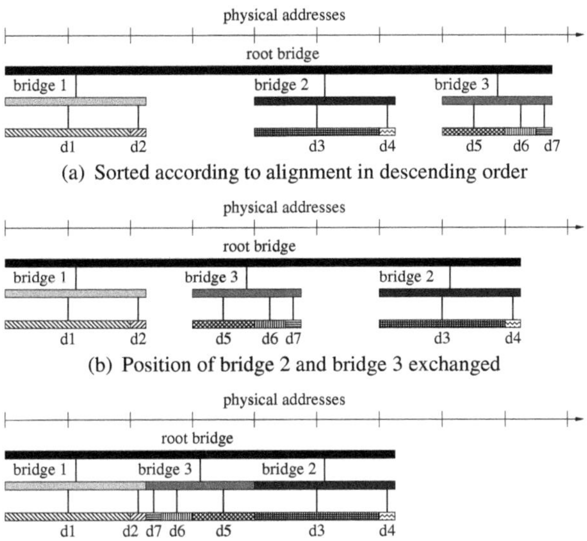


(a) Sorted according to alignment in descending order

(b) Position of bridge 2 and bridge 3 exchanged

(c) Devices under bridge 3 reordered

**Figure 2.** Alternative PCI configurations (only memory space resources are shown)

In summary, a host CPU accesses a PCI device by issuing a transaction on the system interconnect with a physical address that lies in a region decoded by the root bridge of the corresponding PCI tree. This is routed down the tree by bridges; at each level, each bridge on a bus compares the address issued by the CPU to the ranges defined by its base and limit registers. If it matches, the bridge forwards the request to its secondary bus. Each device on a bus compares the address to the regions defined by its BARs, and if the address matches, consumes it and generates a reply.

The PCI programming problem is to configure the base and limit registers of every bridge, and the BARs of every device function, to allow all the hardware registers for every device to be accessible from a CPU. As Figure 2 shows, this can be achieved in many different ways, leading to different usage of the available physical address space and different device locations in that space.

We can now specify the requirements for any PCI programming solution, starting with the basic properties of a solution in the "ideal" case, and progressively refining the list by adding real-world complications.

### 2.2 Basic PCI configuration requirements

Every bridge in a correctly-configured PCI tree decodes a subrange of the addresses visible on its parent bus. In order for all devices behind a bridge to be reachable, PCI requires that:

1. The *bridge window*, defined by its base and limit registers, must include all address regions decoded by all devices and bridges on the secondary bus.

In order that a request is forwarded by at most one bridge, sibling bridges sharing a bus must decode disjoint address ranges. Since a bus may contain both bridges and devices, all bridges and devices on a given bus must decode disjoint address ranges within the range of the parent bridge. This applies in all of the address spaces:

2. Bridges and devices at the same tree level (siblings) must not overlap in either memory or I/O address space.
3. The prefetchable and non-prefetchable memory regions decoded by a bridge or device must not overlap.

Regions of addresses in PCI must also be aligned. For a BAR, the base address must be "naturally" aligned at a multiple of the region's size. Similarly, a bridge's base and limit registers also have limited granularity, giving us the following alignment constraints:

4. BAR base addresses must be naturally aligned according to the BAR size.
5. Bridge base and limit register values for both memory regions must be aligned to 1MB boundaries.
6. Bridge base and limit register values for the I/O region must be aligned to 4kB boundaries.

These requirements constrain the possible locations of device BARs and child bridge base and limit registers within the region decoded by the parent bridge, potentially leading to gaps in address space for padding, as in Figures 2(a) and 2(b).

As described so far, configuring a PCI tree is a non-trivial problem, but can still be efficiently programmed by, for example, executing a post-order traversal of the PCI tree, sorting devices and bridges by descending alignment granularity, and allocating the lowest suitable address range in the appropriate address space at each step. Unfortunately, a number of real-world characteristics of modern computers, like for example the requirement to align addresses naturally, make this simple approach unworkable. Therefore, the simple post-order traversal results in a solution like that in Figure 2(a) where big padding holes need to be inserted between devices.

### 2.3 Non-PCI devices

The first problem is that certain non-PCI devices (e.g. IOAPICs and other platform devices) appear at fixed physical memory addresses, inside the region allocated to a PCI root complex. The locations of these devices may be discovered through platform-specific mechanisms such as ACPI [12], and no PCI device may decode such an address region.

7. Devices must not decode reserved regions of physical address space given by, for example, ACPI, or used by other known non-PCI devices such as IOAPICs.

### 2.4 Fixed-location PCI devices

Some PCI devices may be initialized and enabled by platform firmware at early boot time, for example USB controllers, network interfaces, or other boot devices. Naïvely reprogramming the BARs of such devices may lead to machine check exceptions or crashes since the device may be active, and performing DMA operations. Most operating systems avoid reprogramming the BARs of such devices, which means that their existing address assignment must be preserved. This further constrains the address ranges usable by parent bridges.

8. Certain PCI devices determined at boot cannot change location, and must retain addresses assigned to them by the BIOS.

### 2.5 Quirks

Hardware has bugs, and both devices and bridges can report incorrect information, fail to support valid resource assignments, or behave incorrectly when specific register values are programmed. These problems are known as PCI "quirks" and affect a wide range of shipping devices – the Linux 2.6.34 kernel lists 546 quirks – leading to a collection of workarounds in commodity operating systems. Common quirks include:

- devices that provide incorrect information about their identity as bridges or non-bridges;

- devices which decode more address range than advertised, or which decode address regions not assigned to them;
- standard devices which are hidden by platform firmware, but could otherwise be normally used;
- undefined device behavior (data loss on the bus, reduced bandwidth, system hangs, etc.) when particular values are written to configuration registers.

In the latter case, the PCI configuration process must ensure the problematic register values are never written, which imposes additional constraints on valid address assignments. Thus:

9. Configurations that would cause problematic values to be written to registers on specific devices must be avoided.
10. Incorrect information from PCI discovery must be corrected before calculating address assignment.

### 2.6 Device hotplug

Hotplugging, the addition or removal of PCI devices at runtime, raises another challenge. When a device is plugged in, the OS is notified by an interrupt from the root bridge, and must allocate resources to the BARs of the newly-installed device before it can be used. However, this may require reconfiguring and/or moving the address allocation of bridges and other devices in order to make enough address space available for the device, since it was not present at system boot. Changing the resource allocation of existing devices requires the driver to temporarily disable the device potentially save its current state first. After the new resources are programmed to the BARs, the driver needs to restart the device using the newly allocated resources. Depending on the device, it may need to bring the device to the saved state. This is a disruptive process and may not be supported by all devices, so the reallocation of resources which occurs on hotplug typically attempts to move the fewest possible existing devices and bridges.

11. Configuration should minimize the disruption caused by future hotplug events as much as possible.
12. Hotplug events should cause the minimal feasible reconfiguration of existing devices and bridges.
13. Hotplug-triggered reconfiguration may not move devices whose drivers do not support relocation of address ranges.

### 2.7 Discussion

It should by now be clear that PCI configuration is a somewhat messy problem characterized by a large (and growing) number of hardware-specific constraints which nonetheless have effects which propagate up and down the PCI tree. Consequently, most "clean" solutions written imperatively in a language like C sooner or later fall foul of an exception which can greatly complicate the code, compromise its correctness, reduce the efficiency with which it can manage physical address spaces, and in some cases prevent it from supporting the full PCI feature set.

Most current operating systems, including Linux [25, 29] and FreeBSD [5] on x86-based platforms, rely on platform firmware (BIOS or EFI) to allocate resources to most devices before the OS starts, and then run one or more post-allocation routines [4] to correct any problems in the allocation, allocate resources to devices left unconfigured by the firmware, and handle known quirks as devices are discovered and started.

This approach cannot guarantee success (though it often works): if a bridge is programmed with an address region that is too small to allocate all the devices behind it, there may be no way to grow the size of the bridge's address region without moving other bridges, and thus some devices behind the bridge will be rendered unusable despite sufficient address space being available overall. This problem is exacerbated by device hotplug, as it is impossible to predict at start-up the required size of all devices.

Even so, this simplistic allocation strategy leads to substantial code complexity: the complete PCI drivers of x86 Linux and FreeBSD account for approximately 10k and 6.5k lines of C code respectively, and device-specific quirks account for an additional 3k lines of code in Linux.

On other hardware platforms (such as Alpha/AXP), the firmware does not implement PCI configuration, and Linux instead performs a complete allocation using a greedy approach: devices are sorted by their requested size in ascending order, and resources allocated for each device in that order [25]. This can also lead to unusable devices behind a bridge, due to a suboptimal ordering of devices causing a shortage of address space. Note also that very little code is shared between this implementation and that for the PC platform: bug fixes or feature enhancements for one architecture may not be easily applied to another.

Until recently, Microsoft Windows used a similar strategy to x86 Linux and FreeBSD for PCI configuration, running a fix-up procedure to correct deficiencies in the firmware allocation. As with Linux and FreeBSD, this was unable to resize or change the address regions decoded by bridges, leading to potentially unusable devices [21]. Windows Vista and Server 2008 introduced a new rebalancing algorithm [20], allowing a bridge's resources to be modified according to the needs of its secondary bus, and increasing the likelihood that all PCI devices could be configured. However, this requires additional driver support for re-balancing, and the iterative approach can lead to highly complex multi-level re-balancing. Multi-level re-balancing might potentially need a long time, because increasing a bridge's window size may require to move the bridge to a new big enough free region. This may require more space from the parent bridge because of address alignment requirements, which again may be a problem. In the worst case, multi-level re-balancing may lead to a complete permutation of the PCI tree.

## 3. PCI resource allocation

The previous section detailed the PCI configuration problem and current approaches to solving it. In this section, we describe our implementation of PCI configuration in Barrelfish, and in the following Section 4, a solution to the closely-related problem of interrupt allocation, before evaluating both in Section 5.

Barrelfish [7,8] is a research operating system developed at ETH Zurich and Microsoft Research to address the related problems of scaling and system diversity in future heterogeneous multicore computers. As such, it provides a convenient testbed for our ideas.

PCI resource configuration can be viewed as a constraint satisfaction problem: for a given system, the variables are the base address allocated to each device BAR, and the base and limit of each bridge for each memory region it decodes, and a correct solution may be expressed as an assignment of integer values to these variables satisfying a series of constraints: alignment, sizes, and non-overlap of regions.

The difficulty in PCI resource allocation arises from satisfying these complex constraints. Such complexity is difficult to manage in a low-level systems language like C, but fortunately its runtime performance is not critical to the functioning of the system as a whole. This allows us the freedom to reformulate it in a declarative language, where the challenge becomes closer to defining *what* result we require, than *how* the result is to be produced.

We implemented the PCI resource configuration algorithm as a constraint logic program. This program operates on a high-level data structure representing the PCI tree, consisting of numeric variables and constraints between them that determine the possible solutions. Rather than worrying about how to allocate concrete addresses to bridges and devices, we instead concern ourselves with specifying the correct set of constraints to guide the CLP solver. We begin by describing the separation between C and CLP code, before explaining the constraint logic in detail.

### 3.1 Approach

We explicitly separate the PCI configuration algorithm, expressed in CLP and running in a user-space service, from the register access and device programming mechanisms, implemented in the usual C code as part of the PCI subsystem of the OS. This has several advantages. First, it decouples the details of the configuration algorithm from the device access code, allowing us to exchange and evolve the algorithm independently of the device access mechanisms. Second, the algorithm is expressed only in terms of the generic PCI bus – all architecture-specifics are confined to the device access code.

The CLP solver we use is the Barrelfish system knowledge base [26], a port of the open-source ECL$^i$PS$^e$ CLP system. The SKB is a service which is started early in the Barrelfish boot sequence and runs initially from a RAM disk image, enabling it to function without any device support. It is passive and event-driven, responding to requests from the PCI driver.

At start-up, the PCI driver performs device discovery. The location of root bridges is determined by platform-specific mechanisms such as ACPI [12]. The driver then walks the entire bus hierarchy, determining the complete set of bridges, devices and BARs that are present, and assigning bus numbers to un-numbered bridges. As part of this pass, the PCI driver inserts Prolog *facts* in the SKB. Those facts describe the set of present bridges, devices and BARs, according to the following schema:

```
rootbridge(addr(Bus, Dev, Fun), childbus(MinBus, MaxBus),
    mem(Base, Limit)).
bridge(pcie | pci, addr(Bus, Dev, Fun), VendorID, DevID,
    Class, SubClass, ProgIf, secondary(BusNr)).
device(pcie | pci, addr(Bus, Dev, Fun), VendorID, DevID,
    Class, SubClass, ProgIf, IntPin).
bar(addr(Bus, Dev, Fun), BARNr, Base, Size, mem | io,
    prefetchable | non-prefetchable, 64 | 32).
```

These facts encode all information needed to run the PCI configuration algorithm. A root bridge is identified by its PCI configuration address (bus, device and function number), the range (minimum and maximum) of bus numbers of its children, and its assigned physical memory region. Bridges and devices are identified by their address, and carry standard identifiers for their vendor, device ID, device class and subclass, and programming interface. A bridge also includes the bus number of its secondary bus, and a device the interrupt pin which it will raise (which is used by the interrupt allocation routines described in Section 4). Finally, for a BAR we store its base address (which may have been previously assigned by firmware), required size, region type, and whether it is a 64-bit or 32-bit BAR.

After creating the facts, the PCI driver causes the SKB to run the configuration algorithm to compute a valid allocation. The initialization algorithm we use is described in the following section. Its output is a list of addresses for every device BAR and every bridge, which can be directly programmed into the corresponding registers by the driver. For example:

```
buselement(device, addr(6,0,0), 0, C0000000, D0000000,
        10000000, mem, prefetchable, pcie, 64),
buselement(bridge, addr(0,15,0), secondary(6), B0100000,
        D0000000, 1FF00000, mem, prefetchable, pcie, 0)
```

In this example, the 64-bit PCIe device at bus 6, device 0, function 0 requests a physical address range of 256MB in prefetchable memory space for BAR 0. The base allocated to the device is 0xC0000000 and the limit will thus be 0xD0000000. The bridge at which the device is attached has a base of 0xB0100000 and a limit of 0xD0000000 in the prefetchable memory space, clearly including this device (along with others, not shown here).

The PCI driver takes the addresses and BAR numbers as well as bridge base and limit values from the output, and programs the specified registers. While reprogramming devices and bridges, they are disabled to prevent transient address conflicts. Once reprogramming is complete, the bus is completely configured and device drivers can be started.

### 3.2 Formulation in CLP

We now turn to the configuration algorithm in constraint logic. Its first step is to convert the facts generated by the PCI driver to a suitable data structure, and declare the necessary constraint variables. The data structure used is a tree mirroring the hardware topology, whose inner nodes correspond to bridges, and leaf nodes to device BARs or other unpopulated bridges. The constraints are then naturally expressible through recursive tree traversal. The variables of the CLP program are the base address, limit and size of every bridge and device BAR, and the relationship between them may be expressed by the constraint `Limit $= Base + Size`, which we later apply.

At a high-level, our algorithm performs the following steps for each PCI root bridge:

1. Convert `bridge` and `device` facts for the given root bridge to a list of `buselement` terms, while declaring constraint variables for the base address, limit and size of each element.
2. Construct a tree of `buselement` terms, mirroring the PCI tree.
3. Recursively walk the tree, constraining the base, limit and size variables according to the PCI configuration rules and quirks.
4. Convert the tree back to a list of elements.
5. Invoke the ECL$^i$PS$^e$ constraint solver to compute a solution for all base, limit and size variables satisfying the constraints.

The core logic of the algorithm resides in step 3 above, and we implement this by a direct translation of the rules described in Section 2.2 to constraint logic, as described in the following sections.

#### Bridge windows

**Rule 1** states that all bridge windows must include all address regions decoded by devices and bridges attached to the secondary bus. This means that the bridge's memory and IO base addresses must be smaller or equal to the smallest base of any bridge or device on the secondary bus, and the corresponding limits must be greater than or equal to the highest address used by any device or bridge on the secondary bus.

Although we do not yet have concrete values for the relevant base and limit variables, CLP allows us to constrain them using a recursive walk of the tree, implemented as shown below.
Note that a tree is expressed as `t(Root,Children)`, where `Root` is the root node, and `Children` is a (possibly empty) list of child trees – ECL$^i$PS$^e$ uses conventional Prolog syntax whereby identifiers starting with an uppercase character (e.g. `Node`) denote free variables, and all others denote constants. Also note the ECL$^i$PS$^e$ operations `ic_global:sumlist`, `ic:minlist` and `ic:maxlist` which operate on lists of constraint variables that may not have a concrete value assigned, allowing complex constraints to be introduced between them.

```
setrange(Tree,SubTreeSize,SubTreeMin,SubTreeMax) :-
  % match Tree into current node and list of children
  t(Node,Children) = Tree,
  % match node to get its base, limit and size variables
  buselement(_,_,_,Base,Limit,Size,_,_,_,_) = Node,

  % recursively collect lists of sizes, minimum and
  % maximum addresses for children of this node
  ( foreach(El,Children),
    foreach(Sz,SizeList),
    foreach(Mi,MinList),
    foreach(Ma,MaxList)
    do
      setrange(El,Sz,Mi,Ma)
  ),

  % compute sum of children's sizes as SizeSum
  ic_global:sumlist(SizeList,SizeSum),
  % constrain the size of this node >= SizeSum
  Size $>= SizeSum,

  % if there are any children...
  ( not Children=[] ->
      % determine min base and max limit of children
      ic:minlist(MinList,Min),
      ic:maxlist(MaxList,Max),
      % constrain this node's base and limit accordingly
      Min $>= Base,
      Max $=< Limit
    ; true
  ),

  % constrain this node's limit
  Limit $= Base + Size,

  % output values
  SubTreeSize $= Size,
  SubTreeMin $= Base,
  SubTreeMax $= Limit.

setrange([],0,_,_). % base case of recursion
```

### Non-overlap of bridges and devices

**Rule 2** states that siblings must not overlap at any level of the tree. In other words, all regions allocated to bridges and devices at the same level must be disjunctive. The following goal ensures this, by making use of the `disjunctive` constraint, which ensures that regions specified as lists of base addresses and sizes do not overlap:

```
% convenience functions / accessors
root(t(R,_),R).
base(buselement(_,_,_,Base,_,_,_,_,_,_),Base).
size(buselement(_,_,_,_,_,Size,_,_,_,_),Size).

nonoverlap(Tree) :-
  % collect direct children of this node in ChildList
  t(_ ,Children) = Tree,
  maplist(root,Children,ChildList),

  % if there are children...
  ( not ChildList=[] ->
      % determine base and size of each child
      maplist(base,ChildList,Bases),
      maplist(size,ChildList,Sizes),

      % constrain the regions they define not to overlap
      disjunctive(Bases,Sizes)
    ; true
  ),

  % recurse on all children
  ( foreach(El, Children) do nonoverlap(El) ).
```

### Non-overlap of prefetchable/non-prefetchable memory

**Rule 3** requires that prefetchable and non-prefetchable regions do not overlap. The two regions do not need to be contiguous. Therefore we implemented this by inserting an artificial level in the top of the tree containing two separate bridges, one with all prefetchable memory ranges and another with all non-prefetchable memory ranges of the tree. This gives some freedom to the solver, because the order of the two regions is not explicitly specified by our allocation code, and allows the previously-described logic to operate independently of memory prefetchability. Treating the two regions as completely separate trees causes the prefetchable and non-prefetchable window of every bridge to be at completely different locations, which is fine.

### Alignment constraints

**Rules 4, 5** and **6** require a specific alignment for devices and bridges. In the following, we constrain the alignment of each element, using natural alignment for device BARs, and a fixed alignment for bridge windows (e.g. 1MB in the case of memory regions).

```
naturally_aligned(Tree, BridgeAlignment, LMem, HMem) :-
  t(Node,Children) = Tree,

  % determine required alignment for bridge or device BAR
  ( buselement(device,_,_,Base,_,Size,_,_,_,_) = Node ->
      Alignment is Size; % natural alignment
    buselement(bridge,_,_,Base,_,_,_,_,_,_) = Node ->
      Alignment is BridgeAlignment % from argument
  ),

  % constrain Base mod Alignment = 0
  suspend(mod(Base, Alignment, 0), 0, Base->inst),

  % recurse on children
  ( foreach(El, Children),
      param(BridgeAlignment), param(LMem), param(HMem)
    do naturally_aligned(El, BridgeAlignment, LMem, HMem)
  ).
```

### Reserved regions

**Rule 7** requires that reserved memory regions are not allocated to PCI devices. In other words, memory regions allocated to PCI devices should always be disjunctive with any reserved region. The following goal ensures this requirement, by recursively processing a list of bus elements against a list of reserved memory ranges, specified as `range(Base,Size)` terms:

```
% recursive stopping case
not_overlap_mem_ranges([], _).

% bridges may overlap: no special treatment
not_overlap_mem_ranges(
  [buselement(bridge,_,_,_,_,_,_,_,_,_)|T], MemRanges) :-
    not_overlap_mem_ranges(T, MemRanges).

% device BARs match this pattern
not_overlap_mem_ranges([H|T], MemRanges) :-
  % for each reserved memory range...
  ( foreach(range(RBase,RSize),MemRanges), param(H)
    do
      % match base and size variable from bus element
      buselement(device,_,_,Base,_,Size,_,_,_,_) = H,
      % constrain this BAR not to overlap with it
      disjunctive([Base,RBase], [Size,RSize])
  ),
  % recurse on list tail
  not_overlap_mem_ranges(T, MemRanges).
```

#### Fixed-location devices

We must also avoid moving various initialized boot devices, as in **rule 8**. The following goal shows one such example: given a device class (specified by its class, subclass and programming interface identifiers) that should not be moved, it constrains the possible choice of the base address to the one value which is its initial allocation.

```
keep_orig_addr([], _, _, _).
keep_orig_addr([H|T], Class, SubClass, ProgIf) :-
  ( % if this is a device BAR...
    buselement(device,Addr,BAR,Base,_,_,_,_,_,_) = H,
    % and its device is in the required class...
    device(_,Addr,_,_,Class, SubClass, ProgIf,_),
    % lookup the original base address of the BAR
    bar(Addr,BAR,OrigBase,_,_,_,_) ->
      % constrain the Base to equal its original value
      Base $= OrigBase
    ; true
  ),
  % recurse on remaining devices
  keep_orig_addr(T, Class, SubClass, ProgIf).
```

### 3.3 Quirks

Declarative logic programming provides an elegant solution to the problem of quirks. Quirks require us to correct wrong information as well as apply possible extra constraints to workaround misbehaving devices. In CLP we can easily define a database of facts for devices needing special treatment. Those facts are implicitly matched against the data structure before the configuration algorithm runs, causing incorrect information to be corrected, and additional constraints on the allocation to be defined, without changing any of the core logic of the algorithm.

### 3.4 Device hotplug

In principle, the allocation of resources for hotplugged devices can be handled simply by adding facts for the new device and its BARs, and then re-running the allocation algorithm. However, this may cause all existing address assignments to change (excluding those whose location is fixed, as in Section 3.2), and is thus undesirable due to the performance impact of interrupting running device drivers.

Adding artificial devices to the PCI tree before computing the first allocation helps to produce gaps which can later be used for hotplugged devices. Figure 3 shows that the CLP solution can deal with an almost completely filled region. This means, that the available space can almost be filled completely with artificial devices to provide space for later hotplugs. With CLP this is particularly easy, because the artificial devices get placed around the real ones. Later, when a device gets hotplugged, the algorithm should try to move the least possible number of BARs of other devices. CLP allows to define an objective function for the constraint solver, minimizing the number of BARs which have to be reallocated. Moreover, the CLP solution is better placed to handle complex reconfiguration that may be required by device hotplug, as it specifies the complete set of feasible configurations which will be explored by the solver. Section 5.4 presents the results of a benchmark showing the theoretical limits of the CLP approach in handling device hotplug, in comparison to a traditional postorder traversal.

## 4. Interrupt allocation

We now move from PCI bus configuration to the closely-related problem of interrupt allocation, which we have also implemented in CLP, and which is also evaluated in Section 5.

### 4.1 Problem overview

Interrupts are another important resource that must to be allocated to devices by the OS. Most PCI devices can raise one or more interrupts. To avoid shared interrupt handlers, the OS should try to allocate unique interrupt vectors to every device. Modern systems, and some modern devices, support message signaled interrupts (MSIs). These map interrupts into the physical address space, and therefore the only requirement is choosing a different interrupt address for every device. However many systems and many PCI devices do not yet support MSIs, and thus correctly and efficiently configuring PCI interrupt allocation remains a critical OS task.

Each PCI device signals interrupts by asserting one of up to four available interrupt lines (INTA, INTB, INTC and INTD, represented in our solution as the integers 0–3). On PC-based platforms, these signals are routed via PCI bridges and configurable *link devices* to global system interrupt numbers (GSIs). This routing is encoded in and configured via platform firmware, using a set of ACPI tables [12].

Starting from a given device and interrupt pin, the mapping is determined as follows:

1. Consult the ACPI interrupt routing tables for the current bus, device and pin number. If there is a mapping for the given pin:
   (a) If the entry names a GSI, the interrupt line is fixed.
   (b) Otherwise, the entry names a link device, and the interrupt is selectable from set of GSIs.
2. Otherwise, compute the new interrupt pin on the parent bus, using the formula (*device number* + *pin*) mod 4, and repeat.

The goal of the interrupt allocation code is to assign unique interrupt vectors to every device. Interrupt sharing is to be avoided wherever possible [14]. It can severely impact performance, since the drivers for devices sharing an interrupt must essentially poll their devices to determine if the interrupt is for them. Furthermore, many device drivers do not handle shared interrupts correctly at all. As well as avoiding sharing among PCI devices, specific GSIs are also assigned to legacy (non-PCI) devices and other system devices, which should also be avoided by the allocation code.

We can summarize the requirements for interrupt configuration as follows:

1. assign and configure a GSI (possible translated by bridges and link devices) for every enabled PCI device,
2. ensure that all allocated GSIs are unique.
3. avoid reassigning legacy pre-allocated GSIs.

This problem is not as hard as the PCI address allocation problem and could be implemented in C. However there are still some benefits from using CLP. First, storing and querying information about possible GSIs and prototyping the algorithm in CLP is convenient. Second, ensuring that allocated GSIs are globally unique can easily be done using the built-in goal `alldifferent` (see 4.2). We therefore implemented interrupt allocation in the SKB.

### 4.2 Solution in CLP

At start-up, the PCI/ACPI driver code populates the system knowledge base with a fact for every PCI interrupt routing table entry, mapping a device address and interrupt pin to a source, using the schema:

```
prt(addr(Bus, Dev, _), Pin, pir(Pir) | gsi(Gsi)).
```

These facts include addresses of PCI devices without function number, because the same mapping applies for all functions on a multi-function device. The interrupt source is either a name (ACPI object path) identifying the interrupt link device or a direct GSI number, indicating that this interrupt's allocation is fixed.

For each link device, `pir` facts are added describing the possible GSIs that may be selected for a given device:

```
pir(Pir, GSI).
```

In this relation, `Pir` defines the link device name, and `GSI` one of the selectable GSIs for this device (so each link device has multiple facts, one for each configuration).

The CLP code operates on these facts, and the PCI device facts described in the previous section. At the top-level, it determines the interrupt pin used by a specific device, and passes it to `assignirq` to allocate a unique GSI:

```
assigndeviceirq(Addr) :-
  device(_, Addr, _, _, _, _, _, Pin),
  % require a valid Pin
  Pin >= 0 and Pin < 4,
  ( % check for an exising allocation
    assignedGsi(Addr, Pin, Gsi),
    usedGsi(Gsi, Pir)
  ; % otherwise assign a new GSI
    assignirq(Pin, Addr, Pir, Gsi),
    assert(assignedGsi(Addr, Pin, Gsi))
  ),
  printf("%s %d\n", [Pir, Gsi]).
```

`assignirq` takes the PCI address and interrupt pin for the device as inputs, and chooses a possible GSI for the device. It uses `findgsi` (described below) to determine the available GSIs for the device, and the `alldifferent` goal to avoid overlaps:

```
assignirq(Pin, Addr, Pir, Gsi) :-
  % determine usable GSIs for this device
  findgsi(Pin, Addr, Gsi, Pir),
  ( % flag value for a fixed GSI (i.e. meaningless Pir)
    Pir = fixedGsi
  ;
    % don't change a previously-configured link device
    setPir(Pir, _) -> setPir(Pir, Gsi)
  ;
    true
  ),
  % find all GSIs currently in use
  findall(X, usedGsi(X,_), AllGsis),
  % constrain GSIs not to overlap
  ic:alldifferent([Gsi|AllGsis]),
  % allocate one of the possible GSIs
  indomain(Gsi),
  % store settings for future reference
  ( Pir = fixedGsi ; assert(setPir(Pir,Gsi)) ),
  assert(usedGsi(Gsi,Pir)).
```

Finally, the following CLP function matches the device's address and interrupt pin with the `prt` and `pir` facts to find the possible GSIs (multiple solutions may be found). If no match is found, it recursively performs bridge swizzling until a routing table entry matches (which is always true at the root bridge).

| | Devices | BARs | Bridges | Runtime (ms) |
|---|---|---|---|---|
| sys1 | 7 | 11 | 12 | 2.0 |
| sys2 | 13 | 20 | 6 | 14.7 |
| sys3 | 13 | 20 | 6 | 14.4 |
| sys4 | 14 | 22 | 6 | 36.4 |
| sys5 | 12 | 18 | 5 | 10.0 |
| sys6 | 7 | 9 | 6 | 19.0 |
| sys7 | 9 | 14 | 6 | 22.2 |
| sys8 | 15 | 25 | 4 | 6.7 |
| sys9 | 15 | 25 | 4 | 31.2 |

**Table 1.** System complexity and execution times for the PCI configuration algorithm

```
findgsi(Pin, Addr, Gsi, Pir) :-
  ( % lookup routing table to see if we have an entry
    prt(Addr, Pin, PrtEntry)
  ;
    % if not, compute standard swizzle through bridge
    Addr = addr(Bus, Device, _),
    NewPin is (Device + Pin) mod 4,

    % recurse, looking up mapping for the bridge itself
    bridge(_, BridgeAddr, _, _, _, _, _, secondary(Bus)),
    findgsi(NewPin, BridgeAddr, Gsi, Pir)
  ),
  ( % is this a fixed GSI, or a link device?
    PrtEntry = gsi(Gsi),
    Pir = fixedGsi
  ;
    PrtEntry = pir(Pir),
    pir(Pir, Gsi)
  ).
```

## 5. Evaluation

Picking suitable metrics to evaluate a PCI programming solution is something of challenge. We focus here on code complexity, execution time, and efficiency of resultant solutions, but some of the evaluation necessarily remains subjective in its comparison with current approaches.

### 5.1 Test platforms

We evaluated the PCI configuration and interrupt allocation algorithms on nine different x86 PC and server systems, with a mixture of built-in and expansion devices including network, storage and graphics cards installed. We refer to these as sys1 through sys9, and show the number of PCI elements they include in Table 1. All systems have two PCI root bridges with the exception of sys1, which has one. Here we show the totals for the whole system, as our algorithm allocates resources to all PCI trees in a single invocation.

All of these systems support USB keyboards in the BIOS, and thus the system initializes the USB controller in firmware at boot time. Consequently, our solutions implement this fixed device requirement using the `keep_orig_addr` constraint from Section 3.2 to prevent the USB controllers from being reprogrammed, and also avoid any memory regions marked as reserved by ACPI or in use by IOAPIC devices. The computation does not include handling other quirks, since our hardware does not exhibit them and consequently does not exercise that part of our CLP code. Our implementation is successful in configuring all PCI buses and devices on all the test systems.

| | C LOC | CLP LOC |
|---|---|---|
| Register access | 235 | |
| Data structure | 817 | 31 |
| Algorithm | | 224 |
| ACPI | 360 | |
| Interrupts | 660 | 28 |
| Miscellaneous | 109 | |
| Total | 2181 | 283 |

**Table 2.** Lines of code in PCI configuration and interrupt allocation

| | C LOC |
|---|---|
| Register access | 897 |
| Data structure | 1686 |
| Resource management | 706 |
| ACPI | 121 |
| Interrupts | 521 |
| Miscellaneous | 45 |
| Total | 3976 |

**Table 3.** Lines of code for equivalent functionality in Linux

### 5.2 Performance

We measured the time for PCI configuration on our test systems, and show the results in Table 1. This time is for the CLP algorithm and does not include the initial bus walk, nor programming of device registers. As discussed in Section 3, these remain in C as part of the PCI driver, and the CLP time dominates the overall runtime.

Compared to the performance of a hard-coded allocation in C, which in existing OSes typically requires less than a millisecond, our solution is substantially slower, but the additional overhead of 10–30ms is only incurred at boot time or after a hotplug event, and so is arguably insignificant to the end user. This computation can be run in parallel with other tasks, and since the PCI configuration changes rarely, the computed configuration can be cached and reapplied during the next boot process. In those cases, no additional overhead is added to the boot time.

### 5.3 Code size

In this section we compare the complexity, measured in lines of code (LOC), of our CLP-based approach to the comparable portions of the Linux x86 PCI driver. Such a comparison can never be precise, and must be preceded by several qualifications. First, in both cases we consider the code related to PCI resource configuration, interrupt allocation, PCI device discovery, maintenance of the data structures representing the PCI bus hierarchy, and the corresponding hardware access mechanisms. Second, we exclude some PCI-related mechanisms (such as the legacy PCI BIOS interface) that are currently unsupported by our solution. Third, because we do not handle quirks yet, we exclude the hardware quirk-handling code, but retain handling of other special cases. Finally, the Linux code implements the solution that attempts to fix up the initial BIOS configuration, whereas our code does a full allocation of addresses. Note that our goal is to reduce the complexity of the source code and therefore the number of source lines of code, rather than the number of generated machine statements.

We summarize the results for our solution in Table 2 and for Linux in Table 3. The relevant Linux code is located in the kernel in drivers/pci. Overall, our approach uses 2464 lines of code, compared to 3976 for the pure C-based Linux version.

Breaking this down, we use much less code for register access, as our access to hardware is highly regular and independent of allocation. Building and manipulating data structures is also simpler for us: representing lists and trees is highly concise in Prolog, and allows us to build much simpler structures in the C domain, resulting in about half the code size. We use more code for ACPI, since we explicitly handle ACPI reserved regions, whereas Linux relies on the BIOS initialization for this. Code for interrupt assignment is about the same size. Finally, the "core" of the configuration code (in as much as it can be isolated in the Linux case) is 224 lines of Prolog versus 706 lines of C.

The largest class of code in both implementations is used for maintaining data structures. This is because PCI data must be queried from either ACPI or directly from the hardware, transformed to a meaningful internal representation, and added to a structure. Finally, configuration proceeds by traversing this structure, accessing and mutating it. The corresponding data structure in our implementation consists mostly of Prolog facts which are generated by C but traversed/accessed entirely in CLP, and thus require fewer lines of code than Linux. Despite being large in size in both systems, such code is not the most complex in its logic.

The more complex logic in the PCI configuration algorithm uses 224 lines of CLP code in our implementation. This not only produces a correct and complete allocation, it also handles special constraints such as avoiding reserved regions as well as not moving certain devices. In comparison, the Linux C implementation uses more lines of code for less functionality (it does not perform full bus configuration).

Besides the usual benefits arising from a smaller, simpler, codebase in terms of source lines of code, the separation of concerns between low-level hardware-specific device access code and a high-level declarative resource configuration algorithm enhances the system's maintainability and adaptability to changing hardware requirements. Complex device- and system-specific constraints, such as quirks, can be incorporated without changing the device access code or core algorithm, and it can easily be ported to other PCI-based platforms. We return to this discussion in Section 6.

### 5.4 Postorder traversal comparison

To evaluate the quality of the solutions found, we investigated how they compare to the style of simple postorder traversal used in current operating systems. When allocating resources to a device tree where the size of each device is known in advance, one might expect this approach to be sufficient. We first describe why that is not the case, and then show experimentally the advantage of a declarative CLP solution against such a traversal.

Starting with the base address given by the root bridge, such an algorithm traverses down the left-most branch of the tree first, assigning the current base address to each bridge and finally the left-most leaf device, while satisfying alignment constraints. For each device allocation, the device size is added to the base value, plus any padding required for alignment. The algorithm next traverses all child devices of the bridge, before moving up the tree to the next-upper parent bridge, and updating the bridge's limit register in the process, before continuing with the remaining devices and bridges.

Such an algorithm can be simply described and implemented, and ensures that all bridges are allocated a window including their children and that alignment constraints are satisfied. However, the algorithm is insufficient for PCI configuration for two reasons:

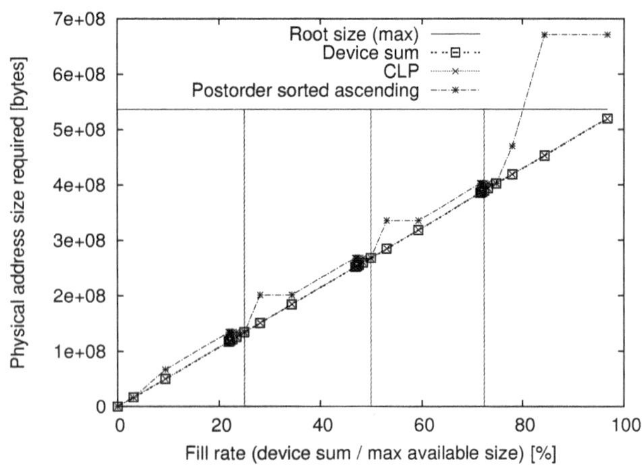


**Figure 3.** Address space utilization of CLP algorithm vs. simple postorder traversal as devices and bridges are added to a simulated system. The CLP algorithm reorders devices as needed, exactly following the *DeviceSum* line, which shows the lower bound. The postorder traversal, which sorts the devices according to size, cannot fit the PCI tree into the given root bridge window. Vertical lines indicate when a new bridge is added; the horizontal line indicates the maximum size of the root bridge window.

1. It fails to include constraints that require keeping devices at a fixed address. This requires all parent bridges to decode the fixed device window. Because all parent bridges have to decode a fixed address, all children of every bridge decoding a fixed address have to be placed close to a predetermined address region. This cannot be easily expressed in a postorder traversal of the device tree.
2. Satisfying alignment constraints leads to potentially large amounts of address space wasted in padding, preventing successful configuration when not all devices fit into the root bridge's address range.

To learn how or CLP-based algorithm behaves when resources are consumed more and more by additional devices, we stressed the configuration algorithm in an offline experiment by adding progressively more devices and bridges to a simulated PCI system. Starting with zero devices and bridges, we added either a device or a bridge on every round and measured the consumed resources by the configuration derived by the algorithm. This scenario is not purely artificial, because it simulates what can happen when devices are hotplugged. We compared our CLP-based algorithm with an improved postorder traversal algorithm, which sorts devices according to their requested size in ascending order. The results are shown in Figure 3.

The horizontal line *Root size (max)* indicates the given root bridge window size, which must not be exceeded for a successful configuration. The vertical lines in the figure indicate where a bridge has been added to the PCI tree. The *DeviceSum* line indicates the sum of the requested size of all installed devices without padding or alignment constraints; this is the absolute lower bound of address space utilization. The data points indicate the address space consumption after having added the next device.

The figure shows that our CLP-based allocation algorithm exactly follows the device sum. Its constraints give it the freedom to reorder bridges and devices, so that no address space is wasted for alignment constraints and a solution can always be found. The best postorder traversal algorithm, which does not respect fixed device requirements, cannot fit the devices into the given root bridge window beyond 80% utilization, indicating that such a simple approach cannot work in general.

# 6. Discussion

We set out to evaluate declarative languages as a way of expressing hardware configuration algorithms, as part of a wider project to build a new operating system for heterogeneous multicore systems. Our hypothesis was that such an approach would reduce the complexity of the code we would have to write, and in the long term would provide a good foundation for reasoning about the complexity and heterogeneity of modern and future hardware.

Our experience so far has been mostly positive, but not without challenges. In this section we describe both the advantages and disadvantages of the approach that we have encountered.

## 6.1 Advantages

***Clear policy/mechanism separation:*** Maintaining a sharp distinction between the algorithm used to find a suitable hardware configurations and the mechanism to configure the hardware by writing values to registers has a number of strong benefits.

First, the algorithm can be clearly understood in isolation from hardware access, making it easier to both debug and maintain. Indeed, much of the debugging, testing, and evaluation of our PCI programming code was carried out "offline" in a vanilla ECL$^i$PS$^e$ running on Linux using PCI configurations obtained from a variety of machines around our lab, before being put into service at boot time in Barrelfish. It is also useful to be able to test this code by writing correctness conditions in Prolog which are then validated automatically.

Second, the hardware access code is simplified, since it is no longer threaded through the configuration algorithm. Verifying (by inspection) that the C code correctly accesses PCI devices and bridges becomes a simpler task, and the chances of breaking this code when changing the configuration algorithm itself are greatly reduced.

***Separation of special cases:*** PCI quirks, fixed PCI devices, reserved non-PCI address ranges, and the like can be handled entirely in the declarative domain through Prolog statements, and do not pollute the C register access code.

Furthermore, adding new quirks or special cases can be done simply by adding such cases as assertions to the declarative specification of the algorithm, *without* modifying the mainline algorithm code in any way. For the most part, additional constraints are one-line references to existing functions, and hence easy to add to the system. It is often sufficient merely to add a device's ID to a list, which is passed to a function applying a specific constraint to the elements. All of this results in a clear separation within the declarative code between special cases and the solution description.

***Flexibility of data structures:*** Device information in traditional operating systems is typically represented by a set of simple, ad-hoc data structures (tables, trees, hash tables) whose design is determined largely (and rightly so) by performance concerns in the kernel. In our approach we retain such structures where needed on the fast path, but represent most of the hardware information as facts in the logic language.

This greatly facilitates reasoning about the information in ways not foreseen at design time. For example, information from ACPI about non-PCI device locations can be transformed easily into regions of memory reserved from the normal PCI allocation process. The logical unification mechanism provided in languages like Prolog makes this expressible in a single rule. Furthermore, this representation can be changed over time without concern for disturbing critical kernel code.

***Late-binding of algorithm:*** ECL$^i$PS$^e$ allows for adding new functionality as well as replacing functionality at runtime. This feature provides considerable flexibility. In the concrete case of PCI programming, we can run the normal allocation algorithm for a complete allocation and later at runtime load an allocation algorithm which is more suited to hotplug scenarios. Whether the algorithm is replaced at runtime or boot time, the mechanism code to access the hardware need not change.

***Platform independence:*** As we have mentioned, PCI code in Linux varies almost completely between, for example, the x86 and Alpha/AXP platforms. In contrast, with our approach the configuration logic is identical across all architectures using PCI. What changes is the register access code in C – for example, most non-x86 architectures replace I/O instructions with memory-mapped I/O. This makes our code highly portable. Furthermore, only short mechanism code has to be ported, reducing the chance of introducing bugs when porting.

***Reuse of functionality:*** While CLP may be regarded as a somewhat heavyweight approach (see below), the functionality provided is close to that required by many other parts of a functional OS – in some ways, the system knowledge base might be regarded as analogous to parts of the Windows Registry, albeit with a much more powerful type system, data model, and query language. Barrelfish uses this functionality for, among other things, representing the memory hierarchy to performance-conscious parallel applications, and as a name server for other system services. Along with the authors of Infokernel [3], we argue for making a rich representation of system information available for online reasoning, and CLP provides a powerful tool for achieving this.

## 6.2 Disadvantages

Unsurprisingly, the approach also has some significant drawbacks.

***Constraint satisfaction is no silver bullet:*** A hardware configuration problem like PCI, with all its special cases, is very natural to express as a constraint satisfaction problem. However, this does not automatically lead to a solution in a reasonable time. Constraint solvers have a well-known tendency to explode in complexity (and, consequently, time of execution) without careful specification of the problem, and our use of CLP is no exception in this regard.

Part of this is due to ECL$^i$PS$^e$ being a relatively simple solver by modern standards, but much of the complexity is inherent. In practice, the onus is on the programmer to guide the solver by careful annotation of the problem. This makes the source code more complex than a simple specification of the constraints - our Prolog code is carefully written to avoid an explosion in complexity and/or runtime.

For example, in our PCI case we sort the variables to be instantiated according to the requesting size of the device in an ascending order. The solver starts probing the last element of the list of variables. This causes it to try to place the device with the biggest size requirement first, which is generally more difficult. If small devices would be placed first, the solver would most likely later need to reallocate them, to free up a large continuous address range in order to place a bigger device. This would potentially lead to a whole permutation of the tree.

To take another example, the natural-alignment property is best expressed by a modulo division of the base address by the size, as shown in Section 3.2. If the remainder is zero, the address is aligned according to the size. However using this implementation, when the solver tries to instantiate the base address variable, it searches all integers one by one until it finds a value with a zero remainder. In case some other constraints cannot be met, the solver must try another solution and repeat searching for values with a remainder of zero, leading to a huge execution time. We therefore modified the associated goal slightly, by letting the solver choose an integer from a (typically small) precomputed range which is multiplied by the device's size to determine the base address. The upper bound of the range is chosen so that the maximum base lies just beyond the fixed window of the root bridge, therefore including all possible naturally-aligned base addresses for the device, while substantially reducing the search space.

***Increased resource usage:*** Even with the heuristics described above, ECL$^i$PS$^e$ CLP is an interpreted, high-level language with high execution time overhead compared to C. Additionally, a CLP algorithm works by propagating constraints and then probing values rather than assigning values in a straight-forward iterative way. Clearly this leads to longer execution times.

For some classes of problem, such as the PCI programming case we discuss in this paper, the execution time overhead is not critical as long as it remains under a second or so. Additionally, the PCI configuration changes rarely and the previous solution can be cached and reapplied without the need of starting the CLP system. In general, boot time is only increased when the PCI configuration changed since the algorithm ran last time. However, the performance penalty clearly rules out a class of other, time-critical hardware-related tasks.

For this work we used a relatively slow language runtime. Using a faster language might significantly improve execution time.

For resource constrained devices such as small battery powered sensor nodes or embedded systems this solution might be inappropriate. However those systems usually have a simple and fixed PCI configuration without hotplug support. They can either be programmed in C or by running the solver once, offline, on a standard PC with PCI data from the embedded system. The solution found can then be added to the device's boot image and applied at every boot-up of the system.

***Large code base:*** While we use considerably less PCI-specific code (C and Prolog) to implement our solution, we do employ a large body of code in the form of the CLP solver. The port of ECL$^i$PS$^e$ we use in Barrelfish consists of 16242 lines of C[1], plus a handful of assembly-language lines. In addition, the core CLP libraries add 1042 lines of Prolog, many of them quite long. The complete solver executable (statically linked) consists of 1.5MB for a 64-bit x86 OS. Additionally, a compressed RAM disk of 600kB provides the necessary Prolog files. This is clearly significant, and adding this amount of code to the boot image of an OS raises at least two concerns.

First, there is the issue of code bloat. On modern hardware, the boot process is unduly impacted by the overhead, but the difference in start-up performance is noticeable compared with the (considerably less functional) hard-coded PCI solution we used in the early stages of OS development. On the other hand, as mentioned above, the CLP solver does provide a valuable data management service to other parts of the OS as a general name server and policy engine, and so the cost in code size should be amortized over the whole set of client subsystems which use it.

Second, there is the extent to which we can trust the CLP solver itself. We rely on ECL$^i$PS$^e$ behaving correctly. Since it is a mature, general-purpose system, we might expect it to be reliable and relatively bug-free. However, it is unlikely that a complex piece of code like ECL$^i$PS$^e$ will be formally verified, which makes our approach less attractive for high-assurance operating systems. However, such systems typically are written to specific hardware platforms, obviating the need for complex configuration logic.

For high-assurance, formally verified systems, a better application of this approach would be to apply the ideas at compile time,

[1] LOC counts were generated using "SLOCCount" by David A. Wheeler.

which would integrate with the seL4 approach [17] of modeling the entire OS in a high-level language, which is then translated (in a way that preserves the verified properties) to C.

***Boot sequence:*** Configuring hardware at OS boot time in a high-level language like CLP means that the language runtime has to be started early in the boot process. Barrelfish may be unique in loading a full CLP system before configuring PCI hardware.

Perhaps surprisingly, this imposes very few requirements on the OS. The SKB, like most of the components, executes in user space as in a classical microkernel design. However, CLP requires very little of the OS to be functional beyond basic (non-paged) virtual memory and a simple file system, initially from a RAM disk passed as a GRUB multiboot module at boot. The dynamic nature of the solution allows us to load further functionality after an initial PCI configuration when disks, networking interfaces, etc. come online.

***Learning curve:*** Most OS programmers use C rather than Prolog to implement algorithms, and the learning curve for a language like Prolog is almost certainly steeper than for C. However, we feel someone with a basic knowledge of Prolog will find it easier to understand our code than a complex, imperative C version.

Furthermore, we are by no means the first people to try using logic programming in operating systems – for example, Prolog has been successfully used to provide network configuration logic in Windows [13].

## 7. Related work

This paper has considered a new approach to hardware programming, focusing on the specific problem of PCI resource configuration. The PCI specification [9, 23] describes the mechanisms and requirements for correct configuration of a PCI system, but does not specify any particular algorithm to be used in this process, leading to a variety of different (usually incomplete) solutions in current systems, as described in Section 2.7. These solutions are being iteratively refined and improved to handle more complex scenarios such as device hotplug [20, 29], leading to greater complexity.

A resource allocation algorithm for a hierarchical tree structure such as PCI has been patented by Dunham [10]. This algorithm sorts devices with fixed requirements according to their base address in ascending order, and all other devices according to their alignment requirements (size) in descending order. It then allocates resources to devices and bridges using a first-fit strategy starting at the lowest-level secondary bus, allowing it to determine the size requirement for the lowest-level bridge. Once its size is set, a bridge is then treated as a fixed-size device for allocation at the upper levels, and placed using the same first-fit allocation. Bridges are considered to have fixed address requirements if a device at any level below the bridge has a fixed requirement. As it encodes a specific traversal of the resource tree, this algorithm is roughly comparable to the postorder traversal discussed in Section 5.4 and used in varying forms by several current systems.

Rather than encode device configuration logic in low-level systems languages, we argue for wider use of declarative programming techniques. In this work, we specifically use constraint logic programming [15], a technique derived from logic programming and used to allocate resources in many fields. Prior applications of CLP include room allocation, task and job scheduling [2, 24], and indeed in our implementation we reused ECL$^i$PS$^e$ primitives originally intended for task scheduling. Prolog has also been used in commercial systems such as Windows NT [13] to derive network configurations: a backtrack-based binding algorithm takes facts about interfaces of network modules and derives valid configurations, including the correct load order of modules, which it then stores to the registry. DEC developed a series of expert systems to ensure that selected component configurations that include CPUs and other hardware as well as software are valid and components are compatible to each other [6]. Hippodrome uses a solver to automatically configure minimal and still performant storage systems by analyzing workloads and iteratively searching a global minimum [1]. Declarative specifications of resources and resource requirements have also been used successfully by systems such as Condor [18, 28]. In the context of the Semantic Web, the resource description format (RDF) [30] is widely used to represent and reason online about resources. RDF is expressively almost equivalent to the logic programming approach we present here (ignoring the constraint and optimization extensions we employ), and might form the basis for a viable alternative to ECL$^i$PS$^e$.

Declarative language techniques have also been applied to operating systems, to date largely in the area of resource allocation. The Infokernel [3] was an early advocate in the OS arena of making a rich representation of system information available for online reasoning. Singularity [27] uses XML manifests to reason about the resources used by a device driver. These manifests may be analyzed at driver install time to checking for resource conflicts. They also ensure the correctness of a driver's interaction with the OS through contracts on message channels. The related system Helios [22] also uses manifests, to define preferred affinities of message channels to other processes, and thus guide the placement of processes to CPUs in a heterogeneous system. Similarly, the Hydra framework [31] uses a declarative approach to reason about available resources in a heterogeneous system consisting of host CPUs and programmable offload devices. Using an XML-based description language, the Hydra runtime selects suitable offload processors, thus achieving greater utilization of processor resources while reducing complexity for the programmer.

The complexity of hardware access can also be reduced through declarative approaches. Devil [19], an IDL for hardware programming, uses a declarative specification of device ports (base addresses), registers and their interpretation to generate low-level code for device access. This leads to simpler and more understandable code for device drivers, in an attempt to improve driver reliability. ATARE [16] uses a series of regular expressions to extract IRQ routing information from ACPI, without the need for the usual complex byte code interpreter.

Finally, SQCK [11] uses declarative queries to concisely implement a complete file-system consistency checker, which is also able to handle complex repairs. Together with the previous work, this signals what we see as a promising trend towards applying high-level declarative techniques to simplifying the construction of traditionally complex and error-prone systems software.

## 8. Conclusion and future work

In this paper we have investigated the case for applying declarative language techniques to low-level configuration of hardware in modern machines. In our initial experiments, we have shown that we can implement a solution to the complex PCI resource allocation problem using CLP with few lines of code, written in a natural and easy-to-evolve manner.

In addition, the approach provides considerable benefit from a clean division between policy and mechanism, and the further separation of general solution specification from the numerous special cases which inevitably occur when dealing with real software. However, care still must be taken when formulating the problem in CLP to avoid unacceptable explosions in execution time when searching for a solution.

The principle disadvantage of our approach is that it is heavyweight, in terms of memory footprint, execution time, and (when also considering the CLP runtime) total lines of code. Much of this is an artifact of our particular choice of a powerful, general purpose, but also mature (and therefore slower than the current state of the art) constraint logic programming system. While this choice has allowed us great freedom to explore the design space, a more appropriate solution for a product would compile the search algorithm into an efficient form when the OS was built, resulting in much faster execution and a smaller memory footprint.

Our view is therefore that the approach shows promise, and our experience in building an OS and delegating much hardware configuration functionality to the CLP engine has been positive so far. In our view, industry trends such as heterogeneous multicore, intelligent peripheral devices, sophisticated and reconfigurable interconnects, and partial cache coherence, combined with increasingly diverse platform configurations, strongly motivate a new and more systematic approach to reasoning about hardware configuration.

In our ongoing work, we are applying declarative techniques to other aspects of Barrelfish – in particular, more complete representations of the memory hierarchy than are available in typical OS NUMA support – and also applying logic programming techniques to naming and addressing the various processing elements in heterogeneous multicore systems.

## Acknowledgments

We would like to thank our shepherd Michael Swift for his many helpful suggestions and the Barrelfish team at ETH Zurich and Microsoft Research, in particular Tim Harris, for numerous helpful suggestions for improving this paper.

## References

[1] Anderson, E., Hobbs, M., Keeton, K., Spence, S., Uysal, M., and Veitch, A. Hippodrome: Running circles around storage administration. In *Proceedings of the 1st USENIX Conference on File and Storage Technologies* (Berkeley, CA, USA, 2002), FAST '02, USENIX Association.

[2] Apt, K. R., and Wallace, M. G. *Constraint Logic Programming using ECL$^i$PS$^e$*. Cambridge University Press, 2007.

[3] Arpaci-Dusseau, A. C., Arpaci-Dusseau, R. H., Burnett, N. C., Denehy, T. E., Engle, T. J., Gunawi, H. S., Nugent, J. A., and Popovici, F. I. Transforming policies into mechanisms with Infokernel. In *Proceedings of the 19th ACM Symposium on Operating System Principles* (Oct. 2003), pp. 90–105.

[4] Baldwin, J. H. Multiple passes of the FreeBSD device tree. In *BSDCan Conference* (May 2009). http://www.bsdcan.org/2009/schedule/attachments/83_article.pdf.

[5] Baldwin, J. H. About hot-plugging support in FreeBSD. http://www.mavetju.org/mail/view_message.php?list=freebsd-arch&id=3106757, Feb. 2010.

[6] Barker, V. E., O'Connor, D. E., Bachant, J., and Soloway, E. Expert systems for configuration at digital: Xcon and beyond. *Commun. ACM 32* (March 1989), 298–318.

[7] The Barrelfish Research Operating System. http://www.barrelfish.org/, December 2010.

[8] Baumann, A., Barham, P., Dagand, P.-E., Harris, T., Isaacs, R., Peter, S., Roscoe, T., Schüpbach, A., and Singhania, A. The multikernel: a new OS architecture for scalable multicore systems. In *Proceedings of the 22nd ACM Symposium on Operating System Principles* (Oct. 2009).

[9] Budruk, R., Anderson, D., and Shanley, T. *PCI Express System Architecture*. Addison Wesley, 2004.

[10] Dunham, S. N. Method for allocating system resources in a hierarchical bus structure, July 1998. US patent 5,778,197.

[11] Gunawi, H. S., Rajimwale, A., Arpaci-Dusseau, A. C., and Arpaci-Dusseau, R. H. SQCK: A declarative file system checker. In *Proceedings of the 8th USENIX Symposium on Operating Systems Design and Implementation* (Dec. 2008).

[12] Hewlett-Packard, Intel, Microsoft, Phoenix, Toshiba. *Advanced Configuration and Power Interface Specification, Rev. 4.0a*, Apr. 2010. http://www.acpi.info/.

[13] Hovel, D. Using Prolog in Windows NT network configuration. In *Proceedings of the Third Annual Conference on the Practical Applications of Prolog* (1995).

[14] The Importance of Implementing APIC-Based Interrupt Subsystems on Uniprocessor PCs. http://www.microsoft.com/whdc/archive/apic.mspx, January 2003.

[15] Jaffar, J., and Lassez, J.-L. Constraint logic programming. In *POPL '87: Proceedings of the 14th ACM SIGACT-SIGPLAN Symposium on Principles of Programming Languages* (1987), pp. 111–119.

[16] Kauer, B. ATARE: ACPI tables and regular expressions. Tech. Rep. TUD-FI09-09, TU Dresden, Faculty of Computer Science, Dresden, Germany, Aug. 2009.

[17] Klein, G., Elphinstone, K., Heiser, G., Andronick, J., Cock, D., Derrin, P., Elkaduwe, D., Engelhardt, K., Kolanski, R., Norrish, M., Sewell, T., Tuch, H., and Winwood, S. seL4: Formal verification of an OS kernel. In *Proceedings of the 22nd ACM Symposium on Operating System Principles* (Oct. 2009).

[18] Livny, M., Basney, J., Raman, R., and Tannenbaum, T. Mechanisms for high throughput computing. *SPEEDUP Journal 11*, 1 (June 1997).

[19] Mérillon, F., Réveillère, L., Consel, C., Marlet, R., and Muller, G. Devil: an IDL for hardware programming. In *Proceedings of the 4th USENIX Symposium on Operating Systems Design and Implementation* (2000), pp. 17–30.

[20] Microsoft. PCI multi-level rebalance in Windows Vista. http://www.microsoft.com/whdc/archive/multilevel-rebal.mspx, Nov. 2003.

[21] Microsoft. Firmware allocation of PCI device resources in Windows. http://www.microsoft.com/whdc/connect/PCI/pci-rsc.mspx, Oct. 2006.

[22] Nightingale, E. B., Hodson, O., McIlroy, R., Hawblitzel, C., and Hunt, G. Helios: heterogeneous multiprocessing with satellite kernels. In *Proceedings of the 22nd ACM Symposium on Operating System Principles* (2009), pp. 221–234.

[23] PCI-SIG. *PCI Express Base 2.1 Specification*, Mar. 2009. http://www.pcisig.com/.

[24] Reis, L. P., and Oliveira, E. A constraint logic programming approach to examination scheduling. In *Proceedings of the 10th Irish Conference on Artificial Intelligence and Cognitive Science* (1999).

[25] Rusling, D. A. The Linux kernel. http://tldp.org/LDP/tlk/tlk.html, 1999.

[26] Schüpbach, A., Peter, S., Baumann, A., Roscoe, T., Barham, P., Harris, T., and Isaacs, R. Embracing diversity in the Barrelfish manycore operating system. In *Proceedings of the 1st Workshop on Managed Multi-Core Systems* (June 2008).

[27] Spear, M. F., Roeder, T., Hodson, O., Hunt, G. C., and Levi, S. Solving the starting problem: device drivers as self-describing artifacts. In *Proceedings of the EuroSys Conference* (2006), pp. 45–57.

[28] Thain, D., Tannenbaum, T., and Livny, M. Distributed computing in practice: the Condor experience. *Concurrency: Practice and Experience 17*, 2–4 (2005), 323–356.

[29] TJ. PCI dynamic resource allocation management. http://tjworld.net/wiki/Linux/PCIDynamicResourceAllocationManagement, June 2008.

[30] W3C. Resource description framework, Feb. 2004. http://www.w3.org/RDF.

[31] Weinsberg, Y., Dolev, D., Anker, T., Ben-Yehuda, M., and Wyckoff, P. Tapping into the fountain of CPUs: on operating system support for programmable devices. In *Proceedings of the 13th International Conference on Architectural Support for Programming Languages and Operating Systems* (2008), pp. 179–188.

# Improved Device Driver Reliability Through Hardware Verification Reuse

Leonid Ryzhyk[1,2] John Keys[3] Balachandra Mirla[1,2] Arun Raghunath[3]
Mona Vij[3] Gernot Heiser[1,2]

[1] NICTA * [2] University of New South Wales [3] Intel Corporation

leonid.ryzhyk@nicta.com.au john.keys@intel.com balachandra.mirla@nicta.com.au
arun.raghunath@intel.com mona.vij@intel.com gernot.heiser@nicta.com.au

## Abstract

Faulty device drivers are a major source of operating system failures. We argue that the underlying cause of many driver faults is the separation of two highly-related tasks: device verification and driver development. These two tasks have a lot in common, and result in software that is conceptually and functionally similar, yet kept totally separate. The result is a particularly bad case of duplication of effort: the verification code is correct, but is discarded after the device has been manufactured; the driver code is inferior, but used in actual device operation. We claim that the two tasks, and the software they produce, can and should be unified, and this will result in drastic improvement of device-driver quality and reduction in the development cost and time to market.

In this paper we propose a device driver design and verification workflow that achieves such unification. We apply this workflow to develop and test drivers for four different I/O devices and demonstrate that it improves the driver test coverage and allows detecting driver defects that are extremely hard to find using conventional testing techniques.

***Categories and Subject Descriptors*** D.4.4 [*Operating Systems*]: Input/Output; B.4.2 [*Input/Output and Data Communications*]: Input/Output Devices

***General Terms*** Reliability, Verification

***Keywords*** Device Drivers, Reliability, RTL Testbenches, Automated Testing, Co-verification.

## 1. Introduction

Device drivers are critical components of an operating system (OS), as they are the software that controls peripheral hardware, such as disks, network interfaces or graphics displays. They make up a large fraction of OS code, e.g., around 70 % in Linux.

Drivers are also important for another reason: they are the leading reliability hazard in modern OSes. Drivers are known to be responsible for the majority of OS failures[9], and have been shown to have 3–7 times the defect density of other OS code [5].

Our recent study [21] has shown that the leading class of driver defects, comprising about 40 % of all driver bugs, are *device protocol violations*, i.e., situations where the driver incorrectly handles the software interface of the device. Common examples of such defects include incorrect use of device registers, sending commands to the device in the wrong order, incorrectly interpreting device responses, etc.

Device protocol violations are easy to introduce but hard to detect and eliminate. They are easy to introduce because driver developers often lack adequate documentation describing how the device should be controlled from software. Available documentation provided by hardware designers in the form of a device datasheet is usually incomplete and inaccurate, leading to numerous driver defects.

Device protocol violations are hard to detect due to limitations of the conventional quality assurance process based on testing. In order to thoroughly test the interaction between the driver and the device, the test harness must exercise the driver under various combinations of inputs from the OS and the device. Existing device driver testing kits [16, 25] do a good job of exercising the OS interface of the driver by generating various sequences of I/O requests that model real application scenarios. Testing different hardware operating conditions is a much harder task. For instance, the behaviour of a network controller device depends on the Ethernet line speed, data throughput, collision rate, inter-packet gap, hardware flow control, and numerous other parameters. The device driver must be able to correctly handle the device under any combination of these parameters.

The problem is that controlling the values of these parameters requires special hardware, firmware, and software support on the remote host. While such support can be provided in principle [25], this is rarely done in practice due to the high complexity of this approach. As a result, many driver defects escape even seemingly thorough testing that does not model different environments that the device can be placed into.

Other components of the system that affect the device behaviour include the CPU, the I/O bus, and the OS scheduler. All of these components influence the timing of communication between the driver and the device in ways that are beyond the control of the testing software, which further limits the achievable test coverage. For example, I/O bus contention in a system with multiple active I/O devices can reduce the device-to-memory data transfer speed and lead to internal device buffer overflow, which must be carefully

* NICTA is funded by the Australian Government's Department of Communications, Information Technology, and the Arts and the Australian Research Council through Backing Australia's Ability and the ICT Research Centre of Excellence programs


*ASPLOS'11,* March 5–11, 2011, Newport Beach, California, USA.

handled by the driver. Since such uncommon scenarios cannot be easily triggered in a directed fashion, they often remain untested.

In addition to the lack of control over the driver's execution environment, the conventional driver testing methodology also suffers from the lack of observability of the device behaviour. Every I/O request sent to the driver must result in certain events occurring at the external interface of the device. For instance, a request to send a network packet must result in the correct data, with valid CRC and padding fields being sent through the Ethernet interface of the device. Since the testing code cannot directly monitor this external device interface, it must rely on indirect evidence to make sure that the driver completed the operation correctly. This is not always sufficient, since an incorrect behaviour is often concealed by timing delays or by hardware reliability mechanisms.

In summary, conventional driver testing suffers from serious limitations that reduce its effectiveness in detecting driver defects. The problem is exacerbated by the inadequate device documentation, leading to the overall poor quality of driver code.

We argue that the underlying cause of these difficulties is the separation of two highly-related tasks: *device verification* and *driver development*. As explained in more detail in the following sections, these two tasks have a lot in common, and result in software that is conceptually and functionally similar. The main difference is that the hardware verification code is built around a simulated model of the device and thus has complete control over all components of the simulated environment, including the I/O bus, the external physical medium, and the thread scheduler, which enables thorough testing of the device as well as device control logic. In contrast, the driver is developed in the OS environment running on top of the real hardware, which does not allow tight control over the testing process.

The result is a particularly bad case of useless duplication of effort: the verification code is correct, but is discarded after the device has been manufactured; the driver code is inferior, but used in actual device operation.

Our central claim is that the two tasks, and the software they produce, can and should be unified, and this will result in a drastic improvement of device-driver quality. To support this claim, we have developed a workflow in which the driver developer implements and tests the driver in the context of the device verification environment. The resulting driver is then transferred without modifications to the OS environment. The workflow guarantees that code that works correctly in the verification environment results in a correct driver.

In the proposed workflow, driver testing is performed in parallel with hardware verification, months before the actual hardware is manufactured. As a result, driver testing is no longer in the critical path to product delivery, which enables shorter product development times and encourages more thorough testing.

We evaluate this workflow by applying it to develop and test drivers for 4 different I/O devices. The results are encouraging: we were able to find 9 driver defects, all of which would have been extremely hard to find using conventional driver testing techniques. Furthermore, we demonstrate that this approach allows improving the quality of hardware verification by finding two hardware design defects in one of the devices.

The rest of the paper is structured as follows. Section 2 gives an overview of the hardware verification workflow. We introduce the main ideas behind our approach to verification reuse in Section 3. Section 4 discusses potential advantages and limitations of this approach. Section 5 presents design and implementation details. We evaluate the proposed approach in Section 6, survey related work in Section 7 and draw conclusions in Section 8.

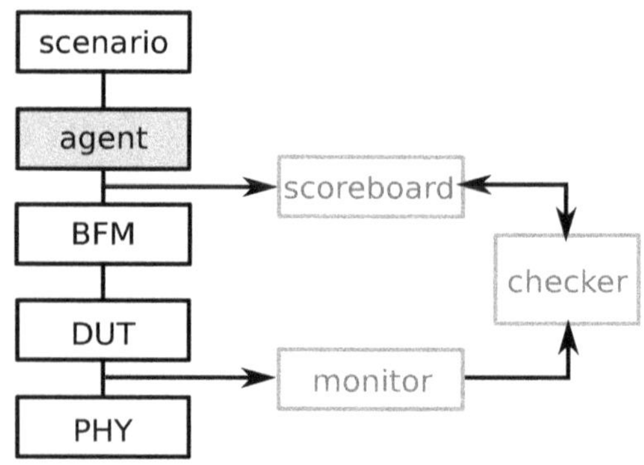


**Figure 1.** The RTL testbench architecture.

## 2. Hardware verification

This section provides an overview of the hardware verification process used in the majority of modern hardware designs.

In current industrial practice, design and testing of a device are tightly integrated. Starting from a formal or informal description of the desired device functionality, the hardware engineer develops a register transfer level (RTL) design of the device. As mistakes are expensive and time-consuming to fix once the design has been fabricated in silicon, much effort is put into verifying the design in a simulated environment prior to producing hardware. The software infrastructure for such verification, called the RTL *testbench*, is developed in parallel with the design of the device.

The testbench is designed to exercise the RTL design and validate its behaviour under a wide range of operating conditions. Most modern testbenches follow the layered architecture shown in Figure 1, which models the hardware and software structure of a real computer system. It is built around a simulated model of the device, called the *design under test* (DUT). The DUT is connected to a *bus functional model* (BFM), which simulates the I/O bus the device is connected to. It accepts bus-read and -write commands from higher layers and translates them into bus transactions at the device interface. The *agent* module consists of functions and associated state that implement high-level device transactions such as sending network packets, changing device configuration, handling interrupts, etc.

The *scenario* layer consists of test scenarios designed to thoroughly test the device in various modes. Finally, the bottom layer of the testbench simulates the physical medium that the device controls. For instance, if the DUT is an Ethernet Medium Access Control (MAC) controller, this layer simulates an Ethernet physical transceiver (PHY) chip.

In addition to the above modules that model components of a computer system, a complete testbench contains modules responsible for monitoring and validating the device operation. The *scoreboard* module keeps track of requests sent by the agent to the DUT and predicts the results of these requests. The *monitor* module records input and output signals at the physical interface of the device and groups them into high-level transactions. The *checker* compares transactions observed by the monitor against predicted ones recorded in the scoreboard. Finally, coverage points (not shown in the figure) are used to measure the progress of the testbench in fulfilling the verification plan requirements.

The testbench is usually designed to operate in the directed and randomised modes. In the directed mode, the testbench validates device responses to pre-defined sequences of input stimuli. In the randomised mode, the testbench generates random sequences of stimuli subject to a set of constraints. Randomisation applies to the ordering, timing, and content of messages sent to the DUT via

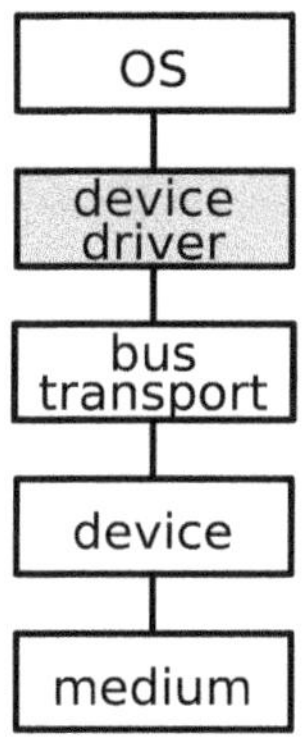


**Figure 2.** The operating system I/O stack architecture.

the bus and the PHY interfaces. Since the testbench has complete control over device interfaces, the test coverage is only limited by the duration of the testing run.

Constructing such a testbench involves substantial engineering effort. It is not uncommon for an RTL testbench to be larger and more complicated than the design that it is intended to test. This complexity can be somewhat reduced by using domain-specific languages such as SystemC and SystemVerilog that provide support for common tasks arising in testbench design, such as generation of constrained-random stimuli and interfacing with RTL. In order to further reduce the effort involved in testbench development, electronic design automation (EDA) tool vendors provide verification class libraries that facilitate the construction of layered designs similar to the one shown in Figure 1. Examples of such libraries include the Verification Methodology Manual (VMM) [2] library from Synopsys and the Open Verification Methodology (OVM) [17] library from Mentor and Cadence.

## 3. A co-verification approach to driver reliability

This section presents our proposed approach to driver quality assurance. In particular, we argue that the hardware verification ecosystem described in the previous section can be reused for driver development and testing.

We observe that the agent component of the testbench (Figure 1) provides similar functionality to a device driver and could in principle use the same implementation.

The agent accepts high-level I/O and configuration requests from the scenario layer and turns these requests into sequences of device-register read and write operations. Examples of requests handled by the agent include sending a network packet, performing a USB bus transaction, or writing a block of data to the disk. The agent also receives interrupt notifications from the DUT, reads device status registers, and informs the scenario layer about the completion status of requested operations.

For comparison, consider the operating system I/O stack architecture shown in Figure 2. It consists of the hardware device connected to the physical medium, the I/O bus transport comprised of the physical I/O bus and the OS bus framework, and the device driver providing services to the rest of the OS.

Similarly to the agent component of the testbench, the driver converts high-level requests from the OS into low-level interactions with the device over the bus transport. Yet, the agent is developed in a more supportive environment than the driver. Firstly, verification engineers have complete access to all device specifications and design internals. As such, they are in a good position to implement device control logic correctly. In contrast, driver developers only have access to the (frequently incorrect) datasheet.

Secondly, the device-control logic can be tested in the context of the RTL testbench more exhaustively than in the context of a driver. The testbench is specifically designed to expose various corner cases in the device behaviour. It has complete control over all components of the simulated environment and can model unusual situations like bus contention, network collisions, etc. As a side effect, such testing also exposes defects in other testbench components, including the agent, since such defects are likely to cause failures in verification scenarios.

Given the conceptual similarity between testbench and driver code, it seems promising to reuse the former for developing the latter. However, achieving this in practice faces significant challenges.

While the agent and the device driver serve a similar purpose in their respective environments, the exact interface they implement can be different. Adapting the agent implementation to the driver interface enforced by a particular OS may involve significant refactoring, e.g., splitting one operation into several or adding calls to OS-specific services. In addition, such adaptation requires writing device-specific glue code to translate OS requests into calls to agent functions. The need for these time-consuming and error-prone steps compromises the purpose of code reuse.

Instead of trying to adapt existing testbench code to work in the OS environment, we propose unifying the device driver interface across the OS and the testbench. A correct implementation of this interface is guaranteed to work correctly in both environments. We call such a reusable implementation an *environment-independent device driver.*

One way to achieve driver interface unification is to simulate the existing device driver API defined by the OS in the testbench environment. This way, a driver developed and tested in the context of a testbench can be reused directly in the OS kernel without the need for any modifications or wrapper code. Moreover, it is also possible to incorporate an existing OS driver in the testbench environment. This is useful for testing drivers developed using the conventional methodology.

The downside of this approach is that the resulting driver is only compatible with one OS. This is often acceptable, in particular for embedded devices that are designed for use with a specific system.

An alternative approach that allows producing reliable drivers for multiple OSes is to define a single, unified driver interface to be supported by the testbench as well as by each target OS. The resulting testbench and OS architectures are shown in Figure 3. In both environments, the device is managed by the environment-independent device driver, which implements two standardised interfaces: the *generic device-class interface* shared by all similar devices (e.g. all Ethernet controllers or all SCSI adapters) and the *generic bus interface* that provides generic methods for access to a specific bus type (PCI, USB, etc). The environment-independent driver is developed and tested in the context of the testbench and is reused without modifications inside the OS.

In the testbench environment, the driver interacts directly with the scenario layer and the BFM, which are designed to be compatible with the generic device-class and bus interfaces. In the OS environment, additional wrappers are required to translate between OS-specific driver interfaces and the corresponding generic interfaces. These wrappers only need to be implemented once for each OS and each generic interface. This way the environment-independent driver can be reused not only between the testbench and the OS environment but also across different OSes.

This architecture enables driver verification reuse across multiple operating systems at the cost of having to provide interface wrappers for each supported OS. In addition, it is not compatible with existing OS-specific device drivers.

In this paper we experiment with both OS-specific and OS-independent driver interfaces and demonstrate that both approaches

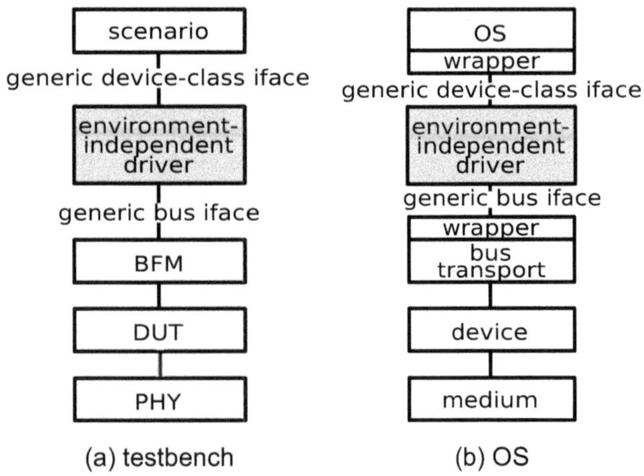


**Figure 3.** The testbench and OS architecture using a common implementation of the environment-independent device driver.

work in practice. The choice of the optimal solution is left to the user and depends on whether they require support for multiple OSes as well as how much effort they are prepared to invest in the driver verification infrastructure.

Interface compatibility is not sufficient to ensure that a driver developed in the testbench environment will work correctly in the OS environment. In particular, some of the implicit assumptions about the environment incorporated in the driver code may not hold inside the OS. The OS may perform various operations in a different order than the testbench, or issue concurrent calls to operations that the testbench executes sequentially. As a result, the driver based on this code may contain defects even though the code was thoroughly tested in the testbench environment.

In order to avoid such defects, we associate a detailed behavioural *contract* with the device-class interface. The contract defines constraints on the ordering of driver requests and responses as well as operations that the device must complete to satisfy each request. A correct driver must handle any sequence of requests permitted by the contract. Any valid environment must use the driver in a way that satisfies all constraints of the contract.

In case the driver implements an OS-specific interface, the contract must capture constraints imposed by the OS on driver behaviour. Such a contract can be derived from OS documentation and source code. Alternatively, if an OS-independent interface is used, the contract must be defined together with the interface. Section 5.2 discusses contracts in more detail.

In order to test the environment-independent driver against constraints of the contract, we implement a *contract conformance tester* as an extension of the testbench environment. The tester consists of two parts. The first part is a testing scenario that randomly generates valid sequences of requests to the driver. The second part consists of monitoring and checking components that keep track of outstanding requests, driver responses, and operations performed by the device and validate them against constraints of the contract.

In summary, our proposed driver development and testing workflow consists of the following steps.

1. The driver developer implements an environment-independent driver for the device in question. The driver must comply with the appropriate device-class and bus interface specifications. These interfaces can be OS-specific or OS-independent.
2. The verification engineer constructs a co-verification environment for the driver. To this end they either modify an existing device testbench or, if one does not exist, build a new testbench for use as a co-verification environment from the ground up. Refactoring an existing testbench that has not been designed for co-verification involves replacing the agent component of the testbench with the environment-independent driver. It also requires modifying the scenario layer and the BFM to support appropriate driver interfaces. The rest of the testbench infrastructure, including PHY, DUT, monitor, checker, and scoreboard modules, are reused with minimal or no changes.
3. The verification engineer extends the resulting testbench with the contract conformance tester, which provides additional testing scenarios to check that the driver correctly implements the device-class contract. The contract conformance tester needs to be implemented once for a class of devices.
4. Once the driver has been tested in the co-verification environment, it undergoes final testing in the target OS environment.

Note that this workflow does not attempt to shift the task of driver development from system programmers to hardware verification engineers, but rather enables them to work together in order to improve the quality of both the driver and the device.

# 4. Analysis

The hardware/software co-verification technique introduced in the previous section has the potential to significantly improve driver reliability by performing driver testing earlier in the product life cycle and by achieving better test coverage. On the other hand, the need to change current hardware verification practices may impede the practical application of this technique. In this section we analyse potential advantages and limitations of the proposed approach.

## 4.1 Improved driver test coverage

We start with analysing how hardware/software co-verification improves the likelihood of detecting various types of driver defects. To this end, we adopt the taxonomy of driver defects developed in our earlier work [21]. We distinguish four categories of defects:

1. *Device protocol violations* occur when the driver incorrectly handles the device interface by issuing an invalid sequence of requests to the device or incorrectly interpreting data received from the device.
2. *OS protocol violations* occur when the driver violates the ordering, content, or timing of interactions with the OS.
3. *Concurrency defects* occur when a driver incorrectly synchronises multiple threads of control executing within it, causing a race condition or a deadlock.
4. *Generic programming faults* include common coding errors, such as memory allocation errors and typos.

Device protocol violations account for about 40% of all driver defects, with the remaining defects distributed evenly across the other three groups [21].

### 4.1.1 Device protocol violations

As discussed in Section 1, the conventional driver testing environment has insufficient control and visibility of the device behaviour, which limits its ability to detect situations where the driver incorrectly uses the device interface.

In contrast, the device testbench built around the simulated model of the device can control device inputs and observe its outputs and its internal state at the clock-cycle granularity. In order to exhaustively test the device under a wide range of operating conditions, the testbench is equipped with stimuli generators that feed various patterns of input signals to the device, monitors that interpret device outputs, and checkers that validate these outputs.

Importantly, testing the driver requires the same generators and monitors as testing the device. This allows leveraging the significant effort invested in the hardware-verification infrastructure for driver testing. For example, the Ethernet PHY model used in testing the Ethernet MAC controller device (Figure 1) should be able to simulate network traffic to the device with a broad range of parameters. On the one hand, this is necessary for testing the controller operation under various network traffic conditions. At the same time, this also allows thoroughly testing how the driver handles data exchange with the device.

The fine-grained visibility of the device behaviour enables end-to-end validation of driver-device interactions. This validation is carried out by the contract conformance tester, which checks that every I/O request issued to the driver is successfully completed by the device. For example, it monitors the network interface of the device to make sure that packets sent to the driver appear at the network interface in the right order and that none of the packets are dropped or delayed. Note that such validation cannot be achieved during conventional driver testing, where the test harness can only observe driver's responses to I/O requests but not the matching device behaviours.

#### 4.1.2 OS protocol violations

Device-class contracts are also the main means of testing OS protocol compliance of a device driver. The contract conformance tester is designed to randomly simulate all possible sequences of requests that the driver can get from the OS and to validate driver responses against contract requirements.

#### 4.1.3 Concurrency defects and generic programming errors

The co-verification methodology that we present here does not provide special means to detect generic programming errors and concurrency defects. However, generic programming errors, such as bugs in bit-level arithmetic, often lead to device or OS protocol violations, in which case they can be detected using mechanisms described above.

In contrast, concurrency defects are unlikely to be detected in the co-verification environment. In order to achieve deterministic execution, device testbenches are usually designed around the co-operative threading model. As a result, most thread interleavings that may cause race conditions in the OS kernel environment do not occur in the testbench environment.

Concurrency defects and generic programming errors can be mitigated using complementary techniques, including static analysis [12] and software fault isolation [26].

#### 4.1.4 Hardware defects

While the co-verification approach is primarily intended to detect device-driver defects, it also has the potential to improve the quality of hardware testing.

Most device testbenches derive their testing scenarios from the specification of the device being tested. These scenarios represent the hardware designer's idea of how the device is going to be used, rather than the actual usage patterns that occur in a real system.

Contract-based testing closes this gap. By testing the device driver for adherence to the contract, we simultaneously test the device under a wide range of scenarios that model how the device will be used in a real OS. This helps uncover hardware-design defects missed by other testing scenarios before the device is implemented in silicon.

### 4.2 Impact on the testbench architecture

The proposed co-verification methodology relies on hardware verification engineers to incorporate environment-independent device drivers and device-class contracts in their testbenches. The need to change well-established verification practices may complicate the industrial adoption of this methodology.

For the approach to be practical, such changes must be kept to a minimum. In particular, modifications required to the existing verification infrastructure to make it compatible with environment-independent driver interfaces only affect the BFM and the scenario layer, which comprise a small fraction of the testbench code. We argue that such modifications are not only acceptable, but that they improve the testbench architecture: interface unification helps avoid reinventing the same interface for every device and facilitates code reuse across testbenches.

### 4.3 Impact on driver development and maintenance

In current OSes, driver development follows one of two dominating models. In the first model the driver is created and maintained by the hardware-device vendor. This approach is standard for Windows drivers. The co-verification methodology fits well into this model, as both the initial version of the driver and all subsequent releases can be tested by the hardware vendor in the co-verification environment.

In the second model, used for the majority of Linux drivers, driver maintenance is the responsibility of OS developers. The initial version of the driver is often provided by the hardware vendor. However, subsequent support, including bug fixing and adaptation to kernel API changes is performed by one of the kernel developers. In this model the driver maintainer does not have access to the device testbench; hence co-verification can only be performed by the device vendor on the initial version of the driver.

In the worst-case scenario, the device vendor does not provide even the initial driver implementation. The driver is written by OS developers based on the device datasheet or by reverse engineering an existing driver for another OS. In this scenario, the driver developer does not have access to the device RTL and its testbench; hence co-verification is not applicable to such drivers.

The use of OS-independent driver interfaces allows improving this process. Instead of implementing drivers for multiple OSes, the device vendor can publish the co-verified OS-independent implementation of the driver. OS developers only need to build and maintain interface wrappers for relevant interfaces.

### 4.4 Simulation speed

The quality of testing is related to its duration: longer test runs detect more defects and result in more reliable drivers. One limitation of testing in the simulated testbench environment is that simulated devices typically run three to four orders of magnitude slower than real hardware. As a result, fewer tests can be run in the given time frame.

Low simulation speed is compensated for by higher testing precision: while conventional driver testing ends up hitting the same common-case execution paths most of the time, the testbench uses its fine-grained control over device interfaces to drive the device into various corner-case situations. To this end, it relies on randomisation and careful choice of testing scenarios.

The problem can be further mitigated using techniques for improving simulation speed. These include FPGA-based testing [3] and replacing low-level RTL device models with more abstract models that simulate faster [27]. Finally, testing in the co-verification environment can be complemented by faster, but less accurate, conventional OS-based testing.

### 4.5 Unified driver-OS interface

Generic device-class and bus interfaces enable the reuse of verification results across multiple OSes: a driver tested in the testbench environment should work correctly in the context of any OS that provides wrappers for the appropriate generic interfaces.

Unfortunately, previous attempts to introduce a unified driver interface [20] were not successful, because major OS vendors were reluctant to give up the competitive advantage of having better hardware support than less popular systems. In addition, open-source systems like Linux continuously evolve their driver interfaces, so that drivers are not even portable across Linux kernel releases. Cross-OS interface unification looks problematic in these settings. Therefore, in the short term the use of OS-specific interfaces in co-verification is likely to be a more practical approach.

### 4.6 Handling non-standard device features

The co-verification methodology described so far assumes that all devices of the same type provide equivalent functionality and can be accessed via a common interface. This allows the reuse of the entire co-verification infrastructure, including the contract conformance tester and OS wrappers, for all devices of the same class.

In practice, many I/O devices support non-standard features that are not covered by the existing device-class interface. Often these features distinguish the product among competitors; therefore reliable software support for them is important.

In order to support such non-standard devices, a custom version of the device-class interface and the associated contract conformance tester must be produced for the device. In addition, the OS wrappers also need to be modified to support the new behaviours. We expect such modifications to be strictly incremental in most cases, since non-standard devices are usually compatible with all features of the standard ones.

Thus, the reuse of the verification environment can be extended even to non-standard devices, although additional per-device effort is required in such cases.

Note that the problem is not unique to the co-verification methodology. Inherently, devices with non-standard features require special testing code. However, with our approach, existing device-class contract testers can be immediately reused to test the generic functionality of non-standard devices, since such devices must still support all the features present in simpler devices.

## 5. Design and implementation

### 5.1 Interface specifications

Before starting on the implemention of the driver and its co-verification environment, one must obtain specifications of the driver interfaces. In case OS-specific interfaces are used, their specifications can be extracted from OS header files. Alternatively, if the co-verification environment is constructed around generic OS-independent interfaces, these interfaces need to be defined first.

Ideally, generic driver interfaces should be standardised across the industry, which will facilitate the reuse of the associated testbench components. In practice, however, different vendors are likely to define their own generic interfaces and develop the entire co-verification infrastructure in-house. In either case, these interfaces must be designed by system programmers, who have in-depth understanding of how the OS interacts with hardware.

Generic interfaces resemble analogous driver interfaces defined by an OS. Unlike OS-specific interfaces, however, generic driver interfaces must allow implementation in any OS, i.e., it should be possible to build an efficient wrapper to translate between the OS-specific and the generic interface.

```
1 virtual class ethernet_mac;
2     virtual task mac_enable (...);
3     virtual task mac_disable (...);
4     virtual task tx_queue_packet (...);
5     ...
6 endclass: ethernet_mac
7
8 virtual class ethernet_mac_cb;
9     virtual task tx_packet_sent (...);
10    ...
11 endclass: ethernet_mac_cb
```

**Figure 4.** A fragment of the Ethernet controller device-class interface specification in SystemVerilog.

We start defining a generic device-class interface by identifying the set of I/O operations that this particular device class must support. These include data transfer requests (e.g., sending and receiving packets), configuration requests, power management requests, etc. We analyse how each of these operations is implemented in several existing OSes in order to come up with a design that is efficient, e.g., avoids unnecessary data copying and blocking, and that can be mapped onto existing OS interfaces. Based on this analysis, we determine whether the given operation should be implemented as a single, potentially blocking, method or as a request-completion chain and define the list of its arguments and their types.

A generic interface specification can be written in either a system programming language, e.g., C or C++, or in a hardware-verification language, e.g., SystemVerilog or SystemC. It can then be automatically translated into any other supported language. To this end, language subsets that allow mapping to other languages must be used.

Figure 4 shows a fragment of the generic interface specification for the Ethernet MAC controller device class, written in SystemVerilog. This interface must be implemented by any environment-independent Ethernet device driver. The first part of the specification (lines 1 through 6) lists methods that an Ethernet driver must provide to the OS, including methods to enable and disable the controller, add a new packet to the device transmit queue, etc. The second part (lines 8–11) defines the callback interface that the OS must provide to the driver. The driver uses this interface to report device status changes and I/O request completions to the OS. For instance, the `tx_packet_sent` callback notifies the OS about successful transmission of a packet.

In addition to generic device-class interfaces, one must also specify generic bus interfaces (see Figure 3) for various types of I/O buses as well as generic interfaces to common OS services such as timers, synchronisation, and DMA buffer management.

In particular, design of the DMA buffer management interface raises some interesting issues due to the different ways in which the testbench and the OS manage devices' access to physical memory. In the OS environment, access to memory is mediated by address-translation hardware, including the MMU and the IOMMU. In contrast, in the testbench environment the driver and the device both have direct access to a simulated RAM.

In order to abstract away the differences between the two models, we designed a generic DMA buffer management API that allows efficient implementation in the testbench environment as well as in any OS kernel. The API exports two simple abstractions: the *iospace* abstraction that represents the device's view of the physical RAM, and the *iobuffer* abstraction that represents a data buffer. All mapping, translation, and coherency issues are handled transparently by the internal implementation of the API.

### 5.2 Device-class contracts

A device-class contract extends the device testbench with a specification of how the OS interacts with the device. It defines constraints on the ordering of requests and responses exchanged by the driver and the OS. It also defines the semantics of each request in terms of its effect on the device behaviour.

The following is a simplified example of a rule defined by the Ethernet controller device-class contract:

1. When the controller is enabled, the OS can call the `tx_queue_packet` method of the driver to transmit a network packet.
2. The driver must transmit packets received from the OS over the network in FIFO order.
3. Once a packet has been transmitted, the driver must notify the OS via the `tx_packet_sent` callback.

The second clause of the rule is the most interesting one, as it relates OS requests to the expected device behaviour. By enforcing this rule at run time, the co-verification environment makes sure that the driver correctly completes all transmit requests. This is in contrast to conventional driver testing where the test program cannot directly observe whether the device has really performed the requested operation.

A device class contract must be sufficiently restrictive to rule out any illegal behaviours, yet sufficiently liberal to allow a range of possible valid behaviours. For example, the network controller is not allowed to drop an incoming packet when its receive buffer is empty and the packet is received without an error. A failure to deliver such a packet to the OS indicates a defect in either the device or the driver. On the other hand, the controller may or may not drop the packet if the inter-packet gap is too short, the receive buffer is full, or the packet is longer than the currently configured threshold. To complicate things further, if several such packets arrive in a row, the controller can accept any subset of them.

Error handling is another source of complexity in contract specifications. The driver must correctly report the status of completed I/O requests to the OS. For example, if hardware CRC checking is enabled and the device receives a packet with invalid CRC field, the driver must report a CRC error.

Finally, a contract must capture various interleavings of hardware and software events. For example, when the network controller is disabled, it must drop all incoming packets. After the OS enables the controller, it must deliver incoming packet to the OS. However, depending on the implementation of the driver and the device, they can keep receiving packets while the disable or enable request in in progress.

At the moment, device-class contracts are written as informal documents. Based on this document, the verification engineer implements a contract conformance tester that is integrated into the device testbench and checks the driver's contract compliance. The tester consists of three modules shown in Figure 5. The *contract scenario* module simulates the most general contract-compliant environment that the driver can be placed into by randomly issuing requests to the driver according to the constraints of the contract. It is designed in such a way that any valid sequence of requests will be generated eventually with probability one.

The *contract scoreboard* module keeps track of outstanding requests issued to the driver and the driver's responses to these requests. It operates at a higher level of abstraction than conventional scoreboards used in hardware verification (see Figure 1). While the hardware scoreboard records individual bus transactions, the contract scoreboard records high-level I/O requests to the driver.

Finally, the *contract checker* module observes the device behaviour and validates it against requests recorded in the scoreboard.

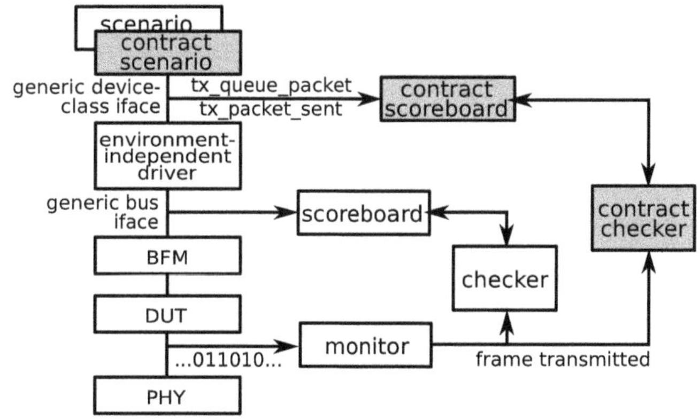


**Figure 5.** Ethernet controller co-verification environment with the contract conformance tester.

As a concrete example, consider how the rule cited above is enforced by the Ethernet device-class contract conformance tester. The contract scenario module implements the first clause of the rule by randomly generating transmit requests to the driver (along with other types of requests) whenever the controller is enabled. The contract scoreboard records each packet sent to the driver in its internal queue. The contract checker receives notifications about transactions that occur at the PHY interface of the device from the monitor module. In particular, it is notified whenever the device transmits a complete Ethernet frame on the wire. It checks that packets are transferred in FIFO order by comparing the payload of this frame with the packet at the head of the internal queue maintained in the scoreboard (clause 2). The checker also gets notified by the contract scoreboard when the driver invokes the `tx_packet_sent` callback and verifies that this only happens *after* the successful transmission of the packet (clause 3). Finally, it makes sure that the driver does not lose packets by checking that every packet recorded in the scoreboard is sent on the network and acknowledged by the driver within a certain time period.

The contract scoreboard and checker modules are incorporated in the device testbench alongside the conventional scoreboard and checker used in device verification (Figure 5). Likewise, the contract scenario module is used along with potentially many other scenarios developed by verification engineers to test the device functionality.

Implementing a contract conformance tester is a complex task; therefore it is desirable to reuse the same implementation with multiple testbenches for different devices of the same type. To this end, all interfaces between the tester modules and the rest of the testbench must be standardised. Inputs to the contract scoreboard module are already standardised as part of the the device-class interface specification. The only remaining interface that needs to be defined is the one between the monitor and the contract checker. For Ethernet devices, for example, this interface consists of methods that notify the checker about frames sent and received by the controller, network collisions, aborted transfers, etc.

### 5.3 Environment-independent drivers

The task of implementing an environment-independent device driver is similar to that of writing a normal driver. One complication involved in sharing the driver implementation between the testbench and the OS environment is that testbenches are written in hardware verification languages such as SystemC and SystemVerilog, whereas OS kernels can only host code written in C or C++. One possible solution is to implement the environment-independent driver in C or C++ and incorporate it into a SystemVerilog or SystemC testbench using inter-language bindings. Alternatively, the driver can be written in the same language as the rest of the testbench and automatically translated into C. We expect the former approach to be the more common one, as C and C++ are currently languages of choice for driver developers. If the latter approach is taken, the use of the verification language must be restricted to a subset that allows automatic translation to C. In case of SystemVerilog, this mainly implies avoiding features that require automatic garbage collection.

Detailed investigation of automatic SystemVerilog-to-C translation is beyond the scope of this research. Only one of the case studies presented in Section 6 uses a SystemVerilog implementation of the driver. For this driver, the translation to C was performed manually.

### 5.4 OS wrappers

OS wrappers implement the translation between OS-specific and generic driver interfaces. This translation must be implemented efficiently to avoid performance degradation. In particular, operations that involve data copying and synchronisation should be avoided in the performance-critical data path.

Avoiding copying means that data buffers passed by the OS to the driver should be converted from the OS-specific representation into the generic iobuffer representation in place, i.e., without copying their data payload. To this end, we provide several implementations of the iobuffer interface on top of different data buffer primitives supported by the OS. For example, Linux has separate primitives for simple buffers, scatter-gather buffers, and network buffers; hence three different iobuffer implementations are required.

## 6. Evaluation

In this section we evaluate the proposed co-verification methodology with respect to the following criteria:

- *Feasibility.* We demonstrate that this methodology enables the creation of device drivers that can be used without modifications in both the OS and the testbench environment. Furthermore, implementing a device driver using this methodology is comparable in terms of required time and effort to conventional driver development.
- *Reliability.* We show that hardware/software co-verification helps improve driver reliability by detecting driver defects that are extemely hard to find during conventional driver testing.
- *Performance.* We provide evidence that the improved driver reliability does not come at the cost of performance degradation.

### 6.1 Case studies

Our evaluation was performed as a series of case studies where we implemented and tested drivers for four different devices. The choice of devices was limited to open-source designs for which RTL specifications are publicly available, and a limited selection of designs used inside Intel.

In one of the case studies we built a co-verification environment around an existing Linux driver. In the three other case studies we defined OS-independent driver interfaces for respective device classes and implemented drivers and their co-verification environments around these interfaces.

Three of the case studies were accomplished by refactoring existing device testbenches, whereas in the fourth case study we implemented a testbench from scratch.

#### 6.1.1 Case study 1: Ethernet controller

In the first case study we implemented and tested a driver for the 100Mb/s Ethernet controller device from the OpenCores project [18]. Our co-verification environment is based on an existing open-source testbench for this device developed using the Synopsys VMM methodology [2].

This is the only case study where the environment-independent driver was implemented in SystemVerilog and then manually translated into C. The translation was performed in a mechanical way that mimicked the work of an automatic translator. In the other case studies drivers were implemented in C from the beginning and integrated in the verification environment using SystemVerilog-to-C bindings.

#### 6.1.2 Case study 2: High-speed UART

The device used in this case study is a high-speed Intel UART controller with an integrated DMA engine.

Our co-verification environment for this device is based on the existing proprietary testbench, developed using the OVM methodology [17].

#### 6.1.3 Case study 3: USB host controller

The third case study is based on an existing Linux driver for the OpenCores USB 1.1 host controller device [19]. We implemented the co-verification environment for this device on top of the existing custom testbench that does not rely on any standard verification methodology.

#### 6.1.4 Case study 4: USB slave controller

Our final case study is based on an Intel USB slave controller device . Since we did not have access to an existing device testbench, we implemented our own testbench from scratch.

#### 6.1.5 Summary of case studies

Table 1 summarises the four case studies. For each case study it shows:

- The size of the native Linux driver for the given device.
- The size of the environment-independent driver used in co-verification.
- The size of the co-verification infrastructure, excluding the driver, the DUT, and the contract conformance tester (see Figure 5).
- The size of the contract conformance tester.

The last two columns represent the reusable part of the co-verification environment that can be applied to test multiple devices of the same type and their drivers. As can be seen from the table, this reusable part is an order of magnitude larger than the driver that is being tested. The only exception is the last case study, where we only implemented a minimal rudimentary testbench. Another observation that can be drawn from the table is that the size of environment-independent device drivers is on par with equivalent native Linux drivers.

### 6.2 Feasibility

We start with evaluating the feasibility of developing and testing device drivers using the co-verification methodology.

Our case studies did not produce any surprises here: writing an environment-independent driver was quite similar to writing a regular OS-based driver, and involved a comparable amount of labour.

Refactoring an existing testbench into a co-verification environment also proved a straightforward task. The main effort involved in such refactoring is implementing various OS services required by the driver, which took several days in our case studies. This is

| # | Case study | Lines of code | | | |
|---|---|---|---|---|---|
| | | Linux driver | Env-independent driver | Co-verification environment | Contract conformance tester |
| 1 | Ethernet controller | 1,189 | 957 | 10,032 | 1,794 |
| 2 | High-speed UART | 1,554 | 2,077 | 18,418 | 5,622 |
| 3 | USB host controller | 1,147 | 1,052 | 7,909 | 1,892 |
| 4 | USB slave controller | 3,333 | 2,705 | 427 | 1,230 |

**Table 1.** Summary of case studies.

a one-off effort, since the resulting implementation can be reused when building a co-verifciation environment for a new device.

The next step is to introduce the contract conformance tester into the testbench in order to thoroughly test the driver functionality against OS requirements. Implementing this tester is the most complicated and time consuming step in the co-verification workflow. Modelling and checking the outcomes of I/O requests under various combinations of hardware and software inputs requires involved logic. This logic is particularly difficult to get right given that it must handle events from three concurrent sources: the driver, the DUT, and the PHY module. In addition, it must reflect the non-determinism in the driver and the device behaviour where the same sequence of inputs can cause multiple valid outputs. The contract conformance tester must be carefully implemented to allow all legal outputs, while detecting any illegal ones.

The effort of developing a device-class contract conformance tester could hardly be justified it it had to be done afresh for each device. Fortunately, this work is amortised across many drivers of the same class that can be tested using the common tester.

The effectiveness of the co-verification methodology can be further improved by automating the task of writing contract conformance testers. As mentioned in Section 5.2, device-class contracts are currently written as informal documents. If contract constraints are specified formally, one can in principle generate a contract conformance tester automatically from this specification. Our ongoing work is focusing on languages and tools for automatic generation of contract conformance testers.

In our case studies, we implemented co-verification environments on top of VMM and OVM testbenches, which represent the two most popular hardware verification methodologies nowadays, as well as on top of a custom testbench. This gives us confidence that our approach to the reuse of the hardware verification infrastructure in driver testing applies to the majority of current device testbenches.

Another encouraging observation is that the testbench provides a better debugging environment for drivers than real hardware. Driver developers are only too familiar with the frustrating situation where a device simply refuses to behave as expected, a situation which frequently requires a trial-and-error approach to resolve. It is a consequence of the inability to inspect the internal state of the device. In the testbench environment, the programmer has complete access to the source code and the runtime state of the simulated device, which helps tremendously in diagnosing difficult problems.

Driver debugging is further simplified due to the fact that the testbench executes as a user-level program. This enables the use of program debugging and analysis tools that are not available in the kernel environment.

### 6.3 Reliability

For evaluating the impact of co-verification on driver reliability, we set out to answer the following questions. Firstly, what types of defects that are hard to find during conventional driver testing can be detected using co-verification? Secondly, what types of defects does co-verification fail to detect?

In order to answer the first question, we invert the normal co-verification workflow: we start with developing and testing the driver in the OS environment before moving to the co-verification environment. Additional defects found during co-verification are analysed to determine why they escaped detection during the initial testing. In some cases, the analysis showed that the defect could have potentially been discovered in the OS environment by running additional tests. In other cases, even extensive additional OS-based testing would have been unlikely to find the defect. These defects represent the classes of defects that can be eliminated or substantially reduced using co-verification.

We followed this approach in case studies 2 and 4. Case study 3 takes a similar approach, but instead of implementing and testing our own Linux driver we used an existing Linux driver for the device that had been used in several working designs. We ported this driver to the co-verification environment with minimal changes.

Finally, case study 1 implemented the normal co-verification workflow, i.e., it started with developing and testing the driver in the co-verification environment before moving to the kernel environment. As we discovered defects in our implementation of the driver, we compared them against the existing Linux driver for the same device. This way we found a potentially dangerous runaway DMA defect in the Linux driver.

Case study 1 also revealed two hardware-design defects in the Ethernet controller RTL. These defects were triggered in situations which occur in a real OS, but which the original device testbench failed to model, such as disabling the controller while there is a packet transfer in progress. As a result, they had not been detected during conventional hardware verification. This is a common problem in hardware verification: verification engineers do not have a good understanding how the device under test must interact with the OS and as a result fail to implement relevant test cases. These defects also had not come up during conventional driver testing, because their effect was masked by TCP/IP error recovery mechanisms.

Table 2 summarises software and hardware defects that were discovered during our case studies and that would have been difficult to detect using conventional testing techniques. These include device and OS protocol violations, generic programming defects, and hardware design errors.

These defects can be further partitioned into three groups. The first group includes defects that depend on system parameters that cannot be controlled by the testing software, such as I/O bus speed or BIOS-defined device configuration (defects #4, 6). The second group contains defects that escape detection during testing because their effect cannot be directly observed by the test program (defects #1, 2, 3, 5, 9, 10). The third group is comprised of defects triggered by software request sequences that are difficult to generate in a directed way in the OS environment (defects #7, 8, 11).

As discussed in Section 1, the fundamental problem that prevents these defects from being detected during conventional OS-based testing is that the OS lacks means to directly control and observe the device behaviour. In contrast, the co-verification environment can generate arbitrary input signals to the device and observe

| # | Description | Type | Comments |
|---|---|---|---|
| | | | Case study 1: Ethernet |
| 1 | Runaway DMA: the device continued accessing DMA buffers after they have been deallocated by the driver. The defect was caused by an undocumented device behaviour where the device, when disabled, did not immediately stop its transmit and receive engines. | dev | The defect was identified by the contract checker when it received a packet transmission notification after the driver had reported that the transmitter had been disabled. It was not found during conventional testing, since runaway DMA cannot be detected by the OS until it causes a memory corruption and even then tracing down the root cause of the problem is difficult. |
| 2 | Hardware race condition: disabling the device and later re-enabling it causes the hardware to skip the first DMA descriptor in the transmit queue. | h/w | These hardware design defects are triggered in situations which occur in a real OS, but which the original device testbench failed to model, such as disabling the controller while there is a packet transfer in progress. As a result, they were not detected during conventional hardware verification. |
| 3 | Hardware race condition: disabling only the receiver part of the device caused corruption of the next transmitted packets. | h/w | |
| | | | Case study 2: High-speed UART |
| 4 | The HS UART implements an extended register set that is only available in the memory-mapped device configuration. The driver, however, attempted to access these extended registers in both the memory-mapped and the I/O-space mapped mode. | dev | The driver was tested on a platform that configured the device in the memory-mapped mode. In contrast, the co-verification environment simulated both modes, which allowed detection of the error. |
| 5 | The driver did not disable software flow control interrupts when running with hardware flow control enabled. This did not affect its functional correctness, but resulted in an increased CPU load due to excessive flow control interrupts generated by the device. | dev | The defect did not cause any functional errors and therefore could not be easily detected during OS-based testing. In the co-verification environment, the UART device-class contract defines constraints on UART interrupt generation, which were violated when the defect was triggered during co-verification. |
| | | | Case study 3: USB host controller |
| 6 | The driver is required to wait for a few microseconds after issuing a write to the device reset register and before reading or writing any other device registers. The Linux driver was missing this delay. As a result, the device failed to initialise correctly. | dev | This defect did not come up during conventional driver testing due to the slow I/O bus on the development board, which introduced sufficient delay between register accesses for the device to complete the reset. It would, however, prevent the device from working correctly in a system with a faster bus. |
| 7 | A typo in bit-vector arithmetic prevented the driver from correctly setting the USB hub port speed during port power-up. | gen | This defect was not detected while testing the driver in Linux, because Linux usually resets the hub port immediately after powering it up. The reset routine set the port speed correctly, thus undoing the effect of the power-up routine. The defect was discovered in the co-verification environment by the contract checker, which checks the connection status after port power-up. |
| 8 | The driver incorrectly assumed that the OS never submits more than one request to a USB control endpoint at a time. When such a situation occurred, the driver's USB transfer abort function aborted the wrong transfer. | os | Multiple outstanding control transfers are uncommon in USB devices, which is why this defect was not discovered during driver testing. Our USB host-controller contract scenario simulates such behaviour and therefore was able to detect this error. |
| | | | Case study 4: USB slave |
| 9 | Upon a USB disconnect, the driver generated numerous bogus disconnect, suspend, and resume notifications for 300ms. The problem was caused by the USB suspend signal in the device status register, which started floating after a disconnect, causing fake interrupt notifications. | dev | The defect was not detected during conventional testing, because the OS is unable to distinguish a bogus disconnect notification from a real one. |
| 10 | When aborting a partially transferred packet, the driver returned incorrect count of transferred bytes. The problem was caused by the driver not properly updating the transfer length field of the packet in the abort path. | gen | This defect could not be detected during conventional testing, because the OS does not know the actual number of bytes transferred and is therefore unable to validate the value returned by the driver. |
| 11 | The driver violated the USB endpoint abort protocol expected by the OS by failing to mark the endpoint as stopped before aborting the first transfer associated with it. As a result, the OS could immediately requeue the transfer, potentially entering an infinite loop. | os | The infinite loop scenario is possible, but rarely occurs in practice and was never encountered during conventional driver testing. |

**Table 2.** Driver defects discovered using co-verification that would have been difficult to detect using conventional testing techniques. The third column describes the type of defect: *dev* – device protocol violation, *os* – OS protocol violation, *gen* – generic programming error, *h/w*–hardware design error.

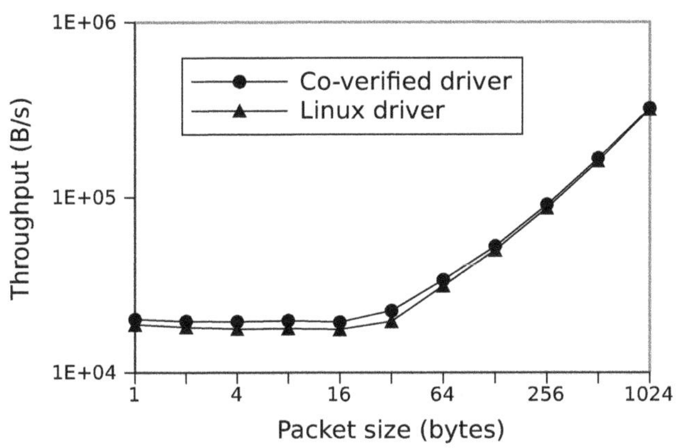


**Figure 6.** OpenCores Ethernet controller UDP throughput benchmark results.

device output signals at the wire level, which makes the detection of this kind of defects straightforward.

To answer the second question about faults missed by co-verification, we place the Ethernet controller driver from case study 1, which has been tested in the co-verification environment, into the Linux kernel environment and keep testing it there. As a result, we uncovered two additional defects that were missed in the co-verification environment.

The first defect was a race condition between the packet transmission function and the interrupt handler. As mentioned in Section 4.1.3, our methodology is not effective against concurrency errors; therefore the discovery of this kind of defect in a co-verified driver did not come as a surprise.

The second defect was caused by the driver not initialising one of its state variables to 0, which prevented it from correctly sending network packets. The defect could have been detected during co-verification if our environment had randomised the content of dynamically allocated memory.

Overall, these results confirm our analysis presented in Section 4: the co-verification methodology is effective in dealing with most types of driver defects, including defects that are difficult to detect using conventional testing techniques.

### 6.4 Performance

For our performance evaluation, we use the Ethernet controller driver from case study 1. The controller hardware runs on a 25MHz FPGA board with an OpenRISC CPU. On such a slow platform, driver performance can have critical impact on both I/O througput and CPU utilisation, especially under heavy network traffic.

We compare the performance of the driver developed using the co-verification methodology against the native Linux driver for this device. To this end we measure network throughput and CPU utitlisation when receiving streams of UDP packets of various sizes.

In all experiments, both drivers generated CPU utilisation of about 100%. Throughput results are shown in Figure 6. The two drivers achieved similar throughput for all packet sizes. In fact, the co-verified driver sustains up to 8% higher throughput than the Linux driver. Our analysis showed that the additional overhead in the Linux driver was caused by an extra data copy operation that it performed in the receive path.

These results indicate that our approach to driver development does not result in a noticeable performance overhead.

## 7. Related Work

Previous research on device driver reliability has mainly focused on detecting [1, 6, 7], isolating [8, 10, 13, 14, 24, 28, 29], and avoiding [21, 23] driver defects. Another approach, implemented in tools like Devil [15] and Termite [22] reduces the number of defects in drivers by generating a partial or complete implementation of a driver from a formal specification of the device interface.

All of these techniques, however, suffer from serious limitations. Existing static analysis tools are capable of detecting a limited subset of errors, such as common OS API rule violations [1] and certain memory allocation and synchronisation errors [7]. Stronger correctness properties, such as memory safety, race-freedom, and correct use of device interfaces, are currently beyond the reach of these tools. Runtime isolation architectures are capable of detecting broader classes of errors; however many of these systems incur intolerably high overhead. In addition, isolation doesn't remove the need for testing, as a bug in an isolated driver can still lead to a complete of partial system failure. Finally, automatic code generation tools are limited by the availability of correct device specifications.

Due to these limitations, driver testing remains the most important technique for ensuring driver correctness.

Recently, Kuznetsov et al. [11] proposed a symbolic execution technique for improving the test coverage of device drivers. Their approach allows detecting generic programming errors, concurrrency errors and, potentially, OS protocol violations; however it is not effective against device protocol violations, which is the most common type of driver defects. We believe that our techniques are complementary: by using symbolic execution rather than randomisation to steer drive testing in the co-verification environment, it is possible to achieve better precision in detecting device protocol violations.

In the hardware design world, virtual prototypes [27] are widely used for software and hardware testing. A virtual prototype is a fully functional model of a complete hardware platform, including the CPU and I/O devices, capable of running the complete system software stack. It enables testing of device drivers as part of the OS before the actual device hardware is available. Virtual prototypes are primarily intended for integration testing and do not provide mechanisms for fine-grained control and monitoring of the device behaviour, which are necessary for thorough testing of device drivers.

Bombieri et al. [4] propose a method for generating a device driver from an existing device testbench by converting the testbench to a state machine representation and manually identifying sequences of commands that correspond to driver operations. One problem with this approach is that the required manual step is error-prone. More importantly, as discussed in Section 3, testbench code that is not designed for reuse in the OS environment is unlikely to be reusable without substantial modification.

## 8. Conclusions

We argue that the lack of cooperation between hardware and software designers is a major source of driver reliability problems and propose an architectural framework to enable such cooperation. This framework allows most of the driver code to be developed and tested at the hardware verification stage, before the device is implemented in silicon.

The benefits are:

- significant improvement of driver reliability, since the driver is identical to the code used to debug the hardware, and is more thoroughly exercised than feasible in an OS environment;

- reduced development cost due to code reuse across the device driver and the device testbench;
- reduced time to market as driver development and testing proceed in parallel with device verification.

## Acknowledgments

We would like to thank Julius Baxter for his help in getting the OpenCores development board up and running. We also thank Anton Burtsev, Thomas Sewell, Simon Winwood, and the anonymous reviewers for helpful comments.

NICTA is funded by the Australian Government's Department of Communications, Information Technology, and the Arts and the Australian Research Council through Backing Australia's Ability and the ICT Research Centre of Excellence programs.

## References

[1] T. Ball, E. Bounimova, B. Cook, V. Levin, J. Lichtenberg, C. McGarvey, B. Ondrusek, S. K. Rajamani, and A. Ustuner. Thorough static analysis of device drivers. In *Proceedings of the 1st EuroSys Conference*, pages 73–85, Leuven, Belgium, Apr. 2006.

[2] J. Bergeron, E. Cerny, A. Hunter, and A. Nightingale. *Verification Methodology Manual for SystemVerilog*. Springer-Verlag, Inc., 2005.

[3] Bluespec, Inc. Emulation: enabling it on every desktop, 2008.

[4] N. Bombieri, F. Fummi, G. Pravadelli, and S. Vinco. Correct-by-construction generation of device drivers based on RTL testbenches. In *Proceedings of the 45th ACM/IEEE Conference on Design, Automation and Test in Europe*, pages 1500–1505, Apr. 2009.

[5] A. Chou, J.-F. Yang, B. Chelf, S. Hallem, and D. Engler. An empirical study of operating systems errors. In *Proceedings of the 18th ACM Symposium on Operating Systems Principles*, pages 73–88, Lake Louise, Alta, Canada, Oct. 2001.

[6] A. Chou, B. Fulton, and S. Hallem. Linux kernel security report, 2005.

[7] D. R. Engler, B. Chelf, A. Chou, and S. Hallem. Checking system rules using system-specific, programmer-written compiler extensions. In *Proceedings of the 4th USENIX Symposium on Operating Systems Design and Implementation*, pages 1–16, San Diego, CA, Oct. 2000.

[8] U. Erlingsson, M. Abadi, M. Vrable, M. Budiu, and G. C. Necula. XFI: software guards for system address spaces. In *Proceedings of the 7th USENIX Symposium on Operating Systems Design and Implementation*, pages 75–88, Seattle, Washington, Nov. 2006.

[9] A. Ganapathi, V. Ganapathi, and D. Patterson. Windows XP kernel crash analysis. In *Proceedings of the 20th USENIX Large Installation System Administration Conference*, pages 101–111, Washington, DC, USA, 2006.

[10] J. N. Herder, H. Bos, B. Gras, P. Homburg, and A. S. Tanenbaum. MINIX 3: A highly reliable, self-repairing operating system. *ACM Operating Systems Review*, 40(3):80–89, July 2006.

[11] V. Kuznetsov, V. Chipounov, and G. Candea. Testing closed-source binary device drivers with DDT. In *Proceedings of the 2010 USENIX Annual Technical Conference*, Boston, MA, June 2010.

[12] S. K. Lahiri, S. Qadeer, and Z. Rakamari'c. Static and precise detection of concurrency errors in systems code using SMT solvers. In *Proceedings of the 21st International Conference on Computer Aided Verification*, pages 509–524, June 2009.

[13] B. Leslie, P. Chubb, N. Fitzroy-Dale, S. Götz, C. Gray, L. Macpherson, D. Potts, Y. R. Shen, K. Elphinstone, and G. Heiser. User-level device drivers: Achieved performance. *Journal of Computer Science and Technology*, 20(5):654–664, Sept. 2005.

[14] J. Liedtke, U. Bartling, U. Beyer, D. Heinrichs, R. Ruland, and G. Szalay. Two years of experience with a $\mu$-kernel based OS. *ACM Operating Systems Review*, 25(2):51–62, Apr. 1991.

[15] F. Mérillon, L. Réveillère, C. Consel, R. Marlet, and G. Muller. Devil: An IDL for hardware programming. In *Proceedings of the 4th USENIX Symposium on Operating Systems Design and Implementation*, pages 17–30, San Diego, CA, USA, Oct. 2000.

[16] Microsoft Corporation. Network Driver Interface Specification Test. http://www.microsoft.com/whdc/DevTools/tools/NDIStest.mspx.

[17] OVM. OVM class reference. Version 2.1.1, Mar. 2010.

[18] Project OpenCores. 10/100 Mbps Ethernet MAC core. http://www.opencores.org/project,ethmac, .

[19] Project OpenCores. USBHostSlave IP core. http://www.opencores.org/project,usbhostslave, .

[20] Project UDI. UDI core specification. Version 1.01, Feb. 2001.

[21] L. Ryzhyk, P. Chubb, I. Kuz, and G. Heiser. Dingo: Taming device drivers. In *Proceedings of the 4th EuroSys Conference*, Nuremberg, Germany, Apr. 2009.

[22] L. Ryzhyk, P. Chubb, I. Kuz, E. L. Sueur, and G. Heiser. Automatic device driver synthesis with Termite. In *Proceedings of the 22nd ACM Symposium on Operating Systems Principles*, Big Sky, MT, USA, Oct. 2009.

[23] L. Ryzhyk, Y. Zhu, and G. Heiser. The case for active device drivers. In *Proceedings of the 1st Asia-Pacific Workshop on Systems*, New Delhi, India, Aug. 2010.

[24] M. M. Swift, B. N. Bershad, and H. M. Levy. Improving the reliability of commodity operating systems. In *Proceedings of the 19th ACM Symposium on Operating Systems Principles*, Bolton Landing (Lake George), New York, USA, Oct. 2003.

[25] usbtest. USB testing on Linux. http://www.linux-usb.org/usbtest/.

[26] R. Wahbe, S. Lucco, T. E. Anderson, and S. L. Graham. Efficient software-based fault isolation. In *Proceedings of the 14th ACM Symposium on Operating Systems Principles*, pages 203–216, Asheville, NC, USA, Dec. 1993.

[27] M. Willems and F. Schirrmeister. Virtual prototypes for software-dominated communication system designs. *IEEE Communications Magazine*, 48:37–43, June 2010.

[28] D. Williams, P. Reynolds, K. Walsh, E. G. Sirer, and F. B. Schneider. Device driver safety through a reference validation mechanism. In *Proceedings of the 8th USENIX Symposium on Operating Systems Design and Implementation*, pages 241–254, San Diego, CA, USA, Dec. 2008.

[29] F. Zhou, J. Condit, Z. Anderson, I. Bagrak, R. Ennals, M. Harren, G. Necula, and E. Brewer. SafeDrive: Safe and recoverable extensions using language-based techniques. In *Proceedings of the 7th USENIX Symposium on Operating Systems Design and Implementation*, pages 45–60, Seattle, WA, USA, Nov. 2006.

# A Case for Neuromorphic ISAs

Atif Hashmi Andrew Nere James Jamal Thomas Mikko Lipasti

Department of Electrical and Computer Engineering, University of Wisconsin-Madison, Madison, WI, USA

{ahashmi, nere, jjthomas3}@wisc.edu, mikko@engr.wisc.edu

## Abstract

The desire to create novel computing systems, paired with recent advances in neuroscientific understanding of the brain, has led researchers to develop *neuromorphic architectures* that emulate the brain. To date, such models are developed, trained, and deployed on the same substrate. However, excessive co-dependence between the substrate and the algorithm prevents portability, or at the very least requires reconstructing and retraining the model whenever the substrate changes. This paper proposes a well-defined abstraction layer – the Neuromorphic instruction set architecture, or NISA – that separates a neural application's algorithmic specification from the underlying execution substrate, and describes the Aivo[1] framework, which demonstrates the concrete advantages of such an abstraction layer. Aivo consists of a NISA implementation for a rate-encoded neuromorphic system based on the cortical column abstraction, a state-of-the-art integrated development and runtime environment (IDE), and various profile-based optimization tools. Aivo's IDE generates code for emulating cortical networks on the host CPU, multiple GPGPUs, or as boolean functions. Its runtime system can deploy and adaptively optimize cortical networks in a manner similar to conventional just-in-time compilers in managed runtime systems (e.g. Java, C#).

We demonstrate the abilities of the NISA abstraction by constructing a cortical network model of the mammalian visual cortex, deploying on multiple execution substrates, and utilizing the various optimization tools we have created. For this hierarchical configuration, Aivo's profiling based network optimization tools reduce the memory footprint by 50% and improve the execution time by a factor of 3x on the host CPU. Deploying the same network on a single GPGPU results in a 30x speedup. We further demonstrate that a speedup of 480x can be achieved by deploying a massively scaled cortical network across three GPGPUs. Finally, converting a trained hierarchical network to C/C++ boolean constructs on the host CPU results in 44x speedup.

***Categories and Subject Descriptors*** C.0 [*General*]: Instruction Set Design; C.0 [*General*]: Hardware/Software Interfaces; I.5.0 [*General*]

***General Terms*** Algorithms, Design, Performance

***Keywords*** Cortical Learning Algorithms, Neuromorphic Architectures, GPGPU

[1] Aivo is the Finnish word for *brain*



*ASPLOS'11,* March 5–11, 2011, Newport Beach, California, USA.



## 1. Introduction

Biological and neuroscientific understanding of the structural and operational aspects of various components of the human brain has significantly increased over the past few decades. This has led to the development of a number of biologically-inspired software and hardware based computational models [5, 16, 43]. Most of these rely on the neocortex, the part of the brain that is evolutionarily the most recent and is unique to mammals, as their biological basis. These models implement some of the basic properties of the neocortex, including uniformity of structure, hierarchical arrangement, invariant representation of features, and feedback based prediction. Even more impressive is the fact that successful learning algorithms are now being deployed on specially designed hardwares which attempts to capture the physical properties of the brain [1, 11, 39].

Although these models show success at various learning tasks, they also suffer from a number of problems. First, the intrinsic complication of modeling the brain can make such models quite hard to understand. Second, many such models require explicit definition of network connectivity and hierarchical arrangements, often using low-level programming techniques. Third, given that many such models scale to large sizes, debugging can become quite cumbersome. Finally, as will be explained further in Section 5, many neuromorphic architectures strongly tie the proposed learning algorithm to the execution substrate. As such, these models can be quite difficult to port and are unable to take advantage of automated profile-driven and machine-specific optimizations to improve performance, reduced resource utilization, and improved robustness.

Historically, general-purpose Von Neumann computer systems suffered from a similar set of challenges until the introduction of standardized instruction set architectures (ISAs). An ISA creates a valuable layer of abstraction between an application's algorithmic specification (software) and it's execution substrate (hardware), enabling separate development in each domain, including automated tools for generating and optimizing machine code while allowing the same software to run on multiple generations of hardware. This paper advocates the adoption of a similar abstraction layer for neurally-inspired cortical models or neuromorphic computing systems and shows many of the same benefits follow.

Cortical models typically rely on some variant of Hebbian learning (rather than explicit programming) to train themselves to perform complex computational tasks. They encode the results of this training as a collection of synaptic weights, thresholds, connectivity, and other key parameters of neural components. Once the model has learned the values for these parameters, it can be deployed on an appropriate execution substrate. In the conventional approach to developing and deploying learning algorithms, the development and deployment substrates are the same, which leads to difficulties and/or compromises in the design and efficiency of both. Any changes to the execution substrate require reconfiguring, retraining, and possibly redesigning the entire network at the algorithmic level, while any attempts to optimize the network to better match the characteristics of the execution substrate must be done manually, in a cumbersome and error-prone manner.

Instead, following the example of well-defined ISAs in conventional computing systems—which separate the algorithm from the execution hardware— this paper proposes adoption of a Neuromorphic Instruction Set Architecture (NISA), which forms an analogous implementation independent abstraction layer for neuromorphic systems.

As a case study of a NISA-based approach for developing neuromorphic systems, this paper introduces Aivo, a neuromorphic framework which consists of a well defined NISA, an integrated development environment (IDE), and several compelling optimization tools, as seen in Figure 1. The Aivo NISA defines an implementation of a cortically-inspired computational model proposed by Hashmi et al. [14, 15]. The key enabling mechanism that Aivo provides over prior approaches for modeling cortical networks is the NISA, which is used for specifying the structure, connectivity, semantics, state, and profile metadata of the cortical network. The NISA is implemented as a *virtual* ISA, and is deployed as an easily readable XML schema. This common intermediate representation allows the various components of the Aivo system to communicate and inter-operate smoothly, while providing a user-friendly, human-readable, self-documenting, and easily-extensible persistent store for all cortical network structure and state. Using the Aivo IDE, this paper shows how such learning models can be easily built, trained, and debugged through a user-friendly interface. Since the NISA approach allows a trained network to exist as a persistent contract between the learning algorithm and the execution substrate, we show how we are able to deploy our model on a single-core CPU, multiple GPGPUs, and even as functional boolean logic. Furthermore, the profiling information about the cortical network stored in the NISA, as well as knowledge of the deployment substrate, open up a number of optimizations for resource utilization and performance improvements. It should be noted that, as multiple ISAs exist in traditional computing systems, multiple NISAs may be developed to accommodate specific requirements of significantly different neuromorphic systems.

The contributions of this paper are as follows:

- We propose the NISA as a virtual ISA which serves as a meaningful layer of abstraction between cortically-inspired learning algorithms and available execution substrates.
- We implement Hashmi et al.'s cortical column model as the Aivo NISA to demonstrate the ability of this abstraction layer.
- We present the Aivo IDE as a useful tool for building, debugging, and deploying large neocortically-inspired networks.
- We demonstrate how the NISA allows for many algorithmic and substrate specific optimizations and guarantees that such translations are safe.
- Finally, we show how the NISA allows for easy deployment on CPU, GPGPU, or simple logic substrates.

The rest of the paper is organized as follows: Section 2 examines work related to learning models and development environments. Section 3 provides some basic background information about the structure and functionality of the neocortex. Section 4 details the biologically inspired computational model. Section 5 provides a detailed discussion of the proposed Neuromorphic ISA abstraction. Section 6 describes the Aivo integrated development environment. Section 7 demonstrates how the NISA abstraction allows us to deploy our learning algorithm on a host CPU, GPGPU, or as boolean logic. Section 8 presents some of the high level optimizations the NISA enables. Section 9 describes our experimentation methodology the results. Section 10 concludes the paper and proposes our future work.

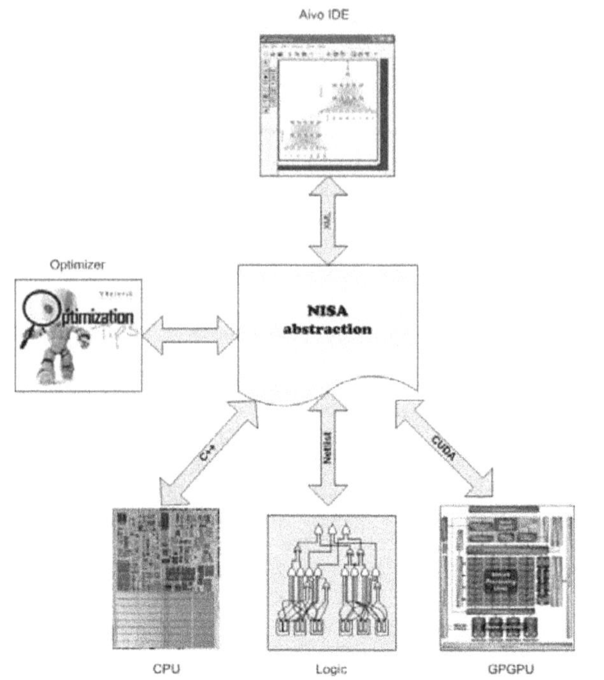


**Figure 1.** *Overview of how the NISA allows independent development and high level optimizations of the learning algorithm, capable of deployment across multiple available substrates.*

## 2. Related Work

Because the brain is so extraordinarily good at tasks such as image recognition, pattern classification, and motor skills, it has been the focus of artificial intelligence and neural network research for decades, and various learning models motivated by the properties of the brain have been proposed. Several models realize the properties of the brain at a very high level of abstraction. They do not model detailed neuron level behavior, but rather focus on how neurons as a group can realize functions like spatial and temporal pooling and developing invariant representations. Recently, Hierarchical temporal memories (HTM) [16] have gained recognition as a very high level computational model of the human brain. HTMs mainly construct a hierarchy of various nodes that learn to associate various spatial and temporal patterns with each other, thus learning complex patterns.

Convolutional neural networks trained with back-propagation are a well studied class of learning algorithm [25, 33] and have shown a degree of success in several applications. Spiking neural network models are another variation, and these models can be even further subdivided according to the biophysiological properties they emulate. One class of spiking neural model may simply incorporate the integrate-and-fire behavior of biological neurons, while another class may include the neural conductances and ion channels in their model [20].

Such learning algorithms have also been deployed on a variety of substrates. Both neural networks and deep belief networks have benefited from the parallel computational power of GPGPUs [21, 35]. FPGAs have even been used for deployment of learning algorithms, as their reconfigurability properties provide the flexibility to more closely resemble the structural properties of the brain [11, 23]. There have even been numerous hardware implementations of artificial neural networks, both past designs such as the Intel ETANN [17], or more recently the FACETS project [39]. Recent developments in memristor technology bring with them the hope of creating online, on-chip plasticity for future neuromorphic hardware designs [9, 34].

Furthermore, there have been several attempts to create user-friendly development environments for developing, connecting, and testing various neurally inspired learning models. Matlab's Neural Network Toolbox [2] is a highly developed software application that has been used for both research and business applications, and Neuroph [3] is another similar tool with an open source development community. Both feature a user-friendly GUI interface, allow user's to import new training data sets, and feature a host of built-in neural network types.

These are just a sample of the ongoing research relating to learning algorithms, their deployment substrates, and the set of tools available for developing, optimizing, and deploying neurally inspired models. However, to the best of our knowledge we believe this paper is the first to advocate a complete abstraction of the underlying learning model. The Aivo development framework uses the NISA abstraction to independently develop cortical learning algorithms, deploy the algorithm across multiple substrates, and utilize various optimizations, while guaranteeing these translations are safe by using the NISA abstraction. In Section 5, we will provide more detail in regard to the benefits of using the NISA.

## 3. The Neocortex

The human brain can be divided into two main parts: the old brain and the new brain. The old brain constitutes the parts that developed early in evolution, including pathways from sensory modalities to the new brain, spinal cord, and other parts that deal with instinctual behavior. The new brain, also referred to as the *neocortex*, is unique to mammals and is highly developed for humans; it accounts for about 77% of the human brain (in volume). The neocortex is responsible for perception, language, mathematics, planning, and all the other aspects necessary for an intelligent system. It contains virtually all our memories, knowledge, skills, and experiences.

A very intriguing property of the neocortex is its apparent *structural and functional uniformity* [31]. Because of this property, the regions of the neocortex that process auditory inputs, for instance, appear very similar to the regions that handle visual processing. This uniformity suggests that even though different regions specialize in different tasks, they employ the same underlying algorithm. In essence, the neocortex is a hierarchy of millions of seemingly-identical functional units known as *cortical columns*. The concept of cortical columns was introduced by the neuroscientist Mountcastle in his seminal paper in 1978 [30]. Since then, this concept has been widely accepted and studied. Later studies showed that cortical columns could further be classified into *minicolumns* and *hypercolumns* [8]. A hypercolumn contains about 50 to 100 minicolumns, and each of these minicolumns consists of around 200 to 300 neurons. The minicolumns within the same hypercolumn share the same input and output connections and are strongly connected with each other through *inhibitory lateral connections*. Studies [18] hypothesize that the minicolumns use these connections to aid in learning unique and independent features from set of inputs they are exposed to. Hypercolumns are arranged in the form of a hierarchy throughout the neocortex. Information flows up this hierarchy via *excitatory feedforward paths* and flows down the hierarchy through *feedback paths*.

The arrangement and functionality of the hypercolumns and minicolumns has been studied in detail in the visual cortex [7, 18, 31]. These studies suggest that minicolumns at the lower levels of the hierarchy learn to identify very basic features (like edges of different orientation) and communicate their responses to minicolumns at the upper levels. Cortical regions operate by progressively abstracting and manipulating increasingly complex notions throughout the neural hierarchy. For instance, the visual cortex hierarchy will first identify segments, then elementary shapes such as angles and intersections, and increasingly complex combinations, such as objects found in our environment [13]. This automatic abstraction capability for various inputs (visual, auditory, olfactory, etc.) partly explains why the neocortex still outperforms traditional computers for a number of tasks, such as face recognition, language learning, and motor control. Emulating such capability is thus a major step in building computing systems that can compete with the processing characteristics of the brain.

## 4. A Biologically Plausible Learning Model

While the structures and functions of the brain have been investigated for a long time, quantitative models consistent with physiological data and capable of accounting for complex tasks have been proposed only recently [40, 41]. In this section, we describe the learning model which uses hyercolumns as the basic computational unit. Later, we describe how the NISA abstraction captures the important semantics and components of this algorithm.

This cortical network model draws inspiration directly from the organization and structures of the primate visual cortex. First, our model implements the preprocessing transformations that affect the visual input as it propagates from the retina to the primary visual cortex through the optical pathways. Second, we create a competitive learning based hierarchical network that uses the preprocessed visual data as input. This results in a biologically plausible system that learns to recognize various visual stimuli and shows partial rotation and scale invariance, as observed in mammals. Other competitive learning models [6, 10, 28] have been proposed in the past, but these models either ignore the important properties of the hypercolumns (discussed in Section 3) or have very high computational requirements.

Figure 2 shows the architecture of the basic functional unit in our competitive learning model, the hypercolumn (left side), in comparison to a biological hypercolumn (right side). We see in biology as well as our model, each hypercolumn contains multiple minicolumns that share the same receptive field. These minicolumns are strongly connected to neighboring minicolumns via inhibitory connections (solid lines in Figure 2).

### 4.1 Input and Receptive Field

In mammals, visual scenes are projected onto the retina. The activations of the retinal cells in response to the visual scene are transfered via the optical nerve to the Lateral Geniculate Nucleus (LGN) cells [24]. The LGN cells are contrast sensitive i.e. they react strongly to an illuminated point surrounded by darkness (known as on-off cells) or conversely to a dark point surrounded by light (off-on) cells. These cells are spatially distributed in such a way that on-off and off-on cells are intertwined [37] and receive inputs from neighboring retinal cells referred to as the *receptive field* of the LGN cells. Cells respond only to input changes that occur within their receptive field. Finally, the activations of the LGN cells become the input to the primary visual cortex.

In our model, all the inputs are preprocessed using the LGN transform [37] as well. For preprocessing, we consider a regular spatial distribution of LGN cells (one on-off and one off-on per pixel), but have also experimented with more random distributions without noticeable differences.

### 4.2 Random Activations and Initial Learning

In our cortical model, all the minicolumns within a hypercolumn are initialized with very weak random weights, thus showing no initial preference for any particular pattern. A key feature of our learning model is random neocortical firing behavior [12, 38]. The minicolumns exhibit high activations over random intervals, mimicking the stochastic nature of biological neurons in the presence of

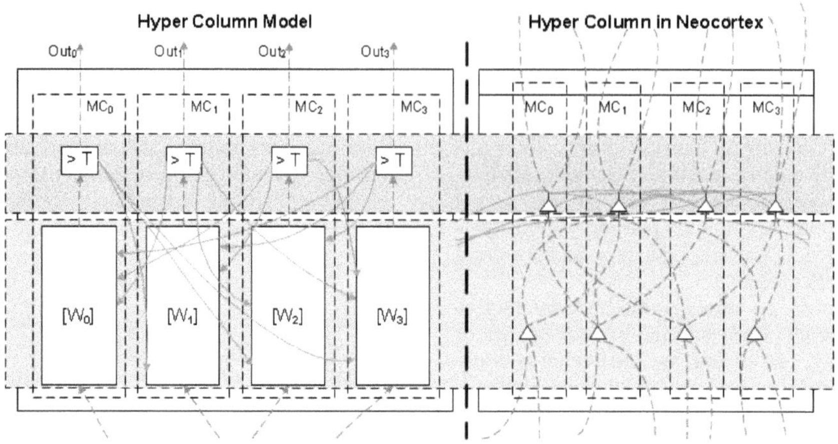


**Figure 2.** *Left: The hypercolumn model as defined by the cortical learning algorithm. Right: The structure of a typical biological hyppercolumn. MC=Minicolumn, T=Threshold of Activation Function. Dashed lines are feedforward paths, while solid lines are lateral inhibitory paths.*

noise. When the random activation of a specific minicolumn coincides frequently with various occurrences of the same pattern, the minicolumn adjusts its synaptic weights to correlate with the input pattern (described in detail in Section 4.4). Thus over time, that minicolumn develops a preference for that specific pattern. While this random activation of minicolumns may not intuitively seem productive, this behavior is harnessed to make the model fault-tolerant, improves the model's training time, and mimics the behavior of its biological inspirations.

### 4.3 Execution of Minicolumns

During each training epoch, each of the minicolumns evaluates the dot-product $DP = \sum_{i=1}^{N} X_i.W_i$ between its weights $\vec{W}$ and the input $\vec{X}$. The result of the dot-product becomes the input to the activation function given by,

$$\frac{1.0}{1.0 + e^{(-\frac{DP - cutoff}{\beta})}} + \alpha \times \sum |W_i| \quad (1)$$

Here, $cutoff = \phi \times \sum |W_i|$. $\phi$ determines the error tolerance of the minicolumn. $\beta$ defines the sharpness of the activation function while $\alpha$ controls the effect of weight strength of a minicolumn on its output. The minicolumn is said to be active or to fire if the value of its activation function is greater than a determined threshold. At the same time, each minicolumn inhibits neighboring minicolumns from firing for the pattern it has learned to recognize via lateral inhibitory connections. Minicolumns also form a competitive learning network, and when multiple minicolumns fire at the same time, the one with the strongest response inhibits the ones with weaker responses. The inhibited minicolumns then weaken their weights corresponding to active $X_i$. As a result of this process, the hypercolumn network is able to recognize unique patterns without supervision.

### 4.4 Weight Update Rules

When a minicolumn fires, it strengthens its weights to increase correlation with the current pattern. Weights of a minicolumn corresponding to active inputs are strengthened with the following update rule"

$$W_i = \left( W_i + \left( C_1 + \gamma \times \frac{1.0}{1.0 + e^{(-\frac{W_i - C_2}{\beta})}} \right) \right) \quad (2)$$

Here, $C_1$ defines the minimum amount of strength added to the current $W_i$, and $C_2$ defines how the present $W_i$ will affect the weight update. The update added to $W_i$ is dependent upon the present value of $W_i$ as well. This means that if $W_i$ is strong it will get a higher update value, as observed in biological data [38]. When a minicolumn is inhibited, it modifies the weights corresponding to active inputs using the following update rule.

$$W_i = (W_i - \delta) \quad (3)$$

Here, $\delta$ defines the weight update rate in the presence of inhibition. It should be noted that other complex update rules for inhibition could also be used here.

### 4.5 Hierarchy of Hypercolumns

Much of the brain's ability comes from its hierarchical organization, which uses different processing levels to perform complicated tasks. Similarly, the modeled hypercolumns can be arranged in a multilevel hierarchy, which we refer to as a cortical network (see Figure 3). Lower hierarchical levels identify simple features and communicate their output to the higher levels which learn progressively more complex features [13]. In this manner the activations flow up the cortical network and the minicolumns in the top-level hypercolumns learn to identify the full complex input pattern.

For pattern recognition tasks, we modeled our hierarchy according to the known properties of the mammalian visual cortex. Once the input images are preprocessed using the LGN/Log-polar transform, they are exposed to a layer of hypercolumns with properties similar to Gabor filter banks [22], which models the organization of the first level of the visual cortex hierarchy. Each of the minicolumns within the Gabor hypercolumns learns to identify edges of different orientations and shows a rotational invariance of 12 degrees, which is in accordance with the neuroscientific experiments on monkeys [42]. The outputs of the Gabor hypercolumns propagate to the cortical network hierarchy, which learns progressively more complex features at each higher level.

### 4.6 Supervised Feedback and Pooling

The feedforward learning process enables our hierarchical cortical network to learn unique features from the input patterns in a completely unsupervised environment. Minicolumns consistently fire for small variations in their learned patterns, depending on their error tolerance parameter. However, if a single pattern can be represented by two very different variations, it is likely that a hypercolumn (and ultimately an entire cortical network) will recognize these as two different patterns. To resolve this issue and generate invariant representation for variations of the same pattern, we make use of a supervised feedback processing algorithm.

To illustrate how this feedback processing is useful, we consider a single handwritten digit from two individuals with very different handwriting styles. From the unsupervised feedforward processing, the cortical network will distinguish the differences between these different input patterns. As a result, the top level hypercolumn will have two trained minicolumns, each of which represents the same digit but are composed of different lower level features. However, for training sets such as handwritten digits, we want to be able to classify objects into categories rather than have the top level hypercolumn dedicate a minicolumn to every variation of a pattern. Here, the supervisory feedback signal of the model is used to notify the top level hypercolumn that it should pool together two variations of a single pattern. The minicolumn receiving excitatory feedback adjusts its weights so that it fires for both variation and inhibits any minicolumn firing for the new variation. The inhibited minicolumn changes its weights so that it does not fire for that input pattern, freeing itself to recognize a truly novel pattern. Thus over multiple exposures, the minicolumn firing for the original pattern will also consistently fire for the new variation.

This feedback pooling process will continue down through the cortical network's hierarchy. Once the top level minicolumn starts to give a stable activation for both variations, it will send a feedback signal down so that lower level minicolumns can also create invariant representations. The amount of feedback sent to each of the lower level minicolumns is proportional to its firing history, with more active columns receiving stronger feedback. The intuition of this proportional feedback is that objects in the visual field likely exhibit some amount of object permanence, so temporally related patterns are more likely variations of a single pattern. Thus, over time the most active minicolumns pool the inputs received from lower level minicolumns which results in invariant representations of an object as well as significant resource optimization. We note that this feedback process differs from back-propagation in neural networks since, rather than altering weights to reduce the error of the classification function, we are simply teaching the cortical network which features can be considered similar. Furthermore, the feedback process in our algorithm relies on spatial locality of the features and synaptic weights being pooled, where synaptic connections in most neural networks do not contain spatial information.

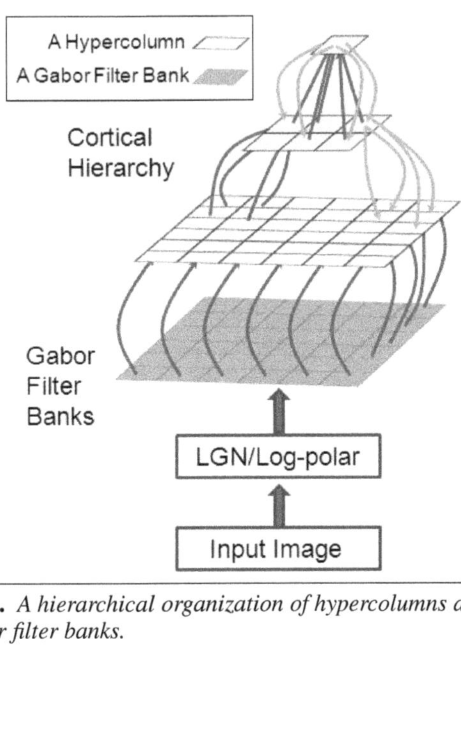


**Figure 3.** *A hierarchical organization of hypercolumns along with the gabor filter banks.*

The process of generating invariant representations within a minicolumn using feedback is explained in the pseudo-code provided in Algorithm 1. It invokes code to update synaptic weights as described in Equation 2 and 3.

**Algorithm 1** Pseudo code for generating invariant representations within a minicolumn using supervised feedback.

```
if feedback > 0 then
  if hasNotFired then
    if hasMaxFiringHistory then
      UpdateSynapticWtsExcitatory(feedback)
    end if
  else
    if hasMaxFiringHistory then
      UpdateSynapticWtsExcitatory(feedback)
      if isStable then
        for i = 1 to N do
          if IsActive(child[i]) then
            SendFBToChild(i, feedback)
          end if
        end for
      end if
    else
      UpdateSynapticWtsInhibitory(feedback)
    end if
  end if
end if
```

## 5. Neuromorphic ISA

Neuromorphic architectures attempt to emulate the function, organization, and processing power of the the brain by combining a learning algorithm together with some type of execution substrate. The learning algorithms themselves may vary quite drastically in terms of the level of detail at which they model the brain, whether they are integrate-and-fire neurons that simply mimic spiking behavior, or highly complex algorithms such as the Hodgkin-Huxley model which includes details about the chemistry and conductances of neurons. The execution substrates on which neuromorphic architectures are deployed also vary widely from model to model. While traditional CPUs, GPGPUs, and even supercomputers have been utilized as the execution substrate for many of these models, research has also explored creating silicon chips that more closely resemble neurons and synapses in the brain [1, 19, 39]. While such projects are both interesting and ambitious, a number of challenges arise from the way these current neuromorphic architectures are designed.

First of all, present neuromorphic architectures strongly tie the learning algorithm to the execution substrate. The Blue Brain Project, which emulates the brain with the highly detailed and complicated Hodgkin-Huxley model, simulates on a Blue Gene supercomputer using the MPI programming interface. While not all researchers may wish to use such a detailed learning algorithm, the nature of tying the implementation of their algorithm so closely with deployment on a supercomputer makes it highly difficult for researchers without such resources to implement or expand on their work. Integrate-and-fire neural networks can be finely tuned for execution on modern day GPGPUs [21], though to achieve fast processing performance, considerable effort may be required to alter or tune the learning algorithms themselves to properly take advantage of the graphics processor architecture. Finally, special-purpose neuromorphic hardware may attempt to model the structure and plasticity of the brain, but limitations in such hardware designs may limit the number of properties that can be presently implemented. These are just some examples of how hardware limitations in turn influence the development of the learning algorithms, which ultimately can defeat the purpose of developing computers that resemble the unique properties of the brain.

Furthermore, strictly tying a learning algorithm to an execution substrate limits the portability of the algorithm across platforms. For example, a learning algorithm like a neural network may be highly tuned to take advantage of GPGPU optimizations, though the same code will not be easily, or at least efficiently, executed on a commodity CPU. Tuning algorithms to optimally execute on novel neuromorphic hardwares may only exacerbate such problems.

Considering the history of the Von Neumann computer architecture, we are able to easily relate to such challenges. Originally, computer architectures and the programs that were executed on them were developed in concert, sacrificing portability and making independent development of hardware and software impossible. Such problems persisted until the introduction of the instruction set architecture (ISA) with the IBM System 360 [4]. The ISA was introduced as a persistent contract between the computer hardware and the software that would execute on it. Essentially, the ISA separated the algorithm from the deployment substrate, allowing each to be developed independently, as well as guaranteeing portability between hardware generations. The introduction of the ISA abstraction furthermore allowed the development of automated tools to allow the production and optimization of machine code, letting software take advantage of the specific benefits of different hardware generations or designs.

Borrowing from the lesson of the ISA, we advocate a Neuromorphic ISA (NISA) as a persistent contract between the learning algorithm and execution substrate. In our current implementation, the NISA serves as a virtual ISA which forms a level of abstraction between these two layers, allowing the independent development of both.

Traditional ISAs specify the *state*, *structure*, and *semantics* of the abstract machine they represent, including register and memory maps, supported data types, and details of operations for data handling, memory access, logic and arithmetic computation, control flow, and so on. Similarly, a neuromorphic ISA should precisely specify state, structure, and semantics for the abstract machine it represents. In most neuromorphic systems, *state* is present in at least two forms: the current level of activation of a component (e.g. is a neuron firing, or how much time has elapsed since it last fired) and the magnitude of the connections that influence its firing (e.g. a neuron's synaptic weights). This state is distributed across the elements (each neuron has local state), rather than being stored in a centralized memory or register file. As a consequence, the aggregate amount of state grows as the system grows, and there is no direct, memory-like, way of accessing this state. The *structure* of a neural system is determined by connections between components (dendritic and axonal projections that intersect), as well as any higher-level structural abstractions included in a particular model (for example, the cortical minicolumns and hypercolumns described in Section 4). Some models may also require representation of physical structure, rather than just logical connectivity, to represent entities such as cortical feature maps. Finally, the *semantics* of a neural system are determined by the rules that govern the activation and plasticity of the components of the system. Activation is typically determined by a thresholding function following a spatial and/or temporal integration of activity at synaptic inputs, while plasticity most often follows Hebbian learning rules to modify synaptic weights. A neuromorphic ISA must then provide primitives that are capable of expressing these characteristics at a level of abstraction that suits the particular neuromorphic system being developed. As is true for traditional ISAs, if neuromorphic system specifications significantly differ from each other, new NISAs may be developed to express them. The benefit of using the NISA abstraction are quite intuitive and clear. By separating the algorithm from the deployment substrate, each can be developed independently without one placing restrictions or limitations on the other. We can, in effect, write *neuromorphic programs* using an existing NISA, and can expect those programs to operate correctly on any current or future execution substrate that is compatible with our NISA.

```
<Hierarchy inputColumns="78" inputRows="24">
    <Grouping ID="6" Nodes="10">
        <Grouping ID="4" Nodes="10">
            <Grouping ID="0" Nodes="10"/>
                <Node>
                        <Status firing="1"/>
                        <Weights>0.093 0.078 ... </Weights>
                        <Threshold limit=".57"/>
                </Node>
                        .
                        .
                        .
            <Grouping ID="1" Nodes="10"/>
        </Grouping>
        <Grouping ID="5" Nodes="10">
                        .
                        .
                        .
        </Grouping>
        <Node>
                <Status firing="0"/>
                <Weights>0.091 0.079 ... </Weights>
                <Threshold limit=".84"/>
        </Node>
    </Grouping>
</Hierarchy>
```

**Figure 4.** *The XML-based Aivo NISA describes a cortical network.*

Given the characteristics of our cortical network model, we have developed a NISA that meets these requirements. Using this NSIA, we can develop a neuromorphic program today and deploy it on a GPGPU cluster, but as future neuromorphic hardwares becomes available, we can directly retarget the neuromorphic program to them by simply adding the new primitives to our NISA abstraction. A simplified example of a cortical network defined by the Aivo NISA, in XML, can be seen in Figure 4.

## 6. Aivo IDE

Throughout the development of the cortical learning model, it was necessary to have a method to create and train large networks, debug their behavior, and further develop the underlying learning algorithm. With these goals in mind, we developed the Aivo integrated development environment (IDE). The Aivo IDE streamlines the process of creating cortical networks by allowing networks to be built in two different ways. First, a network can be built by dragging and dropping hypercolumns onto the main screen of the GUI (see Figure 5). From the GUI, the user can then simply connect the network they desire for the task of interest. Second, a cortical network can also be imported from a previously created XML file, which also adheres to the syntax of the Aivo NISA. From the Aivo IDE, the user can select to deploy the network on either the CPU or the available CUDA enabled GPGPUs.

At any point in creation, debugging, or training, the Aivo IDE allows a cortical network design to be checkpointed to an XML file using the NISA. XML was chosen for this task due to its hierarchical format and the ability to be easily read or hand-coded by the designer. Furthermore, the NISA abstraction allows us to connect components such as the Aivo IDE and Cortical Network Optimizer without creating unnecessary dependencies between such modules.

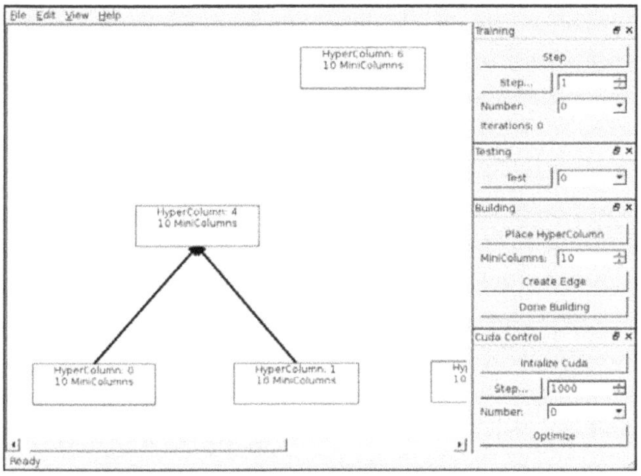


**Figure 5.** *Building a cortical network using the Aivo IDE.*

This file is useful for check-pointing network state and metadata that can be examined for specific information, reloaded for further training, or used for optimization purposes.

The Aivo IDE also features several options we have found useful for training, executing, and debugging a cortical network. Deployment of a cortical network on the host CPU allows a more precise control over the training process. From the Aivo IDE, the user can single-step through each training iteration or batch-train several chosen inputs for longer periods of time. Training on the CPU also allows the user to visually debug a cortical network by simply clicking on hypercolumns and minicolumns to display information should as synaptic weights and firing histories. While having the ability to interactively train and debug a network has its advantages, the Aivo IDE also allows for deployment and training on a CUDA enabled GPGPU substrate. Deployment on the GPGPU lends to some significant speedups in training times, though it loses the ease of user interaction. Section 7 describes the deployment substrates we have investigated in more detail.

## 7. Substrates and Code Generation

In conventional computer systems, a major advantage of having a well-defined ISA is that it allows the same software programs to run correctly on multiple generations of hardware, even with radically different implementations. In this section, we show how the NISA enables the same benefit, making the investigated cortical learning algorithm easily deployable on a commodity CPU, a GPGPU, and even as boolean logic.

### 7.1 Deployment on Commodity CPUs

The initial version of Aivo software was developed for a commodity CPU, and that remains the default deployment substrate. The Aivo IDE also runs on the CPU substrate to develop, initialize, and debug new cortical networks, as well as make changes to the specifics of the learning algorithm. Furthermore, as described in Section 8, execution on the CPU substrate allows us to create high-level optimizations that enhance the model, whether in terms of execution time or robustness. Presently, the learning algorithm is deployed as a single thread on the CPU. However in future work, we plan to utilize multicore processors to take advantage of the performance benefits of parallel execution.

### 7.2 Deployment on GPGPUs

In order to build a neocortical model that can perform comparably to the neocortex, the scale of these models must be significantly large. In fact, many researchers have proposed using supercomputers to affectively scale neocortical models to interesting problems [27, 36]. However, modern GPUs have gained considerable popularity as commodity available hardware accelerators for highly parallel applications. GPGPUs have even been used to speed up biologically-inspired computing models like cortical architectures and neural networks [21, 32]. In particular, Nvidia's CUDA framework has become a popular and affordable method for application acceleration and we have employed it to accelerate cortical networks.

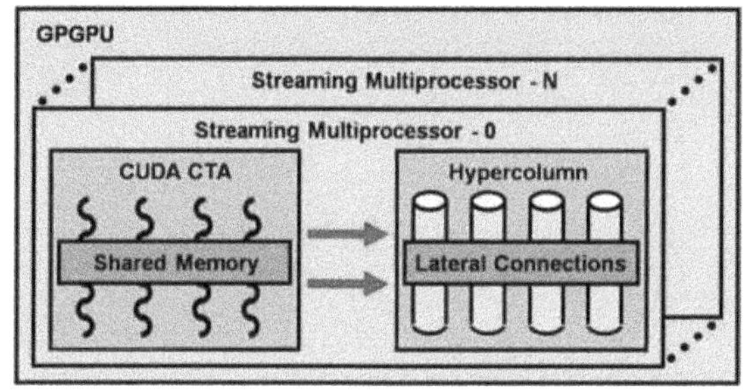


**Figure 6.** *Mapping a hypercolumn to a CUDA CTA.*

To deploy a network on a GPGPU, the Aivo IDE generates CUDA code to be executed on available Nvidia GPGPUs. Nvidia's CUDA framework is built around several hierarchically organized components which can be configured by the programmer. The CUDA-thread is the basic unit of execution, organized into thread-blocks, or *Cooperative Thread-Arrays* (CTAs). Within a CTA, the threads are able to both quickly synchronize using hardware primitives as well as communicate via a fast-access shared memory space. CTAs are then grouped into kernel-launches, or grids, for concurrent execution on the GPGPU.

From the Aivo IDE, the user can choose to deploy a created cortical network on the GPGPU. To these ends, we have created a template CUDA version of the learning model. The Aivo NISA is used to generate the complete CUDA code/binary using this template.

This CUDA-enabled version of our learning model takes advantage of the inherent parallelism of the cortical network. In Section 4, we described the cortical network as having different hierarchically organized components, composed of minicolumns, hyper columns, and cortical networks. The GPU-accelerated code translates the components of the cortical network to the CUDA framework, modeling each minicolumn as a CUDA-thread and each hypercolumn as a CTA, as seen in Figure 6. With such an organization on CUDA, the minicolumns within a hypercolumn can take advantage of a CTA's synchronization and fast memory sharing abilities. As an example of machine-specific optimization, the Aivo code generator organizes the synaptic weights of each minicolumn into a strided pattern that maximizes memory coalescing on the GPGPU, leading to significant performance improvement.

From the Aivo IDE, the user can easily train a cortical hierarchy on any available CUDA-enabled GPUs. Because the cost of transferring the cortical network's weights and inputs can become quite expensive in terms of performance, utilizing GPU acceleration is most beneficial for batch training a large amount of different inputs for many training iterations. After training on the GPU, the cortical network's state information will be copied back to the GUI and saved in an XML file using the proper NISA syntax.

### 7.3 Logic Generation

The NISA abstraction provided by Aivo also supports deployment of a cortical network in the form of logic functions that can later be converted to netlists. For now, the logic level representation of

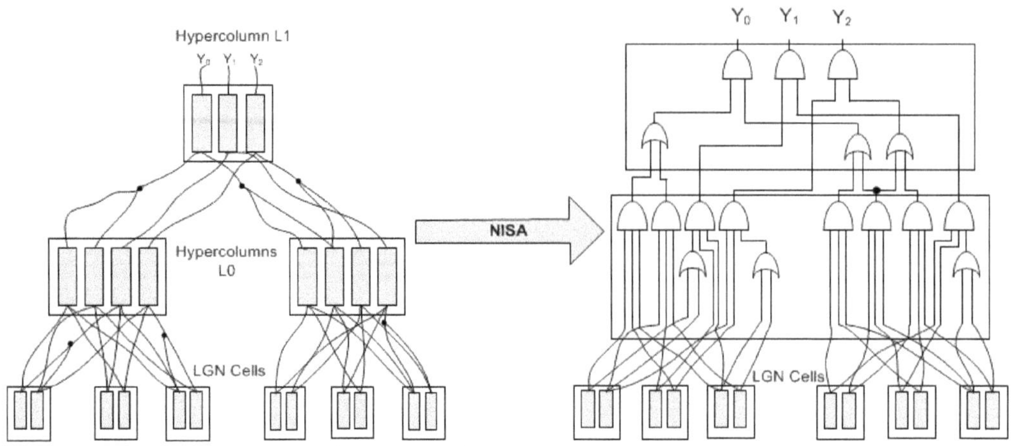


**Figure 7.** *A simple fully trained cortical network and corresponding logic network.*

a cortical network is generated as functional logic blocks in C++. AND- and OR-operations are hierarchically connected to represent the structure of the corresponding cortical network. Once a network is fully trained (i.e. 100% recognition rate on the training dataset), it can be converted to a logic representation for efficient execution. To achieve this, the Aivo IDE exports the state of the hypercolumns and minicolumns of the fully trained network using the Aivo NISA syntax. The Aivo NISA code is then processed to generate the logic representation of the cortical network.

Once a minicolumn has concretely learned a particular feature, its weights can be considered as binary synapses, i.e. it has a strong synaptic connection or no synaptic connection to a particular input. In terms of boolean logic, the output 'Y' of such a minicolumn can be represented as:

$$Y_i = \forall_{k \in S} AND(k)$$

Here, 'S' is the set of inputs to the minicolumn corresponding to high weights.

If a minicolumn has pooled different variations of an input as described in Section 4, then its output can be represented as:

$$Y_i = \forall_j AND(O_j)$$
$$O_j = \forall_{k \in M} OR(k)$$

Here, 'M' is the set of inputs corresponding to high weights that pool different variations of the same pattern.

Figure 7 illustrates the logic generation process using a simple trained cortical network as an example. In this example, the two levels of hypercolumns are replaced with logic equations that perform the equivalent detection or classification function. However, since the LGN cells in this circuit perform a type of analog-to-digital conversion of the input image, they are not simplified to boolean logic.

Even though converting the cortical network to boolean representation results in significant reduction in execution time for a learned task, it comes with a trade-off: this boolean network cannot learn new tasks or features. Rather, it can only detect the features it has already learned, and will not respond to new features appearing in the input. To address this shortcoming, The Aivo runtime monitor is used to detect when a boolean logic equivalent network is not sufficient for the learning task at hand. This runtime monitor relies on a simple property of the competitive learning-based cortical column model: a fully-trained cortical network should evoke a single winning response for every input (i.e. one minicolumn in each hypercolumn should fire). Aivo monitors the firing rate of each boolean circuit hypercolumn, and once it falls below a given threshold, Aivo's runtime will revert the boolean circuit back to a computational model that is able to learn the new features in the input. After the cortical network learns the new features, Aivo can regenerate a new boolean circuit and regain the efficiencies of this approach. Again, all conversions between hypercolumn models and boolean logic circuits occur as an offline process. This process is very similar to profile-driven re-optimization of machine code in managed runtime systems with just-in-time compilers (e.g. Java, C#).

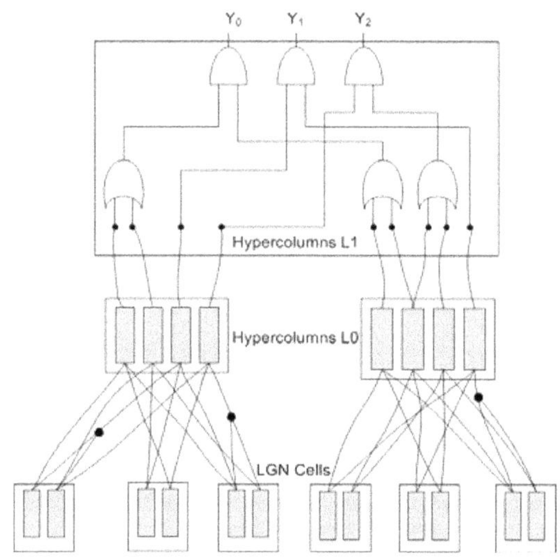


**Figure 8.** *An example of a hybrid network created using the NISA abstraction.*

### 7.4 Code/Logic Hybrid Generation

The NISA abstraction also supports generation of cortical networks using a code/logic hybrid approach. As describe in Section 7.3, once a network is fully converted to logic, it is unable to learn new features. Therefore, the cortical network should achieve 100% recognition rate on the training dataset before it may be converted into an equivalent functional logic representation. This means that during the training period, the cortical network cannot benefit from the logic generation capability of the NISA abstraction, as recognition has not stabilized. To avoid this dilemma, we extend the NISA abstraction to allow cortical networks to be partially converted as they stabilize, which we refer to as Code/Logic hybrid networks. This addition lets the NISA abstraction to partially convert a cortical network into logic (i.e. some of the hypercolumns are converted into their functional logic representation while others are not). To achieve this, the NISA abstraction can store the state activity of

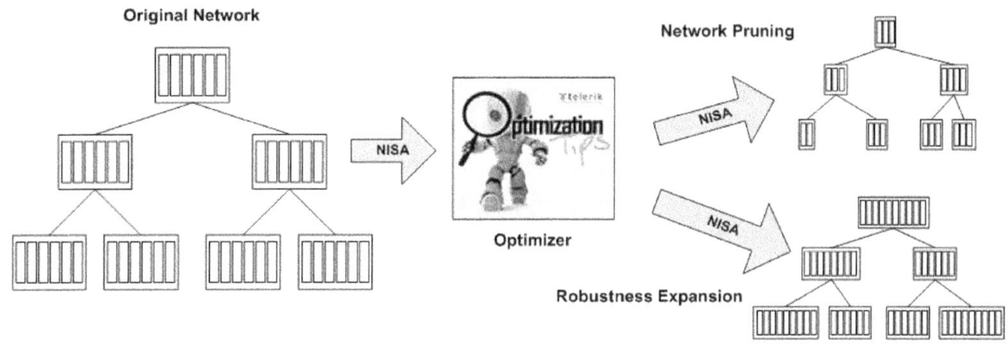


**Figure 9.** *The Cortical Network Optimizer optimizes a trained cortical network for resources utilization or for robustness.*

the hypercolumns in the network. If after a significant number of training epochs no new minicolumns within a hypercolumn learn to recognize any new features, the hypercolumn may be considered stabilized and can be safely converted to a functional logic representation.

The NISA abstraction also allows the programmer to explicitly control the conversion of a hypercolumns to a logic function (i.e. the programmer can mark certain hypercolumns so that they are not converted to logic). For example, the program may configure an explicit hybrid network where the upper levels of the hierarchy are converted to logic functions while the hypercolumns in the lower levels are not. Typically, this type of hybrid conversion is useful for robust recognition of input patterns in the presence of noise. Since the lower levels execute the hypercolumn learning algorithm, they exhibit more resilience to noise or slight variations present in the inputs while the logic converted upper level hypercolumns identify complex objects with computational efficiency. Figure 8 demonstrates this hybrid approach.

## 8. High Level Optimizations

Because the NISA provides a well described abstraction of the cortical learning algorithm we are investigating, we are able to create high level optimizations to improve performance, enhance the robustness of the network being trained, and reduce resource utilization. In this section we will describe some of the optimizations developed thus far.

### 8.1 Cortical Network Optimization

The Aivo Cortical Network Optimizer (CNO) is a high level optimization tool developed to improve the structure of the cortical network, either by expanding the structure to improve learning robustness, or reducing the structure to reduce required processing time. When a user initially creates a cortical network using the Aivo IDE, the correct number of resources (hypercolumns and minicolumns) required to achieve a particular task (e.g. robust recognition of the entire feature set) is probably unknown. Thus, it is likely that resources have been either over allocated or under allocated for the network to learn a particular task. When the resources are over allocated, the cortical network requires more computation than is necessary for each learning iteration. On the other hand, an under-allocated cortical network may not contain enough minicolumns to learn the full number of features in the dataset.

In the case when the cortical network resources are over allocated, all of the unique features of the dataset will be fully recognized after a sufficient amount of learning epochs. However, there will be a number of minicolumns that will not perform useful work, even though they must still evaluate at each learning iteration. While the evaluation of these minicolumns will not affect the activations propagated to the next level of the network, they still contribute to the total execution time. In such cases, the Aivo CNO can be invoked to perform network pruning and remove unnecessary minicolumns. First, the state and structure of the trained cortical network is exported using the Aivo NISA in the form of XML files. Then, the Aivo CNO parses these files and deletes the unnecessary minicolumns. A minicolumn is declared unnecessary if all its synaptic weights are close to zero, which suggests that it has not learned any interesting features from the training dataset; thus it is not required to robustly perform the learned task. Along with pruning unnecessary minicolumns, the CNO will regenerate the netlist that defines the connections between the minicolumns at various levels in the hierarchy to account for the deleted minicolumns and their connections.

Conversely, an under-allocated cortical network may not possess enough minicolumns to robustly recognize all of the features of the dataset. After a significant amount of learning epochs, the Aivo CNO may be invoked to perform a robustness expansion of the cortical network. The trained network's state is again exported in the Aivo NISA format, which the CNO parses, and then allocates more resources for under-allocated hypercolumns, as determined by a defined threshold (i.e. if 90% of minicolumns within a hypercolumns are doing useful computations, CNO allocates more minicolumns to this hypercolumn). Minicolumns are useful if they contain strong weights corresponding to the input activations. This feature is quite useful because the CNO will add minicolumns only to the necessary hypercolumns. Thus, using multiple invocations, Aivo generates cortical network that is sufficient in terms of resource allocation and execution time for the given input dataset. Figure 9 provides a pictorial representation of the CNO's operations.

We use an offline optimization approach for the CNO rather than performing such major structural changes to cortical network during runtime. Such offline structural changes can be considered biologically plausible as well, since there is evidence that memory-consolidations and translations that occur in the brain during sleep have a significant impact on how and where memories are stored [29]. In Aivo, changing the cortical network structure during runtime would result in both code complications and a drastic increase in the execution time for each learning epoch. Furthermore, the structure does not significantly change on an iteration by iteration basis, so it makes sense to optimize after a large number of training epochs.

### 8.2 Optimized Networks on GPGPUs

The Aivo CNO is also able to optimize cortical networks deployed for execution on a GPGPU. However, one limitation of CUDA-enabled GPGPUs is the *warp size*. The scalar multiprocessors in current generation Nvidia GPGPUs issue instructions in SIMD style for groups of 32 threads, known as a warp. The warp size essentially sets a minimum limit to the number of threads (and for the cortical network algorithm, the number of minicolumns) that will execute in parallel in a hypercolumn. With such a limitation, a hypercolumn with only 3 minicolumns will not necessarily execute any faster than a hypercolumn with 32 minicolumns, though it may save some memory space. For this reason, when optimizing the cortical network for the GPGPU, resource allocation or resource recovery is only performed with a granularity of 32 minicolumns.

### 8.3 Utilizing Multi-GPU Systems

For systems with multiple CUDA-enabled devices, Aivo allows cortical networks to be distributed and trained across multiple GPGPUs in parallel. While these sub-hierarchies must synchronize and communicate data at points of convergence, this overhead can be minimized by properly partitioning the hierarchy. Since a system may have a heterogeneous collection of CUDA-enabled devices, we have employed a heuristic to split a cortical hierarchy based on each device's ability, specifically the number of Streaming-Multiprocessors. If multiple GPUs are selected to train a network, the Aivo IDE performs a device query (using a CUDA API call) to determine the number of SMs for each device. Each sub-network is then sized in proportion to each device's SM count, as in Figure 10. When the upper levels of the cortical hierarchy are executed, the GPGPUs must synchronize and copy data to a single GPGPU, though with large-scale networks this is typically negligible when compared to the overall execution time. In practice, this heuristic has shown to be quite effective for the GPGPUs we have available. We leave it to future work to investigate other heuristics for distributing cortical networks across multiple GPGPUs.

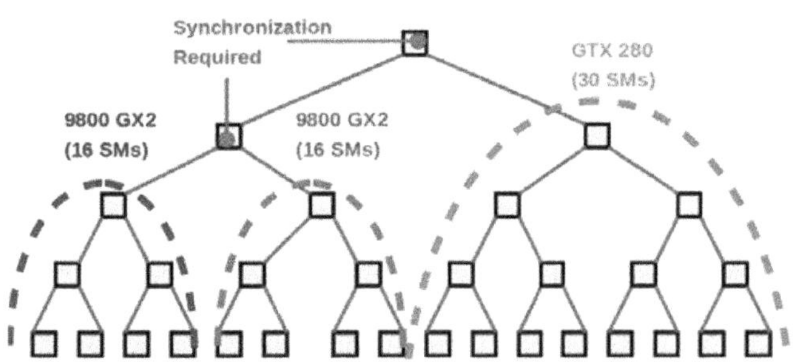


**Figure 10.** *A cortical network is proportionally split across two GPUs.*

## 9. Experimental Case Study

In this section, we perform several case studies to validate the various components of Aivo. We examine using the NISA abstraction for deployment on the CPU, GPGPUs, and logic substrates, as well as Aivo's various optimizations. We tested our model with a sample of handwritten digits (0-9) obtained from the MNIST Database (http://yann.lecun.com/exdb/mnist) [26].

### 9.1 Hardware

The performance results for the experiments are gathered from a AMD Phenom Quad-Core at 2.39 GHz and 8 GB of DRAM. Three CUDA-enabled GPGPUs are also used in these experiments. The first is an NVIDIA GeForce GTX 280, with 30 SMs operating at 1.46 GHz and 1 GB of global memory available. We also use an NVIDIA GeForce 9800 GX2, which contains two GPGPUs, each with 16 SMs operating at 1.5 GHz and 512 MB of memory each.

### 9.2 Recognition Performance

While it is beyond the scope of this paper to rigorously compare the cortical network to other learning algorithms, we include some performance recognition results to demonstrate how our biologically-inspired cortical network compares with more traditional but less

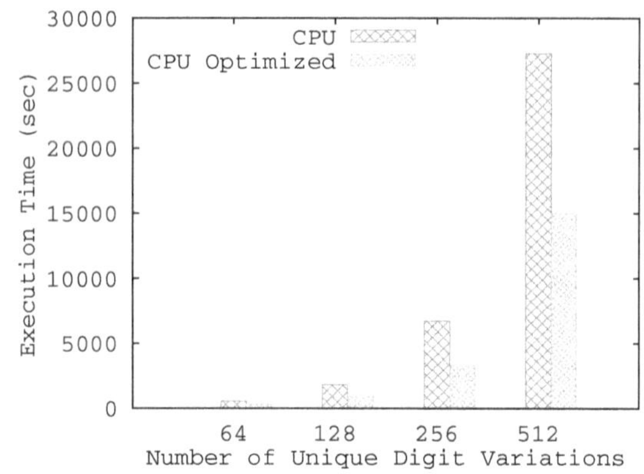


**Figure 11.** *Performance of original and CNO optimized networks on CPU.*

biologically-plausible implementations. Furthermore, since our cortical model is constantly changing due to the addition of new features, it is unfair to compare it with current state-of-the-art neural network models. However, we still compare the cortical network with an existing state-of-the-art convolutional neural network (CNN) based digit recognition system implemented by O'Neil [33] and proposed by LeCun et. al. [25]. O'Neil's implementation is able to achieve a recognition rate of 99.26% on a 10,000 handwritten digit test set, though to achieve such performance the network is trained using multiple distortions of a 60,000 character training set. However, it seems improbable that the human brain requires this many training examples to recognize digits 0 to 9. Requiring such a large number of training inputs seems like over-fitting the problem of digit recognition.

To compare our cortical network with O'Neil's implementation, we trained both the networks with just 1000 training digits (100 variations per digit chosen randomly) and tested it with the full 10,000 digit test set. With 100 variations of each digit, our model achieves a recognition rate of 87.5% which is slightly better than O'Reily's CNN implementation (86%). Unlike the CNN, our model does not use any carefully-tuned parameters, and is arguably more generalizable than the CNN. Overall we see that a competitive recognition can be achieved using a model that much more closely resembles the biological visual cortex.

### 9.3 Network Optimization using CNO

In our second experiment, we create four variations of cortical network to be deployed on the CPU and trained on images of handwritten digits from the MNIST database. Each of these networks consist of 47 hypercolumns, but the number of initial minicolumns is varied depending on the number of training digits. The network trained with 64 images is initialized with 64 minicolumns per hypercolumn, the network learning 128 images began with 128 minicolumns, and so on. In this experiment, we do not provide the supervisory feedback signal, so features are not pooled throughout the hierarchy. Figure 11 shows the execution time of each of the network configurations deployed on the CPU. As can be seen, the execution time grows substantially as the number of minicolumns is increased in each hypercolumn. After Aivo profiles and optimizes the network with CNO, we can clearly see the performance benefit of removing the unused minicolumns whose evaluation adds to the overall execution time, but not to the recognition of the dataset. These optimizations result in nearly 2x speedup for each of the network configurations tested.

These same four variations of the 47-hypercolumn cortical network are also deployed and trained on the GTX 280. In Figure 12, we see that executing the cortical network on the GPGPU can ren-

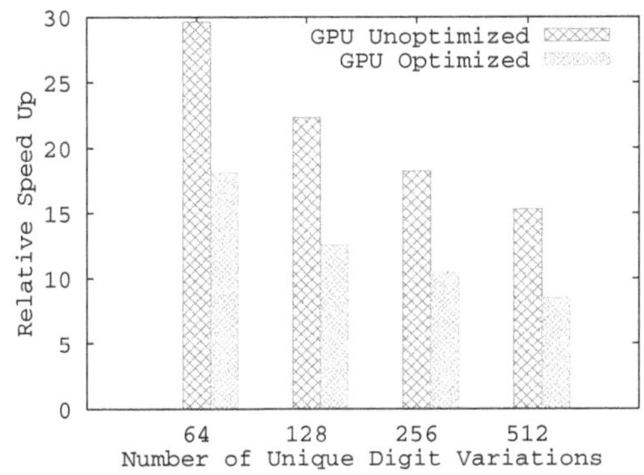


**Figure 12.** *Speedup of GPU vs. CPU cortical networks.*

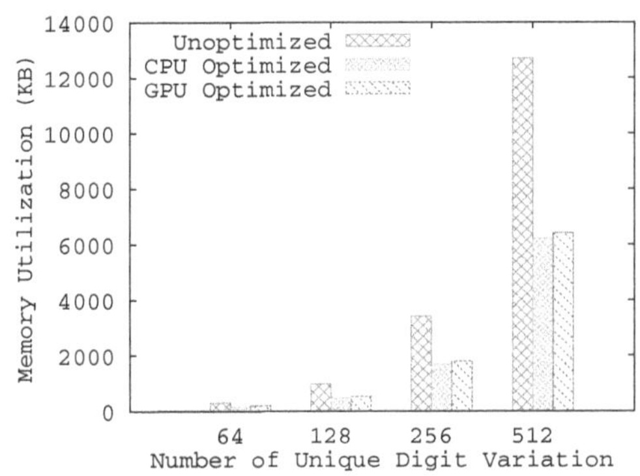


**Figure 13.** *Memory footprint of minicolumns before and after optimization.*

der significant speedups for both baseline and resource-optimized configurations. Executing large and unoptimized cortical network on the GPGPU intuitively exhibits a greater performance benefit since evaluating useless minicolumns does not affect the execution time if all minicolumns are evaluated in parallel. For the cortical network configurations examined, a maximum speedup of nearly 30x can be achieved when comparing an unoptimized cortical network on the CPU vs. the GTX 280 GPGPU. We also notice that the speedup for the GPGPU is maximal for the cortical network initialized with fewer minicolumns per hypercolumn. Since the minicolumns in a hypercolumn rely on the GPGPU's shared memory space for lateral communication and data sharing, smaller hypercolumns require less of this resource bottleneck. As a result, multiple hypercolumns can concurrently execute on each multiprocessor, resulting in more parallelism and better overall performance.

We also examine the amount of resources recovered by the CNO in terms of system memory in Figure 13. When the number of minicolumns is reduced across various hypercolumns, the receptive field size of higher level hypercolumns is also reduced. As this receptive field size is reduced, the number of synaptic weights needed for these upper level hypercolumns is in turn minimized as well. This results in nearly halving the amount of memory required to store the state of the overall cortical network. The optimized network deployed on the CPU recovers slightly more memory resources than the network deployed on the GPGPU. Again, we note that this is because the granularity of optimization is a result of hardware limitations of the GPGPU, and no performance benefit is achieved by reducing minicolumns at granularity less than 32 minicolumns per hypercolumn.

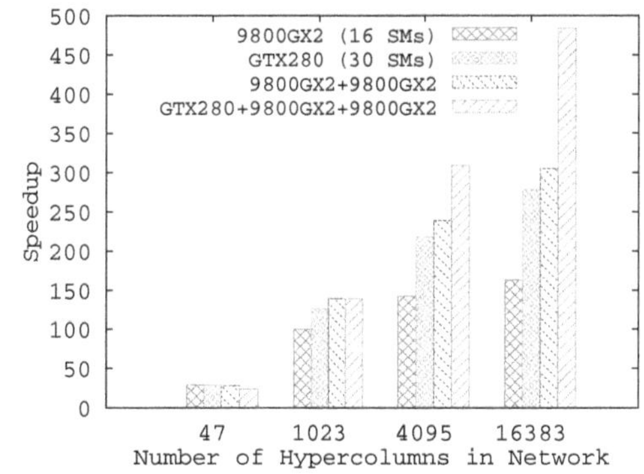


**Figure 14.** *Speedup of multi-GPU configurations vs. an unoptimized single-thread CPU implementation.*

| | Original Network | Optimized Network | Logic Network |
|---|---|---|---|
| **Execution Time / Iteration** | 3000 us | 1080 us | 68 us |
| **Speedup** | 1x | 2.78x | 44.12x |

**Table 1.** *The NISA abstraction provides performance benefits for equivalent optimized networks and boolean logic conversion.*

### 9.4 Scaling Across Multiple GPGPUs

In our third experiment, we examine the speedups achieved by deploying the learning model on the GPGPU. The number of minicolumns per hypercolumn fixed at 64 and the number of hypercolumns in the cortical network is varied. We compare the performance of the serialized cortical network deployed on the CPU to the same network deployed on a single 9800 GX2 (16 SMs), a single GTX 280 (30 SMs), a network split across both GPGPUs in the 9800 GX2s, and finally across all 3 GPUs. In Figure 14 we see that the cortical network's inherent parallelism fits well to the GPU architecture, and the achievable speedups improve with the addition of more GPU resources. The resulting speedups range from 30x to 480x for a massive cortical network proportionally split across three CUDA-enabled GPUs. We also note that the GTX 280 and the paired 9800 GX2s perform very similarly across the configurations tested, as they have a comparable number of total SMs (30 SMs compared to two GPUs with 16 SMs each). For the 47-hypercolumn cortical network, we notice a degradation in performance for the multiple GPU configuration relative to the single GPUs. This is because synchronization accounts for a larger portion of the execution time in smaller networks. It should be noted that these speedups are only achievable when batch training a set of inputs for many iterations, as frequently transferring data to and from the GPU quickly increases execution time.

### 9.5 Boolean Logic Generation Performance

In this experiment, we examine Aivo's ability to interpret a trained cortical network exported using the NISA abstraction and translate it into a boolean logic equivalent. Currently, the boolean logic equivalent cortical networks are simply deployed on the CPU as highly efficient C++ code, though in the future we plan to investigate these translations further, possibly creating equivalent netlists to be deployed on an FPGA or another substrate. We initialize a cortical network with 47 hypercolumns containing 20 minicolumns each, and train the network with 10 variations of a single digit until 100% recognition rate is achieved. We also provide the supervisory feedback signal to the top level of the cortical network, so features are robustly pooled throughout the hierarchy. Aivo then performs the necessary translations to convert the trained network

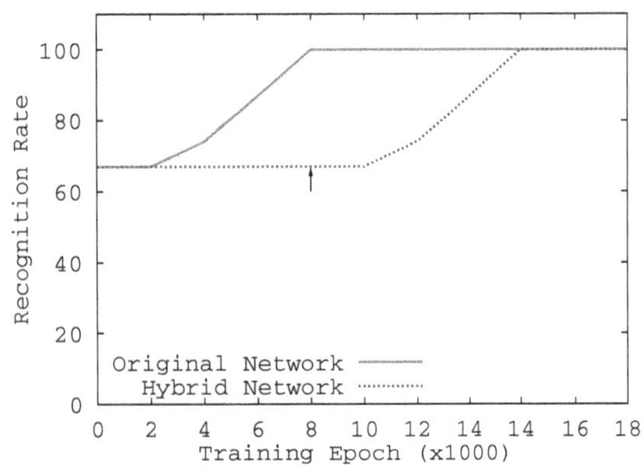


**Figure 15.** *Recognition performance of the original cortical network and its logic based equivalent. At 8000 learning epochs (arrow), Aivo recognizes the logic network is not firing and replaces it with a hypercolumn network.*

to its equivalent boolean logic equations, and also invokes the CNO to create an optimized version of the cortical network. Table 1 compares the performance of the optimized cortical network deployed on the CPU with the translated logic equivalent (also deployed on the CPU). We see that removing useless minicolumns provides a nearly 3x speedup, and deploying an equivalent network using boolean logic results in a 44x speedup for this 47 hypercolumn network.

### 9.6 Aivo's Runtime Monitoring

In this final experiment, we study Aivo's ability to revert the highly optimized boolean logic network back to a network of hypercolumns when new features are introduced into the learning dataset. If the boolean logic network deployed on the CPU does not exhibit any activity for a large number of epochs, Aivo's monitoring system detects it and reverts back to a network of hypercolumns in an effort to learn new features. For this experiment, we create a similar hierarchy as described in Section 9.5 and expose it to 10 variations of a single digit until it achieves 100% recognition rate. Once Aivo generates the optimized boolean logic network for the trained cortical network, we introduce five new variations of the same digit to the original network and optimized boolean logic network. For the sake of this experiment, we run both the hypercolumn network and boolean logic translated network alongside to observe their corresponding recognition rates.

In Figure 15, we see that initially, the new variations are not recognized by either networks. Thus, both the original and the converted logic network exhibit a recognition rate of 67%, i.e. 10 out of 15 digit variations are recognized. Since the original network of hypercolumns has enough resources available to learn new features, after 3000 training epochs, it starts to learn the new variations added to the training dataset. On the other hand, the optimized logic network does not show any improvement in the recognition rate since it can only perform the initial task it was trained to do. Aivo's runtime monitoring eventually recognizes that the logic network has not been active for a large number of epochs. As a result, Aivo translates the boolean logic network to a trainable hypercolumn network. Once the logic network is replaced with a hypercolumn network (at around 8000 epochs of no activity), we see improvement in the recognition rate of the hybrid network.

## 10. Conclusions and Future Work

This paper introduces the concept of a Neuromorphic Instruction Set Architecture (NISA), which separates the algorithmic description, learning, and optimization of cortical networks from their execution substrate. As a case study to demonstrate the abilities and usefulness of the NISA abstraction for neuromorphic architectures, we presented the Aivo framework. Aivo describes a NISA implementation for a rate-encoded neuromorphic systems based on modeled cortical columns, an integrated development and runtime environment, and several optimizations made possible by the NISA abstraction. The Aivo IDE simplifies the task of developing cortical networks by providing an interface to create, debug, train, checkpoint, profile, optimize, and deploy using the NISA abstraction, coded as a virtual ISA in XML. We demonstrated how the Aivo NISA is able to deploy cortical networks on general purpose CPUs as well as multiple CUDA-enabled Nvidia GPGPUs. We also showed how a trained network can be deployed as a third execution substrate, boolean logic, which is presently executed on the host CPU, though future work will investigate exporting a trained networks netlist for deployment on an FPGA or other appropriate hardware substrate. Finally, we demonstrated how the Aivo Cortical Network Optimizer performs high level optimizations to either enhance performance by removing unused modules or expand feature recognition robustness by adding more cortical modules.

The Aivo CNO showed significant performance and resource utilization improvements, resulting in a hypercolumn based cortical network with a 50% memory footprint reduction and up to a 3x speedup. Deploying a trained network as its boolean logic equivalent exhibited even more impressive runtime performance, resulting in a 44x speedup over the original hypercolumn based network. The same hypercolumn based cortical network exhibited a 30x speedup when executed on a GPGPU. Finally, a similarly structured but massively scaled cortical network exhibited up to a 480x speedup when properly distributed over three GPGPUs.

We plan to extend this work to much larger scales of networks that are capable of tackling complex classification problems like image and object recognition, and we expect deployment on GPGPU accelerators to provide the impressive speedups as evidenced in the results. As previously mentioned, we also plan to extend the role of translating a fully trained cortical network to its boolean logic equivalent, as well as hybrid networks, for deployment on an FPGA or other appropriate substrate. Finally, we plan on enhancing the NISA abstraction so other learning algorithms, such as spiking neural networks, can take advantage of the same benefits we have achieved for the cortical column model using the Aivo NISA.

## Acknowledgments

We wish to thank our collaborators Olivier Temam and Hugues Berry for many fruitful discussions on cortical models, as well as the paper's anonymous reviewers and shepherds for their helpful comments. This work was supported in part by National Science Foundation award CCF-0702272, as well as equipment donations from Hewlett Packard.

## References

[1] Systems of neuromorphic adaptive plastic scalable electronics (synapse). 2008. URL `http://www.darpa.mil/dso/solicitations/baa08-28.htm`.

[2] Matlab neural network toolbox, July 2010. URL `http://www.mathworks. com/ products/ neuralnet/`.

[3] Java neuroph, July 2010. URL `http://neuroph. sourceforge. net/ index.html`.

[4] G. M. Amdahl, G. A. Blaauw, and F. P. Brooks. Architecture of the ibm system/360. *IBM Journal of Research and Development*, 8(2):87 –101, 1964. ISSN 0018-8646. doi: 10.1147/rd.82.0087.

[5] J. Arthur and K. Boahen. Learning in silicon: Timing is everything. In *Proceedings of Advances in Neural Information Processing Systems*, volume 18, pages 75–82. Advances in Neural Information Processing Systems, 2006.

[6] R. K. B. Awerbuch. Competitive collaborative learning. *Journal of Computer and System Sciences*, 74(8):1271 –1288, 2008.

[7] T. Binzegger, R. Douglas, and K. Martin. A quantitative map of the circuit of cat primary visual cortex. *J. Neurosci.*, 24(39):8441–8453, Sep 2004.

[8] W. Calvin. Cortical columns, modules, and hebbian cell assemblies. In M. A. Arbib, editor, *The Handbook of Brain Theory and Neural Networks*, pages 269–272. MIT Press, Cambridge, MA, 1998.

[9] L. Chua. Memristor–the missing circuit element. *IEEE Transactions on Circuit Theory*, 18(5):507–519, 1971.

[10] D. DeSieno. Adding a conscience to competitive learning. In *International Conference on Neural Networks, ICNN*, volume 1, pages 117 –124, 1988.

[11] F. Folowosele, R. Vogelstein, and R. Etienne-Cummings. Real-time silicon implementation of v1 in hierarchical visual information processing. In *Biomedical Circuits and Systems Conference, 2008. BioCAS 2008. IEEE*, pages 181 –184, 2008. doi: 10.1109/BIOCAS.2008.4696904.

[12] W. Freeman. Random activity at the microscopic neural level in cortex ("noise") sustains and is regulated by low-dimensional dynamics of macroscopic activity ("chaos"). *International Journal of Neural Systems*, 7(4):473–480, 1996.

[13] K. Grill-Spector, T. Kushnir, T. Hendler, S. Edelman, Y. Itzchak, and R. Malach. A sequence of object-processing stages revealed by fmri in the human occipital lobe. *Hum. Brain Map.*, 6:316–328, 1998.

[14] A. Hashmi and M. Lipasti. Discovering cortical algorithms. In *Proceedings of the International Conference on Neural Computation (ICNC 2010)*, 2010.

[15] A. Hashmi, H. Berry, O. Temam, and M. H. Lipasti. Leveraging progress in neurobiology for computing systems. In *Proceedings of the Workshop on New Directions in Computer Architecture held in Conjunction with 42nd Annual IEEE/ACM International Symposium on Microarchitecture (MICRO-42)*, 2009.

[16] J. Hawkins and D. George. Hierarchical temporal memory. 2006. URL `www.numenta.com/Numenta_HTM_Concepts.pdf`.

[17] M. Holler, S. Tam, H. Castro, and R. Benson. An electrically trainable artificial neural network (etann) with 10240 'floating gate' synapses. In *Neural Networks, 1989. IJCNN., International Joint Conference on*, pages 191 –196 vol.2, June 1989. doi: 10.1109/IJCNN.1989.118698.

[18] D. Hubel and T. Wiesel. Receptive fields and functional architecture of monkey striate cortex. *Journal of Physiology*, 195:215–243, 1968.

[19] K. Hynna and K. Boahen. Silicon neurons that burst when primed. *Circuits and Systems, 2007. ISCAS 2007. IEEE International Symposium on*, pages 3363–3366, May 2007. doi: 10.1109/ISCAS.2007.378288.

[20] E. Izhikevich. Which model to use for cortical spiking neurons? *Neural Networks, IEEE Transactions on*, 15(5):1063 –1070, 2004. ISSN 1045-9227. doi: 10.1109/TNN.2004.832719.

[21] H. Jang, A. Park, and K. Jung. Neural network implementation using cuda and openmp. In *DICTA '08: Proceedings of the 2008 Digital Image Computing: Techniques and Applications*, pages 155–161, Washington, DC, USA, 2008. IEEE Computer Society. ISBN 978-0-7695-3456-5. doi: http://dx.doi.org/10.1109/DICTA.2008.82.

[22] J. Jones and L. Palmer. An evaluation of the two-dimensional gabor filter model of simple receptive fields in cat striate cortex. *Journal of Neurophysiology*, 58(6):1233–1258, December 1987.

[23] S. Jung and S. su Kim. Hardware implementation of a real-time neural network controller with a dsp and an fpga for nonlinear systems. *Industrial Electronics, IEEE Transactions on*, 54(1):265 –271, 2007. ISSN 0278-0046. doi: 10.1109/TIE.2006.888791.

[24] E. Kandel, J. Schwartz, and T. Jessell. *Principles of Neural Science*. McGraw-Hill, 4 edition, 2000.

[25] Y. LeCun, L. Bottou, Y. Bengio, and P. Haffner. Gradient-based learning applied to document recognition. *Proceedings of the IEEE*, 86(11):2278–2324, 1998.

[26] Y. LeCun, L. Bottou, Y. Bengio, and P. Haffner. Gradient-based learning applied to document recognition. *Proceedings of the IEEE*, 86(11):2278–2324, November 1998.

[27] H. Markram. The blue brain project. In *SC '06: Proceedings of the 2006 ACM/IEEE conference on Supercomputing*, page 53, New York, NY, USA, 2006. ACM. ISBN 0-7695-2700-0. doi: http://doi.acm.org/10.1145/1188455.1188511.

[28] T. Martinetz. Competitive hebbian learning rule forms perfectly topology preserving maps. In *International Conference on Artificial Neural Networks, ICANN*, pages 427 –434, 1993.

[29] M. Matthias and J. Born. Hippocampus whispering in deep sleep to prefrontal cortex for good memories? *Neuron*, 61:496–498, 2009.

[30] V. Mountcastle. An organizing principle for cerebral function: The unit model and the distributed system. In G. Edelman and V. Mountcastle, editors, *The Mindful Brain*. MIT Press, Cambridge, Mass., 1978.

[31] V. Mountcastle. The columnar organization of the neocortex. *Brain*, 120:701–722, 1997.

[32] A. Nere and M. Lipasti. Cortical architectures on a gpgpu. In *GPGPU '10: Proceedings of the 3rd Workshop on General-Purpose Computation on Graphics Processing Units*, pages 12–18, New York, NY, USA, 2010. ACM. ISBN 978-1-60558-935-0. doi: http://doi.acm.org/10.1145/1735688.1735693.

[33] M. O'Neil. Neural network for recognition of handwritten digits, October 2010. URL `http://www.codeproject.com/KB/library/NeuralNetRecognition.aspx`.

[34] Y. V. Pershin, S. La Fontaine, and M. Di Ventra. Memristive model of amoeba learning. *Phys. Rev. E*, 80(2):021926, Aug 2009. doi: 10.1103/PhysRevE.80.021926.

[35] R. Raina, A. Madhavan, and A. Ng. Large-scale deep unsupervised learning using graphics processors. In *Proceedings of the 26th Annual International Conference on Machine Learning*, pages 873–880. ACM, 2009. ISBN 978-1-60558-516-1.

[36] K. L. Rice, T. M. Taha, and C. N. Vutsinas. Scaling analysis of a neocortex inspired cognitive model on the cray xd1. *J. Supercomput.*, 47(1):21–43, 2009. ISSN 0920-8542. doi: http://dx.doi.org/10.1007/s11227-008-0195-z.

[37] D. Ringach. Haphazard wiring of simple receptive fields and orientation columns in visual cortex. *J. Neurophysiol.*, 92(1):468–476, Jul 2004.

[38] U. Rokni, A. Richardson, E. Bizzi, and H. Seung. Motor learning with unstable neural representations. *Neuron*, 64:653–666, 2007.

[39] J. Schemmel, J. Fieres, and K. Meier. Wafer-scale integration of analog neural networks. In *Neural Networks, 2008. IJCNN 2008. (IEEE World Congress on Computational Intelligence). IEEE International Joint Conference on*, pages 431 –438, 2008. doi: 10.1109/IJCNN.2008.4633828.

[40] T. Serre, A. Oliva, and T. Poggio. A feedforward architecture accounts for rapid categorization. *Proc. Natl. Acad. Sci. USA*, 104(15):6424–6429, Apr 2007. doi: 10.1073/pnas.0700622104.

[41] T. Serre, L. Wolf, S. Bileschi, M. Riesenhuber, and T. Poggio. Robust object recognition with cortex-like mechanisms. *IEEE Trans. Pattern Anal. Mach. Intell.*, 29(3):411–426, Mar 2007. doi: 10.1109/TPAMI.2007.56.

[42] R. Vogels and G. Orban. How well do response changes of striate neurons signal difference in orientation: a study in the discriminating monkey. *Journal of Neuroscience*, 10(11):3543–3558, 1990.

[43] H. Wersing and E. Korner. Learning optimized features for hierarchical models of invariant object recognition. *Neural Computation*, 15: 1559–1588, 2003.

# Mementos: System Support for Long-Running Computation on RFID-Scale Devices

Benjamin Ransford
Department of Computer Science
University of Massachusetts Amherst
ransford@cs.umass.edu

Jacob Sorber
Institute for Security, Technology, and Society
Dartmouth College
jacob.m.sorber@dartmouth.edu

Kevin Fu
Department of Computer Science
University of Massachusetts Amherst
kevinfu@cs.umass.edu

## Abstract

Transiently powered computing devices such as RFID tags, kinetic energy harvesters, and smart cards typically rely on programs that complete a task under tight time constraints before energy starvation leads to complete loss of volatile memory. *Mementos* is a software system that transforms general-purpose programs into interruptible computations that are protected from frequent power losses by automatic, energy-aware state checkpointing. Mementos comprises a collection of optimization passes for the LLVM compiler infrastructure and a linkable library that exercises hardware support for energy measurement while managing state checkpoints stored in nonvolatile memory. We evaluate Mementos against diverse test cases in a trace-driven simulator of transiently powered RFID-scale devices. Although Mementos's energy checks increase run time when energy is plentiful, they allow Mementos to safely suspend execution when energy dwindles, effectively spreading computation across zero or more power failures. This paper's contributions are: a study of the runtime environment for programs on RFID-scale devices; an energy-aware state checkpointing system for these devices that is implemented for the MSP430 family of microcontrollers; and a trace-driven simulator of transiently powered RFID-scale devices.

***Categories and Subject Descriptors*** C.3 [*SPECIAL-PURPOSE AND APPLICATION-BASED SYSTEMS*]: Real-time and embedded systems

***General Terms*** Design, Experimentation

***Keywords*** Mementos, RFID-Scale Devices, Computational RFID, Energy-Aware Checkpointing

## 1. Introduction

Demand for tiny, easily deployable computers has driven the development of general-purpose *transiently powered computers* that lack both batteries and wired power, operating exclusively on energy harvested from remote supplies or the environment. Such devices range from *computational RFIDs* [36]—microcontroller-based devices that harvest RF from readers and communicate via RFID protocols—to general-purpose batteryless sensor devices [45].

Computing under transient power conditions is a challenge. Transiently powered RFID tags use simple state machines instead of supporting general-purpose computation. Contactless smart cards perform more complicated special-purpose computations (e.g. cardholder authentication); however, they offer no execution guarantees, and instead rely on the user to provide the needed RF power for a sufficient period of time. When energy consumption outpaces energy harvesting, these computations fail and must restart from scratch, when adequate energy becomes available.

With ultra-low-power microcontrollers (MCUs), tiny *programmable* devices can perform computation and sensing under RFID-scale energy constraints; however, these MCUs consume more power than conventional RFID circuitry, and energy consumption can easily outpace harvesting, resulting in frequent power loss.

Today, programs that run CPU-intensive operations like cryptography on these devices are pessimistically and painstakingly hand-tuned to complete within a short time window (often under 100 ms) [7, 9]. The usefulness and power of RFID-scale devices can be dramatically improved if designers can confidently write programs without being limited by power failures.

*Mementos* is a software system that enables long-running computations to span power loss events by combining compile-time instrumentation and run-time energy-aware state checkpointing [1]. At compile time, Mementos inserts function calls that estimate available energy. At run time, Mementos predicts power losses and, when appropriate, saves program state to nonvolatile memory. After a failure, program state is restored and execution continues rather than restarting from scratch.

This paper makes the following contributions: (1) An energy-aware state checkpointing system that splits program execution across multiple lifecycles on transiently powered RFID-scale devices. The system is implemented for the MSP430 family of microcontrollers, requires no hardware modifications to existing devices, and operates automatically at run time without user intervention. (2) A suite of compile-time optimization passes that insert energy checks at control points in a program. The optimization passes employ three different instrumentation strategies that favor different program structures. (3) A trace-driven simulator to evaluate the behavior of programs on transiently powered RFID-scale devices. The simulator, modeled after a prototype hardware device with an off-the-shelf microcontroller, takes executable code as input and simulates power loss events during runs. We evaluate the simulator's accuracy and Mementos's performance under simulation in Section 5.

[1] In the indie film *Memento*, the main character would unpredictably lose short-term memory, especially when sleeping. He checkpointed state with notes and tattoos in an attempt to execute long-running tasks.


*ASPLOS'11,* March 5–11, 2011, Newport Beach, California, USA.

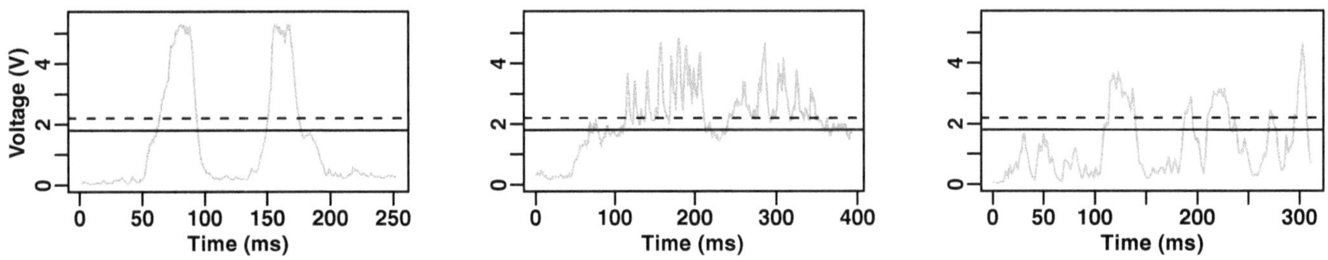


**Figure 1.** Energy availability under RF harvesting is difficult to predict on a transiently powered computer (TPC), threatening the successful completion of long-running programs. These plots show the output of a prototype TPC's energy-harvesting frontend during three different smooth movements within 2 m of an RFID reader. The dashed line at 2.2 V represents this prototype's nominal minimum voltage for flash writes. The solid line at 1.8 V depicts the prototype's nominal minimum operating voltage, below which it loses volatile state.

The compile-time analysis and program transformation components of Mementos are built on the LLVM compiler infrastructure [21]. Our simulation of a transiently powered device is implemented as a set of enhancements to MSPsim [14] and is guided by the hardware parameters of a WISP [39] (Revision 4.1) prototype computational RFID.

**Applications.** Mementos enables long-running or computationally intensive applications on RFID-scale devices. Moving computing into environments that are ill-suited to batteries and tethered power, promising applications include environmental monitoring where battery replacement is not practical, insect-scale wildlife tracking where batteries are too heavy, and implantable medical devices [29] where battery recharging might heat and damage surrounding tissue. Mementos aims to enable these new applications by extending the computational capabilities of transiently powered computers beyond simple programs.

An example of a long-running application that could benefit from Mementos's automatic checkpointing is compressive sensing [8]. RFID-scale devices can measure environmental phenomena—like temperature, acceleration, and light—that may exhibit informative trends over time spans larger than a few seconds. Compressive sensing maintains a set of frequently updated variables that collectively represent a sparse, compressible signal, preserving the structure and information of the signal with high probability. By providing automatic state checkpointing, Mementos would enable a compressive sensing program to accumulate measurements over many lifecycles separated by power loss events. Section 5 includes an evaluation of Mementos on a simplified sensing application that cannot complete under reasonable assumptions in a single lifecycle of our trace-driven simulator or the platform it models.

## 2. Computing on Transient Power

Multiple platforms at various stages of maturity enable battery-less, RFID-scale, transiently powered computing. The WISP [39] uses an MSP430 microcontroller [43] for computation and harvests energy from off-the-shelf RFID readers. A system-on-chip variant, the SoCWISP [46], is small (2.0 mm$^2$) and light enough to attach to insects in flight. The Blue Devil WISP [44] improves performance for RF harvesting and communication. The UMass WISP under development provides increased storage and supports more peripherals (`http://www.cs.umass.edu/~zhangh/`). The EnHANTs [16] platform under development aims to behave like an RFID tag and a sensor mote. All share the goal of enabling sensing and general-purpose computation under transient power.

Previously proposed applications for transiently powered computers include environmental monitoring [17], activity recognition [6], and cryptographic protocols [9]. Mote-class devices (e.g. Telos [35], TinyNode [12]) offer similar capabilities and can also be used in these applications, but their size, weight, and maintenance cost (i.e., dependence on batteries) significantly limits their deployability. Transiently powered devices potentially provide the benefits of programmability and general-purpose computing without the drawbacks associated with more powerful mote-class devices.

Despite their benefits, designing and deploying these systems is challenging. By definition, these systems cannot depend on continuous power. Figure 1 illustrates typical fluctuations in supply voltage that occur under RF energy harvesting. Prototype systems like the WISP use capacitors as short-term energy buffers. For a sense of scale, consider that a WISP's 10 $\mu$F capacitor can store roughly 100 $\mu$J, whereas a Telos sensor mote's two AA batteries can store over 20,000 J—eight orders of magnitude more.

The amount of energy harvested from RF, solar, and other sources varies widely and is difficult to predict [31, 47]—a problem often compounded by device mobility. Consequently, unlike traditional computing systems, transiently powered systems frequently lose power and computational state as a rule, not as a rare exception. Experience with the WISP has shown that power failures every ~100 ms are a reasonable expectation [9, 36]. Existing lightweight operating systems like TinyOS [22] boot too slowly—in an informal test, TinyOS on a TinyNode booted in 253 ms, and 193 ms without clock calibration—to provide robustness via OS services on an RFID-scale device. Under these conditions, long-running programs may never complete, as they restart their work after each failure. In the context of transiently powered devices, we refer to such long-running programs as *Sisyphean tasks*.[2]

A key to solving the problem of Sisyphean tasks on RFID-scale devices is that many general-purpose microcontrollers, notably the MSP430 found on WISP-derived devices, feature nonvolatile memory that can be written to at run time. The most common form of on-chip nonvolatile memory is *flash memory*, typically available on prototype RFID-scale devices in the amount of several kilobytes. Four complications make it nontrivial to use flash memory for checkpoint storage. First, even small flash memories are coarsely divided into segments, 512 bytes each on the MSP430. Each segment must be erased all at once, and erasing a segment requires energy comparable to filling the entire segment with data. Second, flash memories have a *one-way* property: once a bit is set to `0`, the only way to set it back to `1` is to erase the entire segment that contains it. Third, flash reads are nearly as fast as volatile RAM reads, but flash writes are two orders of magnitude slower (and correspondingly more energy intensive) than RAM writes. Fourth, many microcontrollers use flash memory for program storage, which limits the amount of nonvolatile storage available for other purposes.

[2] In Greek mythology, Sisyphus was the first king of Corinth and a conniving malefactor. His punishment in Tartarus was forever to repeat the task of rolling a boulder to the top of a hill only to have it roll back to the bottom.

## 3. Design of Mementos

The key observation motivating the design of Mementos is that it is difficult to predict the behavior of energy harvesting on a transiently powered RFID-scale computer. For example, devices that harvest energy from RFID readers are subject to fluctuations in voltage (Figure 1) that are highly dependent on the operating environment and the device's physical orientation. With the advent of *programmable, general-purpose* transiently powered computing comes a need for general-purpose power failure recovery mechanisms. Without general-purpose mechanisms, programs on these devices must either finish quickly—not always an option—or include potentially complicated application-specific logic to manage their own computational state. Mementos aims to remove both of these obstacles.

Mementos has two parts: a set of program transformation passes that insert energy-measurement code at control points in a program, and a compact library that provides state checkpointing and recovery functions. Mementos can be integrated into a project's build system via standard means (e.g. a Makefile). Following are Mementos's high-level design goals and guiding design principles. Given the constraints of RFID-scale devices, we consider the goals of minimizing overhead and maximizing efficiency to be self-evident. Section 5 evaluates Mementos against our design goal.

**Goal: Split programs across multiple lifecycles.** Mementos must, at run time, automatically suspend and resume programs without user intervention. This program splitting aims to expand the range of applications suitable for RFID-scale devices.

*Principle #1: Run on existing hardware.* Mementos requires no special hardware support other than the ability to measure the voltage of the platform's energy buffer. Circuitry for voltage measurement is common on computing devices that operate on finite energy supplies (e.g. batteries).

*Principle #2: Reason minimally about energy at compile time, maximally at run time.* Past work has demonstrated that even expert programmers cannot be trusted to reason correctly about energy [40]. Reasoning about run-time energy availability at compile time may be impossible because of inconsistent harvesting and limited computation available for prediction. Mementos estimates available energy at run time and inserts energy checks at compile time, obviating the need for complex logic to deal with changing energy conditions.

### 3.1 Compile-Time Instrumentation

Mementos modifies programs in two ways at compile time. First, it places *trigger points*—calls to a Mementos library function that estimates available energy—at control points in the program. Second, it wraps the program's `main()` function with code that restores execution from an available checkpoint.

To suspend execution in time for a checkpoint to complete, Mementos should insert enough energy measurements at compile time so that run-time energy trends are effectively sampled; however, it should not insert so many that measurement cost predominates over execution. To satisfy our goal of supporting a wider range of applications, Mementos must also be compatible with programs that are structured in different ways. To these ends, Mementos offers three different instrumentation strategies that enable it to instrument common structures—loops and function calls. In *loop-latch mode*, Mementos places a trigger point at each loop latch (the backedge from the bottom to the top of a loop), resulting in an energy check for each iteration of each loop in the program. In *function-return mode*, Mementos places a trigger point after each call instruction, resulting in an energy check each time a function returns. In *timer-aided mode*, which is designed to reduce the frequency of energy-intensive checkpointing operations, Mementos adds to either the loop-latch or function-return mode a hardware timer interrupt that raises a flag at predetermined intervals. Each trigger point then checks the flag and proceeds with an energy check only if the flag is up. The flag is lowered again for the next trigger point.

Besides offering three strategies for automatic trigger-point placement, Mementos supports application-specific customization by providing a simple API. A programmer can opt not to run any of Mementos's instrumentation passes and instead insert trigger points manually, simply by including a header file and placing function calls in the program. She can similarly insert her own calls to Mementos functions to skip energy checks and force checkpointing.

### 3.2 Run-Time Energy Estimation

At run time, Mementos estimates the energy remaining in the device's energy buffer by measuring its voltage. Microcontrollers suitable for RFID-scale devices typically have on-chip analog-to-digital converters (ADCs) that sample voltage as a proxy for any number of environmental phenomena (e.g. temperature and physical orientation); Mementos simply makes use of this subsystem.

For an ideal capacitor, the amount of energy it presently contains ($E$) is determined by the capacitor's present voltage ($V$) and its fixed capacitance ($C$), via the following equation: $E = CV^2/2$. However, since calculating energy from voltage may require computationally intensive operations such as squaring or floating-point arithmetic, Mementos uses the ADC's voltage measurement directly when making checkpointing decisions: it compares the measured voltage to a *checkpoint threshold voltage* ($V_{\text{thresh}}$). Above this voltage, Mementos assumes that it does not need to write a state checkpoint. It interprets a voltage below the threshold as indicating that power failure is imminent and begins checkpointing state.

Ideally, program state should be saved at the last practicable opportunity before a power failure in order to minimize unsaved computation. However, unpredictable energy harvesting and the variations in the cost of saving checkpoints make perfect failure prediction infeasible.

Mementos predicts future power failures *conservatively* by assuming that no energy will be harvested between the trigger point and a power failure. Worst-case run times can be calculated as follows. The charge on a capacitor is $Q = CV$. Under a constant current draw $I$, the charge decreases as $\frac{dQ}{dt} = I$, and the time between two voltage levels $V_{\text{max}}$ and $V_{\text{min}}$ is $\Delta t = C(V_{\text{max}} - V_{\text{min}})/I$. If, for example, an MSP430 draws 238 $\mu$A in active mode, fails to write to flash below 2.2 V, and needs 17.5 ms to write a 200-byte checkpoint, Mementos should start checkpointing *at the latest* when supply voltage falls to 2.62 V. However, two factors complicate the task of checkpointing at the last moment: checkpoint sizes and times may vary at run time depending on stack depth; and Mementos's ability to precisely time a checkpoint depends on the frequency of trigger points. Section 4 describes the mechanisms that help a programmer choose a reasonable checkpoint threshold voltage above the lower bound.

Because it may suffer power loss during a checkpointing operation, Mementos exhibits defensive behavior that ensures correctness at a cost of time—i.e., its precautions err on the conservative side and may increase the amount of redundant computation during a complete execution. Mementos's first precaution is that it writes checkpoints *head first* and *tail last*: the first word of data it writes to nonvolatile memory contains enough length information for a complete checkpoint to be reconstructed and an incomplete checkpoint to be detected; the last word it writes is the magic number that ends every valid checkpoint. Second, if Mementos detects an incomplete checkpoint during recovery or next-checkpoint location, it refuses to write any more information to the containing segment of nonvolatile memory and marks the segment for deletion. Mementos erases such marked segments immediately after boot when available energy is guaranteed to be above a predefined threshold.

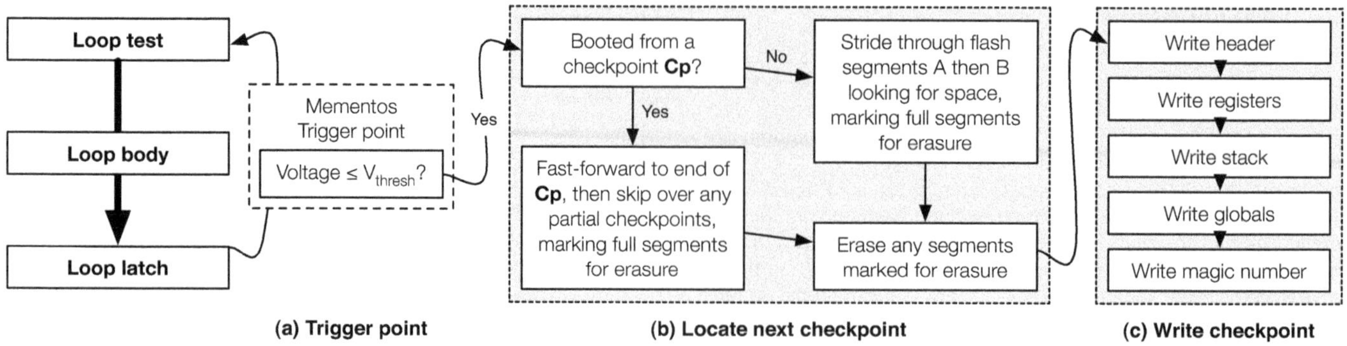


**Figure 2.** Overview of run-time checkpointing in Mementos. This diagram depicts the *loop-latch mode* in which Mementos instruments loop back-edges with energy checks that conditionally trigger checkpointing.

### 3.3 Run-Time Checkpointing

Mementos links trigger-point instrumented programs with a run-time checkpointing library. When a trigger point initiates a checkpoint, Mementos copies relevant program state to nonvolatile memory along with meta-information (Figure 2). After a power failure, Mementos searches for a restorable checkpoint and, if it finds one, copies the stored state into RAM and resumes execution.

Checkpointing on RFID-scale devices is more difficult than checkpointing on more powerful platforms. With no operating system, Mementos must be linked into a deployed program. Mementos shares all of the program's resources and must perform *in-place* checkpointing to capture the state of the program as it was immediately before entering the trigger point. Additionally, the limitations of flash memory (discussed in Section 2 and below) complicate checkpoint management.

**In-place checkpointing.** Most checkpointing systems are designed to run on multiprogrammed operating systems (e.g. the MPI checkpointing of Bronevetsky et al. [3]) or in hardware environments that support the issuance of commands by other devices (e.g. the sensornet checkpointing of Österlind et al. [30]). Mementos runs on RFID-scale devices without resources to run conventional operating systems and may have no electrical connection to their environs. It interacts with its host program via function calls and shares the program's address space, stack, registers, and globals.

Flash writes are slow and energy intensive relative to volatile memory writes, so instead of blindly copying the entire contents of RAM in each checkpoint, Mementos captures only the regions of RAM that are in use at the time the trigger point is called. These comprise the stack, whose depth can be calculated via the stack pointer; the global variables, captured by Mementos in an analysis pass at compile time; and the register file, which includes the stack pointer, program counter, and a status register. Mementos does not capture the program's executable code because this code is typically already stored in nonvolatile memory.

Keeping with a convention generally followed by programs targeting memory-limited mote-class devices, none of our test cases allocates memory dynamically. This allows our implementation of Mementos to sidestep the problem of checkpointing a fragmented heap by not checkpointing the heap at all; we note instead that the feasibility of efficient heap checkpointing depends on the quality of the dynamic memory allocator and its internal state at the time of checkpointing. `setjmp` and `longjmp` operations are unsupported for similar reasons; exception-style control flow is not typically used in embedded software. Notably, the Embedded C++ standard lacks support for exceptions [34]. However, Mementos *is* compatible with interrupt service routines (ISRs) that behave like normal function calls, as they do on MSP430. Finally, Mementos does not currently provide special support for reentrant code or threading libraries; its checkpointing operation is non-reentrant.

At checkpoint time, Mementos first pushes all of the registers onto the stack; registers tend to change during program execution. (On the MSP430, the register file includes the status register `R2`; Mementos takes minor precautions to avoid affecting this register's value before saving it.) It stores the value of the stack pointer, adjusted for the function call that initiated the checkpoint, and sets the stored value of the program counter to the return address from the checkpoint function's own stack frame. It then finds space for a new checkpoint (details below), and writes at the beginning of the free space a checkpoint size header that includes the adjusted stack depth. Mementos then writes the saved registers, stack, and globals to flash. Finally, it writes a magic number to indicate the end of the checkpoint. The location of the magic number is trivial to calculate from the size header, allowing Mementos to detect incomplete checkpoints that are due to power failures during checkpointing.

At boot, Mementos searches for an active checkpoint (details below), then copies its contents into RAM. As when checkpointing, it must copy carefully so that it restores the saved state rather than a mixture of the saved state and its own state. For example, on the MSP430 architecture, it restores the register file in descending numeric order, leaving the stack pointer (`R1`) and the program counter (`R0`) for last. Restoring the program counter from the checkpoint implicitly transfers control to the program where it left off.

**Idempotent actions.** Some code cannot be re-executed safely. For example, an RFID-scale device may contain an actuator that toggles a property of another device. To enable programmers to work with non-idempotent code, Mementos allows programmers to selectively disable instrumentation on a per-loop or per-function basis. Appending the token `_mnotp` (mnemonic: "Mementos, no trigger points!") to any function's name causes Mementos to skip the function, i.e., not instrument its loops or a return from it. A programmer can disable instrumentation even for inline functions, which means she can direct Mementos to ignore any piece of code she wishes. We implemented an optional additional pass that emits compile-time warnings upon encountering possibly non-idempotent actions such as volatile writes—e.g. a write to a memory address that is mapped to a hardware output pin. The warning messages suggest points at which the programmer might profitably disable checkpointing.

**Checkpoint management.** Unlike prior systems that rely on OS facilities to simply dump process memory to a file system (e.g. *libckpt* [33]), Mementos must manage its own checkpoint storage. Its strategy approximates a circular buffer, but the characteristics of flash memory require special care.

Mementos is designed to facilitate the execution of programs from beginning to end; as a result, once a checkpoint is successfully written to nonvolatile memory, all previous checkpoints are *superseded*. Mementos maintains at most one *active* checkpoint at any given time. At boot or when searching for free space, Mementos uses a simple active-checkpoint search algorithm: it walks a reserved region of flash memory, skipping over sequentially stored valid checkpoints (those that end with correct magic numbers) and stopping when it discovers a valid checkpoint that is followed by a byte in the erase state (`0xFF` for flash).

Flash is erasable only segment-by-segment. To erase old or invalid checkpoints without destroying active checkpoints, Mementos reserves two segments of flash memory to checkpoint storage. When a checkpoint is completely written to one of these segments, it supersedes all checkpoints stored in the other, and Mementos marks the other segment erasable by zeroing its first word—an operation that can be reversed in flash only by erasing a whole segment. Mementos erases segments marked erasable at two times: at boot, when energy is likely to be plentiful, and when it cannot find space for a new checkpoint in either segment (i.e., when one segment is marked for erasure and the other is full of checkpoints).

**Energy polling versus interrupts.** A natural question is why Mementos polls the hardware energy supply instead of waiting for an interrupt to occur when voltage falls below a threshold. Voltage supervisors are common circuit components, but most—crucially, including existing prototype RFID-scale devices—do not feature an *adjustable* threshold voltage. Mementos is designed to work on existing devices without design modifications, so it polls for supply voltage. However, if such a device featured an adjustable or multilevel voltage supervisor, Mementos could avoid polling and simply associate itself with the appropriate interrupt(s). The checkpointing routine is designed to be called as a subroutine and works equally well as an interrupt handler (which is how the *checkpointing oracle* described in Section 5 works).

# 4. Implementation

Mementos formulates its program transformations as LLVM [21] optimization passes. These passes operate on intermediate LLVM bitcode before LLVM's MSP430 backend generates target-specific assembly. They are implemented in C++ and comprise a total of 601 lines of code including whitespace, comments and header files. Mementos's run-time library comprises an additional 761 lines of C and inline MSP430 assembly.

We provide a build harness that instruments an existing C program with Mementos and builds multiple MSP430 ELF executables per input program: one version for each of Mementos's three instrumentation strategies and an uninstrumented version for comparison. A script repeatedly calls the build harness with different parameters, varying the checkpointing voltage threshold $V_{\text{thresh}}$ and, when applicable, the timer interval used for timer-aided checkpointing. Finally, another script allows a programmer to compare the performance of all the variants in a simulator. Section 5 details our use of this simulator for evaluation.

**Implementation tradeoffs.** Instrumenting programs at the level of LLVM's intermediate representation allows Mementos to use simple, target-agnostic transformations, but it limits Mementos's visibility into later compilation stages. In particular, Mementos's LLVM passes do not have access to the results of code generation, so they cannot, for example, leverage empirically measured instruction-energy estimates [36]. We originally considered static analysis to count post–code-generation instructions and simply tag basic blocks with energy estimates, but that simple approach proved inadequate because of the complexity of calculating at run time the amount of work remaining until program completion; such calculations necessarily occur at trigger points, which may be frequent.

# 5. Evaluation

This section evaluates Mementos's ability to correctly and efficiently preserve computational state across frequent power failures. To simulate the energy conditions a deployed device might face, we feed voltage traces from a hardware prototype's analog energy-harvesting frontend into a trace-driven, cycle-accurate simulation of an RFID-scale device. We consider three distinct workloads that exercise different computational resources found on prototype RFID-scale devices: computation, sensing, and storage. We evaluate executions of these workloads with each of Mementos's instrumentation strategies and compare the results to baseline measurements taken against predictable energy conditions and uninstrumented programs. Finally, we offer the results of running Mementos on hardware instances of the model we simulate.

## 5.1 Mementos in Simulation

Mementos is designed with RFID-scale devices in mind, so we developed a flexible, trace-driven testbed featuring a simulated microcontroller (MCU) and energy supply modeling those found on a hardware device (a prototype WISP [39], revision 4.1). While the WISP supports interactive debugging via a standard JTAG interface, the simulator adds several key features: the ability to perform repeatable experiments against recorded traces of RF energy harvesting; the ability to vary hardware parameters (e.g. available memory) to overcome limitations of the prototype device; and the ability to obtain exact profiling information such as cycle counts. We therefore primarily present results obtained in simulation.

We augmented MSPsim [14], a cycle-accurate MSP430 simulator that accepts MSP430 ELF binaries, with a simulated capacitor of our design that obeys the basic capacitor equations for charging and discharging.[3] The simulated capacitor halts execution whenever its voltage falls below the MCU's nominal minimum operating level and resets the MCU when the voltage returns to an operable level after a power failure. We also added to MSPsim a notion of electrical current, which governs the speed at which a capacitor's energy is depleted, and associated each of the simulated MCU's operating modes (active mode, flash write, analog-to-digital conversion, and five low-power modes) with current values measured from a hardware WISP. We made other minor changes to MSPsim to simulate power failures (e.g. preserving nonvolatile memory contents across resets).

Our simulator optionally accepts a voltage trace that governs energy availability over time. On a physical RF-harvesting device that buffers energy in a capacitor, such as a WISP, the capacitor's voltage increases when the analog frontend gathers energy from an oscillating radio wave and sends charge through a diode; the voltage decreases as a factor of both time (via leakage) and current draw (via circuit usage). To capture voltage traces from real hardware, we isolated a WISP's RF-harvesting analog frontend, attached it to a $\sim 10\ \text{K}\Omega$ resistor that approximated the electrical load of the WISP's microcontroller during active computation, and recorded ten traces of voltage across the resistor (sequences of *time, voltage* pairs) corresponding to ten different patterns of motion near an RFID reader. Figure 1 shows several of these traces.

As for the simulated capacitor, we tested it under the simulator's suite of simulated electrical currents (drawn from our measurements of a real MSP430 in its various modes) and confirmed that its decay time under each regime was accurate to within 5 ms. Figure 3 compares the voltage trends exhibited by both a hardware WISP and our simulated WISP after each was charged to 4.5 V and allowed to discharge to 2.2 V (the voltage threshold for flash writes) while executing an infinite loop in *active* mode.

[3] We refer the reader to Horowitz and Hill [18] for a detailed discussion of capacitor behavior.

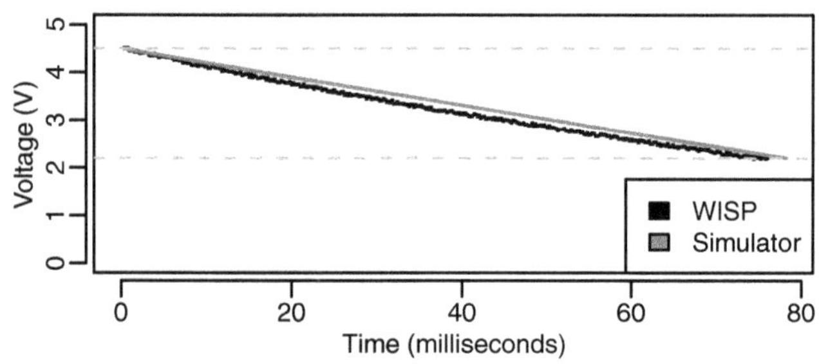


**Figure 3.** Simulated capacitor's voltage approximates the discharge time and voltage drop of a hardware WISP's capacitor. Both were charged to 4.5 V and allowed to discharge while executing an infinite loop at 1 MHz in active mode. Both traces end at 2.2 V, the nominal minimum voltage for flash writes on an MSP430.

The WISP and our simulator are instantiations of the same model: both are transiently powered computational platforms. We tuned the simulator according to empirical measurements of WISP devices, including current consumption in every power mode and the timing and current consumption of flash and ADC operations. However, the only properties of the simulator that bear directly on our design goal of spreading program execution across multiple lifecycles are: (1) our simulations of the hardware peripherals Mementos employs—ADC and flash memory—must incur realistic time and energy costs (Section 5.1.2), and (2) the time and energy available between Mementos's checkpointing threshold $V_{\text{thresh}}$ and the power cutoff threshold must be realistic (Section 5.1.3).

| WISP property | Simulator mechanism |
|---|---|
| MSP430 MCU | MSPsim fully supports MSP430 ISA |
| RF harvesting | Sim. accepts voltage trace recorded on hardware WISP's analog frontend |
| Low-power modes | Sim. obeys low-power setting, changes simulated MCU's current consumption |
| Electrical current | Tracks *(power mode, voltage)* $\rightarrow$ *current* mapping measured empirically |
| Dynamic power | Sim. capacitor obeys capacitor equation for discharging under load |
| Quiescent power | Sim. capacitor obeys exponential decay equation |
| Flash, ADC | Simulated current tracks empirical time and current measurements |
| Radio | (Not simulated) |

**Table 1.** Mapping of WISP hardware properties to simulator mechanisms.

Table 1 maps simulation mechanisms to the hardware features they simulate. The simulator does not simulate the cost of using radio for two reasons: (1) the device being simulated has no active radio, instead using backscatter to reflect radio waves; and (2) backscatter modulation operates on the same radio waves that provide energy, making communication effectively free on backscattering devices. The simulator also makes no attempt to account for environmental parameters such as temperature because the variations they induce are typically small.

### 5.1.1 Test cases

Our evaluation of Mementos considers three test cases representing common tasks for low-power embedded systems.

The `rsa64` test case uses iterative left-to-right modular exponentiation of multiple-precision integers to encrypt a 64-bit message under a 64-bit public key and 17-bit exponent. (Larger sizes cause the computation to exceed the RAM capacity of a WISP.) The program's data segment comprises 124 bytes of globals. Mementos instruments 24 loop latches in loop-latch mode and 51 call sites in function-return mode, in both cases primarily inside the multiple-precision integer library underlying the RSA implementation.

The `sense` test case takes 64 consecutive ADC samples of a simulated accelerometer and computes the minimum, maximum, mean, and standard deviation of the samples, then stores these statistics to nonvolatile memory. Such computations are common in sensing applications that sample environmental phenomena. The program stores raw sensor readings in a 128-byte global in RAM. Mementos instruments three loop latches in loop-latch mode and four call sites in function-return mode.

The `crc` test case, drawn directly from WISP firmware, computes a CRC16–CCITT checksum over a 2 KB region of on-chip flash memory. The WISP firmware computes CRC checksums to send along with responses to an RFID reader. CRC also provides a mechanism for data-integrity checks; we imagine such a check being important for future in-place firmware updates on RFID-scale devices. The program comprises a tight CRC nested loop and an outer loop that repeatedly calls the CRC function; Mementos instruments three loop latches in loop-latch mode and two call sites in function-return mode. Because the CRC loop is tight, we use the `crc` test case to evaluate the `_mnotp` mechanism for selectively disabling checkpoints (Section 3), reducing the number of loop latches instrumented to one.

A testbed provided with Mementos compiles each test case against a variety of Mementos configurations, varying by instrumentation strategy and static checkpoint threshold voltage $V_{\text{thresh}}$. It runs each variant against two modes of the simulator: trace-driven mode and decay-only mode. In trace-driven mode, a voltage trace from real hardware governs simulated energy availability. In decay-only mode, the simulated capacitor's voltage begins at a fixed value and strictly decreases with time and use; it starts at the same voltage in subsequent lifecycles. In both modes, trigger points induce checkpointing below $V_{\text{thresh}}$ and simulated power loss occurs at the platform's nominal minimum voltage for flash writes (2.2 V). Finally, the simulator collects baseline measurements by running each variant without instrumentation, then without energy constraints, and finally in an "oracle" mode that predicts power losses and checkpoints at the last practicable opportunity (Section 5.1.2).

### 5.1.2 Baselines and Metrics for Comparison

Programs instrumented with Mementos differ in several key ways from their uninstrumented counterparts. First, they include additional code that provides checkpointing and restoration mechanisms. This extra code endows programs with robustness properties at a cost of storage space and available cycles at run time. Second, they can execute over multiple device lifecycles instead of restarting from the beginning with each failure. Third, they exhibit different behavior under different energy conditions; checkpoint sizes vary with stack size, and the point at which checkpointing begins varies with supply voltage. With these differences in mind, we adopt the metrics shown in Table 2.

A natural question is *what is the smallest number of CPU cycles in which a program can complete?* To determine the minimum number of CPU cycles required to execute each test case variant, we consider a scenario in which the simulated capacitor's voltage is held in the CPU's normal operating range. Under these circumstances, Mementos's voltage checks never trigger checkpointing and the program completes in a single lifecycle. It is easy to see that, for a given program, its run time against unlimited energy is a lower bound on its run time against any energy scenario. Table 3 gives results for all three test cases. For the instrumented variants,

| Metric | Description |
|---|---|
| Lifecycles | The number of reboots (including initial boot) required to complete the program |
| Total cycle count | The number of CPU cycles required to complete the program over all lifecycles |
| Mementos cycles | Percentage of total cycle count spent in Mementos code |
| Waste | Percentage of total cycles that occurred between the last checkpoint in a lifecycle and the subsequent power loss |

**Table 2.** Metrics for evaluation.

the program spends a nonzero number of cycles executing energy checks at trigger points. The differences in percentage of cycles spent in Mementos are due to the prevalence of different control-flow structures in the test cases.

| Instr. Type | `crc` / % | `sense` / % | `rsa64` / % |
|---|---|---|---|
| Uninstr. | 575,315 / — | 157,635 / — | 70,218 / — |
| Loop latches | 619,450 / 6.9 | 284,795 / 44.3 | 303,250 / 76.2 |
| Fn. returns | 577,702 / 0.2 | 201,151 / 21.9 | 214,177 / 66.5 |
| Timer+latches | 598,171 / 3.4 | 166,375 / 4.5 | 78,914 / 8.6 |

**Table 3.** Cycle counts (and percentage of cycles spent in Mementos code) for three Mementos test cases under an *unlimited-energy* scenario, i.e., voltage always above $V_{\text{thresh}}$. This table illustrates the base cost of Mementos's energy checks at run time.

**Versus an Energy Oracle.** Another natural question is *what is the minimum number of lifecycles over which a program's execution can spread?* If energy is scarce, lifecycles may occur infrequently and the difference between $k$ and $k+1$ lifecycles may be vast. To establish a baseline for evaluation, we implemented an *oracle mode* for the simulator. In oracle mode, the simulator accepts an *uninstrumented* program that has been linked against Mementos. It monitors the simulated capacitor's voltage during the program's execution and, for each power lifecycle, initiates checkpointing at the last practicable opportunity—i.e., when allowing the voltage to fall any farther would result in an incomplete checkpoint. Given the difficulty of predicting power loss events at run time (Section 3), the simulator uses a binary search strategy to adjust its notion of "last practicable" over repeated executions of each lifecycle.

Because programs executed in oracle mode are uninstrumented, they contain no trigger points and no automatically inserted calls to the checkpointing function. The build process splices Mementos's restoration code in front of the program's original `main()` function to enable boot-time restoration from saved checkpoints.

The oracle mode's main benefit is establishing a lower bound on the number of lifecycles and CPU cycles a program needs to complete under a given energy condition, e.g. a trace in the simulator. An ancillary benefit is that the oracle mode guides the implementer in selecting a fixed voltage threshold $V_{\text{thresh}}$. As the simulator runs in oracle mode, it reports the last practicable threshold voltage discovered for each lifecycle. If the implementer can provide a representative voltage trace to the simulator, then choosing a $V_{\text{thresh}}$ suitable for the application is a matter of observing the oracle mode's reported cutoff voltages and choosing a slightly higher value.

Table 4 shows results obtained in oracle mode under *variable voltage* (rather than the fixed high voltage of Table 3). The cycle counts and lifecycle counts in the table should be considered lower bounds on those metrics for instrumented versions.

**Fixed overhead.** Mementos adds space overhead in two ways: by increasing code size and by reserving two flash segments (1 KB total on the MSP430) for checkpoint storage. Without compiler optimizations for code size, Mementos increases executable size

| | `crc` | `sense` | `rsa64` |
|---|---|---|---|
| Decay-only | 621,501 (8) | 197,215 (3) | 70,886 (1) |
| Trace #1 | 685,555 (15) | 308,986 (7) | 179,626 (4) |
| #2 | 685,150 (15) | 304,678 (6) | 158,187 (3) |
| #3 | 685,801 (15) | 308,724 (7) | 219,970 (5) |
| #4 | 685,641 (15) | 288,063 (6) | 157,438 (3) |
| #5 | 685,096 (15) | 840,594 (16) | 153,181 (3) |
| #6 | 685,099 (15) | 287,876 (6) | 139,211 (3) |
| #7 | 683,884 (15) | 287,573 (6) | 180,195 (4) |
| #8 | 685,005 (15) | 287,741 (6) | 139,840 (3) |
| #9 | 685,608 (15) | 287,422 (6) | 157,613 (3) |
| #10 | 685,045 (15) | 287,927 (6) | 158,805 (3) |

**Table 4.** Oracle-mode lower bounds [CPU cycles (lifecycles)] for three test cases against ten voltage traces and decay-only mode. For the `crc` test case, the mean proportion of cycles spent in Mementos code was $24.5 \pm 1.3\%$; for `sense`, $49.1 \pm 11.0\%$; for `rsa64`, $56.6 \pm 5.6\%$.

by a constant amount (just under 2.4 KB) plus 4 bytes per trigger point. While a 2.4 KB increase in code size accounts for 30% of the code memory on our prototype, the sibling chips used in newer RFID-scale devices have much more code space (up to 116 KB) and nearly identical energy characteristics.

We used an oscilloscope to precisely time flash and ADC operations on a WISP prototype, then confirmed that the simulator matched the measured values exactly. Each trigger point that uses the ADC to check voltage consumes 647 clock cycles (647 $\mu$s at 1 MHz). Checkpoint operations consume 105 $\mu$s per 16-bit word written, plus the aforementioned ADC cost for the trigger point, plus several hundred cycles for bookkeeping (depending on the number of currently stored checkpoints). When Mementos must erase a flash segment, the erasure takes 13,062 $\mu$s. Matching these timings with corresponding electrical current measurements gives us confidence that the simulator's behavior is accurate.

### 5.1.3 Performance and Overhead

Via experiments on our test cases in the simulator and on WISP hardware, we find that Mementos satisfies the design goal of splitting program execution across multiple lifecycles with intervening power losses.

For a given voltage trace and test case, the performance of Mementos along all of our metrics depends on the compile-time choice of voltage threshold $V_{\text{thresh}}$. There are natural bounds on practicable values for this variable. From above, $V_{\text{thresh}}$ is practically bounded by the wakeup threshold $V_{\text{w}}$ at which the platform boots after a power failure. If $V_{\text{thresh}} \geq V_{\text{w}}$, Mementos will in the worst case begin checkpointing the first time a trigger point is encountered. From below, $V_{\text{thresh}}$ is strictly bounded by the minimum flash-write voltage, but a higher application-specific threshold effectively lower-bounds $V_{\text{thresh}}$ because incomplete checkpoints are not restorable.

For an example of how the above bounds apply, consider the `crc` test case and a particular voltage trace (#9). Uninstrumented, the test case fails to complete against the trace because it cannot sustain computation for long enough. According to the simulator's oracle mode (Table 4), the minimum number of lifecycles required to run the test case to completion against trace #9 is 15. With loop latches instrumented, the test case runs to completion in 17 or more lifecycles depending on the fixed voltage value $V_{\text{thresh}}$. With function-return instrumentation, the test case fails to complete against the trace: the computation's work loop does not use function calls to transfer control flow, so there are no function returns to instrument until the main loop completes. With timer-controlled loop-latch instrumentation, the test case fails to complete against

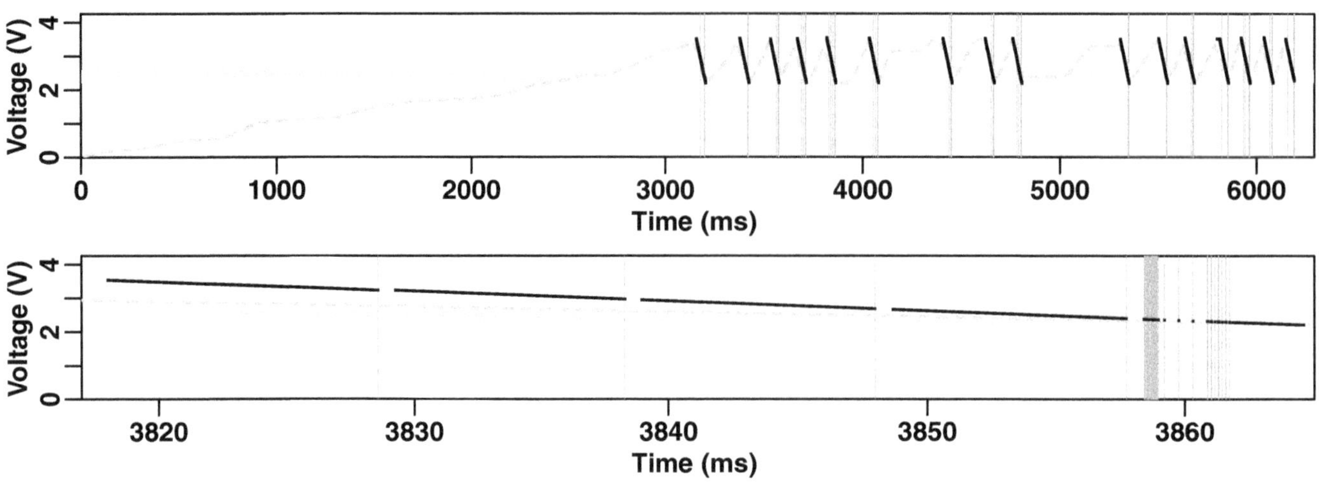


**Figure 4.** Simulated voltage versus time as Mementos spreads the execution of the `crc` test case across 17 power lifecycles (16 resets) against a voltage trace (#9). The bottom plot highlights a single power lifecycle from the top plot.

the trace because of infelicitous timing (the voltage when the timer fired was too low for a subsequent checkpoint to complete).

Figure 4 depicts a complete execution of the `crc` test case against the same voltage trace (#9) in the simulator. The simulated capacitor charges (dotted gray line) when the input voltage increases and discharges (solid black line) during computation and storage. When capacitor voltage falls into the shaded region between $V_{\text{thresh}}$ (set to 2.6 V at compile time) and the CPU's minimum voltage for flash writes (2.2 V), Mementos checkpoints. Mementos uses the CPU (vertical lines) to check energy, find space for checkpoints, collect state, and write state to flash. Gaps in the trace are due to waiting for hardware peripherals (flash and ADC).

Table 5 shows the relationships among $V_{\text{thresh}}$, Mementos's share of CPU cycles, and waste for the `sense` test case instrumented in each of Mementos's modes. For brevity, we delve into detail for only a single test case and only two energy conditions. The top half of the table gives results for *decay-only* mode, in which the capacitor's energy is set to a fixed level and no more energy is delivered until the next lifecycle. The bottom half of the table gives results for a voltage trace (#9) that elicits representative behavior. Without Mementos instrumentation and given unlimited energy, the `sense` test case requires 157,635 CPU cycles to complete. However, when run against any of our voltage traces, the uninstrumented program cannot complete because it never receives enough energy to run for long enough; this uninstrumented program satisfies our definition of a *Sisyphean task.*

Mementos spreads the `sense` task across multiple lifecycles, but it increases the total number of CPU cycles needed for program completion. In oracle mode, the simulator reports that, if Mementos checkpoints at the last practicable opportunity in each lifecycle, the program can complete in 3 lifecycles and 197,215 CPU cycles, an increase of 25.1% over the uninstrumented program. Varying the compile-time $V_{\text{thresh}}$ and (in timer-aided mode) the timer interval, we find that Mementos adds between 65.4% and 360.0% CPU cycles over the uninstrumented program. We infer from Table 5 that $V_{\text{thresh}}$ is effectively lower-bounded by 2.6 V; the oracle-mode log confirms that the oracle began its last-minute checkpointing at 2.61 and 2.64 V in the two lifecycles before program completion. The evident difference between loop-latch and function-return modes in this scenario is that, while loop-latch mode can accommodate a lower $V_{\text{thresh}}$ with its more frequent trigger points on this loop-structured program, function-return mode requires fewer CPU cycles and lifecycles when it is applicable. We also see that timer mode, in which trigger points at loop latches are activated only when a timer interrupt raises a flag, offers a tradeoff: a program may require less time to complete, but a suboptimal value for the timer interval can introduce unexpected timing-related failures.

Against a specific voltage trace (#9), oracle mode reports that the `sense` test case requires at least 6 lifecycles and 287,422 CPU cycles; the last-minute checkpointing voltage thresholds it found were between 2.58 V and 2.62 V. Table 5 shows the effects of automatically varying the instrumentation mode and timer interval over a series of simulated runs. It shows that Mementos adds at least 64.7% CPU cycles over the uninstrumented program. Table 5 also illustrates a hazard of choosing a fixed $V_{\text{thresh}}$ value too close to upper bound of the oracle's reported last-minute voltage threshold choices: at $V_{\text{thresh}} = 2.6$ V, the latch-instrumented program makes progress only when it runs against certain felicitous portions of the voltage trace; none of the other instrumentation modes allow the program to complete. At $V_{\text{thresh}} = 2.8$ V, the program completes in all tested instrumentation modes, and it becomes evident that the program's structure lends itself to function-return instrumentation as well as loop-latch instrumentation. At $V_{\text{thresh}} = 3.0$ V, the program's run time increases because Mementos begins checkpointing earlier in any given lifecycle, and the timer-aided latch-instrumented program begins to evince an advantage over the plain latch-instrumented program because of less-frequent checkpointing. At higher $V_{\text{thresh}}$ values, the non-timer-aided modes fail to complete in fewer than 500 lifecycles because the time between checkpoint restoration and subsequent checkpointing leaves little time for computational progress. A reasonable interpretation of Table 5 is that a fixed value of 3.0 V for $V_{\text{thresh}}$ is appropriate for the `sense` test case if energy conditions are not known in advance; in this case a programmer can reasonably expect the Mementos-instrumented computation to complete within twice the number of lifecycles that the oracle reports.

### 5.2 Mementos on Hardware

We have tested Mementos on a WISP (revision 4.1) prototype like those described in Section 4. Running Mementos on this prototype device required only one small hardware change: we substituted a readily available 2.8 V voltage regulator for the supplied 1.8 V regulator in order to meet the nominal minimum voltage requirement to write to the MSP430's on-chip flash memory. (Other prototype

| $V_{thresh}$ | Loop-latch mode *lifecycles (cycles / %waste / %M)* | Function-return mode | Timer-aided mode interval ($\mu$s) 20,000 | 40,000 |
|---|---|---|---|---|
| 2.4 V | — | — | — | — |
| 2.6 | — | — | — | — |
| 2.8 | 7 (502,576 / 6.8 / 63.9) | — | 4 (298,890 / 52.8 / 21.2) | — |
| 3.0 | 8 (586,788 / 12.6 / 68.6) | 5 (368,255 / 13.0 / 52.9) | 4 (298,890 / 52.8 / 21.2) | — |
| 3.2 | 9 (671,849 / 7.2 / 72.1) | 6 (429,754 / 2.6 / 58.4) | 4 (260,796 / 2.6 / 34.5) | — |
| 3.4 | 9 (725,214 / 15.9 / 73.3) | 6 (453,827 / 16.5 / 59.8) | 5 (361,471 / 4.6 / 49.1) | 4 (314,181 / 20.4 / 27.8) |
| 2.4 | — | — | — | — |
| 2.6 | 89 (5,235,399 / 89.4 / 64.2) | — | — | — |
| 2.8 | 13 (708,641 / 10.5 / 71.3) | 11 (557,164 / 10.8 / 63.7) | 53 (2,779,635 / 70.7 / 32.8) | 22 (1,044,242 / 70.8 / 29.5) |
| 3 | 46 (2,852,111 / 20.4 / 81.6) | 16 (843,093 / 22.6 / 73.4) | 10 (473,396 / 13.8 / 55.1) | 31 (1,421,150 / 77.9 / 29.7) |
| 3.2 | — | — | 10 (489,739 / 13.5 / 55.3) | 15 (702,151 / 56.6 / 29.4) |
| 3.4 | — | — | — | 22 (1,194,221 / 30.0 / 58.3) |

**Table 5.** In decay-only mode (top half) and against a voltage trace (#9, bottom half), the `sense` test case exhibits behavior that is dependent on the voltage threshold $V_{\texttt{thresh}}$ and, in timer-aided mode, the timer interval. *%M* refers to the portion of CPU cycles spent within Mementos code. This table illustrates the key differences among Mementos's various instrumentation modes.

RFID-scale devices, including others in the WISP family, regulate the chip's voltage at the required level, so we expect this substitution to be unnecessary except in the case of this prototype.)

We added to Mementos a simple hardware signaling mechanism using several of the WISP's general-purpose I/O pins; toggling these pins at run time allowed us to observe Mementos's basic activity at run time. We observe via the signaling mechanism that Mementos successfully completes simple computations that span multiple lifecycles, but we omit results comparing hardware runs of our test cases to simulator runs because the poorly suited 2.8 V regulator dominates the platform's energy consumption—its high static power consumption roughly halves the lifecycle duration.

### 5.3 Improvements

We suggest—but do not evaluate, for brevity—several improvements to Mementos that may improve its performance. Code for these improvements is available with the Mementos distribution unless noted otherwise.

**Techniques to reduce trigger point frequency.** As we observed above for the `crc` test case, Mementos's loop latch instrumentation can result in excessively frequent trigger points when applied to loops with small bodies and large trip counts. Detecting small loop bodies and large trip counts, whether via static analysis or profiling or a combination, may prove useful toward reducing Mementos's share of CPU cycles.

**Compression.** Reducing checkpoint sizes has been a concern for previous checkpointing systems; past approaches have included memory exclusion [32] and straightforward file compression via external programs. On an RFID-scale device with flash memory that is expensive to write and erase, Mementos should minimize checkpoint sizes to minimize the cost of writing them (and the amortized cost of erasing them). However, Mementos is designed to run without an operating system or file system, and we found that most implementations of well-known compression algorithms were too large to fit in our devices' limited code space.

Because many programs do not use all available registers, one promising but not fully implemented scheme compresses the register file by using a 16-bit bitmask to indicate which of the CPU's 16 registers are zero valued. During checkpointing, Mementos walks the register file, builds the bitmap, and avoids storing any registers that are zero valued.

We have also considered compressing full checkpoints instead of just the register file; all of the options predictably trade checkpoint size for run time. Our simulator saves checkpoints to files as it validates them, so we used checkpoint files as inputs to compression algorithms running in a separate MSP430 simulator. We implemented a reduced variant of the WK compression algorithm [19] but found that, while it reduced checkpoint sizes by an average of 55% for the `crc` example, it required 3.5 times as many CPU cycles as it would have taken to write the full checkpoint to flash. We implemented a variant of the popular LZ compression algorithm and found that it reduced checkpoint sizes 30% more than WK but was 18 times slower than simply writing the checkpoint to flash.

A third type of compression, not yet implemented, is incremental compression of checkpoints. We have not yet implemented incremental compression because of the complexity of computing incremental updates in a small memory footprint at run time, but the idea is promising—often the changes between two successive loop iterations, for example, are small. Additional compile-time analysis combined with per-trigger-point adjustments might make incremental checkpointing feasible in a future version of Mementos.

**Run-time adaptations.** As the rest of Section 5 illustrates in detail, compile-time tuning of Mementos's parameters can significantly change its behavior. We have designed several schemes by which Mementos could adapt its behavior at run time based on its measurement of key metrics. For example, to avoid executing time- and energy-intensive flash erasures at the beginning of lifecycles, Mementos could decrease the frequency of failed checkpoints by including in each checkpoint header the current value of the checkpoint threshold voltage. If Mementos notices an aborted checkpoint, it can adjust the checkpoint threshold voltage as appropriate. A similar technique might enable Mementos to gradually minimize the amount of wasted work at run time to approach the results of oracle-mode simulations.

We have not designed an energy prediction model for Mementos's run-time system because we assume that such a scheme would be prohibitively time intensive. Relaxing some of our assumptions about unpredictability might lead us to develop lightweight prediction schemes—integer versions of first- and second-order voltage trend approximations, for example—that could allow Mementos to avoid checkpointing if it believes power failure is not imminent.

**Sleeping when appropriate.** Most microcontrollers have RAM-retention modes that retain processor state and the contents of volatile memory. Such modes typically require two orders of magnitude less electrical current than active-mode computation, which slows—but does not stop—capacitor drain. We designed Mementos to be useful when energy delivery is arbitrarily sporadic. Some energy-harvesting mechanisms, such as solar panels, exhibit sudden or prolonged periods of harvesting nothing; in this case, Mementos's strategy of checkpointing to nonvolatile memory would be more suitable than simply entering RAM-retention mode. However, we suspect that a hybrid approach incorporating both RAM retention and nonvolatile checkpoints would be a fruitful avenue for improvements to Mementos.

# 6. Discussion and Future Work

In this section, we discuss some alternatives to Mementos that an application developer might consider. We then suggest some future extensions to Mementos.

## 6.1 Alternative approaches

As discussed previously, traditional RFID-scale devices provide system designers with three options: use only trivially simple programs, require users to provide adequate power, or add state-saving logic to application code. Mementos uses automatic checkpointing to expand the use of RFID-scale devices beyond simplistic computation—without placing additional requirements on the user or the programmer. In addition to checkpointing, we have also considered other approaches to attain these goals.

Applications permitting, computations might instead be shortened using profiling and quality-of-service (QoS) information [1, 28]. These techniques make sense only for applications that tolerate lossy or noisy results, and would require more accurate predictions of power failures. To remain general, Mementos does not include these program transformations, though they are trivially compatible provided that Mementos's instrumentation points are preserved.

Another approach would perform long-running computation on a more powerful device (e.g. a Linux-based RFID reader), rather than the more constrained RFID-scale device. While this removes many impediments, it imposes others. To save power, prototype RFID-scale devices use low-throughput radio mechanisms, including software-controlled backscatter, that limit radio throughput. In security-sensitive applications, outsourcing cryptographic operations may violate security requirements, and existing techniques for outsourcing computation to untrusted infrastructure [15] still require a nontrivial amount of work on the client.

Finally, some CPU-intensive computations such as cryptography can be executed on dedicated peripheral hardware instead of a general-purpose microcontroller. Hardware acceleration allows some operations to complete more quickly but removes the flexibility afforded by reprogrammable microcontrollers. To remain general, Mementos does not assume that such peripherals are available.

## 6.2 Future Hardware

Moore's Law does not have an analogue for batteries [31], and increasing energy storage will likely continue to add significant bulk and weight. Since larger energy storage also makes devices less responsive—they take more time to charge—we expect RFID-scale devices to continue to have small energy buffers akin to today's capacitors.

While Mementos is currently implemented to use widely available flash memory, other types of nonvolatile memory may be better suited to frequent checkpointing in the future. Flash cells can tolerate 10,000 to 1 million erasures before becoming unusable. Information coding schemes that allow rewrites without erasures [4] might extend a system's lifetime; however, alternatives like phase-change memory (PCM), magneto-resistive RAM (MRAM) and ferroelectic RAM (FeRAM) all promise fewer complications. Our initial experiments with EEPROM storage on a prototype WISP indicate that its energy characteristics are similar to flash memory's, but EEPROM reads are significantly slower. Still, EEPROM or other auxiliary storage may be useful for storing small pieces of metadata without necessitating coarse-grained erasures.

## 6.3 Future Work

A key opportunity for improvement lies in making Mementos more adaptive. Each binary linked against Mementos is currently subject to a single set of checkpointing parameters—checkpoint threshold voltage $V_{\text{thresh}}$ and (if applicable) timer interrupt interval—chosen by the programmer prior to run time based on simulation results. Instead of using a fixed configuration that may perform poorly when program behavior is highly variable or depends on environmental factors, future versions of Mementos will adaptively tune checkpointing behavior as described in Section 5.3.

# 7. Related Work

A wealth of research on checkpointing exists at various levels of computer systems. Most related approaches adopt a similar (if broader) approach to Mementos's: capture relevant program state. A key difference between Mementos and previous work is that, on RFID-scale devices, Mementos must consider catastrophic failure to be the *common case* and not an *occasional event*. We group related work into general checkpointing papers and papers related to tolerating failures on small-scale devices.

**Checkpointing.** We borrow our definition of *checkpointing* from Bernstein et al. [2], who define it as "an activity that writes information to stable storage during normal operation in order to reduce the amount of work [the system] has to do after a failure." Automatic checkpointing has long provided insurance against occasional failures. Systems in the 1980s and 1990s explored checkpointing for distributed systems [20, 26, 27], particularly for process migration or high-assurance computing. Checkpointing is especially useful for systems that handle precious data or make promises about fidelity, such as databases [2, 25] or file systems [37, 42].

Plank et al. [33] discuss checkpointing strategies in detail. Their portable *libckpt* library for UNIX implements both automatic (periodic, checkpoint-on-write) and user-directed checkpointing strategies. In the terminology of libckpt, Mementos implements *sequential* checkpointing, wherein the checkpointing procedure stops execution of the main program to capture its state. Like Mementos in timer-aided mode, libckpt automatically captures application state (registers and RAM) at a predefined frequency. Unlike Mementos, libckpt also supports *incremental* checkpointing by using page protection mechanisms to keep track of pages dirtied since the last checkpoint operation. We have not implemented a similar system because Mementos is designed to run directly on hardware.

Previous work has considered the use of static analysis and compile-time modifications to facilitate checkpointing. Compiler-assisted checkpointing systems [23, 24] require users to insert checkpointing cues into programs, unlike Mementos, although Mementos shares the notion of using compile-time instrumentation to make programs amenable to checkpointing. The Porch source-to-source compiler [41] enables programs to be suspended, migrated and resumed on different architectures. Porch uses compile-time analysis to generate program-specific checkpoint and resume functions specific to each possible stopping point. We consider Porch to be too heavyweight for Mementos's target platforms (owing to its lofty goals) although the checkpointing mechanism is similar.

Also relevant, perhaps surprisingly, are checkpointing systems that work on large-scale computers. These computers must tolerate frequent node failures, so job migration is a key feature. Bronevetsky et al. [3] propose a compile- and run-time system that modifies shared-memory programs and coordinates checkpointing and recovery among application threads. Their compiler techniques are essentially the same as Porch's and import the same differences versus Mementos.

**Checkpointing for small-scale devices.** Recent work in sensor networks considers the problem of whole-network checkpointing [30], using MSPsim for experimentation on continuously-powered sensor networks running the Contiki OS [13]. Their checkpointing mechanism saves the entire contents of a sensor node's memory, plus the state of several peripherals, via the node's serial port. A master node freezes and restores nodes using serial-port commands. Using an OS thread to save a complete memory dump is considerably simpler than Mementos; however, the required OS support for threads and the size of the resulting checkpoints make this approach impractical for RFID-scale devices.

The Neutron operating system [10], based on TinyOS [22], uses selective software restarts to mitigate the effects of software errors. Neutron allows programmers can mark "precious" state that must be preserved across software resets—but not across hardware reboots. Rather than requiring programmers to manually mark important state, Mementos favors an automatic approach. Mementos also does not require an operating system like TinyOS or Contiki. In our tests on a MSP430-based TinyNode [12], a vanilla TinyOS instance required $253.4 \pm 1.5$ ms to boot—much too slow to run a device that loses power every $\sim 100$ ms.

Specific to RFID-scale devices, Buettner et al. [5] describe WISP-based *RFID sensor networks* (RSNs) and the difficulty of predicting energy availability. They suggest, but do not implement, program splitting as an approach to execute large programs.

Chae et al. [9] implemented the RC5 block cipher on a WISP by carefully choosing parameters so that computations would finish in a single lifecycle. Mementos, aims to enable such resource-intensive programs to run to completion without requiring modifications to already-complex existing code.

Clark et al. [11] and Gummeson et al. [17] modify the WISP's hardware to increase its ability to survive power outages. Specifically, they experiment with larger capacitor sizes—which store more energy but take longer to charge—and auxiliary solar panels that together prolong the WISP's ability to retain state in low-power modes. Mementos eschews these hardware modifications for the sake of generality.

The flash storage mechanisms of Salajegheh et al. [38] treat flash memory as probabilistic "half-wits" and provide reliable writes to flash memory at voltages well below the nominal operating voltage specified by microcontrollers such as the MSP430. Mementos currently treats the nominal threshold values as hard boundaries; the half-wits result suggests that Mementos could relax those constraints to reliably write checkpoints to flash memory at voltages significantly below the 2.8 V threshold.

**Scheduling on computational RFIDs.** Buettner et al. integrate a voltage-aware task scheduler into the firmware of a WISP [7]. Given a measured voltage level, their scheduler selects a task from predefined set based on its stated resource requirements; they define tasks as small programs that can run to completion in a single lifecycle under reasonable energy conditions. Mementos instead focuses on completing a single task that might otherwise not complete in a single lifecycle.

## 8. Conclusions

Transiently powered RFID-scale devices enable general-purpose computation in scenarios where energy is scarce. However, the lack of a steady supply of energy results in frequent complete losses of power and state. Today, programmers either write short programs or hand-tune assembly code to ensure that computation finishes before a power loss—severely limiting the application space for these devices and making programming cumbersome and error prone.

Mementos addresses the challenge of enabling long-running programs to make steady progress on transiently powered devices. It instruments programs with energy checks at compile time and provides automatic state checkpointing and recovery at run time. A suite of simulation tools based on MSPsim enables a programmer to evaluate the behavior of Mementos-instrumented programs before deploying them.

Source code for Mementos, the simulator, and voltage traces for testing are available for download via the first author's web page.

## Acknowledgments

This material is supported by a Sloan Research Fellowship and the NSF under CNS-0627529, CNS-0845874, NSF CNS-0923313, and a Graduate Research Fellowship. Any opinions, findings, and conclusions expressed in this material are those of the authors and do not necessarily reflect the views of the NSF.

We thank John Brattin for code and discussions; Shane Clark for help with simulation; Mark Corner for providing resources; Michael Buettner, Chris Erway, and Quinn Stewart for feedback on drafts; Edwin Foo, Anton Korobeynikov, Dmitriy Matveev, and John Regehr for help with LLVM's MSP430 backend; Jeremy Gummeson and John Tuttle for conducting measurements; Scott Kaplan for advice on compression; Emery Berger for discussions; and Joshua Smith and Alanson Sample at Intel Labs Seattle for providing the WISP over the last three years.

We thank our shepherd, David Lie, for guidance and the anonymous ASPLOS reviewers for their helpful comments.

## References

[1] W. Baek and T. Chilimbi. Green: A system for supporting energy-conscious programming using principled abstractions. Technical Report MSR-TR-2009-89, Microsoft Research, July 2009.

[2] P. A. Bernstein, V. Hadzilacos, and N. Goodman. *Concurrency Control and Recovery in Database Systems*. Addison-Wesley, 1987. ISBN 0-201-10715-5.

[3] G. Bronevetsky, D. Marques, K. Pingali, P. K. Szwed, and M. Schulz. Application-level checkpointing for shared memory programs. In *Proc. 11th Int'l Conference on Architectural Support for Programming Languages and Operating Systems (ASPLOS-XI)*, pages 235–247. ACM, Oct. 2004.

[4] J. Bruck, A. Vardy, A. Jiang, E. Yaakobi, J. Wolf, R. Mateescu, and P. Siegel. Storage coding for wear leveling in flash memories. In *IEEE Int'l Symposium on Information Theory (ISIT '09)*, pages 1229–1233, June 2009.

[5] M. Buettner, B. Greenstein, A. Sample, J. R. Smith, and D. Wetherall. Revisiting smart dust with RFID sensor networks. In *Proc. 7th ACM Workshop on Hot Topics in Networks (HotNets-VII)*, Oct. 2008.

[6] M. Buettner, R. Prasad, M. Philipose, and D. Wetherall. Recognizing daily activities with rfid-based sensors. In *Proc. 11th Int'l Conference on Ubiquitous Computing (UbiComp '09)*, pages 51–60. ACM, Sept. 2009.

[7] M. Buettner, B. Greenstein, and D. Wetherall. Dewdrop: An energy-aware task scheduler for computational RFID. In *Proc. 8th USENIX Symposium on Networked Systems Design and Implementation (NSDI '11)*. USENIX Association, Mar. 2011. To appear.

[8] E. Candès, J. Romberg, and T. Tao. Robust uncertainty principles: Exact signal reconstruction from highly incomplete frequency information. *IEEE Transactions on Information Theory*, 52(2):489–509, Feb. 2006.

[9] H.-J. Chae, D. J. Yeager, J. R. Smith, and K. Fu. Maximalist cryptography and computation on the WISP UHF RFID tag. In *Proc. Conference on RFID Security*, July 2007.

[10] Y. Chen, O. Gnawali, M. Kazandjieva, P. Levis, and J. Regehr. Surviving sensor network software faults. In *Proc. ACM SIGOPS 22nd Symposium on Operating Systems Principles (SOSP '09)*, pages 235–246, Oct. 2009.

[11] S. S. Clark, J. Gummeson, K. Fu, and D. Ganesan. Towards autonomously-powered CRFIDs. In *Workshop on Power Aware Computing and Systems (HotPower '09)*, Oct. 2009.

[12] H. Dubois-Ferrière, L. Fabre, R. Meier, and P. Metrailler. TinyNode: a comprehensive platform for wireless sensor network applications. In *Proc. 5th Int'l Conference on Information Processing in Sensor Networks (IPSN '06)*, pages 358–365. ACM, Apr. 2006.

[13] A. Dunkels, B. Grönvall, and T. Voigt. Contiki—a lightweight and flexible operating system for tiny networked sensors. In *Proc. First IEEE Workshop on Embedded Networked Sensors (Emnets-I)*. IEEE Computer Society, Nov. 2004.

[14] J. Eriksson, A. Dunkels, N. Finne, F. Österlind, and T. Voigt. MSPsim—an extensible simulator for MSP430-equipped sensor boards. In *Proc. 4th European Conference on Wireless Sensor Networks (EWSN '07), Poster/Demo session*. Springer, Jan. 2007.

[15] R. Gennaro, C. Gentry, and B. Parno. Non-interactive verifiable computing: Outsourcing computation to untrusted workers. In *Advances in Cryptology—CRYPTO 2010*, volume 6223 of *Lecture Notes in Computer Science*, pages 465–482. Springer, Aug. 2010.

[16] M. Gorlatova, P. Kinget, I. Kymissis, D. Rubenstein, X. Wang, and G. Zussman. Challenge: Ultra-low-power Energy-Harvesting Active Networked Tags (EnHANTs). In *Proc. 15th Annual Int'l Conference on Mobile Computing and Networking (MobiCom '09)*, pages 253–260. ACM, Sept. 2009.

[17] J. Gummeson, S. S. Clark, K. Fu, and D. Ganesan. On the limits of effective micro-energy harvesting on mobile CRFID sensors. In *Proc. 8th Annual ACM/USENIX Int'l Conference on Mobile Systems, Applications, and Services (MobiSys '10)*. ACM, June 2010.

[18] P. Horowitz and W. Hill. *The Art of Electronics*. Cambridge University Press, 1989. ISBN 0-521-37095-7.

[19] S. F. Kaplan. *Compressed caching and modern virtual memory simulation*. PhD thesis, University of Texas at Austin, Dec. 1999.

[20] R. Koo and S. Toueg. Checkpointing and rollback-recovery for distributed systems. In *Proceedings of 1986 ACM Fall Joint Computer Conference (ACM '86)*, pages 1150–1158. IEEE Computer Society, 1986.

[21] C. Lattner and V. Adve. LLVM: A compilation framework for lifelong program analysis & transformation. In *Proc. 2004 Int'l Symposium on Code Generation and Optimization (CGO'04)*. ACM, Mar. 2004.

[22] P. Levis, S. Madden, J. Polastre, R. Szewczyk, K. Whitehouse, A. Woo, D. Gay, J. Hill, M. Welsh, E. Brewer, and D. Culler. TinyOS: An operating system for sensor networks. In *Ambient Intelligence*. Springer Verlag, 2004.

[23] C. Li and W. Fuchs. CATCH—Compiler-assisted techniques for checkpointing. In *Digest of Papers, 20th Int'l Symposium on Fault-Tolerant Computing (FTCS-20)*, pages 74–81. IEEE, June 1990.

[24] C. Li, E. Stewart, and W. Fuchs. Compiler-assisted full checkpointing. *Software: Practice & Experience*, 24(10):871–886, 1994.

[25] J.-L. Lin, M. H. Dunham, and M. A. Nascimento. A survey of distributed database checkpointing. *Distributed and Parallel Databases*, 5(3):289–319, July 1997.

[26] M. J. Litzkow, M. Livny, and M. W. Mutka. Condor—a hunter of idle workstations. In *Proc. 8th Int'l Conference on Distributed Computing Systems (ICDCS '88)*, pages 104–111. IEEE Computer Society, June 1988.

[27] J. A. McDermid. Checkpointing and error recovery in distributed systems. In *Proc. 2nd Int'l Conference on Distributed Computing Systems (ICDCS '81)*, pages 271–282. IEEE Computer Society, 1981.

[28] S. Misailovic, S. Sidiroglou, H. Hoffman, and M. C. Rinard. Quality of service profiling. In *Proc. 32nd ACM/IEEE Int'l Conference on Software Engineering (ICSE '10)*. ACM, May 2010.

[29] J. Olivo, S. Carrara, and G. D. Micheli. Energy harvesting and remote powering for implantable biosensors. *IEEE Sensors Journal*, PP(99), October 2010.

[30] F. Österlind, A. Dunkels, T. Voigt, N. Tsiftes, J. Eriksson, and N. Finne. Sensornet checkpointing: Enabling repeatability in testbeds and realism in simulators. In *Proc. 6th European Conference on Wireless Sensor Networks (EWSN '09)*. Springer, Feb. 2009.

[31] J. A. Paradiso and T. Starner. Energy scavenging for mobile and wireless electronics. *IEEE Pervasive Computing*, 4(1):18–27, 2005.

[32] J. S. Plank, M. Beck, and G. Kingsley. Compiler-assisted memory exclusion for fast checkpointing. *IEEE Technical Committee on Operating Systems and Application Environments*, 7(4):10–14, Winter 1995.

[33] J. S. Plank, M. Beck, G. Kingsley, and K. Li. Libckpt: Transparent checkpointing under Unix. In *Proc. USENIX 1995 Technical Conference on UNIX and Advanced Computing Systems*, pages 213–223, Jan. 1995.

[34] P. Plauger. Embedded C++: An Overview. *Embedded Systems Programming*, 10:40–53, 1997.

[35] J. Polastre, R. Szewczyk, and D. Culler. Telos: Enabling ultra-low power wireless research. In *Proc. 4th Int'l Symposium on Information Processing in Sensor Networks: Special track on Platform Tools and Design Methods for Network Embedded Sensors (IPSN/SPOTS '05)*. IEEE, Apr. 2005.

[36] B. Ransford, S. Clark, M. Salajegheh, and K. Fu. Getting things done on computational RFIDs with energy-aware checkpointing and voltage-aware scheduling. In *USENIX Workshop on Power Aware Computing and Systems (HotPower '08)*, Dec. 2008.

[37] M. Rosenblum and J. K. Ousterhout. The design and implementation of a log-structured file system. *ACM Transactions on Computer Systems (TOCS)*, 10(1):26–52, 1992.

[38] M. Salajegheh, Y. Wang, K. Fu, A. A. Jiang, and E. Learned-Miller. Exploiting half-wits: Smarter storage for low-power devices. In *Proc. 9th USENIX Conference on File and Storage Technologies (FAST '11)*, Feb. 2011. To appear.

[39] A. P. Sample, D. J. Yeager, P. S. Powledge, A. V. Mamishev, and J. R. Smith. Design of an RFID-based battery-free programmable sensing platform. *IEEE Transactions on Instrumentation and Measurement*, 57(11):2608–2615, Nov. 2008.

[40] J. Sorber, A. Kostadinov, M. Garber, M. Brennan, M. D. Corner, and E. D. Berger. Eon: A language and runtime system for perpetual systems. In *Proceedings of The Fifth Int'l ACM Conference on Embedded Networked Sensor Systems (SenSys '07)*, pages 161–174, Nov. 2007.

[41] V. Strumpen. Portable and fault-tolerant software systems. *IEEE Micro*, 18(5):22–32, 1998.

[42] S. Sundararaman, S. Subramanian, A. Rajimwale, A. C. Arpaci-Dusseau, R. H. Arpaci-Dusseau, and M. M. Swift. Membrane: Operating system support for restartable file systems. In *Proc. 8th USENIX Conference on File and Storage Technologies (FAST '10)*, Feb. 2010.

[43] Texas Instruments Incorporated. MSP430 Ultra-Low Power Microcontrollers. http://www.ti.com/msp430.

[44] S. Thomas, J. Teizer, and M. Reynolds. Electromagnetic energy harvesting for sensing, communication, and actuation. In *Proc. 27th Int'l Symposium on Automation and Robotics in Construction (ISARC '10)*. IAARC, June 2010.

[45] Y. Yang, L. Wang, D. K. Noh, H. K. Le, and T. F. Abdelzaher. SolarStore: Enhancing data reliability in solar-powered storage-centric sensor networks. In *Proc. 7th Annual Int'l Conference on Mobile Systems, Applications, and Services (MobiSys '09)*, pages 333–346. ACM, 2009.

[46] D. Yeager, F. Zhang, A. Zarrasvand, N. George, T. Daniel, and B. Otis. A 9 $\mu$a, addressable Gen2 sensor tag for biosignal acquisition. *IEEE Journal of Solid-State Circuits*, 45(10):2198–2209, Oct. 2010.

[47] E. Yeatman. Advances in power sources for wireless sensor nodes. In *Proc. Int'l Workshop on Wearable and Implantable Body Sensor Networks (BSN '04)*, pages 20–21. IEEE Computer Society, Apr. 2004.

# Pocket Cloudlets

Emmanouil Koukoumidis
Princeton University
Princeton, NJ, USA
ekoukoum@princeton.edu

Dimitrios Lymberopoulos
Microsoft Research
Redmond, WA, USA
dlymper@microsoft.com

Karin Strauss
Microsoft Research
Redmond, WA, USA
kstrauss@microsoft.com

Jie Liu
Microsoft Research
Redmond, WA, USA
liuj@microsoft.com

Doug Burger
Microsoft Research
Redmond, WA, USA
dburger@microsoft.com

## Abstract

Cloud services accessed through mobile devices suffer from high network access latencies and are constrained by energy budgets dictated by the devices' batteries. Radio and battery technologies will improve over time, but are still expected to be the bottlenecks in future systems. Non-volatile memories (NVM), however, may continue experiencing significant and steady improvements in density for at least ten more years. In this paper, we propose to leverage the abundance in memory capacity of mobile devices to mitigate latency and energy issues when accessing cloud services.

We first analyze NVM technology scaling trends, and then propose a cloud service cache architecture that resides on the mobile device's NVM (pocket cloudlet). This architecture utilizes both individual user and community access models to maximize its hit rate, and subsequently reduce overall service latency and energy consumption.

As a showcase we present the design, implementation and evaluation of PocketSearch, a search and advertisement pocket cloudlet. We perform mobile search characterization to guide the design of PocketSearch and evaluate it with 200 million mobile queries from the search logs of `m.bing.com`. We show that PocketSearch can serve, on average, 66% of the web search queries submitted by an individual user without having to use the slow 3G link, leading to 16x service access speedup.

Finally, based on experience with PocketSearch we provide additional insight and guidelines on how future pocket cloudlets should be organized, from both an architectural and an operating system perspective.

***Categories and Subject Descriptors*** H.4 [*Information Systems Applications*]: Miscellaneous

***General Terms*** Design, Experimentation

***Keywords*** Mobile Search, Mobile Cloud, Flash Storage



## 1. Introduction

The wide availability of internet access on mobile devices, such as phones and personal media players, has allowed users to access various cloud services while on the go. Currently, there are 54.5 million mobile internet users and market analysis shows that this number will increase to 95 million by 2013 [22], indicating that mobile devices are quickly becoming the dominant computing platform. As a result, optimizing these devices to better support access to cloud services becomes critical.

Although most cloud services have been designed to transparently support a wide range of client devices, the end user experience for these services can vary significantly across devices. Conversely to the desktop domain where the connection to any cloud service takes place over very fast and almost always available links (*i.e.*, ethernet), in the mobile domain users rely on cellular radios that tend to exhibit higher latency and unpredictability. For instance, most desktop computers can submit a search query to the search engine and successfully receive the search results in less than a second. The same task on a high-end smartphone with a 3G connection can take at least one order of magnitude more time (3 to 10 seconds depending on location, device and operator used). When the 3G radio is not connected or only Edge connectivity is available, this time can be doubled or even tripled.

Even as the throughput of radio links on mobile devices increases (*e.g.*, 4G), the user response time for the various cloud services will not be drastically improved for two reasons. First, while higher throughput links can be particularly effective for bulk transfers, recent studies [8] have shown that users tend to exchange small data packets, making link latency be the major bottleneck. Second, the radio link needs between 1.5 and 2 seconds to wake up from its standby mode even if it is already connected to the cell tower. This high startup cost is independent of the radio's throughput and is expected to hold even for future generations of radio links.

Radio links impose not only a latency bottleneck, but also a power bottleneck. Mobile devices are battery operated and the cellular radio, along with the processor and the screen, is one of the most power hungry components. The more data is exchanged and the more time the radio link is active, the lower the battery lifetime of the mobile device becomes, creating a negative user experience.

While there is such a large speed gap in accessing the internet between mobile devices and desktops, the traditional memory/storage gap between these two classes of devices is rapidly fading away. Phones and personal music players currently support up to 64GB of flash memory and future flash technologies

**Figure 1.** The GUI of the PocketSearch prototype. Local search results/ads are instantly displayed in the auto-suggest box as the user types the query. The GUI of the web search prototype is not shown due to space constraints.

promise much higher capacities (Section 2). The increasingly available memory resources on these devices can transform the way mobile cloud services are structured. As more and more information can be stored on mobile devices, specific parts of or even full cloud services could be transferred to the actual mobile devices, transforming them into *pocket cloudlets*.

Pocket cloudlets could drastically improve the mobile user experience in three major ways. First, since all or portions of the information resides on the phone, users can instantly get access to the information they are looking for, eliminating, when possible, the latency and power bottleneck introduced by the cellular radio. Furthermore, by serving user requests on the actual device, pocket cloudlets can mitigate pressure on cellular networks, which is expected to be a critical resource as mobile internet grows. Second, since most of the interactions between the user and the service take place on the mobile device, it is easier to personalize the service according to the behavior and usage patterns of individual users. Third, since the service resides on the phone, all the personalization information could also be stored on the phone and possibly protect the privacy of individual users.

For instance, in the case of a search engine, a large part of the web index, ad index and local business index can be stored on the phone enabling users to instantly access search results locally without having to use the cloud. In essence, a mini search engine could be running on the phone providing real-time search results to the mobile user. In another setting, the actual web content could also be cached on the mobile device to provide an instant browsing experience. Web content that might be of interest to the user could be automatically downloaded to the user's phone overnight and become available during the course of the day.

Independently of what cloud service is replicated on the mobile device, pocket cloudlets enable a fast and personalized mobile user experience. In this paper we describe a new architecture of mobile cloud services that takes advantage of the increasing non-volatile memory sizes to alleviate the latency and power bottlenecks introduced by cellular radios on mobile devices. First, we show an analysis on how NVM capacity is expected to increase in the future. Then we propose the pocket cloudlet architecture that leverages both community and user behavior to provide an instant mobile user experience reducing, when possible, overall service latency and energy consumption.

We then present in detail the design, implementation and evaluation of PocketSearch, a pocket cloudlet that replicates a search and advertisement engine on an actual phone. We analyze 200 million queries to understand how mobile users search on their phones, and then utilize the results of this analysis to guide the design of PocketSearch. Using a prototype implementation (Figure 1) and real search query streams extracted from mobile search logs of `m.bing.com`, we show that PocketSearch is able to successfully serve, on average, 66% of all web search queries submitted by an individual user. The benefits are twofold. From the user perspective,two thirds of the queries can be answered within 400ms, which is 16 times faster when compared to querying through the 3G link. From the search engine perspective, two thirds of the query load can be eliminated resulting in significant cost savings and easier query load balancing during peak times.

| | Flash | | | | Other NVM technology | | | | |
|---|---|---|---|---|---|---|---|---|---|
| year | '10 | '12 | '14 | '16 | '18 | '20 | '22 | '24 | '26 |
| tech (nm) | 32 | 22 | 16 | 11 | 11 | 8 | 5 | 5 | 5 |
| scaling factor | 1 | 2 | 4 | 8 | 8 | 16 | 32 | 32 | 32 |
| chip stack | 4 | 4 | 6 | 6 | 8 | 8 | 12 | 12 | 16 |
| cell layers | 1 | 1 | 1 | 2 | 2 | 4 | 4 | 8 | 8 |
| bits per cell | 2 | 3 | 2 | 2 | 2 | 1 | 1 | 1 | 1 |

**Table 1.** Technology scaling trends.

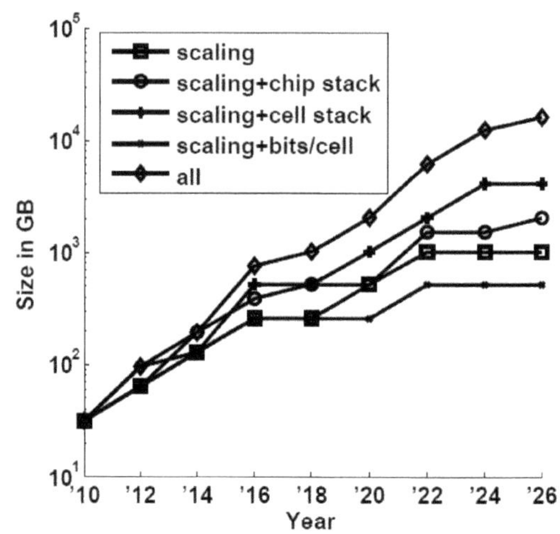


**Figure 2.** Memory size evolution for high-end smartphones assuming the trends shown in Table 1.

## 2. Mobile NVM Scaling Trends

When it comes to pocket cloudlets, the first question we need to answer is: "what capacities of NVMs are likely to be available in future mobile devices?" A closer look at technology scaling trends helps understand how the capacity of NVM memories in mobile devices is expected to evolve and get so abundant that it fundamentally changes the balance of cloud service implementation and makes the concept of proactively pushing large amounts of information into mobile devices appealing.

Table 1 shows our somewhat *conservative* technology scaling projections in the NVM market over the next 16 years. We assume that flash will dominate this market until it runs into charge-based storage scaling issues in the 2016/2018 time frame. At this point, we assume it will be replaced with another NVM technology more resilient to smaller feature sizes, such as resistive (*e.g.*, PCM [5], RRAM [14]) or magneto-resistive memories (*e.g.*, STT-MRAM [12]).

The first data row of Table 1 shows a projection of how the number of cells per layer in NVM memory devices is expected to scale in the form of a scaling factor. During the period in which flash is used as the NVM technology of choice, it is projected to double in capacity every two years [9].

In 2018, flash may lose traction due to increasing challenges in storing state (*i.e.*, electrons) in charge-based cells. A new technology providing more stable cells at smaller features may at that point replace flash. Single-layer PCM is already being productized

| Pocket Cloudlet | Single Item | Number of Items |
|---|---|---|
| Web Search | 100 KB (search result page) | ≈ 270,000 |
| Mobile Ads | 5 KB (ad banner) | ≈ 5,500,000 |
| Yellow Business | 5 KB (map tile with business info) | ≈ 5,500,000 |
| Web Content | 1.5 MB (www.cnn.com) | ≈ 17,500 |
| Mapping | 5 KB (128x128 pixels map tile) | ≈ 5,500,000 |

**Table 2.** Number of data items that can be stored in 25.6GB (10% of the projected NVM size available on low-end smartphones) for different pocket cloudlets.

as replacement for NOR flash in mobile devices, so it is a good candidate. The shift from flash to another technology could cause significant disruption in fabrication processes and would likely cause scaling to stall for one generation. Scaling is likely to resume in subsequent years until it finally stops in 2022 when industry is expected to hit $5nm$ technology. The second row shows chip stacking projections. Two layers are added every four years until 2022, when the technology may be mature enough to start making increments of four layers every four years. The third row shows a progression of number of layers when cell stacking is employed. Cell stacking is a technique by which devices are fabricated in multiple layers on the same silicon base (instead of in independently fabricated chips that are then combined, as in chip stacking) [6]. The process of taking a technology from academic demostration to initial production is typically five years. Given that this technology was demonstrated in 2009, this technology is likely to be adopted circa 2016 and the number of layers is likely to double every four years. Finally, the fourth row shows number of bits per memory cell. This number should increase in the next few years for flash, but then start to decrease as feature sizes get smaller, process variation increases and the average number of electrons per cell drops. In such a setting, even small electron losses may cause cell state to be corrupted, which in turn forces designers to reduce the number of logic levels, and therefore bits per cell, to increase the distance between these levels and better distinguish stored values.

Assuming the trends described above, Figure 2 presents various evolution scenarios for NVM parts used in smartphones. Our projections start with the NVM storage found in a high-end smartphone in 2010. We then apply different combinations of scaling and other capacity-increasing techniques to make a projection of total NVM capacity in future smartphones. Figure 2 shows that high-end phones may reach 1 TB of NVM as early as 2018. Considering that low-end smartphones today have 512 MB of NVM, a ratio of 64-to-1 when compared to high-end smartphones, we can calculate that low-end phones may eventually reach 256 GB (16 GB in 2018), still a respectable amount of storage.

Dedicating only 10% of a 256 GB NVM memory to caching services results in 25.6 GB of storage available in a mobile device. This storage could be used by various cloud services to offer an instant mobile user experience through pocket cloudlets. Table 2 shows the number of data items (*i.e.*, search result pages, web sites, etc.) that can be stored in 25.6 GB of space for various pocket cloudlets. A low-end smartphone is projected to be able to store more than 5 million map tiles or 17000 web sites. To put these numbers in perspective, our search log analysis indicated that more than 90% of mobile users visit fewer than 1000 URLs over a period of several months, which is 17 times fewer than the number of web sites that we can actually store on the phone. For the mapping service, assuming that each map tile covers 300x300 meters of actual earth surface, 5.5 million map tiles can cover the area of a whole state in the United States. As a result, the projected memory resources for smartphones could easily sustain the web browsing and mapping needs of a typical mobile user.

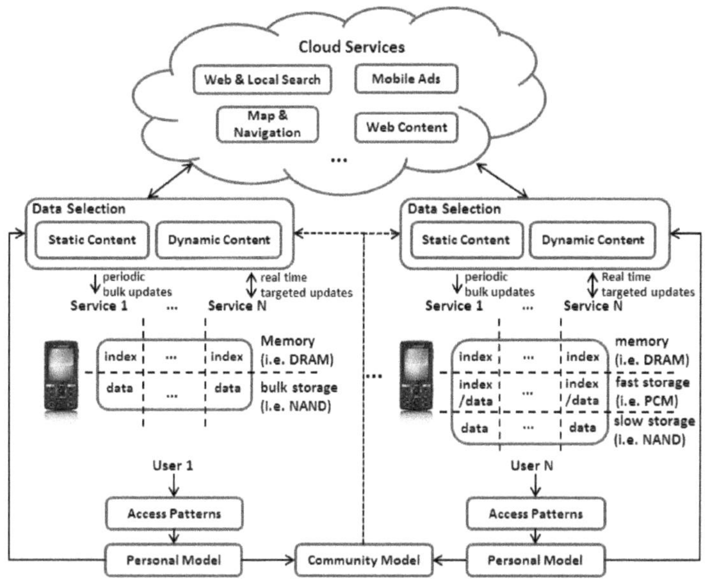


**Figure 3.** The envisioned architectural support required to transform mobile devices into pocket cloudlets.

## 3. Pocket Cloudlet Architecture

Enabling mobile devices to efficiently host cloud services poses various challenges. First, the amount of data to be stored locally on the device needs to be determined for each cloud service. Even though the analysis in Section 2 shows that memory resources on mobile devices will be abundant in the next decade, the amount of data available on the internet and across the different cloud services may exceed the available memory resources on a typical smartphone. Second, a mechanism to manage the locally stored cloud data is required as this data might change over time (*e.g.*, web content changes over time). Third, a storage architecture for efficiently storing and accessing this large amount of data is needed. Mobile users need to be able to quickly search and access data across services while still having enough space to store their personal data. Figure 3 shows the infrastructure required to transform mobile devices into pocket cloudlets.

### 3.1 Data Selection

At a higher level, the data stored locally on the mobile device is selected based on both personal and community access models. The access patterns of the individual user to a specific service (*i.e.*, web content or web search) are recorded and used to construct a personal model (*e.g.*, favorite web pages or search topics). At the same time, the personal models across users are combined together into a community model that identifies the most popular parts of the cloud service data across all users. Both personal and community models are then used to identify the most frequently accessed parts of the cloud service data that is or might be of interest to the individual user.

### 3.2 Data Management

The locally cached cloud service data needs to get updated periodically (*e.g.*, nightly, weekly or monthly). Updates occur when the device has access to power resources and high bandwidth links (*i.e.*, charging and connected to WiFi or tethered to a desktop computer). Periodic updates based on the charging state of the device are appealing, but can only be effective for relatively static data. That is, data that is not very frequently updated. For instance, the search index or the map tiles used for search and mapping services

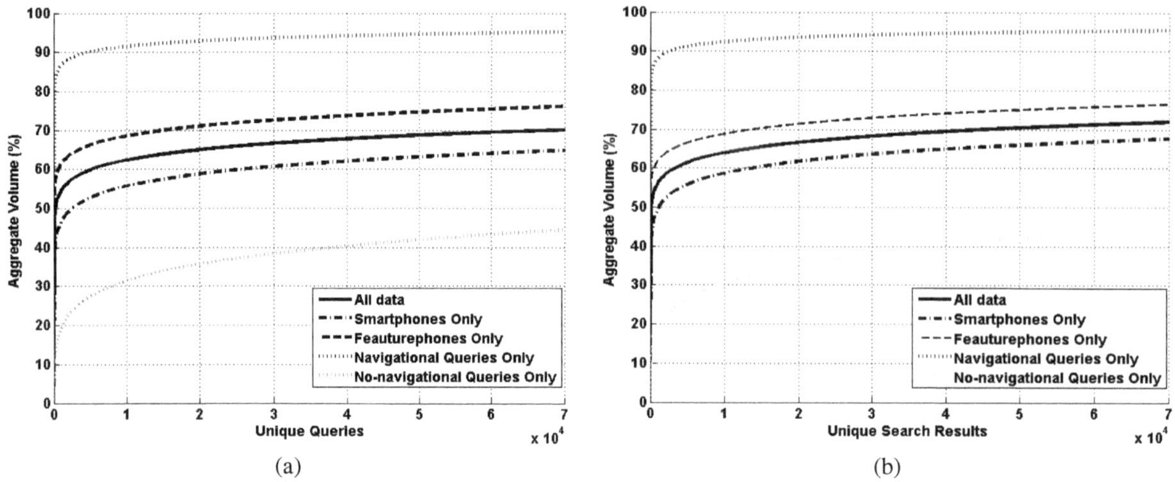


**Figure 4.** CDF plots of the (a) query volume and (b) clicked search result volume.

are examples of static data that could be updated periodically and only when the mobile device is charging without hurting the quality of the cloud service. However, not all cached data tend to be static. For instance, web content such as news and stock prices is dynamic in nature and tends to be accessed by individual users several times within a day. For this type of pocket cloudlets, real time updates over the radio link are required to guarantee freshness of the cached data. However, performing bulk updates over power hungry and bandwidth limited radio links is inefficient, if not impossible. Luckily, it turns out that the amount of dynamic data that is repeatedly accessed by mobile users tends to be small. For example, the analysis of 200 million mobile search queries submitted by hundreds of thousands of users showed that 70% of web visits tend to be revisits to less than a couple of tens of web pages for more than 50% of the users. As a result, instead of enforcing inefficient bulk updates over the radio link, only the small set of most frequently visited data (identified by the access patterns of the individual user) is updated in real time.

### 3.3 Architectural Implications

At a lower level, each cloud service owns its own storage space on the mobile device and uses it to store the necessary data. For instance, the storage can mirror web pages in the case of the web content service, and map tile snapshots and local business information in the case of mapping and navigation services. Since the amount of data required by these services is expected to be large and should always be available on the device even after a power down, bulk non-volatile storage such as NAND flash is a suitable memory technology. Besides storing the actual data on the mobile device's NVM, each cloud service also maintains an index of its data in fast volatile memory (DRAM). The index enables instant retrieval of the required data from bulk storage. Given the characteristics of current memory technologies, the main memory of the phone (*i.e.*, DRAM) is able to provide the necessary performance and density for storing the different indexes.

However, as new memory technologies such as PCM mature, this two-tier memory structure might slowly evolve into a three-tier structure as shown in Figure 3. PCM memory could become the intermediate tier by filling the performance and storage density gap between DRAM and NAND flash. In practice, PCM could be seen as fast bulk storage when compared to NAND flash, making it an ideal technology for storing the data indexes. While slower than DRAM, PCM has the advantage of being non-volatile and significantly faster than NAND flash. Being able to store data indexes in PCM eliminates the need to commit to and load the index from NAND after each power cycle of the mobile device. Given that the data required by the cloud services might be in the order of tens or even hundreds of gigabytes, the size of the data indexes can reach gigabytes, making its transfer between flash and main memory extremely time consuming. By introducing a PCM-based layer, all data indexes could become instantly available on the device at boot time offering a much faster user experience. At the same time, the DRAM tier could be used to cache the most frequently accessed parts of the data indexes in order to provide the fastest user experience when possible.

Figure 3 only shows the high level architectural requirements to enable mobile cached cloud services. In practice, however, several lower level challenges and design tradeoffs can arise. In the next sections, we present these challenges and tradeoffs for an example cloud service that focuses on mobile search and advertisement.

## 4. Cacheability of Mobile Search

Before designing and implementing a pocket cloudlet for a cloud service, it is important to study its cacheability. For instance, the real impact of a search pocket cloudlet depends on the fraction of the query volume that can be successfully served locally on the device. To answer this question we analyzed 200 million queries, submitted to `m.bing.com` over a period of several consecutive months in 2009. The query volume consisted of web search queries submitted from mobile devices such as phones and personal music players. Every entry in the search logs we analyze contains the raw query string that was submitted by the mobile user as well as the search result that was selected as a result of the submitted query. No personal information, such as location, is included in the logs.

### 4.1 The Mobile Community Effect

First, we examine the community of mobile users as a whole to discover caching opportunities across users. From the web search logs, we extract the most popular queries submitted and the most popular search results clicked by the mobile users. Figures 4(a) and 4(b) show the cumulative query and search result volume as a function of the number of most popular queries and search results respectively. When looking across all data, it turns out that the 6000 most popular queries and the 4000 most popular search results are responsible for approximately 60% of the query and search result volumes respectively. In other words, there is a small set of queries and search results that is popular across all mobile users. This suggests that if we store these 6000 queries and 4000 search results locally on the phone we could theoretically answer 60% of

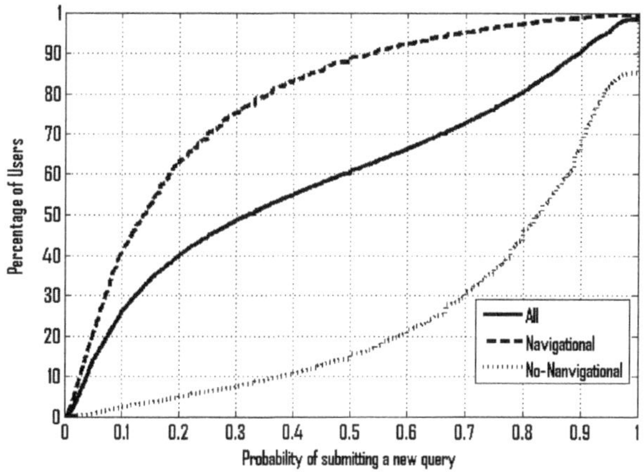


**Figure 5.** CDF plot of the repeatability of mobile search queries across individual users over a 1-month period.

the overall queries submitted by mobile users without having to use the radio link.

Note that these 4000 search results might not always point to static web pages. However, while some web content might be highly dynamic, the search results and queries that point to it can be relatively static. For instance, the CNN web page (`www.cnn.com`) is updated every minute and sometimes even more frequently. However, the way mobile users reach this dynamic web page is relatively static (*e.g.*, search for "cnn" or "news" and then click on the static search result that points to the CNN web page).

Similar popularity trends exist for desktop queries. However, mobile queries are significantly more concentrated than desktop queries. For instance, the first 6000 queries represent 60% of the query volume in the mobile domain but less than 20% of the query volume in the desktop domain [19].

We further divide the queries in two different categories, navigational[1] (*i.e.*, "youtube" or "facebook") and non-navigational (*i.e.*, "michael jackson"), and we study the same trends for each category. As Figure 4 shows, both query types follow the same trends but navigational queries are significantly more concentrated compared to non-navigational queries. For instance, the first 5000 navigational queries are responsible for 90% of the navigational query volume while the same number of non-navigational queries accounts for less than 30% of the non-navigational query volume.

Another interesting observation comes from comparing the results between Figures 4(a) and 4(b). To achieve a cumulative volume of 60%, 50% more queries are required compared to the number of search results (6000 queries vs 4000 search results). The search logs show that users search for the same web page in many different ways. For instance, mobile users often either misspell their queries because of the small keyboards they have to interact with (*i.e.*, "yotube" instead of "youtube") or purposely change the query term to reduce typed characters (*i.e.*, "boa" instead of "bank of america"). However, even though a misspelled or altered query is submitted, the search engine successfully provides the correct search result and thus a successful click through is recorded. As a result, a popular webpage is, in general, reached through multiple search queries.

Figures 4(a) and 4(b) also show the same information when considering the queries and search results that were submitted by featurephone (low-end mobile devices with limited browsers and internet capabilities) and smartphone users in isolation. Even though the exact same observations hold in both cases, queries and search results that are accessed over feature-phones are in general more concentrated when compared to smartphones. This is an artifact of the limited user interfaces found on feature-phones that make web access a challenging task.

[1] A query is classified as navigational when the actual query string is a substring of the clicked URL (*i.e.*, "youtube" and `www.youtube.com`)

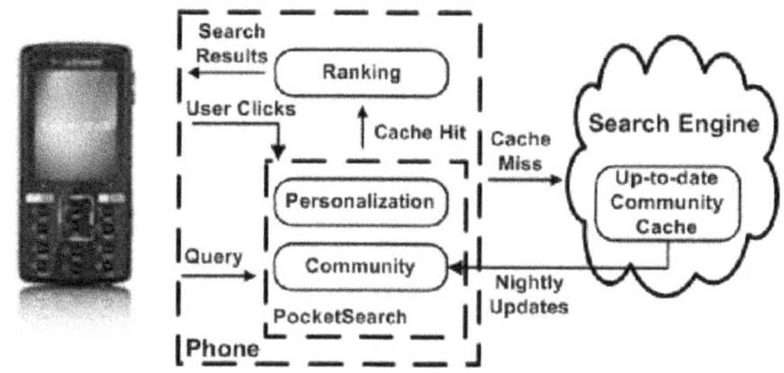


**Figure 6.** Overview of the PocketSearch cloudlet.

### 4.2 The Individual Mobile User Effect

Next, we examine personal query traces to discover caching opportunities within the search habits of individual users. In particular, we study how often individual users repeat queries. We call a query a repeated query only if the user submits the same query and clicks on the exact same search result. Figure 5 shows the percentage of individual mobile users as a function of the probability of submitting a new query within a month. Approximately 50% of mobile users will submit a new query at most 30% of the time. Thus, at least 70% of the queries submitted by half of the mobile users are repeated queries. Figure 5 also shows this trend for both navigational and non-navigational queries.

Consequently, knowing what the user searched in the past provides a very good indication of what the user will search for in the future. Again, this trend of repeating queries is not unique to mobile queries. Desktop users also tend to repeat queries, but not as frequently as mobile users. Recent studies have shown that desktop users will repeat queries on average 40% of the time [28] as opposed to 56.5% for mobile users (Section 4.2.1).

## 5. PocketSearch Architecture

Given the mobile search trends that the analysis of the web search logs highlighted, we designed and implemented PocketSearch, a mobile search pocket cloudlet that lives on the phone and is able to answer queries locally without having to use the 3G link[2]. The goal of the PocketSearch architecture is to capture the locality of mobile search as demonstrated in Section 4, and to be computationally tractable so that it can efficiently run on a mobile device. PocketSearch accomplishes both of these goals making its underlying architecture a template for other pocket cloudlet services.

Note that PocketSearch is not aiming to replace the actual search engine. Instead, its goal is to assist the search engine to provide a much faster mobile search experience in a way that is transparent to the user. For instance, most of the high-end smartphones today can automatically provide query suggestions to the user almost instantly and as the user is typing his query. PocketSearch's ability to retrieve search results fast, can make this experience richer by enabling the display of actual search results along with auto-suggest query terms in the auto-suggest box in real time (Figure 1). If users are not interested in any of these search results, they can access the latest set of search results through the 3G radio by

[2] PocketSearch only stores search results and not the actual web content that these results point to. Another cloudlet responsible for web content caching/pre-fetching (*i.e.*, PocketWeb) running along with PocketSearch could be used to serve the actual web content.

| Query | Search Result | Volume |
|---|---|---|
| michael jackson | www.imdb.com/name/nm0001391/bio | $10^6$ |
| movies | www.fandango.com | $95 * 10^4$ |
| michael jackson | www.azlyrics.com/j/jackson.html | $90 * 10^4$ |
| ringtones | www.myxer.com | $50 * 10^4$ |
| pof | www.plentyoffish.com | $20 * 10^4$ |
| ... | ... | ... |
| | **Total Volume** | $50 * 10^5$ |

**Table 3.** A list of query-search result pairs sorted by their volume is generated by processing the mobile web search logs over a time window (*i.e.*, a month). The volume numbers used in this table are hypothetical.

selecting the query term provided by auto-suggest or by entering the full query term on their own.

The PocketSearch cloudlet can be used to store web search results, local businesses as well as mobile advertisements (Figure 1). However, in the interest of space and to describe the underlying architecture in greater clarity, we limit this paper into describing the proposed caching system in the context of web search caching.

PocketSearch consists of two discrete but strongly interrelated components; the community and the personalization components (Figure 6). The community part of the cache is responsible for storing the small set of queries and search results that are popular across all mobile users. This information is automatically extracted from the search logs and is updated overnight every time the mobile device is recharging, making sure that the latest popular information is available on the mobile device. The community part serves as a warm start for the cache and enables PocketSearch to instantly provide search results without requiring any previous knowledge of the user.

The personalization part of the cache monitors the queries entered as well as the search results clicked by the user and performs two discrete tasks. First, it expands the cache to include all those queries and search results accessed by the user that did not initially exist in the community part of the cache. In that way, the cache can take advantage of the repeatability of the queries submitted by the mobile users to serve as many queries as possible locally on the mobile device. Second, it collects information about user clicks, such as when and how many times the user clicks on a search result after a query is submitted, to customize ranking of search results to user's click history.

When a query is submitted, PocketSearch will first perform a lookup in the cache to find out if there are locally available search results for the given query. In the case of a cache hit, the search results are fetched from the local storage, ranked based on the past user access patterns recorded by the personalization part of the cache, and immediately displayed to the user. In the case of a cache miss, the query is submitted to the search engine over the 3G radio link.

Realizing the architecture shown in Figure 6 on an actual mobile device poses several challenges:

**Content Generation**: A methodology is required to decide which and how many queries and search results should be included in the cache.

**Storage Architecture**: An efficient way to store and quickly retrieve the search results on the mobile device is needed. Memory overhead should be minimized to prevent performance degradation on the device and provide ample storage space for user's personal files. At the same time, PocketSearch should be able to quickly locate and retrieve the search results to minimize user response time.

**Personalized Ranking**: The user's search patterns provide important information about the individual user's interests. PocketSearch should record and leverage this information over time to personalize the search experience.

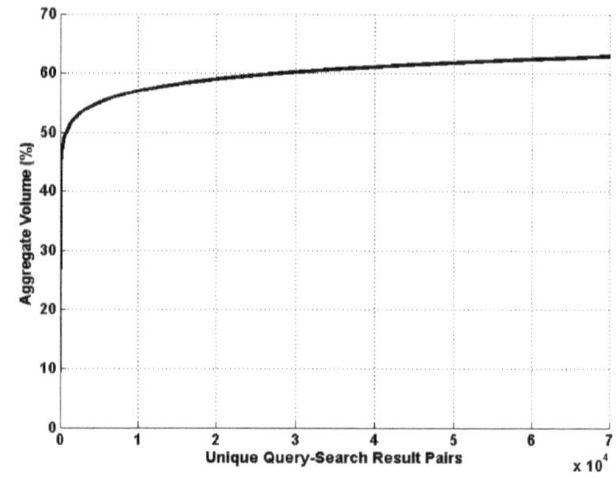


**Figure 7.** Cumulative query-search result volume as a function of the most popular query-search result pairs.

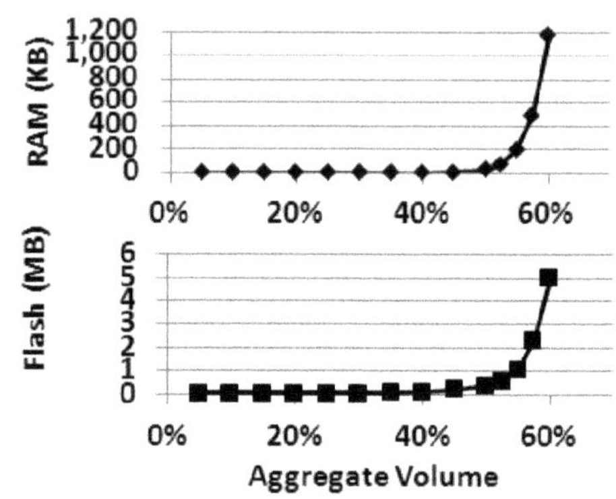


**Figure 8.** PocketSearch's DRAM and flash overhead for different *query-search result* aggregate volumes.

**Cache Management**: A scalable mechanism for regularly updating the cache contents is required. Having available the most up-to-date set of popular queries and search results on the phone is necessary for maximizing the number of queries that can be served by PocketSearch.

## 5.1 Cache Content Generation

The search results stored in the cache are extracted directly from the mobile search logs. The goal of this process is to identify the most popular queries and search results that are of interest to the mobile community.

A set of triplets in the form <query, search result, volume> are extracted from the search logs and sorted based on *volume* (Table 3). The term *query* corresponds to the query string submitted to the search engine, the term *search result* corresponds to the search result that was selected after entering the query, and the term *volume* represents the number of times in the search logs that the specific *search result* was selected after entering the query string *query*. For instance, the first row in Table 3 can be interpreted as follows: *In the last month, there were 1 million searches where the search result www.imdb.com/name/nm0001391/bio was selected after the query "michael jackson" was submitted.*

The number of triplets in Table 3 can be in the order of tens or hundreds of millions. Storing all of them would require significant memory resources that a phone might not be able to provide or a user might not be willing to sacrifice.

Deciding which entries to store is straightforward. To maximize the query volume that can be served by the cache, we should always store the most popular pairs of queries and search results indicated by the top entries of Table 3.

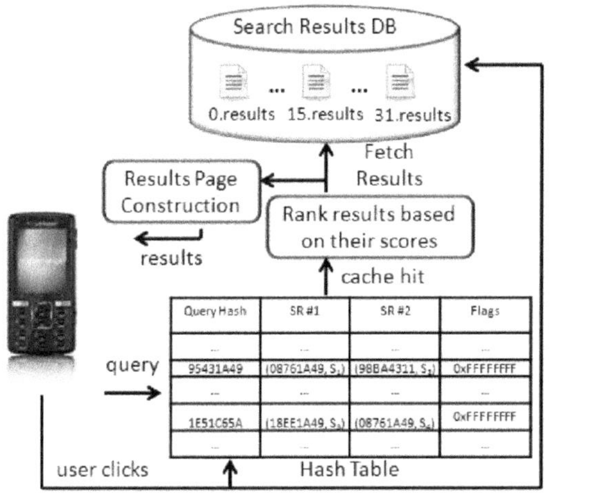


**Figure 9.** Overview of PocketSearch's storage architecture.

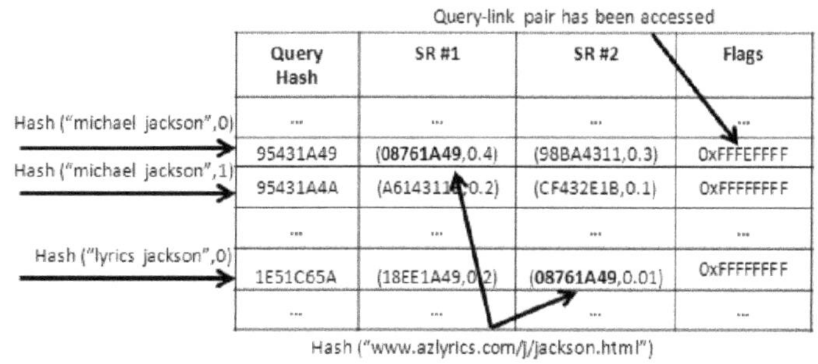


**Figure 10.** The hash table data structure used to link queries to search results.

Deciding how many of the most popular *query-search result* pairs to store is a more complicated process. We select the number of *query-search result* pairs to cache based on either a memory or cache saturation threshold.

**Memory (NAND flash or DRAM) Threshold**: Starting from the top entry in Table 3, we run down through its entries and continuously add *query-search result* pairs until a specific flash or DRAM memory size threshold $M_{th}$ is reached. This threshold can be set by either the phone itself based on its available memory resources or by the user, depending on how much storage space and memory the user is willing to sacrifice for PocketSearch.

**Cache Saturation Threshold**: Starting from the top entry in Table 3, we run down through its entries and continuously add *query-search result* pairs until we reach a *query-search result* pair with a normalized volume lower than a predetermined threshold $V_{th}$. The normalized volume of a *query-search result* pair is generated by dividing this pair's volume by the total volume of all *query-search result* pairs in the search logs. For instance, the *normalized volume* of the first query-search result pair in Table 3 is equal to: $10^6/5 * 10^6 = 0.2$.

The value of the cache saturation threshold is illustrated in Figure 7. It is apparent that the value of adding *query-search result* pairs quickly diminishes. In particular, slightly increasing the aggregate volume from 58% to 62% requires to double the amount of *query-search result* pairs from 20000 to 40000.

In practice, the mobile web search log analysis we performed showed that the cache saturation threshold will be quickly reached before PocketSearch stretches the memory or storage resources available on the phone. This can be seen in Figure 8 that shows the size of DRAM and flash required by PocketSearch as a function of the aggregate *query-search result* volume represented by all the pairs stored in the cache. It is clear that the saturation point of the cache is quickly reached when the most popular *query-search result* pairs that correspond to approximately 55% of the cumulative *query-search result* volume has been cached. At this point, the cache requires approximately 1MB of flash and 200KB of DRAM, which accounts for less than 1% of the available memory and storage resources on a typical smartphone.

Independently of which threshold is used (memory or cache saturation), this methodology identifies the $n$ top entries in Table 3. Each of these n top *query-search result* pairs is then associated with a ranking score that is produced by normalizing its volume across all search results that correspond to the query. For instance, in the case of query "michael jackson" in Table 3, the ranking score for the $imdb$ search result is equal to $10^6/1.9 * 10^6 = 0.53$ and the score for the $azlyrics$ is $9 * 10^5/1.9 * 10^6 = 0.47$. The generated <query,search result,score> triplets can now be used to build the cache on the phone.

Extracting PocketSearch's cache contents directly from the mobile search logs provides several advantages. First, even though there might be tens or even hundreds of search results available for a given query, we only cache these search results that are popular across all mobile users, limiting the amount of memory resources required. Second, each query and search result pair extracted from the search logs is associated to a ranking score, enabling the phone to rank search results locally. Third, by processing the mobile search logs we automatically discover the most common misspellings and shortcuts of popular queries, enabling PocketSearch to cache search results for these cases. As a result, queries such as "pof", and "boa" can now be served locally on the phone by instantly displaying search results such as `www.plentyoffish.com` and `www.bankofamerica.com` respectively.

### 5.2 Storage Architecture

The extracted set of <query,search result,score> triplets must be efficiently stored on the phone. Storage efficiency is defined in two ways. First, the memory resources required to store the search results should be as low as possible to permit many pocket cloudlet services to concurrently run. Second, the time it takes to retrieve, rank and display search results after the user enters a query should be as low as possible.

Figure 9 provides an overview of PocketSearch's storage architecture. It consists of two components, a hash table and a custom database of search results. The hash table lives in main memory and its role is to link queries to search results. Given a query the hash table can quickly identify if we have a cache hit or a cache miss. In the case of a cache hit, the hash table provides pointers to the database where the search results for the submitted query are located. Along with each search result pointer, the hash table provides its ranking score, enabling PocketSearch to properly rank search results on the phone.

The custom database of search results resides in flash and its role is to store all the available search results so that they occupy the least possible space and they can be quickly retrieved. The data stored in the database for each search result includes all the necessary information for generating the same search user experience with the search engine: the actual web address, a short description of the website and the human readable form of the web address.

Over time and as the user submits queries and clicks on search results, PocketSearch updates both the hash table and the database of search results. Every time the user clicks on a search result, its ranking score is properly updated in the hash table. In addition, if a new query or a new search result is selected that does not exist in the cache, both the hash table and the database are properly updated so that this query and search result can be retrieved from the cache in the future.

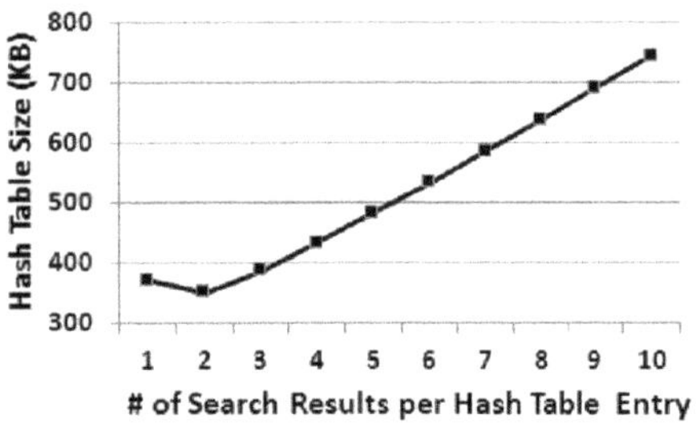


**Figure 11.** The memory footprint of the hash table for different number of search results per hash table entry.

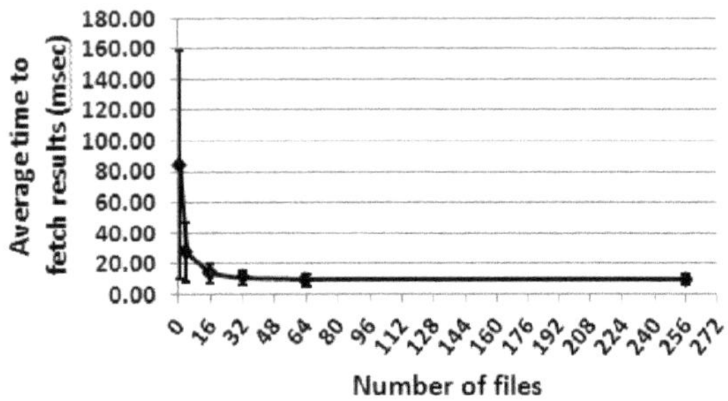


**Figure 12.** Average time to retrieve two search results from the database as a function of the number of files used to store the search results. The vertical bars represent the deviation of the access time over 10 consecutive experiments.

### 5.2.1 Query Hash Table

Figure 10 shows the structure of the hash table used to link queries to search results. Every entry in the hash table corresponds to one and only one query and has 4 fields. The first field contains the hash value of the query string that this entry corresponds to. The next two fields are of identical type and represent two search results associated to the query (SR #1 and SR #2 in Figure 10.). As it is explained later in detail, only two search results are stored per entry to minimize hash table's memory footprint. Each search result in the hash table is represented by a pair of numbers. The first number corresponds to the hash value of the web address of the search result. This value is used to uniquely identify a search result and, as it will be described in the next section, is used as a pointer to retrieve the information associated to the search result (short description, web address etc.) from the database. The second number corresponds to the ranking score of the search result. The last field of each entry in the hash table is a 64-bit number that is used to log information about the two search results in this entry. Currently, we use only one bit for each search result to indicate if the user has ever accessed the specific *query-search result* pair. The rest of the flag bits are reserved for future purposes.

In general, given a set of <query,search result,score> triplets the hash table is generated as follows. For every unique query in the set of triplets we identify all the search results associated to this query. An entry is created in the hash table for the query and search results are added in descending order of score. If more than two search results are associated to the same query, additional entries are created in the hash table by properly setting the second argument of the hash function (*i.e.*, "michael jackson" query in Figure 10).

This approach of linking queries to search results highlights two important design decisions that were influenced by the properties of the <query,search result,score> triplets extracted from the mobile web search logs. First, the number of search results linked to a query in a hash table entry affects the memory footprint of the hash

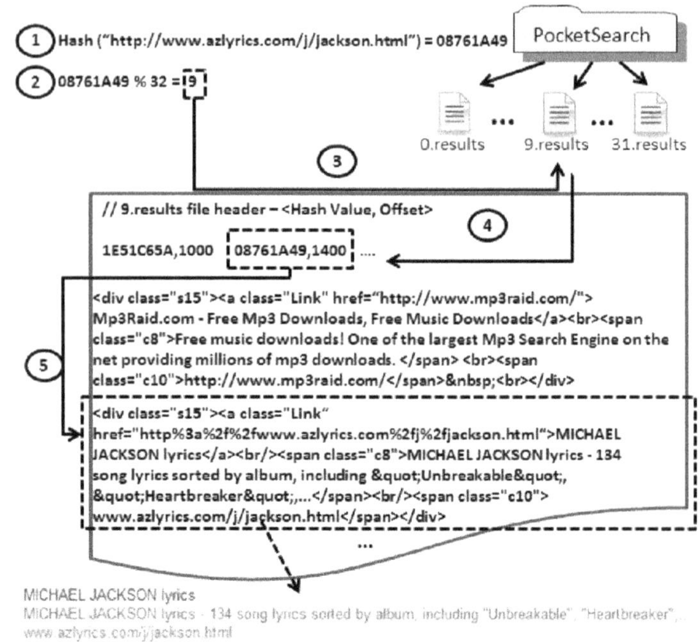


**Figure 13.** The 32-file custom database and illustration of the process of retrieving a search result.

table. This is illustrated in Figure 11 that shows the memory footprint of the hash table for different numbers of search results stored per hash table entry. The smallest memory footprint is achieved when two search results are stored per hash table entry.

Second, the way queries are linked to search results can affect the storage requirements of the database of search results. The simplest and fastest approach to retrieving and displaying search results to the user would be to store them in a single HTML file. Even though this approach would simplify the structure of the hash table, it would significantly increase the flash memory required to store them. The reason is that most of the search results are shared across a large number of queries. The analysis of the logs indicates that only 60% of the search results in PocketSearch are unique. If a single search result page were to be stored for every query, then 40% of the search results would have to be stored at least twice. To avoid wasting flash resources, we opted to store each search result once and then link individual queries to each search result independently. Besides saving space, this approach also enables PocketSearch to easily add/remove search results to/from the hash table and update the ranking score of search results over time. As it will be shown in Section 6, the overhead introduced by this approach in terms of user response time is negligible.

### 5.2.2 Search Results Organization

Search results are stored in flash using a custom database of plain text files to ensure portability of PocketSearch across different mobile platforms. For every search result, we store its title, which serves as the hyperlink to the landing page, a short description of the landing page and the human readable form of the hyperlink (Figure 13).

The amount of memory required to store the information associated to a search result into a file is, on average, 500 bytes. However, the actual memory space required might be significantly higher due to the internal structure of flash chips. Flash memories are organized in blocks of fixed size that are usually equal to 2KB, 4KB or 8KB depending on the size of the chip. If we store a 500 bytes file containing a single search result in flash memory, then this file

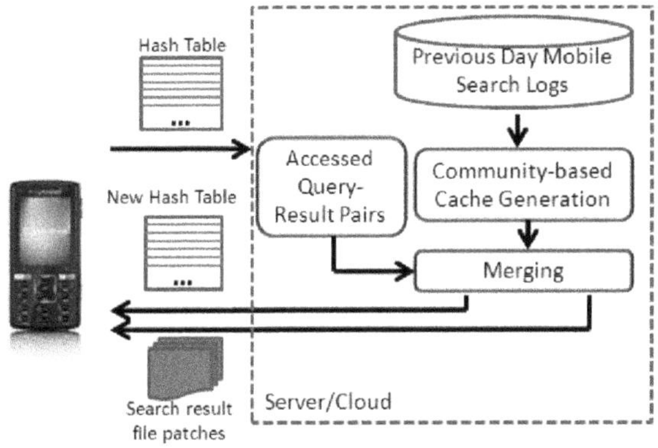


**Figure 14.** Overview of PocketSearch's updating process.

will occupy 4, 8 or 16 times more flash space than its actual size depending on the block size that is used.

In order to avoid flash fragmentation, multiple search results should be aggregated and stored into as few files as possible. However, storing a large number of search results into a single file could increase the time it takes PocketSearch to locate and retrieve a search result and, thus it could hurt the response time of the cache. As a result, the way search results are aggregated into files and organized within a file is critical for minimizing both, flash fragmentation and cache response time. By evaluating different database organizations (Figure 12) we found that a number of 32 database files constitutes the best tradeoff between flash fragmentation and user response time.

Figure 13 shows how search results are organized within a database file when 32 database files are used. Each search result is assigned to one of the 32 files based on the hash value of its web address. In particular, the remainder of the division of the hash value with the number of files in the database (a number between 0 and 31) is used to identify the file where the search result should be stored.

The first line in each of the 32 database files contains pairs of the form $(hash\,value,\ offset)$. The *offset* represents the actual offset from the beginning of the file where the information for the search result represented by the *hash value* is located. By parsing the first line of a database file we can identify where each search result stored in this file is located. Whenever the user clicks on a search result that is not already cached, PocketSearch will add the search result at the end of the database file and augment the header of this file with the $(hash\,value,\ offset)$ pair for this search result.

### 5.3 Personalized Ranking

By monitoring user clicks over time, the personalization component of the cache is aware of when and how many times the user selects a search result after a given query is submitted. PocketSearch uses this information to incrementally update the ranking score of the cached search results to offer a personalized search experience.

Assume that for a query $Q$ there are two search results $R_1$ and $R_2$ available in the cache. Every time the user submits the query $Q$ and clicks on the search result $R_1$, PocketSearch updates the scores $S_1$ and $S_2$ for the two search results $R_1$ and $R_2$ respectively, as follows:

$$S_1 = S_1 + 1 \tag{1}$$

$$S_2 = S_2 * e^{-\lambda} \tag{2}$$

The ranking score of the selected search result is increased by 1 (Equation (1)), the maximum possible score of a search result extracted from the mobile search logs. In that way, we always favor search results that the user has selected. Note that if this search result did not initially exist in the cache (selected after a cache miss), then a new entry in the hash table is created that links the submitted query to the selected search result and its score becomes equal to 1. At the same time, the ranking score for the unselected search result is exponentially decreased [3] (Equation (2)). This enables PocketSearch to take into account the freshness of user clicks. For instance, if search result $R_1$ was clicked 100 times one month ago and search result $R_2$ was clicked 100 times during last week, then the ranking score for $R_2$ will be higher.

Using Equations (1) and (2), the ranking score of the search results, at any given time, reflects both the number and freshness of past user clicks. In practice, any personalization ranking algorithm [27],[28] could be used with the proposed cache.

### 5.4 Cache Management

Figure 14 provides an overview of the mechanism used to update the community component of the cache. The phone transmits to the server its current version of the hash table. The server runs through the hash table and removes all the *query-search result* pairs that have not been accessed by the user in the past. This can be easily done by examining the *flags* column in the hash table (Figure 10). The *query-search result* pairs that have been accessed by the user in the past are only removed from the cache when their ranking score becomes lower than a predetermined threshold (*i.e.*, the user hasn't accessed the search result over the last 3 months).

At the same time, the server periodically (*i.e.*, daily) extracts the most popular queries and search results from the mobile search logs as described in Section 5.1, and adds them to the hash table. During this process, conflicts might arise in the sense that a *query-search result* pair that already exists in the hash table (previously accessed by the user) might re-appear in the popular set of queries and search results extracted on the server. The conflict is caused when the ranking score stored in the hash table is different from the new ranking score computed on the server based on the search log analysis. PocketSearch resolves these conflicts by always adopting the maximum ranking score.

After the hash table has been updated, the server creates the necessary patch files for the database files that live on the phone. The new hash table and the 32 patch files are transmitted to the phone and the new cache becomes available to the user. Note that the amount of data exchanged between the phone and the server will usually be less than 1.5MB given that PocketSearch requires, on average, approximately 200KB for storing the hash table and 1MB for storing the search results (Figure 8).

## 6. PocketSearch Evaluation

First, we use the prototype implementation to quantify the amount of time required to serve a search query through PocketSearch and compare its performance to that of the different radio links available on the phone. Second, we extract anonymized search query streams from the `m.bing.com` search logs and run them against PocketSearch to quantify what fraction of the query volume of an actual user can be served locally on the phone.

### 6.1 Cache Hit Performance

All of the measurements presented in this section were acquired using the prototype PocketSearch implementation on a Sony Ericsson Experia X1a cell phone running Windows Mobile 6.1 connected to AT&T's network. (Figure 1). To measure how fast queries are served using PocketSearch and the different radios available on the phone (Edge, 3G, 802.11g), we randomly selected 100 different queries for which cached search results were available. In every experiment, each of the 100 queries was submitted 100 times and the average user response time was calculated.

[3] The parameter $\lambda$ controls how fast the ranking score is decayed.

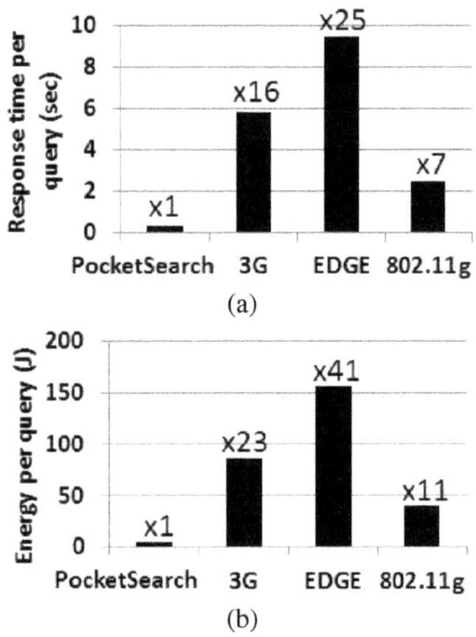


**Figure 15.** (a) Average search user response time per query. (b) Average energy per query.

| Operation | Average Time (ms) | Percentage |
|---|---|---|
| Hash Table Lookup | 0.01 | ≈ 0% |
| Fetch Search Results | 10 | 2.7% |
| Browser Rendering | 361 | 96.7% |
| Miscellaneous | 7 | 1.7% |
| **Total** | 378 | 100% |

**Table 4.** PocketSearch's user response time breakdown

User response time is defined as the elapsed time from the moment that the query is submitted (search button is clicked in Figure 1) to the moment that the embedded browser object in the application has completed rendering the search results web page.

In the experiments where the PocketSearch cache was used to serve queries, a cache containing all the *query-search result* pairs that account for 55% of the cumulative *query-search result* volume over a period of several months was used (Figures 7 and 8). This cache included approximately 2500 search results occupying 1MB of flash space as described in Section 5.2.2.

### 6.1.1 Search User Response Time

Figure 15(a) shows the average user response time per query when the PocketSearch cache or one of the radios on the phone is used. On average, PocketSearch is able to serve a query 16 times faster than 3G, 25 times faster than Edge and 7 times faster than 802.11g. Note that even though 802.11g can provide a low user response time that is slightly higher than 2 seconds, it has a major drawback. Due to its high power consumption, 802.11g is rarely turned on and connected to an access point on a continuous basis. As a result, in practice, 802.11g is not instantly available and requires extra steps that introduce delay and unnecessary user interaction.

Table 4 shows the breakdown of PocketSearch's user response time in the case of a cache hit. 96.7% of the time it takes PocketSearch to serve a query is spent at the browser while rendering the search results web page. The time it takes the cache to locate and retrieve search results is approximately 10ms and it accounts for only 3.3% of the overall user response time.

Furthermore, the time it takes PocketSearch to look up its hash table and determine if a query is a cache hit or a cache miss is only $10\mu s$ (Table 4). Therefore, in the case of a cache miss, the overall user response time will only be increased by $10\mu s$, a negligible increase given that any radio on the phone requires several seconds to serve a search query.

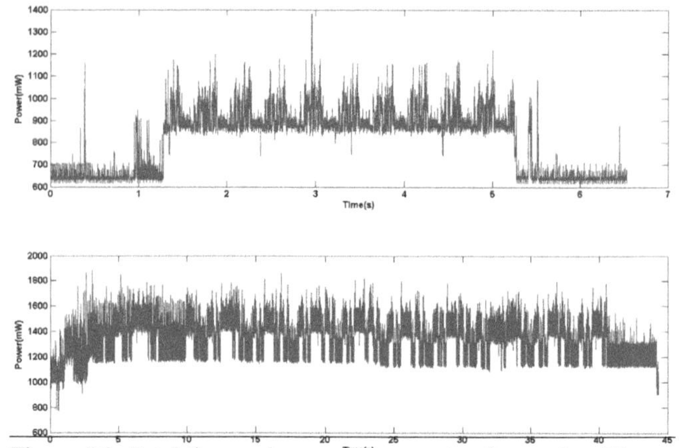


**Figure 16.** Total time and power consumption for serving 10 consecutive queries through PocketSearch (top) and the 3G radio (bottom).

| | Navigation user response time | | |
|---|---|---|---|
| | PocketSearch | 3G | Speedup over 3G |
| Lightweight Page | 15.378s | 21.048s | 28.7% |
| Heavyweight Page | 30.378s | 36.048s | 16.7% |

**Table 5.** Navigation user response time for PocketSearch and 3G for two example webpage load times.

### 6.1.2 Navigation User Response Time

By reducing search user response time, PocketSearch manages to also improve the overall navigation user response time, that includes both the time it takes the user to first search the web as well as the time to download the actual webpage. Table 5 shows the actual navigation time for two representative pages, a lightweight version and a heavyweight version that take 15 seconds and 30 seconds respectively to be downloaded and rendered over 3G. When PocketSearch serves the search results, the user can access the desired webpage up to approximately 29% faster than when querying through the 3G link.

### 6.1.3 Energy Consumption

Figure 15(b) shows the average energy consumed by the phone per query when PocketSearch or one of the radios on the phone is used. PocketSearch is on average 23 times more energy efficient than 3G, 41 times more energy efficient than Edge and 11 times more energy efficient that 802.11g. Note that the gap in the energy efficiency between PocketSearch and the different radios on the phone is larger than the corresponding gap in the user response time shown in Figure 15(a). This performance gap is justified by PocketSearch's ability to conserve energy in two ways (Figure 16). First, no data are being transmitted or received in the case of a cache hit, and thus the overall power consumption of the phone remains low (900mW vs 1500mW in Figure 16). Second, since PocketSearch achieves a user response time that is an order of magnitude lower compared to when the radios on the phone are used (4 seconds vs 40 seconds in Figure 16), the per query energy dissipation is significantly lower for PocketSearch.

## 6.2 Cache Hit Rate Performance

To quantify the cache hit rate achieved by PocketSearch for a typical user, we used anonymized search query streams from the mo-

| User Class | Monthly Query Volume | % of Users |
|---|---|---|
| Low Volume | [20,40) | 55% |
| Medium Volume | [40,140) | 36% |
| High Volume | [140,460) | 8% |
| Extreme Volume | [460,∞) | 1% |

**Table 6.** Classes of users and their characteristics.

bile search logs. To ensure a representative and unbiased selection of search query streams, we classified users in 4 different classes based on their monthly query volume. Table 6 shows the different user classes and the percentage of users in the mobile search logs that belongs to each class. Note that we ignore users that submit fewer than 20 queries per month for two reasons. First, PocketSearch is targeting users that frequently access the internet and search the web. Second, as higher-end smartphones with advanced browsing capabilities become more and more available, the average monthly query volume submitted by individual users will increase beyond the threshold of 20 queries per month.

For the experiments described in this section, we randomly selected 100 anonymized users from each class shown in Table 6 and extracted their search query streams from the mobile search logs over a period of one month. Each of the 400 search query streams was replayed against the PocketSearch cache that was generated using the mobile search logs of the preceding month. The resulting cache contained approximately 2500 search results that corresponded to 55% of the cumulative *query-search result* volume in the search logs. Note that the data used to build the cache and the data used to extract the 400 query streams were non-overlapping.

### 6.2.1 Hit Rate Results

Figure 17 shows the average hit rate for each user class described in Table 6. On average, 65% of the queries that an individual user submits are cache hits, and can be served 16 times faster. By examining Figure 17, it becomes apparent that the cache hit rate increases with the monthly query volume. PocketSearch achieves a cache hit rate of approximately 60% for the low volume class which immediately jumps to 70% for the medium volume class and to 75% for the high and extreme volume classes.

Figure 17 also shows the average cache hit rate for every user class in the cases where PocketSearch is using only either the community or personalization component of the cache. When only the community component of the cache is used, new queries and search results selected by the user are not cached over time and therefore, the cache cannot take advantage of the repeatability of mobile queries. When only the personalization component of the cache is used, the cache is initially empty and therefore cache hits are achieved only from repeated queries.

As Figure 17 illustrates, when only the community part of the cache is used, the average hit rate across all user classes is reduced from 65% to 55%. What is even more interesting is the fact that the hit rate seems to increase monotonically with the monthly query volume. Even though the exact same cache is used across all classes (since personalization is not used), the users that submit more queries seem to also experience higher hit rates.

When only the personalization part of the cache is used, the average hit rate across all user classes is reduced from 65% to 56.5%. Note that for every user class, the personalization part of the cache achieves the same or higher hit rate compared to the case where only the community part of the cache is used. This is another indication of the high repeatability of mobile queries that the personalization part of the cache is able to capture. In addition, the fact that the cache hit rate increases for users with higher query volumes due to the personalized component of the cache, shows

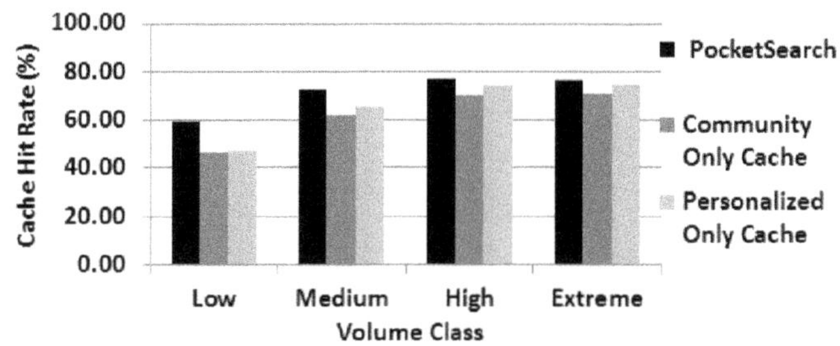


**Figure 17.** PocketSearch's average cache hit rate.

that users with higher query volumes repeat the same queries more often.

Even though users repeat mobile queries frequently, the community part of the cache is still very important for the overall user experience. Figure 18 shows the average hit rate for the different user classes during the first week (Figure 18(a)) and first two weeks (Figure 18(b)) of the one-month long query streams. Note, that after the first week, the hit rate of the personalization component of the cache remains lower than that of the community component of the cache. In particular, the fewer queries a user submits, the more time it takes the personalization component to warm up and be able to take advantage of the repeated queries. However, even during the first week, PocketSearch cache is able to provide the same hit rate with the one achieved in Figure 18 after a month. The community part of the cache provides a warm start for PocketSearch and the best possible out of the box search user experience.

The breakdown of the queries that result into a cache hit can be seen in Figure 19. On average and across all user classes, 59% of the cache hits are navigational queries[4] (*e.g.*, facebook, youtube, etc.) and the rest 41% are non-navigational queries that. The non-navigational hit rates are significantly increased or even doubled when compared to the medium volume class for both the high and extreme volume classes. This trend indicates that higher volume users tend to submit more diversified queries. However, even for this type of users PocketSearch is able to achieve high hit rates by taking advantage of the repeatability of mobile queries with its personalization component.

### 6.2.2 Daily Cache Updates

To understand how changes on the set of popular queries and search results on the server affect PocketSearch's cache hit rate, we repeated the same experiments while updating the PocketSearch cache on a daily basis as described in Section 5.4. On average, across all user classes PocketSearch achieves a cache hit rate of 66% when daily updates are used (we omit the graphs in the interest of space). This incremental improvement of 1.5% (66% vs 65% hit rate when daily updates are not used) is due to the fact that the popular set of queries and search results did not change significantly over the one month period we examined.

## 7. Architectural Considerations

The design and implementation of PocketSearch highlights the impact that the pocket cloudlet architecture can have on mobile user experience. Using only a couple of hundreds of KB of DRAM and a couple of MB of flash memory, PocketSearch can instantly serve 66% of the query volume that an average user submits. At the same time, Pocketsearch prevents 66% of the query volume across all users from hitting the cellular radio and the search engine servers, mitigating pressure on both cellular links and datacenters.

[4] these are queries that current browser cache substring matching techniques could also serve.

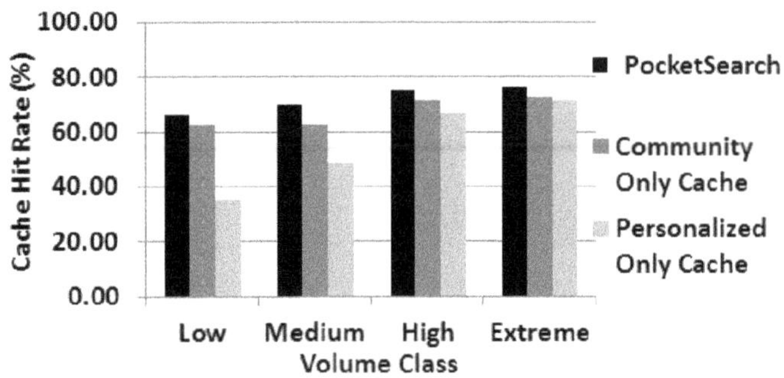


(a)

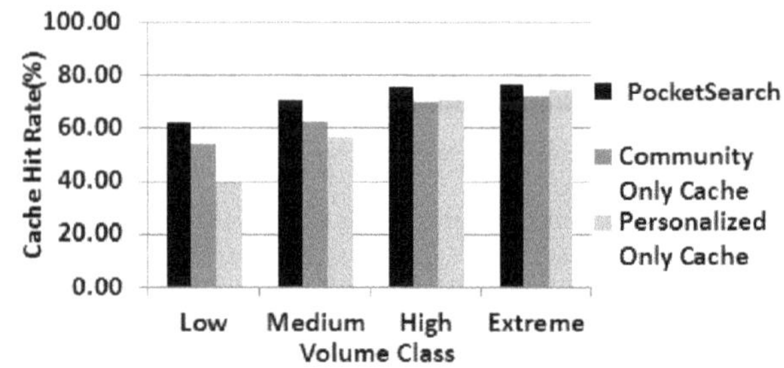


(b)

**Figure 18.** Average cache hit rate across the 4 user classes for (a) the first week and (b) the first two weeks of the month.

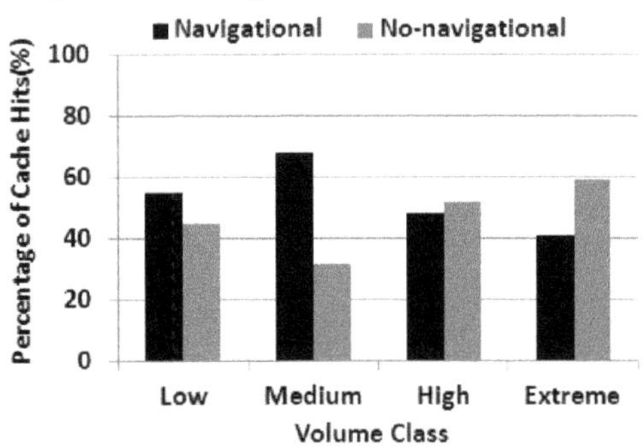


**Figure 19.** Breakdown of PocketSearch's cache hits into navigational and non-navigational across the 4 user classes.

Even though PocketSearch focuses on search services, we believe that the proposed architecture can serve as a template architecture for a broader family of cloudlets. Several other mobile cloud services beyond web search could leverage the same pocket cloudlet architecture, but each service eventually imposes its own memory requirements that might be very different when compared to PocketSearch. For instance, as the data in Table 2 shows, a mapping service cloudlet would require approximately 25 GB to cache all the map tiles for the user's state. Furthermore, creating a yellow pages cloudlet requires storing information about 23 million businesses across the United States, which according to Table 2 corresponds to approximately 100 GB. Similarly, web content, mobile ads and other pocket cloudlets impose their own requirements.

Even though each pocket cloudlet might share the same architecture and design principles, when multiple cloudlets with different requirements run on the same device, they naturally compete for resources within themselves and with other user applications. Managing the system resources properly across multiple cloudlets poses several architectural challenges.

**User versus pocket cloudlets**:The operating system will need to limit memory consumption such that enough memory is available to user data and applications. The more content cloudlets cache, the larger their indexes become. These indexes are stored in main memory and compete with regular user application memory usage. Pushing the indexes (or part of them) into slow storage-class memory would significantly affect cloudlet performance. We suggest the adoption of an intermediate tier consisting of fast storage-class memory, as described in Section 3, to address this problem.

**Pocket cloudlet interactions**: Many pocket cloudlet services cache related data. For example, when the user performs a web search, both search and ad cloudlets are invoked for the same query. In addition, the results will point to related web content, map tiles and yellow page entries. Different cloudlets have distinct storage requirements, and their relative storage allocation should take this into account. In addition, we believe that when memory needs to be reclaimed and cache entries evicted, it should be done in a coordinated fashion. If a particular query misses in the local search cache, there is not much benefit in hitting the ad cache because the latency bottleneck to service this query will be waking up the radio. Cache eviction policies should be managed by the operating system and coordinated such that closely related items are evicted together.

**Security**: Some cloudlets may include sensitive user and/or application data in their caches. Consequently, other cloudlets should not be allowed unrestricted access to those cache contents. For example, a map cloudlet shouldn't be allowed to access information regarding a user's recent bank transactions. We envision the operating system will provide such isolation and access control.

## 8. Related Work

The concept of caching information on client devices has been applied in the past in the context of web content [24], [21], [23], [25], [13] and advertisement [11] caching. The work presented in this paper differs in three ways. First, we describe a generalized mobile caching architecture that can be applied to various cloud services. Second, PocketSearch is complimentary to these efforts, in the sense that focuses on caching search results and not web content. Third, conversely to the previous work, PocketSearch was designed and implemented on an actual smartphone, addressing the challenges of building such an architecture on a mobile device.

File server caching systems, such as Coda [2], have focused on remote/offline access of files. Such schemes do not distinguish between a search result and a standard webpage HTML file let alone allow for personalized ranking of results within a page. Since these systems have no notion of search results, they don't take into account search trends into designing optimal client-side caching strategies. For instance, our data-driven approach indicated that by storing individual search results, storage requirements can be reduced by a factor of 8. In addition, PocketSearch combines both personal and community access characteristics to decide what search results to cache.

Approaches focusing on client side database caching have been combined with web browser caches to locally serve dynamic pages [1, 10]. Such approaches, however, aim to reproduce the exact same dynamic page as the servers (*e.g.*, search engines). They do not focus on assessing the popularity and cacheability of individual objects (*e.g.*, search results) within the dynamic page (*e.g.*, search results page) let alone personalize their ranking.

Content delivery or distribution networks (CDNs), such as the commercially available Akamai (`www.akamai.com`), aim to minimize user access time to content but they are complementary to PocketSearch. CDNs have great impact on wired networks where the latency between the client device and the nearby CDN node is low. However, on mobile devices, the bottleneck is the wireless link. By properly combining Pocket Cloudlets and CDNs, distributed cloud services that provide instant user experience can be created.

There have been several research efforts on understanding mobile search behavior through search log analysis [4], [3], [15], [16], [17], [18], [19], [30]. These efforts have analyzed search query volumes that vary from hundreds of thousands to several tenths of millions of queries. The search log analysis presented in this paper differs in two fundamental ways. First, we analyze 200 million mobile search queries, a query volume that is at least one order of magnitude larger than the query volume used in any other mobile search log study; volumes that large have been studied before only for desktop search [26]. Second, besides reporting similar observations on the locality of queries across mobile users, we also study in detail the repeatability of mobile queries for individual users.

The locality and repeatability of queries in the desktop search domain has been studied extensively and used to propose a server-side search caching scheme to reduce the load of search engines and improve user response time [20], [29], [7]. In the mobile domain though, the performance bottleneck is not the search engine but the slow radio link. Conversely to these approaches, PocketSearch is a client-based search cache that lives on the phone and enables search results to be displayed instantaneously as the user enters a query.

Previous work has also used mobile search log analysis findings to provide keyword auto-completion services on mobile devices [18] and thus facilitate and speed up query string entry. Such services are already popular on smartphone browsers and other mobile search applications and are complementary to PocketSearch, which focuses on providing fast search results and not query suggestions.

Recently, browsers and dedicated search applications on high-end smartphones such as Android and iPhone, have enabled web site suggestions as the user types a query. This is done in two ways.

First, for every new letter typed in the search box, a query is submitted in the background to the server for the partially entered query term and the most popular search result is returned as a website suggestion to the user. Note, that in this case a regular search query has to be submitted to the server over the radio link and therefore the usual slow mobile search experience is taking place.

Second, as the user types a query, a substring matching algorithm between the partial query string and all the website addresses in browser's cache can instantly provide the most relevant website that has been previously visited by the user. Unfortunately, this approach only works for a portion of the navigational queries.

## 9. Conclusions

In this paper, we proposed pocket cloudlets, an effective architecture that leverages abundant NVM in mobile devices to significantly improve user experience, both in terms of latency and battery life, by avoiding expensive radio wakeups and transmissions to access cloud services. We presented a case study of a search pocket cloudlet, and showed a surprising result: such service is viable even in today's mobile devices. We also explored other services that could benefit from a pocket cloudlet architecture and provided recommendations on how to build a system that supports multiple pocket cloudlets.

## References


[1] E. Benson, A. Marcus, D. Karger, and S. Madden. Sync Kit: a persistent client-side database caching toolkit for data intensive websites. In *Proceedings of WWW*, pages 121–130, 2010.

[2] P. J. Braam. The CODA distributed file system. *Linux J.*, 1998, June 1998. ISSN 1075-3583.

[3] K. Church, B. Smyth, P. Cotter, and K. Bradley. Mobile information access: A study of emerging search behavior on the mobile internet. *ACM Trans. Web*, 1(1), 2007.

[4] K. Church, B. Smyth, K. Bradley, and P. Cotter. A large scale study of european mobile search behaviour. In *MobileHCI*, 2008.

[5] S. R. et al. Phase-change random access memory: A scalable technology. *IBM Journal of Reseach and Development*, 52(4/5), 2008.

[6] D. K. et all. A stackable cross point phase change memory. In *2009 International Electron Device Meeting*, Dec 2009.

[7] T. Fagni, R. Perego, F. Silvestri, S. Orlando, U. Ca, and F. Venezia. Boosting the performance of web search engines: Caching and prefetching query results by exploiting historical usage data. *ACM Trans. Inf. Syst*, 24, 2006.

[8] H. Falaki, R. Mahajan, S. Kandula, D. Lymberopoulos, G. Ramesh, and D. Estrin. Diversity in smartphone usage. In *MobiSys*, 2010.

[9] I. T. R. for Semiconductors Working Group. International technology roadmap for semiconductors 2009 report. Technical report, International Technology Roadmap for Semiconductors, 2009.

[10] M. J. Franklin, M. J. Carey, and M. Livny. Local disk caching for client-server database systems. In *Proceedings of the 19th International Conference on Very Large Data Bases*, VLDB '93.

[11] S. Guha, A. Reznichenko, K. Tang, H. Haddadi, and P. Francis. Serving ads from localhost for performance, privacy, and profit. In *Hotnets*, 2009.

[12] Y. Huai. Spin-transfer torque mram (stt-mram): challenges and prospects. *AAPPS Bulletin*, 18(6):33–40, Dec 2008.

[13] S. Isaacman and M. Martonosi. The C-LINK system for collaborative web usage: A real-world deployment in rural nicaragua. In *NSDR '09*.

[14] R. C. Johnson. Memristors ready for prime time. http://www.eetimes.com/electronics-news/4077811/Memristors-ready-for-prime-time, Jul 2008.

[15] M. Kamvar and S. Baluja. A large scale study of wireless search behavior: Google mobile search. In *CHI*, 2006.

[16] M. Kamvar and S. Baluja. Deciphering trends in mobile search. *Computer*, 40(8):58–62, 2007.

[17] M. Kamvar and S. Baluja. The role of context in query input: using contextual signals to complete queries on mobile devices. In *Mobile-HCI*, 2007.

[18] M. Kamvar and S. Baluja. Query suggestions for mobile search: understanding usage patterns. In *CHI*, 2008.

[19] M. Kamvar, M. Kellar, R. Patel, and Y. Xu. Computers and iphones and mobile phones, oh my! In *WWW*, 2009.

[20] E. Markatos. On caching search engine query results. In *Computer Communications*, 2000.

[21] E. P. Markatos and C. E. Chronaki. A top-10 approach to prefetching on the web. In *Proceedings of INET*, 1998.

[22] Mobile Search Trends Report, `http://www.marketingcharts.com/interactive/mobile-local-search-ad-revenues-to-reach-13b-by-2013-8092/`.

[23] A. Nanopoulos, D. Katsaros, and Y. Manolopoulos. A data mining algorithm for generalized web prefetching. *IEEE Trans. on Knoweledge and Data Engineering*, 2003.

[24] V. N. Padmanabhan and J. C. Mogul. Using predictive prefetching to improve world wide web latency. *SIGCOMM Comput. Commun. Rev.*, 26(3), 1996.

[25] J. Pitkow and P. Pirolli. Mining longest repeating subsequences to predict world wide web surfing. In *USENIX*, pages 139–150, 1999.

[26] C. Silverstein, H. Marais, M. Henzinger, and M. Moricz. Analysis of a very large web search engine query log. *SIGIR Forum*, 33(1), 1999.

[27] J. Teevan, S. T. Dumais, and E. Horvitz. Personalizing search via automated analysis of interests and activities. In *SIGIR*, 2005.

[28] J. Teevan, E. Adar, R. Jones, and M. A. S. Potts. Information re-retrieval: repeat queries in yahoo's logs. In *SIGIR*, 2007.

[29] Y. Xie and D. O'Hallaron. Locality in search engine queries and its implications for caching. In *Infocom*, 2002.

[30] J. Yi, F. Maghoul, and J. Pedersen. Deciphering mobile search patterns: a study of yahoo! mobile search queries. In *WWW*, 2008.

# Blink: Managing Server Clusters on Intermittent Power

Navin Sharma, Sean Barker, David Irwin, and Prashant Shenoy

Department of Computer Science
University of Massachusetts, Amherst
{nksharma,sbarker,irwin,shenoy}@cs.umass.edu

## Abstract

Reducing the energy footprint of data centers continues to receive significant attention due to both its financial and environmental impact. There are numerous methods that limit the impact of both factors, such as expanding the use of renewable energy or participating in automated demand-response programs. To take advantage of these methods, servers and applications must gracefully handle intermittent constraints in their power supply. In this paper, we propose blinking—metered transitions between a high-power active state and a low-power inactive state—as the primary abstraction for conforming to intermittent power constraints. We design Blink, an application-independent hardware-software platform for developing and evaluating blinking applications, and define multiple types of blinking policies. We then use Blink to design BlinkCache, a blinking version of memcached, to demonstrate the effect of blinking on an example application. Our results show that a load-proportional blinking policy combines the advantages of both activation and synchronous blinking for realistic Zipf-like popularity distributions and wind/solar power signals by achieving near optimal hit rates (within 15% of an activation policy), while also providing fairer access to the cache (within 2% of a synchronous policy) for equally popular objects.

***Categories and Subject Descriptors*** C.5.0 [*Computer System Implementation*]: General
***General Terms*** Design, Management, Performance
***Keywords*** Power, Intermittent, Renewable Energy, Blink

## 1. Introduction

Energy-related costs have become a significant fraction of total cost of ownership (TCO) in modern data centers. Recent estimates attribute 31% of TCO to both purchasing power and building and maintaining the power distribution and cooling infrastructure [15]. Consequently, techniques for reducing the energy footprint of data centers continue to receive significant attention in both industry and the research community. We categorize these techniques broadly as being either primarily *workload-driven* or *power-driven*. Workload-driven systems reconfigure applications as their workload demands vary to use the least possible amount of power to satisfy demand. Examples include consolidating load onto a small number of servers, e.g., using request redirection [8, 17] or VM migration, and powering down the remaining servers during off-peak hours, or balancing load to mitigate thermal hotspots and reduce cooling costs [3, 23, 24]. In contrast, power-driven systems reconfigure applications as their power supply varies to achieve the best performance possible given the power constraints.



*ASPLOS'11,* March 5–11, 2011, Newport Beach, California, USA.


While prior work has largely emphasized workload-driven systems, power-driven systems are becoming increasingly important. For instance, data centers are beginning to rely on intermittent renewable energy sources, such as solar and wind, to partially power their operations [14, 35]. Intermittent power constraints are also common in developing regions that experience "brownouts" where the electric grid temporarily reduces its supply under high load [8, 38]. Price-driven optimizations, due to either demand-response incentives or market-based pricing, introduce intermittent constraints as well, e.g., if multiple data centers coordinate to reduce power at locations with high spot prices and increase power at locations with low spot prices [29]. Variable pricing is an important tool for demand-side power management of future smart electric grids. The key challenge in power-driven systems is optimizing application performance in the presence of power constraints that may vary significantly and frequently over time. Importantly, these power and resource consumption constraints are *independent of workload demands*.

In this paper, we present *Blink*, a new energy abstraction for gracefully handling intermittent power constraints. Blinking applies a duty cycle to servers that controls the fraction of time they are in the active state, e.g., by activating and deactivating them in succession, to gracefully vary their energy footprint. For example, a system that blinks every 30 seconds, i.e., is on for 30 seconds and then off for 30 seconds, consumes half the energy, modulo overheads, of an always-on system. Blinking generalizes the extremes of either keeping a server active (a 100% duty cycle) or inactive (a 0% duty cycle) by providing a spectrum of intermediate possibilities. Blinking builds on prior work in energy-aware design. First, several studies have shown that turning a server off when not in use is the most effective method for saving energy in server clusters. Second, blinking extends the PowerNap [21] concept, which advocates frequent transitions to a low-power sleep state, as an effective means of reducing idle power waste.

An application's *blinking policy* decides when each node is active or inactive at any instant based on both its workload characteristics and energy constraints. Clearly, blinking impacts application performance, since there may not always be enough energy to power the nodes necessary to meet demand. Hence, the goal of a blinking policy is to minimize performance degradation as power varies. In general, application modifications are necessary to adapt traditional server-based applications for blinking, since these applications implicitly assume always-on, or mostly-on, servers. Blinking forces them to handle regular disconnections more often associated with weakly connected [36] environments, e.g., mobile, where nodes are unreachable whenever they are off or out of range.

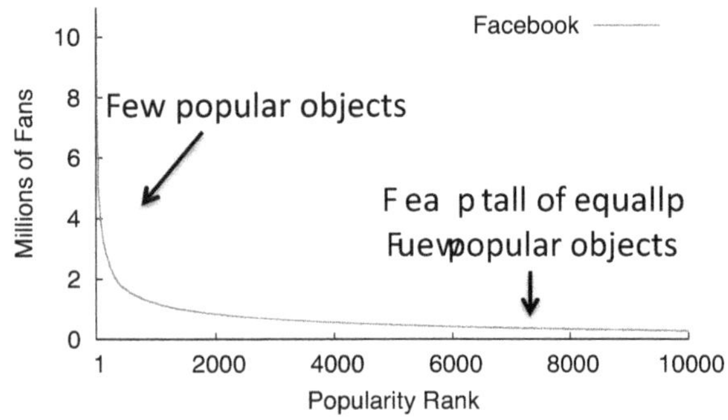


Figure 1: The popularity of web data often exhibits a long heavy tail of equally unpopular objects. This graph ranks the popularity of Facebook group pages by their number of fans.

### 1.1 Example: BlinkCache

To demonstrate how blinking impacts a common data center application, we explore the design of BlinkCache—a blinking version of *memcached* that gracefully handles intermittent power constraints—as a proof-of-concept example. Memcached is a distributed memory cache for storing key-value pairs that many prominent Internet sites, including LiveJournal, Facebook, Flikr, Twitter, YouTube, and others, use to improve their performance.

Memcached is a natural first application to optimize for variable power constraints for two reasons. First, a memcached cluster is energy-intensive, since it requires continuous operation of high-memory nodes to ensure instant access to in-memory state. Second, since memcached is performance supplement that is not necessary for correctness, it does not preclude a constrained power source that may offer little or no power over some time periods. A blinking memcached cluster also exploits the increasing trend toward elevating memory in the storage hierarchy, and using it as the primary storage substrate in cloud data centers [26]. An important consequence of this trend is that applications increasingly use memory less like a cache that only stores a small set of popular objects, and more like a storage system that also stores a long heavy tail of unpopular objects. However, unpopular objects are not unimportant.

For Internet services that store user-generated content, the typical user is often interested in the relatively unpopular objects in the heavy tail, since these objects represent either their personal content or the content of close friends and associates. As one example, Figure 1 depicts a popularity distribution for Facebook group pages in terms of their number of fans. While the figure only shows the popularity rank of the top 10,000 pages, Facebook has over 20 million group pages in total. Most of these pages are nearly equally unpopular. For these equally unpopular objects, blinking nodes synchronously to handle variable power constraints results in fairer access to the cache. While fair cache access is important, maximizing memcached's hit rate requires prioritizing access to the most popular objects. We explore these performance tradeoffs in-depth for a memcached cluster with intermittent power constraints.

### 1.2 Contributions

In designing, implementing, and evaluating BlinkCache as a proof-of-concept example, this paper makes the following contributions.

- **Make the Case for Blinking Systems**. We propose blinking systems to deal with variable power constraints in server clusters. We motivate why blinking is a beneficial abstraction for dealing with intermittent power constraints, define different types of blinking policies, and discuss its potential impact on a range of distributed applications.
- **Design a Blinking Hardware/Software Platform**. We design Blink, an application-independent hardware/software platform to develop and evaluate blinking applications. Our small-scale prototype uses a cluster of 10 low-power motherboards connected to a programmable power meter that replays custom power traces and variable power traces from a solar and wind energy harvesting deployment.
- **Design, Implement, and Evaluate BlinkCache**. We use Blink to experiment with blinking policies for BlinkCache, a variant of memcached we optimize for intermittent power constraints. Our hypothesis is that a load-proportional blinking policy, which keeps nodes active in proportion to the popularity of the data they store, combined with object migration to group together objects with similar popularities, results in near optimal cache hit rates, as well as fairness for equally unpopular objects. To validate our hypothesis, we compare the performance of activation, synchronous, and load-proportional policies for realistic Zipf-like popularity distributions. We show that a load-proportional policy is significantly more fair than an optimal activation policy for equally popular objects (4X at low power) while achieving a comparable hit rate (over 60% at low power).

Section 2 provides an overview of blinking systems and potential blinking policies. Section 3 presents Blink's hardware and software architecture in detail, while Section 4 presents design alternatives for BlinkCache, a blinking version of memcached. Section 5 then evaluates BlinkCache using our Blink prototype. Finally, Section 6 discusses related work and Section 7 concludes.

## 2. Blink: Rationale and Overview

Today's computing systems are not energy-proportional [6]—a key factor that hinders data centers from effectively varying their power consumption by controlling their utilization. Designing energy-proportional systems is challenging, in part, since a variety of server components, including the CPU, memory, disk, motherboard, and power supply, now consume significant amounts of power. Thus, any power optimization that targets only a single component is not sufficient, since it reduces only a fraction of the total power consumption [6, 19]. As one example, due to the power consumption of non-CPU components, a modern server that uses dynamic voltage and frequency scaling in the CPU at low utilization may still operate at over 50% of its peak power [5, 37]. Thus, deactivating entire servers, including most of their components, remains the most effective technique for controlling energy consumption in server farms, especially at low power levels that necessitate operating servers well below 50% peak power on average.

However, data centers must be able to rapidly activate servers whenever workload demand increases. PowerNap [21] proposes to eliminate idle power waste and approximate an energy-proportional server by rapidly transitioning the entire server between a high-power active state and a low-power inactive state. PowerNap uses the ACPI S3 state, which places the CPU and peripheral devices in sleep mode but preserves DRAM memory state, to implement inactivity. Transition latencies at millisecond-scale, or even lower, may be possible between ACPI's fully active S0 state and its S3 state. By using S3 to emulate the inactive "off" state. [1] PowerNap is able to consume minimal energy while sleeping. Typical high-end servers draw as much as 40x less power in S3.

Blink extends PowerNap in important ways. First, PowerNap is a workload-driven technique that eliminates idle server power waste—it uses rapid transitions in a workload-driven fashion to activate each server when work arrives and deactivate it when idle.

[1] We use "active" and "on" interchangeably to reference ACPI's S0 state, and inactive and "off" interchangeably to represent ACPI's S3 state.

| Type | Model | S3 Transition Time (s) |
|---|---|---|
| Desktop | Optiplex 745 | 13.8 |
| Desktop | Dimension 4600 | 12.0 |
| Laptop | Lenovo X60 | 11.7 |
| Laptop | Lenovo T60 | 9.7 |
| Laptop | Toshiba M400 | 9.1 |
| Laptop | OLPC-XO (w/ NIC) | 1.6 |
| Laptop | OLPC-XO (no NIC) | 0.2 |

Table 1: Latencies for several desktop and laptop models to perform a complete S3 cycle (suspend and resume). Data from both [2] and our own measurements of Blink's OLPC-X0.

In contrast, Blink is a *power-driven* technique that regulates average node power consumption independent workload demands. Second, the PowerNap mechanism applies to each server independently, while Blink applies to collections of servers. Blinking policies, which we formally define next, are able to capture, and potentially exploit, cross-server dependencies and correlations in distributed applications. Finally, unlike workload-driven transitions, blinking provides benefits even for the non-ideal S3 transition latencies on the order of seconds that are common in practice, as we show in Section 5.1.3. [2] Table 1 shows S3 transition latencies for a variety of platforms, as reported in [2], with the addition of Blink's OLPC-X0 nodes. The latencies include both hardware transitions as well as the time to restart the OS and reset its IP address.

DEFINITION 1. *The* blink state *of each node $i$ is defined by two parameters that determine its duty cycle $d_i$,* (i) *length of the ON interval $t_{on}$ and* (ii) *length of the OFF interval $t_{off}$, such that* $d_i = \frac{t_{on}}{t_{on}+t_{off}} \cdot 100\%$

DEFINITION 2. *A* blink policy *defines the* blink state *of each node in a cluster, as well as a* blink schedule *for each node.*

The blink schedule defines the clock time at which a specified node transitions its blink state to active, which in turn dictates the time at which the node turns on and goes off. The schedule allows nodes to synchronize their blinking with one another, where appropriate. For example, if node $A$ frequently accesses disk files stored on node $B$, the blink policy should specify a schedule such that the nodes synchronize their active intervals. To illustrate how a data center employs blinking to regulate its aggregate energy usage, consider a scenario where the energy supply is initially plentiful and there is sufficient workload demand for all nodes. In this case, a feasible policy is to keep all nodes continuously on.

Next assume that the power supply drops by 10%, and hence, the data center must reduce its aggregate energy use by 10%. There are several blink policies that are able to satisfy this 10% drop. In the simplest case, 10% of the nodes are turned off, while the remaining nodes continue to stay on. Alternatively, another blink policy may specify a duty cycle of $d_i = 90\%$ for every node $i$. There are also many ways to achieve a per-server duty cycle of 90% by setting different $t_{on}$ and $t_{off}$ intervals, e.g., $t_{on} = 9s$ and $t_{off} = 1s$ or $t_{on} = 900ms$ and $t_{off} = 100ms$. Yet another policy may assign different blink states to different nodes, e.g., depending on their loads, such that aggregate usage decreases by 10%.

We refer to the first policy in our example above as an *activation* policy. An activation policy only varies the number of active servers at each power level [8, 37] such that some servers are active, while others are inactive; the energy supply dictates the size of the active server set. In contrast, *synchronous policies* toggle all nodes between the active and inactive state in tandem. In this case, all servers are active for $t_{on}$ seconds and then inactive for $t_{off}$ seconds, such that total power usage over each duty cycle matches the available power. Of course, since a synchronous policy toggles all servers to active at the same time, it does not reduce peak power, which has a significant impact on the cost of energy production. An *asynchronous* policy may randomize the start of each node's active interval to decrease peak power without changing the average power consumption across all nodes. Finally, an *asymmetric* policy may blink different nodes at different rates, while ensuring the necessary change in the energy footprint. For example, an asymmetric policy may be *load-proportional* and choose per-node blink states that are a function of current load.

All of the policies above are equally effective at capping the average power consumption for a variable power signal over any time interval. However, the choice of the blink policy greatly impacts application performance. To see why, consider two common applications: a simple cluster-based web server [8, 17] and an Hadoop cluster [20]. An activation policy is well-suited for a cluster-based web server where each node serves static content replicated on each node—by turning off a subset of nodes and evenly redirecting incoming web requests to active servers, the application is able to regulate its energy usage to match its supply. Since any node is able to service any request, transitioning a subset of the nodes to the inactive state does not pose a problem. In this case, the application requires only minimal changes to accommodate dynamic changes in the set of active servers.

However, an activation policy presents a problem for applications that maintain memory or disk state on specific nodes and exhibit inter-node dependencies. In this case, deactivating nodes will render some application-specific state unavailable. Hadoop is one example, since Hadoop's HDFS file system [31] replicates and stores data chunks of each file across many different nodes to improve both performance and data availability. As a result, simply powering down some nodes for long periods is not effective, since inactive nodes may store data necessary for a job to continue execution [4, 16, 20]. One, potentially non-optimal, option for addressing the problem without incurring the overhead of changing the data layout or migrating state prior to deactivating nodes is to leverage a synchronous blinking policy, where all nodes have the same duty cycle. Since all nodes blink between the active and inactive state in tandem, all disk state is accessible during the active periods. While the synchronous policy is not necessarily optimal for all applications and maximizes peak power demand, it does eliminate the complexities of dealing with application-specific communication patterns when determining the blink schedule. However, dealing with application-specific complexities may improve performance: an asynchronous blinking policy may reduce costs by reducing peak power or an asymmetric blinking policy may improve performance by prioritizing nodes that store heavily-accessed data.

In general, distributed applications that store per-node state require application modifications to gracefully handle blinking, and ensure the state is available at the proper times. However, since intermittent power scenarios may yield little or no power during certain periods, it is not appropriate in all application scenarios. For instance, intermittent power is not appropriate for applications that make performance guarantees. The approach is applicable in many scenarios, such as for best-effort batch jobs, including Hadoop/MapReduce jobs, or for performance optimizations that augment an always-on infrastructure. In this paper, we focus on the latter example by developing a version of memcached, called BlinkCache, that gracefully handles intermittent power constraints via blinking. While memcached's design explicitly avoids the type of inter-node dependencies present in Hadoop, and other tightly-coupled distributed applications, it is able to benefit from an

[2] PowerNap's on-demand transitions show little benefit once latencies exceed 100 milliseconds [21].

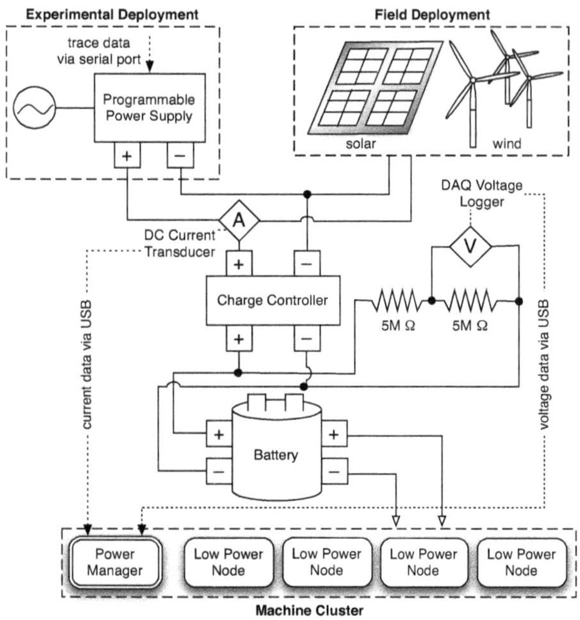


Figure 2: Hardware architecture of the Blink prototype.

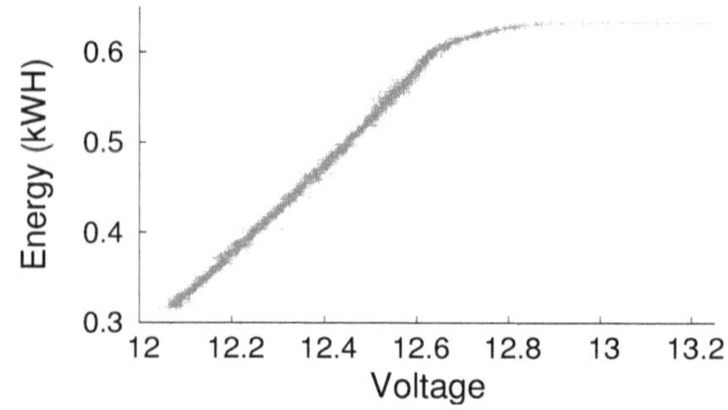


Figure 3: Empirically-measured battery capacity as a function of voltage for our deep-cycle battery. We consider the battery empty below 12V, since using it beyond this level will reduce its lifetime.

asymmetric load-proportional policy, as we describe in Section 4. Additionally, nodes dedicated to memcached deployments do not require disks. Mechanical disks pose an additional constraint for blinking due to both performance and reliability concerns with frequently spinning disks up and down [41]. The effect of power cycling on the lifetime of CPUs, memory, and motherboards is an open question; we know of no prior work that addresses the issue.

## 3. Blink Prototype

Blink is a combined hardware/software platform for developing and evaluating blinking applications. This section describes our prototype's hardware and software architecture in detail.

### 3.1 Blink Hardware Platform

Blink's current hardware platform consists of two primary components: (i) a low-power server cluster that executes Blink-aware applications and (ii) a variable energy source constructed using an array of micro wind turbines and solar panels. We use renewable energy to expose the cluster to intermittent power constraints.

#### 3.1.1 Energy Sources

We deployed an array of two wind turbines and two solar panels to power Blink. Each wind turbine is a SunForce Air-X micro-turbine designed for home rooftop deployment, and rated to produce up to 400 watts in steady 28 mph winds. However, in our measurements, each turbine generates approximately 40 watts of power on windy days. Our solar energy source uses Kyocera polycrystalline solar panels that are rated to produce a maximum of 65 watts at 17.4 volts under full sunlight. Although polycrystalline panels are known for their efficiency, our measurements show that each panel only generates around 30 watts of power in full sunlight and much less in cloudy conditions.

We assume blinking systems use batteries for short-term energy storage and power buffering. Modern data centers and racks already include UPS arrays to condition power and tolerate short-term grid disruptions. We connect both renewable energy sources in our deployment to a battery array that includes two rechargeable deep-cycle ResourcePower Marine batteries with an aggregate capacity of 1320 watt-hours at 12V, which is capable of powering our entire cluster continuously for over 14 hours. However, in this paper we focus on energy-neutral operation over short time intervals, and thus use the battery array only as a small 5-minute buffer. We connect the energy sources to the battery pack using a TriStar T-60 charge controller that provides over-charging circuitry. We deployed our renewable energy sources on the roof of a campus building in September 2009 and used a HOBO U30 data logger to gather detailed traces of current and voltage over a period of several months under a variety of different weather conditions.

While our energy harvesting deployment is capable of directly powering Blink's server cluster, to enable controlled and repeatable experiments we leverage two Extech programmable power supplies. We use the programmable power supplies, instead of the harvesting deployment, to conduct repeatable experiments by replaying harvesting traces, or emulating other intermittent power constraints, to charge our battery array. [3]

Since the battery's voltage level indicates its current energy capacity, we require sensors to measure and report it. We use a data acquisition device (DAQ) from National Instruments to facilitate voltage measurement. As shown in Figure 2, the prototype includes two high-precision 5MOhm resistors between the battery terminals and employs the DAQ to measure voltage across each resistor. We then use the value to compute the instantaneous battery voltage, and hence, capacity. Figure 3 shows the empirically-derived capacity of our prototype's battery as a function of its voltage level. In addition to battery voltage, we use DC current transducers to measure the current flowing from the energy source into the battery, and the current flowing from the battery to the cluster. The configuration allows Blink to accurately measure these values every second.

#### 3.1.2 Low-power Server Cluster

Our Blink prototype uses a cluster of low-power server nodes. Since our energy harvesting deployment is only capable of producing 100-140 watts of power, a cluster of traditional high-power servers, such as Xeon servers that consume roughly 500W each, is not feasible. As a result, we construct our prototype from low-power nodes that use AMD Geode processor motherboards. Each motherboard, which we scavenge from OLPC-XO laptops, consists of a 433 MHz AMD Geode LX CPU, 256 MB RAM, a 1GB solid-state flash disk, and a Linksys USB Ethernet NIC. Each node runs the Fedora Linux distribution with kernel version 2.6.25. We con-

[3] We are able to set the initial battery level for each experiment using a separate charge controller in load-control mode.

| Blinking Interface |
|---|
| `setDutyCycle(int nodeId, int onPercentage)` |
| `setBlinkInterval(int nodeId, int interval)` |
| `syncActiveTime(int node, long currentTime)` |
| `forceSleep(int nodeId, int duration)` |

Table 2: Blink APIs for setting per-node blinking schedules.

| Measurement Interface |
|---|
| `getBatteryCapacity()` |
| `getBatteryEnergy()` |
| `getChargeRate(int lastInterval)` |
| `getDischargeRate(int lastInterval)` |
| `getServerLoadStats(int nodeId)` |

Table 3: Blink's measurement APIs that applications use to inform their blinking decisions.

nect our 10 node cluster together using 2 energy-efficient 8-port Rosewill 100 Mbps switches. Each low-power node consumes a maximum of 8.6W, and together with the switch, the 10 node cluster has a total energy footprint of under 100 watts, which closely matches the energy generated from our renewable energy sources.

Similar clusters of low-power nodes, e.g., using Intel Atom processors, are currently being considered by data centers for energy-efficient processing of I/O-intensive workloads [5]. Our low-power Blink design should also scale to traditional Xeon-class servers for appropriately sized energy sources, although, as we discuss in Section 5, an application's performance may differ for higher-power nodes. An advantage of using XO motherboards is that they are specifically optimized for rapid S3 transitions that are useful for blinking. Further, the motherboards use only 0.1W in S3 and 8.6W in S0 at full processor and network utilization. The wide power range in these two states combined with the relatively low power usage in S3 makes these nodes an ideal platform for demonstrating the efficacy of Blink's energy optimizations.

### 3.2 Blink Software Architecture

Blink's software architecture consists of an application-independent control plane that combines a power management service with per-node access to energy and node-level statistics. Blink-aware applications interact with the control plane using Blink APIs to regulate their power consumption. The power management service consists of a power manager daemon that runs on a gateway node and a power client daemon that runs on each cluster node. The architecture separates mechanism from policy by exposing a single simple interface for applications to control blinking for each cluster node.

The power manager daemon has access to the hardware sensors, described above, that monitor the battery voltage and current flow. Each Blink power client also monitors host-level metrics on each cluster node and reports them to the power manager. These metrics include CPU utilization, network bandwidth, and the length of the current active period. The power client exposes an internal RPC interface to the power manager that allows it to set a node's blinking pattern. To set the blinking pattern, the power client uses the timer of the node's real-time clock (RTC) to automatically sleep and wake up, i.e., transition back to S0, at specific intervals. Thus, the power client is able to set repetitive active and inactive durations. For example, the power manager may set a node to repeatedly be active for 50 seconds and inactive for 10 seconds. In this case, the blink interval is 60 seconds with the node being active 83% of the time and inactive 17% of the time. We assume that nodes synchronize clocks using a protocol such as NTP to enable policies that coordinate blink schedules across cluster nodes.

The impact of clock synchronization is negligible for our blink intervals at the granularity of seconds, but may become an issue for blink intervals at the granularity of milliseconds or less. Note that clock synchronization is not an issue for applications, such as memcached, that do not perform inter-node communication. Transitioning between S0 and S3 incurs a latency that limits the length of the blink interval. Shorter blink intervals are preferable since they allow each node to more closely match the available power, more rapidly respond to changes in supply, and reduces the battery capacity necessary for short term buffering. The XO motherboard yields S3 sleep latencies that range from roughly 200 milliseconds to 2 seconds depending on the set of active devices and drivers (see Table 1). For instance, since our USB NIC driver does not implement the ACPI `reset_resume` function, we must unload and load its driver when transitioning to and from S3. As a result, the latency for our experiments is near 2 seconds. Unfortunately, inefficient and incorrect device drivers are commonplace, and represent one of the current drawbacks to blinking in practice.

The Blink control plane exposes an RPC interface to integrate with external applications as shown in Tables 2 and 3. Applications use these APIs to monitor input/output current flow, battery voltage, host-level metrics and control per-node blinking patterns. Since Blink is application-independent, the prototype does not report application-level metrics. In such cases, an application must monitor itself. For instance, for some policies in our blinking version of memcached, a proxy monitors per-key hit rates, as described in Section 4.3.1.

## 4. Blinking Memcached

Memcached is a distributed in-memory cache for storing key-value pairs that significantly reduces both the latency to access data objects and the load on persistent disk-backed storage. Memcached has become a core component in Internet services that store vast amounts of user-generated content, with services maintaining dedicated clusters with 100s to 1000s of nodes [26]. Since end users interact with these services in real-time through web portals, low-latency access to data is critical. High page load latencies frustrate users and may cause them to stop generating new content [25], which is undesirable since these services' primary source of revenue derives from their content, e.g., by selling targeted ads.

### 4.1 Memcached Overview

Memcached's design uses a simple and scalable client-server architecture, where clients request a key value directly from a single candidate memcached server with the potential to store it. Clients use a built-in mapping function to determine the IP address of this candidate server. Initial versions of memcached determined the server using the function `Hash(Key)%NumServers`, while the latest versions use the same consistent hashing approach popularized in DHTs, such as Chord [34]. In either case, the key values randomly map to nodes without regard to their temporal locality, i.e., popularity. Since all clients use the same mapping function, they need not communicate with other clients or servers to compute which server to check for a given key. Likewise, Memcached servers respond to client requests (gets and sets) without communicating with other clients or servers. This lack of inter-node communication enables Memcached to scale to large clusters.

Importantly, clients maintain the state of the cache, including its consistency with persistent storage. As a result, applications are explicitly written to use memcached by (i) checking whether an object is resident in the cache before issuing any subsequent queries, (ii) inserting a newly referenced object into the cache if it is not already resident, and (iii) updating a cached object to reflect

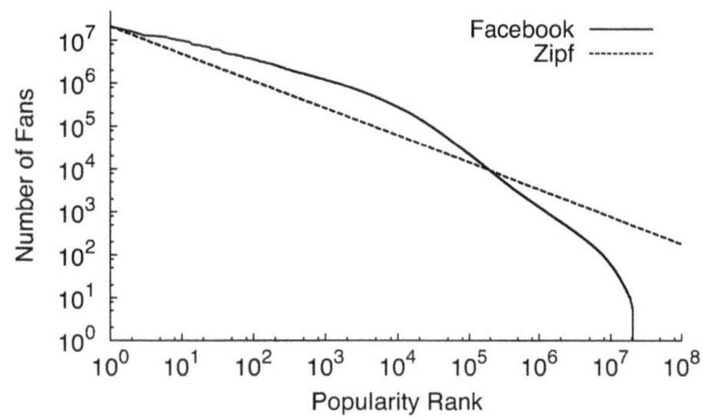


Figure 4: The popularity rank, by number of fans, for all 20 million public group pages on Facebook follows a Zipf-like distribution with $\alpha = 0.6$.

a corresponding update in persistent storage. Each memcached server uses the Least Recently Used (LRU) replacement policy to evict objects. One common example of a cached object is an HTML fragment generated from the results of multiple queries to a relational database and other services. Since a single HTTP request for many Internet services can result in over 100 internal, and potentially sequential, requests to other services [10, 26], the cache significantly decreases the latency to generate the HTML.

### 4.2 Access Patterns and Performance Metrics

The popularity of web sites has long been known to follow a Zipf-like distribution [7, 39], where the fraction of all requests for the $i$-th most popular document is proportional to $1/i^{\alpha}$ for some constant $\alpha$. Previous studies [7, 39] have shown that $\alpha$ is typically less than one for web site popularity. The key characteristic of a Zipf-like distribution is its heavy tail, where a significant fraction of requests are for relatively unpopular objects. We expect the popularity of user-generated content for an Internet service to be similar to the broader web, since, while some content may be highly popular, such as a celebrity's Facebook page, most users are primarily interested in either their own content or the content of close friends and associates.

As a test of our expectation, we rank all 20 million user-generated fan pages on Facebook by their number of fans. We use the size of each page's fan base as a rough approximation of the popularity of its underlying data objects. Figure 4 confirms that the distribution is Zipf-like with $\alpha$ approximately 0.6. Recent work also states that Facebook must store a significant fraction of their data set in massive memcached cluster, i.e., on the order of 2000 nodes, to achieve high hit rates, e.g., 25% of the entire data set to achieve a 96.5% hit rate [26]. This characteristic is common for Zipf-like distributions with low $\alpha$ values, since many requests for unpopular objects are inside the heavy tail. Thus, the distribution roughly divides objects into two categories: the few highly popular objects and the many relatively unpopular objects. As cache size increases, it stores a significant fraction of objects that are unpopular compared to the few popular objects, but nearly uniformly popular compared to each other. These mega-caches resemble a separate high-performance storage tier [26] for all data objects, rather than a small cache for only the most popular data objects.

Before discussing different designs alternatives for BlinkCache, we define our performance metrics. The primary cache performance metric is hit ratio, or hit rate, which represents the percentage of object requests that the cache services. A higher hit rate indicates both a lower average latency per request, as well as lower load on the back-end storage system. In addition to hit rate, we argue that fairness should be a secondary performance metric for large memcached clusters that store many objects of equal popularity. A fair cache distributes its benefits—low average request latency—equally across objects. Caches are usually unfair, since their primary purpose is to achieve high hit rates by storing more popular data at the expense of less popular data. However, fairness increases in importance when there are many objects with a similar level of popularity, as in today's large memcached clusters storing data that follows a Zipf-like popularity distribution. An unfair cache results in a wide disparity in the average access latency for these similarly popular objects, which ultimately translates to end-users receiving vastly different levels of performance. We use the standard deviation of average request latency per object as our measure of fairness. The lower the standard deviation the more fair the policy, since this indicates that objects have average latencies that are closer to the mean.

### 4.3 BlinkCache Design Alternatives

We compare variants of three basic memcached policies for variable power constraints: an activation policy, a synchronous policy, and an asymmetric load-proportional policy. In all cases, any get request to an inactive server always registers as a cache miss, while any set request is deferred until the node becomes active. We defer a discussion of the implementation details using Blink to the next section.

- **Activation Policy**. An activation policy ranks servers $1...N$ and always keeps the top $M$ servers active, where $M$ is the maximum number of active servers the current power level supports. We discuss multiple activation variants, including a *static* variant that does not change the set of available servers in each client's built-in mapping function to reflect the current set of active servers, and a *dynamic* variant that does change the set. We also discuss a *key migration* variant that continuously ranks the popularity of objects and migrates them to servers $1...N$ in rank order.
- **Synchronous Policy**. A synchronous policy keeps all servers active for time $t$ and inactive for time $T - t$ for every interval $T$, where $t$ is the maximum duration the current power level supports and $T$ is short enough to respond to power changes but long enough to mitigate blink overhead. The policy does not change the set of available servers in each client's built-in mapping function, since all servers are active every interval.
- **Load-Proportional Policy**. A load-proportional policy monitors the aggregate popularity of objects $P_i$ that each server $i$ stores and keeps each server active for time $t_i$ and inactive for time $T - t_i$ for every interval $T$. The policy computes each $t_i$ by distributing the available power in the same proportion as the aggregate popularity $P_i$ of the servers. The load-proportional policy also migrates similarly popular objects to the same server.

#### 4.3.1 Activation Policy

A straightforward approach to scaling memcached as power varies is to activate servers when power is plentiful and deactivate servers when power is scarce. One simple method for choosing which servers to activate is to rank them $1...N$ and activate and deactivate them in order. Since, by default, memcached maps key values randomly to servers, our policy for ranking servers and keys is random. In this case, a static policy variant that does not change each client's built-in mapping function to reflect the active server set arbitrarily favors keys that happen to map to higher ranked servers, regardless of their popularity. As a result, requests for objects that map to the top-ranked server will see a significantly lower average latency than requests for objects that happen to map to the bottom-ranked

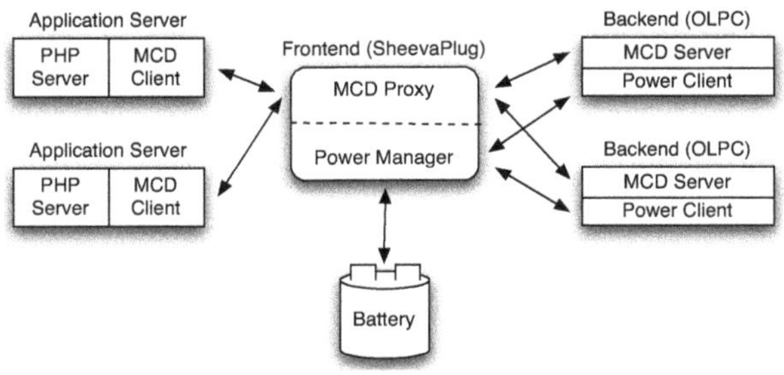


Figure 5: To explicitly control the mapping of keys to servers, we interpose always-active request proxies between memcached clients and servers. The proxies are able to monitor per-key hit rates and migrate similarly popular objects to the same nodes.

server. One way to correct the problem is to dynamically change the built-in client mapping function to only reflect the current set of active servers. With constant power, dynamically changing the mapping function will result in a higher hit rate since the most popular objects naturally shift to the current set of active servers.

**Hash-based Key Mapping**. Memcached recently added support for consistent hashing to reduce the disruption from changing a cluster's size. The original function (`Hash(Key)%NumServers`) invalidates nearly every key when adding or removing a single server from a cluster of size $n$. Only the keys that have both the old `NumServers` and the new `NumServers` as common factors do not change mappings. The approach is clearly not scalable, since each change, regardless of size, flushes nearly the entire cache, which abruptly increases load on the back-end storage system, as well as request latency, until the cache re-populates itself.

Consistent hashing, originally popularized [34] by DHTs, significantly improves the situation, since adding or removing each server only invalidates $1/n^{th}$ of the keys for a cluster of size $n$. The approach scales gracefully, since the percentage of keys the cache invalidates by changing a single server in the active set decreases as cluster size increases. However, consistent hashing is not a panacea when power varies either frequently or significantly. For instance, if the available power doubles, thereby doubling the number of active servers, a consistent hashing approach will still invalidate 50% of its resident objects. With a dynamic approach, frequent variations in power repeatedly incur this steep invalidation penalty.

Thus, while our dynamic variant results in a higher hit rate than a static variant under constant power, the opposite is true, due to invalidation penalties, for power that varies frequently or significantly. One option for eliminating invalidation penalties entirely is to explicitly control the mapping of individual keys to servers, and pro-actively migrate the most popular objects to the most popular servers. Figure 5 illustrates a memcached design that interposes an always-active proxy between memcached clients and servers to control the mapping. In this design, clients issue requests to the proxy, which maintains a hash table that stores the current mapping of keys to servers, issues requests to the appropriate back-end server, and returns the result to the client.

**Table-based Key Mapping**. Since all requests pass through the proxy, it is able to continuously monitor and sort the popularity of objects in the background and dynamically change the server mappings as popularities change. Note that to migrate an object the proxy need only change its key→server mapping. After the change, the next key request for the object will incur one cache miss on the new server, which results in application-level code re-generating and re-inserting the object at the new location. The proxy may either pro-actively evict the object from the old server or simply allow LRU replacement to evict the object. This strategy eliminates invalidation penalties, since popularity-based migration always places the most popular objects on the highest-ranked servers. The design requires no changes to either memcached clients or servers.

Deactivating lower-ranked servers invalidates objects that are already less popular than objects on the higher-ranked active servers, while activating additional servers grows the size of the cache without invalidating the more popular objects that are already resident. The approach does introduce the overhead of monitoring and sorting keys by popularity, as well as proxying requests through an intermediary server. However, these overhead costs are independent of power variations and amortized over time, rather than imposed abruptly at each change in the power level. The proxy approach scales to multiple proxies by allowing memcached clients to use their original built-in mapping function to map keys to a set of proxies instead of a set of servers, such that each proxy is responsible for a random subset of keys.

In a multi-proxy design, the proxies periodically send popularity statistics to a central server that sorts them in the background and distributes each proxy a new server mapping. The period between re-mappings is a function of both how fast key popularity is changing and the number of keys in the cache, since drastic popularity changes require re-mappings and more keys increase the time to gather, sort, and distribute new mappings. Changes to server mappings need not be highly synchronized across all proxies, though, since memcached provides no guarantees that data is present or consistent with a back-end database. A multi-proxy design allows the proxies to share the bandwidth and processing load of issuing client requests to servers, while maintaining the ability to explicitly control key mappings.

We expect a few-to-many relationship between proxies and memcached servers, although highly-loaded memcached clusters may require a mapping as low as one-to-one. In this case, the argument for using proxies instead of the nodes themselves mirrors Somniloquy's argument for using low-power, augmented network interfaces to perform simple application functions on behalf of sleeping nodes [2]. Another consideration for a proxy-based migration approach is the load imposed on the highest-ranked memcached servers. If the highest-ranked servers become overloaded, the re-mapping process may need to place a few less popular keys on high-ranked nodes to ensure they are not overloaded. The technique is analogous to Popularity-based Data Concentration (PDC) for disk arrays that must be careful not to deactivate too many disks and then overload the remaining active disks [28].

### 4.3.2 Synchronous Policy

The migration-enabled activation policy, described above, approaches the optimal policy for maximizing the cache's hit rate, since ranking servers and mapping objects to them according to popularity rank makes the distributed cache operate like a centralized cache that simply stores the most popular objects regardless of the cache's size. We define optimal as the hit rate for a centralized cache of the same size as the distributed Memcached instance under the same workload. However, the policy is unfair for servers that store similarly popular objects, since these servers should have equal rankings. The activation policy is forced to arbitrarily choose a subset of these equally ranked servers to deactivate. In this case, a synchronous policy is significantly more fair and results in nearly the same hit rate as the optimal activation policy. To see why, consider the simple 4-node memcached cluster in Figure 6 with enough available power to currently activate half the cluster. There is enough power to support either (i) our activation policy with migration that keeps two nodes continuously active or (ii) a

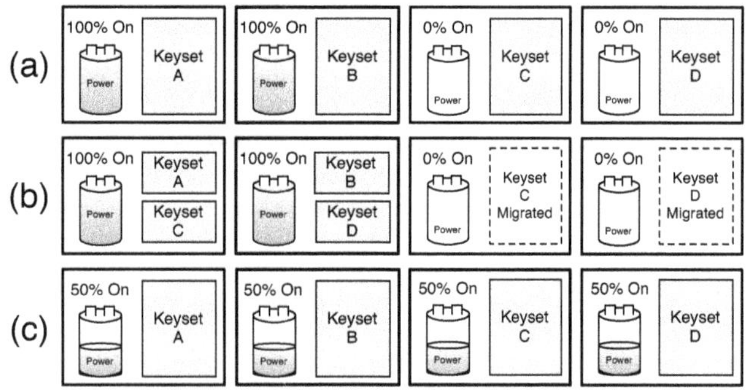


Figure 6: Graphical depiction of a static/dynamic activation blinking policy (a), an activation blinking policy with key migration (b), and a synchronous blinking policy (c).

synchronous policy that keeps four nodes active half the time but synchronously blinks them between the active and inactive state.

For now we assume that all objects are equally popular, and compare the expected hit rate and standard deviation of average latency across objects for both policies, assuming a full cache can store all objects at full power on the 4 nodes. For the activation policy, the hit rate is 50%, since it keeps two servers active and these servers store 50% of the objects. Since all objects are equally popular, migration does not significantly change the results. In this case, the standard deviation is 47.5ms, assuming an estimate of 5ms to access the cache and 100ms to regenerate the object from persistent storage. For a synchronous policy, the hit rate is also 50%, since all 4 nodes are active half the time and these nodes store 100% of the objects. However, the synchronous policy has a standard deviation of 0ms, since all objects have a 50% hit probability, if the access occurs when a node is active, and a 50% miss probability, if the access occurs when a node is inactive. Rather than half the objects having a 5ms average latency and half having a 100ms average latency, as with activation, a synchronous policy ensures an average latency of 52.5ms across all objects.

Note that the synchronous policy is ideal for a normal memcached cluster with a mapping function that randomly maps keys to servers, since the aggregate popularity of objects on each server will always be roughly equal. Further, unlike an activation policy that uses the dynamic mapping function, the synchronous policy does not incur invalidation penalties and is not arbitrarily unfair to keys on lower-ranked servers.

#### 4.3.3 Load-Proportional Policy

A synchronous policy has the same hit rate as an activation policy when keys have the same popularity, but is significantly more fair. However, an activation policy with migration is capable of a significantly higher hit rate for highly skewed popularity distributions. A proportional policy combines the advantages of both approaches for Zipf-like distributions, where a few key values are highly popular but there is a heavy, but significant, tail of similarly unpopular key values. As with our activation policy, a proportional policy ranks servers and uses a proxy to monitor object popularity and migrate objects to servers in rank order. However, the policy distributes the available power to servers in the same proportion as the aggregate popularity of their keys.

For example, assume that in our 4 server cluster after key migration the percentage of total hits that go to the first server is 70%, the second server is 12%, the third server is 10%, and the fourth server is 8%. If there is currently 100W of available power then the first server ideally receives 70W, the second server 12W, the third server 10W, and the fourth server 8W. These power levels then translate directly to active durations over each interval $T$. In practice, if the first server's maximum power is 50W, then it will be active the entire interval, since its maximum power is 70W. The extra 20W is distributed to the remaining servers proportionally. If all servers have a maximum power of 50W, the first server receives 50W, the second server receives 20W, i.e., 40% of the remaining 50W, the third server receives 16.7W, and the fourth server receives 13.3W. These power levels translate into the following active durations for a 60 second blink interval: 60 seconds, 24 seconds, 20 seconds, and 16 seconds, respectively.

The hit rate from a proportional policy is only slightly worse than the hit rate from the optimal activation policy. In this example, we expect the hit rate from an activation policy to be 85% of the maximum hit rate from a fully powered cluster, while we expect the hit rate from a proportional policy to be 80.2%. However, the policy is more fair to the 3 servers—12%, 10%, and 8%—with similar popularities, since each server receives a similar total active duration. The Zipf distribution for a large memcached cluster has similar attributes. A few servers store highly popular objects and will be active nearly 100% of the time, while a large majority of the servers will store equally unpopular objects and blink in proportion to their overall unpopularity.

| *Metric* | *Workload* | *Best Policy* |
|---|---|---|
| Hit Rate | Uniform | Synchronous |
| Hit Rate | Zipf | Activation (Migration) |
| Fairness | Uniform/Zipf | Synchronous |
| Fairness + Hit Rate | Zipf | Load-Proportional |

Table 4: Summary of the best policy for a given performance metric and workload combination.

### 4.4 Summary

Table 4 provides a summary of the best policy for each performance metric and workload combination. In essence, an activation policy with key migration will always have the highest hit rate. However, for distributions with equally popular objects, the synchronous policy achieves a similar hit rate and is more fair. A load-proportional policy combines the best attributes of both for Zipf-like distributions, which include a few popular objects but many similarly unpopular objects.

## 5. Implementation and Evaluation

We implement and evaluate the BlinkCache design alternatives from the previous section using our small-scale Blink prototype. The purpose of our evaluation is not to maximize the performance of our particular memcached deployment or improve on the performance of the custom memcached server deployments common in industry. Instead, our goal is to explore the effects of churn on memcached caused by power fluctuations for different BlinkCache designs. Our results will differ across platforms according to the specific blink interval, CPU speed, and network latency and bandwidth of the servers and the network. Since our prototype uses low-power CPUs and motherboards, the request latencies we observe in our prototype are not representative of those found in high performance servers.

Each node in Blink connects to a low-power (2.4W/switch) 100 Mbps switch and runs an instance of Blink's power client and an unmodified memcached server. We wrote a memcached client workload generator to issue key requests at a configurable, but steady, rate according to either a Zipf popularity distribution, parameterized by $\alpha$, or a uniform popularity distribution. As in a typical application, the workload generator fetches any data not resi-

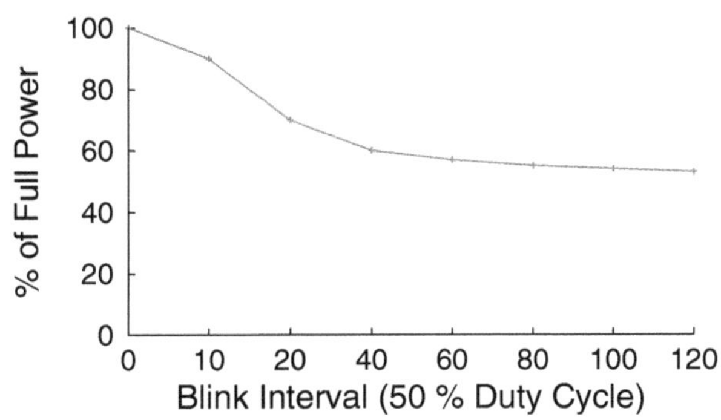


Figure 7: The near 2 second latency to transition into and out of S3 in our prototype discourages blinking intervals shorter than roughly 40 seconds. With a 50% duty cycle we expect to operate at 50% full power, but with a blink interval of less than 10 seconds we operate near 100% full power.

dent in the cache from a MySQL database and places it in the cache. Since we assume the MySQL server provides always-available persistent storage, it runs off the power grid and not variable power. Note that for our benchmarks we take the conservative approach of simply fetching key values directly from MySQL with a single query, and do not imitate the sequential, multi-query nature of production web applications. While we do not model or evaluate the impact of workloads that include multi-get memcached requests that issue gets for multiple keys in parallel, blinking with key migration should not impact the performance of multi-get requests for keys with similar popularities, e.g., part of the same HTML page, since our proxy will migrate these keys to the same server.

Unless otherwise noted, in our experiments, we use moderate-size objects of 10 kilobytes, Facebook-like Zipf $\alpha$ values of 0.6, and memcached's consistent hashing mapping function. Each experiment represents a half-hour trace, we configure each memcached server with a 100MB cache to provide an aggregate cache size of 1GB, and we use our programmable power supply to drive each power trace. Since each node has only 256MB of memory, we scale our workloads appropriately for evaluation. We modify magent, a publicly available memcached proxy, [4] to implement the design alternatives in the previous section, including table-based key mapping and popularity-based key migration. Our modifications are not complex: we added or changed only 300 lines of code to implement all of the BlinkCache design variants from Section 3. Since all requests pass through the proxy, it is able to monitor key popularity. The proxy controls blinking by interacting with Blink's power manager, which in our setup runs on the same node, to monitor the available power and battery level and set per-node blinking patterns. We also use the proxy for experiments with memcached's default hash-based key mappings, rather than modifying the memcached client. Since our always-on proxy is also subject to intermittent power constraints, we run it on a low-power (5W) embedded SheevaPlug with a 1.2 GHz ARM CPU and 512 MB of memory.

We first use our workload generator to benchmark the performance of each blinking policy for both Zipf-like and uniform popularity distributions at multiple power levels with varying levels of oscillation. We then demonstrate the performance for an example web application—tag clouds in GlassFish—using realistic traces from our energy harvesting deployment that have varying power and oscillation levels.

[4] `http://code.google.com/p/memagent/`

### 5.1 Benchmarks

We measure the maximum power of each node, at 100% CPU and network utilization, in S0 to be 8.6W and its minimum power in S3 to be 0.2W. We use these values in the proxy to compute the length of active and inactive periods to cap power consumption at a specific level. We also measure the impact of our node's near 2 second transition latency for blink intervals $T$ between 10 seconds and 2 minutes. Figure 7 shows the results for a duty cycle of 50%. In this case, the blinking interval must be over 40 seconds before average power over the interval falls below 55% of the node's maximum power, as we expect. The result shows that on-demand transitions that occur whenever work arrives or departs are not practical in our prototype. Further, even blinking intervals as high as 10 seconds impose significant power inefficiencies. As a result, we use a blinking interval of 60 seconds for our experiments. Our 60 second blink interval is due solely to limitations in the Blink prototype. Note that there is an opportunity to significantly reduce blink intervals through both hardware and software optimizations. Since server clusters do not typically leverage ACPI's S3 state, there has been little incentive to optimize its transition latency.

Next, we determine a baseline workload intensity for memcached, since, for certain request rates and key sizes, the proxy or the switch becomes a bottleneck. In our experiments, we use a steady request rate (1000 get requests/sec) that is less than the maximum request rate possible once the proxy or switch becomes a bottleneck. Note that our results, which focus on hit rates, are a function of the popularity of objects rather than the distribution of request inter-arrival times. Our goal is to evaluate how blinking affects the relative hit rates between the policies, and not the performance limitations of our particular set of low-power components. Figure 8 demonstrates the maximum performance, in terms of total throughput and request latency for different key values sizes, of an unmodified memcached server, our memcached proxy, and a MySQL server. As expected, the memcached server provides an order of magnitude higher throughput and lower request latency than MySQL. Further, our proxy implementation imposes only a modest overhead to both throughput and latency, although the latency impact of proxy-based redirections will be greater on faster CPUs since less relative request time is spent in the OS and network. Our subsequent experiments focus on request hit rates rather than request latencies, since latencies vary significantly across platforms and workloads. Further, the wide disparity in latency between serving a request from memory and serving it from disk would show a larger, and potentially unfair, advantage for a blinking system. Thus, we consider hit rate a better metric than latency for evaluating a blinking memcached instance.

#### 5.1.1 Activation Blinking and Thrashing

An activation policy for an unmodified version of memcached must choose whether or not to alter the hash-based mapping function as it activates and deactivates servers. For constant power, a dynamic mapping function that always reflects the currently active set of servers should provides the best hit rate, regardless of the popularity distribution, since applications will be able to insert the most popular keys on one of the active servers. Figure 9 demonstrates this point for a workload with a Zipf popularity distribution ($\alpha = 0.6$), and shows the hit rates for both static and dynamic activation variants at multiple constant power levels. While at high power levels the approaches have similar hit rates, as power level decreases, we see that the static variant incurs a higher penalty under constant power. However, Figure 10 demonstrates that the opposite is true for highly variable power. The figure reports hit rates for different levels of power oscillation, where the average power for each experiment is 45% of the power necessary to run all nodes concurrently. The $x$-axis indicates oscillation level as a percentage,

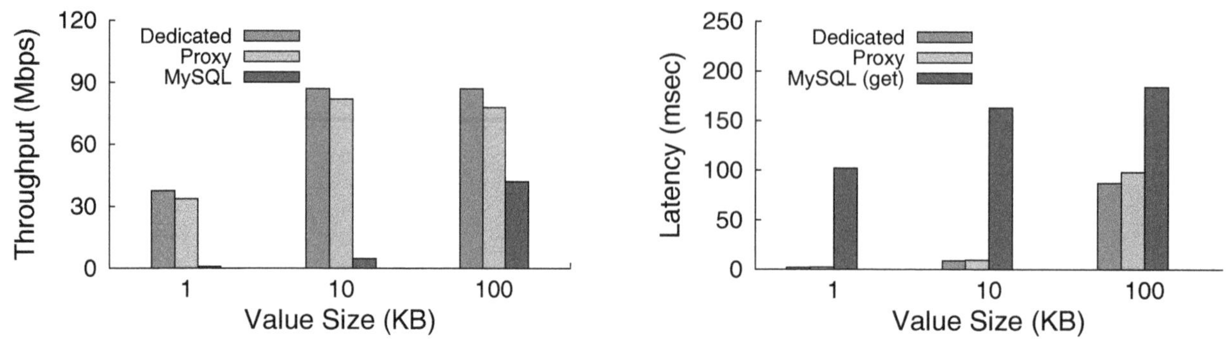


(a) Throughput

(b) Latency

Figure 8: Maximum throughput (a) and latency (b) for a dedicated memcached server, our memcached proxy, and a MySQL server. Our proxy imposes only a modest overhead compared with a dedicated memcached server.

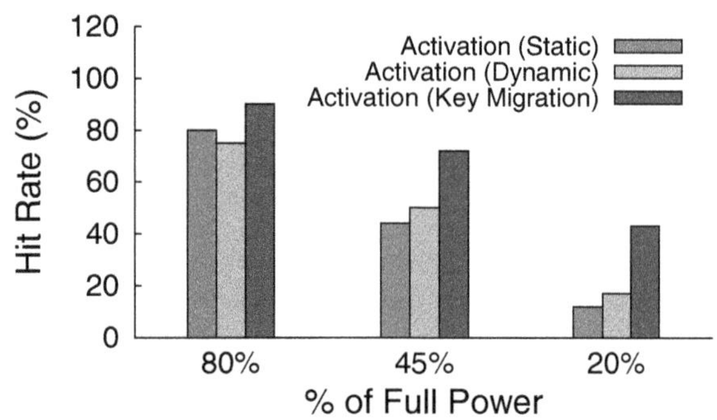


Figure 9: Under constant power for a Zipf popularity distribution, the dynamic variant of the activation policy performs better than the static variant as power decreases. However, the activation policy with key migration outperforms the other variants.

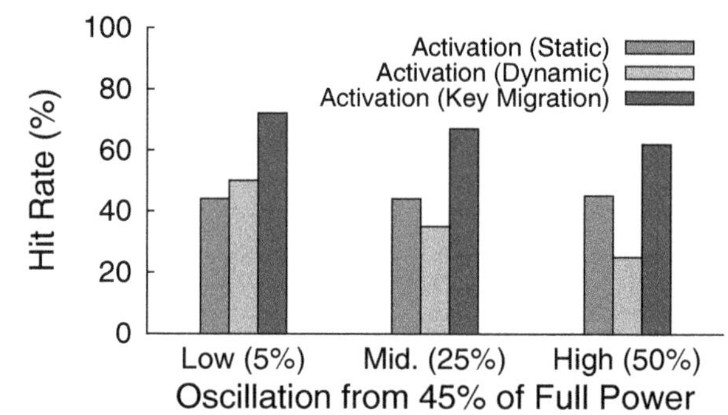


Figure 10: Under oscillating power for a Zipf popularity distribution, the static variant of the activation policy performs better than the dynamic variant as the oscillation increases. Again, the activation policy with key migration outperforms the other variants.

such that 0% oscillation holds power steady throughout the experiment and $N\%$ oscillation varies power between $(45 + 0.45N)\%$ and $(45 - 0.45N)\%$ every 5 minutes.

We see that dynamic changes in the active server set of memcached's hash-based mapping function incur an invalidation penalty. Since the invalidation penalty does not occur when memcached does not change the mapping function, the static variant provides a significantly better hit rate as the oscillations increase. Although not shown here, the difference with the original modulo approach is much greater, since each change flushes nearly the entire cache. The hash-based mapping function forces a choice between performing well under constant power or performing well under variable power. A table-based approach that uses our proxy to explicitly map keys to servers and uses key migration to increase the priority of popular keys performs better in both scenarios. That is, the approach does not incur invalidation penalties under continuously variable power, or result in low hit rates under constant power, as also shown in Figure 9 and Figure 10. Note that oscillation has no impact on other policies, e.g. those using key migration or the synchronous policy.

### 5.1.2 Synchronous Blinking and Fairness

While the activation policy with key migration results in the highest hit rate overall, it is unfair when many servers store equally popular objects since the policy must choose some subset of equally popular servers to deactivate. Figure 11 quantifies the fairness of the dynamic activation policy, the activation policy with key migration, and the synchronous policy, as a function of standard deviation in average per-object latency, at multiple constant power levels for a uniform popularity distribution where all objects are equally popular. Note that for distributions where all objects are equally popular, key migration is not necessary and is equivalent to using the static variant of hash-based mapping.

The synchronous policy is roughly 2X more fair than the activation policy with key migration at all power levels. While the dynamic hash-based mapping is nearly as fair as the synchronous policy, it has a worse hit rate, especially in high-power scenarios, as shown in Figure 12. Thus, the synchronous policy, which is more fair and provides lower average latency, is a better choice than any variant of the activation policy for uniform popularity distributions. Note that the key popularity distribution across servers in *every* memcached cluster that uses a hash-based mapping function is uniform, since keys map to servers randomly. Thus, the synchronous policy is the best choice for a heavily-loaded memcached cluster that cannot tolerate the throughput penalty of using proxies.

### 5.1.3 Balancing Performance and Fairness

Activation with key migration results in the maximum hit rate for skewed popularity distributions where some objects are significantly more popular than others, while the synchronous policy re-

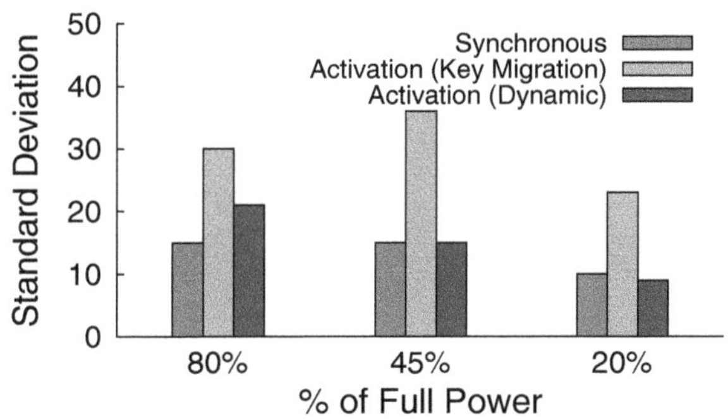


Figure 11: For a uniform popularity distribution, both the synchronous policy and the dynamic variant of the activation policy are significantly more fair, i.e., lower standard deviation of average per-object latency, than the activation policy with key migration.

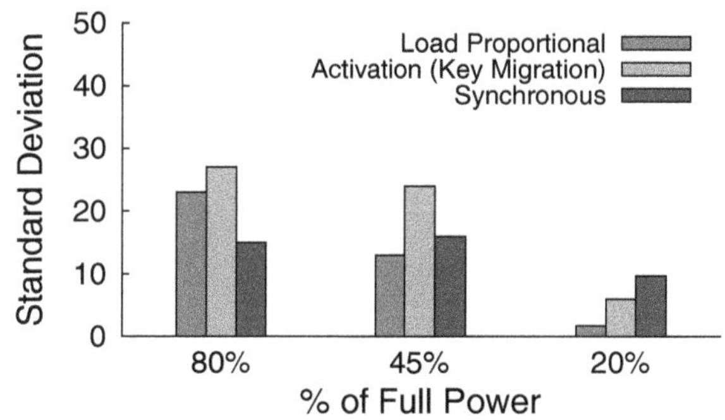


Figure 13: The load-proportional policy is more fair to the unpopular objects, i.e. bottom 80% in popularity, than the activation policy with key migration for Zip popularity distributions, especially in low-power scenarios.

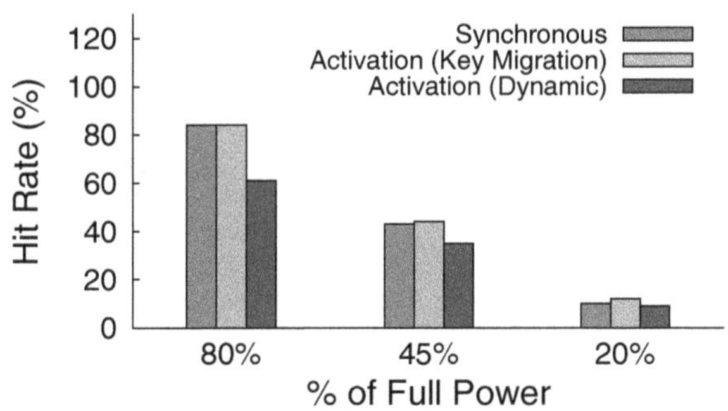


Figure 12: For a uniform popularity distribution, the synchronous policy and the activation policy with key migration achieve a similar hit rate under different power levels. Both policies achieve a better hit rate than the dynamic variant of the activation policy.

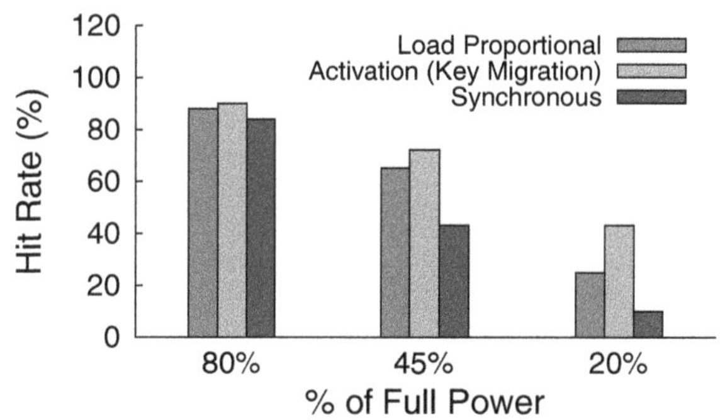


Figure 14: The load-proportional policy has a slightly lower hit rate than the activation policy with key migration.

sults in the best overall performance, in terms of both hit rate and fairness, for uniform popularity distributions. The proportional policy combines the advantages of both and works well for Zipf-like distributions with a few popular objects but a long tail of similarly (un)popular objects, since the long heavy tail in isolation is similar to the uniform distribution. Figure 14 shows the hit rate for the proportional policy, the activation policy with migration, and the synchronous policy for a Zipf popularity distribution with $\alpha = 0.6$ at different power levels. The synchronous policy performs poorly, especially at low power levels, in this experiment, since it does not treat popular objects different than unpopular objects.

However, the proportional policy attains nearly the same hit rate as the activation policy at high power levels, since it also prioritizes popular objects over unpopular objects. Even at low power levels its hit rate is over 60% of the activation policy's hit rate. Further, the proportional policy is significantly more fair to the many unpopular objects in the distribution. Figure 13 reports fairness, in terms of the standard deviation in per-object latency, at different power levels for the unpopular keys, i.e., keys ranked in the bottom 80th percentile of the distribution. The activation policy's unfairness is nearly 4X worse at low power levels. Thus, the proportional policy strikes a balance between performance and fairness when compared against both the synchronous and activation policies.

Finally, Figure 15 shows how the S3 transition overhead affects our results at a moderate power level. The figure shows that the overhead has only a modest effect on the load-proportional policy's hit rate. The overhead does not affect the relative fairness of the policies. Note that all of our previous experiments use our prototype's 2 second transition overhead. A shorter transition overhead would improve our results, and even a longer transition would show some, albeit lesser, benefits.

### 5.2 Case Study: Tag Clouds in GlassFish

While our prior experiments compare our blinking policies for different power and oscillation levels, we also conduct an application case study using traces from our energy harvesting deployment. The experiment provides a glimpse of the performance tradeoffs for realistic power signals. GlassFish is an open source Java application server from Sun, which includes a simple example application that reuses parts of the Java PetStore multi-tier web application, used in prior research, e.g., [9], to create tag clouds for pets. Tag clouds are a set of weighted tags that visually represent the most popular words on a web page. We modify the default web application to generate HTML for per-user tag cloud pages and cache them in memcached. The data to construct each HTML page comes from a series of 20 sequential requests to a MySQL database.

For these experiments, we measure the latency to load user tag cloud pages, which incorporates MySQL and HTML regeneration latencies whenever HTML pages are not resident in the cache.

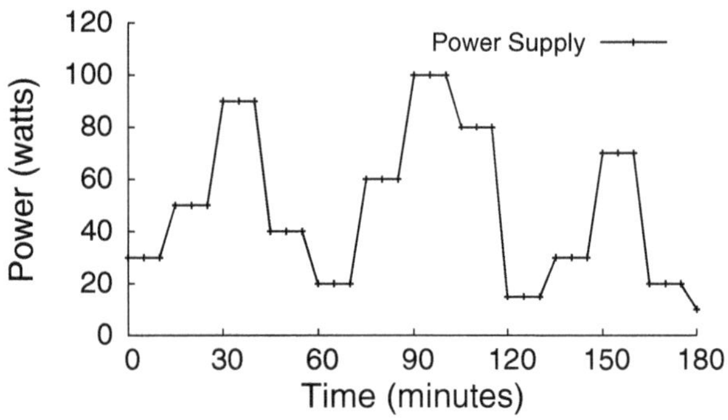

(a) Power

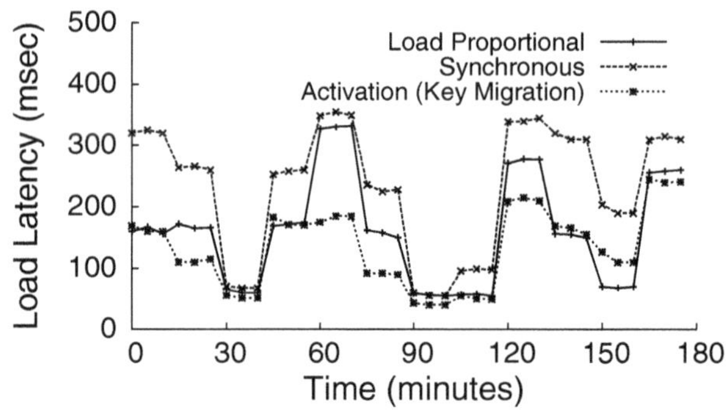

(b) Page Load Latency

Figure 16: Power signal from a combined wind/solar deployment (a) and average page load latency for that power signal (b).

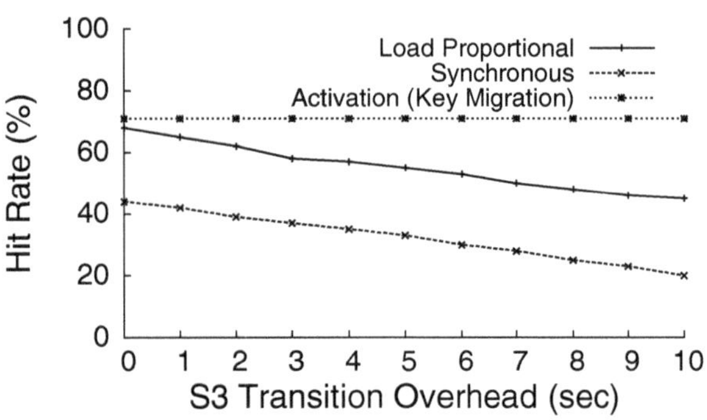


Figure 15: As S3 transition overhead increases, the hit rate from the load-proportional policy decreases relative to the activation policy with key migration for a Zipf distribution at a moderate power level.

The MySQL latency for our simple table-based data is typically 30ms per database query. While page load latency follows the same trend as hit rate, it provides a better application-level view of the impact of different policies. Figure 16(b) shows the average latency to load user web pages across 40,000 users for our three different policies—activation with key migration, proportional, and synchronous—for a combined solar and wind trace, assuming the popularity of each user's tag cloud page follows a Zipf distribution with $\alpha = 0.6$. We derive the power signal, shown in Figure 16(a), by compressing a 3-day energy harvesting trace to 3 hours.

As expected, the activation policy with key migration and the load-proportional policy exhibit comparable page load latencies at most points in the trace. For this trace, the load-proportional policy is within 15% of the activation policy's hit rate. The activation policy is slightly better at low energy levels, since it tends to strictly ensure that more popular content is always cached. Also as expected, the synchronous policy tends to perform poorly across all power levels. Also as expected, we measure the standard deviation of page load latencies for the load-proportional policy to be within 2% to the synchronous policy for the vast majority, i.e., bottom 80%, of the equally unpopular objects.

## 6. Related Work

The sensor network community has studied strategies for dealing with variable sources of renewable power, since these systems often do not have access to the power grid. However, since sensor networks are geographically distributed, each node must harvest its own energy, resulting in network-wide energy imbalances [11], whereas data center nodes share a common power delivery infrastructure. Further, the primary performance metric for a sensor network is the amount of data the network collects. As a result, much of the energy harvesting work is not directly applicable to data centers. Similarly, mobile computing generally focuses on extending battery life by regulating power consumption [40], rather than modulating performance to match energy production.

The increasing energy consumption of data centers [1] has led companies to invest heavily in renewable energy sources [22, 35]. For example, the goal of Google's RE<C initiative is to make large-scale renewable power generation cheaper than coal-based production. As a result, researchers have started to study how to incorporate renewables into a data center's power delivery infrastructure [33]. As one example, Lee et al. [18] use request redirection to control the carbon footprint of data centers by redirecting load to servers powered by renewable energy sources. While not directly related to energy harvesting, Power Routing [27] proposes shuffled power delivery topologies that allow data centers to control how much power each rack receives. While the topologies are well-suited for delivering variable amounts of power to racks based on aggregate demand, they are also useful for flexible routing of a variable power supply. Prior research on workload-driven approaches to improve data center energy efficiency is orthogonal to our work. Examples include designing platforms that balance CPU and I/O capacity [5, 32], routing requests to locations with the cheapest energy [29], and dynamically activating and deactivating nodes as demand rises and falls [8, 17, 37]. PowerNap's node-level energy proportional technique has also been viewed as a workload-driven optimization [21]. We show that a similar technique is useful for controlling per-node power consumption in a power-driven system.

Power capping has also been studied previously in data centers to ensure collections of nodes do not exceed a worst-case power budget [12, 30]. However, the work assumes exceeding the power budget is a rare transient event that does not warrant application-specific modifications, and that traditional power management techniques, e.g., DVFS, are capable of enforcing the budget. These assumptions may not hold in many scenarios with intermittent power constraints, as with our renewable energy power source. Gandhi et al. cap CPU power by forcing CPU idle periods [13]. While similar, blinking focuses on capping per-node power where the CPU is only one component of the total power draw. Improving the energy-efficiency of storage is also a related research area. While Memcached does not offer persistent storage, our modifications for blinking adapt similar ideas from prior storage research, such as migrating popular objects to more active nodes [28, 41]. Additionally, power-aware caching algorithms focus on maximizing the idle time between disk accesses to reduce disk power consumption, while our work focus on controlling the power consumption of the cache itself [42].

Blinking introduces regulated churn into data center applications as nodes switch from the active to inactive state. Churn has been well-studied in decentralized, self-organizing distributed hash tables [34]. However, the type of churn experienced by DHTs is different than the churn caused by blinking, which motivates our different approach to the problem. In the former case, nodes arrive and depart unexpectedly based on autonomous user behavior and network conditions, while in the latter case, nodes switch between the active and inactive states in a regular and controllable fashion. Finally, RAMCloud [26] proposes using memory for low-latency persistent storage, and cites as motivation the increasingly large memcached clusters used in production data centers. The size of these clusters motivates our observation that fairness for the large number of equally unpopular objects, in addition to hit rate, is an important performance metric.

## 7. Applicability of Blinking

While we apply blinking to a memcached cluster powered by renewable energy in this paper, we believe blinking is applicable to other applications with intermittent power constraints. There are a range of scenarios beyond renewable energy where imposing intermittent constraints may be attractive. For example, data centers may wish to participate in automated demand-response programs with the electric grid. Automated demand-response, which is a cornerstone of a future smart electric grid, decreases power levels at participating consumers when the electric grid is under stress in exchange for lower power rates. Data centers are well-positioned to benefit from automated demand-response, since servers, as opposed to other types of electrical appliances, already include sophisticated power management mechanisms and are remotely programmable. Blink simply uses these pre-existing mechanisms to gracefully scale application performance as power varies. Additionally, data centers consume significant quantities of power, and demand-response programs typically target large power consumers first. Thus, addressing intermittent constraints in data centers may contribute to a more flexible and efficient electric grid.

In addition to automated demand-response programs, data center operators may wish to cap energy bills or power consumption at a fixed level for a variety of reasons, which also imposes intermittent power constraints. For instance, capping energy bills imposes variable power constraints when energy prices vary, as with wholesale energy prices which vary at intervals as low as every 5 minutes [29]. Thus, as market prices vary, the amount of power a fixed budget purchases will also vary. Capping power is also necessary during "brownout" scenarios, more common in developing countries, where the electric grid is not always able to fully meet demand. Further, Ranganathan et al. [30], as well as others [12], point out the benefits of oversubscribing a data center's power delivery infrastructure, including the possibility of using dense clusters of lower-cost, but higher-power, components and then capping power to prevent damage.

Finally, we believe blinking is applicable to applications beyond memcached. As with memcached, applying blinking will likely require application-level modifications to handle regular and periodic disconnections. One particularly interesting case is leveraging blinking to run distributed storage systems under intermittent power constraints, such as in "brownout" scenarios. Persistent storage presents a different problem than memcached, since there is not an alternative always-on option to fallback on to retrieve data. The problems memcached presents stem from its process of mapping keys to nodes that is sensitive to power-level changes, which necessitate changing the active set of servers. Since distributed storage systems explicitly control the mapping of data to nodes they do not present the same problem. However, while we measure memcached's performance primarily as a function of hit rate and fairness, a blinking storage system's performance is primarily a measure of data availability, including both the latency and throughput to access data. As a result, a blinking storage system may need to judiciously replicate data to increase availability and ensure consistency across replicas, despite regular and frequent node transitions between the active and inactive states.

## 8. Conclusion

In this paper, we focus on managing server clusters running on intermittent power. We propose blinking as the primary abstraction for handling intermittent power constraints, and define multiple types of blinking policies. We then design an application-independent platform for developing and evaluating blinking applications, and use it to perform an in-depth study of the effects of blinking on one particular application and power source: memcached operating off renewable energy. We find that while an activation policy with key migration results in the best hit rates, it does not distribute the benefits of the cache equally among equally popular objects. As in-memory caches continue grow in size, they will store a greater fraction of equally popular objects for Zipf-like object popularity distributions. We then propose and evaluate an asymmetric load-proportional policy to increase fairness without significantly sacrificing the cache's hit rate. We are currently studying how blinking applies to other types of data center applications, including distributed storage layers and data-intensive batch systems.

**Acknowledgements**. We would like to thank our shepherd Thomas Wenisch and the anonymous reviewers for their insightful comments that improved this paper. This work was supported in part by NSF grants CNS-0855128, CNS-0834243, CNS-0916577, and EEC-0313747.

## References

[1] U.S. Environmental Protection Agency. Report To Congress On Server And Data Center Energy Efficiency. August 2nd 2007.

[2] Y. Agarwal, S. Hodges, R. Chandra, J. Scott, P. Bahl, and R. Gupta. Somniloquy: Augmenting Network Interfaces To Reduce PC Energy Usage. In *Proceedings of the Conference on Networked Systems Design and Implementation*, pages 365-380, April 2009.

[3] F. Ahmad and T. Vijaykumar. Joint Optimization of Idle and Cooling Power in Data Centers while Maintaining Response Time. In *Proceedings of the Conference on Architectural Support for Programming Languages and Operating Systems*, pages 243-256, March 2010.

[4] H. Amur, J. Cipar, V. Gupta, M. Kozuch, G. Ganger, and K. Schwan. Robust and Flexible Power-Proportional Storage. In *Proceedings of the Symposium on Cloud Computing*, June 2010.

[5] D. Anderson, J. Franklin, M. Kaminsky, A. Phanishayee, L. Tan, and V. Vasudevan. FAWN: A Fast Array Of Wimpy Nodes. In *Proceedings of the Symposium on Operating Systems Principles*, pages 1-14, October 2009.

[6] L. Barroso and U. Hölzle. The Case For Energy-proportional Computing. In *Computer*, 40(12):33-37, December 2007.

[7] L. Breslau, P. Cao, L. Fan, G. Phillips, and S. Shenker. Web Caching And Zipf-like Distributions: Evidence And Implications. In *Proceedings of the International Conference on Computer Communications*, pages 126-134, June 1999.

[8] J. Chase, D. Anderson, P. Thakar, A. Vahdat, and R. Doyle. Managing Energy And Server Resources In Hosting Centres. In *Proceedings*

*of the Symposium on Operating Systems Principles*, pages 103-116, October 2001.

[9] I. Cohen, J. Chase, M. Goldszmidt, T. Kelly, and J. Symons. Correlating Instrumentation Data To System States: A Building Block For Automated Diagnosis And Control. In *Proceedings of the Symposium on Operating System Design and Implementation*, pages 231-234, December 2004.

[10] G. DeCandia and D. Hastorun and M. Jampani and G. Kakulapati and A. Lakshman and A. Pilchin and S. Sivasubramanian and P. Vosshall and W. Vogels. Dynamo: Amazon's Highly Available Key-value Store. In *Proceedings of the Symposium on Operating Systems Principles*, pages 205-220, October 2007.

[11] K. Fan, Z. Zheng, and P. Sinha. Steady And Fair Rate Allocation For Rechargeable Sensors In Perpetual Sensor Networks. In *Proceedings of the Conference on Embedded Networked Sensor Systems*, pages 239-252, November 2008.

[12] X. Fan, W. Weber, and L. Barroso. Power Provisioning for a Warehouse-Sized Computer In *Proceedings of the International Symposium on Computer Architecture*, pages 13-23, June 2007.

[13] A. Gandhi, M. Harchol-Balter, R. Das, J. Kephart, and C. Lefurgy. Power Capping via Forced Idleness. In *Proceedings of the Workshop on Energy-efficient Design*, June 2009.

[14] P. Gupta. Google To Use Wind Energy To Power Data Centers. In *New York Times*, July 20th 2010.

[15] J. Hamilton. Overall Data Center Costs. In *Perspectives* at http://perspectives.mvdirona.com/. September 18, 2010.

[16] R. Kaushik and M. Bhandarkar. GreenHDFS: Towards an Energy-Conserving Storage-Efficient, Hybrid Hadoop Compute Cluster. In *Proceedings of the USENIX Annual Technical Conference*, June 2010.

[17] A. Krioukov, P. Mohan, S. Alspaugh, L. Keys, D. Culler, R. Katz. NapSAC: Design And Implementation Of A Power-Proportional Web Cluster. In *Proceedings of the Workshop on Green Networking*, August 2010.

[18] K. Lee and O. Bilgir and R. Bianchini and M. Martonosi and T. Nguyen Managing the Cost, Energy Consumption, and Carbon Footprint of Internet Services. In *Proceedings of the SIGMETRICS Conference*, June 2010.

[19] E. Le Sueur and Gernot Heiser. Dynamic Voltage and Frequency Scaling: The Laws of Diminishing Returns. In *Proceedings of the Workshop on Power Aware Computing and Systems*, October 2010.

[20] J. Leverich and C. Kozyrakis. On The Energy (In)efficiency Of Hadoop Clusters. In *ACM SIGOPS Operating Systems Review*, 44(1):61-65, January 2010.

[21] D. Meisner, B. Gold, and T. Wenisch. PowerNap: Eliminating Server Idle Power. In *Proceedings of the Conference on Architectural Support for Programming Languages and Operating Systems*, pages 205-216, March 2009.

[22] R. Miller. Microsoft To Use Solar Panels In New Data Center. In *Data Center Knowledge*, September 24th 2008.

[23] J. Moore, J. Chase, and P. Ranganathan. Weatherman: Automated, Online, And Predictive Thermal Mapping And Management For Data Centers. In *Proceedings of the International Conference on Autonomic Computing*, pages 155-164, June 2006.

[24] J. Moore, J. Chase, P. Ranganathan, and R. Sharma. Making Scheduling "Cool": Temperature-Aware Resource Assignment In Data Centers. In *Proceedings of the USENIX Annual Technical Conference*, April 2005.

[25] F. Nah. A Study On Tolerable Waiting Time: How Long Are Web Users Willing To Wait? In *Behaviour and Information Technology*, 23(3), May 2004.

[26] J. Ousterhout, P. Agarwal, D. Erickson, C. Kozyrakis, J. Leverich, D. Mazieres, S. Mitra, A. Narayanan, G. Parulkar, M. Rosenblum, S. Rumble, E. Stratmann, and R. Stutsman. The Case For RAMClouds: Scalable High-performance Storage Entirely In DRAM. In *ACM SIGOPS Operating Systems Review*, 43(5):92-105, December 2009.

[27] S. Pelley, D. Meisner, P. Zandevakili, T. Wenisch, and J. Underwood. Power Routing: Dynamic Power Provisioning In The Data Center. In *Proceedings of the Conference on Architectural Support for Programming Languages and Operating Systems*, pages 231-242, March 2010.

[28] E. Pinheiro and R. Bianchini. Energy Conservation Techniques for Disk Array-based Servers. In *Proceedings of the International Conference on Supercomputing*, pages 68-78, July 2004.

[29] A. Qureshi, R. Weber, H. Balakrishnan, J. Guttag, and B. Maggs. Cutting The Electric Bill For Internet-scale Systems. In *Proceedings of the SIGCOMM Conference*, pages 123-134, August 2009.

[30] P. Ranganathan, P. Leech, D. Irwin, and J. Chase. Ensemble-level Power Management for Dense Blade Servers. In *Proceedings of the International Symposium on Computer Architecture*, pages 66-77, June 2006.

[31] S. Shvachko, H. Kuang, S. Radia, and R. Chansler. The Hadoop Distributed File System. In *Proceedings of the Symposium on Mass Storage Systems and Technologies*, pages 1-10, May 2010.

[32] S. Rivoire, M. Shah, P. Ranganathan, and C. Kozyrakis. JouleSort: A Balanced Energy-efficiency Benchmark. In *Proceedings of the SIGMOD Conference*, pages 365-376, June 2008.

[33] C. Stewart and K. Shen. Some Joules Are More Precious Than Others: Managing Renewable Energy In The Datacenter. In *Proceedings of the Workshop on Power-Aware Computer Systems*, October 2009.

[34] I. Stoica, R. Morris, D. Karger, F. Kaashoek, and H. Balakrishnan. Chord: A Scalable Peer-to-peer Lookup Service For Internet Applications. In *Proceedings of the SIGCOMM Conference*, pages 149-160, August 2001.

[35] B. Stone. Google's Next Frontier: Renewable Energy. In *New York Times*, November 28th 2007.

[36] D. Terry, M. Theimer, K. Petersen, A. Demers, M. Spreitzer, and C. Hauser. Managing Update Conflicts In Bayou, A Weakly Connected Replicated Storage System. In *Proceedings of the Symposium on Operating Systems Principles*, pages 172-183, December 1995.

[37] N. Tolia, Z. Wang, M. Marwah, C. Bash, P. Ranganathan, and X. Zhu. Delivering Energy Proportionality With Non Energy-proportional Systems: Optimizing The Ensemble. In *Proceedings of the Workshop on Power-Aware Computer Systems*, San Diego, California, December 2008.

[38] A. Verma, P. De, V. Mann, T. Nayak, A. Purohit, G. Dasgupta, and R. Kothari. BrownMap: Enforcing Power Budget In Shared Data Centers. IBM, Technical Report RI09016, December 2009.

[39] A. Wolman, G. Voelker, N. Sharma, N. Cardwell, A. Karlin, and H. Levy. On The Scale And Performance Of Cooperative Web Proxy Caching. In *Proceedings of the Symposium on Operating Systems Principles*, pages 16-31, December 1999.

[40] H. Zeng and C. Ellis and A. Lebeck and A. Vahdat. ECOSystem: Managing Energy As A First Class Operating System Resource. In *Proceedings of the Conference on Architectural Support for Programming Languages and Operating Systems*, pages 123-132, October 2002.

[41] Q. Zhu and Z. Chen and L. Tan and Y. Zhou and K. Keeton and J. Wilkes. Hibernator: Helping Disk Arrays Sleep Through the Winter. In *Proceedings of the Symposium on Operating Systems Principles*, pages 177-190, October 2005.

[42] Q. Zhu and Z. Chen and L. Tan and Y. Zhou and K. Keeton and J. Wilkes. Power-Aware Storage Cache Management. In *IEEE Transactions on Computers*, 54(5):587-602, May 2005.

# Dynamic Knobs for Responsive Power-Aware Computing

Henry Hoffmann * Stelios Sidiroglou* Michael Carbin Sasa Misailovic
Anant Agarwal Martin Rinard

Computer Science and Artificial Intelligence Laboratory
Massachusetts Institute of Technology
{hank,stelios,mcarbin,misailo,agarwal,rinard}@csail.mit.edu

## Abstract

We present PowerDial, a system for dynamically adapting application behavior to execute successfully in the face of load and power fluctuations. PowerDial transforms static configuration parameters into *dynamic knobs* that the PowerDial control system can manipulate to dynamically trade off the accuracy of the computation in return for reductions in the computational resources that the application requires to produce its results. These reductions translate directly into performance improvements and power savings.

Our experimental results show that PowerDial can enable our benchmark applications to execute responsively in the face of power caps that would otherwise significantly impair responsiveness. They also show that PowerDial can significantly reduce the number of machines required to service intermittent load spikes, enabling reductions in power and capital costs.

***Categories and Subject Descriptors*** C.4 [*Performance of Systems*]: Reliability, availability, and serviceability

***General Terms*** Performance, Reliability, Experimentation

***Keywords*** Accuracy-aware Computing, Power-aware Computing, Self-aware Systems

## 1. Introduction

Many applications exhibit a trade-off between the accuracy of the result that they produce and the power and/or time that they require to produce that result. Because an application's optimal operating point can vary depending on characteristics of the environment in which it executes (for example, the delivered computational capacity of the underlying computing platform), developers often provide a static interface (in the form of configuration parameters) that makes it possible to choose different points in the trade-off space for different executions of the application. Configured at startup, the application operates at the selected point for its entire execution.

But phenomena such as load fluctuations or variations in available power can change the optimal operating point of the application as it is executing. Static configuration leaves the application with two unappealing choices: either continue its execution at a suboptimal point in the trade-off space (potentially impairing properties such as responsiveness to users) or terminate its current execution and restart at a new operating point (and incur service interruptions as it drops its current task and restarts).

### 1.1 Dynamic Knobs and Adaptive Response

We present a new system, PowerDial, for dynamically adapting the behavior of running applications to respond to fluctuations in load, power, or any other event that threatens the ability of the underlying computing platform to deliver adequate capacity to satisfy demand:

- **Dynamic Knob Insertion:** PowerDial uses dynamic influence tracing to transform static application configuration parameters into dynamic control variables stored in the address space of the running application. These control variables are made available via a set of *dynamic knobs* that can change the configuration (and therefore the point in the trade-off space at which it executes) of a running application without interrupting service or otherwise perturbing the execution.
- **Dynamic Knob Calibration:** PowerDial explores the underlying accuracy versus performance trade-off space (originally available via the configuration parameters) to characterize the accuracy and performance of each dynamic knob setting. It uses a quality of service (QoS) metric to quantify the accuracy of each setting.
- **Dynamic Knob Control:** PowerDial is designed for applications that are deployed to produce results at a target frequency (with performance measured as the time between results). It uses the Application Heartbeats framework [24] to dynamically monitor the application. An existing control strategy [35] is combined with a novel actuation mechanism to maintain performance. When the performance either drops below target (i.e., the time between results exceeds a given threshold) or rises above target (i.e., the time between results drops below the threshold), the PowerDial system uses the calibrated dynamic knobs to move the application to a more appropriate point in its trade-off space (the new point may, for example, give up some accuracy in return for increased performance and decreased power consumption). The goal is to maximize accuracy while preserving responsiveness in the face of fluctuations in the capabilities of the underlying computing platform.

### 1.2 Summary of Experimental Results

We evaluate PowerDial's ability to control the behavior of four benchmark applications (the x264 video encoder, the bodytrack human tracking application, the swaptions financial analysis application, and the swish++ search engine) dynamically in environments with fluctuating load and power characteristics. Our results show:

* Henry Hoffmann and Stelios Sidiroglou contributed equally to the research presented in this paper.



*ASPLOS'11,* March 5–11, 2011, Newport Beach, California, USA.

- **Trade-Off Space:** All of the applications exhibit a large viable trade-off space — three of the applications (x264, bodytrack, and swaptions) can execute from four to six times faster than their baseline (which defines the default quality of service) with acceptable quality of service losses. swish++ can execute approximately 1.5 times faster than its baseline (at the cost of dropping lower-ranked search results).
- **Power Capping:** Systems often respond to power caps (reductions in the delivered power imposed, for example, in response to cooling system failures) by dynamic voltage/frequency scaling (DVFS) (reducing the frequency and voltage at which the system operates [51]). The ensuing reduction in the delivered computational capacity of the system can make it difficult or impossible for applications to continue to deliver responsive service.

  Our results show that PowerDial enables applications to adapt effectively as a power cap (which reduces the processor frequency from 2.4 GHz to 1.6 GHz) is first imposed, then lifted. When the power cap is imposed, PowerDial preserves responsiveness by moving the applications to new Pareto-optimal points with less computational demands and slightly lower quality of service. When the power cap is lifted, PowerDial restores the original quality of service by moving the applications back to the baseline.
- **Peak Load Provisioning:** Systems are often provisioned to service the peak anticipated load. Common workloads often contain intermittent load spikes [9]. The system therefore usually contains idle machines that consume power but perform no useful work.

  Our results show that PowerDial can reduce the number of machines required to successfully service time-varying workloads. When a load spike overwhelms the ability of the system to service the load with the baseline application configuration, PowerDial preserves responsive performance by dynamically reconfiguring the application to use less computation to produce (slightly) lower quality results. Specifically, our results show that PowerDial can make it possible to reduce (by a factor of 3/4 for x264, bodytrack, and swaptions and by a factor of 1/3 for swish++) the number of machines required to provide responsive service in the face of intermittent load spikes. The system provides baseline quality of service for the vast majority of tasks; during peak loads, the system provides acceptable quality of service and (at most) negligible performance loss.

PowerDial is not designed for all applications — it is instead designed for applications that 1) have viable performance versus QoS trade-off spaces and (as is evident in the availability of appropriate configuration parameters) have been engineered to operate successfully at multiple points within those spaces and 2) operate in contexts where they must satisfy responsiveness requirements even in the face of fluctuations in the capacity of the underlying computing platform. In this paper we focus on fluctuations in power and load, but PowerDial can enable applications to adapt dynamically to any change that affects the computational capacity delivered to the application.

### 1.3 Contributions

This paper makes the following contributions:

- **Dynamic Knobs:** It presents the concept of dynamic knobs, which manipulate control variables in the address space of a running application to dynamically change the point in the underlying performance versus quality of service trade-off space at which the application executes.
- **PowerDial:** It presents PowerDial, a system that transforms static configuration parameters into calibrated dynamic knobs and uses the dynamic knobs to enable the application to operate successfully in the face of fluctuating operating conditions (such as load spikes and power fluctuations).
- **Analysis and Instrumentation:** It presents the PowerDial analysis and instrumentation systems, which dynamically analyze the application to find and insert the dynamic knobs.
- **Control:** It presents the PowerDial control system, which uses established control techniques combined with novel actuators to automatically maintain the application's desired performance while minimizing quality of service loss.
- **Resource Requirements:** It shows how to use dynamic knobs to reduce the number of machines required to successfully service peak loads and to enable applications to tolerate the imposition of power caps. It analyzes the resulting reductions in the amount of resources required to acquire and operate a computational platform that can successfully deliver responsive service in the face of power and load fluctuations.
- **Experimental Results:** It presents experimental results characterizing the trade-off space that dynamic knobs make available in our benchmark applications. It also presents results demonstrating PowerDial's ability to enable automatic, dynamic adaptation of applications in response to fluctuations in system load and power.

## 2. Dynamic Knobs

Dynamic knobs are designed for applications that 1) have static configuration parameters controlling performance versus QoS trade-offs and 2) use the Application Heartbeats API [24] (our system can automatically insert the required API calls, see Section 2.3). These applications typically exhibit the following general computational pattern:

- **Initialization:** During initialization the application parses and processes the configuration parameters, then computes and stores the resulting values in one or more control variables in the address space of the running application.
- **Main Control Loop:** The application executes multiple iterations of a main control loop. At each iteration it emits a heartbeat, reads the next unit of input, processes this unit, produces the corresponding output, then executes the next iteration of the loop. As it processes each input unit, it reads the control variables to determine which algorithm to use.

With this computational pattern, the point in the performance versus QoS trade-off space at which the application executes is determined by the configuration parameters when the application starts and does not change during its execution. A goal of PowerDial, as illustrated in Figure 1, is to augment the application with the ability to dynamically change the point in the trade-off space at which it is operating. At a high level, PowerDial accomplishes this goal as follows:

- **Parameter Identification:** The user of the program identifies a set of configuration parameters and a range of settings for each such parameter. Each combination of parameter settings corresponds to a different point in the performance versus QoS trade-off space.
- **Dynamic Knob Identification:** For each combination of parameter settings, PowerDial uses dynamic influence tracing (which traces how the parameters influence values in the running application) to locate the control variables and record the values stored in each control variable.
- **Dynamic Knob Calibration:** Given a set of representative inputs and a QoS metric, PowerDial executes a training run for each input and combination of parameter settings. For each training run it records performance and QoS information. It then processes this information to identify the Pareto-optimal points in the explored performance versus QoS trade-off space.

- **Dynamic Knob Insertion:** PowerDial inserts callbacks that the PowerDial control system can use to set the control variables to values previously recorded during dynamic knob identification, thereby moving the application to a different Pareto-optimal point in the performance versus QoS trade-off space. Subsequent iterations of the main control loop will read the updated values in the control variables to (in effect) process further input as if the configuration parameters had been set to their corresponding different settings at application startup.

The result is an application that enables the PowerDial control system to dynamically control the point in the performance versus QoS trade-off space at which the application executes. In standard usage scenarios PowerDial is given a target heart rate. If the application's dynamically observed heart rate is slower than the target heart rate, PowerDial uses the calibrated dynamic knobs to move the application to a new point in the trade-off space with higher performance at the cost, typically small, of some QoS. If the observed heart rate is higher than the target, PowerDial moves the application to a new point with lower performance and better QoS.

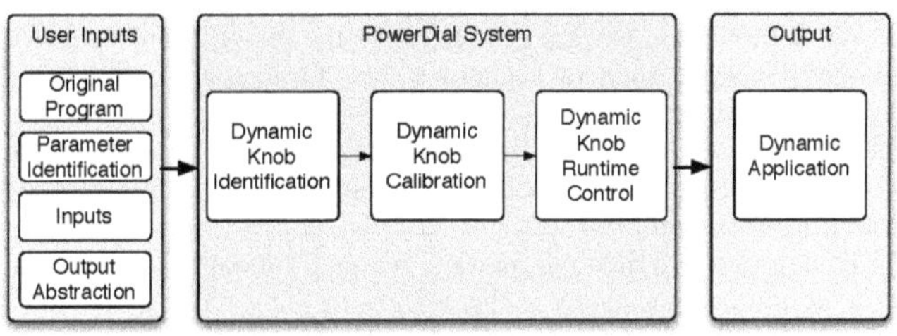


Figure 1: Dynamic Knob work flow.

### 2.1 Dynamic Knob Identification

For PowerDial to transform a given set of configuration parameters into dynamic knobs, it must identify a set of control variables that satisfy the following conditions:

- **Complete and Pure:** All variables whose values are derived from configuration parameters during application startup (before the application emits its first heartbeat) are control variables. The values of control variables are derived only from the given set of configuration parameters and not from other parameters.
- **Relevant and Constant:** During executions of the main control loop, the application reads but does not write the values of the control variables.

PowerDial uses influence tracing [11, 19] to find the control variables for the specified configuration parameters. For each combination of configuration parameter settings, PowerDial executes a version of the application instrumented to trace, as the application executes, how the parameters influence the values that the application computes. It uses the trace information to find the control variables and record their values, applying the above conditions as follows:

- **Complete and Pure Check:** It finds all variables that, before the first heartbeat, contain values influenced by the specified configuration parameters. It checks that these values are influenced only by the specified configuration parameters.
- **Relevance Check:** It filters out any variables that the application does not read after the first heartbeat — the values of these variables are not relevant to the main control loop computation.
- **Constant Check:** It checks that the execution does not write a control variable after the first heartbeat.

Finally, PowerDial checks that the control variables are *consistent*, i.e., that the different combinations of parameter settings all produce the same set of control variables. If the application fails any of these checks, PowerDial rejects the transformation of the specified configuration parameters into dynamic knobs.

For each combination of parameter settings, PowerDial records the value of each control variable. The PowerDial control system uses this information to automatically change the values of the control variables at runtime. Note that because PowerDial uses a dynamic influence analysis to find the control variables, it is possible for unexercised execution paths to violate one or more of the above conditions. The influence analysis also does not trace indirect control-flow or array index influence. To enable a developer to (if desired) check that neither of these potential sources of imprecision affects the validity of the control variables, PowerDial produces a control variable report. This report lists the control variables, the corresponding configuration parameters from which their values are derived, and the statements in the application that access them. We have examined the reports for all of our benchmark applications (see Section 4) and verified that all of the automatically computed control variables are valid.

Our influence tracing system is implemented as a static, source-based instrumentor for C and C++. It is built on the LLVM compiler framework [11, 30] and inserts code to trace the flow of influence through the values that the application computes. For each value, it computes the configuration parameters that influenced that value. The currently implemented system supports control variables with datatypes of int, long, float, double, or STL vector. It augments the production version of the application with calls to the PowerDial control system to register the address of each control variable and read in the previously recorded values corresponding to the different dynamic knob settings. This mechanism gives the PowerDial control system the information it needs to apply a given dynamic knob setting.

### 2.2 Dynamic Knob Calibration

In this step, PowerDial explores the performance versus QoS trade-off space available to the application via the specified configuration parameters. The user provides an application, a set of representative inputs, a set of specified configuration parameters, a range of values for each parameter, and a QoS metric. Given these values, PowerDial produces, for each combination of parameter settings, a specification of the point in the trade-off space to which the parameter settings take the application. This point is specified relative to the baseline performance and QoS of the parameter setting that delivers the highest QoS (which, for our set of benchmark applications, is the default parameter setting).

The PowerDial calibrator executes all combinations of the representative inputs and configuration parameters. For each parameter combination it records the mean (over all representative inputs) speedup of the application. It computes the speedup as the execution time of the application running with the default parameter settings divided by the execution time of the application with the current parameter combination. In a separate instrumented execution, it also records the values of the control variables (see Section 2.1).

For each combination of configuration parameters PowerDial also records the mean (over all representative inputs) QoS. The QoS metric works with a user-provided, application-specific *output abstraction* which, when provided with an output from the program, produces a set of numbers $o_1, \ldots, o_m$. The output abstraction typically extracts relevant numbers from the output or computes a measure of output quality (such as, for example, the peak signal-to-noise ratio of the output). Given the output abstraction from the baseline execution $o_1, \ldots, o_m$ and an output abstraction $\hat{o}_1, \ldots, \hat{o}_m$ from the execution with the current parameter settings, we compute the QoS loss as the *distortion* [43]:

$$qos = \frac{1}{m}\sum_{i=1}^{m} w_i \left|\frac{o_i - \hat{o}_i}{o_i}\right| \quad (1)$$

Here each weight $w_i$ is optionally provided by the user to capture the relative importance of the $i$th component of the output abstraction. Note that a $qos$ of zero indicates optimal QoS, with higher numbers corresponding to worse QoS. PowerDial supports caps on QoS loss — if a specific parameter setting produces a QoS loss that exceeds a user-specified bound, the system can exclude the corresponding dynamic knob setting from further consideration.

## 2.3 The PowerDial Control System

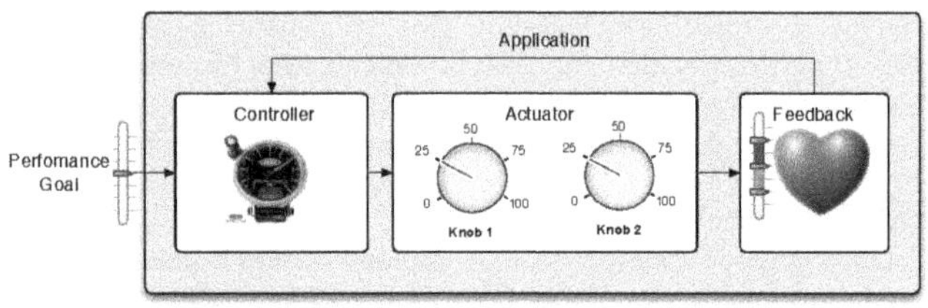


Figure 2: The PowerDial Control System.

The PowerDial control system automatically adjusts the dynamic knobs to appropriately control the application. As shown in Figure 2, the PowerDial control system contains the following components: a feedback mechanism that allows the system to monitor application performance, a control component which converts the feedback into a desired speedup, and an actuator which converts the desired speedup into settings for one or more dynamic knobs.

### 2.3.1 Feedback Mechanism

PowerDial uses the Application Heartbeats framework as its feedback mechanism [24]. In general, PowerDial can work with any application that has been engineered using this framework to emit heartbeats at regular intervals and express a desired performance in terms of a target minimum and maximum heart rate. For our set of benchmark applications, the PowerDial instrumentation system automatically inserts the API calls that emit heartbeats — it profiles each application to find the most time-consuming loop (in all of our applications this is the main control loop), then inserts a heartbeat call at the top of this loop. In general, the PowerDial control system is designed to work with any target minimum and maximum heart rate that the application can achieve. For our experiments (see Section 4), the minimum and maximum heart rate are both set to the average heart rate measured for the application using the default configuration parameters.

We use Application Heartbeats as a feedback mechanism for several reasons. First, this interface provides direct measurement of a specific application's performance, obviating the need to infer this measure from low-level metrics such as hardware performance counters or high-level metrics such as total system throughput. Second, Application Heartbeats are applicable to a variety of applications as they are more general than other common metrics such as flop rate (which is not designed to measure the performance of integer applications) and instructions per clock (which is not designed to measure the true performance of I/O bound applications or applications lacking instruction-level parallelism). Third, the interface is simple and can easily be customized by users who want to control the placement of heartbeat calls or the target performance. Finally, heartbeat-enabled applications can be controlled using a general and extensible control framework.

### 2.3.2 Control Strategy

PowerDial employs an existing, general control strategy which can work with any application that uses Application Heartbeats as a feedback mechanism [35]. This controller monitors the heartbeat data and determines both when to speed up or slow down the application as well as how much speedup or slowdown to apply. As described in [35], the control system models application performance as

$$h(t+1) = b \cdot s(t) \quad (2)$$

where $h(t)$ is the application's heart rate at time $t$, $b$ is the speed of the application when all knobs are set to their baseline values, and $s(t)$ is the speedup applied at time $t$.

Given this model of application behavior, the control system computes the speedup $s(t)$ to apply at time $t$ as

$$e(t) = g - h(t) \quad (3)$$

$$s(t) = s(t-1) + \frac{e(t)}{b} \quad (4)$$

where $e(t)$ is the error at time $t$ and $g$ is the target heart rate.

We demonstrate several properties of the steady-state behavior for the system defined in Equations 2–4. First, we show that the system converges, i.e., the performance reaches the desired heart rate, $g$. Second, we show that it is stable and does not oscillate around the desired heart rate. Third we show that the convergence time is bounded and fast.

To demonstrate these properties, we use standard control theoretic techniques and analyze the system in the Z-domain [23]. To begin, we compute the Z-transforms $F(z)$ and $G(z)$ of the systems defined in Equations 2 and 4, respectively as[1]:

$$G(z) = \frac{H(z)}{S(z)} = \frac{b}{z} \quad (5)$$

$$F(z) = \frac{S(z)}{E(z)} = \frac{z}{b(z-1)} \quad (6)$$

Using Equations 5 and 6 we compute the transfer function $F_{loop}(z)$ of the closed-loop system which drives the current heart rate, $h(t)$, to the target heart rate $g$ as

$$F_{loop}(z) = \frac{F(z)G(z)}{1 + F(z)G(z)} \quad (7)$$

$$F_{loop}(z) = \frac{1}{z} \quad (8)$$

We use standard techniques [23, 35] to demonstrate the desired properties of the system whose Z-transform is given by Equation 8. To show that the system converges, we show that it has a unit steady state gain, i.e., $F_{loop}(1) = 1$. Clearly, when $z = 1$, $F_{loop}(z) = 1$, so the system converges to the desired heart rate. To demonstrate that the system is stable and does not oscillate, we must ensure that the poles[2] of $F_{loop}(z)$ are less than 1. $F_{loop}(z)$ has a single pole $p$ at 0, so it is stable and will not oscillate. The time $t_c$ required for the system to converge is estimated as $t_c \approx -4/\log(|p_d|)$, where $p_d$ is the dominant pole of the system [23]. As the only pole for $F_{loop}(z)$ is $p = 0$, the system will converge almost instantaneously. In practice, the convergence time will be limited by a time quantum used to convert the continuous speedup signal into a discrete knob setting as described in the next section.

[1] A Z-transform converts an infinite list of values (e.g. $s(t)$ for all $t \geq 0$) into an infinite sum. In many cases, this infinite sum has a compact representation which is easier to analyze than the infinite list representation.

[2] A pole is a point $p$ such that $\lim_{z \to p} F(z) = \infty$.

### 2.3.3 Actuation Policy

The PowerDial actuator must convert the speedup specified by the controller into a dynamic knob setting. The controller is a continuous linear system, and thus, the actuator must convert the continuous signal into actions that can be realized in the application's discrete, potentially non-linear, dynamic knob system. For example, the controller might specify a speedup of 1.5 while the smallest speedup available through a knob setting is 2. To resolve this issue, the actuator computes a set of actions to take over a time quantum. We heuristically establish the time quantum as the time required to process twenty heartbeats. In the example, the actuator would run with a speedup of 2 for half the time quantum and the default speedup of 1 for the other half. Therefore, the average speedup over the time quantum is 1.5, the desired value.

The actuator determines which actions to take for the next time quantum by optimizing a system of linear constraints. Let $b$ be the heart rate in the baseline configuration, while $g$ is the target heart rate of the system. Let $s_{max}$ be the maximum achievable speedup for the application given its dynamic knobs, and let $s_{min}$ be the minimum speedup corresponding to a knob setting such that $s_{min} \geq g/b$. Let unknowns $t_{max}, t_{min}$, and $t_{default}$ correspond to the percentage of time during the next quantum to run with the application's knobs set to the maximum speedup, the minimum required speedup, and the default settings, respectively. The following system of constraints captures the behaviors considered for the next time quantum.

$$s_{max} \cdot t_{max} + s_{min} \cdot t_{min} + \frac{b}{g} \cdot t_{default} = 1 \quad (9)$$

$$t_{max} + t_{min} + t_{default} \leq 1 \quad (10)$$

$$t_{max}, t_{min}, t_{default} \geq 0 \quad (11)$$

While there are many solutions to this system of constraints, two are of particular interest for making power versus performance versus QoS trade-offs. First, for platforms with sufficiently low idle power consumption (for more detail see Section 3), PowerDial supports *race-to-idle* execution by setting $t_{min} = t_{default} = 0$, which forces the application to run at the highest available speedup. If $t_{max} < 1$ the system can idle for the remaining $1 - t_{max}$ portion of the time quantum to save power. The second solution PowerDial considers results from setting $t_{max} = 0$ and requiring $t_{min} + t_{default} = 1$. This solution will run the application at the lowest obtainable speedup that will enable the application to meet its heart rate target and delivers the lowest feasible QoS loss. Having determined values for $t_{max}, t_{min}$, and $t_{default}$ for the next time quantum, the PowerDial controller executes the corresponding plan, then computes a new plan when the quantum expires.

## 3. Analytical Models

Data center power consumption is experiencing significant growth. By 2011, U.S. data centers are predicted to use 100 Billion kWh, at a cost of $7.4 billion per year [50]. Of particular concern is the low average data center utilization, typically around 20-30% [9, 37], which coupled with high idle power consumption (at idle, current servers use about 60% of peak power), leads to significant waste.

The combination of brief but frequent bursts of activity with latency requirements results in underutilized machines remaining online. Server consolidation through the use of virtual machines, commonly used for non-critical services, cannot react quickly enough to maintain the desired level of service [37]. Turning idle systems off (even in low power mode), has similar problems.

To deal with idle power waste, researchers have proposed that system components be designed to consume energy proportional to their use [9]. Dynamic voltage and frequency scaling (DVFS) is a power management technique commonly found in modern processors [1, 3] that demonstrates this concept.

Beyond direct energy costs, data centers also incur capital costs (e.g. power provisioning, cooling, etc.,). Over the lifetime of the facility, these capital costs may exceed energy costs. To reduce such costs, researchers have proposed techniques that aim to operate facilities as close to maximum power capacity as possible, sometimes guaranteeing availability using various forms of *power capping* [18, 31, 41]. Power capping throttles server performance during utilization spikes to ensure that power budgets are satisfied. As a consequence of power capping, applications may experience increased latency due to the lower operating frequency. This increased latency may violate latency service level agreements.

We next present several analytical models that characterize the effectiveness of dynamic knobs in enabling applications to respond to dynamic voltage/frequency scaling (caused, for example, by the imposition or lifting of power caps) and in reducing the number of machines required to maintain responsiveness in the face of intermittent load spikes.

**DVFS and Dynamic Knobs:** Figure 3 shows how operating at lower power states can enable systems to reduce power consumption at the cost of increased latency. The area within the boxes represents the total energy required to complete a workload. For a task which takes time $t$ and consumes average power of $P_{avg}$, the total energy can be calculated as: $E_{task} = P_{avg} \cdot t$. Without DVFS (Figure 3 (a)), the workload consumes power $P_{nodvfs}$ for time $t_1$ and power $P_{idle}$ for the remaining time $t_{delay}$. With DVFS (Figure 3 (b)), the consumed power is reduced to $P_{dvfs}$ but the execution time increases to $t_2 = t_1 + t_{delay}$. To accurately calculate DVFS energy savings, the idle power consumed by the non-DVFS system ($P_{idle}$) must be included. Thus the energy savings due to DVFS can be computed as:

$$E_{dvfs} = (P_{nodvfs} \cdot t_1 + P_{idle} \cdot t_{delay}) - (P_{dvfs} \cdot t_2) \quad (12)$$

For CPU-bound applications, $t_2$ can be predicted by the change in operating frequency as: $t_2 = \frac{f_{nodvfs}}{f_{dvfs}} \cdot t_1$. We note that any power savings here come at the cost of added latency.

Dynamic knobs can complement DVFS by allowing systems to save power by reducing the amount of computational resources required to accomplish a given task. There are two cases to consider depending on the idle power of the system $P_{idle}$ as illustrated in Figure 4. Figure 4(a) illustrates the first case. This case applies to systems with low idle power consumption (i.e., small $P_{idle}$). In this case, the best energy savings strategy is to complete the task as quickly as possible, then return to the low-power idle state, a strategy known as *race-to-idle*. Dynamic knobs can facilitate race-to-idle operation by decreasing the amount of computational resources required to complete the task (in return for some QoS loss), thereby reducing $t_1$. Figure 4(b) illustrates the second case, which applies to systems with high idle power consumption (i.e., large $P_{idle}$), common in current server class machines. In this case, dynamic knobs can allow the system to operate at a lower power state for the time $t_2$ allocated to complete the task.

In both cases the energy savings available through combining DVFS and dynamic knobs can be calculated as:

$$t_1' = \frac{t_1}{S(QoS)}, \quad t_{delay}' = t_{delay} + t_1 - \frac{t_1}{S(QoS)} \quad (13)$$

$$E_1 = P_{nodvfs} \cdot t_1' + P_{idle} \cdot t_{delay}' \quad (14)$$

$$t_2' = \frac{t_2}{S(QoS)}, \quad t_{delay}'' = t_2 - \frac{t_2}{S(QoS)} \quad (15)$$

$$E_2 = P_{dvfs} \cdot t_2' + P_{idle} \cdot t_{delay}'' \quad (16)$$

$$E_{elasticdvfs} = \min(E_1, E_2) \quad (17)$$

$$E_{dvfs} = \min(P_{nodvfs} \cdot t_1 + P_{idle} \cdot t_{delay}, P_{dvfs} \cdot t_2) \quad (18)$$

$$E_{savings} = E_{dvfs} - E_{elasticdvfs} \quad (19)$$

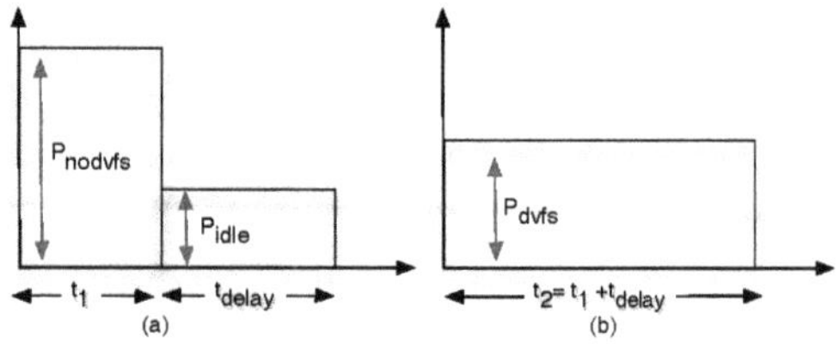


Figure 3: Power Consumption with DVFS

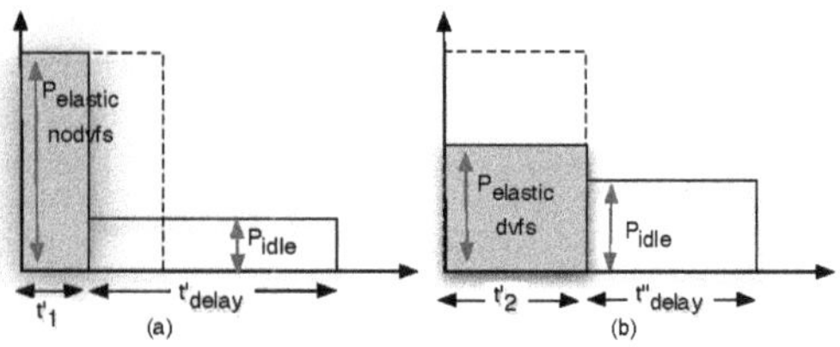


Figure 4: Power Consumption with DVFS and Dynamic Knobs

where $S(QoS)$ represents the speedup available as a function of acceptable QoS loss (i.e., the desired level of accuracy). In the power cap scenario discussed in Section 5.4, $t_{delay} = 0$ and the control objective is to find a point that maximizes delivered quality of service for a given constant $t_2$.

**Server Consolidation:** Dynamic knobs can also enable power savings by reducing the total number of machines required to meet peak load without increasing latency. This is achieved by increasing the throughput of each individual machine (by trading QoS for performance) thus reducing the number of machines that are needed to service peak demand. The resulting reduction in computational resources required to service the load enables the system to service the load spike without increasing the service time. The reduction in the number of machines improves server utilization during normal operation and reduces energy wasted on idle resources. It can also provide significant extra savings in the form of reduced cooling costs.

To quantify how dynamic knobs can help improve server consolidation, we need to examine the total work required to meet system peak load requirements. This can be calculated as follows:

$$W_{total} = (W_{machine} \cdot N_{orig}) \tag{20}$$

$W_{total}$ represents the total work, where $W_{machine}$ represents the work per machine and $N_{orig}$ is the total number of machines. Let $S(QoS)$ be the speedup achieved as a function of the reduction in QoS. For the default QoS (obtained with the default knob settings) the speedup is 1. The number of machines required to meet peak load with some loss of accuracy can be computed as:

$$N_{new} = \left\lceil \frac{W_{total}}{S(QoS)} \cdot \frac{1}{W_{machine}} \right\rceil \tag{21}$$

Here $N_{new}$ is the new, lower number of machines that can be used to meet peak load requirements after consolidation. To measure the savings achieved by this consolidation let $U_{new} = N_{orig}/N_{new}$ be the average utilization of the consolidated system and $U_{orig}$ be the average utilization in the original system. Further assume that the two systems both use machines that consume power $P_{load}$ under load and $P_{idle}$ while idle. Let $P_{orig}$ be the average power in the original system, while $P_{new}$ is the average power in the smaller consolidated system. Then we can calculate the average power savings of the consolidated system as:

$$P_{orig} = N_{orig}(U_{orig} \cdot P_{load} + (1 - U_{orig})P_{idle}) \tag{22}$$

$$P_{new} = N_{new}(U_{new} \cdot P_{load} + (1 - U_{new})P_{idle}) \tag{23}$$

$$P_{save} = P_{orig} - P_{new} \tag{24}$$

This power savings can reduce both the power required to operate the system and indirect costs such as cooling and conversion costs. It can also reduce the number of machines and therefore the capital cost of acquiring the system.

## 4. Benchmarks and Inputs

We report results for four benchmarks. swaptions, bodytrack, and x264 are all taken from the PARSEC benchmark suite [10]; swish++ is as open-source search engine [48]. For each application we acquire a set of representative inputs, then randomly partition the inputs into *training* and *production* sets. We use the training inputs to obtain the dynamic knob response model (see Section 2) and the production inputs to evaluate the behavior on previously unseen inputs. Table 1 summarizes the sources of these inputs. All of the applications support both single- and multi-threaded execution. In our experiments we use whichever mode is appropriate.

### 4.1 swaptions

**Description:** This financial analysis application uses Monte Carlo simulation to solve a partial differential equation that prices a portfolio of swaptions. Both the accuracy and the execution time increase with the number of simulations — the accuracy approaches an asymptote, while the execution time increases linearly.

**Knobs:** We use a single command line parameter, `-sm`, as the dynamic knob. This integer parameter controls the number of Monte Carlo simulations for each swaption. The values range from 10, 000 to 1, 000, 000 in increments of 10, 000; 1,000,000 is the default value for the PARSEC native input.

**Inputs:** Each input contains a set of parameters for a given swaption. The native PARSEC input simply repeats the same parameters multiple times, causing the application to recalculate the same swaption price. We augment the evaluation input set with additional randomly generated parameters so that the application computes prices for a range of swaptions.

**QoS Metric:** Swaptions prints the computed prices for each swaption. The QoS metric computes the distortion of the swaption prices (see Equation 1), weighting the prices equally to directly measuring the application's ability to produce accurate swaption prices.

### 4.2 x264

**Description:** This media application encodes a raw (uncompressed) video according to the H.264 standard [53]. Like virtually all video encoders, it uses lossy encoding, with the visual quality of the encoding typically measured using continuous values such as peak signal-to-noise ration.

**Knobs:** We use three knobs: `--subme` (an integer parameter which determines the algorithms used for sub-pixel motion estimation), `--merange` (an integer which governs the maximum search range for motion estimation), and `--ref` (which specifies the number of reference frames searched during motion estimation). `--subme` ranges from 1 to 7, `--merange` ranges from 1 to 16, and `--ref` ranges from 1 to 5. In all cases higher numbers correspond to higher quality encoded video and longer encoding times. The PARSEC native defaults for these are 7, 16, and 5, respectively.

**Inputs:** The native PARSEC input contains a single high-definition (1080p) video. We use this video and additional 1080p inputs from xiph.org [5].

**QoS Metric:** The QoS metric is the distortion of the peak signal to noise ratio (PSNR, as measured by the H.264 reference de-

| Benchmark | Training Inputs | Production Inputs | Source |
|---|---|---|---|
| swaptions | 64 swaptions | 512 swaptions | PARSEC & randomly generated swaptions |
| x264 | 4 HD videos of 200+ frames | 12 HD videos of 200+ frames | PARSEC & xiph.org [5] |
| bodytrack | sequence of 100 frames | sequence of 261 frames | PARSEC & additional input from PARSEC authors |
| swish++ | 2000 books | 2000 books | Project Gutenberg [2] |

Table 1: Summary of Training and Production Inputs for Each Benchmark

coder [22]) and bitrate (as measured by the size of the encoded video file), with the PSNR and bitrate weighted equally. This QoS metric captures the two most important attributes of encoded video: image quality and compression.

### 4.3 bodytrack

**Description:** This computer vision application uses an annealed particle filter and videos from multiple cameras to track a human's movement through a scene [15]. bodytrack produces two outputs: a text file containing a series of vectors representing the positions of body components (head, torso, arms, and legs) over time and a series of images graphically depicting the information in the vectors overlaid on the video frames from the cameras. In envisioned usage contexts [15], a range of vectors is acceptable as long as the vectors are reasonably accurately overlaid over the actual corresponding body components.
**Knobs:** bodytrack uses positional parameters, two of which we convert to knobs: `argv[5]`, which controls the number of annealing layers, and `argv[4]`, which controls the number of particles. The number of layers ranges from 1 to 5 (the PARSEC native default); the number of particles ranges from 100 to 4000 (the PARSEC native default) in increments of 100.
**Inputs:** bodytrack requires data collected from four carefully calibrated cameras. We use a sequence of 100 frames (obtained from the maintainers of PARSEC) as the training input and the PARSEC native input (a sequence of 261 frames) as the production input.
**QoS Metric:** The QoS metric is the distortion of the vectors that represent the position of the body parts. The weight of each vector component is proportional to its magnitude. Vector components which represent larger body components (such as the torso) therefore have a larger influence on the QoS metric than vectors that represent smaller body components (such as forearms).

### 4.4 swish++

**Description:** This search engine is used to index and search files on web sites. Given a query, it searches its index for documents that match the query and returns the documents in rank order. We configure this benchmark to run as a server — all queries originate from a remote location and search results must be returned to the appropriate location.
**Knobs:** We use the command line parameter `--max-results` (or `-m`, which controls the maximum number of returned search results) as the single dynamic knob. We use the values 5, 10, 25, 50, 75, and 100 (the default value).
**Inputs:** We use public domain books from Project Gutenberg [2] as our search documents. We use the methodology described by Middleton and Baeza-Yates [38] to generate queries for this corpus. Specifically, we construct a dictionary of all words present in the documents, excluding stop words, and select words at random following a power law distribution. We divide the documents randomly into equally-sized training and production sets.
**QoS Metric:** We use F-measure [36] (a standard information retrieval metric) as our QoS metric. F-measure is the harmonic mean of the *precision* and *recall*. Given a query, precision is the number of returned documents that are relevant to the query divided by the total number of returned documents. Recall is the number of relevant returned documents divided by the total number of relevant documents (returned or not). We examine precision and recall at different cutoff values, using typical notation **P @N**.

### 4.5 Discussion

These applications are broadly representative of our target set of applications — they all have a performance versus quality of service trade-off and they all make that trade-off available via configuration parameters. Other examples of applications with appropriate trade-off spaces include most sensory applications (applications that process sensory data such as images, video, and audio), most machine learning applications, many financial analysis applications (especially applications designed for use in competitive high-frequency trading systems, where time is critically important), many scientific applications, and many Monte-Carlo simulations. Such applications (unlike more traditional applications such as compilers or databases) are typically inherently approximate computations that operate largely without a notion of hard logical correctness — for any given input, they instead have a range of acceptable outputs (with some outputs more accurate and therefore more desirable than others). This broad range of acceptable outputs, in combination with the fact that more accurate outputs are often more computationally expensive to compute, gives rise to the performance versus quality of service trade-offs that PowerDial enables the applications to dynamically navigate.

There are a variety of reasons such applications would be deployed in contexts that require responsive execution. Applications that process soft real-time data for human users (for example, video-conferencing systems) need to produce results responsively to deliver an acceptable user experience. Search and information retrieval applications must also present data responsively to human users (although with less stringent response requirements). Other scenarios involve automated interactions. Bodytrack and similar probabilistic analysis systems, for example, could be used in real-time surveillance and automated response systems. High-frequency trading systems are often better off trading on less accurate results that are available more quickly — because of competition with other automated trading systems, opportunities for lucrative trades disappear if the system does not produce timely results.

## 5. Experimental Evaluation

We next discuss the experimental platform and each of the experiments used to evaluate PowerDial. Our first set of experiments explores the performance versus QoS trade-off space for each of our benchmark applications. Next, we explore the (closely related) power versus QoS trade-off spaces. We then investigate how PowerDial enables applications to respond to the imposition of power caps using dynamic knobs. Finally, we investigate the use of PowerDial to reduce the number of machines required for servicing workloads with intermittent load spikes. This reduction can, in turn, reduce the cost of acquiring and operating the system.

For each application, our experimental evaluation works with two data sets: a training data set used to characterize the application's performance versus QoS trade-off space, and a production data set used to evaluate how well the obtained characterization

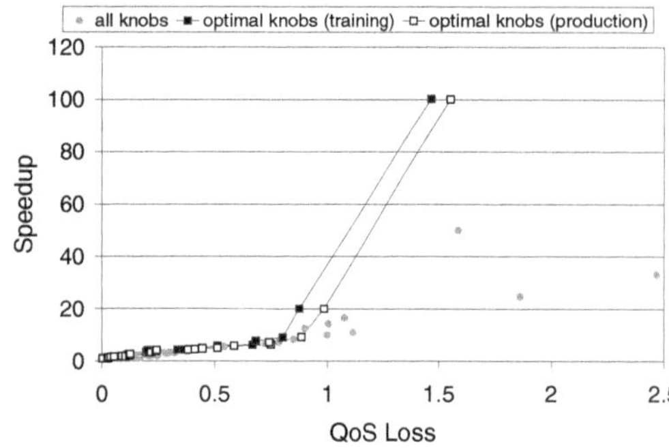


(a) swaptions

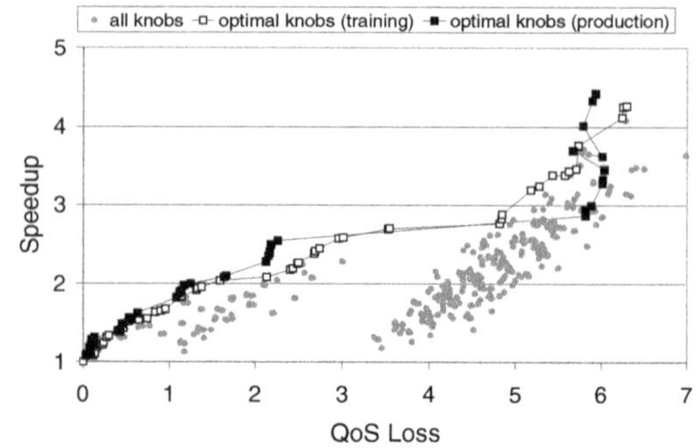


(b) x264

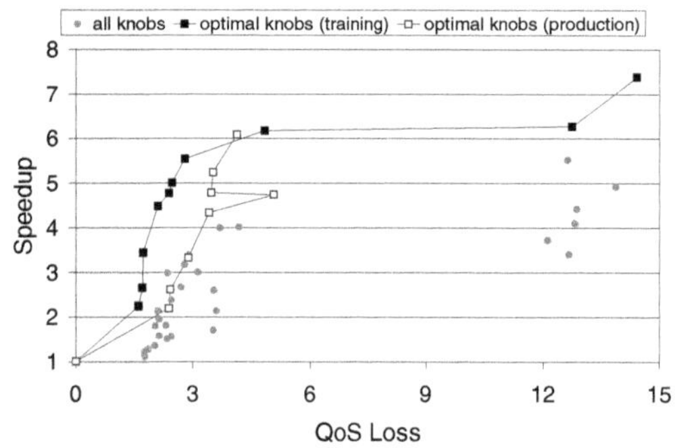


(c) bodytrack

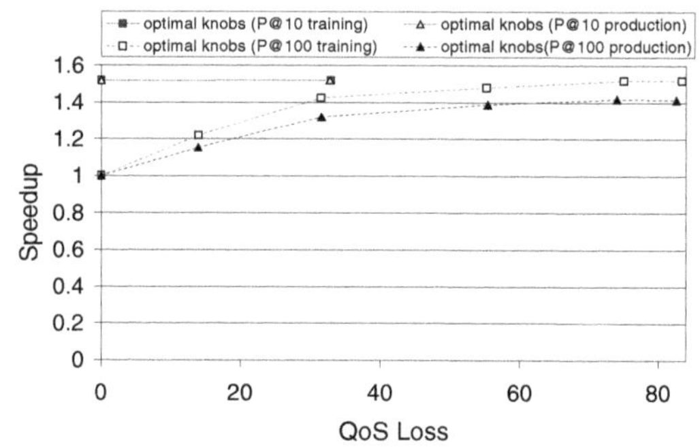


(d) swish++

Figure 5: QoS loss versus speedup for each benchmark.

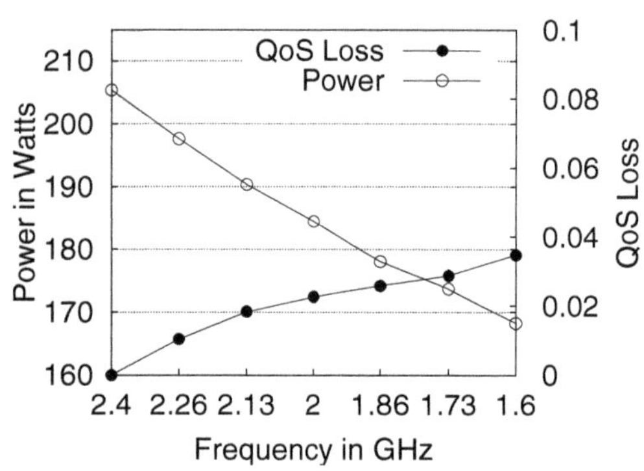


(a) swaptions

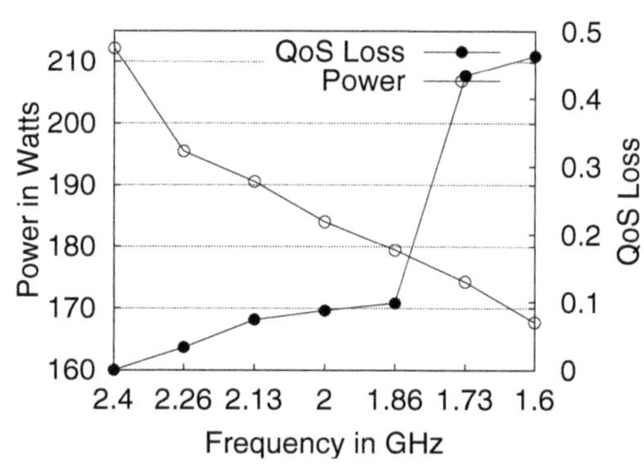


(b) x264

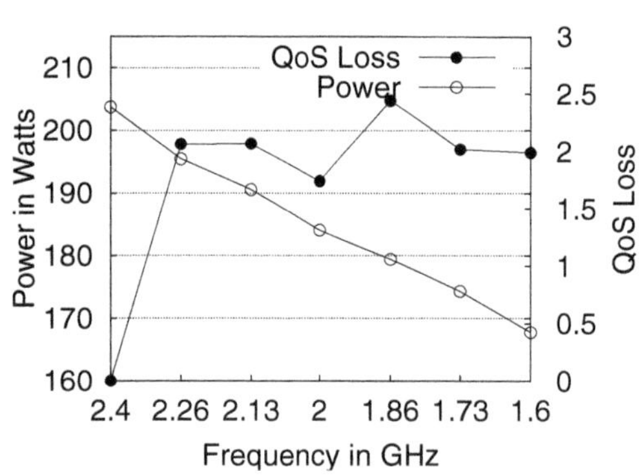


(c) bodytrack

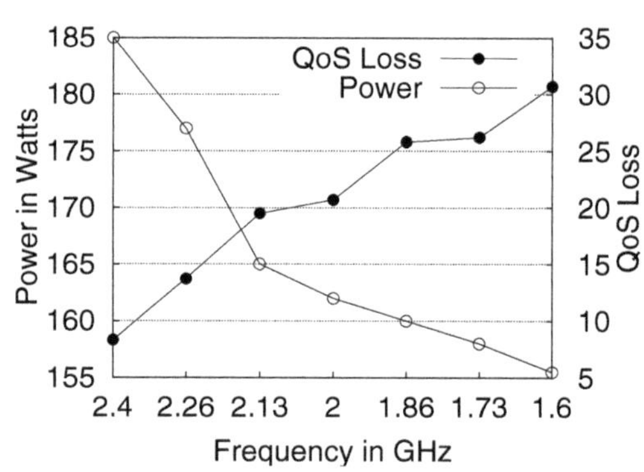


(d) swish++

Figure 6: Power versus QoS trade-offs for each benchmark.

generalizes to other inputs. We obtain a set of inputs for each application, then randomly divide this set of inputs into training and production sets.

### 5.1 Experimental Platform

We run all our experiments on a Dell PowerEdge R410 server with two quad-core Intel Xeon E5530 processors running Linux 2.6.26. The processors support seven power states with clock frequencies from 2.4 GHz to 1.6 GHz. The `cpufrequtils` package enables software control of the clock frequency (and thus the power state). We use a WattsUp device to sample and store the consumed power at 1 second intervals [4]. All benchmark applications run for significantly more than 1 second. The measured power ranges from 220 watts (at full load) to 80 watts (idle), with a typical idle power consumption of approximately 90 watts. The WattsUp device measures full system power and all results reported here are based on this measurement.

We measure the overhead of the PowerDial control system by comparing the performance of the benchmarks with and without the control system. The overhead of the PowerDial control system is insignificant and within the run-to-run variations in the execution times of the benchmarks executing without the control system.

### 5.2 Performance Versus QoS Trade-Offs

Dynamic knobs modulate power consumption by controlling the amount of computational work required to perform a given task. On a machine that delivers constant baseline performance (i.e., no clock frequency changes), changes in computational work correspond to changes in execution time.

Figures 5a–5d present the points that dynamic knobs make available in the speedup versus QoS trade-off space for each benchmark application. The points in the graphs plot the observed mean (across the training or production inputs as indicated) speedup as a function of the observed mean QoS loss for each dynamic knob setting. Gray dots plot results for the training inputs, with black squares (connected by a line) indicating Pareto-optimal dynamic knob settings. White squares (again connected by a line) plot the corresponding points for these Pareto-optimal dynamic knob settings for the production inputs. All speedups and QoS losses are calculated relative to the dynamic knob setting which delivers the highest QoS (and consequently the largest execution time). We observe the following facts:

- **Effective Trade-Offs:** Dynamic knobs provide access to operating points across a broad range of speedups (up to 100 for swaptions, 4.5 for x264, and 7 for bodytrack). Moreover, QoS losses are acceptably small for virtually all Pareto-optimal knob settings (up to only 1.5% for swaptions, 7% for x264, and, for speedups up to 6, 6% for bodytrack).
  For swish++, dynamic knobs enable a speedup of up to approximately a factor of 1.5. The QoS loss increases linearly with the dynamic knob setting. The effect of the dynamic knob is, however, very simple — it simply drops lower-priority search results. So, for example, at the fastest dynamic knob setting, swish++ returns the top five search results.
- **Close Correlation:** To compute how closely behavior on production inputs tracks behavior on training inputs, we take each metric (speedup and QoS loss), compute a linear least squares fit of training data to production data, and compute the correlation coefficient of each fit (see Table 2). The correlation coefficients are all close to 1, indicating that behavior on training inputs is an excellent predictor of behavior on production inputs.

| Benchmark | Speedup | QoS Loss |
|---|---|---|
| x264 | 0.995 | 0.975 |
| bodytrack | 0.999 | 0.839 |
| swaptions | 1.000 | 0.999 |
| swish++ | 0.996 | 0.999 |

Table 2: Correlation coefficient of observed values from training with measured values on production inputs.

### 5.3 Power Versus QoS Trade-offs

To characterize the power versus QoS trade-off space that dynamic knobs make available, we initially configure each application to run at its highest QoS point on a processor in its highest power state (2.4 GHz) and observe the performance (mean time between heartbeats). We then instruct the PowerDial control system to maintain the observed performance, use `cpufrequtils` to drop the clock frequency to each of the six lower-power states, run each application on all of the production inputs, and measure the resulting performance, QoS loss, and mean power consumption (the mean of the power samples over the execution of the application in the corresponding power state). We verify that, for all power states, PowerDial delivers performance within 5% of the target.

Figures 6a–6d plot the resulting QoS loss (right y axis, in percentages) and mean power (left y axis) as a function of the processor power state. For x264, the combination of dynamic knobs and frequency scaling can reduce system power by as much as 21% for less than 0.5% QoS loss. For bodytrack, we observe a 17% reduction in system power for less than 2.3% QoS loss. For swaptions, we observe an 18% reduction in system power for less than .05% QoS loss. Finally, for swish++ we observe power reductions of up to 16% for under 32% QoS loss. For swish++ the dynamic knob simply truncates the list of returned results — the top results are the same, but swish++ returns fewer total results.

The graphs show that x264, bodytrack, and swaptions all have suboptimal dynamic knob settings that are dominated by other, Pareto-optimal dynamic knob settings. The exploration of the trade-off space during training is therefore required to find good points in the trade-off space. The graphs also show that because the Pareto-optimal settings are reasonably consistent across the training and production inputs, the training exploration results appropriately generalize to the production inputs.

### 5.4 Elastic Response to Power Capping

The PowerDial system makes it possible to dynamically adapt application behavior to preserve performance (measured in heartbeats) in the face of *any* event that degrades the computational capacity of the underlying platform. We next investigate a specific scenario — the external imposition of a temporary power cap via a forced reduction in clock frequency. We first start the application running on a system with uncapped power in its highest power state (2.4 GHz). We instruct the PowerDial control system to maintain the observed performance (time between heartbeats). Approximately one quarter of the way through the computation we impose a power cap that drops the machine into its lowest power state (1.6 GHz). Approximately three quarters of the way through the computation we lift the power cap and place the system back into its highest power state (2.4 GHz).

Figures 7a–7d present the dynamic behavior of the benchmarks as they respond to the power cap and corresponding processor frequency changes. Each graph plots the observed performance (computed as the sliding mean of the last twenty times between heartbeats times normalized to the target heart rate of the application) of the application (left y axis) as a function of time. We present the

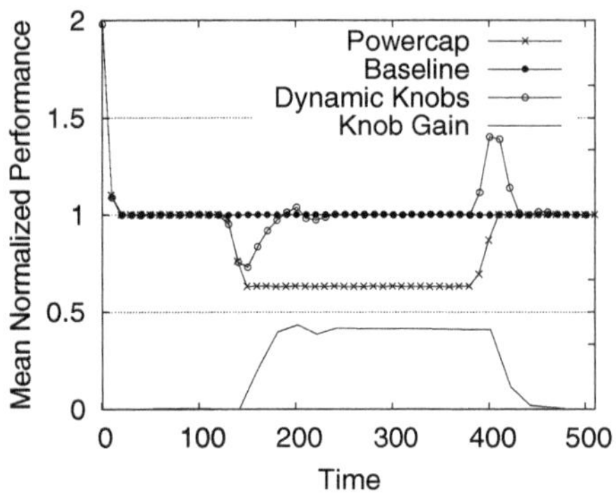


(a) swaptions

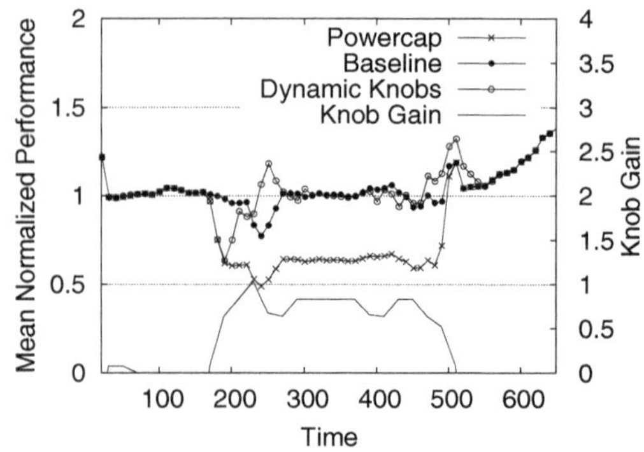


(b) x264

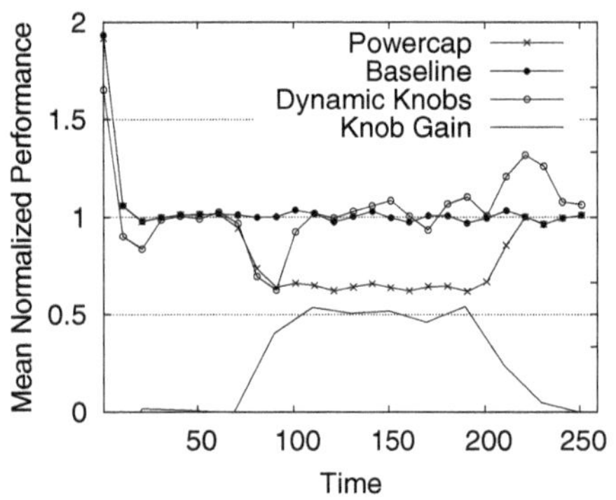


(c) bodytrack

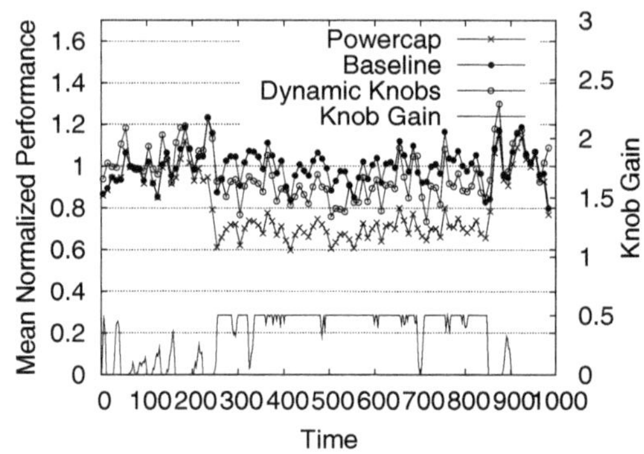


(d) swish++

Figure 7: Behavior of benchmarks with dynamic knobs in response to power cap.

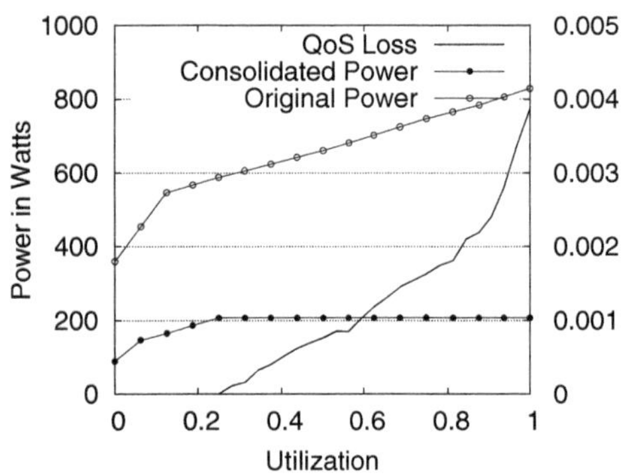


(a) swaptions

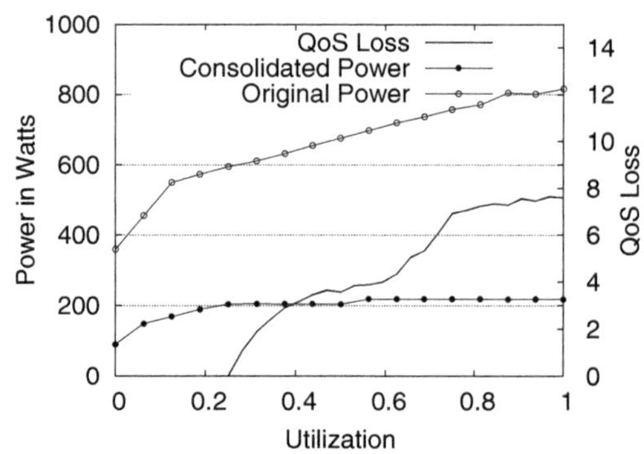


(b) x264

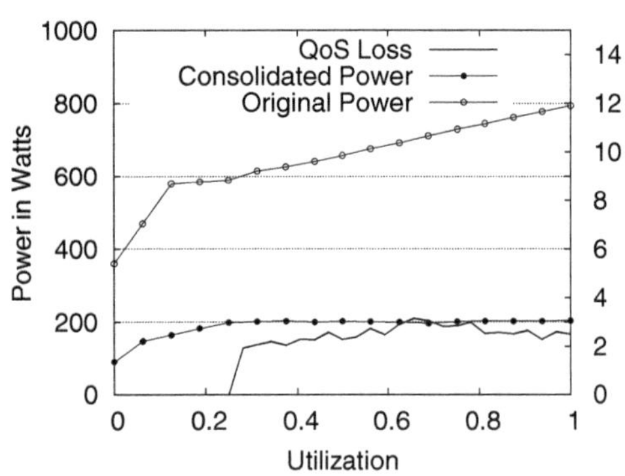


(c) bodytrack

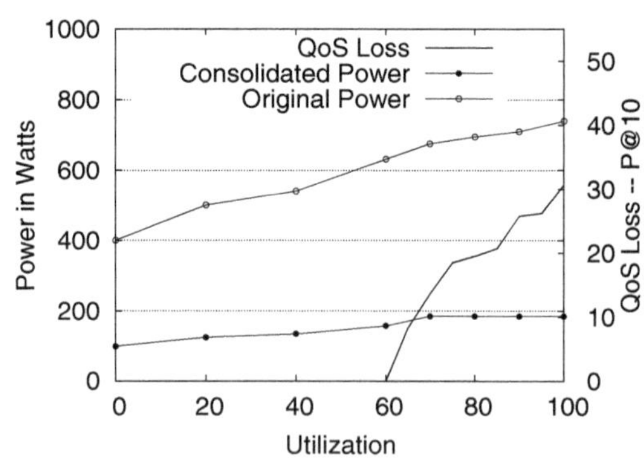


(d) swish++

Figure 8: Using dynamic knobs for system consolidation.

performance of three versions of the application: a version without dynamic knobs (marked with an ×), a baseline version running with no power cap in place (black points), and a version that uses dynamic knobs to preserve the performance despite the power cap (circles). We also present the knob "gain" or the instantaneous speedup achieved by the dynamic knob runtime (right y axis).

All applications exhibit the same general pattern. At the imposition of the power cap, PowerDial adjusts dynamic knobs, the gain increases (Knob Gain line), and the performance of the application first spikes down (circles), then returns back up to the baseline performance. When the power cap is lifted, the dynamic knobs adjust again, the gain decreases, and the application performance returns to the baseline after a brief upward spike. For most of the first and last quarters of the execution, the application executes with essentially no QoS loss. For the middle half of the execution, the application converges to the low power operating point plotted in Figures 6a–6d as a function of the 1.6 GHz processor frequency. Without dynamic knobs (marked with ×), application performance drops well below the baseline as soon as the power cap is imposed, then rises back up to the baseline only after the power cap is lifted.

Within this general pattern the applications exhibit varying degrees of noise in their response. Swaptions exhibits very predictable performance over time with little noise. swish++, on the other extreme, has relatively unpredictable performance over time with significant noise. x264 and bodytrack fall somewhere in between. Despite the differences in application characteristics, our dynamic adaptation mechanism makes it possible for the applications to largely satisfy their performance goals in the face of dynamically fluctuating power requirements.

### 5.5 Peak Load Provisioning

We next evaluate the use of dynamic knobs to reduce the number of machines required to service time-varying workloads with intermittent load spikes, thereby reducing the number of machines, power, and indirect costs (such as cooling costs) required to maintain responsive execution in the face of such spikes:

- **Target Performance:** We set the target performance to the performance achieved by running one instance of the application on an otherwise unloaded machine.
- **Baseline System:** We start by provisioning a system to deliver target performance for a specific peak load of the applications running the baseline (default command line) configuration. For the three PARSEC benchmarks we provision for a peak load of 32 (four eight-core machines) concurrent instances of the application. For swish++ we provision for a peak load of three concurrent instances, each with eight threads. This system load balances all jobs proportionally across available machines. Machines without jobs are idle but not powered off.
- **Consolidated System:** We impose a bound of either 5% (for the PARSEC benchmarks) or 30% (for swish++) QoS loss. We then use Equation 21 to provision the minimum number of machines required for PowerDial to provide baseline performance at peak load subject to the QoS loss bound. For the PARSEC benchmarks we provision a single machine. For swish++ we provision two machines.
- **Power Consumption Experiments:** We then vary the load from 0% utilization of the original baseline system (no load at all) to 100% utilization (the peak load). For each load, we measure the power consumption of the baseline system (which delivers baseline QoS at all utilizations) and the power consumption and QoS loss of the consolidated system (which uses PowerDial to deliver target performance. At low utilizations the consolidated system will configure the applications to deliver maximum QoS. As the utilization increases, PowerDial will progressively manipulate the dynamic knobs to maintain the target performance at the cost of some QoS loss.

Figures 8a–8d presents the results of these experiments. Each graph plots the mean power consumption of the original (circles) and consolidated (black dot) systems (left y axis) and the mean QoS loss (solid line, right y axis) as a function of system utilization (measured with respect to the original, fully provisioned system). These graphs show that using dynamic knobs to consolidate machines can provide considerable power savings across a range of system utilization. For each of the PARSEC benchmarks, at a system utilization of 25% consolidation can provide an average power savings of approximately 400 Watts, a reduction of 66%. For swish++ at 20% utilization, we see a power savings of approximately 125 Watts, a reduction of 25%. These power savings come from the elimination of machines that would be idle in the baseline system at these utilization levels.

Of course, it is not surprising that reducing the number of machines reduces power consumption. A key benefit of the dynamic knob elastic response mechanism is that even with the reduction in computational capacity, it enables the system to maintain the same performance at peak load while consuming significantly less power. For the PARSEC benchmarks at a system utilization of 100%, the consolidated systems consume approximately 75% less power than the original system while providing the same performance. For swish++ at 100% utilization, the consolidated system consumes 25% less power.

The consolidated systems save power by automatically reducing QoS to maintain performance. For swaptions, the maximum QoS loss required to meet peak load is 0.004%, for x264 it is 7.6%, and for bodytrack it is 2.5%. For swish++ with P@10, the QoS loss is 8% at a system utilization of 65%, rising to 30% at a system utilization of 100%. We note, however, that the majority of the QoS loss for swish++ is due to a reduction in recall — top results are generally preserved in order but fewer total results are returned. Precision is not affected by the change in dynamic knob unless the P@N is less than the current knob setting. As the lowest knob setting used by PowerDial is five, precision is always perfect for the top 5 results.

For common usage patterns characterized by predominantly low utilization punctuated by occasional high-utilization spikes [9], these results show that dynamic knobs can substantially reduce overall system cost, deliver the highest (or close to highest) QoS in predominant operating conditions, and preserve performance and acceptable QoS even when the system experiences intermittent load spikes. Note that system designers can use the equations in Section 3 to choose a consolidation appropriate for their envisioned usage pattern that minimizes costs yet still delivers acceptable QoS even under the maximum anticipated load spike.

## 6. Related Work

Adaptive, or self-aware, computing systems have the flexibility to meet multiple goals in changing computing environments. A number of adaptive techniques have been developed for both software [45] and hardware [6]. Adaptive hardware techniques are complementary to the Dynamic Knobs approach for developing adaptive applications. If such hardware chooses to save power by reducing computational capacity, Dynamic Knobs can enable the software to respond and maintain performance. This section focuses on related software techniques.

Trading accuracy of computation for other benefits is a well-known technique. It has been shown that one can trade off accuracy for performance [16, 32, 40, 43, 44], energy consumption [12, 13, 16, 20, 34, 43, 47] and fault tolerance [13, 43, 47]. The Dynamic Knobs system presented in this paper, along with loop perforation [26, 39] and task skipping [43, 44], is unique in that it enables applications to adaptively trade accuracy for performance and does so without requiring a developer to change the application source code.

Autotuners explore a range of equally accurate implementation alternatives to find the alternative or combination of alternatives that deliver the best performance on the current computational platform [17, 52, 54]. Researchers have also developed APIs that an application can use to expose variables for external control (by, for example, the operating system) [29, 42, 49]. This paper presents a system (PowerDial) that transforms static configuration parameters into dynamic knobs and contains a control system that uses the dynamic knobs to maintain performance in the face of load fluctuations, power fluctuations, or any other event that may impair the ability of the application to successfully service its load with the given computational resources. It also presents experimental results that demonstrate the effectiveness of its approach in enabling server consolidation and effective execution through power reductions (imposed, for example, by power caps).

Researchers have developed several systems that allow programmers to provide multiple implementations for a given piece of functionality, with different implementations occupying different points in the performance versus accuracy trade-off space. Such systems include the *tunability interface* [14], Petabricks [7], Green [8], and Eon [46]. Chang and Karamcheti's tunability interface allows application developers to provide multiple configurations of an application (specified by the programmer through compiler directives). A tunable application is then modeled in a *virtual execution environment*, to determine which configuration is best suited for different system states. Petabricks is a parallel language and compiler that developers can use to provide alternate implementations of a given piece of functionality. Green also provides constructs that developers can use to specify alternate implementations. The alternatives typically exhibit different performance and QoS characteristics. PetaBricks and Green both contain algorithms that explore the trade-off space to find points with desirable performance and QoS characteristics. Eon [46] is a coordination language for power-aware computing that enables developers to adapt their algorithms to different energy contexts. In a similar vein, energy-aware adaptation for mobile applications [16], adapts to changing system demands by dynamically adjusting application input quality. For example, to save energy the system may switch to a lower quality video input to reduce the computation of the video decoder.

Each of these systems requires the developer to intervene directly in the source code to provide or specify multiple implementations of the same functionality. They can therefore increase the size and development cost of the application and require the presence of a developer who understands the internal structure of the implementation and can appropriately modify the implementation. These systems are therefore of little or no use when such a developer is unavailable, either because the original developers are no longer with the organization or are dedicated to other projects; the organization that originally developed the software no longer exists, is no longer developing or maintaining the application, or is simply unwilling to incorporate the functionality into their code base; or when the cost of performing the modifications is prohibitively expensive.

In contrast, PowerDial works directly on unmodified and unannotated applications. It automatically transforms existing configuration parameters into dynamic knobs and automatically inserts the appropriate Application Heartbeats API calls into the application. It can therefore enable third-party users to automatically augment their applications with desirable dynamic adaptation properties without the need to involve knowledgeable developers or the organization that originally developed the application.

None of Petabricks, Green, or Eon provides a control mechanism which can react to changes that affect performance. Petabricks does not have a dynamic control component. Green uses heuristic control to manage quality of service but does not control or even monitor performance. Similarly, Eon uses a heuristic control system to manage the energy consumption of the system, but does not directly control performance. Both control systems are completely heuristic, with no guaranteed convergence or predictability properties whatsoever. The Chang/Karamcheti approach does directly control performance using a heuristic decision mechanism. This controller monitors system state and attempts to select a configuration appropriate for the current state, but does not use direct feedback from the application.

In contrast, PowerDial uses a decision mechanism grounded in control science with provably good convergence and predictability properties [35]. By relying on a modeling phase to discover Pareto-optimal knob settings, the PowerDial control system is able to solve constrained optimization problems to dynamically maintain performance while minimizing quality loss. In addition, the PowerDial control system uses Heartbeats as its feedback mechanism. By using direct feedback from the application the control system is able to operate maintain performance without having to infer application performance from low measurements of system state.

Researchers have also explored the use of loop perforation (which automatically transforms loops to skip loop iterations) to augment applications with the ability to operate at different points in an induced performance versus quality of service trade-off space [26, 39]. The results show that loop perforation can help developers find computations that are suitable for further optimization [39] and enables applications to adapt to fluctuations in the delivered computational resources [26]. Task skipping [43, 44] has also been shown to automatically augment applications with the ability to trade off quality of service in return for increased performance. This paper presents a system that uses dynamic knobs instead of loop perforation, has a control system with guaranteed performance and predictability properties, and more fully demonstrates how to use dynamic knobs to solve power management issues.

Hellerstein et al [23] and Karamanolis et al [28] have both identified standard control theoretic techniques as a general solution for managing dynamic behavior in computing systems. Other authors have shown how control techniques can be generalized allowing software developers to incorporate them without having to develop expertise in control science [21, 25, 33, 35, 55]. The PowerDial control system furthers this idea, showing how standard control techniques can be automatically embedded into an application to dynamically manage performance. The control system presented in this paper uses Application Heartbeats as a feedback mechanism (or sensor) combined with a novel actuation strategy which converts static configuration options into dynamically tunable parameters. Control theory provides predictable behavior, making it a good match for applications with performance constraints.

## 7. Conclusion

The PowerDial system augments applications with dynamic knobs that the PowerDial control system can use to adapt the behavior of the application to execute successfully in the face of load spikes, power fluctuations, or (in general) any event that changes the balance between the computational demand and the resources available to meet that demand. Our results demonstrate that PowerDial can enable applications to maintain responsive execution in the face of power caps and load spikes (thereby reducing or even eliminating the over-provisioning otherwise required to service these spikes). We see PowerDial as an early example of an emerging class of management systems that will enable applications to operate successfully in complex modern computing environments characterized by fluctuations in power, load, and other key operating characteristics.


### Acknowledgements

Henry Hoffmann and Anant Agarwal are grateful for support from DARPA, the NSF, and Quanta Computer. Stelios Sidiroglou, Michael Carbin, Sasa Misailovic, and Martin Rinard are supported in part by the National Science Foundation under Grant Nos. 0937060 to the Computing Research Association for the CIFellows Project, Nos. CNS-0509415, CCF-0811397 and IIS-0835652, DARPA under Grant No. FA8750-06-2-0189 and Massachusetts Institute of Technology. We note our earlier technical reports on performance versus QoS trade-offs [26, 27].


## References


[1] Intel Xeon Processor. http://www.intel.com/technology/Xeon.

[2] Project Gutenberg. http://www.gutenberg.org/.

[3] Intel Atom Processor. http://www.intel.com/technology/atom.

[4] Wattsup .net meter. http://www.wattsupmeters.com/.

[5] Xiph.org. http://xiph.org.

[6] D. H. Albonesi, R. Balasubramonian, S. G. Dropsho, S. Dwarkadas, E. G. Friedman, M. C. Huang, V. Kursun, G. Magklis, M. L. Scott, G. Semeraro, P. Bose, A. Buyuktosunoglu, P. W. Cook, and S. E. Schuster. Dynamically tuning processor resources with adaptive processing. *Computer*, 36:49–58, December 2003.

[7] J. Ansel, C. Chan, Y. L. Wong, M. Olszewski, Q. Zhao, A. Edelman, and S. Amarasinghe. Petabricks: A language and compiler for algorithmic choice. In *ACM SIGPLAN Conference on Programming Language Design and Implementation*, Dublin, Ireland, June 2009.

[8] W. Baek and T. Chilimbi. Green: A framework for supporting energy-conscious programming using controlled approximation. In *ACM SIGPLAN Conference on Programming Language Design and Implementation*, June 2010.

[9] L. Barroso and U. Holzle. The case for energy-proportional computing. *COMPUTER-IEEE COMPUTER SOCIETY-*, 40(12):33, 2007.

[10] C. Bienia, S. Kumar, J. P. Singh, and K. Li. The PARSEC benchmark suite: Characterization and architectural implications. In *PACT-2008: Proceedings of the 17th International Conference on Parallel Architectures and Compilation Techniques*, October 2008.

[11] M. Carbin and M. Rinard. Automatically Identifying Critical Input Regions and Code in Applications. In *Proceedings of the International Symposium on Software Testing and Analysis*, 2010.

[12] L. N. Chakrapani, B. E. S. Akgul, S. Cheemalavagu, P. Korkmaz, K. V. Palem, and B. Seshasayee. Ultra-efficient (embedded) soc architectures based on probabilistic cmos (pcmos) technology. In *Proceedings of the conference on Design, automation and test in Europe*, DATE, pages 1110–1115, 2006.

[13] L. N. Chakrapani, K. K. Muntimadugu, A. Lingamneni, J. George, and K. V. Palem. Highly energy and performance efficient embedded computing through approximately correct arithmetic: a mathematical foundation and preliminary experimental validation. In *Proceedings of the 2008 international conference on Compilers, architectures and synthesis for embedded systems*, CASES, pages 187–196, 2008.

[14] F. Chang and V. Karamcheti. Automatic configuration and run-time adaptation of distributed applications. In *Proceedings of the International ACM Symposium on High Performance Parallel and Distributed Computing*, HPDC, pages 11–20, 2000.

[15] J. Deutscher and I. Reid. Articulated body motion capture by stochastic search. *International Journal of Computer Vision*, 61(2):185–205, 2005.

[16] J. Flinn and M. Satyanarayanan. Energy-aware adaptation for mobile applications. In *Proceedings of the seventeenth ACM symposium on Operating systems principles*, page 63. ACM, 1999.

[17] M. Frigo and S. G. Johnson. FFTW: An adaptive software architecture for the FFT. In *Proc. 1998 IEEE Intl. Conf. Acoustics Speech and Signal Processing*, volume 3, pages 1381–1384. IEEE, 1998.

[18] A. Gandhi, M. Harchol-Balter, R. Das, C. Lefurgy, and J. Kephart. Power capping via forced idleness. In *Workshop on Energy-Efficient Design*, June 2009.

[19] V. Ganesh, T. Leek, and M. Rinard. Taint-based directed whitebox fuzzing. In *Proceedings of the 2009 IEEE 31st International Conference on Software Engineering*, pages 474–484. IEEE Computer Society, 2009.

[20] J. George, B. Marr, B. E. S. Akgul, and K. V. Palem. Probabilistic arithmetic and energy efficient embedded signal processing. In *Proceedings of the 2006 international conference on Compilers, architecture and synthesis for embedded systems*, CASES, pages 158–168, 2006.

[21] A. Goel, D. Steere, C. Pu, and J. Walpole. Swift: A feedback control and dynamic reconfiguration toolkit. In *2nd USENIX Windows NT Symposium*, 1998.

[22] H.264 reference implementation. http://iphome.hhi.de/suehring/tml/download/.

[23] J. L. Hellerstein, Y. Diao, S. Parekh, and D. M. Tilbury. *Feedback Control of Computing Systems*. John Wiley & Sons, 2004.

[24] H. Hoffmann, J. Eastep, M. D. Santambrogio, J. E. Miller, and A. Agarwal. Application Heartbeats: A Generic Interface for Specifying Program Performance and Goals in Autonomous Computing Environments. In *7th International Conference on Autonomic Computing*, ICAC, 2010.

[25] H. Hoffmann, M. Maggio, M. D. Santambrogio, A. Leva, and A. Agarwal. SEEC: A Framework for Self-aware Computing. Technical Report MIT-CSAIL-TR-2010-049, CSAIL, MIT, October 2010.

[26] H. Hoffmann, S. Misailovic, S. Sidiroglou, A. Agarwal, and M. Rinard. Using Code Perforation to Improve Performance, Reduce Energy Consumption, and Respond to Failures . Technical Report MIT-CSAIL-TR-2009-042, CSAIL, MIT, September 2009.

[27] H. Hoffmann, S. Sidiroglou, M. Carbin, S. Misailovic, A. Agarwal, and M. Rinard. Power-Aware Computing with Dynamic Knobs. Technical Report TR-2010-027, CSAIL, MIT, May 2010.

[28] C. Karamanolis, M. Karlsson, and X. Zhu. Designing controllable computer systems. In *Proceedings of the 10th conference on Hot Topics in Operating Systems*, pages 9–15, Berkeley, CA, USA, 2005. USENIX Association.

[29] P. J. Keleher, J. K. Hollingsworth, and D. Perkovic. Exposing application alternatives. In *Proceedings of the 19th IEEE International Conference on Distributed Computing Systems*, ICDCS, page 384, Washington, DC, USA, 1999. IEEE Computer Society.

[30] C. Lattner and V. Adve. LLVM: A Compilation Framework for Lifelong Program Analysis & Transformation. In *Proceedings of the 2004 International Symposium on Code Generation and Optimization* , CGO, Palo Alto, California, March 2004.

[31] C. Lefurgy, X. Wang, and M. Ware. Power capping: a prelude to power shifting. *Cluster Computing*, 11(2):183–195, 2008.

[32] J. Letchner, C. Re, M. Balazinska, and M. Philipose. Approximation trade-offs in markovian stream processing: An empirical study. In *2010 IEEE 26th International Conference on Data Engineering*, ICDE, pages 936 –939, 2010.

[33] B. Li and K. Nahrstedt. A control-based middleware framework for quality-of-service adaptations. *Selected Areas in Communications, IEEE Journal on*, 17(9):1632 –1650, September 1999.

[34] S. Liu, K. P. amd Thomas Moscibroda, and B. G. Zorn. Flicker: Saving Refresh-Power in Mobile Devices through Critical Data Partitioning. Technical Report MSR-TR-2009-138, Microsoft Research, Oct. 2009.

[35] M. Maggio, H. Hoffmann, M. D. Santambrogio, A. Agarwal, and A. Leva. Controlling software applications via resource allocation within the Heartbeats frame work. In *49th IEEE Conference on Decision and Control*, pages 3736 –3741, December 2010.

[36] J. Makhoul, F. Kubala, R. Schwartz, and R. Weischedel. Performance measures for information extraction. In *Broadcast News Workshop'99 Proceedings*, page 249. Morgan Kaufmann Pub, 1999.

[37] D. Meisner, B. Gold, and T. Wenisch. PowerNap: eliminating server idle power. *ACM SIGPLAN Notices*, 44(3):205–216, 2009.

[38] C. Middleton and R. Baeza-Yates. A comparison of open source search engines. Technical report, Universitat Pompeu Fabra, Department of Technologies, October 2007.

[39] S. Misailovic, S. Sidiroglou, H. Hoffmann, and M. Rinard. Quality of service profiling. In *Proceedings of the 32nd ACM/IEEE International Conference on Software Engineering*, ICSE, pages 25–34. ACM, 2010.

[40] R. Narayanan, B. Ozisikyilmaz, G. Memik, A. Choudhary, and J. Zambreno. Quantization error and accuracy-performance tradeoffs for embedded data mining workloads. In *Proceedings of the 7th international conference on Computational Science*, ICCS, pages 734–741, Berlin, Heidelberg, 2007. Springer-Verlag.

[41] S. Pelley, D. Meisner, P. Zandevakili, T. Wenisch, and J. Underwood. Power routing: dynamic power provisioning in the data center. *ACM SIGPLAN Notices*, 45(3):231–242, 2010.

[42] R. Ribler, J. Vetter, H. Simitci, and D. Reed. Autopilot: adaptive control of distributed applications. In *High Performance Distributed Computing*, July 1998.

[43] M. Rinard. Probabilistic accuracy bounds for fault-tolerant computations that discard tasks. In *Proceedings of the 20th annual international conference on Supercomputing*, pages 324–334. ACM New York, NY, USA, 2006.

[44] M. C. Rinard. Using early phase termination to eliminate load imbalances at barrier synchronization points. In *Proceedings of the 22nd annual ACM conference on Object-oriented programming systems and applications*, OOPSLA, pages 369–386, New York, NY, USA, 2007. ACM.

[45] M. Salehie and L. Tahvildari. Self-adaptive software: Landscape and research challenges. *ACM Transactions on Autonomous and Adaptive Systems*, 4(2):1–42, 2009.

[46] J. Sorber, A. Kostadinov, M. Garber, M. Brennan, M. D. Corner, and E. D. Berger. Eon: a language and runtime system for perpetual systems. In *Proceedings of the 5th international conference on Embedded networked sensor systems*, SenSys, New York, NY, USA, 2007. ACM.

[47] P. Stanley-Marbell, D. Dolech, A. Eindhoven, and D. Marculescu. Deviation-Tolerant Computation in Concurrent Failure-Prone Hardware. Technical Report ESR-2008-01, Eindhoven University of Technology, January 2008.

[48] SWISH++. `http://swishplusplus.sourceforge.net/`.

[49] C. Tapus, I. Chung, and J. Hollingsworth. Active harmony: Towards automated performance tuning. In *Proceedings of the 2002 ACM/IEEE Conference on Supercomputing*, pages 1–11, Los Alamitos, CA, USA, 2002. IEEE Computer Society Press.

[50] U.S. Environmental Protection Agency. EPA report to congress on server and data center energy efficiency, 2007.

[51] M. Weiser, B. Welch, A. Demers, and S. Shenker. Scheduling for reduced CPU energy. *Mobile Computing*, pages 449–471, 1996.

[52] R. Whaley and J. Dongarra. Automatically tuned linear algebra software. In *Proceedings of the 1998 ACM/IEEE conference on Supercomputing*, pages 1–27. IEEE Computer Society, 1998.

[53] x264. `http://www.videolan.org/x264.html`.

[54] J. Xiong, J. Johnson, R. W. Johnson, and D. Padua. SPL: A language and compiler for DSP algorithms. In *Proceedings of the ACM SIGPLAN 2001 conference on Programming language design and implementation*, PLDI, pages 298–308, 2001.

[55] R. Zhang, C. Lu, T. Abdelzaher, and J. Stankovic. Controlware: A middleware architecture for feedback control of software performance. In *Proceedings of the 22nd International conference on Distributed Computing Systems*. IEEE computer society, 2002.

# Flikker: Saving DRAM Refresh-power through Critical Data Partitioning


Song Liu
Northwestern University
sli646@eecs.northwestern.edu

Karthik Pattabiraman
University of British Columbia
karthikp@ece.ubc.ca

Thomas Moscibroda Benjamin G. Zorn
Microsoft Research
{moscitho, zorn}@microsoft.com



## Abstract

Energy has become a first-class design constraint in computer systems. Memory is a significant contributor to total system power. This paper introduces *Flikker*, an application-level technique to reduce refresh power in DRAM memories. Flikker enables developers to specify critical and non-critical data in programs and the runtime system allocates this data in separate parts of memory. The portion of memory containing critical data is refreshed at the regular refresh-rate, while the portion containing non-critical data is refreshed at substantially lower rates. This partitioning saves energy at the cost of a modest increase in data corruption in the non-critical data. Flikker thus exposes and leverages an interesting trade-off between energy consumption and hardware correctness. We show that many applications are naturally tolerant to errors in the non-critical data, and in the vast majority of cases, the errors have little or no impact on the application's final outcome. We also find that Flikker can save between 20-25% of the power consumed by the memory sub-system in a mobile device, with negligible impact on application performance. Flikker is implemented almost entirely in software, and requires only modest changes to the hardware.



***Categories and Subject Descriptors*** B.3.4 [*Hardware*]: Memory Structures-Reliability, Testing, and Fault-Tolerance; C.0 [*Computer Systems Organization*]: General-Hardware/software interfaces

***General Terms*** Design, Management, Reliability

***Keywords*** Power savings, DRAM refresh, soft errors, critical data, allocation


## 1. Introduction

Energy has become a first-class design constraint in many computer systems, particularly in mobile devices, clusters, and server-farms [5, 11, 27]. In a mobile phone, saving energy can extend battery life and enhance mobility. Recently, mobile phones have morphed into general-purpose computing platforms, often called smartphones. Smartphones are typically used in short-bursts over extended periods of time [21], i.e., they are idle most of the time. Nonetheless, they are "always-on" as users expect to resume their applications in the state they were last used. Hence, even when the phone is not being used, application state is stored in the phone's memory to maintain responsiveness. This wastes power because Dynamic Random Access Memories (DRAMs) leak charge and need to be refreshed periodically, or else they will lose data.

Memory is a major part of overall system power in smartphones. Measures of DRAM power as a fraction of overall power range from 5-30% [6, 14] and depend on the application model, operating system, and underlying hardware. Some smartphone application programming models, such as Android's, emphasize reducing application DRAM usage in idle mode [30]. Further, the memory capacity of smartphones has been steadily increasing and, as a result, memory power consumption will be even more important in the future. Memory consumes power both when the device is active (active mode) and when it is suspended (standby mode). In standby mode, the refresh operation is the dominant consumer of power, and hence we focus on reducing refresh power in this paper.

This paper proposes *Flikker*,[1] a software technique to save energy by reducing refresh power in DRAMs. DRAM manufacturers typically set the refresh rate to be higher than the leakage rate of the fastest-leaking memory cells. However, studies have shown that the leakage distribution of memory-cells follows an exponential distribution [22], with a small fraction of the cells having significantly higher leakage rates than other cells. Hence, the vast majority of the cells will retain their values even if the refresh rate of the memory chip is significantly reduced. Flikker leverages this observation to obtain power-reduction in DRAM memories at the cost of knowingly introducing a modest number of errors in application data.

Typical smartphone applications include games, audio/video processing and productivity tasks such as email and web-browsing. These applications are insensitive to errors in all but a small portion of their data. We call such data *critical data*, as it is important for the overall correctness of the application [7, 8, 32]. For example, in a video processing application, the data-structure containing the list of frames is more important than the output buffer to which frames are rendered (as the human eye is tolerant to mild disruptions in a frame). Therefore, this data structure would be considered as critical data.

Flikker enables the programmer to distinguish between critical and non-critical data in applications. At runtime, Flikker allocates the critical and non-critical data in separate memory pages and reduces the refresh rate for pages containing non-critical data at the cost of increasing the number of errors in these pages. Pages containing critical data are refreshed at the regular rate and are hence free of errors. This differentiated allocation strategy enables Flikker to achieve power savings with only marginal degradation of the application's reliability.

[1] CRT monitors occasionally exhibited flickering, i.e., loss of resolution, when their refresh rates were lowered—hence the name.




*ASPLOS'11,* March 5–11, 2011, Newport Beach, California, USA.

Our approach in Flikker fundamentally differs from existing solutions for saving energy in low-power systems. In these solutions, energy reduction is achieved by appropriately trading-off performance metrics, such as throughput/latency, Quality-of-Service (QoS), or user response time, e.g. [17, 37, 39]. In contrast, our approach explores a largeley unexplored trade-off in system design, namely *trading off energy consumption for data integrity at the application level.* By intentionally lowering hardware correctness in an application-aware manner, we show that it is possible to achieve significant power-savings at the cost of a negligible reduction in application reliability.

*To the best of our knowledge, Flikker is the first software technique to intentionally introduce hardware errors for memory power-savings based on the characteristics of the application.* While we focus on mobile applications in this paper, we believe that Flikker approach can also be applied to data-center applications (Section 9).

Aspects of Flikker make it appealing for use in practice. First, Flikker allows programmers to control what errors are exposed to the applications, and hence explicitly specify the trade-off between power consumption and reliability. Programmers can define what parts of the application are subject to errors, and take appropriate measures to handle the introduced errors. Second, Flikker requires only minor changes to the hardware in the form of interfaces to expose refresh rate controls to the software. Current mobile DRAMs already allow the software to specify how much of the memory should be refreshed (Partial Array Self-Refresh (PASR) [18]), and we show that it is straightforward to enhance the PASR architecture to refresh different portions of the memory at different rates. Finally, legacy applications can work unmodified with *Flikker*, as it can be selectively enabled or disabled on demand. Hence, Flikker can be incrementally deployed on new applications.

We have evaluated Flikker both using analytical and experimental methods on five diverse applications representative of mobile workloads. We find that Flikker can save between 20% to 25% of the total DRAM power in mobile applications, with negligible degradation in reliability and performance (less than 1%). Based on previous study of DRAM power as a fraction of total power consumption, this 20-25% corresponds to 1% of total power savings in a smartphone [6]. We also find that the effort required to deploy Flikker is modest (less than half-a-day per application) for the applications considered in the paper.

## 2. Flikker: Design Overview

We start with a brief overview of Flikker. Flikker requires a modest set of simple changes to both hardware and software. For the *hardware* portion, Flikker enhances existing DRAM architectures that allow for a partial refresh of DRAM memory by allowing different *refresh rates* for different sections in memory. For the *software* portion, Flikker (1) introduces a new programming language construct that allows application programmers to mark non-critical data, and (2) provides OS and runtime support to allocate the data to its corresponding portion in the DRAM memory. The hardware and software components of Flikker are explained in detail in Sections 3 and 4, respectively.

The changes required by Flikker are justified for several reasons. First, the software changes required to deploy Flikker can be easily made by application developers, who already distinguish between critical and non-critical data implicitly (see Section 4). Further, hardware is becoming less reliable due to trends in silicon manufacturing, and hence it is important to write software that can degrade gracefully in the presence of hardware faults [4]. The software changes to partition the application into critical and non-critical portions can also provide resilience against naturally occurring hardware faults.

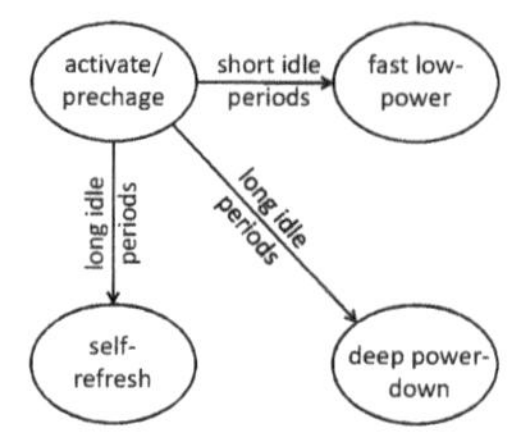


**Figure 1.** Simplified Diagram of DRAM Operating States.

Secondly, small hardware changes are not an inherent showstopper in terms of practical deployment, given that mobile phone architectures (both hardware and software) are still in a state of flux, with new hardware and software models being developed and put to market regularly. For example, the Partial-Array Self-Refresh Mode (PASR) mode on which we base Flikker was a relatively recent introduction in mobile DRAMs (in 2002). We show in Section 3 that the hardware changes we propose are relatively minor and only involve the memory controller.

Finally, our approach allows us to explore a novel and fundamental trade-off in system design. Traditionally, the hardware/software boundary in computer systems (and specifically the hardware memory) has provided a clear abstraction layer. The hardware was assumed to provide a resilient and "correct" substrate based on which the operating system and application can run. In Flikker, we re-examine this assumption and consciously allow the DRAM to violate data integrity (to a limited degree) in order to save energy.

## 3. Flikker Hardware

This section presents the hardware architecture of Flikker, i.e., the Flikker DRAM (§3.2) and the impact of lowering the refresh rate on DRAM error-rates (§3.3). We present an analytical model to evaluate the power-savings of the Flikker DRAM in §3.4. This model is used to determine the best refresh rates in our system design (§3.5), and to estimate power savings in our evaluations (§5).

### 3.1 Background on mobile DRAMs

Mobile phones have traditionally used SRAMs (Static Random Access Memories) for memory. However, as memory capacity increases, conventional SRAM becomes more expensive, and hence, smartphones have adopted DRAM (Dynamic RAMs). A DRAM memory system consists of three major components: (1) multiple DRAM banks that store the actual data, (2) the DRAM controller (scheduler) that schedules commands to read/write data from/to the DRAM banks, and (3) DRAM address/data/command buses that connect banks and the controller. The organization into multiple banks allows memory requests issued to different banks to be serviced in parallel. Each DRAM bank has a two-dimensional structure, consisting of multiple rows and columns. The usual memory mapping is for consecutive addresses in memory to be located in consecutive columns in the same row, and consecutive memory rows to be located in different banks. The size of a row varies between 1 to 32 kilobytes in commodity DRAMs. In mobile DRAMs, the row size varies from 1 to 4 kilobyes.

Figure 1 shows a simplified diagram of DRAM operating states. DRAM could only be accessed in active states (activate/precharge). Beside active states, several low-power states are used in different system scenarios. Fast low-power states, which have good responsiveness (short wakeup time), are used in idle period during application executions. In systems with light DRAM traffic, utilizing these fast low-power states is usually a good power-performance tradeoff. On the other hand, self-refresh state and deep power-down state are used when the whole system is in standby mode. Com-

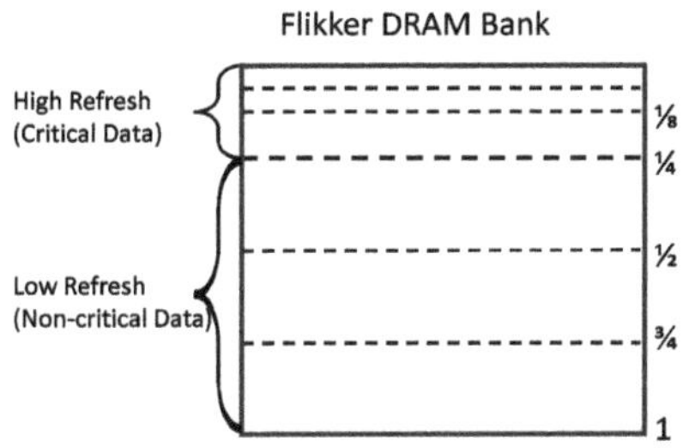


**Figure 2.** Flikker Bank Architecture. The DRAM bank is partitioned into two parts, the high refresh part, which contains critical data, and the low refresh part, which contains non-critical data. The high refresh / low refresh partition can be assigned at discrete locations, as shown by the dashed lines. The curly brackets on the left show a partition with 1/4 high refresh rows and 3/4 low refresh rows.

pared with fast low-power states, self-refresh and deep power-down has lower power consumption as well as longer wakeup time. Unlike the self-refresh, the deep power-down mode will stop all refresh operations and hence the DRAM will lose data in deep power-down state. In the following, we will discuss details of these low-power states.

**Self-refresh:** *Self-refresh* is a feature of low power mobile DRAMs in which the DRAM array is periodically refreshed even if the processor is in sleep mode. The self-refresh operation is performed by dedicated hardware on the DRAM chip. The self-refresh mode is activated only when the mobile device is in standby and the processor is put to sleep as it incurs considerable latencies to transition in and out of self-refresh mode. The Operating System (OS) needs to activate self-refresh before putting the mobile device to sleep.

**Partial Array Self Refresh (PASR)** is an enhancement of the self-refresh low power state [18] in which only a portion of the DRAM array is refreshed. DRAM cells that are not refreshed will lose data in PASR. In a system with PASR, before switching to self-refresh mode, the OS needs to specify the portion of the memory array to refresh. In Micron's mobile DDR SDRAM [18] with 4 banks, there are five different options for PASR, full array (4 banks), half array (2 banks), quarter array (1 bank), 1/8 array (1/2 bank), and 1/16 array (1/4 bank).

The main difference between Flikker DRAM and PASR is that instead of discarding the data in a part of the memory array, Flikker lowers the reliability of the data. As a result, Flikker is able to achieve similar levels of power savings as PASR, without compromising on the amount of memory available to applications.

**Fast Low-power States**: Mobile DRAMs also employ low-power states during active mode to conserve power. These low-power modes are activated even when there are brief periods of no DRAM traffic as the latency of transitioning out of these states is only around 10 nano-seconds. The transition to/from these modes is performed by the DRAM controller and does not need OS intervention. The power consumption in these low-power states is typically less than half of the DRAM power-consumption without any memory accesses.

### 3.2 Flikker DRAM Architecture

Figure 2 illustrates a Flikker DRAM bank. In Flikker DRAM, each bank is partitioned into two different parts, the *high refresh fault-free part* and the *low refresh faulty part*. DRAM rows in the high refresh part are refreshed at a regular refresh cycle time $T_{regular}$ (64 milliseconds or 32 milliseconds in most systems). The error rate of data in these high refresh parts is negligible (similar to data in state-of-the-art DRAM chips). On the other hand, the low refresh part is refreshed at a much lower rate (longer refresh cycle time $T_{low}$) and its error rate is a function of the refresh cycle time (see Section 3.3).

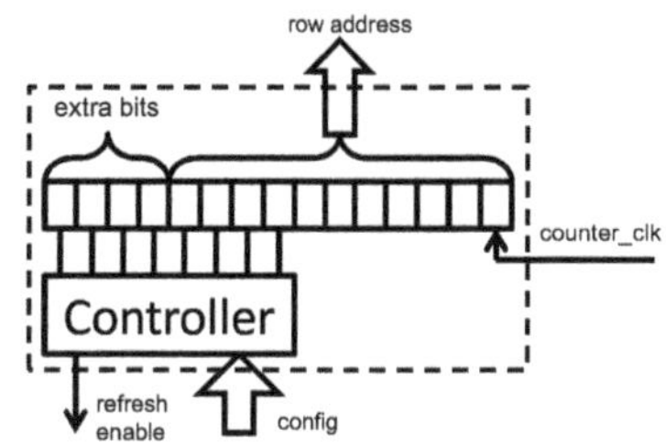


**Figure 3.** Self-refresh counter in the Flikker DRAM.

Mobile DRAMs use a hardware counter during the self-refresh operation to remember which row to refresh next, known as the self-refresh counter. Flikker DRAM extends this counter by a few extra bits (see Figure 3.2) in order to support two refresh rates. The Flikker self-refresh counter also has an additional "refresh enable" output. The DRAM row is refreshed only when the refresh enable bit is set to "1". A configurable controller sets different values to refresh enable bit based on higher bits of the row address and the extra bits, and thus control the refresh rate of different DRAM rows.

The number of additional bits required in the self-refresh counter is given by the ratio of $T_{low}$ to $T_{regular}$. For example, in a system where $T_{low} = 16 \times T_{regular}$, the Flikker self-refresh counter requires 4 extra bits. The refresh enable bit is always set to "1" when the row address is a high refresh row. For low refresh rows, the refresh enable bit is set to "1" only when the extra bits has a predefined value (say "1111"). In the case of 1/8 high refresh, when the extra bits are "0000" through "1110", the refresh enable bits is only set for row addresses with highest three bits of "000". When the extra bits are "1111". The refresh enable bits is set for all row addresses. With this configuration, the low refresh rows (rows with "001" through "111" in highest bits of row address) are refreshed 16 times less frequently than the high refresh rows.

### 3.3 Flikker DRAM Error Rates

Previous work [3, 36] has measured DRAM error rate as a function of refresh cycle time. Bhalodia presents the per cell DRAM error rate under different temperatures and different refresh cycles [3]. Venkatesan et al. measure the percentage of DRAM rows that are free from errors with a low refresh rate [36]. Although these two measurements are at different granularity (per cell versus per row), their results are consistent with each other.

Table 1 shows the DRAM error rates used in our experiments which are based on Bhalodia's measurements [3]. The retention time of DRAM cells decrease with temperature. Therefore, under a given refresh cycle, the DRAM error rate increases with ambient temperature. We assume an operating temperature of 48°C, which is higher than the operating temperatures of most smartphones, and hence our error-rates are higher than those likely to be experienced under real conditions.

Note that the above error-rates are only a function of the refresh period and temperature. In particular, *the error-rates do not depend on the duration of low refresh mode.* This is because errors in DRAM cells are primarily caused by manufacturing variations among their retaining capacities. Thus, under a given temperature and refresh rate, a fraction of DRAM cells loses their charge, and this fraction is independent of how long the refresh rate is applied.

### 3.4 Flikker DRAM Power Model

We use an analytical model to estimate the power consumption of the Flikker DRAM. The model is based on real power measurements in mobile DDR DRAMs with PASR [18]. The self-refresh power consumption is calculated as follows:

| Refresh Cycle [s] | Error Rate | Bit Flips per Byte |
|---|---|---|
| 1 | $4.0 \times 10^{-8}$ | $3.2 \times 10^{-7}$ |
| 2 | $2.6 \times 10^{-7}$ | $2.1 \times 10^{-6}$ |
| 5 | $3.8 \times 10^{-6}$ | $3.0 \times 10^{-5}$ |
| 10 | $2.0 \times 10^{-5}$ | $1.6 \times 10^{-4}$ |
| 20 | $1.3 \times 10^{-4}$ | $1.0 \times 10^{-3}$ |

**Table 1.** Error rate under different refresh cycle (under 48°C, data derived from [3]).

| High Refresh Size | Self-Refresh Current [mA] | | | |
|---|---|---|---|---|
| | PASR | Flikker | | |
| | | 1s | 10s | 100s |
| 1 | 0.5 | 0.5 | 0.5 | 0.5 |
| 3/4 | 0.47* | 0.4719 | 0.4702 | 0.4700 |
| 1/2 | 0.44 | 0.4438 | 0.4404 | 0.4400 |
| 1/4 | 0.38 | 0.3877 | 0.3807 | 0.3801 |
| 1/8 | 0.35 | 0.3596 | 0.3509 | 0.3501 |
| 1/16 | 0.33 | 0.3409 | 0.3310 | 0.3301 |

**Table 2.** Self-refresh current in different PASR and Flikker configurations (PASR current values are from [18]). * This value is derived from linear interpolation of full array (1) and half array(1/2) cases.

$$\begin{aligned} P_{Flikker} =& P_{refresh} + P_{other} \\ =& P_{refresh\_low} + P_{refresh\_high} + P_{other} \\ =& \underline{P_L \times \frac{T_{regular}}{T_{low}}} + \underline{\underline{P_{refresh\_high} + P_{other}}} \\ =& \underline{(P_{full} - P_{PASR}) \times \frac{T_{regular}}{T_{low}}} + \underline{\underline{P_{PASR}}} \end{aligned} \quad (1)$$

As shown in Eq. 1, $P_{Flikker}$ has two components, $P_{refresh}$, which is the power consumed by refresh operations, and $P_{other}$, which is the power consumed by other parts of the DRAM (e.g. the control logic) in standby. $P_{refresh}$ is proportional to the refresh rate; while $P_{other}$ is independent of the refresh rate and is constant. Then we divide $P_{refresh}$ into $P_{refresh\_high}$ and $P_{refresh\_low}$, which correspond to the refresh power consumed by the high and low refresh parts respectively (as shown in second line of Eq. 1). We further explicate the relationship between refresh power and refresh cycle time by representing $P_{refresh\_low}$ as $P_L$ (which is a constant) times $T_{regular}/T_{low}$ (third line in Eq. 1).

In order to evaluate $P_{Flikker}$, we consider the DRAM with PASR and DRAM with full array refreshed (i.e., regular DRAM) as two extreme cases of Flikker. We calculate $P_{PASR}$ and $P_{full}$ by assigning $T_{low} = \infty$ and $T_{low} = T_{regular}$ in the third line of Eq. 1. With these two extremes cases, we rewrite the third line of Eq. 1 with $P_{PASR}$ and $P_{full}$ (as shown in the fourth line of Eq. 1). The underlined and double-underlined parts of the third line in Eq. 1 are equal to the corresponding parts in the fourth line.

Table 2 summarizes the self-refresh current of different PASR configurations and Flikker DRAM with different refresh cycle times for the low refresh part. The self-refresh power is calculated as self-refresh current times power supply voltage (1.8V in our experiments). It is important to understand that the self-refresh power comprises the power consumed in refreshing the DRAM array, and the power consumed to control the refresh operations of the DRAM chip. The former is proportional to the refresh rate, while the latter is a constant. Therefore, the self-refresh power does not decrease linearly with the refresh rate, but decreases and saturates at about 33%.

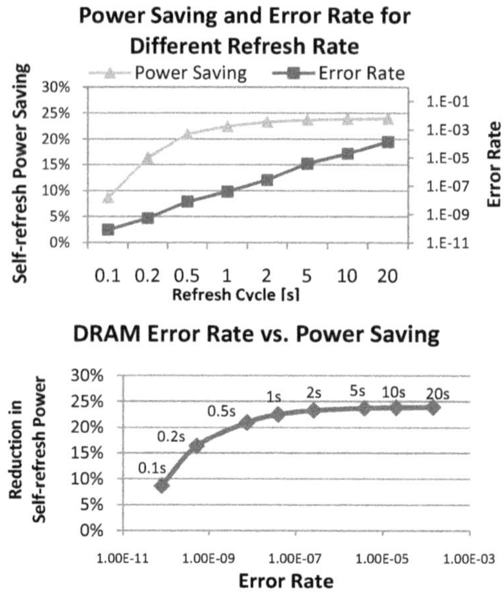


**Figure 4.** Error rate and power saving for different refresh cycles. The high refresh part is 1/4 of DRAM array .

### 3.5 Power-Reliability Trade-off

The models derived in the two previous sections are used to derive a suitable refresh rate for Flikker. Figure 4 shows the self-refresh power saving and DRAM error rate of different refresh cycles in a system with 1/4 of the memory array at the high refresh rate. In Figure 4 (top), the X-axis represents the refresh cycle time, the Y-axis on the left represents the power-savings in self-refresh mode, while the Y-axis on the right represents the error-rate on a logarithmic scale. It can be observed that the DRAM error rate increases exponentially with the DRAM refresh cycle. However, the self-refresh power saving saturates to about 25% at a refresh cycle time of about 1 second.

Increasing the refresh cycle beyond 1 second leads to significant increase in the error rates (the graph is draw to log-scale). For example, from 1 to 20 seconds, the error rate increases over 3000 times, from $4.0 \times 10^{-8}$ to $1.3 \times 10^{-4}$. However, the improvement in power saving corresponding to the refresh cycle increase is small (22.5% to 23.9%). On the other hand, reducing refresh cycle time from 1 second to 0.5 seconds leads to a steep decrease in power saving. This finding is also substantiated in Figure 4 (bottom), which shows the power-savings as a function of the error-rate (in log scale). Therefore, we believe that *a refresh cycle of 1 second is near-optimal, as it achieves a desirable tradeoff between power savings and reliability*. This is the value we use in our experiments.

## 4. Flikker Software

In this section, we describe the changes that need to be made to software so that it can use the Flikker DRAM. Figure 5 shows the steps involved in the operation of Flikker. First, the programmer marks application data as critical or non-critical. Second, the runtime system allocates critical and non-critical data to separate pages in memory, and places the pages in separate regions of memory (i.e., high-refresh and low-refresh respectively). Third, the Operating System (OS) configures the DRAM self-refresh counter before switching to the self-refresh mode. Finally, the self-refresh controller refreshes different rows of the DRAM bank at different rates depending on the OS-specified parameters. Based on Figure 5, modifications need to be made to the application, the runtime system and the Operating System (OS).

### 4.1 Application Changes

Critical data is defined as any data that if corrupted, leads to a catastrophic failure of the application. It includes any data that cannot be easily recreated or regenerated and has a significant impact on the output. The concept of critical data has been used in prior work [7, 8, 32] on error recovery. However, to the best of our knowledge, our work is the first to leverage critical data in applications for power savings.

Earlier studies have shown that it is intuitive for developers to identify critical data in applications [8, 32]. This is consistent with our observations in this paper as each application considered in the paper took us less than a day to partition (including the time we spent understanding it).

**Reason for ease of critical data separation**: We posit that application developers make a natural distinction between critical and non-critical data. Such a distinction is important for three reasons. First, application developers typically partition their code into modules based on functionality. Some modules may be responsible for the application's core functionality and separating the data manipulated by such modules from the rest of the application's data makes it easier to reason about their correctness. Secondly, software fails due to a variety of different reasons (in production use), and application developers may provide recovery and restart mechanisms for such failures. While the operating system may provide limited support, it is typically up to the application developer to store the important state of the application periodically and to restart the application from the stored state upon a failure [7]. Finally, programs typically separate the data structures storing different parts of their input/output space. For example, a video application will likely store its non-critical video data separate from the critical meta-data describing the video file.

**How to identify critical data**: In Flikker, the programmer marks program variables as "critical" or "non-critical" through type-annotations in the program's source code. We assume that the default type of a variable is critical, so that we can run an unmodified (legacy) application safely. An application's memory footprint has four components, code, stack, heap, and global data. Errors in the code or the stack are likely to crash the application and hence, we place code and stack data on the critical pages. Global data and heap data, on the other hand, contain both critical and non-critical parts. For global data, the programmer uses special keywords to designate the non-critical part. This requires support from the compiler and linker, which we currently do not have (we emulate such support). For heap data, the programmer allocates non-critical objects with a custom allocator, which involves modifying malloc calls in the program where non-critical data objects are allocated.

**Limitations**: Failure to identify critical data correctly may lead to corrupted states of applications and/or loss of data. As a result, Flikker may not be suitable for safety critical applications, such as bio-medical devices. However, there are a large class of applications that do not require such stringent correctness guarantees. To protect data during application failures, programmers of many applications already identify and protect critical data. Specifically, some applications periodically dump critical data to persistent storage (e.g., a file), while other applications introduce redundancy in the critical data. For these applications, Flikker may not require substantial effort from programmers. However, in many other applications, the separation between critical and non-critical data may not be as obvious. In particular, applications in which the critical state it tightly intertwined with the non-critical state are not good candidates for Flikker. In such applications, there are two difficulties with deploying Flikker. One is that the programmer may miss identifying critical data, leading to corruption of critical state and failure of the application. The second difficulty is that the programmer may over-annotate critical data, thereby marking non-critical data as critical. This leads to lost opportunities for power savings, though the application's reliability is not impacted. Identifying the most effective way for the programmer to partition critical data is outside the scope of this paper and is a topic of future work.

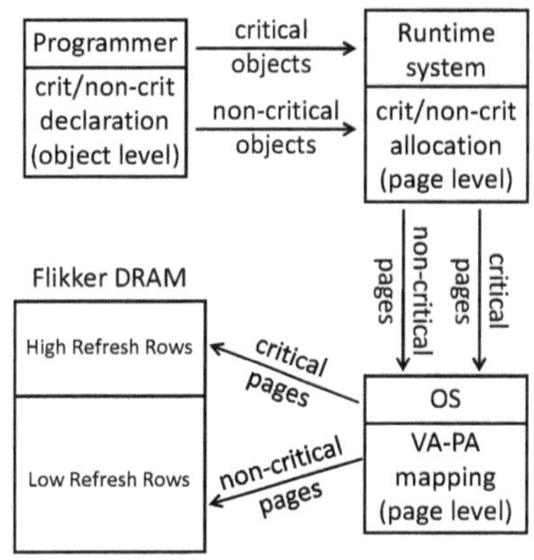


**Figure 5.** Flikker system diagram.

### 4.2 Runtime System Support

Flikker utilizes a custom allocator that allocates critical and non-critical heap data on different pages. The allocator marks pages containing non-critical data using a special bit in the page-table entry. The allocator also ensures that either all the data in a page is critical or all of it is non-critical, i.e., there is not mixing of critical and non-critical data within a page.

Ideally, both heap and global data should be partitioned into critical/non-critical parts. Our current version of Flikker does not implement partitioning of global data as this requires compiler support. However, as we will show in the experimental results (Section 6), there is strong evidence that global data has similar characteristics as heap data in terms of the relative proportion of critical to non-critical data.

### 4.3 Operating System Support

In a system with Flikker, the OS is responsible for managing critical and non-critical pages. A "criticality bit" is added to the page table entry of each page. This bit is set by the custom allocator when allocating any data from the page, unless the data has been designated as non-critical by the programmer. Based on the criticality bit, the OS maps critical pages to the high refresh part of the bank (top down in Figure 2), and non-critical pages to the low refresh part (bottom up in Figure 2). Before switching to the self-refresh mode, the OS configures DRAM registers that control the self-refresh controller based on the amount of critical data.

Ideally, the high refresh rate portion in the bank covers only pages containing critical data. However, this may not always be possible due to discretization in the self-refresh mode (Section 3.4). Therefore, the OS may end up placing more DRAM banks in high-refresh state than absolutely necessary, leading to wasted power. We show in Section 5 that this discretization does not significantly impact the power-savings of Flikker.

## 5. Experimental Setup

In this section, we present the applications and experimental methods used to evaluate Flikker. As mentioned in Section 3, Flikker requires minor changes to the hardware and hence we do not evaluate it directly on a mobile device. Instead, we use hardware simulation based on memory traces from real applications to evaluate the performance overheads and active power consumption of Flikker. Further, we evaluate the error-resilience of these applications by injecting representative faults in the applications' memory with an error-rate corresponding to the expected rate of errors from Section 3.3. The fault-injection experiments are carried out during the execution of each application (to completion) on a real system. We inject thousands of faults in each application and observe their final outputs in order to evaluate the reliability degradation due to Flikker. Finally, we evaluate the total power consumed by combining the active power consumption with the idle power consumption from the analytical model.

### 5.1 Selected Applications

We choose a diverse range of applications to evaluate Flikker, based on typical application categories for smartphones. Each application's output is evaluated using custom metrics based on its characteristics. For each application, we describe the application, the choice of critical data and the metrics for evaluating its output.

**mpeg2**: Multimedia applications are important for smartphones. Many multimedia applications utilize lossy compression / decompression algorithms, which are naturally error resilient. We select mpeg2 decoder from MediaBench [26] to represent multimedia applications. We mark the input file pointer, video information, and output file name as critical because corrupting these objects will cause unrecoverable failures in the application. We use the Signal-to-Noise-Ratio (SNR) to evaluate the output of the mpeg2 application, which is a commonly-used measure of video/audio fidelity in multimedia applications.

**c4**: Computer games constitute an important class of smartphone applications. Games usually have a save mechanism to store their state to files. Since the game can be recovered entirely from the saved files, the data stored to these files constitute the critical data. We select c4 [13] (known as connect 4 or four-in-a-row), which is a turn-based game similar to chess. c4 stores its moves in a heap-allocated array, which we mark as critical. We modify c4 to save its moves at the end of each game, and use the saved moves to check its output.

**rayshade**: Rayshade [24] is an extensible system for creating ray-traced images. Rayshade represents a growing class of mobile 3D applications. In rayshade, objects that model articles in the scene are marked critical as errors in these objects impact large ranges of the output figure. As was the case with mpeg2, we use the SNR to evaluate the output of rayshade.

**vpr**: Optimization algorithms may be executed on mobile phones for a variety of common tasks, e.g., calculating driving directions. We select vpr from SPEC2000 [35] to represent these algorithms, as it employs a graph routing algorithm for optimizing the design of Field-Programmable Gate Arrays (FPGAs). We choose the graph data structure as critical because any error in this structure will crash the program. We evaluate the output of vpr by perfoming a byte-by-byte comparison with the fault-free outputs.

**parser**: Natural language parsing is used in applications such as word processing and translation. The parser application from SPEC2000 [35] is chosen to represent this class of applications. Parser translates the input file into the output file based on a dictionary. Errors in the dictionary data are likely to affect multiple lines in the output and hence the dictionary is marked critical. Similar to vpr, we evaluate the results of parser by comparing the output file with the fault-free output.

Table 3 summarizes the characteristics and evaluation metrics of these applications.

### 5.2 Experimental Framework

We introduce the main components of our experimental infrastructure in this section.

**Memory Footprint Analyzer**: We analyze the memory footprint of each application in order to calculate the proportion of critical data. This foot-print is used to calculate power-consumption in idle-mode. These measurements were performed by enhancing the Pin dynamic-instrumentation framework [29].

| Application | LoC | Input | Metric |
|---|---|---|---|
| mpeg2 | 10,000 | mei16v2.m2v | output SNR |
| c4 | 6100 | N/A | saved moves |
| rayshade | 24,200 | balls.ray | output SNR |
| vpr | 24,600 | ref/test | output file |
| parser | 11,500 | ref/test | output file |

**Table 3.** Application characterizations and the output criteria used for evaluating Flikker. (LoC = Lines of Code)

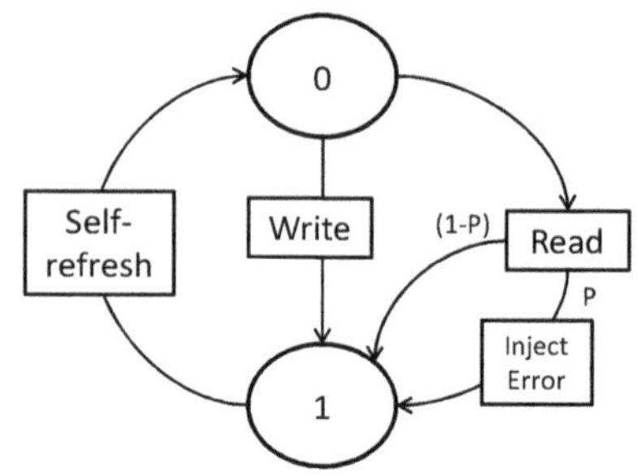


**Figure 6.** State transition diagram of "modified" bit in fault-injection. Error is injected to the DRAM with probability "P".

**Architectural simulator**: We use a cycle-accurate architectural simulator for evaluating the Flikker hardware. The simulator contains a functional front-end based on Pin [29] and a detailed memory system model. A DRAM power model based on the system-power calculator [19] is incorporated into the simulator. We do not specify the physical allocation of pages among different banks in the simulator—this is implicitly assigned depending on whether the page is critical. The simulator takes instruction traces as inputs, and produces as outputs estimates of the total power consumed and the total number of processor cycles and instructions executed in the trace. Table 4 shows the main processor and DRAM parameters used by the simulator. These parameters are chosen to model a typical smartphone with a 1GHz processor and 128 Mega-bytes of DRAM memory.

**Fault-injector**: We built a fault-injector based on the Pin [29] dynamic instrumentation framework. The injector starts the application and executes it for an initial period. No errors are injected during this period. Then a self-refresh period is inserted, after which errors are injected to the non-critical memory pages to emulate the effect of lowering their refresh rate. In order to keep track of the errors injected during the self-refresh period, the injector maintains a "modified" bit for each byte in the low refresh pages denoting whether this byte has been accessed after the self-refresh period. Before a low refresh byte is read, the corresponding modified bit is checked. If it is "0", meaning that the byte has not been accessed after self-refresh, a single bit is flipped in the byte with a pre-computed probability (third column of Table 1).[2] Modified bits that correspond to target bytes of memory read or write operations are set to "1" to prevent future injections into these bytes. Figure 6 shows the state transition diagram of the "modified" bit.

### 5.3 Experimental Methodology

We evaluate the performance overhead, power savings, and reliability degradation due to Flikker. Figure 7 demonstrates our overall evaluation methodology. The main steps are as follows:

[2] Given the low error rates in Table 1, the probability of multiple bit flips in each byte is extremely low, and are hence ignored.

| Parameter | Value |
|---|---|
| Processor | single core, 1GHz |
| Cache | 32KB IL1 and 32KB DL1, 4-way set associative, 32-byte block, 1-cycle latency |
| DRAM | 1Gb, 4 banks, 200MHz (see [18]) |
| Low power scheme | precharge row buffer after 100ns idle; switch to fast low power state 100ns after precharge |
| Cache miss delay | row-buffer-hit: 40ns, row-buffer-close: 60ns, row-buffer-conflict: 80ns |

**Table 4.** Major architectural simulation parameters.

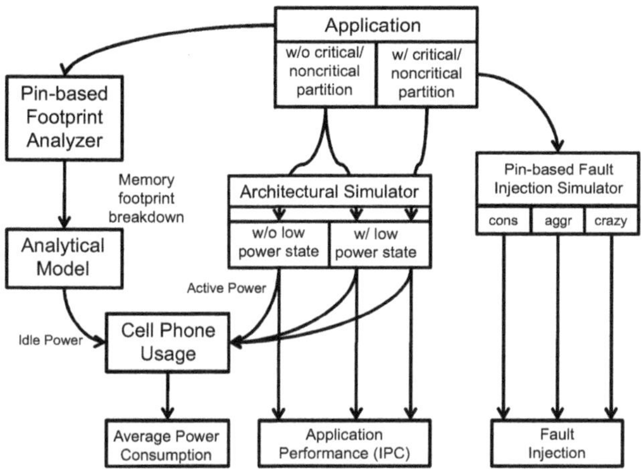


**Figure 7.** Evaluation Framework.

1. First partition each application's data into critical and non-critical (top box of Fig. 7).
2. Obtain the memory footprint of each application and use the analytical model to calculate the idle DRAM power consumption with and without Flikker (left portion of Fig. 7).
3. Apply architectural simulation for measuring the performance degradation and active DRAM power consumed by the application (middle portion of Fig. 7).
4. Calculate average DRAM power consumption and the total DRAM power saving achieved by Flikker (bottom left portion of Fig. 7).
5. Use fault-injection to evaluate the application's reliability under Flikker (right portion of Fig. 7).

In the following, we describe each of the above steps in detail.

**Critical Data Partitioning**: We modify all 5 applications to use Flikker's custom allocator for allocating heap data. Our experimental infrastructure does not allow us to partition the global data into critical and non-critical parts. To understand the impact of global data partitioning, we consider two configurations: "conservative", in which all global data is critical, and "aggressive", in which all global data is non-critical. The configurations bound the performance benefit and the reliability impact of partitioning the global data. We anticipate that partitioning global data yields a power-savings close to that of aggressive and has reliability impact close to that of the conservative configuration, provided that the critical data is a small fraction of all global data (in Section 6.4, we present experimental evidence that this is indeed the case).

In the above discussion, we assumed that stack data is placed in high-refresh state. However, in some applications, the stack data may also be amenable to being partitioned into critical and non-critical. To emulate this condition, we consider a third-configuration "crazy", where the stack and critical data are also placed in low-refresh state. Table 5 summarizes the configurations used for evaluating each application.

| Configuration | High Refresh | Low Refresh |
|---|---|---|
| conservative | Code, Stack<br>Crit-Heap, Global | Noncrit-Heap |
| aggressive | Code, Stack<br>Crit-Heap | Global<br>Noncrit-Heap |
| crazy | Code | Stack, Global<br>Crit/Noncrit-Heap |

**Table 5.** Configurations used to evaluate Flikker

| App. | Code | Stack | Global | Crit Heap | Noncrit Heap |
|---|---|---|---|---|---|
| mpeg2 | 79 | 31 | 181 | 1 | 618 |
| c4 | 473 | 21 | 10062 | 1 | 0 |
| rayshade | 97 | 10 | 603 | 2 | 541 |
| vpr | 114 | 713 | 4271 | 1739 | 2888 |
| parser | 88 | 544 | 1570 | 27 | 7688 |

**Table 6.** Memory footprint breakdown (number of 4kB pages).

**Memory foot-print and idle-power calculator**: Table 6 summarizes the memory footprint break down for code, stack, global data, critical, and non-critical heap pages. For stack and heap data, we report the maximum number of pages used during the execution. Hence, these measurements form an upper-bound on the total memory foot-print of the application.

We calculate the power consumed by the system in idle mode based on the analytical model derived in Section 3.4 and the data presented in Table 6. The refresh cycle in the low refresh portion of memory is assumed to be 1 second. This calculation is based on the results of the analytical model in Section 3.4. Further, the high refresh portions in each application are rounded up to the discrete levels in Table 2 to emulate their real-world behavior.

**Architectural Simulation**: We evaluate the performance and power consumption in active mode using the hardware simulator described in Section 5.2. For evaluating performance, we measure the Instructions Per Cycle (IPC) of the system, and for evaluating the power consumption, we measure the total energy consumed by each DRAM bank and divide it by the simulation time.

All 5 applications are compiled with Microsoft Visual Studio 2008. The simulations are performed with application traces consisting of 100 million instructions chosen from the approximate middle of the execution of each application. For vpr and parser, we use the SPEC ref inputs in architectural simulations, while for the other applications, we choose inputs representative of typical usage scenarios.

The main source of performance overhead due to Flikker stems from the partitioning of application data, which can potentially impact locality and bank-parallelism. Therefore, the overhead of Flikker is evaluated by considering a system that employs data partitioning (Part) with one that does not (Base). Note that the refresh rate of Flikker plays no part in the measurement of active power. In both cases, we assume that the DRAM aggressively transitions to low-power states when not in use, as mentioned in Section 3.1.

| Application | Scenario | IPC | Active Power [mW] |
|---|---|---|---|
| mpeg2 | Base | 1.462 | 4.17 |
| | Part | 1.462 | 4.18 |
| c4 | Base | 1.057 | 5.06 |
| | Part | 1.068 | 5.03 |
| rayshade | Base | 1.734 | 4.15 |
| | Part | 1.734 | 4.15 |
| vpr | Base | 1.772 | 4.14 |
| | Part | 1.772 | 4.14 |
| parser | Base | 1.694 | 4.17 |
| | Part | 1.695 | 4.16 |

**Table 7.** Performance (IPC) and Active Power Consumption of Flikker

**Power-savings calculation**: We assume a mobile DRAM device having a capacity of 128 megabytes, which is conservative compared to the memory capacity of current smartphones (e.g., the iPhone). [3] Most of the selected applications will use far less RAM than this space. However, in a realistic scenario, multiple applications will share the RAM space and hence it is important to account for power-savings on a per-application basis. Therefore, we compute the proportion of critical and non-critical data for the application, and scale it to the size of the entire DRAM. This allows us to emulate the multiple-application scenario while considering only one application at a time. In order to evaluate overall DRAM power reduction, we assume that the cell phone usage profile is 5% busy versus 95% in standby mode (self-refresh state) as assumed in prior work [36].

**Fault-injection**: The fault-injection experiments are performed using the fault-injector described in Section 5.2. Note that the inputs used for each application during fault-injection are the same as those used for performance evaluation and active-power calculation (the only exceptions are vpr and parser, where we use the SPEC test inputs for fault-injection due to the large number of trials performed). When performing the fault-injection experiments, we monitor the applications for failures, i.e., crashes and hangs. If the application does not fail, its final output is evaluated using application-specific metrics shown in Table 3. We classify the fault-injection results into three categories as follows, (1) perfect (the output is identical to an error-free execution), (2) degraded (program finishes successfully with different output), and (3) failed (program crashes or hangs).

## 6. Experimental Results

We now discuss the results of experiments used to evaluate the power savings, reliability and performance degradation with Flikker.

### 6.1 Performance & Active Power

Table 7 (column 2) shows the performance and active power consumption of the Base and Part system scenarios. Recall that Base represents the non-partitioned version of the application, while Part represents the partitioned version. The results in Table 7 show that the IPC of the Base and Part scenarios are similar for all applications (both within 1% of each other). Therefore, the performance overhead of Flikker is negligible for the applications considered. Further, Flikker does not significantly increase the active power consumption of the application. In some cases, the active power consumption is actually reduced due to the partitioning because it increases the bank-parallelism by laying out memory differently.

[3] The higher the memory capacity, the greater the power savings achieved by Flikker.

### 6.2 Power Reduction

Figure 8 shows the reduction in DRAM standby power for different applications and the three configurations in Table 5. Figure 9 shows the overall power reduction for different applications, which are obtained by combining the results in Figure 8 with the active power measurements in Table 7. The following trends may be observed from Figures 8 and 9.

- Both the standby and overall power consumed vary with the application and the configuration. For all applications, the crazy configuration achieves the highest power savings (25-32% standby and 20-25% overall), followed by the aggressive configuration (10-32 % standby and 9-25% overall) and finally the conservative configuration (0-25% standby and 0-17% overall).
- The aggressive configuration achieves significant power savings in all applications except vpr. This is because the applications' memory foot-print is dominated by global and non-critical data, whereas in vpr the stack, code and critical data pages constitute a sizable fraction of the total memory pages (over 35% according to Table 6). However, the crazy configuration achieves significant power savings for vpr, as the stack and critical pages are placed in the low-refresh state.
- For mpeg2, c4 and rayshade, the aggressive and crazy configurations yield identical power savings (both standby and overall) as these applications have very few stack and critical data pages.
- Among all applications in the conservative configuration, parser exhibits the maximum reduction in both standby and overall power consumption (22% and 17% respectively). This is because parser has the largest proportion of non-critical heap data among the applications considered, and this data is placed in low-refresh state in the conservative configuration.
- The power savings for the c4 application in the conservative configuration is 0% as its memory footprint is dominated by global data pages (according to Table 6), which are placed in high-refresh mode in the conservative configuration.

From Figure 8 and 9, Flikker achieves substantial DRAM power savings. The actual reduction in the overall system power consumption depends on the relative fraction of memory power to total system power. Previous work [6] shows that DRAM contributes about 4% of overall power consumption of the Openmoko Neo Freerunner (revision A6) mobile phone. In this case, Flikker would only yield 1% reduction of total system energy consumption. Nevertheless, as DRAM power is and will continue to be a significant component of computer systems, Flikker savings can be obtained across the spectrum of systems, ranging from the very small (mobile devices) to the very large (datacenters).

### 6.3 Fault Injection Results

In this section, we present the results of fault-injection experiments to evaluate the reliability of Flikker. We first present overall results corresponding to the error-rate for a low-refresh period of one second, which we showed represents the optimal refresh period for power-reliability trade-off in Section 3.4. We further evaluate the output degradation for each application under faults. Finally, we demonstrate the importance of protecting critical data by performing targeted fault-injections into the critical heap data.

#### 6.3.1 Injections in both critical and non-critical data

Figure 10 shows the result of the fault-injection experiments for five applications and three configurations with an error-rate corresponding to a 1 second refresh period. Each bar in the figure represents

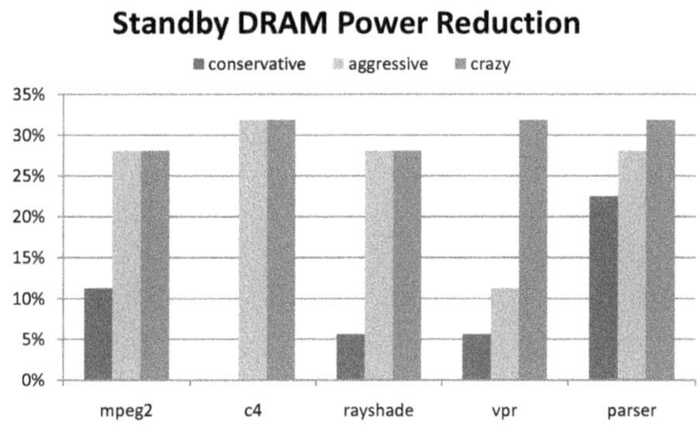


**Figure 8.** Standby DRAM power reduction for different applications.

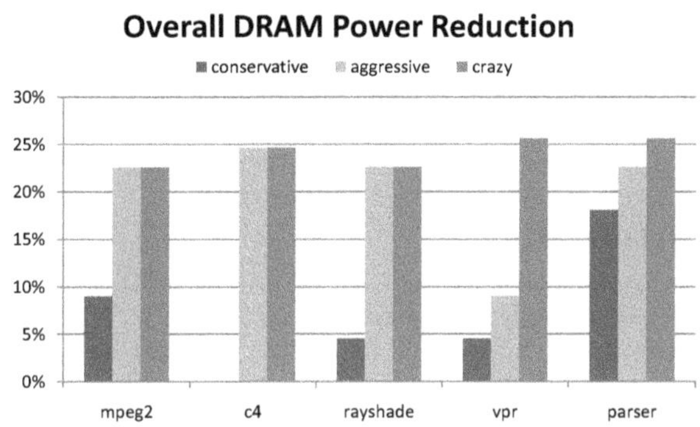


**Figure 9.** Overall DRAM power reduction for different applications.

the result of 1000 fault-injection trials. The results are normalized to 100% for ease of comparison.

The main results from Figure 10 are summarized as follows:

- No application exhibits failures in the conservative configuration. In fact, c4, vpr, and parser, have perfect outputs in the conservative configuration. However, mpeg2 and rayshade have a few runs with degraded results (about 33% for mpeg2 and 4% for rayshade), but as we show later in the section, the degradation is marginal. The degradation accurs because mpeg2 and rayshade maintain a large output buffer in DRAM, which is likely to accumulate errors during the self-refresh period.
- Both aggressive and crazy configurations yield worse results than conservative for all applications. The only exception is c4, which has a very small proportion of critical pages. These pages are unlikely to get corrupted given the relatively low error rate corresponding to the 1 second refresh period.
- The difference between the aggressive and crazy configurations is small, with aggressive having slightly fewer failures and degraded outputs. This is because the proportion of critical heap and stack pages is relatively small, and hence the probability of corrupting objects in these pages is very low.
- Finally, the aggressive configuration exhibits a very small number of failures across applications (except parser). This confirms our earlier intuition (see Section 5.3) that global data is likely to contain a very small proportion of critical data.

As mentioned above, the conservative configuration yields degraded outputs in about 33% of mpeg2 executions and in about 4% of rayshade executions. The aggressive and crazy configurations also yield degraded output in about 40% and 20% of mpeg2 executions and 21% and 23% of rayshade executions respectively.

To further understand the extent of output degradation, we measure the quality of the video or image using measures such as the

| Configuration | mpeg2 | rayshade |
|---|---|---|
| conservative | 95 | 101 |
| aggressive | 88 | 72 |
| crazy | 88 | 73 |

**Table 8.** Average SNR of degraded output for mpeg2 and rayshade [dB]. Larger values indicate better output quality.

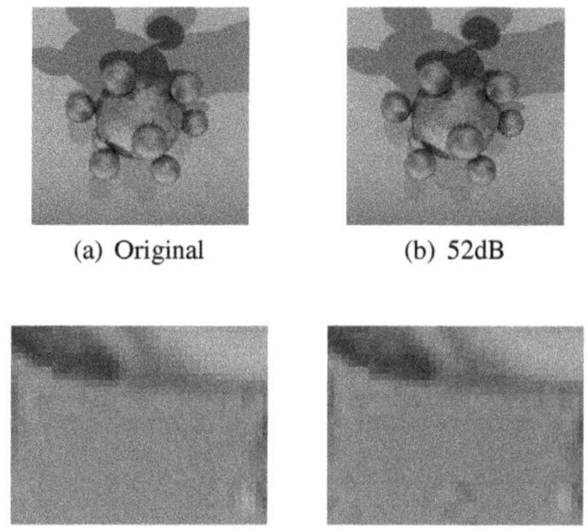

(a) Original (b) 52dB

(c) Magnified orig. (d) Magnified 52dB

**Figure 11.** Rayshade output figures with different SNRs.

Signal-to-Noise Ratio (SNR). Table 8 shows the average SNR measurements for the outputs averaged across all trials exhibiting degraded outputs. Note that SNR is measured in decibels (dB), a logarithmic unit of measurement. As can be seen from the table, the conservative configuration yields over 95 decibels of output quality for mpeg2 and over 100 decibels for rayshade on average. The aggressive and crazy configurations both yield SNRs of over 80 decibels for mpeg2 and over 70 decibels for rayshade.

In order to understand better the qualitative impact of output degradation in mpeg2, we take a raw video, encode it with the mpeg2 encoder, and decoded the result with the mpeg2 decoder. Compared with the original video, the final output video has an SNR of 35 decibels. This demonstrates that an SNR of 80 or above in fact represents a video of high-quality, which we believe is acceptable for a mobile smartphone with a limited display resolution.

For rayshade, we attempt to understand the output degradation by studying the rendered images. Figures 11 a and 11 b show the original image and the corresponding degraded image (with a SNR of 52 decibels). The latter is generated during a faulty execution of rayshade. These figures are shown with a scale factor of 0.25. As can be seen from the figure, it is almost impossible to tell the difference between the original image and the degraded image. However, when we magnify the images to a factor of two of the original (Figures 11 c and 11 d), small differences among the pixels become discernible. Therefore, even for a significantly degraded image with SNR considerably below 70 decibels, the differences become discernible only at high resolutions.

### 6.3.2 Injections into critical data only

Based on the results presented in the previous section, one may ask whether it is indeed necessary to partition applications in order to prevent errors in the non-critical data. We attempt to answer this question by performing targeted injections into the critical data. If we do not observe any failures in these experiments, then we can conclude that preventing errors in the critical data (and hence partitioning of data) is unnecessary for achieving high reliability.

In these experiments, we inject a single error into the critical data during each trial because the proportion of critical data in each

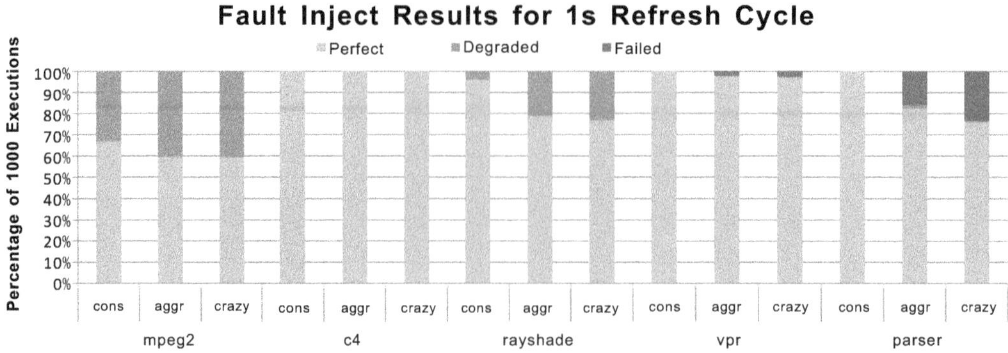


**Figure 10.** Fault-injection result for systems with low refresh rate of 1 second.

| Application | Perfect | Degraded | Failed | SNR |
|---|---|---|---|---|
| mpeg2 | 0% | 0% | 100% | N/A |
| rayshade | 42% | 58% | 0% | 39.37dB |
| vpr | 7% | 0% | 93% | N/A |
| parser | 52% | 10% | 38% | N/A |

**Table 9.** Results of injecting a single error in the critical heap data.

application is relatively small. Further, we perform fewer trials (50-100) than previous experiments as we obtained converging results even within these trials.

Table 9 shows the results of these experiments normalized to 100%. We exclude c4 from the experiments, because its only critical heap data is the game record, and this is precisely the output used for comparison. Therefore, all injections into the critical data of c4 will result in failures.

From Table 9, mpeg2 always fails (crashes) due to the injected errors because its output path or file pointer gets corrupted. On the other hand, rayshade does not fail but its output quality with even a single error in the critical data is 39 decibels on average, which is considerably worse than the quality with errors in non-critical data (over 70 decibels). Both parser and vpr experience high failure rates due to a single error in the critical data - vpr even more so than parser. The above results illustrate the importance of protecting critical data in applications and underline the need for data partitioning to prevent reliability degradation due to lowering of refresh rates.

### 6.4 Optimal Configurations

In this section, we combine the fault-injection results (Figure 10) with the power-savings results (Figures 8 and 9) to find the optimal configuration in terms of the power-reliability trade-off for each application. The main results are as follows:

- mpeg2, c4 and rayshade exhibit high overall power savings (20-25%) and no failures in the aggressive configuration. Further, the output quality is high (measured in SNR) for both rayshade and mpeg2 in the aggressive configuration. Hence, the best configuration for these applications is aggressive, suggesting that they have a large proportion of non-critical global data (see Section 5.3).
- For parser, the best results are achieved in the conservative configuration. This is because parser has a large proportion of non-critical data pages, and hence significant power savings (about 25%) can be achieved by putting these pages in the low-refresh mode. Further, parser experiences quite a few failures in the aggressive configuration, which suggests that it has a sizable chunk of critical global data.
- Finally, for vpr, the crazy configuration achieves the best overall power savings (nearly 25%) compared to the other two configurations. Further, even under the crazy configuration, the number of failures in vpr is marginal (less than 3%). This is because vpr has a significant proportion of stack data due to recursive calls, which is not critical to its correct execution.

## 7. Related Work

This section discusses related work in the areas of both hardware and software techniques for power reduction.

**Hardware Techniques:** Traditionally, hardware design techniques over-provision for the worst-case behavior of the platform. However, in the majority of common usage scenarios, the worst-case behavior is rarely exhibited, and the approach is often wasteful. Therefore, a new class of techniques have emerged that provision for the average case and treat the worst case behavior as an exception. This paradigm is referred to as *Better-Than-Worst-Case* (BTWC) [1]. Razor is one of the best known examples of the BTWC paradigm [12]. Razor reduces the energy consumption of processors by progressively lowering their voltage until such a point that the processor starts to experience errors due to timing violations.

At a high-level, Flikker is also a BTWC technique. However, unlike Razor and other BTWC technique which attempt to correct the introduced errors in hardware, Flikker exposes the errors all the way up the system stack to the application, thereby leveraging power-saving opportunities that were unexposed or infeasible at the architectural level alone. This is because many applications are naturally resilient to errors [28, 38], and this resilience can be exploited for power-savings through application-level techniques such a Flikker.

*RAPID* [36] is a hardware-software technique that applies the BTWC principle for DRAM refresh-power reduction. The main idea is to characterize the leakage behavior of each physical page and partition the pages into different classes based on their DRAM leakage characteristics. Applications preferentially use pages from the leakage class with the lowest leakage rate and the overall refresh rate is set based on the highest leakage class of pages allocated by the application (thereby preserving data integrity). In order for RAPID to be effective, applications must have substantial slack in memory usage. However, this assumption often does not hold for smartphone applications which are memory-constrained and typically operate near their peak memory capacities.

A number of other techniques modify the memory controller hardware to reduce unnecessary or redundant refreshes of DRAM cells [15, 23, 31]. These techniques however, require substantial changes to the memory controller's hardware compared to Flikker.

Finally, ESKIMO [20] is a hardware mechanism to save DRAM power using knowledge of application semantics. Similar to Flikker,

ESKIMO modifies the memory allocator to expose details of the application's allocation patterns to the hardware. However, in terms of refresh-power reduction, ESKIMO differs from Flikker in two ways. First, ESKIMO focuses on reducing the refresh power of unused memory areas, while Flikker focuses on reducing the refresh power of the used memory areas. Second, ESKIMO attempts to preserve data integrity in the allocated areas, and hence has only limited opportunities for saving refresh-power (6 to 10%).

**Software Techniques**: Recently, a number of software-based techniques have been proposed that trade-off reliability for energy savings [2, 10, 16, 34]. These techniques share the same goal as Flikker, namely to reduce hardware reliability in an application-specific manner in order to achieve power savings. We discuss the techniques further in this section and then discuss the differences with Flikker.

Fluid-NMR [34] performs N-way replication of applications in a multi-core processors for tolerating errors due to reductions in voltage-levels of processors. The parameter N is varied based on the application's ability to tolerate errors. Relax is a technique to save computational power by exposing hardware errors to software in specified regions of code [10]. Relax allows programmers to mark certain regions of the code as "relaxed", and lowers the processor's voltage and frequency below the critical threshold when executing such regions, thereby allowing errors to occur during computation. Green [2] trades off Quality-of-Service (QoS) for energy efficiency in server and high-performance applications respectively. Green allows programmers to specify regions of code in which the application can tolerate reduced precision. Based on this information, the Green system attempts to compute a principled approximation of the code-region (loop or function body) to reduce processor power. Code perforation [16] is similar to Green, except that it attempts to infer the approximation code regions based on acceptance criteria provided by the user. Further, code perforation monitors the application at runtime and adapts the inference mechanism based on the application's behavior.

The above techniques are very similar to Flikker in their overall objectives. However, they differ from Flikker in two ways. First, they are task-centric and/or code-centric whereas Flikker is data-centric. In other words, the techniques require programmers to identify regions of code where errors are allowed (code perforation infers such regions automatically [16]), while Flikker requires programmers to identify data items where errors are allowed, i.e., non-critical data. We believe that it is more intuitive for programmers to identify non-critical data as data items often map directly to applications' outputs. Second, the above techniques target processor power reduction, while Flikker targets memory power reduction, which involves a different set of trade-offs and is hence orthogonal to the techniques.

In work submitted concurrently with our own, Salajegheh et al. propose "Half-wits" to save Flash power consumption by operating Flash chips at a lower voltage level and correcting errors with software techniques [33]. However, Half-wits fail to exploit the full potential of power reduction because it provides same level of reliability to both critical and non-critical data. The combination of Half-wits and Flikker will achieve more power savings.

## 8. Alternatives to Flikker

In this section, we consider alternative technologies to Flikker and qualitatively discuss the relative costs and benefits of the Flikker technique vis-a-vis these technologies.

**Flash memory** is predominantly used in smartphones as secondary storage. Flash memory is durable and does not need to be periodically refreshed. Hence it can be used to store the application's data before the smartphone transitions into sleep mode. Unfortunately, Flash memory read and write times are an order of magnitude higher than DRAM's, with the result that it is considerably slower read/write the contents of entire DRAM to memory. For a smartphone with 128 megabytes of DRAM and 16 megabytes per second effective Flash bandwidth, paging the whole main memory from Flash requires 8 seconds. Since memory capacity scales faster than bandwidth, this delay is likely to increase in future smartphones. While it is possible to accelerate the process by writing out only selected portions of the memory state, the challenges in doing so are similar to those faced by Flikker. In particular, the programmer must identify critical data in the application and be prepared to restore the application based only on the critical data.

**Phase-Change Memory (PCM)** is an emerging technology that offers better write performance and longer lifetime than Flash. Some recent proposals [25] have called for the partial replacement of DRAMs with PCMs in mobile devices. However, due to its overhead in dynamic power and access latency, PCM is not expected to completely replace DRAMs, but instead to be used for high-endurance but infrequently accessed data [25]. Flikker can also be applied in this context by storing the critical data only on PCM memory. This will allow the refresh rate of the entire DRAM array to be reduced rather than partition the array into the high-refresh and low-refresh part as done by Flikker. This is an avenue for future investigation.

**ECC memory** is widely used in systems that require extreme relibility. To enable error correction, ECC memory employs both extra storage and logic, which consumes power. As a result, ECC memory is not suitable for power-constrained systems. To the best of our knowledge, fault-tolerant refresh reduction [22] is the only technique that utilizes ECC memory for refresh power reduction. However, this technique targets the system scenario where only idle power consumption is considered. Hence, dynamic power consumed in the logic circuit is eliminated from the power overhead of ECC in this technique. An additional factor to consider is the increased cost of ECC memory, which may be a significant bottleneck to its adoption in commodity systems. Studies have shown that this cost may be as high as 25% in some systems [9].

## 9. Conclusion and Future Work

We present Flikker, a novel technique to save refresh power in DRAMs. Flikker enables programmers to partition the application data based on its criticality and lowers the refresh rate of the part of memory containing the non-critical data to save power. This separation introduces a modest amount of data corruption in the non-critical data, which is tolerated by the natural error-resilience of many applications. We prototyped the Flikker approach on a mobile device (using simulation), and find that it saves between 20-25% of total DRAM power in memory systems with less than 1% performance degradation and almost no loss in application reliability. Flikker represents a novel tradeoff in systems design, namely trading off hardware reliability for power-savings in an application-aware manner, as hardware only needs to be as reliable as the software requires.

Flikker can also be applied to data-center applications because they, (1) exhibit high variations in workloads and have considerable periods of inactivity, (2) consume significant power in idle-mode due to over-engineering, and (3) are inherently error-resilient and do not have to be 100% accurate [2]. Understanding the benefits of Flikker in this domain is a direction for future research.

**Acknowledgements**: We thank Emery Berger, Martin Burtscher, Shuo Chen, Trishul Chilimbi, John Douceur, Erez Petrank, Martin Rinard, Karin Strauss, Nikhil Swamy and David Walker for useful comments and discussions about this work. We also thank our shepherd, Luis Ceze, and the anonymous reviewers for their constructive feedback.

## References


[1] T. Austin, V. Bertacco, D. Blaauw, and T. Mudge. Opportunities and challenges for better than worst-case design. In *Proceedings of the Asia South Pacific design automation conference*, pages 2–7, 2005.

[2] W. Baek and T. M. Chilimbi. Green: a framework for supporting energy-conscious programming using controlled approximation. In *ACM SIGPLAN Conference on Programming language design and implementation*, PLDI '10, pages 198–209, 2010.

[3] Vimal Bhalodia. SCALE DRAM subsystem power analysis. Master's thesis, Massachusetts Institute of Technology, 2005.

[4] S. Borkar. Microarchitecture and design challenges for gigascale integration. In *Proceedings of the International Symposium on Microarchitecture (MICRO)*, 2004.

[5] Kirk W. Cameron, Rong Ge, and Xizhou Feng. High-performance, power-aware distributed computing for scientific applications. *Computer*, 38:40–47, 2005.

[6] A. Carroll and G. Heiser. An analysis of power consumption in a smartphone. *Usenix Annual Technical Conference (ATC)*, 2010.

[7] S. Chandra and P.M. Chen. The impact of recovery mechanisms on the likelihood of saving corrupted state. In *International Symposium on Software Reliability Engineering (ISSRE)*, page 91, 2002.

[8] Y. Chen, O. Gnawali, M. Kazandjieva, P. Levis, and J. Regehr. Surviving sensor-networks software faults. In *Proceedings of the International Symposium on Operating Systems Design (SOSP)*. ACM New York, NY, USA, 2009.

[9] Tezzaron corporation. Soft errors in electronic memory (white paper), 2005. Available from `http://www.tezzaron.com/about/papers/Papers.htm`.

[10] Marc de Kruijf, Shuou Nomura, and Karthikeyan Sankaralingam. Relax: an architectural framework for software recovery of hardware faults. *International Symposium on Computer Architecture (ISCA)*, pages 497–508, 2010.

[11] C. Ellis, A. Lebeck, and A. Vahdat. System support for energy management in mobile and embedded workloads (white paper). Technical report, Duke University, 1999.

[12] D. et al. Ernst. Razor: A low-power pipeline based on circuit-level timing speculation. In *Proceedings of the 36th annual IEEE/ACM International Symposium on Micro-architecture (MICRO)*, 2003.

[13] Martin Fierz. 4 in a row. Available from `http://www.fierz.ch/4inarow.htm`.

[14] J. Flinn, K.I. Farkas, and J. Anderson. Power and energy characterization of the Itsy pocket computer (version 1.5). *Compaq Western Research Laboratory, Tech. Rep*, 2000.

[15] M. Ghosh and H.H.S. Lee. Smart refresh: An enhanced memory controller design for reducing energy in conventional and 3D die-stacked DRAMs. In *Proceedings of the 40th Annual IEEE/ACM International Symposium on Micro-architecture(MICRO)*.

[16] H. Hoffmann, S. Misailovic, S. Sidiroglou, A. Agarwal, and M. Rinard. Using code perforation to improve performance, reduce energy consumption, and respond to failures. Technical report, Technical Report Massachusets Institute for Technology, 2009.

[17] Henry Hoffmann, Stelios Sidiroglou, Michael Carbin, Sasa Misailovic, Anant Agarwal, and Martin Rinard. Dynamic knobs for responsive power-aware computing. In *Proceedings of the 16th International Conference on Architectural Support for Programming Languages and Operating Systems (ASPLOS'11)*, March 2011.

[18] Micron Technology Inc. 1gb mobile LPDDR. Available from `http://www.micron.com/products/partdetail?part=MT46H32M32LFCG-5IT`.

[19] Micron Technology Inc. System power calculator. Available from `http://www.micron.com/support/designsupport/tools/powercalc/powercalc`.

[20] Ciji Isen and Lizy John. Eskimo - energy savings using semantic knowledge of inconsequential memory occupancy for DRAM subsystem. In *Proceedings of the International Conference on Microarchitecture (MICRO)*. IEEE, 2009.

[21] A.K. Karlson, B.R. Meyers, A. Jacobs, P. Johns, and S.K. Kane. Working Overtime: Patterns of Smartphone and PC Usage in the Day of an Information Worker. In *Pervasive Computing: 7th International Conference, Pervasive 2009, May 11-14, 2009, Proceedings*, page 398. Springer, 2009.

[22] Y. Katayama, E.J. Stuckey, S. Morioka, and Z. Wu. Fault-Tolerant Refresh Power Reduction of DRAMs for Quasi-Nonvolatile Data Retention. In *International Symposium on Defect and Fault Tolerance in VLSI Systems (DFT-VLSI)*, volume 311, page 318, 1999.

[23] J. Kim and MC Papaefthymiou. Block-based multiperiod dynamic memory design for low data-retention power. *IEEE Transactions on Very Large Scale Integration (VLSI) Systems*, 11(6):1006–1018, 2003.

[24] Craig Kolb. Rayshade graphics program. Available from `http://www-graphics.stanford.edu/~cek/rayshade`.

[25] Benjamin C. Lee, Engin Ipek, Onur Mutlu, and Doug Burger. Architecting phase change memory as a scalable DRAM alternative. *International Symposium on Computer Architecture (ISCA)*, 2009.

[26] Chunho Lee, Miodrag Potkonjak, and William H. Mangione-Smith. Mediabench: a tool for evaluating and synthesizing multimedia and communicatons systems. In *Proceedings of the 30th annual ACM/IEEE International Symposium on Microarchitecture*, 1997.

[27] C. Lefurgy, K. Rajamani, F. Rawson, W. Felter, M. Kistler, and T.W. Keller. Energy management for commercial servers. *Computer*.

[28] Xuanhua Li and Donald Yeung. Application-level correctness and its impact on fault tolerance. *International Symposium on High-Performance Computer Architecture (HPCA)*, 0:181–192, 2007.

[29] Chi-Keung et. al. Luk. Pin: Building customized program analysis tools with dynamic instrumentation. In *ACM SIGPLAN Conference on Programming Language design and implementation (PLDI)*, pages 190–200, New York, NY, USA, 2005. ACM.

[30] M. Murphy. *Beginning Android*. Apress, 2009.

[31] K. Patel, E. Macii, M. Poncino, and L. Benini. Energy-Efficient Value Based Selective Refresh for Embedded DRAMS. *Lecture Notes in Computer Science (LNCS)*, 3728:466, 2005.

[32] Karthik Pattabiraman, Vinod Grover, and Benjamin G. Zorn. Samurai: protecting critical data in unsafe languages. In *Eurosys '08: Proceedings of the 3rd ACM SIGOPS/EuroSys European Conference on Computer Systems 2008*, 2008.

[33] Mastooreh Salajegheh, Yue Wang, Kevin Fu, Anxiao (Andrew) Jiang, and Erik Learned-Miller. Exploiting half-wits: Smarter storage for low-power devices. In *Proceedings of the 9th USENIX Conference on File and Storage Technologies (FAST '11)*, February 2011.

[34] John Satori, Joseph Sloan, and Rakesh Kumar. Fluid NMR-performing power/reliability tradeoffs for applications with error tolerance. *Workshop on Power Aware Computing and Systems (HotPower'09)*, 2009.

[35] SPEC. SPEC CPU2000. Available from `http://www.spec.org/cpu2000`.

[36] Ravi K. Venkatesan, Stephen Herr, and Eric Rotenberg. Retention-aware placement in DRAM (RAPID): software methods for quasi-non-volatile DRAM. In *Proceedings of the International Symposium on High-Performance Computer Architecture (HPCA)*, 2006.

[37] M. Weiser, B. Welch, A. Demers, and S. Shenker. Scheduling for reduced CPU energy. *Kluwer International Series in Engineering and Computer Science*, pages 449–472, 1996.

[38] V. Wong and M. Horowitz. Soft Error Resilience of Probabilistic Inference Applications. *SELSE II*, 2006.

[39] W. Yuan, K. Nahrstedt, SV Adve, DL Jones, and RH Kravets. GRACE-1: Cross-layer adaptation for multimedia quality and battery energy. *IEEE Transactions on Mobile Computing*, 5(7).

# MemScale: Active Low-Power Modes for Main Memory *


Qingyuan Deng
Dept. of Computer Science
Rutgers University
qdeng@cs.rutgers.edu

David Meisner
Advanced Computer Architecture Lab
University of Michigan
meisner@umich.edu

Luiz Ramos
Dept. of Computer Science
Rutgers University
luramos@cs.rutgers.edu

Thomas F. Wenisch
Advanced Computer Architecture Lab
University of Michigan
twenisch@umich.edu

Ricardo Bianchini
Dept. of Computer Science
Rutgers University
ricardob@cs.rutgers.edu



## Abstract

*Main memory is responsible for a large and increasing fraction of the energy consumed by servers. Prior work has focused on exploiting DRAM low-power states to conserve energy. However, these states require entire DRAM ranks to be idled, which is difficult to achieve even in lightly loaded servers. In this paper, we propose to conserve memory energy while improving its energy-proportionality by creating active low-power modes for it. Specifically, we propose MemScale, a scheme wherein we apply dynamic voltage and frequency scaling (DVFS) to the memory controller and dynamic frequency scaling (DFS) to the memory channels and DRAM devices. MemScale is guided by an operating system policy that determines the DVFS/DFS mode of the memory subsystem based on the current need for memory bandwidth, the potential energy savings, and the performance degradation that applications are willing to withstand. Our results demonstrate that MemScale reduces energy consumption significantly compared to modern memory energy management approaches. We conclude that the potential benefits of the MemScale mechanisms and policy more than compensate for their small hardware cost.*



***Categories and Subject Descriptors*** C.5 [*Computer System Implementation*]: Miscellaneous

***General Terms*** Design, experimentation, performance

***Keywords*** Memory subsystem, energy conservation, dynamic voltage and frequency scaling


## 1. Introduction

Over the last several years, it has become clear that the massive energy consumption of datacenters represents a serious burden on their operators and on the environment [12]. Concern over energy waste has led to numerous academic (e.g., [35, 37, 39]) and industrial efforts to improve the efficiency of datacenter infrastructure. As a result, in state-of-the-art facilities, over 80% of power is now consumed by servers themselves [15].

Historically, within the server, the processor has dominated energy consumption. However, as processors have become more energy-efficient and more effective at managing their own power consumption, their contribution has been decreasing. In contrast, main memory energy consumption has been growing [5, 25, 28], as multi-core servers are requiring increasing main memory bandwidth and capacity. Making matters worse, memory energy management is challenging in the context of servers with modern (DDR*[1]) DRAM technologies. Today, main memory accounts for up to 40% of server energy [5]—comparable to or slightly higher than the processors' contribution. In reality, the fraction attributable to memory accesses may be even higher, since these estimates do not consider the memory controller's energy consumption.

The early works on memory energy conservation focused on creating memory idleness through scheduling, batching, and layout transformations, so that idle low-power states could be exploited [10, 13, 20, 24, 27, 36]. Those studies generally assumed the rich, chip-level power management permitted in older technologies, such as RDRAM [8]. More recent works have considered reducing the number of DRAM chips that are accessed at a time (rank subsetting) [1, 44] and even changing the microarchitecture of the DRAM chips themselves to improve energy efficiency [43]. A common theme of these works is to reduce the number of chips or bits actually touched as a result of a memory access, thereby reducing the dynamic memory energy consumption.

We argue that none of these approaches is ideal. Creating enough idleness is difficult in modern DDR* memories, since power management is available only at coarse granularity (entire ranks spanning multiple chips). Thus, deep idle low-power states can rarely be used without excessively degrading performance. For this reason, today, even the most aggressive memory controllers use only shallow, fast-exit power-down states to conserve energy while idle. Rank subsetting requires changes to the architecture of the memory DIMMs (Dual In-Line Memory Modules), which are expensive and increase latency. Changing DRAM chip microarchitecture may have negative implications on capacity and yield.


* This research has been partially supported by NSF under grants #CCF-0916539, #CSR-0834403, #CCF-0811320, and Google.


[1] DDR* refers to the family of Double Data Rate memory devices.




*ASPLOS'11,* March 5–11, 2011, Newport Beach, California, USA.

In contrast, we propose MemScale, a set of low-power modes, hardware mechanisms, and software policies to conserve energy while respecting the applications' performance requirements. Specifically, MemScale creates and leverages *active* low-power modes for the main memory subsystem (formed by the memory devices and the memory controller). Our approach is based on the key observation that server workloads, though often highly sensitive to memory access latency, only rarely demand peak memory bandwidth. To exploit this observation, we propose to apply dynamic voltage and frequency scaling (DVFS) to the memory controller and dynamic frequency scaling (DFS) to the memory channels and DRAM devices. By dynamically varying voltages and frequencies, these mechanisms trade available memory bandwidth to conserve energy when memory activity is low. Although lowering voltage and frequency causes increases in channel transfer time, controller latency, and queueing time at the controller, other components of the memory access latency are essentially not affected. As a result, these overheads have only a minor impact on average latency. Also importantly, MemScale requires only limited hardware changes—none involving the DIMMs or DRAM chips—since most of the required mechanisms are already present in current memory systems. In fact, many servers already allow one of a small number of memory channel frequencies to be statically selected at boot time.

To leverage the new memory DVFS/DFS modes, we further propose a management policy for the operating system to select a mode using online profiling and memory power/performance models that we have devised. The models incorporate the current need for memory bandwidth, the potential energy savings, and the performance degradation that applications would be willing to withstand. We assume that the degradation limit is defined by users on a per-application basis.

MemScale's low-power modes and performance-aware energy management policy have several advantages. Because the modes are active, there is no need to create or rely on memory idleness. Not relying on idleness improves memory energy-proportionality [6]. In fact, even when the memory is idle, scaling can lower power consumption further. Because MemScale does not require changes to DIMMs or DRAM chips and largely exploits existing hardware mechanisms, it can be implemented in practice at low cost. Because MemScale's energy-management policy is driven by the operating system (at the end of each time quantum), the memory controller can remain simple and efficient. Finally, MemScale can be combined easily with rank subsetting, since each addresses complementary aspects of energy management (memory controller energy and background energy vs. dynamic energy, respectively).

We evaluate MemScale using detailed simulations of a large set of workloads. Our base results demonstrate that we can reduce memory energy consumption between 17% and 71%, for a maximum acceptable performance degradation of 10%. In terms of system-wide energy savings, our approach produces energy savings ranging from 6% to 31%. For comparison, a system that uses aggressive transitions to fast-exit powerdown for energy management conserves only between 0.3% and 7.4% system energy. In contrast, Decoupled DIMMs [45], the closest prior work, conserves between -0.8% and 11% system energy. MemScale can save almost a factor of 3x more system energy on average than Decoupled DIMMs, without exceeding the allowed performance degradation.

We also perform an extensive sensitivity analysis to assess the impact of key aspects of our memory system design and management policy: the number of memory channels, the contribution of the memory subsystem to overall power consumption, the power proportionality of the memory controller and DIMMs, the maximum acceptable performance degradation, and the length of MemScale epochs and profiling phases. This analysis demonstrates that the fraction of memory power and the power proportionality have the largest impact on our results. MemScale's energy savings grow with a decrease in power proportionality or an increase in the memory subsystem's contribution to overall power, while still maintaining performance within the allowed degradation bound.

Based on our experience and results, we conclude that the potential benefits of MemScale are significant and more than compensate for its small hardware and software costs.

**Summary of contributions.** We propose dynamic memory frequency scaling, or "MemScale", a new approach to enable memory active low-power modes. We further examine varying memory controller voltage and frequency in response to memory demand, an opportunity that has been overlooked by previous energy management studies. This paper describes the few additional hardware mechanisms that are required by dynamic scaling, as well as an operating system policy that leverages the mechanisms. Finally, we present extensive results demonstrating that we can conserve significant energy while limiting performance degradation based on a user-selected performance target.

## 2. Background

We provide a brief overview of modern memory subsystems and the impact of dynamic scaling on their performance and power consumption.

### 2.1 Memory System Technology

First, we discuss memory organization, timing, and power consumption. Although there have been numerous memory architectures, DRAM technologies and variations, we restrict ourselves to today's pervasive JEDEC-style DDR* SDRAM (Synchronous DRAM) memory subsystems [23]. A more detailed and complete treatment of memory subsystems can be found in [22].

**DRAM organization.** Figure 1 illustrates the multiple levels of organization of the memory subsystem. To service memory accesses, the *memory controller* (MC) sends commands to the *DIMMs* on behalf of the CPU's last-level cache across a *memory bus*. As shown, recent processors have integrated the MC into the same package as the CPU. To enable greater parallelism, the width of the memory bus is split into multiple *channels*. These channels act independently and can access disjoint regions of the physical address space in parallel.

Multiple DIMMs may be connected to the same channel. Each DIMM comprises a printed circuit board with register devices (for buffering address and control signals), a Phase Lock Loop device (for maintaining frequency and phase synchronization), and multiple *DRAM chips* (for data storage). The DRAM chips are the ultimate destination of the MC commands. The subset of DRAM chips that participate in each access is called a *rank*. The number of chips in a rank depends on how many bits each chip produces/consumes at a time. For example, the size of the rank is 8 DRAM chips (or 9 chips for DIMMs with ECC) when each chip is x8 (pronounced "by 8"), since memory channels are 64 bits wide (or 72 bits wide with ECC). Each DIMM can have up to 16 chips (or 18 chips with ECC), organized into 1-4 ranks.

Each DRAM chip contains multiple *banks* (typically 8 banks nowadays), each of which contains multiple two-dimensional memory *arrays*. The basic unit of storage in an array is a simple capacitor representing a bit—the *DRAM cell*. Thus, in a x8 DRAM chip, each bank has 8 arrays, each of which produces/consumes one bit at a time. However, each time an array is accessed, an entire multi-KB row is transferred to a row buffer. This operation is called an "ac-

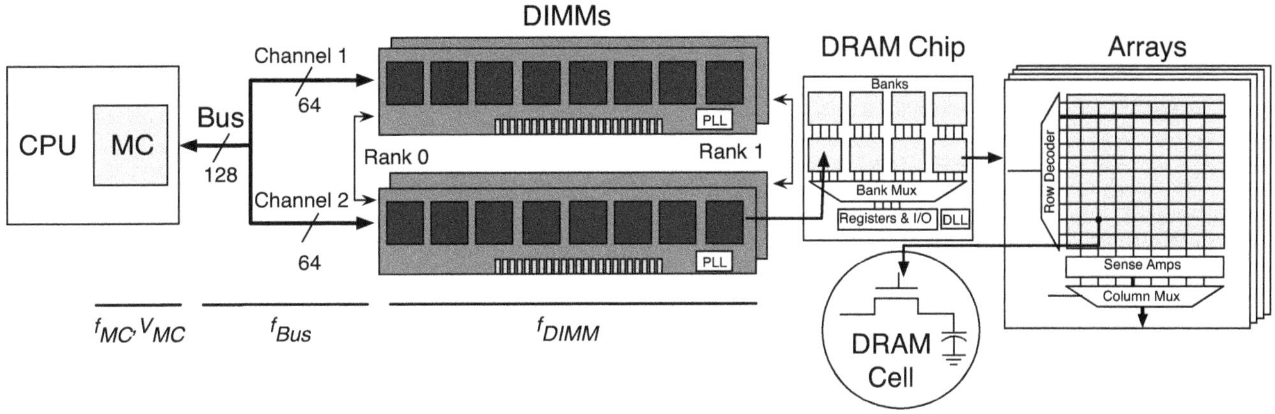


**Figure 1: Organization of a modern memory subsystem.** The parameters that our control mechanisms impact are highlighted. The parameters $V_{MC}$ and $f_{MC}$ control the memory controller (MC) voltage and frequency respectively. $f_{Bus}$ and $f_{DIMM}$ are the memory bus frequency and DIMM frequency, respectively; the DIMMs' PLL allows interfacing of these components at different frequencies (i.e., $f_{Bus} = f_{DIMM}$).

tivation" or a "row opening". Then, any column of the row can be read/written over the channel in one burst. Because the activation is destructive, the corresponding row eventually needs to be "pre-charged", that is, written back to the array. Under a closed-page management scheme, the MC pre-charges a row after every column access, unless there is another pending access for the same row. Prior studies suggest that closed-page management typically works better than open-page management for multi-core systems [40]. The DIMM-level Phase-Lock Loop (PLL) and chip-level Delay-Lock Loop (DLL) devices are responsible for synchronizing signal frequency and phase across components.

**DRAM timing.** For the MC to access memory, it needs to issue a number of commands to the DRAM chips. These commands must be properly ordered and obey a number of timing restrictions. For example, a row activation first requires a pre-charge of the data in the row buffer, if the row is currently open. If the row is closed, the activation can proceed without any delay. An example timing restriction is the amount of time between two consecutive column accesses to an open row.

In DRAM lingo, a pre-charge, an activation, and a column access are said to take $T_{RP}$, $T_{RCD}$, and $T_{CL}$ times, respectively. The latest DDR3 devices perform each of these operations in around 10 memory cycles at 800MHz. At this frequency, transferring a 64-byte cache line over the channel takes 4 cycles ($T_{BURST}$), since data is transferred on both edges of the clock in DDR technology.

**MC and DRAM power.** Because an increasing fraction of a server's power budget is dedicated to the memory subsystem [5, 25, 28], it is important to understand where power is consumed in this subsystem. We categorize the power breakdown into three major categories: DRAM, register/PLL, and MC power. The DRAM power can be further divided into background, activation/pre-charge, read/write, and termination powers. The background power is independent of activity and is due to the peripheral circuitry, transistor leakage, and refresh operations. The activation/pre-charge power is due to these operations on the memory arrays. The read/write power is due to these column accesses to row buffers. The termination power is due to terminating signals of other ranks on the same channel. The three latter classes of DRAM power are often referred to as "dynamic DRAM power", but they also include a level of background power.

Figure 2 quantifies the average power breakdown for three categories of workloads: memory-intensive (MEM), compute-intensive

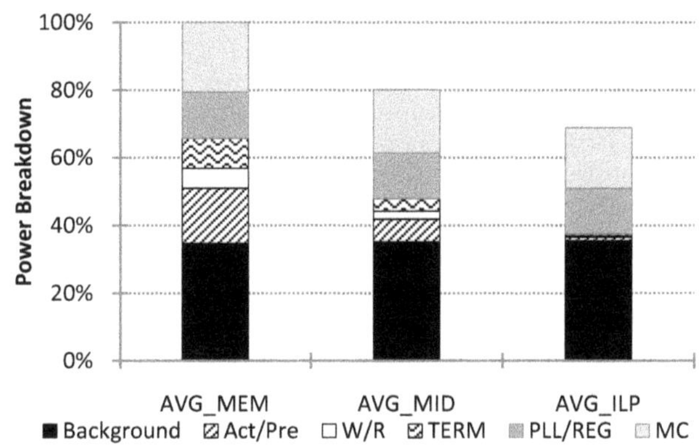


**Figure 2: Conventional memory subsystem power breakdown.** There is substantial opportunity for MemScale: it can reduce Background, PLL/REG, and MC power.

(ILP), and balanced (MID). The results are normalized to the average power of the MEM workloads. (We explain the details of our workloads and simulation methodology in Section 4.)

We make four main observations from this figure: (1) background power is a significant contributor to power consumption, especially for the ILP and MID workloads (upcoming feature size reductions will make the background power an even larger fraction of the total); (2) activation/pre-charge and read/write powers are significant only for MEM workloads; (3) despite the fact that register/PLL power is often disregarded by researchers, this category of power consumption also contributes significantly to the total; and (4) despite the fact that the MC has not been included in previous studies of memory subsystem energy, it contributes a significant amount to overall consumption.

### 2.2 Impact of Voltage and Frequency Scaling

Figure 2 suggests that any mechanism that can lower the background, register/PLL, and MC powers without increasing other power consumptions or degrading performance excessively could be used to conserve significant energy. As it turns out, modern servers already embody one such mechanism. Specifically, in these servers, the voltage and frequency of MCs and the frequency of memory buses, DIMMs, and DRAM chips are configurable (in tandem, since incompatible frequencies would require additional synchronization devices). Unfortunately, these parameters must currently be set *statically* at boot time, typically through the BIOS.

To exploit this mechanism for energy conservation, one has to understand the effect of lowering frequency on both power and performance. Lowering frequency affects performance by making data bursts longer and the MC slower, both by linear amounts. (The wall-clock performance of other operations is unaffected, despite the fact that their numbers of cycles increase linearly with decreases in frequency.) Because of these delays, queues at the MC may become longer, increasing memory access times further. Nevertheless, note that these latency increases in certain stages of the memory access process do *not* translate into linear increases in overall memory access time. In fact, our detailed simulations show only minor increases in average memory access time.

Lowering frequency affects power consumption in many ways. First, it lowers background and register/PLL powers linearly. Second, it lowers MC power approximately by a cubic factor. The reason for this large benefit is two-fold: (1) lowering the MC frequency is accompanied by lowering its voltage; and (2) MC DVFS provides similar dynamic power advantages to CPU DVFS ($Power \propto Voltage^2 \times frequency$). In fact, note that, even though the MC is in the CPU chip nowadays, it is often in a voltage domain that is separate from those of the cores. Third, lowering frequency increases read/write and termination energy almost linearly (power is not affected but accesses take longer). Finally, if lowering frequency causes a degradation in application performance, the energy consumed by the server's non-memory-subsystem components will increase accordingly.

## 3. MemScale

In this section, we describe the MemScale design and the OS-level control algorithm to use it. First, we describe our proposed mechanisms to allow dynamic control of the memory subsystem leveraging underlying hardware capabilities. Next, we provide an overview of the control policy used to maximize the energy-efficiency of the system, while adhering to a performance goal. We then detail performance and energy models used by our control policy. Finally, we address the MemScale implementation costs.

### 3.1 Hardware and Software Mechanisms

Our system utilizes two key mechanisms: (1) our dynamic frequency scaling method, MemScale; and (2) performance counter-based monitoring to drive our control algorithm.

**MemScale.** The key enhancement we add to modern memory systems is the ability to adjust MC, bus, and DIMM frequencies during operation. Furthermore, we propose to adjust the supply voltage of the MC (independently of core/cache voltage) in proportion to frequency.

Though commercially-available DIMMs support multiple frequencies already, today, switching frequency typically requires system reboot. The JEDEC standard provides mechanisms for changing frequency [23]; the operating frequency of a DIMM may be reset while in the precharge powerdown or self-refresh state. Accordingly, we propose a mechanism wherein the system briefly suspends memory operation and can reconfigure itself to run at a new power-performance setting. For DIMMs, we leverage precharge powerdown for frequency re-calibration because the latency overhead is significantly less than self-refresh. The majority of re-calibration latency is due to DLL synchronization time, $t_{DLLK}$ [32], which consumes approximately 500 memory cycles. Although our system adjusts the frequency of the MC, bus and DIMM together, from now on we shall simply refer to adjusting the bus frequency. The DIMM clocks lock to the bus frequency (or a multiple thereof), while the MC frequency is fixed at double the bus frequency.

**Performance counter monitoring.** Our management policies require input from a set of performance counters implemented in the on-chip MC. Specifically, we require counters that track the amount of work pending at each memory bank and channel (i.e., queue depths). *Counters similar to those we require already exist in most modern architectures, and are often already accessible through the CPU's performance-monitoring interface.* Under our scheme, the operating system reads the counters, like any other performance register, during each control epoch. We use the following counters:

- **Instruction counts** – For each core, we need a counter for the *Total Instructions Committed* (`TIC`), and *Total LLC (Last-Level Cache) Misses* (`TLM`). These counters increment each time any instruction is retired and any instruction causes an LLC miss, respectively. Our control algorithm uses these counters to determine the fraction of CPI attributable to memory operations.
- **Transactions-outstanding accumulators** – To estimate the impact of queueing delays, our performance model requires counters that track the number of requests outstanding at banks and channels. The *Bank Transactions Outstanding* (`BTO`) and *Channel Transactions Outstanding* (`CTO`) accumulators are incremented by the number of already-outstanding requests to the same bank when a new request arrives for a bank/channel. We also require a *Bank Transaction Counter* (`BTC`) and *Channel Transactions Counter* (`CTC`) that increment by one for each arriving request. The ratio of BTO/BTC (or CTO/CTC) gives the average number of requests an arriving request sees ahead of it queued for the same bank/channel. Note that only a single set of counters is needed regardless of the number of banks/channels, as only the average (rather than per-bank or per-channel) counts are used in our performance model.
- **Row buffer performance** – To estimate the average DRAM device access latency, our model requires a *Row Buffer Hit Counter* (`RBHC`), which tracks accesses that hit on an open row; an *Open Row Buffer Miss Counter* (`OBMC`), which counts the number of accesses that miss an open row and require the row to be closed; a *Closed Row Buffer Miss Counter* (`CBMC`), which counts accesses that occur when the corresponding bank is closed (since we use a closed-page access policy, this case is the most common for our multiprogrammed workloads; a row buffer hit occurs only when the next access to a row is already scheduled while the previous access is performed); and an *Exit PowerDown Counter* (`EPDC`), which counts the number of exits from powerdown state. As noted above, only a single set of these counters is needed, since average counts are enough to compute accurate DRAM access latencies.
- **Power modeling** – To instantiate our memory power model [33], we need a *Precharge Time Counter* (`PTC`) to count the percentage of time that all banks of a rank are precharged; a *Precharge Time With CKE Low* (`PTCKEL`) to count the percentage of time that all banks are precharged (PTC) when the clock enable signal is low; an *Active Time With CKE Low* (`ATCKEL`) to count the percentage of time that some bank is active (1 - PTC) when the clock enable signal is low; and a *Page Open/Close Counter* (`POCC`) to count the number of page open/close command pairs. The other information required by the power model can be derived from the other counters. Again, only a single set of these counters is needed to model power accurately [33].

Of these counters, only BTO, CTO, PTC, PTCKEL, and ATCKEL are not currently available (or not easily derived from other coun-

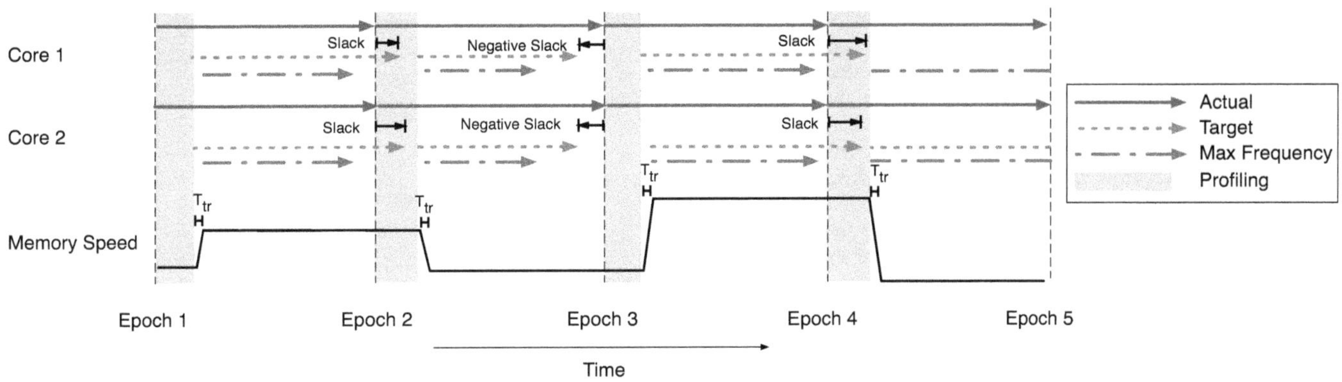


**Figure 3: Memscale operation:** In this example, we illustrate the operation of MemScale for two cores. The best-case execution time is calculated at each epoch ("Max Frequency"). The target time is a fixed percent slower than this best case. Slack is the time difference between the target and current execution; it is accumulated across epochs.

ters) in the latest Intel processors [21]. In fact, although some of these counters track events in off-chip structures, the counters themselves are already implemented in the MC hardware. Finally, note that counters EPDC, PTCKEL, and ATCKEL are only needed when we combine MemScale with a policy that transitions devices to powerdown. We consider such a combined policy in Section 4.

### 3.2 Energy Management Policy

Given these mechanisms, we now describe the energy management policy that controls frequency changes.

**Performance slack.** Our control algorithm is based upon the notion of program *slack*: the difference between a baseline execution and a target latency penalty that a system operator is willing to incur on a program to save energy (similar to [9, 27]). Without energy management, a given program would execute at a certain base rate. By reducing the memory subsystem performance, the overall rate of progress is reduced. To constrain the impact of this performance loss, we allow no more than a fixed maximum performance degradation. Our control algorithm uses this allowance to save energy. The target is defined such that each executing program incurs no more than a pre-selected maximum slowdown relative to its execution without energy management (i.e., at maximum frequency). Given this target, the slack is then the difference in time of the program's execution ($T_{\text{Actual}}$) from the target ($T_{\text{Target}}$).

$$\begin{aligned} \text{Slack} &= T_{\text{Target}} - T_{\text{Actual}} \\ &= T_{\text{MaxFreq}} \cdot (1+\gamma) - T_{\text{Actual}} \end{aligned} \qquad (1)$$

The quantity $\gamma$ defines the target maximal execution time increase.

**Operation.** Our control algorithm is based upon fixed sized-epochs. We typically associate an epoch with an OS-level time quantum. During each epoch, we profile the system and select a memory subsystem frequency that (1) minimizes *overall system* energy, while (2) maintaining performance within the target given the accumulated slack from prior epochs. Each epoch proceeds in four stages:

1. **Profile applications online** – At the beginning of each epoch, the system is profiled by collecting statistics using the performance counters described above. By default, we profile for 300 $\mu$s, which we have found to be sufficient to predict the memory subsystem resource requirements for the remainder of the epoch. Our default epoch length is 5 ms.
2. **Control algorithm invocation** – After the profiling phase (i.e., collecting performance counters), the operating system uses the profiling information to calculate a new memory frequency based on the models described in the next subsection.
3. **Bus frequency re-locking** – We transition the memory subsystem to its new operating frequency. To accomplish this adjustment, memory accesses are temporarily halted and PLLs and DLLs are resynchronized. Since the resynchronization overhead ($< 1$ $\mu$s) is so small compared to our epoch size ($> 1$ ms), the penalty is negligible.
4. **Slack update** – The epoch executes to completion at the new memory speed. At the end of the epoch, we again query the performance counters and estimate what performance would have been achieved had the memory subsystem operated at maximum frequency, and compare this to the achieved performance. The difference between these is used to update the accumulated slack and carried forward to calculate the target performance in the next epoch.

Note that our policy queries the performance counters both at the end of each epoch and at the end of each profiling phase. Although we could rely solely on end-of-epoch accounting, we opt to profile for two main reasons. First, an epoch is relatively long compared to the length of some applications' execution phases; a short profiling phase often provides a more current picture of the applications' behaviors. Second, because it may not be possible to monitor all the needed counters at the same time, the profiling phase can be used to measure just the power-related counters (while only the performance-related counters would be measured the rest of the time). In this paper, we assume that all counters are monitored at the same time.

**Frequency selection.** We select a memory frequency to achieve two objectives. First, we wish to select a frequency that maximizes full-system energy savings. The energy-minimal frequency is not necessarily the lowest frequency—as the system continues to consume energy when the memory subsystem is slowed, lowering frequency can result in a net energy loss if the program slowdown is too high. Our models explicitly account for the system-vs.-memory energy balance. Second, we seek to observe the bound on allowable CPI degradation for each running program. Because multiple programs execute within a single system, the selected frequency must satisfy the needs of the program with the greatest memory performance requirements.

**MemScale example.** We illustrate the operation of MemScale in Figure 3. Each epoch begins with a profiling phase, shown in gray. Using the profiling output, the system estimates the performance at the highest memory frequency ("Max Frequency"), and then sets a target performance ("Target") via Equation 1 above. Based on the target, a memory speed is selected and the system transitions to the new speed. In Epoch 1, the example shows that the actual execution ("Actual") is faster than the target. Hence, the additional slack is carried forward into Epoch 2, slightly widening the gap between Max Frequency and Target, allowing the memory speed to be lowered. However, at the end of Epoch 2, performance falls short of the target, and the negative slack must be made up in Epoch 3 (or later epochs, if necessary) by raising memory frequency. By adjusting slack from epoch to epoch, MemScale tries to ensure that the desired performance target (given by $\gamma$) is met over time.

### 3.3 Performance and Energy Models

Now, we describe the performance and energy models that the control algorithm uses to make smart decisions about frequency.

**Performance model.** Our control algorithm relies on a performance model to predict the relationship between CPU *cycles per instruction* (CPI) of an application and the memory frequency. The purpose of our model is to determine the runtime and power/energy implications of changing memory performance. Given this model, the OS can set the frequency to both maximize energy-efficiency and stay within the predefined limit for CPI loss.

We model an in-order processor with one outstanding LLC miss per core. We do so for three reasons: (1) these processors translate any increases in memory access time due to frequency scaling directly to execution time; (2) we expect server cores to become simpler as the number of cores per CPU increases; and (3) the modeling of these processors is simpler than their more sophisticated counterparts, making it easier to demonstrate our ideas. We approximate the effect of greater memory traffic (e.g., resulting from prefetching or out-of-order execution) by varying the number of memory channels and cores in Section 4.2.4.

For our processors, the runtime of a program can be defined as:

$$\begin{aligned} t_{\text{total}} &= t_{\text{CPU}} + t_{\text{Mem}} \\ &= I_{\text{CPU}} \cdot E[TPI_{\text{CPU}}] + I_{\text{Mem}} \cdot E[TPI_{\text{Mem}}] \end{aligned} \tag{2}$$

Here, $I_{\text{CPU}}$ represents the number of instructions and $I_{\text{mem}}$ is the number of instructions that cause an LLC miss to main memory. $TPI_{\text{CPU}}$ represents the average time that instructions spend on the CPU, whereas $TPI_{\text{Mem}}$ represents the average time that a LLC-missing instruction spends in main memory.

Since runtime is not known a priori, our system models the rate of progress of an application in terms of CPI. The average CPI of a program is defined as:

$$E[\text{CPI}] = (E[TPI_{\text{CPU}}] + \alpha \cdot E[TPI_{\text{Mem}}]) \cdot F_{\text{CPU}} \tag{3}$$

Where $\alpha$ is the fraction of instructions that miss the LLC and $F_{\text{CPU}}$ is the operating frequency of the processor. The value of $\alpha$ can easily be calculated as the ratio of `TLM` and `TIC`.

While the expected time per CPU operation is insensitive to changes in memory speed (for simplicity, we assume it is fixed), the CPI of LLC-missing instructions varies with memory subsystem frequency. To model the time per cache miss, we decompose the expected time as:

$$\begin{aligned} E[TPI_{\text{Mem}}] &= E[T_{\text{Bank}}] + E[T_{\text{Bus}}] \\ E[T_{\text{Bank}}] &= E[S_{\text{Bank}}] + E[W_{\text{Bank}}] \\ E[T_{\text{Bus}}] &= E[S_{\text{Bus}}] + E[W_{\text{Bus}}] \end{aligned} \tag{4}$$

Here, $E[S_{\text{Bank}}]$ is the average time, excluding queueing delays, to access a particular bank (including precharge, row access and column read, etc). $E[S_{\text{bus}}]$ is the average data transfer (burst) time

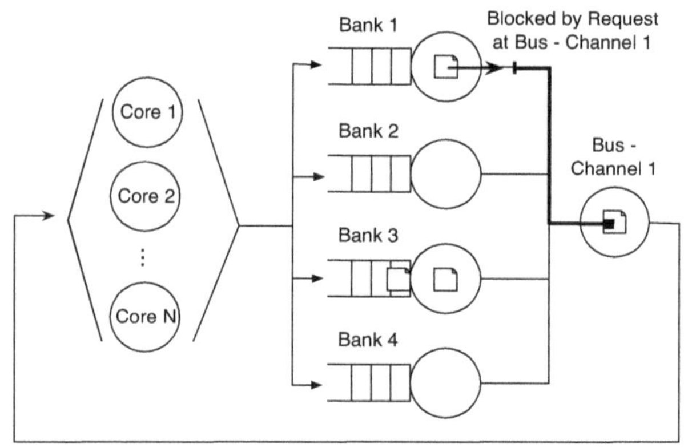


**Figure 4: Memory subsystem queuing model:** Banks and channels are represented as servers. The cores issue requests to bank servers, which proceed to the channel server upon completion. Because of DRAM operation, requests are held at the bank server until a request frees from the channel server (the channel server has a queue depth of 0). In our example, the request that finishes at bank 1 cannot proceed to the bus until the request already there leaves. This example shows only a single channel.

across the bus. Finally, the average waiting time to service previous request (i.e., queueing delays due to contention for the bank and bus) are represented by $E[W_{\text{Bank}}]$ and $E[W_{\text{Bus}}]$.

$S_{\text{Bank}}$ can be further broken down as:

$$E[S_{\text{Bank}}] = E[T_{\text{MC}}] + E[T_{\text{Device}}] \tag{5}$$

$T_{\text{MC}}$ varies as a function of MC frequency. In our MC design, each request requires five MC clock cycles to process (in the absence of queueing delays). $T_{\text{Device}}$ is a function of DRAM device parameters and applications' row buffer hit/miss rates and does not vary significantly with frequency, as we do not alter the operation or timing of the DRAM chips' internal DRAM arrays. During the profiling phase, we estimate $E[T_{\text{Device}}]$ for the epoch using row buffer performance counters via:

$$\begin{aligned} \text{Row hit time} &= T_{\text{hit}} = T_{\text{CL}} \cdot \texttt{RHBC} \\ \text{Closed-bank miss time} &= T_{\text{cb}} = [T_{\text{RCD}} + T_{\text{CL}}] \cdot \texttt{CBMC} \\ \text{Open-bank miss time} &= T_{\text{ob}} = [T_{\text{RP}} + T_{\text{RCD}} + T_{\text{CL}}] \cdot \texttt{OBMC} \\ \text{Powerdown exit time} &= T_{\text{pd}} = T_{\text{XP}} \cdot \texttt{EPDC} \\ E[T_{\text{Device}}] &= \frac{T_{\text{hit}} + T_{\text{cb}} + T_{\text{ob}} + T_{\text{pd}}}{\texttt{RHBC} + \texttt{CBMC} + \texttt{OBMC}} \end{aligned} \tag{6}$$

$T_{\text{CL}}$, $T_{\text{RP}}$, $T_{\text{RCD}}$, and $T_{\text{XP}}$ are characteristics of a particular memory device and are obtained from datasheets. To simplify the above equations, we have subsumed some aspects of DRAM access timing that have smaller impacts.

Whereas modeling $S_{\text{Bank}}$ and $S_{\text{Bus}}$ is straight-forward given manufacturer data sheets, modeling the wait times due to contention $E[W_{\text{Bank}}]$ and $E[W_{\text{Bus}}]$ is more challenging. Ideally, we would like to model the memory system as a queuing network to determine these quantities. Figure 4 shows the queuing model corresponding to our system. Queueing delays arise due to contention for a bank and the memory bus. (Delayed requests wait at the MC; there are typically no queues in the DRAM devices themselves). The in-order CPUs act as users in a closed queuing network (each issuing a single memory access at a time). Memory requests are serviced by the various banks, each represented by a queue. The bus is modeled as a server with no queue depth; when a request completes service at a bank, it must wait at the bank (blocking further requests) until it is accepted by the bus. This blocking behavior models the activate-access-precharge command sequence used to access a DRAM bank—the bank remains blocked until the sequence is complete.

Unfortunately, this queueing network is particularly difficult to analyze. Specifically, because the system exhibits *transfer blocking* behavior [2, 4] (disallowing progress at the bank due to contention at the bus), product form solutions of networks of this size are infeasible. Most approaches to this problem rely on approximations that have errors as high as 25% [2, 4]. Instead of using a typical queuing model, we now describe how a simple counter-based model can yield accurate predictions. We find that the accuracy afforded by the counters justify their implementation cost.

Our approach is to define counters that track the number of preceding requests that each arriving request finds waiting ahead of it for a bank/bus. We then take the expectation of this count over all arrivals to obtain an expression for the expected wait time for each request. We implement the necessary counters directly in hardware as described in Section 3.1.

We first illustrate our derivation for bus time. For a single request $k$, the bus time can be expressed as $E[S_{\text{Bus}}] \cdot \sum_{l=1}^{k} \text{BusServiceLeft}(l, k)$. The function $\text{BusServiceLeft}(l, k)$ is defined as the fraction (between 0 and 1) of service time remaining for request $l$ at the arrival time of request $k$ (it is 0 for requests that are complete and 1 for requests that are queued but not yet in service). The summation adds together the remaining service for all jobs arriving before $k$, thereby yielding the total number of requests in queue at the time request $k$ arrives, including request $k$. To obtain average bus time, we average over all requests:

$$\begin{aligned} E[T_{\text{bus}}] &= \frac{\sum_{k=1}^{n} \sum_{l=1}^{k} \text{BusServiceLeft}(l, k)}{n} \cdot E[S_{\text{Bus}}] \\ &= \xi_{\text{Bus}} \cdot E[S_{\text{Bus}}] \end{aligned} \quad (7)$$

The variable $\xi$ represents the average work in the queue, including *residual* work from prior requests, when a new request arrives. In our hardware design, $\xi_{\text{Bus}}$ is approximated by the performance counters CTO/CTC, which track the average number of requests waiting for a bus channel. Our estimate of $\xi_{\text{Bus}}$ is an approximation because we use the values of CTO and CTC measured at one frequency (the frequency in use during profiling) and assume the value holds at all other frequencies. In reality, the degree of bank and channel queueing can vary across frequencies. However, we have found that, in practice, this approximation works well, because deep bank/bus queues are rare for our workloads and small estimation errors are corrected through the slack mechanism. Nevertheless, our approach can easily be modified to tackle deep queues, by profiling at one more frequency and interpolating the queue size results for the others.

Using a similar construction, we can derive an expression for the expected bank time:

$$\begin{aligned} E[T_{\text{bank}}] &= \frac{\sum_{i=1}^{n} \sum_{j=1}^{i} \text{BankServiceLeft}(j, i)}{n} \cdot [E[S_{\text{Bank}}] + E[T_{\text{Bus}}]] \\ &= \xi_{\text{Bank}} \cdot [E[S_{\text{Bank}}] + E[T_{\text{Bus}}]] \end{aligned} \quad (8)$$

where $\xi_{\text{Bank}}$ is approximated by BTO/BTC. Note that $E[T_{\text{Bus}}]$ appears as a term within $E[T_{\text{Bank}}]$, as a request arriving at a bank remains blocked till all preceding requests are able to drain over the bus. It is precisely this construction that captures the transfer blocking behavior and allows us to sidestep the difficulties of queuing analysis.

Noting that, under this construction, $E[TPI_{\text{Mem}}] = E[T_{\text{bank}}]$ (bus time has been folded into the expression for the bank time), we condense our analysis to the equation:

$$E[TPI_{\text{Mem}}] = \xi_{\text{bank}} \cdot (S_{\text{Bank}} + \xi_{\text{bus}} \cdot S_{\text{bus}}) \quad (9)$$

**Full-system energy model.** Simply meeting the CPI loss target for a given workload does not necessarily maximize energy-efficiency. In other words, though additional performance degradation may be allowed, it may save more energy to run faster. To determine the best operating point, we construct a model to predict full-system energy usage. For memory frequency $f_{\text{mem}}$, we define the *system energy ratio* (SER) as:

$$\text{SER}(f_{\text{mem}}) = \frac{T_{f_{\text{Mem}}} \cdot P_{f_{\text{Mem}}}}{T_{\text{Base}} \cdot P_{\text{Base}}} \quad (10)$$

$T_{f_{\text{Mem}}}$ is the performance estimate for an epoch at frequency $f_{\text{Mem}}$. $P_{f_{\text{Mem}}} = P_{\text{Mem}}(f_{\text{Mem}}) + P_{\text{NonMem}}$, where $P_{\text{Mem}}(f)$ is calculated according to the model for memory power in [33], and $P_{NonMem}$ accounts for all non-memory system components and is assumed to be fixed. $T_{\text{Base}}$ and $P_{\text{Base}}$ are corresponding values at a nominal frequency. At the end of the profiling phase of each epoch, we calculate SER for all memory frequencies that can meet the performance constraint given by Slack, and select the frequency that minimizes SER. As we consider only ten frequencies, it is reasonable to exhaustively search the possibilities and choose the best. In fact, given that this search is only performed once per epoch (5 ms by default), its overhead is negligible.

### 3.4 Hardware and Software Costs

We now consider the implementation cost of MemScale. The core features in our system are already available in commodity hardware. Although real servers do not exploit this capability, existing DIMMs already support multiple frequencies and can switch among them by transitioning to powerdown or self-refresh states [23]. Moreover, integrated CMOS MCs can leverage existing voltage and frequency scaling technology. One necessary change is for the MC to have separate voltage and frequency control from other processor components. In the most recent Intel architecture, this would require separating last-level cache and MC voltage control [21]. Though processors with multiple frequency domains are common, there have historically been few voltage domains; however, recent research has shown this is likely to change soon [17].

Whereas modifying the operating voltage of DIMMs and DRAM circuitry may be possible, devices with this capability have not yet been marketed commercially. There are substantial challenges in operating a DRAM array at multiple voltages, as many circuits in the DRAM access path require precisely tuned timing and transistor sizing that is specific to the operating voltage. Since we observe significant energy savings from frequency scaling alone, we restrict our first study to a single voltage level in DIMMs. Nevertheless, we will consider more aggressive approaches in our future work.

Our design also may require enhancements to hardware performance counters in some processors. Most processors already expose a set of counters to observe processing, caching and memory-related performance behaviors (e.g., row buffer hits/misses, row pre-charges). In fact, the latest Intel architecture already exposes a number of MC counters for queues [26]. However, the existing counters may not conform precisely to the specifications required for our models. As discussed above, the time overhead of our OS-level policy is negligible, since it is only incurred at the multi-millisecond granularity.

Table 1: Workload descriptions.

| Name | RPKI | WPKI | Applications (x4 each) | | | |
|---|---|---|---|---|---|---|
| ILP1 | 0.37 | 0.06 | vortex | gcc | sixtrack | mesa |
| ILP2 | 0.16 | 0.01 | perlbmk | crafty | gzip | eon |
| ILP3 | 0.27 | 0.01 | sixtrack | mesa | perlbmk | crafty |
| ILP4 | 0.24 | 0.06 | vortex | mesa | perlbmk | crafty |
| MID1 | 1.72 | 0.01 | ammp | gap | wupwise | vpr |
| MID2 | 2.61 | 0.09 | astar | parser | twolf | facerec |
| MID3 | 2.41 | 0.16 | apsi | bzip2 | ammp | gap |
| MID4 | 2.11 | 0.07 | wupwise | vpr | astar | parser |
| MEM1 | 17.03 | 3.03 | swim | applu | art | lucas |
| MEM2 | 8.62 | 0.25 | fma3d | mgrid | galgel | equake |
| MEM3 | 15.6 | 3.71 | swim | applu | galgel | equake |
| MEM4 | 8.96 | 0.33 | art | lucas | mgrid | fma3d |

Table 2: Main system settings.

| Feature | | Value |
|---|---|---|
| CPU cores | | 16 in-order, single thread, 4GHz<br>6 IntALU, 2 IntMul, 4FpALU, 2FpMulDiv |
| L1 I/D cache (per core) | | 64KB, 2-way, 1 CPU cycle hit |
| L2 cache (shared) | | 16MB, 4-way, 10 CPU cycle hit, 1 miss/core |
| Cache block size | | 64 bytes |
| Memory configuration | | 4 DDR3 channels, 8 2GB DIMMs with ECC |
| Time | tRCD, tRP, tCL | 15ns, 15ns, 15ns |
| | tFAW | 20 cycles |
| | tRTP | 5 cycles |
| | tRAS | 28 cycles |
| | tRRD | 4 cycles |
| | Exit fast pd (tXP) | 6ns |
| | Exit slow pd (tXPDLL) | 24ns |
| | Refresh period | 64ms |
| Current | Row buffer read, write | 250 mA, 250 mA |
| | Activation-precharge | 120 mA |
| | Active standby | 67 mA |
| | Active powerdown | 45 mA |
| | Precharge standby | 70 mA |
| | Precharge powerdown | 45 mA |
| | Refresh | 240 mA |
| VDD | | 1.575 V |

# 4. Evaluation

## 4.1 Methodology

**Simulator and workloads.** Since the few hardware mechanisms we propose are not yet available, our evaluation is based on simulations. To reduce simulation times, our simulations are done in two steps. In the first step, we use M5 [7] to collect memory access (LLC misses and writebacks) traces from a variety of workloads running on a 16-core server.

Table 1 lists the main characteristics of our 12 workloads. The workloads are formed by combining applications from the SPEC 2000 and SPEC 2006 suites. As in [45], we classify the workloads into three categories: memory-intensive workloads (MEM), computation-intensive workloads (ILP), and balanced workloads (MID). We use the same workload mixes as the prior study [45] with two exceptions: two workloads they classify as balanced behave like memory-intensive workloads in our environment. For this reason, we replaced those two workloads with our MID3 and MID4 workloads. The rightmost column of Table 1 lists the composition of each workload.

We analyze the best 100M-instruction simulation point for each application (selected using Simpoints 3.0 [38]). The workload terminates when the slowest application has executed 100M instructions. We report the LLC misses per kilo instruction (RPKI) and LLC writebacks per kilo instruction (WPKI) observed during trace generation in Table 1.

In the second step, we replay the traces using our own detailed memory system simulator. This simulator models all aspects of the OS, memory controller, and memory devices that are relevant to our study, including behavior profiling, memory channel and bank contention, memory device power and timing, and row buffer management. The memory controller exploits bank interleaving and uses closed-page row buffer management, where a bank is kept open after an access only if another access for the same bank is already pending. Closed-page management is known to lead to lower energy consumption and better performance for multi-core CPUs [40]. Memory read requests (cache misses) are served on an FCFS basis. Reads are given priority over writebacks until the writeback queue is half-full. More sophisticated memory scheduling is not necessary for these single-issue multiprogrammed workloads, as opportunities to increase bank hit rate via scheduling are rare, and such improvements are orthogonal to our study.

Regarding energy management, the simulator implements our mechanisms and policy in great detail. For comparison, we also simulate scenarios in which the memory controller immediately transitions a rank to fast-exit powerdown or slow-exit powerdown upon closing all banks of the rank. We also simulate a scenario in which a fixed frequency for the entire memory subsystem (memory controller, channels, DIMMs, and DRAM devices) is selected statically. As a final baseline for comparison, our simulator implements the Decoupled DIMMs approach to conserving memory system energy [45].

**Parameter settings.** Table 2 lists our main parameter settings. Recall that one of the reasons we study in-order cores is to expose any performance degradations resulting from frequency scaling directly to running time. We compensate for their lower bus utilization by simulating a large number of cores. Our baseline memory subsystem has 4 DDR3 channels, each of which is populated with two registered, dual-ranked DIMMs with 18 DRAM chips each. Each DIMM also has a PLL device. Each DRAM chip has 8 banks. We study the impact of the most important aspect of the memory subsystem configuration (the number of memory channels) in Section 4.2.4. This study also allows us to approximate the effect of the greater memory traffic.

The timing and power parameters of the DRAM chips, register, PLL, and memory controller are also shown in Table 2 [33]. These data are for devices running at 800 MHz. We also consider frequencies of 733, 667, 600, 533, 467, 400, 333, 267, and 200 MHz.

The timing parameters at frequencies other than 800 MHz were computed in the obvious way, according to the aspects of performance that are affected by scaling (Section 2). The current parameters at other frequencies were scaled according to Micron's power calculator [33]. The transitions between frequencies are assumed to take 512 memory cycles plus 28 ns. This assumes that frequency can only be changed after going into fast-exit pre-charge powerdown state and locking the DLLs, as specified in [23]. The power consumptions of some components also vary with the utilization. Specifically, the powers of registers and memory controller scale with their respective utilization linearly from idle to peak power; the PLL power does not scale with utilization. The register power ranges from 0.25W to 0.5W as a function of utilization, whereas the memory controller power ranges from 7.5W to 15W [16, 21]. This maximum memory controller power was taken from [3]. We study the impact of the power proportionality of the register and the memory controller in Section 4.2.4. We assume that the voltage of the memory controller varies over the same range as the cores (0.65V-1.2V), as its frequency changes. Some year-2010 Xeons have an even wider range (e.g., core voltages in the 7500 series range from 0.675V to 1.35V). In current Xeons, the uncore voltage range is narrower than that of the cores. However, the uncore domain cur-

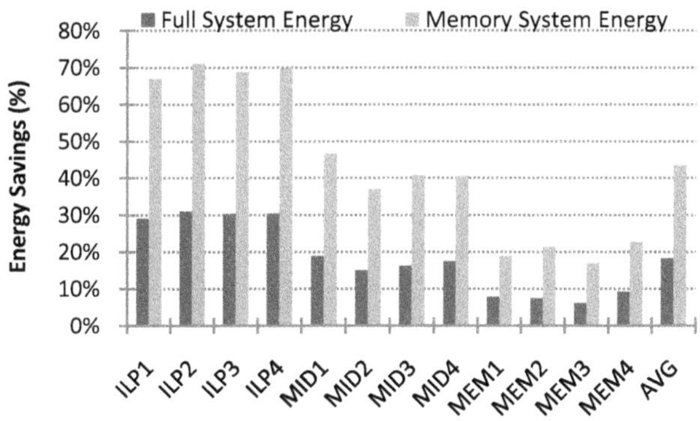


**Figure 5: Energy savings.** Memory and full-system energies are significantly reduced, particularly for the ILP workloads.

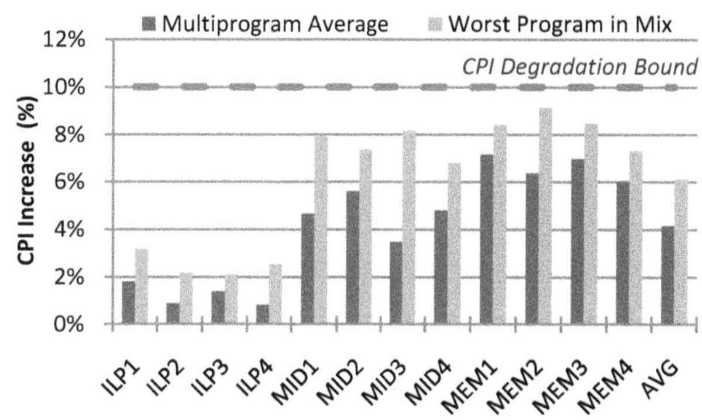


**Figure 6: CPI overhead.** Both average and worst-case CPI overheads fall well within the target degradation bound.

rently includes SRAM, which is typically more difficult to voltage-scale than logic. The power of the memory controller scales with both voltage and frequency. The PLL and register powers scale linearly with channel frequency.

We do not model power consumption in the non-memory system components in detail. Rather, we assume that the average power consumption of the DIMMs accounts for 40% of the total system power, and compute a fixed average power estimate (the remaining 60%) for all other components. This ratio has been identified as the current contribution of DIMMs to entire server power consumption [5, 6, 42]. We study the impact of this ratio in Section 4.2.4.

For the static-frequency baseline, we select the frequency (467 MHz) that achieves the highest energy savings on average, without violating the performance target for any workload. Similarly, our implementation of Decoupled DIMMs assumes that the memory channels run at 800 MHz, whereas the DRAM devices operate at the static frequency (400 MHz) that achieves the highest energy savings on average, without violating the performance target for any workload. In addition, we optimistically neglect any power overhead for the synchronization buffer required by Decoupled DIMMs.

### 4.2 Results

In this subsection, we present the quantitative evaluation of our performance-aware energy management policy.

#### 4.2.1 Energy and Performance

We start by studying the impact of our policy on the energy and performance of our workloads, assuming a maximum allowable performance degradation of 10%.

Figure 5 shows the memory and system energy savings we achieve for each workload, compared to a baseline system that keeps the memory subsystem at its highest voltage and frequency. The memory energy savings range from 17% to 71%, whereas the system energy savings range from 6% to 31%. As one would expect, the ILP workloads achieve the highest gains (system energy savings of at least 30%). These workloads can keep the voltage and frequency of the memory system at their lowest possible value all the time. The savings achieved by the MID workloads are lower but still significant (system energy savings of at least 15%). The MEM workloads achieve the smallest energy savings (system energy savings of at least 6%), since their greater memory channel traffic reduces the opportunities for significant voltage and frequency scaling.

Figure 6 shows that these energy savings can be achieved without violating the maximum allowable performance degradation for any application in the workloads. The figure shows the average and maximum percent CPI losses across the applications in each of our workloads, again compared to the vanilla baseline. The results demonstrate that our policy indeed limits the maximum CPI increase to the acceptable range; no application is ever slowed down more than 9.2%. The results also demonstrate that, when we average the performance degradations of all the applications in each workload, this average is never higher than 7.2%. Again, as one would expect, the degradations are smallest for the ILP workloads, followed by the MID workloads, and then the MEM workloads.

One might think that the policy could produce even higher energy savings, if it could keep voltage and frequency low longer and approximate the maximum allowable degradation more closely. This would increase the memory energy savings. However, remember that increasing running time also involves consuming more system energy. Thus, our policy degrades performance only up to the point that this translates into overall system energy savings.

These energy and performance results are very positive. The ILP workloads can achieve up to 31% system energy savings for only a maximum performance degradation of 3.2%. The MID results also exhibit substantial benefits. Even the challenging MEM workloads achieve up to 9% system energy savings within the allowable performance degradation. Overall, we observe that MemScale produces average system energy savings of 18.3% for an average performance degradation of only 4.2%.

#### 4.2.2 Dynamic Behavior

To understand the results above more deeply, let us consider an example workload and the dynamic behavior of our policy. Figure 7 plots (a) the memory subsystem frequency selected by our policy for workload MID3, (b) the CPI of each application in the workload (averaged over the 4 instances of the application), and (c) the resulting scaled channel utilization, as a function of execution time.

The figure shows a few interesting frequency transitions. After the start of the workload, our policy quickly reduces the frequency to the minimum value and keeps it there until it detects the massive phase change of application apsi. As Figure 7(b) illustrates, the phase change occurred during the 46 ms quantum. Because our policy is OS-driven, the system only detected the phase change and increased the frequency at the next quantum boundary (around 51 ms). Despite this short reaction delay, our policy still keeps the performance degradation for apsi (8.2%) well under the allowable limit. As Figure 7(c) depicts, the two frequencies selected by our policy for the two phases of the workload keep the scaled channel utilization around 25%.

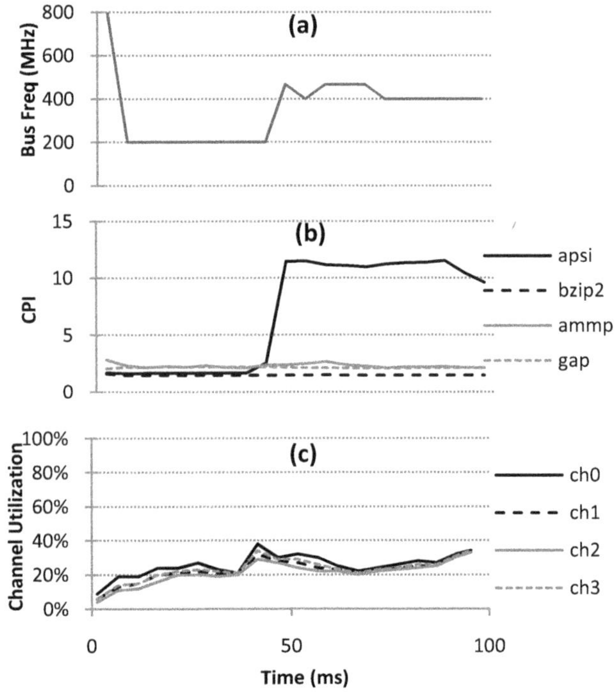


**Figure 7: Timeline of MID3 workload.** MemScale adjusts memory system frequency rapidly in response to the phase change in apsi.

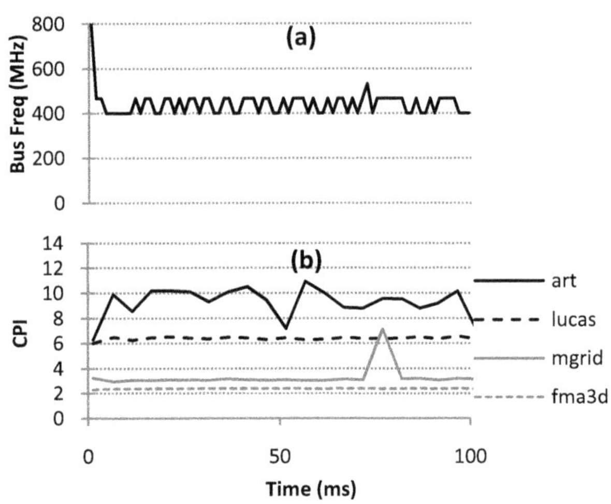


**Figure 8: Timeline of MEM4 workload.** MemScale approximates a "virtual frequency" by oscillating between two neighboring frequencies.

Figure 8 shows another interesting dynamic behavior, this time for workload MEM4 on an 8-core system. Note that our policy alternates between two frequencies throughout most of the execution. (Recall that frequency transitions are fast and we only initiate transitions on quantum boundaries.) The reason for this behavior is that the space of usable frequencies is not continuous; the ideal frequency is really between the two usable frequencies. In essence, our policy defines a "virtual frequency" by alternating between the two frequencies.

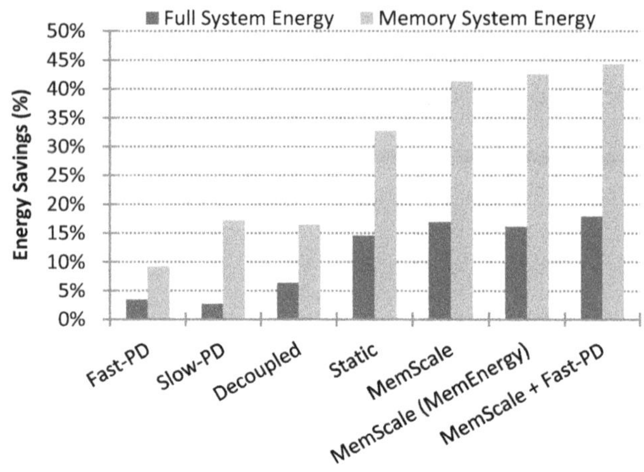


**Figure 9: Energy savings.** MemScale provides greater full-system and memory system energy savings than alternatives.

### 4.2.3 Comparison with Other Policies

In this subsection, we compare our MemScale policy ("MemScale") to six alternatives. The first alternative ("Fast-PD") represents today's aggressive memory controllers, which immediately transition a rank to fast-exit precharge powerdown state whenever the last open bank of the rank is closed. The second alternative ("Slow-PD") is even more aggressive in that it transitions the rank to slow-exit precharge powerdown state. The third alternative ("Decoupled") is the decoupled DIMM approach to energy conservation, which combines low-frequency memory devices with high-frequency channels. The fourth alternative ("Static") represents the scenario in which the frequency for the memory controller, channels, DIMMs, and DRAM devices is selected statically before the workloads are started. The fifth and sixth alternatives are actually variations of our policy. The fifth ("MemScale (MemEnergy)") considers only the memory energy (rather than the overall system energy) in making decisions. The sixth ("MemScale + Fast-PD") is our full policy combined with fast-exit powerdown.

Figure 9 shows the average energy savings achieved by all alternatives, across the MID workloads. For these same workloads, Figure 10 breaks down the average system power of each alternative between its DRAM, PLL/register, memory controller, and rest-of-the-system (everything but the memory subsystem) components. Figure 11 shows the average and maximum performance degradations for all the alternatives, again across the same workloads. All results are computed with respect to the baseline, which keeps the memory subsystem at its highest frequency at all times.

These results demonstrate that Fast-PD achieves small energy savings at small performance degradations. The energy savings come from reductions in the power consumption of the DRAM chips. For the MEM and ILP workloads, Fast-PD achieved system energy savings between 0.3% (MEM2) and 7.4% (ILP3). Being more aggressive with Slow-PD actually hurts performance so much that the workloads consume more system energy than the baseline system. In fact, the performance of one of the applications actually degrades by 15%. Both of these results match expectations.

In contrast, Decoupled does better than Fast-PD or Slow-PD. It achieves higher energy savings at moderate performance degradations for the MID workloads. The energy savings come from reductions in the power consumed by the DRAM devices. Decoupled also does well for the ILP workloads, achieving a maximum energy savings of 11%. However, it actually *increases* the energy

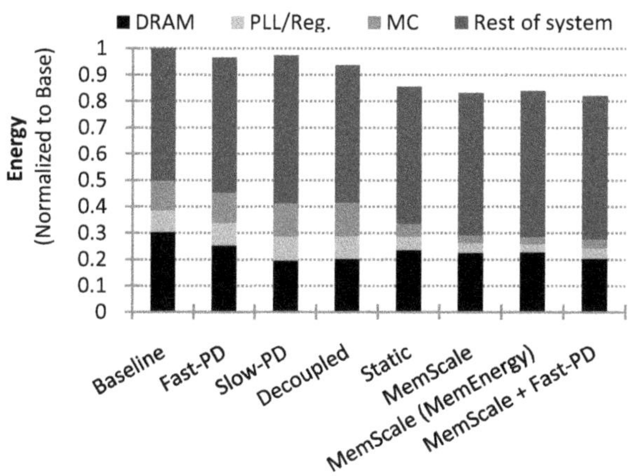


**Figure 10: System energy breakdown.** MemScale reduces DRAM, PLL/Reg, and MC energy more than alternatives.

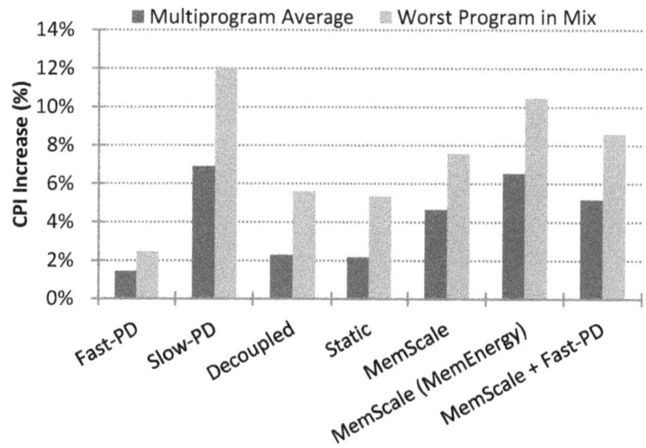


**Figure 11: CPI overhead.** MemScale's CPI increases are under 10%. MemScale (MemEnergy) slightly exceeds the bound.

consumption for one of the MEM workloads (MEM3) by 0.8%. This result is due to a significant performance degradation for this workload.

Static conserves more memory and system energy than Decoupled (for roughly the same performance degradations), despite the fact that the frequency of the DRAM devices is lower under Decoupled than Static (400 vs 467 MHz). This arises because Static decreases the energy consumption of the memory controller and the PLL/register devices. Decoupled does not address these sources of energy consumption. DRAM device energy is indeed lower under Decoupled, as one would expect. Static also does well for the ILP and MEM workloads, achieving average system energy savings of 19.1% and 7.8%, respectively, always within the allowed performance degradation.

MemScale easily outperforms Decoupled. We achieve almost 3x higher energy savings, while keeping degradation within the allowed range. The reason for this result is that MemScale can dynamically adjust frequencies and achieve energy gains in the memory controller and PLL/register as well.

MemScale is also superior to Static in both memory and system energy savings, but leads to slightly (2%) higher performance degradations. Specifically, MemScale's average system energy savings is 30.2% for the ILP workloads and 16.9% for the MID workloads, whereas Static achieves only 19.1% and 14.5% savings, respectively. (Their savings for the MEM workloads are comparable.) Our greater energy savings come from MemScale's ability to dynamically adjust frequency to the exact conditions of each workload. Under the *unrealistic* assumption that the user would (1) manually select the best frequency for each workload, and (2) somehow instruct the server to reboot to the new frequency before running the workload, Static and MemScale would differ little for the workloads that do not exhibit dynamic phase changes. For those that do, MemScale would still surpass Static through dynamically adjusting the frequency, as seen in the MID3 workload, for example.

As we suggested before, when our policy is set to consider memory energy and not system energy (MemScale (MemEnergy)), the system conserves more memory energy but at the cost of system energy and performance. Moreover, note that MemScale (MemEnergy) exceeds the performance target by just 0.8% for two applications, each in a different workload. The reason is that MemScale sometimes mispredicts the queue lengths of the highest memory frequency. These mispredictions affect MemScale's computation of the performance slack.

Interestingly, note that adding Fast-PD to MemScale does not meaningfully improve its results; the average system energy savings stay roughly the same (lower DRAM chip power but higher rest-of-the-system power), whereas the performance degradations worsen slightly.

### 4.2.4 Sensitivity Analysis

In this section, we investigate the effect of our main simulation and policy parameters: the maximum allowable performance degradation, the configuration of the channels and DIMMs, the fraction of the memory power with respect to the whole server power, the power proportionality of the memory controller and DIMMs' registers, the length of the OS quantum, and the length of the profiling period. We again perform these studies using the MID workloads.

**Maximum performance degradation.** This parameter is important in that higher allowable degradations could enable greater energy savings. To understand the impact of this parameter, Figure 12 illustrates the energy savings (bars on the left) and maximum *achieved* degradations (bars on the right), for maximum *allowable* degradations of 1%, 5%, 10%, and 15%. Recall that our default maximum allowable degradation is 10%. All other parameters remain at their defaults. It is interesting to observe that 1% and 5% degradations indeed produce lower energy savings. However, allowing 15% degradation does not improve our savings: beyond a certain point, lengthening the execution to conserve more memory energy actually increases overall energy. At that point, our policy stops lowering frequency.

**Amount of memory traffic.** As far as MemScale is concerned, the number of channels is the most important aspect of the memory subsystem configuration. The number of channels directly affects how heavily utilized each channel is and, thus, our opportunities to lower frequency without excessively degrading performance. In fact, decreasing the number of channels approximates the effect of greater memory traffic that could result from prefetching or out-of-order execution. Figure 13 depicts the energy savings (left) and maximum achieved performance degradation (right) for 2, 3, and 4 channels. Recall that our default results assumed 4 channels. The figure shows that increases in the number of channels indeed increase the benefits of MemScale by non-trivial amounts, without affecting our ability to limit performance losses. Interestingly, the figure also shows that doubling the channel traffic (from 4 to 2 channels) still leads to system energy savings of roughly 14%.

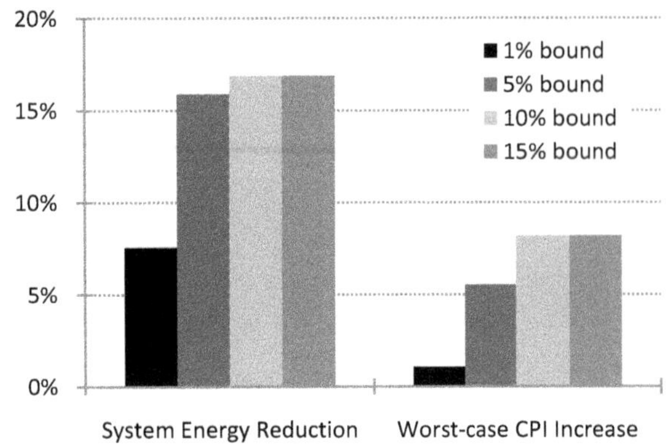


**Figure 12: Impact of CPI bound.** Increasing the bound beyond 10% does not yield further energy savings.

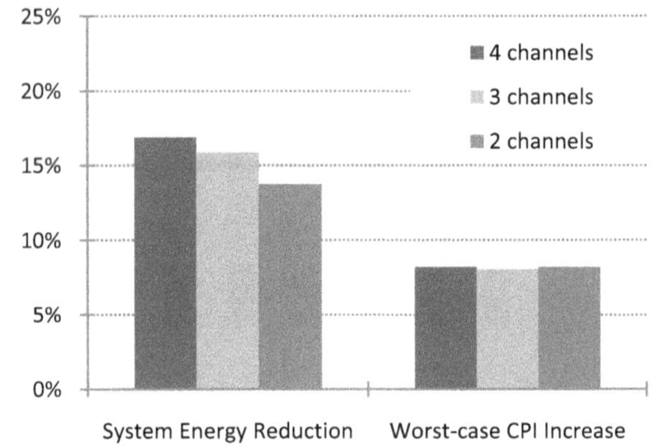


**Figure 13: Impact of number of channels.** MemScale provides greater savings when there are more, less-utilized channels.

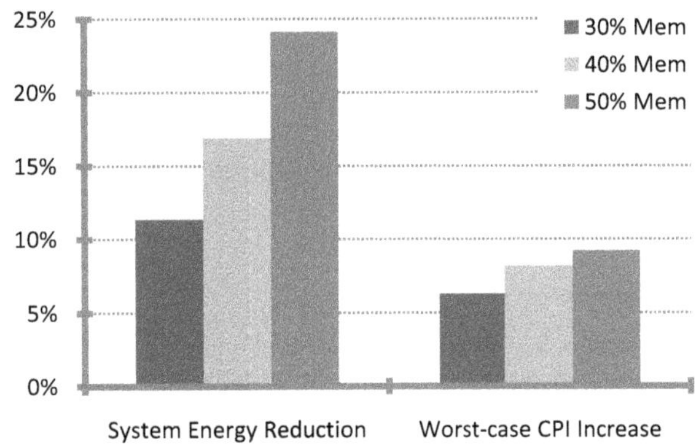


**Figure 14: Impact of fraction of memory power.** Increasing the fraction increases energy savings.

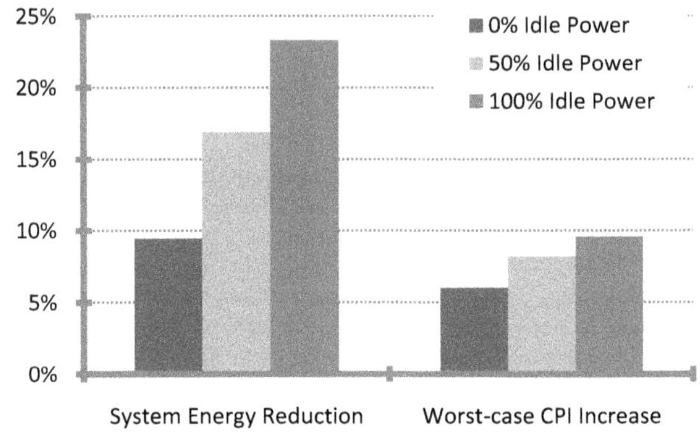


**Figure 15: Impact of power proportionality of MC and registers.** Decreasing proportionality increases energy savings.

Another approach for studying the effect of greater memory traffic is to increase the number of cores, while keeping the LLC size the same. Thus, we performed experiments with 32 cores and 4 memory channels. For the MID workloads, the larger number of cores causes 2x-4x increases in traffic. These increases translate into system energy savings ranging from 7.6% to 10.4%, without any violations of the performance bound.

**Fraction of memory system power with respect to server power.** Because MemScale seeks to reduce whole-system energy consumption by reducing the memory subsystem energy, the contribution of the memory subsystem to the overall power consumption of the server becomes a crucial parameter. Intuitively, the larger this fraction, the larger our percentage energy savings. Furthermore, recall that the non-memory-subsystem power consumption affects our energy management policy. Intuitively, the lower the non-memory-subsystem contribution, the lower the frequencies that our policy can select. Figure 14 quantifies the impact of 30%, 40%, and 50% fractions of memory power on the system energy savings. Recall that our baseline assumes a fraction of 40%.

The figure shows that the fraction of memory power has a significant effect on the system energy savings. Increasing the fraction from 30% to 50% (or, equivalently, reducing the rest-of-the-system contribution from 70% to 50%) more than doubles the savings (11% vs 24%). The maximum CPI degradation increases by a few percent as well, but stays within the allowed range.

**Power proportionality of the memory controller and DIMMs' registers.** Since the memory controller and DIMM register designs are vendor- and model-dependent, we studied a wide range of power proportionality possibilities for these components. Specifically, we varied their idle power consumption from 0% (perfect proportionality) to 100% (no proportionality) of their peak power consumption. Recall that our default assumption is 50% idle power for these components. For this analysis (and our other results), we assume that their power consumption changes linearly with utilization between idle and peak loads. Figure 15 depicts the results.

The figure shows that the power proportionality of these components has a significant impact on the system energy savings. Interestingly, decreasing proportionality actually increases our savings significantly to 23%. As the memory subsystem's idle power increases (decreasing proportionality), the scope of MemScale to reduce register and memory controller power grows. Importantly, MemScale achieves these benefits without violating the allowed performance degradation.

**Length of the OS quantum (epoch) and profiling period.** We studied the effect of (1) the epoch length by considering quanta of 1, 5, and 10ms; and (2) the length of the profiling period by considering periods of 0.1, 0.3, and 0.5ms. The first study sought to assess our ability to stay within the performance requirement, even when our decisions could not be changed for long periods of time. Similarly, the goal of the second study was to assess the need for long profiling periods before making decisions. Overall, these studies revealed that MemScale is essentially insensitive to reasonable values of these parameters.

## 5. Related Work

To the best of our knowledge, this paper is the first to propose active low-power modes for main memory. It is also the first to create such modes for the memory controller. Finally, it is the first to propose operating system policies to leverage these modes to conserve energy without excessive performance degradation. We discuss various classes of related works next.

**Processor DVFS.** Our work is most closely related to processor DVFS. While there is a large body of work on this topic, these techniques have only been applied to the CPU, e.g. [17, 19, 34].

**Lowering DRAM frequency.** The memory-related approach that is most closely related to ours is to run the DRAM devices at a lower frequency than the memory channel, using *Decoupled DIMMs* [45]. Like MemScale, this technique reduces DRAM power. However, our work differs from Decoupled DIMMs in three main ways. First, a Decoupled DIMM requires a power-hungry synchronization buffer to bridge the gap between the DRAM and channel speeds. Second, we allow *dynamic* adjustment of frequencies by the operating system to match the needs of workloads online; the frequencies of the memory channels and DRAM devices were set statically in Decoupled DIMMs. Third, MemScale not only reduces DRAM power, but also memory bus, non-DRAM DIMM, and MC powers as well.

**Rank subsetting and DRAM reorganization.** Recently, there have been several proposals to improve the efficiency of the memory system by reducing the number of chips or bits accessed at a time [1, 43, 44]. Udipi *et al.* proposes to do so by re-architecting the DRAM devices [43]. Unfortunately, although highly beneficial, such re-architecting is likely to incur significant costs and may affect yield as well.

In contrast, other proposals reduce the number of chips in a rank by modifying DIMMs but not the DRAM chips [1, 44]. For example, Multicore DIMMs [1] allow the creation of Virtual Memory Devices (VMDs) comprising a small number of DRAM chips. This approach divides a physical channel into as many logical buses as there are VMDs. In addition, it requires a demux register in each rank, which routes signals to the correct VMD.

MemScale is orthogonal to and can easily be combined with these approaches; we target background, register/PLL, and MC power consumptions, whereas they target dynamic power. In addition, our work leverages existing commodity DIMM and DRAM parts and proposes extending existing hardware mechanisms to dynamically scaling MCs, channels, DIMMs, and DRAM devices.

**DRAM idle low-power states.** DRAM technologies often expose a small number of idle low-power states that greatly reduce DRAM power, but preclude access until the DRAM returns to the active state. Because servers do not typically exhibit enough memory idleness, researchers have proposed many approaches to create idleness and conserve energy using these states [10, 11, 13, 20, 24, 27, 36]. Unfortunately, these techniques are very difficult to exploit when the granularity of power management is a rank of DRAM chips, as in DDR* technology.

**Leveraging ensembles for energy savings.** A few proposals have used ensemble-level techniques [28, 31, 41] to amortize the impact of memory energy. At this point, it is not clear if these techniques apply to all workloads. Nevertheless, our approach is orthogonal to ensembles and could be applied to them as well.

**Managing peak power and temperature.** Recent research has proposed techniques to limit the peak power consumption and/or manage temperature [11, 14, 18, 29, 30]. Among them, memory throttling has been receiving significant attention. Throttling limits power consumption by limiting the number of requests to memory in each time period. MemScale differs from throttling in two main regards. First, our goal is to conserve energy, not to limit peak power or prevent thermal overload. Second, we reduce the speed of the memory subsystem, instead of delaying memory accesses.

## 6. Conclusion

In this paper, we proposed the MemScale approach to managing memory energy under performance constraints. MemScale creates and leverages active low-power modes that result from dynamically scaling the frequency of memory channels and DRAM devices, and dynamically scaling the voltage and frequency of the memory controller. We also proposed a small set of mechanisms and an operating system policy to determine the best power mode at each point in time. Our evaluation demonstrated that MemScale conserves significant memory and system energy, while staying within pre-set performance limits. Our results also showed that MemScale is superior to four competing energy management techniques. We conclude that MemScale's potential benefits far outweigh its small hardware costs.

Our future work will consider selecting different frequencies for different channels, OS-level scheduling to increase the potential benefits of MemScale, coordinating CPU and memory DVFS, combining MemScale with rank-subsetting techniques, and voltage scaling parts of DIMMs as well.


## Acknowledgements

We would like to thank Eugene Gorbatov and our shepherd Onur Mutlu for comments on many aspects of this work.


## References


[1] J. H. Ahn, N. P. Jouppi, C. Kozyrakis, J. Leverich, and R. S. Schreiber. Future scaling of processor-memory interfaces. *SC '09 - Super Computing*, 2009.

[2] I. Akyildiz. On the exact and approximate throughput analysis of closed queuing networks with blocking. *IEEE Transactions on Software Engineering*, 14(1):62–70, 1988.

[3] AMD. ACP – The Truth About Power Consumption Starts Here, 2009. http://www.amd.com/us/Documents/43761C_ACP_WP_EE.pdf.

[4] S. Balsamo, V. D. N. Persone, and R. Onvural. *Analysis of Queuing Networks with Blocking*. 2001.

[5] L. A. Barroso and U. Hölzle. The Datacenter as a Computer: An Introduction to the Design of Warehouse-Scale Machines. *Synthesis Lectures on Computer Architecture*, Jan. 2009.

[6] L. A. Barroso and U. Hölzle. The Case for Energy-Proportional Computing. *IEEE Computer*, 40(12):33–37, December 2007.

[7] N. Binkert, R. Dreslinski, L. Hsu, K. Lim, a.G. Saidi, and S. Reinhardt. The M5 Simulator: Modeling Networked Systems. *IEEE Micro*, 26(4):52–60, July 2006.

[8] R. Crisp. Direct Rambus Technology: The New Main Memory Standard. *IEEE Micro*, 1997.

[9] R. Das, O. Mutlu, T. Moscibroda, and C. R. Das. Aérgia : Exploiting Packet Latency Slack in On-Chip Networks. *ISCA '10: International Symposium on Computer Architecture*, 2010.

[10] V. Delaluz, M. Kandemir, N. Vijaykrishnan, A. Sivasubramaniam, and M. J. Irwin. Hardware and Software Techniques for Controlling DRAM Power Modes. *IEEE Transactions on Computers*, 50(11), 2001.

[11] B. Diniz, D. Guedes, W. M. Jr, and R. Bianchini. Limiting the Power Consumption of Main Memory. *ISCA '07: International Symposium on Computer Architecture*, 2007.

[12] EPA. Report to Congress on Server and Data Center Energy Efficiency Public Law 109-431, 2007.

[13] X. Fan, C. Ellis, and A. Lebeck. Memory Controller Policies for DRAM Power Management. In *Proceedings of the International Symposium on Low-Power Electronics and Design*, August 2001.

[14] W. Felter, K. Rajamani, T. Keller, and C. Rusu. A Performance-Conserving Approach for Reducing Peak Power Consumption in Server Systems. *ICS '05: International Conference on Supercomputing*, 2005.

[15] Google. Going Green at Google, 2010.

[16] E. Gorbatov, 2010. Personal communication.

[17] M. S. Gupta, G.-Y. Wei, and D. Brooks. System level analysis of fast, per-core DVFS using on-chip switching regulators. *HPCA '08: High Performance Computer Architecture*, 2008.

[18] H. Hanson and K. Rajamani. What Computer Architects Need to Know About Memory Throttling. *WEED '10: Workshop on Energy-Efficient Design*, 2010.

[19] S. Herbert and D. Marculescu. Analysis of Dynamic Voltage/Frequency Scaling in Chip-Multiprocessors. *ISLPED '07: International Symposium on Low Power Electronics and Design*, 2007.

[20] H. Huang, P. Pillai, and K. G. Shin. Design and Implementation of Power-Aware Virtual Memory. In *Proceedings of the USENIX Annual Technical Conference*, June 2003.

[21] Intel. Intel Xeon Processor 5600 Series, 2010.

[22] B. Jacob, S. W. Ng, and D. T. Wang. *Memory Systems: Cache, DRAM, Disk.* Morgan Kaufmann Publishers, 2007.

[23] JEDEC. DDR3 SDRAM Standard, 2009.

[24] A. R. Lebeck, X. Fan, H. Zeng, and C. Ellis. Power Aware Page Allocation. *ASPLOS '00: Architectural Support for Programming Languages and Operating Systems*, 2000.

[25] C. Lefurgy, K. Rajamani, F. Rawson, W. Felter, M. Kistler, and T. W. Keller. Energy Management for Commercial Servers. *IEEE Computer*, 36(12), December 2003.

[26] D. Levinthal. Performance Analysis Guide for Intel Core i7 Processor and Intel Xeon 5500 processors, 2009.

[27] X. Li, Z. Li, F. M. David, P. Zhou, Y. Zhou, S. V. Adve, and S. Kumar. Performance-directed energy management for main memory and disks. In *Proceedings of the 11th International Conference on Architectural Support for Programming Languages and Operating Systems*, October 2004.

[28] K. Lim, J. Chang, T. Mudge, P. Ranganathan, S. K. Reinhardt, and T. F. Wenisch. Disaggregated Memory for Expansion and Sharing in Blade Servers. *ISCA '09: International Symposium on Computer Architecture*, 2009.

[29] J. Lin, H. Zheng, Z. Zhu, H. David, and Z. Zhang. Thermal Modeling and Management of DRAM Memory Systems. *ISCA '07: International Symposium on Computer Architecture*, 2007.

[30] J. Lin, H. Zheng, Z. Zhu, E. Gorbatov, H. David, and Z. Zhang. Software Thermal Management of DRAM Memory for Multicore Systems. *SIGMETRICS*, pages 337–348, 2008.

[31] D. Meisner, B. T. Gold, and T. F. Wenisch. PowerNap: Eliminating Server Idle Power. *ASPLOS '09: Architectural Support for Programming Languages and Operating Systems*, Feb. 2009.

[32] Micron. 1Gb: x4, x8, x16 DDR3 SDRAM, 2006.

[33] Micron. Calculating Memory System Power for DDR3, July 2007.

[34] A. Miyoshi, C. Lefurgy, E. V. Hensbergen, R. Rajamony, and R. Rajkumar. Critical Power Slope : Understanding the Runtime Effects of Frequency Scaling. *ICS '02: International Conference on Supercomputing*, 2002.

[35] J. Moore, J. S. Chase, and P. Ranganathan. Weatherman: Automated, Online and Predictive Thermal Mapping and Management for Data Centers. *ICAC '06: International Conference on Autonomic Computing*, 2006.

[36] V. Pandey, W. Jiang, Y. Zhou, and R. Bianchini. DMA-Aware Memory Energy Management. *HPCA '06: High-Performance Computer Architecture*, 2006.

[37] S. Pelley, D. Meisner, P. Zandevakili, T. F. Wenisch, and J. Underwood. Power Routing : Dynamic Power Provisioning in the Data Center. *ASPLOS '10: Architectural Support for Programming Languages and Operating Systems*, 2010.

[38] E. Perelman, G. Hamerly, M. V. Biesbrouck, T. Sherwood, and B. Calder. Using SimPoint for Accurate and Efficient Simulation Erez Perelman. *SIGMETRICS*, 2003.

[39] L. Ramos and R. Bianchini. C-Oracle: Predictive thermal management for data centers. *HPCA '08: High Performance Computer Architecture*, Feb. 2008.

[40] K. Sudan, N. Chatterjee, D. Nellans, M. Awasthi, Rajeev Balasubramonian, and A. Davis. Micro-Pages : Increasing DRAM Efficiency with Locality-Aware Data Placement. *ASPLOS '10: Architectural Support for Programming Languages and Operating Systems*, 2010.

[41] N. Tolia, Z. Wang, M. Marwah, C. Bash, P. Ranganathan, and X. Zhu. Delivering Energy Proportionality with Non Energy-Proportional Systems Optimizing the Ensemble. *HotPower*, 2008.

[42] D. Tsirogiannis, S. Harizopoulos, and M. A. Shah. Analyzing the energy efficiency of a database server. *SIGMOD*, 2010.

[43] A. N. Udipi, N. Muralimanohar, N. Chatterjee, Rajeev Balasubramonian, A. Davis, and N. P. Jouppi. Rethinking DRAM Design and Organization for Energy-Constrained Multi-Cores. *ISCA '10: International Symposium on Computer Architecture*, 2010.

[44] H. Zheng, J. Lin, Z. Zhang, E. Gorbatov, H. David, and Z. Zhu. Mini-rank: Adaptive DRAM architecture for improving memory power efficiency. *MICRO '08: Symposium on Microarchitecture*, Nov. 2008.

[45] H. Zheng, J. Lin, Z. Zhang, and Z. Zhu. Decoupled DIMM : Building High-Bandwidth Memory System Using Low-Speed DRAM Devices. *ISCA '09: International Symposium on Computer Architecture*, 2009.

# 2ndStrike: Toward Manifesting Hidden Concurrency Typestate Bugs


Qi Gao *
Facebook Inc.
gao@fb.com

Wenbin Zhang
The Ohio State University
zhangwen@cse.ohio-state.edu

Zhezhe Chen
The Ohio State University
chenzhe@cse.ohio-state.edu

Mai Zheng
The Ohio State University
zhengm@cse.ohio-state.edu

Feng Qin
The Ohio State University
qin@cse.ohio-state.edu



## Abstract

Concurrency bugs are becoming increasingly prevalent in the multi-core era. Recently, much research has focused on data races and atomicity violation bugs, which are related to low-level memory accesses. However, a large number of concurrency typestate bugs such as "invalid reads to a closed file from a different thread" are under-studied. These concurrency typestate bugs are important yet challenging to study since they are mostly relevant to high-level program semantics.

This paper presents 2ndStrike, a method to manifest hidden concurrency typestate bugs in software testing. Given a state machine describing correct program behavior on certain object typestates, 2ndStrike profiles runtime events related to the typestates and thread synchronization. Based on the profiling results, 2ndStrike then identifies bug candidates, each of which is a pair of runtime events that would cause typestate violation if the event order is reversed. Finally, 2ndStrike re-executes the program with controlled thread interleaving to manifest bug candidates.

We have implemented a prototype of 2ndStrike on Linux and have illustrated our idea using three types of concurrency typestate bugs, including invalid file operation, invalid pointer dereference, and invalid lock operation. We have evaluated 2ndStrike with six real world bugs (including one previously unknown bug) from three open-source server and desktop programs (i.e., MySQL, Mozilla, pbzip2). Our experimental results show that 2ndStrike can effectively and efficiently manifest all six software bugs, most of which are difficult or impossible to manifest using stress testing or active testing techniques that are based on data race/atomicity violation. Additionally, 2ndStrike reports no false positives, provides detailed bug reports for each manifested bug, and can consistently reproduce the bug after manifesting it once.


* This work was done while the author was a Ph.D. student at The Ohio State University




*ASPLOS'11,* March 5–11, 2011, Newport Beach, California, USA.





***Categories and Subject Descriptors*** D.2.5 [*Testing and Debugging*]: Testing Tools

***General Terms*** Reliability

***Keywords*** Software Testing, Typestate Bugs, Concurrency Bugs


## 1. Introduction

Concurrency bugs are becoming increasingly prevalent in the multi-core era as more programs are written or rewritten in a multi-threaded fashion for better utilizing multi-core systems. However, it is extremely difficult for developers to reason about all possible orders of accessing shared objects from multiple threads. This is especially true for multi-threaded programs with complex semantics. Consequently, concurrency bugs hidden in corner cases are inevitable and cause runtime errors.

Unfortunately, concurrency bugs are notoriously difficult to pinpoint in testing due to their non-deterministic nature. The *de facto* way to expose and detect concurrency bugs is stress testing, i.e., running a multi-threaded program repetitively for a long time with test inputs. While easy to conduct, stress testing is inefficient due to large consumption of computing resources. Furthermore, stress testing is usually ineffective in exposing concurrency bugs because it exercises only a fraction of possible thread interleavings [39, 47].

Much research has been conducted on detecting two types of concurrency bugs, i.e., data races [14, 56, 72] and atomicity violations [24, 33, 67]. These approaches focus on detecting memory accesses to shared variables that are not protected by common locks or not serializable under exercised thread interleavings. While these methods are effective in detecting concurrency bugs that are triggered, they cannot handle concurrency bugs hidden in un-exercised thread interleavings. To address this issue, several active testing techniques [46, 47, 57] are recently proposed. Based on information from external detectors or runtime profilers, these testing techniques actively control the thread scheduling to favor the interleavings that may trigger data races [57] or atomicity violations [46, 47]. As a result, these tools help expose data races or atomicity violations hidden in uncommon thread interleavings.

However, previous studies have shown that large system programs contain a significant number of concurrency bugs that involve neither data races nor atomicity violations [36]. Figure 1 shows a real-world concurrency bug of this type in MySQL, a popular database server [1]. In this example, Thread 1 reads data from a file at statement $A$ and Thread 2 closes the same file at statement $B$. As shown in Figure 1(a), the correct thread interleaving

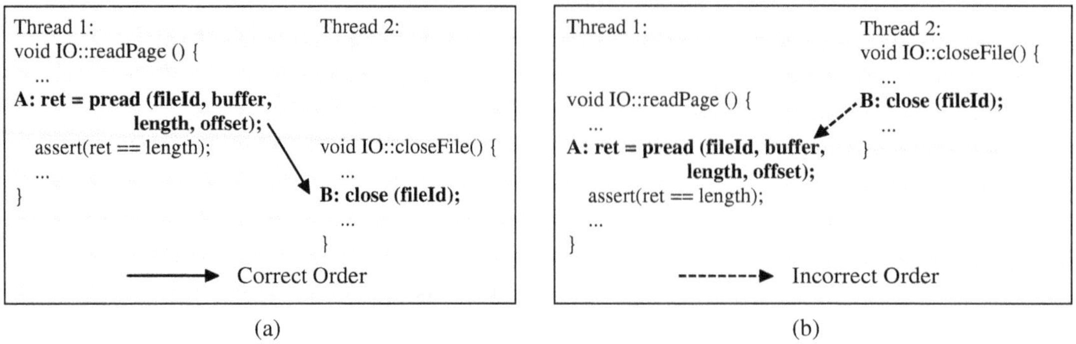


**Figure 1.** A real-world concurrency typestate bug extracted from MySQL

is reading the file from Thread 1 followed by closing the file from Thread 2, which is the common case for program execution. However, due to improper synchronization, Thread 2 can potentially, although rarely, close the file before Thread 1 accesses the same file, which is shown in Figure 1(b). This synchronization error violates file semantics instead of causing data races or atomicity violation.

This type of concurrency bugs are related to high-level program semantics, and can be captured by *typestates* [62]. A typestate is the state associated to an object of a given type (e.g., a file descriptor, a lock, or a memory object). At each typestate, an object is permitted to be applied with a subset of operations. Among the permitted operations, some may alter the typestate of the object, while others preserve the typestate of the object. *Concurrency typestate bugs* occur when typestate-altering operations from one thread are not well synchronized with other operations from different threads, causing the object being applied with un-permitted operations in some typestate, i.e., *typestate violation*. Figure 1(b) demonstrates such concurrency typestate bug. The operation `close` in Thread 2 changes the typestate of the file object to `CLOSED`. Then, the operation `pread` in Thread 1 is performed in the same file object with the typestate of `CLOSED`, which is not permitted.

Concurrency typestate bugs are important yet challenging to address. Similar to typestate bugs in sequential programs, which have been studied extensively [6, 7, 11, 12, 17, 18, 25, 62], concurrency typestate bugs are common yet under-studied mistakes in large multi-threaded system programs [36]. In these programs, many stateful objects, such as connections for Internet servers and tables for databases, are shared among multiple threads. With complex business logic, it is easy for programmers to make mistakes in reasoning about object states with thread synchronization, often leading to concurrency typestate bugs. Furthermore, existing approaches that detect or expose data races or atomicity violations [14, 24, 33, 46, 47, 56, 57, 67, 72] cannot deal with this type of bugs. The main reason is that these methods focus on the synchronization at the memory access level without taking program semantics into consideration. Even if data races or atomicity violations may co-exist in some concurrency typestate bugs, existing methods can provide few insights for understanding the root causes of bugs due to lack of high-level program semantics. Recently-proposed approaches Falcon [49] and Bugaboo [37] can detect order violation bugs, which may be relevant to concurrency typestates. However, these approaches focus on detecting instead of exposing concurrency bugs.

**Our Contributions:** In this paper, we propose a general and extensible testing framework called *2ndStrike* to manifest potential concurrency typestate bugs hidden in multi-threaded programs. By using user-defined state machines to capture semantic-related typestate information in the program, 2ndStrike performs runtime profiling specific to typestate properties. Based on the profiling results, 2ndStrike identifies the potential synchronization errors that could lead to typestate violation. Then 2ndStrike re-executes the program with controlled thread scheduling for manifesting the potential errors. This work flow can be fully automated and easily integrated with existing test harnesses.

The brief process of applying 2ndStrike to the previous bug example goes as follows. First, 2ndStrike profiles runtime events that are related to file operations and thread synchronization. The event orders in the log are most likely generated by common scenarios as shown in Figure 1(a). By analyzing the log, 2ndStrike identifies the pair of events, i.e., `pread` from Thread 1 and `close` from Thread 2, as a candidate of potential typestate violation. This is because `pread` from Thread 1 is not permitted to be applied to a file object with the typestate of `CLOSED`, which is the result of applying `close` from Thread 2 to the same file object with the typestate of `OPEN`. Then, 2ndStrike attempts to manifest this potential concurrency typestate bug by re-executing the program with a different thread scheduling, i.e., `close` from Thread 2 is scheduled before `pread` from Thread 1.

Based on the above idea, we have implemented a prototype of 2ndStrike on Linux for manifesting three common types of concurrency typestate bugs, including invalid file operation, invalid pointer dereference, and invalid lock operation. We chose these three typestate properties for illustrating the idea since they are easy to understand without requiring much domain knowledge. We do not see any particular technical difficulties to extend 2ndStrike for application-specific typestates.

We have evaluated 2ndStrike with six real-world concurrency typestate bugs of three types from three open-source server and desktop programs, including MySQL [1], Mozilla [2], and pbzip2 [3]. Our experimental results show that 2ndStrike can effectively and efficiently manifest all six concurrency typestate bugs. Additionally, it provides detailed bug reports and can consistently reproduce the bugs after manifesting them once. Compared to existing approaches, 2ndStrike has one or more of the following advantages:

- 2ndStrike is effective. To the best of our knowledge, 2ndStrike is the first offline testing method to *manifest concurrency typestate bugs* by exploiting semantics-related information and thread scheduling. Our experimental results show that it can manifest all six tested concurrency typestate bugs. These bugs are difficult to trigger by stress testing and five of them will be missed by data race or atomicity violation directed active testing techniques [47, 57].
- 2ndStrike is efficient. With typestate specific instrumentation, users can instrument a small set of semantics-related runtime events. This incurs much smaller runtime overhead than many existing tools that instrument every memory accesses (by a

factor of 3-50). Furthermore, 2ndStrike's stand-alone analyzer runs in parallel with the program being tested and analyzes the runtime logs on-the-fly without saving them to disk, which reduces both storage and runtime overhead.

- 2ndStrike is extensible. 2ndStrike is a general testing framework to perform typestate specific profiling, analysis, and scheduling control for manifesting concurrency typestate bugs. As examples, three 2ndStrike modules have been built for manifesting three common types of concurrency typestate bugs.
- 2ndStrike is easy to use. It does not require source code changes and can be easily integrated with existing test harnesses packaged with software programs. Additionally, it does not report false positives. Moreover, it provides reproducibility and bug reports to facilitate developers to diagnose the manifested bugs.

The rest of this paper is organized as follows. Section 2 presents the background of concurrency typestate bugs and compares them with data race/atomicity violation bugs. Section 3 provides an overview of 2ndStrike, followed by detailed description on each step in the work flow. Section 4 discusses design issues. After that, Section 5 presents the evaluation methodology, followed by the experimental results in Section 6. Then Section 7 discusses related work and Section 8 concludes the paper.

## 2. Concurrency Typestate Bugs

### 2.1 Typestates, State Machines, and Concurrency Typestate Bugs

First introduced in [62], typestate is a temporal extension of the concepts of types in programming languages. Each type has an associated set of typestates. At each program point, an object of a given type is in one of the typestates associated with its type. In essence, typestate determines a set of operations that are permitted to be applied to the corresponding objects.

In 2ndStrike, we use a finite state machine to model typestates for objects of a given type, defining which operations are permitted to be applied to the objects in which typestates. There are several ways to provide state machines for a object type. Generally, programmers can provide such state machines since they know high-level program semantics better than others. To reduce programmers' manual effort, researchers have proposed static methods [59] as well as dynamic methods [5] for automatically inferring the likely typestate property of objects. Furthermore, we can derive certain state machines based on common programming rules, such as "cannot read on a closed file handler" and "cannot dereference an invalid pointer".

Figure 2(a), (b), and (c) show the state machines for objects of the types as files, pointers, and locks, respectively. As shown in Figure 2(a), a file has two states: `OPEN` and `CLOSED`. A file in `OPEN` state indicates that its content is ready for being accessed, while the file content cannot be accessed when it is in `CLOSED` state. More specifically, the operations such as `Read`, `Write`, `Seek`, and `Close` are permitted on the file in `OPEN` state, and the operation `Open` is permitted on the `CLOSED` state. Among these operations, `Read`, `Write`, and `Seek` do not change the file's typestate, while `Open` changes the file state to `OPEN` and `Close` changes the file state to `CLOSED`. Similarly, Figure 2(b) and (c) show the state machines for pointers and locks, respectively.

A *typestate violation* occurs when a non-permitted operation is applied to an object in certain states. For example, when the operation `Read` is performed on a file object with the state of `CLOSED`, it incurs a typestate violation.

In this paper, a *concurrency typestate bug* refers to a synchronization error among multiple threads where one thread applies a state-changing operation to an object followed by another thread apply operations to the same object that causes a typestate violation. As shown in Figure 1, the order between the operation `pread` by Thread 1 and the operation `close` by Thread 2 is not strictly enforced. Therefore in some rare cases, the file state could first change to `CLOSED` before the operation `pread` is applied, resulting in a typestate violation.

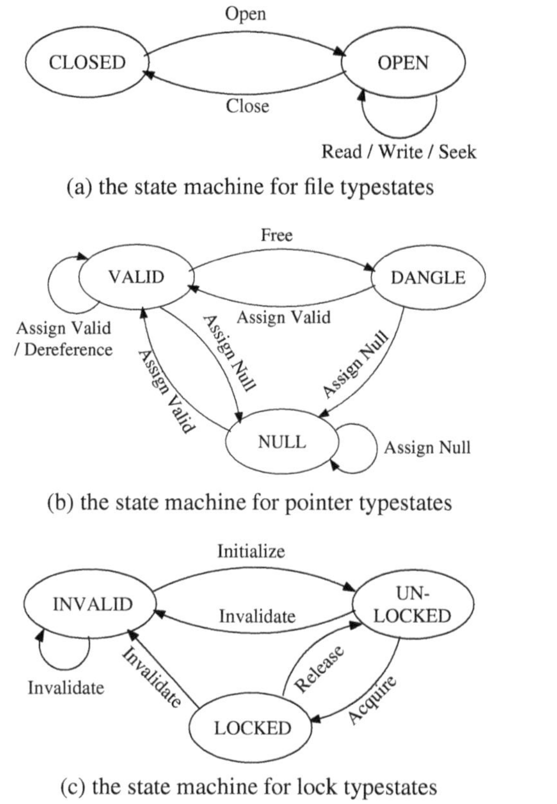


**Figure 2.** The state machines for files, pointers, and locks

To illustrate how 2ndStrike works, we use three state machines as shown in Figure 2(a), (b), and (c) for three types of concurrency typestate bugs, including invalid file operation, invalid pointer dereference, and invalid lock operation, respectively. We chose them because they are simple state machines suitable for illustrating the idea.

### 2.2 Concurrency Typestate Bugs versus Data Race/Atomicity Violation Bugs

Concurrency typestate bugs are relevant to, yet quite different from data race/atomicity violation bugs. They are relevant because the synchronization errors causing typestate violations can be data races and/or atomicity violations in some cases. However, the key difference between them is that data race and atomicity violation bugs focus on low-level memory accesses, while concurrency typestate bugs focus on high-level object typestates, which are related to program semantics.

The philosophy behind data race and atomicity violation bugs is that programmers should protect the accesses to shared variables via locks and achieve atomicity in order to guarantee the correctness. Indeed, many concurrency bugs occur because mutual exclusion property and/or atomicity property are not enforced by the code. Ultimately, mutual exclusion and atomicity are properties to distinguish between correct and incorrect execution orders in multithreaded programs. For example, the atomicity property for two

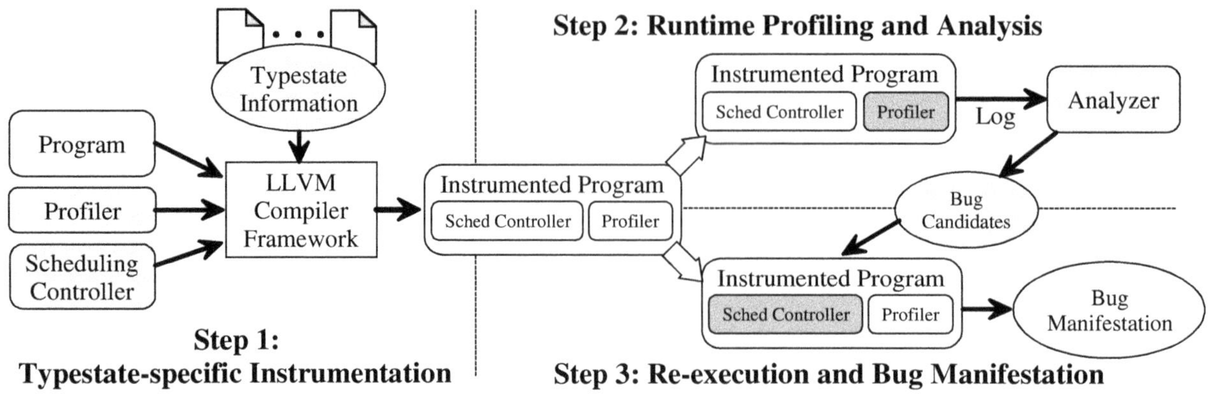


**Figure 3.** 2ndStrike Overview

consecutive reads on an object $a$ from one thread ($R_a^{l1}$, $R_a^{l2}$) with a remote write on the same object from another thread ($W_a^r$) is to distinguish the incorrect order, i.e., $R_a^{l1}\ W_a^r\ R_a^{l2}$, from the correct orders, i.e., $W_a^r\ R_a^{l1}\ R_a^{l2}$ and $R_a^{l1}\ R_a^{l2}\ W_a^r$.

Concurrency typestate bugs are directly related to the orders of runtime operations on objects and thus can capture the general order violation bugs [36], which cannot be considered as atomicity violations or simple data races. By associating semantic information to runtime variables, the notion of concurrency typestate bugs is helpful for detecting concurrency bugs that are related to program semantics.

## 3. 2ndStrike Design and Implementation

### 3.1 Overview

2ndStrike performs three steps to manifest hidden concurrency typestate bugs in testing scenarios. As shown in Figure 3, it first performs typestate-specific instrumentation to the program, then executes the program with runtime profiling and analysis, and lastly attempts to manifest the potential bugs with controlled scheduling during program re-execution.

The first step is to instrument the program being tested so that the events related to the typestates can be monitored and further actions can be performed. Different concurrency typestate bugs are related to different aspects of program semantics, users (e.g. programmers or testing engineers) can select one or more defined state machines for a typestate to test in this step. Depending on object types and typestates, the instrumentation can range from very light-weight to somewhat heavy-weight. The idea is to allow users to define the semantics and to control what they want in testing. The profiler and scheduling controller are also linked as shared library in this step.

The second step is to execute the instrumented program with test inputs for profiling typestate related events and to analyze these events for identifying *bug candidates*. A bug candidate is a pair of operations from different threads that can cause a concurrency typestate bug if the order of the operation pair is reversed. For better performance, the analyzer works in parallel with the profiler for processing the log stream.

After finishing the steps of profiling and analysis, 2ndStrike re-executes the program with controlled thread scheduling to manifest the potential bugs indicated by the analyzer. If a bug is successfully manifested, a bug report is generated with the candidate information to help programmers reproduce and diagnose the bug.

### 3.2 Typestate-Specific Instrumentation

In order to monitor the typestates of runtime objects and to control scheduling, 2ndStrike first instruments the multi-threaded program. The instrumentation is typestate-specific since it is for manifesting a given type of concurrency typestate bugs. For example, for invalid file operation bugs, 2ndStrike instruments the file related library calls such as `open`, `read`, and `close`. Similarly, for invalid pointer dereference bugs, 2ndStrike instruments: a) allocation and de-allocation of runtime objects, such as `malloc` and `free`, to determine the validity of a memory address, b) assignment that involves pointers, and c) dereference of pointers. For invalid lock operation bugs, 2ndStrike instruments lock initialization and invalidation, as well as lock acquire and release operations.

The runtime overhead incurred by the instrumentation largely depends on the targeted typestate. For example, monitoring pointer typestate involves instrumenting a large number of pointer dereference events, and such heavy instrumentation generally results in larger runtime overhead. On the other hand, instrumentation for file typestate is much lighter weight since file operations in a program usually are much less than pointer operations. Users can balance the manifestation benefit and runtime overhead in their own testing environments. Note that since the instrumentation is targeted, even for instrumenting the heavy-weight typestate such as pointer typestate, the runtime overhead is still less than instrumenting each memory access, which is required for data race and atomicity violation detectors (See our evaluation results in Section 6 for details).

Additionally, 2ndStrike keeps track of general synchronization events to prune false bug candidates in the subsequent analysis step (Section 3.3.2). For this purpose, it instruments: a) thread fork/join, b) lock activities, and c) semaphore or condition variable activities.

In our prototype, we use LLVM compiler framework [32] to perform static instrumentation in a code transformation pass. More specifically, the program source code is first fed into the compiler front-end to generate LLVM intermediate representation (IR). Then the 2ndStrike pass is applied to transform the original IR into the instrumented IR. After that, the code generation part of LLVM is used to generate assembly code of the instrumented program. The whole process can be fully automated by modifying the build scripts of the software. Since 2ndStrike simply performs instrumentation, the running time for code transformation is small, ranging from a few seconds for small programs to a few minutes for large programs. We choose static instrumentation over dynamic instrumentation because IR has more semantic information and can make event tracking easier and more accurate.

Our goal for instrumentation is to enable both profiling and scheduling control at program points of interest. To do so, we introduce the concept of *instrumentation point (InstPt)* to perform these two tasks. An InstPt is a specific source code location where 2ndStrike either emits a log entry via profiler or potentially inserts delay via scheduling controller. At each InstPt, 2ndStrike inserts a call to an external library, which performs the actual profiling and scheduling control. In this way, 2ndStrike can easily switch its function between profiling and scheduling without reinstrumenting the code.

### 3.3 Runtime Profiling and Analysis

#### 3.3.1 Design of Runtime Profiling and On-the-fly Analysis

During the profiling execution, 2ndStrike logs every typestate-related operation and synchronization event. Each log entry includes the following information: a) event type, such as "file close" and "pointer dereference", b) the thread ID on which the event happens, c) additional event information, e.g. file descriptor that is closed or pointer that is dereferenced, d) the InstPt number corresponding to the event, and e) the callsite that indicates the runtime context of the event.

2ndStrike analyzes the log to generate bug candidates. Each candidate is a pair of operations, from different threads, whose order needs to be flipped for manifesting a potential typestate violation. In each bug candidate, the detailed information on the operations is included for 2ndStrike scheduling controller to accurately identify the runtime operation pair. More specifically, each operation in the bug candidate includes its InstPt and the callsite information. Additionally it can be configured to include the thread ID and the object ID for matching. The algorithm of identifying bug candidates is described in Section 3.3.2.

In 2ndStrike workflow, the analyzer processes log entries in parallel with the profiler generating them. The main reason for the on-the-fly analysis is to reduce storage and runtime overhead. Saving the log to disk may incur non-trivial storage overhead, and also slows down the testing. This is especially true for profiling heavy-weight typestates, e.g., pointer typestate. Therefore, 2ndStrike analyzer runs in a separate process which connects to the program being tested via socket, so that it can consume the generated logs without saving them to disk.

#### 3.3.2 Analysis Algorithm to Identify Bug Candidates

**Criteria for Potential Concurrency Typestate Bugs.** To manifest concurrency typestate bugs, 2ndStrike needs to identify the potential problems in the synchronization between a state-transition operation (referred to as *OP-transit*) and an operation that is only permitted on a subset of typestates (referred to as *OP-limit*). A bug candidate is a pair of OP-transit and OP-limit in two threads, respectively, that may cause typestate violation if the order of these two operations is reversed.

Figure 4 shows two scenarios where 2ndStrike identifies bug candidates. As shown in Figure 4(a), the first scenario goes as follows. Thread $T_1$ first performs an operation OP-limit on an object of the state $S_p$, where OP-limit is not permitted in state $S_q$. Then another thread $T_2$ performs an operation OP-transit, which causes the state of the object to transit from $S_p$ to $S_q$. This is a correct order between these two events in $T_1$ and $T_2$, respectively. If the program does not enforce such correct order between the two events, 2ndStrike identifies them as a potential bug. This is because if the order of the two events is reversed, i.e., OP-transit happens before OP-limit, there would be a typestate violation when the OP-limit is performed in the object of the state $S_q$. Similarly, a bug candidate can also be an OP-transit operation followed by an OP-limit operation that is not permitted in the previous state, as shown in Figure 4(b).

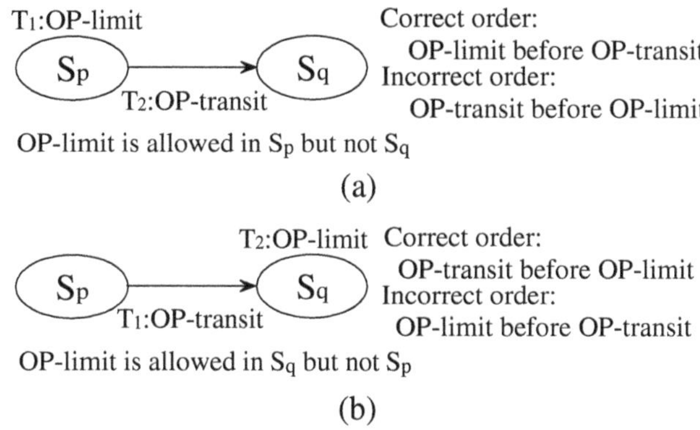


**Figure 4.** Two scenarios of bug candidates

**Algorithm 1** Analysis algorithm

```
 1: // For each incoming event evt, do the following
 2: candidates ← ∅
 3: if evt is OP-transit then
 4:     set ← QueryOPlimit(evt → objId, evt → tid,
                           evt → oldState)
 5:     matchSet ← ∅
 6:     for each OP-limit event evtPrev in set do
 7:         if NotPermitted(evtPrev, evt → newState) then
 8:             matchSet ← matchSet ∪ {evtPrev}
 9:         end if
10:     end for
11:     cands ← FormCandidates(evt, matchSet)
12: end if
13: candidates ← candidates ∪ cands
14: if evt is OP-limit then
15:     set ← QueryOPtransit(evt → objId, evt → tid,
                             evt → state)
16:     matchSet ← ∅
17:     for each OP-transit event evtPrev in set do
18:         if NotPermitted(evt, evtPrev → oldState) then
19:             matchSet ← matchSet ∪ {evtPrev}
20:         end if
21:     end for
22:     cands ← FormCandidates(evt, matchSet)
23: end if
24: candidates ← candidates ∪ cands
25: if evt is OP-transit then
26:     InsertOPtransit(evt)
27: end if
28: if evt is OP-limit then
29:     InsertOPlimit(evt)
30: end if
```

**Identifying Bug Candidates.** In order to support the on-the-fly analysis, 2ndStrike analyzer uses a one-pass algorithm that treats the incoming log as a stream. The analyzer keeps track of the typestates of each object and temporarily stores the runtime events in hash tables according to the event type and indexes them by object IDs. For a specific typestate bug, it maintains two hash tables, one for OP-transit and the other for OP-limit.

Algorithm 1 shows how 2ndStrike identifies bug candidates. For each incoming OP-transit event, the analyzer checks the OP-limit table, looking for previous OP-limit events from a different thread on the same object in its old state (line 4). Then, among the resulting OP-limit events, it looks for the ones that are not permitted in the new state to form bug candidates with the OP-transit event (line 5-11). This is for identifying bug candidates in the first scenario as shown in Figure 4(a). Similarly, for each incoming OP-limit event, the analyzer looks up the OP-transit table and identifies the OP-transit events whose previous states do not permit OP-limit to form bug candidates (line 15-22). This is for identifying bug candidates in the second scenario as shown in Figure 4(b). After forming the bug candidates, the event is stored into the corresponding tables (line 25-30). Note that one event can be both OP-transit and OP-limit, e.g., the event `Close` is OP-transit because it causes state transition from the state `OPEN` to the state `CLOSED`, and it is also OP-limit because it is only permitted in the state `OPEN`. In this case, such event will be handled twice–one as OP-transit event and the other as OP-limit event.

Some optimizations can be applied to reduce the number of events in the tables. For example, if the operations permitted in the previous state of an OP-transit include the operations permitted in the new state, the OP-transit is not kept in the table (line 26) because it will never be matched (line 18). In addition, the old events that are outside of a certain window is periodically cleaned up to reduce the memory usage and maintain table lookup efficiency. Therefore, the worst case time complexity for the algorithm is $O(N^2)$, where $N$ is the total number of operations bounded by the window size.

**Pruning False Bug Candidates.** With identified bug candidates, there could be cases where the two operations cannot be re-ordered. One main reason is that there could be strict order between the operations enforced by thread synchronization events. A technique from previous work [47] is adapted to filter out such strictly-ordered operation pairs. Specifically, 2ndStrike profiles general synchronization events, such as thread fork/join and condition variable wait/ signal. Based on this information, it computes a vector clock associated with each operation and forms happens-before relation between operations. In some cases, threads may synchronize each other in customized ways, e.g., using arbitrary shared variables as flags (See Section 4 for details), which results in false bug candidates generated by 2ndStrike. Fortunately, these false candidates will not cause false positives in our final bug reports because if a candidate cannot be manifested by 2ndStrike, it will not be reported to users. Furthermore, a recently-proposed technique [65] can help reduce false candidates by identifying such ad-hoc synchronization in a program.

2ndStrike can prune more false bug candidates by exploiting history information. The observation is that a test suite usually have many inputs and these test inputs tend to cause a similar set of false candidates in the common part of a program such as initialization. To address this issue, 2ndStrike maintains a list of bug candidates that it have attempted but failed to manifest in previous executions. These candidates are likely to be the false ones whose event orders are protected by customized synchronization. For future program execution with different test inputs, 2ndStrike prunes the bug candidates that are in the maintained history list. This design helps increasing the testing efficiency in the long run.

After pruning, 2ndStrike ranks the remaining bug candidates. Similar to previous work [47], our ranking algorithm selects the low-probability candidates since they are more likely to be hidden mistakes. More specifically, our algorithm uses a combination of two metrics, the distance between the two events and the number of occurrence of the event pair at runtime. The candidates with longer distance between two events and smaller number of occurrence are ranked higher.

### 3.4 Re-execution and Bug Manifestation

After bug candidates being generated, 2ndStrike performs one round of program re-execution for each bug candidate to try to manifest the bug. As each bug candidate consists of two events, we call them *preceding event* and *subsequent event*, reflecting the correct order in normal execution. In the re-execution, 2ndStrike attempts to reorder them by inserting delay before the preceding event.

Specifically, a bug manifesting run uses the same input for the instrumented program with the scheduling controller being activated. At each InstPt, 2ndStrike checks whether the current program location matches the program location of the preceding event in the bug candidate by comparing their InstPt ids and callsites. If they match, 2ndStrike blocks the thread on a semaphore before the operation, allows other threads to proceed as normal, and looks for the matching subsequent event at each InstPt. In addition to matching InstPt ids and callsites with the subsequent event in the bug candidate, the object id in the operation has to match the one in the delayed operation. If any thread has an event matching the subsequent event in the bug candidate, it means the previous thread would commit a typestate violation if it resumes the delayed operation. In this case, 2ndStrike unblocks the previously-blocked thread immediately after the subsequent event occurs in another thread. Additionally, 2ndStrike blocks all other threads so that the previously-blocked thread can get scheduled and commit the typestate violation. At this point, 2ndStrike successfully manifests the bug candidate. Note that 2ndStrike records the runtime information at both preceding event and subsequent event in the bug report.

It is also possible that the matching subsequent event never happens after one thread is blocked before the operation in the preceding event. This is mainly because other synchronization mechanisms such as flag variables are used in the program to prevent such reordering. In this case, 2ndStrike will unblock the previously-blocked thread and keep looking for the preceding event for this bug candidate after a certain time threshold. After a certain number of such timeouts, 2ndStrike will abort the reordering attempt and stop re-execution for this bug candidate.

## 4. Issues and Discussion

**Un-monitored synchronization.** Similar to previous active testing tools [47, 57], 2ndStrike does not monitor all possible synchronizations occurring in the program execution, especially the ones based on shared flag variables. This will cause 2ndStrike analyzer to generate some operation pairs that are impossible to be reordered as bug candidates. Although these candidates will be pruned later since 2ndStrike cannot manifest them, they do reduce the test efficiency. To address this issue, we can either ask developers for hints on their customized synchronization mechanisms or derive such information using techniques proposed in [65]. How to more accurately capture the synchronization behavior for exposing concurrency typestate bugs are left for our future work.

**Non-determinism.** Multi-threaded programs are naturally non-deterministic in their execution, which means the profiling information based on previous executions may not be valid for subsequent executions. Similar to previous active testing tools [47, 57], 2ndStrike assumes that the program execution paths at different runs are mostly the same for a given test input. In practice, unfortunately, there are certain degree of non-determinism involved in program executions especially for large complex software. Therefore, for some program executions that are very different from the profiling execution, 2ndStrike may fail to manifest the concurrency typestate bugs because the object may not be operated in the same way. To address this issue, one way is to integrate 2ndStrike with existing deterministic replay tools [15, 22] for replaying the program execution as much as possible until the scheduling change has to be made.

| App. | Bug id | Bug description |
|---|---|---|
| MySQL | MySQL-file | A file descriptor was accessed after being closed, causing assertion failure |
| MySQL | MySQL-ptr1 | An invalid pointer dereference causing crash when handling transactions |
| MySQL | MySQL-ptr2 | An invalid pointer dereference causing crash on accessing recovery objects |
| MySQL | MySQL-ptr3* | An invalid pointer dereference causing crash on accessing a freed table index |
| Mozilla | Mozilla-ptr | An invalid pointer dereference causing crash when destroying contexts |
| pbzip2 | pbzip2-lck | An invalid lock usage causing crash when decompressing a file |

**Table 1.** Evaluated applications and concurrency typestate bugs. ***MySQL-ptr3 was previously unknown and manifested by 2ndStrike**.

**Input coverage.** 2ndStrike's capability for manifesting bugs depends on test inputs. Although the ability to integrate with existing test harnesses and use existing test suites can alleviate this issue, 2ndStrike does not provide systematic coverage as model checking tools (e.g., CHESS [40]) do. To address this issue, we hope to integrate 2ndStrike with symbolic execution techniques [10, 26, 58] for generating test inputs to cover interesting program paths in the future.

**False negatives.** Although 2ndStrike guarantees there is no false positives in final results, it may have false negatives. Two main sources for false negatives are above-mentioned inadequate input coverage and non-determinism. In addition, history-based bug candidate pruning could also cause false negatives since one failed attempt to manifest a bug cannot rule out the possibility of the bug. Furthermore, users may choose to only try a limited number of bug candidates as allowed by resources, in which case users need to balance the risk of potential false negatives and the testing overhead.

## 5. Evaluation Methodology

We have implemented a prototype of 2ndStrike on Linux and conducted the experiments on a Intel Xeon machine with four 2GHz processing cores (eight logical processors with hyper-threading enabled). The L2 cache is 12MB and the DRAM size is 16GB. The Linux kernel version is 2.6.16.

We have evaluated 2ndStrike with three different types of multithreaded applications, including MySQL [1], a database server, Mozilla [2], a web browser, and pbzip2 [3], a utility program for file compression and decompression, as shown in Table 1. These applications contain six real-world concurrency typestate bugs of three different types, including invalid file operation, invalid pointer dereference, and invalid lock operation. For MySQL, we test its Falcon storage engine, a new storage engine for highly concurrent workloads. For Mozilla, we test its JavaScript engine with concurrent workloads.

To evaluate the effectiveness, we run 2ndStrike with the test inputs that can potentially trigger (but do not trigger) the bug cases. Whenever possible, we use the default testing frameworks for the applications such as `mysql-test`, and the default testing inputs such as JavaScript files provided in the Mozilla JavaScript engine release package. This allows us to evaluate how 2ndStrike integrates with existing test harnesses, which we consider as an important issue for usability. For pbzip2, since it does not have test inputs included in the package, we use a Linux kernel tarball as input (40MB bz2 file decompressed into 224MB tar file).

For comparison, we have performed a stress testing by running the tested programs with the same inputs repetitively. Furthermore, in order to evaluate whether the active testing tools proposed in RaceFuzzer [57] and CTrigger [47] are effective in detecting the bugs in tested programs, we have conducted data race detection and atomicity violation detection with the same inputs. We implement the hybrid race detection technique [45] (used by RaceFuzzer) to detect races and implement the unserializable access detection idea [33] (used by CTrigger) to detect atomicity violation.

| Bug id | 2ndStrike | Stress | Data race directed | Atomicity violation directed |
|---|---|---|---|---|
| MySQL-file | 20.4 | No | No | No |
| MySQL-ptr1 | 137.0 | 45,535 | No | No |
| MySQL-ptr2 | 103.7 | No | No | No |
| MySQL-ptr3 | 160.8 | No | No | No |
| Mozilla-ptr | 85.0 | No | No | No |
| pbzip2-lck | 9.8 | No | Yes | Yes |

**Table 2.** Overall effectiveness of 2ndStrike: The '2ndStrike' and 'Stress' columns show the time in seconds needed to manifest the bug for 2ndStrike and stress testing, respectively. 'No' means a bug cannot be manifested within 24 hours. The last two columns show whether the data race and atomicity violation directed tools can effectively manifest the bugs. 'Yes' and 'No' indicate whether they can or cannot manifest the bugs, based on experimental results from data race detection and atomicity violation detection.

To evaluate the efficiency of 2ndStrike, we have conducted experiments for measuring both profiling/analyzing overhead and bug manifesting overhead (i.e., for controlled thread interleavings). For profiling/analyzing overhead, we measure the program execution time under the following four configurations:

- Baseline, executing the programs natively without 2ndStrike.
- 2ndStrike's profiling only, executing the programs with 2ndStrike's profiling enabled, but logs not recorded (fed into `/dev/null`).
- 2ndStrike's profiling and analyzing, executing the programs with 2ndStrike profiling enabled and running the analyzer in parallel for generating bug candidates.
- Memory access profiling, executing the programs with profiling every memory access and logs not recorded. This is for comparing 2ndStrike's profiling overhead with existing active testing tools based on memory accesses.

For bug manifesting overhead, we measure the execution time for a manifesting run with the bug successfully manifested, and the execution time for bug manifesting run without bug being manifested, e.g., the tested bug candidate is not corresponding to a real bug.

Moreover, we have evaluated the reproducibility of 2ndStrike for each bug. With the bug candidate identified by 2ndStrike after initial successful manifestation, we execute the 2ndStrike in manifesting mode for 30 times to measure how well the bug can be reproduced. High reproducibility can greatly improve developers' efficiency of understanding and fixing a bug.

## 6. Experimental Results

### 6.1 Effectiveness

Table 2 describes our evaluation results on effectiveness of 2ndStrike. The second column shows the total time in seconds for profiling the program, analyzing the log, and manifesting the bug for each bug case. The third column shows the time in seconds for manifesting the bug via stress testing. 'No' in this column means

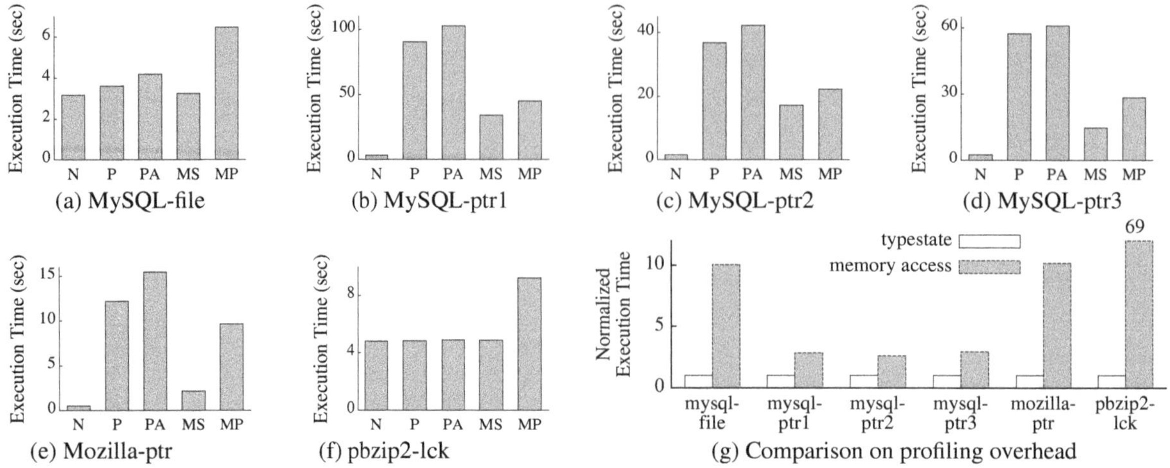


**Figure 5.** Efficiency of 2ndStrike: (a) to (f) show the performance results for 2ndStrike. (g) compares the profiling overhead for 2ndStrike with profiling every memory access. In (a) to (f), 'N' means normal execution without 2ndStrike being applied; 'P' means execution with 2ndStrike profiling only and logs are fed into `/dev/null`; 'PA' means execution with both 2ndStrike profiling and on-the-fly analysis enabled; 'MS' means bug manifesting run that successfully manifests the bug; 'MP' means bug manifesting run that passes without manifesting any bug.

the bug cannot be manifested by stress testing within 24 hours. The last two columns show whether the data race and atomicity violation directed tools can effectively manifest the bug.

Our results show that 2ndStrike is effective in manifesting the tested concurrency typestate bugs. With 2ndStrike, all six tested bugs are manifested within 160.8 seconds. The main reason of 2ndStrike's effectiveness is that it focuses on the semantic errors instead of only on memory accesses. For example, instead of only observing accesses to file descriptors and pointers, 2ndStrike considers the operations close and deallocation as OP-transit, and the operations read and dereference as OP-limit. This allows 2ndStrike to identify the potential typestate violations and manifest them during re-execution. We expect 2ndStrike enabling programmers to manifest more semantic-related bugs by manually defining or automatically inferring more application-specific typestate models.

In our experiments, 2ndStrike discovers one unknown bug referred to as MySQL-ptr3. The bug occurs when a database frontend thread is altering a table and freeing an old index, immediately followed by an operation execution and the index access from a back-end thread. This concurrency behavior does not involve traditional data races since both critical sections are protected by locks. However, it does violate the typestate property: accessing a freed index. In fact, this type of bugs can be caught more easily if 2ndStrike is based on more application-specific typestate instead of generic ones on pointers.

On the contrary, the stress testing cannot manifest five out of the six bugs, at least within 24 hours. For MySQL-ptr1, stress testing is 331 times slower than 2ndStrike for manifesting the bug. This is mainly because stress testing tend to focus on only a fraction of possible thread interleavings.

Our experimental results from data race detection and atomicity violation detection also show that the active testing tools based on them cannot manifest five of the six bugs. This is because the bug-triggering object is not involved in data races or unserializable accesses from multiple threads for these bugs. For example, in MySQL-file case, both `pread` and `close` read the file descriptor but do not write. Similarly, for the dangling pointer bugs, both dereference and deallocation only read the pointer. In fact, Mozilla-ptr was categorized as 'order violation' in a previous study [36] because it does not involve unserializable accesses to shared variables. Due to this reason, these tools are unable to manifest these five bugs. For pbzip2-lck, the data race detector can catch the error because the lock variable is involved in data race. Similarly, the unserializable access detector can also detect the error in the pbzip2-lck case. However, the profiling on every memory access incurs much larger overhead than 2ndStrike does and there are many benign data races reported by the race detector.

## 6.2 Efficiency

Figure 5 shows the detailed performance results when using 2ndStrike to manifest the six concurrency typestate bugs.

We can observe that by using typestate specific instrumentation, 2ndStrike incurs tolerable runtime overhead incurred by profiling and analysis for software testing purposes. The profiling overhead highly depends on the typestate being profiled. For example, profiling file typestate for MySQL-file and lock typestate for pbzip2-lck only incur 13% and 1% overhead, respectively. However, profiling pointer typestate incurs 22x to 27x overhead, which is largely due to frequent pointer dereference events. Figure 5 (g) compares 2ndStrike's profiling overhead with the overhead incurred by profiling every memory access. We can see that 2ndStrike profiling incurs 61% to 98% less overhead.

Moreover, the results show that 2ndStrike's on-the-fly analysis design helps reduce the profiling and analysis overhead. Performing analysis along with profiling only makes the execution time a little longer, by 1.4% to 16.1% with an average 13.2% (see column 'PA' versus column 'P'). In comparison, performing analysis alone with the log from disk takes about the same time as profiling and performing on-the-fly analysis. In addition, on-the-fly analysis totally avoids saving the log to disk, which otherwise would cause substantial space overhead for the heavy-weight typestate profiling.

Table 3 shows the detailed results on typestate-specific profiling versus memory access profiling. The second column and the third column show the number of static instrumentation points for 2ndStrike and memory access profiling, respectively. The last two columns show the number of dynamically profiled events for 2ndStrike and memory access profiling, respectively. This table clearly indicates the reason why 2ndStrike incurs small overhead for lightweight typestates such as file and lock. Taking MySQL-file as an example, 2ndStrike only instruments at 654 program locations, which combines file typestate profiling with general synchronization. On the contrary, 58,033 program locations must be instru-

| Bug id | 2ndStrike InstPt | Memory access InstPt | 2ndStrike events | Memory access events |
|---|---|---|---|---|
| MySQL-file | 654 | 58,033 | 164,702 | 12,147,265 |
| MySQL-ptr1 | 27,525 | 59,541 | 26,541,228 | 78,651,987 |
| MySQL-ptr2 | 27,379 | 59,301 | 9,522,145 | 28,381,980 |
| MySQL-ptr3 | 30,378 | 72,608 | 16,699,980 | 51,135,709 |
| Mozilla-ptr | 18,194 | 172,409 | 3,360,687 | 29,054,798 |
| pbzip2-lck | 163 | 1,479 | 11,016 | 165,005,902 |

**Table 3.** Statistics of instrumentation and runtime events by 2ndStrike in comparison with memory access instrumentation and profiling

| Bug id | Generated | After pruning | Rank |
|---|---|---|---|
| MySQL-file | 9 | 5 | 3 |
| MySQL-ptr1 | 568 | 36 | 1 |
| MySQL-ptr2 | 751 | 204 | 3 |
| MySQL-ptr3 | 2013 | 16 | 4 |
| Mozilla-ptr | 176 | 60 | 8 |
| pbzip2-lck | 11 | 11 | 1 |

**Table 4.** Effectiveness of pruning and ranking bug candidates in 2ndStrike

mented to profile memory access, which also generates orders-of-magnitudes more runtime log entries.

Pruning and ranking bug candidates is also critical to 2ndStrike's efficiency. Table 4 shows the results of pruning and ranking. The second column shows the total number of bug candidates generated. The third column shows the number of bug candidates after pruning based on the strong synchronization order and history information. The last column shows the rank of the bug-triggering candidate, or the highest rank in the case where multiple candidates can trigger the bug. We can observe that the pruning and ranking algorithm can effectively reduce the number of false bug candidates tried in re-execution, and therefore improve testing efficiency.

### 6.3 Usability

**Integration with testing framework.** 2ndStrike can be easily integrated with existing testing frameworks and inputs. It does not require source code change or special dynamic instrumentation environments. All it requires is changing the build scripts for the software component. In addition, it is flexible to be applied only to a subset of components in a large software package. In our experiments with MySQL and Mozilla, we only apply 2ndStrike to MySQL's Falcon storage engine and Mozilla's JavaScript engine. We believe that this flexibility can help developers perform more targeted testing and is very important for large software with many components.

**Bug reporting.** After manifesting a bug, 2ndStrike generates an accurate and detailed bug report, which includes following pieces of information: a) the test input that can potentially trigger the bug, b) the typestate violation manifested, c) the bug candidate, and d) the runtime 'preceding event' and 'subsequent event' that happened during bug manifesting execution. Note that since the bug is manifested when the order between the 'preceding event' and the 'subsequent event' is flipped, the 'subsequent event' actually happens first in the buggy run while the 'preceding event' happens after. For both events, the bug report includes: a) the InstPt information, which corresponds to a unique source code location, b) the runtime callsite, including multiple levels of function names, c) the thread id, and d) the object id. This information can be very helpful for developers to diagnose the bug and pinpoint the root cause.

| Bug id | MySQL-file | MySQL-ptr1 | MySQL-ptr2 |
|---|---|---|---|
| Reproduce rate | 100% | 86.67% | 93.33% |
| Bug id | MySQL-ptr3 | Mozilla-ptr | pbzip2-lck |
| Reproduce rate | 100% | 100% | 100% |

**Table 5.** Reproducibility of the manifested concurrency typestate bugs in 2ndStrike

**No false positives.** In addition, 2ndStrike reports no false positives in its final results. This is because all bug candidates that are not corresponding to real bugs are pruned automatically in the bug manifesting executions. Only the bug candidates that can trigger real concurrency typestate bugs are reported in the final results. This feature is also critical to developers, who are generally very reluctant to spend efforts in vain on spurious errors.

**Bug reproducing.** Moreover, 2ndStrike helps developers by reproducing a manifested bug easier. As shown in Table 5, a candidate of concurrency typestate bug can be reproduced by 2ndStrike with a high probability after it is being manifested once. The reason why some are not 100% reproducible is the non-deterministic nature of multi-threaded program executions (see Section 4 for details). In some of these multi-threaded program executions, the exercised code path is different from that in the profiling run.

## 7. Related Work

Our work is related to concurrent program testing, typestate bug detection, concurrency bug detection, concurrency bug diagnosis, and concurrency bug prevention or avoidance.

**Concurrent program testing.** Researchers have conducted many studies on testing concurrent programs, including generating input test cases to execute certain regions of concurrent programs [58], devising interleaving coverage criteria to measure the coverage of concurrency testing [27, 30, 34, 63, 69], and exposing potential memory level errors including data races or atomicity violation bugs [8, 39, 40, 47, 57]. Recently-proposed ConMem [75] detects concurrency bugs that can cause severe memory errors. Techniques for generating input test cases is complementary to our work for testing concurrent programs because concurrency bug manifestation requires both certain inputs and certain thread/process interleaving. Furthermore, interleaving coverage criteria can be used to guide our work for improving the coverage. As discussed in Section 1 and Section 2.2, existing active testing techniques focus on memory accesses and mainly to expose data races or atomicity violation bugs. Unlike these approaches, our work can manifest concurrency typestate bugs, ranging from the memory level (e.g., NULL pointer dereferences) to high-level program semantics (e.g., file operation errors). PCT [9] is a randomized scheduler for manifesting concurrency bugs. 2ndStrike can improve PCT by guiding the assignment of thread priorities and identifying priority change points.

**Typestate bug detection.** There are plenty of studies on detecting typestate bugs in programs. Some approaches detect typestate bugs via program analysis [18, 25, 62] or symbolic execution [17], while others checks typestate properties at runtime [6, 7, 11, 12]. These approaches are proposed for detecting typestate bugs in sequential programs.

PRETEX [28] is close to our work. It detects potential race-related typestate bugs in multi-threaded Java programs by analyzing correct program executions combined with other possible execution paths indicated by race conditions. However, it does not attempt to construct an execution to manifest the detected potential typestate bugs. Along with the fact that PRETEX is based on inferred typestate properties, it may cause a large number of false positives reported to programmers. Unlike this tool, our work attempts to manifest the non-exposed concurrency typestate bug candidates via system methods, therefore all false positives are automatically pruned. Furthermore, our work can handle the concurrency typestate bugs that are not related with race conditions. Yang et al. have proposed typestate-guide static analysis for detecting data races and atomicity violations [70]. This method may report false positives since it utilizes static methods to model threading interleavings.

**Concurrency bug detection.** Many studies have been conducted on detecting concurrency bugs, including static methods [19, 23, 54, 61] and dynamic approaches [14, 20, 43, 44, 50, 51, 56, 72] for race detection, and techniques [33, 35] for atomicity violation detection. Complementary to these detection methods, which depend on manifestation of concurrency bugs, our work helps manifest hidden concurrency bugs, belonging to the same category as previous active testing work [8, 39, 40, 47, 57].

**Concurrency bug diagnosis.** With the assistance of deterministic replay [21, 22, 41, 42, 55, 60, 66, 68] or execution sketching [48], bug diagnosis techniques such as delta debugging [13, 16, 74] and program slicing [4, 64, 76] can be used for understanding concurrency bugs. Recent work on execution synthesis [73] helps inferring a buggy input and the related thread interleaving by extracting information from coredump/callstack and the source code. Similar to concurrency bug detection tools, these diagnosis methods also depend on bug manifestation, which our work can help.

**Concurrency bug avoidance.** Recently, several studies have been proposed for avoiding concurrency bugs. Programming on transactional memory [31] prevents data races. Isolator [52] and ToleRace [53] exploit data replication to tolerate data races. Atomaid [38] leverages transactional memory for surviving atomicity violation bugs during production runs. Yu et al. have proposed a shared-memory multi-processor design to avoid untested thread interleavings that may cause concurrency bugs [71]. Dimmunix [29] prevents programs from re-encountering previously-seen deadlocks. Unlike these production-phase tools, our work is applied in testing phase.

## 8. Conclusions

In summary, this paper presents a general testing framework called 2ndStrike for manifesting concurrency typestate bugs in multi-threaded programs in the testing phase. To do so, 2ndStrike profiles runtime events that are related to object typestates described by a given state machine along with synchronization events. Then 2ndStrike identifies bug candidates by checking the profiled events against the state machine with different orders of possible thread interleavings. Finally 2ndStrike re-executes the program with controlled thread interleaving for manifesting the bug candidates.

Our evaluation of 2ndStrike prototype with six real world bugs from three open-source server and desktop programs (i.e., MySQL, Mozilla, pbzip2) has shown that 2ndStrike can effectively and efficiently manifest concurrency typestate bugs, which are otherwise difficult to be manifested using stress testing or data race/atomicity violation based active testing techniques. Additionally, 2ndStrike provides detailed bug reports and can consistently reproduce the bugs after manifesting the bugs once.

## Acknowledgments

We would like to thank David August, our shepherd, and anonymous reviewers for their insightful feedback. We also thank Min Xu for early discussions. This research is supported in part by NSF grant#CCF-0953759 (CAREER Award).

## References

[1] Mysql. `http://www.mysql.com/`.

[2] Mozilla. `http://www.mozilla.org/`.

[3] Parallel bzip2. `http://compression.ca/pbzip2/`.

[4] H. Agrawal, R. A. DeMillo, and E. H. Spafford. An execution-backtracking approach to debugging. *IEEE Software*, 8(3):21–26, 1991.

[5] G. Ammons, R. Bodík, and J. R. Larus. Mining specifications. In *POPL '02: Proceedings of the 29th ACM SIGPLAN-SIGACT symposium on Principles of Programming Languages*, 2002.

[6] M. Arnold, M. Vechev, and E. Yahav. Qvm: an efficient runtime for detecting defects in deployed systems. In *OOPSLA '08: Proceedings of the 23rd ACM SIGPLAN conference on Object-Oriented Programming Systems Languages and Applications*, 2008.

[7] P. Avgustinov, J. Tibble, and O. de Moor. Making trace monitors feasible. In *OOPSLA '07: Proceedings of the 22nd ACM SIGPLAN conference on Object-Oriented Programming Systems and Applications*, 2007.

[8] A. Bron, E. Farchi, Y. Magid, Y. Nir, and S. Ur. Applications of synchronization coverage. In *PPoPP '05: Proceedings of the tenth ACM SIGPLAN symposium on Principles and Practice of Parallel Programming*, 2005.

[9] S. Burckhardt, P. Kothari, M. Musuvathi, and S. Nagarakatte. A randomized scheduler with probabilistic guarantees of finding bugs. In *ASPLOS '10: Proceedings of the 15th International Conference on Architectural Support for Programming Languages and Operating Systems*, 2010.

[10] C. Cadar, D. Dunbar, and D. Engler. Klee: Unassisted and automatic generation of high-coverage tests for complex systems programs. In *OSDI '08: Proceedings of Operating System Design and Implementation*, 2008.

[11] P. Centonze, G. Naumovich, S. J. Fink, and M. Pistoia. Role-based access control consistency validation. In *ISSTA '06: Proceedings of the 2006 International Symposium on Software Testing and Analysis*, 2006.

[12] F. Chen and G. Roşu. Mop: an efficient and generic runtime verification framework. In *OOPSLA '07: Proceedings of the 22nd ACM SIGPLAN conference on Object-Oriented Programming Systems and Applications*, 2007.

[13] J.-D. Choi and A. Zeller. Isolating failure-inducing thread schedules. In *ISSTA '02: Proceedigns of the International Symposium on Software Testing and Analysis*, 2002.

[14] J.-D. Choi, K. Lee, A. Loginov, R. O'Callahan, V. Sarkar, and M. Sridharan. Efficient and precise datarace detection for multithreaded object-oriented programs. In *PLDI '02: Proceedings of the ACM SIGPLAN 2002 Conference on Programming Language Design and Implementation*, 2002.

[15] J. Chow, D. Lucchetti, T. Garfinkel, G. Lefebvre, R. Gardner, J. Mason, S. Small, and P. M. Chen. Multi-stage replay with crosscut. In *VEE '10: Proceedings of the 2010 ACM SIGPLAN/SIGOPS International Conference on Virtual Execution Environments*, 2010.

[16] H. Cleve and A. Zeller. Finding failure causes through automated testing. In *Proceedings of the Fourth International Workshop on Automated Debugging*, 2000.

[17] M. Das, S. Lerner, and M. Seigle. ESP: path-sensitive program verification in polynomial time. In *PLDI '02: Proceedings of the ACM SIGPLAN 2002 Conference on Programming Language Design and Implementation*, 2002.

[18] R. DeLine and M. Fahndrich. Typestates for objects. In *ECOOP '04: Proceedings of the 18th European Conference on Object-Oriented Programming*, 2004.

[19] D. L. Detlefs, K. R. M. Leino, K. Rustan, M. Leino, G. Nelson, and J. B. Saxe. Extended static checking. Technical report, TR SRC-159, COMPAQ SRC, 1998.

[20] A. Dinning and E. Schonberg. An empirical comparison of monitoring algorithms for access anomaly detection. In *PPoPP '90: Proceedings of the second ACM SIGPLAN symposium on Principles and Practice of Parallel Programming*, 1990.

[21] G. W. Dunlap, S. T. King, S. Cinar, M. A. Basrai, and P. M. Chen. Revirt: enabling intrusion analysis through virtual-machine logging and replay. In *OSDI '02: Proceedings of the 5th symposium on Operating Systems Design and Implementation*, 2002.

[22] G. W. Dunlap, D. G. Lucchetti, M. A. Fetterman, and P. M. Chen. Execution replay of multiprocessor virtual machines. In *VEE '08: Proceedings of the fourth ACM SIGPLAN/SIGOPS International Conference on Virtual Execution Environments*, 2008.

[23] D. Engler and K. Ashcraft. Racerx: effective, static detection of race conditions and deadlocks. In *SOSP '03: Proceedings of the nineteenth ACM Symposium on Operating Systems Principles*, 2003.

[24] C. Flanagan and S. N. Freund. Atomizer: a dynamic atomicity checker for multithreaded programs. In *POPL '04: Proceedings of the 31st ACM SIGPLAN-SIGACT symposium on Principles of Programming Languages*, 2004.

[25] J. S. Foster, T. Terauchi, and A. Aiken. Flow-sensitive type qualifiers. In *PLDI '02: Proceedings of the ACM SIGPLAN 2002 Conference on Programming Language Design and Implementation*, 2002.

[26] P. Godefroid, M. Y. Levin, and D. Molnar. Automated whitebox fuzz testing. In *NDSS '08: Proceedings of the 16th Annual Network and Distributed System Security Symposium*, 2008.

[27] M. Harrold and B. Malloy. Data flow testing of parallelized code. In *ICSM '92: Proceedings of International Conference on Software Maintenance*, 1992.

[28] P. Joshi and K. Sen. Predictive typestate checking of multithreaded jave programs. In *ASE '08: Proceedings of the 23rd IEEE/ACM International Conference on Automated Software Engineering*, 2008.

[29] H. Jula, D. Tralamazza, C. Zamfir, and G. Candea. Deadlock immunity: Enabling systems to defend against deadlocks. In *OSDI '08: Proceedings of the 8th USENIX Symposium on Operating Systems Design and Implementation*, 2008.

[30] P. V. Koppol and K.-C. Tai. An incremental approach to structural testing of concurrent software. In *ISSTA '96: Proceedings of the 1996 ACM SIGSOFT International Symposium on Software Testing and Analysis*, 1996.

[31] J. R. Larus and R. Rajwar. Transactional memory. *Morgan & Claypool*, 1(1):1–226, 2006.

[32] C. Lattner and V. Adve. Llvm: A compilation framework for lifelong program analysis & transformation. In *CGO '04: Proceedings of the International Symposium on Code Generation and Optimization*, 2004.

[33] S. Lu, J. Tucek, F. Qin, and Y. Zhou. Avio: detecting atomicity violations via access interleaving invariants. In *ASPLOS '06: Proceedings of the 12th International Conference on Architectural Support for Programming Languages and Operating Systems*, 2006.

[34] S. Lu, W. Jiang, and Y. Zhou. A study of interleaving coverage criteria. In *ESEC-FSE companion '07: The 6th Joint Meeting on European software engineering conference and the ACM SIGSOFT symposium on the Foundations of Software Engineering*, 2007.

[35] S. Lu, S. Park, C. Hu, X. Ma, W. Jiang, Z. Li, R. A. Popa, and Y. Zhou. Muvi: automatically inferring multi-variable access correlations and detecting related semantic and concurrency bugs. In *SOSP '07: Proceedings of twenty-first ACM SIGOPS Symposium on Operating Systems Principles*, 2007.

[36] S. Lu, S. Park, E. Seo, and Y. Zhou. Learning from mistakes: a comprehensive study on real world concurrency bug characteristics. In *ASPLOS '08: Proceedings of the 13th International Conference on Architectural Support for Programming Languages and Operating Systems*, 2008.

[37] B. Lucia and L. Ceze. Finding concurrency bugs with context-aware communication graphs. In *Micro'09: Proceedings of the 42nd Annual IEEE/ACM International Symposium on Microarchitecture*, 2009.

[38] B. Lucia, J. Devietti, K. Strauss, and L. Ceze. Atom-aid: Detecting and surviving atomicity violations. In *ISCA '08: Proceedings of the 35th International Symposium on Computer Architecture*, 2008.

[39] M. Musuvathi and S. Qadeer. Iterative context bounding for systematic testing of multithreaded programs. In *PLDI '07: Proceedings of the 2007 ACM SIGPLAN conference on Programming Language Design and Implementation*, 2007.

[40] M. Musuvathi, S. Qadeer, T. Ball, and G. Basler. Finding and reproducing heisenbugs in concurrent programs. In *OSDI '08: Proceedings of the 8th USENIX Symposium on Operating Systems Design and Implementation*, 2008.

[41] S. Narayanasamy, G. Pokam, and B. Calder. Bugnet: Continuously recording program execution for deterministic replay debugging. In *ISCA '05: Proceedings of the 32nd annual International Symposium on Computer Architecture*, 2005.

[42] S. Narayanasamy, C. Pereira, and B. Calder. Recording shared memory dependencies using strata. In *ASPLOS '06: Proceedings of the 12th International Conference on Architectural Support for Programming Languages and Operating Systems*, 2006.

[43] R. H. B. Netzer and B. P. Miller. Improving the accuracy of data race detection. In *PPoPP '91: Proceedings of the third ACM SIGPLAN symposium on Principles and Practice of Parallel Programming*, 1991.

[44] R. O'Callahan and J.-D. Choi. Hybrid dynamic data race detection. In *PPoPP '03: Proceedings of the ninth ACM SIGPLAN symposium on Principles and Practice of Parallel Programming*, 2003.

[45] R. O'Callahan and J.-D. Choi. Hybrid dynamic data race detection. In *PPoPP '03: Proceedings of the ninth ACM SIGPLAN symposium on Principles and Practice of Parallel Programming*, 2003.

[46] C.-S. Park and K. Sen. Randomized active atomicity violation detection in concurrent programs. In *FSE '08: Proceedings of the 16th ACM SIGSOFT International Symposium on Foundations of Software Engineering*, 2008.

[47] S. Park, S. Lu, and Y. Zhou. CTrigger: exposing atomicity violation bugs from their hiding places. In *ASPLOS '09: Proceeding of the 14th International Conference on Architectural Support for Programming Languages and Operating Systems*, 2009.

[48] S. Park, Y. Zhou, W. Xiong, Z. Yin, R. Kaushik, K. H. Lee, and S. Lu. Pres: probabilistic replay with execution sketching on multiprocessors. In *SOSP '09: Proceedings of the ACM SIGOPS 22nd Symposium on Operating Systems Principles*, 2009.

[49] S. Park, R. W. Vuduc, and M. J. Harrold. Falcon: Fault localization in concurrent programs. In *ICSE'10: Proceedings of the 32nd ACM/IEEE International Conference on Software Engineering*, 2010.

[50] D. Perkovic and P. J. Keleher. Online data-race detection via coherency guarantees. In *OSDI '96: Proceedings of the Second Symposium on Operating Systems Design and Implementation*, 1996.

[51] E. Pozniansky and A. Schuster. Efficient on-the-fly data race detection in multithreaded c++ programs. In *PPoPP '03: Proceedings of the ninth ACM SIGPLAN symposium on Principles and Practice of Parallel Programming*, 2003.

[52] S. Rajamani, G. Ramalingam, V. P. Ranganath, and K. Vaswani. Isolator: dynamically ensuring isolation in comcurrent programs. In *ASPLOS '09: Proceeding of the 14th International Conference on*

*Architectural Support for Programming Languages and Operating Systems*, 2009.

[53] P. Ratanaworabhan, M. Burtscher, D. Kirovski, B. Zorn, R. Nagpal, and K. Pattabiraman. Detecting and tolerating asymmetric races. In *PPoPP '09: Proceedings of the 14th ACM SIGPLAN symposium on Principles and Practice of Parallel Programming*, 2009.

[54] K. Rustan, M. Leino, G. Nelson, and J. B. Saxe. Esc/java users manual. Technical report, Compaq Systems Research Center, 2001.

[55] Y. Saito. Jockey: a user-space library for record-replay debugging. In *AADEBUG'05: Proceedings of the sixth International Symposium on Automated Analysis-driven Debugging*, 2005.

[56] S. Savage, M. Burrows, G. Nelson, P. Sobalvarro, and T. Anderson. Eraser: a dynamic data race detector for multithreaded programs. *ACM Trans. Comput. Syst.*, 15(4):391–411, 1997.

[57] K. Sen. Race directed random testing of concurrent programs. In *PLDI '08: Proceedings of the 2008 ACM SIGPLAN conference on Programming Language Design and Implementation*, 2008.

[58] K. Sen and G. Agha. Automated systematic testing of open distributed programs. In *FASE '06: Proceedings of Fundamental Approaches to Software Engineering*, 2006.

[59] S. Shoham, E. Yahav, S. Fink, and M. Pistoia. Static specification mining using automata-based abstractions. In *ISSTA '07: Proceedings of the 2007 International Symposium on Software Testing and Analysis*, 2007.

[60] S. M. Srinivasan, S. Kandula, C. R. Andrews, and Y. Zhou. Flashback: A lightweight extension for rollback and deterministic replay for software debugging. In *Proceedings of the 2004 USENIX Technical Conference*, 2004.

[61] N. Sterling. Warlock: A static data race analysis tool. In *Proceedings of the 1993 USENIX Winter Technical Conference*, 1993.

[62] R. E. Strom and S. Yemini. Typestate: A programming language concept for enhancing software reliability. *IEEE Trans. Softw. Eng.*, 12(1):157–171, 1986.

[63] R. Taylor, D. Levine, and C. Kelly. Structural testing of concurrent programs. *IEEE Transactions on Software Engineering*, 18:206–215, 1992.

[64] M. Weiser. Programmers use slices when debugging. *Commun. ACM*, 25(7):446–452, 1982.

[65] W. Xiong, S. Park, J. Zhang, Y. Zhou, and Z. Ma. Ad hoc synchronization considered harmful. In *OSDI '10: Proceedings of the 9th USENIX Symposium on Operating Systems Design and Implementation*, 2010.

[66] M. Xu, R. Bodik, and M. D. Hill. A "flight data recorder" for enabling full-system multiprocessor deterministic replay. In *ISCA '03: Proceedings of the 30th Annual International Symposium on Computer Architecture*, 2003.

[67] M. Xu, R. Bodík, and M. D. Hill. A serializability violation detector for shared-memory server programs. In *PLDI '05: Proceedings of the 2005 ACM SIGPLAN conference on Programming Language Design and Implementation*, 2005.

[68] M. Xu, M. D. Hill, and R. Bodik. A regulated transitive reduction (rtr) for longer memory race recording. In *ASPLOS '06: Proceedings of the 12th International Conference on Architectural Support for Programming Languages and Operating Systems*, 2006.

[69] C.-S. D. Yang, A. L. Souter, and L. L. Pollock. All-du-path coverage for parallel programs. In *ISSTA '98: Proceedings of the 1998 ACM SIGSOFT International Symposium on Software Testing and Analysis*, 1998.

[70] Y. Yang, A. Gringauze, D. Wu, and H. Rohde. Detecting data race and atomicity violation via typestate-guided static analysis. Technical report, Microsoft Research, 2008.

[71] J. Yu and S. Narayanasamy. A case for an interleaving constrained shared-memory multi-processor. In *ISCA '09: Proceedings of the 36th annual International Symposium on Computer architecture*, 2009.

[72] Y. Yu, T. Rodeheffer, and W. Chen. Racetrack: efficient detection of data race conditions via adaptive tracking. In *SOSP '05: Proceedings of the twentieth ACM Symposium on Operating Systems Principles*, 2005.

[73] C. Zamfir and G. Candea. Execution synthesis: a technique for automated software debugging. In *EuroSys '10: Proceedings of the 5th European Conference on Computer Systems*, 2010.

[74] A. Zeller. Yesterday, my program worked. today, it does not. why? In *ESEC-FSE '99: The Joint Meeting on European software engineering conference and the ACM SIGSOFT symposium on the Foundations of Software Engineering*, 1999.

[75] W. Zhang, C. Sun, and S. Lu. Conmem: detecting severe concurrency bugs through an effect-oriented approach. In *ASPLOS '10: Proceedings of the fifteenth edition of ASPLOS on Architectural Support for Programming Languages and Operating Systems*, 2010.

[76] X. Zhang, R. Gupta, and Y. Zhang. Precise dynamic slicing algorithms. In *ICSE '03: Proceedings of the 25th International Conference on Software Engineering*, 2003.

# ConSeq: Detecting Concurrency Bugs through Sequential Errors

Wei Zhang[1] Junghee Lim[1] Ramya Olichandran[1] Joel Scherpelz[1] Guoliang Jin[1]
Shan Lu[1] Thomas Reps[1,2]

[1]Computer Sciences Department, University of Wisconsin–Madison [2]GrammaTech,Inc
{wzh,junghee,ramya,scherpel,aliang,shanlu,reps}@cs.wisc.edu

## Abstract

Concurrency bugs are caused by non-deterministic interleavings between shared memory accesses. Their effects propagate through data and control dependences until they cause software to crash, hang, produce incorrect output, etc. The lifecycle of a bug thus consists of three phases: (1) triggering, (2) propagation, and (3) failure.

Traditional techniques for detecting concurrency bugs mostly focus on phase (1)—i.e., on finding certain structural patterns of interleavings that are common triggers of concurrency bugs, such as data races. This paper explores a consequence-oriented approach to improving the accuracy and coverage of state-space search and bug detection. The proposed approach first statically identifies potential failure sites in a program binary (i.e., it first considers a phase (3) issue). It then uses static slicing to identify critical read instructions that are highly likely to affect potential failure sites through control and data dependences (phase (2)). Finally, it monitors a single (correct) execution of a concurrent program and identifies suspicious interleavings that could cause an incorrect state to arise at a critical read and then lead to a software failure (phase (1)).

ConSeq's backwards approach, (3)→(2)→(1), provides advantages in bug-detection coverage and accuracy but is challenging to carry out. ConSeq makes it feasible by exploiting the empirical observation that phases (2) and (3) usually are short and occur within one thread. Our evaluation on large, real-world C/C++ applications shows that ConSeq detects more bugs than traditional approaches and has a much lower false-positive rate.

***Categories and Subject Descriptors*** D.2.5 [*Testing and Debugging*]: Testing Tools

***General Terms*** Languages, Reliability

***Keywords*** Software testing, concurrency bugs

## 1. Introduction

### 1.1 Motivations

Concurrency bugs are caused by non-deterministic interleavings between shared memory accesses. They exist widely (e.g., 20% of driver bugs examined in a previous study [50] are concurrency bugs) and are among the most difficult bugs to detect and diagnose. They have caused real-world disasters such as the Therac-25 medical accident [29] and the 2003 Northeast blackout [52]. Today, they are of increasing concern due to the pervasiveness of multi-core machines. Effective approaches to detecting concurrency bugs *before* software is released are sorely desired.

Reliability research for sequential software has made tremendous progress recently [9, 17, 41]. However, these successes have not translated to the world of concurrency software, because concurrency bugs are caused by a feature (namely, interleavings) not found in sequential programs.

Interleavings are not only complicated to reason about, but they also dramatically increase the state space of software. For large real-world applications, each input easily maps to billions of execution interleavings, and a concurrency bug may only be exposed by one specific interleaving. How to analyze this huge space *selectively* and expose hidden bugs is an open problem for static analysis, model checking, and software testing.

To address this challenge, existing techniques for detecting concurrency bugs are mostly guided by certain structural patterns of interleavings that most frequently cause concurrency bugs. These patterns include data races (conflicting accesses to a shared variable) [12, 19, 42, 51, 64], simple atomicity violations (unserializable interleavings of two small code regions) [33, 44, 56, 62], context-switch bounded interleavings [7, 27, 38, 39], etc. Although much progress has been made in this direction, fundamental limitations remain:

(1) False negatives (*are there other patterns of buggy interleavings?*). Many patterns have been proposed, while common real-world bugs that cannot be covered by traditional patterns keep popping up, such as multi-variable concurrency bugs [25, 31, 34] and order violations [32, 63], as shown in Figure 1.

(2) False positives (*are these interleavings truly harmful?*). Only about 2–10% of *true* data races are harmful [8, 40]. A similar rate holds for other interleaving patterns [44, 66]. Although innovative training [11, 31, 33] and testing [39, 44, 53] can mitigate this problem, lots of machine time and manual effort can be wasted on false positives.

(3) User unfriendliness. Interleavings are complicated to reason about. It is usually difficult for developers to judge whether a suspicious-looking interleaving snippet is truly a bug, and if so, how severe it is. Some commercial bug-detection tools choose not to flag concurrency errors solely because the reported buggy interleavings are too difficult to explain to developers [5]!



*ASPLOS'11,* March 5–11, 2011, Newport Beach, California, USA.

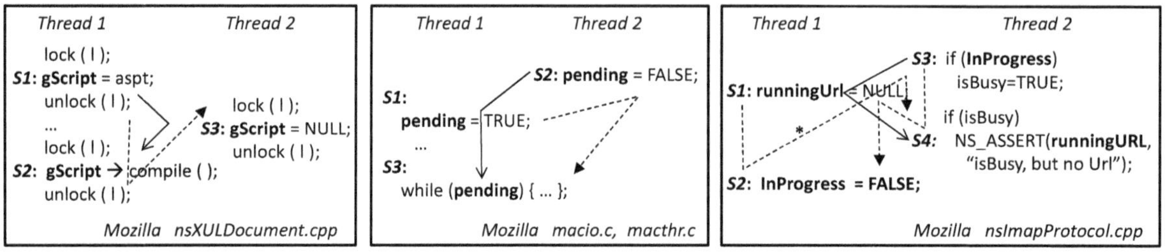


(a) This bug is not a race; it is an atomicity violation [33,56] ⟶ (b) This bug is not atomicity violation or race; it is an order violation [32] ⟶ (c) This is not a traditional bug; it is a multi-variable synchronization problem [31,35]

**Figure 1.** Bugs caused by various types of interleavings. (Solid and dotted arrows represent incorrect and correct interleavings, respectively. *: In (c), S1→S2→S3→S4 is a correct and feasible execution order, because `InProgress` could be set to TRUE and `runningURL` to a non-NULL URL string in between the execution of S2 and S3 by code not shown in the figure.)

### 1.2 Going beyond interleavings

ConSeq uses potential software failures to guide its search of the interleaving space. It uses a consequence-oriented approach to bug detection, which starts from the following observation [1]:

> *Concurrency and sequential bugs have drastically different causes but have mostly similar consequences.*

For example, the three bugs in Figure 1 all start with complicated interleavings, which cannot be detected by many existing detectors [31], and end up as common errors and failures similar to sequential bugs. The bug in Figure 1(a) is caused by an atomicity violation and cannot be detected by race detectors [33]; it causes a NULL-pointer dereference, and crashes in thread 1. The bug in Figure 1(b) is caused by an order violation: S2 could unexpectedly execute before S1, in which case the `FALSE` value of `pending` would be overwritten too early. This problem cannot be fixed by locks, and cannot be correctly detected by atomicity-violation or race detectors [32]. It causes an infinite loop in thread 1. The bug in Figure 1(c) has a different cause from the above two bugs. Since S1→S2→S3→S4 and S3→S4→S1→S2 are both correct interleavings, the specific order between S1's and S4's accesses to `runningUrl` is not responsible for the software failure. Similarly, the specific order between S2 and S3 does not matter. It is the unsynchronized accesses to *two* correlated shared variables that lead to an assertion failure. Sophisticated multi-variable concurrency-bug detectors [31] were designed to detect this type of bug.

To better understand the above observation, Figure 2 depicts the three-phase life cycle of a concurrency bug [28, 47]. After being *triggered* by an incorrect execution order across multiple threads, a concurrency bug usually *propagates* in *one* thread through a short data/control-dependence chain, similar to one for a sequential bug [21]. The erroneous internal state is propagated until an externally visible failure occurs. At the end, concurrency and sequential bugs are almost indistinguishable: no matter what the cause, a crash is often preceded by a thread touching an invalid memory location or violating an assertion; a hung thread is often caused by an infinite loop; incorrect outputs are emitted by one thread, etc. The only major class of concurrency errors that have substantially different characteristics is deadlocks, which fortunately have been thoroughly studied [24, 57].

Given the above observation and the trouble presented by the enormous space of interleavings, we naturally ask, "How can we leverage the sequential aspects of concurrency bugs? Can we reverse the bug-propagation process and start bug detection from the potential points of failure?" This approach, if doable, has the potential to leverage common error-propagation patterns shared between concurrency and sequential bugs:

- In terms of false positives, the questions 'is this a bug?' and 'how harmful is this bug?' are easier to answer with this technique, because causing a failure is the criterion used for deciding whether or not to report a bug.
- In terms of false negatives, it can provide a nice complement to existing cause/interleaving-oriented detectors, because what ConSeq detects is not limited to any specific interleaving pattern.
- ConSeq's reports are likely to be more accessible to developers who are familiar with the effects/symptoms of sequential bugs. Moreover, developers can now contribute to the bug-detection process by writing per-thread consistency checks, and by specifying which potential failures are worth more attention.

The consequence-oriented approach to bug detection presents many challenges. Backward analysis might be straightforward for failure replay and diagnosis [1, 15, 46, 58, 65] when the failure has already occurred. However, it is much more difficult for bug-detection and testing, where we need to identify *potential* points of bugs and failures. The problem we face is more similar to proving whether a specific property in a concurrent program could be violated. This is known to be a hard problem in software verification, even when attempted on small programs, and explains why little work has been done in this direction. In this paper, we show that it is possible to apply such techniques to large, real-world C/C++ programs (with millions of lines of source code and object files tens of megabytes long).

### 1.3 Contributions

This paper proposes ConSeq, a consequence-oriented backward-analysis framework to detect concurrency bugs. ConSeq starts its detection by identifying potential failure sites in the program. It then uses static analysis and run-time information collected from correct runs to decide whether these failures could occur under other interleavings. It can automatically and accurately detect concurrency bugs—with various types of root causes—before they occur, including atomicity violations, order violations, anti-atomicity violations, multi-variable synchronization problems, and others.

To carry out consequence-oriented bug-detection, ConSeq addresses two major challenges:

**Challenge I**: how to automatically identify *potential* error sites *before* an error occurs? Naive solutions will identify either too many (theoretically, every instruction could generate or acquire an incorrect value) or too few (if limited to specific patterns) and cause accuracy and coverage problems.

To fully leverage the similarity between concurrency and sequential bugs' error/failure patterns, ConSeq statically identifies **five** types of potential error sites that cover almost all major types

[1] All the observations and characteristics mentioned here are discussed in more detail in Section 3.

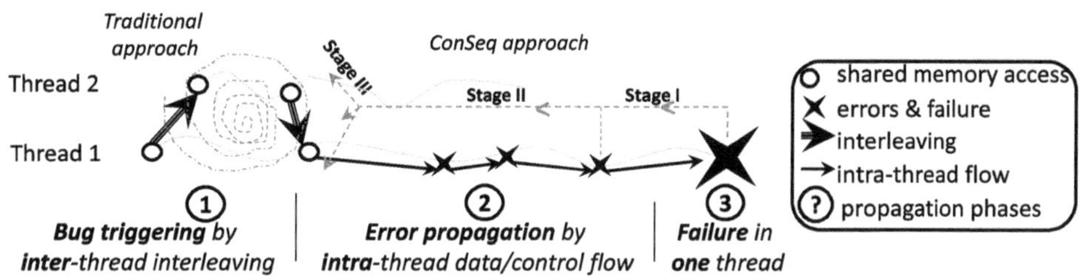


**Figure 2.** The common three-phase error-propagation process for most concurrency bugs.

| Concurrency Bug Propagation & Characteristics | | ConSeq Bug Detection |
|---|---|---|
| Phase 1: Triggering | •involving a small # of shared memory accesses | Step 3: Find and test suspect interleavings (trace-based synchronization analysis) |
| Phase 2: Propagation | •mostly within one thread •mostly a short distance | Step 2: Identify error-inducing reads (static program slicing) |
| Phase 3: Errors & Failures | •mostly within one thread •common error patterns | Step 1: Identify potential errors (thread-local static analysis) |

**Table 1.** Observations about concurrency bugs and corresponding components of ConSeq.

of concurrency bug failures (**Stage I** of ConSeq as shown in Figure 2):[2] (1) calls to assertions in the software (for assertion crashes); (2) back-edge in loops (for infinite loop hangs); (3) calls to output functions (for incorrect functionality failures), (4) calls to error-message functions in the software (for various types of internal errors); (5) reads on global variables where important invariants likely hold according to Daikon [17], a tool for inferring program invariants (for miscellaneous errors and failures).

**Challenge II**: how to predict whether a potential error could occur in a *future interleaving*? Checking whether a specific property can be violated in concurrent programs is an NP-hard problem [23] and cannot be used for large real-world applications.

ConSeq addresses this challenge by exploiting two characteristics of concurrency bugs: first, the error-propagation distance is usually short in terms of data/control-dependence edges [21] (more validation in Section 3); second, the cause of a concurrency bug usually involves a specific ordering of just a few (two or three) shared memory accesses [7, 32].

Specifically, ConSeq first uses static slicing to identify shared memory reads that can impact each potential error site through a short chain of control/data dependences (**Stage II** of ConSeq in Figure 2). Then, after monitoring a correct run, ConSeq uses execution-trace analysis and perturbation-based interleaving testing to explore potential non-determinism around these reads (**Stage III** of ConSeq in Figure 2). Non-determinism that could affect the values acquired at those reads and lead to eventual errors and failures will be exposed effectively.

Overall, our work makes the following contributions:

(1) We report the results of a study of concurrency bugs' error-propagation characteristics. In a sample of 70 real-world concurrency bugs, we find that most non-deadlock concurrency bugs have short propagation distances (59 out of 70). In addition, failures in most concurrency bugs involve only one thread (66 out of 70).

(2) The work provides a new perspective on concurrency-bug detection and testing, which is to start from potential consequences and work backwards. It provides alternative interpretations for some concurrency bugs with complicated causes that are difficult to detect using traditional approaches, and sets up a nice connection with sequential bug-detection research, such as Daikon [17].

(3) We present a three-stage bug-detection framework that leverages characteristics from all three phases of the concurrency-bug propagation process (Table 1). This design separates the complexity of inter-thread interleaving analysis and intra-thread propagation analysis, and makes it easy to leverage advanced static-analysis techniques, such as slicing and loop analysis. Each stage of the framework can be easily extended. In particular, programmers can assist ConSeq by putting more consistency checks into their code, such as assertions and error messages.

(4) We implemented these ideas in a bug-detection tool that can analyze one correct run of a concurrent program and detect possible bugs that could occur in the future.

We evaluated ConSeq on 11 real-world concurrency bugs in seven widely used C/C++ open-source server and client applications. Results show that ConSeq is able to detect 10 out of 11 tested concurrency bugs, which cover a wide range of root causes, from simple races and single-variable atomicity-violations to order-violations, anti-atomicity violation bugs, multi-variable synchronization problems, etc. For comparison, we evaluated a race detector and an atomicity-violation detector and found that they could only detect 3 and 4 bugs, respectively. ConSeq detects these bugs with high accuracy: it has about one-tenth the false-positive rate of the race detector and the atomicity-violation detector.

We also found 2 new bugs in Aget, 2 new bugs in Click, and one output non-determinism in Cherokee, for which bugs have not been previously reported. We found a known infinite-loop bug in a version of MySQL for which the bug had not been previously reported. Experiments in which we used ConSeq together with Daikon [17] show that ConSeq can detect complicated concurrency bugs that previous tools cannot (e.g., a bug involving 11 threads and 21 shared variables). The performance of ConSeq is suitable for in-house testing.

## 2. Background

A concurrent program's execution is a mix of inter-thread communication and intra-thread calculation. Consequently, in rough terms the error-propagation of concurrency bugs consists of three phases, as shown in Figure 3.

*Phase 1* is the triggering phase. A concurrency bug is triggered by a specific execution order among a set of shared memory accesses (referred to as a *buggy interleaving*).

*Phase 2* is the propagation phase. It starts with some read instructions that fetch problematic values from shared memory locations as a result of the buggy interleaving. In this paper, we will refer to these instructions as **critical reads**. The effect of these val-

[2] We skip two types of failures that have been thoroughly studied: deadlocks [24, 65] and crashes with memory errors [66].

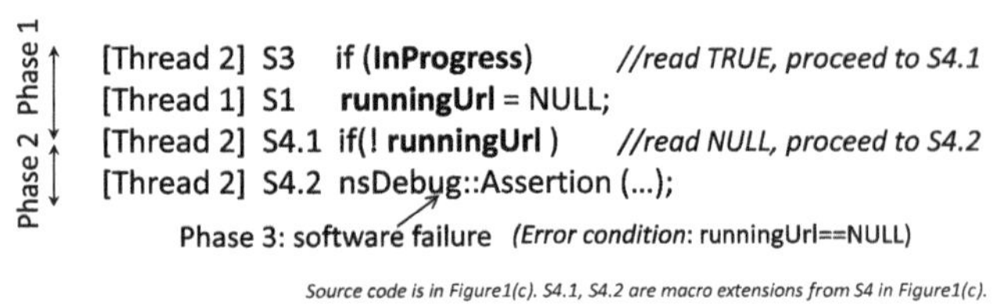


**Figure 3.** Error propagation in a concurrency bug.

ues begins to propagate, usually within one thread, through data and control dependences. Note that the corresponding thread may read many shared variables during the error-propagation phase, but only those that impact the failure through control/data dependences are considered to be 'critical'. In this paper, we measure the **distance** of error propagation through data- or control-dependence edges. During this phase, some variable values begin to deviate from the correct program state. These are called *errors*. Note that races and atomicity violations do not belong to our definition of an error.

*Phase 3* is the failure phase. Propagation leads to more severe errors, and finally to an error with an externally visible symptom (i.e., a **failure**) such as a crash or a hung process.

To simplify the discussion, the rest of the paper will refer to instructions where failures/errors occur as **failure/error sites**. We refer to the same set of instructions as **potential error/failure sites** during correct runs, because they indicate sites of errors that might occur in a different interleaving. We sometimes do not differentiate failure sites from error sites, because failures can be considered to be externally visible errors. Finally, we refer to the conditions that judge whether a program has deviated from its correct states as **error conditions**, as depicted in Figure 3.

## 3. Error-propagation study

This section reports on a study of the error-propagation process of real-world concurrency bugs, which have not been well-studied previously. The characteristics presented here have guided our design of ConSeq.

We manually studied a set of 70 non-deadlock concurrency bugs that have been collected in previous work [32] from four widely used open-source C/C++ applications (Mozilla, MySQL database server, Apache web server, and OpenOffice), and made the following observations.

<u>Observation 1</u> Concurrency bugs' failures mostly occur in one thread. This is true for 66 out of the 70 examined bugs. The only exceptions are four MySQL bugs that cause inconsistent behavior between two threads: the thread that completes a database operation first finishes its logging second. The behavior of each thread is correct. Only when comparing them with each other would we notice the misbehavior—the global log puts them in a different order from what really happened. For most bugs, propagation starts with multiple threads and ends with one thread, as shown in Figure 2.

Observation 1 implies that bug detection can be divided into separate stages of concurrency analysis and sequential analysis.

<u>Observation 2</u> The failure patterns of concurrency bugs are similar to those of sequential bugs. We see five patterns—assertion-violation, error-message, incorrect outputs, infinite loop, and memory bugs—that contribute to 65 out of 70 failures. Errors become externally visible for reasons similar to ones for sequential bugs.

Observation 2 implies that it is easy to identify potential failure sites for concurrency bugs.

<u>Observation 3</u> The propagation distance is usually short (referred to as the 'short-propagation heuristic'). For 59 out of the 70 bugs, after the last critical read, failure occurs before the current function exits. This trend is consistent across different applications and different types of failures. Of course, the distance is also frequently more than one data/control dependence step.

The rationale behind this observation is that there are usually operations within a few dependence steps that have the potential to cause an internal error to be visible externally. These include pointer operations, I/Os, and sanity checks inserted by programmers. Our observation about concurrency bugs is consistent with previous observations about other types of software/system defects [21, 30] that have guided previous work on failure recovery [49] and software replay [46].

Observation 3 implies that it is not difficult to look for causes based on consequences. Of course, we can also see that the approach of looking for causes from consequences is not a panacea for the challenges involved in detecting concurrency bugs. Those concurrency bugs that have long propagation distances will be challenging to detect.

## 4. Overview of ConSeq

As shown in Figure 4, ConSeq uses a combination of static and dynamic analyses. It uses the following modules to create an analyzer that works backwards along potential bug-propagation chains.

**Error-site identifier**: this static-analysis component processes a program binary and identifies instructions where certain errors might occur. For example, a call to `__assert_fail` is a potential assertion-violation failure site. Currently, ConSeq identifies potential error sites for five types of errors (Section 5). Developers can adjust the bug-detection coverage and performance of ConSeq by specifying specific types of error sites on which to focus.

**Critical-read identifier**: this component uses static slicing to find out which instructions that read shared memory are likely to impact a potential error site. Note that static analysis is usually not scalable for multi-threaded C/C++ programs. By leveraging the short-propagation characteristic of concurrency bugs and the staged design of ConSeq, our module is scalable to large C/C++ programs (Section 6).

**Suspicious-interleaving finder**: this dynamic-analysis module monitors one run of the concurrent program, which is usually a correct run, and analyzes what alternative interleavings could cause a critical read to acquire a different and dangerous value (Section 7). By leveraging the characteristics of concurrency bugs' root causes, this module is effective for large applications. Via this module, ConSeq generates a bug report, which provides a list of critical reads that can potentially read dangerous writes and lead to software failures. Critical reads, dangerous writes, and the potential failure sites are represented by their respective program counters in the bug report. Additionally, the stack contents are provided to facilitate programmers' understanding of the bug report.

**Suspicious-interleaving tester**: this module tries out the detected suspicious interleavings by perturbing the program's re-execution (Section 8). It helps expose concurrency bugs and thereby improves programmers' confidence in their program. Via this module, ConSeq prunes false positives from the bug report, and extends the report of each true bug with how to perturb the execution and make the bug manifest.

Note that the boundaries of ConSeq's static and dynamic analysis are not fixed. Making the bug-detection technique scalable and applicable to large C/C++ applications is a principle in ConSeq's design. ConSeq uses dynamic analysis to refine static-analysis results, and static analysis also takes feedback from run-time information.

Before diving into the technical details of ConSeq, we use the multi-variable concurrency bug shown in Figure 1(c) as an example to demonstrate the work flow of ConSeq. When we apply ConSeq to the binary of the Mozilla mail client, ConSeq's *error-site identifier* identifies 200 assertions. One of them is the instruction

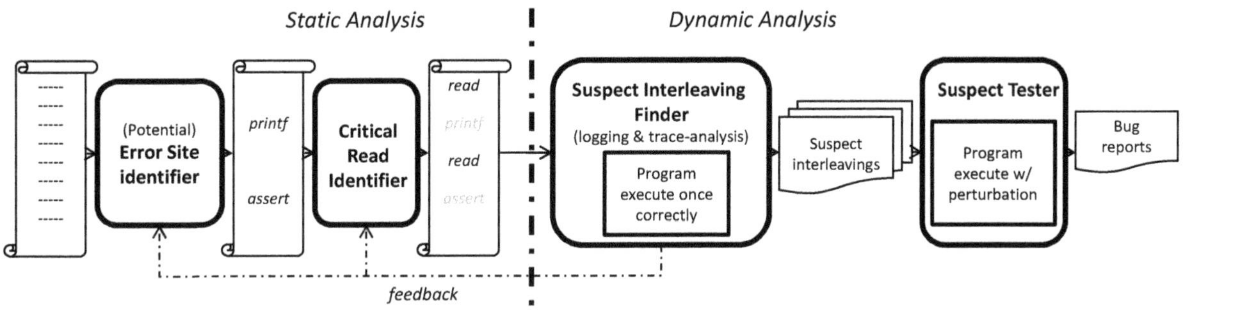


**Figure 4.** An overview of the ConSeq architecture.

0x4f81d (i.e., the assertion-failure call site corresponding to S4 in Figure 1(c)). Next, ConSeq's *critical-read identifier* statically analyzes the control/data dependences leading to each assertion identified above. In particular, instruction 0x4f7f2 (i.e., the read of `runningUrl` in statement S4 in Figure 1(c)) is identified for the assertion site 0x4f81d. The application is then executed. Not surprisingly, no error occurs during the execution. ConSeq analyzes the 31 executed critical reads one by one. It identifies an alternative interleaving that might cause instruction 0x4f7f2 to read an assertion-violating value, `NULL`, defined by instruction 0x8062e5 (S1 in Figure 1(c)). Finally, ConSeq's *suspicious-interleaving tester* executes the program again and triggers a failure. In terms of users' involvement, ConSeq only requires a user to provide one thing: a test suite. Users are also allowed to provide a list of function names of interest (such as the customized error-message function). ConSeq then will automate the whole bug-finding process described above.

## 5. Identify potential error sites

The error-site identification module has three goals: (i) to identify potential error sites automatically, (ii) to identify them before an error occurs, and (iii) to accomplish (i) and (ii) with good accuracy and coverage. This module provides the starting points for ConSeq's backward concurrency-bug detection strategy and directly affects the false-positive and false-negative rates of ConSeq. To achieve its goals, ConSeq follows two design principles:

(1) Use static analysis instead of dynamic analysis. Errors rarely occur during monitored runs of concurrent programs. Static analysis can go beyond what occurs during a single execution.

(2) Exploit the failure patterns of software bugs. Concurrency bugs, fortunately, have similar failure patterns as sequential bugs, which are well-studied and well-understood.

### 5.1 Identifying explicit failure sites

Failures of non-deadlock concurrency bugs can be covered by five patterns that they share with sequential bugs (Section 3). ConSeq identifies each pattern as follows.

**Infinite Loop**: For non-deadlock bugs, infinite loops in one thread are the main causes of hangs (an example is shown in Figure 1(b)). Every back-edge in a loop is a potential site for this type of failure. ConSeq identifies strongly connected components (SCCs) that are potential failure sites for infinite-loop hangs by checking whether any shared-memory read is included in the backward slice of each back-edge in an SCC. To identify nested loops, CodeSurfer/x86 implements *Bourdoncle*'s algorithm [6], which recursively decomposes an SCC into sub-SCCs, etc.

**Assertion Violations**: Assertion violations (Figure 1 (c)) are a major source of program crashes. Fortunately, it is a common practice of developers to place assertions in their code. Moreover, assertions are able to specify certain other types of errors. In C/C++ programs, a call to gcc's `assert` library function is translated to an if statement whose else-branch contains a call to `__assert_fail`. The call sites on `__assert_fail` are considered to be potential failure sites. Some applications use customized assertions, such as `nsDebug::Assertion` in Mozilla. ConSeq also considers those call sites to be potential failure sites.

**Memory Errors**: Invalid memory accesses are another major source of program crashes, especially in C/C++ programs (e.g., the NULL-pointer dereference shown in Figure 1(a)). ConSeq incorporates a module to identify every pointer dereference as a potential memory-error site. Because this specific type of error has been thoroughly studied in recent work [66], we focus on other types of failures and corresponding concurrency bugs in this paper.

**Incorrect Outputs**: Most non-fail-stop software failures occur when the software generates incorrect outputs or totally misses an output. ConSeq considers a call to an output function, such as `printf` and `fprintf`, as a potential incorrect-output failure site. Some applications have special output functions, such as MySQL's `BinLog::Write`. ConSeq allows developers to specify application-specific output functions in a text file. ConSeq reads the text file and identifies call sites on the specified functions.

**Error Messages (consistency-check sites)**: Consistency checks have an interesting role in concurrency bugs. They are usually **not** designed for catching synchronization bugs, and simply reflect a developer's wish to enforce some important correctness property. Luckily, however, for many complicated concurrency bugs, there are warning signs long before the ultimate failure arises. As a result, the error-propagation distance is greatly shortened and backward bug-detection becomes much easier due to error messages. *Writing such consistency checks has been a common practice of programmers for a long time [28], and the presence of consistency checks can greatly help the approach taken by ConSeq.*

ConSeq identifies calls to functions that print error messages as potential failure sites. These include both library functions, such as `fprintf(stderr,...)`, and application-specific routines, such as the `NS_WARNING` in Mozilla and `tr_err` in Transmission (a BitTorrent client). ConSeq allows developers to specify these error-reporting functions in a file. ConSeq reads this file and identifies call sites on all these functions. In our experience, most applications only have a few (usually just one or two) error-reporting routines. Therefore, we believe it will not be a big burden for developers to write down these functions.

In the case of assertion failures and error messages, a condition that indicates whether the value acquired at a given site is correct or not is obtained as a by-product. This condition is used to improve the accuracy of ConSeq's bug-detection capabilities (Section 7).

### 5.2 Inferring implicit error sites

As discussed above, consistency checks added by developers are very helpful in ConSeq's method for bug detection. What if developers did not provide any consistency checks?

Interestingly, a lot of research on sequential programs has faced this problem before, and some solutions have been proposed. For instance, Daikon [17] is a tool that infers likely program invariants based on evidence provided by (correct) training runs. Daikon's most advanced features allow for inference among derived variables, as well as set relations and arithmetic relations between array elements. In this respect, Daikon can automatically provide information that is similar to the consistency checks manually added by developers. We can treat those places where Daikon identifies program invariants to be potential error sites.

Specifically, we first apply Daikon to the target software. Daikon's frontend logs run-time variable values at program points selected by Daikon. Daikon's backend processes the log and outputs a list of {program-point, invariant} pairs.

ConSeq checks every global read instruction $I$ that reads global variable $v$. If Daikon has identified an invariant involving $v$ right before $I$, ConSeq identifies $I$ as a potential invariant-violation site.

One implementation challenge we encountered is that the default frontend, kvasir-dtrace, of Daikon's academic version only collects information at function entries and exits. As a result, we cannot obtain invariants at the granularity of individual instructions. With the help of the Daikon developers, we tried two ways to get around this problem. For small applications in our experiments, we manually inserted dummy functions before every global-variable read. For large applications in our experiments, we replaced Daikon's default front-end with our own PIN tool. This PIN tool collects run-time information before every global-variable read, and outputs this information in the input format used by kvasir-dtrace. By this means, the Daikon backend can process the Pin tool's output and generate invariants.

For large applications, one potential concern is that Daikon could identify a huge number of invariants, which could impose a large burden on ConSeq's critical-read identifier, suspicious-interleaving finder, and suspicious-interleaving tester. Fortunately, Daikon provides ranking schemes [18] to identify important invariants. ConSeq leverages the ranking mechanism to focus on the most important invariants.

In summary, ConSeq currently focuses on five types of potential failure/error sites. Except for the potential error sites inferred by Daikon, all sites are identified by statically analyzing the program.

# 6. Identifying critical reads

The goal of the critical-read identification module is to identify *critical-read* instructions that are likely to impact potential error sites through data/control dependences. It uses static slicing to approximate (in reverse) the second propagation phase of a concurrency bug, as shown in Figure 2. There are two major design principles for this module:

1. Use *static* analysis rather than dynamic analysis to identify which instructions *may* affect an error site. ConSeq is different from failure-diagnosis tools. It aims to expose concurrency bugs **without any knowledge of how they may arise or even if they exist**, so its analysis cannot be limited to any specific monitored run. Specifically, ConSeq uses *static slicing* for this purpose.
2. Only report instructions with short propagation distances as critical reads. Computing the complete program slice, e.g., all the way back to an input, is complicated and also unnecessary for ConSeq. ConSeq leverages the short-propagation characteristic of concurrency bugs (Section 3) to improve bug-detection efficiency and accuracy.

## 6.1 General issues

We had to make several design decisions that are general to all types of error sites:

*Must critical-read instructions access shared memory?* Instructions that read thread-local variables could be of interest for sequential bug detection, but not for concurrency bug detection, because their values cannot be directly influenced by interleavings. To get rid of these instructions, ConSeq first uses static analysis to filter out as many stack accesses as possible. ConSeq's run-time monitoring will proceed to prune out the rest of the stack accesses. Of course, it is possible for threads to share values using the stack, although it is rare in practice. Escape analysis would be able to identify these special stack accesses, and make ConSeq more accurate. We leave this as future work.

*Shall we consider inter-thread control/data dependences?* Multi-thread static slicing is much more difficult than single-thread slicing. Fortunately, because ConSeq's design separates the propagation steps in a concurrency bug into inter-thread and intra-thread phases, here only single-thread dependence analysis is needed to identify critical reads. All analyses involving multi-thread interleavings will be conducted in the suspicious-interleaving finder (Section 7).

*How to set the propagation-distance threshold?* In accordance with the short-propagation heuristic, ConSeq only reports read instructions whose return values can affect the error sites through a short sequence of data/control dependences. Our static-slicing tool provides the slice, together with the value of the shortest distance to the starting point of the slice, for each instruction of the slice. An example is shown in Figure 5. ConSeq provides a tunable threshold *MaxDistance* for users to control the balance between false negatives and false positives. By default, ConSeq uses 4 as *MaxDistance*. A detailed evaluation is presented in Section 10. We will explore other metrics for propagation distance in the future.

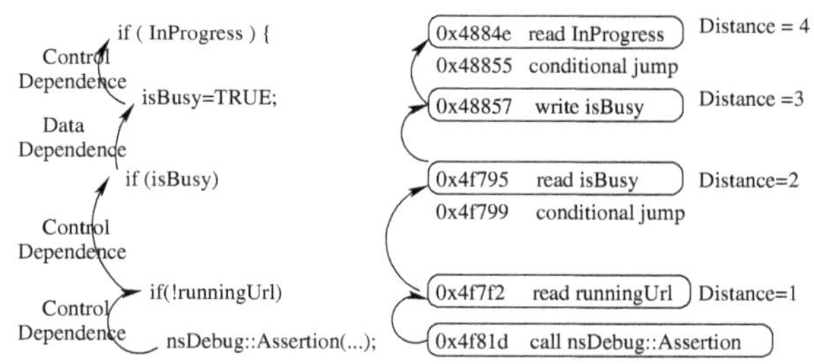


**Figure 5.** Static slicing of machine code (right) and the distance calculation.

*How to reuse the analysis results across inputs?* Because ConSeq uses static instead of dynamic analyses, the results from this module, as well as those from the error-site identifier, can be reused for different inputs. Our current static slicer analyzes one object file at a time. To speed up the analysis when there are only a few inputs, we first process those object files that these inputs would touch.

**Customization for different types of error sites**

ConSeq customizes the analysis for each type of error site:

- Each consistency-check error site is a 'call' instruction that calls a standard or custom error-reporting routine. ConSeq directly applies slicing for that instruction. For a 'call' instruction, the first step backward is always through a control dependence, followed by a sequence of control and data dependences.
- Each assertion-failure site is a 'call' to the `__assert_fail` library routine. We handle it in the same way as a consistency-check error site.
- Each invariant-violation failure site is an instruction that reads heap or global variables. No customization is needed. ConSeq directly applies control-and-data slicing for each of these instructions.
- Each incorrect-output site is a '`call`' instruction to output functions. Before applying static slicing, we first use a simple

static analysis to identify all instructions that push argument values onto the stack (sometimes via `push` and sometimes via `mov`).[3] We add those instructions into the slice (at distance 1) and apply slicing to these instructions and the original `call`

- Each infinite-loop site involves a jump instruction that conditionally jumps out of a loop. Among instructions that are on the slice, we only keep those that are repeatedly executed inside the loop body, because only those instructions could lead to the loop executing repeatedly.

### 6.2 Static slicing details

*Program slicing* is an operation that identifies semantically meaningful decompositions of programs, where the decompositions may consist of elements that are not textually contiguous [59]. A *backward slice* of a program with respect to a set of program elements $S$ consists of all program elements that might affect (either directly or transitively) the values of the variables used at members of $S$. Slicing is typically carried out using *program dependence graphs* [22].

**CodeSurfer/x86.** ConSeq uses backward slicing to identify shared memory reads that might impact each potential error site. To obtain the backward slice for each potential error site, it uses CodeSurfer/x86 [2], which is a static-analysis framework for analyzing the properties of x86 executables. Various analysis techniques are incorporated in CodeSurfer/x86, including ones to recover a *sound approximation* to an executable's variables and dynamically allocated memory objects [3]. CodeSurfer/x86 tracks the flow of values through these objects, which allows it to provide information about control/data dependences transmitted via memory loads and stores.

**Side-Stepping Scalability Problems.** To avoid the possible scalability problems that can occur with CodeSurfer/x86 due to the size of the applications used in evaluating ConSeq, we set the starting point of each analysis in CodeSurfer/x86 to the entry point of the function to which a given potential error site belongs, instead of the main entry point of the program. By doing so, CodeSurfer/x86 only needs to analyze the functions of interest and their transitive calls rather than the whole executable. Thus the static analyses time grows roughly linearly in the number of functions that contain error sites. This makes ConSeq much more scalable, as will be illustrated in Section 10.

This approach is applicable in ConSeq because—based on the observation that the error-propagation distance is usually short, as discussed in Section 3—ConSeq only requires a *short* backward slice that can be covered in one procedure. The backward-slicing and other analysis operations in CodeSurfer/x86 are, however, still context-sensitive and *interprocedural* [22]. Moreover, to obtain better precision from slices, each of the analyses used by CodeSurfer/x86 is also performed interprocedurally: calls to a subprocedure are analyzed with the (abstract) arguments that arise at the call-site; calls are not treated as setting all the program elements to $\top$.

**Analysis Accuracy.** To obtain static-analysis results that over-approximate what can occur in any execution run, all the program elements (memory, registers, and flags) in the initial state with which each analysis starts are initialized to $\top$, which represents any value. Such an approximation makes sure that no critical read will be missed by ConSeq at run time. Of course, some instructions could be mistakenly included in the backward slice and be wrongly treated as critical reads. Fortunately, our short-propagation-distance heuristic minimizes the negative impact of over-approximation. In practice, we seldom observe the inaccuracy caused by this over-approximation.

Finally, the CodeSurfer/x86 framework has information about every direct calls' call-sites. Therefore, if needed, it can also support backward slicing that starts at the entry of a procedure and backs up into the callers.

[3] Figuring out the parameters to a call in the binary is easy for the CDECL calling convention. If we need to process GCC __fastcalls, we will need to go back to analyzing the source code. The current implementation of ConSeq does not handle __fastcalls.

## 7. Identifying suspicious interleavings

The module for finding suspicious interleavings focuses on the first phase of concurrency-bug propagation. ConSeq monitors a program's (correct) execution, collects a trace using binary instrumentation, and analyzes the trace to decide whether a different interleaving could change the dynamic control/data dependence graph and generate a potentially incorrect value at a critical read.

Because it is impractical to check all potential interleavings and all potential dynamic control/data dependence graphs [23], ConSeq leverages the short-propagation characteristic (Section 3) and the widely used shallow-depth heuristic (i.e., the manifestation of most concurrency bugs involves only two or three shared-memory accesses) [7, 38, 39, 44]. It examines writes that are *one data-dependence step backward* from each critical read $r$, and looks for suspicious interleavings that could make $r$ obtain a potentially incorrect value written by a write access that is different from the one that occurred in the monitored run. The algorithm in ConSeq is neither sound nor complete. Rather, ConSeq tries to balance generality, simplicity, and accuracy.

### 7.1 The core analysis

We formalize the key question this portion of ConSeq has to answer as follows: in a concurrent program's execution trace $T$, a read instruction $r$ gets a value defined by a write access $w$; we ask whether $r$ can read a value defined by a different write $w'$ in an alternative interleaving.

To realize a $w'$–$r$ data-dependence, three conditions have to be satisfied. First, $w'$ and $r$ need to access the same memory location $m$. This condition is fairly easy to check, as long as ConSeq records the addresses of the locations touched by memory accesses.

Second, $w'$ needs to execute before $r$. This condition can be prohibited by barrier-style synchronizations. Therefore, ConSeq monitors `pthread_create/join`, `pipe`, and `barrier` at run-time to maintain vector-clock time-stamps for each thread and hence each access. A $w'$–$r$ dependence is infeasible if $r$ has a smaller time-stamp than $w'$. ConSeq computes the vector-clock time-stamps in a similar way as traditional happens-before race detectors [42]. ConSeq does not update time-stamps according to `lock/unlock` operations, because these operations do not provide any execution-order guarantees.

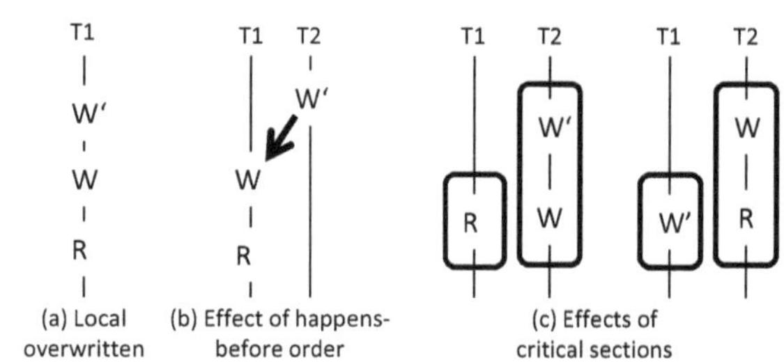


**Figure 6.** A value written by W' may never reach R

Third, the value written by $w'$ to $m$ is not overwritten before it reaches $r$. There are three situations in which an overwrite always happens, as demonstrated in Figure 6. The first is due to intra-thread program logic, when there is another write $w$ to $m$ between $w'$ and $r$ in the same thread as shown in Figure 6(a). The second is due to barrier-style synchronization, as shown in Figure 6(b). That is, synchronization operations, such as `barrier` or `pthread_create/join`, force $w'$ to always execute before another write $w$ and $w$ to always execute before $r$. The third is due to mutual exclusion, as shown in Figure 6(c). When $w'$ is followed by $w$ in a critical section from which $r$ excluded, the result of $w'$ can never reach $r$. The situation is similar when $r$ is preceded by $w$ in a critical section from which $w'$ is excluded. As long as the trace includes sufficient information about lock operations, ConSeq can analyze all of these situations.

Pseudo-code for the method described above is given as Algorithm 1.

**Algorithm 1** ConSeq identify suspicious interleavings

**Require:** write access $w$
**Require:** write access $w'$
**Require:** read access $r$
**Require:** $w$,$w'$,$r$ access the same shared memory address
**Ensure:** return true if r can read a value from $w'$, false if not

/*
Time-stamp comparison is based on the happens-before relationship and vector-clock time-stamps
*/
**if** $r$.time-stamp $<$ $w'$.time-stamp **then**
  /*$r$ happens before $w'$ */
  **return** false
**end if**
**if** $w'$.time-stamp $<$ $w$.time-stamp $<$ $r$.time-stamp **then**
  /*$w'$ is overwritten by $w$ */
  **return** false
**end if**
**if** $w$ is executed before $r$ in a critical section $CS1$, $w'$ is in critical section $CS2$, $CS1$ and $CS2$ are from different threads, **and** $CS1$ is mutually exclusive from $CS2$ **then**
  **return** false
**end if**
**if** $w'$ is executed before $w$ in a critical section $CS1$, $r$ is in critical section $CS2$, $CS1$ and $CS2$ are from different threads, **and** $CS1$ is mutually exclusive from $CS2$ **then**
  /*$w'$ is overwritten by $w$ */
  **return** false
**end if**
/*Report feasible in all the other cases */
**return** true

### 7.2 The complete algorithm and extensions

ConSeq uses binary instrumentation to monitor three types of operations at run-time: critical-read instructions, instructions that write global and heap variables, and synchronization operations. For each memory-access instruction, ConSeq records the program counter, the address of the accessed memory, and the value of the accessed memory location before the read or after the write. For each lock operation (`pthread_mutex_(un)lock`), ConSeq records the address of the lock variable. For each barrier-style synchronization (`pthread_create/join`, `pipe`, `barrier`,etc.), ConSeq updates the vector time-stamps of every thread. ConSeq uses one trace file for each thread to avoid slow global synchronization. Given these pieces of information, ConSeq can easily analyze the trace and find out all feasible $w'$–$r$ dependences.

ConSeq also extends the basic algorithm in three ways.

First, ConSeq records the values read by $r$ and written by $w'$ during the correct run, denoted by $v'$ and $v$, respectively. If the two values are the same, ConSeq does not report a suspicious interleaving. To further prune false positives, ConSeq also evaluates $v'$ against the assertion/error-condition before reporting a suspicious interleaving, using a symbolic-execution module inside ConSeq.

Second, the basic algorithm cannot be directly applied for detecting infinite loops. Suppose that $r$ is a critical read that is associated with a potential infinite-loop site. During the monitored run, ConSeq records the write $w$ and its value $v$ that are read by the last dynamic instance of $r$ right before the loop terminates. Now suppose that the basic algorithm identifies an alternative interleaving in which this specific instance of $r$ can receive a different value from an alternative write $w'$. This condition is insufficient to conclude that this interleaving is suspicious. If $w$ is executed after $w'$, another instance of $r$ in a later iteration of the loop can still receive $v$ from $w$ and terminate the loop. Therefore, for each alternative write $w'$ identified by the basic algorithm, ConSeq further compares the happens-before time-stamps between $w$ and $w'$. An infinite-loop suspect is reported when $w'$ is strictly ordered after $w$ and when $w'$ is concurrent with $w$.

Third, interleavings could make a critical read $r$ execute too early and receive an uninitialized value. ConSeq also reports these cases as suspicious interleavings.

**Discussion.** There are several sources of inaccuracy in our analysis that can cause false positives and negatives. One is that the value written by a write $w'$ might vary in different runs. Another is that interleavings could change the control flow and cause inaccuracy of our analysis. Finally, ad-hoc synchronization has been a problem for almost all predictive concurrency-bug-detection tools. We leverage our static analysis component, which identifies loops, back-edge jumps, and backward slices of back-edge jumps, to identify one type of common ad-hoc synchronization (one thread spins on a while-flag to wait for another thread). The identification algorithm is similar to previous work [61]. After identifying this type of ad-hoc synchronization, ConSeq treats occurrences as traditional barrier-style synchronizations.

## 8. Exercising suspicious interleavings

The input to ConSeq-tester, the module for testing suspicious interleavings, is a list of data dependences, represented as write/read pairs ($w_{bad}$–$r$). The goal is to exercise suspicious interleavings that can realize these suspicious data dependences, so that we can either reliably trigger the bugs or prune them as false positives.

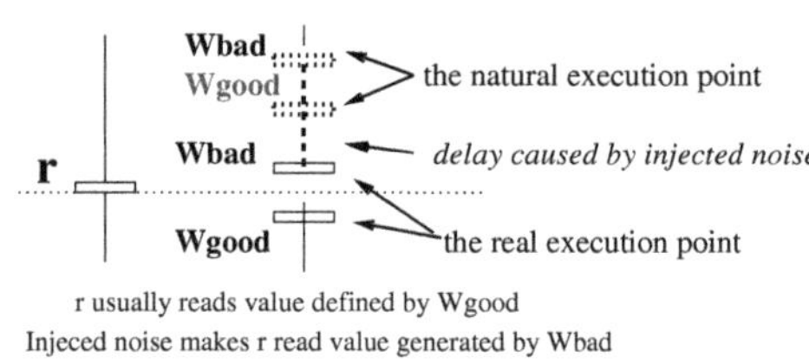


**Figure 7.** Exercising a suspicious interleaving.

To achieve this goal, ConSeq uses a testing technique that has been used in several previous bug-detection tools [44, 53]. Specifically, ConSeq instruments the program binary and inserts conditional delays with time-outs before every $r$ and $w_{bad}$ instructions. ConSeq then re-executes the program with the original input. Because ConSeq is used during in-house testing, the input is available. At run time, the instrumented code either suspends for a while the thread that is going to execute $w_{bad}$, to wait for the arrival of $r$ in another thread, or suspends for a while the thread that is going to execute $r$, to wait for the arrival of $w_{bad}$. When both $w_{bad}$ and $r$ are ready to execute, the instrumented code will force the program to execute $w_{bad}$ immediately followed by $r$. Therefore, the probability that those $w_{bad}$–$r$ dependences occur is significantly improved. An example of how ConSeq-tester exercises a suspicious interleaving is shown in Figure 7.

We have encountered two interesting issues in ConSeq.

First, $w_{bad}$ and $r$ might be from the same thread. The basic scheme shown in Figure 7 does not work for this case, because ConSeq will not see $r$ coming when it blocks a $w_{bad}$ operation that is from the same thread as $r$. ConSeq's suspicious-interleaving identification module marks these cases during trace analysis. During testing, instead of blocking $w_{bad}$, ConSeq will let it proceed and block any following writes that touch the same memory location that $w_{bad}$ accesses, until $r$ is executed. Second, sometimes $w_{bad}$ and $r$ are protected by the same lock. In those cases, ConSeq inserts a delay before the thread enters the corresponding critical section.

Like many previous concurrency-bug validation tools [40, 44, 66], ConSeq can significantly increase the probability that a concurrency bug manifests, but it cannot provide a 100% guarantee to provoke every bug. In Section 10, however, we will see that ConSeq performs well in practice.

# 9. Experimental Methodology

| Bug-ID | Symptoms | Application | LOC |
|---|---|---|---|
| Aget1* | Wrong output | Aget-0.4.1 | 1.1K |
| FFT | Wrong output | FFT | 1.2K |
| MySQL1 | Miss log | MySQL-4.0.12 | 681K |
| Moz1 | Assertion | Mozilla-1.7 | 1.2M |
| MySQL2 | Assertion | MySQL-4.0.16 | 654K |
| Trans | Assertion | Transmission | 95K |
| Moz2 | Error message | Mozilla JS-1.5 | 87K |
| Moz3 | Error message | Mozilla | N/A |
| MySQL3 | Error message | MySQL-5.0.16 | 1.6M |
| MySQL4 | infinite-loop | MySQL-5.0.41 | 1.6M |
| OO | infinite-loop | OpenOffice | N/A |
| Cherokee-0.99.48*, web server | | | 96K |
| Click-1.8.0*, modular router | | | 290K |

**Table 2.** Applications and Bugs (Mozilla-JS is the Mozilla Javascript Engine; Cherokee-0.99.48 and Click-1.8.0 are both the latest versions and previously had no known buggy inputs; Moz3 and OO are extracted from old versions of Mozilla and OpenOffice that can no longer compile. ***:ConSeq detected new bugs in Aget, Cherokee, and Click.**)

ConSeq's dynamic modules are implemented using the PIN [37] binary-instrumentation framework. The experiments are carried out on an 8-core Intel Xeon machine running Linux version 2.6.18.

We evaluated ConSeq on 8 widely used C/C++ applications. This includes two server applications (the MySQL database and the Cherokee web server), two client applications (Transmission BitTorrent client and Mozilla), two desktop applications (Aget file downloader and OpenOffice), one router (Click [13]), and one scientific application kernel (FFT [60]).

Input design is usually out of the scope of dynamic bug detection [33, 51] and interleaving testing [39, 44, 53], and ConSeq is no different. The intended usage scenario is that ConSeq will be applied to a test suite during in-house testing to expose hidden interleaving errors from (apparently) non-buggy runs on inputs provided by developers or testers. Our experiments were designed to provide insight on the following two questions:

(1) Can ConSeq handle a wide range of types of concurrency bugs? To address this question, and to evaluate ConSeq's bug-detection capability in comparison with traditional bug-detection tools, we used a large set of concurrency bugs that cover different failure symptoms from different applications. In particular, we took 11 concurrency bugs—which cover assertion failures, hangs, wrong outputs, and error-message problems—from the change logs and bug databases of 6 applications (the first 11 lines of Table 2). In these experiments, to drive ConSeq's bug-detection process we used inputs that were known to have the *potential* of triggering the bug. Our experiments did not leverage any information about the bugs, other than the known inputs. In fact, **none** of the bugs *ever* manifested during the runs that ConSeq performs to generate execution traces for subsequent bug-detection analysis. This methodology is consistent with that used in many previous studies [44, 53]. We will see that ConSeq was able to handle a wide range of types of concurrency bugs (detecting 10 of the 11 bugs).

(2) Can ConSeq find new bugs in the setting of in-house testing (i.e., bugs are not previously known, and inputs are supplied by knowledgeable users)? To mimic the setting of in-house testing, we applied ConSeq to the latest versions of the Cherokee web server [10] and the Click [13] modular router, using test inputs provided by their developers. We were not aware of any concurrency bugs in these two programs. We will see that ConSeq found concurrency bugs in them. Note that these experiments were not started until ConSeq's design and implementation were completely finished. The ability of ConSeq to detect such unknown concurrency bugs also demonstrates the effectiveness of heuristics like the short-propagation heuristic.

Our evaluation of false positives and performance overhead completely executes each input (or set of client requests) from the beginning to the end. The reported performance numbers are the average across 5 runs. The reported false-positive numbers are stable across the multiple runs that we tried. By default, we set *MaxDistance* to 4. We also evaluate false-positive and false-negative results under different *MaxDistance* settings. ConSeq-Daikon demands special setup, and is discussed separately in Section 10.5.

For comparison, we also evaluated two state-of-the-art cause-oriented approaches to detecting concurrency bugs under the same setting. *Race* is a lock-set–happens-before hybrid race detector, commonly known as Helgrind, implemented as part of the open-source bug-detection tool Valgrind [41]. *Atom* [44] detects the most common type of atomicity bug (two accesses in one thread unserializably interleaved by another thread [32, 33, 56]). Similar to ConSeq, these two detectors aim to detect bugs from correct runs.

# 10. Experimental Results

## 10.1 Overall bug-detection results

Table 3 shows the overall bug-detection results. As we can see, ConSeq has good coverage in bug detection. It detected 10 out of the 11 bugs. *Race* and *Atom* only correctly detected 3 and 4 bugs, respectively.

Aside from the bug in Aget listed in the Table 2, ConSeq detected two new bugs in Aget that have never been reported before (one by tracing back from a `printf` call site and one by finding a violation of a (candidate) invariant identified by ConSeq-Daikon). In MySQL-5.0.16, ConSeq detected an infinite-loop concurrency bug initially reported in MySQL-5.0.41, which shows that the bug actually existed in the older version and can be triggered using a different input. Our analysis of Cherokee-0.99.48 and Click-1.8.0 used the basic inputs provided in the applications' test suites, and ConSeq discovered bugs in them as we will see in Section 10.3.

*Atom* targets single-variable atomicity violations that involve three accesses, and cannot detect concurrency bugs caused by other interleaving patterns, such as the bugs in Moz-1 (a multi-variable atomicity violation), MySQL-2 and OO (anti-atomicity violations where the software behaves correctly only when a certain code region in a thread is not atomic), Moz-3 (an atomicity violation

| Bug-ID | ConSeq Detected | *Race* Detected | *Atom* Detected |
|---|---|---|---|
| Aget1 | | | |
| FFT | ✓ | | ✓ |
| MySQL1 | ✓ | | ✓ |
| Moz1 | ✓ | | |
| MySQL2 | ✓ | | |
| Trans | ✓ | | |
| Moz2 | ✓ | ✓ | ✓ |
| Moz3 | ✓ | ✓ | |
| MySQL3 | ✓ | ✓ | ✓ |
| MySQL4 | ✓ | | |
| OO | ✓ | | |

**Table 3.** Bug detection results (✓: detected; Blank: not).

involving more than three accesses), MySQL-4 and Trans (order violation), etc. *Race* suffers from a similar source of false negatives as *Atom*: the root cause of many of these bugs has nothing to do with locks, and many buggy code fragments did use locks correctly (e.g., OO, MySQL-4). In addition, *Race* uses some heuristics to lower the false-positive rate (e.g., not reporting a race when earlier races are already reported on that variable), which leads to some false negatives.

ConSeq's consequence-oriented approach means that its bug-detection capabilities are not limited to any specific interleaving pattern, and thus ConSeq can detect bugs that *Race* and *Atom* cannot. Section 4 has already discussed how ConSeq detects Moz-1, the **multi-variable bug** illustrated in Figure 1(c). Figure 8 shows an **anti-atomicity** example (MySQL2). *S*3 from the slave thread wants to use the value of `pos` defined by the master thread (*S*2) to read the log. Unfortunately, *S*3 could non-deterministically execute before *S*2 and mistakenly read a value defined by its own thread, leading to the MySQL failure. The bug is obviously not a race, because all accesses are well-protected. The bug is also not an atomicity-violation bug, because MySQL executes *correctly* when the atomicity between *S*1 and *S*3 is *violated*! Furthermore, it is not a simple order-violation bug, because there are many dynamic instances of *S*1, *S*2, and *S*3. No order between *S*2–*S*1 or *S*2–*S*3 can guarantee failure. With a cause-oriented approach [34, 55], more sophisticated interleaving patterns and a large number of training runs are needed to detect this bug. In contrast, with ConSeq's consequence-oriented approach, this bug presents no special challenges. MySQL developers already put a sanity check before each log read: `assert(pos_in_file + pos == req_pos)`. Analyzing backwards from that check, ConSeq easily discovers the bug.

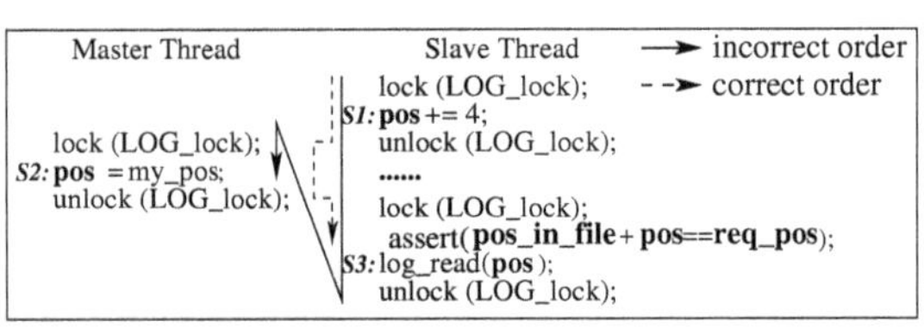


**Figure 8.** An example showing that ConSeq can detect a non-race, non-atomicity-violation bug (simplified for purposes of illustration).

**New bugs detected by ConSeq:** Apart from detecting the bugs described above, ConSeq also detected two more concurrency bugs that we were unaware of in Aget, and a known infinite-loop bug in a different version of MySQL than originally reported.

More interestingly, ConSeq found an output non-determinism in Cherokee and two bugs in Click. For example, one bug in Click can cause locks to be destroyed when they are still in use. ConSeq can detect this bug using any input provided in Click's test suite. Specifically, after a correct run of Click, ConSeq reported that an error message `"Spinlock:: Spinlock(): assertion '_depth == 0' failed"` could be triggered under a different interleaving. The report accurately points us to the bug. In terms of the root cause, this bug is a non-datarace order-violation bug. Neither *Race* nor *Atom* is able to detect this bug.

**False negatives:** There is one bug in Aget that evaded detection by all three tools. The bug is an atomicity violation that involves 11 threads and 21 shared variables. ConSeq failed to detect it because the bug involves a long propagation distance. However, with the support of Daikon, ConSeq can successfully detect it, see (Section 10.5).

ConSeq and traditional tools look at concurrency bugs from different perspectives and can miss bugs in different ways. *Race* and *Atom* have false negatives in the examples discussed above because they cannot cover certain interleaving patterns. ConSeq will inevitably miss some bugs due to missing certain types of failure sites or due to error-propagation distances that exceed the threshold used in the short-propagation heuristic. Of course, the coverage of ConSeq could be further improved in the future by adding more failure templates or tuning the *MaxDistance* threshold. It could also be helped by the use of additional invariant-inference techniques and by developers who are comfortable with adding consistency checks. In summary, ConSeq can well complement existing bug-detection approaches.

### 10.2 False positives

**Before suspicious-interleaving testing.** False positives have always been a problem in concurrency bug detection, especially for predictive bug detectors that need to analyze a huge number of potential interleavings, such as ConSeq, *Race*, and *Atom*.

| Bug-ID | ConSeq OUT | ASS | ERR | LOOP | *Race* | *Atom* | Base |
|---|---|---|---|---|---|---|---|
| Aget1 | 0 | 0 | 0 | 0 | 2 | 4 | 0 |
| FFT | 0 | 0 | 0 | 0 | 8 | 16 | 20 |
| MySQL1 | 0 | 0 | 0 | 0 | 127 | 51 | 77 |
| Moz1 | 0 | 0 | 0 | 0 | 26 | n/a | OM |
| MySQL2 | 0 | 4 | 2 | 5 | 163 | 402 | OM |
| Trans | 0 | 2 | 0 | 0 | 42 | 33 | 136 |
| Moz2 | 1 | 4 | 0 | 0 | 20 | 279 | 244 |
| Moz3 | 0 | 0 | 0 | 0 | 0 | 0 | 0 |
| MySQL3 | 0 | 4 | 3 | 7 | 714 | 1026 | OM |
| MySQL4 | 0 | 1 | 3 | 0 | 180 | 552 | 197 |
| OO | 0 | 0 | 0 | 0 | 0 | 0 | 0 |
| Cherokee | 0 | 0 | 1 | 3 | 40 | 296 | OM |
| Click | 0 | 1 | 0 | 0 | 13 | 20 | 37 |

**Table 4.** False positives in bug detection. (OM means analysis runs out of memory before finish.)

As shown in Table 4, ConSeq has much better accuracy than *Race* and *Atom*,[4] exhibiting only about one-tenth the false-positive rate of the latter two. For 11 out of the 13 cases, ConSeq only has 0–5 false positives. Compared to traditional predictive bug-detection tools, ConSeq can save a lot of testing resources and manual effort by developers.

The main reason that ConSeq reports fewer false positives than traditional approaches is that its consequence-oriented approach has made it much more focused. To validate this, we also measured the false-positive rate for ConSeq with identification of critical reads turned off. The numbers are roughly comparable to the ones

[4] We conducted manual validation for randomly sampled *Race* and *Atom* bug reports.

for *Atom*, as shown by the last column ('Base') in Table 4. Actually, if not guided by potential failure sites and critical reads, the analysis runs out of memory before finishing for several MySQL and Mozilla workloads, because the interleaving space is huge. This is exactly why ConSeq identifies critical read instructions based on potential failure patterns.

The false positives of ConSeq are of two types: (1) Unidentified customized synchronization operations make a suspicious interleaving infeasible. This reason is responsible for all but 3 cases. (2) A different but still correct value is read at a critical read *r*. This is responsible for 3 false positives.

**After suspicious-interleaving testing.** ConSeq-tester prunes out all the false positives discussed above with one false negative. Specifically, ConSeq-tester successfully makes the 9 bugs detected by ConSeq in Table 3 manifest. Unfortunately, of the two new bugs detected by ConSeq in Click, one cannot be automatically exposed by ConSeq-tester. Its manifestation requires a complicated sequence of branches to be followed, involving multiple branch points in Click.

For those bugs that can be automatically exposed by ConSeq-tester, their manifestation can all be reliably repeated by inserting delays at the same places recorded by ConSeq-tester, which can help programmers perform further diagnoses.

### 10.3 Detailed bug-detection results

**Sensitivity of MaxDistance:** In ConSeq, the *MaxDistance* threshold affects how many read instructions are considered 'critical'. We measured the false positives and false negatives of ConSeq under different *MaxDistance* settings. The total number of false positives gradually increases, as does the bug-detection capability. Adding all 13 bug-detection runs together, ConSeq reports 25, 33, 37, 41, 61 false positives in total, with *MaxDistance* set to 1, 2, 3, 4, and 5, respectively. ConSeq detects 6, 8, 9, 10, and 10 out of the tested 11 bugs, with *MaxDistance* set to 1, 2, 3, 4, and 5, respectively. These numbers demonstrate the usefulness of static slicing in ConSeq: if ConSeq only looks at shared variables right at the failure site, almost half of the bugs will be missed.

| | Object File Size | # of Error Sites | # of Critical Reads |
|---|---|---|---|
| Aget1 | 56K | 86 | 49 |
| FFT | 33K | 52 | 111 |
| MySQL1 | 15M | 2137 | 8562 |
| Moz1 | 4.9M | 142 | 397 |
| MySQL2 | 14M | 487 | 1369 |
| Trans | 1.2M | 158 | 232 |
| Moz2 | 1.4M | 856 | 929 |
| Moz3 | 5.7K | 1 | 1 |
| MySQL3 | 25M | 1349 | 2020 |
| MySQL4 | 27M | 867 | 2341 |
| OO | 13K | 26 | 75 |
| Cherokee | 2.6M | 424 | 1261 |
| Click | 24M | 386 | 1365 |

**Table 5.** Potential error sites and critical reads.

**Potential error sites and critical reads.** Table 5 shows the size of the object files processed by our static-slicing tool and the number of potential failure sites and critical reads identified. As we can see, our static-analysis component can handle large applications whose object files are tens of mega-bytes.

### 10.4 Performance results

ConSeq is designed for in-house testing and goes through three phases. The first phase of ConSeq uses static analysis to identify potential failure sites and critical reads. This step is *not* performance-critical, because it is conducted only *once* for each piece of code. It can be re-used across different testing runs and different inputs. Even after a code modification, ConSeq only needs to re-analyze those object files that have been changed. In our experiments, the static analysis is scalable. It can finish within a couple of hours for most applications. Processing MySQL3 takes the longest time — 18392 seconds or about 5 hours.

The second phase of ConSeq takes a test input, runs it once to collect a trace, and analyzes the trace to report suspicious interleavings. At the end of this step, concurrency bugs are reported as shown in Table 3 and 4. This step would be repeated many times during in-house testing and is the most important for ConSeq's performance. Table 6 shows the results for this phase. ConSeq's run-time overheads for the four types of failure patterns are similar, so for each application in the table we only present the worst-case performance and largest trace size among these four cases. Adding the run-time and the time for off-line analysis of the trace together, ConSeq introduces execution overhead of 1.26X — 38.5X for each test input, which is suitable for in-house use. ConSeq's trace sizes are reasonably small. The biggest trace size is about 115MB in our experiments, as shown in Table 6. The peak memory consumption of ConSeq at run-time is less than 100 MB for all applications.

At the end, ConSeq also has an optional step of suspicious-interleaving testing. This step imposes less than 10–55% execution overhead for validating each bug report. Given the small false-positive rate of ConSeq, this step does not take a long time and can be omitted by developers. In our experiments, MySQL3 had the largest accumulated overhead at this step, because it has the largest number of false positives. The baseline run of MySQL3 finishes in 0.46 seconds. In total, ConSeq took 10.6 seconds for the validation step for all 15 reported suspicious interleavings and pruned out 14 false positives.

| | Base Line | Run-Time Overhead (%) | Trace Analysis | Trace Size |
|---|---|---|---|---|
| Aget1 | 12.45s | 26% | 0.01s | 24.7K |
| FFT | 0.05s | 2724% | 0.01s | 1.2M |
| MySQL1 | 0.18s | 21.1% | 0.27s | 2.9M |
| Moz1 | 0.18s | 444% | 1.57s | 36M |
| MySQL2 | 0.13s | 157% | 0.27s | 18M |
| Trans | 1.17s | 210% | 0.01s | 132K |
| Moz2 | 12.0s | 1065% | 0.01s | 490K |
| MySQL3 | 0.46s | 130.2% | 6.77s | 67M |
| MySQL4 | 0.10s | 135.5% | 0.13s | 17M |
| Cherokee | 11.26s | 21.28% | 11.45s | 115M |
| Click | 0.02s | 3846% | 0.01s | 80K |

**Table 6.** Performance of trace collection and analysis (Base Line is the time for the original test run w/o any instrumentation.)

### 10.5 Experience with ConSeq-Daikon

As discussed in Section 5, we played some tricks to get around the granularity limitations of Daikon's frontend. For MySQL, we replaced the default frontend with our own PIN tool. Daikon's backend generates invariants from the log dumped by our PIN tool. For Aget, a relatively small program, we manually inserted dummy functions before *every* global-variable read and then instructed Daikon's frontend kvasir-dtrace to record all global variables at the exit of these dummy functions. Note that this is not a fundamental limitation of Daikon. In fact, the commercial version of Daikon can provide invariants at instruction-level granularity, and could have been used straight out of the box.

**MySQL1:** After a training phase with a mix of 50 INSERT, 25 SELECT, and 25 DELETE queries to MySQL server, Daikon produced a total of 338 equality invariants, each associated with one instruction that reads a global variable. ConSeq considers these instructions as critical reads and detects that 13 out of these 338 invariants could be violated by pure interleaving changes. Among these 13, one of them points to a read of `binlog::log_type` inside function `MySQL::insert`. Daikon observes that this variable's value is always 3 (i.e., `LOG_OPEN`), while ConSeq finds that the value could become 0 (i.e., `LOG_CLOSED`) under an alternative interleaving. This turns out to be exactly the MySQL-1 bug. The abnormal `LOG_CLOSED` value would cause MySQL to miss some logging entries.

Among the other 12 possible violations reported by ConSeq, ten of them are false positives that cannot actually occur due to custom synchronization. The other two can truly occur and violate the candidate invariants proposed by Daikon. However, they are not bugs and do not lead to software failures.

**Aget:** Aget contains a concurrency bug that involves 11 threads and 21 shared variables (1 scalar and 20 entries in an array of structs), as shown in Figure 9. For purposes of illustration, we only show 11 involved variables here.

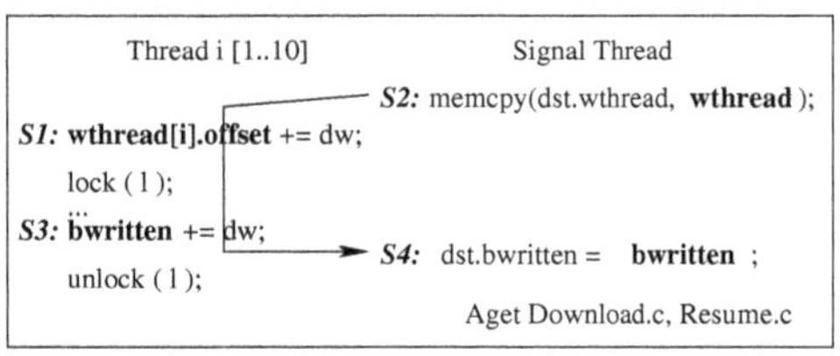


**Figure 9.** A multi-variable atomicity-violation bug that involves 11 threads and many shared variables.

After 50 training runs, Daikon generates equality invariants at 20 program locations. Based on that information, ConSeq reports 2 bugs. **The first bug is Aget1, which cannot be accurately detected by any previous tool. The second is a new bug in Aget that has never been reported.** Specifically, Daikon showed the following invariants just before S4 in Figure 9:

```
..dummy_bwritten_005():::EXIT
::bwritten == sum(::wthread[].bwritten)
```

It means the sum of each thread's `wthread[i].bwritten` fields (across all 10 worker threads) should be equal to `bwritten`, a global variable representing the total number of bytes that have been written by all threads. ConSeq then reports a suspicious interleaving (Figure 9) that could violate this invariant.

One point to note about the new Aget bug that ConSeq found is that it could be triggered by fewer than 11 threads (e.g., two worker threads and one signal thread would suffice). However, when the user does not specify the number of worker threads on the command line, the default is 10. We used the default in the Aget experiment to simulate an in-house tester who wishes to test a system's default configuration. Note that if a (user-supplied) test provokes a complicated situation in the initial run, that is what ConSeq must work with. It has no automatic way of "reducing" the run down to a minimal-size example. Fortunately, Daikon will work with any number of threads and does not have a major scaling problem; Daikon's work remains roughly the same, because each thread does less work when there are more threads. In summary, the Aget experiment illustrates the usage scenario of an in-house tester wishing to test a system's default configuration, and shows that ConSeq has the capability to detect bugs even when the input used generates a complicated interleaving scenario.

## 11. Related Work

**Concurrency bug detection** Sections 1 and 10 have already compared ConSeq with race detectors and atomicity-violation detectors. Recent work has studied multi-variable bugs [25, 31, 35, 63] and order problems [34]. In general, ConSeq complements these tools by starting from consequences rather than causes. ConSeq has a smaller false-positive rate than most traditional tools, and can effectively detect many concurrency bugs caused by complicated interleavings that are difficult for traditional tools to detect.

Recently, several invariant-based tools have been proposed for debugging concurrency bugs with complicated causes, such as definition-use violations and order violations [45, 55]. These tools rely on observing many training runs to identify abnormal interleavings. As a result, insufficient training will cause false positives for them. Furthermore, they cannot report bugs until the buggy interleavings are observed.

Another recent tool, ConMem [66], focuses on concurrency bugs that directly lead to memory errors, such as NULL-pointer dereferences on shared pointer variables. In terms of design philosophy, traditional detectors focus on certain interleaving patterns, which is one end of a spectrum of techniques that can be used to identify concurrency bugs whereas ConMem focuses on the other end (certain failure patterns). ConSeq takes matters even further: ConSeq starts from the failure and analyzes backwards through the error-propagation process. ConSeq is much more general than ConMem. It not only covers all major types of failure patterns (ConMem only covers one), but it also provides a general solution for bugs with various types of error propagation. ConMem does not consider the propagation process at all, and only considers buggy interleavings that directly cause memory bugs (i.e., the critical reads must be exactly the memory error sites)– a strategy that would be difficult to apply to other types of bugs. In terms of techniques, ConSeq is not a direct extension of previous work. To balance generality, analysis simplicity, and bug-report accuracy, ConSeq fully leverages the characteristics of concurrency bugs, and combines advanced static analyses with dynamic analyses.

**Interleaving testing** ConSeq shares the same goals of interleaving-testing tools [16, 39, 44, 53]. Such tools all try to explore the *interleaving* space for each *input* provided by developers during in-house testing. ConSeq uses synchronization analysis and perturbation-based interleaving enforcement in common with some of these tools [44]. The difference between ConSeq and previous tools is that ConSeq uses different methods to guide its exploration of the interleaving space.

RaceFuzzer [53] and CTrigger [44] use race/atomicity-violation detection results to guide their interleaving testing. ConSeq can complement them by exposing concurrency bugs that cannot be detected by race/atomicity detectors, as shown in Section 10. In terms of performance, the high false-positive rates of these bug-detection tools determine that RaceFuzzer and CTrigger will need to test many more interleavings than ConSeq for *each* input. On the other hand, ConSeq needs extra static analysis to identify critical reads. Fortunately, because ConSeq only needs to perform static analysis once for *all* inputs and *all* testing runs, the overhead will easily be offset by the interleaving testing time that is associated with *specific* inputs.

CHESS [39] guides its interleaving testing by bounding the number of preempting context switches. Although this is an effective heuristic, CHESS still faces the challenge of balancing coverage and performance, because its testing space increases polynomially in the number of potential context-switch points during the whole execution. If it considers each shared memory access to be a potential context-switch point, CHESS still cannot effectively explore the large interleaving space of applications like MySQL, as shown in previous work [58]. Therefore, CHESS often limits context switches only to synchronization points. This constraint will fail to expose many concurrency bugs, including many bugs discussed in this paper. Recently, people also proposed using randomized schedulers [7] to probabilistically expose concurrency bugs.

It works very well for simple concurrency bugs, such as many order-violation bugs, but will be ineffective for many other bugs in large applications, such as atomicity-violations or more complicated bugs.

In general, ConSeq and previous interleaving-testing tools complement each other by looking at the interleaving space from different perspectives.

**Failure-diagnosis and repeating** The consequence-oriented approach in ConSeq is similar in flavor to failure-diagnosis/replay tools [1, 15, 46, 58, 65]. For example, slicing is a useful technique in both cases [15, 58, 65]. The heuristic of paying more attention to the code close to a (potential) failure site is also widely used [46, 58, 65].

However, ConSeq and failure-diagnosis tools have different design purposes. ConSeq looks for unknown interleaving errors that can cause previously unobserved failures, while diagnosis tools try to repeat/diagnose a failure after it occurred. The different design purposes present different resource and scalability challenges.

Diagnosis tools come into play after a failure has occurred and been observed. Therefore, they usually assume complete knowledge about the failure core-dump, and sometimes also run-time information collected from the failure. They can spend a lot of resources on repeating and understanding one specific failure. On the contrary, ConSeq simply applies itself to every test input and does not know where failures might occur. It needs to prune out unlikely failure sites as quickly as possible, and expose hidden failures using limited testing resources. For example, in our experiments, ConSeq's trace analysis needs to triage hundreds of potential failure sites within seconds, while diagnosis tools frequently need a couple of hours or more to repeat one failure caused by a concurrency bug in a large application [1, 58], unless they have sufficient information from production runs [46]. Of course, ConSeq's scalability comes with a cost. ConSeq might miss some failures involving long propagation distances that diagnosis tools can successfully diagnose.

**Input generation and symbolic execution** Most failure-diagnosis tools assume full knowledge of bug-triggering inputs. ConSeq and other interleaving-testing tools [16, 39, 44, 53] also rely on input test-case generation to provide good test suites. Recently, symbolic execution [9, 20, 54, 65] has been used to generate high-coverage inputs for unit testing. DDT [26] and ESD [65] further extended this approach for concurrent programs. Using symbolic execution, DDT can detect synchronization problems caused by untimely interrupts in device drivers, and ESD can generate bug-triggering inputs and interleavings based on core-dumps from deadlock situations. These inspiring works can potentially help all testing and diagnosis tools, including ConSeq. However, due to the scalability constraints of symbolic execution and theorem provers, previous work only experimented with relatively small applications or relatively simple interleaving problems. Remember that exposing deadlocks is usually easier than exposing non-deadlock bugs, because it only needs to explore the different orders among lock acquisitions and releases, instead of the orders among all shared memory accesses. Further research is needed on how to scale symbolic execution to expose general concurrency bugs that go beyond simple lock-discipline issues; symbolic execution is currently not able to address concurrency bugs that are caused by arbitrary interleavings among arbitrary code segments in large, real-world applications.

**Model-checking** Model-checking research aims to verify properties of concurrent programs. Recently, a lot of progress has been made [27, 39, 48]. However, the state-explosion problem still exists. ConSeq has a different design goal and makes different trade-offs from model-checking tools. ConSeq does not try to obtain sound or complete results. ConSeq leverages the characteristics of concurrency bugs, especially the short-propagation heuristic, and uses a combination of static and dynamic analysis to make backward bug-detection feasible for large applications.

**Run-time avoidance** has also been studied for concurrency bugs. Dimmunix [24] learns lessons from previous deadlocks to avoid future deadlocks. Atom-Aid [36] and PSet [63] provide ways to survive concurrency bugs by prohibiting certain patterns of interleavings at run-time through hardware support. Deterministic execution [14] pushes this to an extreme. Software-only tools like Grace [4] and Kendo [43] achieve similar goals for certain types of multi-threaded programs at run-time. ConSeq complements such tasks by exposing concurrency bugs before they manifest in a production run.

## 12. Conclusions

This paper explores a backward, consequence-oriented approach to concurrency-bug detection. Our evaluation showed that ConSeq can detect 10 out of 11 tested concurrency bugs by monitoring correct testing runs. These bugs cover various types of failures and root causes, many of which cannot be detected by traditional race detectors and atomicity-violation detectors. ConSeq also found previously unknown bugs in open-source applications. Due to its consequence-oriented approach, ConSeq also has much better accuracy than traditional tools.

We believe ConSeq provides a nice complement to traditional concurrency-bug-detection tools. It demonstrates that we can leverage tools designed for sequential programs and sequential bugs, such as Daikon, to detect complicated concurrency bugs. Application developers can easily extend and adjust ConSeq by inserting sequential-style assertions and error messages in their code.

Of course, ConSeq still has limitations. First, similar to other dynamic bug-detection tools, ConSeq depends on test inputs for code coverage. Second, ConSeq currently focuses on the failure types detailed in this paper; while these failure types cover a large subset of all software failures, they are certainly not comprehensive. Third, ConSeq uses the short-propagation-distance heuristic; while this heuristic has proven to be effective in our rather inclusive benchmarks, it will inevitably cause some bugs that have long propagation distances to be missed by ConSeq.

Future work on ConSeq will concern several aspects. First, we plan to apply it to more applications and inputs. Second, we plan to extend it with more failure patterns. Third, we plan to try alternative distance metrics and use better customized synchronization-pruning techniques to further improve its accuracy.

## 13. Acknowledgments

We would like to thank our shepherd, Shimin Chen, and the anonymous reviewers for their invaluable feedback. We thank Bill Harris for many helpful discussions. We thank people from Daikon research group for providing much needed help. We also thank Mark Hill for his feedback and suggestions. Shan Lu is supported by a Claire Boothe Luce faculty fellowship, and her research group is supported by NSF grant CCF-1018180. Thomas Reps's research group is supported by NSF under grants CCF-0810053 and CCF-0904371, by ONR under grants N00014-09-1-0510 and N00014-10-M-0251, by ARL under grant W911NF-09-1-0413, and by AFRL under grants FA9550-09-1-0279 and FA8650-10-C-7088. Thomas Reps has an ownership interest in GrammaTech, Inc., which has licensed elements of the technology reported in this publication.

## References

[1] G. Altekar and I. Stoica. ODR: output-deterministic replay for multicore debugging. In *SOSP*, 2009.

[2] G. Balakrishnan, R. Gruian, T. Reps, and T. Teitelbaum. CodeSurfer/x86 – A platform for analyzing x86 executables, (tool demonstration paper). In *CC*, 2005.
[3] G. Balakrishnan and T. Reps. Analyzing memory accesses in x86 executables. In *Compiler Construction*, 2004.
[4] E. D. Berger, T. Yang, T. Liu, and G. Novark. Grace: safe multithreaded programming for C/C++. In *OOPSLA*, 2009.
[5] A. Bessey, K. Block, B. Chelf, A. Chou, B. Fulton, S. Hallem, C. Henri-Gros, A. Kamsky, S. McPeak, and D. Engler. A few billion lines of code later: using static analysis to find bugs in the real world. *Commun. ACM*, 53(2):66–75, 2010.
[6] F. Bourdoncle. Efficient chaotic iteration strategies with widenings. In *Int. Conf. on Formal Methods in Prog. and their Appl.*, 1993.
[7] S. Burckhardt, P. Kothari, M. Musuvathi, and S. Nagarakatte. A randomized scheduler with probabilistic guarantees of finding bugs. In *ASPLOS*, 2010.
[8] J. Burnim and K. Sen. Asserting and checking determinism for multithreaded programs. In *FSE*, 2009.
[9] C. Cadar, D. Dunbar, and D. R. Engler. Klee: Unassisted and automatic generation of high-coverage tests for complex systems programs. In *OSDI*, 2008.
[10] Cherokee. Cherokee: The Fastest free Web Server out there! http://www.cherokee-project.com/.
[11] L. Chew and D. Lie. Kivati: Fast detection and prevention of atomicity violations. In *EuroSys*, 2010.
[12] J.-D. Choi et al. Efficient and precise datarace detection for multithreaded object-oriented programs. In *PLDI*, 2002.
[13] Click. The Click Modular Router Projec. http://read.cs.ucla.edu/click/click.
[14] J. Devietti, B. Lucia, L. Ceze, and M. Oskin. DMP: deterministic shared memory multiprocessing. In *ASPLOS*, 2009.
[15] M. Dimitrov and H. Zhou. Anomaly-based bug prediction, isolation, and validation: an automated approach for software debugging. In *ASPLOS*, 2009.
[16] O. Edelstein, E. Farchi, Y. Nir, G. Ratsaby, and S. Ur. Multi-threaded Java program test generation. *IBM Systems Journal*, 2002.
[17] M. Ernst, A. Czeisler, W. G. Griswold, and D. Notkin. Quickly detecting relevant program invariants. In *ICSE*, 2000.
[18] M. D. Ernst, J. H. Perkins, P. J. Guo, S. McCamant, C. Pacheco, M. S. Tschantz, and C. Xiao. The daikon system for dynamic detection of likely invariants. *Sci. Comput. Program.*, 69(1-3):35–45, 2007.
[19] C. Flanagan and S. N. Freund. FastTrack: efficient and precise dynamic race detection. In *PLDI*, 2009.
[20] P. Godefroid, N. Klarlund, and K. Sen. Dart: directed automated random testing. In *PLDI*, 2005.
[21] W. Gu, Z. Kalbarczyk, R. K. Iyer, and Z.-Y. Yang. Characterization of Linux kernel behavior under errors. In *DSN*, 2003.
[22] S. Horwitz, T. Reps, and D. Binkley. Interprocedural slicing using dependence graphs. In *TOPLAS*, 1990.
[23] R. Jhala and R. Majumdar. Software model checking. *Computing Surveys*, 41(4), 2009.
[24] H. Jula, D. Tralamazza, C. Zamfir, and G. Candea. Deadlock immunity: Enabling systems to defend against deadlocks. In *OSDI*, 2008.
[25] N. Kidd, P. Lammich, T. Touilli, and T. Reps. A static technique for checking for multiple-variable data races. *Software Tools for Technology Transfer*, 2010.
[26] V. Kuznetsov, V. Chipounov, and G. Candea. Testing closed-source binary device drivers with DDT. In *USENIX*, 2010.
[27] A. Lal and T. Reps. Reducing concurrent analysis under a context bound to sequential analysis. *Form. Methods Syst. Des.*, 2009.
[28] I. Lee and R. K. Iyer. Faults, symptoms, and software fault tolerance in the Tandem GUARDIAN90 Operating System. *IEEE*, pages 20–29, 1993.
[29] N. G. Leveson and C. S. Turner. An investigation of the therac-25 accidents. *Computer*, 26(7):18–41, 1993.
[30] X. Li and D. Yeung. Application-level correctness and its impact on fault tolerance. In *HPCA*, 2007.
[31] S. Lu, S. Park, C. Hu, X. Ma, W. Jiang, Z. Li, R. A. Popa, and Y. Zhou. MUVI: Automatically inferring multi-variable access correlations and detecting related semantic and concurrency bugs. In *SOSP*, October 2007.
[32] S. Lu, S. Park, E. Seo, and Y. Zhou. Learning from mistakes – a comprehensive study of real world concurrency bug characteristics. In *ASPLOS*, 2008.
[33] S. Lu, J. Tucek, F. Qin, and Y. Zhou. AVIO: detecting atomicity violations via access interleaving invariants. In *ASPLOS*, 2006.
[34] B. Lucia and L. Ceze. Finding concurrency bugs with context-aware communication graphs. In *MICRO*, 2009.
[35] B. Lucia, L. Ceze, and K. Strauss. Colorsafe: architectural support for debugging and dynamically avoiding multi-variable atomicity violations. In *ISCA*, 2010.
[36] B. Lucia, J. Devietti, K. Strauss, and L. Ceze. Atom-aid: Detecting and surviving atomicity violations. In *ISCA*, 2008.
[37] C.-K. Luk, R. Cohn, R. Muth, H. Patil, A. Klauser, G. Lowney, S. Wallace, V. J. Reddi, and K. Hazelwood. Pin: building customized program analysis tools with dynamic instrumentation. In *PLDI*, 2005.
[38] M. Musuvathi and S. Qadeer. Iterative context bounding for systematic testing of multithreaded programs. In *PLDI*, 2007.
[39] M. Musuvathi, S. Qadeer, T. Ball, G. Basler, P. A. Nainar, and I. Neamtiu. Finding and reproducing heisenbugs in concurrent programs. In *OSDI*, 2008.
[40] S. Narayanasamy, Z. Wang, J. Tigani, A. Edwards, and B. Calder. Automatically classifying benign and harmful data races using replay analysis. In *PLDI*, 2007.
[41] N. Nethercote and J. Seward. Valgrind: a framework for heavyweight dynamic binary instrumentation. In *PLDI*, 2007.
[42] R. H. B. Netzer and B. P. Miller. Improving the accuracy of data race detection. In *PPoPP*, 1991.
[43] M. Olszewski, J. Ansel, and S. P. Amarasinghe. Kendo: Efficient deterministic multithreading in software. In *ASPLOS*, 2009.
[44] S. Park, S. Lu, and Y. Zhou. Ctrigger: Exposing atomicity violation bugs from their finding places. In *ASPLOS*, 2009.
[45] S. Park, R. W. Vuduc, and M. J. Harrold. Falcon: fault localization in concurrent programs. In *ICSE '10*, 2010.
[46] S. Park, Y. Zhou, W. Xiong, Z. Yin, R. Kaushik, K. H. Lee, and S. Lu. PRES: probabilistic replay with execution sketching on multiprocessors. In *SOSP*, 2009.
[47] D. K. Pradhan. *Fault-Tolerant Computer System Design*. Prentice-Hall, Incorporated, 1996.
[48] S. Qadeer and D. Wu. Kiss: keep it simple and sequential. In *PLDI*, 2004.
[49] F. Qin, J. Tucek, J. Sundaresan, and Y. Zhou. Rx: Treating bugs as allergies c a safe method to survive software failures. In *SOSP*, 2005.
[50] L. Ryzhyk, P. Chubb, I. Kuz, and G. Heiser. Dingo: taming device drivers. In *EuroSys*, 2009.
[51] S. Savage, M. Burrows, G. Nelson, P. Sobalvarro, and T. Anderson. Eraser: A dynamic data race detector for multithreaded programs. *ACM TOCS*, 1997.
[52] SecurityFocus. Software bug contributed to blackout. http://www.securityfocus.com/news/8016.
[53] K. Sen. Race directed random testing of concurrent programs. In *PLDI*, 2008.
[54] K. Sen, D. Marinov, and G. Agha. Cute: a concolic unit testing engine for c. In *ESEC/SIGSOFT FSE*, 2005.
[55] Y. Shi, S. Park, Z. Yin, S. Lu, Y. Zhou, W. Chen, and W. Zheng. Do i use the wrong definition? defuse: Definition-use invariants for detecting concurrency and sequential bugs. In *OOPSLA*, 2010.
[56] M. Vaziri, F. Tip, and J. Dolby. Associating synchronization constraints with data in an object-oriented language. In *POPL*, 2006.
[57] Y. Wang, T. Kelly, M. Kudlur, S. Lafortune, and S. A. Mahlke. Gadara: Dynamic deadlock avoidance for multithreaded programs. In *OSDI*, 2008.
[58] D. Weeratunge, X. Zhang, and S. Jagannathan. Analyzing multicore dumps to facilitate concurrency bug reproduction. In *ASPLOS*, 2010.
[59] M. Weiser. Program slicing. In *IEEE Transactions on Software Engineering*, 1984.
[60] S. C. Woo, M. Ohara, E. Torrie, J. P. Singh, and A. Gupta. The SPLASH-2 programs: Characterization and methodological considerations. In *ISCA*, 1995.
[61] W. Xiong, S. Park, J. Zhang, Y. Zhou, and Z. Ma. Ad hoc synchronization considered harmful. In *OSDI*, 2010.
[62] M. Xu, R. Bodík, and M. D. Hill. A serializability violation detector for shared-memory server programs. In *PLDI*, 2005.
[63] J. Yu and S. Narayanasamy. A case for an interleaving constrained shared-memory multi-processor. In *ISCA*, 2009.
[64] Y. Yu, T. Rodeheffer, and W. Chen. Racetrack: Efficient detection of data race conditions via adaptive tracking. In *SOSP*, 2005.
[65] C. Zamfir and G. Candea. Execution synthesis: A technique for automated software debugging. In *EuroSys*, 2010.
[66] W. Zhang, C. Sun, and S. Lu. ConMem: Detecting severe concurrency bugs through an effect-oriented approach. In *ASPLOS*, 2010.

# S2E: A Platform for In-Vivo Multi-Path Analysis of Software Systems

Vitaly Chipounov, Volodymyr Kuznetsov, George Candea

School of Computer and Communication Sciences
École Polytechnique Fédérale de Lausanne (EPFL), Switzerland
{vitaly.chipounov,vova.kuznetsov,george.candea}@epfl.ch

## Abstract

This paper presents $S^2E$, a platform for analyzing the properties and behavior of software systems. We demonstrate $S^2E$'s use in developing practical tools for comprehensive performance profiling, reverse engineering of proprietary software, and bug finding for both kernel-mode and user-mode binaries. Building these tools on top of $S^2E$ took less than 770 LOC and 40 person-hours each.

$S^2E$'s novelty consists of its ability to scale to large real systems, such as a full Windows stack. $S^2E$ is based on two new ideas: *selective symbolic execution*, a way to automatically minimize the amount of code that has to be executed symbolically given a target analysis, and relaxed *execution consistency models*, a way to make principled performance/precision trade-offs in complex analyses. These techniques give $S^2E$ three key abilities: to simultaneously analyze entire families of execution paths, instead of just one execution at a time; to perform the analyses in-vivo within a real software stack—user programs, libraries, kernel, drivers, etc.—instead of using abstract models of these layers; and to operate directly on binaries, thus being able to analyze even proprietary software.

Conceptually, $S^2E$ is an automated path explorer with modular path analyzers: the explorer drives the target system down all execution paths of interest, while analyzers check properties of each such path (e.g., to look for bugs) or simply collect information (e.g., count page faults). Desired paths can be specified in multiple ways, and one can either combine existing analyzers to build a custom analysis tool, or write new analyzers using the $S^2E$ API.

***Categories and Subject Descriptors*** D.2.4 [*Software/Program Verification*]

***General Terms*** Reliability, Verification, Performance, Security

## 1. Introduction

System developers routinely need to analyze the behavior of what they build. One basic analysis is to *understand observed behavior*, such as why a given web server is slow on a SPECweb benchmark. More sophisticated analyses aim to *characterize future behavior* in previously unseen circumstances, such as what will a web server's maximum latency and minimum throughput be, once deployed at a customer site. Ideally, system designers would also like to be able to do quick *what-if analyses*, such as determining whether aligning a certain data structure on a page boundary will avoid all cache misses and thus increase performance. For small programs, experienced developers can often reason through some of these questions based on code alone. The goal of our work is to make it feasible to answer such questions for large, complex, real systems.

We introduce in this paper a platform that enables easy construction of analysis tools (like oprofile, valgrind, bug finders, reverse engineering tools) while simultaneously offering the following three properties: (1) efficiently analyze entire families of execution paths; (2) maximize realism by running the analyses within a real software stack; and (3) ability to handle binaries. We explain these properties below.

First, predictive analyses often must reason about entire *families of paths* through the target system, not just one path. For example, security analyses must check that there exist no corner cases that could violate a desired security policy; recent work has employed model checking [28] and symbolic execution [11] to find bugs in real systems—these are all multi-path analyses. One of our case studies demonstrates multi-path analysis of performance properties: instead of profiling solely one execution path, we derive performance envelopes that characterize the performance of entire families of paths. Such analyses can check real-time requirements (e.g., that an interrupt handler will never exceed a given bound on execution time), or can help with capacity planning (e.g., determine how many web servers to provision for a web farm). In the end, properties shown to hold for *all* paths constitute proofs, which are in essence the ultimate prediction of a system's behavior.

Second, an accurate estimate of program behavior often requires taking into account the *whole environment* surrounding the analyzed program: libraries, kernel, drivers, even CPU architecture—in other words, it requires in-vivo[1] analysis. Even small programs interact with their environment (e.g., to read/write files or send/receive network packets), so understanding program behavior requires understanding the nature of these interactions. Some tool execute the real environment, but allow calls from different execution paths to interfere inconsistently with each other [12, 18]. Most approaches abstract away the environment behind a model [2, 11], but writing abstract models is labor-intensive (taking in some cases multiple person-years [2]), they are rarely 100% accurate, and they

[1] *In vivo* is Latin for "within the living" and refers to experimenting using a whole live system; *in vitro* uses a synthetic or partial system. In life sciences, in vivo testing—animal testing or clinical trials—is often preferred, because, when organisms or tissues are disrupted (as in the case of in vitro settings), results can be substantially less representative. Analogously, in-vivo program analysis captures all interactions of the analyzed code with its surrounding system, not just with a simplified abstraction of that system.



*ASPLOS'11,* March 5–11, 2011, Newport Beach, California, USA.

tend to lose accuracy as the modeled system evolves. It is therefore preferable that analyzed programs interact directly with their real environment in a way that is consistent with multi-path analysis.

Third, real systems are made up of many components from various vendors; access to all corresponding source code is rarely feasible and, even when source code is available, building the code exactly as in the shipped software product is difficult [5]. Thus, in order to be practical, analyses ought to operate *directly on binaries*.

Scalability is the key challenge of performing analyses that are in-vivo, multi-path, and operate on binaries. Going from single-path analysis to multi-path analysis turns a linear problem into an exponential one, because the number of paths through a program increases exponentially in the number of branches—the "path explosion" problem [7]. It is therefore not feasible today to execute fully symbolically an entire software stack (programs, libraries, OS kernel, drivers, etc.) as would be necessary if we wanted consistent in-vivo multi-path analysis.

We describe in this paper $S^2E$, a general platform for developing multi-path in-vivo analysis tools that are practical even for large, complex systems, such as an entire Windows software stack. First, $S^2E$ simultaneously exercises entire families of execution paths in a scalable manner by using *selective* symbolic execution and *relaxed* execution consistency models. Second, $S^2E$ employs virtualization to perform the desired analyses in vivo; this removes the need for the stubs or abstract models required by most state-of-the-art symbolic execution engines and model checkers [3, 11, 18, 28, 35]. Third, $S^2E$ uses dynamic binary translation to directly interpret x86 machine code, so it can analyze a wide range of software, including proprietary systems, even if self-modifying or JITed, as well as obfuscated and packed binaries.

The $S^2E$ platform offers an automated path exploration mechanism and modular path analyzers. The explorer drives in parallel the target system down all execution paths of interest, while analyzers check properties of each such path (e.g., to look for bugs) or simply collect information (e.g., count page faults). An analysis tool built on top of $S^2E$ glues together path selectors with path analyzers. *Selectors* guide $S^2E$'s path explorer by specifying the paths of interest: all paths that touch a specific memory object, paths influenced by a specific parameter, paths inside a target code module, etc. *Analyzers* can be pieced together from $S^2E$-provided analyzers, or can be written from scratch using the $S^2E$ API.

$S^2E$ comes with ready-made selectors and analyzers that provide a wide range of analyses out-of-the-box. The typical $S^2E$ user only needs to define in a configuration file the desired selector(s) and analyzer(s) along with the corresponding parameters, start up the desired software stack inside the $S^2E$ virtual machine, and run the $S^2E$ launcher in the guest OS, which starts the desired application and communicates with the $S^2E$ VM underneath. For example, one may want to verify the code that handles license keys in a proprietary program, such as Adobe Photoshop. The user installs the program in the $S^2E$ Windows VM and launches the program using *s2e.exe C:\Program Files\Adobe\Photoshop*. From inside the guest OS, the *s2e.exe* launcher communicates with $S^2E$ via custom opcodes (described in §4). In the $S^2E$ configuration file, the tester may choose a memory checker analyzer along with a path selector that returns a symbolic string whenever Photoshop reads *HKEY_LOCAL_MACHINE\Software\Photoshop\LicenseKey* from the Windows registry. $S^2E$ then automatically explores the code paths in Photoshop that are influenced by the value of the license key and looks for memory safety errors along those paths.

Developing a new analysis tool with $S^2E$ takes on the order of 20-40 person-hours and a few hundred LOC. To illustrate $S^2E$'s generality, we present here three very different tools built using $S^2E$: a multi-path in-vivo performance profiler, a reverse engineering tool, and a tool for automatically testing proprietary software.

This paper makes the following four contributions:

- ***Selective symbolic execution***, a new technique for automatic bidirectional symbolic–concrete state conversion that enables execution to seamlessly and correctly weave back and forth between symbolic and concrete mode;
- ***Execution consistency models***, a systematic way to reason about the trade-offs involved in the approximation of paths in analyses that employ mixed concrete/symbolic execution;
- A ***general platform*** for performing diverse in-vivo multi-path analyses in a way that scales to large real systems;
- The first use of ***symbolic execution in performance analysis***.

In the rest of the paper, we describe selective symbolic execution (§2), present the execution consistency models (§3), the use of $S^2E$ for developing analysis tools (§4), the $S^2E$ prototype (§5), evaluation (§6), related work (§7), and conclusions (§8).

## 2. Selective Symbolic Execution

In devising a way to efficiently exercise entire families of paths, we were inspired by the successful use of symbolic execution [21] in automated software testing [11, 18]. The idea is to treat a program as a superposition of possible execution paths. For example, a program that is all linear code except for one conditional statement *if* $(x > 0)$ *then ... else ...* can be viewed as a superposition of two possible paths: one for $x > 0$ and another one for $x \leq 0$. To exercise all paths, it is not necessary to try all possible values of $x$, but rather just one value greater than 0 and one value less than 0.

We unfurl this superposition of paths into a *symbolic execution tree*, in which each possible execution corresponds to a path from the root of the tree to a leaf corresponding to a terminal state. The mechanics of doing so consist of marking variables as symbolic at the beginning of the program, i.e., instead of allowing a variable $x$ to take on a concrete value 5, it is viewed as a superposition $\lambda$ of all possible values $x$ could take. Then, any time a branch instruction conditioned on predicate $p$ depends (directly or indirectly) on $x$, execution is split into two executions $E_i$ and $E_k$, two copies of the program's state are created, and $E_i$'s path remembers that the variables involved in $p$ must be constrained to make $p$ true, while $E_j$'s path remembers that $p$ must be false.

The process repeats recursively: $E_i$ may further split into $E_{i_i}$ and $E_{i_k}$, and so on. Every execution of a branch statement creates a new set of children, and thus what would normally be a linear execution (if concrete values were used) now turns into a tree of executions (since symbolic values are used). A node $s$ in the tree represents a program state (a set of variables with formulae constraining the variables' values), and an edge $s_i \rightarrow s_j$ indicates that $s_j$ is $s_i$'s successor on any path satisfying the constraints in $s_j$. Paths in the tree can be pursued simultaneously, as the tree unfurls; since program state is copied, the paths can be explored independently. Copy-on-write is used to make this process efficient.

$S^2E$ is based on the key observation that often *only some* families of paths are of interest. For example, one may want to exhaustively explore all paths through a small program, but not care about all paths through the libraries it uses or the OS kernel. This means that, when entering that program, $S^2E$ should split executions to explore the various paths, but whenever it calls into some other part of the system, such as a library, multi-path execution can cease and execution can revert to single-path. Then, when execution returns to the program, multi-path execution must be resumed.

Multi-path execution corresponds to *expanding* a family of paths by exploring the various side branches as they appear; switching to single-path mode is like *corseting* the family of paths. When multi-path exploration is on, the tree grows in width and depth;

when off, the tree only grows in depth. It is for this reason that we think of S$^2$E's multi-path exploration as being *elastic*. S$^2$E turns multi-path off whenever possible, to trim the execution tree so as to only include paths that are of interest for the target analysis.

S$^2$E's elasticity of multi-path exploration is key in being able to perform in-vivo multi-path exploration of programs inside complex systems, like Windows. By combining elasticity with virtualization, S$^2$E offers the illusion of symbolically executing a full software stack, while actually executing symbolically only select components. In particular, by concretely (i.e., non-symbolically) executing libraries and the OS kernel, S$^2$E allows a program's paths to be explored efficiently without having to model its surrounding environment. We refer to this as *selective symbolic execution.*

Interleaving of symbolic execution phases with concrete phases must be done carefully, to preserve the meaningfulness of the explored execution. For example, say we wish to analyze a program $P$ in multi-path (symbolic) mode, but none of its libraries $L_i$ are to be explored symbolically. If $P$ has a symbolic variable $n$ and calls `strncpy(dst,src,n)` in $L_k$, S$^2$E must convert $n$ to some concrete value and invoke `strncpy` with that value. This is straightforward: solve the current path constraints with a constraint solver and get some legal value for $n$ (say $n$=5) and call `strncpy`. But what happens to $n$ after `strncpy` returns? Variable *dst* will contain $n$=5 bytes, whereas $n$ prior to the call was symbolic—can $n$ still be treated symbolically? The answer is yes, if done carefully.

In S$^2$E, when a symbolic value is converted to concrete ($n$: $\lambda \rightarrow 5$), the family of executions is corseted. When a concrete value is converted to symbolic ($n : 5 \rightarrow \lambda$), the execution family is allowed to expand. The process of doing this back and forth is governed by the rules of an execution consistency model (§3). For the above example, one might require that $n$ be constrained to value 5 in all executions following the return from `strncpy`. However, doing so may exclude a large number of paths from the analysis. In §3, we describe systematic and safe relaxations of execution consistency.

We now describe the mechanics of switching back and forth between multi-path (symbolic) and single-path (concrete) execution in a way that execution stays consistent. We know of no symbolic execution engine that has the machinery for efficiently and flexibly crossing the symbolic/concrete boundary both back and forth.

Fig. 1 provides a simplified example of using S$^2$E: an application *app* uses a library *lib* on top of an OS *kernel*. The target analysis requires to symbolically execute *lib*, but not *app* or *kernel*. Function *appFn* in the application calls a library function *libFn*, which eventually invokes a system call *sysFn*. Once *sysFn* returns, *libFn* does some further processing and returns to *appFn*. When execution crosses into the symbolic domain (shaded) from the concrete domain (white), the execution tree (right side of Fig. 1) expands. When execution returns to the concrete domain, the execution tree is corseted and does not add any new paths, until execution returns to the symbolic domain. Some paths may terminate earlier than others (e.g., due to a crash or a successful return) and not split further.

We now describe the two directions in which execution can cross the concrete/symbolic boundary.

### 2.1 Concrete → Symbolic Transition

When *appFn* calls *libFn*, it does so by using concrete arguments; the simplest conversion is to use an S$^2$E selector to change the concrete arguments into symbolic ones, e.g., instead of *libFn(10)* call *libFn($\lambda$)*. One can additionally opt to constrain $\lambda$, e.g., $\lambda \leq 15$.

Once this transition occurs, S$^2$E executes *libFn* symbolically using the (potentially constrained) argument(s) and simultaneously executes *libFn* with the original concrete argument(s) as well. Once exploration of *libFn* completes, S$^2$E returns to *appFn* the concrete return value resulting from the concrete execution, but *libFn* will have been explored symbolically as well. In this way, the execution

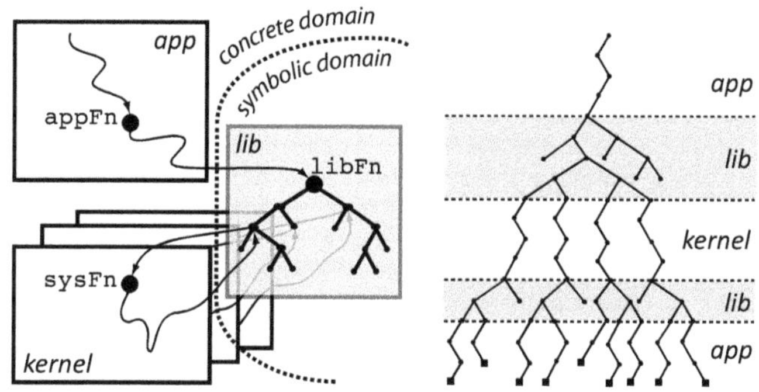


**Figure 1:** Multi-path/single-path execution: three different modules (left) and the resulting execution tree (right). Shaded areas represent the multi-path (symbolic) execution domain, while the white areas are single-path.

of *app* is consistent, while at the same time S$^2$E exposes to the analyzer plugins those paths in *lib* that are rooted at *libFn*. The concrete domain is unaware of *libFn* being executed in multi-path mode. All paths execute independently, and it is up to the S$^2$E analyzer plugins to decide whether, besides observing the concrete path, to also look at the symbolic paths.

### 2.2 Symbolic → Concrete Transition

Dealing with the *libFn→sysFn* call is more complicated. Say *libFn* has the code shown in Fig. 2, and was called with an unconstrained symbolic value $x \in (-\infty, +\infty)$. At the first *if* branch instruction, execution forks into one path along which $x \in (-\infty, 5)$ and another path where $x \in [5, +\infty)$. These are referred to as *path constraints*, as they constrain the values that $x$ can take on that path. Along the then-branch, a call to *sysFn(x)* must be made. This requires $x$ to be concretized, since *sysFn* is in the concrete domain. Thus, S$^2$E chooses a value, say $x = 4$, that is consistent with the $x \in (-\infty, 5)$ constraint and performs the *sysFn(4)* call.

```
int  M=...;
void libFn(int x) {
  if (x<5) {
    buf=sysFn(x);
    if (x<0)
      M=M/2;
  }
}
```

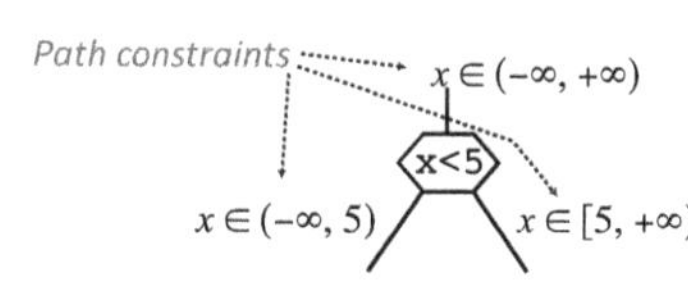


**Figure 2:** The *libFn* function makes a system call *sysFn*.

Note that S$^2$E actually employs *lazy concretization*: it converts the value of $x$ from symbolic to concrete on-demand, only when the concretely running code *branches* on $x$. This is an important optimization when doing in-vivo symbolic execution, because much data can be carried through the layers of the software stack without conversion. For example, when a program writes a buffer of symbolic data to the filesystem, there are usually no branches in the kernel or the disk device driver that depend on this data, so the buffer can pass through unconcretized and be written in symbolic form to the virtual disk, from where it will eventually be read back in its symbolic form. For the sake of clarity, we will assume in the remainder of this section eager (non-lazy) concretization.

Once *sysFn* completes, execution returns to *libFn* in the symbolic domain, and the path constraints must be updated to reflect that now $x = 4$. This is not only because $x$ has been concretized, but also because *sysFn*'s return value is correct only under this constraint (i.e., all computation in *sysFn* was done assuming $x = 4$). Furthermore, *sysFn* may also have had side effects that are equally intimately tied to the $x = 4$ constraint. With this constraint, execution of *libFn* can continue, and correctness is fully preserved.

The problem, however, is that this constraint corsets the family of *future* paths that can be explored from this point on: $x$ can no longer take all values in $(-\infty, 5)$ so, if subsequently there is a branch of the form *if* $(x < 0)$ ..., the then-branch will no longer be feasible due to the added $x = 4$ constraint. This is referred to as "overconstraining": the constraint is not introduced by features of *libFn*'s code, but rather as a result of concretizing $x$ to call into the concrete domain. We think of $x = 4$ as a soft constraint imposed by the symbolic/concrete boundary, while $x \in (-\infty, 5)$ is a hard constraint imposed by *libFn*'s code. Whenever a branch in the symbolic domain is disabled because of a soft constraint, it is possible to go back in the execution tree and pick another value for the soft constraint that would enable that branch. As will be explained later, $S^2E$ can track branch conditions in the concrete domain, which helps redo the call in a way that re-enables subsequent branches.

The "overconstraining" problem has two components: (a) the loss of paths that results directly from the concretization of $x$, and (b) the loss of paths that results indirectly via the constrained return value and side effects. Due to the fact that $S^2E$ implements VM state in a way that is shared between the concrete and symbolic domain (more details in §5), return values and side effects can be treated using identical mechanisms. We now discuss how the constraints are handled under different consistency models.

## 3. Execution Consistency Models

The traditional assumption about system execution is that the state at any point in time is consistent, i.e., there exists a feasible path from the start state to the current state. However, there are many analyses for which this assumption is unnecessarily strong, and the cost of providing such consistency during multi-path exploration is often prohibitively high. E.g., when doing unit testing, one typically exercises the unit in ways that are consistent with the unit's interface, without regard to whether all those paths are indeed feasible in the integrated system. This is both because testing the entire system in a way that exercises all paths through the unit is too expensive, and because exercising the unit as described above offers higher confidence in its correctness in the face of future use.

$S^2E$ aims to be a general platform for system analyses, so it provides several levels of execution consistency, to enable users to make the right trade-offs. In this section, we take a first step toward systematically defining alternate execution consistency models (§3.1), after which we explain how these different models dictate the conversions applied upon transition between the analyzed unit and environment (§3.2). In §3.3 we survey some of the ways in which consistency models are implemented in other analysis tools.

### 3.1 Model Definitions

The key distinction between execution consistency models is which execution paths are admissible under that model. Choosing an appropriate consistency model is a trade-off between how "realistic" the admitted paths are vs. the cost of enforcing the required model. The appropriateness of the trade-off is determined by the nature of the analysis, i.e., by how the feasibility of different paths affects completeness and soundness of the analysis.

In this section we use the term *system* to denote the complete software system under analysis, including the application programs, libraries, and the operating system. We use the term *unit* to denote the part of the system that is to be analyzed. A unit could encompass different parts of multiple programs, libraries, or even parts the operating system itself. We use the term *environment* to denote everything in the system except the unit. Informally, the system is the union of the environment and the target unit of interest.

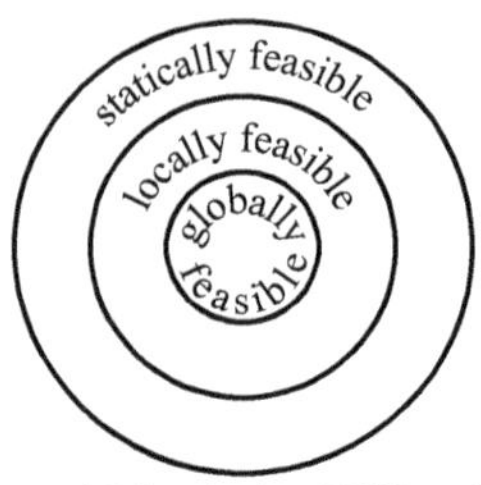


When defining a model, we think in terms of which paths it included vs. excludes. Following the circle diagram on the right, an execution path can be *statically feasible*, in the sense that there exists a path in the control flow graph (CFG) corresponding to the execution in question. A subset of the statically feasible paths are *locally feasible* in the unit, in the sense that the execution is consistent with both the CFG and with the restrictions on control flow imposed by the data-related constraints within the unit. Finally, a subset of locally feasible paths is *globally feasible*, in the sense that their execution is additionally consistent with control flow restrictions imposed by data-related constraints in the environment. Observing only the code executing in the unit, with no knowledge of code in the environment, it is impossible to tell apart locally feasible from globally feasible paths.

We say that a model is *complete* if every path through the unit, that corresponds to some globally feasible path through the system, will eventually be discovered by exploration done under that model. A model is *consistent* if, for every path through the unit admissible by the model, there exists a corresponding globally-feasible path through the system (i.e., the system can run concretely that way).

We now define several points that we consider of particular interest in the space of possible consistency models, progressing from strongest to weakest consistency. They are summarized in Fig. 3 using a "feasibility circles" representation. Their completeness and consistency are summarized in Table 1. We invite the reader to follow Fig. 3 while reading this section.

| Model | Consistency | Completeness | Use Case |
|---|---|---|---|
| SC-CE | consistent | incomplete | Single-path profiling/testing of units having a limited number of paths |
| SC-UE | consistent | incomplete | Analysis of units that generate hard-to-solve constraints (e.g., cryptography) |
| SC-SE | consistent | complete | Sound and complete verification without false positives/negatives, testing of tightly-coupled systems with fuzzy unit boundaries. |
| LC | locally consistent | incomplete | Testing and profiling while avoiding false positives in the unit |
| RC-OC | inconsistent | complete | Reverse engineering: extract consistent path segments |
| RC-CC | inconsistent | complete | Quick traversal of the CFG for dynamic disassembly of a binary |

**Table 1:** $S^2E$ consistency models: completeness, consistency and use cases. Each use case is assigned to the weakest model it can be accomplished with.

#### 3.1.1 Strict Consistency (SC)

The strongest form of consistency is one that admits only the globally consistent paths. For example, the concrete execution of a program always obeys the strict consistency (SC) model. Moreover, every path admitted under the SC model can be mapped to a certain concrete execution of the system starting with certain concrete inputs. Sound analyses produce no false positives under SC.

We define three subcategories of SC based on what information is taken into account when exploring new paths.

***Strictly-Consistent Concrete Execution (SC-CE)*** Under the SC-CE model, the entire system is treated as a black box: no internal information is used to explore new paths. The only explored paths are the paths that the system follows when executed with the sample input provided by the analysis. New paths can only be explored by blindly guessing new inputs. Classic fuzzing (random input testing) falls under this model.

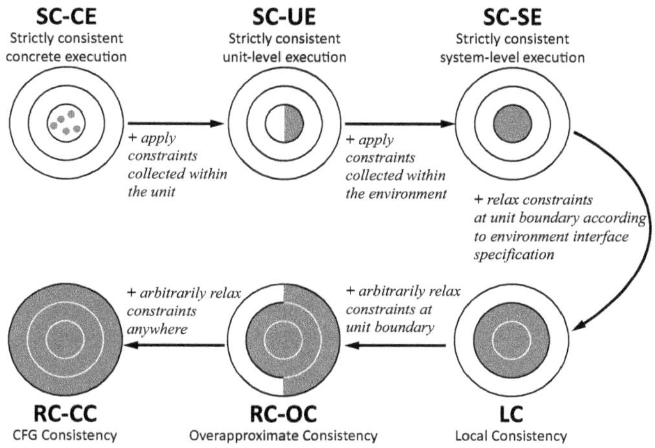


**Figure 3:** Different execution consistency models cover different sets of feasible paths. The SC-CE model corresponds to the concrete execution. The SC-UE and SC-SE models are obtained from the previous ones by using increasingly more information about the system execution to explore new states. The LC, RC-OC and RC-CC models are obtained through progressive relaxation of constraints.

***Strictly-Consistent Unit-level Execution (SC-UE)*** Under the SC-UE model, an exploration engine is allowed to gather and use information internal to the unit (e.g., by collecting path constraints while executing the unit). The environment is still treated as a black box, i.e., path constraints generated by environment code are not tracked. Not every globally feasible path can be found with such partial information (e.g., paths that are enabled by branches in the environment can be missed). However, the exploration engine saves time by not having to analyze the environment, which is typically orders of magnitude larger than the unit.

This model is widely used by symbolic and concolic execution tools [11, 12, 18]. Such tools usually instrument only the program but not the operating system code (sometimes such tools replace parts of the OS by models, effectively adding a simplified version of it as a part of the program). Whenever such tools see a call to the OS, they execute the call uninstrumented, selecting some concrete arguments for the call. Such "blind" selection of concrete arguments might cause some paths through the unit to be missed (e.g., paths that are enabled only be specific values of the arguments).

***Strictly-Consistent System-level Execution (SC-SE)*** Under the SC-SE model, an exploration engine gathers and uses information about all parts of the system, to explore new paths through the unit. Such exploration is not only sound but also complete, provided that the engine can solve all constraints it encounters. In other words, every path through the unit that is possible under a concrete execution of the system will be eventually found by SC-SE exploration, making SC-SE the only model that is both strict and complete.

However, the implementation of SC-SE is limited by the path explosion problem: the number of globally feasible paths is roughly exponential in the size of the whole system. As the environment is typically orders of magnitude larger than the unit, including its code in the analysis offers an unfavorable trade-off given today's technology.

### 3.1.2 Local Consistency (LC)

The local consistency (LC) model aims to combine the performance advantages of the SC-UE model with the completeness advantages of the SC-SE model. The idea behind LC is to replace the results of executing selected parts of the environment with symbolic values that represent any possible valid result of the execution.

For example, when a program calls the `write(fd, buf, count)` function of a POSIX OS, the function can return any integer value between -1 and `count`, depending on the state of the system. The exploration engine can discard the actual value returned by the system and treat it as a symbolic integer between -1 and `count`. This allows exploring all paths through the program, enabled by different return values of the `write` function, without having to find concrete inputs to the overall system that would enable those paths. This however introduces global inconsistency into the system, because in no concrete execution is it possible, for instance, that `count` bytes be written to the file yet the `write` function return 0. However, unless the program explicitly checks the file (e.g., by reading its content), this inconsistency can never lead to any locally infeasible paths.

More precisely, the LC model allows the exploration engine to introduce inconsistencies into the environment, while keeping the state of the unit internally consistent. However, the exploration engine must track the propagation of the inconsistencies inside the environment and abort a path as soon as these inconsistencies influence the internal state of the unit on that path.

This keeps the internal state of the unit internally consistent on all explored paths: for each explored path, there exists some concrete execution of the system that would lead to exactly the same internal state of the unit along that path—except the engine does not need to incur the cost of actually finding that path. Consequently, any sound analysis that takes into account only the internal state of the unit produces no false positives under the LC model. For this reason, we call the LC model "locally consistent".

The set of paths explored by such a strategy corresponds to the set of locally feasible paths, as defined earlier. However, some paths could be aborted before completion, or even be missed completely, due to the propagation of inconsistency. This means that the LC model is not complete. In practice, the less coupled the unit is to the environment, the fewer paths are aborted or missed.

Technically speaking, the LC model is inconsistent, thus it ought to be a sub-model of the RC model, described next. However, since the LC model is equivalent to a SC model for a large class of analyses, we devoted to it an independent category.

### 3.1.3 Relaxed Consistency (RC)

Admitting locally infeasible paths in the analysis (or, equivalently, allowing the internal state of the unit to be inconsistent) makes most analyses prone to false positives because some of the paths they operate on are globally infeasible. This might be acceptable if the analysis is itself unsound anyway, or if the analysis only relies on a subset of the state that could be kept consistent (similar to the LC model, but here the subset of the state can be different from the state of the unit).

We loosely define relaxed consistency (RC) to admit every path through the program, even those that are not allowed by the SC and LC models. The RC model is therefore inconsistent by definition.

In theory, as the RC model enables more paths, it should slow down the exploration. This can be mitigated, however, by decreasing the precision of the analysis. Another possibility is to limit the impact of this problem by enabling only certain infeasible paths and aborting these paths early on. These infeasible paths allow the engine to effectively bypass large parts of the system that would otherwise be difficult to analyze, letting the engine to reach specific code of interest much faster.

We distinguish two subcategories of the RC model that we found useful in practice.

***Overapproximate Consistency (RC-OC)*** In the RC-OC model, the exploration engine is allowed to ignore both the values produced by selected parts of the environment and the constraints that are always imposed on these values by the environment. Whenever the unit invokes these parts, the engine discards the actual return values and treats them as being completely arbitrary, even if this breaks the API contracts between the environment and the unit. Being strictly weaker than the SC-SE model, though using the same information to explore new paths, the RC-OC model is complete, but obviously not consistent.

The RC-OC model is useful, for example, for reverse engineering. It explores and allows to reverse engineer all the behaviors of the unit that are possible under a valid environment, plus some extra behaviors that are possible only when the environment behaves unexpectedly. For instance, if reverse engineering a device driver, the RC-OC model allows the hardware to return symbolic values; in this way, the resulting reverse engineered paths include some of those that correspond to allegedly impossible hardware behaviors. This makes the reverse engineering only more precise as it also reverse engineers the reactions of the original code to the unexpected behavior of the environment [13].

***CFG Consistency (RC-CC)*** In the RC-CC model, the exploration engine is allowed to change any part of the system state as long as the explored paths remain feasible in the control flow graph of the unit. This roughly corresponds to the consistency provided by static program analyzers that are dataflow-insensitive and analyze completely unconstrained paths. Being strictly weaker than the SC-SE model, though using the same information to explore new paths, the RC-CC model is complete.

The RC-CC model is useful for disassembly of obfuscated and/or encrypted code: the engine can let the code decrypt itself while running in LC mode, in order to ensure the correctness of decryption. Then, the engine switches to the RC-CC model to reach high coverage of the decrypted code and disassemble as much of it as possible.

### 3.2 Implementing Consistency Models

We now explain how the consistency models can be implemented by a selective symbolic execution engine (SSE), namely the specifics of symbolic ↔ concrete conversion as execution goes from the unit to the environment and then back again.

We illustrate the different implementations with the case of a kernel-mode device driver (Fig. 4). The driver reads and writes from/to hardware I/O ports and calls the `write_usb` function, which is implemented in a kernel-mode USB library, as well as `alloc`, implemented by the kernel itself.

```
   int send_packet(buffer, size) {
1.  packet *pkt;
2.  status = alloc(&pkt, size);
3.  if (status == FAIL) {
4.      assert(pkt == NULL);
5.      return;
6.  }
  ...
7.  if(read_port(STATUS) == READY)
8.     if (!write_usb(pkt))
9.         return FAIL;
}                                DRIVER
```

```
int write_usb(pkt) {
  if (usb_ready())
     return do_send(pkt);
  return 0;
}                          USBLIB
```

```
int alloc (*ptr, size);
...                        KERNEL
```

Unit (solid box) / Environment (dashed box)

**Figure 4:** Example of a "unit" (device driver) interacting with the "environment" (kernel-mode library and OS kernel itself).

#### 3.2.1 Implementing Strict Consistency (SC)

***Strictly-Consistent Concrete Execution (SC-CE)*** For this model, an SSE allows only concrete input to enter the system. This leads to executing a single path through the unit and the environment. The SSE can execute the whole system natively without having to track or solve any constraints, because there is no symbolic data.

***Strictly-Consistent Unit-level Execution (SC-UE)*** To implement this model, the SSE converts all symbolic data to concrete values when the unit calls the environment. The conversion is consistent with the current set of path constraints. No other conversion is performed. The environment is treated as a black box, and no symbolic data can flow into it.

In the example of Fig. 4, the SSE concretizes the content of packet `pkt` when calling `write_usb` and, from there on, this soft constraint (see §2.2) is treated as a hard constraint on the content of `pkt`. The resulting paths trough the driver are globally feasible paths, but exploration is not complete, because treating the constraint as hard can curtail globally feasible paths during the exploration of the driver (e.g., paths that depend on the packet type).

***Strictly-Consistent System-level Execution (SC-SE)*** Under SC-SE, the SSE lets symbolic data cross the unit/environment boundary. As a result, the entire system is executed symbolically, while preserving global execution consistency.

Consider the `write_usb` function: This function gets its input from the USB host controller. Under strict consistency, the USB host controller (being "outside the system") can return a symbolic value, which in turn propagates through the USB library, eventually causing `usb_ready` to return a symbolic value as well.

State explosion caused by large environments can make SC-SE hard to use in practice. The paths that go through the environment can outnumber those that go through the unit of interest, possibly delaying useful exploration. An SSE can heuristically prioritize the paths to explore, or employ *incremental symbolic execution*, which executes parts of the environment as much as necessary to discover interesting paths in the unit quicker. We describe this next.

The execution of `write_usb` proceeds as if it was executed symbolically, but only one globally feasible path is pursued in a depth-first manner, while all other the forked paths are stored in a wait list. This simulates a concrete, single-path execution through a symbolically executing environment. After returning to `send_packet`, the path being executed carries the constraints that were accumulated in the environment, and symbolic execution continues in `send_packet` as if `write_usb` had executed symbolically. The return value $x$ of `write_usb` is constrained according to the depth-first path pursued in the USB library, and so are the side effects. If, while executing `send_packet`, a branch that depends on $x$ becomes infeasible due to the constraints imposed by the call to `write_usb`, the SSE returns to the wait list and resumes execution of a wait-listed path that, e.g., is likely to eventually execute line 9.

#### 3.2.2 Implementing Local Consistency (LC)

In this model, an SSE converts concrete values generated at interface boundaries inside the environment to properly-constrained symbolic data that conforms to the interface specifications. To satisfy the definition of LC, the SSE tracks the propagation of the converted data through the system, to detect violations of LC. For this, the SSE monitors the execution of each path and signals a violation whenever any converted data is read again by the system.

For the driver in Fig. 4, SSE turns the concrete `alloc`'s return value $v$ into a symbolic value $s$ constrained to equal $v$ or to equal `FAIL`. The SSE also constrains `pkt` to be null in case $v$ is `FAIL`, to respect the OS API contract.

For the driver, the global state can be inconsistent, since the driver explores a failure path when no failure occurred. However, this inconsistency has no effect on the execution, as long as the OS does not make assumptions about whether or not buffers are still allocated after the driver's failure. LC would have been violated had the OS read the symbolic value of `pkt`, e.g., if the driver stored it in an OS-specific structure.

#### 3.2.3 Implementing Relaxed Consistency (RC)

***Overapproximate Consistency (RC-OC)*** In this model, the SSE converts concrete values at interface boundaries to unconstrained symbolic values, regardless of the interface contract. E.g., when returning from `alloc`, both `pkt` and `status` are marked symbolic.

This model brings completeness at the expense of substantial overapproximation. No feasible paths are ever excluded from the symbolic execution of `send_packet`, but since `pkt` and `status` are completely unconstrained, there could be many locally infeasible paths when exploring `send_packet` after the call to `alloc`.

For example, the `assert` on line 4 would fail, which is normally impossible, because `alloc` is guaranteed to set `pkt` to null whenever it returns `FAIL`. The assertion failure occurs because `status` is unconstrained on line 3, enabling the execution of line 4. On line 4, `pkt` is also unconstrained, which triggers the exploration of both outcomes of the `assert` statement. Under stronger consistency models, `pkt` must be null if `status==FAIL` holds.

***CFG Consistency (RC-CC)*** Finally, SSE can implement RC-CC by further allowing the unconstraining of branch conditions. This enables an SSE to follow all the edges of the unit's control flow graph. This is useful in the case of a dynamic disassembler: running with stronger consistency models may leave uncovered (i.e., non-disassembled) code. Instead, RC-CC forces the disassembly of the missing code. Implementing RC-CC requires program-specific knowledge to avoid exploring non-existing edges, as in the case of an indirect jump pointing to an unconstrained memory location.

### 3.3 Consistency Models in Existing Tools

We illustrate now the consistency models by surveying some existing tools that implement similar levels of consistency.

Most dynamic analysis tools use the SC-CE model. Examples include Valgrind [37], PIN [26], and Eraser [32]. These tools execute and analyze programs along a single path, generated by user-specified concrete input values. Being significantly faster than multi-path exploration, analyses performed by such tools are, for instance, useful to characterize or explain program behavior on a small set of developer-specified paths (i.e., test cases). However, such tools cannot provide any confidence that results of the analyses extend beyond the concretely explored paths.

Dynamic test case generation tools usually employ either the SC-UE or the SC-SE models. For example, DART [18] uses the SC-UE model. It executes the program concretely (starting with random inputs) but instruments the code to collect path constraints on each execution. DART uses these constraints to produce new concrete inputs that would drive the program along a different path on the next run. However, DART does not instrument the environment and hence cannot use information from it when generating new concrete inputs, thus missing feasible paths as indicated by SC-UE.

As another example, KLEE [11] uses either the SC-SE or a form of the SC-UE model, depending on whether the environment is modeled or not. In the former case, both the unit and the model of the environment are executed symbolically. In the latter case, whenever the unit calls the environment, KLEE executes the environment with concrete arguments. However, KLEE does not track the side effects of the environment, allowing them to propagate across otherwise independent execution paths, thus making the corresponding program states inconsistent. Because of this limitation, the implementation of the SC-UE model in KLEE is not exact.

Static analysis tools usually implement some forms of the RC model. For example, SDV [2] converts a program into a boolean form, which is an over-approximation of the original program. Consequently, every path that is feasible in the original program would be found by SDV, but it also finds additional infeasible paths.

## 4. System Analysis with $S^2E$

$S^2E$ is a platform for rapid prototyping of custom system analyses. It offers two key interfaces: the *selection* interface, used to guide the exploration of execution paths (and thus implement arbitrary consistency models), and the *analysis* interface, used to collect events or check properties of execution paths. Both interfaces accept modular selection and analysis plugins. Underneath the covers, $S^2E$ consists of a customized virtual machine, a dynamic binary translator (DBT), and an embedded symbolic execution engine, as shown in Fig. 5. The DBT decides which guest machine instructions to execute natively on the physical CPU vs. which ones to execute symbolically using the embedded symbolic execution engine.

$S^2E$ provides many plugins out of the box for building custom analysis tools—we describe these plugins in §4.1. One can also extend $S^2E$ with new plugins, using $S^2E$'s developer API (§4.2).

### 4.1 User Interface

**Path Selection:** The first step in using $S^2E$ is deciding on a policy for which part of a program to execute in multi-path (symbolic) mode vs. single-path (concrete) mode; this policy is encoded in a selector. $S^2E$ provides a default set of selectors for the most common types of selection. They fall into three categories:

Data-based selection provides a way to expand an execution path into a multi-path execution by introducing symbolic values into the system—any time $S^2E$ encounters a branch predicate involving a symbolic value, it will fork the execution. Symbolic data can enter the program from various sources, and $S^2E$ provides a selector for each: *CommandLine* for symbolic command-line arguments, *Environment* for environment variables, *MSWinRegistry* for Microsoft Windows-specific registry entries, etc.

Often it is useful to introduce a symbolic value at an internal interface. For example, say a server program calls a library function `libFn`$(x)$ almost always with $x = 10$, but may call it with $x < 10$ in strange corner cases that are hard to induce via external workloads. The developer might therefore be interested in exploring the behavior of `libFn` for all values $0 \leq x \leq 10$. For such analyses, we provide an *Annotation* plugin, which allows direct injection of custom-constrained symbolic values anywhere they are needed.

Code-based selection enables/disables multi-path execution depending on whether the program counter is or not within a target code area; e.g., one might focus cache profiling on a web browser's SSL code, to see if it is vulnerable to side channel attacks. The *CodeSelector* plugin takes the name of the target program, library, driver, etc. and a list of program counter ranges. Each such range can be an inclusion or an exclusion range, indicating that code within that range should be explored in multi-path mode or single-path mode, respectively. *CodeSelector* is typically used in conjunction with data-based selectors to constrain the data-selected multi-path execution to within only code of interest.

Priority-based selection is used to define the order in which paths are explored within the family of paths defined with data-based and code-based selectors. $S^2E$ includes some obvious choices, such as *Random*, *DepthFirst*, and *BreadthFirst*. The *MaxCoverage* selector works in conjunction with coverage analyzers to heuristically select paths that maximize coverage. The *PathKiller* selector monitors the executed program and deletes paths that are determined to no longer be of interest to the analysis. For example, paths can be killed if a fixed sequence of program counters repeats more than $n$ times; this avoids getting stuck in polling loops.

**Path Analysis:** Once the selectors define a family of paths, $S^2E$ executes these paths and exposes each one of them to the analyzer plugins. One class of analyzers are bug finders, such as *DataRaceDetector* and *MemoryChecker*, which look for the corresponding bug conditions and output an executable execution trace

| | |
|---|---|
| onInstrTranslation | DBT is about to translate a machine instruction |
| onInstrExecution | VM is about to execute an instruction |
| onExecutionFork | $S^2E$ is about to fork execution |
| onException | The VM interrupt pin has been asserted |
| onMemoryAccess | VM is about to execute a memory access |

**Table 2:** Core events exported by the $S^2E$ platform.

| | |
|---|---|
| multiPathOn/Off() | turn on/off multi-path execution |
| readMem(*addr*) | read contents of memory at address *addr* |
| writeReg(*reg, val*) | write *val* (symbolic or concrete) to *reg* |
| getCurTransBlock() | currently executing code block from DBT |
| raiseInterrupt(*irq*) | assert the interrupt line for *irq* |

**Table 3:** Subset of the *ExecState* object's interface.

every time they encounter a bug. Another type of analyzer is *ExecutionTracer*, which selectively records the instructions executed along a path, along with the memory accesses, register values, and hardware I/O. It can be used to measure coverage with offline tools. Finally, the *PerformanceProfile* analyzer counts cache misses, TLB misses, and page faults incurred along each path—this can be used to obtain a performance envelope of an application, and we describe it in more detail in the evaluation section (§6).

While most plugins are OS-agnostic, $S^2E$ comes with a set of analyzers that expose Windows-specific events using undocumented interfaces or other hacks. For example, the *WinDriverMon* analyzer parses OS-private data structures and notifies other plugins when the Windows kernel loads a driver. The *WinBugCheck* plugin catches "blue screen of death" events and kernel hangs.

### 4.2 Developer Interface

We now describe the interface that can be used to write new plugins or to extend the default plugins described above. Both selectors and analyzers use the same interface; the only distinction between selectors and analyzers is that selectors influence the execution of the program, whereas analyzers are passive observers. $S^2E$ also allows writing of plugins that arbitrarily modify the execution state.

$S^2E$ has a modular plugin architecture, in which plugins communicate via events in a publish/subscribe fashion. $S^2E$ events are generated either by the $S^2E$ platform or by other plugins. To register for a class of events, a plugin invokes *onEventX(callbackPtr)*. An event callback is invoked every time *EventX* occurs. Callbacks have different parameters, depending on the type of event.

Table 2 shows the *core events* exported by $S^2E$ that arise from regular code translation and execution. We chose these core events because they correspond to the lowest possible level of abstraction of execution: instruction translation, execution, memory accesses, and state forking. It is possible to build any state manipulation and analysis on top of them, as we will show in the evaluation.

**The ExecState object** captures the current state of the entire virtual machine *along a specific path*. It is the first parameter of every event callback. *ExecState* gives plugins read/write access to the entire VM state, including the processor, VM physical memory, and virtual devices. Plugins can also toggle multi-path execution and read/write VM memory and registers (see Table 3 for a short list of API functions). A plugin can obtain the PID of the running process from the page directory base register, can read/write page tables and physical memory, can change the control flow by modifying the program counter, and so on.

For each path being explored, there exists a distinct *ExecState* object instance; when execution forks, each child execution receives its own private copy of the parent *ExecState*. Aggressive use of copy-on-write reduces the memory overhead substantially (§5).

Plugins partition their own state into per-path state (e.g., number of cache misses along a path) and global state (e.g., total number of basic blocks touched). The per-path state is stored in a *PluginState* object, which hangs off of the *ExecState* object. *PluginState* must implement a *clone* method, so that it can be cloned together with *ExecState* whenever $S^2E$ forks execution. Global plugin state can live in the plugin's own heap.

The dynamic binary translator (DBT) turns blocks of guest code into corresponding host code; for each block of code this is typically done only once. During the translation process, a plugin may be interested in marking certain instructions (e.g., function calls) for subsequent notification. It registers for *onInstrTranslation* and, when notified, it inspects the *ExecState* to see which instruction is about to be translated; if it is of interest (e.g., a `CALL` instruction), the plugin marks it. Whenever the VM executes a marked instruction, it raises the *onInstrExecution* event, which notifies the registered plugin. For example, the *CodeSelector* plugin is implemented as a subscriber to *onInstrTranslation* events; upon receiving an event, it marks the instruction depending on whether it is or not an entry/exit point for a code range of interest. Having the *onInstrTranslation* and *onInstrExecution* events separate leverages the fact that each instruction gets translated once, but may get executed millions of times, as in the body of a loop. For most analyses, *onInstrTranslation* ends up being raised so rarely that using it introduces no runtime overhead (e.g., catching the kernel panic handler requires instrumenting only the first instruction of that handler).

**$S^2E$ opcodes** are custom guest machine instructions that are directly interpreted by $S^2E$, and they provide a communication channel that circumvents all plugins. $S^2E$ has an extensible set of opcodes for creating symbolic values (`S2SYM`), enabling/disabling multi-path execution (`S2ENA` and `S2DIS`) and logging debug information (`S2OUT`). These give developers even finer grain control over multi-path execution and analysis; they can be injected into the target programs using tools like PIN [26]. In practice, opcodes are the easiest way to mark data symbolic and get started with $S^2E$.

The interface presented here was sufficient for all the multi-path analyses we attempted with $S^2E$. Selectors can enable or disable multi-path execution based on arbitrary criteria and can manipulate machine state. Analyzers can collect information about low-level hardware events all the way up to program-level events, they can probe memory to extract any information they need, and so on.

## 5. $S^2E$ Prototype

The $S^2E$ platform prototype (Fig. 5) reuses parts of the QEMU virtual machine [4], the KLEE symbolic execution engine [11], and the LLVM tool chain [24]. To these, we added 23 KLOC of C++ code written from scratch, not including third party libraries[2]. We added 1 KLOC of new code to KLEE and modified 1.5 KLOC; in QEMU, we added 1.5 KLOC of new code and modified 3.5 KLOC of existing code. $S^2E$ currently runs on MacOS X, Windows, and Linux, it can execute any guest OS that runs on x86, and can be easily extended to other CPU architectures, like ARM or PowerPC. $S^2E$ can be downloaded from `http://s2e.epfl.ch`.

$S^2E$ explores paths by running the target system in a virtual machine and selectively executing small parts of it symbolically. Depending on which paths are desired, some of the system's machine instructions are dynamically translated within the VM into an intermediate representation suitable for symbolic execution, while the rest are translated to the host instruction set. Underneath the covers, $S^2E$ transparently converts data back and forth as execution weaves between the symbolic and concrete domains, so as to offer the illusion that the full system (OS, libraries, applications, etc.) is executing in multi-path mode.

$S^2E$ mixes concrete with symbolic execution in the same path by using a representation of machine state that is shared between the VM and the embedded symbolic execution engine. $S^2E$ shares the

[2] All reported LOC measurements were obtained with SLOCCount [38].

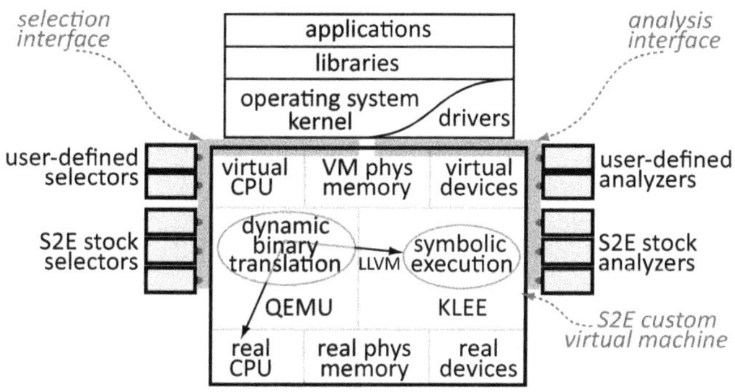


**Figure 5:** S²E architecture.

state by redirecting reads and writes from QEMU and KLEE to the common machine state—VM physical memory, virtual CPU state, and virtual device state. In this way, S²E provides distinct copies of the entire machine state to distinct paths and can transparently convert data between concrete and symbolic. S²E reduces the memory footprint of all these states using copy-on-write optimizations.

In order to achieve transparent interleaving of symbolic and concrete execution, we modified QEMU's DBT to translate the instructions that depend on symbolic data to LLVM and dispatch them to KLEE. Most instructions, however, run natively; this is the case even in the symbolic domain, because most instructions do not operate on symbolic state. We wrote an x86-to-LLVM back-end for QEMU, so neither the guest OS nor KLEE are aware of the x86 to LLVM translation. S²E redirects all guest physical memory accesses, including MMIO devices, to the KLEE memory state object.

Besides VM physical memory, S²E must also manage the internal state of the virtual devices when switching between execution paths. We use QEMU's snapshot mechanism to automatically save and restore virtual devices and CPU states when switching execution states. The shared representation of memory and device state between the concrete and symbolic domains enables S²E to do on-demand concretization of data that is stored as symbolic. A snapshot can range from hundreds of MBs to GBs; we use aggressive copy-on-write to transparently share common state between snapshots of physical memory and disks. Some state need not be saved—for example, we do not snapshot video memory, so all paths share the same framebuffer. As an aside, this makes for intriguing visual effects on screen: multiple erratic mouse cursors and BSODs blend chaotically, providing free entertainment to the S²E user.

Interleaved concrete/symbolic execution and copy-on-write are transparent to the guest OS, so all guest OSes can run out of the box. Sharing state between QEMU and KLEE allows the guest to have a view of the system that is consistent with the chosen execution consistency model. It also makes it easy to replay execution paths of interest, e.g., to replay a bug found by a bug-detection analyzer.

Conversion from x86 to LLVM gives rise to complex symbolic expressions. S²E sees a much lower level representation of the programs than what would be obtained by compiling source code to LLVM (as done in KLEE): it actually sees the code that simulates the execution of the original program on the target CPU architecture. Such code typically contains many bitfield operations (e.g., `and`, `or`, `shift`, masking to extract or set bits in the `eflags` register).

We therefore implemented a bitfield-theory expression simplifier to optimize these expressions. The simplifier relies on the observation that, if parts of symbolic variables are masked away by bit operations, there is an opportunity to simplify the corresponding expressions. First, the simplifier starts from the bottom of the expression (represented as a tree) and propagates information about individual bits whose value is known. If an expression has all bits known, we replace it with the constant result. Second, the simplifier propagates top-down information about bits that are ignored by the upper part of the expression—when an operator modifies only bits that are ignored later, the simplifier removes that entire operation.

Symbolic expressions can also appear in pointers (e.g., as array indices or jump tables generated by compilers for switch statements). When a memory access with a symbolic pointer occurs, S²E determines the pages referenced by the pointer, before passing their contents to the constraint solver. Alas, large page sizes can lead to exponential complexity that bottlenecks the solver, so S²E splits the memory into small pages of configurable size (e.g., 128 bytes), so that the constraint solver need not reason about large areas. In §6.2 we show how much this helps in practice.

Finally, S²E must carefully handle time. Each system state has its own virtual time, which freezes when that state is not being run (i.e., is not in an actively explored path). Since running code symbolically is slower than native, S²E slows down the virtual clock when symbolically executing a state. If it didn't do this, the (relatively) frequent VM timer interrupts would overwhelm execution and prevent progress. S²E also offers an opcode to completely disable interrupts for a section of code to further reduce the overhead.

## 6. Evaluation

We now answer three key questions: Is S²E truly a general platform for running diverse analysis tools (§6.1)? Does S²E perform these analyses with reasonable performance (§6.2)? What are the measured trade-offs involved in choosing different execution consistency models on both kernel-mode and user-mode binaries (§6.3)? Unless otherwise specified, the reported results were obtained on a $2 \times$ 4-core Intel Xeon E5405 2GHz machine with 20 GB of RAM.

### 6.1 Three Use Cases

First, we used S²E to build three vastly different tools: an automated tester for proprietary drivers (§6.1.1), a reverse engineering tool for binary drivers (§6.1.2), and a multi-path in-vivo performance profiler (§6.1.3). The first two use cases are complete rewrites of two systems that were built previously in an ad-hoc manner: RevNIC [13] and DDT [22]. The third use case is brand new.

One of S²E's main goals is to enable rapid prototyping of useful analysis tools. Before looking at the individual use cases, we show in Table 4 the substantial productivity advantage of using S²E compared to writing these tools from scratch. For the tools we built, S²E engendered two orders of magnitude improvement in both development time and resulting code volume. This justifies our efforts to create general abstractions for multi-path in-vivo analyses, and to centralize them into one platform.

| Use Case | Development Time [ person-hours ] | | Tool Complexity [ lines of code ] | |
|---|---|---|---|---|
| | *from scratch* | *with S²E* | *from scratch* | *with S²E* |
| Testing of proprietary device drivers | 2,400 | 38 | 47,000 | 720 |
| Reverse engineering of closed-source drivers | 3,000 | 40 | 57,000 | 580 |
| Multi-path in-vivo performance profiling | n/a | 20 | n/a | 767 |

**Table 4:** Comparative productivity when building analysis tools from scratch (i.e., without S²E) vs. using S²E. Reported LOC include only new code written or modified; any code that was reused from QEMU, KLEE, or other sources is not included. For reverse engineering, 10 KLOC of offline analysis code is used in both versions. For performance profiling, we do not know of any equivalent non-S²E tool, hence the lack of comparison.

#### 6.1.1 Automated Testing of Proprietary Device Drivers

We used S²E to build DDT⁺, a tool for testing closed-source Windows device drivers. This is a reimplementation of DDT [22], an ad-hoc combination of changes to QEMU and KLEE, along with hand-written interface annotations: 35 KLOC added to QEMU, 3 KLOC added to KLEE, 2 KLOC modified in KLEE, and 7 KLOC modified in QEMU. By contrast, DDT$^+$ has 720 LOC of C++ code, which glues together several exploration and analysis plugins, and provides the necessary kernel/driver interface annotations.

DDT$^+$ combines several plugins: the *CodeSelector* plugin restricts multi-path exploration to the target driver, while the *MemoryCheck*, *DataRaceDetector*, and *WinBugCheck* analyzers look for bugs. To collect additional information about the quality of testing (e.g., coverage), we use the *ExecutionTracer* analyzer plugin. Additional checkers can be easily added. DDT$^+$ implements local consistency (LC) via interface annotations that specify where to inject symbolic values while respecting local consistency—examples of annotations appear in [22]. In the absence of annotations, DDT$^+$ reverts to strict consistency (SC-SE), where the only symbolic input comes from hardware. None of the reported bugs are false positives, indicating the appropriateness of local consistency for bug finding.

We run DDT$^+$ on two Windows network drivers, RTL8029 and AMD PCnet. DDT$^+$ finds the same 7 bugs reported in [22], including memory leaks, segmentation faults, race conditions, and memory corruption. Of these bugs, 2 can be found when operating under SC-SE consistency; relaxation to local consistency (via annotations) helps find 5 additional bugs. DDT$^+$ takes <20 minutes to complete testing of each driver and explores thousands of paths in each one.

For each bug found, DDT$^+$ outputs a crash dump, an instruction trace, a memory trace, a set of concrete inputs (e.g., registry values and hardware input) and values that where injected according to the LC model that trigger the buggy execution path.

As DDT$^+$ uses the LC model, the traces may are globally infeasible. Indeed, while it is always possible to produce concrete inputs for the system that would lead it to the same local state (i.e., to reproduce the bug) along a globally feasible path, the exploration engine does not do it in a LC model. Consequently, replaying execution traces provided by DDT$^+$ requires replaying the injection into the system that was made in accordance to the LC model. Such replaying could be done in S$^2$E itself. Despite being only locally consistent, the replay is still useful for debugging: the execution of the driver during the replay is valid and consistant, injected correspond to the values that the kernel could have passed to the driver under different conditions.

S$^2$E generates crash dumps readable by Microsoft WinDbg. Developers can thus inspect the crashes using their existing tools, scripts, and extensions for WinDbg. They can also compare crash dumps from different execution paths to better understand the bugs.

### 6.1.2 Reverse Engineering of Closed-Source Drivers

We also built REV$^+$, a tool for reverse engineering binary Windows device drivers; it is a reimplementation of RevNIC [13]. REV$^+$ takes a closed-source binary driver, traces its execution, and then feeds the traces to an offline component that reverse engineers the driver's logic and produces new device driver code that implements the exact same hardware protocol as the original driver. In principle, REV$^+$ can synthesize drivers for any OS, making it easy to port device drivers, without any vendor documentation or source code.

Adopting the S$^2$E perspective, we cast reverse engineering as a type of behavior analysis. As in DDT$^+$, the *CodeSelector* plugin restricts the symbolic domain to the driver's code segment. The *ExecutionTracer* plugin is configured to log the driver's executed instructions, memory and register accesses, hardware I/O, and writes them to a file. The existing RevNIC's offline analysis tool processes these traces to synthesize a new driver.

REV$^+$ uses overapproximate consistency (RC-OC). The main goal of the tracer is to merely see each basic block execute, in order to extract its logic—full path consistency is not necessary. The trace interpreter only needs fragments of paths in order to reconstruct the original control flow graph—details appear in [13]. By using RC-OC, REV$^+$ sacrifices consistency in favor of obtaining coverage fast.

| | RevNIC | REV$^+$ | Improvement |
|---|---|---|---|
| PCnet | 59% | 66% | +7% |
| RTL8029 | 82% | 87% | +5% |
| 91C111 | 84% | 87% | +3% |
| RTL8139 | 84% | 86% | +2% |

**Table 5:** REV$^+$ obtains better coverage than RevNIC.

We run REV$^+$ on the same drivers reported in [13], and REV$^+$ reverse engineers them with better coverage than RevNIC (see Table 5) in less than an hour. Fig. 6 shows how coverage evolves over time during reverse engineering. By inspecting the covered basic blocks, we found the resulting drivers to be equivalent to those generated by RevNIC.

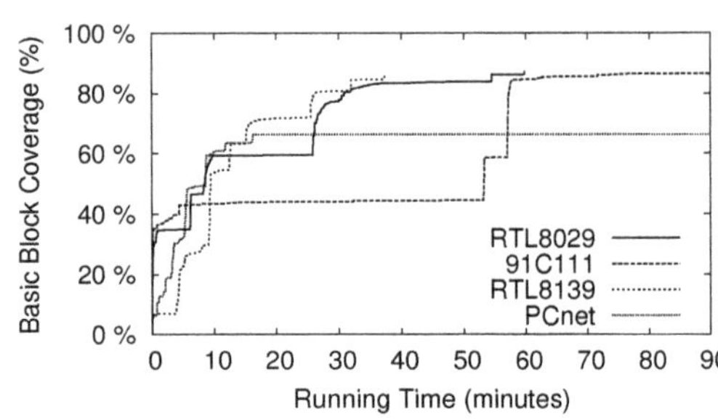


**Figure 6:** Basic block coverage over time for REV$^+$.

### 6.1.3 Multi-Path In-Vivo Performance Profiling

To further illustrate S$^2$E's generality, we used it to develop PROF$_S$, a multi-path in-vivo performance profiler and debugger. To our knowledge, such a tool does not exist today, and this use case is the first in the literature to employ symbolic execution for performance analysis. In this section, we show through several examples how PROF$_S$ can be used to predict performance for certain classes of inputs. To obtain realistic profiles, performance analysis can be done under local consistency or any stricter consistency models.

PROF$_S$ allows users to measure instruction count, cache misses, TLB misses, and page faults for arbitrary memory hierarchies, with flexibility to combine any number of cache levels, size, associativity, line sizes, etc. This is a superset of the cache profiling functionality found in Valgrind [37], which can only simulate L1 and L2 caches, and can only measure cache misses.

To build PROF$_S$, we developed the *PerformanceProfile* plugin. It counts the number of instructions along each path and, for read and write operations, it simulates the behavior of the desired cache hierarchy and counts hits and misses. This plugin is a generalization of the logic contained in Valgrind. The path exploration in PROF$_S$ is tunable, allowing the user to choose any execution consistency model. We configured PROF$_S$ with 64 KB I1 and D1 caches with 64-byte cache lines and associativity 2. We also configured a 1 MB L2 cache with 64-byte cache lines and associativity 4.

The first PROF$_S$ experiment analyzes the distribution of instruction counts and cache misses for Apache's URL parser. In particular, we were interested to see whether there is any opportunity for a denial-of-service attack on the Apache web server via carefully constructed URLs. The analysis ran under local consistency for 9.5 hours and explored 5,515 different paths through the code. Of the 9.5 hours, 2.5 hours were spent in the constraint solver and 6 hours were spent running concrete code. In this experiment, the analysis carries high overhead, because it simulates a TLB and 3 caches.

We found each path involved in parsing a URL to take on the order of $4.3 \times 10^6$ instructions, with one interesting feature: for every additional "/" character present in the URL, there are 10 extra instructions being executed. We found no upper bound on the execution of URL parsing: a URL containing $n + k$ "/" characters will take $10 \times k$ more instructions to parse than a URL with $n$ "/" characters. The total number of cache misses on each path was predictable at $15,984 \pm 20$. These are examples of behavioral insights one can obtain with a multi-path performance profiler. Such insights can help developers fine-tune their code or make it more secure (e.g., by checking that password processing time does not depend on the password itself, to avoid side channel attacks).

We also set out to measure the page fault rate experienced by the Microsoft IIS web server inside its SSL modules while serving a static page workload over HTTPS. Our goal was to check the distribution of page faults in the cryptographic algorithms, to see if there is any opportunity for side channel attacks. We found no page faults in the SSL code along any of the paths, and only a small number of them in gzip.dll. This suggests that counting page faults should not be the first choice if trying to break IIS's SSL encryption.

Next, we aimed to establish a performance envelope in terms of instructions executed, cache misses, and page faults for the ubiquitous `ping` program. This program has on the order of 1.3 KLOC. The performance analysis ran under local consistency LC, explored 1,250 different paths, and ran for 5.9 hours. Unlike the URL parsing case, almost 5.8 hours of the analysis were spent in the constraint solver—the first 1,000 paths were explored during the first 3 hours, after which the exploration rate slowed down.

The analysis did not find a bound on execution time, and pointed to a path that could go around a loop without bound. This happens when the reply packet to `ping`'s initial packet has the record route (RR) flag set and the option length is 3 bytes, leaving no room to store the IP address list. `ping` finds that the list of addresses is empty and, instead of `break`-ing out of the loop, it does `continue` without updating the loop counter. This is an example where performance analysis can identify a performance bug that some may consider a security bug. Once we patched `ping`, we found the performance envelope to consist of a minimum of 1,645 and a maximum of 129,086 instructions executed. When the bug was still present, the maximum had reached $1.5 \times 10^6$ and continued growing.

PROF$_S$ can also find inputs for which we get best-case performance, without enumerating all paths. For this, we modify slightly the *PerformanceProfile* plugin to keep track of the current lower bound (for instructions, page faults, etc.) across all paths being explored at the moment; any time a path exceeds this minimum, its exploration is automatically abandoned. This modification makes use of the *PathKiller* selector, described in §4. This type of functionality can be used, e.g., to efficiently and automatically determine workloads that make a system perform at its best; it is an example of something that can only be done using multi-path analysis.

We wanted to compare our results to what a combination of existing tools could achieve: run KLEE to obtain inputs for paths through the program, then run each such test case in Valgrind (for multi-path analysis) and with Oprofile (for in-vivo analysis). This is not possible for `ping`, because KLEE's networking model does not support ICMP packets. It is not possible for binary drivers either, because KLEE cannot fork kernel state and requires source code. These difficulties illustrate the benefits of having a platform like S$^2$E that does not require models and can automatically cross back and forth the boundary between symbolic and concrete domains.

To conclude, we used S$^2$E to build a thorough multi-path in-vivo performance profiler that achieves better path coverage (and therefore more precise results) than classic profilers. Valgrind [37] is thorough, but only single-path and not in-vivo. Unlike Valgrind-type tools, PROF$_S$ performs its analyses along multiple paths at a time, not just one, and can measure the effects of the OS kernel on the program's cache behavior and vice versa, not just the program in isolation. Although tools like Oprofile [29] can perform in-vivo measurements, but not multi-path, they are based on sampling, so they lack the precision of PROF$_S$—it is impossible, for instance, to count the exact number of cache misses in an execution. Such improvements over state-of-the-art tools come "for free" with S$^2$E.

#### 6.1.4 Other Uses of S$^2$E

S$^2$E can be used for pretty much any type of system-wide analysis. We describe here four additional ideas: energy profiling, hardware validation, certification of binaries, and privacy analysis.

First, S$^2$E could be used to profile energy use of embedded applications: given a power consumption model, S$^2$E could find energy-hogging paths and help the developer optimize them. Second, S$^2$E could serve as a hardware model validator: S$^2$E can symbolically execute a SystemC-based model together with the real driver and OS; when there is enough confidence in the correctness of the hardware model, the chip can be synthesized. Third, S$^2$E could perform end-to-end certification of binaries—S$^2$E alleviates the need to trust a compiler, since it performs all analysis on the final binary. For instance, S$^2$E could check that memory safety holds along all critical paths. Finally, S$^2$E could be used to analyze binaries for privacy leaks: by monitoring the flow of symbolic input values (e.g., credit card numbers) through the software stack, S$^2$E could tell whether any of the data leaks outside the system.

### 6.2 Implementation Overhead

S2E introduces ~6× runtime overhead over vanilla QEMU when running in concrete mode, and ~78× in symbolic mode. Concrete-mode overhead is mainly due to checks for accesses to symbolic memory (for lazy concretization), while the overhead in symbolic mode is due to interpretation and handling of symbolic expressions.

The overhead of symbolic execution is mitigated in practice by the fact that the symbolic domain is much smaller than the concrete domain. All the system code (e.g., page fault handler, timer interrupt, system calls) that is called frequently, as well as all the software that is running (e.g., services and daemons) are in concrete mode. Furthermore, S$^2$E can distinguish inside the symbolic domain instructions that can execute concretely (e.g., when they do not touch symbolic data) and run them natively. For instance, for the `ping` experiments, S$^2$E executed $3 \times 10^4$ times more x86 instructions concretely than it did symbolically. These 4 orders of magnitude provide a *lower* bound on the amount of savings selective symbolic execution brings over classic symbolic execution: by executing concretely those paths that would otherwise run symbolically, S$^2$E saves the overhead of further forking (e.g., on branches inside the concrete domain) paths that are ultimately not of interest.

Another source of overhead comes from symbolic pointers. We compared the performance of symbolically executing the `unlink` utility's x86 binary in S$^2$E vs. symbolically executing its LLVM version in KLEE. Since KLEE recognizes all memory allocations performed by the program, it can pass to the constraint solver memory arrays of exactly the right size; in contrast, S$^2$E must pass entire memory pages. In 1 hour, with a 256-byte page size, S$^2$E explores 7,082 paths, compared to 7,886 paths in KLEE. Average constraint solving time is 0.06 sec for both. With 4 KB pages, though, S$^2$E explores only 2,000 states and averages 0.15 sec per constraint.

We plan to reduce this overhead in two ways: First, we can instrument the LLVM bitcode generated by S2E with calls to the symbolic execution engine, before JITing it into native machine code, to avoid the overhead of interpreting each instruction in KLEE. This is similar in spirit to what QEMU does vis-a-vis the Bochs [6] emulator: while the latter interprets instructions in one giant switch

| Consistency | 91C111 Driver | PCnet Driver | Lua |
|---|---|---|---|
| RC-OC | 1,400 | 3,300 | 1,103 |
| LC | 1,600 | 3,200 | 1,114 |
| SC-SE | 1,700 | 1,300 | 1,148 |
| SC-UE | 5 | 7 | - |

**Table 6:** Time (in sec) under different consistencies: overapproximate (RC-OC), local (LC), system-level strict (SC-SE), and unit-level strict (SC-UE).

statement, the former JITs them to native code, which results in a significant speedup. Second, we plan to add support for directly executing native LLVM binaries inside S$^2$E, which would reduce significantly the blowup resulting from x86-to-LLVM translation and would reduce the overhead of symbolic pointers.

### 6.3 Execution Consistency Model Trade-Offs

Having seen the ability of S$^2$E to serve as a platform for building powerful analysis tools, we now experimentally evaluate the trade-offs involved in the use of different execution consistency models. In particular, we measure how total running time, memory usage, and path coverage efficiency are influenced by the choice of models. We illustrate the tradeoffs using both kernel-mode binaries—the SMSC 91C111 and AMD PCnet network drivers—and a user-mode binary—the interpreter for the Lua embedded scripting language [25]. The 91C111 closed-source driver binary has 19 KB, PCnet has 35 KB; the symbolic domain consists of the driver, and the concrete domain is everything else. Lua has 12.7 KLOC; the concrete domain consists of the lexer+parser (2 KLOC) and the environment, while the symbolic domain is the remaining code (e.g., the interpreter). Parsers are the bane of symbolic execution engines, because they have many possible execution paths, of which only a small fraction are paths that pass the parsing/lexing stage [19]. The ease of separating the Lua interpreter from its parser in S$^2$E illustrates the benefit of selective symbolic execution.

We use a script in the guest OS to call the entry points of the drivers. Execution proceeds until all paths have reached the `unload` entry point. We configure a selector plugin to exercise the entry points in steps. If S$^2$E has not discovered any new basic block for some time (60 sec), this plugin kills all paths but one at random. The plugin chooses the remaining path so that execution can proceed to the next entry point.

The selector plugin also discards redundant subtrees when entry points return and makes it possible to exercise entire drivers. Without path selection, drivers would remain stuck in the early initialization phase, because of the state explosion problem. E.g., the tree rooted at the initialization entry point may have several thousand leaves (paths) when its exploration completes. Yet, calling the next entry point in the context of these execution states will mostly exercise the same paths, because these states have few differences.

For Lua, we provided a symbolic string as the input program in the Lua language, under SC-SE consistency. Under local consistency, the input is concrete, and we insert a suitably constrained symbolic Lua opcode after the parser stage. Finally, in RC-OC mode, we make the opcode completely unconstrained. We average results over 10 runs for each consistency model on a 4×6-core AMD Opteron 8435 machine, 2.6 GHz, 96GB of RAM. Table 6 shows running times for different execution consistencies.

Weaker (more relaxed) consistency models help achieve higher basic block coverage, as shown in Fig. 7. For PCnet, coverage varies from 14% to 66%, while 91C111 ranges from 10% to 88%. The stricter the model, the fewer sources of symbolic values, hence the fewer explorable paths and discoverable basic blocks in a given amount of time. In the case of our Windows drivers, system-level strict consistency (SC-SE) keeps all registry inputs concrete, which prevents several configuration-dependent parts from being explored. In unit-level strict consistency (SC-UE), concretizing symbolic inputs to arbitrary values prevents the driver from loading, thus yielding poor coverage.

In the case of Lua, the local consistency model allows bypassing the lexer component, which is especially difficult to symbolically execute due to its loops and complex string manipulations. RC-OC exceptionally yielded less coverage because execution got stuck in complex crash paths reached due to incorrect Lua opcodes.

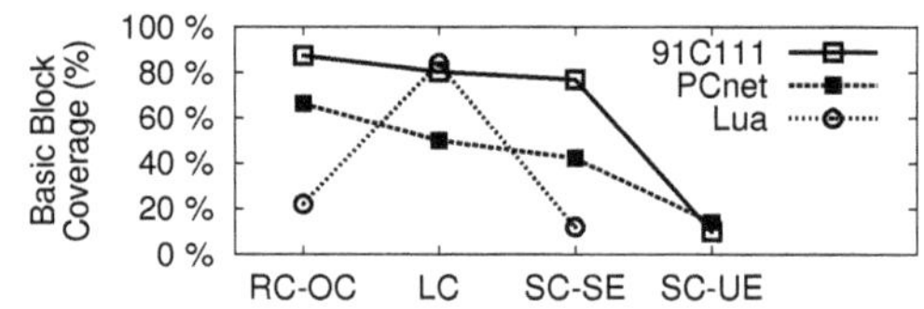


**Figure 7:** Effect of consistency models on coverage.

Path selection together with adequate consistency models optimize memory usage (Fig. 8). In local consistency, the PCnet driver spends 4 minutes in the initialization method, exploring ~7,000 paths and using 8 GB of memory. In contrast, it spends only 2 minutes (~2,500 paths) and 4 GB under RC-OC consistency. Under LC consistency, the `CardType` registry setting is symbolic, causing the initialization entry point to call in parallel several functions that look for different card types. Under LC consistency, S$^2$E explores these functions slower than under RC-OC consistency, where we liberally inject symbolic values to help these functions finish quicker. Slower exploration leads to less frequent timeout reset, hence longer exploration, more paths, and more memory consumption. Under SC-SE and SC-UE consistency, registry settings are concrete, exploring only functions for one card type.

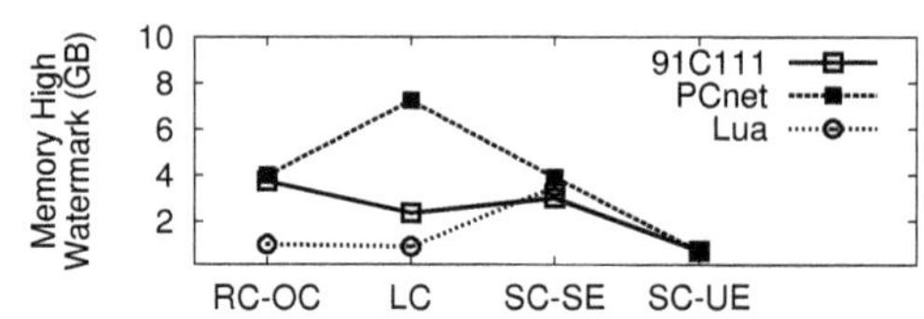


**Figure 8:** Effect of consistency models on memory usage.

Finally, consistency models affect constraint solving time (Fig. 9). The relationship between consistency model and constraint solving often depends on the structure of the system being analyzed—generally, the deeper a path, the more complex the corresponding path constraints. We observe that, for our targets, solving time decreases with stricter consistency, because stricter models restrict the amount of symbolic data. For 91C111, switching from local to overapproximate consistency increases solving time by 10×. This is mostly due to the unconstrained symbolic inputs passed to the `QueryInformationHandler` and `SetInformationHandler` entry points, which results in complex expressions being generated by switch statements. In Lua, the structure of the constraints causes S$^2$E to spend most of its time in the constraint solver.

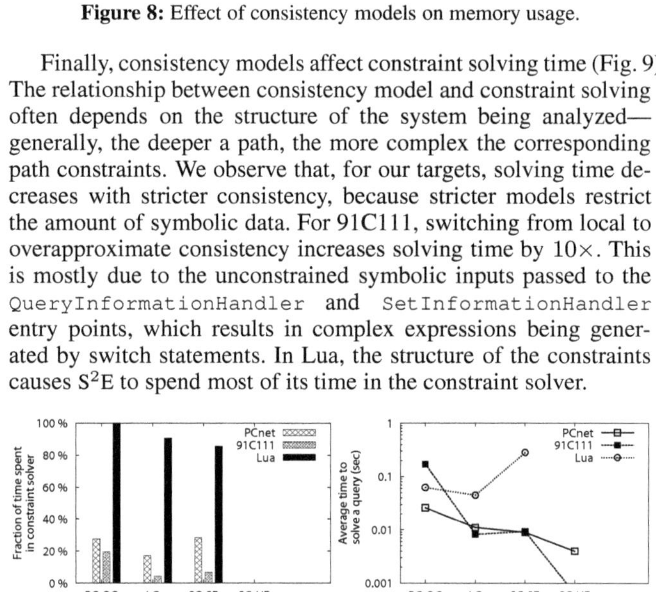


**Figure 9:** Impact of consistency models on the constraint solver

As in §6.1.3, we wished to include in these results a comparison to vanilla KLEE. Besides the problems faced in the case of drivers, we expected that the Lua interpreter, being completely in user-mode and not having any complex interactions with the environment, could be handled by KLEE. However, KLEE does not model some operations. For example, the Lua interpreter makes use of `setjmp` and `longjmp`, which become calls into `libc` that manipulate the PC and other registers in a way that confuses KLEE. Unlike S²E, engines like KLEE do not have a unified representation of the hardware, so all these details must be explicitly coded for (e.g., detect that `setjmp` / `longjmp` is being used, and ensure that KLEE's view of the execution state is appropriately adjusted). In S²E, this comes "for free," because the CPU registers, memory, I/O devices, etc. are shared between the concrete and symbolic domain.

## 7. Related Work

We are not aware of any platform that can offer the level of generality in terms of dynamic analyses and execution consistency models that S²E offers. Nevertheless, a subset of the ideas behind S²E did appear in various forms in earlier work.

BitBlaze [36] is the closest dynamic analysis framework to S²E. It combines virtualization and symbolic execution for malware analysis and offers a form of local consistency to introduce symbolic values into API calls. In contrast, S²E brings four additional consistency models and different generic path selectors that trade accuracy for exponentially improved performance in more flexible ways. To our knowledge, S²E is the first to handle all aspects of hardware communication, which consists of I/O, MMIO, DMA, and interrupts. This enables symbolic execution across the entire software stack, down to hardware, resulting in richer analyses.

One way to tackle the state explosion problem is to use models and/or relax execution consistency. File system models have allowed, for instance, KLEE to test UNIX utilities without involving the real filesystem. However, based on our own experience writing models for KLEE, doing so is labor-intensive and error-prone. Writing and maintaining a model for the kernel/driver interface of a modern OS takes several person-years [2].

Other bodies of work have chosen to execute the "outside world" concretely, with various levels of consistency that were appropriate for the specific analysis in question, most commonly bug finding. For instance, CUTE [35] can run concrete code consistently (unlike KLEE) without modeling, but it is limited to strict consistency and code-based selection. SJPF [31] can switch from concrete to symbolic domains, but does not track constraints when switching back, so it cannot preserve consistency.

Another approach to tackle state explosion is compositional symbolic execution [17]. This approach aims to save the result of exploration of parts of the program and reuse them when those parts are called again in a different context. We are investigating how to implement this approach in S²E, to further improve scalability.

Non-VM based approaches cannot control the environment outside the analyzed program. E.g., both KLEE and EXE allow a symbolically executing program to call into the concrete domain (e.g., perform a system call), but they cannot fork the global system state. As a result, different paths clobber each other's concrete domain, with unpredictable consequences. Concolic execution [34] runs everything concretely and scales to full systems (and is not affected by state clobbering), but may result in lost paths when execution crosses program boundaries. Likewise, CUTE, KLEE, and others cannot track the branch conditions in the concrete code (unlike S²E), and thus cannot determine how to redo calls in order to enable overconstrained but feasible paths.

In-situ model checkers [16, 20, 28, 34, 39, 40] can directly check programs written in a common programming language, usually with some simplifications such as data-range reduction, without requiring the creation of a model. Since S²E directly executes the target binary, one could say it is an in-situ tool. However, S²E goes further and provides a consistent separation between the "outside world" (whose symbolic execution is not necessary) and the target code to be tested (which is typically orders of magnitude smaller than the rest)—this is what we call in-vivo in S²E: analyzing the target code in-situ, while transparently facilitating its interaction with that code's unmodified, real environment. Murphy et al. propose a technique [27] to inject test suites with concrete inputs in a forked version of a process to preserve the consistency of the original run. Our definition differs from theirs, where in-vivo stands for executing tests in *production* environments.

Several static analysis frameworks have been proposed. Saturn [14] and `bddbddb` [23] prove the presence or absence of bugs using a path-sensitive analysis engine to decrease the number of false positives. Saturn uses function summaries to scale to larger programs and looks for bugs described in a logic programming language. `bddbddb` stores programs in a database as relations that can be searched for buggy patterns using Datalog. Besides detecting bugs, `bddbddb` helped optimizing locks in multi-threaded programs. Static analysis tools rely on source code for accurate type information and cannot easily verify run-time properties and reason about the entire system. Both `bddbddb` and Saturn require to learn a new language.

Dynamic analysis frameworks alleviate the limitations of static analysis tools. In particular, they allow the analysis of binary software. Theoretically, one could statically convert an x86 binary to, say, LLVM and run it in a system like KLEE, but this faces the classic undecidable problems of disassembly and decompilation [33]: disambiguating code from data, determining the targets of indirect jumps, unpacking code, etc.

S²E adds multi-path analysis abilities to all single-path dynamic tools, while not limiting the types of analysis. PTLsim [41] is a VM-based cycle-accurate x86 simulator that selectively limits profiling to user-specified code ranges to improve scalability. Valgrind [37] is a framework best known for cache profiling tools, memory leak detectors, and call graph generators. PinOS [9] can instrument operating systems and unify user/kernel-mode tracers. However, PinOS relies on Xen and a paravirtualized guest OS, unlike S²E. PTLsim, PinOS, and Valgrind implement cache simulators that model multi-level data and code cache hierarchies. S²E allowed us to implement an equivalent *multi-path* simulator with little effort.

S²E complements classic single-path, non VM-based, profiling and tracing tools. For instance, DTrace [15] is a framework for troubleshooting kernels and applications on production systems in real time. DTrace, and other techniques for efficient profiling, such as continuous profiling [1], sampling-based profiling [10], and data type profiling [30] trade accuracy for low overhead. They are useful in settings where the overhead of precise instrumentation is prohibitive. Other projects have also leveraged virtualization to achieve goals that were previously prohibitively expensive. These tools could be improved with S²E by allowing them to witness multi-path executions.

Finally, S²E reuses mixed-mode execution as an optimization, to increase efficiency. This idea first appeared in DART [18], CUTE [35], and EXE [12], and later in Bitscope [8]. However, automatic bidirectional data conversions across the symbolic-concrete boundary did not exist in previous work, and is key to S²E's scalability.

To summarize, S²E embodies numerous ideas that were fully or partially explored in earlier work. What is unique in S²E is its generality for writing various analyses, the availability of multiple user-selectable (as well as definable) consistency models, automatic bidirectional conversion of data between the symbolic and concrete domains, and its ability to operate without any modeling or modification of the (concretely running) environment.

## 8. Conclusions

This paper described $S^2E$, a new platform for *in-vivo multi-path analysis* of systems, which scales even to large, proprietary, real-world software stacks, like Microsoft Windows. It is the first time virtualization, dynamic binary translation, and symbolic execution are combined for the purpose of generic behavior analysis. $S^2E$ simultaneously analyzes entire *families of paths*, operates directly on *binaries*, and operates *in vivo*, i.e., includes in its analyses the entire software stack: user programs, libraries, kernel, drivers, and hardware. $S^2E$ uses automatic bidirectional symbolic–concrete data conversions and relaxed execution consistency models to achieve scalability. We showed that $S^2E$ enables rapid prototyping of a variety of system behavior analysis tools with little effort. $S^2E$ can be downloaded from `http://s2e.epfl.ch/`.

## Acknowledgments

We thank Jim Larus, our shepherd, and Andrea Arpaci-Dusseau, Herbert Bos, Miguel Castro, Byung-Gon Chun, Petros Maniatis, Raimondas Sasnauskas, Willy Zwaenepoel, Johannes Kinder, the $S^2E$ user community, and the anonymous reviewers for their help in improving our paper. We are grateful to Microsoft Research for supporting this work through a PhD Fellowship starting in 2011.

## References

[1] J. Anderson, L. Berc, J. Dean, S. Ghemawat, M. Henzinger, S.-T. Leung, D. Sites, M. Vandevoorde, C. A. Waldspurger, and W. E. Weihl. Continuous profiling: Where have all the cycles gone? In *Symp. on Operating Systems Principles*, 1997.

[2] T. Ball, E. Bounimova, B. Cook, V. Levin, J. Lichtenberg, C. McGarvey, B. Ondrusek, S. K. Rajamani, and A. Ustuner. Thorough static analysis of device drivers. In *ACM SIGOPS/EuroSys European Conf. on Computer Systems*, 2006.

[3] T. Ball, E. Bounimova, V. Levin, R. Kumar, and J. Lichtenberg. The static driver verifier research platform. In *Intl. Conf. on Computer Aided Verification*, 2010.

[4] F. Bellard. QEMU, a fast and portable dynamic translator. In *USENIX Annual Technical Conf.*, 2005.

[5] A. Bessey, K. Block, B. Chelf, A. Chou, B. Fulton, S. Hallem, C. Henri-Gros, A. Kamsky, S. McPeak, and D. Engler. A few billion lines of code later: using static analysis to find bugs in the real world. *Communications of the ACM*, 53(2), 2010.

[6] Bochs IA-32 Emulator. http://bochs.sourceforge.net/.

[7] P. Boonstoppel, C. Cadar, and D. R. Engler. RWset: Attacking path explosion in constraint-based test generation. In *Intl. Conf. on Tools and Algorithms for the Construction and Analysis of Systems*, 2008.

[8] D. Brumley, C. Hartwig, M. G. Kang, Z. L. J. Newsome, P. Poosankam, D. Song, and H. Yin. BitScope: Automatically dissecting malicious binaries. Technical Report CMU-CS-07-133, Carnegie Mellon University, 2007.

[9] P. P. Bungale and C.-K. Luk. PinOS: a programmable framework for whole-system dynamic instrumentation. In *Intl. Conf. on Virtual Execution Environments*, 2007.

[10] M. Burrows, U. Erlingson, S.-T. Leung, M. T. Vandevoorde, C. A. Waldspurger, K. Walker, and W. E. Weihl. Efficient and flexible value sampling. In *Intl. Conf. on Architectural Support for Programming Languages and Operating Systems*, 2000.

[11] C. Cadar, D. Dunbar, and D. R. Engler. KLEE: Unassisted and automatic generation of high-coverage tests for complex systems programs. In *Symp. on Operating Systems Design and Implementation*, 2008.

[12] C. Cadar, V. Ganesh, P. M. Pawlowski, D. L. Dill, and D. R. Engler. EXE: Automatically generating inputs of death. In *Conf. on Computer and Communication Security*, 2006.

[13] V. Chipounov and G. Candea. Reverse engineering of binary device drivers with RevNIC. In *ACM SIGOPS/EuroSys European Conf. on Computer Systems*, 2010.

[14] I. Dillig, T. Dillig, and A. Aiken. Sound, complete and scalable path-sensitive analysis. In *Conf. on Programming Language Design and Implementation*, 2008.

[15] Dtrace. `http://www.sun.com/bigadmin/content/dtrace/index.jsp`.

[16] P. Godefroid. Model checking for programming languages using Verisoft. In *Symp. on Principles of Programming Languages*, 1997.

[17] P. Godefroid. Compositional dynamic test generation. In *Symp. on Principles of Programming Languages*, 2007. Extended abstract.

[18] P. Godefroid, N. Klarlund, and K. Sen. DART: Directed automated random testing. In *Conf. on Programming Language Design and Implementation*, 2005.

[19] P. Godefroid, M. Y. Levin, and D. Molnar. Automated whitebox fuzz testing. In *Network and Distributed System Security Symp.*, 2008.

[20] Java PathFinder. http://javapathfinder.sourceforge.net, 2007.

[21] J. C. King. Symbolic execution and program testing. *Communications of the ACM*, 1976.

[22] V. Kuznetsov, V. Chipounov, and G. Candea. Testing closed-source binary device drivers with DDT. In *USENIX Annual Technical Conf.*, 2010.

[23] M. S. Lam, J. Whaley, V. B. Livshits, M. C. Martin, D. Avots, M. Carbin, and C. Unkel. Context-sensitive program analysis as database queries. In *Symp. on Principles of Database Systems*, 2005.

[24] C. Lattner and V. Adve. LLVM: A compilation framework for lifelong program analysis and transformation. In *Intl. Symp. on Code Generation and Optimization*, 2004.

[25] Lua: A lightweight embeddable scripting language. `http://www.lua.org/`, 2010.

[26] C.-K. Luk, R. Cohn, R. Muth, H. Patil, A. Klauser, G. Lowney, S. Wallace, V. J. Reddi, and K. Hazelwood. PIN: building customized program analysis tools with dynamic instrumentation. In *Conf. on Programming Language Design and Implementation*, 2005.

[27] C. Murphy, G. Kaiser, I. Vo, and M. Chu. Quality assurance of software applications using the in vivo testing approach. In *Intl. Conf. on Software Testing Verification and Validation*, 2009.

[28] M. Musuvathi, S. Qadeer, T. Ball, G. Basler, P. A. Nainar, and I. Neamtiu. Finding and reproducing Heisenbugs in concurrent programs. In *Symp. on Operating Systems Design and Implementation*, 2008.

[29] Oprofile. http://oprofile.sourceforge.net.

[30] A. Pesterev, N. Zeldovich, and R. T. Morris. Locating cache performance bottlenecks using data profiling. In *ACM SIGOPS/EuroSys European Conf. on Computer Systems*, 2010.

[31] C. Păsăreanu, P. Mehlitz, D. Bushnell, K. Gundy-Burlet, M. Lowry, S. Person, and M. Pape. Combining unit-level symbolic execution and system-level concrete execution for testing NASA software. In *Intl. Symp. on Software Testing and Analysis*, 2008.

[32] S. Savage, M. Burrows, G. Nelson, P. Sobalvarro, and T. Anderson. Eraser: a dynamic data race detector for multithreaded programs. *ACM Transactions on Computer Systems*, 15(4), 1997.

[33] B. Schwarz, S. Debray, and G. Andrews. Disassembly of executable code revisited. In *Working Conf. on Reverse Engineering*, 2002.

[34] K. Sen. Concolic testing. In *Intl. Conf. on Automated Software Engineering*, 2007.

[35] K. Sen, D. Marinov, and G. Agha. CUTE: a concolic unit testing engine for C. In *Symp. on the Foundations of Software Eng.*, 2005.

[36] D. Song, D. Brumley, H. Yin, J. Caballero, I. Jager, M. G. Kang, Z. Liang, J. Newsome, P. Poosankam, and P. Saxena. Bitblaze: A new approach to computer security via binary analysis. In *Intl. Conf. on Information Systems Security*, 2008.

[37] Valgrind. http://valgrind.org/.

[38] D. Wheeler. SLOCCount. `http://www.dwheeler.com/sloccount/`, 2010.

[39] J. Yang, T. Chen, M. Wu, Z. Xu, X. Liu, H. Lin, M. Yang, F. Long, L. Zhang, and L. Zhou. MODIST: Transparent model checking of unmodified distributed systems. In *Symp. on Networked Systems Design and Implementation*, 2009.

[40] J. Yang, C. Sar, and D. Engler. EXPLODE: a lightweight, general system for finding serious storage system errors. In *Symp. on Operating Systems Design and Implementation*, 2006.

[41] M. T. Yourst. PTLsim: A cycle accurate full system x86-64 microarchitectural simulator. In *IEEE Intl. Symp. on Performance Analysis of Systems and Software*, 2007.

# Ensuring Operating System Kernel Integrity with OSck

Owen S. Hofmann Alan M. Dunn Sangman Kim Indrajit Roy* Emmett Witchel

The University of Texas at Austin *HP Labs

{osh,adunn,sangmank,witchel}@cs.utexas.edu indrajitr@hp.com

## Abstract

Kernel rootkits that modify operating system state to avoid detection are a dangerous threat to system security. This paper presents OSck, a system that discovers kernel rootkits by detecting malicious modifications to operating system data. OSck integrates and extends existing techniques for detecting rootkits, and verifies safety properties for large portions of the kernel heap with minimal overhead. We deduce type information for verification by analyzing unmodified kernel source code and in-memory kernel data structures.

High-performance integrity checks that execute concurrently with a running operating system create data races, and we demonstrate a deterministic solution for ensuring kernel memory is in a consistent state. We introduce two new classes of kernel rootkits that are undetectable by current systems, motivating the need for the OSck API that allows kernel developers to conveniently specify arbitrary integrity properties.

***Categories and Subject Descriptors*** D.4.6 [*Operating Systems*]: Security and Protection—Invasive software

***General Terms*** Security, Verification

***Keywords*** Rootkit detection

## 1. Introduction

Rootkits are software packages left on an exploited system to facilitate further malicious access. They compromise operating system security in ways that are difficult for modern tools to detect. Increasingly dangerous are *kernel rootkits* that use access to kernel memory to subvert the integrity of kernel code or data structures, giving control of critical resources (such as processing, the file system, or the network) to a malicious entity [29].

Kernel rootkits are difficult to detect because operating systems have complicated data structures with no explicit integrity constraints, providing a large and growing attack surface to rootkit authors. In addition, user- or kernel-level security tools should not trust a compromised operating system kernel to correctly execute security checks. To efficiently and reliably detect rootkits, we propose OSck[1], a hypervisor-based system to specify and enforce the integrity of operating system data structures. Kernel rootkits change the state of operating system data structures in order to gain unauthorized access to computer resources and to prevent detection. OSck detects when the state of kernel data structures violates the integrity properties specified to the hypervisor. If a rootkit compromises kernel integrity, the hypervisor can take appropriate action, such as terminating the operating system or alerting an administrator.

We extend previous work in hypervisor-based monitoring in four important directions:

1. OSck verifies type-safety properties for the kernel heap through a linear scan of memory, rather than traversing a data structure graph. This approach is based on extracting assumptions about kernel memory layout from memory management data structures. It is more efficient than graph traversal in both time and space, and facilitates incremental verification.
2. OSck correctly handles concurrency between the running kernel and verification process. Previous systems assumed that any inconsistencies caused by concurrency would be transient. We show this assumption incorrect through user code that causes these errors frequently enough so as to appear persistent.
3. OSck exports an expressive API for specifying ad-hoc integrity checks. With OSck, integrity checks are written as if the code executes in a kernel thread, with full access to all kernel data structures, even though the code executes in the context of an unprivileged hypervisor address space.
4. We design and implement two new classes of rootkits and implement new versions of known attacks, demonstrating that defeating new rootkit exploits with OSck is simple, often requiring fewer than 100 lines of code. One of our new attacks would evade detection by all previous monitoring systems because it modifies data that is not reachable by traversing kernel data structures from global roots.

OSck supports a rich API for writing kernel integrity checks. We give three examples of integrity properties that vary in complexity and require different levels of support from OSck. First, the dbgreg rootkit sets up the x86 debugging registers to transfer control to it when the kernel executes the code to demultiplex a system call. OSck prevents this rootkit's operation simply by verifying that x86 hardware debug registers do not reference kernel text. Second, most in-the-wild kernel rootkits modify kernel state by directing function pointers to custom functions [23]. OSck detects such rootkits by verifying type-safety for kernel data structures—the property that each pointer points to an object of the correct type. This is a complex property that must be checked concurrently with kernel execution, and OSck extracts rules about data structure allocations from the kernel source. Third, integrity constraints may require coordination between the kernel and hypervisor to prevent false positives due to race conditions. For instance, the Linux kernel maintains both a tree and list representation of the run queue. Rootkit tasks can avoid being listed by system utilities like `ps` by removing themselves from the list representation, while remaining in the tree representation allows them to be scheduled. However, because

[1] Like `fsck`, but for operating system state.



*ASPLOS'11,* March 5–11, 2011, Newport Beach, California, USA.

the kernel updates these data structures on every scheduling event, workloads that involve significant scheduling activity may require synchronization to coordinate the OS modification with the hypervisor's checking.

We demonstrate a new class of rootkit exploits that modify specific return addresses on the stack. The new attack covertly executes by replacing return addresses from the `schedule` function for currently sleeping processes. Previous integrity monitoring systems could not prevent this attack because they check data structures by traversing them, pointer by pointer, from global variables. However, kernel stacks are large regions of untyped memory with potentially unspecified bounds and are thus resistant to traversal. Even software defenses for stack smashing attacks [2] cannot prevent this attack since such defenses detect overwrites to a region of stack space including a compiler inserted sentinel value. These defenses do not work when only the return address is overwritten.

The rest of this paper is organized as follows: §2 describes how OSck detects kernel rootkits. §4 describes our implementation of OSck as part of the KVM hypervisor. §5 describes kernel rootkits we used to evaluate OSck and the associated integrity properties these rootkits violate. We evaluate OSck in §6, discuss related work in §7, and conclude in §8.

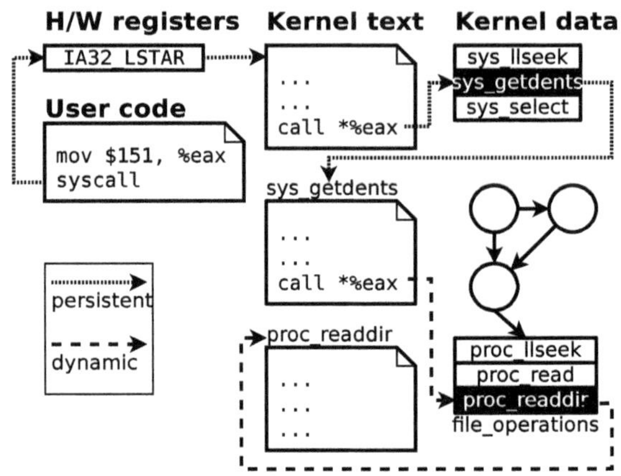


**Figure 1.** Control transfers in kernel invocation of a `getdents` system call. Static control transfers occur within blocks of kernel text. Persistent and dynamic control transfers use values in hardware registers and kernel memory to determine the next instruction executed.

## 2. Detecting kernel rootkits

Rootkits obscure signs of their presence, such as files in the filesystem or running processes, using a variety of techniques. There are three main techniques that rootkit writers use to hide the presence of a rootkit.

- Diverting control to code that hides presence of the rootkit.
- Executing code or storing data outside of a traditional process or file context.
- Modifying operating system data structures to conceal the presence of the rootkit.

A rootkit can divert control flow to modify queries about the state of the kernel, such as by hiding entries in the Linux `proc` filesystem by replacing pointers to functions implementing the filesystem with versions that conceal malicious running processes. It can also divert control flow so that the rootkit code runs outside of a context visible to the system administrator, such as running as a frequently invoked kernel callback rather than a traditional process. Additionally, rootkits can modify non-control data structures in a way that conceals its presence in the system. For example, a rootkit may remove a malicious process from kernel data structures used to list active processes in a system utility such as `ps`, but not from the data structures used to schedule processes.

### 2.1 Protecting control flow

A rootkit may modify operating system control flow to hide resources visible to user level monitoring tools. For instance, the adore-ng rootkit substitutes its own implementation of the Linux Virtual File System (VFS) `readdir` method for the `/proc` filesystem. The custom implementation hides certain entries from user queries about the contents of `/proc`, preventing a system administrator from viewing the full set of running processes. Alternately, a rootkit may modify control flow to run its code in a context undetectable by users. Our new "return-to-schedule" rootkit (§5), executes code in the context of every running process by modifying descheduled processes' stacks.

To detect rootkits that modify control flow, OSck verifies *control-flow integrity*, the property that execution of the kernel follows a predetermined control-flow graph [1]. We divide control transfers into three categories: *static*, *persistent*, and *dynamic*. Figure 1 illustrates these categories in a common system call.

***Static and persistent control transfers*** *Static control transfers* consist of branches and function calls determined at kernel compile time, and are encoded in kernel text. *Persistent control transfers* are established by the kernel during initialization and remain constant while the kernel is executing, such as a system call invocation that is directed to the correct kernel text location via the values of hardware registers and the contents of the system call table (an in-memory table of function pointers). These register values and the contents of the table do not change once the kernel is initialized. OSck forces these transfers to remain immutable, by write-protecting kernel text, read-only data, and the values of special machine registers (§4.1).

***Dynamic control transfers*** The kernel makes significant use of *dynamic control transfers*, which consist of indirect jumps and function calls based on pointers in writable kernel memory. The object-oriented design of the kernel encourages the use of function pointers to implement common interfaces to similar functionality. For example, virtual file system (VFS) modules associate tables of function pointers with kernel objects representing inodes and open files. To invoke the correct function for a given file, a generic kernel routine dereferences one of these pointers to perform a filesystem-specific function.

Unlike static and persistent control transfers, determining the valid target for a dynamic control transfer instruction in the running kernel may not be possible. For instance, two invocations of the same filesystem function on separate objects may result in different functions being invoked from the same call instruction in kernel text. The validity of the targeted function depends on a significant amount of context, such as the filesystem that contains the object and the type of filesystem object referenced. Instead of attempting to verify these complex correctness properties, OSck instead restricts rootkits' ability to execute arbitrary code by ensuring that dynamic control transfers will target functions that are *safe* for that particular callsite. Safe functions are part of known kernel or module text and share the desired function's *type signature*: the return type, and number and types of arguments.

The function pointer dereferenced in a dynamic control transfer is determined by a complex traversal of kernel data structures from some globally accessible root data structure. Because the exact traversal is only specified by the dynamic execution of kernel code, OSck must verify that all paths the kernel could traverse from

```
bool check_pidmap(){
  for_each_process(ptask){
    // bitmap entry for each process
    // should be set
    if(!test_bit(ptask->pid, pidmap))
      return false;
  }
  return true;
}
```

**Figure 2.** Simplified code that checks integrity of non-control data.

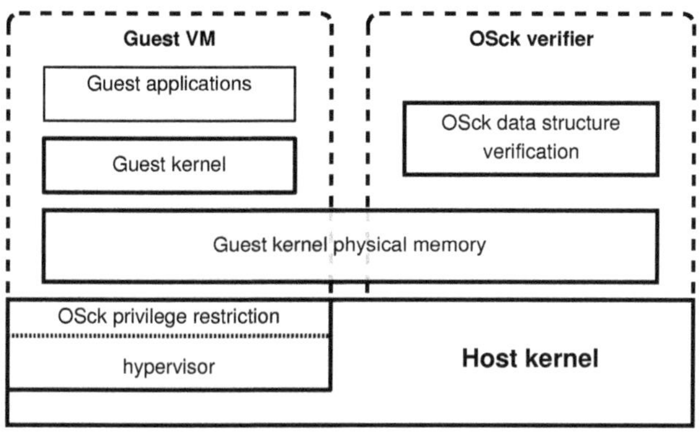


**Figure 3.** OSck architecture. Most of OSck's verification runs in a thread at the same privilege level as the guest OS, isolated by process and VM boundaries.

a global root to a function pointer will result in calling a safe function. OSck verifies this property by checking certain type-safety properties of the kernel heap (§3.2).

### 2.2 Protecting non-control data

In addition to modifying kernel control flow, a rootkit may also conceal system resources from the user by modifying non-control data in the kernel heap. For instance, rootkits based on direct kernel object modification [15] exploit the fact that kernels keep different data structures for enumerating and scheduling processes. In Linux, a rootkit can hide a process just by removing it from a hash table used for process enumeration. The hidden process is still scheduled normally.

Unlike type-safety of a graph of data structures, modifications to non-control data structures violate constraints that in many cases cannot be extracted from raw kernel source. In the example above, the invariant violated by the rootkit is that the hash table should contain the same set of processes as those in the process descriptor list and the run queue. Extracting such an invariant from source requires an understanding of code semantics that is beyond the scope of current and foreseeable tools.

Figure 2 is an example of code that checks the integrity of non-control data to protect the kernel from the `pidmap-hide` rootkit (§5) that hides itself from `/proc`.

For non-control data, OSck focuses on exporting a convenient interface for writing integrity checks. OSck extracts data structure definitions from kernel source and automatically generates an API for writing integrity checks as if they are code that would execute within a kernel thread, automatically handling translation of kernel addresses (§4.4).

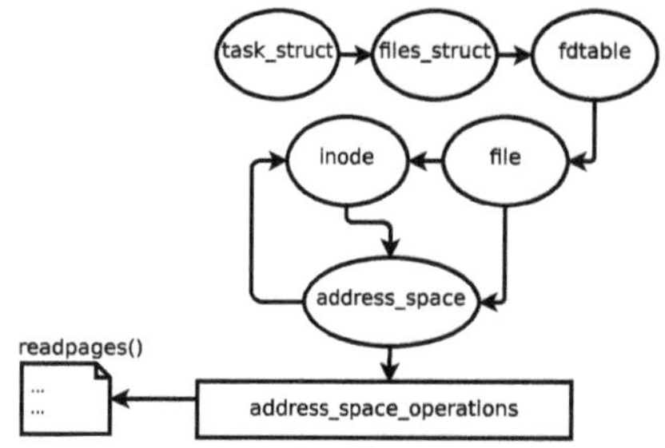


**Figure 4.** A subset of the kernel type graph. The kernel's traversal of this graph will result in the execution of the safe function `readpages`.

## 3. Design

OSck must verify the integrity of the running kernel, remaining safe even if the kernel is compromised. OSck runs as an independent thread at the same privilege level as the guest OS, but isolated from the guest by the hypervisor. Although it does not run as part of the hypervisor, the hypervisor must trust it (like domain 0 in Xen). Figure 3 summarizes the organization. OSck shares access to the guest OS' physical memory. Coordinating access to guest OS memory is the most hypervisor-specific part of OSck.

Many of OSck's integrity checks are based on verifying correctness properties of in-memory kernel data structures, so the most natural way to express integrity checks would be as code that could run in a kernel thread. Integrity checks should be allowed to reference kernel data structures using the same programming interface as kernel code. OSck extracts full type information from the kernel (§4) to support access to all kernel data structures (§4.3).

OSck detects rootkits by preventing or detecting modifications to static, persistent, and dynamic control transfers, and by verifying properties of non-control data. OSck protects static and persistent control transfers by restricting the guest kernel's ability to modify these values once they are installed. Dynamic control transfers are protected by verifying the type safety properties described in §2.1. OSck provides a programming environment identical to writing kernel code to make the job of verifying non-control data as easy as possible. Finally, OSck has the ability to quiesce the running kernel for any property whose verification fails due to the guest OS modifying data structures concurrently with OSck's checks.

### 3.1 Determining which code to trust

OSck detects malicious code in a running OS kernel by verifying that the hardware and memory values used to transfer control adhere to certain safety properties. For these checks to provide meaningful safety, OSck must ensure that both the code invoking control transfers and the code that the transfers target is code that is part of the original, non-malicious kernel implementation.

As a result, OSck must manage the regions of memory that are considered to be valid kernel code. We assume a trusted boot process via a technology such as TPM [31], to bring the system from a potentially untrusted kernel image on disk to executing a trusted kernel that may then be subject to OSck's verification. Modules dynamically loaded into the kernel must also become a part of the memory regions that OSck considers to be valid code. Currently, OSck relies on a whitelist and cryptographic hash of trusted modules. We believe that this solution is reasonable for a high-security setting. However, more robust solutions such as modules signed by a distributor are possible.

### 3.2 Verifying heap safety

Once the kernel is loaded in memory, it must not transfer control to malicious code while executing at the OS privilege level. OSck verifies this property by ensuring that any sequence of dereferences the kernel performs to reach a function pointer will result in a pointer to a safe function (defined in §2.1). OSck considers each node (a kernel data structure in memory) separately, verifying that the pointers contained in the data structure are consistent with the *type graph* specified by kernel code. A subset of the type graph for the Linux kernel is shown in Figure 4. OSck asserts that each pointer field within an object must point to the data type specified by that pointer, and all function pointers must point to safe functions.

***Type information from an untrusted kernel*** OSck's type analysis maps arbitrary regions of kernel memory to kernel data types, often using kernel state that could be corrupted. A key challenge is to show that using type information from a possibly compromised kernel, it is possible to verify that any dereference path from a kernel root object to a function pointer must result in invoking a safe function. Here, we outline an argument that even a malicious kernel cannot evade detection by corrupting OSck's map of type information.

We consider two mappings of kernel addresses to data types, the *effective* mapping and the *bound* mapping. The effective mapping is the mapping implicitly created by the actions of kernel code. For a memory address, the effective mapping uses the type that kernel code implicitly assumes at that address, based on a sequence of pointer dereferences. That is, if the kernel traverses a `struct page` pointer to arrive at memory address 0x100, then memory at address 0x100 is of type `struct page`. We assume that the effective mapping is consistent with the kernel's type graph — the kernel does not typecast pointers to an unrelated type as it traverses them. A rootkit seeks to modify the effective map, changing kernel pointers such that the kernel believes a malicious function is legitimate, because a function pointer points to it.

The *bound* mapping is the map that OSck creates, starting with type information from the kernel source code, and augmented with potentially unreliable information on heap-allocated types. Memory locations in the kernel image (such as functions and static data structures) are bound to a type at link time, when a symbol name (with an associated type in the source code) is assigned an address. The type of memory locations on the heap are bound when dynamically allocated memory is scanned during runtime, through analysis of kernel memory data structures described in §4.2. The bound mapping and the effective mapping will agree for all global roots. Global roots are symbols compiled into the kernel, and they are protected by OSck by write-protecting the kernel text that uses those symbols as constant values. In addition, the bound mapping maps the entry points of all safe functions to their type signature. For both global roots and safe functions, a compromised kernel cannot change the bound mapping, since OSck does not rely on dynamic kernel state for those addresses.

In the presence of a rootkit, the bound mapping must differ from the effective mapping in at least one place: the malicious function. The kernel believes the memory at the malicious function is a valid function, while OSck, which binds the addresses of safe functions when the kernel is linked, and does not rely on the values of mutable function pointers, will not.

If a rootkit inserts malicious functionality into the kernel by modifying a function pointer, there is a traversal of the data structures in the kernel's effective map that begins at a global root and ends at the malicious function. At the global root, the effective map and bound map must be consistent, since OSck protects the global roots. At the malicious function, the effective and bound maps must be inconsistent. Thus, there must be a step in the traversal, a pointer in object $A$ to a destination location $B$, for which the maps have $A$ mapped consistently, and $B$ mapped inconsistently with each other. We assume that the effective map is consistent with the type graph. Then for OSck, which uses the bound map, the pointer from $A$ to $B$ must be inconsistent with the type graph. If it were consistent, then $B$ would be mapped to the same type as in the effective map. This pointer will fail OSck's verification process, and OSck will detect the presence of a rootkit.

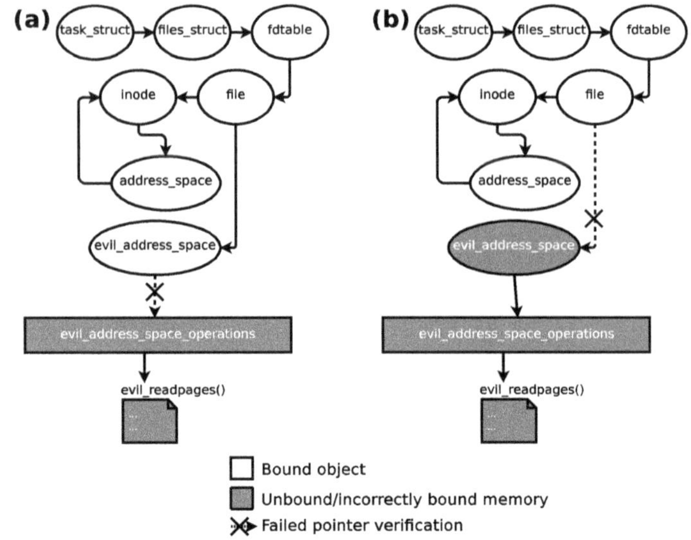


**Figure 5.** Modified type graph created by a malicious modification to the kernel heap, with two possible bindings from object to type. Regardless of binding, malicious modification will cause verification to fail.

***Type-safety example*** Consider a typical Linux file read that traverses the data structure graph from a `file` object to the associated `address_space` to the table of `address_space_operations`, and finally to the `readpages` method. The type graph on which this traversal operates is illustrated in Figure 4. A kernel rootkit may divert this traversal in several ways that result in the kernel invoking an unsafe function. One possible modification is illustrated in Figure 5. A rootkit may allocate a duplicate `evil_address_space` that points to a duplicate `evil_address_space_operations`, which contains a pointer to the rootkit's custom code. If OSck binds the `evil_address_space` to the `address_space` type, as in Figure 5(a), but the `evil_address_space_operations` remains unbound or is bound (based on incorrect information from the kernel) to some other type, verification will fail because the pointer to the `evil_address_space_operations` is not type-safe. If neither object is bound, as in Figure 5(b), verification will fail because the pointer from the `file` object to the `evil_address_space` is not type-safe. OSck uses kernel memory management data structures to bind kernel memory to data types without requiring developer interaction. §4.2 describes this process in detail.

OSck verifies the entire heap in a linear scan of kernel memory. This approach has several advantages. First, a linear scan is efficient: in the common case, checking pointer targets is a read-only operation. It does not require marking objects as visited, updating queues of unvisited objects, or making recursive calls. In our benchmarks, checking type-safety for much of the kernel heap requires at most around 300ms, and as little as 50ms (§6.2). Second, our approach facilitates incremental verification. A performance-sensitive system, or a system unable to concurrently run kernel and verification code may require that the heap be verified in stages. OSck's linear scan facilitates easy recording of the position in the heap to be resumed later.

### 3.3 Handling concurrency

A key goal of OSck is to minimize the performance impact of monitoring kernel state by interleaving execution of OSck's verification process and the kernel's execution as much as possible. However, running the kernel verifier concurrently with the kernel presents several synchronization issues. In general, OSck's verification process may attempt to check kernel state that the kernel is in the process of updating by means of a code region that it believes to be atomic. For example, OSck could read a pointer from a structure that is incompletely initialized and whose contents could point anywhere, or it could observe a red-black tree in the process of rebalancing and conclude that an integrity constraint has been violated.

Although OSck's access to kernel memory could allow it to correctly synchronize with the running kernel, doing so would significantly increase complexity and reduce performance. OSck frequently scans large portions of the kernel heap. Correct synchronization would require acquiring and holding a large number of locks, and adhering to the locking discipline of the existing kernel. In addition, there are synchronization requirements in the kernel that can depend on the order in which data structures are accessed, adding additional undue complexity and requiring OSck to follow numerous rules specified only through comments and a particular kernel implementation. OSck is designed to minimize effort when porting to successive kernel versions. Incorporating details of kernel synchronization into OSck would require additional expertise to verify that OSck's synchronization conventions accurately track the kernel's.

Instead, we make two assumptions that allow OSck to verify the state of the kernel with no synchronization in the common case. First, we assume that false negatives due to unsynchronized accesses are transient. OSck detects persistent modifications to kernel state, and it is unlikely that malicious code could consistently modify kernel state to be correct when observed by OSck, but incorrect when viewed by the kernel. Second, we assume that false positives due to unsynchronized accesses are rare. OSck may then employ a heavyweight synchronization mechanism in the event of an integrity violation to bring the system to consistent state and re-verify. In the common case that the event reflects an actual integrity violation, performance is not critical. In the rare case of a false positive, that heavyweight synchronization will have negligible performance impact. This assumption is validated by our experiments. While we are able to construct microbenchmarks in which false positives are frequent, we did not observe any false positives in any of the benchmarks that we ran (§6.4).

In the event of an integrity violation, OSck performs two steps before alerting the user about the possible rootkit infection:

- Immediately re-verify the state of the kernel. Kernel atomic regions are short, so re-running the check should resolve many integrity violations due to concurrent accesses.
- Enforce *quiescence*. OSck halts the kernel at a point at which all data structures should be consistent, and then re-verifies kernel state.

Choosing an effective point at which to enforce quiescence is an important part of OSck's design. An effective quiescence point should have two key properties. First, it should be a point where kernel data structures are consistent. Second, a multi-processor system requires enforcing quiescence for each processor. A processor should not quiesce in a place where it holds resources required by another processor (such as a lock), thus preventing quiescence for the second processor and creating deadlock. Our implementation is discussed in §4.5.

### 3.4 Discussion

As with other systems that attempt to detect security violations by inspecting the state of a potentially insecure system (e.g. a virus scanner), it may be possible for a sufficiently advanced rootkit to evade detection by OSck. OSck currently detects the attack vectors used by all of the Linux rootkits that we were able to locate. In this section, we discuss our assumptions, and ways in which a sufficiently advanced rootkit might evade detection.

***Threat model*** The threat model we consider for OSck is that of an attacker with temporary read-write access to kernel memory. For example, an attacker might gain access to kernel memory through a bug in the kernel, or by exploiting a setuid program and accessing the (now-deprecated) `/dev/kmem` interface. An attacker with access to kernel memory could corrupt kernel state and cause the kernel to crash. OSck does not protect against these modifications, or similar attempts to deny service. Instead, the goal of OSck is to detect *meaningful* malicious modifications to kernel state: modifications that facilitate further malicious activity in a way that will not be detected by a system administrator. For instance, an attacker could spawn a daemon as the root user, and then use modifications to kernel memory to hide that daemon from the list of running processes. The attacker must modify kernel memory carefully enough that queries into system state return a reasonable set of results while hiding some set of information.

***Type-safety*** A majority of kernel rootkits (see §5) implement malicious behavior by subverting kernel control flow. Many control transfers within the kernel are relatively simple to protect by protecting modifications to low-level state, such as the contents of kernel code and architectural registers.

The kernel makes extensive use of function pointers to transfer control, thus OSck must also protect the values of function pointers in writable kernel memory. OSck protects function pointers by ensuring that any function pointer used by the kernel points to a function that is a part of already trusted code, and has the correct type signature. This policy prevents all current attacks on function pointers, which direct pointers to custom rootkit functionality.

An attacker that wishes to remain undetected may only swap pointers with other functions that share the same type signature. We believe that implementing meaningful malicious behavior (such as hiding a single entry in the `/proc` filesystem) under these constraints is unlikely to be successful.

***Kernel data structures*** In addition to subverting kernel control flow, an attacker can hide evidence of malicious activity by subverting implicit invariants between kernel data structures, for example in the Linux kernel the assumed equivalence between the tree used to schedule processes and the linked list used to display them. OSck protects these data structure relationships through ad-hoc checks on kernel state.

For a large production kernel such as Linux, specifying the complete set of invariants is not likely to be tractable. However, to provide effective security, OSck need only check invariants that rootkits can violate to implement meaningful malicious behavior. In addition, adding a new integrity check to OSck's library is significantly less intrusive than fixing a kernel exploit, and does not require restarting a system. Checks in OSck can be implemented in a handful of lines of code, and do not need to be as thoroughly tested as patches to a production kernel: a crash in OSck requires only that it be restarted, without affecting the running kernel.

***Concurrency*** OSck's checking code runs concurrently, and in the common case unsynchronized, with kernel code. We make

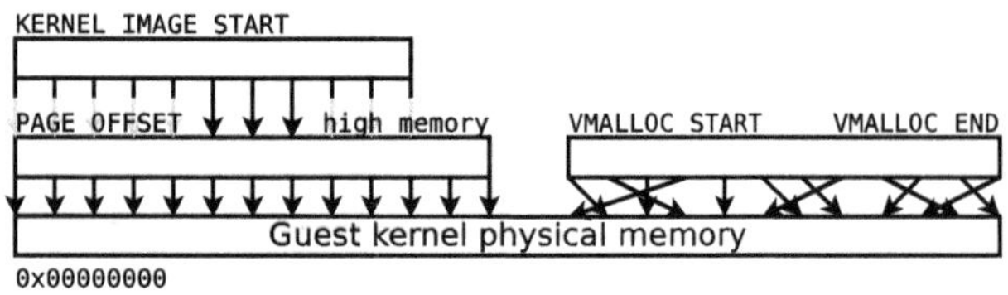


**Figure 6.** Mapping guest OS memory into the OSck verifier address space.

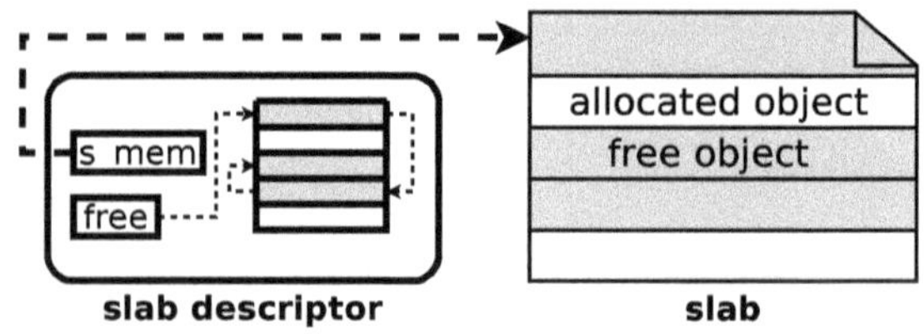


**Figure 7.** Slab organization of kernel memory allocations. Information about allocated and free objects within a slab is contained in a slab descriptor's internal list.

two main assumptions regarding concurrency. For performance, we assume false positives (detecting a violation of some invariant due to concurrent modification and not malicious behavior) are rare. Our experiments (§6) support this assumption. For security, we assume that false negatives are rare and not reproducible by an attacker. We recognize that race conditions form a significant body of attack vectors on a wide variety of systems. However we note that in general a race must happen once to violate security, while in OSck an attacker would have to win every race for the lifetime of the system to evade detection. We also assume that an attacker cannot accurately predict when an OSck check will run, so attack code cannot repair kernel data structures just in time for the OSck check, and then corrupt them again after the check.

## 4. Implementation

We implement OSck as part of the KVM hypervisor [20]. KVM virtualizes a guest kernel within a host Linux kernel. A user-level *launcher* binary allocates a region of memory to serve as the guest's physical memory, loads the guest kernel, and then calls into the host kernel to run the virtualized guest. OSck runs as a separate process, communicating over a socket with the launcher binary. OSck reads guest state by mapping the same memory region as the launcher.

OSck integrity checks are written as if they were executed in a guest OS kernel thread, although they are isolated from the guest kernel by the hypervisor. This is possible by mapping several virtually contiguous memory segments from the guest kernel into the OSck verifier address space, as shown in Figure 6. The majority of kernel data structures are addressed in a large portion of the virtual address space that linearly maps physical memory. In the 32-bit x86 Linux kernel, this consists of the last gigabyte of a 4GB address space. On the 64-bit kernel, a 64TB region starting from `0xFFFF880000000000` maps physical memory. A second region (the same region in 32-bit Linux) maps text and data in the kernel image.

In addition to the linearly mapped region, several kernel data structures (such as the list of kernel modules) reside in a region of memory allocated by the `vmalloc` function, which may contain non-linear mappings of physical memory. The OSck verifier translates addresses in this area by reading guest page tables from physical memory. Although reading page tables in software is inefficient, few kernel data structures reside in this area, and so this does not noticeably increase OSck's overhead. These memory mappings give the OSck verifier the same view of kernel data structures as a kernel thread. Our original OSck prototype was developed for 32-bit Linux. Porting OSck to a 64-bit architecture required few changes other than redefining a few aspects of the kernel's memory layout and interpreting a different page table format.

Both automatic and manual integrity checks in OSck make significant use of data structure definitions and properties extracted from kernel source code. As part of kernel compilation, OSck translates the kernel into the C intermediate language (CIL)[22]. We use CIL to output sanitized kernel type definitions for use in manual checks and to automatically generate functions to verify type-safety for each data type. The executed kernel is compiled directly using `gcc`; the CIL processing step is only to generate code that executes as part of OSck integrity checks.

This section explains how OSck protects static and persistent control transfers by restricting guest privilege (§4.1). Dynamic control transfers are protected by verifying type-safety properties (§2.1). Verifying these properties requires a mapping from locations in kernel memory to the data structure type. §4.2 describes how we use existing kernel memory management structures to efficiently construct a mapping. OSck provides a convenient interface to kernel data structures that is used both by automatic verification code (§4.3) and system programmers specifying custom integrity properties (§4.4). §4.5 discusses the synchronization protocol between the guest kernel and OSck.

### 4.1 Restricting guest privilege

A query about the state of the system, in the form of a system call, begins with a user executing the `syscall` instruction with a system call number specified in the x86 `eax` register, or an `int 0x80` instruction with the values contained in the x86 interrupt descriptor table. Either way, the path of control from user-level to the kernel implementation of the system call is determined by the value of hardware registers, kernel data, and kernel text. These control transfers remain fixed once they are installed by the booting kernel.

OSck protects the static and persistent control transfers on system call entry by restricting the guest operating system's privilege to modify certain registers and regions of memory once their values are set during boot. Modifying hardware registers that determine the transfer of control flow from user to kernel mode (such as x86 machine-specific registers that determine the operation of the `syscall` instruction) is a privileged operation, and must be implemented through a call to the hypervisor. OSck modifies the hypervisor to prevent updates to these registers after the initial values are installed.

After a user system call traps into the kernel text segment, code transfers control to the service routine corresponding to the desired system call number by indexing the *system call table*, an array of function pointers in kernel memory. The kernel does not modify the system call table once it has been created. OSck protects the system call table through hardware page protection and a hypervisor call ensuring that once the table is initialized the guest operating system may not modify it. Similarly, the implementations of kernel functions, such as the routines that implement individual system calls, remain static once the kernel is running. As with the system call table, OSck freezes read-only hardware page protections on pages containing kernel text, preventing the guest kernel from modifying their contents.

### 4.2 Slabs for efficient type safety

Efficiently constructing an accurate mapping between kernel memory and data type is key to both OSck's integrity guarantees and performance. Most important data structures in the Linux kernel are allocated via *slab allocation*, which provides *caches*, or specialized per-type allocators [7]. Kernel caches allocate memory from groups of pages called *slabs* containing a single type of object. Important kernel data structures that are dynamically allocated from caches include directory entry (`dentry`) structures used by kernel filesystem lookup routines, `buffer_head` structures that describe on-disk locations of blocks that make up a memory page, and `radix_tree_node` structures that comprise radix trees used, for example, in indexing pages in page caches.

OSck can determine the type of memory allocated within each page by determining the type allocated by a kernel cache. The Linux kernel maintains data structures that allow a given memory address to be associated with metadata about its containing page. For pages that are part of a slab, the metadata contains a pointer to the *slab descriptor*. The slab descriptor, shown in Figure 7 specifies the cache that contains the given slab, alignment information for objects within the slab, and a list of free objects.

OSck uses this kernel-provided information to perform efficient mapping between memory and data type. OSck associates each cache with a data type, and binds every allocated object in the slab to that data type. Objects that are not allocated or not part of a slab are unbound.

OSck associates individual kernel caches with data types by analyzing kernel source code during compilation of the kernel binary. The addresses of most kernel caches are stored and accessed through global variables. To allocate an object from a kernel cache, a cache variable is passed to a generic allocation function, and the resulting untyped pointer is cast to the desired type. OSck's analysis of kernel source code detects these sequences and associates the cache variable with the type that it allocates.

### 4.3 Automatic type-safety checks

The wealth of data types within the kernel requires that OSck automatically generate per-type checks for verifying the type safety of the kernel heap. For each data type, OSck generates a C function that takes a pointer to kernel memory as input. For each pointer within the data type, OSck outputs a call to our pointer-based type safety verifier. For each nested data type, OSck outputs a call to the function responsible for verifying that data type.

Most kernel type definitions are unambiguous. However, some types include a C `union` to pack multiple fields of information within a single region of memory. Without higher-level information, OSck is unable to disambiguate the different fields of a union to call the correct verifying function. Instead, OSck considers a union correct if at least one of its fields verifies correctly.

### 4.4 Manual integrity checks

Although many rootkits violate kernel control flow in a way that may be detected by automatically generated type-safety verification, there are many integrity properties important to kernel operation that cannot be automatically extracted from kernel code. For instance, the relationship between the bitmap of allocated process ids and the list of running tasks is unlikely to be extracted from kernel source code. For these properties, OSck exports an interface for writing verification code that is convenient for those who understand kernel internals best: kernel developers. We believe that hand-written code for checking data structures should resemble as closely as possible code that runs within a kernel-level thread.

There are two challenges to allowing developers to write natural verification code within a user-space program. First, the wide variety of data structures within the kernel must be made available, without the complication of including kernel header files in user code. Second, authors of integrity checks should be able to seamlessly use pointers within kernel data structures, without considering the translation necessary to reflect the kernel address space within a user process.

As part of its analysis phase, OSck automatically generates a convenient API for writing kernel integrity checks. OSck collects kernel type definitions and performs a source to source translation, generating a header file containing type definitions with memory layouts identical to those in the kernel, without preprocessor and other complexities common to kernel header files. OSck sanitizes identifiers for safe usage within C++, and transforms all pointers within data structures to smart pointers. These pointers automatically translate from kernel addresses to addresses in the user-level reflection of the kernel address space, illustrated in Figure 6. Pointers within the linearly-mapped region of kernel memory translate directly to the launcher process' map of guest physical memory. Pointers within the `vmalloc` region translate to the launcher process' map of the kernel virtual address space.

We have found OSck's automatically generated kernel data structure API useful in practice. Kernel convenience functions and macros, such as for iterating through kernel lists, may be copied without modification and perform correctly on a more complex translation of the kernel address space. Nearly all of the verification code in OSck is written using this API, including the large amount of code dedicated to caching kernel type information and verifying type-safety for kernel pointers.

### 4.5 Quiescence

To minimize checking overhead, OSck verifies kernel data structure integrity in a thread that runs concurrently with guest execution. In the common case, when OSck does not synchronize with the guest kernel, data races are possible. OSck must manage errors and false positives due to races efficiently and safely. First, OSck maximizes performance when data structures are not being updated, or inconsistencies due to races are transient. Second, OSck provides a means for the hypervisor to synchronize with the guest to check properties that are violated because of guest activity.

It is possible for the guest OS's workload to prevent an integrity check from succeeding. For example, we present an experiment in Section 6.4 where several user programs are constantly yielding the CPU, making it difficult for the OSck hypervisor to verify that the rbtree representation of the run queue contains the same processes as the list representation (the kernel assumes the same processes are in both representations). To check this property, the hypervisor must quiesce the system, which suspends execution of the virtual processors of the guest OS.

As discussed in §3.3, OSck attempts to verify data structures and when it fails, it quickly re-verifies (to see if the problem was transient and has disappeared). If the re-verification fails, it enforces *quiescence*.

The guest's virtual processors must be suspended while kernel data structures are consistent, otherwise it will look to the hypervisor like a transient problem is persistent. There are locations in the guest where all guest data structures are consistent, and these are potential points at which the hypervisor can suspend virtual processors. However, it is also important only to select points such that all kernel threads can reach quiescence. If a guest kernel thread on a suspended virtual processor held locks that were necessary for another kernel thread to reach a quiescence point, then attempting to induce quiescence would instead induce deadlock.

OSck quiesces the kernel at the start of the `schedule` function. The function is called frequently, minimizing the response latency of the guest when the hypervisor requires quiescence. Although some kernel locks may be held when `schedule` is called, all such

| Type | Name | Data structures exploited |
|---|---|---|
| Control flow-related | ret-to-sched* | Return address of suspended kernel thread's stack |
| | extable* | Exception table of the inserted module |
| | adore-ng% | `file_operations` table of `/proc` |
| | enyelkm% | Kernel text and page table |
| | dbg-reg | Debug registers and the `notifier` chain |
| | net3 | Protocol handlers and netfilter filters |
| | proc-hide | `file_operations` table of `/proc` |
| Non-control | hideme† | Thread list for a process id |
| | pidmap-hide† | Bitmap for PID allocation |

**Table 1.** Summary of rootkits used in our evaluation. Asterisks (*) indicate new classes of rootkits proposed in this paper. Percent signs (%) indicate actual rootkit code, ported to the latest 2.6 kernel. Daggers (†) indicate new implementations of known attack techniques.

locks are *blocking*. If another kernel thread attempts to acquire a lock held by a virtual processor that has quiesced in the `schedule` function, it will yield the processor by calling `schedule` itself. Instead of deadlocking, the processor attempting to acquire the lock will similarly quiesce.

OSck enforces quiescence in two stages. First, it interrupts the guest kernel to halt its execution. OSck overwrites the beginning of `schedule` with a hypercall after ensuring no guest thread is in the midst of executing the replaced instructions, and allows the guest to resume. When the guest attempts to call `schedule`, the hypercall transfers control to OSck. OSck verifies the entire state of the quiesced kernel, restores the original instructions in `schedule`, and resumes execution at the beginning of the function. The guest the continues as if it had completed a simple call to `schedule`.

## 5. Rootkits

We evaluate OSck with several publicly-available Linux rootkits, that corrupt the integrity of a running kernel via several vectors. The source code of many of these are specific to the 2.4 version of the kernel. We ported existing rootkits to work with the latest 2.6 kernel, sometimes specializing them to separate out different attack vectors.

In addition, we present several kernel exploits that to the best of our knowledge are not currently used by rootkits. These are Linux exploits developed out of our familiarity with the kernel. While having the source code of Linux was valuable in writing these exploits, we believe that programmers who work with the APIs of a closed source operating system like Windows would be able to create similarly creative exploits. Table 1 summarizes the rootkits used in this study.

***Return to schedule*** The ret-to-sched rootkit overwrites the return address on the stack of every process blocked for I/O. Rather than return to the `schedule` function, processes return to the rootkit code, which then returns to `schedule`. This exploit is undetectable by all previous integrity checking systems we are aware of. It does not modify any kernel data structure reachable from pointers in the kernel heap. By modifying a single stack location, there is no "collateral damage" (overwrites of compiler-placed sentinel values) that techniques like StackGuard [10] rely on to detect a stack smashing attack.

The ret-to-sched rootkit runs in the context of many processes by rescanning the I/O queues on each invocation and reinfecting any processes that are blocked. The attack depends on the rootkit understanding the stack layout of the compiler, though in the case of Linux there are few compilers besides `gcc` that can compile a functioning kernel.

Because ret-to-sched does not create or perceptibly alter the number or state of running processes, it is not detectable by any system administration utilities. Listing the system's active processes will not detect anything out of the ordinary. OSck detects this attack by ensuring that the return addresses on the stacks of descheduled processes correspond with valid kernel code regions. Stacks are not currently checked to determine if they represent a valid call stack, so a sufficiently advanced attacker could construct a return-oriented program [28]. However, OSck could be extended to add this property, by including information on the valid kernel call graph in its analysis.

***extable*** The extable rootkit uses the kernel's exception handling mechanism to subvert control flow. The exception table is a necessary kernel feature that speeds up the common case of copying data to and from the user. On every page fault, the Linux page fault handler searches the exception table of the kernel and loaded modules using the faulting PC as the key. If a match is found, control is transferred to the value in the exception table. The extable rootkit inserts an entry that associates a faulting address in the kernel text section with a fixup address within the module text section (or dynamically allocated kernel memory). Any page fault at the specified kernel PC will cause execution flow to resume at the fixup PC that is specified by the module.

The rootkit corrupts a kernel global variable that is dereferenced in a single location in kernel code, and is never copied into another data structure. The variable is dereferenced whenever a workqueue (a Linux mechanism used to defer work in interrupt handlers) is created. On this common event, the kernel faults, the rookit executes and finishes by patching up the machine registers to make it appear as if the dereference succeeded. The pointer remains corrupt, so the rootkit can be called again.

***adore-ng*** adore-ng modifies structures that contain sets of function pointers used by Linux's Virtual File System (VFS) layer to accommodate many different filesystems within one uniform directory hierarchy. adore-ng has a user-controllable security password, and a lookup of `<password>-fullprivs` as a filename within `/proc` will call adore-ng's `lookup` function, giving the task performing the lookup root privileges. This is used as a method of obtaining root privileges on subsequent login after an initial intrusion.

The Linux developers have taken steps to make this exploit more difficult. Beginning in kernel version 2.6.16, data marked `const` is placed on write-protected pages, and all data structures containing these function pointers were marked `const`. Writes to these structures are no longer possible without modifying permissions in page tables. However, when used through VFS, the operations are actually referenced via pointers from directory lookup cache entries (`dentry`). We modified adore-ng to change the pointers within `dentry` structures to point to rootkit allocated VFS function pointer structures with malicious function pointers. This example indicates how difficult it is to defeat rootkits from within the kernel. OSck ensures the integrity of individual function pointers, and will detect the malicious pointers in adore-ng.

***enyelkm*** enyelkm hides files and processes by modifying code that dispatches to the system call table. The system call code is patched to redirect system calls to modified versions. A new version of `getdents` conceals directory entries, such as those in the `/proc` filesystem used to enumerate running processes. In addition, enyelkm modifies the `read` system call to not return portions from files that are contained within specially delimited sections.

As a result, enyelkm can survive reboot by allowing an adversary to modify startup configuration files in a way such that the enyelkm module loads on boot, while the configuration file changes will then be subsequently invisible due to the modified `read` system call. Detectors that examine the system call table contents themselves will not detect this rootkit.

In order to be able to modify the system call dispatch code on recent version of Linux, we modified enyelkm to change the page table permissions for the system call code region. OSck detects this modification and flags it for violating the integrity of the system call table.

***dbg-reg*** dbg-reg is a specialized version of the mood_nt rootkit that uses x86 debugging registers and breakpoint notifiers to alter kernel control flow.

The x86 has four debug registers that can hold addresses which, when executed, cause breakpoint exceptions. Linux handles breakpoint exceptions using a chain of callbacks, named notifiers. On a breakpoint exception, the notifiers on the chain are called one by one until the end of the chain is reached, or one of the callbacks returns a special return code.

dbg-reg registers a notifier and puts the address of the `call` instruction that dispatches function pointers from the system call table into a debug register. The rootkit dispatches from a modified system call table that contains pointers to malicious functions. The control register (DR7) has a protection bit which helps disguise the rootkit. When the general detect enable bit is set, any attempt to read or write the debug registers causes a debug exception, which transfers control to the dbg-reg handler. In this case, the handler emulates the read or write and returns a code preventing other handlers from running. Code that reads or writes the registers believes it has succeeded. OSck defeats this rootkit by disallowing the guest OS to set debug registers with kernel addresses. In a production setting where security is paramount, debugging support for the kernel is not necessary.

***net3*** net3 implements an attack [26] where protocol handlers and netfilter filters take arbitrary action upon receiving network traffic (specifically, ICMP traffic). The rootkit netfilters pass the ICMP traffic, but can be configured to drop incoming or outgoing traffic that matches arbitrary criteria. Dropping incoming traffic can disguise input used to signal the rootkit. Dropping outgoing traffic can disrupt a component of a distributed application executing on the machine.

This rootkit can be stopped by ensuring that functions called by protocol handlers and netfilter filters are in legitimate address regions—either within kernel text or within the text of a set of allowed modules. OSck is notified when the kernel loads modules, so it verifies that the netfilters function pointers are legitimate.

***Non-control flow based rootkits*** hideme and pidmap-hide directly manipulate the relationship among kernel data structures instead of altering control flow. Both rootkits hide a process from the `/proc` directory. When the user lists the contents of the `/proc` directory, the kernel enumerates all processes, creating a directory for each PID. hideme removes the target process from the `pid_hash`, hiding it from the PID enumeration.

Because PID use is sparse, the kernel first checks the `pid_hash` table when enumerating PIDs, and then uses the `pidmap` bitmap to find the next in-use PID. pidmap-hide clears the bit in `pidmap` that corresponds to the target process. But the kernel looks in `pid_hash` first without looking at `pidmap`. To hide PID $p$, the rootkit must prevent any running process from having PID $p-1$, which it does by running several processes in quick succession to get two with adjacent PIDs. The cleared bit in `pidmap` will be detected and corrected by the kernel when PID allocation overflows. The rootkit delays PID overflow by setting the last allocated PID to $p+1$ where $p$ is the PID for the process hidden by the rootkit.

| Rootkit | OSck action | Detection time (s) |
|---|---|---|
| ret-to-sched | Detected | 0.51 |
| extable | Detected | 0.51 |
| adore-ng | Detected | 0.50 |
| enyelkm-1.3 | Prevented | - |
| dbg-reg | Prevented | - |
| net3 (protocol handler) | Detected | 0.44 |
| net3 (netfilter filter) | Detected | 0.48 |
| proc-hide | Detected | 0.46 |
| hideme | Detected | 0.56 |
| pidmap-hide | Detected | 0.74 |

**Table 2.** Rootkits detected by OSck

| Integrity check | LOC | Rootkits |
|---|---|---|
| Guest privilege restriction | | enyelkm, dbg-reg |
| Heap type-safety | 504 | adore-ng, proc-hide |
| ck_extable | 64 | extable |
| ck_net_filter | 74 | net3 |
| ck_prot_handlers | 64 | net3 |
| ck_proc_namespace | 99 | hideme, pidmap-hide |
| ck_stacks | 40 | ret-to-sched |

**Table 3.** Kernel integrity checks implemented by OSck. Lines of code for each check are reported as calculated by SLOCCount [33].

# 6. Evaluation

In this section we measure the performance and detection capability of our OSck prototype implemented in the KVM hypervisor. All experiments were performed on a Intel 2.80GHz Core i7 860 CPU, with 8GB memory and running the 64-bit Linux 2.6.32.9 kernel. We ran virtualized guests with 2GB memory, and in 1- and 4-core configurations.

## 6.1 Rootkit detection

Table 2 shows the set of rootkits we created or ported, and the average time OSck takes to detect them. Rootkits listed as "Detected" were detected by OSck's periodic integrity checks. Rootkits listed as "Prevented" were prevented from modifying the kernel by OSck's restriction of guest privilege. We ran each rootkit a minimum of 5 times to make sure OSck detected it each time, and report the average detection latency for those detected by integrity checks. Our experiments show that OSck detects rootkits reliably and promptly. We observed no false positives: every non-rootkit benchmark run with OSck did not report a rootkit.

Table 3 lists OSck's integrity checks. Heap type-safety requires about 500 lines of code, but all other checkers were less than 100 lines. The largest checker, `ck_proc_namespace`, verifies two independent properties of the `/proc` filesystem, and detects two rootkits. In general, integrity violations caused by a wide class of kernel rootkits are defeated with very small checking functions.

## 6.2 Performance of OSck integrity checks

To illustrate the low overhead of OSck's integrity checks, we measured the time necessary to complete an iteration of the full set of checking code, including verifying type-safety for much of the kernel heap (Table 4). The amount of time to check the integrity of kernel data structures varies by the number of data structures a given benchmark creates on the heap. Our kernel compile benchmark requires on average 126ms to complete a complete iteration of OSck's checking code. RAB, which can create 10 times as many

| Benchmark | Avg. check time (ms) | Max. check time (ms) |
|---|---|---|
| SPEC INT | 76 | 123 |
| SPEC FP | 43 | 109 |
| RAB | 109 | 316 |
| Kernel compile | 126 | 324 |

**Table 4.** Execution times for a single iterations of OSck's complete integrity checks for each single core benchmark.

| Single core | | | |
|---|---|---|---|
| | host | guest | OSck |
| SPEC 2006 | | | |
| INT | 1.00 | 1.03 | 1.05 (2%) |
| FP | 1.00 | 1.03 | 1.03 (0%) |
| PARSEC | | | |
| raytrace | 13.2 | 13.4 | 13.5 (1%) |
| swaptions | 11.5 | 11.5 | 11.5 (0%) |
| x264 | 2.76 | 2.87 | 2.87 (0%) |
| RAB | | | |
| mkdir | 5.62 | 5.87 | 5.98 (2%) |
| copy | 17.68 | 44.07 | 45.15 (2%) |
| du | 0.29 | 0.39 | 0.40 (3%) |
| grep/sum | 2.51 | 1.89 | 1.86 (-2%) |
| Kernel compile | | | |
| 2.6.32.9 | 515 | 471 | 473 (0%) |

| Multiple core | | | |
|---|---|---|---|
| | host | guest | OSck |
| PARSEC | | | |
| raytrace | 7.87 | 8.05 | 8.17 (2%) |
| swaptions | 3.43 | 4.24 | 4.11 (-3%) |
| x264 | 0.97 | 1.20 | 1.17 (-3%) |
| Kernel compile | | | |
| 2.6.32.9 | 145 | 179 | 189 (6%) |

**Table 5.** Benchmark execution time (slowdown of OSck checks over guest execution in parentheses). SPEC reports the weighted geometric mean of slowdown, the remainder report seconds.

objects as an idle system, requires an average of 110ms over the entire benchmark. We report the average and maximum times for any iteration of OSck's checks to describe the range of the latency.

For a given checking latency, a user can set the checking interval to achieve a particular performance level. For example, if OSck checks take about 50ms, then running them every 5s will slow down the workload by 1%. Rootkit detection on the order of seconds is the goal of OSck. If a multiprocessor host has a free CPU, OSck checks can mostly be overlapped with guest computation. Quiescence is rare in our benchmarks (§6.4), so its latency can be safely ignored.

### 6.3 Benchmarks

Table 5 compares the execution time of several benchmarks on the host machine, executing within the KVM hypervisor, and executing on KVM with OSck integrity checks run every 0.5 seconds. All results are the average of 5 runs.

We first describe the slowdown for several compute-intensive workloads. For SPEC 2006 [14], we report the weighted geometric mean for the slowdown of integer and floating point workloads. The results show that OSck has less than a 2% or lower performance overhead over KVM at this checking interval.

We ran a subset of the PARSEC [6] benchmark suite to verify that OSck continues to minimally impact performance in a multicore setting. We report the average of 5 runs for three different applications: a ray-tracer, a securities market simulator, and an H.264 encoder. We used a four core VM for this benchmark. OSck exhibited a maximum of 2% overhead in any one application.

As an I/O bound benchmark, we ran the reimplemented andrew benchmark (RAB) [24], a scalable version of the Andrew benchmark [16] that uses several phases to stress the file system. In our configuration RAB initially creates 100 files of 1024B each and measures the time for the following four operations: (1) creation of 20,000 directories, (2) copying each of the 100 initial files to 500 directories, (3) executing the du command to calculate disk usage, and (4) searching for a short string and checksumming all the files. Our experiments show that OSck imposes a maximum overhead of 3% compared to the guest OS running in the unmodified KVM. This workload has over an order of magnitude more kernel objects than the other workloads.

Finally, we report the performance of a kernel compile, a workload that balances I/O and CPU demands. In the single core case, execution time does not change compared with unmodified KVM, and for four cores, the overhead is 6%.

| Num procs | Failed checks |
|---|---|
| 5 | 14% |
| 10 | 19% |
| 50 | 23% |

**Table 6.** Percent of OSck's runqueue integrity checks that fail for different numbers of user processes that do nothing but yield the processor.

### 6.4 OSck and concurrency

A key goal of OSck is behaving correctly in the face of concurrency. Previous systems have assumed that any false positives when monitoring the kernel heap due to data races would be transient. However, we present a user-level benchmark that consistently violates an integrity property due to concurrency. One technique for hiding malicious processes is to create inconsistency between structures used for scheduling processes, and those used for listing processes. We run an integrity checker that compares the list and rbtree representations of the scheduler runqueue, as several user-level programs continuously yield the CPU. This creates a steady stream of updates to the kernel's runqueue data structures. Because OSck checks the integrity of these data structures while they are being modified, it can see an inconsistent view. Table 6 shows that as the number of user programs increases, the likelihood of seeing an inconsistent view rises. Many previous integrity checking systems simply reverify a failed check a fixed number of times (e.g., 3), and this data shows that such a strategy is not sufficient. Even with 5 processes, 14% of checks find an inconsistent view making a false positive from 3 consecutive inconsistent views an eventual certainty.

OSck only quiesces if two consecutive checks fail, so a mechanism to deal with repeated failures is necessary in practice, though rare enough that a heavy-weight mechanism is acceptable. There were no false positives—all checks passed after quiescence in this concurrency stress-test. We found no occurrences of quiescence in our other non-rootkit benchmarks.

## 7. Related work

Since the time that VMM-based introspection was originally proposed [13], there has been significant progress on techniques for monitoring kernel integrity from a hypervisor. OSck integrates many of these techniques into a single practical package that stresses cooperation between the hypervisor and the monitored kernel. Just as paravirtualization [5] modifies kernel device drivers to make virtualization more efficient, OSck integrates type information and an understanding of the kernel memory allocators to make integrity checking comprehensive and efficient. OSck requires only minimal modification to the guest kernel, generally to communicate boot time parameters like when to begin enforcing immutability of protection on kernel text page table entries.

VMM-based approaches to security can be categorized by the types of guarantees that they provide for a guest VM. Systems like Terra [12] attest, via a chain of trust, that the VMs are initialized to a desired state. Terra [12] guarantees that its virtual machines cannot be inspected or modified by other VMs. Attested VM initialization and its counterparts like secure boot [3, 19] are orthogonal to the design goals of OSck. OSck is instead concerned with the continued maintenance of guest OS integrity after initialization, and Terra provides no such guarantee.

After correct initialization, the next guarantee is that of guest kernel code integrity. SecVisor [27] protects kernel code from modification thus defeating certain attacks. However, merely protecting code segments is insufficient to guarantee correct kernel operation, as shown by return-to-libc [30] and return-oriented programming [17, 28] attacks that make use of unmodified, non-malicious code to accomplish malicious goals. Kernel code integrity is the foundation on which the more stringent guarantees of control-flow integrity [1] and data integrity [4, 8, 11] are layered.

Unlike OSck, that maintains the guest OS integrity against malicious applications, Overshadow [9] ensures secrecy and integrity for application memory against a compromised OS kernel. Overshadow enforces that application code and data pages appear encrypted to the OS, thus ensuring application integrity. However, Overshadow does not protect guest OSes from corruption, hence it is possible for applications to receive incorrect yet consistent responses from a compromised OS. For example, an application may believe it is reading a configuration file and yet actually be reading a fabricated version.

### 7.1 Control-flow integrity

Petroni and Hicks [23] describe a VMM-based approach to maintaining control-flow integrity (execution follows a predetermined control-flow graph [1]) They perform periodic scans of kernel memory, verifying *state-based control-flow integrity*, a property similar to that verified by OSck. They compute a type graph from kernel source, and use this graph to determine a set of global roots for kernel data, the fields of kernel data structures that are function pointers, and the fields that point to other structures. Periodically, their integrity checking monitor executes and traverses the kernel's object graph starting from the set of global roots, successively following pointers to examine all allocated kernel data structures. For each object, the system verifies that all function pointers have desired properties, for example, that they point to a specific set of allowed functions. This requires a breadth-first search of the data structure graph, while OSck verifies type safety via a linear scan of kernel memory.

The Petroni/Hicks system does not consider the stack, though they assert that attacks on the stack are generally transient. Our "return to schedule" rootkit demonstrates a non-transient stack-based attack that would not be caught by their system. Furthermore, their system does not address inconsistencies that can occur because their checks are performed as they scan through a tree of kernel data structures that can be concurrently modified by the OS. OSck avoids these inconsistencies by quiescing when integrity is in question after preliminary checks.

HookSafe [32] protects function pointers (often called hooks) by moving them to a write-protected area. Instructions that access these pointers within the kernel are detected with a profiling run, and then rewritten via binary translation to access the new hook locations. Any accesses to function pointers not present in the profiling run are not correctly translated during runtime. OSck verifies a larger class of integrity properties than properties about kernel function pointers. When possible, it protects function pointers by placing them in hardware-protected memory (whose access policy is determined by the hypervisor), otherwise, it periodically verifies that function pointers point to legitimate code targets according to a flexible policy.

### 7.2 Data Integrity

KernelGuard [25] protects kernel data structures by selectively interposing on memory writes. KernelGuard checks the kernel function that writes a guarded memory region against explicit sets of allowed functions per region. While specifying what functions can modify which regions is a powerful primitive, it does not prevent large classes of attacks where (for example) a function that is permitted to modify a region does so maliciously. For example, protocol handler and netfilter filter registration functions need to be able to install new filters—the latter is used in the firewalling tool `iptables`. OSck enforces OS integrity guarantees on the data structures themselves—in this case, that the functions for protocol handlers and netfilter filters are contained within kernel or allowed module text. Indirect guarantees do not ensure OS integrity.

LiveDM [18] is a system for tracking the types of dynamically allocated kernel memory. It operates by interposing on guest VM operation, waiting until the VM reaches any of a set of kernel memory allocation functions. For these functions, the VMM keeps a "shadow stack" of pending return addresses that it uses to determine when a particular call returns so it can associate call sites (kernel code locations) with return values. The types of return values can then be inferred by static analysis of surrounding code regions; an instrumented version of `gcc` is used to generate an AST for static analysis. While OSck focuses on typing slab allocation, it only uses CIL for static analysis and does not require instrumenting a compiler. No performance measurements are given for LiveDM, but OSck's cache scanning mechanism has low system impact.

Loscocco et. al. present the Linux kernel integrity monitor (LKIM) [21] which is a hypervisor component that intelligently hashes kernel data structures for integrity. LKIM does not provide advanced features like type-checking the kernel heap or providing an interface to kernel programmers to write their own integrity checks.

## 8. Conclusion

OSck is a virtual machine based system that detects rootkits by determining violations to operating system invariants. OSck introduces new mechanisms for bulk verification of types, and consistent data structure views to provide practical and efficient detection. Our deployment of OSck can efficiently detect many kinds of rootkits including two new classes that cannot be handled by any previous rootkit detection system.

## Acknowledgments

We thank our shepherd, Mendel Rosenblum, as well as the anonymous reviewers for their comments on earlier versions of this paper. This research is supported by NSF CNS-0905602, NSF CAREER CNS-0644205, the NSF Graduate Research Fellowship Program, and a Google research award.

## References

[1] M. Abadi, M. Budiu, U. Erlingsson, and J. Ligatti. Control-flow integrity. In *Proceedings of the 12th ACM Conference on Computer and Communications Security*, CCS '05, pages 340–353, New York, NY, USA, 2005. ACM.

[2] Aleph One. Smashing the stack for fun and profit. *Phrack*, 7(49), Nov 1996.

[3] W. A. Arbaugh, D. J. Farber, and J. M. Smith. A secure and reliable bootstrap architecture. In *SP '97: Proceedings of the 1997 IEEE Symposium on Security and Privacy*, page 65, Washington, DC, USA, 1997. IEEE Computer Society.

[4] A. Baliga, P. Kamat, and L. Iftode. Lurking in the shadows: Identifying systemic threats to kernel data. In *Proceedings of the 2007 IEEE Symposium on Security and Privacy*, SP '07, pages 246–251, Washington, DC, USA, 2007. IEEE Computer Society.

[5] P. Barham, B. Dragovic, K. Fraser, S. Hand, T. Harris, A. Ho, R. Neugebauer, I. Pratt, and A. Warfield. Xen and the art of virtualization. In *Proceedings of the nineteenth ACM Symposium on Operating Systems Principles*, SOSP '03, pages 164–177, New York, NY, USA, 2003. ACM.

[6] C. Bienia. *Benchmarking Modern Multiprocessors*. PhD thesis, Princeton University, January 2011.

[7] J. Bonwick. The slab allocator: an object-caching kernel memory allocator. In *Proceedings of the USENIX Summer 1994 Technical Conference*, pages 6–6, Berkeley, CA, USA, 1994. USENIX Association.

[8] S. Chen, J. Xu, E. C. Sezer, P. Gauriar, and R. K. Iyer. Non-control-data attacks are realistic threats. In *Proceedings of the 14th conference on USENIX Security Symposium - Volume 14*, pages 12–12, Berkeley, CA, USA, 2005. USENIX Association.

[9] X. Chen, T. Garfinkel, E. C. Lewis, P. Subrahmanyam, C. A. Waldspurger, D. Boneh, J. Dwoskin, and D. R. Ports. Overshadow: a virtualization-based approach to retrofitting protection in commodity operating systems. In *Proceedings of the 13th international conference on Architectural support for programming languages and operating systems*, ASPLOS XIII, pages 2–13, New York, NY, USA, 2008. ACM.

[10] C. Cowan, C. Pu, D. Maier, H. Hintony, J. Walpole, P. Bakke, S. Beattie, A. Grier, P. Wagle, and Q. Zhang. Stackguard: automatic adaptive detection and prevention of buffer-overflow attacks. In *Proceedings of the 7th conference on USENIX Security Symposium - Volume 7*, pages 5–5, Berkeley, CA, USA, 1998. USENIX Association.

[11] A. Cozzie, F. Stratton, H. Xue, and S. T. King. Digging for data structures. In *Proceedings of the 8th USENIX conference on Operating systems design and implementation*, OSDI'08, pages 255–266, Berkeley, CA, USA, 2008. USENIX Association.

[12] T. Garfinkel, B. Pfaff, J. Chow, M. Rosenblum, and D. Boneh. Terra: a virtual machine-based platform for trusted computing. In *Proceedings of the nineteenth ACM Symposium on Operating Systems Principles*, SOSP '03, pages 193–206, New York, NY, USA, 2003. ACM.

[13] T. Garfinkel and M. Rosenblum. A virtual machine introspection based architecture for intrusion detection. In *Procedings of the Network and Distributed Systems Security Symposium*, pages 191–206, 2003.

[14] J. L. Henning. SPEC CPU2006 benchmark descriptions. *SIGARCH Comput. Archit. News*, 34(4):1–17, 2006.

[15] G. Hoglund and J. Butler. *Rootkits: Subverting the Windows Kernel*. Addison-Wesley Professional, 2005.

[16] J. H. Howard, M. L. Kazar, S. G. Menees, D. A. Nichols, M. Satyanarayanan, R. N. Sidebotham, and M. J. West. Scale and performance in a distributed file system. *ACM Transactions on Computer Systems*, 6:51–81, February 1988.

[17] R. Hund, T. Holz, and F. C. Freiling. Return-oriented rootkits: bypassing kernel code integrity protection mechanisms. In *Proceedings of the 18th conference on USENIX security symposium*, SSYM'09, pages 383–398, Berkeley, CA, USA, 2009. USENIX Association.

[18] D. X. Junghwan Rhee. LiveDM: Temporal mapping of dynamic kernel memory for dynamic kernel malware analysis and debugging. Technical report, 2 2010.

[19] B. Kauer. OSLO: improving the security of trusted computing. In *Proceedings of 16th USENIX Security Symposium on USENIX Security Symposium*, pages 16:1–16:9, Berkeley, CA, USA, 2007. USENIX Association.

[20] A. Kivity. kvm: The Linux Virtual Machine Monitor. In *The 2007 Ottawa Linux Symposium*, OLS '07, pages 225–230, July 2007.

[21] P. A. Loscocco, P. W. Wilson, J. A. Pendergrass, and C. D. McDonell. Linux kernel integrity measurement using contextual inspection. In *Proceedings of the 2007 ACM workshop on Scalable trusted computing*, STC '07, pages 21–29, New York, NY, USA, 2007. ACM.

[22] G. C. Necula, S. McPeak, S. P. Rahul, and W. Weimer. Cil: Intermediate language and tools for analysis and transformation of c programs. In *Proceedings of the 11th International Conference on Compiler Construction*, CC '02, pages 213–228, London, UK, 2002. Springer-Verlag.

[23] N. L. Petroni, Jr. and M. Hicks. Automated detection of persistent kernel control-flow attacks. In *Proceedings of the 14th ACM Conference on Computer and Communications Security*, CCS '07, pages 103–115, New York, NY, USA, 2007. ACM.

[24] D. E. Porter, O. S. Hofmann, C. J. Rossbach, A. Benn, and E. Witchel. Operating system transactions. In *Proceedings of the ACM SIGOPS 22nd Symposium on Operating Systems Principles*, SOSP '09, pages 161–176, New York, NY, USA, 2009. ACM.

[25] J. Rhee, R. Riley, D. Xu, and X. Jiang. Defeating dynamic data kernel rootkit attacks via vmm-based guest-transparent monitoring. *International Conference on Availability, Reliability and Security*, 0:74–81, 2009.

[26] J. Rutkowska. Linux kernel backdoors and their detection. In *ITUnderground*, Oct 2004.

[27] A. Seshadri, M. Luk, N. Qu, and A. Perrig. Secvisor: a tiny hypervisor to provide lifetime kernel code integrity for commodity oses. In *Proceedings of twenty-first ACM SIGOPS Symposium on Operating Systems Principles*, SOSP '07, pages 335–350, New York, NY, USA, 2007. ACM.

[28] H. Shacham. The geometry of innocent flesh on the bone: return-into-libc without function calls (on the x86). In *Proceedings of the 14th ACM Conference on Computer and Communications Security*, CCS '07, pages 552–561, New York, NY, USA, 2007. ACM.

[29] A. Shevchenko. Rootkit evolution. `http://www.securelist.com/en/analysis?pubid=204792016`.

[30] Solar Designer. Getting around non-executable stack (and fix). 1997. http://seclists.org/bugtraq/1997/Aug/63.

[31] Trusted Computing Group. *TPM Main Specification*, 2007. `http://www.trustedcomputinggroup.org/resources/tpm_main_specification`.

[32] Z. Wang, X. Jiang, W. Cui, and P. Ning. Countering kernel rootkits with lightweight hook protection. In *Proceedings of the 16th ACM Conference on Computer and Communications Security*, CCS '09, pages 545–554, New York, NY, USA, 2009. ACM.

[33] D. Wheeler. SLOCCount. `http://www.dwheeler.com/sloccount/`, 2001.

# Rethinking the Library OS from the Top Down

Donald E. Porter[†], Silas Boyd-Wickizer[‡], Jon Howell, Reuben Olinsky, Galen C. Hunt

Microsoft Research
One Microsoft Way
Redmond, WA 98052

[†] Department of Computer Science
Stony Brook University
Stony Brook, NY 11794

[‡] MIT CSAIL
32 Vassar Street
Cambridge, MA 02139

*"There is nothing new under the sun, but there are a lot of old things we don't know."*

– *Ambrose Bierce,* The Devil's Dictionary

## Abstract

This paper revisits an old approach to operating system construction, the *library OS*, in a new context. The idea of the library OS is that the personality of the OS on which an application depends runs in the address space of the application. A small, fixed set of abstractions connects the library OS to the host OS kernel, offering the promise of better system security and more rapid independent evolution of OS components.

We describe a working prototype of a Windows 7 library OS that runs the latest releases of major applications such as Microsoft Excel, PowerPoint, and Internet Explorer. We demonstrate that desktop sharing across independent, securely isolated, library OS instances can be achieved through the pragmatic reuse of networking protocols. Each instance has significantly lower overhead than a full VM bundled with an application: a typical application adds just 16MB of working set and 64MB of disk footprint. We contribute a new ABI below the library OS that enables application mobility. We also show that our library OS can address many of the current uses of hardware virtual machines at a fraction of the overheads. This paper describes the first working prototype of a full commercial OS redesigned as a library OS capable of running significant applications. Our experience shows that the long-promised benefits of the library OS approach—better protection of system integrity and rapid system evolution—are readily obtainable.

***Categories and Subject Descriptors*** D.4 [**Operating Systems**]: Organization and Design.

***General Terms*** Experimentation, Performance.

## 1. Introduction

The *library OS* approach to OS construction was championed by several operating system designs in the 1990s [3, 10, 13, 21]. The idea of the library OS is that the entire *personality* of the OS on which an application depends runs in its address space as a library. An OS personality is the implementation of the OS's application programming interfaces (APIs) and application visible semantics; the OS services upon which applications are built. Early proponents of the library OS approach argued primarily that it could enable better performance through per-application customization. For example, a disk-I/O bound application with idiosyncratic file access patterns can realize better performance by using a custom file system storage stack rather than using the default sequential prefetching heuristics.

Like many of its contemporaries, the library OS approach is largely forgotten, a casualty of the rise of the modern virtual machine monitor (VMM) [8]. While most new OS designs of the time—including library OS designs—ran only a handful of custom applications on small research prototypes, VMM systems proliferated because they could run major applications by reusing existing feature-rich operating systems. The performance benefits offered by library OS designs did not overcome the need for legacy compatibility. On the other hand, the need for security and independent system isolation has increased since the 1990s due to the rise of the Internet.

We revisit the library OS approach to OS construction, prioritizing application compatibility, security isolation, and independent system evolution benefits. Our goal is to realize the benefits of a VMM, but with order-of-magnitude lower overheads. This paper shows for the first time that it is possible to build a library OS running major applications from a feature-rich, commercial OS. We describe a Windows 7 library OS, called *Drawbridge*, running the latest commercial releases of a large set of applications, including Microsoft Excel, PowerPoint, Internet Explorer, and IIS. Windows applications running on Drawbridge have access to core Windows features and enhanced APIs including the .NET common language runtime (CLR) and DirectX.

This paper describes a new top-down approach to building library OSes—an approach that prioritizes application compatibility and high-level OS code reuse and avoids low-level management of the underlying hardware by the library OS. Drawbridge demonstrates that a small set of OS abstractions—threads, virtual memory, and I/O streams—are sufficient to host a Windows 7 library OS and a rich set of applications. This small set of abstractions helps simplify protection of system integrity, mobility of applications, and independent evolution of the library OS and the underlying kernel components. Despite being strongly isolated, Drawbridge applications can still share resources, including the screen, keyboard, mouse, and user clipboard, across independent library OS instances through the pragmatic reuse of networking protocols.

As a structuring principle, we identify three categories of services in OS implementations: *hardware services*, *user services*, and *application services*. Hardware services include the OS kernel and device drivers, which abstract and multiplex hardware, along with file systems and TCP/IP networking stack (see Figure 1). User services in the OS include the graphical user interface (GUI) shell and desktop, clipboard, search indexers, etc. Application services in the OS include the API implementation; to an application, these


*ASPLOS'11* March 5–11, 2011, Newport Beach, California, USA.

comprise the OS personality. Applications services include frameworks, rendering engines, common UI controls, language runtimes, etc. The application communicates with application services, which in turn communicate with hardware and user services.

We use these service categories to drive the refactoring of Windows into the Drawbridge library OS. Drawbridge packages application services into the *library OS* and leaves user and hardware services in the *host OS* (see Figure 2). The library OS communicates with hardware services in the host OS through a narrow *application binary interface* (ABI), which is implemented by a *platform adaptation layer* and a *security monitor*. The library OS communicates with user services in the host OS using the *remote desktop protocol* (RDP) [28] tunneled through the ABI. Each application runs in its own address space with its own copy of the library OS. The security monitor virtualizes host OS resources through its ABI with the library OS and maintains a consistent set of abstractions across varying host OS implementations. For example, the file system seen by an application is virtualized by the security monitor from file systems in the host OS.

Previous library OS designs aimed to provide application-customized performance enhancement, and thus exposed low-level hardware abstractions to applications. Cache Kernel, Exokernel, and Nemesis innovated by providing applications with fine-grained, customized control of hardware resources, such as page tables, network packets, and disk blocks [10, 13, 21]. In contrast, Drawbridge's differing goals (security, host independence, and migration) free it to offer higher-level abstractions. These higher-level abstractions make it easier to share underlying host OS resources such as buffer caches, file systems, and networking stacks with the library OS. By making low-level resource management an independent concern from OS personality, each can evolve more aggressively.

One can view a modern VMM as a mechanism for automatically treating a conventional OS as a library OS, but the facility incurs significant overheads. Each isolated application runs in a different dedicated VM, each of which is managed by a separate OS instance. The OS state in each VM leads to significant storage overheads. For example, a Windows 7 guest OS in a Hyper-V VM consumes 512MB of RAM and 4.8GB of disk. In contrast, Drawbridge refactors the guest OS to extract just those APIs needed by the application; it adds less than 16MB of working set and 64MB of disk.

The Drawbridge approach could significantly impact desktop computing by enabling fine-grain packaging of self-contained application. The VMM approach allowed the construction of self-contained application packages comprised of an application and OS, with minimal dependencies on the underlying VMM or hardware. VMM-based application packaging enabled a huge shift in server computing through server consolidation and cloud computing [1, 25], all despite huge overheads. We believe that the finer-grained, higher-performance application and OS packages that are now possible with library OSes could precipitate similar shifts in desktop and mobile computing; for example, snapshots of running Drawbridge applications could easily move from device to device and to the cloud because they are so small—a compressed process snapshot of Excel is under 4MB for Drawbridge, versus nearly 150MB for a similar VM snapshot.

In summary, this paper describes the first refactoring of a widely used, monolithic OS into a functionally-rich library OS. It contributes a set of heuristics for refactoring a monolithic kernel into a library as well as a new ABI for separating library OS from host

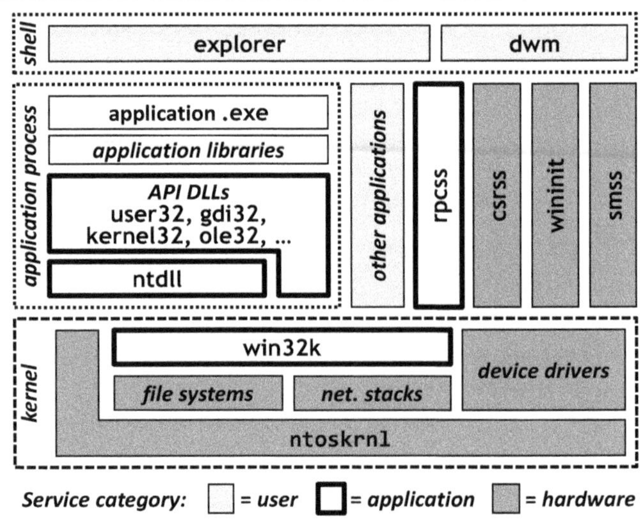


**Figure 1.** Windows 7 OS Architecture.

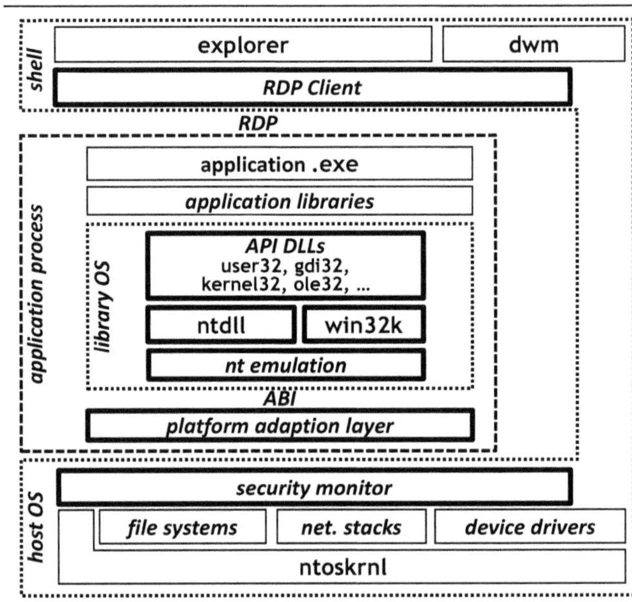


**Figure 2.** Drawbridge Architecture.

OS. The benefits of this design include: 1) strong encapsulation of the host OS from the library OS, enabling rapid and independent evolution of each; 2) migration of running state of individual applications across computers; and 3) better protection of system and application integrity (i.e., strongly isolated processes).

The remainder of the paper is structured as follows. Section 2 provides helpful background on the Windows 7 OS architecture as it exists prior to Drawbridge. Section 3 describes our approach for separating the Win32 personality from the rest of Windows to create a library OS. Section 4 describes the security monitor and the ABI it presents to the library OS. Section 5 describes our implementation of the Windows 7 library OS. Section 6 evaluates the scalability, complexity, update surface, and overheads of our approach through examination of the current implementation.

Section 7 places Drawbridge into context with related work. In Section 8 we discuss possible impacts of the library OS approach on end-user computing. Finally, we summarize our contributions in Section 9.

## 2. Windows 7 Architecture

Refactoring a general-purpose, commercial operating system away from its long-evolved roots into a library OS is a significant challenge. This section outlines the key features of the Windows 7 architecture, drawing analogies between elements in Windows and corresponding elements common to such Unix systems as Linux. We draw these analogies to help the reader appreciate that similar challenges exist in other large-scale OSes.

Windows is architecturally divided into *dynamic link libraries* (DLLs) that load into an application's address space, *services* that run as daemon processes, the *NT kernel*, and *drivers*, which are dynamically loaded kernel-mode components (see Figure 1). DLLs are similar to shared object (.so) files in Unix systems. The NT kernel implements the usual core of a monolithic operating system: resource management, scheduling, I/O services, a hierarchical object namespace, and the *registry*, a key-value store for configuration data. Replaceable kernel-mode components, such as the networking stack and file systems, are loaded as drivers.

In practice, all Windows applications are programmed to the Win32 API. While there is no official count, Win32 is known to include over 100,000 API functions. The API is implemented as a large collection of in-process DLLs. These DLLs access the NT kernel indirectly through a runtime DLL, ntdll, which the kernel inserts into every process during creation. ntdll implements the dynamic loader for DLLs along with functionality roughly equivalent to the Unix libc, including stubs for the 401 functions in the NT system-call table. Commonly used Win32 API DLLs include: kernel32, which provides access to kernel operations for process control, threading, virtual memory, registry, and block and character device I/O functionality; user32 and gdi32, which provide the basics of windowing, drawing, and GUI; ws2_32, which provides a sockets interface to the networking stack; and ole32, which provides access to the Component Object Model (COM) and Object Linking and Embedding (OLE) APIs for constructing multi-component application experiences (e.g., a PowerPoint presentation with an embedded Excel chart). These DLLs correspond to libraries such as libX11 and the libraries that make up the GNOME or KDE frameworks on Unix systems.

The core of Win32 is implemented in the Windows subsystem. Divided into a kernel-mode component (win32k) and a user-mode daemon (csrss), the Windows subsystem provides roughly the analogue of an X server, a print server, and audio support. Most of the implementation resides in win32k, which implements windowing event message queues, overlapping windows, rasterization, font management and rendering, the mouse and keyboard input event queues, and a shared clipboard. csrss coordinates system initialization, shutdown, and application error reporting. Prior to Windows NT 4.0 (1996), functionality now in win32k ran in the csrss service daemon, but was moved to kernel mode to improve performance and to simplify the implementation of accelerated graphics drivers. User-mode API DLLs access win32k indirectly through stubs in user32 and gdi32; the stubs trap into a secondary system-call table of 827 functions from win32k.

In addition to the Windows subsystem, the implementation of the Win32 API depends on multiple service daemons. smss performs a role similar to Unix init, handling startup and shutdown. wininit creates read-only shared data structures, which are subsequently mapped into most processes and used by win32k to cache such common objects as default fonts, internationalization tables, and cursors. wininit also launches the components of the user's desktop upon login, the analogue of an X session manager. rpcss implements shared services for high-level inter-process communication, including COM and OLE, similar to D-Bus [24] in Linux. explorer, the Windows GUI shell, launches programs and provides shared services for drag-and-drop, "open" and "save" dialogs, and file preview. dwm implements the Windows 7 compositing window manager.

## 3. Approach

To maximize application compatibility while minimizing dependencies outside the library OS, we refactored Windows 7 by applying four high-level heuristics: inclusion of API DLLs based on their usage in a representative set of applications, reuse of virtualized host OS resources, resolution of dependencies through inclusion or alternative implementations, and device driver emulation. One insight we applied repeatedly in our work is the recognition that much of the code in an OS kernel and major OS subsystems is not relevant in the context of a library OS. For example, much OS code ensures security and consistency when sharing resources—either physical or virtual—between multiple applications and multiple users. In a library OS, these concerns are greatly diminished as library OS state is not shared by multiple applications or users.

Our first heuristic was to identify the API DLLs required by a representative set of applications. Those DLLs account for over 14,000 functions of the Win32 API. We used static analysis on the application binaries to roughly approximate the required set of API DLLs, and then refined the set with dynamic instrumentation by monitoring DLL load operations issued during a test runs. In our experience, static analysis alone is either insufficient—DLLs can be loaded without static stubs through calls to LoadLibrary (equivalent to dlopen on Unix) with a dynamically generated string—or overly conservative—including delay-bound DLLs loaded only for specific OS versions.

Second, for kernel-mode dependencies, we implemented an NT kernel emulation layer at the bottom of the library OS. This emulation layer is quite thin, as many complex parts of a kernel—like threading, virtual memory, file system, and networking—are provided by the host OS through the security monitor. The security monitor virtualizes host resources according to a well-defined high-level ABI independent of host OS version. Other parts of the library OS are simpler because multi-user multiplexing is no longer required; for this reason the Drawbridge registry implementation is $1/50^{th}$ the lines of code of the Windows 7 equivalent. While our emulation provides most of the interfaces of the NT kernel, many calls return failure, including all requests to access or modify other processes, and almost all ioctl requests. In theory the "holes" in our emulation of the NT kernel could cause an application to fail unexpectedly due to an unimplemented corner case. In practice, we find that most applications either don't use the unimplemented interfaces, or respond gracefully when a rarely-used API returns a failure result.

Third, for dependencies on service daemons and the Windows subsystem, we either moved code into the library OS, or altered the API DLL to remove the dependency. As a rule of thumb, we included code where most of the service was relevant when running a single application, and replaced code where it was needlessly complicated by the security or consistency demands of supporting multiple applications and/or multiple users. For example, we included almost all of win32k and rpcss, as these services provide core functionality for applications. By contrast, we wrote custom library OS code to replace csrss, smss, and wininit, which primarily aid cross-application sharing of state.

Fourth, for console and human interface device dependencies, we provide emulated device drivers. We emulate the keyboard and mouse drivers required by the Windows subsystem with stub drivers that provide simple input queues, and the display driver with a stub driver that draws to an in-process frame buffer. I/O from the emulated devices is tunneled to the desktop and the user through stateless RDP connections. Our implementation of RDP reuses code from the Windows 7 kernel-mode RDP server but not the RDP device drivers, which are replaced by simpler stubs.

## 4. Security Monitor

The library OS interacts with the host OS through the Drawbridge ABI, which is implemented by the security monitor. The Drawbridge ABI is designed to provide a small set of functions with well-defined semantics easily supported across a wide range of host OS implementations. The ABI's design enables the host OS to expose virtualized resources to the library OS with minimal duplication of effort. We describe here first the ABI and then the implementation of the security monitor.

In providing the ABI, the security monitor enforces a set of external policies governing the host OS resources available to the application. Inspired by previous work in Singularity [33], we encode policy in manifest files associated with the application. The manifest whitelists the host OS resources that an application may access, identified by URI path. We also use the manifest as a convenient place to store per-application configuration settings.

### ABI Description

The ABI includes three calls to allocate, free, and modify the permission bits on page-based virtual memory. Permissions include read, write, execute, and guard. Memory regions can be unallocated, reserved, or backed by committed memory:

```
VOID *DkVirtualMemoryAlloc(Addr, Size, AllocType, Prot);
DkVirtualMemoryFree(Addr, Size, FreeType);
DkVirtualMemoryProtect(Addr, Size, Prot);
```

The ABI supports multithreading through five calls to create, sleep, yield the scheduler quantum for, resume execution of, and terminate threads, as well as seven calls to create, signal, and block on synchronization objects:

```
DKHANDLE DkThreadCreate(Addr, Param, Flags);
DkThreadDelayExecution(Duration);
DkThreadYieldExecution();
DkThreadResume(ThreadHandle);
DkThreadExit();
DKHANDLE DkSemaphoreCreate(InitialCount, MaxCount);
DKHANDLE DkNotificationEventCreate(InitialState);
DKHANDLE DkSynchronizationEventCreate(InitialState);
DkSemaphoreRelease(SemaphoreHandle, ReleaseCount);
BOOL DkEventSet(EventHandle);
DkEventClear(EventHandle);
ULONG DkObjectsWaitAny(Count, HandleArray, Timeout);
```

The primary I/O mechanism in Drawbridge is an I/O stream. I/O streams are byte streams that may be memory-mapped or sequentially accessed. Streams are named by URIs. The stream ABI includes nine calls to open, read, write, map, unmap, truncate, flush, delete and wait for I/O streams and three calls to access metadata about an I/O stream. The ABI purposefully does not provide an ioctl call. Supported URI schemes include file:, pipe:, http:, https:, tcp:, udp:, pipe.srv:, http.srv, tcp.srv:, and udp.srv:. The latter four schemes are used to open inbound I/O streams for server applications:

```
DKHANDLE DkStreamOpen(URI, AccessMode, ShareFlags,
        CreateFlags, Options);
ULONG DkStreamRead(StreamHandle, Offset, Size, Buffer);
ULONG DkStreamWrite(StreamHandle, Offset, Size, Buffer);
DkStreamMap(StreamHandle, Addr, ProtFlags, Offset, Size);
DkStreamUnmap(Addr);
DkStreamSetLength(StreamHandle, Length);
DkStreamFlush(StreamHandle);
DkStreamDelete(StreamHandle);
DkStreamWaitForClient(StreamHandle);
DkStreamGetName(StreamHandle, Flags, Buffer, Size);
DkStreamAttributesQuery(URI, DK_STREAM_ATTRIBUTES *Attr);
DkStreamAttributesQueryByHandle(StreamHandle,
        DK_STREAM_ATTRIBUTES *Attr);
```

The ABI includes one call to create a child process and one call to terminate the running process. A child process does not inherit any objects or memory from its parent process and the parent process may not modify the execution of its children. A parent can wait for a child to exit using its handle. Parent and child may communicate through I/O streams provided by the parent to the child at creation:

```
DKHANDLE DkProcessCreate(URI, Args, DKHANDLE *FirstThread);
DkProcessExit(ExitCode);
```

Finally, the ABI includes seven assorted calls to get wall clock time, generate cryptographically-strong random bits, flush portions of instruction caches, increment and decrement the reference counts on objects shared between threads, and to coordinate threads with the security monitor during process serialization:

```
LONG64 DkSystemTimeQuery();
DkRandomBitsRead(Buffer, Size);
DkInstructionCacheFlush(Addr, Size);
DkObjectReference(Handle);
DkObjectClose(Handle);
DkObjectsCheckpoint();
DkObjectsReload();
```

We believe the brevity of the Drawbridge ABI enables tractable coding-time and run-time review of its isolation boundary. Our largest implementation of the ABI in a security monitor is 17KLoC.

We recognize that the Drawbridge ABI could be smaller. While size matters, we have in a few cases opted for exposing a slightly larger set of abstractions than was strictly necessary in order to ease porting of Windows code into the library OS. Our experience is that a slightly larger ABI (say with a dozen more calls) makes it easier to port existing code and makes the ported code easier to maintain. For example, instead of exposing semaphores, notification events, and synchronization events, we could have exposed only a single synchronization primitive. In fact, the initial version of the ABI had just 19 calls, with synchronization objects and I/O streams being coalesced into a single pipe abstraction; for example, lock release was implemented in the library OS as a one-byte send on a pipe and acquire as a one-byte write. The ABI was smaller, but reasoning about library OS implementation was more torturous. The slightly larger ABI allows the security monitor to implement virtualized resources with resources that the host OS can more efficiently support.

### Implementation

The Drawbridge ABI is implemented through two components: the security monitor, dkmon, and the platform adaptation layer, dkpal. The primary job of dkmon is to virtualize host OS resources into the application while maintaining the security isolation boundary between the library OS and the host OS. Although implementations of dkmon and dkpal vary across different host systems, these components are responsible for maintaining strict compatibility with the ABI specification. We currently have implementations of dkmon that run Drawbridge applications as processes on Windows 7 and Windows Server 2008 R2, on MinWin [36] built from Windows 7, and on a pre-release of the next version of Windows. We also have a version of dkmon that runs Drawbridge applications in ring 0 in a raw Hyper-V VM partition, while relying on I/O streams served from a Windows Server 2008 R2 host. Applications using the Drawbridge library OS run identically on all of these platforms.

A Drawbridge process accesses the ABI by calling dkpal. We have three implementations of dkpal: the first, which requires no changes to the host OS kernel, and uses four host OS calls to issue requests over an anonymous named pipe to dkmon; the second, which replaces the NT system-call service table on a per-process basis using techniques developed for Xax [11]; and the third, which makes Hyper-V hypercalls. dkmon services ABI requests by modifying the address space and host OS handle table of the calling process with standard Windows cross-process manipulation APIs (ReadProcessMemory, VirtualAllocEx, VirtualFreeEx, and DuplicateHandle). As an optimization, dkpal implements a few simple ABI calls (e.g., blocking wait, thread yield) by directly invoking compatible, host OS system calls; this is safe, as the Drawbridge process cannot create host OS handles. dkpal currently calls 15 distinct host OS system calls. Eventually, we expect to move the data paths dkmon into the host kernel to avoid the cost of a complete address space change to service some ABI calls, and to harden the boundary around Drawbridge processes; this will require an update to dkpal, but no changes in the Drawbridge library OS.

dkmon uses host NT threads and synchronization objects—semaphores, notification events, and synchronization events—to implement the scheduling objects exposed through the ABI. As a result, Drawbridge threads reside in the host kernel's scheduling queues and avoid unnecessary scheduling overheads.

I/O streams are used by the library OS to implement such higher-level abstractions as files, sockets, and pipes. The security monitor filters access to I/O streams by URI based on a manifest policy; where access is allowed, it directs I/O to the mapped resources. This indirection enables run-time configuration of the application's virtual environment, and prevents applications from inadvertently or maliciously accessing protected resources within the host system's file namespace. Unless overridden, the monitor's default policy only allows a Drawbridge process to access files within the same host directory as its application image.

As an example, our library OS leverages I/O streams to emulate NT file objects and named pipe objects, as well as a proxied interface to networking sockets. In the latter case, the library OS includes a minimal version of ws2_32 that use I/O streams identified by tcp: and udp: URIs. The security monitor backs these streams with sockets provided by the host system's ws2_32. The current approach was taken as an implementation expediency; Drawbridge could provide better isolation by offering an IP-packet stream interface and moving the implementation of TCP and UDP into the library OS.

## 5. Windows Library OS

Refactoring Windows 7 into a library OS constituted the largest portion of the work to realize Drawbridge. The main challenges included: orchestrating process bootstrap with minimal changes to existing components, emulating host kernel interfaces in user mode on the Drawbridge ABI, porting system-wide application services to run in-process, and enabling process serialization and deserialization. We believe that these challenges would be typical of the refactoring effort required to convert any complex, modern operating system into a library OS for desktop applications, and that our solutions would apply elsewhere. However, we also recognize that our task was made significantly easier because most Windows applications seldom use child processes and the Windows API has no fork primitive.

### OS Library Bootstrap

Bootstrapping is a challenging task in any OS, balancing the demands of efficiency and good engineering. For example, should one first initialize the lock manager, which requires memory for storage, or the memory manager, which requires locks for synchronization? Some of these complexities remain for the library OS, which aggregates per-process code and state with formerly system-wide OS code and state.

***Process Bootstrap*** To create a Drawbridge process, dkmon uses the host OS's native facilities to create a suspended process containing a bootstrap loader (dkinit). Every NT process is created with the ntdll library mapped copy-on-write, because the kernel uses fixed offsets in the library as up-call entry points for exceptions. Before allowing a new process to execute, dkmon maps its own dkntdll library into the new process's address space and overwrites upcall entry points in the host-provided ntdll with jumps to dkntdll, eviscerating ntdll to a jump table and replacing it as the dynamic loader. dkmon writes a parameter block into the new process's address space to communicate initialization parameters, such as a reference to the pipe to be used for communication with dkmon. dkmon then resumes the suspended process, with execution starting in ntdll and immediately jumping to dkntdll, which sets up initial library linkage (to itself) and transfers control to dkinit. dkinit invokes dkntdll to initialize the win32k library (described next) and to load the application binary and its imported libraries. When loading is complete, dkinit jumps to the application's entry point.

***Win32k Bootstrap*** Converting win32k from a kernel subsystem to a user-mode library required reformulating its complicated, multi-process initialization sequence. In standard Windows, first, the single, system-wide instance of win32k is initialized in kernel mode. Second, wininit initiates the preloading of win32k's caches with shared public objects such as fonts and bitmaps. Because win32k makes upcalls to the user32 and gdi32 user-mode libraries to load an object into its cache, these libraries must be loaded before filling the cache. Third, when a normal user process starts, it loads its own copies of user32 and gdi32, which connect to win32k and provide GUI services.

We considered refactoring the initialization of win32k, but rejected that idea as it required a deeper fork of the source code than desired and prevented sharing of code between full Windows and Drawbridge. Instead, we opted for an approach that simulates the full win32k bootstrapping sequence within a single process. We exported entry points from win32k, user32, and gdi32, which are called by dkinit for each of the boot steps.

Much of the effort described here can be viewed as unwinding the complexity of the multi-server architecture of Windows into an in-process library OS. On a full Windows system, csrss creates a read-only, shared-memory segment to share cached bitmaps and fonts, which is replaced in the library OS with heap allocated objects, since all components that access it now share the same address space and protection domain. The upcalls that torture the win32k initialization sequence were needed only because a shared, trusted win32k must avoid being confused into loading one principal's objects on behalf of another; in Drawbridge, that responsibility is removed, and the corresponding complexity can be reduced. Likewise, we removed many other access checks over shared state from win32k, and eliminated the Windows logon session abstraction, wininit, and csrss.

### Emulating NT Kernel Interfaces

To support binary compatibility with existing Windows 7 API DLLs, we provide user-mode implementations of approximately 150 NT kernel system calls. The majority of these functions are stubs that either trivially wrap the Drawbridge ABI (e.g., virtual memory allocation, thread creation, etc.), return static data, or always return an error (i.e., STATUS_NOT_IMPLEMENTED).

The remaining system calls produce higher-level NT abstractions, such as files, locks, and timers, built entirely inside the library OS using Drawbridge primitives. The most challenging part of this work was building compatible semantics for the NT I/O model, including synchronous and asynchronous I/O, "waitable" file handles, completion ports, and asynchronous procedure calls.

Additional NT emulation calls were required to win32k from kernel mode to user mode. The interfaces provided to kernel-mode libraries by the NT kernel are largely disjoint from those provided to user-mode libraries; we added roughly 6.3KLoC to emulate these kernel-mode calls.

### Shared System Services

Windows applications depend on shared system services, accessible either through system calls or IPCs to trusted service daemons. These include services such as the Windows registry and OLE. In order to confine the state and dependencies of Drawbridge processes, our library OS implements the functionality of several such services using two design patterns: providing simple alternate implementations of service functionality, and hosting extant library code in-process.

***Alternative Implementations*** Many Windows system services are backed by complex and robust implementations, tuned and hardened for a wide variety of use cases. For a few such services like the registry, it proved more practical to reimplement the services' advertised interfaces within the library OS rather than port their existing implementations.

The *registry* is a system-wide, hierarchical, key-value store, accessible to Windows processes through system calls. The traditional Windows registry is implemented in kernel mode with 61 KLoC; its complexity is required to implement fine-grained access control and locking as well as transactional semantics. While we might have replicated code for the kernel registry into the library OS, we found that registry code is inseparably connected to code for the kernel object namespace and the kernel scheduler. The Drawbridge library OS instead includes a private, in-process reimplementation of the registry, significantly simpler than the shared kernel registry. Drawbridge's NT emulation layer supplies a simple 1.3 KLoC interface to this implementation, with coarse locking and no support for transactions.

***Importing Implementations*** In several cases, we encountered shared Windows services whose implementations could be ported largely intact. As an example, Drawbridge's support for COM required functionality traditionally provided by rpcss. Supporting COM is an absolute requirement for rich applications in Windows; a significant number of desktop- and server-class applications are formed by composing multiple COM objects through the OLE protocol. With one exception (Reversi) each of our test applications uses OLE.

Refactoring COM followed the same basic pattern used with other system services: shared, out-of-process components were ported to run privately in-process and bound directly to application-side libraries. For example, a key component of OLE is the running object table (ROT), which provides inter- and intra-process name resolution for COM objects. While only one instance of the ROT is maintained per system within rpcss, in Drawbridge it runs directly within the application process and only manages local objects. Fewer than 500 lines out of 318 KLoC were changed in the COM runtime (ole32) to make these changes.

### Process Serialization

The volatile state associated with a traditional Windows process is distributed across the NT kernel and kernel-mode drivers; shared, out-of-process, user-mode service daemons; and the process's own address space. Serializing the running state of a Windows process would require the careful cooperation of each of these components, and significant changes to the OS. However, with Drawbridge process isolation, a process's transient state is either confined to pages in its address space or can be reconstructed from data maintained within its address space.

Due to careful design of the ABI and library OS, serializing a Drawbridge process is relatively simple. Running win32k as a user-mode library vastly reduced the amount of kernel state associated with the process. The remaining out-of-process state consists of resources managed by the host OS, such as files and synchronization objects. To account for this, our implementation of the ABI inserts indirection between Drawbridge system objects and host NT system objects. This distinction enables the library OS to easily unbind and rebind these objects at deserialization time. Because the metadata for host kernel objects are stored within a process's address space, serialization only requires quiescing the threads and serializing the contents of the address space. The thread contexts need not be serialized, as the active register contents are stored on their stacks during quiescence. The application serializes itself with no involvement from the host, beyond the I/O stream to which the serialized state is saved.

In order to quiesce the threads within a Drawbridge process, the security monitor signals a notification event to indicate a serialization request. Threads blocked on Drawbridge ABIs are woken via the notification event, outstanding I/O requests are completed, and other threads are interrupted with an exception. Once notified of the pending serialization, all threads, except one, yield indefinitely. The final thread begins serializing the process to a monitor-provided I/O stream, recording virtual memory bookkeeping information and the contents of the process's address space. Files on which the process depends must be migrated with the application or accessed through a distributed file system. Network sockets are terminated on migration causing applications to reestablish their network connections. In a world of migrating laptops, we find that applications are robust to network interruptions. After serialization is complete, the yielding threads are woken and the process continues normal execution.

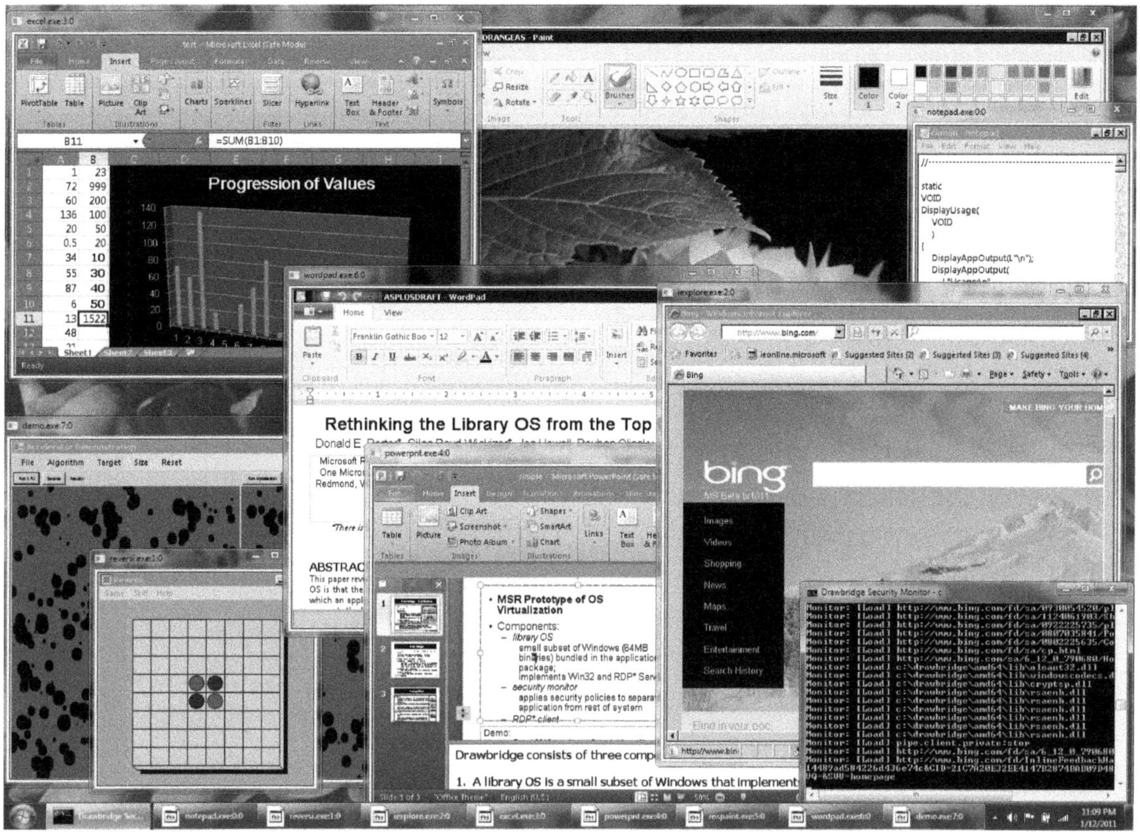


**Figure 3.** Screenshot of Drawbridge Applications: Clockwise from the top-left: Excel, Paint, Notepad, dkmon, Internet Explorer, WordPad, PowerPoint, Reversi, and a CLR Demo.

Reconstructing a Drawbridge process from its serialized state requires adjustments to its initialization sequence. Instead of loading the application binary, serialized virtual memory data are used to restore the contents of the process's address space, including heap and stack memory as well as memory-mapped I/O streams. Code in dkpal rebinds host system objects to ABI objects without involvement from the library OS or the application. After recreating the process, the threads quiesced during serialization are unblocked and continue normal execution.

**Limitations**

The present Drawbridge system is a research prototype; it is far from a production system. While Drawbridge supports over 14,000 Win32 API functions, this is a fraction of the total Win32 API. At the time of writing, Microsoft has no plans to productize any of the concepts prototyped in Drawbridge.

The two holes in the current implementation are support for printing and support for multi-process applications that communicate through shared state. The challenge of printing is that most Windows printer drivers actually load in-process with the application. As our design requires leaving hardware drivers within the host OS, they can't be loaded into the library OS without creating undesirable dependencies. A possible solution is to reuse the approach of RDP 7.0, which employs a universal application printer driver that prints to a common format, XPS, and then asks the RDP client's printer to print the XPS.

Solving the problem of multi-process applications is much harder, particularly for applications that communicate through shared state in win32k, as is done in many OLE scenarios. For example, Microsoft Outlook can be configured to use Microsoft Word as a text editor with the shared state passing through win32k message queues. We have considered, but not implemented, two possible designs. One is to load multiple applications into a single address space. Another is to run win32k in a separate user-mode server process that can be shared by multiple applications in the same isolation container. The latter approach follows a pattern commonly used by microkernel designs.

A third weakness in the present implementation is that code paths in many Win32 APIs ultimately lead to NT APIs that are not implemented by our emulation layer. We have ported the most frequently used subset of a very large API space. As we have run new applications, the number of additions to the library OS has diminished, but not completely disappeared. For example, after Excel ran, getting PowerPoint to run on Drawbridge took only two days: one to fix a bug we had introduced in win32k, and one to implement an additional API in the NT emulation layer.

Finally, there are classes of applications that, by design, will probably never run in Drawbridge. For example, administration tools, that manipulate the host OS, or development tools such as debuggers, which need unfiltered access to the environment, cannot be run without creating hard dependencies on the host OS.

## 6. Experiments

This section evaluates the theses of the Drawbridge project: that a library OS can run rich desktop applications, that such refactoring is feasible, that it is suitable for isolating large numbers of applications in a single computer, that it protects the integrity of the host OS at least as well as a VMM, that it provides greater mobility for running applications, and that it enables independent evolution of host OS from library OS. We also measure the servicing implications of the library OS.

All data were collected on an HP z800 Workstation with dual 2.4GHz Intel Xeon E5530 Quad-Core CPUs with hyper-threads disabled, 16GB of RAM, and dual 10,000 RPM hard drives. All Windows experiments use 64-bit Windows 7, Ultimate Edition, with the page file disabled. All Hyper-V experiments run on 64-bit Windows Server 2008 R2, Enterprise Edition, which shares the same code base as Windows 7. Drawbridge and all applications are 64-bit binaries. Windows 7 and Hyper-V were tuned for maximum scalability according to published best practices [27].

For most experiments, we present results for three applications: Excel, a canonical desktop application; Internet Explorer, a web browser and network client application; and IIS, a canonical server application. Unless stated otherwise: Excel experiments used small (11KB), large (20MB), and huge (100MB) spreadsheets; Internet Explorer rendered research.microsoft.com, and IIS was serving up the default Visual Studio 2010 ASP.NET application using CLR 4.0.

### Running Applications

The primary hypothesis of Drawbridge is that a legacy OS can be refactored into a resource-efficient library OS that supports a large class of rich, desktop applications. Figure 3 shows a sample screenshot with output from dkmon and seven applications running in Drawbridge: Microsoft Excel 2010, Windows 7 Paint, Notepad, Internet Explorer 8, PowerPoint 2010, Windows 7 WordPad, a CLR demo application, and Reversi, the first game to run on Windows. Other applications we have tested include IIS 7.5, DirectX 11 demos, and a number of in-house applications. With the exception of disabling software licensing in Excel and PowerPoint, all application binaries are unmodified.

To run on Drawbridge, applications were "sequenced", by running their setup programs on a desktop copy of Windows 7, and capturing the file-system and registry changes made by the setup program into a Drawbridge package. Tools for collecting file-system and registry changes are well understood and deployed with products such as Microsoft Application Virtualization (App-V) and VMWare ThinApp [37].

### Cost of Refactoring

Our hypothesis maintains that the refactoring task is tractable. Of the 93 binaries containing executable code in the Drawbridge library OS, 62 come directly from Windows 7 with no modifications, 12 are alternative implementations (mostly machine generated stubs), and 19 contain modifications. The changes are generally quite small when compared with the number of lines of code that remain unchanged (see Table 1). The most significant changes were in: gdi32, ntdll, and user32, which no longer trap, but now directly call either win32k or the NT emulation layer; dxapi, dxg, and win32k, which were kernel-mode drivers now modified to run as user-mode DLLs; and ole32 and wininet, in which we removed dependencies on external services. Supporting our hypothesis, repurposing 5.6 MLoC of Windows 7 into a library OS required less than 16 KLoC of changes (0.3% of code base) and 36 KLoC of new code; the entire project was completed in fewer than two person-years.

| Binary | #if's | Changed LoC | Total LoC | Size (KB) |
|---|---|---|---|---|
| advapi32.dll | 18 | 720 | 61,975 | 655 |
| dxapi.dll | 88 | 294 | 3,225 | 18 |
| dxg.dll | 110 | 449 | 12,706 | 85 |
| dxgi.dll | 4 | 20 | 46,347 | 616 |
| dxgkrnl.dll | 1 | 8 | 518 | 9 |
| gdi32.dll | 9 | 70 | 43,711 | 374 |
| kernel32.dll | 37 | 262 | 153,905 | 944 |
| kernelbase.dll | 21 | 188 | 40,734 | 312 |
| msvcrt.dll | 1 | 5 | 70,201 | 590 |
| ntdll.dll | 83 | 4,274 | 148,327 | 1,484 |
| ole32.dll | 188 | 915 | 196,706 | 1,907 |
| oleaut32.dll | 5 | 34 | 84,331 | 763 |
| rdp4vs.dll | 5 | 647 | 50,312 | 261 |
| rdpclip.dll | 18 | 111 | 21,306 | 128 |
| rdpvdd.dll | 1 | 666 | 4,312 | 30 |
| rpcrt4.dll | 5 | 34 | 135,812 | 959 |
| user32.dll | 68 | 497 | 60,161 | 935 |
| win32k.dll | 685 | 5,341 | 343,082 | 2,845 |
| winhttp.dll | 15 | 1,146 | 6,225 | 40 |
| **New Implementations:** clbcatq.dll, ddraw.dll, dwmapi.dll, iphlpapi.dll, msi.dll, netapi32.dll, sechost.dll, secur32.dll, wininet.dll, winspool.drv, ws2_32.dll, wtsapi32.dll | | | 25,984 | 251 |
| **Unchanged:** atl.dll, comctl32.dll, comdlg32.dll, comsvcs.dll, crypt32.dll, cryptbase.dll, cryptsp.dll, d3d10.dll, d3d10_1.dll, d3d10_1core.dll, d3d10core.dll, d3d10level9.dll, d3d10ref.dll, d3d10sdklayers.dll, d3d10warp.dll, d3d11.dll, d3d11ref.dll, d3d11sdklayers.dll, d3d8thk.dll, d3d9.dll, d3dcompiler_42.dll, d3dx10_42.dll, d3dx11_42.dll, d3dx9_42.dll, dbghelp.dll, ddrawex.dll, dui70.dll, duser.dll, explorerframe.dll, fms.dll, gdiplus.dll, iertutil.dll, imagehlp.dll, mfc42u.dll, mlang.dll, msasn1.dll, msftedit.dll, msls31.dll, mswsock.dll, odbc32.dll, oleacc.dll, profapi.dll, propsys.dll, psapi.dll, rdpd3d.dll, rgb9rast.dll, rsaenh.dll, shell32.dll, shfolder.dll, shlwapi.dll, sspicli.dll, uiribbon.dll, urlmon.dll, userenv.dll, usp10.dll, uxtheme.dll, version.dll, windowscodecs.dll, winmm.dll, wintrust.dll, wsock32.dll, xmllite.dll | | | 3,995,244 | 57,912 |
| **Totals** | **1,362** | **15,681** | **5,505,124** | **71,118** |

**Table 1.** Summary of changes to Windows 7 executable binaries to produce the Drawbridge library OS.

### Overheads

To validate the hypothesis that Drawbridge has modest resource overheads, we measure committed memory and start times for

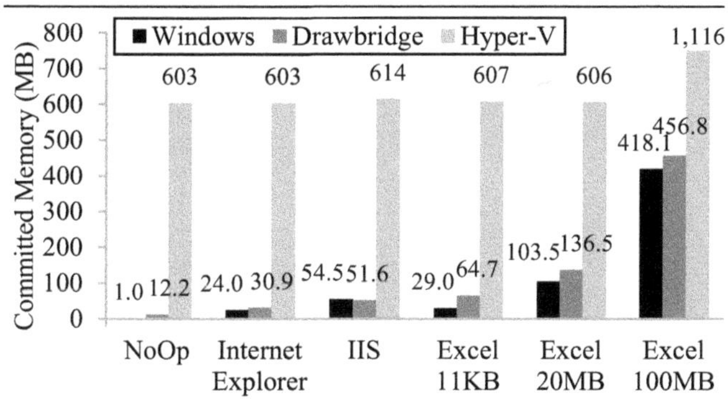


**Figure 4.** Memory per application (including memory used by library OS or guest OS).

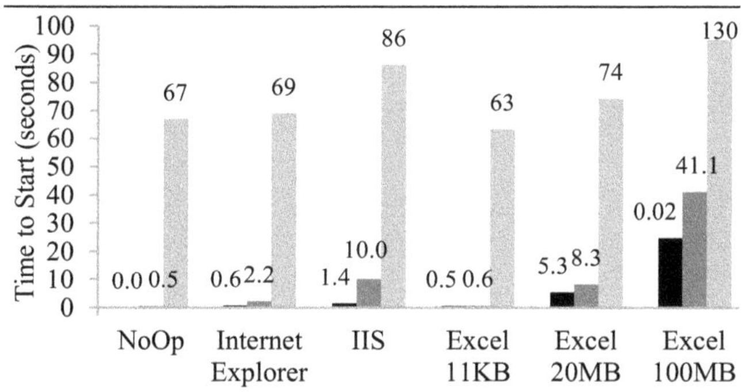


**Figure 5.** Time to start application (including time to start library OS or guest OS).

applications running natively on Windows, on Drawbridge, and on Hyper-V. Figure 4 shows the amount of committed memory required for each OS configuration and application. All VMs were configured with 512MB of RAM, except Excel 100MB test, which has 1024MB to avoid excessive paging. With 512MB, the startup time is over 260 seconds. The additional committed memory of Drawbridge is basically the cost of each application running a private copy of win32k, including its fonts and graphic object caches. Running the application in a VMM, on the other hand, incurs the full cost of running a complete guest OS. Similarly, startup times for a full guest OS are much higher than for a library OS (see Figure 5). Ongoing execution overheads are only slightly higher with Hyper-V (for our applications typically less than 1%).

Figure 6 shows the aggregate effect of memory for Excel. While Hyper-V can host only 23 isolated copies of Excel (each with a 20MB spreadsheet loaded), Drawbridge can host 104 instances on the same hardware, compared to 142 instances if Excel is run as a native Windows application with no isolation. Drawbridge is sufficiently efficient that every application can be run in its own isolation container. For Internet Explorer, we found that Drawbridge can host 527 instances, Windows can host 138, and Hyper-V can host 22 (see Figure 7). In the case of Windows, Internet Explorer exhausts the hard limit on GDI handles per logon session in win32k, not physical memory. Drawbridge does not have this limit as each library OS has its own private win32k. Finally, for IIS, we found that Drawbridge can host 287 instances, Windows can host 266 and Hyper-V can host 21 (see Figure 8).

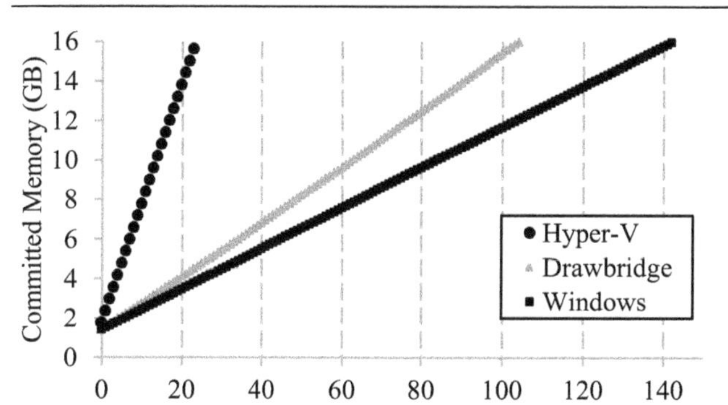


**Figure 6.** Memory committed for increasing copies of Excel, each with a 20MB spreadsheet loaded.

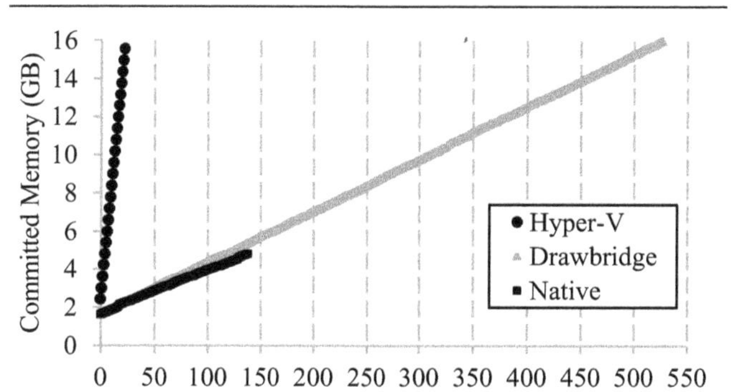


**Figure 7.** Memory committed for increasing copies of Internet Explorer rendering research.microsoft.com.

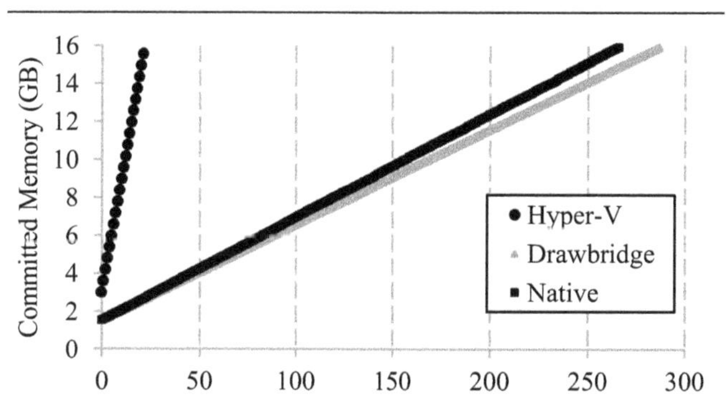


**Figure 8.** Memory committed for increasing copies of IIS.

In terms of disk footprint, the Drawbridge library OS is 64MB (or 83MB with DirectX 11 support) compared to 4.2GB for a guest OS copy of Windows 7. If desired, the library OS can be further reduced to meet the needs of a single application; a copy of the library OS reduced to its minimum for running Reversi is under 16MB.

### Protecting System Integrity

To illustrate that Drawbridge applications are isolated and cannot harm the host OS, we performed two simple experiments and conducted a case study based on a recently-published Internet Explorer exploit [20]. First, we ran a toy malware program that deletes every registry key, which would normally leave a system unusable, and found that only the malware was affected. Second, we wrote a simple key logger using the SetWindowsHookEx function. When run outside of Drawbridge, the key logger collected every keystroke issued. Inside Drawbridge, the key logger was unable to obtain keystrokes in other applications.

Keetch [20] documents a set of attack vectors and attack patterns to exploit possible weaknesses in the protected mode of Internet Explorer. Protected mode runs a copy of Internet Explorer in a process with restricted OS permissions. Among other restrictions, in protected mode, Internet Explorer should not be able to write to persistent storage. The idea of protected mode is that even if an attacker is able to run exploit code within Internet Explorer, the code cannot escape the low privilege process and therefore no permanent harm can be done to the system. Keetch identifies five attack vectors for exploit code to escape protected mode: name squatting on the NT kernel object namespace, leaked or duplicated handles, objects deliberately shared between low- and fully-privileged processes, clipboard content spoofing, and spoofing of a web server in the local-domain trusted zone through the loop-back interface.

Drawbridge mitigates all five of the attack vectors identified by Keetch. Each application runs with its own library OS that doesn't share an emulated kernel namespace, doesn't share handles, and doesn't share kernel objects. Drawbridge applications can access the clipboard and act as network servers, but only if the ability has been whitelisted for the application. Internet Explorer on Drawbridge is not permitted to act as a web server, thus preventing network spoofing. Access to the clipboard in Drawbridge is set by RDP policy and can also be prevented. By comparison, Windows 7 running in a VMM doesn't share its kernel namespace, doesn't share handles, and doesn't share kernel objects. Furthermore, like Drawbridge, a VMM guest OS can access the desktop clipboard and the local network only if permitted.

### Migrating Applications

One benefit of Drawbridge's ABI is that it enables the migration of running applications between computers and across OS reboots. For most Windows applications, the only alternative to Drawbridge is to use a VMM to migrate the application and its full operating system. To compare the cost of migration of an application using Drawbridge versus a Windows 7 guest VM using Hyper-V, we ran five application scenarios on each system, triggered a memory snapshot, and then compressed the snapshot to determine the smallest image. We disabled the page file in Windows 7 on Hyper-V to avoid including the additional size of a page file in the snapshot.

As Table 2 shows, Drawbridge snapshots are significantly smaller, because it doesn't serialize the OS with the application. In practice, we find that application snapshots for Drawbridge are typically in the 3-4MB range; roughly the size of an MP3, they are easily moved over network connections. Application serialization and deserialization generally takes less than 1 second on Drawbridge, and more than 10 seconds for Hyper-V.

### Evolving the OS Kernel

By factoring the OS into three components (high-level user shell, library OS, and low-level kernel), Drawbridge enables their independent evolution. To validate this assertion we wrote a version of dkpal designed to run as a Hyper-V partition in ring-0, replacing the low-level Windows 7 kernel implementation.

| Application | Drawbridge Snapshot | Hyper-V Snapshot |
|---|---|---|
| Excel: 11KB file opened | 3.1 MB | 148.6 MB |
| Excel: 20MB file opened | 21.2 MB | 155.8 MB |
| Excel: 100MB file opened | 86.9 MB | 313.2 MB |
| Internet Explorer | 3.9 MB | 184.8 MB |
| IIS: no site pre-loaded | 1.1 MB | 193.4 MB |

**Table 2.** Comparison of compressed memory snapshots.

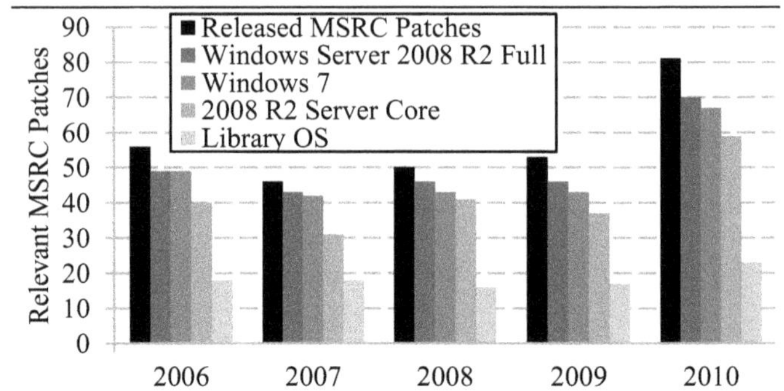


**Figure 9.** Security patches affecting binaries in Windows Server 2008 R2, Windows 7, Windows Server 2008 R2 Server Core, and Drawbridge.

hvdkpal is essentially a small OS kernel that implements the Drawbridge ABI described in Section 4. hvdkpal implements threading and preemptive scheduling by multiplexing Hyper-V virtual CPUs. hvdkpal includes an implementation of futexes [14], which it uses to provide Drawbridge events and semaphores. Since hvdkpal runs in ring-0, it is able to manipulate page tables directly in order to manage virtual memory. hvdkpal does not implement a file system or networking stack; to support I/O streams, it forwards I/O-related ABI calls to the host Windows Server 2008 R2 kernel running in Hyper-V's root partition. The hvdkpal implementation is about 6,000 lines of C.

Despite the large differences between the hvdkpal kernel and the Windows kernel applications expect, hvdkpal runs our entire suite of unmodified Windows applications with an unmodified library OS and an unmodified high-level user shell. The applications are oblivious to the fact that they are running in ring-0.

We also ran our set of unmodified applications and library OS on a MinWin [36] build of Windows. MinWin is a minimal build of Windows with less than 48MB of binaries; it consists of the NT kernel, the NTFS file system, TCP/IP stack, and the storage and network drivers for a specific computer. It does not include a shell. For our experiments, we connected the RDP client directly to a graphics frame buffer driver. One of our colleagues has begun to experiment with Windows 7 applications on the Barrelfish OS [6] using the Drawbridge ABI to explore extreme hardware configurations. Our experiments indicate that Drawbridge's approach to factoring OS components enables independent evolution of the low-level kernel from the library OS and applications.

### Servicing the Library OS

Once a month, on "Patch Tuesday", Microsoft issues security bulletins (MSRCs) describing software security vulnerabilities and releases patches to those vulnerabilities. The amount of code inside the library OS is smaller than the code in the full OS, so one would expect fewer patches to affect the library OS. This intuition is validated by an analysis of which binaries were affected by each security-related patch from 2006 to 2010.

As Figure 9 shows, the library OS requires significantly fewer security updates due to its smaller code size. Compared with Windows 7, Windows Server 2008 R2, and Windows Service 2008 R2 Server Core, the Drawbridge library OS has a much smaller servicing footprint. Of 286 security bulletins, 254 have resulted in patches to OS computers. Just 36% of patches, 92, affect the library OS; the rest affect code found only in the host OS. Furthermore, some of the patches in the library OS might be redundant if they prevent one application from compromising another. The comparison with Server Core installation of Windows Server 2008 R2 is interesting because Server Core is positioned as a way to reduce the attack surface of servers by removing "client" components such as the GUI shell. Drawbridge is affected by roughly half as many MSRC issues as Server Core over the same time period.

# 7. Related work

This section surveys related work, primarily: previous library OSes, which adopt similar designs in service of different goals, and virtual machines, which provide many similar benefits at a higher cost. We briefly discuss other approaches to achieving strongly isolated processes.

### Previous Library Operating Systems

Anderson [3] initially proposed that larger portions of the OS be factored into application libraries, primarily to improve performance. A general-purpose OS often applies resource management heuristics that can work at cross-purposes with a particular application. For instance, file read-ahead is a common optimization that is useful in the common case (sequential file access), but can harm performance of an application that accesses its data randomly. This idea was brought to fruition in the Cache kernel [10], Nemesis [21], and Exokernel [13]. The Cache kernel design focused on allowing applications fine-grained control over thread scheduling and memory swapping. The Nemesis OS was particularly focused on eliminating scheduling and performance interference through shared resources, in order for multimedia applications to meet real-time deadlines. The Exokernel design is closest to the bare hardware interface of a modern VMM.

Although previous library OS systems focused on performance, rather than encapsulation of the OS personality, Drawbridge shares with them several design points. At a high-level, the Drawbridge design is similar to the original Exokernel design, which had a kernel responsible for controlling access to the low-level hardware, and the rest of the functionality in the application library. The interface between the Exokernel and library OS was much closer to the hardware interface of a modern virtual machine, whereas Drawbridge provides higher-level APIs of threads and virtual memory, similar to the Cache or Nemesis kernels. The Exokernel also allowed applications to load constrained (or "safe") extensions into the kernel for management of hardware resources that could not be reasonably exported into a non-privileged address space. For instance, Exokernel library OSes would install packet filters into the lower-level kernel to multiplex the network. In contrast, both Drawbridge and the Cache kernel delegate low-level resource management to the kernel and neither system permits a library OS to load code into the kernel.

Relative to previous library OS designs, the first contribution of our work is to show that a large commercial OS can in fact be refactored into a library OS; this is in contrast to the minimal library OS implementations of previous systems. Second, Drawbridge incorporates an ABI design that streamlines the library OS implementation without compromising security isolation or unduly exposing implementation details of the underlying host OS. As a proof of this point, Drawbridge is the first library OS system of which we are aware that supports either process serialization or migration of the guest application across diverse host systems. Finally, the Drawbridge ABI presents higher-level abstractions that trivially share host OS resources, such as the CPU and buffer caches. We believe the Drawbridge ABI offers a better starting point for library OS construction.

### Virtual Machines

Virtual machines [35] are the primary success story for packaging an application and its dependencies on a fully-featured OS into a single self-contained unit. Research systems, such as The Collective [31], use a single virtual machine per application to encapsulate an application and its OS. Treating a complete legacy operating system, including the kernel, as a library for a single application wastes substantial memory and computation. This waste comes from an "impedance mismatch" that causes lost sharing opportunities, lost statistical multiplexing opportunities, and allocation strategies designed for physical resources running against virtual ones. Only through significant research and development effort has this waste been reduced.

New *paravirtualization* approaches, which warp the VM interface gradually farther away from a raw hardware interface, expose instead resources that a guest operating system can use more efficiently [5, 12, 17, 38, 39]. Despite significant research effort, however, running a full legacy operating system in a VM still incurs substantial overhead, as the legacy operating system brings with it system management processes and large allocations of kernel memory. Each guest can demand gigabytes of disk storage and hundreds of megabytes of physical RAM (perhaps reduced by clever sharing). Ultimately, paravirtualization is only chipping away at the margins; paravirtualized VMs will not scale to the same level as OS processes without more drastic measures.

A key contribution of Drawbridge is judicious selection of extremely paravirtualized VM abstractions in the Drawbridge ABI. This ABI demonstrably alleviates the overheads of hardware virtualization without unduly constraining OS design or compromising isolation. Roscoe *et al* [30] argued for research into higher-level hypervisor abstractions, Drawbridge answers that call.

### Other Approaches to Library OS Goals

***OS customization*** Like previous library OSes, Libra [2] allows applications to customize their OS within a virtual machine in order to improve application performance. In Libra, an application that needs to extend the OS runs in a separate VM. The default OS functionality is provided by a sibling virtual machine over a shared memory protocol, and applications can selectively service their own requests from a custom implementation.

The performance concerns of Libra and other library OSes are largely complementary to Drawbridge; one could imagine customizing versions of the Drawbridge library OS with application-specific performance optimizations. More than optimizing performance, Drawbridge is concerned with encapsulating the personality of a library OS and enabling applications to run on future host OSes.

***Xax and NaCl*** Recent research on isolating untrusted web applications demonstrated that a limited set of OS abstractions were sufficient for porting large libraries of legacy code, albeit not entire interactive GUI applications [11]. The isolation technique proposed in Xax, namely hardware memory protection and a limited system call table, is shared by Drawbridge; NaCl [40] uses alternate techniques based on software fault isolation..

***Stronger isolation in monolithic kernels*** The monolithic organization of conventional operating systems makes them difficult to secure. In order to avoid the loss of functionality and performance, a number of systems have attempted to augment monolithic systems with additional security checks in a minimally disruptive manner. For instance, the Linux VServer [32] adds additional access control list checks and imposes a separate namespace for kernel objects used by an isolated process. All kernel data, however, reside within a shared, monolithic kernel address space. This approach of adding security checks and/or replicated kernel data structures is also exemplified by SELinux [23], zones [29], jails [34] and containers [7], however it suffers several drawbacks.

First, it is difficult to know that the job of inserting additional checks is done, or that the set of hooks is complete in a complex and rapidly growing kernel. Second, the abstractions to which the hooks must be added are exactly those that were not designed to express restrictions; therefore, the resulting mechanisms may not lend themselves to a reasonable policy calculus. For instance, a simple policy such as "Do not allow the contents of file X to leave the machine" must be translated into a perilous series of decisions on whether to allow innocuous-looking accesses to local system resources [15, 41].

It is tempting to try to paint a layer of isolation functionality onto an existing monolithic system, but the result is hard to trust since it requires maintaining properties across a large interface to a large and evolving code base. Often, the structure of a monolithic system makes it difficult even to rigorously specify isolation. Therefore, Drawbridge avoids a monolithic organization in favor of a library OS design, which lifts much OS functionality into the application's strongly isolated address space.

We hypothesize that library OSes will prove a more amenable platform for strong security isolation than a monolithic kernel, with a potentially simpler mapping of policies onto concrete decisions that must be made in the security monitor. Previous systems have explored policies much more thoroughly than this work, and we defer their design to future work.

***Compatibility through API emulation*** Several research systems have attempted to provide compatibility with legacy OSes by emulating their APIs [4, 16, 18]. Although emulation can work for common, heavily used functions, it is highly prone to subtle inconsistencies in the less used functions. Emulating the Windows API on Unix has required a colossal effort and consistently remained several releases behind Windows in terms of compatibility [30]. Even among Unix implementations, calls such as `setuid` are prone to compatibility issues [9]. In terms of compatibility, there is simply no substitute for bundling an application with the appropriate components of the original OS.

***Application Virtualization*** The need to robustly package applications without the high cost of VMM solutions has driven development of at least two commercial products. Both App-V [26] and ThinApp [37] virtualize calls to the file system and registry. By doing so, they allow users to run desktop application like Microsoft Office without running a setup program. Because they virtualize only a subset of the file system and registry, they are easily circumvented or broken by new OS releases, and provide no migration for live applications. However, the application "sequencing" techniques used by these systems to create application packages are complementary to Drawbridge.

## 8. Discussion

The library OS allows a new model for packaging applications and new opportunities to reshape the computing experience. The fundamental problem of application packaging is deciding how to separate an application and its dependencies from their environment so the application can run predictably across a nearly infinite variety of user deployments. An ideal packaging technology makes it easy to deploy an application, continue the application across changes such as an OS upgrade, relocate the application from one computer to another, prevent the application from corrupting its host, and prevent the host from corrupting the application.

The library OS offers a new way to package applications. Applications can either be packaged with their dependent library OS, or can contain metadata informing the host OS of their required library OS. With the latter approach, a vendor could distribute and service a number of library OS images—say Windows XP, Windows Vista, and Windows 7 library OSes—with a single host OS.

For researchers and developers, the library OS approach offers the ability to rapidly evolve OS kernels, shells, and APIs independently without breaking other OS components or applications. Easily serialized applications offer opportunities to improve debugging and testing through techniques such as time-travel debugging, easy cloning of running application instances, and easy release of experimental OS components. For example, colleagues at Microsoft Research have used Drawbridge to deploy prototypes of new Win32 APIs that enable distributed user experiences.

### Application Compatibility

Maintaining compatibility with application binaries across multiple OS releases is a significant challenge. While OS vendors expend significant resources maintaining compatibility, each OS release inevitably results in a large number of broken applications. Techniques for maintaining application compatibility in Windows 7 include one-off code in APIs; application compatibility shims, which load as intermediate code between application and API to alter input or output parameters; and Windows XP mode, which is a complete VM image of the latest release of Windows XP.

Application compatibility is particularly onerous for enterprises where one-off line-of-business (LOB) applications are abundant. The recourses available to an enterprise when a LOB application is broken by a new OS release are often limited as programming staff has moved to other projects and source code may be missing.

By encapsulating the portions of the OS most likely to break application compatibility, the library OS offers a new technique to resolve application compatibility problems. Each application could run with the library OS of its choice. Programmers or IT administrators could bind an application to a known good library OS, which would continue to run correctly on top of new host OS releases. For example, an application packaged with a Windows XP library OS could continue to run correctly on Windows XP, Windows Vista, or Windows 7 host OSes. Conversely, an update to Windows 7 could ship with library OSes for Windows XP and Windows Vista. Users could upgrade to new OS releases unconstrained by the complex calculus of application compatibility.

Applications might even run on down-level OS releases. For example, an application with the Windows 7 library OS could run on Windows XP. Reverse compatibility is particularly useful for developers of new applications as they can target the library OS with the latest features rather than anticipating adoption curves.

**Dynamic Application Relocation**

With process serialization and deserialization, a running application needs no longer be tied to the OS instance on which it started. An application could be moved to a new OS instance by serializing its state, moving the state to a new computer as needed, and then deserializing the state to restore the application. Drawbridge enables new opportunities for distributed computing, cycle harvesting, and applications running across OS-servicing reboots.

We are currently experimenting with a distributed computing environment based on Drawbridge in which running applications move from computer to computer to follow the user. For example, an application might start running a user's desktop, then move to the user's smartphone during their commute (which might be facilitated by dynamic instruction-set recompilation), and then move to the user's home computer. Running applications might also move from a laptop or smartphone to the cloud or a local server to conserve battery. While such migration is possible in theory with VMMs, VM images are too large to make it practical.

Process checkpointing has long been used to harvest spare CPU cycles in systems such as Condor [22] by moving background computations to under-utilized workstations. While systems like Condor were limited to applications without interactive user interfaces, with Drawbridge mainstream applications could be moved under the control of a resource manager system to create a "virtual desktop cloud" within an institution. Users could connect to their mobile applications through RDP proxies. Running applications could be cloned to multiple machines or staged to disk, to improve availability and to accommodate hardware failures or periods of peak load. With Drawbridge's per-application granularity, a virtual desktop infrastructure could be created much more cheaply than with VMM-based alternatives.

Serialization and deserialization of running processes offer end users new functionality even if applications are never migrated to a new machine. For example, instead of closing applications for an OS reboot, the applications could be serialized to persistent storage and then restored after the reboot.

**Reducing Security Risks**

The modern Internet is a place of nearly constant danger. Technical and social attacks often exploit the fact that OS security is oriented toward protecting users from each other, and not from their own software. While the risks of running untrusted software can be mitigated through the use of "sandbox VMs", in practice the resource and administrative costs of a VM image are generally too high to afford each application its own sandbox, so typical users do not employ VMs to isolate software [19]. With the substantially lower overheads of the Drawbridge library OS design, every desktop application could be run within its own sandbox. Running a sandbox per application would mitigate many exploits that attack specific application weaknesses because the exploit could damage at most the single application in the sandbox. Drawbridge might also reduce a large class of social exploits—those which trick users into downloading programs—if downloaded programs always ran within a sandbox with a read-only copy of the library OS.

Cloud hosting services, such as EC2 and Windows Azure, might use the library OS design to substantially lower their per-sandbox costs. While VMMs offer the benefits of a complete OS, and thus will likely always have their place in server consolidation, the library OS uses far fewer resources and thus offers lower costs, particularly for cloud applications with low CPU utilization.

# 9. Conclusion

This paper provides the first existence proof that a feature-rich operating system can be refactored to produce a library OS that is compatible with desktop applications. Drawbridge provides a Windows 7 library OS that can run a large set of rich desktop and server applications such as Excel 2010, PowerPoint 2010, Internet Explorer 8, and IIS 7.5. With the exception of changes to licensing code, Windows 7 applications run in Drawbridge using unmodified binaries.

We described our heuristics for separating the "OS personality", as captured in the API implementation layer, from the rest of Windows 7 to produce a library OS that is $1/50^{th}$ the size of the full desktop OS, yet still provides rich application compatibility. We believe our techniques are efficient, as we produced the entire Drawbridge system in less than two person-years, and that the same techniques could be applied to other operating systems.

We described our implementation and demonstrated through experiments that Drawbridge can provide increased system security, more aggressive system evolution, and greater application mobility through process serialization and deserialization. We have provided experimental data showing that the library OS design offers significant scalability advantages over VMMs. We demonstrated the improved flexibility for independent evolution by running the same library OS across four host OS releases.

The library OS is very relevant today. It offers new opportunities to significantly improve end-user computing: redefining application packaging, increasing application compatibility across OS releases, enabling running applications to persist across OS reboots and relocations, and reducing the security risks of running untrusted software.

# Acknowledgements

We wish to thank our colleagues at MSR, including Andrew Baumann, Barry Bond, David Molnar, and Ed Nightingale who have improved this work by contributing code, experience, and ideas. The anonymous reviewers and our shepherd, Orran Krieger, provided valuable feedback that significantly improved the presentation of our work.

# References

[1] Amazon. *Amazon Elastic Compute Cloud (EC2)*. Seattle, WA, 2006.

[2] Ammons, G., Appavoo, J., Butrico, M., Da Silva, D., Grove, D., Kawachiya, K., Krieger, O., Rosenburg, B., Van Hensbergen, E. and Wisniewski, R.W. Libra: A Library OS for a JVM in a Virtualized Execution Environment. In *Proceedings of the 3rd International Conference on Virtual Execution Environments*, 2007.

[3] Anderson, T.E. The Case for Application-Specific Operating Systems. In *Proceedings of the 3rd Workshop on Workstation Operating Systems*, 1992.

[4] Appavoo, J., Auslander, M., Da Silva, D., Edelsohn, D., Krieger, O., Ostrowski, M., Rosenburg, B., Wisniewski, R.W. and Xenidis, J. Providing a Linux API on the Scalable K42 Kernel. In *Proceedings of the 2003 USENIX Annual Technical Conference*, 2003.

[5] Barham, P., Dragovic, B., Fraser, K., Hand, S., Harris, T., Ho, A., Neugebauer, R., Pratt, I. and Warfield, A. Xen and the Art of Virtualization. In *Proceedings of the 19th ACM Symposium on Operating Systems Principles*, 2003.

[6] Baumann, A., Barham, P., Dagand, P.-E., Harris, T., Isaacs, R., Peter, S., Roscoe, T., Schüpbach, A. and Singhania, A. The Multikernel: a new OS architecture for scalable multicore systems. In *Proceedings of the 22nd ACM Symposium on Operating Systems Principles*, 2009.

[7] Bhattiprolu, S., Biederman, E.W., Hallyn, S. and Lezcano, D. Virtual servers and checkpoint/restart in mainstream Linux. *SIGOPS Operating Systems Review*, *42* (5), 2008.

[8] Bugnion, E., Devine, S., Govil, K. and Rosenblum, M. Disco: Running Commodity Operating Systems on Scalable Multiprocessors. *ACM Transactions on Computer Systems*, *15* (4), 1997.

[9] Chen, H., Wagner, D. and Dean, D. Setuid Demystified. In *Proceedings of the 11th USENIX Security Symposium*, USENIX Association, 2002.

[10] Cheriton, D.R. and Duda, K.J. A Caching Model of Operating System Kernel Functionality. In *Proceedings of the 1st USENIX Symposium on Operating Systems Design and Implementation*, 1994.

[11] Douceur, J.R., Elson, J., Howell, J. and Lorch, J.R. Leveraging Legacy Code to Deploy Desktop Applications on the Web. In *Proceedings of the 8th USENIX Symposium on Operating Systems Design and Implementation*, 2008.

[12] Eiraku, H., Shinjo, Y., Pu, C., Koh, Y. and Kato, K. Fast Networking with Socket-Outsourcing in Hosted Virtual Machine Environments. In *Proceedings of the 24th ACM Symposium on Applied Computing*, 2009.

[13] Engler, D.R., Kaashoek, M.F. and O'Toole, J., Jr. Exokernel: an Operating System Architecture for Application-Level Resource Management. In *Proceedings of the 15th ACM Symposium on Operating Systems Principles*, 1995.

[14] Franke, H., Russel, R. and Kirkwood, M. Fuss, Futexes and Furwocks: Fast Userlevel Locking in Linux. In *Proceedings of the Ottawa Linux Symposium*, 2002.

[15] Garfinkel, T. Traps and Pitfalls: Practical Problems in System Call Interposition based Security Tools. In *Proceedings of the Network and Distributed Systems Security Symposium*, 2003.

[16] Gerard Malan, R.R., David Golub, and Robert Brown. DOS as a Mach 3.0 Application. In *Proceedings of the USENIX Mach Symposium*, 1991.

[17] Gupta, D., Lee, S., Vrable, M., Savage, S., Snoeren, A.C., Varghese, G., Voelker, G.M. and Vahdat, A. Difference Engine: Harnessing Memory Redundancy in Virtual Machines. In *Proceedings of the 8th USENIX Symposium on Operating Systems Design and Implementation*, 2008.

[18] Helander, J., *Unix under Mach: The Lites Server*. Helsinki University of Technology, Helsinki, 1994.

[19] Howell, J., Hunt, G.C., Molnar, D. and Porter, D.E., *Living Dangerously: A Survey of Software Download Practices*. MSR-TR-2010-51, Microsoft Research, 2010.

[20] Keetch, T., *Escaping from Protected Mode Internet Explorer – Evaluating a potential security boundary*. Verizon Business, London, UK, 2010.

[21] Leslie, I., McAuley, D., Black, R., Roscoe, T., Barham, P., Evers, D., Fairbairns, R. and Hyden, E. The Design and Implementation of an Operating System to Support Distributed Multimedia Applications. *IEEE Journal on Selected Areas In Communications*, *14* (7), 1996.

[22] Litzkow, M., Tannenbaum, T., Basney, J. and Livny, M., *Checkpoint and Migration of UNIX Processes in the Condor Distributed Processing System*. University of Wisconsin-Madison, 1997.

[23] Loscocco, P. and Smalley, S. Integrating flexible support for security policies into the Linux operating system. In *Proceedings of the 2001 USENIX Annual Technical Conference*, 2001.

[24] Love, R. Get on the D-BUS. *Linux Journal*, 2005.

[25] Microsoft. *Internet Information Services 7.5*. Redmond, WA, 2009.

[26] Microsoft. *Microsoft Application Virtualization (App-V)*. Redmond, WA, 2006.

[27] Microsoft *Performance Tuning Guidelines for Windows Server 2008 R2*, Redmond, WA, 2009.

[28] Microsoft, *Remote Desktop Protocol: Basic Connectivity and Graphics Remoting Specification*. Redmond, WA, 2010.

[29] Price, D. and Tucker, A. Solaris zones: operating system support for server consolidation. In *Proceedings of the Large Installation Systems Administration Conference*, 2004.

[30] Roscoe, T., Elphinstone, K. and Heiser, G. Hype and virtue. In *Proceedings of the 11th USENIX Workshop on Hot Topics in Operating Systems*, 2007.

[31] Sapuntzakis, C., Brumley, D., Chandra, R., Zeldovich, N., Chow, J., Lam, M.S. and Rosenblum, M. Virtual Appliances for Deploying and Maintaining Software. In *Proceedings of the Large Installation Systems Administration Conference*, 2003.

[32] Soltesz, S., Pötzl, H., Fiuczynski, M.E., Bavier, A. and Peterson, L. Container-based Operating System Virtualization: A Scalable, High-Performance Alternative to Hypervisors. In *Proceedings of the 2nd ACM SIGOPS/EuroSys European Conference on Computer Systems 2007*, ACM, 2007.

[33] Spear, M.F., Roeder, T., Hodson, O., Hunt, G.C. and Levi, S., Solving the Starting Problem: Device Drivers as Self-Describing Artifacts. In *Proceedings of the EuroSys 2006 Conference*, Leuven, Belgium, 2006.

[34] Stokely, M. and Lee, C. *The FreeBSD Handbook 3rd Edition, Vol. 1: User's Guide*. FreeBSD Mall, Inc., Brentwood, CA, 2003.

[35] Sugerman, J., Venkitachalam, G. and Lim, B.-H. Virtualizing I/O Devices on VMware Workstations Hosted Virtual Machine Monitor. In *Proceedings of the 2001 USENIX Annual Technical Conference*, 2001.

[36] Torre, C. Mark Russinovich: Inside Windows 7. *Channel 9*, Redmond, WA, January, 2009.

[37] VMWare. *ThinApp*. Palo Alto, CA, 2008.

[38] Waldspurger, C.A. Memory Resource Management in VMware ESX Server. In *Proceedings of the 5th USENIX Symposium on Operating Systems Design and Implementation*, 2002.

[39] Whitaker, A., Shaw, M. and Gribble, S.D. Scale and Performance in the Denali Isolation Kernel. In *Proceedings of the 5th USENIX Symposium on Operating Systems Design and Implementation*, 2002.

[40] Yee, B., Sehr, D., Dardyk, G., Chen, J.B., Muth, R., Orm, T., Okasaka, S., Narula, N., Fullagar, N. and Inc, G. Native Client: A Sandbox for Portable, Untrusted x86 Native Code. In *Proceedings of the 30th IEEE Symposium on Security and Privacy*, 2009.

[41] Zeldovich, N., Boyd-Wickizer, S., Kohler, E. and Mazières, D. Making information flow explicit in HiStar. In *Proceedings of the 8th USENIX Symposium on Operating Systems Design and Implementation*, 2006.

# Faults in Linux: Ten Years Later

Nicolas Palix *
DIKU, University of Copenhagen
npalix@diku.dk

Gaël Thomas
INRIA Regal/LIP6
Gael.Thomas@lip6.fr

Suman Saha
INRIA Regal/LIP6
Suman.Saha@lip6.fr

Christophe Calvès
INRIA Regal/LIP6
Christophe.Calves@lip6.fr

Julia Lawall
INRIA Regal/LIP6,
University of Copenhagen
julia@diku.dk

Gilles Muller
INRIA Regal/LIP6
Gilles.Muller@lip6.fr

## Abstract

In 2001, Chou *et al.* published a study of faults found by applying a static analyzer to Linux versions 1.0 through 2.4.1. A major result of their work was that the `drivers` directory contained up to 7 times more of certain kinds of faults than other directories. This result inspired a number of development and research efforts on improving the reliability of driver code. Today Linux is used in a much wider range of environments, provides a much wider range of services, and has adopted a new development and release model. What has been the impact of these changes on code quality? Are drivers still a major problem?

To answer these questions, we have transported the experiments of Chou *et al.* to Linux versions 2.6.0 to 2.6.33, released between late 2003 and early 2010. We find that Linux has more than doubled in size during this period, but that the number of faults per line of code has been decreasing. And, even though `drivers` still accounts for a large part of the kernel code and contains the most faults, its fault rate is now below that of other directories, such as `arch` (HAL) and `fs` (file systems). These results can guide further development and research efforts. To enable others to continually update these results as Linux evolves, we define our experimental protocol and make our checkers and results available in a public archive.

***Categories and Subject Descriptors*** D.4 [*Operating Systems*]: Reliability

***General Terms*** Reliability, Experimentation, Measurement

***Keywords*** Linux, fault-finding tools

## 1. Introduction

The Linux operating system is widely used, on platforms ranging from embedded systems, to personal computers, to servers and supercomputers. As an operating system (OS) with a traditional monolithic kernel, Linux is responsible for the security and integrity of the interactions between software and the underlying hardware. Therefore, its correctness is essential. Linux also has a large developer base, as it is open source, and is rapidly evolving. Thus, it is critical to be able to continually assess and control the quality of its code.

Almost 10 years ago, in 2001, Chou *et al.* published a study of the distribution and lifetime of certain kinds of faults[1] in OS code, focusing mostly on the x86 code in the Linux kernel [5], in versions up to 2.4.1. The ability to collect fault information automatically from such a large code base was revolutionary at the time, and this work has been highly influential. Indeed, their study has been cited over 360 times, according to Google Scholar, and has been followed by the development of a whole series of strategies for automatically finding faults in systems code [1, 16, 33, 36, 38]. The statistics reported by Chou *et al.* have been used for a variety of purposes, including providing evidence that driver code is unreliable [12, 35], and evidence that certain OS subsystems are more reliable than others [10].

Linux, however, has changed substantially since 2001, and thus it is worth examining the continued relevance of Chou *et al.*'s results. In 2001, Linux was a relatively young OS, having first been released only 10 years earlier, and was primarily used by specialists. Today, well-supported Linux distributions are available, targeting servers, embedded systems, and the general public [11, 37]. Linux code is changing rapidly, and only 30% of the Linux 2.6.33 code is more than five years old [7, 8]. Linux now supports 23 architectures, up from 13 in Linux 2001, and the developer base has grown commensurately. The development model has also changed substantially. Until Linux 2.6.0, which was released at the end of 2003, Linux releases were split into stable versions, which were installed by users, and development versions, which accommodated new features. Since Linux 2.6.0 this distinction has disappeared; releases in the 2.6 series occur every three months, and new features are made available whenever they are ready. Finally, a number of fault finding tools have been developed that target Linux code. Patches are regularly submitted for faults found using checkpatch [4], Coccinelle [24], Coverity [9], smatch [36] and sparse [31].

In this paper, we transport the experiments of Chou *et al.* to the versions of Linux 2.6, in order to reevaluate their results in

* Now at Joseph Fourier University and INRIA Sardes, Grenoble, nicolas.palix@inria.fr

[1] Chou *et al.* used the terminology "errors." In the software dependability literature [13], however, this term is reserved for incorrect states that occur during execution, rather than faults in the source code, as were investigated by Chou *et al.* and are investigated here.


*ASPLOS'11,* March 5–11, 2011, Newport Beach, California, USA.

the context of the current state of Linux development. Because Chou *et al.*'s fault finding tool and checkers were not released, and their results were released on a local web site but are no longer available, it is impossible to exactly reproduce their results on recent versions of the Linux kernel.[2] To provide a baseline that can be more easily updated as new versions are released, we propose an experimental protocol based on the open source tools Coccinelle [24], for automatically finding faults in source code, and Herodotos [25], for tracking these faults across multiple versions of a software project. We validate this protocol by replicating Chou *et al.*'s experiments as closely as possible on Linux 2.4.1 and then apply our protocol to all versions of Linux 2.6. To ensure the perenity of our work, our tools and results are available in a public archival repository [27].

The contributions of our work are as follows:

- We provide a repeatable methodology for finding faults in Linux code, based on open source tools, and a publicly available archive containing our complete results.
- We show that the faults kinds considered 10 years ago by Chou *et al.* are still relevant, because such faults are still being introduced and fixed, in both new and existing files. These fault kinds vary in their impact, but we have seen many patches for all of these kinds of faults submitted to the Linux kernel mailing list [17] and have not seen any receive the response that the fault was too trivial to fix.
- We show that while the rate of introduction of such faults continues to rise, the rate of their elimination is rising slightly faster, resulting in a kernel that is becoming more reliable with respect to these kinds of faults. This is in contrast with previous results for earlier versions of Linux which found that the number of faults was rising with the code size.
- We show that the rate of the considered fault kinds is falling in the `drivers` directory, which suggests that the work of Chou *et al.* and others has succeeded in directing attention to driver code. The directories `arch` (HAL) and `fs` (file systems) now show a higher fault rate, and thus it may be worthwhile to direct research efforts to the problems of such code.
- We show that the lifespan of faults in Linux 2.6 is comparable to that observed for previous versions, at slightly under 2 years. Nevertheless, we find that fault kinds that are more likely to have a visible impact during execution have a much shorter average lifespan, of as little as one year.
- Although fault-finding tools are now being used regularly in Linux development, they seem to have only had a small impact on the kinds of faults we consider. Research is thus needed on how such tools can be better integrated into the development process. Our experimental protocol exploits previously collected information about false positives, reducing one of the burdens of tool use, but we propose that approaches are also needed to automate the fixing of faults, and not just the fault finding process.

The rest of this paper is organized as follows. Section 2 briefly presents our experimental protocol based on Coccinelle and Herodotos. Section 3 gives some background on the evolution of Linux. Section 4 establishes a baseline for our results, by comparing our results for Linux 2.4.1 with those of Chou *et al.* Section 5 presents a study of Linux 2.6, considering the kinds of code that contain faults, the distribution of faults across Linux code, the lifetime of faults, and effect of the use of fault-finding tools. Section 6 presents some limitations of our approach. Finally, Section 7 describes related work and Section 8 presents our conclusions.

[2] Chou *et al.*'s work did lead to the development of the commercial tool Coverity, but using it requires signing an agreement not to publish information about its results (`http://scan.coverity.com/policy.html#license`).

## 2. Experimental protocol

In laboratory sciences there is a notion of experimental protocol, giving all of the information required to reproduce an experiment. For a study of faults in operating systems code, such a protocol should include the definition of the fault finding tools and checkers, as well as the strategies for identifying false positives, as each of these elements substantially affects the results. In this section, we first present our checkers, both for finding faults and for assessing the fault rate, and then describe the tools that we have used in the fault finding and validation process. All of our results, as well as the scripts used and the source code of the Coccinelle and Herodotos tools are available on the open access archive HAL [28] and on the project website [29].

### 2.1 Fault finding checkers

Based on the descriptions of Chou *et al.*, we have implemented our interpretations of their **Block**, **Null**, **Var Inull**, **Range**, **Lock**, **Intr**, **LockIntr**, **Float**, and **Size** checkers. We omit the **Real** checker, related to the misuse of `realloc`, and the **Param** checker, related to dereferences of user-level pointers, as in both cases, we did not have enough information to define checkers that found any faults. In the description of each checker, the initial citation in italics is the description provided by Chou *et al.*

***Block*** *"To avoid deadlock, do not call blocking functions with interrupts disabled or a spinlock held."* Implementing this checker requires knowing the set of functions that may block, the set of functions that disable interrupts, and the set of functions that take spinlocks. These functions vary across Linux versions. Identifying them precisely requires a full interprocedural analysis of the Linux kernel source code, including a precise alias analysis, as these operations may be performed via function pointers. To our knowledge, Chou *et al.*'s tool `xgcc` did not provide these features in 2001, and thus we assume that these functions were identified based on their examination of the source code and possibly heuristics for collecting functions with particular properties. We take the same approach, but add a simple interprocedural analysis, based on the iterative computation of a transitive closure though the call graph. This iterative analysis implies that our **Block** checker automatically takes into account the new blocking functions that are added in each version.

To identify blocking functions, we consider two kinds of functions as the starting point of our interprocedural analysis. First, we observe that basic memory allocation functions, such as the kernel function `kmalloc`, often take as argument the constant `GFP_KERNEL` when they are allowed to block until a page becomes available. Thus, we consider that a function that contains a call with `GFP_KERNEL` as an argument may block. Second, we observe that blocking is directly caused by calling the function `schedule`. Given this initial list of blocking functions, we then iteratively augment the list with the names of functions that call functions already in the list without first explicitly releasing locks or turning on interrupts, until reaching a fixed point.

To identify functions that turn off interrupts and take locks, we rely on our knowledge of a set of commonly used functions for these purposes, listed in the appendix. However, we observe that blocking with interrupts turned off is not necessarily a fault, and indeed core Linux scheduling functions, such as `interruptible_sleep_on`, call `schedule` with interrupts turned off. Thus, we only consider the case where a blocking function is called while holding a spinlock, which is always a fault. We refer to this checker as **BlockLock** to highlight the different design.

***Null*** *"Check potentially NULL pointers returned from routines."* To collect a list of the functions that may return NULL, we follow the same iterative strategy as for the **Block** checker, with the starting point of the iteration being the set of functions that explicitly return NULL. Once the transitive closure is computed, we check the call sites of each collected function to determine whether the returned value is compared to NULL before it is used.

***Var*** *"Do not allocate large stack variables (> 1K) on the fixed-size kernel stack."* Our checker looks for local variables that are declared as large arrays, *e.g.*, 1,024 or more elements for a `char` array. Many array declarations express the size of the array using macros, or even local variables, rather than explicit constants. Because Coccinelle does not expand macros, and indeed some macros may have multiple definitions across different architectures, we consider only array declarations where the size is expressed as an explicit constant.

***Inull*** *"Do not make inconsistent assumptions about whether a pointer is NULL."* We distinguish two cases: **IsNull**, where a null test on a pointer is followed by a dereference of the pointer, and **NullRef**, where a dereference of a pointer is followed by a null test on the pointer. The former is always an error, while the latter may be an error or may simply indicate overly cautious code, if the pointer can never be NULL. Still, at least one **NullRef** fault has been shown to allow an attacker to obtain root access [34].

***Range*** *"Always check bounds of array indices and loop bounds derived from user data."* We recognize the functions `memcpy_fromfs`, `copy_from_user` and `get_user` as giving access to user data. Possible faults are cases where a value obtained using one of these functions is used as an array index, with no prior test on its value, and where some value is checked to be less than a value obtained using one of these functions, as would occur in validating a loop index.

***Lock and Intr*** *"Release acquired locks; do not double-acquire locks (**Lock**)." "Restore disabled interrupts (**Intr**)."* In early versions of Linux, locks and interrupts were managed separately: typically interrupts were disabled and reenabled using `cli` and `sti`, respectively, while locks were managed using operations on spinlocks or semaphores. In Linux 2.1.30, however, functions such as `spin_lock_irq` were introduced to combine locking and interrupt management. Our **Lock** checker is limited to operators that only affect locks (spinlocks and, from Linux 2.6.16, mutexes), our **Intr** checker is limited to operators that only disable interrupts, and for the combined operations, we introduce a third checker, **LockIntr**. The considered functions are listed in the appendix.

***Free*** *"Do not use freed memory."* Like the **Null** checker, this checker first iteratively collects functions that always apply `kfree` or some collected function to some parameter, and then checks each call to `kfree` or a collected function for a use of the freed argument after the call.

***Float*** *"Do not use floating point in the kernel."* Most uses of floating point in kernel code are in computations that are performed by the compiler and then converted to an integer or in code that is part of the kernel source tree, but is not actually compiled into the kernel. Our checker only reports a floating point constant that is not a subterm of an arithmetic operation involving another constant.

***Size*** *"Allocate enough memory to hold the type for which you are allocating."* Because our checker works at the source code level without first invoking the C preprocessor, it is not aware of the sizes of the various data types on a particular architecture. We thus focus on the information apparent in the source code, considering the following two cases. In the first case, one of the basic memory allocation functions, `kmalloc` or `kzalloc`, is given a size argument involving a `sizeof` expression defined in terms of a type that is different from the type of the variable storing the result of the allocation. To reduce the number of false positives, the checker ignores cases where one of the types involved represents only one byte, such as `char`, as these are often used for allocations of unstructured data. We consider as a fault any case where there is no clear relationship between the types, whether the allocated region is too large or too small. In the second case, there is an assignment where the right hand side involves taking the size of the left hand side expression itself, rather than the result of dereferencing that expression. In this case, the allocated region has the size of a pointer, which is typically significantly smaller than the size intended.

| | Find | Fix | Impact |
|---|---|---|---|
| Block | Hard | Hard | Low |
| Null | Hard | Hard | Low |
| Var | Easy | Easy | Low |
| IsNull | Easy | Easy | Low |
| NullRef | Easy | Hard | Low |
| Range | Easy | Easy | Low |
| Lock | Easy | Easy | High |
| Intr | Easy | Easy | High |
| LockIntr | Easy | Easy | High |
| Free | Hard | Easy | High |
| Size | Easy | Easy | High |
| Float | Easy | Hard | High |

**Table 1.** Assessment of the difficulty of finding and fixing faults, and the potential of a fault to cause a crash or hang at runtime

These faults vary in how easy they are to find in the source code, how easy they are to fix once found, and the likelihood of a runtime impact. Table 1 summarizes these properties for the various fault kinds, based on our observations in studying the code. Faults involving code within a single function are often easy for both maintainers and tools to detect, and thus we designate these as "Easy." Finding "Hard" faults requires an interprocedural analysis to identify functions that have specific properties. Interprocedural analysis requires more effort or expertise from a maintainer, or more complexity in a tool. Fixing a fault may require only an easy local change, as in **Size**, where the fix may require only changing the argument of `sizeof` to the type of the allocated value. Cases that require creating new error handling code, such as **Null**, or choosing between several alternative fixes (*e.g.*, moving a dereference or dropping an unnecessary null test), such as **NullRef**, are more difficult. Instances of fault kinds that entail more difficult fixes may benefit less from the use of tools, as the tool user may not have enough expertise to choose the correct fix. Finally, we indicate a low impact when a crash or hang is only likely in an exceptional condition, and high when it is likely in normal execution.

### 2.2 Assessing the fault rate

The maximum number of faults that code can contain is the number of occurrences of code relevant to the fault, *i.e.* where a given kind of fault may appear. For example, the number of **Block** faults is limited by the number of calls to blocking functions. We follow Chou *et al.* and refer to these occurrences of relevant code as *notes*. Then,

$$\textit{fault rate} = \textit{faults}/\textit{notes}$$

We find the notes associated with each of our checkers as follows. For **Block**, **Null**, and **Free**, a note is a call to one of the functions collected as part of the transitive closure in the fault-finding process. For **Var**, a note is a local array declaration. For **Inull** (**IsNull** and **NullRef**), a note is a null test of a value that is derefenced elsewhere in the same function. For **Range** and for **Lock**, **Intr**, or **LockIntr**, a note is a call to one of the user-level access functions or locking functions, respectively. For **Size**, a note is a use of `sizeof` as an argument to one of the basic memory allocation functions `kmalloc` or `kzalloc` when the argument is a type, or a use of `sizeof` where the argument is an expression. In the former case, as for the checker, we discard some cases that are commonly false positives such as when the argument to `sizeof` is a one-byte type such as `char`. Finally, we do not calculate the number of notes for **Float**, because we consider that every occurrence of a float in a context where it may be referenced in the compiled code is a fault, and thus the number of notes and faults is the same.

### 2.3 Tools

Our experimental protocol relies on two open-source tools: Coccinelle (v0.2.2), to automatically find potential faults and notes in the Linux kernels [24], and Herodotos (v0.6.0), to correlate the fault reports between versions [25]. We store the resulting data in a PostgreSQL database (v8.4), and analyze it using SQL queries.

Coccinelle performs control-flow based pattern searches in C code. It provides a language, the Semantic Patch Language (SmPL), for specifying searches and transformations and an engine for performing them. Coccinelle's strategy for traversing control-flow graphs is based on the temporal logic CTL [2], while that of the tool used by Chou *et al.* is based on automata. There are technical differences between these strategies, but we do not expect that they are relevant here.

A notable feature of Coccinelle is that it does not expand preprocessor directives. We have only found this feature to be a limitation in the **Var** case, as noted in Section 2.1. On the other hand, this feature has the benefit of making the fault-finding process independent of configuration information, and thus we can find faults across the entire Linux kernel source tree, rather than being limited to a single architecture.

To be able to understand the evolution of faults in Linux code, it is not sufficient to find potential faults in the code base; we must also understand the history of individual fault occurrences. To do so, we must be able to correlate potential fault occurrences across multiple Linux versions, even in the presence of code changes in the files, and manage the identification of these occurrences as real faults and false positives. For these operations, we use Herodotos. To correlate fault occurrences, Herodotos first uses `diff` to find the changes in each pair of successive versions of a file for which Coccinelle has produced fault reports. If a pair of reports in these files occur in the unchanged part of the code, at corresponding lines, they are automatically considered to represent the same fault, with no user intervention. Otherwise, if only one of a pair of reports occurs in the unchanged part of the code, then the reports are automatically considered to be unrelated. Finally, if both of a pair of reports occur in the changed part of the code, then their status is considered to be unknown, and the user must indicate, via an interface based on the emacs "org" mode, whether they represent the same fault or unrelated ones. Once the correlation process is complete, a similar interface is provided to allow the user to classify each group of correlated reports as representing either a fault or a false positive. Further details about the process of using Herodotos are provided elsewhere [25, 26].

Once the fault reports are correlated and assessed for false positives, we import their histories into the database, along with the associated notes. The database also contains information about Linux releases such as the release date and code size, and information about Linux files (size, number of modifications between releases) and functions (starting and ending line numbers). The complete database, including both the reports and the extra information, contains 1.5 GB of data. To analyze the collected data, we wrote over 2,000 lines of PL/pgSQL and SQL queries that extract and correlate information.

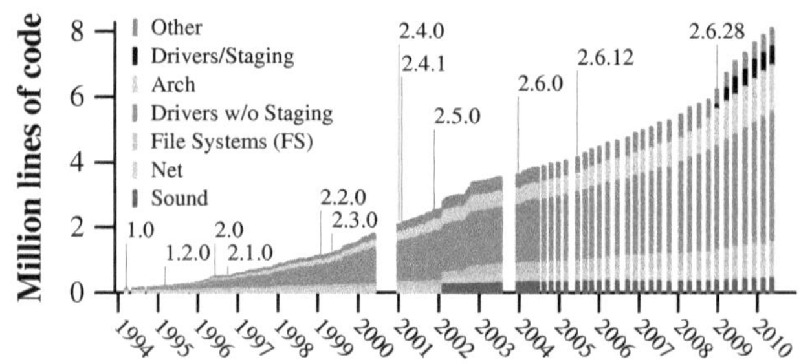


**Figure 1.** Linux directory sizes (in MLOC)

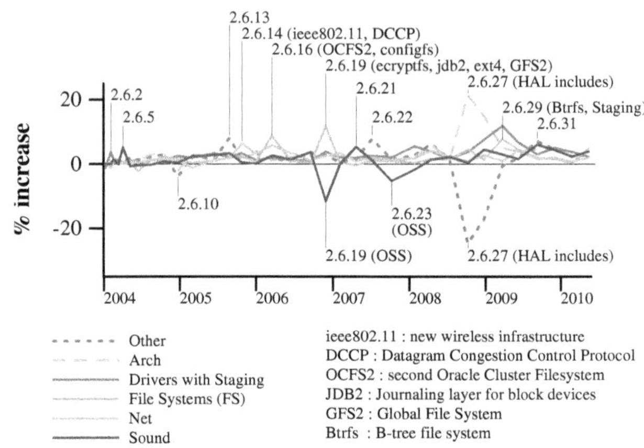


**Figure 2.** Linux directory size increase

***Extending the results to new versions*** A benefit of our experimental protocol is that it makes it easy to extend the results to new versions of Linux. When a new version of Linux is released, it is only necessary to run the checkers on the new code, and then repeat the correlation process. As our collected data contains information not only about the faults that we have identified, but also about the false positives, Herodotos automatically annotates both faults and false positives left over from previous versions as such, leaving only the new reports to be considered by the user.

## 3. Evolution of Linux

To give an overview of the complete history of Linux, we first consider the evolution in code size of the Linux kernel between version 1.0, released in March 1994, and version 2.6.33, released in February 2010, as shown in Figure 1. This figure shows the size of the development versions, when available, as it is in these versions that new code is added, and this added code is then maintained in the subsequent stable versions. Code sizes are computed using David A. Wheeler's 'SLOCCount' (v2.26) [39] and include only the ANSI C code. The code sizes are broken down by directory, highlighting the largest directories: `drivers/staging`, `arch`, `drivers`, `fs` (file systems), `net`, and `sound`. `Drivers/staging` was added in Linux 2.6.28 as an incubator for new drivers that are not yet mature enough to be used by end users. Code in `drivers/staging` is not compiled as part of the default Linux configuration, and is thus not included in standard Linux distributions. `Sound` was added in Linux 2.5.5, and contains sound drivers that were previously in the `drivers` directory. The largest directory is `drivers`, which, including `drivers/staging`, has made up 57% of the source code since Linux 2.6.30.

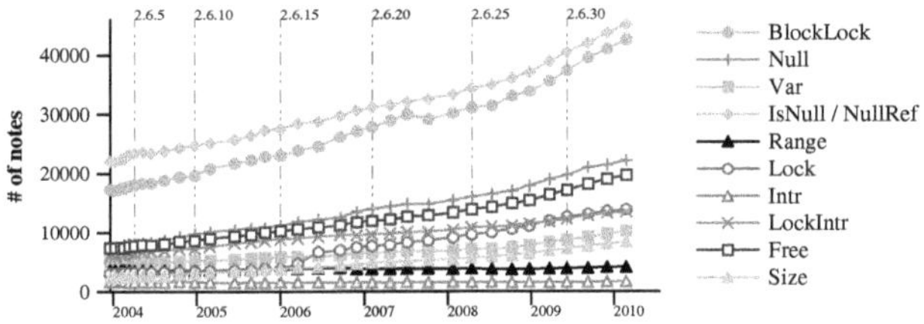


**Figure 3.** Notes through time per kind

For most directories, the code growth has been roughly linear since Linux 1.0. Some exceptions are highlighted in Figure 2, which shows the percentage code size increase in each directory from one version to the next. We have marked some of the larger increases and decreases. Many of the increases involve the introduction of new services, such as new file systems. In Linux 2.6.19 and 2.6.23, old OSS drivers already supported by ALSA were removed from `sound`, decreasing its size. In Linux 2.6.27, `arch` was reorganized, and received some large header files from `include`, adding around 180,000 lines of C code. Finally, `staging` grew substantially in 2.6.29. All in all, these changes have resulted in code growth from 2MLOC in 2001 to more than 8MLOC in 2010.

In our study, we are less interested in the absolute number of lines of code than the amount of code relevant to our fault kinds. As shown in Figure 3, the increase in code size has induced an almost linear increase in the number of notes, as defined in Section 2.2, in almost all cases. In fact, across all of Linux 2.6, the number of notes per line of code is essentially constant, between 0.027 and 0.030.

## 4. Linux 2.4.1

Linux 2.4.1 was the latest version of Linux considered by Chou *et al.* [5]. To validate our experimental protocol, we have used our checkers to find faults and notes in this version, and we compare our results to those provided in their paper. We focus on the results that are specific to Linux 2.4.1, rather than those that relate to the history of Linux up to that point, to avoid the need to study earlier versions that are of little relevance today.

### 4.1 What code is analyzed?

For the results of fault finding tools to be comparable, the tools must be applied to the same code base. Chou *et al.* focus only on x86 code, finding that 70% of the Linux 2.4.1 code is devoted to drivers. Nevertheless, we do not know which drivers, file systems, etc. were included. To calibrate our results, we use SLOCCount to obtain the number of lines of ANSI C code in the Linux kernel and in the `drivers` directory, considering three possibilities: all code in the Linux 2.4.1 kernel source tree ("All code"), the set of `.c` files compiled when using the default x86 configuration ("Min x86"),[3] and all 2.4.1 code except the `arch` and `include` subdirectories that are specific to non-x86 architectures ("Max x86"). Max x86 gives a result that is closest to that of Chou *et al.*, although the proportion of driver code is slightly higher than 70%. This is reasonable, because some driver code is associated with specific architectures and cannot be compiled for x86. Nevertheless, these results show that we do not know the precise set of files used in Chou *et al.*'s tests.

In our experiments, we consider the entire kernel source code, and not just the code for x86, as every line of code can be assumed to be relevant to some user.

[3] This configuration was automatically generated using `make menuconfig` without any modification of the proposed configuration. To collect the `.c` files, we compiled Linux 2.4.1 according to this configuration using a Debian 3.1 (Sarge) installation in a virtual machine, with `gcc` version 2.95.4 and `make` version 3.80.

| | All code | Min x86 | Max x86 |
|---|---|---|---|
| Drivers LOC | 1,248,930 | 71,938 | 1,248,930 |
| Total LOC | 2,090,638 | 174,912 | 1,685,265 |
| Drivers % | 59% | 41% | 74% |

**Table 2.** Percentage of Linux code found in **drivers** calculated according to various strategies

### 4.2 How many faults are there?

For the entire Linux 2.4.1 kernel, using the checkers described in Section 2.1, we obtain 600 reports, of which we have determined that 467 represent faults and the remainder represent false positives. Chou *et al.*'s checkers find 1,025 faults in Linux 2.4.1. They have checked 602 of these reports; the remainder are derived from what they characterize as low false positive checkers. We have checked all of the reports included in our study.

Table 3 compares the number of faults found per checker. In most cases, we find fewer faults. This may be due to different definitions of the checkers, or different criteria used when identifying false positives. In the case of **Var**, we find fewer faults because we consider only cases where the size is explicitly expressed as a number. In a few cases, we find more faults. For example, Chou *et al.*'s **Inull** checker can be compared to our **IsNull** and **NullRef** checkers. We find fewer **IsNull** faults than their **Inull** faults, but far more **NullRef** faults. We also find slightly more **Free** faults. This may derive from considering a larger number of files, as we have found that only one of our **Free** faults occurs in a file that is compiled using the default x86 configuration. Results from Chou *et al.*'s checkers were available at a web site interface to a database, but Chou has informed us that this database is no longer available. Thus, it is not possible to determine the precise reasons for the observed differences.

| Checker | Chou *et al.* checked | Chou *et al.* unchecked | Our results |
|---|---|---|---|
| Block | 206 | 87 | N/A |
| BlockLock | N/A | N/A | 43 |
| Null | 124 | 267 | 98 |
| Var | 33 | 69 | 13 |
| Inull | 69 | 0 | N/A |
| IsNull | N/A | N/A | 36 |
| NullRef | N/A | N/A | 221 |
| Range | 54 | 0 | 11 |
| Lock | 26 | 0 | 5 |
| Intr | 27 | 0 | 2 |
| LockIntr | N/A | N/A | 6 |
| Free | 17 | 0 | 21 |
| Float | 10 | 15 | 8 |
| Size | 3 | 0 | 3 |
| Total | 569 | 438 | 467 |

**Table 3.** Comparative fault count

### 4.3 Where are the faults?

Chou *et al.* find that the largest number of faults is in the `drivers` directory and that the largest number of these faults are in the categories **Block**, **Null**, and **Inull**, with around 180, 95, and 50 faults in `drivers`, respectively.[4] As shown in Figure 4(a), we also observe that the largest number of faults is in the `drivers` directory, with the largest number of these faults also being in **BlockLock**, **Null**, and **Inull** (**IsNull** and **NullRef**), although in different proportions.

A widely cited result of Chou *et al.* is that the `drivers` directory contains almost 7 times as many of a certain kind of faults (**Lock**) as all other directories combined. They computed this ratio using

[4] These numbers are approximated from the provided graphs.

the following formula for each directory *d*, where *d* refers to the directory *d* itself and $\overline{d}$ refers to all of the code in all other directories:

$$\mathit{fault\ rate}_d / \mathit{fault\ rate}_{\overline{d}}$$

Figure 4(b) shows the values of the same formula, using our results. We obtain a similar ratio with a relative rate of over 8 for **Lock** in `drivers`, as compared to all other directories combined. We also find that the `drivers` directory has a rate of **Free** faults that is almost 8 times that of all other directories combined. Chou *et al.*, however, found a fault rate of only around 1.75 times that of all other directories combined in this case. With both approaches, however, the absolute number of **Free** faults is rather small. Like Chou *et al.*, we also observe a high fault rate in the `arch` directory for the **Null** checker, in both cases about 4.8 times that of all other directories combined. Finally, unlike Chou *et al.*, we observe a high rate of **Var** faults in both `arch` and *other*. In the `arch` case, all of the **Var** faults found are for architectures other than x86. Indeed, overall for `arch`, we find 60 faults, but only 3 (all **Null**) in the x86 directory.

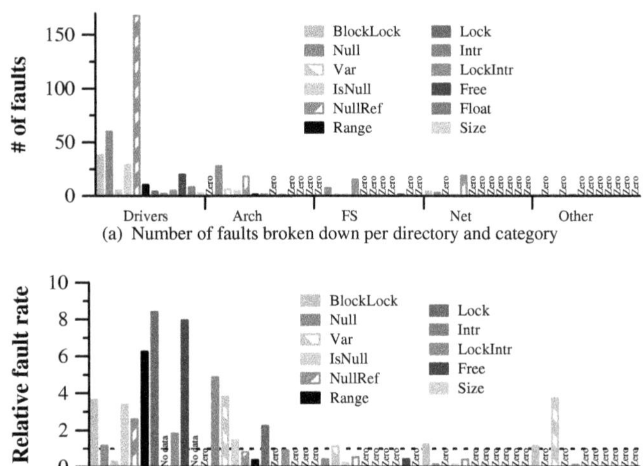


(a) Number of faults broken down per directory and category

(b) Rate of faults compared to all other directories

**Figure 4.** Faults in Linux 2.4.1

### 4.4 How are faults distributed?

Chou *et al.* plot numbers of faults against the percentage of files containing each number of faults and find that for all of the checkers except **Block**, the resulting curve fits a log series distribution, with a $\theta$ value of 0.567 and a degree of confidence (p-value) as measured by the $\chi^2$ test of 0.79 (79%). We observe a $\theta$ value of 0.562 and a p-value of 0.234 without **Block**. We conjecture that this low p-value is due to the fact that two files have 5 and 6 faults while three files have 7 faults each; such an increase for larger values is not compatible with a log series distribution. Nevertheless, the values involved are very small, and, as shown in Figure 5, the curve obtained from our experimental results fits well with the curve obtained using the corresponding calculated $\theta$ value. The curve obtained from Chou *et al.*'s value of $\theta$ is somewhat lower, because they found a smaller number of faulty files, probably due to having considered only the x86 architecture.

Chou *et al.* also find that younger files and larger functions have a higher fault rate, of up to 3% for the **Null** checker. We also find fault rates of around 3% for the **Null** checker, for files of all ages and for larger functions. Overall, we find that younger files have a fault rate of 0.8% while middle aged files, *i.e.*, those with an average age of over 6 years, have a significantly higher fault rate, of 0.4%. We also find a definite increase in fault rate as function size

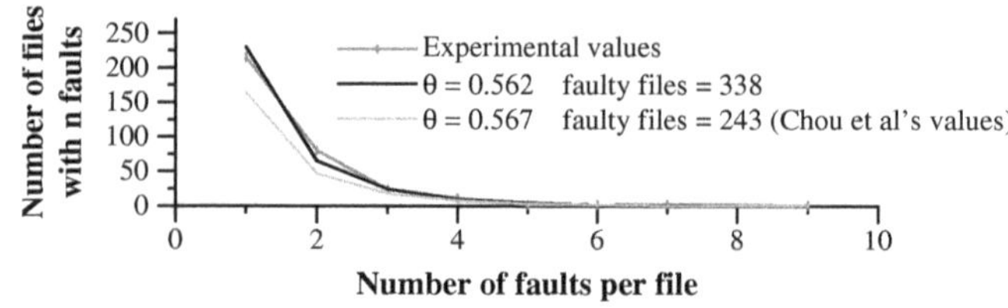


**Figure 5.** Comparison of the error distributions

increases: from 0.2% for functions containing up to 16 lines, to 0.6% for functions containing between 17 and 36 lines, to 0.8%-1.0% for larger functions.

### 4.5 Assessment

In this section, we have seen that our checkers do not find the same number of faults in Linux 2.4.1 code as those of Chou *et al.* We recall that Chou *et al.*'s checkers are not very precisely described, and thus we expect that most of the differences are in how the checkers are defined. Furthermore, we do not consider exactly the same set of files. Nevertheless, the distribution of these faults among the various directories is roughly comparable, and their distribution among the files is also comparable. We thus conclude that our checkers are sufficient to provide a basis for comparison between Linux 2.6 and previous versions studied by Chou *et al.*

## 5. Linux 2.6 kernels

We now assess the extent to which the trends observed for Linux 2.4.1 and previous versions continue to apply in Linux 2.6, and study the points of difficulty in kernel development today. We consider what has been the impact of the increasing code size and the addition of new features on code quality, and whether drivers are still a major problem.

Concretely, we study a period of over 6 years, beginning with the release of Linux 2.6.0 at the end of 2003 and ending in early 2010 with the release of Linux 2.6.33. For the entire Linux 2.6 kernel, using the checkers described in Section 2.1, we obtain 3,915 different reports (after correlation), of which we have determined that 2,370 represent faults and the rest represent false positives. We also consider some new checkers related to the use of the recently added RCU locking API. Finally, because one of our goals is to provide a means of repeating our work, we consider how our experimental protocol eases the extension of the results to new Linux versions.

### 5.1 How many faults are there?

We first analyze the relation between the code growth and the total number of faults in Linux 2.6. As shown in Figure 6(a), the number of the faults considered has held roughly steady over this period, with an overall increase of only 7%, and indeed a decrease of 11% from 2.6.0 to 2.6.28. This is quite remarkable given that the code size has more than doubled since Linux 2.6.0 (Figure 1). Indeed, the rate of faults per line of code has significantly decreased, by 50%, as shown in Figure 6(b). These observations are quite different from those for versions up through Linux 2.4.1: there was a code size increase of over 17 times between Linux 1.0 and Linux 2.4.1 and a corresponding increase in the number of the faults considered of over 33 times [5]. Figure 6(c) shows that faults are still introduced, indeed at a growing rate. But in most versions even more faults are eliminated.

Figure 7 shows the number of each kind of fault found in Linux 2.6, separated for readability into those that have increased in number between the beginning and the end (Figure 7(a)) and those

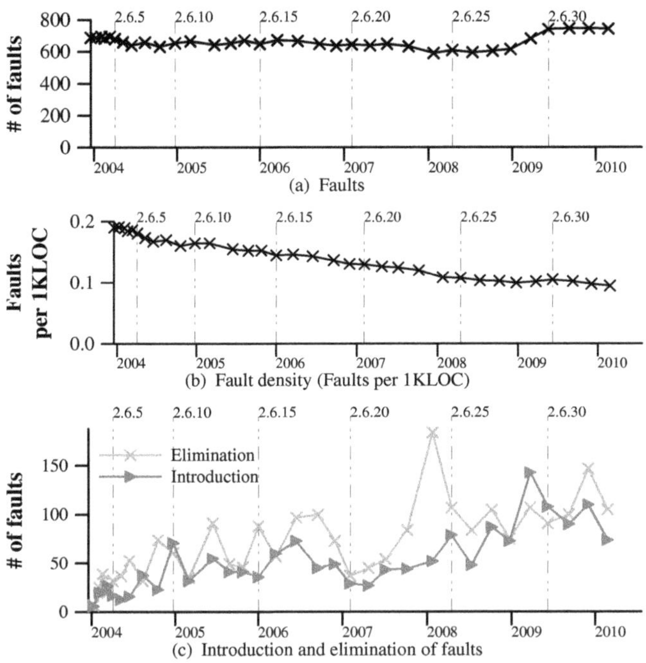


**Figure 6.** Faults in Linux 2.6.0 to 2.6.33

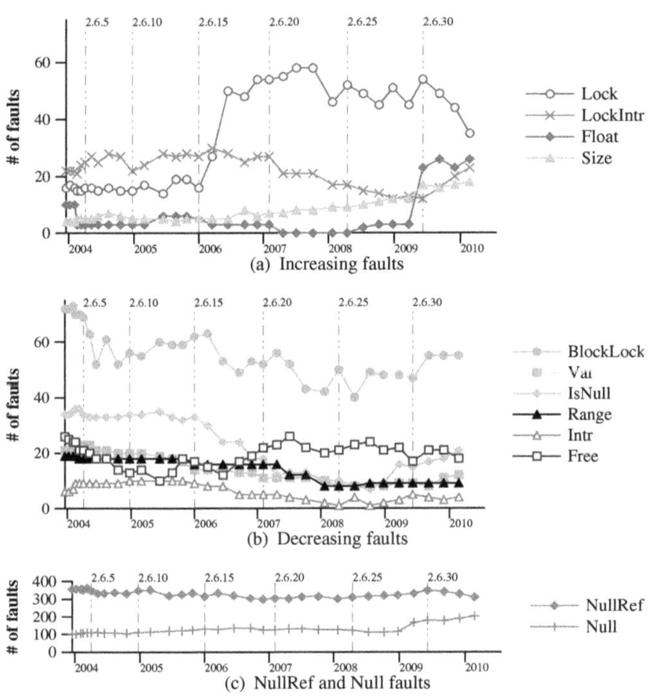


**Figure 7.** Faults through time

that have decreased in number in the same versions (Figure 7(b)). **NullRef** and **Null** are further separated from the others. For many fault kinds, the number of faults is essentially constant over the considered period.

Three notable exceptions to the stability in the number of Linux 2.6 faults are **Lock**, **Null**, and **Float**, in Linux 2.6.16 and 2.6.17, Linux 2.6.29, and Linux 2.6.30, respectively (Figures 7(a) and 7(c)). In Linux 2.6.16, the functions `mutex_lock` and `mutex_unlock` were introduced to replace mutex-like occurrences of the semaphore functions `down` and `up`. 9 of the 11 **Lock** faults introduced in Linux 2.6.16 and 23 of the 25 **Lock** faults introduced in Linux 2.6.17 were in the use of `mutex_lock`. In Linux 2.6.29, the `btrfs` file system was introduced, as seen in Figure 2. 33 **Null** faults were added with this code. 7 more **Null** faults were added in `drivers/staging`, which more than tripled in size at this time. 29 other **Null** faults were also added in this version. Finally, in Linux 2.6.30 there was a substantial increase in the number of Comedi drivers [6] in `drivers/staging`. All of the 21 **Float** faults introduced in this version were in two Comedi files. These faults are still present in Linux 2.6.33. Recall, however, that `staging` drivers are not included in Linux distributions.

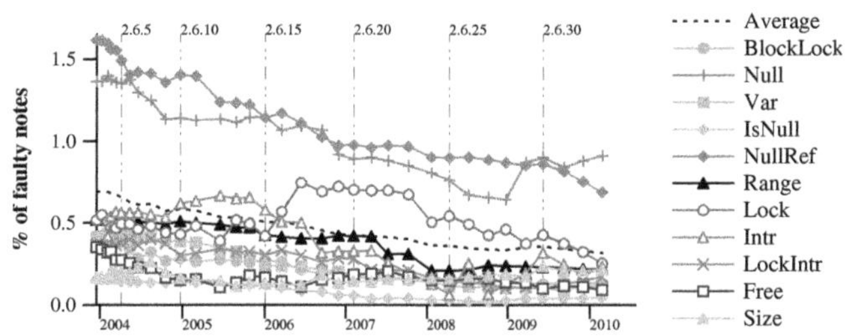


**Figure 8.** Fault rate per fault kind

As shown in Figure 8, the fault rate, *i.e.*, the ratio of observed faults to the number of notes, for the considered fault kinds confirms the increase in reliability (Float is omitted, as described in Section 2.2). As the number of notes increases roughly with the size of the Linux kernel while the number of faults is relatively stable, the fault rate tends to decline. The main increases, in **Lock** and **Null**, are due to the introduction of `mutex_lock` and the `btrfs` file system, respectively, as mentioned previously.

## 5.2 Where are the faults?

The presence of a high rate of faults in a certain kind of code may indicate that this kind of code overall needs more attention. Indeed, Chou *et al.*'s work motivated studies of many kinds of driver faults, going beyond the fault kinds they considered. Many properties of the Linux kernel have, however, changed since 2001, and so we reinvestigate what kind of code has the highest rate of faults, to determine whether attention should now be placed elsewhere.

As shown in Figure 9, the largest number of faults is still in `drivers`, which indeed makes up over half of the Linux kernel source code. The second-largest number of faults is in `arch`, accompanied by `fs` and `drivers/staging` in recent versions. In contrast to the case of Linux 2.4.1, however, as shown in Figure 10, `drivers` no longer has the largest fault rate, and indeed since Linux 2.6.19 its fault rate has been right at the average. There was not a large increase in the number of `drivers` notes at that time, so this decrease is indicative of the amount of attention drivers receive in the peer reviewing process. `Arch` on the other hand has many faults and relatively little code, and so it has the highest fault rate throughout most of Linux 2.6. Around 30% of the `arch` faults are **Null** faults, although there appears to be no pattern to their introduction. Over 90% of the `arch` faults are outside of the `x86/i386` directories, with many of these faults being in the `ppc` and `powerpc` code. The largest numbers of faults in `fs` are in `cifs`, with over 40 faults in Linux 2.6.0 but a decreasing number after, in `ocfs2`, with 10-15 faults per version starting in Linux 2.6.17, and in `btrfs`, with 36 in Linux 2.6.29 and 38 in Linux 2.6.30 and gradually fewer after that. All of these are recently introduced file systems: `cifs` was introduced in

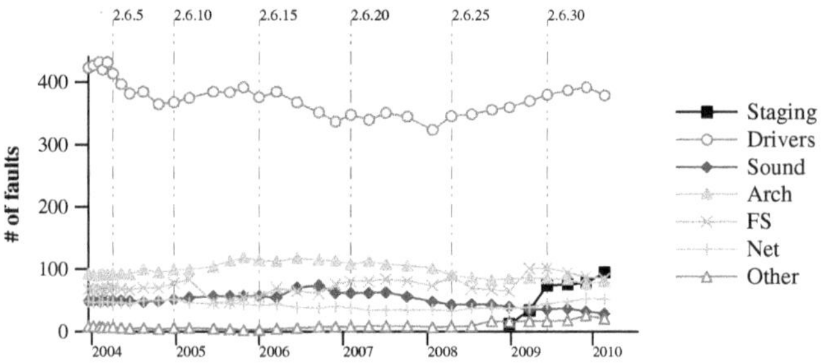


**Figure 9.** Faults per directory

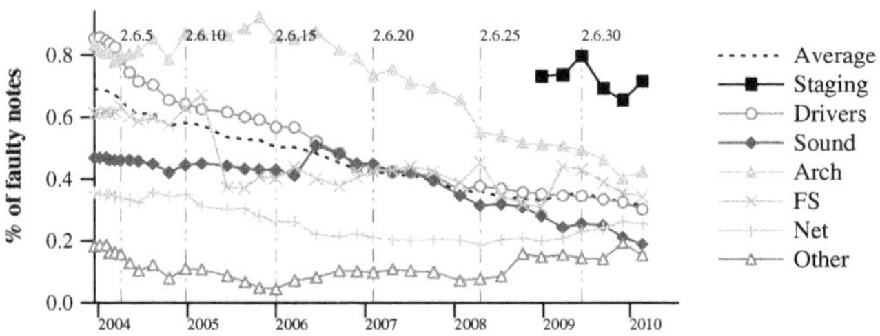


**Figure 10.** Fault rate per directory

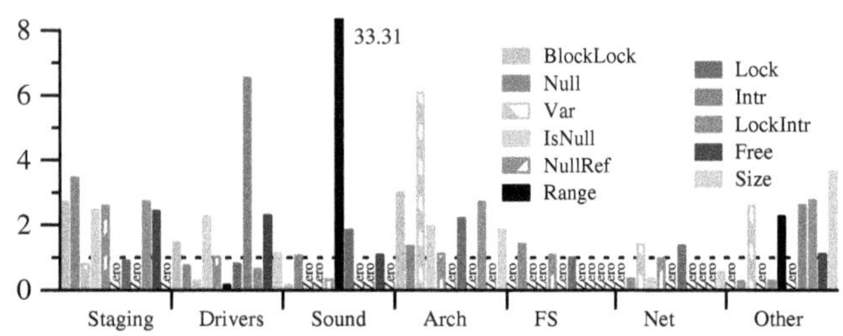


**Figure 11.** Fault rates compared to other directories (Linux 2.6.33)

Linux 2.5.42, **ocfs2** in Linux 2.6.16, and **btrfs** in Linux 2.6.29. **Drivers/staging**, introduced in Linux 2.6.28, also has a high fault rate, exceeding that of **arch**. This directory is thus receiving drivers that are not yet mature, as intended. The introduction of **drivers/staging**, however, has no impact on the fault rate of **drivers**, as **drivers/staging** accommodates drivers that would not otherwise be accepted into the Linux kernel source tree. Such drivers benefit from the expertise of the Linux maintainers, and are updated according to API changes with the rest of the kernel.

For Linux 2.4.1, we observed that **drivers** had a much higher fault rate for certain kinds of faults than other directories. Figure 11 shows that **drivers** has a high rate of **Intr** faults in Linux 2.6.33 as compared to other directories, but there are very few **Intr** fault in this version. **Sound**, which was part of **drivers** in 2.4.1, has a high rate of **Range** faults, as compared to the other directories, but again the actual number of faults is relatively small. Overall, while **drivers** has a high rate as compared to other directories for some fault kinds, it is more common that **drivers/staging**, **arch**, or *other* has the highest fault rate, indicating again that the drivers that are intended for use in the Linux kernel are no longer the main source of faults.

Finally, in Figure 12, we consider the number of faults per file that contains at least one fault. The highest average number of faults per faulty file is for **fs** in the versions prior to 2.6.12. In this case, there was a single file with many **NullRef** faults, as many as 45 in Linux 2.6.11. In later versions, the highest average is for

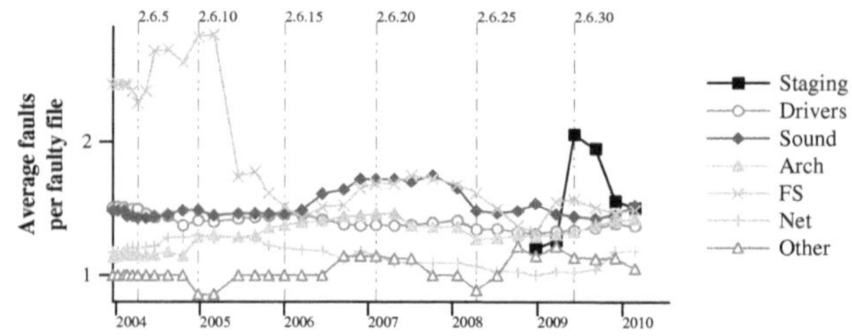


**Figure 12.** Faults per faulty file per directory

**drivers/staging**, for which the average was over 2 in Linux 2.6.30. At that point, a large number of drivers had recently been introduced in this directory. Many of these faults have been corrected and the rate of entry of new drivers has slowed, and thus the average has dropped to around 1.5, close to that of other directories. **Sound** had a relatively high number of faults per faulty file starting in Linux 2.6.16 with the introduction of **mutex_lock**; faulty functions often contain more than one **mutex_lock**, and thus a single omitted **mutex_unlock** may result in multiple **Lock** reports.

### 5.3 How long do faults live?

Eliminating a fault in Linux code is a three step process. First, the fault must be detected, either manually or using a tool. Then it must be corrected, and a patch submitted to the appropriate maintainers. Then, the patch must be accepted by a hierarchy of maintainers, ending with Linus Torvalds. Finally, there is a delay of up to 3 months until the next release. The lifespan of a fault, modulo this three month delay, is an indication of the efficiency of this process.

***Fault lifespans*** Figure 13 presents the average lifespan of faults across Linux 2.6, by directory and by fault kind. We omit **drivers/-staging** because it was only introduced recently. Some faults were present before Linux 2.6.0 and some faults were still present in Linux 2.6.33. For the average lifespan calculation, in the former case, we assume that the fault was introduced in Linux 2.6.0 and in the latter case, we assume that the fault was eliminated in Linux 2.6.34, thus potentially underestimating the lifespan of such faults.

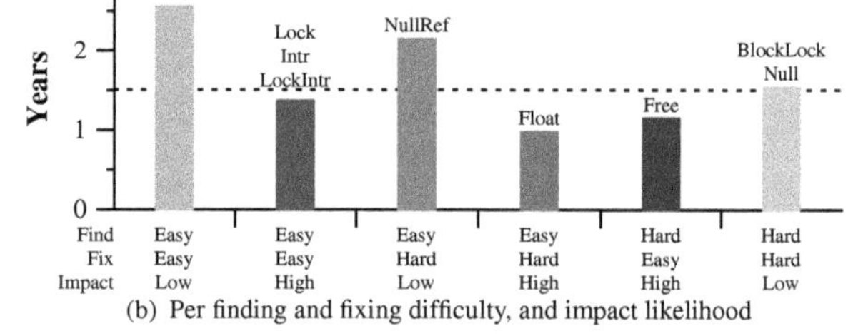


**Figure 13.** Average fault lifespans (without staging)

The average fault lifespan across all files of Linux 2.6 is 1.5 years, as indicated by the horizontal dotted line in Figure 13 The lifespans vary somewhat by directory. As shown in Figure 13(a), the average lifespan of faults in the **drivers** directory is the same as the average lifespan of all faults, and indeed is less than the average lifespan of faults in the **sound** and **arch** directories. **Sound** faults now have the longest average lifespan. **Sound** used to be part of **drivers**; it may be that the sound drivers are no longer benefiting from the attention that other drivers receive.

For the fault kinds, Figure 13(b) shows that the average lifespans correspond roughly to our assessment of the difficulty of finding and fixing the faults and their likelihood of impact (Table 1). In particular, all of the fault kinds we have designated as having high impact, meaning that the fault is likely to have an observable effect if the containing function is executed, are fixed relatively quickly. On the other hand, the ease of finding and fixing the faults has little impact on their lifespan, showing that developers are willing to invest in tracking down any faults that cause obvious problems.

Figure 14 examines the fault lifetimes in more detail, by showing the number of faults that have been fixed in less than each amount of time. Again we include the faults already present in Linux 2.6.0 and the faults still remaining in Linux 2.6.33. While half of the faults we found where fixed within just under one year, it took about 5.5 years (almost half of the period studied) to fix 80% of the faults. For the **drivers** and **fs** directories, half of the faults were fixed within just under one year, while 2.5 years were required for **sound**. On the other hand, half of the **staging** and *other* faults were fixed within 6 months.

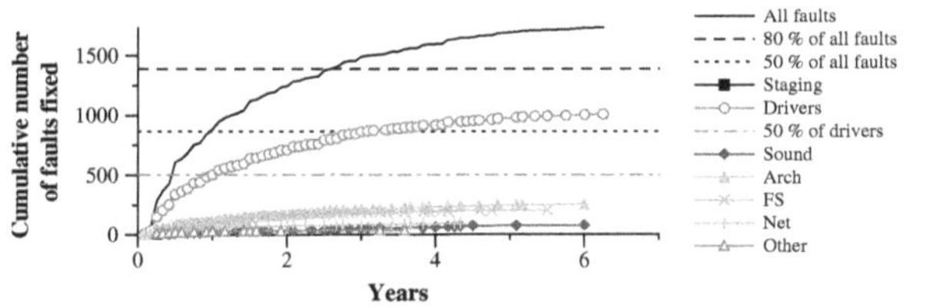


**Figure 14.** Cumulative number of fixed faults per amount of elapsed time

***Origin of faults*** Figure 15 shows the lifetime of all of the Linux 2.6 faults in our study, with Linux 2.6.1 at the bottom of the graph and Linux 2.6.33 at the top. The 689 faults in Linux 2.6.0 are omitted to save space; their lifetime within Linux 2.6 can be seen later as the leftmost curve in Figure 16. They may, however, have been introduced earlier. Of the faults introduced and eliminated within the period considered, 36% of the faults introduced in or after Linux 2.6.0 were introduced with the file and 12% of the faults eliminated before Linux 2.6.33 were eliminated with the file.[5]

While we have seen that the total number of faults is essentially constant across the versions, Figure 15 shows that since Linux 2.6.27 a significantly larger number of faults have been introduced. **Null** and **NullRef** faults predominate, with for example 51% of the added faults in Linux 2.6.27 being **NullRef** faults, most of which were introduced in various drivers. In Linux 2.6.30 and Linux 2.6.32, 43% and 26% of the introduced faults were in **drivers/staging**. In each case, about half of the introduced faults were fixed within a few versions.

Figure 16 shows the number of faults in each version that are still present in each of the previous and successive versions. Except for the increase at Linux 2.6.29 and 2.6.30, as previously noted, the height and angle of all of the lines is fairly similar, indicating that the rate of introductions and eliminations of faults across the versions is relatively stable. These facts indicate a maturity in the Linux code and its development model.

[5] The degree to which this is visible depends on the image quality. It may be useful to print this page rather than view it on a screen.

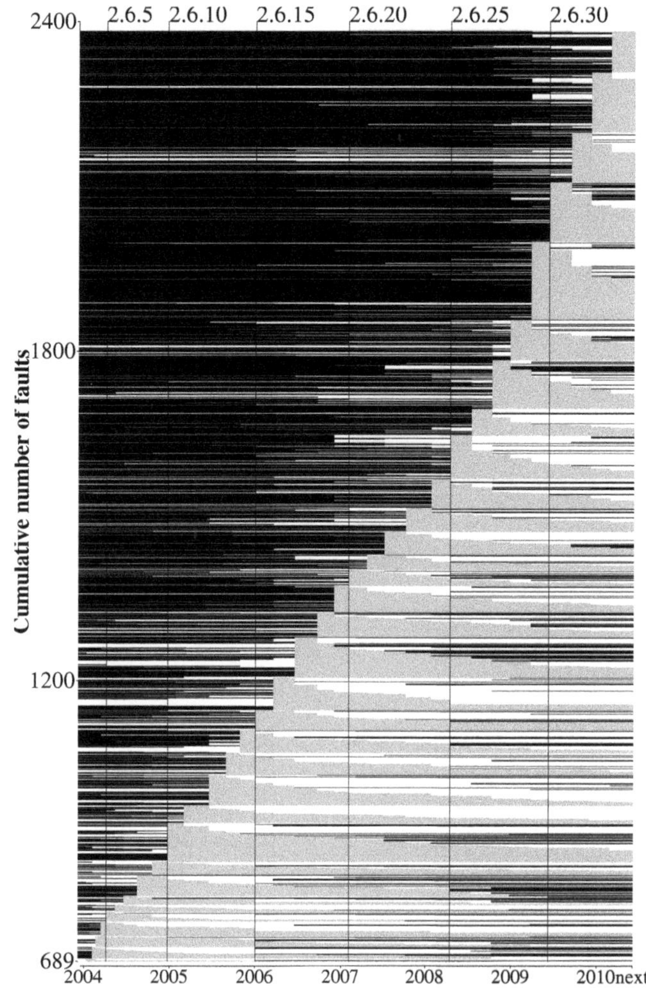


**Figure 15.** Lifetime of faults. Each row represents a separate fault. Blue (grey) lines indicate the periods where the fault is present. Black lines indicate the period where the file containing the fault does not exist and white lines indicate the period where the file does exist but the fault does not. The 689 faults in Linux 2.6.0 are omitted.

***Developer and maintainer activity*** In the Linux development model, anyone (an *author*) can submit a patch, and the patch is then picked up by a maintainer, who *commits* it into his git repository that is then propagated to Linus Torvalds. The number of patch authors is thus an indicator of the number of participants in the Linux development process, and the number of committers is an indicator of the amount of manpower that is available to begin the integration of patches into a release. Figure 17 shows the number of authors and committers associated with the patches included in each version, both in total and broken down by directory.

For **drivers**, the numbers of authors and committers are rising at the same rate, roughly at the rate of the increase in the code size. For **arch** and **fs**, however, where we have previously noted a higher fault rate, the number of authors is rising significantly more slowly than the number of committers. The lower number of authors may suggest that potential authors are not able to develop adequate expertise to keep up with the number of new architectures and file systems (Figure 2). Finally, the small number of **sound** authors may explain the previously observed long life of **sound** faults (Figure 13(a)).

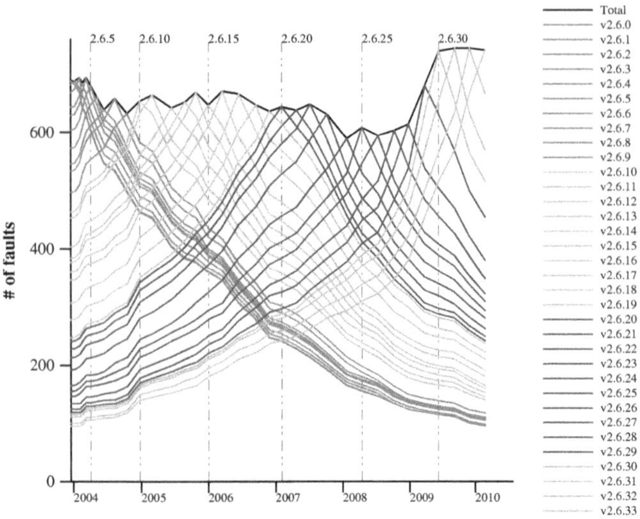


**Figure 16.** Lifetime of faults across versions

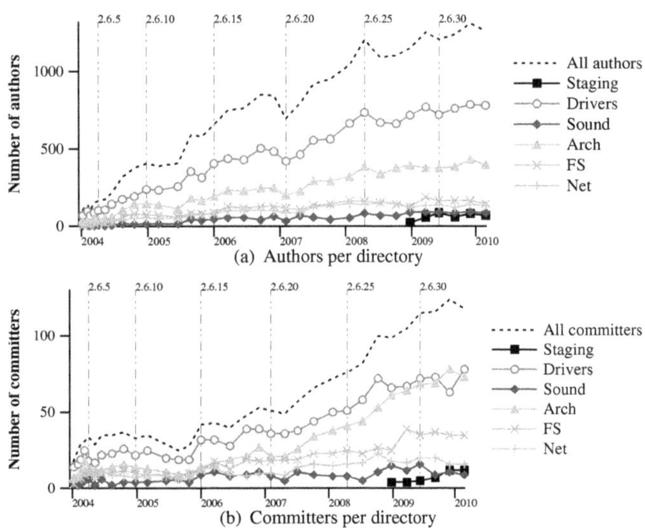


**Figure 17.** Authors and committers per version

***Use of tools*** In principle, since the work of Chou *et al.*, it has been possible to find all of the considered faults using tools. Figure 18 shows the number of patches in each Linux version that mention one of the fault-finding tools Coccinelle [24] (used in this paper), Coverity [9] (the commercial version of Chou *et al.*'s `xgcc` tool), sparse [31, 33], and smatch [36]. As developers are not obliged to mention the tools they use, these results may be an underestimation.

The use of the various tools is somewhat variable across the different versions. In the case of Coverity, the main use occurred between 2006 and 2009, when its application to open-source software, including Linux, was funded by the US Department of Homeland Security [3]. Sparse usage shows several peaks, at 2.6.25 and at 2.6.29-30. No particular pattern emerges for 2.6.25. For versions 2.6.29 and 2.6.30, a single developer was responsible for 140 of the 253 sparse-related patches. He fixed faults across the entire kernel. The tools have also been used to find a wider range of faults than those considered in this paper. For example, in Linux 2.6.24, only about half of the patches that mention Coverity relate to the kinds of faults we consider, particularly **Null**, **IsNull**, **NullRef**, and **Free**. Overall, despite the variability in usage, the results show a willingness on the part of the Linux developers to use fault-finding tools and to pay attention to the kinds of faults that they find.

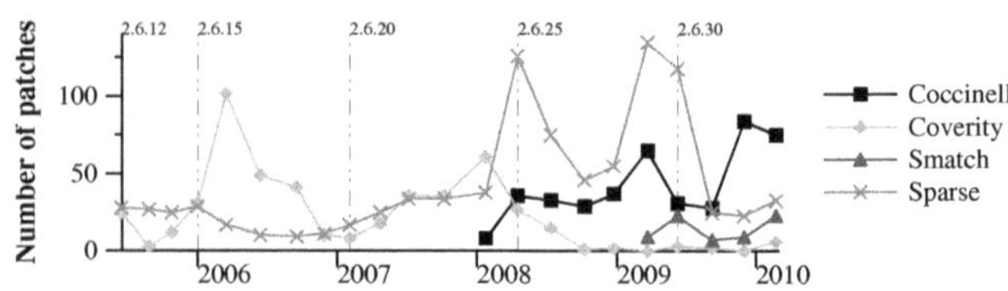


**Figure 18.** Tool usage since the introduction of git

### 5.4 Is code quality predictable?

In the software engineering community, substantial work has been done on identifying metrics that predict code quality. We consider three possible metrics: code churn, file age, and function size. We also evaluate the quality of Linux code in light of the conjecture that open source code is more reliable because it can be examined by many people.

***Churn*** Elbaum and Munson observed that code churn, *i.e.*, the number of times a file is modified, is a good predictor of fault rate [21]. Nagappan and Ball reached a similar conclusion in a study that used metrics relating to the development of Windows Server 2003 to predict SP1's fault rate [22]. Figure 19 shows the relationship between the average churn per day preceding the release of each version and the number of the considered faults added in that version. The relationship between churn and fault rate is similar. There is an overall tendency of high-churn versions to contain more new faults, even if some high-churn versions have a smaller number of faults than lower churn versions. Recall, however, that in most versions, more faults were eliminated than added; the churn includes the elimination of faults as well.

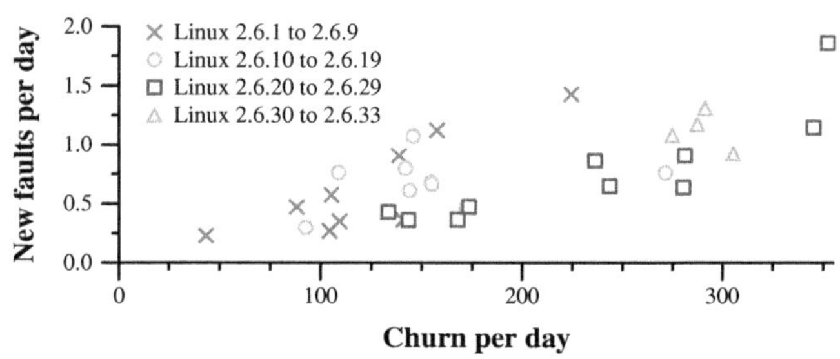


**Figure 19.** Churn vs. new faults

***Kernel configuration*** In *"The Cathedral and the Bazaar"* [30], Eric S. Raymond formalized Linus' law: "given enough eyeballs, all bugs are shallow." But, in practice, code that is frequently executed, or at least frequently compiled, is more likely to be reviewed than the rest. When code is frequently executed, many users are likely to encounter any faults, and some may fix the faults themselves or submit a request that the faults be fixed by a kernel maintainer. When code is frequently compiled, even if it is not frequently executed, it can easily be submitted to fault-finding tools that are integrated with the kernel compilation process. "Eyeballs" may also focus on fixing faults in code that they are able to compile, as even standard compilers such as `gcc` perform some sanity checks that provide some confidence that a fix has not *e.g.*, introduced a typographical error, even if the code cannot be tested.

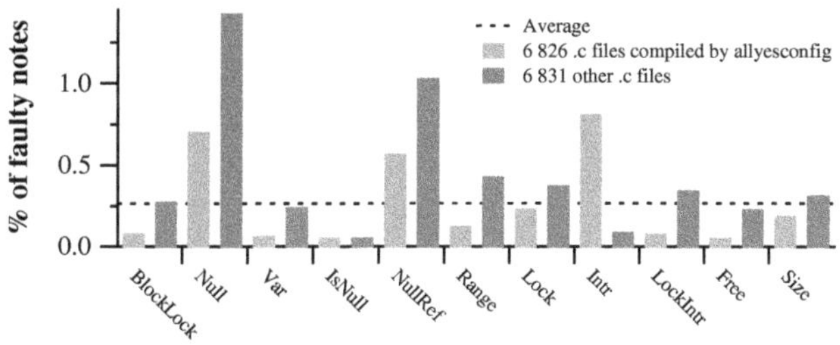


**Figure 20.** Fault rate compared between configurations (Linux 2.6.33)

Figure 20 compares the number of faults found in the `.c` files that are compiled using the configuration generated on an x86 architecture by the Linux Makefile argument `allyesconfig` to the number of faults found in the `.c` files found in the rest of the Linux kernel.[6] The Makefile argument `allyesconfig` creates a configuration file for the given architecture that includes as many options as possible without causing a conflict and without including `drivers/staging`. Thus, it can be assumed to trigger the compilation of a set of well-tested files and a superset of what is normally included with a Linux distribution, and thus what is executed by ordinary users. In most cases, we do find that the `allyesconfig` files have a lower fault rate than the other files. The only exception is for **Intr** faults, but there are only 4 faults in this case.

***File age and function size*** One may expect that as a file ages the number of faults would decrease, and that large functions would tend to harbor more faults. Indeed, Chou *et al.* found these trends in Linux 2.4.1, to a varying degree for the different fault kinds. Figure 21 considers the relationship between file age or function size and fault rate in Linux 2.6.33. Files and functions are organized by increasing age or size, respectively, then collected into buckets containing an exponentially decreasing number of elements, from the smallest age or size to the largest. This strategy permits a fine degree of granularity for the files with smaller ages or sizes, respectively. Each graph then shows the average age or size of the files or functions in each bucket and their average fault rate.

Figure 21 shows that in Linux 2.6.33, the youngest half of the files, represented by the leftmost point, has a fault rate about twice that of the next youngest quarter of the files. For older files, however, the relation between age and fault rate is less clear, as the rate first increases and then decreases as the file age increases. On the other hand, the average fault rate clearly increases as the function size increases. Indeed, the bucket with the smallest functions (up to 14 lines) has a significantly lower fault rate than the next bucket. There is also an increase at 54 lines. This suggests that larger functions, although there are relatively fewer of them, may need more attention. As shown by our exponential bucketing strategy, there are relatively few large functions, meaning that it should be feasible to check them more carefully, either manually or using tools.

### 5.5 How does the fault rate in new APIs compare

The fault kinds that we have considered until now involve code structures that are either common to all C code or that have been present in Linux for a long time. To give an alternate perspective on the robustness of Linux 2.6 code, we consider the use of a more recent and specialized locking API: the one that implements the Read-Copy-Update (RCU) mechanism [20]. RCU is a lightweight synchronization mechanism that protects readers against writers.

[6] Compilation was done on an Ubuntu 10.04 (Lucid Lynx) installation with `gcc` 4.4.3 and `make` 3.81.

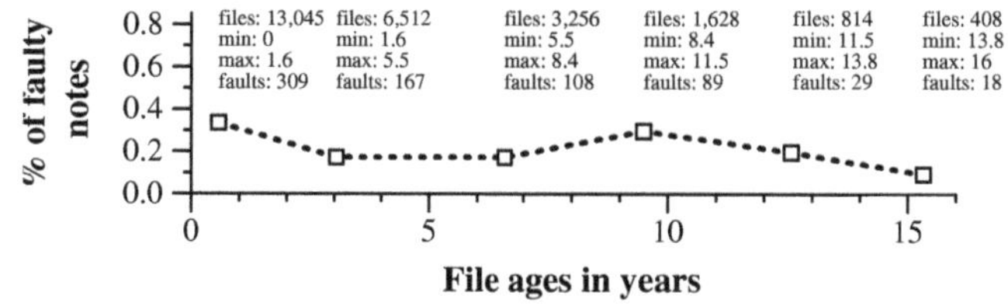


(a) Fault rate by file age in 2.6.33

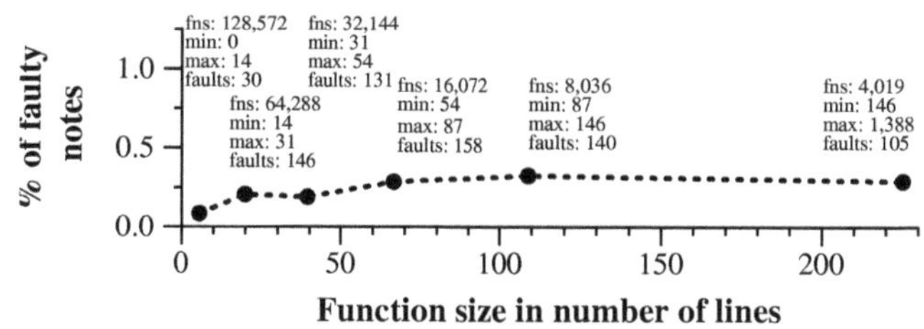


(b) Fault rate by function size in 2.6.33

**Figure 21.** Impact of file age and function size. Each point represents twice as many files or functions as the next point. At each point, "files" and "fns" refers respectively to the number of files and functions considered to compute the point, "min" and "max" refer to the minimal or maximal age or size represented by the point, and faults indicates the number of faults that occur in the code in that range

Reads are wait-free with very low overhead while writes are more expensive. Therefore, RCU particularly favors workloads that mostly read shared data rather than updating it. RCU has been increasingly used in Linux 2.6, but is still used less often than spinlocks and mutexes, as shown in Figure 22.

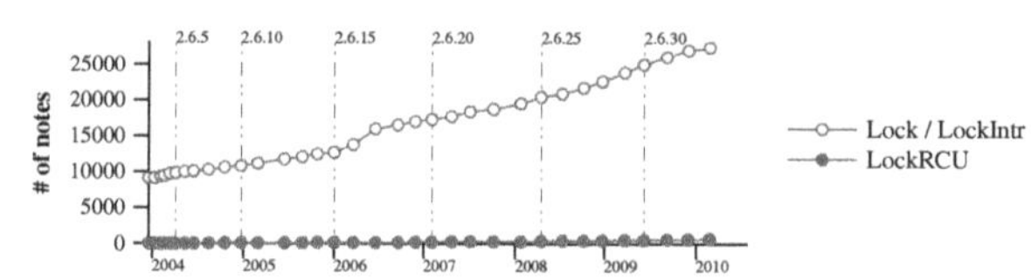


**Figure 22.** The use of spinlock and mutex locking functions as compared to the use of RCU locking functions

The main functions that we consider in the RCU API are the locking functions: `rcu_read_lock`, `srcu_read_lock`, `rcu_read_lock_bh`, `rcu_read_lock_sched`, and `rcu_read_lock_sched_notrace`. We identify as faults any cases where a blocking function is called while a RCU lock is held (**BlockRCU**) and where a RCU lock is taken but not released (**LockRCU**). These are analogous to the previously considered **BlockLock** and **Lock** fault kinds, respectively. Double-acquiring an RCU lock is allowed, and thus this is not considered to be a fault. Finally, we identify as a fault any case where shared data is accessed using `rcu_dereference` when an RCU lock is not held (**DerefRCU**).

The largest number of uses of the RCU lock functions is in `net`, followed by `drivers` in earlier versions and *other* in later versions, with `kernel`, `include`, `mm`, and `security` being the main *other* directories where it is used. Correspondingly, as shown in Figure 23, most faults are found in `net`, and the few remaining faults are found in *other*. The average lifespan of the `net` faults is around a year, while that of the *other* faults is a few months longer. As shown in Figure 24, most of the faults are **BlockRCU** faults, and the largest number of faults per version is only 10, in Linux 2.6.26. Thus, overall, the fault rates are substantially below the fault rates observed for any of the previously considered fault kinds, and in particular far below the rates observed for the various locking faults (**Lock**, **Intr**, and **LockIntr**). Nevertheless, the developers who have added calls to the various RCU locking functions are relatively experienced, having at the median 123 patches accepted between Linux 2.6.12 and Linux 2.6.33. Still, these results suggest that Linux developers can be successful at adopting a new API and using it correctly.

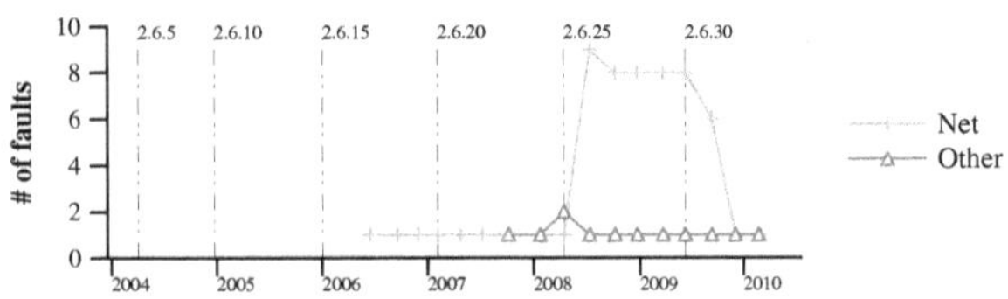


**Figure 23.** RCU faults per directory

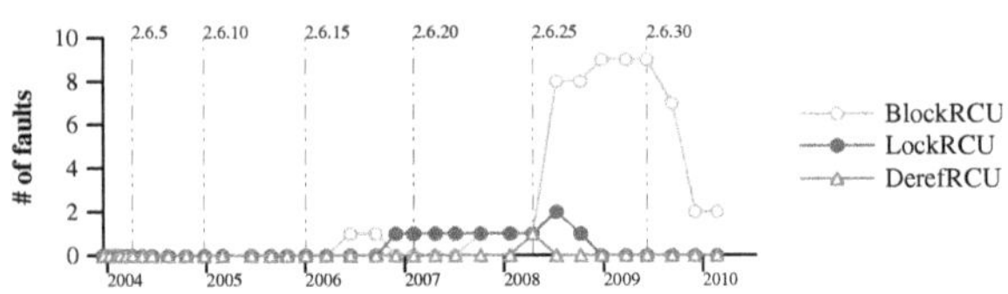


**Figure 24.** RCU faults through time

### 5.6 Processing New Versions

As presented in Section 2, the automatic report correlations provided by Herodotos make it easy to extend an existing set of results to the next version of Linux. For example, for the **BlockLock** checker, suppose one starts with a set of already annotated reports for at least Linux 2.6.32. For Linux 2.6.33, as shown in Figure 25, the checker produces 70 reports of potential faults of which 51 are faults inherited from Linux 2.6.32, and 14 are false positives also present in that version. Herodotos would annotate these reports automatically, leaving only five reports to be annotated by the user. In this case, four are faults. Overall, for Linux 2.6.33 there are 232 new reports to consider. Half of these are for **Float**, but of these most follow the same pattern, and can be dealt with in a few minutes.

## 6. Limitations

The main limitations of our work are in the choice of faults considered and the definition of the checkers. We have focused on the same kinds of faults as Chou *et al.*, to be able to assess the changes in Linux since their work. Current fault finding tools, including Coccinelle, are able to find other kinds of faults, such as memory leaks. The considered set of faults also does not include concurrency faults, which are becoming increasingly important with the prevalence of multicore architectures. A recent study of concurrency faults in infrastructure software, however, has shown that over 20% of deadlocks are caused by a thread reacquiring a resource it already holds [18], amounting to a double lock, as detected by our **Lock** checker.

Our checkers could also be improved to reduce the number of false positives. In particular, as we have seen for **Float** in Section 5.6, some kinds of false positives are due to recurring patterns specific to certain Linux files. Taking these patterns into account in the checkers would avoid generating large numbers of trivial false positive reports. Finally, we have tried to be conservative in our identification of real faults, and this may have lead to an underestimation of their number. By making our results available in a public archive, we hope to benefit from feedback from the Linux community to improve our classification strategies.

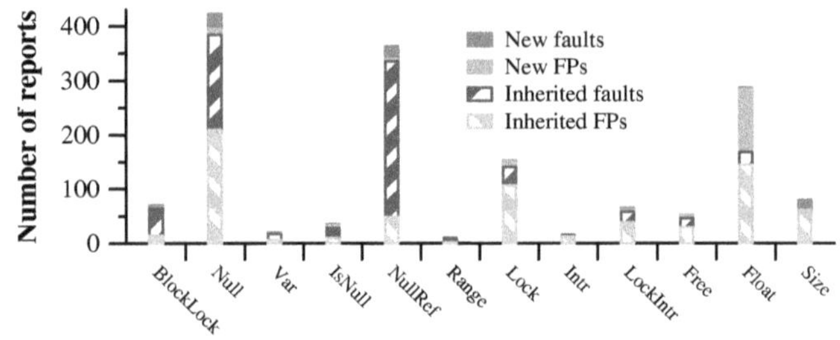


**Figure 25.** Reports generated for Linux 2.6.33

## 7. Related Work

Chou *et al.* briefly considered OpenBSD, as well as Linux [5]. Because of its wider use and more active development, we have focused only on Linux instead, comparing the properties of old and new versions.

In previous work, Palix *et al.* have used Coccinelle to conduct a study of faults in versions of Linux and several other open source projects released between 2005 and 2009 [25]. They proposed Herodotos, in order to correlate the faults between releases. They did not consider fault kinds requiring an interprocedural analysis, nor did they consider lock-related faults. As shown in Figure 7, these are among the most prevalent and also have high impact. Lawall *et al.* proposed a methodology allowing to find interprocedural faults in Linux code, but consider only a single Linux version [15].

Israeli and Feitelson have studied 810 versions of the Linux kernel, from Linux 1.0 to Linux 2.6.25 [14]. They considered traditional source-code metrics to measure complexity [19] and maintainability [23], rather than actual numbers of faults. They found that the complexity per Linux function is decreasing, and the maintainability is increasing. Nevertheless, they did find that `arch` and `drivers` do contain some very high complexity functions, typically interrupt handlers or `ioctl` functions, and that `arch` and `drivers` code is somewhat less maintainable than the code in other parts of the kernel. Their work is complementary to ours, and reaches some of the same conclusions.

Song *et al.* have studied the reasons for software hangs in open source infrastructure software, such as MySQL and Apache [32]. They focused on bug reports rather than analysis of the source code. They found that most types of concurrency faults are fixed on average within 100 days. Nevertheless, they did not take into account the time elapsed between the introduction of the fault and the time when it was first detected, and so the actual fault lifetime may be more in line with what we have observed. Lu *et al.* also considered concurrency faults in infrastructure software, primarily focusing on the kinds of tools that would be helpful to address them [18].

## 8. Conclusion

During the last 10 years, much of the research in operating system reliability has been predicated on the assumption that drivers are the main problem. The first major result of our study is that while `drivers` still has the largest number of faults in absolute terms, it no longer has the highest fault rate in Linux kernel code, having been supplanted by the HAL. The second major result of our study is that even though faults are continually being introduced, the overall code quality is improving. Our work thus shows the importance of being able to periodically repeat the study of faults in source code in order to revise research priorities as the fault patterns change in response to research efforts. Because the priorities of individuals and individual institutions change over time, the need to repeat such studies implies that the tools and other data required must be available in an public archival repository.

Our study also shows that tools, while used, are under-exploited. Tools are indeed available to find all of the fault kinds considered in this paper. The fact that these kinds of faults remain and have a relatively long lifespan suggests that research is needed on how to design tools that are better integrated into the Linux development process. Another potential problem is the reactiveness of maintainers. Indeed, some services have no maintainer, but remain in the kernel source tree. This may somewhat artificially increase the number of faults. Still, any such faults can impact anyone who uses the code.

Our study has identified 736 faults in Linux 2.6.33, including RCU faults, some of which have not yet been corrected in the current developer snapshot, `linux-next`. We have submitted a number of patches based on our results.

## Acknowledgments

We thank the anonymous reviewers and our shepherd, Frans Kaashoek, for their feedback. We also thank Emmanuel Cecchet and Willy Zwaenepoel for comments on an earlier version of this paper. This work was partially supported by the Agence Nationale de la Recherche (France) under the contract ANR-09-BLAN-0158-01 and the Danish Research Council for Technology and Production Sciences.

## References

[1] A. Aiken, S. Bugrara, I. Dillig, T. Dillig, B. Hackett, and P. Hawkins. An overview of the Saturn project. In *Proceedings of the 7th ACM SIGPLAN-SIGSOFT Workshop on Program Analysis for Software Tools and Engineering, PASTE'07*, pages 43–48, San Diego, CA, June 2007.

[2] J. Brunel, D. Doligez, R. R. Hansen, J. Lawall, and G. Muller. A foundation for flow-based program matching using temporal logic and model checking. In *The 36th annual ACM SIGPLAN-SIGACT Symposium on Principles of Programming Languages*, pages 114–126, Savannah, GA, USA, Jan. 2009.

[3] How is the department of homeland security involved?, 2009. `http://scan.coverity.com/faq.html#how-department-homeland-security-involved`.

[4] Checkpatch. `http://www.codemonkey.org.uk/projects/checkpatch/`.

[5] A. Chou, J. Yang, B. Chelf, S. Hallem, and D. Engler. An empirical study of operating systems errors. In *Proceedings of the 18th ACM Symposium on Operating System Principles*, pages 73–88, Banff, Canada, Oct. 2001.

[6] Comedi: Linux Control and Mesurement Device Interface. `http://www.comedi.org/`.

[7] J. Corbet. The age of kernel code in various subsystems, Feb. 2010. `http://lwn.net/Articles/374622/`.

[8] J. Corbet. How old is our kernel?, Feb. 2010. `http://lwn.net/Articles/374574/`.

[9] Static source code analysis, static analysis, software quality tools by Coverity Inc. `http://www.coverity.com/`, 2008.

[10] A. Depoutovitch and M. Stumm. Otherworld – giving applications a chance to survive OS kernel crashes. In *ACM EuroSys*, pages 181–194, Paris, France, Apr. 2010.

[11] Fedora project, 2010. `http://fedoraproject.org/`.

[12] J. N. Herder, H. Bos, B. Gras, P. Homburg, and A. S. Tanenbaum. Fault isolation for device drivers. In *2009 IEEE/IFIP International Conference on Dependable Systems and Networks (DSN)*, pages 33–42, Estoril, Portugal, June 2009.

[13] IEEE std 982.2-1988 IEEE guide for the use of IEEE standard dictionary of measures to produce reliable software, 1988.

[14] A. Israeli and D. G. Feitelson. The Linux kernel as a case study in software evolution. *Journal of Systems and Software*, 83(3):485–501, 2010.

[15] J. L. Lawall, J. Brunel, R. R. Hansen, H. Stuart, G. Muller, and N. Palix. WYSIWIB: A declarative approach to finding protocols and bugs in Linux code. In *The 39th Annual IEEE/IFIP International Conference on Dependable Systems and Networks*, pages 43–52, Estoril, Portugal, June 2009.

[16] Z. Li and Y. Zhou. PR-Miner: automatically extracting implicit programming rules and detecting violations in large software code. In *Proceedings of the 10th European Software Engineering Conference held jointly with 13th ACM SIGSOFT International Symposium on Foundations of Software Engineering*, pages 306–315, Lisbon, Portugal, Sept. 2005.

[17] Lkml: The Linux kernel mailing list. `http://lkml.org/`.

[18] S. Lu, S. Park, E. Seo, and Y. Zhou. Learning from mistakes: a comprehensive study on real world concurrency bug characteristics. In *Architectural Support for Programming Languages and Operating Systems (ASPLOS)*, pages 329–339, Seattle, WA, USA, Mar. 2008.

[19] T. J. McCabe. A complexity measure. *IEEE Transactions on Software Engineering*, 2(4):308–320, July 1976.

[20] P. E. McKenney and J. Walpole. Introducing technology into the Linux kernel: a case study. *ACM SIGOPS Operating Systems Review*, 42(5):4–17, 2008.

[21] J. C. Munson and S. G. Elbaum. Code churn: A measure for estimating the impact of code change. In *International Conference Software Maintenance (ICSM)*, pages 24–31, 1998.

[22] N. Nagappan and T. Ball. Use of relative code churn measures to predict system defect density. In *27th International Conference on Software Engineering (ICSE)*, pages 284–292, St. Louis, Missouri, USA, May 2005.

[23] P. Oman and J. Hagemeister. Construction and testing of polynomials predicting software maintainability. *Journal of Systems and Software*, 24(3):251–266, 1994.

[24] Y. Padioleau, J. Lawall, R. R. Hansen, and G. Muller. Documenting and automating collateral evolutions in Linux device drivers. In *EuroSys 2008*, pages 247–260, Glasgow, Scotland, Mar. 2008.

[25] N. Palix, J. Lawall, and G. Muller. Tracking code patterns over multiple software versions with Herodotos. In *Proc. of the ACM International Conference on Aspect-Oriented Software Development, AOSD'10*, pages 169–180, Rennes and Saint Malo, France, Mar. 2010.

[26] N. Palix, J. L. Lawall, and G. Muller. Herodotos: A tool to expose bugs' lives. Research report RR-6984, INRIA, July 2009.

[27] N. Palix, S. Saha, G. Thomas, C. Calvès, J. Lawall, and G. Muller. Database of Faults in Linux: Ten Years Later, Aug. 2010. `http://hal.inria.fr/docs/00/50/92/56/ANNEX/10years.sql.pg_dump`.

[28] N. Palix, S. Saha, G. Thomas, C. Calvès, J. Lawall, and G. Muller. Faults in Linux: Ten years later. Research report RR-7357, INRIA, Aug. 2010.

[29] N. Palix, S. Saha, G. Thomas, C. Calvès, J. Lawall, and G. Muller. Website of Faults in Linux: Ten Years Later, Dec. 2010. `http://faultlinux.lip6.fr/`.

[30] E. S. Raymond. *The Cathedral and the Bazaar: Musings on Linux and Open Source by an Accidental Revolutionary.* O'Reilly & Associates, Inc., 2001.

[31] D. Searls. Sparse, Linus & the Lunatics, Nov. 2004. Available at `http://www.linuxjournal.com/article/7272`.

[32] X. Song, H. Chen, and B. Zang. Why software hangs and what can be done with it. In *International Conference on Dependable Systems and Networks (DSN 2010)*, Chicago, IL, USA, June 2010.

[33] Sparse. `https://sparse.wiki.kernel.org/index.php/Main_Page`.

[34] B. Spencer. Local kernel exploit in /dev/net/tun. `http://grsecurity.net/~spender/cheddar_bay.tgz`.

[35] M. M. Swift, M. Annamalai, B. N. Bershad, and H. M. Levy. Recovering device drivers. *ACM Transactions on Computer Systems*, 24(4):333–360, 2006.

[36] The Kernel Janitors. Smatch, the source matcher, 2010. Available at `http://smatch.sourceforge.net`.

[37] Ubuntu, 2010. `http://www.ubuntu.com/`.

[38] D. Wheeler. Flawfinder home page. Web page: `http://www.dwheeler.com/flawfinder/`, Oct. 2006.

[39] D. A. Wheeler. SLOCCount. `http://www.dwheeler.com/sloccount/`.


## Appendix

***Locking functions:*** {mutex,spin,read,write}_lock, {mutex,spin,read,write}_trylock

***Interrupt disabling functions:*** cli, local_irq_disable

***Functions combining both:*** {read,write,spin}_lock_irq, {read,write,spin}_lock_irqsave, local_irq_save, save_and_cli

# Looking Back on the Language and Hardware Revolutions: Measured Power, Performance, and Scaling *

Hadi Esmaeilzadeh† Ting Cao‡ Xi Yang‡ Stephen M. Blackburn‡ Kathryn S. McKinley§

†University of Washington ‡Australian National University §The University of Texas at Austin

hadianeh@cs.washington.edu {Ting.Cao,Xi.Yang,Steve.Blackburn}@anu.edu.au mckinley@cs.utexas.edu

## Abstract

This paper reports and analyzes *measured* chip power and performance on five process technology generations executing 61 diverse benchmarks with a rigorous methodology. We measure representative Intel IA32 processors with technologies ranging from 130nm to 32nm while they execute sequential and parallel benchmarks written in native and managed languages. During this period, hardware and software changed substantially: (1) hardware vendors delivered chip multiprocessors instead of uniprocessors, and independently (2) software developers increasingly chose managed languages instead of native languages. This quantitative data reveals the extent of some known and previously unobserved hardware and software trends. Two themes emerge.

(I) *Workload:* The power, performance, and energy trends of native workloads do not approximate managed workloads. For example, (a) the SPEC CPU2006 native benchmarks on the i7 (45) and i5 (32) draw significantly less power than managed or scalable native benchmarks; and (b) managed runtimes exploit parallelism even when running single-threaded applications. The results recommend architects always include native and managed workloads when designing and evaluating energy efficient hardware.

(II) *Architecture:* Clock scaling, microarchitecture, simultaneous multithreading, and chip multiprocessors each elicit a huge variety of power, performance, and energy responses. This variety and the difficulty of obtaining power measurements recommends exposing on-chip power meters and when possible structure specific power meters for cores, caches, and other structures. Just as hardware event counters provide a quantitative grounding for performance innovations, power meters are necessary for optimizing energy.

***Categories and Subject Descriptors*** D.3.4 [*Programming Languages*]: Processors—Native & Managed Languages; Performance; Power

***General Terms*** Experimentation, Languages, Performance, Power, Measurement

* This work is supported by ARC DP0666059 and NSF CSR-0917191. Any opinions, findings and conclusions expressed herein are the authors' and do not necessarily reflect those of the sponsors.



*ASPLOS'11,* March 5–11, 2011, Newport Beach, California, USA.



## 1. Introduction

Quantitative performance analysis serves as a foundation for computer system design and innovation. In their now classic paper [9, 10], Emer and Clark noted that "A lack of detailed timing information impairs efforts to improve performance." They pioneered the quantitative approach by characterizing the instruction mix and cycles per instruction on real timesharing workloads. In fact, they surprised their reviewers by demonstrating the VAX-11/780 was a .5 MIPS machine, not a 1 MIPS machine! Using this data, their team, academics, and other industrial architects subsequently used a more principled approach to improving performance, or in other words [10]: "Boy, you ruin all our fun—you have data." This paper extends the quantitative approach to measured power on modern workloads. This work is timely because the past decade heralded the era of power and energy (power × execution time) constrained computer architecture design. A lack of detailed power measurements is impairing efforts to reduce energy consumption on real modern workloads.

From 2003 to 2010, technology shrank from 130nm to 32nm, following Moore's law. However, physical on-chip power limits and design complexity forced architects to stop using clock scaling as the primary means of improving performance. In this period, Dennard scaling slowed significantly [6]; reductions in process technology are no longer yielding both power and performance gains at historical rates; and wire delay hit its physical limit. For example, single-cycle cross-chip access times are not possible with typical chip areas. Because of technology constraints, computing entered the Chip MultiProcessor (CMP) era, in which architects are delivering more processors on each chip. On a broader scale, explosive demand for power and energy efficient large-scale computing [13] and mobile devices continues unabated. Consequently, power is a first-order design constraint in all market segments.

A commensurate explosion of software applications make these devices useful. Demands such as complexity management, reliability, correctness, security, mobility, portability, and ubiquity have pushed developers in many market segments away from native compiled ahead-of-time programming languages. Developers are increasingly choosing *managed* programming languages, which provide safe pointer disciplines, garbage collection (automatic memory management), extensive standard libraries, and portability through dynamic just-in-time compilation. For example, web services are increasingly using PHP on the server side and JavaScript on the client side. Java and its virtual machine are now mature technologies and are the dominant choice in markets as diverse as financial software and cell phone applications. This software trend, which is independent of the CMP hardware trend, motivates including managed workloads in architecture analysis.

This paper examines power, performance, and scaling in this period of software and hardware changes. We use eight representative Intel IA32 processors from five technology generations introduced in 2003 through 2010 that range from 130nm to 32nm. These processors have an isolated processor power supply on the motherboard with a stable voltage. We use a Hall effect sensor to measure the power supply current, and hence processor power. We calibrate and validate our sensor data. We find that actual power measurements vary widely with benchmarks. Furthermore, relative performance, power, and energy are not well predicted by core count, clock speed, or reported Thermal Design Power (TDP), i.e., the nominal amount of power the chip is designed to dissipate without exceeding the maximum junction temperature.

We execute 61 diverse sequential and parallel benchmarks written in native C, C++, and Fortran languages and in the managed Java language. We draw these benchmarks from SPEC CINT2006, SPEC CFP2006, PARSEC, SPECjvm, DaCapo 06-10-MR2, DaCapo 9.12, and pjbb2005. We use Java as our representative of managed languages because it is the most widely used managed language [33], has publicly available real-world sophisticated benchmarks, and has mature Virtual Machine (VM) technology. We classify the benchmarks into four groups and weight the groups equally: native non-scalable benchmarks (Native Non-scalable), native scalable benchmarks (Native Scalable), Java non-scalable benchmarks (Java Non-scalable), and Java scalable benchmarks (Java Scalable).

We explore the energy impact of a variety of hardware features using hardware configuration to perform controlled experiments. We explore the effects of simultaneous multithreading (SMT), core count (CMP), clock frequency, die shrink, gross microarchitectural changes, Turbo Boost,[1] software parallelism, and workload. We perform a historical analysis and a Pareto energy efficiency analysis, which identifies the most power and performance efficient designs in this architecture configuration space of real processors. We make all our data publicly available to encourage others to use it and perform further analysis. The individual benchmark results, experiments, and analysis described in this paper are in the ACM Digital Library in csv and excel formats as a companion to this paper [12]. To the best of our knowledge, this study is the first systematic exploration of power and performance across technology generations using measured processor power, controlled configuration, and diverse workloads.

This quantitative data reveals the extent, with precision and depth, of some known workload and hardware trends and some previously unobserved trends. We call out four workload and nine architecture findings from our data and analysis. Two themes emerge.

**Workload Findings** *The power, performance, and energy trends of native workloads do not approximate managed workloads well.* For example, (a) the SPEC CPU2006 native benchmarks executing on the i7 (45) and i5 (32) are outliers with respect to power because they draw significantly less power than managed or scalable native benchmarks; (b) the addition of SMT *slows down* non-scalable Java on the Pentium 4 (130), and (c) managed runtimes exploit parallelism, even when managed applications do not. For example, single-threaded Java workloads run on average about 10% faster and up to 60% faster on two cores when compared to one core. This result is not due to better code from more aggressive just-in-time compilation on unutilized cores. This speedup comes directly from parallelism in the VM and reductions in VM and application interference when the VM performs its computation and data accesses elsewhere. Native single-threaded workloads *never* experience performance or energy improvements from CMPs or SMT, and sometimes consume a small amount of additional power on CMPs. While measuring and simulating managed workloads does require additional methodologies, prior work resolves them (see Sections 2 and 5). *These results recommend that architects always include native and managed workloads when designing and evaluating energy efficient designs.*

**Architectural Findings** *A huge variety of processor power, performance, and energy responses due to features such as clock scaling, microarchitecture, Turbo Boost, SMT, and CMP reveal a complex and poorly understood energy efficiency design space.* Consider these three sample findings. (a) Halving the clock rate of the i5 (32) increases its energy consumption around 4%, whereas it decreases the energy consumption of the i7 (45) and Core 2D (45) by around 60%, i.e., running the i5 (32) at its *peak* clock rate is as energy efficient as running it as its lowest, whereas running the i7 (45) and Core 2D (45) at their *lowest* clock rate is substantially more energy efficient than their peak. (b) Two pairs of our processors observe the effect of a die-shrink. On the Core and Nehalem families, the die shrink is remarkably effective at reducing energy consumption, *even when controlling for clock speed.* (c) We disable and enable SMT and find that on more modern processors it is a remarkably energy efficient mechanism for exploiting software parallelism. Although it was originally designed for wide-issue out-of-order processors, SMT provides the most energy benefits for the dual-issue in-order Atom (45). Modern processors include power management techniques that monitor power sensors to minimize power usage and boost performance, for example. However, these sensors are not currently exposed. *The wide variety of performance and power responses to workload and architectural features, and the difficulty of obtaining power measurements recommends exposing on-chip power meters and when possible, structure-specific power meters for cores, caches, and other structures. Coupling these measurements with hardware event performance counters will provide a quantitative basis for optimizing power and energy for future system design.*

Measurement is key to understanding and optimization.

## 2. Methodology

This section describes our benchmarks, compilers, Java Virtual Machines, operating system, hardware, power measurement methodologies, and performance measurement methodologies.

### 2.1 Benchmarks

The following methodological choices in part prescribe our choice of benchmarks. (1) *Individual benchmark performance and average power:* We measure execution time and average power of individual benchmarks in isolation and aggregate them by workload type. While multi-programmed workload measurements, such as SPECrate can be valuable, the methodological and analysis challenges they raise are beyond the scope of this paper. (2) *Language and parallelism:* We systematically explore native / managed, and scalable / non-scalable workloads. We create four benchmark groups in the cross product and weight each group equally.

**Native Non-scalable**: C, C++ and Fortran single-threaded benchmarks from SPEC CPU2006.

**Native Scalable**: Multithreaded C and C++ benchmarks from PARSEC.

**Java Non-scalable**: Single and multithreaded benchmarks that do not scale well from SPECjvm, DaCapo 06-10-MR2, DaCapo 9.12, and pjbb2005.

**Java Scalable**: Multithreaded benchmarks from DaCapo 9.12, selected because their performance scales similarly to Native Scalable on the i7 (45).

Native and managed applications embody different tradeoffs between performance, reliability, portability, and deployment. In this

[1] Intel Turbo Boost technology automatically increases frequency beyond the default frequency when the chip is operating below power, current, and temperature thresholds [19].

| Grp | Src | Name | Time | Description |
|---|---|---|---|---|
| Native Non-scalable | | perlbench | 1037 | Perl programming language |
| | | bzip2 | 1563 | bzip2 Compression |
| | | gcc | 851 | C optimizing compiler |
| | | mcf | 894 | Combinatorial opt/singledepot vehicle scheduling |
| | | gobmk | 1113 | AI: Go game |
| | | hmmer | 1024 | Search a gene sequence database |
| | SI | sjeng | 1315 | AI: tree search & pattern recognition |
| | | libquantum | 629 | Physics / Quantum Computing |
| | | h264ref | 1533 | H.264/AVC video compression |
| | | omnetpp | 905 | Ethernet network simulation based on OMNeT++ |
| | | astar | 1154 | Portable 2D path-finding library |
| | | xalancbmk | 787 | XSLT processor for transforming XML |
| | | gamess | 3505 | Quantum chemical computations |
| | | milc | 640 | Physics/quantum chromodynamics (QCD) |
| | | zeusmp | 1541 | Physics/Magnetohydrodynamics based on ZEUS-MP |
| | | gromacs | 983 | Molecular dynamics simulation |
| | | cactusADM | 1994 | Cactus and BenchADM physics/relativity kernels |
| | | leslie3d | 1512 | Linear-Eddy Model in 3D computational fluid dynamics |
| | | namd | 1225 | Parallel simulation of large biomolecular systems |
| | SF | dealII | 832 | PDEs with adaptive finite element method |
| | | soplex | 1024 | Simplex linear program solver |
| | | povray | 636 | Ray-tracer |
| | | calculix | 1130 | Finite element code for linear and nonlinear 3D structural applications |
| | | GemsFDTD | 1648 | Solves the Maxwell equations in 3D in the time domain |
| | | tonto | 1439 | Quantum crystallography |
| | | lbm | 1298 | Lattice Boltzmann Method for incompressible fluids |
| | | sphinx3 | 2007 | Speech recognition |
| Native Scalable | | blackscholes | 482 | Prices options with Black-Scholes PDE |
| | | bodytrack | 471 | Tracks a markerless human body |
| | | canneal | 301 | Minimizes the routing cost of a chip design with cache-aware simulated annealing |
| | | facesim | 1230 | Simulates human face motions |
| | PA | ferret | 738 | Image search |
| | | fluidanimate | 812 | Fluid motion physics for realtime animation with SPH algorithm |
| | | raytrace | 1970 | Uses physical simulation for visualization |
| | | streamcluster | 629 | Computes an approximation for the optimal clustering of a stream of data points |
| | | swaptions | 612 | Prices a portfolio of swaptions with the Heath-Jarrow-Morton framework |
| | | vips | 297 | Applies transformations to an image |
| | | x264 | 265 | MPEG-4 AVC / H.264 video encoder |
| Java Non-scalable | | compress | 5.3 | Lempel-Ziv compression |
| | | jess | 1.4 | Java expert system shell |
| | | db | 6.8 | Small data management program |
| | SJ | javac | 3.0 | The JDK 1.0.2 Java compiler |
| | | mpegaudio | 3.1 | MPEG-3 audio stream decoder |
| | | mtrt | 0.8 | Dual-threaded raytracer |
| | | jack | 2.4 | Parser generator with lexical analysis |
| | D6 | antlr | 2.9 | Parser and translator generator |
| | | bloat | 7.6 | Java bytecode optimization and analysis tool |
| | | avrora | 11.3 | Simulates the AVR microcontroller |
| | | batik | 4.0 | Scalable Vector Graphics (SVG) toolkit |
| | | fop | 1.8 | Output-independent print formatter |
| | D9 | h2 | 14.4 | An SQL relational database engine in Java |
| | | jython | 8.5 | Python interpreter in Java |
| | | pmd | 6.9 | Source code analyzer for Java |
| | | tradebeans | 18.4 | Tradebeans Daytrader benchmark |
| | | luindex | 2.4 | A text indexing tool |
| | JB | pjbb2005 | 10.6 | Transaction processing, based on SPECjbb2005 |
| Java Scalable | | eclipse | 50.5 | Integrated development environment |
| | | lusearch | 7.9 | Text search tool |
| | D9 | sunflow | 19.4 | Photo-realistic rendering system |
| | | tomcat | 8.6 | Tomcat servlet container |
| | | xalan | 6.9 | XSLT processor for XML documents |

**Table 1.** Benchmark Groups; Source: SI: SPEC CINT2006, SF: SPEC CFP2006, PA: PARSEC, SJ: SPECjvm, D6: DaCapo 06-10-MR2, D9: DaCapo 9.12, and JB: pjbb2005; Source, Name, and reference run times in seconds.

| | Execution Time | | Power | |
|---|---|---|---|---|
| | average | max | average | max |
| Average | 1.2% | 2.2% | 1.5% | 7.1% |
| Native Non-scalable | 0.9% | 2.6% | 2.1% | 13.9% |
| Native Scalable | 0.7% | 4.0% | 0.6% | 2.5% |
| Java Non-scalable | 1.6% | 2.8% | 1.5% | 7.7% |
| Java Scalable | 1.8% | 3.7% | 1.7% | 7.9% |

**Table 2.** Aggregate 95% confidence intervals for measured execution time and power, showing average and maximum error across all processor configurations, and all benchmarks.

setting, it is impossible to meaningfully separate language from workload. We therefore offer no commentary on the *virtue* of a language choice, but rather, reflect the measured reality of two workload classes that are ubiquitous in today's software landscape.

We draw 61 benchmarks from six suites to populate these groups. We weight each group equally in our aggregate measurements; see Section 2.6 for more details on aggregation. We use Java to represent the broader class of managed languages. Table 1 shows the benchmarks, their groupings, the suite of origin, the *reference running time* (see Section 2.6) to which we normalize our results, and a short description. In the case of native benchmarks, all single-threaded benchmarks are non-scalable and all parallel multithreaded native benchmarks are scalable on up to eight hardware contexts, the maximum we explore. By scalable, we mean that adding hardware contexts improves performance. Bienia et al. show that the PARSEC benchmarks scale up to 8 hardware contexts [2]. To create a comparable group of scalable Java programs, we put multithreaded Java programs that do not scale well in the non-scalable category.

***Native Non-scalable Benchmarks*** We use 27 C, C++, and Fortran codes from the SPEC CPU2006 suite [31] for Native Non-scalable and all are *single-threaded*. The 12 SPEC CINT benchmarks represent compute-intensive integer applications that contain sophisticated control flow logic, and the 15 SPEC CFP benchmarks represent compute-intensive floating-point applications. These native benchmarks are compiled ahead-of-time. We chose Intel's *icc* compiler because we found that it consistently generated better performing code than *gcc*. We compiled all of the Native Non-scalable benchmarks with version 11.1 of the 32-bit Intel compiler suite using the `-o3` optimization flag, which performs aggressive scalar optimizations. This flag does not include any automatic parallelization. We compiled each benchmark once, using the default Intel compiler configuration, without setting any microarchitecture-specific optimizations, and used the *same* binary on all platforms. We exclude 410.bwaves and 481.wrf because they failed to execute when compiled with the Intel compiler. Three executions are prescribed by SPEC. We report the mean of these three successive executions. Table 2 shows that aggregate 95% confidence intervals are low for execution time and power: 1.2% and 1.5% respectively.

***Native Scalable Benchmarks*** The Native Scalable benchmarks consists of 11 C and C++ benchmarks from the PARSEC suite [2]. The benchmarks are intended to be diverse and forward looking parallel algorithms. All but one uses POSIX threads and one contains some assembly code. We exclude freqmine because it is not amenable to our scaling experiments, in part, because it does not use POSIX threads. We exclude dedup from our study because it has a large working set that exceeds the amount of memory available on the 2003 Pentium 4 (130). The multithreaded PARSEC benchmarks include *gcc* compiler configurations, which worked correctly. The icc compiler failed to produce correct code for many of the PARSEC benchmarks with similar configurations. We used the PARSEC default gcc build scripts with gcc version 4.4.1. The gcc scripts use `-O3` optimization. We leave systematic comparisons using both icc and gcc to future work. We report the mean of five successive executions of each benchmark. We use five executions, which as Table 2 shows, gives low aggregate 95% confidence intervals for execution time and power: 0.9% and 2.1% on average.

***Java Non-scalable Benchmarks*** The Java Non-scalable group includes benchmarks from SPECjvm, both releases of DaCapo, and pjbb2005 that do not scale well. It includes both single-threaded and multithreaded benchmarks. SPECjvm is intended to be representative of client-side Java programs. Although the SPECjvm benchmarks are over ten years old and Blackburn et al. have shown that they are simple and have a very small instruction cache and data footprint [4], many researchers still use them. The DaCapo Java benchmarks are intended to be diverse, forward-looking, and non-trivial [4, 32]. The benchmarks come from major open source projects under active development. Researchers have not reported extensively on the 2009 release, but it was designed to expose richer behavior and concurrency on large working sets. We exclude tradesoap because its heavy use of sockets suffered from timeouts on the slowest machines. We use pjbb2005, which is a fixed-workload variant of SPECjbb2005 [30] that holds the workload, instead of time, constant. We configure pjbb2005 with 8 warehouses and 10,000 transactions per warehouse. We include the following multithreaded benchmarks in Java Non-scalable: pjbb2005, avrora, batik, fop, h2, jython, pmd, and tradebeans. As we show below, these applications do not scale well. Section 2.2 discusses the measurement methodology for Java. Table 2 indicates low aggregate 95% confidence intervals for execution time and power: 1.6% and 1.5%.

***Java Scalable Benchmarks*** We include the multithreaded Java benchmarks in Java Scalable that scale similarly to the Native Scalable benchmarks. Figure 1 shows the scalability of the multithreaded Java benchmarks. The five most scalable are: sunflow, xalan, tomcat, lusearch and eclipse, all from DaCapo 9.12. Together, they speed up on average by a factor of 3.4 given eight hardware contexts compared to one context on the i7 (45). Our Native Scalable benchmarks scale better on this hardware, improving by a factor of 3.8. Although eliminating lusearch and eclipse would improve average scalability, it would reduce the number of benchmarks to three, which we believe is insufficient. Table 2 shows low aggregate 95% confidence intervals for execution time and power: 1.8% and 1.7%.

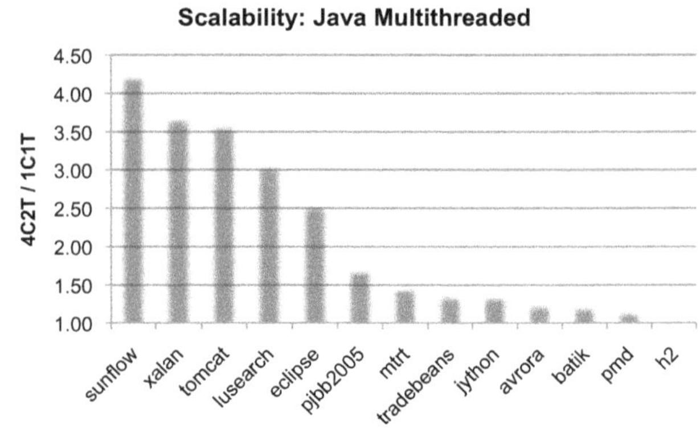


**Figure 1.** Scalability of Java multithreaded benchmarks on i7 (45).

## 2.2 Java Virtual Machines and Measurement Methodology

We use Java as the managed language representative in part because of its mature Java Virtual Machine (JVM) technology, which includes high performance garbage collection, profiling, and dynamic optimizations. We report Oracle (Sun) HotSpot build 16.3-b01 Java 1.6.0 Virtual Machine. We did some additional experiments with Oracle JRockit build R28.0.0-679-130297 and IBM J9 build pxi3260sr8. Their average performance is similar to HotSpot, but individual benchmarks vary substantially. We observe aggregate power differences of up to 10% between JVMs [12]. Exploring the influence of the native compilers and JVMs on power and energy is an interesting avenue for future research.

To measure both Java Non-scalable and Java Scalable, we follow the recommended methodologies for measuring Java [5, 14]. We use the `-server` flag and fix the heap size at a generous 3× the minimum required for each benchmark. We did not set any other JVM flags. We report the fifth iteration of each benchmark within a single invocation of the JVM to capture steady state behavior. This methodology avoids class loading and heavy compilation activity that often dominates the early phases of execution. The fifth iteration may still have a small amount of compiler activity, but has sufficient time to create optimized frequently executed code. We perform this process twenty times and report the mean. Table 2 reports the measured error. We require twenty invocations to generate a statistically stable result because the adaptive JIT compilation and garbage collection induce non-determinism. In contrast to the compiled ahead-of-time native configurations, Java compilers may dynamically produce microarchitecture-specific code.

## 2.3 Operating System

We perform all the experiments using 32-bit Ubuntu 9.10 Karmic with the 2.6.31 Linux kernel. We use a 32-bit OS and compiler builds because the 2003 Pentium 4 (130) does not support 64-bit. Exploring the impact of word size is also interesting future work.

## 2.4 Hardware Platforms

We use eight IA32 processors, manufactured by Intel using four process technologies (130nm, 65nm, 45nm, and 32nm), representing four microarchitectures (NetBurst, Core, Bonnell, and Nehalem). Table 3 lists processor characteristics: uniquely identifying sSpec number, release date / price; CMP and SMT (*n*C*m*T means *n* cores, *m* SMT threads per core), die characteristics; and memory configuration. Intel sells a large range of processors for each microarchitecture—the processors we use are just samples within that space. Most of our processors are mid-range desktop processors. The release date and release price in Table 3 provides the context regarding Intel's placement of each processor in the market. The two Atoms and the Core 2Q (65) *Kentsfield* are extreme points at the bottom and top of the market respectively.

## 2.5 Power Measurements

In contrast to whole system power studies [3, 20, 22], we measure on-chip power. Whole system studies measure AC current to an entire computer, typically with a clamp ammeter. To measure on-chip power, we must isolate and measure DC current to the processor on the motherboard, which cannot be done with a clamp ammeter. We use *Pololu's ACS714* current sensor board, following prior methodology [26]. The board is a carrier for *Allegro's* ±*5A ACS714* Hall effect-based linear current sensor. The sensor accepts a bidirectional current input with a magnitude up to $5A$. The output is an analog voltage ($185mV/A$) centered at $2.5V$ with a typical error of less than 1.5%. The sensor on i7 (45), which has the highest power consumption, accepts currents with magnitudes up to $30A$.

Each of our experimental machines has an isolated power supply for the processor on the motherboard, which we verified by examining the motherboard specification and confirmed empirically. This requirement precludes measuring for example the Pentium M, which would have given us a 90nm processor. We place the sensors on the $12V$ power line that supplies only the processor. We experimentally measured voltage and found it was very stable, varying less than 1%. We send the measured values from the current sen-

| Processor | µArch | Processor | sSpec | Release Date | Price USD | CMP SMT | LLC B | Clock GHz | nm | Trans M | Die $mm^2$ | VID Range V | TDP (W) | FSB MHz | B/W GB/s | DRAM Model |
|---|---|---|---|---|---|---|---|---|---|---|---|---|---|---|---|---|
| Pentium 4 | NetBurst | Northwood | SL6WF | May '03 | — | 1C2T | 512K | 2.4 | 130 | 55 | 131 | — | 66 | 800 | — | DDR-400 |
| Core 2 Duo E6600 | Core | Conroe | SL9S8 | Jul '06 | $316 | 2C1T | 4M | 2.4 | 65 | 291 | 143 | 0.85 - 1.50 | 65 | 1066 | — | DDR2-800 |
| Core 2 Quad Q6600 | Core | Kentsfield | SL9UM | Jan '07 | $851 | 4C1T | 8M | 2.4 | 65 | 582 | 286 | 0.85 - 1.50 | 105 | 1066 | — | DDR2-800 |
| Core i7 920 | Nehalem | Bloomfield | SLBCH | Nov '08 | $284 | 4C2T | 8M | 2.7 | 45 | 731 | 263 | 0.80 - 1.38 | 130 | — | 25.6 | DDR3-1066 |
| Atom 230 | Bonnell | Diamondville | SLB6Z | Jun '08 | $29 | 1C2T | 512K | 1.7 | 45 | 47 | 26 | 0.90 - 1.16 | 4 | 533 | — | DDR2-800 |
| Core 2 Duo E7600 | Core | Wolfdale | SLGTD | May '09 | $133 | 2C1T | 3M | 3.1 | 45 | 228 | 82 | 0.85 - 1.36 | 65 | 1066 | — | DDR2-800 |
| Atom D510 | Bonnell | Pineview | SLBLA | Dec '09 | $63 | 2C2T | 1M | 1.7 | 45 | 176 | 87 | 0.80 - 1.17 | 13 | 665 | — | DDR2-800 |
| Core i5 670 | Nehalem | Clarkdale | SLBLT | Jan '10 | $284 | 2C2T | 4M | 3.4 | 32 | 382 | 81 | 0.65 - 1.40 | 73 | — | 21.0 | DDR3-1333 |

**Table 3.** The eight experimental processors and key specifications.

| | Speedup Over Reference | | | | | | | | Power (W) | | | | | | | |
|---|---|---|---|---|---|---|---|---|---|---|---|---|---|---|---|---|
| Processor | NN | NS | JN | JS | $Avg^w$ | $Avg^b$ | Min | Max | NN | NS | JN | JS | $Avg^w$ | $Avg^b$ | Min | Max |
| Pentium 4 | 0.91 *6* | 0.79 *7* | 0.80 *6* | 0.75 *7* | 0.82 *6* | 0.85 *6* | 0.51 *6* | 1.25 *6* | 42.1 *7* | 43.5 *6* | 45.1 *7* | 45.7 *6* | 44.1 *6* | 43.5 *7* | 34.5 *7* | 50.0 *6* |
| Core 2 Duo E6600 | 2.02 *5* | 2.10 *5* | 1.99 *5* | 2.04 *5* | 2.04 *5* | 2.03 *5* | 1.40 *4* | 2.85 *5* | 24.3 *5* | 26.6 *4* | 26.2 *5* | 28.5 *4* | 26.4 *5* | 25.6 *5* | 21.4 *5* | 32.3 *4* |
| Core 2 Quad Q6600 | 2.04 *4* | 3.62 *3* | 2.04 *4* | 3.09 *3* | 2.70 *3* | 2.41 *4* | 1.39 *5* | 4.67 *3* | 50.7 *8* | 61.7 *8* | 55.3 *8* | 64.6 *8* | 58.1 *8* | 55.2 *8* | 45.6 *8* | 77.3 *7* |
| Core i7 920 | 3.11 *2* | 6.25 *1* | 3.00 *2* | 5.49 *1* | 4.46 *1* | 3.84 *1* | 2.16 *2* | 7.60 *1* | 27.2 *6* | 60.4 *7* | 37.5 *6* | 62.8 *7* | 47.0 *7* | 39.1 *6* | 23.4 *6* | 89.2 *8* |
| Atom 230 | 0.49 *8* | 0.52 *8* | 0.53 *8* | 0.52 *8* | 0.52 *8* | 0.51 *8* | 0.39 *8* | 0.75 *8* | 2.3 *1* | 2.5 *1* | 2.3 *1* | 2.4 *1* | 2.4 *1* | 2.3 *1* | 1.9 *1* | 2.7 *1* |
| Core 2 Duo E7600 | 2.48 *3* | 2.76 *4* | 2.49 *3* | 2.44 *4* | 2.54 *4* | 2.53 *3* | 1.45 *3* | 3.71 *4* | 19.1 *3* | 21.1 *3* | 20.5 *3* | 22.6 *3* | 20.8 *3* | 20.2 *3* | 15.8 *3* | 26.8 *3* |
| Atom D510 | 0.53 *7* | 0.96 *6* | 0.61 *7* | 0.86 *6* | 0.74 *7* | 0.66 *7* | 0.41 *7* | 1.17 *7* | 3.7 *2* | 5.3 *2* | 4.5 *2* | 5.1 *2* | 4.7 *2* | 4.3 *2* | 3.4 *2* | 5.9 *2* |
| Core i5 670 | 3.31 *1* | 4.46 *2* | 3.18 *1* | 4.26 *2* | 3.80 *2* | 3.56 *2* | 2.39 *1* | 5.42 *2* | 19.6 *4* | 29.2 *5* | 24.7 *4* | 29.5 *5* | 25.7 *4* | 23.6 *4* | 16.5 *4* | 38.2 *5* |

**Table 4.** Average performance and power characteristics. The rank for each measure is indicated in small italics.

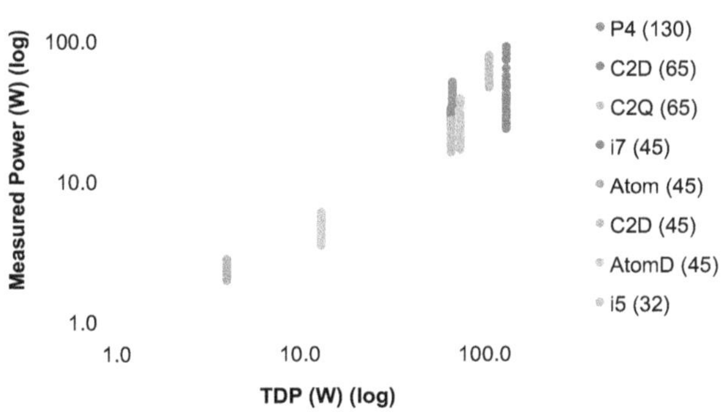


**Figure 2.** Measured benchmark power for each processor.

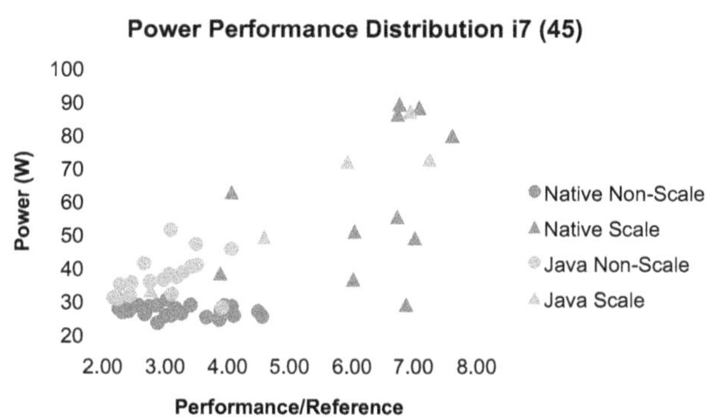


**Figure 3.** Benchmark power and performance on the i7 (45).

sor to the measured machine's USB port using *Sparkfun's Atmel AVR Stick*, which is a simple data-logging device. We use a data-sampling rate of 50Hz. We execute each benchmark, log its measured power values, and then compute the average power consumption over the duration of the benchmark.

To calibrate the meters, we use a current source to provide 28 reference currents between 300mA and 3A, and for each meter record the output value (an integer in the range 400-503). We compute linear fits for each of the sensors. Each sensor has an $R^2$ value of 0.999 or better, which indicates an excellent fit [12]. The measurement error for any given sample is about 1%, which reflects the fidelity of the quantization (103 points).

***Thermal Design Power (TDP)*** TDP is the nominal thermal design power for a processor, i.e., the nominal amount of power the chip is designed to dissipate without exceeding the maximum transistor junction temperature. Table 3 indicates the TDP for each of our processors. Because measuring real processor power is difficult and TDP is readily available, TDP is often substituted for real measured power. Figure 2 shows that this substitution is problematic. It plots measured power for each benchmark on each stock processor as a function of TDP, on a logarithmic scale. Note that for these benchmarks TDP is strictly higher than actual power, and that measured power varies greatly among the benchmarks. This variation is highest on the i7 (45) and i5 (32), which likely reflects the advanced power management integrated into these processors [29]. For example, on the i7 (45), measured power varies between 23W for 471.omnetpp and 89W for fluidanimate! The smallest variation between maximum and minimum is on the Atom (45), but even this is around 30%. Manufacturers sometimes report the same TDP for a family of microarchitectures. For example, Core 2D (65) and Core 2D (45) have the same TDP of 65W as shown in Table 3, yet their measured power differs by around 40-50% as shown in Figure 2. In summary, while TDP loosely correlates with power consumption, it *does not* provide a good estimate for: (1) maximum power consumption of individual processors; (2) comparing among processors; or (3) approximating benchmark-specific power consumption.

### 2.6 Reference Execution Time, Reference Energy, and Aggregation

As is standard, we weight each benchmark equally within each workload group, since the execution time of the benchmark is not necessarily an indicator of benchmark importance. Furthermore, we want to represent each of our benchmark groups equally. These goals require (1) a reference execution time and a reference energy value for normalization, and (2) an average of the benchmarks in each workload group. Since the average power of a benchmark is not directly biased by execution time, we use it directly. We also normalize energy to a reference, since *energy* = *power* × *time*.

Table 1 shows the reference running time we use to normalize the execution time and energy results. To avoid biasing performance measurements to the strengths or weaknesses of one architecture, we normalize individual benchmark execution times to its average execution time executing on four architectures. We choose the Pentium 4 (130), Core 2D (65), Atom (45), and i5 (32) to capture all four microarchitectures and all four technology generations in this study. The reference energy is the average power on these four processors times the average runtime. Given a power and time measurement, we compute energy and then normalize it to the reference energy.

Table 1 shows that the native workloads tend to execute for much longer than the managed workloads. Measuring their code bases is complicated because of the heavy use of libraries by the managed languages and by PARSEC. However, some native benchmarks are tiny and many PARSEC codes are fewer than 3000 lines of non-comment code. These estimates show that the size of the native and managed application code bases alone (excluding libraries) does not explain the longer execution times. There is no evidence that native execution times are due to more sophisticated applications; instead these longer execution times are likely due to more repetition.

The averages equally weight each of the four benchmark groups. We report results for each group by taking the arithmetic mean of the benchmarks within the group. We use the mean of the four groups for the overall average. This aggregation avoids bias due to the varying number of benchmarks within each group (from 5 to 27). Table 4 shows the measured performance and power for each of the processors and each of the benchmark groups. The table indicates the weighted average ($Avg^{w}$), which we use throughout the paper, and for comparison, the simple average of the benchmarks ($Avg^{b}$). The table also records the highest and lowest performance and power measures seen on each of the processors.

### 2.7 Benchmark Power / Performance Diversity

Figure 3 shows the range of power and performance among our benchmarks and among our workload groups. Native / managed is differentiated by color and scalable / non-scalable is differentiated by shape for each benchmark. The graph plots performance of the i7 (45) normalized to the reference performance on the x-axis, and power on the y-axis. Unsurprisingly, the scalable benchmarks perform the best and consume the most power, since the i7 (45) has eight hardware contexts. Non-scalable benchmarks however exhibit a wide range of performance and power characteristics as well. Overall, the benchmarks exhibit a diversity of power and performance characteristics.

### 2.8 Processor Configuration Methodology

We evaluate the eight stock processors and configure them for a total of 45 processor configurations. We produce power and performance data for each benchmark that corresponds to Figure 3 for each configuration [12]. To explore the influence of architectural features, we control for clock speed and hardware contexts. We selectively down-clock the processors, disable cores, disable simultaneous multithreading (SMT), and disable Turbo Boost [19]. Intel markets SMT as Hyper-Threading [18]. The stock configurations of Pentium 4 (130), Atom (45), Atom D (45), i7 (45), and i5 (32) include SMT (Table 3). The stock configurations of the i7 (45) and i5 (32) include Turbo Boost, which automatically increases frequency beyond the base operating frequency when the core is operating below power, current, and temperature thresholds [19]. We control each variable via the BIOS. We experimented with operating system configuration, which is far more convenient, but it was not sufficiently reliable. For example, operating system scaling of hardware contexts often caused power consumption to increase as hardware resources were decreased! Extensive investigation revealed a bug in the Linux kernel [23]. We use all the means at our disposal to isolate the effect of various architectural features using stock hardware, but often the precise semantics are undocumented. Notwithstanding such limitations, these processor configurations help quantitatively explore how a number of features influence power and performance in real processors.

## 3. Feature Analysis

We organize the results into two sections. This first section explores the energy impact of hardware features through controlled experiments. The second section explores historical trends and performs an energy and performance Pareto efficiency analysis at the 45nm technology node. We present two pairs of graphs for feature analysis experiments as shown in Figure 4 for example. The top graph compares relative power, performance, and energy as an average of the four workload groups. The bottom graph breaks down energy by workload group. In these graphs, higher is better for performance. Lower is better for power and energy. Because of the volume of data and analysis, we cannot present all our data and sometimes refer to data that we gathered, but do not present. In these cases, we cite the complete, on line data as appropriate [12]. We organize the analysis by calling out, labeling, and numbering summary points as ARCHITECTURE FINDINGS and WORKLOAD FINDINGS.

### 3.1 Chip Multiprocessors

We measure the effect of enabling one or two cores. We disable Simultaneous Multithreading (SMT) to maximally expose thread-level parallelism to the Chip MultiProcessor (CMP) hardware feature. We also disable Turbo Boost because its power and performance behavior is affected by the number of idle cores. (Section 3.6 explores Turbo Boost.) Figure 4(a) shows the average power, performance, and energy effects of moving from one core to two cores for the i7 (45) and i5 (32) processors. Figure 4(b) breaks down the energy effect as a function of benchmark group. While average energy is reduced by 9% on the i5 (32), it is increased by 12% on the i7 (45). Figure 4(a) shows that the source of this difference is that the i7 (45) experiences twice the power overhead for enabling a core as the i5 (32), while producing roughly the same performance improvement.

> ARCHITECTURE FINDING 1. *When comparing one core to two, enabling a core is not consistently energy efficient.*

Figure 4(b) shows that Native Non-scalable and Java Non-scalable suffer the most energy overhead with the addition of another core on the i7 (45). As expected, performance for Native Non-scalable is unaffected [12]. However, turning on an additional core for Native Non-scalable leads to a power increase of 4% and 14% respectively for the i5 (32) and i7 (45), translating to energy overheads.

More interesting is that Java Non-scalable does not incur energy overhead on the i5 (32). Careful examination reveals that the *single-threaded* Java Non-scalable experience performance gains from CMP on both processors. Figure 6 shows the scalability of the single-threaded subset of Java Non-scalable on the i7 (45), with SMT disabled, comparing one and two cores. We were very surprised that most of the single-threaded Java workloads exhibit measurable speedups with a second core. On the i5 (32), the Java speedups offset the power overhead of enabling additional cores. Although these Java benchmarks themselves are single-threaded, the JVMs on which they execute are not.

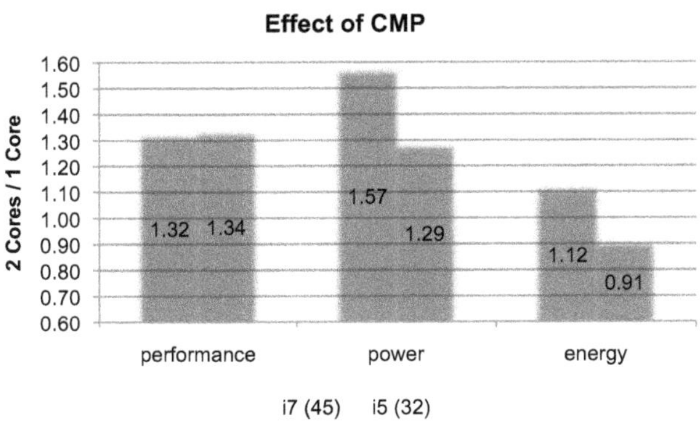


(a) Average impact of doubling cores.

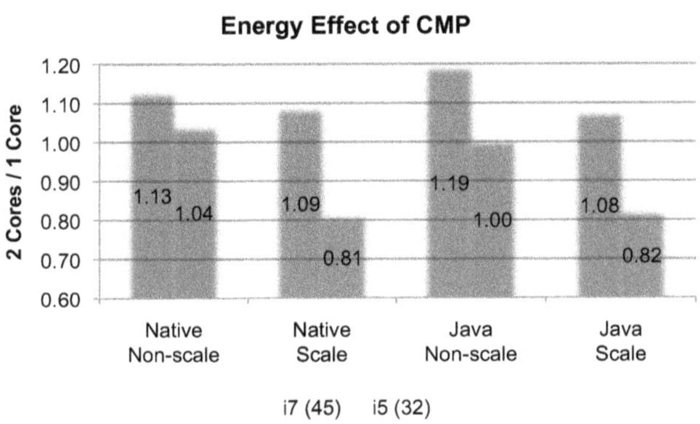


(b) Workload energy impact of doubling cores.

**Figure 4.** Comparing two cores to one *without* SMT or Turbo Boost.

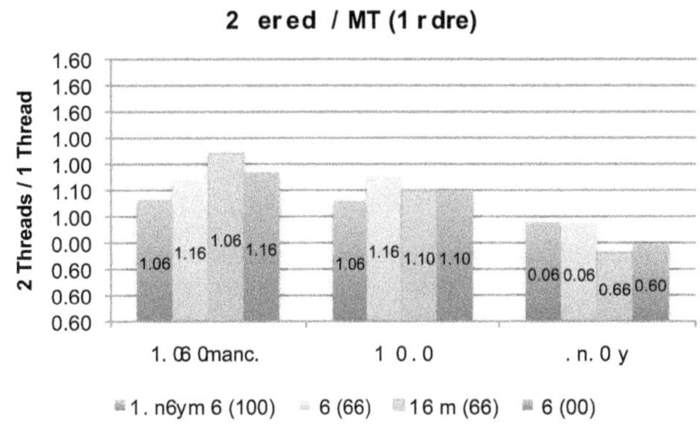


(a) Average impact of two-way SMT.

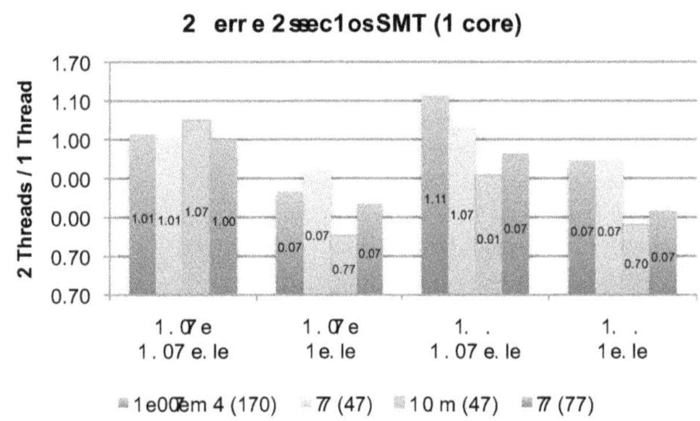


(b) Workload energy impact of two-way SMT.

**Figure 5.** Two-way SMT impact with respect to a single core.

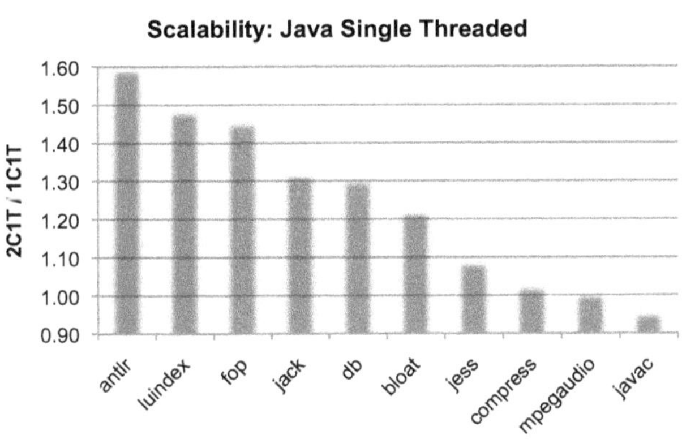


**Figure 6.** CMP impact for single-threaded Java.

WORKLOAD FINDING 1. *The JVM often induces significant amounts of parallelism into the execution of single-threaded Java benchmarks.*

Since the JVM's runtime services, such as profiling, just-in-time (JIT) compilation, and garbage collection, are concurrent and parallel, the JVM provides substantial scope for parallelization, even within these ostensibly sequential applications. To understand these effects better, we instrumented the HotSpot JVM to separately count cycles and retired instructions for the JVM and application. These experiments isolate the sources of parallelism from HotSpot to the JIT compiler and garbage collector.

Most benchmarks spend around 90-99% of their time in the application thread, but for example, antlr spends as much as 50% of its time in the JVM. Although db spends 95% of its instructions in single-threaded application code, it experiences a 30% improvement when it uses two hardware contexts on the i7 (45). Performance counter measurements show that memory system performance improvements were the cause of this surprising result. The DTLB experiences a factor of 2.5 fewer misses when more cores were available. Our hypothesis is that when the garbage collector executes on other cores it dramatically reduces the collector displacement effect on application data in local caches. These memory and cache behaviors are clearly significant but they are very subtle and need further exploration.

### 3.2 Simultaneous Multithreading

We measured the effect of simultaneous multithreading (SMT) [34] by disabling SMT at the BIOS on the Pentium 4 (130), Atom (45), i5 (32), and i7 (45). Each processor supports two-way SMT. On the i5 (32) and i7 (45) multiprocessors, we use only one core to ensure that SMT is the sole opportunity for thread-level parallelism. We disable Turbo Boost since it may vary the clock rate. Each processor is otherwise in its stock configuration. Figure 5(a) shows the overall power, performance, and energy impact of enabling SMT on a single core. Singhal states that the small amount of logic that is exclusive to SMT consumes very little power [29]. Nonetheless, this logic is integrated, so SMT does contribute to total power even when disabled. These results therefore slightly underestimate the power cost of SMT. The performance advantage of SMT is significant. Notably, on the i5 (32) and Atom (45), SMT improves average performance significantly without much cost in power, leading to net energy savings.

ARCHITECTURE FINDING 2. *SMT delivers substantial energy savings for the i5 (32) and Atom (45).*

Given that SMT was motivated and continues to be motivated by the challenge of filling issue slots and hiding latency in wide issue superscalars [29, 34], it appears counter intuitive that performance on the dual-issue Atom (45) should benefit so much more from SMT than the quad-issue i7 (45) and i5 (32). One potential explanation is that the in-order Atom (45) is more restricted in its capacity to fill issue slots. Compared to other in-order processors, the Atom (45) has a relatively deep pipeline. Compared to the other processors in this study, the Atom (45) has much smaller caches. These features accentuate the need to hide latency, and therefore the value of SMT.

The performance improvements on the Pentium 4 (130) due to SMT are half to one third that of the newer processors, and consequently there is no net energy advantage. This result is not so surprising given that the Pentium 4 (130) is among the first commercial implementations of SMT. Furthermore, the i5 (32) and i7 (45) have more issue slots to fill and their much larger cache capacities and memory bandwidth better sustain the demands of SMT.

WORKLOAD FINDING 2. *On the Pentium 4 (130), SMT degrades performance for Java Non-scalable.*

SMT is particularly unhelpful to Java on the Pentium 4 (130) as shown in Figure 5(b). It offers substantially lower performance improvements on Java Scalable and a performance *degradation* on Java Non-scalable [12], the latter leading to an 11% energy overhead. Figure 5(b) shows that, as expected, Native Non-scalable benchmarks experience very little energy overhead due to enabling SMT, whereas Figure 4(b) shows that enabling a core incurs a significant power and thus energy penalty. The scalable benchmarks unsurprisingly benefit most from SMT.

The effectiveness of SMT is impressive on recent processors as compared to CMP, particularly given its 'very low' die footprint [29]. Compare Figure 4 and 5. SMT provides less performance improvement than CMP—SMT adds about half as much performance as CMP on average, but incurs much less power cost—SMT adds just a quarter of the power of CMP on the i7 (45) and one third the power on the i5 (32). These factors lead to greater energy savings on the i7 (45) and i5 (32). These results on the modern processors show SMT in a much more favorable light than in Sasanka et al.'s model-based comparative study of the energy efficiency of SMT and CMP [28].

### 3.3 Clock Scaling

We vary the processor clock on the i7 (45), Core 2D (45), and i5 (32) between their minimum and maximum settings and measure the effect on power and performance. The range of clock speeds are: 1.6 to 2.7GHz for i7 (45); 1.6 to 3.1GHz for Core 2D (45); and 1.2 to 3.5GHz for i5 (32). We uniformly disable Turbo Boost to produce a consistent clock rate for comparison; Turbo Boost may vary the clock rate, but only when the clock is set at its highest value. Each processor is otherwise in its stock configuration. Figures 7(a) and 7(b) express changes in power, performance, and energy with respect to doubling in clock frequency over the range of clock speeds to normalize and compare across architectures.

The three processors experience broadly similar increases in performance of around 80%, but *power differences vary substantially, from 70% to 180%*. On the i7 (45) and Core 2D (45), the performance increases require disproportional power increases—conse-

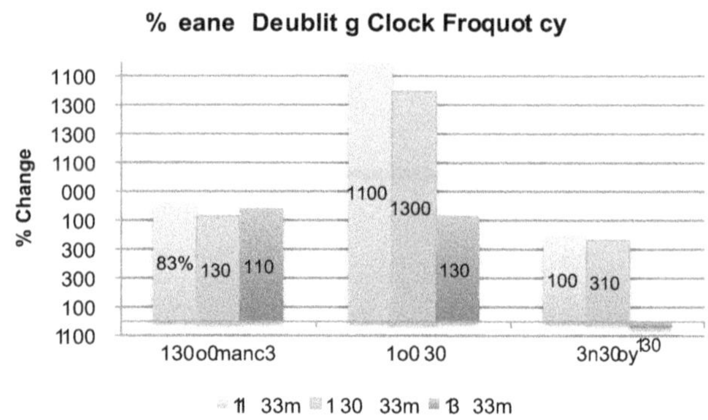


(a) Average impact of doubling clock.

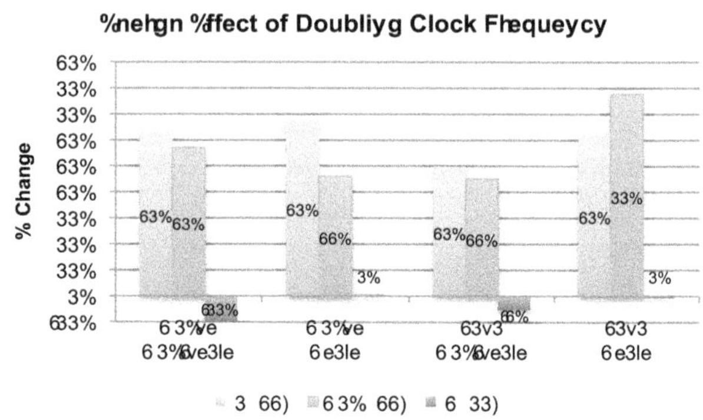


(b) Workload energy impact of doubling clock.

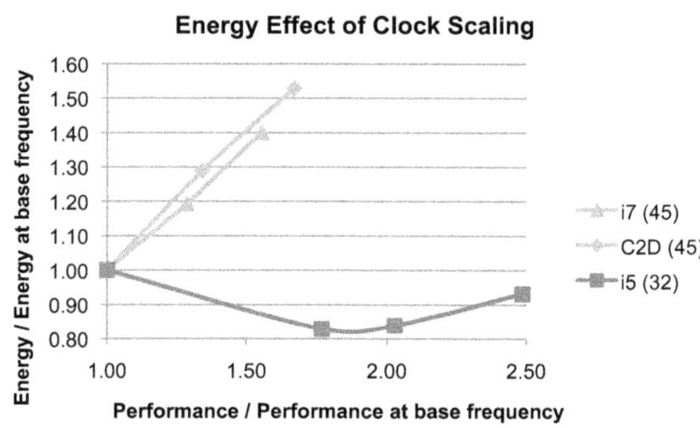


(c) Average energy performance curve, each point is a clock speed.

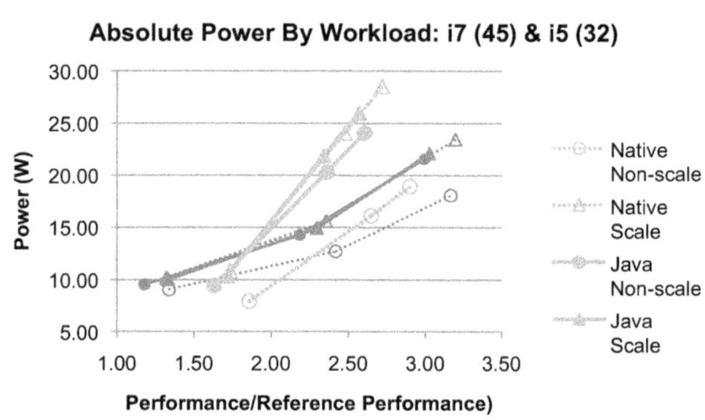


(d) Absolute power (Watts) and performance on the i7 (45) (green) and i5 (32) (red) by benchmark group, each point is a clock speed.

**Figure 7.** The impact of clock scaling in stock configurations.

quently energy consumption increases by about 60% as the clock is doubled. The i5 (32) is starkly different—doubling its clock leads to a slight energy reduction.

ARCHITECTURE FINDING 3. *The i5 (32) does not increase energy consumption as the clock increases, in contrast to the i7 (45) and Core 2D (45).*

Figure 7(c) shows that this result is consistent across the range of i5 (32) clock rates. A number of factors may explain why the i5 (32) performs relatively so much better at its highest clock rate: (a) the i5 (32) is a 32nm process, while the others are 45nm; (b) the power-performance curve is non-linear and these experiments may observe only the upper (steeper) portion of the curves for i7 (45) and Core 2D (45); (c) although the i5 (32) and i7 (45) share the same microarchitecture, the second generation i5 (32) likely incorporates energy improvements; (d) the i7 (45) is substantially larger than the other processors, with four cores and a larger cache.

WORKLOAD FINDING 3. *The power / performance behavior of Native Non-scalable differs from the three other workload groups.*

Figure 7(b) shows that doubling the clock on the i5 (32) roughly maintains or improves energy consumption of all benchmark groups, with Native Non-scalable improving the most. For the i7 (45) and Core 2D (45), doubling the clock raises energy consumption. Figure 7(d) shows that Native Non-scalable has a different power / performance behavior compared to the other workloads and that this difference is largely independent of clock rate. The Native Non-scalable benchmarks draw less power overall, and power increases less steeply as a function of performance increases. Native Non-scalable (SPEC CPU2006) is the most widely studied workload in the architecture literature, but it is the outlier. These results reinforce the importance of including scalable and managed workloads in energy evaluations.

### 3.4 Die Shrink

We used processor pairs from the Core (Core 2D (65)/ Core 2D (45)) and Nehalem (i7 (45)/ i5 (32)) microarchitectures to explore die shrink effects. These stock hardware comparisons are imperfect because they are not straightforward die shrinks. To limit the differences, we control for hardware parallelism by limiting the i7 (45) to two cores, and control for clock speed by running both Cores at 2.4GHz and both Nehalems at 2.66GHz. We also run them at their native speeds. Nonetheless, we cannot control for the cache size and other differences. For the Core, it appears that the die shrink was fairly straightforward, except that the Core 2D (45) uses a 3MB triple-port cache, whereas the Core 2D (65) uses a 4MB dual-port cache. Nehalem's changes are more extensive and include a reduction in the number of cores, the size of the cache, a more limited DMI interconnect instead of QPI, the integration of a PCIe controller in the i5 (32), and the inclusion of a GPU on a separate 45nm die within the same package. The GPU is not exercised by any of our benchmarks, but is nonetheless included in our power measurements. Notwithstanding these caveats, these architectures present an opportunity to compare power and performance across process technologies.

ARCHITECTURE FINDING 4. *A die shrink is remarkably effective at reducing energy consumption, even when controlling for clock frequency.*

Figure 8(a) shows the power and performance effects of the die shrinks with the stock clock speeds for all the processors. The newer processors are significantly faster at their higher stock clock speeds and significantly more power efficient. Figure 8(b) shows the same experiment, but down clocking the newer processors to match the frequency of their older peers. Down clocking the new processors improves their relative power and energy advantage even further. Note that as expected, the die shrunk processors offer no performance advantage once the clocks are matched, indeed the i5 (32) performs 10% slower than the i7 (45). However, power consumption is reduced by 47%. This result is consistent with expectations, given the lower voltage and reduced capacitance at the smaller feature size.

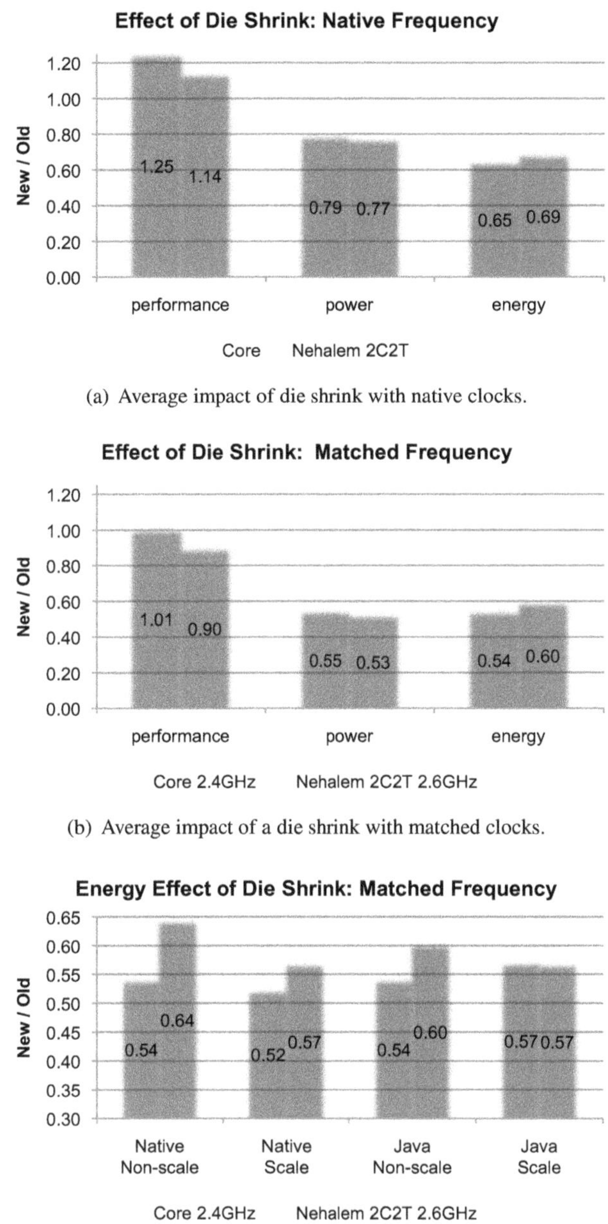


(a) Average impact of die shrink with native clocks.



(b) Average impact of a die shrink with matched clocks.



(c) Workload energy impact of a die shrink with matched clocks.

**Figure 8.** The impact of a die shrink for Core and Nehalem microarchitecture families.

ARCHITECTURE FINDING 5. *Moving from 45nm to 32nm repeated the energy improvements of the previous generation.*

Figures 8(a) and 8(b) reveal a striking similarity in the power and energy savings between the Core (65nm / 45nm) and Nehalem (45nm / 32nm) die shrinks. This data suggests that Intel was able to maintain the same rate of energy reduction across each of these generations. ITRS predicted a 9% increase in frequency and 20% reduction in power from 45nm to 32nm [21]. Figure 8(a) is more encouraging, showing a 14% increase in performance and 23% reduction in power accompanying the 26% increase in stock frequency from the i7 (45) to i5 (32).

### 3.5 Gross Microarchitecture Change

We explore the power and performance effect of gross microarchitectural change through a series of comparisons where we can match architectural features such as processor clock, degree of hardware parallelism, process technology, and cache size. The processors in this study represent only one or two examples of the many processors built in each family. For example, Intel sells over sixty 45nm Nehalems ranging in price from around $190 to over $3700. However, we chose mainstream processors at similar price points for the most part. These microarchitecture comparisons are imperfect, but they provide broader perspective on the processors and workloads.

Figure 9 compares the Nehalem i7 (45) with with the NetBurst Pentium 4 (130), Bonnell Atom D (45), and Core 2D (45) microarchitectures, and it compares the Nehalem i5 (32) with the Core 2D (65). Each comparison configures the Nehalems to match the clock speed, number of cores, and hardware threads of the other architecture. It is pleasing, although unsurprising, to see the i7 (45) performing 2.6× faster than the Pentium 4 (130), while consuming just one third the power, when controlling for clock speed and hardware parallelism. Much of the 50% power improvement is attributable to process technology advances (Architecture Finding 4). However, this comparison does not control for memory speed, nor for three generations of process technology scaling.

> ARCHITECTURE FINDING 6. *Controlling for hardware parallelism and clock speed, Nehalem performs about 14% better than Core.*

Both the i7 (45) and i5 (32) comparisons to the Core show that the move from Core to Nehalem yields a small 14% performance improvement. This finding is not inconsistent with Nehalem's stated primary design goals, i.e., delivering scalability and memory performance. Power increases by 14% when we hold process technology constant (i7 (45) / Core 2D (45)) and reduces 45% when we shift two technology generations (i5 (32) / Core 2D (65)).

> ARCHITECTURE FINDING 7. *Controlling for technology, hardware parallelism, and clock speed, the Nehalem has similar energy efficiency to Core and Bonnell.*

The comparisons between the i7 (45) and Atom D (45) and Core 2D (45) hold process technology constant at 45nm. All three processors are remarkably similar in energy consumption. This outcome is all the more interesting because the i7 (45) is disadvantaged since it uses fewer hardware contexts here than in its stock configuration. Furthermore, the i7 (45) integrates more services on-die, such as the memory controller, that are off-die on the other processors and thus outside the scope of the power meters. The i7 (45) improves upon the Core 2D (45) and Atom D (45) with a more scalable, much higher bandwidth on-chip interconnect, that is not heavily exercised by our workloads. It is impressive that despite all of these factors, the i7 (45) delivers similar energy efficiency to these two 45nm peers.

### 3.6 Turbo Boost Technology

Intel Turbo Boost Technology on Nehalem processors over-clocks cores under the following conditions [19]. With Turbo Boost enabled, *all* cores can run one "step" (133MHz) faster if temperature, power, and current conditions allow. When only one core is active, Turbo Boost may clock it an additional step faster. Turbo Boost is only enabled when the processor executes at its default highest clock setting. This feature requires on-chip power sensors which are currently not exposed to the programmer. We verified empirically on the i7 (45) and i5 (32) that all cores ran 133MHz faster with Turbo Boost. When only one core was active, the core ran 266MHz faster. Since the i7 (45) runs at a lower clock (2.67GHz) than the i5 (32) (3.46GHz), it experiences a relatively larger boost.

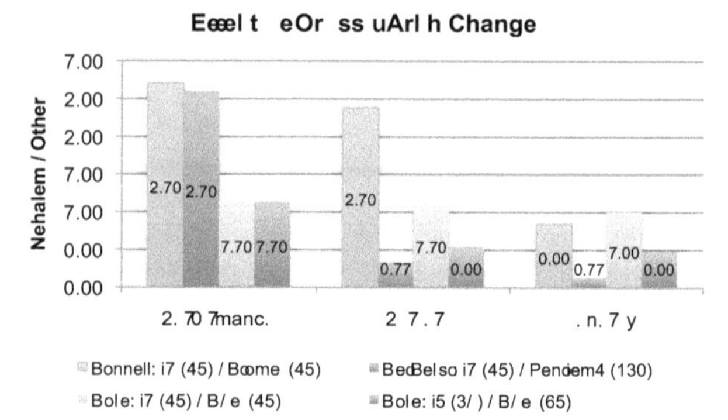

(a) Average impact of a gross $\mu$arch change.

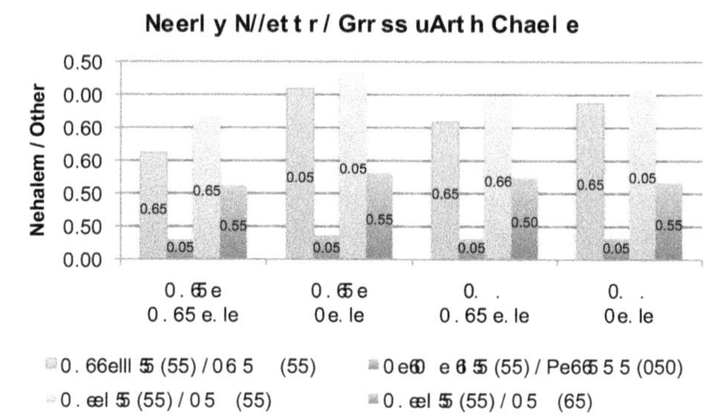

(b) Workload energy impact of a gross $\mu$arch change.

**Figure 9.** The impact of gross microarchitectural change.

> ARCHITECTURE FINDING 8. *Turbo Boost is not energy efficient on the i7 (45).*

Figure 10(a) shows the effect of disabling Turbo Boost at the BIOS on the i7 (45) and i5 (32) in their stock configurations (dark) and when we limit each machine to a single hardware context (light). With the single hardware context, Turbo Boost will increment the clock by two steps if thermal conditions permit. The actual performance changes are well predicted by the clock rate increases. The i7 (45) clock step increases are 5 and 10%, and the actual performance increases are 4 and 7%. The i5 (32) clock step increases are 4 and 8%, and the actual performance increases are 3 and 5%. However, the i7 (45) responds with a substantially higher power increase and consequent energy overhead, while the i5 (32) is essentially energy-neutral.

Figure 10(b) shows that when all hardware contexts are available (dark), the non-scalable benchmarks consume relatively more energy than scalable benchmarks on the i7 (45) in its stock configuration. Because the non-scalable native and sometimes Java utilize only a single core, Turbo Boost will likely increase the clock by an additional step. Figure 10(a) shows that this technique is power-hungry on the i7 (45).

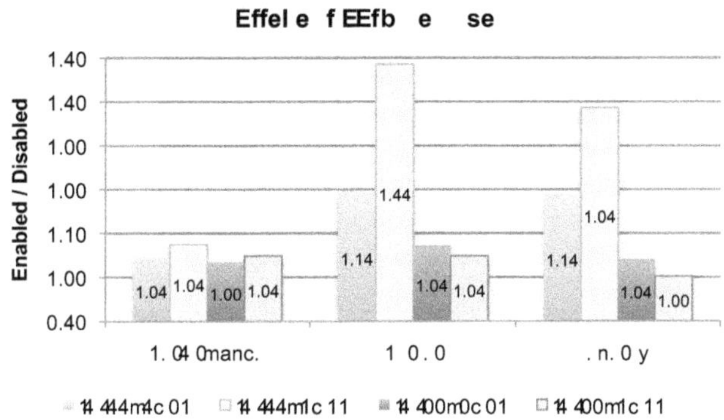


(a) Average impact of Turbo Boost.

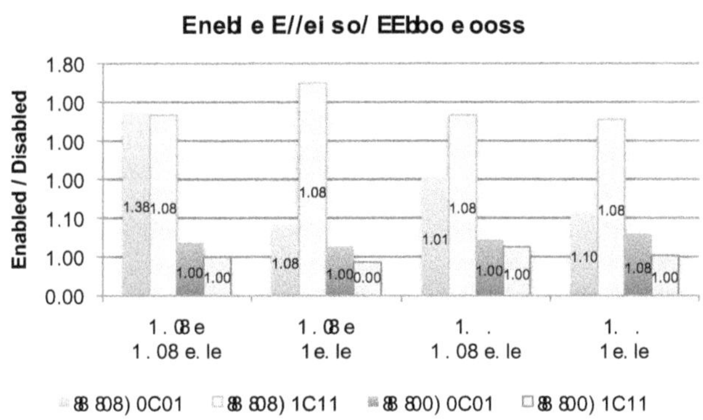


(b) Workload energy impact of Turbo Boost.

**Figure 10.** Workload impact of enabling Turbo Boost.

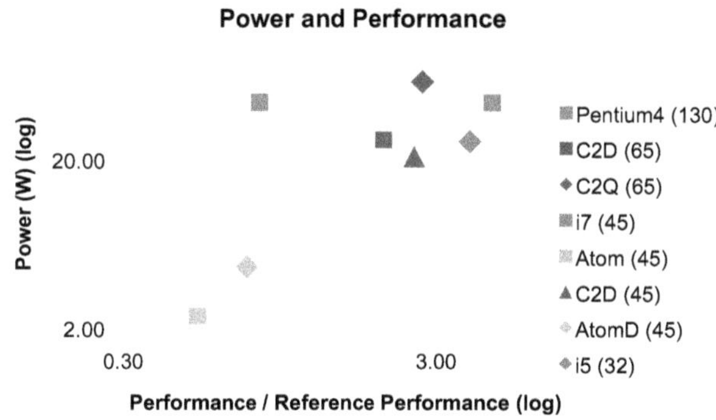


(a) Power / performance tradeoff by processor.

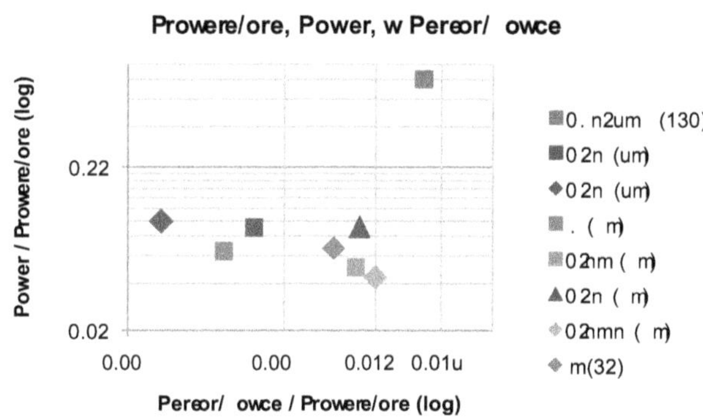


(b) Power / performance tradeoff as a function of transistors.

**Figure 11.** Power / performance tradeoff by processor.

# 4. Perspective

To give a broader view, this section: (1) examines the energy tradeoffs made by each processor over time, (2) examines the energy tradeoffs as a function of transistors count, and (3) conducts a Pareto energy efficiency analysis for our benchmarks running on the 45nm processors. This section presents processor performance relative to the reference performance for each benchmark shown in Table 1 and described in Section 2.6. We use the same methodology for energy, but because power is not dependent on benchmark length, we present measured power directly.

## 4.1 Historical Overview

Figure 11(a) plots the power and performance for each processor in their stock configuration relative to the reference performance, using a log / log scale. Both graphs in Figure 11 use the same color for all the experimental processors in the same family. The shapes encode release age: a square is the oldest, the diamond is next, and the triangle is the youngest, smallest technology in the family.

While mobile devices have historically optimized for power, general purpose processor design has not. Several results stand out that illustrate that power is now a first-order design goal and trumps performance in some cases. (1) The Atom (45) and Atom D (45) are designed as low power processors for a different market, however they do run all these benchmarks, and indeed they are the most power efficient processors. Compared to the Pentium 4 (130), they degrade performance modestly and reduce power enormously, consuming as little as one twentieth the power. (2) Comparing one generation between 65nm and 45nm with the Core 2D (65) and Core 2D (45) shows only a 25% increase in performance, but a 35% drop in power. (3) Comparing the most recent two generations with the i7 (45) and i5 (32), the figure shows that the i5 (32) delivers about 15% less performance, while consuming about 40% less power. This result has three root causes: (a) the i7 (45) has four cores instead of two on the i5 (32), (b) since half the benchmarks are scalable multithreaded benchmarks, the software parallelism benefits more from the additional two cores, increasing the advantage to the i7 (45), and (c) the i7 (45) has significantly better memory performance. Comparing the Core 2D (45) to the i5 (32) where the number of processors are matched, the i5 (32) delivers 50% better performance, while consuming around 25% more power than the Core 2D (45).

Contemporaneous comparisons also reveal the tension between power and performance. For example, the contrast between the Core 2D (45) and i7 (45) shows that the i7 (45) delivers 75% more performance than the Core 2D (45), but this performance is very costly in power with an increase of nearly 100%. These processors thus span a wide range of energy tradeoffs within and across the generations. Overall, these result indicate that optimizing for both power and performance is so far considerably more challenging than optimizing for performance alone.

ARCHITECTURE FINDING 9. *Power per transistor is relatively consistent within a microarchitecture family.*

Figure 11(b) explores the effect of transistors on power and performance by dividing them by the number of transistors in the *package* for each processor. We include all transistors because our power measurements occur at the level of the package, not the die. This measure is rough and will downplay results for the i5 (32) and Atom D (45), each of which have GPUs within the package.

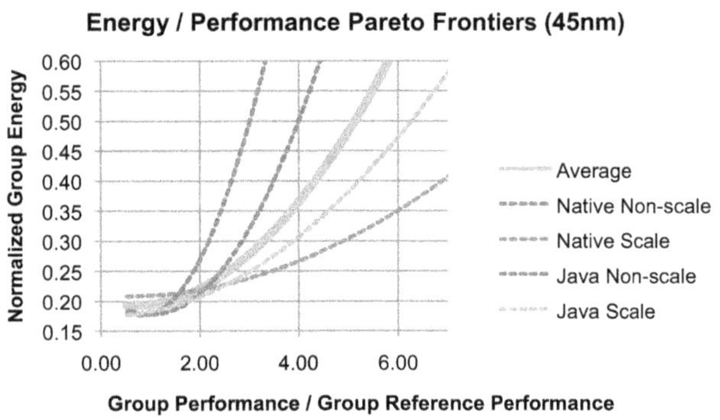


**Figure 12.** Energy / performance Pareto frontiers for our selection of 45nm processors executing at both stock and at clock and hardware context scaled configurations.

| | **Atom (45) 1C2T @ 1.7GHz** | Core 2D (45) 2C1T @ 1.6GHz | **Core 2D (45) 2C1T @ 3.1GHz** | i7 (45) 1C1T @ 2.7GHz No TB | i7 (45) 1C1T @ 2.7GHz | i7 (45) 1C2T @ 1.6GHz | i7 (45) 1C2T @ 2.4GHz | i7 (45) 2C1T @ 1.6GHz | i7 (45) 2C2T @ 1.6GHz | i7 (45) 4C1T @ 2.7GHz No TB | i7 (45) 4C1T @ 2.7GHz | i7 (45) 4C2T @ 1.6GHz | i7 (45) 4C2T @ 2.1GHz | i7 (45) 4C2T @ 2.7GHz No TB | **i7 (45) 4C2T @ 2.7GHz** |
|---|---|---|---|---|---|---|---|---|---|---|---|---|---|---|---|
| **Average** | ✔ | | | | | | | | ✔ | | | ✔ | ✔ | ✔ | ✔ |
| Native Non-scalable | | | | ✔ | ✔ | ✔ | ✔ | | | | | | | | |
| Native Scalable | ✔ | ✔ | | | | | | | | | | ✔ | ✔ | ✔ | ✔ |
| Java Non-scalable | ✔ | | ✔ | | | | ✔ | ✔ | | ✔ | ✔ | | | | ✔ |
| Java Scalable | ✔ | | | | | | | | ✔ | | | ✔ | ✔ | ✔ | ✔ |

**Table 5.** Pareto efficient processor configurations for each benchmark group. Stock configurations are indicated in bold.

Even though our benchmarks do not exercise the GPUs, we include them in the totals because the GPU transistor counts on the Atom D (45) are undocumented. Note the similarity between the Atom (45), Atom D (45), Core 2D (45), and i5 (32), which at the bottom right of the graph, are the most efficient processors by the transistor metric. Even though the i5 (32) and Core 2D (45) have five to eight times more transistors than the Atom (45), they all eek out very similar performance and power per transistor.

The left-most processors yield the smallest amount of performance per transistor. Among these processors, the Core 2D (65) and i7 (45) yield the least performance per transistor. These two machines correspond to the ones with the largest (8MB) caches among our set. This result is consistent with Patt's observation that very large caches are a waste of transistors [27], but this result does not hold for all workloads.

The Pentium 4 (130) is perhaps most remarkable—it yields the most performance per transistor and consumes the most power per transistor by a considerable margin. Consider applying the die shrink parameters from Finding 4 to the Pentium 4 (130) design across four generations from 130nm to a 32nm. The resulting microarchitecture would reduce power four fold and increase performance two fold, sliding it down and to the right on the graph.

Performance per transistor is inconsistent across microarchitectures, but power per transistor is consistent. Power per transistor correlates well with microarchitecture, regardless of technology generation.

### 4.2 Pareto Analysis at 45nm

The Pareto frontier defines a set of choices that are most Pareto efficient in a tradeoff space, and identifies the most optimal choices within the space. Prior research uses the Pareto frontier to explore tradeoffs of power and performance using *models* and then derives potential architectural designs on the frontier [1, 17]. Instead of models, we present a Pareto frontier derived from *measured performance and power* on contemporary real processors. We hold the process technology constant and use the four 45nm processors: Atom (45), Atom D (45), Core 2D (45), and i7 (45). We expand the number of processors from four to twenty-nine by configuring the number of hardware contexts (SMT and CMP), by clock scaling, and by disabling Turbo Boost. We use the same data as analyzed in Section 3. We use the twenty-five non-stock configurations as proxies for alternative design points. We explore processor configurations that are most efficient in the performance $\times$ energy space.

The set of Pareto efficient choices is determined by plotting all choices on an energy / performance scatter graph, and then identifying those choices that are not dominated in performance or energy efficiency by any other choice [12]. Visually these configurations are the bottom-right-most choices on the graphs in a figure such as Figure 12.

Table 5 shows the Pareto efficient processor configurations on the frontier for each of the benchmark groups and the average. Fifteen of the twenty-nine processor configurations are represented in Table 5, the remaining fourteen processors, including all four Atom D (45) configurations, are not Pareto efficient for any of the five groupings. As shown in previous sections, the energy and performance behavior of each benchmark group differs and consequently, the selection of most efficient choices differs for each group. Notice further that: (1) Native Non-scalable shares only one choice with any other group, (2) Java Scalable shares the same choices as the average, and (3) of the eleven choices on the Java Non-scalable and Java Scalable frontiers, only two are common to both.

It is interesting to note that Native Non-scalable does not include the Atom (45) in its frontier. This finding contradicts Azizi et al., who conclude that 2-wide in-order cores and 2-wide out of order cores are Pareto optimal designs with respect to the Native Non-scalable benchmarks [1]. Instead we find that all of the Pareto efficient points for Native Non-scalable are various configurations of the 4-wide out of order i7 (45).

Figure 12 shows the resulting Pareto frontier curves for each benchmark group. The curve for a group is constructed by plotting the energy and performance of the group on each processor and fitting a polynomial curve through those processors that are Pareto efficient according to Table 5.

WORKLOAD FINDING 4. *Pareto analysis shows energy efficient architectural design is very sensitive to workload.*

The curves for each benchmark group deviate substantially from the average. Even when the groups share points in common, the respective points are usually in different places on the graph because each group exhibits a different energy / performance tradeoff. Comparing the scalable and non-scalable benchmarks at 0.40 normalized energy on the y-axis, it is impressive to see how the architectures we evaluate are able to very effectively exploit software parallelism, pushing the curves to the right, increasing performance from about 3 to 7 while holding energy constant. This measured behavior confirms prior model-based observations about the role of software parallelism in extending the energy / performance curve to the right [1, 17].

## 5. Related Work

The processor design literature is full of performance measurement and analysis, a tradition that began in the 1980s [9, 10]. Unfortunately, despite the growing importance of power, power measurements are relatively rare and new [20].

***Measured Power*** Isci and Martonosi introduce a coordinated measurement approach that combines real total power using a clamp ammeter with performance counters for per unit power estimation [20]. They measure total power for an Intel Pentium 4 on the SPEC CPU2000 benchmark suite. Bircher and John [3] perform a detailed study of power and performance on AMD quad core Opteron and Phenom processors. They measure power using a series resistor, sampling the voltage across the resistor at 1KHz. Our work is complimentary. While the prior work takes a very close look at power on two processor cores and off-core resources, we examine trends across microarchitectures and technology generations.

Le Sueur and Heiser study the energy impact of dynamic voltage and frequency scaling (DVFS) on three server-class AMD processors fabricated at 130nm, 90nm, and 45nm using one memory-bound (181.mcf) SPEC CPU2000 benchmark [22]. They measure the whole system power with a RAM disk to prevent the inclusion of hard disk power in the measurements. They conclude that as the technology shrinks to 45nm the energy effectiveness of scaling down the frequency diminishes due to the increase of static power in lower voltages. We measure many benchmarks, processors, and use configuration to understand microarchitecture sensitivity.

Fan et al. study accurately estimating whole system power for large scale data centers [13]. They find that even the most power-consuming workloads draw less than 60% of the 'nameplate' peak power consumption. We measure chip power and support their results by showing that TDP does not predict chip measured power well on a range of workloads.

***Power Models and Simulation*** Li et al. explore the design space of chip multiprocessors under various area and thermal constraints [24]. They combine decoupled trace-driven cache simulation and cycle-accurate execution-driven multicore simulation with detailed single-core simulation to achieve high accuracy in power and performance estimation for chip multiprocessors. While Li et al.'s work uses simulation and is prospective, ours uses direct measures and is retrospective.

Azizi et al. introduce a joint circuit-architecture design space exploration framework [1]. They create statistical architectural models using simple simulations and combine these models with circuit-level energy-performance tradeoff functions to populate the single-core energy and performance design space using a subset of SPEC CPU benchmarks. They use Verilog models synthesized using a CMOS 90nm standard-cell library to generate the circuit-level energy and delay tradeoff functions. The framework uses Pareto optimal tradeoff curves for cycles per instruction versus energy per instruction to determine microarchitectural parameters, circuit implementations, and operating voltage and frequency given performance and energy constraints. Our Pareto analysis uses measurements and is historical rather than predictive.

Charles et al. study and characterize the behavior of Turbo Boost technology using a Core i7 (45nm) processor with SPEC CPU2006 and a subset of PARSEC and multithreaded BLAST benchmarks [8]. They analyze how the rate of memory accesses and the overall processor load affects Turbo Boost activation. They estimate the energy impact of Turbo Boost using a power model derived from the time spent at different frequencies. Their findings are similar to ours—they find Turbo Boost is costly in energy, but we use measurements rather than models. Our Turbo boost study extends theirs by considering two processors, i7 (45) and i5 (32), and a diverse set of workloads.

***Thermal Design Power (TDP)*** TDP is widely used in the literature as an estimate of chip power consumption. Horowitz et al. study energy across different process technologies while using TDP to estimate power and SPECmark to estimate performance for understanding CMOS scaling [17]. Hempstead et al. introduce an early stage modeling framework, Navigo, for CMP architecture exploration across future process technologies from 65nm down to 11nm [16]. Navigo models voltage and frequency scaling based on ITRS [21] and Predictive Technology Models [25]. As the starting point, Navigo uses reported TDP for power and SPECmarks for performance and then predicts the power and performance of processors in future technologies. Chakraborty uses TDP as the power envelope for studying CMP power consumption trends in future technologies [7]. Perhaps it is already well known that TDP is a poor estimate for actual chip power consumption, but our data suggests these studies need to be reconsidered.

We published preliminary data and analysis of TDP, CMP scaling, and historical trends without the Native Scalable benchmarks in a workshop paper [11]. The data and methodology here are more complete and rigorous. For example, the data and analysis include aggregation by benchmark group, Native Scalable benchmarks, more samples of all native benchmarks, sensor calibration, sensor validation, and extensive architecture configuration. Furthermore, all the feature analysis in Section 3 and the Pareto analysis are new here.

***Methodology*** Although the results show conclusively that managed and native workloads have different responses to architectural variations, perhaps this result is not or should not be surprising. However, very few academic publications with processor measurements or simulated designs use Java or any other managed workloads. The evaluation methodologies for real processors that we use here, however, are well developed [5, 14]. Objections to using managed languages in architectural design include lack of simulator support and simulation time. However, prior work shows how to modify simulators to handle Java [4]. The modest execution times of DaCapo were intended to ease experimentation on real processors and simulators, while also providing substantial and diverse workloads [4]. Some additional methodologies are needed to simulate managed workloads, but prior work has addressed these issues as well [15].

## 6. Conclusion

As far as we are aware, this paper is the first to quantitatively study measured power and performance at the chip level across hardware generations using single threaded and multithreaded, native and managed workloads. The volume of data and results do not lend themselves to concise conclusions, but they do offer three recommendations. Manufacturers: (1) Expose on-chip power meters to the community. Researchers: (2) Use both managed and native workloads. (3) Measure power and performance to understand and optimize power, performance, and energy.

## Acknowledgements

A number of people have generously provided us with assistance. We thank Bob Edwards at ANU for helping fabricate and calibrate the current sensors. We thank Daniel Frampton for managing and configuring the machines, and for his feedback. We thank Katherine Coons, Pradeep Dubey, Jungwoo Ha, Laurence Hellyer, Daniel Jiménez, and Bert Maher for their comments and suggestions. We thank our ASPLOS shepherd, David Patterson, and John Hennessy for their feedback and encouragement.

## References


[1] O. Azizi, A. Mahesri, B. C. Lee, S. J. Patel, and M. Horowitz. Energy-performance tradeoffs in processor architecture and circuit design: A marginal cost analysis. In *ACM/IEEE International Symposium on Computer Architecture*, pages 26–36, 2010.

[2] C. Bienia, S. Kumar, J. P. Singh, and K. Li. The PARSEC benchmark suite: Characterization and architectural implications. Technical Report TR-811-08, Princeton University, January 2008.

[3] W. L. Bircher and L. K. John. Analysis of dynamic power management on multi-core processors. In *ACM International Conference on Supercomputing*, pages 327–338, Island of Kos, Greece, 2008.

[4] S. M. Blackburn, R. Garner, C. Hoffman, A. M. Khan, K. S. McKinley, R. Bentzur, A. Diwan, D. Feinberg, D. Frampton, S. Z. Guyer, M. Hirzel, A. Hosking, M. Jump, H. Lee, J. E. B. Moss, A. Phansalkar, D. Stefanović, T. VanDrunen, D. von Dincklage, and B. Wiedermann. The DaCapo benchmarks: Java benchmarking development and analysis. In *ACM SIGPLAN Conference on Object-Oriented Programing, Systems, Languages, and Applications*, pages 169–190, Oct. 2006.

[5] S. M. Blackburn, K. S. McKinley, R. Garner, C. Hoffman, A. M. Khan, R. Bentzur, A. Diwan, D. Feinberg, D. Frampton, S. Z. Guyer, M. Hirzel, A. Hosking, M. Jump, H. Lee, J. E. B. Moss, A. Phansalkar, D. Stefanović, T. VanDrunen, D. von Dincklage, and B. Wiedermann. Wake up and smell the coffee: Evaluation methodologies for the 21st century. *Communications of the ACM*, 51(8):83–89, Aug. 2008.

[6] M. Bohr. A 30 year retrospective on Dennard's MOSFET scaling paper. *IEEE SSCS Newsletter*, pages 11–13, Winter 2007.

[7] K. Chakraborty. *Over-provisioned Multicore Systems*. PhD thesis, University of Wisconsin-Madison, 2008.

[8] J. Charles, P. Jassi, N. S. Ananth, A. Sadat, and A. Fedorova. Evaluation of the Intel® Core™ i7 Turbo Boost feature. In *IEEE International Symposium on Workload Characterization*, pages 188–197, 2009.

[9] J. S. Emer and D. W. Clark. A characterization of processor performance in the VAX-11/780. In *ACM/IEEE International Symposium on Computer Architecture*, pages 301–310, 1984.

[10] J. S. Emer and D. W. Clark. Retrospective: A characterization of processor performance in the VAX-11/780. *ACM 25 Years ISCA: Retrospectives and Reprints 1998*, pages 274–283, 1998.

[11] H. Esmaeilzadeh, S. M. Blackburn, X. Yang, and K. S. McKinley. Power and performance of native and Java benchmarks on 130nm to 32nm process technologies. In *Sixth Annual Workshop on Modeling, Benchmarking, and Simulation*, June 2010.

[12] H. Esmaeilzadeh, T. Cao, X. Yang, S. M. Blackburn, and K. S. McKinley. Source materials in ACM Digital Library for: Looking back on the language and hardware revolutions: Measured power, performance, and scaling. In *International Conference on Architectural Support for Programming Languages and Operating Systems*, Mar. 2011.

[13] X. Fan, W.-D. Weber, and L. A. Barroso. Power provisioning for a warehouse-sized computer. In *ACM/IEEE International Symposium on Computer Architecture*, pages 13–23, San Diego, CA, 2007.

[14] A. Georges, D. Buytaert, and L. Eeckhout. Statistically rigorous Java performance evaluation. In *ACM Conference on Object–Oriented Programming Systems, Languages, and Applications*, pages 57–76, 2007.

[15] J. Ha, M. Gustafsson, S. M. Blackburn, and K. S. McKinley. Microarchitectural Characterization of Production JVMs and Java Workloads. In *IBM CAS Workshop*, Feb. 2008.

[16] M. Hempstead, G.-Y. Wei, and D. Brooks. Navigo: An early-stage model to study power-contrained architectures and specialization. In *Workshop on Modeling, Benchmarking, and Simulations*, June 2009.

[17] M. Horowitz, E. Alon, D. Patil, S. Naffziger, R. Kumar, and K. Bernstein. Scaling, power, and the future of CMOS. In *Proceedings of International Electron Devices Meeting*, pages 7–15, December 2005.

[18] Intel Corporation. Intel Hyper-Threading Technology, 2011. URL `http://www.intel.com/technology/platform-technology/hyper-threading`.

[19] Intel Corporation. Intel Turbo Boost Technology in Intel Core Microarchitecture (Nehalem) Based Processors. White Paper, Nov. 2008.

[20] C. Isci and M. Martonosi. Runtime power monitoring in high-end processors: Methodology and empirical data. In *IEEE International Symposium on Microarchitecture*, pages 93–104, December 2003.

[21] ITRS Working Group. International technology roadmap for semiconductors, 2011. URL `http://www.itrs.net`.

[22] E. Le Sueur and G. Heiser. Dynamic voltage and frequency scaling: The laws of diminishing returns. In *Workshop on Power Aware Computing and Systems*, Vancouver, Canada, Oct. 2010.

[23] S. H. Li. Linux kernel bug 5471, 2011. URL `https://bugzilla.kernel.org/show_bug.cgi?id=5471`.

[24] Y. Li, B. Lee, D. Brooks, Z. Hu, and K. Skadron. CMP design space exploration subject to physical contraints. In *International Symposium on High Performance Computer Architecture*, pages 17–28, Feb 2006.

[25] Nanoscale Integration and Modeling (NIMO) Group. Predictive technology model, 2011. URL `http://ptm.asu.edu`.

[26] V. Pallipadi and A. Starikovskiy. The ondemand governor: Past, present and future. In *Proceedings of Linux Symposium*, volume 2, pages 223–238, July 2006.

[27] Y. Patt. Future microprocessors: Multi-core, mega-nonsense, and what we must do differently moving forward. Distinguished Lecture at UIUC, (April 2010), 2011. URL `http://www.parallel.illinois.edu/presentations/2010_04_30_Patt_Slides.pdf`.

[28] R. Sasanka, S. V. Adve, Y.-K. Chen, and E. Debes. The energy efficiency of CMP vs. SMT for multimedia workloads. In *ACM International Conference on Supercomputing*, pages 196–206, Malo, France, 2004.

[29] R. Singhal. Inside Intel next generation Nehalem microarchitecture. Intel Developer Forum (IDF) presentation (August 2008), 2011. URL `http://software.intel.com/file/18976`.

[30] Standard Performance Evaluation Corp. SPEC Benchmarks, 2010. URL `http://www.spec.org`.

[31] Standard Performance Evaluation Corporation. SPEC CPU2006 benchmark descriptions. *ACM SIGARCH Newsletter, Computer Architecture News*, 34(4), September 2006.

[32] The DaCapo Research Group. The DaCapo Benchmarks, beta-2006-08, 2006. URL `http://www.\-dacapo\-bench.\-org`.

[33] TIOBE Software. TIOBE Programming Community Index for January 2011, 2011. URL `http://www.tiobe.com`.

[34] D. M. Tullsen, S. J. Eggers, and H. M. Levy. Simultaneous multithreading: Maximizing on-chip parallelism. In *ACM/IEEE International Symposium on Computer Architecture*, pages 392–403, Santa Margherita Ligure, Italy, June 1995.

# Synthesizing Concurrent Schedulers for Irregular Algorithms *

Donald Nguyen
Department of Computer Science
The University of Texas at Austin
ddn@cs.utexas.edu

Keshav Pingali
Department of Computer Science
Institute for Computational Engineering and Sciences
The University of Texas at Austin
pingali@cs.utexas.edu

## Abstract

Scheduling is the assignment of tasks or activities to processors for execution, and it is an important concern in parallel programming. Most prior work on scheduling has focused either on static scheduling of applications in which the dependence graph is known at compile-time or on dynamic scheduling of independent loop iterations such as in OpenMP.

In irregular algorithms, dependences between activities are complex functions of runtime values so these algorithms are not amenable to compile-time analysis nor do they consist of independent activities. Moreover, the amount of work can vary dramatically with the scheduling policy. To handle these complexities, implementations of irregular algorithms employ carefully handcrafted, algorithm-specific schedulers but these schedulers are themselves parallel programs, complicating the parallel programming problem further.

In this paper, we present a flexible and efficient approach for specifying and synthesizing scheduling policies for irregular algorithms. We develop a simple compositional specification language and show how it can concisely encode scheduling policies in the literature. Then, we show how to synthesize efficient parallel schedulers from these specifications. We evaluate our approach for five irregular algorithms on three multicore architectures and show that (1) the performance of some algorithms can improve by orders of magnitude with the right scheduling policy, and (2) for the same policy, the overheads of our synthesized schedulers are comparable to those of fixed-function schedulers.

***Categories and Subject Descriptors*** D.3.3 [*Programming Languages*]: Concurrent programming structures

***General Terms*** Algorithms, Performance

***Keywords*** Amorphous data-parallelism, Irregular programs, Multicore processors, Optimistic parallelization, Program synthesis, Scheduling

* This work was supported by NSF grants 0833162, 0719966, 0702353, 0724966, and 0739601, as well as grants from the IBM and Intel Corporations.


*ASPLOS'11,* March 5–11, 2011, Newport Beach, California, USA.


## 1. Introduction

Given a decomposition of a program into activities or tasks, the *scheduling problem* is the *assignment of these activities to processors and the specification of an order in which each processor should execute the activities assigned to it.* Scheduling is important for both sequential and parallel implementations of algorithms since it may affect locality and load balance; it may even effect the total amount of work performed by some programs, as we show in this paper.

Scheduling can be done either statically by a compiler or dynamically by a runtime or operating system. Static scheduling can be used when dependences between activities are known statically and the execution time of each activity can be estimated accurately at compile-time. Stencil computations are the classic examples of algorithms amenable to static scheduling. Dynamic scheduling is useful for problems in which (1) dependences between activities cannot be elucidated statically, or (2) new work is created dynamically so the number of activities is not known statically, or (3) accurate estimates of the time required to execute each activity are not available. The vast majority of algorithms, including almost all *irregular* algorithms (in which the key data structures are sparse graphs) require dynamic scheduling.

For the most part, prior work on dynamic scheduling has focused on problems in which there are no dependences between activities and new work is not created dynamically, so the only problem is that time required to execute an activity cannot be determined accurately. Self-scheduling of DO-ALL loops in OpenMP is the classic example [10]. Activities in this case correspond to iterations of the DO-ALL loop; the number of iterations is known before the loop is executed, and it is assumed that there are no dependences between iterations. However, different iterations may take different and unpredictable amounts of time to execute, so to ensure good load balance, OpenMP provides scheduling policies such as chunked dynamic self-scheduling, in which a processor gets a chunk of $k$ iterations every time it needs work, and guided self-scheduling, in which the chunk size decreases steadily as the loop nears completion. Chunking reduces the overheads of scheduling and may improve locality.

More recently, attention has shifted to "task-parallelism" in which new activities are created dynamically, although it is still assumed that all activities are independent except for fork-join control dependences. In OpenMP 3.0, there is support for different dynamic scheduling policies such as breadth-first and work-first policies [11]. Another popular technique is *work-stealing*. In work-stealing, each thread maintains a local deque that it initially adds and removes activities from. When a thread's local deque is empty, it selects the local deque of another thread, the victim, and tries to steal activities from it. Work-stealing is parameterized by the order maintained in the local deque (usually LIFO) and how a thread selects a victim (usually at random). Work-stealing was implemented in MultiLisp [13] and was later popularized by the Cilk language [4], where it is used to implement fork-join parallelism. It is now available in many programming environments [17, 21, 22].

The key assumptions in this work on task-parallelism are that any dependences between activities are captured by fork-join control dependences and are known statically. While these assumptions are reasonable for regular (dense-array) algorithms and divide-and-conquer algorithms, they do not hold for most irregular graph algorithms because dependences in these algorithms are complex functions of runtime values (*e.g.*, the shape of the graph and the values on nodes and edges), which may themselves change during execution. An abstract description of parallelism in irregular algorithms is the following. At each step of the algorithm, there are certain *active nodes* in the graph where computation needs to be performed. Performing the computation at an active node may require reading or writing other graph nodes and edges, known collectively as the *neighborhood* of that activity (the neighborhood is usually distinct from the neighbors of the active node). In general, there are many active nodes in a graph, so a sequential implementation must pick one of them and perform the appropriate computation. In the *unordered algorithms* considered in this paper, the implementation is allowed to pick *any* active node for execution.[1] The final output may be different for different orders of executing active nodes, but all such outputs are acceptable, a feature known as *don't-care non-determinism.* A parallel implementation of such an algorithm can process active nodes simultaneously, provided their neighborhoods do not overlap (this condition can be relaxed but is sufficient for correct execution). However, the neighborhood of an activity is generally not known until the activity has finished execution. This parallelism is known as *amorphous data-parallelism* [30].

Efficient exploitation of amorphous data-parallelism requires far more sophisticated runtime support than fork-join parallelism or DO-ALL parallelism for the following reasons.

1. In most irregular algorithms, nodes become active dynamically, so the number of activities is not known statically.
2. In general, the neighborhood of an activity may be known only after that activity completes execution. Therefore, it may be necessary to use optimistic or speculative parallelization.
3. Most importantly, the number of activities that are executed by an algorithm may be dramatically different for different schedules.

For these reasons, even *sequential* implementations of irregular algorithms often use handcrafted, algorithm-specific scheduling policies; for example, some mesh refinement algorithms process triangles or tetrahedra in decreasing size order since this can reduce the total amount of refinement work [27]. Section 2 describes some of the more important policies in the literature. However, following these orders strictly can dramatically reduce parallelism, so parallel implementations of irregular algorithms often use more complex scheduling policies that trade off extra work for increased parallelism. These schedulers are themselves concurrent data structures and add to the complexity of parallel programming. In addition, they cannot easily be reused for other applications.

In this paper, we present a flexible and efficient approach for specifying and synthesizing schedulers for sequential and parallel implementations of irregular algorithms. We distinguish between *scheduling policies*, which are descriptions (possibly informal) of the order in which activities should be processed (*e.g.*, LIFO, FIFO, etc.), *scheduling specifications*, which are formal descriptions of scheduling policies, and *schedulers*, which are concrete implementations of scheduling specifications. A *schedule* is a specific mapping of activities to processors in time.

The rest of this paper is organized as follows. In Section 2, we describe several irregular algorithms and scheduling policies studied in the literature. Section 3 describes a language that concisely encodes these policies as scheduling specifications. Section 4 describes how concurrent schedulers are synthesized from these specifications. Our modular and compositional approach can produce efficient schedulers without requiring users to write complex, concurrent code. In Section 5, we evaluate our synthesized schedulers against *fixed-function schedulers* that use work-stealing with local LIFOs, work-stealing with local FIFOs and bulk-synchronous worklists.[2] We show that (1) for the same scheduling policy, fixed-function schedulers and synthesized schedulers have similar performance, and (2) for some algorithms, algorithm-specific schedulers synthesized by our approach outperform fixed-function schedulers. Section 6 compares our approach with previous work in scheduling and synthesis. Finally, Section 7 summarizes our contributions.

## 2. Algorithms

In this section, we describe five algorithms that exhibit amorphous data-parallelism. All the algorithms are unordered, which means that activities can execute in any order, and each algorithm has at least one algorithm-specific scheduling policy that has been proposed in the literature. Pseudocode for these algorithms is written using the Galois programming model [19], which is a sequential, object-oriented programming model augmented with a *Galois unordered-set iterator*, which is similar to set iterators in C++ or Java but permits new items to be added to a set while it is being iterated over.

- **foreach** (e : Set S) {B(e)} — The loop body B(e) is executed for each item e of set S. The order in which iterations execute is indeterminate and can be chosen by the implementation. There may be dependences between the iterations. An iteration may add items to S during execution.

### 2.1 Delaunay Triangulation

Finding the Delaunay triangulation (DT) of a set of points is a classic computational geometry problem. There are many algorithms for finding the triangulation; here, we describe the incremental algorithm of Bowyer and Watson [5, 35]. Each point is associated with the triangle that contains it. We assume points are in 2D. Initially, there is one large triangle that covers all the points. Each point $p$ calculates all triangles whose circumcircles include $p$. This is the cavity of $p$. The cavity is re-triangulated, $p$ is removed and the remaining points of the cavity are redistributed among their corresponding triangles. Figure 1 shows the pseudocode. G is the graph representing the triangulation. Figure 2 shows an example of processing one point.

All orders of processing points lead to the same Delaunay triangulation. Clarkson and Shor have shown that selecting points at random is optimal [8]. Amenta *et al.* present an algorithm called biased randomized insertion order (BRIO) that takes advantage of locality while still maintaining the optimality of randomness [1]. Briefly, let $n$ be the number of points to triangulate. Points are processed in $\log n$ rounds. The probability that a point is processed in the final round is $\frac{1}{2}$. For the remaining points, the probability that

[1] In contrast, *ordered algorithms* have a specific order in which active nodes must be executed.

[2] Fixed-function schedulers and synthesized schedulers are not mutually exclusive. In particular, work-stealing with local LIFOs can be seen as one implementation of a LIFO policy. However, in this paper, we separate the two to clearly delineate our contribution.

```
Workset ws = new Workset(points);
foreach (Point p : ws) {
  Cavity c = new Cavity(p);
  c.expand();
  c.retriangulate();
  G.update(c);
  c.dispatchPoints();
}
```

**Figure 1.** Pseudocode for Delaunay triangulation.

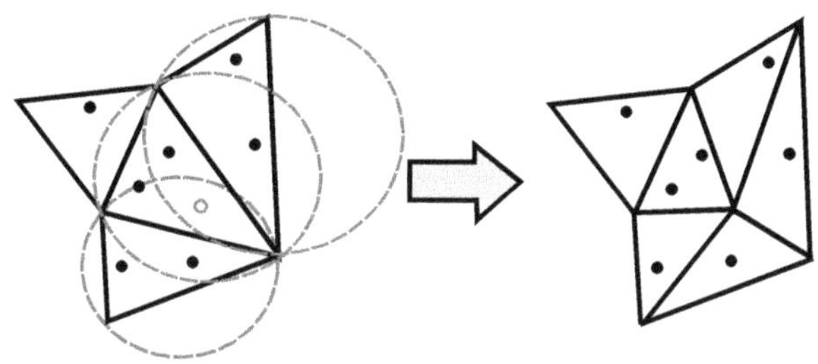

**Figure 2.** Example of processing an active point (hollow and red) for Delaunay triangulation. Circles are circumcircles of triangles containing the active point.

they will be processed in the next-to-last round is $\frac{1}{2}$, and so on until the first round. For the first round, all remaining points are processed with probability one. Within a round, points are processed according to the spatial divisions of an oct-tree.

### 2.2 Delaunay Mesh Refinement

Delaunay mesh refinement (DMR) [7] is an algorithm related to Delaunay triangulation. Given a Delaunay triangulation, triangles may have to satisfy additional quality constraints beyond that guaranteed by triangulation. To improve the quality of a triangulation, Delaunay mesh refinement iteratively fixes "bad" triangles, which do not satisfy the quality constraints, by adding new points to the mesh and re-triangulating. Refining a bad triangle may itself introduce new bad triangles, but it can be shown that, at least in 2D, this iterative refinement process will terminate and produce a guaranteed-quality mesh.

Figure 3 shows the pseudocode for this algorithm. It is similar to Delaunay triangulation, except that activities are centered on triangles rather than points. In both cases, a cavity is expanded and re-triangulated. However, in DMR, new bad triangles can be created that must be processed as well. They are tracked in a workset.[3] Additionally, different orders of processing bad triangles lead to different meshes, but all such meshes satisfy the quality constraints and are acceptable outcomes of the refinement process [7]. In contrast, for Delaunay triangulation, different orders still produce the same triangulation.

Naive implementations of DMR have quadratic worst-case running times [31] although they perform well in practice. Miller proved sub-quadratic worst-case time of a modification of DMR that processes triangles in decreasing circumcircle diameter together with other changes [27]. In Shewchuk's Triangle program, bad triangles are placed into buckets according to their minimum angle, each bucket stores triangles in FIFO order, and buckets are processed in increasing angle order [32]. Kulkarni *et al.* showed that a parallel implementation of DMR that distributes the initial

[3] Throughout this paper, we use the colloquial term workset, although more formally, these objects behave as bags or multisets because they may contain duplicate items.

```
Workset ws = new Workset(G.badTriangles());
foreach (Triangle t : ws) {
  if (!G.contains(t)) continue;
  Cavity c = new Cavity(t);
  c.expand();
  c.retriangulate();
  G.update(c);
  ws.addAll(c.badTriangles());
}
```

**Figure 3.** Pseudocode for Delaunay mesh refinement.

bad triangles among threads and uses thread-local stacks for newly created bad triangles performs well in practice [18].

### 2.3 Inclusion-based Points-to Analysis

Inclusion-based points-to analysis (PTA), also known as Andersen's algorithm [2], is a flow and context-insensitive static analysis that determines the points-to relation for program variables. PTA is a fixpoint algorithm that computes the least solution to a system of set constraints. The basic algorithm maintains a workset of program variables whose points-to relations need to be computed. For each variable in the workset, the algorithm examines the system of constraints to see if the current variable satisfies the constraints. If so, the algorithm continues processing the remaining variables. If not, some set of program variables are modified to satisfy the constraints. These modified variables are then added to the workset, and the algorithm continues until the workset is empty. Hardekopf and Lin showed how the basic fixpoint algorithm augmented with sophisticated cycle-detection can scale to large problem sizes [14]. From this algorithm, Mendez-Lojo *et al.* produced the first parallel implementation of this algorithm [24]. Our results in Section 5 are based on this implementation.

Since this is a fixpoint algorithm, all orders of processing variables will produce the same solution. Many heuristics have been proposed for organizing the workset, such as processing variables in least recently fired (LRF) order [29] or dividing the workset into current and next parts [28]. Variables are processed from the current part, but newly active variables are enqueued onto the next part. When the current part is empty, the roles of the current and next parts are swapped. Hardekopf and Lin report that the divided workset approach performs better in practice [14].

### 2.4 Single-source Shortest-path

Given a weighted, directed graph $G = (V, E)$, a weight function $w : E \rightarrow \mathbb{R}$ mapping edges to real-valued weights, and a source node $s \in V$, the single-source shortest-path (SSSP) problem is to find the least weight path from $s$ to all other nodes in the graph. The Bellman-Ford algorithm solves this problem on graphs with arbitrary weights. In the case of graphs with no negative weight edges, there are specialized algorithms such as Dijkstra's algorithm. In this paper, we consider the case where graphs have no negative weight edges. The Bellman-Ford algorithm can also be optimized for this case by reformulating it as a fixpoint algorithm. Instead of processing each node $|V|$ times, there is a workset that maintains nodes whose distances have changed; only those nodes are processed. One parallel SSSP algorithm is delta-stepping [25].

Each one of these algorithms can be viewed as an instantiation of a generic algorithm with different scheduling policies (see Figure 4). Each node $n$ has a tentative distance estimate $n.dist$ (initialized to $\infty$), and there is a set $ws$ of distance requests $(u, d, light)$ indicating that node $u$ can be updated with distance $d$. The additional $light$ value is only used by the delta-stepping algorithm. If the requested distance $d$ is less than the current distance $u.dist$ at node $u$, the current distance is updated. This generates a set of new

```
Workset ws = new Workset({(u, w(s,n), w(s,n) ≤ Δ) : (s,u) ∈ E})
s.dist = 0
foreach ((u, d, light) : ws) {
  if (d < u.dist) {
    u.dist = d;
    for (Node v : u.neighbors()) {
      float w = G.edgeData(u, v);
      ws.add((v, d + w, w <= Δ))
    }
  }
}
```

**Figure 4.** Pseudocode for generic single-source shortest path algorithm. $\Delta$ parameter and light value are only used by delta-stepping algorithm.

requests based on the new value of $u.dist$ that are then added to $ws$.

The (optimized) Bellman-Ford algorithm processes requests in arbitrary order. Dijkstra's algorithm is an *ordered* algorithm which processes requests in increasing distance order. The delta-stepping algorithm orders requests as follows. The algorithm creates a sequence of buckets, $b_1, b_2, \ldots, b_N$. Bucket $b_i$ contains all requests with distances in the range $[\Delta(i-1), \Delta i)$ where $\Delta$ is an input to the algorithm. Furthermore, requests are divided into light requests, whose distances come from edges with weight less than $\Delta$, and heavy requests otherwise. Requests are processed in increasing bucket order. Within a bucket, light requests are processed before heavy ones.

### 2.5 Preflow-push

Given a directed graph $G = (V, E)$, a capacity function $c : E \rightarrow \mathbb{R}^+$ mapping edges to non-negative values and source and sink nodes $s, t \in V$, the preflow-push algorithm computes the maximal flow from source to sink. Unlike in maxflow algorithms based on augmenting paths, nodes in preflow-push can temporarily have more flow coming into them than going out. Each node $n$ maintains its excess inflow $n.excess$. Each node $n$ also has a label called height, which is an estimate of the distance from $n$ to $t$ in the residual graph induced by unsaturated edges. Nodes with non-zero excess that are not the source or sink are contained in a workset. These nodes are called active nodes. The preflow-push algorithm repeatedly selects a node from the workset. Each node tries to eliminate its excess by pushing flow to a neighbor (see Figure 5). Pushing flow may cause a neighbor to become active. A node can only push flow to a neighbor at a lower height. If a node is active but no neighbors are eligible to receive flow, the node relabels itself, increasing its height to one more than its lowest height neighbor.

Cherkassy and Goldberg show the importance of two heuristics named global relabeling and gap relabeling [6]. Global relabeling is a technique that periodically reassigns heights by performing a breadth-first traversal from the sink. The frequency of global relabeling is determined empirically. Gap relabeling is a technique that preemptively removes from the workset any nodes that cannot push flow to the sink. The key insight is that if no node has height $h$, all nodes with height greater than $h$ cannot push flow to the sink. Cherkassy and Goldberg also consider two orders for processing active nodes: HL order, where nodes are processed in decreasing height order, and FIFO order. The parallel implementation evaluated in Section 5 includes all these heuristics.

## 3. Scheduling Policies

Section 2 demonstrates that many algorithms benefit from scheduling strategies that are more complex than simple strategies like LIFO and FIFO. In this section, we show how the informal policies

```
Workset ws = new Workset({s});
foreach (Node u : ws) {
 L1:
  while (u.excess > 0) {
    for (Node v : u.neighbors()) {
      float cap = G.edgeData(u, v);
      if (cap > 0 && u.height == v.height + 1) {
        pushFlow(u, v, min(cap, u.excess));
        if (v != s && v != t)
          ws.add(v);
        if (u.excess == 0)
          break L1;
      }
    }
    relabel(u);
  }
  if (*)
    globalRelabel()
}
```

**Figure 5.** Pseudocode for preflow-push.

described in the previous section can be encoded in a simple but flexible specification language.

Scheduling specifications are built from *ordering rules*, where an ordering rule specifies a total order on activities or items. Given two items $a$ and $b$, an ordering rule $R$ may specify that $a$ should be processed before $b$ (written as $a <_R b$) or vice versa ($b >_R a$), or it may leave the order unspecified ($a =_R b$). For example, if items have integer priorities, an ordering rule $A_1$ may order them in ascending priority order; the relative order of items with the same priority is left unspecified by $A_1$. Ordering rules can be composed sequentially in a manner similar to lexicographic ordering: a sequence $D = R_1 R_2 R_3 \ldots$ is itself an ordering rule that first orders items according to $R_1$; if two items are not strictly ordered by $R_1$, they are ordered according to $R_2$, etc. For example, if $F_1$ orders items in FIFO order, then $A_1 F_1$ denotes the order in which items are processed in increasing priority order and items with the same priority are processed in FIFO order. For the synthesis procedure described in Section 4, it is convenient to distinguish between *final rules*, which are rules that appear last in an ordering sequence, and *non-final rules*.

As discussed in Section 2, some implementations of irregular algorithms maintain separate global and thread-local worksets, so it is natural to use different ordering rules for them. A scheduling specification can have both a global ordering rule and a local ordering rule. The global rule is applied to the initial set of items, and the local rule is applied to each thread-local workset, which holds items created dynamically by the corresponding thread. A thread accesses the global workset only when its local workset is empty. Continuing the previous example, if $L_1$ is last-in-first-out (LIFO) order, then global order $A_1 F_1$ and local order $L_1$ specify that global items are processed as before, and local items are processed in LIFO order.

Figure 6 gives the syntax rules for scheduler specifications. $\mathbf{T}$ is the type of items. Figure 7 gives the semantics. The meaning of an ordering rule $R$ is given as a function over items $a$ and $b$ that is true iff $a <_R b$ ($<$ is the standard order on integers and reals). For the FIFO and LIFO rules, we define an auxiliary function $\mathbf{time}$ that maps an item to an integer according to when the item is added to the scheduler. For the first item $x_1$ added to the scheduler, $\mathbf{time}(x_1) = 0$; for the second item $x_2$, $\mathbf{time}(x_2) = 1$, and so on. $f_U$ is an injective function mapping items to integers; this function essentially encodes a random permutation of items. The function $f_D$ should be consistent with a total order.

Figure 8 shows the specifications of the scheduling policies discussed in Section 2. When a specification has an empty local ordering, we omit the global and local tags. The BRIO specification

| | | | |
|---|---|---|---|
| $P$ | ::= | Global: $D$ Local: $D$ | *Specification* |
| $D$ | ::= | $R_{NF}^*$ $R_F?$ | *Ordering rule* |
| $R_F$ | ::= | FIFO | *Final rule* |
| | \| | LIFO | |
| | \| | Random | |
| $R_{NF}$ | ::= | ChunkedFIFO($k$) | *Non-final rule* |
| | \| | ChunkedLIFO($k$) | |
| | \| | Ordered($f_D$) | |
| | \| | OrderedByMetric($f_M$) | |
| $k$ | | | *Integer* |
| $f_D$ | | | $\mathbf{T} \times \mathbf{T} \to \mathbf{bool}$ |
| $f_M$ | | | $\mathbf{T} \to \mathbb{R}$ |

**Figure 6.** Scheduler specification syntax.

$$\begin{aligned}
[\![\text{FIFO}]\!](a,b) &= \mathbf{time}(a) < \mathbf{time}(b)\\
[\![\text{LIFO}]\!](a,b) &= \mathbf{time}(a) > \mathbf{time}(b)\\
[\![\text{Random}]\!](a,b) &= f_U(a) < f_U(b)\\
[\![\text{ChunkedFIFO}(k)]\!](a,b) &= \lfloor \mathbf{time}(a)/k \rfloor < \lfloor \mathbf{time}(b)/k \rfloor\\
[\![\text{ChunkedLIFO}(k)]\!](a,b) &= \lfloor \mathbf{time}(a)/k \rfloor > \lfloor \mathbf{time}(b)/k \rfloor\\
[\![\text{Ordered}(f_D)]\!](a,b) &= f_D(a,b)\\
[\![\text{OrderedByMetric}(f_M)]\!](a,b) &= f_M(a) < f_M(b)\\
[\![R_1\, R_2 \ldots]\!](a,b) &= \begin{cases} [\![R_2 \ldots]\!](a,b) & \text{if } a =_{R_1} b \\ [\![R_1]\!](a,b) & \text{otherwise} \end{cases}
\end{aligned}$$

**Figure 7.** Rule semantics.

assumes that items have already been assigned rounds according to the random distribution described previously. To process light requests before heavy ones, the delta-stepping specification splits each bucket into two: one part for the light requests and one part for the heavy requests.

# 4. Synthesis

It is straightforward to implement sequential schedulers for policies specified in the language described in Section 3. Each rule can be implemented by a *workset*, which is an object with the following methods:

- **void** add(**T** t) — adds an item to the workset
- **T** poll () — removes and returns the next item to execute; if there are no items left, returns a **null** value distinct from all items added to the workset

Items are added to the workset by invoking the add method, which returns the value **void** when it completes. To get items from the workset, the poll method is invoked; if this method invocation does not find any items in the workset, it returns a unique **null** value.

The goal of this section is to synthesize *concurrent* worksets that implement this functionality. One approach is to compose a set of library components, each of which is a workset by itself. There is a workset for each final rule; non-final rules are implemented by worksets parameterized by a function that constructs instances of the next workset in the ordering sequence, the inner workset.

However, a naive implementation along these lines can be incorrect in a concurrent setting, as we argue in Section 4.1, and the result may not satisfy any intuitive notion of correctness such as linearizability [16]. To address this problem, we propose a relaxed correctness condition in Section 4.2 that requires modifications to the semantics of worksets and to how they are used by clients.

In Section 4.3, we discuss two important consequences of this relaxed condition: (1) all final scheduling policy rules in Section 3 have implementations that satisfy the relaxed condition, and (2) non-final worksets satisfy the relaxed condition assuming only that their inner worksets satisfy the relaxed condition. This permits compositional construction of worksets.

In Section 4.4, we discuss the implementation of scheduling policies in Java and several optimizations to improve the performance of the synthesized worksets.

## 4.1 Problems with Naive Composition

To understand the issues that arise in composing worksets, consider the implementation of the OrderedByMetric rule in lines 1-23 of Figure 9, and its client, a simple *runtime system*, in lines 24-30. The runtime system manages threads and assigns them work. The workset creates an array of inner worksets and processes each inner workset in ascending order. This workset is essentially an implementation of a priority queue in which the range of keys is known *a priori*; there is one inner workset (bucket) for each key value. Similar worksets have been used in a variety of sequential [1, 6, 32] and parallel implementations [25] of irregular algorithms.

Unfortunately, the workset in Figure 9 can exhibit incorrect behavior because it is possible for items to be inserted into the workset but never retrieved. Consider two threads $T_1$ and $T_2$, where $T_1$ is executing the poll method and $T_2$ is executing the add method. The following sequence of events may take place:

1. $T_1$ executes line 14. The cursor value is $i$, and the the poll method on buckets[i] returns **null**.
2. $T_2$ executes lines 6-8. The value of index $= i$, so an item is added to buckets[i].
3. $T_1$ executes lines 15 and 16 of the poll method, incrementing cursor.

Clearly, the item added by $T_2$ is now lost. The race exists even if each line of the implementation is atomic, so that reading and updating the cursor on line 8 or incrementing its value on line 16 is performed atomically. To use this implementation correctly in a concurrent context, we must ensure that when poll moves to the next bucket, no thread is adding an element to a higher priority bucket. One solution is to use transactional memory [15], but the overhead of software transactional memory systems is high, especially for a performance-critical component like a scheduler. Hardware transactional memory systems exist, but they are not widely available.

We summarize these observations.

- In general, simple compositions of worksets do not produce correct concurrent worksets.
- Composition of concurrent worksets is problematic even in absence of having to maintain a particular order of items.

## 4.2 Relaxed Concurrent Semantics

In this section, we describe a solution to the problem of composing worksets that takes advantage of the fact that scheduling specifications for unordered algorithms are inherently "fuzzy" and are intended as suggestions to the runtime system rather than as commands that must be followed exactly. At a high level, the idea is the following.

- We relax the behavior of the poll method so that in a parallel setting, it may return a different item than the one it would have returned in a sequential setting. In addition, we allow poll to return **null** even when there are still items in the workset. These modifications permit us to implement poll with low overhead.
- To compensate for the relaxed behavior of poll, we introduce a new method poll-s that is similar to poll but is never executed concurrently with other invocations. It returns **null** only when the workset is truly empty.

| Algorithm | Order | Specification | Used by |
|---|---|---|---|
| DMR | Bucketed triangle angle (AS2) | OrderedByMetric($\lambda t$ : minangle($t$)) FIFO | [32] |
| | Local stack (AS1) | Global: ChunkedFIFO($k$) Local: LIFO | [18] |
| DT | BRIO (AS1) | OrderedByMetric($\lambda p : p.round$) ChunkedFIFO($k$) | [1] |
| | Random | Random | [8] |
| PFP | FIFO | FIFO | [12] |
| | HL order (AS1) | OrderedByMetric($\lambda n : -n.height$) FIFO | [6] |
| PTA | LRF | FIFO | [29] |
| | Split worklists (BS-F) | | [14, 28] |
| SSSP | Bellman-Ford | FIFO | [9] |
| | Delta-stepping (AS1) | OrderedByMetric($\lambda n : \lfloor 2 * n.w/\Delta \rfloor + (n.light) ? 0 : 1$) FIFO | [25] |
| | Dijkstra (AS2) | Ordered($\lambda a, b : a.w \leq b.w$) | [9] |

**Figure 8.** Application-specific scheduling specifications.

```
1  class OrderedByMetricWorkset implements Workset {
2    Workset[] buckets;
3    int cursor;
4
5    void add(T t) {
6      int index = floatToInt(f_M(t));
7      buckets[index].add(t);
8      if (index < cursor) cursor = index;
9    }
10
11   T poll() {
12     T retval = null;
13     while (cursor < buckets.length) {
14       retval = buckets[cursor].poll();
15       if (retval == null)
16         cursor++;
17       else
18         break;
19     }
20     return retval;
21   }
22 }
23
24 OrderedByMetricWorkset scheduler;
25 ThreadPool.fork(N); // spawn N threads
26 T item;
27 while ((item = scheduler.poll()) != null) {
28   operator.call(item, scheduler);
29 }
30 ThreadPool.join(N);
```

**Figure 9.** Naive bucketed scheduler and its use in a parallel runtime system.

Intuitively, if most items are retrieved from the workset using the poll method, and poll-s is used infrequently to determine if the workset is truly empty, we get a solution that is both correct and efficient. In this section, we formalize this behavior, and in Section 4.3, we show how this behavior is closed under composition.

We model a workset by its history $H$, which is a finite sequence of *events*, where an event is either (1) a method invocation, (2) a response to a method invocation, or (3) a special termination event, $\langle$term$\rangle$. We write $\langle o.m(a, b, \ldots)\ T\rangle$ for an invocation on object $o$ of method $m$ with arguments $a, b, \ldots$ by thread $T$, $\langle o.m(a, b, \ldots)/r\ T\rangle$ for a response to method $m$ with return value $r$, and **void** for the unit return value. An invocation $\langle o_1.m_1(a_1, b_1, \ldots)\ T_1\rangle$ *matches* a response $\langle o_2.m_2(a_2, b_2, \ldots)/r\ T_2\rangle$ if $o_1 = o_2, m_1 = m_2, a_1 = a_2, b_1 = b_2$ and so on, and $T_1 = T_2$. We omit the object and/or thread if it is clear from context. We use $x_1, x_2, \ldots$ as variables over arguments or return values.

An invocation is *pending* in $H$ if it has no matching response. A history is *whole* if it has no pending invocations and it contains exactly one termination event and that is the last event in the history. A history *restricted to* object $o$ or thread $T$ is the subsequence with only events on $o$ or by $T$ respectively and possibly a termination event. Without loss of generality, we assume items are unique. The notation $a \rightarrow_H b$ denotes that event $a$ precedes event $b$ in history $H$; we write $a \rightarrow b$ when the history is clear from context.

Property 1 is a formal description of the behavior of poll and poll-s. Condition B1 states that (1) items returned by poll and poll-s must have been added earlier by the add method, and (2) a given item can only be returned once. Both requirements are captured by the injective function $M$. Condition B2 states that poll-s cannot be invoked when there are pending method invocations. Condition B3 states that if poll-s returns **null**, all previously added items have been retrieved by poll or poll-s, and the workset is truly empty. This is captured by requiring $M$ to be a bijective function.

**Property 1** (Weak Bag). *A history $H$ models a* weak bag *if the following are true:*

*B1. There is an injective function $M$ from non-***null** *response events $e_1 = \langle poll()/x_1\ T_1\rangle$ or $e_1 = \langle poll\text{-}s()/x_1\ T_1\rangle$ to invocation events $e_2 = \langle add(x_2)\ T_2\rangle$ such that (1) $M(e_1) = e_2$, (2) $x_1 = x_2$, and (3) $e_2 \rightarrow e_1$.*

*B2. For each invocation event $e = \langle poll\text{-}s()\ T\rangle$ of poll-s in $H = H_1, e, H_2$, there are no pending invocations in $H_1$.*

*B3. For each* **null** *response event $e = \langle poll\text{-}s()/\mathbf{null}\ T\rangle$ of poll-s in $H = H_1, e, H_2$, $H_1$ satisfies condition B1 and $M$ is a bijective function.*

A workset is *correct* if it only generates whole histories satisfying Property 1. It is the responsibility of the client to use the workset properly by never invoking poll-s concurrently with other methods. This form of correctness may seem particularly weak since it does not refer to the sequential ordering semantics. However, we have found it useful because it includes many natural compositions of worksets as well as most hand-written schedulers. A linearizable bag is a correct workset if one considers poll-s the same as poll. Likewise, a bag with a single lock guarding all its methods is also a correct workset.[4]

One correct workset and its proper use by a runtime system is the following modification of Figure 9. After line 30, the runtime system should call poll-s; if the returned value is a non-**null** item, the system should process that item and go to line 25 to continue execution. The poll-s method should walk the bucket array calling poll-s on each inner workset and return the first non-**null** item if it exists.

The implementations in the Galois system of the final rules in Figure 6 satisfy Property 1 since the LIFO and FIFO rules are implemented by a linearizable stack and queue respectively, and the

[4] It is possible to introduce deadlock when arbitrarily composing worksets with locks. However, compositions based on Theorem 2 whose implementations are themselves wait-free do not introduce deadlocks.

Random rule is implemented with a resizable array and all method invocations are protected by a single lock.

### 4.3 Workset Composition

We now show how the implementations of the non-final rules in Figure 6 satisfy Property 1, assuming they are parameterized by correct worksets. We give a detailed description for the OrderedByMetric workset, and for lack of space, summarize the reasoning for the other non-final worksets.

Theorem 1 models the behavior of the OrderedByMetric workset by its history with respect to its inner worksets. Theorem 2 shows how objects that generate such histories are correct worksets.

**Theorem 1** (OrderedByMetric). *Let o be an instance of the OrderedByMetric workset in Figure 9 modified so that each thread maintains a thread-local cursor variable and poll-s walks all the buckets calling poll-s on each inner workset. Let* $W = \{w_1, w_2, \ldots, w_n\}$ *be the set of correct worksets contained in the buckets. The workset o only generates whole histories containing the following non-overlapping sequences when restricted to thread T for all threads:*

*D1.* $\langle o.add(x)\rangle$,
$\quad\langle w.add(x)\rangle, \langle w.add(x)/\mathbf{void}\rangle$,
$\langle o.add()/\mathbf{void}\rangle$.

*D2.* $\langle o.poll()\rangle$,
$\quad(\langle w_*.poll()\rangle, \langle w_*.poll()/\mathbf{null}\rangle)^*$,
$\quad\langle w.poll()\rangle, \langle w.poll()/x\rangle$,
$\langle o.poll()/x\rangle$ *where* $x \neq \mathbf{null}$.

*D3. The above with poll() replaced with poll-s().*

*D4.* $\langle o.poll()\rangle$,
$\quad(\langle w_*.poll()\rangle, \langle w_*.poll()/\mathbf{null}\rangle)^*$,
$\langle o.poll()/\mathbf{null}\rangle$.

*D5.* $\langle o.poll\text{-}s()\rangle$,
$\quad\langle w_1.poll\text{-}s()\rangle, \langle w_1.poll\text{-}s()/\mathbf{null}\rangle, \ldots,$
$\quad\langle w_n.poll\text{-}s()\rangle, \langle w_n.poll\text{-}s()/\mathbf{null}\rangle$,
$\langle o.poll\text{-}s()/\mathbf{null}\rangle$.

*Proof.* Omitted due to lack of space. □

**Theorem 2** (OrderedByMetric is correct). *Whole histories H satisfying Theorem 1 model a weak bag.*

*Proof.* We consider each condition of Property 1 in turn.

First, $H$ satisfies condition B1. Without loss of generality, we discuss events of poll; events of poll-s behave similarly. From clauses D2 and D4, the only time the workset $o$ produces a non-**null** response $e_1 = \langle o.\text{poll}()/x_1\rangle$ is when one of its correct worksets $w \in W$ produces a response $f_1 = \langle w.\text{poll}()/x_1\rangle$. There is exactly one event $e_1$ for each event $f_1$ and vice versa. Let $M_1$ be the bijective function from events of the form $e_1$ to events of the form $f_1$. From clause D1, there is exactly one event $f_2 = \langle w.\text{add}(x_2)\rangle$ for each event $e_2 = \langle o.\text{add}(x_2)\rangle$ and vice versa. Let $M_2$ be the bijective function from events of the form $f_2$ to events of the form $e_2$.

We now show there exists an injective function $M_C$ such that $M_C(e_1) = e_2$, $x_1 = x_2$ and $e_1 \nrightarrow e_2$. By definition, $M_1(e_1) = f_1 = \langle w.\text{poll}()/x_1\rangle$. Since $w$ is a correct workset, there exists an injective function $M_w$ such that $M_w(f_1) = f_2 = \langle w.\text{add}(x_1)\rangle$ and $f_2 \nrightarrow f_1$. Let $M$ be the expansion of $M_w$ over the range of all $w \in W$. The ranges of $M_{w_1}, \ldots, M_{w_n}$ are disjoint and each $M_w$ is an injective function so $M$ is also an injective function (see Figure 10). By definition, $M_2(f_2) = e_2 = \langle o.\text{add}(x_1)\rangle$. Let $M_C$ be the composed function $M_2 \circ M \circ M_1$. $M_C$ is injective because $M$ is injective and $M_1$ and $M_2$ are bijective. $M_C(e_1) = e_2$ by function

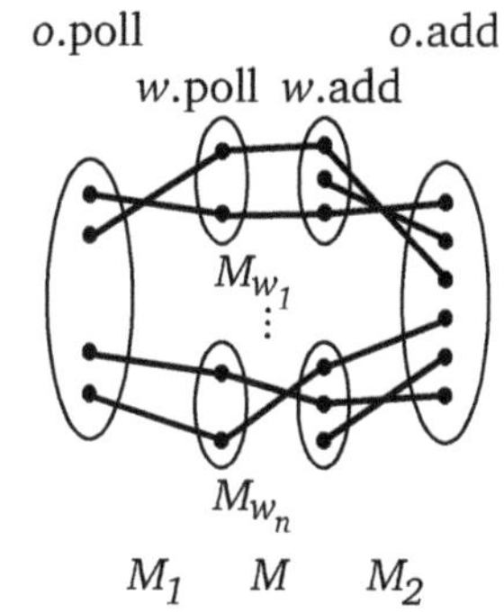


**Figure 10.** Relationship between $M_1$, $M$ and $M_2$ in the proof of Theorem 2

composition. From clauses D1 and D2, $e_2 \rightarrow f_2$ and $f_1 \rightarrow e_1$, and by the correctness of $w$, $f_2 \nrightarrow f_1$; so, by transitivity, $e_2 \nrightarrow e_1$.

Second, $H$ satisfies condition B2. Clients of $o$ do not invoke $o$.poll-s() concurrently. From clauses D3 and D5, it is clear that if there are no pending invocations immediately before $o$.poll-s() is invoked, then there will be no pending invocations immediately before $w$.poll-s() for all $w \in W$.

Finally, $H$ satisfies condition B3. From above, we know that $M_C$ satisfies condition B1 and is an injective function from non-**null** poll and poll-s responses to add invocations on $o$. We now show that when $o$ produces the **null** response $\langle o.\text{poll-s}()/\mathbf{null}\rangle$, $M_C$ is a bijection as well. From clause D5, if $o$ produces a **null** response, all $w \in W$ have produced a **null** response as well. Thus, $M$ is a bijection, and correspondingly, $M_C$ is one as well. □

The ChunkedFIFO rule is implemented with a single linearizable (global) queue whose elements (chunks) are instances of the inner workset. Each inner workset contains at most $k$ items. Each thread maintains a thread-local chunk to poll from. When the chunk is empty, the thread polls from the global queue for the next chunk. Each thread also maintains a thread-local chunk to add to. When the chunk is full, the thread adds it to the global queue and creates a new empty chunk to add to. The poll-s method walks each thread-local chunk and the global queue calling poll-s on each.

Theorem 2 does not immediately apply because chunks are created and discarded dynamically. One modification would be to keep track of all the chunks ever created. However, one observation is that chunks are accessed by at most one thread at a time, and they are discarded when they are empty, which can be determined by invoking poll-s on the chunk. Empty chunks will never contain any more items. Thus, discarded chunks do not affect the eventual correctness of the workset. Only chunks that may contain items matter, which are precisely those traversed by poll-s.

The ChunkedLIFO rule is implemented similarly to ChunkedFIFO except with a linearizable stack.

The Ordered rule is implemented with a concurrent heap with additional locks to protect the inner worksets. Showing the correctness of its implementation is beyond the scope of this paper because it uses commutativity conditions to reduce the granularity of the locking [20].

Although not a rule *per se*, the composition of a global and local rule, used to implement global and local orders in specifications, is implemented with worksets as well. There is one workset that implements the global rule and thread-local worksets that implement the local rule. Initial work is added to the global workset, while newly created work is added to the thread-local workset. New work is retrieved from the thread-local workset, if possible, and from the global workset otherwise. For proving correctness, this implementation can be viewed as a refinement of a chunked workset where

```
Lambda<T, Integer> indexer = new Lambda<T, Integer >() {
  public Integer call(T item) {
    return item.height;
  }
}
Priority.first(OrderedByMetric.class, indexer)
        .then(FIFO.class)
```

**Figure 11.** Concrete syntax of AS1 for PFP.

```
Priority.first(G1.class, args).then(...)
        .thenLocally(L1.class, args).then(...)
```

**Figure 12.** Concrete syntax of Global: $G_1$ ... Local: $L_1$ ....

chunks are never discarded but are instead refilled from the global workset.

### 4.4 Implementation and Optimization

In the Galois system, the specification language is implemented as a library-based domain-specific language in Java. Each rule is represented by a Java class that implements the corresponding workset. Figure 11 gives an example. Figure 12 gives the general form. The sequence of method calls produces an AST that is passed to the workset synthesizer.

Additionally, we take advantage of the semantics of rules to choose optimized workset implementations.

- **Use Serial**: As mentioned in Section 4.3, the inner worksets used by ChunkedFIFO and ChunkedLIFO are thread-local. The worksets generated from the local part of a specification are also thread-local. Thread-local worksets can be implemented with non-concurrent data structures that are typically more efficient than concurrent ones.
- **Ignore Size**: In certain cases, worksets require inner worksets to maintain an estimate of the number of items they contain. The chunked worksets use this to keep track of when a chunk is full. The Ordered workset uses these sizes to implement commutativity conditions. This overhead may be significant in concurrent worksets because keeping track of sizes may require atomic increments. When sizes are not needed, the size metadata and effort maintaining it may be removed.
- **Use Bounded**: When a chunked workset is used, each inner workset can be no larger than the chunk size. The inner worksets can be optimized for a bounded size rather than using dynamically sized data structures.

The synthesizer applies rewrite rules over the AST to detect the above cases and selects, if possible, implementations that are non-concurrent, do not keep track of their size or are bounded. Table 1 summarizes the impact of these optimizations for the PFP application and a synthesized scheduler called BASE (described in more detail in Section 5). Positive numbers indicate how much slower a combination is relative to all optimizations on. We chose to highlight this application and scheduler because all the optimizations described above can be applied and the amount of work done per workset item is small, which increases the relative impact of an efficient workset implementation. From the table, it is clear that these optimizations on worksets have a significant and mostly beneficial impact on single-threaded and multi-threaded performance.

| Ignore Size | Use Serial | Use Bounded | $t = 1$ | $t = 8$ |
|---|---|---|---|---|
| + | + | + | 0.0 | 0.0 |
| - | + | + | 0.8 | 12.1 |
| + | - | + | 2.4 | 5.5 |
| - | - | + | 7.8 | 7.7 |
| + | + | - | 3.6 | 3.5 |
| - | + | - | 11.3 | 11.5 |
| + | - | - | 5.0 | 16.8 |
| - | - | - | 2.9 | 17.5 |

**Table 1.** Relative difference in percent (%) of the runtime of PFP and BASE scheduler on Shanghai machine varying synthesizer optimizations (+: on, -: off) relative to all optimizations on for one and eight threads.

## 5. Evaluation

We implemented the algorithms presented in Section 2 and parallelized them using the Galois system.[5] Figure 13 shows the datasets we used for each application. The shortest-path application uses atomic compare-and-set operations to update distances. The currently distributed implementation uses abstract locks [19], but compare-and-set operations are much faster for this application.

We modified the Galois system to support the scheduler specifications and synthesis algorithm described in Section 4. To evaluate our approach, we ran each algorithm with the following set of schedulers.

- **BASE**: This is the default scheduler used by the Galois system. It is a synthesized ChunkedFIFO with a chunk-size of 32. Each chunk is a thread-local LIFO.
- **FIFO, LIFO, RAND**: These schedulers are synthesized from the final rules FIFO, LIFO and Random. Application-specific schedulers typically use one of these schedulers as their lowest-level (final) scheduler.
- **WS-L, WS-F**: These schedulers are work-stealing with local LIFOs and FIFOs respectively. These schedulers were ported directly from the Fork-Join implementation in JSR166 and should appear in Java JDK 7. WS-L is widely used in many parallel systems.
- **BS-L, BS-F**: These schedulers use a bulk-synchronous strategy with global LIFOs and FIFOs respectively. A barrier is used to safely swap between queues concurrently.
- **AS1, AS2**: These schedulers are synthesized from the application-specific specifications in Figure 8.

We ran our experiments on three architectures:

- **Nehalem**: a Sun Fire X2270 machine running Ubuntu Linux 8.04.4 LTS 64-bit. It contains two 4-core 2.93 GHz Intel Xeon X5570 (Nehalem) processors. The two CPUs share 24 GB of main memory. Each core has a 32 KB L1 cache and a unified 256 KB L2 cache. Each processor has an 8 MB L3 cache that is shared among the cores.
- **Shanghai**: a machine also running Ubuntu Linux 8.04.4 LTS 64-bit. It contains four 4-core 2.7 GHz AMD Opteron 8384 (Shanghai) processors. Each core has a 64 KB L1 cache and a 512 KB L2 cache. Each processor has a 6 MB L3 cache that is shared among the cores.
- **Niagara**: a Sun T5440 machine running SunOS 5.10. It contains four 8-core 1.4 GHz Sun UltraSPARC T2 Plus (Niagara 2) processors. Each processor has a 4 MB L2 cache that is shared among the cores.

[5] Available at `http://iss.ices.utexas.edu/galois`

We used the Sun JDK 1.6.0_21 to compile and run the programs with a heap size of 20 GB. To control for JIT compilation, we ran each application four times within the same JVM instance and report only the last run.

The Galois system uses speculative parallelization, which introduces overheads from (1) using concurrent implementations of data structures and schedulers rather than their sequential counterparts, (2) acquiring locks to guarantee disjointness of neighborhoods, and (3) recording undo actions to implement rollback. The *serial* version of an application uses sequential data structures only and does not acquire locks or perform undo actions. The difference in performance between the serial version and the parallel, one-threaded version is the overhead of enabling speculative execution but never using it. This overhead can be significant for applications with short activities like PFP and SSSP.

Table 2 shows the runtimes for serial applications. Table 3 shows the parallel speedup over the best performing serial scheduler (shown in bold in Table 2). The runtimes for PTA exclude time to read input, perform offline-cycle detection and write results. This differs from the methodology of Mendez-Lojo *et al.*, which includes the time to perform offline-cycle detection [24]. For all other applications, runtimes exclude time to read input data or write results but may include sections of the application that are not parallelized. This portion of time is usually negligible, but for DT with the AS1 scheduler, this includes time to construct the oct-tree.

Empty entries indicate combinations of schedulers and applications that would either be redundant or perform significantly worse (by an order of magnitude or more) than the best serial version. For DT, the performance without randomizing the initial points is much worse than with randomization. Since the application does not create any new tasks, we evaluated the BASE and WS-L schedulers after including a timed phase that randomizes the input points. We omit the other non-random schedulers because they perform similarly after including this phase. For PTA, the RAND, LIFO and WS-L schedulers timed out. For SSSP, only the AS1 and AS2 schedulers are competitive.

An important result is that the best scheduler for serial execution tends to be the best for parallel execution as well. This supports the use case where users experiment with scheduling specifications within a sequential programming model and rely on a synthesis routine to generate efficient, concurrent schedulers that faithfully maintain the desired scheduling. Also, note the large swings between best and worst schedulers and recall that the missing entries for PFP, PTA and SSSP correspond to combinations that perform significantly worse than the recorded times. Choosing the wrong scheduler can have a drastic impact on performance.

Overall, the AS1 schedulers perform as well or better than any fixed-function scheduler for the same application. Surprisingly, the BASE scheduler, which is implemented by a global queue with fixed-size local stacks, performs relatively well across applications. DMR benefits from LIFO policies, while PFP, PTA and SSSP benefit from FIFO policies.

While direct comparison is not possible, these results are similar to previously reported results of application-specific schedulers on similar inputs for PFP [3], PTA [24] and SSSP [23].

Now, we turn to each application in more detail.

***Delaunay Mesh Refinement*** Table 2 shows that for the serial implementation, the best performance is obtained by the LIFO scheduler. When a bad triangle is fixed, it may create a set of new bad triangles whose cavities overlap with the cavity of the original bad triangle. The LIFO scheduler exploits the potential temporal and spatial locality. However, both of the global LIFO scheduling policies, LIFO and BS-L, perform poorly in a parallel setting because the probability of conflicts increases if triangles close to each other in the mesh are processed speculatively in parallel. Figure 14 shows the relative number of aborted to total iterations on Shanghai. The trends are similar for the other two machines. Not surprisingly, global FIFO schedulers behave the same way. The BASE scheduler, which uses a global FIFO, ameliorates this problem to some extent by distributing chunks of work to each thread.

The best performance is obtained with the AS1 scheduler, which is implemented by a global workset processed in chunked FIFO order and local worksets maintained in LIFO order. This enables exploitation of locality while controlling the abort ratio, as can be seen in Figure 14.

***Delaunay Triangulation*** DT does not create any new work. Its performance is governed by the initial work order, which should be randomized for best algorithmic performance. With randomization, the BASE and WS-L schedulers perform similarly. AS1 is significantly faster than the other two schedulers serially, but the performance difference dissipates as the number of threads increases. Recall that the AS1 scheduler is designed to increase spatial locality between activities. In speculative parallel execution, this scheduling strategy causes the abort ratio to increase, as can be seen in Figure 15.

***Preflow-push*** PFP is an example of an algorithm whose performance is highly schedule-dependent because different schedulers result in dramatically different amounts of work. Figure 16 shows the number of iterations committed relative to the best performing serial version on Shanghai. Most schedulers result in twice as many iterations as the best serial version. LIFO and WS-L perform four times more iterations in some cases. Table 2 shows the impact of the varying work on the serial versions. The runtime of the fastest and slowest schedulers differ by a factor of more than three.

For a hand-parallelized implementation of PFP using the heuristics described in Section 2, Bader and Sachdeva reported a maximum speedup of about 2 with eight processors on an UltraSPARC II architecture with an input similar to that used here, which is refered to as an RMF graph [3].

***Inclusion-based Points-to Analysis*** PTA is another example of a highly schedule-dependent algorithm. PTA performs a fixpoint computation, and for these computations, FIFO policies usually perform well because a variable gets to accumulate several updates before its value is propagated down-stream. LIFO policies perform poorly, and most versions time-out. BS-F, which alternates between two queues, does the best on this input. On other inputs, not shown here, BASE outperforms BS-F.

As noted earlier, these results are based on the implementation of Mendez-Lojo *et al.*, the first parallel implementation of PTA [24].

***Single-source Shortest-path*** SSSP is a case where the generally accepted best serial scheduler, which is AS2 and is based on Dijkstra's algorithm, does not perform well in parallel. It has better theoretical algorithmic complexity, but the concurrent priority queue limits performance on most inputs. The difficulty in implementing such queues is one motivation for the delta-stepping order (AS1), which seeks to balance good order with efficient concurrent implementation. From experiments not shown here, it can be shown that the delta-stepping order performs only 1.2 times more work than Dijkstra's algorithm for this input, an overhead that is modest enough to overcome through parallelism.

Madduri *et al.* produced an implementation of delta-stepping for the Cray MTA-2 architecture [23]. On the same input used here, a road network of the western USA, they reported a maximum speedup of about 2 on sixteen processors.

| | BASE | RAND | LIFO | FIFO | WS-L | WS-F | BS-L | BS-F | AS2 | AS1 |
|---|---|---|---|---|---|---|---|---|---|---|
| | | | | | Nehalem | | | | | |
| DMR | 12.88 | 14.80 | **11.45** | 13.09 | 11.51 | 13.27 | 12.76 | 13.17 | 15.56 | 11.62 |
| DT | 25.04 | | | | | 25.42 | | | | **14.78** |
| PFP | 110.93 | 109.77 | 169.86 | 115.40 | 173.47 | 116.44 | 110.18 | 118.59 | | **45.94** |
| PTA | 13.87 | - | - | **12.58** | - | 12.74 | 20.26 | 12.84 | | |
| SSSP | - | - | - | - | - | - | - | - | 7.66 | **4.96** |
| | | | | | Shanghai | | | | | |
| DMR | 16.29 | 19.52 | **13.55** | 16.76 | 13.74 | 16.76 | 16.25 | 16.71 | 19.59 | 13.64 |
| DT | 43.40 | | | | | 43.55 | | | | **27.86** |
| PFP | 237.04 | 210.57 | 320.24 | 237.17 | 314.53 | 234.13 | 216.50 | 217.67 | | **74.26** |
| PTA | 19.99 | - | - | 18.80 | - | **18.79** | 26.44 | 18.82 | | |
| SSSP | - | - | - | - | - | - | - | - | 11.08 | **9.53** |
| | | | | | Niagara | | | | | |
| DMR | 61.76 | 68.10 | 54.79 | 63.51 | **53.84** | 63.31 | 62.86 | 64.17 | 77.81 | 60.33 |
| DT | 178.21 | | | | | 179.00 | | | | **149.42** |
| PFP | 787.05 | 734.27 | 1264.61 | 741.01 | 1297.71 | 775.04 | 720.20 | 827.07 | | **342.41** |
| PTA | 59.17 | - | - | 57.73 | - | 57.30 | 76.16 | **56.99** | | |
| SSSP | - | - | - | - | - | - | - | - | 33.84 | **23.35** |

**Table 2.** Runtimes of serial versions in seconds. In bold are the best serial times, the basis for the speedup numbers in Table 3. Entries with - timed out. Blank entries indicate invalid or redundant combinations.

| | BASE | RAND | LIFO | FIFO | WS-L | WS-F | BS-L | BS-F | AS2 | AS1 |
|---|---|---|---|---|---|---|---|---|---|---|
| | | | | | Nehalem ($t \leq 8$) | | | | | |
| DMR | 5.70 | 4.82 | 0.95 | 3.81 | 4.35 | 5.13 | 2.64 | 3.53 | 2.01 | **6.15** |
| DT | 2.21 | | | | | 2.09 | | | | **2.35** |
| PFP | 1.30 | 0.71 | 0.20 | 1.15 | 0.72 | 2.30 | 0.37 | 0.89 | | **3.35** |
| PTA | 2.83 | - | - | 3.53 | - | 2.05 | 2.37 | **3.77** | | |
| SSSP | - | - | - | - | - | - | - | - | 0.61 | **3.16** |
| | | | | | Shanghai ($t \leq 16$) | | | | | |
| DMR | 7.85 | 3.43 | 0.95 | 3.74 | 6.94 | 7.53 | 1.91 | 3.83 | 2.32 | **10.45** |
| DT | 2.64 | | | | | **2.65** | | | | 2.53 |
| PFP | 1.28 | 0.62 | 0.20 | 1.00 | 0.65 | 2.19 | 0.37 | 0.74 | | **2.56** |
| PTA | 3.69 | - | - | 3.63 | - | 3.08 | 3.25 | **5.03** | | |
| SSSP | - | - | - | - | - | - | - | - | 0.80 | **3.04** |
| | | | | | Niagara ($t \leq 32$) | | | | | |
| DMR | 18.77 | 5.95 | 0.89 | 6.81 | 11.47 | 18.53 | 3.60 | 5.89 | 3.59 | **21.53** |
| DT | 5.43 | | | | | **5.48** | | | | 3.29 |
| PFP | 2.30 | 1.25 | 0.32 | 2.84 | 2.18 | 4.46 | 0.80 | 2.13 | | **5.92** |
| PTA | 4.20 | - | - | 4.49 | - | 5.42 | 4.62 | **6.16** | | |
| SSSP | - | - | - | - | - | - | - | - | 0.50 | **2.33** |

**Table 3.** Speedup over serial versions. In bold are the best speedups for each (application, machine) pair. Entries with - timed out. Blank entries indicate invalid or redundant combinations.

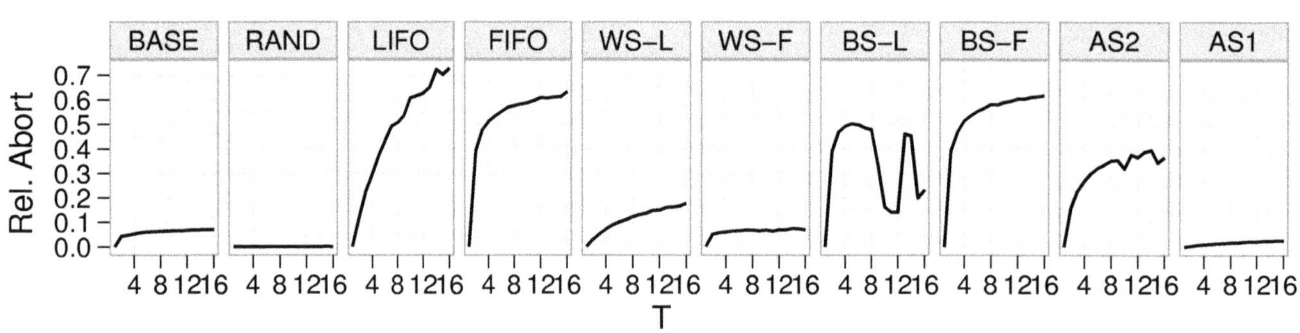


**Figure 14.** Relative number of aborted to total iterations for DMR on Shanghai.

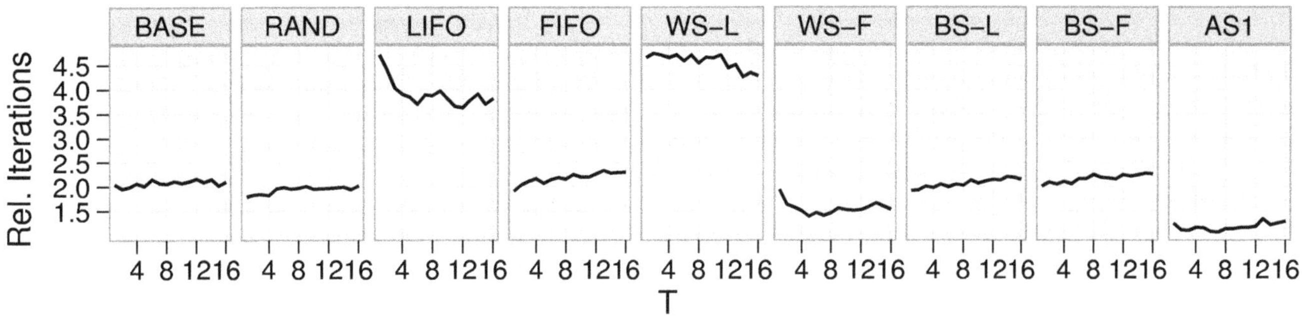


**Figure 16.** Relative number of committed iterations to that of the best performing serial version for PFP on Shanghai.

| | |
|---|---|
| DMR | Triangle mesh of 550,000 triangles of which 261,100 are initially bad |
| DT | 1,733,360 points generated from edge detection of a photograph |
| PFP | A flow network of 526,904 vertices arranged in 14 consecutive 194x194 frames with uniformly random capacities |
| PTA | Analysis of the gimp program |
| SSSP | Road network of western USA, weights are distances between locations: 6,262,104 vertices, 15,119,284 edges |

**Figure 13.** Datasets used for each application.

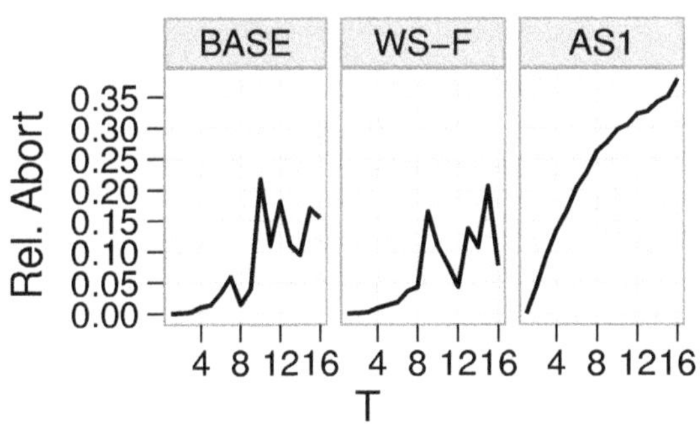


**Figure 15.** Relative number of aborted to total iterations for DT on Shanghai.

## 6. Related Work

Although we synthesize schedulers from specifications, this is not the standard concurrent program synthesis problem considered in the literature [33, 34]. Scheduling specifications for unordered algorithms are inherently "fuzzy" (even FIFO scheduling of the workset can result in different executions depending on the speed of processors). Therefore, scheduling specifications are advice to the runtime system about how to bias scheduling decisions for efficiency, whereas in conventional program synthesis, implementations must satisfy specifications exactly.

Recent work has shown that more efficient workset implementations may be possible if the application is written so that it can tolerate duplicate work items [22, 26]. Exploiting this idempotence property would require changes to the definitions in Sections 3 and 4, but the implementation would be straightforward for final worksets. However, some non-final worksets, such as the chunked worksets, depend on the correspondence between adds and polls, which makes taking advantage of idempotence a challenge in these cases.

Another avenue of further research is to examine more algorithms to see if our current set of rules is adequate. Our FIFO and LIFO workset implementations would benefit from some of the memory-level optimizations.

Previously, Kulkarni *et al.* [18] explored different handwritten scheduling policies in the Galois system. However, the policies were a small number of fixed forms. In contrast, the schedulers described here are synthesized (not handwritten), they include policies studied in the literature such as delta-stepping, and they can be composed arbitrarily, which is important in practice.

The inspector-executor method [36] is a popular approach for parallelizing irregular applications in which dependences can be computed at runtime once the input has been supplied to the program. It is orthogonal to our work since it does not consider scheduling strategies for controlling the amount of work performed by the implementation, for enhancing locality, etc., which are the main considerations of this paper.

## 7. Conclusion

Scheduling order matters even in the sequential implementation of irregular algorithms. In the context of parallel implementations, prior work on scheduling assumed that activities are independent or that dependences are subsumed by fork-join control dependences, so current general-purpose runtime schedulers embody only a few simple scheduling policies. In contrast, handwritten schedulers for parallel implementations of irregular algorithms often use carefully crafted policies that trade-off excess work for increased parallelism, but they increase the burden of parallel programming and may be difficult to reuse for other algorithms.

In this paper, we proposed one solution to this problem by (1) developing a specification language for schedulers and (2) showing how efficient concurrent implementations can be synthesized from these specifications. This allows application programmers to focus on what they do well — coming up with scheduling policies — while delegating the tedious task of implementing the policy to the synthesizer and runtime system.

*Acknowledgements:* We thank David August (Princeton) for being a "good shepherd". We are also grateful to Milind Kulkarni (Purdue) and Roman Manevich (UT Austin) for their suggestions for improving the paper.

## References

[1] N. Amenta, S. Choi, and G. Rote. Incremental constructions con brio. In *Proc. Symp. on Computational Geometry (SCG)*, pages 211–219, 2003.

[2] L. O. Andersen. *Program Analysis and Specialization for the C Programming Language*. PhD thesis, DIKU, University of Copenhagen, May 1994. (DIKU report 94/19).

[3] D. Bader and V. Sachdeva. A cache-aware parallel implementation of the push-relabel network flow algorithm and experimental evaluation of the gap relabeling heuristic. In *Proc. 18th ISCA International Conference on Parallel and Distributed Computing Systems (PDCS)*, September 2005.

[4] R. D. Blumofe, C. F. Joerg, B. C. Kuszmaul, C. E. Leiserson, K. H. Randall, and Y. Zhou. Cilk: an efficient multithreaded runtime system. *SIGPLAN Not.*, 30(8):207–216, 1995.

[5] A. Bowyer. Computing Dirichlet tessellations. *The Computer Journal*, 24(2):162–166, 1981.

[6] B. V. Cherkassy and A. V. Goldberg. On implementing push-relabel method for the maximum flow problem. In *Proc. Intl. Conf. on Integer Programming and Combinatorial Optimization (IPCO)*, pages 157–171, London, UK, 1995.

[7] L. P. Chew. Guaranteed-quality mesh generation for curved surfaces. In *Proc. Symp. on Computational Geometry (SCG)*, 1993.

[8] K. L. Clarkson and P. W. Shor. Applications of random sampling in computational geometry, ii. *Discrete Comput. Geom.*, 4(5):287–421, 1989.

[9] T. Cormen, C. Leiserson, R. Rivest, and C. Stein, editors. *Introduction to Algorithms*. MIT Press, 2001.

[10] L. Dagum and R. Menon. OpenMP: An industry-standard API for shared-memory programming. *IEEE Comput. Sci. Eng.*, 5(1):46–55, 1998.

[11] A. Duran, J. Corbalán, and E. Ayguadé. Evaluation of OpenMP task scheduling strategies. In *Proc. Conf. on OpenMP in a new era of parallelism (IWOMP)*, pages 100–110, 2008.

[12] A. V. Goldberg and R. E. Tarjan. A new approach to the maximum-flow problem. *J. ACM*, 35(4):921–940, 1988.

[13] R. H. Halstead, Jr. MULTILISP: a language for concurrent symbolic computation. *ACM Trans. Program. Lang. Syst.*, 7:501–538, October 1985.

[14] B. Hardekopf and C. Lin. The ant and the grasshopper: fast and accurate pointer analysis for millions of lines of code. In *Proc. Conf. on Programming Language Design and Implementation (PLDI)*, 2007.

[15] M. Herlihy and J. E. B. Moss. Transactional memory: architectural support for lock-free data structures. In *Proc. of International Symposium on Computer Architecture (ISCA)*, 1993.

[16] M. P. Herlihy and J. M. Wing. Linearizability: a correctness condition for concurrent objects. *ACM Trans. Program. Lang. Syst.*, 12(3):463–492, 1990.

[17] Intel Corporation. Intel threading building blocks 3.0. `http://threadingbuildingblocks.org`.

[18] M. Kulkarni, P. Carribault, K. Pingali, G. Ramanarayanan, B. Walter, K. Bala, and L. P. Chew. Scheduling strategies for optimistic parallel execution of irregular programs. In *Proc. Symp. on Parallelism in algorithms and architectures (SPAA)*, pages 217–228, New York, NY, USA, 2008.

[19] M. Kulkarni, K. Pingali, B. Walter, G. Ramanarayanan, K. Bala, and L. P. Chew. Optimistic parallelism requires abstractions. *SIGPLAN Not. (Proceedings of PLDI)*, 42(6):211–222, 2007.

[20] M. Kulkarni, D. Prountzos, D. Nguyen, and K. Pingali. Defining and implementing commutativity conditions for parallel execution. regular rech report TR-ECE-09-11, School of Electrial and Computer Engineering, Purdue University, August 2009.

[21] D. Lea. A Java fork/join framework. In *Proc. Conf. on Java Grande*, pages 36–43, 2000.

[22] D. Leijen, W. Schulte, and S. Burckhardt. The design of a task parallel library. In *Proc. Conf. on object-oriented programming, systems, languages, and applications (OOPSLA)*, pages 227–242, 2009.

[23] K. Madduri, D. Bader, J. Berry, and J. Crobak. Parallel shortest path algorithms for solving large-scale instances. Technical Report GT-CSE-06-19, Georgia Institute of Technology, September 2006.

[24] M. Méndez-Lojo, A. Mathew, and K. Pingali. Parallel inclusion-based points-to analysis. In *Proc. Intl. Conference on Systems, Programming, Languages and Applications: Software for Humanity (SPLASH)*, 2010.

[25] U. Meyer and P. Sanders. Delta-stepping: A parallel single source shortest path algorithm. In *Proc. European Symp. on Algorithms (ESA)*, pages 393–404, 1998.

[26] M. M. Michael, M. T. Vechev, and V. A. Saraswat. Idempotent work stealing. In *Proc. Symp. on Principles and practice of parallel programming (PPoPP)*, pages 45–54, 2009.

[27] G. L. Miller. A time efficient Delaunay refinement algorithm. In *Proc. Symposium on Discrete Algorithms (SODA)*, pages 400–409, New Orleans, 2004.

[28] F. Nielson, H. R. Nielson, and C. Hankin. *Principles of Program Analysis*. Springer-Verlag New York, Inc., Secaucus, NJ, USA, 1999.

[29] D. J. Pearce, P. H. J. Kelly, and C. L. Hankin. Online cycle detection and difference propagation for pointer analysis. In *Intl. IEEE Workshop on Source Code Analysis and Manipulation (SCAM)*, pages 3–12, 2003.

[30] K. Pingali, M. Kulkarni, D. Nguyen, M. Burtscher, M. Mendez-Lojo, D. Prountzos, X. Sui, and Z. Zhong. Amorphous data-parallelism in irregular algorithms. regular tech report TR-09-05, The University of Texas at Austin, 2009.

[31] J. Ruppert. A Delaunay refinement algorithm for quality 2-dimensional mesh generation. *J. Algorithms*, 18(3):548–585, 1995.

[32] J. R. Shewchuk. Triangle: Engineering a 2d quality mesh generator and Delaunay triangulator. In *Applied Computational Geometry: Towards Geometric Engineering*, volume 1148 of *Lecture Notes in Computer Science*, pages 203–222. Springer-Verlag, 1996.

[33] A. Solar-Lezama, C. G. Jones, and R. Bodik. Sketching concurrent data structures. In *Proc. Conf. on Programming Language Design and Implementation (PLDI)*, pages 136–148, New York, NY, USA, 2008.

[34] M. T. Vechev, E. Yahav, D. F. Bacon, and N. Rinetzky. CGCExplorer: a semi-automated search procedure for provably correct concurrent collectors. In *Proc. Conf. on Programming Language Design and Implementation (PLDI)*, pages 456–467, New York, NY, USA, 2007.

[35] D. F. Watson. Computing the $n$-dimensional tessellation with application to Voronoi polytopes. *The Computer Journal*, 24(2):167–172, 1981.

[36] J. Wu, R. Das, J. Saltz, H. Berryman, and S. Hiranandani. Distributed memory compiler design for sparse problems. *IEEE Transactions on Computers*, 44, 1995.

# Exploring Circuit Timing-aware Language and Compilation

Giang Hoang Robert Bruce Findler Russ Joseph

Electrical Engineering and Computer Science
Northwestern University
{gho705,robby,rjoseph}@eecs.northwestern.edu

## Abstract

By adjusting the design of the ISA and enabling circuit timing-sensitive optimizations in a compiler, we can more effectively exploit timing speculation. While there has been growing interest in systems that leverage circuit-level timing speculation to improve the performance and power-efficiency of processors, most of the innovation has been at the microarchitectural level. We make the observation that some code sequences place greater demand on circuit timing deadlines than others. Furthermore, by selectively replacing these codes with instruction sequences which are semantically equivalent but reduce activity on timing critical circuit paths, we can trigger fewer timing errors and hence reduce recovery costs.

***Categories and Subject Descriptors*** D.3.4 [*Programming Languages*]: Processors—code generation, compilers, optimization; C.0 [*General*]: Hardware/software interfaces

***General Terms*** Design, Languages, Performance

***Keywords*** timing speculation, compiler, ISA design

## 1. Introduction

While we can expect Moore's Law to continue to provide increases in transistor density, we know that frequency scaling will not provide the same performance gains that it traditionally has. Power and thermal concerns place first-order constraints that drastically curb frequency. Challenges in semiconductor manufacturing, device reliability, design complexity all play increasingly critical roles in limiting frequency gains. Together these factors have redirected industry toward a future where chip-multiprocessors featuring an increasingly large number of simple cores will be more common. At the same time, Amdahl's law and some recent studies [14] remind us that single-thread performance cannot be neglected. We will still need to extract some gains from clock frequency.

Timing speculative architectures present an increasingly popular research direction which aims at some of the technology challenges to boost clock frequency and extract more performance from meager power budgets [6, 8, 9, 11, 17, 18, 23]. Systems that support timing speculation abandon the traditional worst-case design assumptions about circuit timing constraints and clock-frequency. They instead expect timing faults to occasionally appear during runtime and rely on runtime hardware mechanism to detect and recover from the errors. The error recovery ensures correctness and in exchange the system can operate at a greater clock-frequency or decreased supply voltage, yielding improved overall instruction throughput and energy-efficiency. Previous work has explored many ways to judiciously trade-off error rate for clock-frequency and power [23]. In particular, some recent efforts have shown the benefits for from-the-ground-up support for timing speculation [9, 17]. By considering gate-level timing characteristics and how frequently each path is exercised, circuits can be optimized to improve their error rate curves and improve their suitability for timing speculation. While these proposals view the design of timing speculative systems more holistically, they still focus almost exclusively on innovation below the ISA. They do not consider the role that other layers of the system stack may have on influencing timing errors and hence cannot exploit the capabilities of language design, compilers, binary optimizers, or system software to improve performance.

Given the promise of timing speculation and the prevailing focus downward to the lower portions of the system stack, improvements in code generation offer enticing possibilities. In particular, a compiler which considers how code selection and instruction scheduling influence timing errors could reduce the degree to which timing sensitive paths are exercised in a way analogous to techniques aimed at the circuit-level [9, 17]. By generating binaries specifically targeted for timing speculation, a timing speculation aware compiler will be able to significantly reduce incidence of timing errors. This will allow systems to operate at more aggressive clock frequencies and extend the reach of timing speculation.

In this paper, we take steps toward building systems that are holistically designed for timing speculation. We make the observation that the sequence of instructions in an application binary can have significant impact on timing error rate and introduce code transformations and ISA extensions that improve the efficacy of timing speculation while preserving program semantics. Specifically, computations that risk activating critical paths can often be replaced with those that do not, at either no cost or a small increase in instruction count. In particular, simple loop optimizations targeted specifically for timing speculative designs can have dramatic effects in increasing clock frequency for timing speculative architectures. Given that recovering from a timing error incurs a minimum penalty of a pipeline flush, and potentially more if checkpoints are involved, this is often a significant gain.

We evaluate the potential benefits of timing-aware code by executing code with several different types of optimizations on a complete gate-level timing model for a simple Alpha processor. This paper makes the following contributions:

- We introduce the concept of timing speculation-aware code generation and evaluate a number of simple yet effective code transformations that reduce timing error rate and boost overall performance.



*ASPLOS'11,* March 5–11, 2011, Newport Beach, California, USA.

- We evaluate a number of low cost extensions to the microarchitecture and ISA that allow for even more flexibility in avoiding critical paths during code generation.

The remainder of the paper is structured as follows: In Section 2, we walk through an example that illustrates how compilers can enhance timing speculation. Then, we describe a set of program and architecture optimizations in Section 3. In Section 4, we present an evaluation of our code transformations on a detailed processor model. Section 5 discusses related work. Finally, Sections 6 and 7 discuss some limitations in this our work and conclude.

## 2. Overview

To get a sense of how compiler optimizations, the design of the ISA, and the design of the programming language can all come together to make timing speculation more effective, this section explores how a compiler can generate code for the simplest loop possible in order to maximize the performance gains that timing speculation offers.

Consider this C code that counts from 0 up to 127.

```
#define N 128
for (int x=0; x<N; x++)
  /* empty loop body */ ;
```

With the exception of the **or** instruction, a typical compiler would generate this code for that loop:[1]

```
main:
      addl $31,$31,$1
$L1:
      or $31,$31,$31 # nop
      addq $1,1,$1
      cmple $1,127,$2
      bne $2,$L1
```

The **or** operation serves as a **nop** (register 31 is always zero) corresponding to the empty loop body, but also transitions the inputs and internal nodes in the ALU so that different iterations of the loop are less likely to create happy timing coincidences.

Running this program at 2.2x[2] of the processor's normal frequency causes nearly all of the instructions in the program to fail, making the program finish at 1.28x the time of the original program.[3] Although this program is an efficient implementation of the original C program on an ordinary processor, it demonstrates a number of choices that could be improved to target an architecture with timing speculation.

As a first step to improving the program, consider the use of the **cmple** instruction. Since less than comparison logic at best entails several levels of logic and at worst is implemented via subtraction, this instruction generally requires a long time to complete. The loop termination condition for this program could have been implemented via an equality check, however, which would behave much better with the higher frequency.

Unfortunately, to compile the given code into code that uses an equality check requires a fair amount of sophistication in the compiler. While such compilers do exist, a simpler, more robust idea is to merely change the form of the looping construct in the programming language. That is, if programming language supported a looping construct like this one:[4]

```
#define N 128
for (int x in 0...N)
  /* empty loop body */ ;
```

then the compiler is free to generate a loop termination that better supports timing speculation.

So, rewriting the **cmple** to **cmpeq** yields this program:

```
main:
      addl $31,$31,$1
$L1:
      or $31,$31,$31 # nop
      addq $1,1,$1
      cmpeq $1,128,$2
      beq $2,$L1
```

It still has a lot of failures, but the **cmpeq** instruction no longer fails, so the program runs significantly faster than the previous version, taking 0.86x the time of the original program.

We can further improve the code if we augment standard compiler optimizations with timing speculation smarts. One such optimization, loop unrolling, duplicates the loop body in order to get better pipeline behavior and to expose opportunities for other optimizations that cross iterations of a loop. In addition to that, we can also take advantage of a more efficient increment operation once the loop body has been duplicated. Specifically, in even iterations of the loop, we know that adding one to the index operation can be implemented with **or**, a much faster operation. Usually, in an ALU, **or** and addition are implemented separately, where **or** could be computed using an array of OR gates, while an addition operation is implemented with a high performance adder. While the adder is limited by a potentially long carry chain, an **or** operation is very fast because the result bits can be computed in parallel.

Making these transformations to our example yields this:

```
main:
      addq $31,$31,$1
$L1:
      or $31,$31,$31 # nop
      or $1,1,$1
      cmpeq $1,128,$2
      bne $2,$L2
      or $31,$31,$31 # nop
      addq $1,1,$1
      cmpeq $1,128,$2
      beq $2,$L1
$L2:
```

which clocks in at 0.81x the time of the original program. Applying the loop unrolling optimization alone, i.e., still using the **addq** instruction to increment the loop results in negligible gains. (Our processor model predicts branches are always taken, so the unrolling improves the pipeline behavior, but these savings are swamped by the recovery costs for timing errors.)

Unfortunately, more aggressive loop unrolling does not help us improve performance of the loop index computation when using a standard ISA because implementing the increment operation in the

[1] Technically, a naive compiler would likely generate worse code than this code and a sophisticated compiler would probably notice that the loop has no effect on the computation and thus eliminate it. Nevertheless, if the loop's body had some interesting computation, a sophisticated compiler would likely generate code like the given code to implement the loop's iteration.

[2] We acknowledge that many practical constraints might prevent one from operating at such an extreme frequency in a real system. Since our example loop is very small and simple, it does not exercise the most critical paths in the processor. Running the simulation at 2.2x frequency helps better demonstrate the failure behavior of this simple loop benchmark as well as the effectiveness of our code transformation.

[3] Our precise model and the associated cost of failure are discussed in Section 4.

[4] Using iterators and generators à la Python or Racket [7]

newly exposed cases would require multiple logical operations and thus multiple cycles.

Instead, we introduce the **brinc** instruction, short for "broken increment". Its operands are just like the **addq** instruction, but it only performs the addition in the lowest 4 bits of the operand. For the remaining bits, the first operand is just carried forward to the result. Thus, when adding a big number to a small one which does not create a carry bit from the lower 4 bits, **brinc** behaves just like **addq**, making **brinc** a good candidate for use in an index computation in an unrolled loop.[5]

Exploiting that in our example produces this program:

```
main:
      addl $31,$31,$1
$L1:
      or $31,$31,$31 # nop
      brinc $1,1,$1
      cmpeq $1,128,$2
      bne $2,$L2
      or $31,$31,$31 # nop
      brinc $1,1,$1
      cmpeq $1,128,$2
      bne $2,$L2
      or $31,$31,$31 # nop
      brinc $1,1,$1
      cmpeq $1,128,$2
      bne $2,$L2
      or $31,$31,$31 # nop
      addq $1,1,$1
      cmpeq $1,128,$2
      beq $2,$L1
$L2:
```

which completes in 0.74x the time of the original program. This time, performing the optimization without the timing speculation enhancements (unrolling without adding **brinc**) improves the performance over the original somewhat (to 0.82x), but still represents a slowdown as compared to the simpler unrolling with the **or**.

At this point, most of the failing instructions are the branch instructions, due to the arithmetic they execute to compute the target address from the current PC. A backward branch with **beq** involves subtracting the PC with an offset, which usually results in a long carry chain. The compiler can generate a **bne** instruction instead of the final **beq** instruction, turning a subtraction into an addition, which is more likely to complete at the higher frequency and thus better exploit timing speculation. We call this optimization "branch rerouting".

Applying branch rerouting to our code yields this program

```
main:
      addl $31,$31,$1
      lda  $3,8200($31)
$L1:
      or $31,$31,$31 # nop
      brinc $1,1,$1
      cmpeq $1,128,$2
      bne $2,$L2
      or $31,$31,$31 # nop
      brinc $1,1,$1
      cmpeq $1,128,$2
      bne $2,$L2
      or $31,$31,$31 # nop
      brinc $1,1,$1
      cmpeq $1,128,$2
      bne $2,$L2
      or $31,$31,$31 # nop
      addq $1,1,$1
      cmpeq $1,128,$2
      bne $2,$L2
      jmp $31,($3)
$L2:
```

which runs in 0.76x the time of the original program. Interestingly, branch rerouting alone actually slows the program down slightly when we omit the **brinc** instructions, clocking in a 0.83x the time of the original program.

Finally, if the compiler can prove that the loop index variable is not mutated and that the loop has a number of iterations that is an even multiple of $4^6$, it can remove the intermediate compare and branch instructions in the unrolled version, making our example run much faster. Of course, most of the speedup here comes from the fact that the compiler can eliminate most of the loop itself and thus this speedup will happen only when the loop body is very simple (e.g., initializing an array or similar).

Making that transformation here produces this code

```
main:
      addl $31,$31,$1
      lda  $3,8200($31)
$L1:
      or $31,$31,$31 # nop
      brinc $1,1,$1
      or $31,$31,$31 # nop
      brinc $1,1,$1
      or $31,$31,$31 # nop
      brinc $1,1,$1
      or $31,$31,$31 # nop
      addq $1,1,$1
      cmpeq $1,128,$2
      bne $2,$L2
      jmp $31,($3)
$L2:
```

which runs at 0.37x the time of the original loop.

In short, combining conventional compiler optimizations and judiciously chosen changes to the programming language and the ISA yields results that take advantage of timing speculation much effectively than possible without them.

## 3. Code transformations

In addition to the transformations given in Section 2, there are a number of other speculation-specific enhancements that compilers can take advantage of.

### 3.1 NOP Padding

When a timing error occurs in execution units, it has two immediate consequences on the instructions in the pipeline. First, it produces

[5] One might think that when adding a small number to a large number, the delay of the operation is proportional to the length of the carry chain. That is not always the case because the the delay of the current addition depends not only on the current input values but also on the state of intermediate logic gates that were set by the previous addition. In particular, if a previous addition induces a long carry chain but the current one does not have any carries, the intermediate logic gates representing the propagate and generate signals must change to hold the correct values for the current addition. For example, with an 8-bit Kogge-Stone adder, the delay for the addition of 1 to 11111100, which does not have any carries, can vary greatly depending on the previous inputs. If the previous operation is adding 1 to 11111111, the delay of this current addition can be three times as long as if the previous addition is adding 1 to 11111110.

[6] In theory, the compiler can generate a loop header that runs a small number of iterations to guarantee that the main body of the loop is always an even multiple of 4.

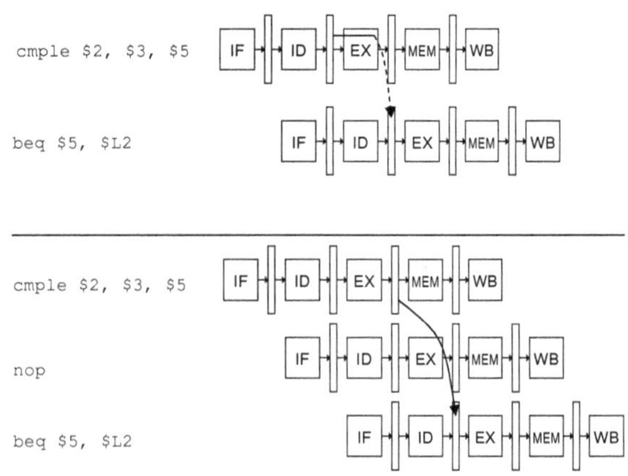


**Figure 1.** Pipeline timing diagram for two code sequences with RAW register dependencies. For the first sequence (above) the `cmple` instruction completes its execution but cannot forward its result to the following `beq` leading to a timing error for the branch. For the second sequence (below), a NOP has been inserted between the two instructions, padding the timing error. Now the result is forwarded a cycle later from a pipeline register. The padded version of this code eliminates timing errors on the forwarding paths.

an incorrect result for the instruction slotted to that execution unit which must be corrected. Under some error recovery mechanisms, this may require replay and has the likely effect of delaying other instructions in the pipeline. Second, errant results are forwarded to dependent instructions elsewhere in the pipeline. To limit the impact of timing errors, both effects need to be addressed.

By padding the instruction sequence with NOPs, we can mitigate the later concern – incorrect forwarded results with no hardware modifications. However, with some small microarchitectural improvements, we can extend pipeline control logic to improve the pipeline error recovery as well. Figure 1 shows a code sequence with a RAW register dependence. At a frequency scaling factor of 2.15x, the clock cycle would be sufficient for the execution hardware to produce the result and capture the value in the stage pipeline registers but due to the time necessary to pass through forwarding logic, it would violate the setup time needed to successfully forward the value to the dependent instruction. As seen in Figure 1, after inserting the NOP, the result is no longer forwarded directly from the execution unit in the EX stage, it instead is forwarded from a pipeline register in the MEM stage. Consequently, all input values arrive at pipeline registers in sufficient time and no timing errors occur.

If the frequency factor is increased to 2.2x then a simple NOP operation is no longer sufficient. Instead, the compare operation itself cannot produce a result. Under timing speculative architectures that apply stage-level checking granularity (e.g. Razor [6]), the pipeline would likely have to recompute the compare operation and then replay the subsequent instructions, a potentially significant recovery penalty. If on the other hand, the microarchitecture could recognize cases where replay was not necessary, it would significantly decrease the error recovery penalty. One way to achieve this would be to add a special NOP operation which we call PAD to the ISA that tells the hardware that replay is unnecessary. The compiler could then insert this PAD instruction in cases where it can statically determine that replay is unnecessary. Figure 2 shows how the hardware to support this might be incorporated into recovery control logic. The key elements are the PAD detection logic and the AND gate which suppress the flush signal.

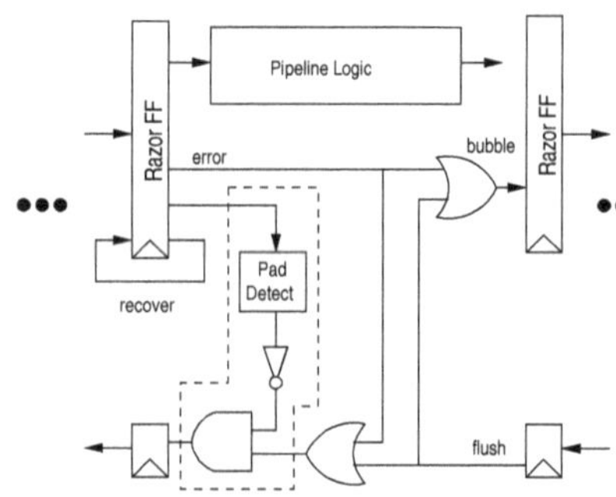


**Figure 2.** Control logic needed to support the PAD operation. The outline shows the modifications to the original Razor control mechanism [6].

### 3.2 Broken Operations

Many of the operations in a standard ISA have hidden addition operations as part of their function. For example, computing the effective address of a load involves an addition of an offset to a register and, in some cases, these additions are amenable to **brinc**.

Consider this snippet of a C program implementing a game with a small number of players. Each player tracks which of the other players are adjacent to in a neighbors struct:

```
#define set int

// recording (as a set of booleans)
// who is in the neighborhood
// of a given player
typedef struct {
  set left;
  set up;
  set right;
  set down;
} neighbors;
```

Using this data structure we can write a function that iterates over all of the neighbors structs and determines the set of players that are adjacent to at least one other player (i.e., the players that are not hiding).

```
int all_vis(neighbors *ns, int size) {
  int i;
  set r=0;
  for (i=0; i<size; i++)
    r |= (ns[i].left  |
          ns[i].up    |
          ns[i].right |
          ns[i].down);
  return r;
}
```

When we compile this code, we get this loop.[7]

```
$L5:
        ldl  $1,0($16)
        ldl  $2,4($16)
        ldl  $3,8($16)
        ldl  $4,12($16)
        addl $5,1,$5
        bis  $0,$1,$0
        bis  $0,$2,$0
```

[7] Indeed, `gcc -O2` produces a loop almost identical to this one when given the above function, but with the operations in a slightly different order.

```
bis $0,$3,$0
bis $0,$4,$0
cmpeq $5,$17,$2
addl $31,$1,$0
lda $16,16($16)
beq $2,$L5
```

If we can arrange the neighbor array such that it begins at a virtual address that is a multiple of 16, then we know that all of the effective address computations in the **ldl** instructions are safe for use with **brinc**.

### 3.3 Multi-instruction Code Substitution

In some cases, it may be possible to replace a multi-instruction sequence with an equivalent set of instructions (i.e., that produce an equivalent result), but place less stress on critical path structures. Consider the following two-instruction sequence that performs multiplication by a constant factor of 6. Note that this code was generated by a circuit timing agnostic compiler (`gcc-4.2`):

```
s8subq $2, $2, $4
subq   $4, $2, $4
```

The first instruction, `s8subq`, scales r2 by 8 and then subtracts r2 from that result (r4 $\leftarrow$ 8 $\times$ r2 - r2 = 7 $\times$ r2). The second instruction performs one more subtraction to produce the result r2 $\times$ 6. By performing constant multiplication with shifts and add/sub instructions, the compiler can produce multiplies that may be faster than some true dedicated multiplier components. Unfortunately, this code begins to generate timing errors at 1.18x of the base frequency when a small or medium value is present in r2 register. This is due to the way that the `subq` sensitizes the adder carry chain. Note that an instruction sequence like this inside an inner loop would severely limit frequency scaling.

However, the above instruction sequence is not the only combination of shifts and arithmetic instructions that can produce r2 $\times$ 6. We could instead produce the same result using:

```
addq   $2, $2, $4
s4addq $2, $4, $4
```

The key benefit of this alternate sequence is that it places much less stress on critical path circuits in the ALU and can tolerate significantly higher clock frequencies.

## 4. Evaluation

In this section, we describe our processor model and application workload. We then present experimental results and evaluate the code optimizations presented in Section 2 and 3.

### 4.1 Models and Methodology

We evaluate the potential of code optimization for timing speculative architectures using the following benchmarks: `bitcount`, `dijkstra`, and `strsearch` from MiBench [12], and a sequential version of `integer sort` (`is`) from NAS benchmark suite [2]. Instead of directly implementing these code optimizations in a compiler backend, we apply the code transformations by hand. We compile the benchmarks with `gcc-4.2` with the `-O2` optimization level and hand tune the assembly code with our techniques before assembling into binary.

We construct a Verilog processor model for a simple in-order five-stage Alpha pipeline. Alpha is an example of a clean, classic RISC architecture, and a simple in-order pipeline is representive of some low power-embedded processors. Our processor implements the vast majority of user-mode integer instructions and supports all forwarding paths. We synthesize the processor model using Synopsys Design Compiler with the FreePDK 45nm gate library [25] and target the design for a 350MHz clock speed suitable for a low-power embedded processor. The optimization effort is set to "high" to produce a design as balanced as possible. The critical paths in this design include the integer ALU, some forwarding paths, and NextPC logic. We do not implement floating-point data paths.

We use the M5 simulator [3] to fast-forward the benchmarks to the start of the main execution loop, then transfer the register and memory states to our gate-level Verilog model. The detailed gate-level simulation allows us to evaluate all of our code transformations and generate error rates that reflect the gate-level transitions inside a real design. Due to the extremely long run-times associated with gate-level simulation, we reduced the size of the input sets. We acknowledge that this may have some impact on data working set size and memory stall time. However, it would not have an impact on factors like instruction mix and control flow which would be more closely related to the optimizations proposed in this paper.

We model a Razor-like per stage dynamic error detection and recovery mechanism. We model a five cycle error recovery penalty which would be appropriate for a shallow in-order pipeline. However, we believe that many of the techniques presented in this paper would also be applicable to architectures which support different checking granularities and correction strategies with alternative recovery latencies. In architectures that feature more punitive recovery latencies, many of our techniques would have a more pronounced benefit.

Our modeled design features an 8KB instruction L1, an 8KB data L1 cache, and a 256 KB unified L2 cache. We do not model timing errors in SRAM structures including the caches and register file. There has been a large amount of recent work on technology-aware cache designs that support overclocking, counter the effects of parameter variation, and tolerate ultra-low voltage scaling [20, 26]. We believe that some of these techniques could be applied to bolster the caches in our design. In addition, the techniques that we apply are orthogonal to any improvements in cache and register file design.

### 4.2 Experimental Results

We apply three of the proposed code optimizations: *branch rerouting*, *nop padding*, and, *loop unrolling w/ brinc conversion.* To evaluate the impact that modifying the ISA can have on timing speculation, we synthesize execution hardware which implements the **brinc** operation described in Section 2. This operation is intended to accelerate addition with small values. We incorporate the additional hardware into our baseline design. We apply all optimizations to each benchmark, with two exceptions. First, we were unable to apply **brinc** conversion in the `bitcount` benchmark because most of the dominant loops were not suitable for unrolling. Second, for `is`, we did not identify enough candidates for selective nop padding. Even when the frequency is doubled, most of the faults observed in the pipeline are due to backward branch address calculation, for which our nop operation does not help. For *nop padding*, we use two methods of insertion. A naive method blindly inserts nop after any instruction that uses the 64 bit adder. This method is very simple, but it doubles the CPI for those instructions padded even when they are not affected by timing speculation. A better method is to compile the application and profile the application with timing speculation to find out the most frequent failing instructions and selectively pad only those instructions with nops.

Figure 3 presents the normalized execution times for all four of our benchmarks as we scale the clock frequency. The individual sub-figures demonstrate that timing speculation performs well on baseline code. For the `is` benchmark, the performance is maximized at around double the frequency. For the others, the baseline achieves peak performance around a frequency of 1.3x the baseline clock (although `dijkstra` reaches its best performance at both

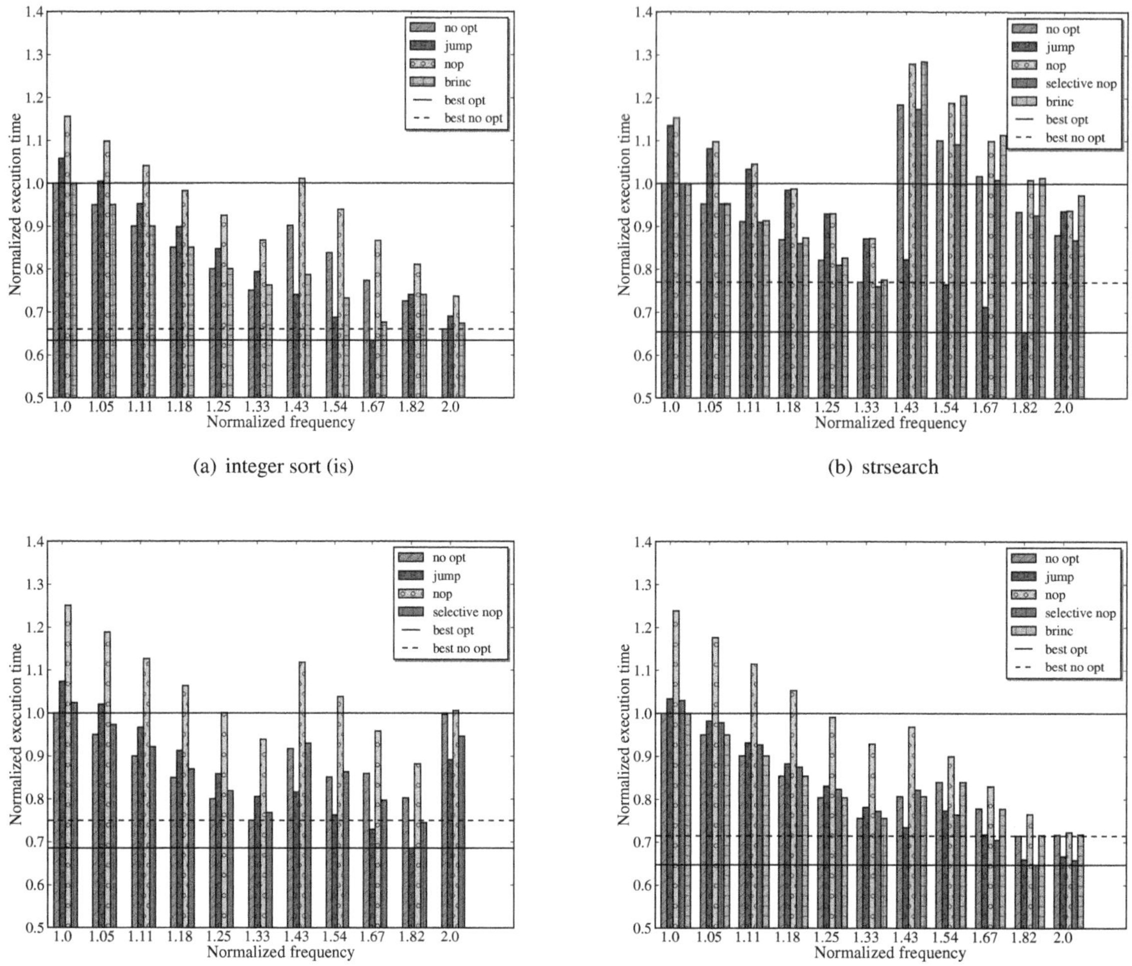


(a) integer sort (is)

(b) strsearch

(c) bitcount

(d) dijkstra

**Figure 3.** Normalized execution time for `is`, `strsearch`, `bitcount`, and `dijkstra`; showing the baseline performance and with three code optimizations: branch-rerouting, nop-padding, and loop unrolling plus brinc conversion. For nop-padding we examine two varieties: *nop* - which applies nop padding following any instruction capable of stressing critical path circuits versus *selective nop*, which inserts nops more judiciously.

points). While this result confirms some of the benefits of timing speculation these figures more importantly show that by specifically optimizing code for timing speculation, the performance can be significantly boosted. Collectively the code optimizations can shift the optimum frequency upwards and elevate performance. However, it is clear from these figures that not all the code optimizations are successful in every case. Branch rerouting is clearly the most consistent as it is capable of increasing the optimum frequency and noticeably improving performance over the baseline in three of the four benchmarks.

As shown in Figures 3(a) and 3(b), compiler optimizations offer the most promising gains for `is` and `strsearch`. For those benchmarks, branch rerouting is extremely effective and is capable of reducing execution time by **37%** and **35%** respectively. In both cases, at higher frequencies a large number of errors in the baseline code can be attributed to calculating PC-relative targets in the backwards branches within inner loops. By eliminating these errors, the optimized code can effectively reshape the error rate curve and tolerate higher frequencies. This effect is especially pronounced in Figure 3(b) because the error rates for non-optimized code increase very rapidly at higher frequencies.

For the remaining benchmarks, `bitcount` and `dijkstra`, there are performance gains from some of the optimizations, but the overall impact is not as strong. In these two cases, the small performance gains stem from very different reasons. For `bitcount`, the error rates become very large for high frequencies. More importantly, the high error rates can be attributed to instructions which we cannot directly address with our current techniques. This leads to limited efficacy. In the case of `dijkstra`, the baseline code achieves excellent performance under extreme frequency scaling. Consequently, it is very difficult for the timing speculative optimizations to contribute additional performance gains.

While branch rerouting works well overall, the remaining techniques have more irregular success. These large differences show that proper selection of nop pad locations is essential. The non-selective nop padding consistently achieves poor perfor-

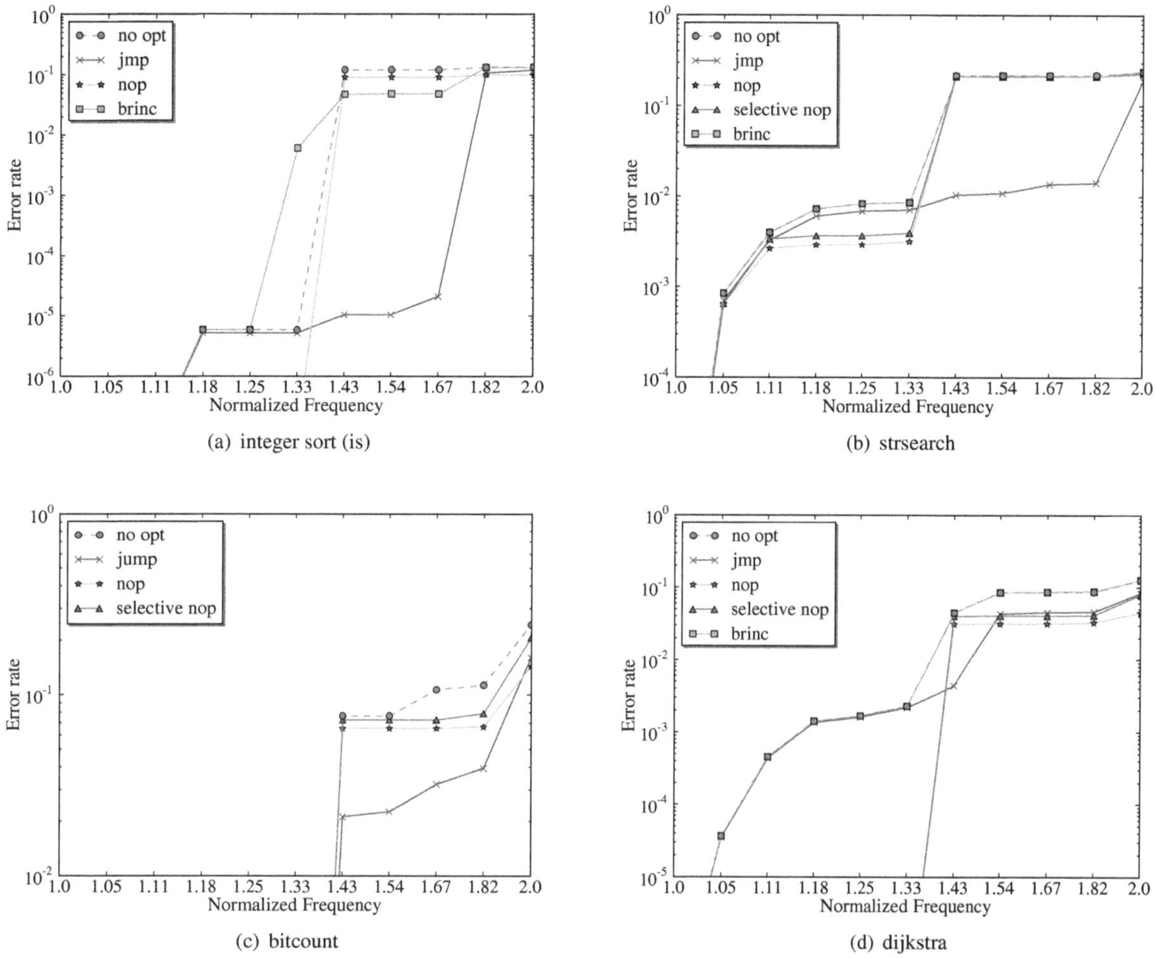


**Figure 4.** Error rates for the same runs as shown in Figure 3

mance while the selective nop padding achieves some small wins in `bitcount` and `dijkstra`. In contrast, as Figure 3(d) shows, the indiscriminate nop padding severely hurts performance for `dijkstra`. This is a benchmark which scales well with frequency, so by definition, there should be few places to apply padding. Once added, the superfluous nops significantly increase runtime.

### 4.3 Error Rates

In many cases, the execution time graphs follow a shape like a reverse sawtooth, slowly improving and then suddenly jumping back up. This behavior is due to the way timing errors suddenly appear at particular clock frequencies. Specifically, consider Figure 4, which shows the error count as a function of the clock frequency. In general, there are several plateaus as various thresholds are crossed, which trigger waves of failures. Comparing these graphs with those in Figure 3, the points where the execution time jumps back up correspond to the beginning of the plateaus. This is where a new class of instructions has failed, inducing a sudden jump in error rate. After that point, the execution time gradually decreases along the plateau of the error rate curves, because no new instructions are failing while frequency is decreasing.

The error rate curves in Figure 4 demonstrate how code optimizations can reshape the error rate curve. Furthermore, they help to explain why some of the optimizations perform better than others. First, branch rerouting is capable of maintaining a dominant error rate (i.e. a curve which is no worse than any of the other optimizations) throughout the frequency scaling window for `is` and `bitcount` as well as large portions of `strsearch` and `dijkstra`. In particular, there are some frequency ranges for `is` and `strsearch` where branch rerouting maintains two or three orders of magnitude lower error rates than the unoptimized code. This is a dramatic difference, which shows the potential for circuit timing aware compilation. Referring back to Figures 3(a) and 3(b), these also correspond to frequency ranges where branch rerouting offers superior performance.

Secondly, the two versions of nop padding follow very similar error rate curves as the frequency scales. The indiscriminant nop padding keeps the error rate slightly lower, but there are no large gaps between the two. This suggests that the selective nop padding is not too selective i.e. it is not missing many opportunities which are exploited by the indiscriminant padding. In addition, there is a small window (1.1x-1.33x frequency scaling factor) in `strsearch` where nop padding does better than the other techniques. Unfortunately, this does not translate into large performance gains as witnessed in Figure 3. This is because the penalties of superfluous nops outweigh of most of the gains offered by the useful nops. Another

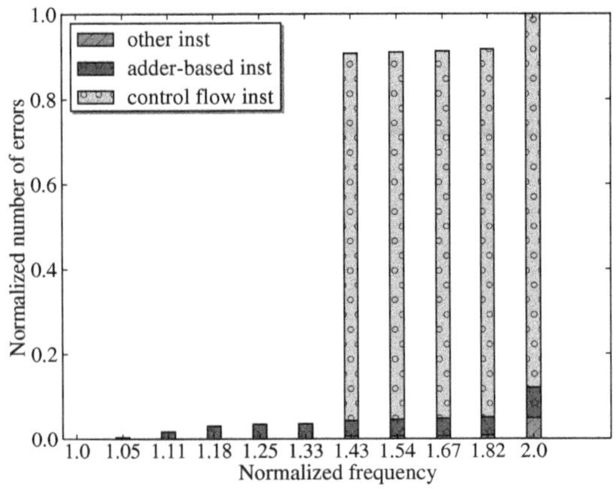


(a)

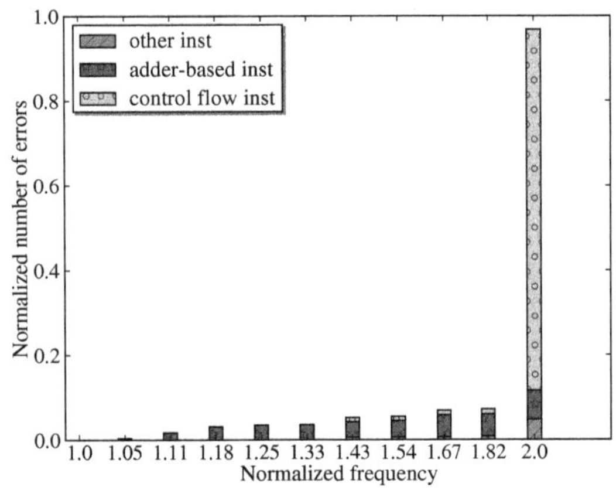


(b)

**Figure 5.** Failure counts categorized by type of failing instruction for the original `strsearch` benchmark and the `strsearch` benchmark with the jump rerouting optimization

way to view this is to say that the degree of nop padding is too high for this part of the error rate curve. In short, nop padding can help reduce error rates in some instances, but it needs to be very selective.

We choose to investigate further the behavior of the branch rerouting technique, the most effective in reducing timing errors. We examine the number of timing errors for `strsearch` before and after branch rerouting is applied. Each error is classified into one of the three categories. Adder-based instructions are arithmetic instructions that rely mainly on the 64-bit adder. These include additions, subtractions, scale-and-add operations. Control flow instructions include conditional branches as well as direct-address jumps. Instructions that do not fit into these two categories are classified as "others". Figure 5(a) shows the error counts for the `strsearch` benchmark, broken down by the type of instruction that fails. The graph shows that 1.33x of the original frequency is the critical point for conditional branches. Beyond that point, a majority of failures are due to conditional branches, and these failures hinder further frequency increase.

Figure 5(b) shows the error count for the same program, but after the branch rerouting optimization has been applied. The conditional branches have been replaced by direct-address jumps. These direct address jumps load the next address directly from a register rather than computing the next address using an adder. Therefore, the delay of a direct-address jump is much shorter than a conditional jump, allowing the processor to operate with very small number of control flow failures until the frequency reaches 2x. At 2x the normal frequency, these direct-address jumps start failing, resulting in massive number of errors due to control flow instructions. These errors put a limit on frequency scaling, however, we can see that the lower latency of direct-address jump already allows significant improvement in frequency scaling of the processor compared to the usual conditional branch.

### 4.4 Processor Model Discussion

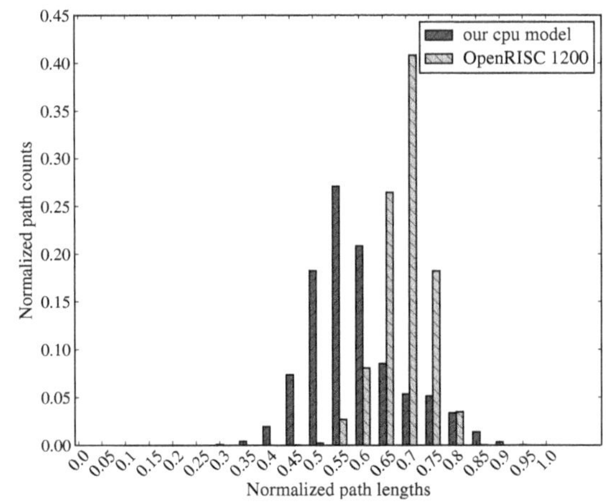


(a) Our CPU model vs. OpenRISC 1200

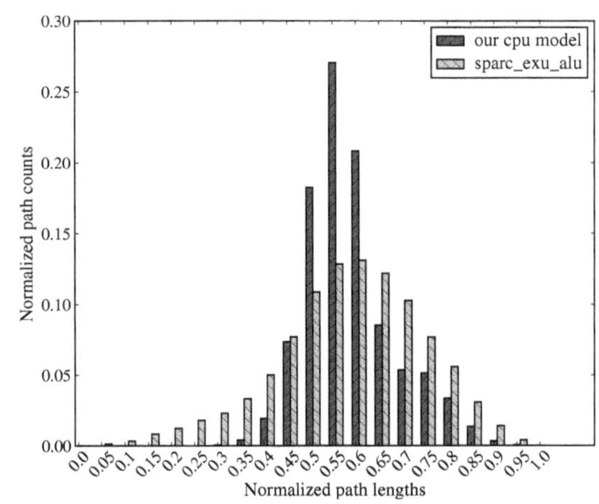


(b) Our CPU model vs. OpenSPARC ALU

**Figure 6.** Path distributions comparison between our CPU model and other existing models.

The high frequency that we are able to achieve with our processor model does raise some questions. To make sure that our processor model is reasonable, we analyze the path distribution of our design and compare it with other freely available designs. Figure 6(a) shows the distribution of all paths in our CPU model and an OpenRISC 1200 core. The OpenRISC 1200 is a simple in-order pipelined IP core, which is very close to the design of our processor model. We synthesized the OpenRISC 1200 with the same gate library and target it for 250MHz frequency. The synthesized gate-level model is used for comparison with our design. We wrote a script which enumerates all paths in the synthesized design to create a path distribution histogram.

The figure shows that the path distribution of our processor model skews more towards the center, meaning that our processor has many paths with medium length. The OpenRISC, being an optimized design, has a majority of path lengths closer to the critical path. This explains why we were able to experiment with higher frequency than what we would expect to achieve with a normal processor. However, the fact that our processor model is not as optimized as the OpenRISC 1200 core does not disqualify the merit of this work. The path distribution of OpenRISC 1200 shows that there is still a large gap between the critical path length and the length of the majority of paths in the core (less than 5% the total number of paths has length greater than 75% of the longest path). We believe that the even though the distribution of paths are not the same, the bottleneck in the designs are the same, which are the adder, nextPC logic. Therefore, our compiler techniques will have positive impacts on a processor such as OpenRISC 1200, although the frequency achieved will not be as high.

Figure 6(b) shows a comparison of our processor model versus a synthesized OpenSPARC T1 ALU. The OpenSPARC T1 ALU also has a majority of paths distributed to the medium length path, which is not too different from our design. This shows that even though our processor design is not as optimized as OpenRISC 1200 core, it is still reasonable to merit the results of our work.

## 5. Related Work

In this section, we discuss the proposed techniques in relation to previous work.

### 5.1 Improving hard fault robustness with the compiler and system software

In recent years, a number of researchers have examined software support to improve system resiliency in the presence of hard faults. These proposals have considered optimizations at the compiler or hypervisor level that either directly prevent architecturally incorrect results from being written to committed state or serve as an assist to hardware which maintains this invariant. The code transformation techniques examined in this work fall into the later category.

Meixner and Sorin introduce *detouring* [19], a software solution which applies code transformations to avoid use of faulty processor components. The authors target this technique for multi-core designs which feature many cores with narrow and shallow pipelines, lacking component-level redundancy. Through a series of code transformations and substitutions applied inside a compiler or binary translator, application software is modified to maintain correct functionality given the presence of known hardware faults. Overall, this technique obtains good fault coverage with zero hardware cost. Consequently, this approach has no performance impact on fault-free cores and may squeeze some performance out of partially functional cores that would otherwise have to be decommissioned.

Gupta *et al.* [10], Hazelwood *et al.* [13], and Reddi *et al.* [27] apply compiler transformations to reduce stress on the power delivery system. The overall goal is to reduce the likelihood of instruction execution patterns [16] that could lead to excitations in the RLC networks which connect the on-chip circuits with the off-chip power supply. In so doing, the system avoids severe droops and ringing on the PWR/GND that would take the circuits out of safe operating range and potentially lead to errors.

System software level has also been focus of investigation for hard-fault detection and recovery mechanisms. In particular, migration and emulation capable virtualization software has been proposed as one means to help reclaim performance from from partially functional cores in a CMP [15]. Recent work has also proposed system-software guided detection of hard faults during processor lifetime [5, 28]. We focus our work at the compiler level and evaluate static code optimization. However, a binary translator or JIT compiler in a level of system software (e.g. virtual machine monitor) may be able to offer many of the same capabilities for generating timing-aware code.

### 5.2 Hardware support for timing speculation and hard fault resilience

Recent work has examined hardware solutions capable of (i) increasingly the utility of processors under marginal operating conditions, (ii) tolerating hard faults in a single core through demapping and redundancy, and (iii) boosting throughput in CMPs with faulty-cores.

First, there has been increasing interest in hardware that can extract additional performance out of real silicon and eliminate dependence on worst-case design margins [1, 6]. Razor introduced a timing speculative microarchitecture that included dynamic detection and recovery for timing errors [6]. Key innovations included the concept of normal computation tolerating a small non-zero error rate, design of double sampling state elements to detect timing violations, and a low-complexity recovery mechanism based on counter-flow pipelining. In exchange for a small non-zero error rate, Razor designs are capable of significantly reduced supply voltage and can yield dramatic power savings.

Recent trends in silicon manufacturing and processor design complexity have fueled continued interest in architectures that can tolerate timing errors [8, 9, 11, 17, 18, 23]. There have been several important innovations in timing speculative architectures. The Circuit-level Timing Speculation scheme [18] speeds up critical blocks such as adder, rename and issue logic by implementing a faster approximation version of each unit. The approximated results are checked in the next cycle using fully implemented blocks and recovery is possible by reissuing the instruction. Paceline introduced dynamic error detection and correction suitable for aggressive out-of-order processors using a dual core leader-checker strategy and checkpoint-based recovery [8]. The EVAL framework applies microarchitectural techniques and run-time control techniques to influence the error rate curve via high-dimensional adaptation [23]. This work demonstrated the idea that error rate curves could be manipulated to tradeoff error rate versus power and processor frequency. Gupta *et al.* developed a micro-architecture capable of globally adapting voltage and frequency to address process, voltage, temperature (PVT), variations [11]. The fine-grained, high-frequency variations that they tackle necessitate local recovery mechanisms which they introduce. Blueshift applies a ground-up based design strategy to maximize the potential of timing speculation [9]. The approach includes gate-level optimizations to decrease the delay of the most frequently sensitized paths at the expense of less frequently utilized paths. Also taking the ground-up design approach, Kahng *et al.* proposes a power-aware slack redistribution algorithm that allows the processor to fail more gracefully and extends the range over which voltage/reliability tradeoff is possible [17].

The second category, includes fine-grained techniques that isolate faulty subcomponents and restrict computation to functional portions of the core. Bower *et al.* describe microarchitectural self-repair techniques that tolerate failures in a variety of array structures. Srinivasan *et al.* demonstrate that microarchitectural redundancy can significantly improve mean time to failure under a variety of lifetime wear mechanisms. Rescue applies very fine-grained logic-level fault-isolation techniques as well as de-mapping of faulty components and leverage of functionally redundant resources to obtain high-fault coverage [24]. As a whole, these techniques target primarily stuck-at-faults and are aimed well-below the ISA. In this paper, we consider joint extensions to the ISA and microarchitecture that create more opportunities for functional isolation and limited duplication of execution hardware. This is useful in cases where the faster hardware can be used to avoid timing faults.

Finally, many techniques attempt to improve the performance of multi-core systems with one or more cores that have some permanent component failures. A common insight is that when a given core has lost functionality due to failure, the lost functionality can be provided by some set of remaining cores. Core Cannibalization [22] leverages cross-core redundancy at the granularity of a pipeline stage. A special interconnect between neighboring cores allows them to share functional resources and bypass faulty components. Powell *et al.* examined more coarse-grained hardware driven core salvaging for CMPs [21]. They advocate use of hardware mechanisms to save and transfer state. This permits computational migration in the presence of failure as an alternative to fine-grained resource sharing. In this work, we focus on core-level timing faults. We believe that in some cases thread migration and cross pipeline resource sharing may offer additional ways to reduce timing violations especially when considering parameter variations [4]. In particular, compile-time knowledge may be useful determining how to schedule these operations. This maybe an interesting avenue for future work.

## 6. Limitations and Future Work

Process variations will be an increasingly significant problem for future processor generations. Prominent process variations could affect our compiler techniques adversely. The variations of path lengths from core to core make the performance of these technique less predictable. First, the difference between a fast path and an equivalent slow path will vary, making the improvement from our techniques more pronounced in one core while less significant in others. It will become harder to decide an optimal set of techniques for each benchmark. We acknowledge that this is a problem but do not address this issue in this work. It will be one of the focuses of our future work.

Our results show that branch rerouting consistently improve performance on all benchmarks. There is not a clear winner, however, among the rest of the techniques. This calls for a methodology to decide where and what techniques should be applied to obtain maximum benefits. We have not addressed this issue in this paper. This is an important item for future work. It will likely involve repeated profile-guided transformations using a compiler.

The introduction of BRINC breaks the ISA abstraction and possibly has consequences with regard to software compatibility. However, we believe that to improve performance, this is a worthwhile tradeoff. With shrinking process technology, future processors will be more likely to be affected by process variations and hard faults. To address these problems effectively, the solutions should involve many layers of the system from software down to the gate level.

## 7. Conclusion

Timing speculation is a promising technique to further improve single-thread performance. In this paper, we have demonstrated that to unleash more potential of timing speculation, we should involve the design at multiple levels from gate level, micro-architectural level, the ISA, the compiler and all the way up to programming language. In particular, we have proposed and demonstrated a few simple compiler transformation techniques that improve code resilience under timing errors. These techniques use simple compiler transformation to replace long delay operations with faster ones, and reduce the number of timing errors significantly. Although the performance of these techniques varies depending on the benchmark, there is always one that outperforms baseline timing speculation by up to 15%.


## Acknowledgments

We would like to thank anonymous reviewers and Antonio Gonzalez for their helpful comments. This work is in part supported by NSF CAREER CCF-0644332 and NSF CNS-0720820.


## References


[1] T. Austin, V. Bertacco, D. Blaauw, and T. Mudge. Opportunities and challenges for better than worst-case design. In *Proceedings of the 2005 Asia and South Pacific Design Automation Conference*, page 7. ACM, 2005.

[2] D. Bailey, E. Barszcz, J. Barton, D. Browning, R. Carter, L. Dagum, R. Fatoohi, P. Frederickson, T. Lasinski, R. Schreiber, et al. The NAS parallel benchmarks. *International Journal of High Performance Computing Applications*, 5(3):63, 1991.

[3] N. L. Binkert, R. G. Dreslinski, L. R. Hsu, K. T. Lim, A. G. Saidi, and S. K. Reinhardt. The m5 simulator: Modeling networked systems. *IEEE Micro*, 26:52–60, 2006. ISSN 0272-1732. doi: http://doi.ieeecomputersociety.org/10.1109/MM.2006.82.

[4] S. Borkar et al. Parameter variations and impact on circuits and microarchitecture. In *Proceedings of the 40th Design Automation Conference (DAC-40)*, 2003.

[5] K. Constantinides, O. Mutlu, T. Austin, and V. Bertacco. Software-based online detection of hardware defects mechanisms, architectural support, and evaluation. In *Proceedings of the 40th Annual IEEE/ACM International Symposium on Microarchitecture*, pages 97–108. IEEE Computer Society, 2007.

[6] D. Ernst et al. Razor: A low-power pipeline based on circuit-level timing speculation. In *The 36th International Symposium on Microarchitecture (MICRO-36)*, November 2003.

[7] M. Flatt and PLT. Reference: Racket. `http://www.racket-lang.org/tr1/`.

[8] B. Greskamp and J. Torrellas. Paceline: Improving single-thread performance in nanoscale cmps through core overclocking. In *Proceedings of the 16th International Conference on Parallel Architecture and Compilation Techniques*, PACT '07, pages 213–224, Washington, DC, USA, 2007. IEEE Computer Society. ISBN 0-7695-2944-5. doi: http://dx.doi.org/10.1109/PACT.2007.52. URL `http://dx.doi.org/10.1109/PACT.2007.52`.

[9] B. Greskamp, L. Wan, U. Karpuzcu, J. Cook, J. Torrellas, D. Chen, and C. Zilles. BlueShift: Designing Processors for Timing Speculation from the Ground Up. In *IEEE 15th International Symposium on High Performance Computer Architecture, 2009. HPCA 2009*, pages 213–224, 2009.

[10] M. Gupta, K. Rangan, M. Smith, G. Wei, and D. Brooks. Towards a software approach to mitigate voltage emergencies. In *Proceedings of the 2007 international symposium on Low power electronics and design*, page 128. ACM, 2007.

[11] M. Gupta, J. Rivers, P. Bose, G. Wei, and D. Brooks. Tribeca: design for PVT variations with local recovery and fine-grained adaptation. In *Proceedings of the 42nd Annual IEEE/ACM International Symposium on Microarchitecture*, pages 435–446. ACM, 2009.

[12] M. Guthaus, J. Ringenberg, D. Ernst, T. Austin, T. Mudge, and R. Brown. MiBench: A free, commercially representative embedded benchmark suite. In *IEEE 4th annual Workshop on Workload Characterization*, 2001.

[13] K. Hazelwood and D. Brooks. Eliminating voltage emergencies via microarchitectural voltage control feedback and dynamic optimiza-

tion. In *Proceedings of the International Symposium on Low Power Electronics and Design (ISLPED)*, August 2004.

[14] M. Hill and M. Marty. Amdahl's law in the multicore era. *Computer*, 41(7):33–38, 2008.

[15] R. Joseph. Exploring salvage techniques for multi-core architectures. In *Workshop on High Performance Computing Reliability Issues (HPCRI) 2005*. Citeseer, 2005.

[16] R. Joseph, D. Brooks, and M. Martonosi. Control techniques to eliminate voltage emergencies in high performance processors. In *Proceedings of the 9th International Symposium on High Performance Computer Architecture (HPCA-9)*, February 2003.

[17] A. Kahng, S. Kang, R. Kumar, and J. Sartori. Designing a Processor From the Ground Up to Allow Voltage/Reliability Tradeoffs. In *IEEE 16th International Symposium on High Performance Computer Architecture, 2010. HPCA 2010*, 2010.

[18] T. Liu and S.-L. Lu. Performance improvement with circuit-level speculation. In *Proceedings of the 33rd annual ACM/IEEE international symposium on Microarchitecture*, MICRO 33, pages 348–355, New York, NY, USA, 2000. ACM. ISBN 1-58113-196-8. doi: http://doi.acm.org/10.1145/360128.360166. URL `http://doi.acm.org/10.1145/360128.360166`.

[19] A. Meixner and D. Sorin. Detouring: Translating software to circumvent hard faults in simple cores. In *IEEE International Conference on Dependable Systems and Networks With FTCS and DCC, 2008. DSN 2008*, pages 80–89, 2008.

[20] S. Ozdemir, D. Sinha, G. Memik, J. Adams, and H. Zhou. Yield-aware cache architectures. In *roceedings of the 39th Annual IEEE/ACM International Symposium on Microarchitecture (MICRO-39)*, December 2006.

[21] M. Powell, A. Biswas, S. Gupta, and S. Mukherjee. Architectural core salvaging in a multi-core processor for hard-error tolerance. In *Proceedings of the 36th annual international symposium on Computer architecture*, pages 93–104. ACM, 2009.

[22] B. Romanescu and D. Sorin. Core cannibalization architecture: improving lifetime chip performance for multicore processors in the presence of hard faults. In *Proceedings of the 17th international conference on Parallel architectures and compilation techniques*, pages 43–51. ACM, 2008.

[23] S. Sarangi, B. Greskamp, A. Tiwari, and J. Torrellas. EVAL: Utilizing processors with variation-induced timing errors. In *Proceedings of the 2008 41st IEEE/ACM International Symposium on Microarchitecture-Volume*, 2008.

[24] E. Schuchman and T. N. Vijaykumar. Rescue: A microarchitecture for testability and defect tolerance. In *Proceedings of the 32nd Annual International Symposium on Computer Architecture (ISCA-32)*, June 2005.

[25] J. Stine, I. Castellanos, M. Wood, J. Henson, F. Love, W. Davis, P. Franzon, M. Bucher, S. Basavarajaiah, J. Oh, et al. Freepdk: An open-source variation-aware design kit. 2007.

[26] C. Wilkerson, H. Gao, A. R. Alameldeen, Z. Chishti, M. Khellah, and S.-L. Lu. Trading off cache capacity for reliability to enable low voltage operation. In *Proceedings of the 35th Annual International Symposium on Computer Architecture*, ISCA '08, pages 203–214, Washington, DC, USA, 2008. IEEE Computer Society. ISBN 978-0-7695-3174-8. doi: http://dx.doi.org/10.1109/ISCA.2008.22. URL `http://dx.doi.org/10.1109/ISCA.2008.22`.

[27] V. J. Reddi, S. Campanoni, M. S. Gupta, K. Hazelwood, M. D. Smith, G.-Y. Wei, and D. Brooks. Eliminating Voltage Emergencies via Software-Guided Code Transformations. *Transactions on Architecture and Code Optimization (TACO)*, 7(2), 2010.

[28] S. Sastry Hari, M. Li, P. Ramachandran, B. Choi, and S. Adve. mSWAT: low-cost hardware fault detection and diagnosis for multicore systems. In *Proceedings of the 42nd Annual IEEE/ACM International Symposium on Microarchitecture*, pages 122–132. ACM, 2009.

# Orchestration by Approximation

## Mapping Stream Programs onto Multicore Architectures

S. M. Farhad[1,3] * Yousun Ko[2] § Bernd Burgstaller[2] § Bernhard Scholz[1] ‡

[1]The University of Sydney
Sydney, Australia
{smfarhad, scholz}@it.usyd.edu.au

[2]Yonsei University
Seoul, Korea
{yousun.ko, bburg}@cs.yonsei.ac.kr

[3]NICTA
Locked Bag 9013
Alexandria NSW 1435, Australia

## Abstract

We present a novel 2-approximation algorithm for deploying stream graphs on multicore computers and a stream graph transformation that eliminates bottlenecks. The key technical insight is a data rate transfer model that enables the computation of a "closed form", i.e., the data rate transfer function of an actor depending on the arrival rate of the stream program. A combinatorial optimization problem uses the closed form to maximize the throughput of the stream program. Although the problem is inherently NP-hard, we present an efficient and effective 2-approximation algorithm that provides a lower bound on the quality of the solution. We introduce a transformation that uses the closed form to identify and eliminate bottlenecks.

We show experimentally that state-of-the art integer linear programming approaches for orchestrating stream graphs are (1) intractable or at least impractical for larger stream graphs and larger number of processors and (2) our 2-approximation algorithm is highly efficient and its results are close to the optimal solution for a standard set of StreamIt benchmark programs.

***Categories and Subject Descriptors*** D.3.4 [*Programming Languages*]: Processors Compilers

***General Terms*** Languages, Algorithms, Performance

***Keywords*** StreamIt, multicore, stream programming

## 1. Introduction

Multicore processors have become the industry standard because the von Neumann computing model [2] of uniprocessor architectures has ceased to scale effectively. Example systems include the IBM Cell BE processor with 9 cores [13], the IBM Power7 with 8 cores [14], the Sun UltraSPARC T3 with 16 cores [26], NVIDIA's GeForce GTX 480 that provides 15 streaming processors each with 32 CUDA cores [23], and the Cisco CRS-1 and CRS-3 routers that utilize Tensilica's Metro and QuantumFlow processors with 188 and 40 4-threaded cores [8, 10]. Intel and AMD are already producing x86 systems with 8 and 12 cores respectively.

Sequential programming languages are ill-suited to multicore architectures, because they assume a single instruction stream and a single, uniform memory system. Identifying coarse-grained parallelism for efficient multicore execution is left to the programmer and the compiler. Multicore architectures vary in their communication primitives and in the number and capabilities of their CPU cores. Sequential programming languages provide insufficient parallel hardware abstractions, which greatly hampers performance and portability of software on multicore architectures.

The stream programming paradigm has turned out to be an effective approach for programming multicore architectures. Stream programming languages facilitate application domains characterized by regular sequences of data, such as digital signal processing, audio, video, graphics and networking. Examples of stream programming languages and language extensions include StreamIt [30], Brook [5], Baker [7], StreamFlex [27], Cg [21] and SPUR [36].

In our work we use StreamIt, which represents a program as a set of actors that interact through FIFO data channels (see Figure 1). During program execution, actors are invoked repeatedly in a periodic schedule [3]. Because each actor has a separate program counter and an independent address space, dependencies between actors are made explicit by the data channels. StreamIt employs the synchronous data-flow model (SDF, [19]), which requires the number of data items produced and consumed by each actor to be known a-priori (with StreamIt this information is already specified in the source code). Compilers can then leverage the static dependence information to orchestrate parallel execution.

The major optimization objective with stream programs is to maximize data throughput. Although stream programs contain an abundance of parallelism, obtaining an efficient mapping onto parallel architectures is nevertheless a challenging problem. The gains obtained from parallel execution are easily overshadowed by the costs of communication and synchronization. Resource limitations of the system must be incorporated into the mapping process to avoid stalls and load-imbalances. Resource limitations of shared-memory multiprocessors include processing capabilities and memory bandwidth. A compiler must take into account the structural properties of actors and actor dependencies to resolve *bottlenecks* that constrain the throughput of a stream program. Stream pro-

* NICTA is funded by the Australian Government as represented by the Department of Broadband, Communications and the Digital Economy and the Australian Research Council through the ICT Centre of Excellence program.

§ Research partially supported by the National Research Foundation of Korea (NRF) grant funded by the Korea government (MEST) (No. 2010-0005234), and the OKAWA Foundation Research Grant (2009).

‡ Research partially supported by the Australian Research Council through ARC DP grant DP1096445.

grams contain task, data and pipeline parallelism, and it is critical for a compiler to leverage a synergistic combination while avoiding the hazards associated with each.

Recently, significant research effort has been spent for orchestrating stream graphs on multicore architectures [6, 7, 11, 12, 16, 18, 28, 31, 32, 34, 35]. It has been shown in [18] how the unfolding and partitioning of actors onto a multicore architecture can be formulated as an Integer Linear Programming (ILP) problem. This ILP formulation does not take into account communication costs between actors. The ILP solution-space for unfolding and partitioning of actors grows exponentially in the number of processors, actors and data channels. Our experiments with existing methods using CPLEX indicate that ILP formulations become intractable or at least impractical already for three or four cores (see also Table 2 where $P\#$ is the number of cores and $t_{ILP}$ is the CPLEX solve time). An approach that approximates the optimal solution of the ILP formulation seems therefore desirable. In contrast to previous work, our work uses a data transfer model that sets in relation the input and output data rates of actors. In our model, we maximize the arrival rate whereas previous work optimizes makespan, i.e., the runtime of the longest running processor, which is an indirect measure of arrival rate and throughput.

This paper makes the following contributions:

- a novel data rate transfer model for stream programs that introduces data rate functions for actors that depend on the arrival rate of the stream program,
- a quantitative analysis to identify bottlenecks and "hot regions" in stream programs,
- a transformation for stream programs that is region based for eliminating bottlenecks and, hence, reduces communication costs, and
- a 2-approximation algorithm that maps actors onto a parallel system by maximizing the arrival rate of the stream program.

Experiments show that our approximation approach solves the orchestration problem instantly (i.e., within milliseconds), with a solution that achieves 95–100% of the throughput obtained by an ILP formulation.

The paper is organized as follows: in Section 2 we motivate problems and optimization opportunities with stream program orchestration on multicore architectures. Section 3 introduces our analytical performance model. In Section 4 we discuss the elimination of bottlenecks. Section 5 contains the actor allocation problem (AAP) and our approximation thereof. In Section 6 we discuss the experimental results. We survey related work in Section 7 and draw our conclusions in Section 8. We provide a glossary in Appendix B.

## 2. Orchestration

The motivation for our approximation algorithm for actor unfolding and partitioning are scalability problems with the existing, optimal ILP formulation. We observed impractical solve times already for a program consisting of 26 actors on 4 processors (see Section 6). However, a recent survey ([29]) on the characteristics of stream programs reports increasing program sizes of up to 2868 actors per program. In conjunction with the semiconductor industry's projected increases in core counts an approach that approximates the optimal solution of the ILP formulation is important.

We motivate our approach using a simple StreamIt program consisting of four actors depicted in Figure 1. Let us assume that actors 1 and 4 are *stateful* and actors 2 and 3 are *stateless*. Only stateless actors may be duplicated to exploit data-parallelism, because a stateful actor propagates local state information between actor invocations. As a result, every invocation of a stateful actor depends on a previous invocation, and hence must not be duplicated.

In Figure 1(a) actor execution times are depicted next to stream graph nodes. Actors 2 and 3 consume more processing time (60 time units each) than actors 1 and 4. The stream program takes 130 time units when executed on a uniprocessor with a single invocation for all actors. Note that actors 2 and 3 will cause a bottleneck if the program is executed on a multicore system due to the high execution costs. We refer to these actors as *hot actors*. To improve the throughput of stream programs on multi-core systems, hot actors are duplicated to spread the load evenly among processors. In this example the hot actors form a *hot region* since they are adjacent to each other.

An optimal allocation is presented in Figure 2(a) following the method described in [18]. Actors 2 and 3 are duplicated two times,

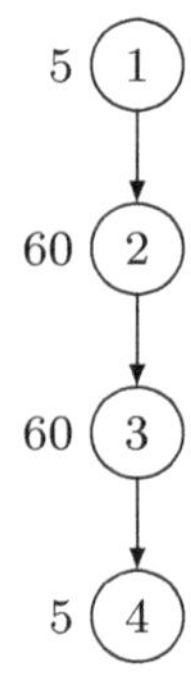


(a)

```
void->void pipeline Program() {
  add IntSource;
  add ID1;
  add ID2;
  add IntPrinter;
}
void->int filter IntSource() {
  int x;
  init {x=0;}
  work push 1 {push (x++); }
}
int->int filter ID1() {
  work push 1 pop 1 {
      push(pop());
      //do expensive work
  }
}
int->int filter ID2() {
  work push 1 pop 1 {
      push(pop());
      //do expensive work
  }
}
int->void filter IntPrinter() {
  work pop 1 { print(pop());}
}
```

(b)

**Figure 1.** (a) Stream graph (b) Corresponding StreamIt source code.

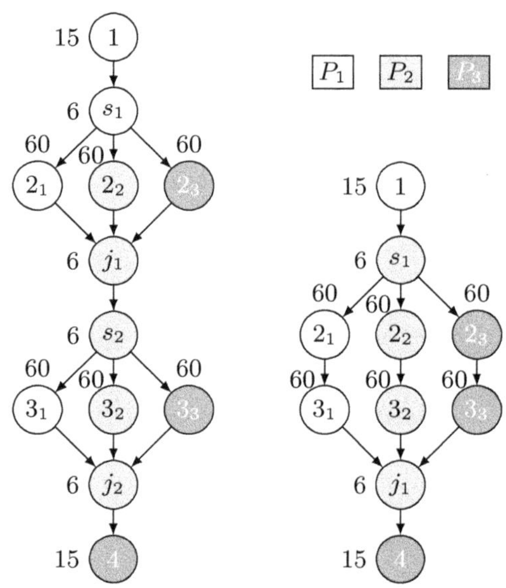

(a) (b)

**Figure 2.** (a) Integrated bottleneck resolution and actor allocation approach of [18] (b) hot region bottleneck resolution.

totaling in three versions each. Splitters $s_1$, $s_2$ and joiners $j_1$, $j_2$ are added to distribute data among the three versions of actors 2 and 3. Nodes $2_1$, $2_2$, $2_3$ constitute the three versions of actor 2 and nodes $3_1$, $3_2$, $3_3$ constitute the three versions of actor 3. Node colors indicate the processor allocation. In this example, the workloads assigned to processors $P_1$, $P_2$ and $P_3$ are 141, 138 and 135 time units, respectively, if we account a workload of 6 time units for splitters and joiners. We calculate speedups by dividing the weighted uniprocessor execution-time by the load on the maximally loaded processor. The weight of the uniprocessor execution-time is 3, since the transformed program represents three invocations of the original program. The maximally loaded processor is processor $P_1$ with 141 time units. Hence, the obtained speedup for the stream graph in Figure 2(a) is $\frac{3\times130}{141} = 2.77$.

In our approach, the solution in Figure 2(a) is further improved by combining actors 2 and 3 into a hot region. The result of duplicating the hot region as a whole is depicted in Figure 2(b). Because the overhead of joiner $j_1$ and splitter $s_2$ is avoided, the speedup increases to $\frac{3\times130}{135} = 2.89$. Our approach separates hot actor identification from actor allocation, which enables the duplication of hot regions. In this way our method can achieve improved bottleneck elimination over existing techniques.

Essential for the hot region transformation is a data transfer model for actors that is able to identify hot actors. The data transfer model permits the computation of closed forms that express the output data rate of an actor as a function that depends solely on the arrival rate of the whole program, i.e., the closed form incorporates all immediate and intermediate data transfer dependencies of an actor. With the closed form the allocation problem simplifies as well since the topology of the graph does not need to be considered. An overview of the proposed approach to statically optimize the throughput of a stream program is illustrated in Figure 3.

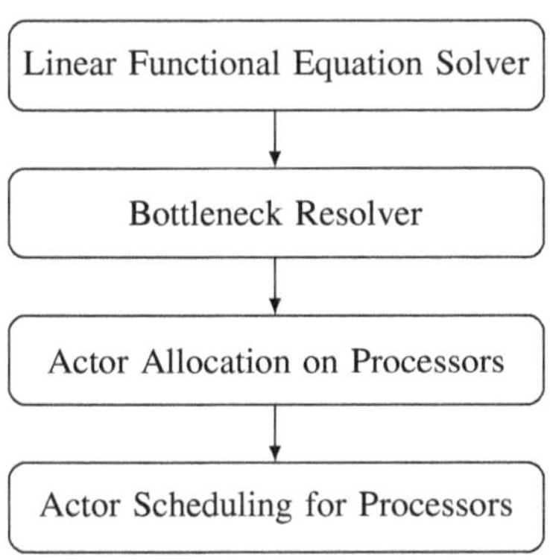


**Figure 3.** Framework overview.

Our static optimization consists of four components: a linear functional equation solver, a bottleneck resolver, actor allocation and actor scheduling. An analytical performance model is created for a stream program that employs a linear functional equation solver to compute the closed form of data transfers rates in the stream program. After computing closed forms, we perform a quantitative analysis to detect bottlenecks and duplicate hot regions. The remaining steps are the mapping of actors to processors via an approximation algorithm and computing the schedule using standard techniques.

## 3. Data Transfer Model

The dataflow model [9] represents a program as a *stream graph* $G(V, E)$ whose vertices $V = \{1, \ldots, n\}$ are called *actors* and whose edges $E \subseteq V \times V$ are called *channels*. A channel $(i, j) \in E$ queues data elements called *tokens* which are passed from the output of computation $i$ to the input of computation $j$. Synchronous dataflow (SDF, [3, 19]) restricts the dataflow model by fixing the number of consumed tokens denoted by $c_i$ and the number of produced tokens denoted by $p_i$ of an actor $i$ at compile time. StreamIt [30] employs the SDF model except for the following differences: (1) StreamIt has a non-consuming read (`peek`) operation from the input channel similar to the computation model introduced in [17], (2) the number of tokens consumed and produced are specified for actors rather than along data channels, and (3) stream graphs in StreamIt are "structured", i.e., they are composites of filters, pipelines, split/joins, and feedback loops.

There is a cornucopia of scheduling work for synchronous dataflow [6, 11, 16, 18, 19, 24, 31, 32] ensuring that a schedule requires finite resources for storing tokens along channels, and that actors do not dead-lock whilst executing the schedule. A *periodic static* schedule [19] consists of a finite sequence of actor invocations; the periodic schedule is computed at compile time, invokes each actor of the stream graph at least once, and produces no net change in the system state, i.e., the number of tokens on each edge is the same before and after executing the schedule. Hence, a periodic schedule can be executed ad-infinitum without exhausting memory, and we refer to the state before and after the execution of a periodic schedule as the *steady-state*.

A periodic schedule has a positive integer vector $\mathbf{q} \in \mathbb{N}^n$ called *repetition vector* [19] whose elements correspond to actors in the stream graph. Element $q_i$ for all $i \in \{1, \ldots, n\}$ is equal to the number of occurrences of actor $i$ in the periodic schedule. Because every actor needs to be invoked at least once in the schedule, $q_i$ is greater than or equal to 1.

A parallel periodic schedule distributes the invocation of actors on a parallel system and has a finite sequence of actor invocations for each processor. Synchronization between processors is necessary to wait for the longest running processor before executing the next iteration of the periodic schedule. We refer to the time duration of the longest running processor as *make span* $\Pi$, which affects the performance (i.e., throughput) of the stream graph.

### 3.1 Performance of a Periodic Static Schedule

The performance of a periodic schedule may be determined by the number of input tokens it can process in time duration $\Pi$. Without loss of generality we assume there is a unique actor that solely reads the input of the program and receives no input from other actors in the stream graph. We refer to this actor as the *start node* and assign it the ordinal number 1.

The *arrival rate* $z$ of a periodic schedule measures the number of input tokens processed in time duration $\Pi$ and is obtained by

$$z = \frac{\iota_1 q_1}{\Pi}, \tag{1}$$

where $\iota_1$ is the number of bytes[1] read from the program input for a single invocation of the start node. Note that $\iota_i$ for all $i \in \{1, \ldots, n\}$, is the product of the size of an input token in bytes times the number of tokens $c_i$ consumed by an invocation of actor $i$. The *output data rate* of actor $i$ is defined by

$$\xi_i = \frac{\omega_i q_i}{\Pi}, \quad \text{for all } i \in \{1, \ldots, n\}, \tag{2}$$

where $\omega_i$ represents the number of bytes produced by a single invocation of actor $i$. Parameter $\omega_i$ is the product of the size of an output token in bytes and the number of tokens $p_i$ produced by actor $i$ for a single invocation.

An alternative measure of performance for stream programs is the notion of *throughput*. Throughput of a stream program may be

[1] SDF semantics implies static push and pop rates of actors.

defined as the sum of output data rates of its actors, i.e., $\sum_{i=1}^{n} \xi_i$. In Section 5, Eq. (14), we show that with an SDF model although arrival rate and throughput are different optimization objectives, the solutions are identical.

In this work, we seek a parallel periodic schedule that maximizes the arrival rate by placing actors on processors and transforming the stream graph. Our approach relies on a performance model of stream graphs that is able to compute the output data rate of an actor as a linear function of the arrival rate, independent of a concrete periodic schedule and the make span $\Pi$.

### 3.2 Model

Actors in the stream graph consume and produce a fixed number of tokens for a single invocation in the schedule. Under the assumption that we know the input data rate of an actor, we can compute the output data rate using *data rate transfer functions* $\Phi_i : \mathbb{R}^+ \rightarrow \mathbb{R}^+$, which are defined as $x \mapsto \alpha_i x$, where $\alpha_i$ is the ratio between the number of bytes produced and consumed for a single invocation of actor $i$, i.e., $\alpha_i = \frac{\omega_i}{\iota_i}$.

For example, all channels in Figure 1 are of type integer. The push and pop rates of the second actor are 1. If we assume a 4-byte integer representation, we get $\iota_2 = 4{\cdot}1$ and $\omega_2 = 4{\cdot}1$, i.e., invoking the second actor once consumes 4 bytes from the input channel and produces 4 bytes on the output channel. Hence, the parameter of the data transfer function is 1, i.e., $\alpha_2 = \frac{\omega_2}{\iota_2} = 1$, which implies that the input data rate of the actor is equal to the output data rate.

An actor may have more than one outgoing channel, and SDF semantics allows a fixed ratio for splitting the output rate of an actor $i$ among its outgoing channels. In our model, the data rate of channel $(i, j) \in E$ is given by term $w_{ij}\Phi_i(x)$, where weight $w_{ij}$ denotes the fraction of the output data rate of actor $i$ that is diverted from actor $i$ to channel $(i, j)$. If $w_{ij}$ is zero, it denotes that there is no dataflow between actor $i$ and actor $j$. To conserve dataflow in a stream program, it must hold that $\sum_{j=1}^{n} w_{ij} = 1$, for all $i \in \{1, \ldots, n\}$.

For example, the weights of the channels in Figure 2(b) are all one except for edges $(s_1, 2_1)$, $(s_1, 2_2)$, and $(s_1, 2_3)$, whose weights are $\frac{1}{3}$.

The input data rate of an actor $i$ is the sum over all data rates of the incoming channels of $i$, i.e., $\sum_{j=1}^{n} w_{ji}x_j$, where $x_j$ is the output data rate of actor $j$. We obtain *data rate equations* by setting the data rate transfer functions of an actor in relation to its input and output data rates.

DEFINITION 1. *The data rate equations of a stream graph are defined as*

$$x_1 = \Phi_1(z) \quad \textit{and}$$

$$x_i = \Phi_i\left(\sum_{j=1}^{n} w_{ji}x_j\right), \qquad \textit{for all } i \in \{2, \ldots, n\}, \tag{3}$$

*where the output data rate for actor $i$ is $x_i \in \mathbb{R}^+$, and $z$ is the arrival rate.*

LEMMA 1. *For a given periodic schedule, the output data rate $\xi$ is a solution of the data rate equations.*

PROOF 1. *To preserve the steady-state of a periodic schedule, the number of consumed tokens $c_i q_i$ of an actor $i$ must be equal to the number of received tokens $\sum_{j=1}^{n} w_{ji}p_j q_j$ for all $i \in \{2, \ldots, n\}$. Hence, the following equations hold for a periodic schedule:*

$$c_i q_i = \sum_{j=1}^{n} w_{ji}p_j q_j, \quad \textit{for all } i \in \{2, \ldots, n\}. \tag{4}$$

*The relationship between $q_i$ and $\xi_i$ is established in Eq. (2) and is transformed to $q_i = \frac{\Pi}{\omega_i}\xi_i$. We rewrite the data rate equations of Eq. (4) to Eq. (3) for all $i \in \{2, \ldots, n\}$ as follows,*

$$\tfrac{c_i\Pi}{\omega_i}\xi_i = \sum_{j=1}^{n} \tfrac{w_{ji}p_j\Pi}{\omega_j}\xi_j \Rightarrow \xi_i = \tfrac{\omega_i}{c_i}\sum_{j=1}^{n} \tfrac{w_{ji}p_j}{\omega_j}\xi_j \Rightarrow$$

$$\xi_i = \alpha_i \sum_{j=1}^{n} w_{ji}\xi_j \Rightarrow \xi_i = \Phi_i\left(\sum_{j=1}^{n} w_{ji}\xi_j\right)$$

*since the ratio $\frac{\omega_j}{p_j}$ is the byte size of an output token of actor $j$, and it is equal among all predecessors $j$ of actor $i$, the inverse $\frac{p_j}{\omega_j}$ can be moved out of the sum reducing the term to $\alpha_i$. Substituting Eq. (1) in Eq. (2) for the start node by eliminating $q_1$ gives the equation $\xi_1 = \Phi_1(z)$ and the lemma follows.*

### 3.3 Closed Form

A *closed-form* $\Phi_i^* : \mathbb{R}^+ \rightarrow \mathbb{R}^+$ of actor $i$ is a data rate transfer function that solely depends on arrival rate $z$ of the dataflow program, i.e., $z \mapsto \alpha_i' z$. With the existence of a closed form, the output rate of an actor can be determined by knowing the arrival rate $z$. In this work, the closed form is fundamental for placing actors on processors and eliminating bottlenecks.

The solution of the simultaneous equation system in Eq. (3) is a set of linear functions that depend on $z$ which can be solved by employing standard linear algebra. We introduce a new matrix $\mathcal{A}$ with elements $a_{ik} = \alpha_i w_{ki}$ and vector $\mathbf{b}$ with elements $b_1 = \alpha_1$, and $b_i = 0$ for all $i \in \{2, \ldots, n\}$.

LEMMA 2. *The closed form of stream graph $G$ is*

$$\alpha' = (\mathcal{I} - \mathcal{A})^{-1}\boldsymbol{b} \tag{5}$$

where $\mathcal{I}$ is the identity matrix.

PROOF 2. *We rewrite the data rate equations of Eq. (3) as*

$$\boldsymbol{x} = \mathcal{A}\boldsymbol{x} + z\boldsymbol{b} \tag{6}$$

*which is reduced to $\mathcal{I}\boldsymbol{x} = \mathcal{A}\boldsymbol{x} + z\boldsymbol{b} \Rightarrow (\mathcal{I} - \mathcal{A})\boldsymbol{x} = z\boldsymbol{b} \Rightarrow \boldsymbol{x} = z(\mathcal{I} - \mathcal{A})^{-1}\boldsymbol{b}$, and the lemma follows.*

For large numbers of actors, the computation of the inverse of matrix $\mathcal{A}$ is expensive. An alternate method that computes the closed form more efficiently is required for practical purposes.

LEMMA 3. *For a program that has a periodic schedule, matrix $(\mathcal{I} - \mathcal{A})$ is nonsingular.*

Due to space limitations we only sketch the proof here. The proof in Lemma 1 establishes a connection between the data rate equations and the equilibrium of consumed and produced tokens of actors. In [19] the equilibrium was expressed in form of a topological matrix mapping the repetition vector to a null vector, and it was shown that if the stream graph is connected, the rank of the topology matrix is $n - 1$. This result can be used to argue that the matrix $(\mathcal{I} - \mathcal{A})$ is nonsingular.

LEMMA 4. *Given the repetition vector $\boldsymbol{q}$ of a stream program, the parameter $\alpha_i'$ of the closed form is given by*

$$\alpha_i' = \frac{\omega_i q_i}{\iota_1 q_1} \tag{7}$$

PROOF 3. *We set in relationship the data output rate of Eq. (1) and the closed form. We substitute the arrival rate $z$ by the right-hand side of Eq. (2), i.e., $\alpha_i'$ as $\frac{\xi_i}{z}$ that further reduces to*

$$\xi_i = \alpha_i' z \Rightarrow \frac{\omega_i q_i}{\Pi} = \alpha_i' \frac{\iota_1 q_1}{\Pi} \Rightarrow \alpha_i' = \frac{\omega_i q_i}{\iota_1 q_1} \tag{8}$$

By Lemma 4, the parameter $\alpha'$ of the closed form may be computed by knowing $\mathbf{q}$, which is a property of the stream graph [19].

Fast solvers for computing the repetition vector of a stream graph are known to compute solutions in linear time complexity for unstructured graphs [3] and structured graphs [15]. Computing the parameter $\alpha'$ by employing linear equation solvers exhibits a higher computational complexity though fast equation solvers as used for data flow analysis [25] might deliver sufficient performance in practice.

For example, the second and third actor in Fig. 1 have data transfer functions whose $\alpha$-parameters are 1, i.e., the input data rate is equal to the output data rate. As stated in the previous sub-section, the output rate of an actor is expressed as a linear functional equation system. Consider the third actor. The equation of the third actor is $x_3 = \Phi_3(x_2)$, which simplifies to $x_3 = x_2$ since $\alpha_3 = 1$. By expanding $x_2$ and so forth, we obtain a closed form $x_3 = z$ which implies that the output data rate of the third actor is the arrival rate. Instead of performing Gaussian elimination which exhibits a cubic runtime complexity to find the closed form of the actor, we employ Eq. (8) that requires a repetition vector. In our example, a most trivial periodic schedule can be found that contains a single invocation for each actor. Hence, the repetition vector of this periodic schedule is $\mathbf{q} = (1\,1\,1\,1)$. Using the formula from Eq. (8), we obtain $\alpha'_3 = \frac{\omega_3 \cdot q_3}{\iota_3 \cdot q_1} = 1$ and $x_3 = \alpha'_3 z = z$.

### 3.4 Processor Utilization

For the bottleneck elimination we require the notion of processor load incurred by the execution of actors depending on the input data rate. We have an underlying assumption that the multi-core system has the same *execution time* $t_i$ of an actor invocation $i$ on all parallel processors, and we obtain the execution time by profiling (see Section 6).

In our model the measurement of utilization is in percentage of the processor load. Assuming that a processor of the multi-core system exclusively executes actor $i$, the load of this processor would become 100% and the input data rate of actor $i$ is $\frac{\iota_i}{t_i}$. Hence, $\frac{\iota_i}{t_i}$ bytes per second constitutes an upper bound for the input data rate of actor $i$, i.e., $\sum_{j=1}^{n} w_{ji} x_j \leq \frac{\iota_i}{t_i}$. This upper bound is used in the following section, which discusses a quantitative model for bottleneck elimination.

For the actor allocation and the bottleneck elimination we introduce a *processor utilization function* $\Gamma_i : \mathbb{R}^+ \to \mathbb{R}^+$, that maps the input data rate of actor $i$ to a processor load which is defined as $x \mapsto \gamma_i x$, where

$$\gamma_i = \frac{t_i}{\iota_i}, \quad \text{for all } i \in \{1, \ldots, n\}.$$

We observe that $\Gamma_i(\frac{\iota_i}{t_i})$ represents a load of 100%, because $\frac{\iota_i}{t_i}$ is the upper bound of the input data rate.

For example, the parameter of the processor utilization function of the second actor in Figure 1 is $\frac{\iota_3}{t_3} = \frac{4}{60} = 0.066$ and therefore the maximal input data rate of actor 3 is 15 bytes per time unit.

For sake of readability, we define the processor load of actor $i$ depending on the arrival rate:

$$U_1(z) = \Gamma_1(z)$$
$$U_i(z) = \Gamma_i\left(\sum_{j=1}^{n} w_{ji} \Phi_j^*(z)\right), \quad \text{for all } i \in \{2, \ldots, n\}.$$

Due to the linearity of the processor utilization function, we obtain

$$U_i(z) = \gamma_i \left(\sum_{j=1}^{n} w_{ji} \alpha'_j\right) z.$$

## 4. Elimination of Bottlenecks

The input data rate $z$ of a stream program is limited by the processor capacity of the cores and the memory bandwidth used by storing tokens along channels. Bottlenecks limit the arrival rate of a stream program although free processing capacity in the parallel system is available. Hence, it is of key importance to eliminate bottlenecks in order to maximize the arrival rate of a stream program.

We perform the elimination of bottlenecks in a stream graph in two steps. In the first step, a quantitative analysis that is based on the performance model described in Section 3 identifies bottlenecks. In the second step, a stream graph transformation duplicates hot-regions, i.e., sub-graphs of the stream graph that cause a bottleneck. After transforming the stream graph the arrival rate is bound by the system resources.

### 4.1 Identification of Hot Actors

A quantitative analysis determines two types of upper bounds for the arrival rate: (1) an upper bound that is imposed by an actor in the stream graph, and (2) an upper bound that is imposed by the processing capacity and memory bandwidth of the parallel system. If the upper bound imposed by an actor is smaller than the upper bound of the parallel system, then the actor is *hot* and causes a bottleneck because free processing capacity is available but cannot be utilized.

The upper bound $\text{ub}_i$ of the arrival rate for an actor $i$ is discussed in the following. Assume that $R$ is the maximum data rate in bytes at which an actor can receive tokens. Data rate $R$ is limited by the memory bandwidth of the underlying hardware; we determine $R$ through profiling. We can state the following inequalities for an actor:

$$\sum_{j=1}^{n} w_{ji} \Phi_j^*(z) \leq R, \quad \text{for all } i \in \{2, \ldots, n\}$$
$$U_i(z) \leq 1, \quad \text{for all } i \in \{1, \ldots, n\}$$

The first constraint limits the data rate of an input stream to $R$ and the second constraint restricts the arrival rate $z$ by the processor capacity of a single core whilst executing a single actor solely. Since the left-hand sides of both constraints are linear functions in $z$, we obtain:

$$z \leq \frac{R}{\sum_{j=1}^{n} w_{ji} \alpha'_j}, \quad \text{for all } i \in \{2, \ldots, n\}$$
$$z \leq \frac{1}{\sum_{j=1}^{n} w_{ji} \alpha'_j \gamma_i}, \quad \text{for all } i \in \{1, \ldots, n\}$$

Hence, the upper bound $\text{ub}_i$ for actor $i \in \{2, \ldots, n\}$ is

$$z \leq \min\left(\frac{R}{\sum_{j=1}^{n} w_{ji} \alpha'_j}, \frac{1}{\sum_{j=1}^{n} w_{ji} \alpha'_j \gamma_i}\right) = \text{ub}_i,$$

whereas for the start node the upper bound is $\text{ub}_1 = \min(R, \frac{1}{\gamma_1})$.

The upper bound $\text{ub}_s$ of the arrival rate imposed by the parallel system is given by

$$\sum_{i=1}^{n} \Phi_i^*(z) \leq pR$$
$$\sum_{i=1}^{n} U_i(z) \leq p,$$

where the first inequality states that the sum of the output data rates of actors cannot exceed $pR$ assuming that each processor has the same memory bandwidth and the second constraint limits the overall load of the system to $p$ times 100%. Since the left-hand sides of the above inequalities are linear, z can be factored out and

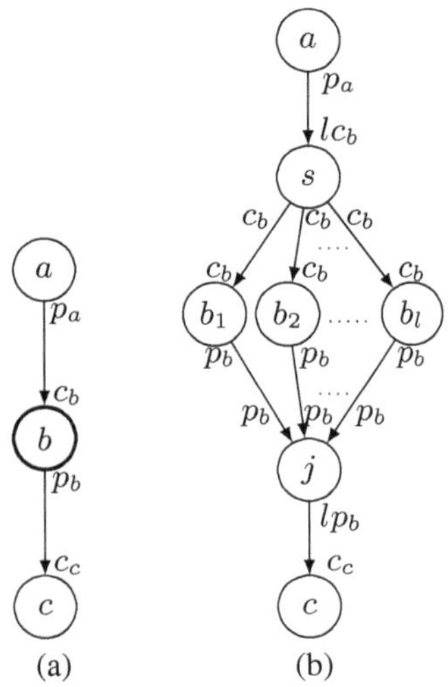


**Figure 4.** Hot actor duplication: (a) A pipeline consists of one hot actor $b$ with duplicity $l$. (b) Duplication of actor $b$.

we obtain

$$z \leq \frac{pR}{\sum_{i=1}^{n} \alpha'_i}$$

$$z \leq \frac{p}{\gamma_1 + \sum_{i=2}^{n} \gamma_i \sum_{j=1}^{n} w_{ji}\alpha'_j}.$$

Hence, the upper bound $\mathrm{ub}_s$ is obtained by

$$z \leq \min\left(\frac{pR}{\sum_{i=1}^{n} \alpha'_i}, \frac{p}{\gamma_1 + \sum_{i=2}^{n} \gamma_i \sum_{j=1}^{n} w_{ji}\alpha'_j}\right) = \mathrm{ub}_s .$$

The upper bound $\mathrm{ub}_i$ of an actor $i$ and the upper bound of the parallel system $\mathrm{ub}_s$ are conservative since a concrete placement can further lower the upper bound.

DEFINITION 2. *An actor $i$ is called hot if $\mathrm{ub}_i < \mathrm{ub}_s$, and cold otherwise.*

If a hot actor is stateless, the stream graph transformation will create new instances of the actor to reduce the data input rate. With the reduced data input rates of the new instances, the bottleneck will be eliminated. Note that actors with a peek-rate that is greater than the pop-rate carry implicit state and hence are treated as stateful actors. For stateful hot actors, there is no simple transformation to overcome the bottleneck.

For the stream graph transformation, we introduce the notion of *duplicity* of an actor $i$ that gives the number of instances required to avoid a bottleneck in the stream graph.

DEFINITION 3. *The duplicity of an actor is defined by*

$$d_i = \lceil U_i(\mathrm{ub}_s) \rceil .$$

A duplicity of one means that the actor is cold; a duplicity greater than one makes an actor hot.

### 4.2 Stream Graph Transformation

If the total processing capacity and the memory bandwidth of the parallel system are the most restricting constraints for the arrival rate $z$, the stream program is called *bottleneck free*, i.e., the processing capacity and/or the memory bandwidth is fully utilized. If a stateless actor $b$ is hot, the stream program has a *bottleneck* and we create new instances of the actor so that the transformed stream program becomes bottleneck free.

The duplication of a hot actor $b$ with duplicity $l$ is depicted in Figure 4. Additional $l - 1$ instances of actor $b$, a new roundrobin splitter $s$ and a joiner $j$ are added to the vertex set $V$ and incoming and outgoing streams for the instances of actor $b$ are duplicated for the new vertices, i.e.,

$$E' = E \cup \{(a,s)|(a,b) \in E\} \cup \{(j,c)|(b,c) \in E\}$$
$$\cup\{(s,b_i)\} \cup \{(b_i,j)\}, \text{for all } i \in \{1,\ldots,l\} \quad (9)$$

The consumed and produced tokens for the newly introduced nodes $s$ and $j$ are adjusted according to the data rates of hot actor $b$ and duplicity $l$.

To minimize the number of data channels introduced by the duplication, we extend the notion of hot actors to *hot regions*. A hot region is a maximal connected subgraph $HR = (V', E')$ in $G$ whose actors are hot and stateless. We assume that splitters and joiners are special nodes which cannot be regarded as hot actors. Hence, a hot region has the shape of a pipeline consisting one or more hot filters. The heuristic approach for region duplication is outlined in Algorithm 1.

**Algorithm 1** Heuristic for Bottlenecks

1: Determine hot regions (*HRs*) in $G$.
2: **for** each $(V', E')$ in *HRs* **do**
3: $\quad d_{HR} = \max_{i \in V'} d_i$
4: $\quad$ Duplicate $(V', E')$ in $G$
5: **end for**

Hot regions are determined by a DFS search (line 1). The duplicity of a hot region *HR* is calculated by taking the maximum duplicity of the actors in the *HR* (line 3). In duplicating *HR* (line 4), we apply the same approach as explained in Figure 4 except that all the internal edges of the *HR* will also be duplicated and the consumed and produced tokens for the newly added nodes $s$ and $j$ are adjusted according to the duplicity of the *HR* and the data rates of the first and last hot actors of the *HR*, respectively.

## 5. Actor Allocation Problem

The *Actor Allocation Problem* (AAP) seeks an actor placement onto processors such that the arrival rate $z$ of the stream program becomes maximal. The actor allocation problem may be expressed as a mathematical program as stated below:

$$max.\ z \quad (10)$$

$$s.t. \sum_{j=1}^{p} y_{ij} = 1 \quad \text{for all } i \in \{1,\ldots,n\} \quad (11)$$

$$\sum_{i=1}^{n} U_i(z) y_{ij} \leq 1 \quad \text{for all } j \in \{1,\ldots,p\} \quad (12)$$

$$y_{ij} \in \{0,1\} \quad \text{for all } i \in \{1,\ldots,n\}, \text{ for all } j \in \{1,\ldots,p\} \quad (13)$$

The binary variable $y_{ij}$ is one if actor $i$ is placed on processor $j$; zero otherwise. The constraint in Eq. (11) ensures that exactly one processor executes actor $i$. The right-hand side of the constraint in Eq. (12) represents the processor load of processor $j$ for an allocation and it is bounded by 100%, i.e., the maximal processor load.

The mathematical program optimizes for the arrival rate rather than the throughput. However, the throughput is a linear function of the arrival rate, i.e.,

$$\sum_{i=1}^{n} \xi_i = \sum_{i=1}^{n} \Phi_i^*(z) = \left(\sum_{i=1}^{n} \alpha'_i\right) z, \quad (14)$$

whose slope $\sum_{i=1}^{n} \alpha_i'$ is positive. Although arrival rate and throughput are different optimization objectives, the solutions are identical.

THEOREM 1. *The actor allocation problem is NP-hard.*

PROOF 4. *The proof is shown in Appendix A.*

In the following we devise an algorithm for AAP that uses an oracle. The oracle tests whether for a given arrival rate $z$, there exists an actor allocation. With the existence of an oracle, binary search can be employed to seek for the largest $z$ for which there exists an actor allocation. The binary search needs an upper and lower bound to commence the search. The lower bound is zero and an upper bound can be derived directly from the AAP problem itself as shown later in this section. Since the problem is NP hard, we cannot hope for an oracle that delivers a precise answer in polynomial time (unless P=NP). Hence, we use an approximate oracle that has no false positives, i.e., if the approximate oracle answers positively, there always exists an allocation, however, if the answer is "no", there might or might not exist an allocation.

As an oracle for AAP we use the bin-packing problem. For a fixed arrival rate $z$, the mathematical program of AAP reduces to the standard bin-packing problem [33].

DEFINITION 4 (**Bin-packing**). *Given a set of items $A$ with sizes $s_i \in (0,1]$ for all $i \in \{1,\dots,n\}$, find a $k$-partitioning $B_1,\dots,B_k$ of $k$ disjoint sets $B_j \subseteq A$ such that $\sum_{s_i \in B_j} s_i \leq 1$, for all $j \in \{1,\dots,k\}$.*

Bin-packing is an NP-complete problem for which approximation algorithms with polynomial runtime complexity and bounded solution quality exist.

OBSERVATION 1. *Bin-packing is an oracle in the arrival rate $z$.*

PROOF 5. *Assume actors in AAP become items and processors in AAP bins, and set the item size to $s_i = U_i(z)$. The bin-packing problem either delivers a packing for AAP limiting the number of bins to p, or it fails.*

The binary search scheme is illustrated in Algorithm 2. Let $\mathrm{ub}_z$ denote an upper bound of the arrival rate. The feasibility test of allocating actors to processors is achieved by using a bin-packing oracle (cf. line 8) for a given arrival rate $m$, whether an allocation for $p$ bins (i.e. processors) and $n$ items (i.e. actors) can be found. In the algorithm we have the invariant that the lower bound $l$ of the arrival rate represents a feasible solution and $u$ represents an infeasible solution. If the initial upper bound of the algorithm represents a feasible solution, we do not enter the loop and terminate with a feasible and optimal solution. If the actor allocation is feasible at the mid point of $u$ and $l$, the lower bound is assigned the midpoint; otherwise the upper bound is assigned the midpoint (see line 7–11 of Algorithm 2). We terminate the binary search when the gap between lower and upper bound is less than or equal to a small value $\epsilon$. In each step $i$ the initial gap of $\mathrm{ub}_z$ between feasible and infeasible solution halves and we gain one bit in precision. Hence, the inequality $\frac{\mathrm{ub}_z}{2^i} \leq \epsilon$ holds after the termination of the algorithm, where $i$ is the number of executed steps. The inequality implies that after $\lceil \lg_2(\frac{\mathrm{ub}_z}{\epsilon}) \rceil$ steps the binary search scheme will terminate.

For achieving an acceptable runtime complexity, an approximate oracle is employed. The approximate oracle is implemented as a greedy approximation algorithm for bin-packing [33] that achieves a packing of $B_{apx} \leq 2B_{opt}$, where $B_{opt}$ is the optimal number of bins required to pack the items, and $B_{apx}$ is the worst-case result of the approximation algorithm for all instances of bin-packing.

**Algorithm 2** Binary Search

**Require:** $n$: the number of actors, $p$: the number of processors

```
1: l ← 0
2: u ← ub_z
3: if ∃ bin-packing allocation for arrival rate u then
4:     return allocation for arrival rate u
5: end if
6: while u − l > ε do
7:     m ← (l + u)/2
8:     if ∃ bin-packing alloc. for p bins and z = m then
9:         l ← m
10:    else
11:        u ← m
12:    end if
13: end while
14: return allocation for arrival rate l
```

The greedy bin-packing algorithm is implemented as follows: At any intermediate step $i$, it has a list of partially packed bins, $B_1,\dots,B_k$. The approximation algorithm picks an item of size $s_i$ and attempts to pack it in one of the partially packed bins of any assumed order. If the item does not fit into any of the partially filled bins, the algorithm opens a new bin $B_{k+1}$ and packs the item in it. If the algorithm requires $B_{apx}$ bins then at least $B_{apx} - 1$ of the bins are more than half filled. Hence, $\frac{B_{apx}-1}{2} < \sum_{i=1}^{n} s_i$ implies $B_{apx} - 1 < 2B_{opt}$ since $\sum_{i=1}^{n} s_i$ is a lower bound and $B_{apx} \leq 2B_{opt}$ follows.

In the following we analyze the quality of the solution obtained by binary search using the approximate oracle.

LEMMA 5. *Given a packing $B_1,\dots,B_k$ of an instance of bin-packing. There exists a packing with $\lceil \frac{k}{2} \rceil$ bins by scaling items by $\frac{1}{2}$, i.e., $s_i' = \frac{s_i}{2}$.*

PROOF 6. *In the packing $B_1,\dots,B_k$ of $k$ bins, $\sum_{s_i \in B_j} s_i \leq 1$, for all $j \in \{1,\dots,k\}$. If all items are scaled by a factor $\frac{1}{2}$, the inequality*

$$\sum_{s_i' \in B_j} s_i' \leq \frac{1}{2} \quad \textit{for all } j \in \{1,\dots,k\}$$

*holds. Hence, two consecutive bins can be packed in a single bin, i.e., $B_j' = B_{2j-1} \cup B_{2j}$ such that $\sum_{s_i' \in B_j} s_i' \leq 1$ for all $j \in \{1,\dots,\lfloor \frac{k}{2} \rfloor\}$. If $k$ is an odd number, then $B'_{\lceil \frac{k}{2} \rceil} = B_k$ of size less than or equal to $\frac{1}{2}$; otherwise this bin is not required.*

COROLLARY 1. *If there exists an optimal packing with $k$ bins, a 2-approximation bin-packing algorithm obtains a packing of $k$ bins with item sizes $s_i' = \frac{s_i}{2}$.*

THEOREM 2. *A 2-approximation for the bin-packing oracle gives a $2 + \epsilon$-approximation for AAP.*

PROOF 7. *W.l.o.g. we assume that p bins are required to pack items of item sizes $s_i = U_i(z_{opt} - \epsilon)$ with a worst-case arrival rate of $z_{opt} - \epsilon$ using a precise oracle. Note that the arrival rate may be reduced by $\epsilon$ due to the halting condition of the binary search and we assume that $U_i(z) \geq \epsilon$.*

*By Corollary 1 we achieve an approximate packing with $p$ bins by scaling the item sizes by $\frac{1}{2}$:*

$$U_i(z_{apx}) \geq \frac{U_i(z_{opt} - \epsilon)}{2} \Rightarrow$$

$$\left(\sum_{j=1}^{n} \alpha'_j w_{ji}\right) z_{apx} \geq \frac{\left(\sum_{j=1}^{n} \alpha'_j w_{ji}\right)(z_{opt} - \epsilon)}{2} \Rightarrow$$

$$\frac{z_{opt}}{z_{apx}} \leq 2 + \frac{\epsilon}{z_{apx}} \leq 2 + \epsilon.$$

For each step in the binary search scheme, we have an invocation of the bin-packing approximation that exhibits a worst-case runtime complexity of $\mathcal{O}(np)$. There are at most $\lg_2 \frac{\mathrm{ub}_z}{\epsilon}$ invocations of the bin-packing heuristic, and, hence, the overall complexity of finding an approximate solution is $\mathcal{O}(np \lg_2 \frac{\mathrm{ub}_z}{\epsilon})$.

An *instance bound* gives an upper bound on the quality of an approximate solution without knowing the optimal solution. An instance bound can be found if an upper bound of the arrival rate is known, i.e.,

$$1 \leq \frac{z_{opt}}{z_{apx}} \leq \frac{\mathrm{ub}_z}{z_{apx}}. \tag{15}$$

We can deduce an upper bound by summing up the left- and right-hand side of Eq. (11) over $j \in 1, \ldots, p$:

$$\sum_{j=1}^{p}\sum_{i=1}^{n} U_i(z) y_{ij} = \sum_{i=1}^{n} U_i(z) \sum_{j=1}^{p} y_{ij} = \sum_{i=1}^{n} U_i(z) \leq p \Rightarrow$$

$$\sum_{i=1}^{n}\left(\gamma_i \sum_{j=1}^{n} \alpha'_j w_{ji}\right) z \leq p \Rightarrow$$

$$z \leq \frac{p}{\sum_{i=1}^{n}\left(\gamma_i \sum_{j=1}^{n} \alpha'_j w_{ji}\right)} = \mathrm{ub}_z \tag{16}$$

The upper bound $\mathrm{ub}_z$ is also employed for initializing the binary search scheme.

## 6. Experiments

We have implemented our proposed mapping technique as an extension to the StreamIt compiler framework [1]. Our backend generates a uniprocessor schedule for profiling actor execution times of a stream program. Profiling uses the x86-64's hardware cycle counters exported by the clock library from [4]. Actor profiles and the stream graph topology information are then used to compute the closed form on the input data rate $z$. Quantitative analysis determines bottleneck actors and their duplicity. After bottleneck removal we compute the periodic schedule for the transformed stream graph and allocate actors to processors. Bottleneck removal and actor allocation are parameterized by the user-supplied number of processors ($p$), and by the memory bandwidth ($R$) that we determine through profiling. Based on the processor allocation our StreamIt compiler backend generates C-code for the parallelized version of the stream program. With the parallelized version the main program will spawn a scheduler thread on each of the $p$ processors. Each scheduler invokes the actors that have been allocated to the corresponding processor. Together, the schedulers execute a steady-state iteration of the parallel periodic schedule. In between iterations, schedulers synchronize at a barrier. Data-channels between actors are implemented as shared-memory FIFO-buffers. Buffer sizes are derived from the periodic schedule and buffers are statically allocated. We employ multi-buffering similar to [11] to remove filter dependencies within a steady-state iteration of the stream graph.

**Table 1.** Benchmark characteristics.

| *Benchmark* | Actors | Stateful | Peeking |
|---|---|---|---|
| `DCT` | 22 | 18 | 16 |
| `FMRadio` | 67 | 23 | 22 |
| `TDE` | 55 | 27 | 2 |
| `FFT` | 26 | 14 | 0 |
| `MergeSort` | 31 | 2 | 0 |
| `FilterBank` | 53 | 34 | 16 |
| `RadixSort` | 13 | 2 | 0 |
| `Equalizer` | 65 | 22 | 20 |
| `BitonicSort` | 452 | 2 | 0 |
| `DES` | 375 | 180 | 1 |
| `MPEG` | 39 | 7 | 0 |
| `MatrixMult` | 52 | 2 | 0 |

To have a comparison for the quality of our achieved solutions we implemented the ILP formulation from [18]. The resulting ILP problems were solved using CPLEX. We evaluated our technique using 12 StreamIt applications depicted in Table 1.

We considered programs which have both stateful and stateless actors and actors with peeking operations (the ILP formulation from [18] was extended to work with stateful actors: we added additional constraints that prevent duplication of stateful actors, which reduces the solution space as well). Note again that actors where the peek-rate is greater than the pop-rate were identified as stateful actors and thus no actor duplication was performed. We encountered only one benchmark, FMRadio, that showed this characteristic.

The details of each benchmark are available online [1]. We have disabled the println statements because they were used in the sink nodes imposing high overheads. Sink nodes are stateful and hence cannot be duplicated. However, having a stateful node with dominating costs makes actor allocation trivial and does not allow a meaningful comparison of the approaches. Each benchmark was compiled and executed on a 2.33GHz dual quad-core Intel Xeon computer with 16GB main memory and Linux kernel version 2.6.23.

Table 2 shows the experimental results on 2–4 processors. The time to solve our actor allocation problem was in the range of milliseconds and we omitted it because it does not provide any useful insight. On the other hand, the ILP solve times vary greatly, with a tendency to grow substantially for larger numbers of processors (column $t_{ILP}$ in Table 2). E.g., with `FFT` the ILP solve time increases from 0.46 seconds to 12 hours when the processor number is increased to three. The solver takes about 70 hours to solve the mapping for four processors.

We compared the input data rates achieved by our method with the data rates from the ILP formulation (the optimal solution). Column $\frac{z_{apx}}{z_{opt}}$ in Table 2 shows that the quality of our solutions stays within 5% of the optimum. The data rates achieved by our method are given in megabytes/second (column $z_{apx}$ of Table 2). The lowest data rate was achieved for the `FFT` benchmark for 4 processors, and it is still 95% of the optimal data rate. The `DCT` and `MergeSort` benchmarks achieve 96% and 97% of the optimal rates respectively. Other than these, our approximation is mostly identical to the optimum. Data rates increase with the number of processors.

Figure 5 presents the speedups obtained by the approximation method for 2, 4, 6 and 8 processors over uniprocessor execution. Our approximation obtains near-linear average speedups of 6.95x for 8 processors. `MPEG`, `RadixSort` and `MatrixMult` achieve lower speedups due to stateful filters that cannot be paral-

**Table 2.** Experimental results for 2–4 processors.

| *Benchmark* | *P#* | $t_{ILP}$ (s) | $\frac{z_{apx}}{z_{opt}}$ | $z_{apx}$ (MB/s) |
|---|---|---|---|---|
| DCT | 2 | 0.27 | 0.99 | 42.56 |
| | 3 | 1585.69 | 0.97 | 62.46 |
| | 4 | 2285.01 | 0.96 | 82.57 |
| FMRadio | 2 | 0.08 | 1.00 | 2.89 |
| | 3 | 3.22 | 1.00 | 4.00 |
| | 4 | 1.29 | 0.99 | 5.34 |
| TDE | 2 | 0.09 | 1.00 | 6.08 |
| | 3 | 0.17 | 1.00 | 19.80 |
| | 4 | 274.69 | 1.00 | 28.81 |
| FFT | 2 | 0.46 | 0.98 | 43.91 |
| | 3 | 44694.25 | 0.98 | 46.85 |
| | 4 | 249240.09 | 0.95 | 95.50 |
| MergeSort | 2 | 0.07 | 1.00 | 26.35 |
| | 3 | 0.09 | 0.99 | 56.24 |
| | 4 | 1.62 | 0.97 | 70.12 |
| FilterBank | 2 | 0.06 | 1.00 | 1.68 |
| | 3 | 0.62 | 0.99 | 2.51 |
| | 4 | 3.56 | 1.00 | 5.29 |
| RadixSort | 2 | 0.64 | 0.99 | 32.91 |
| | 3 | 0.09 | 1.00 | 49.98 |
| | 4 | 0.47 | 0.99 | 66.83 |
| Equalizer | 2 | 0.06 | 1.00 | 0.56 |
| | 3 | 5.29 | 1.00 | 0.83 |
| | 4 | 57553.83 | 0.99 | 1.59 |
| BitonicSort | 2 | 0.3 | 1.00 | 3.16 |
| | 3 | 3.06 | 1.00 | 4.73 |
| | 4 | 16371.99 | 1.00 | 10.14 |
| DES | 2 | 0.51 | 1.00 | 0.12 |
| | 3 | 2.73 | 1.00 | 0.18 |
| | 4 | 11.24 | 1.00 | 0.24 |
| MPEG | 2 | 0.09 | 1.00 | 36.59 |
| | 3 | 1.37 | 0.99 | 54.68 |
| | 4 | 0.44 | 1.00 | 73.22 |
| MatrixMult | 2 | 0.14 | 1.00 | 18.74 |
| | 3 | 4.85 | 1.00 | 28.16 |
| | 4 | 103.00 | 0.99 | 37.37 |

lelized as explained in Section 2. All other benchmarks scale well with increasing numbers of processors.

## 7. Related Work

Unlike classical data flow [9], SDF [20] fixes the number of tokens produced and consumed by an actor already at compile time. The static nature of SDF facilitates static program optimizations wrt. streamgraph transformations, partitioning and scheduling. A wide range of static scheduling algorithms for the SDF model exist [11, 16, 18, 19, 24, 31, 32]. SDF has been fundamental for contemporary stream languages including StreamIt [28, 30].

The StreamIt compiler [11] targets the Raw Microprocessor [22], shared-memory multicore architectures and clusters of workstations. To increase the computation to communication ratio, adjacent actors are fused as long as the result is stateless. A heuristic for actor fission is then applied to increase data-parallelism to the extent that a communication-efficient balance between task and data parallelism is maintained. Coarse-grained software-pipelining of actors eliminates actor dependencies within the same steady-state iteration, which increases flexibility of the program partitioning and scheduling phases. A greedy partitioning heuristic that minimizes the makespan is applied to load-balance actors among processors.

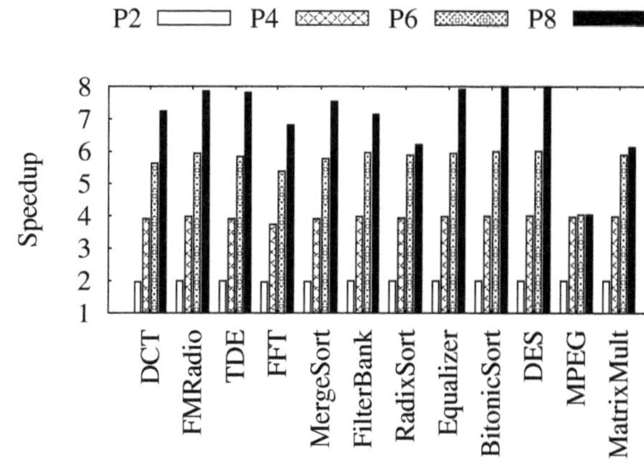


**Figure 5.** Speedups obtained for 2, 4, 6 and 8 processors.

Kudlur and Mahlke's stream graph modulo scheduling [18] employs an ILP formulation to evenly distribute StreamIt actors among the synergistic processing elements of the Cell processor [13]. The ILP formulation consists of an integrated unfolding and partitioning technique that spreads data-parallel actors and maximally packs actors onto cores. Coarse-grained software pipelining is then applied such that computations of the current steady-state iteration are overlapped with data transfers for future iterations. In contrast to our model, (1) no approximation scheme was provided, making the approach intractable for larger problem instances, (2) the mathematical model optimizes makespan rather than arrival rate, (3) the proposed stream graph transformation duplicates single actors rather than regions, which may lead to a larger number of communication channels, and (4) we separate the bottleneck elimination from the actor allocation.

Udupa et al. devised an ILP formulation to partition and software-pipeline StreamIt programs on GPUs. The optimal execution configuration of a stream program in terms of the number of registers per thread and the number of data-parallel actor instances is determined through profiling. A buffer layout technique for GPUs that coalesces accesses to device memory is presented. The proposed approach minimizes makespan.

Orchestrating the execution of stream programs on multicore platforms with accelerators like GPGPUs is examined in [32]. Udupa et al. formulated a communication-aware ILP problem for partitioning computations between CPU cores and GPGPU streaming multiprocessors (SMs). They proposed a heuristic algorithm for the ILP problem, with solutions on average within 9.05% of the optimal solution across the benchmark suite. Partitioned tasks are then software-pipelined to execute on CPU cores and on the SMs of the GPU.

Carpenter et al. [6] present an iterative heuristic partitioning and allocation algorithm that maps Kahn process networks with optional SDF-parts onto heterogeneous multiprocessors. Partitions with short software pipelines are favored to reduce memory, latency and startup overheads that increase with the number of pipeline stages. To shorten software pipelines, generated partitions are convex, i.e., they are connected and without circular dependencies. Partitioning is parameterizable through the provision of basic connected sets, which constitute collections of actors that the compiler is allowed to pairwise merge. Their assumption that partitions need to be convex is not proven to be code optimal.

## 8. Conclusion

In this paper, we presented an approximation algorithm for solving the actor allocation problem, and a data rate transfer model that resolves bottlenecks in stream graphs. In our approach, we separate the bottleneck elimination process from the actor allocation which enables efficient and effective bottleneck elimination and actor allocation for multicore architecture.

Current state-of-the-art approaches rely on integer linear programming that provides optimal solutions for actor allocation (though only sub-optimal ILP models for rewriting the stream graph are currently available). The runtime of commercial ILP solvers makes an ILP approach impractical even for small to moderate benchmark sizes and low numbers of processors. In contrast, our approximation framework performs the task within milliseconds. The quality of our solution is 5% off the optimal solution, and for up to 8 processors achieves a geometric mean speedup of 6.95x over single processor execution across the StreamIt benchmark suite.

## Acknowledgements

We thank Professor Saman Amarasinghe for shepherding this paper. Much gratitude also goes to the anonymous referees who provided excellent feedback on this work.

## References

[1] StreamIt Website. `http://groups.csail.mit.edu/cag/streamit`, retrieved 2010.

[2] J. Backus. Can programming be liberated from the von Neumann style? A functional style and its algebra of programs. *ACM Turing Award Lectures*, 2007.

[3] S. S. Battacharyya, E. A. Lee, and P. K. Murthy. *Software Synthesis from Dataflow Graphs*. Kluwer Academic Publishers, 1996.

[4] R. E. Bryant and D. R. O'Halloran. *Computer Systems: A Programmer's Perspective*. Prentice-Hall, 2003.

[5] I. Buck, T. Foley, D. Horn, J. Sugerman, K. Fatahalian, M. Houston, and P. Hanrahan. Brook for GPUs: Stream computing on graphics hardware. *ACM Trans. Graph.*, 23(3):777–786, 2004.

[6] P. M. Carpenter, A. Ramirez, and E. Ayguade. Mapping stream programs onto heterogeneous multiprocessor systems. In *CASES '09: Proceedings of the 2009 International Conference on Compilers, Architecture, and Synthesis for Embedded Systems*, pages 57–66. ACM, 2009.

[7] M. K. Chen, X. F. Li, R. Lian, J. H. Lin, L. Liu, T. Liu, and R. Ju. Shangri-la: Achieving high performance from compiled network applications while enabling ease of programming. In *PLDI '05: Proceedings of the 2005 ACM SIGPLAN Conference on Programming Language Design and Implementation*. ACM, 2005.

[8] Cisco. The Cisco QuantumFlow processor: Cisco's next generation network processor. White paper, 2008.

[9] J. B. Dennis. First version of a data flow procedure language. In *Programming Symposium, Proceedings Colloque sur la Programmation*, pages 362–376. Springer-Verlag, 1974.

[10] W. Eatherton. The push of network processing to the top of the pyramid, 2005.

[11] M. I. Gordon, W. Thies, and S. Amarasinghe. Exploiting coarse-grained task, data, and pipeline parallelism in stream programs. In *ASPLOS '06: Proceedings of the 2006 International Conference on Architectural Support for Programming Languages and Operating Systems*, 2006.

[12] J. Gummaraju and M. Rosenblum. Stream programming on general-purpose processors. In *MICRO 38: Proceedings of the 38th Annual IEEE/ACM International Symposium on Microarchitecture*, pages 343–354. IEEE Computer Society, 2005.

[13] H. P. Hofstee. Power efficient processor architecture and the Cell processor. In *HPCA '05: Proceedings of the 2005 International Symposium on High-Performance Computer Architecture*, pages 258–262. IEEE Computer Society, 2005.

[14] R. Kalla, B. Sinharoy, W. J. Starke, and M. Floyd. Power7: IBM's next-generation server processor. *IEEE Micro*, 30(2):7–15, 2010.

[15] M. Karczmarek. Constrained and phased scheduling of synchronous data flow graphs for the StreamIt language. Master's thesis, Massachusetts Institute of Technology, 2002.

[16] M. Karczmarek, W. Thies, and S. Amarasinghe. Phased scheduling of stream programs. *LCTES '03: Proceedings of the 2003 ACM SIGPLAN/SIGBED Conference on Languages, Compilers, and Tools for Embedded Systems*, 38(7):1235–1245, 2003.

[17] R. M. Karp and R. E. Miller. Properties of a model for parallel computations: Determinacy, termination, queueing. *SIAM Journal on Applied Mathematics*, 14(6):1390–1411, 1966.

[18] M. Kudlur and S. Mahlke. Orchestrating the execution of stream programs on multicore platforms. In *PLDI '08: Proceedings of the 2008 ACM SIGPLAN Conference on Programming Language Design and Implementation*. ACM, 2008.

[19] E. A. Lee and D. G. Messerschmitt. Static scheduling of synchronous data flow programs for digital signal processing. *IEEE Transactions on Computers*, 36:24–35, 1987.

[20] E. A. Lee and D. G. Messerschmitt. Synchronous data flow. *Proceedings of the IEEE*, 75(9):1235–1245, 1987.

[21] W. R. Mark, R. Steven G., K. Akeley, and M. J. Kilgard. Cg: a system for programming hardware in a C-like language. In *SIGGRAPH '03*. ACM, 2003.

[22] E. W. Michael, M. Taylor, V. Sarkar, W. Lee, V. Lee, J. Kim, M. Frank, P. Finch, S. Devabhaktuni, R. Barua, J. Babb, S. Amarasinghe, and A. Agarwal. Baring it all to software: The Raw machine. *IEEE Computer*, 30:86–93, 1997.

[23] NVIDIA Corporation. CUDA C Programming Guide 3.1, 2010.

[24] S. Robert. A survey of stream processing. *Acta Informatica*, 34(7):491–541, 1997.

[25] B. G. Ryder and M. C. Paull. Elimination algorithms for data flow analysis. *ACM Comput. Surv.*, 18(3):277–316, 1986.

[26] J. L. Shin, K. Tam, D. Huang, B. Petrick, and H. Pham. A 40nm 16-core 128-thread CMT SPARC SoC processor. In *ISSCC '10, Solid-State Circuits Conference Digest of Technical Papers*. IEEE International, 2010.

[27] J. H. Spring, J. Privat, R. Guerraoui, and J. Vitek. StreamFlex: High-throughput stream programming in Java. *OOPSLA '07: Proceedings of the 2007 ACM SIGPLAN Conference on Object-oriented Programming Systems and Applications*, 42(10), 2007.

[28] W. Thies. *Language and Compiler Support for Stream Programs*. PhD thesis, Massachusetts Institute of Technology, USA, 2009.

[29] W. Thies and S. Amarasinghe. An empirical characterization of stream programs and its implications for language and compiler design. In *PACT '10 Proceedings of the 2010 Conference on Parallel Architectures and Compilation Techniques*. ACM, 2010.

[30] W. Thies, M. Karczmarek, and S. P. Amarasinghe. StreamIt: A language for streaming applications. In *CC '02: Proceedings of the 11th International Conference on Compiler Construction*, pages 179–196, London, UK, 2002. Springer-Verlag.

[31] A. Udupa, R. Govindarajan, and M. J. Thazhuthaveetil. Software pipelined execution of stream programs on GPUs. In *CGO '09: Proceedings of the 7th Annual IEEE/ACM International Symposium on Code Generation and Optimization*. IEEE Computer Society, 2009.

[32] A. Udupa, R. Govindarajan, and M. J. Thazhuthaveetil. Synergistic execution of stream programs on multicores with accelerators. *LCTES '09: Proceedings of the 2009 ACM SIGPLAN/SIGBED Conference on Languages, Compilers, and Tools for Embedded Systems*, 44(7), 2009.

[33] V. V. Vazirani. *Approximation Algorithms*. Springer-Verlag, 2001.

[34] H. Wei, J. Yu, H. Yu, and G. R. Gao. Minimizing communication in rate-optimal software pipelining for stream programs. In *CGO '10: Proceedings of the 8th Annual IEEE/ACM International Symposium on Code Generation and Optimization*, pages 210–217. ACM, 2010.

[35] D. Zhang, Q. J. Li, R. Rabbah, and S. Amarasinghe. A lightweight streaming layer for multicore execution. *SIGARCH Comput. Archit. News*, 36(2):18–27, 2008.

[36] D. Zhang, Z. Li, H. Song, and L. Liu. A programming model for an embedded media processing architecture. In *SAMOS '05: Proceedings of the 2005 International Conference on Embedded Computer Systems: Architectures, Modeling, and Simulation*. Springer LNCS, 2005.


## A. NP Hardness

PROOF 8. *(of Theorem 1). We show the NP hardness by reducing the partitioning problem [33] to the actor allocation problem. The partitioning problem has a finite set of integer numbers* $A = \{a_1, \ldots, a_n\}$ *as input and determines whether there exists two disjoint subset* $X_1 \subseteq A$ *and* $X_2 \subseteq A$ *with* $A = X_1 \cup X_2$ *whose sums* $\sum_{a \in X_1} a$ *and* $\sum_{a \in X_2} a$ *are equal.*

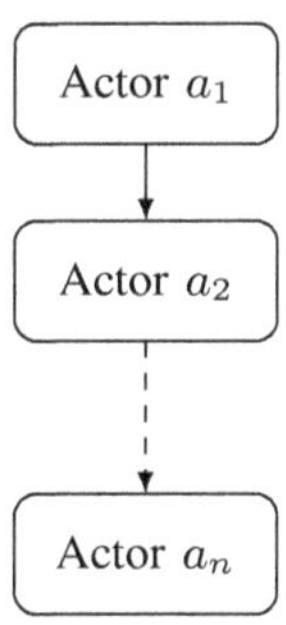


**Figure 6.** Reduction of partition problem to actor allocation problem.

*Let's assume that the parallel system has two processors* $p_1$ *and* $p_2$*. For each element in set A we introduce a vertex* $u \in V$*. Element* $a \in A$ *of associated vertex u is denoted by* $a_u$*. The principle decision whether a number a is either in the subset* $X_1$ *or* $X_2$*, is modeled by placing u on* $p_1$ *otherwise u is placed on* $p_2$*.*

*We chain the filters in a pipeline as depicted in Figure 6 and define following constants for the bandwidth and processor utilization function*

$$\alpha_u = 1$$
$$\gamma_u = \frac{2a_u}{\sum_{a \in A} a}$$

*Hence,* $\alpha'_u = 1$*, and* $U_u(z) = \gamma_u$*. The arrival rate can be at most one, if the AAP problem can pack the load of the actors equally on the two processors constituting a solution to the partitioning problem and the theorem follows.*

## B. Glossary

| | |
|---|---|
| $\alpha_i$ | The ratio between the number of bytes produced and consumed for a single invocation of actor $i$ |
| $\Gamma_i$ | The processor utilization function of actor $i$ |
| $\Gamma_i^{-1}$ | The inverse function the processor utilization function $\Gamma_i$ |
| $\gamma_i$ | $\frac{t_i}{\iota_i}$ |
| $\iota_i$ | The number of bytes read from the program input for a single invocation of actor $i$ |
| $\xi_i$ | The output data rate of actor $i$ in the periodic schedule |
| $\Pi$ | Make span: the time duration of the longest running processor |
| $\Phi_i$ | Data rate transfer function of actor $i$ |
| $\omega_i$ | The number of bytes produced by a single invocation of actor $i$ |
| $(i,j)$ | A channel $(i,j) \in E$ queues data elements which are passed from the output of computation $i$ to the input of computation $j$ |
| $c_i$ | Number of consumed tokens on each execution of actor $i$ |
| $d_i$ | Duplicity of an actor $i$, i.e., how many instances in the stream graph are required to avoid a bottleneck. |
| $E$ | A set of edges |
| $G(V,E)$ | A stream graph consists of $V$ vertices and $E$ edges |
| $\mathcal{I}$ | The identity matrix |
| $n$ | Number of actors in the stream program |
| $p$ | Number of processors in the parallel system |
| $p_i$ | Number of produced tokens on each execution of actor $i$ |
| $\mathbf{q}$ | Repetition vector |
| $q_i$ | The number of occurrences of actor $i$ in the periodic schedule |
| $R$ | Maximum data rate limited by memory bandwidth |
| $t_i$ | The execution time of actor $i$ |
| $U_i$ | Utilization, $U_i = \gamma_i \sum_{j=1}^{n} \left(w_{ji}\alpha'_j\right) z$ |
| $\mathrm{ub}_i$ | The upper bound of the arrival rate for an actor $i$ |
| $\mathrm{ub}_s$ | The upper bound of the arrival rate imposed by the parallel system |
| $\mathrm{ub}_z$ | The upper bound of the arrival rate obtained by quantitative analysis |
| $V$ | A set of vertices |
| $w_{ij}$ | The fraction of the output data rate of actor $i$ that is diverted from actor $i$ to channel $(i,j)$ |
| $x_i$ | The output data rate of actor $i$ |
| $z$ | Arrival rate |

# On-the-Fly Elimination of Dynamic Irregularities for GPU Computing


Eddy Z. Zhang  Yunlian Jiang  Ziyu Guo  Kai Tian  Xipeng Shen

Computer Science Department
The College of William and Mary, Williamsburg, VA, USA
{eddy,jiang,guoziyu,ktian,xshen}@cs.wm.edu



## Abstract

The power-efficient massively parallel Graphics Processing Units (GPUs) have become increasingly influential for general-purpose computing over the past few years. However, their efficiency is sensitive to dynamic irregular memory references and control flows in an application. Experiments have shown great performance gains when these irregularities are removed. But it remains an open question how to achieve those gains through software approaches on modern GPUs.

This paper presents a systematic exploration to tackle dynamic irregularities in both control flows and memory references. It reveals some properties of dynamic irregularities in both control flows and memory references, their interactions, and their relations with program data and threads. It describes several heuristics-based algorithms and runtime adaptation techniques for effectively removing dynamic irregularities through data reordering and job swapping. It presents a framework, *G-Streamline*, as a unified software solution to dynamic irregularities in GPU computing. G-Streamline has several distinctive properties. It is a pure software solution and works on the fly, requiring no hardware extensions or offline profiling. It treats both types of irregularities at the same time in a holistic fashion, maximizing the whole-program performance by resolving conflicts among optimizations. Its optimization overhead is largely transparent to GPU kernel executions, jeopardizing no basic efficiency of the GPU application. Finally, it is robust to the presence of various complexities in GPU applications. Experiments show that G-Streamline is effective in reducing dynamic irregularities in GPU computing, producing speedups between 1.07 and 2.5 for a variety of applications.



***Categories and Subject Descriptors*** D.3.4 [*Programming Languages*]: Processors—optimization, compilers

***General Terms*** Performance,Experimentation

***Keywords*** GPGPU, Thread divergence, Memory coalescing, Thread-data remapping, CPU-GPU pipelining, Data transformation




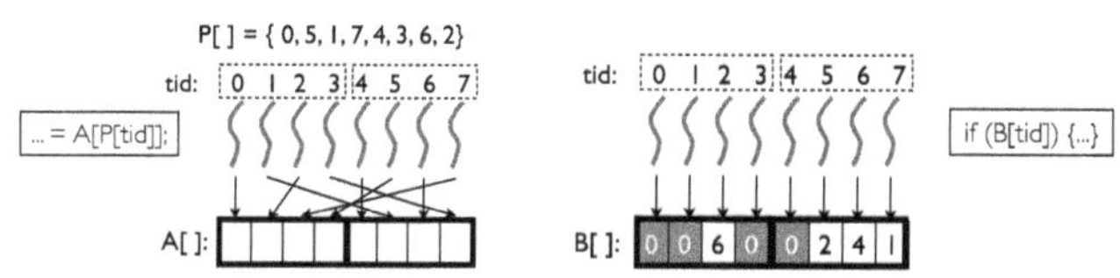


(a) Irregular memory reference (b) Irregular control flow

**Figure 1.** Examples of dynamic irregularities (warp size=4; segment size=4). Graph (a) shows that inferior mappings between threads and data locations cause more memory transactions than necessary; graph (b) shows that inferior mappings between threads and data values cause threads in the same warp diverge on the condition.

## 1. Introduction

Recent several years have seen a quick adoption of Graphic Processing Units (GPU) in general-purpose computing, thanks to their tremendous computing power, and favorable cost effectiveness and energy efficiency. These appealing properties come from the massively parallel architecture of GPU, which, unfortunately, entails a major weakness of GPU: the high sensitivity of their throughput to the presence of irregularities in an application.

The massive parallelism of GPU is embodied by the equipment of a number of streaming multiprocessors (SM), with each containing dozens of cores. Correspondingly, a typical application written in GPU programming models (e.g., CUDA [14] from NVIDIA) creates thousands of parallel threads running on GPU. Each thread has a unique ID, *tid*. These threads are organized into warps[1]. Threads in one warp are assigned to a single SM, and proceed in an SIMD (Single Instruction Multiple Data) fashion. As a result, hundreds of threads may be actively running on a GPU at the same time. Parallel execution of such a large number of threads may well exploit the tremendous computing power of GPU, but not for irregular computations.

***Dynamic Irregularities in GPU Computing*** Irregularities in an application may throttle GPU throughput by as much as an order of magnitude. There are two types of irregularities, one on data references, the other on control flows.

Before explaining irregular data references, we introduce the properties of GPU memory access. (Without noting, "memory" refers to GPU off-chip global memory.) In a modern GPU device (e.g., NVIDIA Tesla C1060, S1070,C2050, S2070), memory is composed of a large number of continuous segments. The size of

[1] This paper uses NVIDIA CUDA terminology.

each segment is a constant[2], denoted as $Z$. One memory transaction can load or store all data in one memory segment. The accesses by a set of threads at one load or store instruction are coalesced into a single memory transaction, if these threads are within a warp and meanwhile the words accessed by them lie in a single memory segment. An *irregular reference* refers to a load or store instruction, at which, the data requested by a warp happens to lie on multiple memory segments, causing more (up to a factor of $W$; $W$ for warp size) memory transactions than necessary. Because a memory transaction incurs latency of hundreds of cycles, irregular references often degrade the effective throughput of GPU significantly.

A special class of irregular data references is *dynamic irregular references*, referring to irregular references whose memory access patterns are unknown (or hard to know) until execution time. Figure 1 (a) shows an example. The memory access pattern of "A[P[tid]]" is determined by the runtime values of the elements in array $P$, whose content causes an irregular mapping between threads and the locations of the requested data, resulting in four memory transactions in total, twice of the minimum. Being dynamic, these references are especially hard to tackle, making effective exploitation of GPU difficult for many applications in various domains, including fluid simulation, image reconstruction, dynamic programming, data mining, and so on [13, 18].

Dynamic irregularities also exist in program control flows, causing *thread divergences*. Thread divergences typically happen on a condition statement. When threads in a warp diverge on which branch to take, their parallel execution turns into a serial execution of the threads that take different branches. Figure 1 (b) illustrates such an example. Consider the first warp in the graph. Due to the values of the data mapped to the threads, only thread 2 takes the "if" branch. During the execution of that thread, all the other threads in that warp have to stay idle and wait. Note that because the warp is not completely idle, no other warps are allowed to run on that SM during that time, causing waste of computing resource. Consider a typical case where each warp contains 32 threads. The waste of the SM throughput is up to 96% (31/32). The problem is especially serious for loops. Consider a loop "for (i=0; i¡A[tid]; i++)" in a kernel and A[0] to A[31] are all zero except that A[13]=100. All threads in the warp have to stay idle until thread 13 finishes the $100^{th}$ iteration.

Dynamic irregularities severely limit the efficiency of GPU computing for many applications. As shown in Figure 2, removing the dynamic irregularities may improve the performance of a set of GPU applications and kernels (detailed in Section 7) by a factor of *1.4* to *5.3*.

There have been some recent explorations on the irregularity issues. Some propose new hardware features [8, 13, 18], others offer software solutions through compiler techniques [3, 4, 11, 20, 21]. Software solutions, being immediately deployable on real GPUs, are the focus of this paper. Previous software solutions mainly concentrate on cases that are amenable to static program analysis. They are not applicable to *dynamic* irregularities, whose patterns remain unknown until execution time. A recent work [22] tackles dynamic irregular control flows, but in a limited setting (as elaborated in Section 8).

Overall, a systematic software solution to address *dynamic* irregularities in GPU computing is yet to be developed. In fact, what remains missing are not just solutions, but more fundamentally, a comprehensive understanding to the problem of irregularity removal itself. For instance, as Figure 1 shows, the two types of irregularities stem from the relations between GPU threads and runtime data values or layouts, but the relations are preliminarily understood. No answers exist to the questions such as what data layouts and thread-data mappings minimize the irregularities, what the computational complexities are for finding desired layouts or mappings, and how they can be effectively approximated.

[2] In real GPU devices, the value of $Z$ varies across data types. The difference is considered in our implementation but elided in discussions for simplicity.

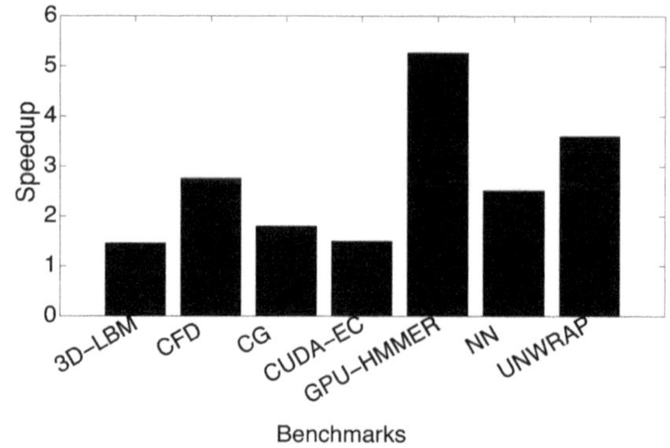


**Figure 2.** Potential performance improvement when dynamic irregularities are eliminated for applications running on an GPU (Tesla 1060).

Moreover, previous explorations (in software) have treated the two kinds of irregularities separately. But in many real applications, both may exist at the same time and connect with each other—optimizing one may influence the other (e.g., *3dlbm* shown in Section 7). It is important to treat them in a holistic fashion to maximize overall performance.

***Overview of This Work*** In this work, we aim to answer these open questions and contribute a comprehensive, practical software solution to both types of dynamic irregularities. First, we unveil some analytical findings on the inherent properties of irregularities in GPU computing. This includes the interactions between irregular control flows and memory references, the NP-completeness of finding the optimal data layouts and thread-job mappings and a set of heuristics-based algorithms, as well as the relations among dynamic irregularities, program data, and GPU threads. These findings substantially enhance the current understanding of the irregularities. Second, we provide a unified framework, named **G-Streamline**, as a comprehensive solution to both types of dynamic irregularities. G-Streamline has several distinctive properties. It is a pure software solution and works on the fly, requiring no hardware extensions or offline profiling. It treats both types of irregularities at the same time in a holistic fashion, maximizing the whole-program performance by resolving conflicts among optimizations of multiple irregularities of the same or different types. Its optimization overhead is transparent to GPU executions, jeopardizing no basic efficiency of the GPU application. Finally, it is robust to the presence of various complexities in the GPU application, including the concealing of the data involved in condition statements, the overlapping of the data involved in irregular data references.

We build G-Streamline based on a perspective illustrated in Figure 1 (a) and (b): Both irregular memory references and control flows essentially stem from an inferior mapping between threads and data (data locations for the former; data values for the latter). This perspective leads to the basic strategy of G-Streamline for irregularity elimination: enhancing the thread-data mappings on the fly. To make this basic strategy work efficiently, we develop a set of techniques organized in three components as shown in Figure 3.

The component, "transformation" (Section 3), includes techniques for the realization of new thread-data mappings. Its core

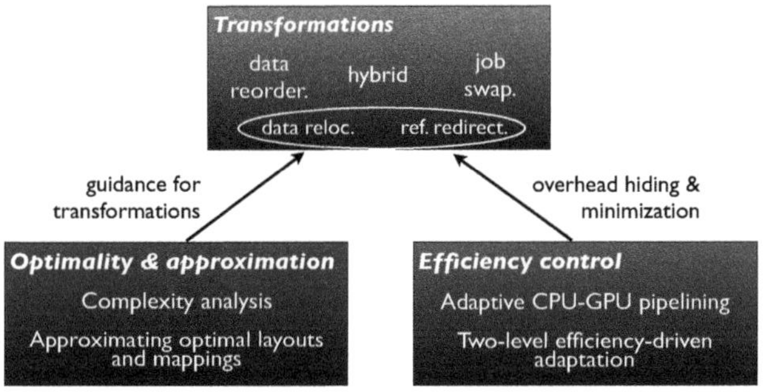


**Figure 3.** Major components of G-Streamline.

consists of two primary mechanisms, data relocation and reference redirection. The former moves data elements on memory to create new data layouts; the latter redirects the references of a thread to new memory locations. Together they lead to three transformation techniques—data reordering, job swapping, hybrid transformation—with respective strengths and weaknesses, suitable for different scenarios. There are two key conditions for the transformations to work effectively: the determination of desirable data layouts or mappings, and the minimization and concealment of transformation overhead.

The second component, "optimality & approximation" (Section 4), helps meet the first condition by answering a series of open questions on the determination of desirable data layouts and mappings for GPU irregularity removal. It proves that finding the optimal data layouts or thread-data mappings in order to minimize the number of memory transactions is NP-complete. For the minimization of thread divergences, it shows that the problem is NP-complete as well but with respect to the number of conditional branches rather than the number of threads. Based on the theoretical insights, this component provides a heuristics-based algorithm for each type of transformations, enabling the computation of near-optimal data layouts or thread-data mappings. Meanwhile, it offers some guidelines for resolving conflicts among the optimizations of different irregularities.

The third component, "efficiency control" (Section 5), addresses overhead issues. On one hand, because the irregularities are dynamic, optimizations must happen during run time. On the other hand, transformations for irregularity removal are usually expensive due to the data movements and relevant computations involved. To address that tension, the "efficient control" component employs two techniques. First, based on a previous proposal [22], it adopts an adaptive CPU-GPU pipelining scheme to offload most transformations to CPU so that the transformations can happen asynchronously with the GPU kernel execution. The scheme effectively hides transformation overhead from kernel execution, and meanwhile, protects the basic efficiency of the program by automatically shutting down transformations when necessary. Second, it uses a multilevel adaptation scheme to reduce transformation overhead. The first level is on the tuning of individual transformations; the second level is on the selection of different transformation methods, according to their distinctive properties and the runtime scenarios.

***Contributions*** In summary, this work makes four-fold contributions:

- It provides the first software solution for handling *dynamic* irregularities in both control flows and memory references for GPU computing.
- It proves the computational complexities of irregularity removal, and reveals the essential properties of the irregularities along with their relations with threads and data, advancing current understanding to GPU irregularity removal substantially.
- It develops a set of transformations, analyzes their properties and applicabilities, and proposes several heuristics-based algorithms to circumvent the NP-completeness of irregularity removal.
- It develops a multilevel efficiency-driven adaptation scheme and integrates it into a CPU-GPU pipelining mechanism, demonstrating the feasibility of on-the-fly software irregularity removal solutions.

## 2. Terms and Abstract Forms

Before describing the three components of G-Streamline, we first present some terms and abstract forms to be used in the following discussions.

A *kernel* is a function executed on GPU. On an invocation of a kernel, thousands of threads are created and execute the same kernel function. They may access different data and behave differently due to the appearances of *tid* in the kernel. Arrays are the major data structure in most GPU kernels, hence the focused data structure in this study. Typically, a GPU kernel takes some arrays as input, conducts certain computations based on their content, and stores results into some other arrays (or scalars) as its final output. We call these arrays *input arrays* and *output arrays* respectively (one array may play both roles).

In the following discussions, we use the abstract form "A[P[tid]]" to represent an irregular reference, and "if (B[tid])" to represent an irregular control flow. The arrays "P" and "B" are both conceptual. In real applications, "P" may appear as an actual input array, or results computed from some input arrays (e.g., "A[X[tid]%2+Y[tid]]"), while, "B" may appear as a logical expression on some input arrays. Using these abstract forms gives conveniences to our discussion, but does not affect the generality of the conclusions (elaborated in Section 6).

## 3. Transformations for Irregularity Removal

G-Streamline contains three main transformation methods for realizing new thread-data mappings. They are all built upon two basic program transformation mechanisms: data relocation and reference redirection. Although the basic mechanisms are classic compilation techniques, it remains preliminarily understood how to use them to remove irregularities in GPU computing—more fundamentally, what are the relations between GPU irregularities and threads and data, how those transformation mechanisms and methods affect the relations, and what the strengths and weaknesses of each transformation method are. This section discusses the mechanisms and transformation methods.

### 3.1 Two Basic Transformation Mechanisms

Data relocation is a transformation that moves data on memory through data copying. It can be either out-of-place (e.g., creating a new array), or in-place (e.g., elements swapping inside an array).

Reference redirection directs a data reference to certain memory location. In G-Streamline, the redirection is through the use of redirection arrays. For instance, we can replace "A[tid]" with "A[D[tid]]"; the redirection array "D" indicates which element in "A" is actually referenced.

### 3.2 Three Transformation Methods

We develop three transformation methods for removing irregular control flows and memory references. Each of them consists of a series of applications of the two basic mechanisms. In the following explanation on how the transformations remove dynamic irreg-

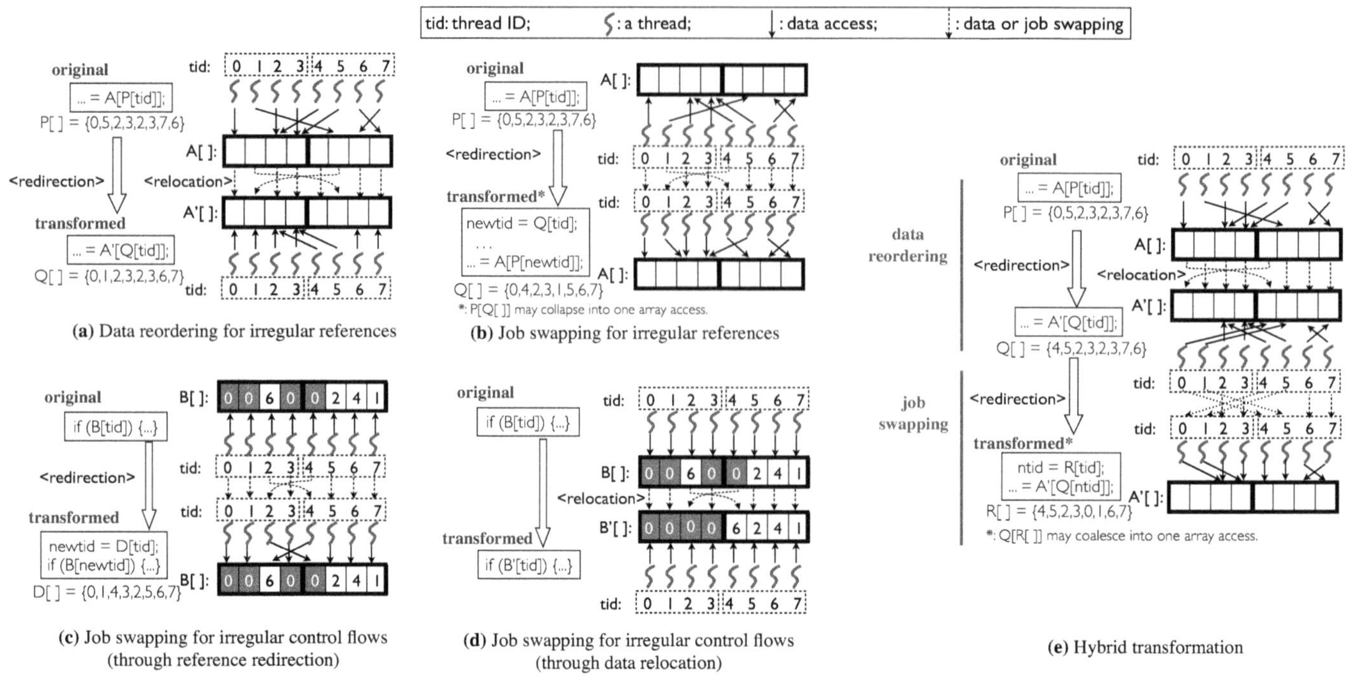


**Figure 4.** Examples for illustrating the uses of data reordering and job swapping for irregularity removal.

ularities, we assume that the desirable mappings between threads and data (locations or values) are known. Section 4 discusses how to determine those mappings.

### 3.2.1 Data Reordering

The first strategy is to adjust data locations on memory to create a new order for the elements of an array. Its application involves two steps, as illustrated in Figure 4 (a). In the first step, data relocation creates a new array $A'$ that contains the same set of elements as the original array $A$ does but in a different order. The new order is created based on a desirable mapping (obtained from $P$ as shown in Section 4) between threads and data locations. In our example, originally, the values of the elements in $P$ cause every warp to reference elements of $A$ on two segments (the top half of the graph). The relocation step switches the locations of $A[5]$ and $A[1]$. The second step of the transformation changes accesses to $A$ in the kernel such that each thread accesses the same data element (likely in a different location) as it does in the original program. The boxes in the left part of Figure 4 (a) illustrates the change: $A[P[tid]]$ is replaced with $A[Q[tid]]$, where $Q$ is a newly produced redirection array. After this transformation, all data accessed by the threads in the first warp lie in the first segment; the total needed memory transactions is reduced from four to three. (Section 3.2.3 will show how to reduce it further to the minimum.)

Data reordering is applicable to various irregular memory references. But as it maintains the original mapping between threads and data values, it is not applicable to the removal of irregular control flows by itself.

### 3.2.2 Job Swapping

The second method for irregularity removal is exchanging jobs among threads. A *job* in this context refers to the whole set of operations a GPU thread conducts and the entire set of data elements it loads and stores in a kernel execution.

As shown in Figure 4 (b), by exchanging the jobs of threads 1 and 4, we make thread 1 access $A[2]$ and thread 4 access $A[5]$. The

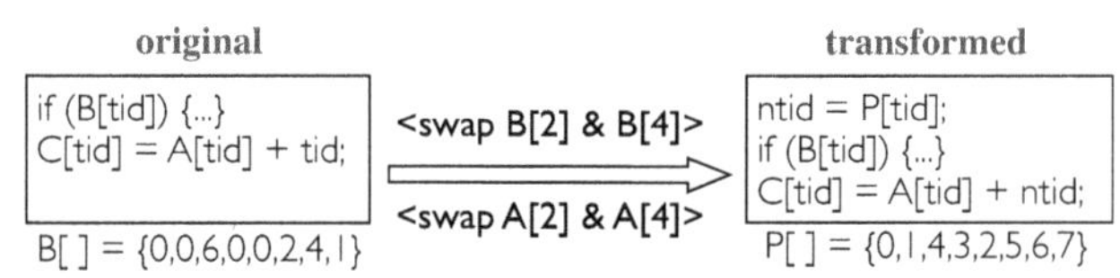


**Figure 5.** Using data relocation for job swapping faces some complexities.

transformation achieves the same reduction of memory transactions as data reordering does (not reaching the optimal either). When applying job swapping, it is important to keep the integrity of each job—that is, the *entire* jobs of thread 2 and thread 4 in our example must be swapped. To do so, one just need to replace all occurrences of $tid$ in the kernel with a new variable (e.g., $newtid$), and inserting a statement like "newtid=Q[tid]" at the beginning of the kernel, where, $Q$ is an array capturing the desired mapping between threads and jobs. The bottom box in Figure 4 (b) exemplifies this process. Apparently, the arrays $Q$ and $P$ can collapse into one $R$ such that $R[tid] = P[Q[tid]]$. The collapse may avoid the additional reference "newtid=Q[tid]", introduced by the transformation.

Job swapping is applicable for removals of irregular control flows as well. Figure 4 (c) shows an example. In the original program, the values of elements in $B$ cause both warps to diverge on the condition statement. By exchanging the jobs of thread 2 and thread 4, the transformation eliminates divergences of both warps on the condition statement. This example exposes a side effect of job swapping: It may change memory access patterns in the kernel. The swapping in Figure 4 (c) impairs the regularity of the accesses to $B$, causing extra memory transactions. This side effect can be avoided by applying the data reordering transformation described in the prior sub-section as a follow-up transformation to job swapping.

Job swapping can be materialized in two ways. Besides through reference redirection as Figures 4 (b) and (c) show, the second way is through data relocation. As shown in Figure 4 (d), when the locations of $B[2]$ and $B[4]$ switch while $tid$ remains unchanged in the kernel, threads 2 and 4 automatically swap their jobs. There are some complexities in applying this job swapping method, exemplified by Figure 5. First, it requires all input arrays in the kernel (e.g., $A$ and $B$ in Figure 5) go through the same data exchanges to maintain the integrity of a job. The incurred data copying may cause large overhead. Second, for this approach to work, it must treat occurrences of $tid$ that are outside array subscripts carefully. For instance, in Figure 5, simply switching $A[2]$ and $A[4]$ on memory would cause the expression "A[tid]+tid" to produce wrong results. A careful treatment to appearances of "tid" that are outside array subscripts can fix the problem, as shown in the transformed code in Figure 5 (where, $P$ is an assistant array created to record the mapping between threads and jobs). Finally, at the end of the kernel, the order of the elements in output arrays (e.g., $C$ in Figure 5) has to be restored (e.g., switch $C[2]$ and $C[4]$) so that the order of elements match with the output of the original program.

Apparently, relocation-based job swapping applies only to the removal of irregular control flows, but not irregular memory references as the mapping between threads and data locations remains the same as the original.

#### 3.2.3 Hybrid Transformations

The third strategy for removing irregularities is to combine data reordering and job swapping. The combination has two benefits. The first has been mentioned in the prior sub-section: A follow-up data reordering helps eliminate the side effects that thread divergence elimination imposes on memory references.

The second benefit is that combined transformations often lead to greater reduction of memory transactions than each individual transformation does. As shown in Figure 4 (a) and (b), data reordering and job swapping both reduce the needed memory transactions to three for the shown example. Figure 4 (e) shows that a combination of the two transformations may reduce the number of memory transactions to two, the minimum. The rationale for the further reduction is that the reordering step creates a data layout that is more amenable for job swapping to function than the original layout is. On the new layout, two threads in warp one reference two data elements in segment two, and meanwhile, two threads in warp two reference two data elements in segment one. Swapping the jobs of the two pairs of threads ensures that the references by each warp fall into one single segment, hence minimizing the number of needed memory transactions.

#### 3.2.4 Comparisons

Both types of irregularities may benefit from multiple kinds of transformations. We briefly summarize the properties of the various transformations. Section 5 describes the selection scheme adopted in G-Streamline.

Irregular reference removal may benefit from all three strategies (except relocation-based job swapping). Data reordering and job swapping each has some unique applicable scenarios. Suppose the segment size and warp size are both 4. For a reference "A[Q[tid]]" with "Q[ ]={0,4,8,12,16,20,24,28}", data reordering works but job swapping does not; a contrary example is "A[Q[tid]]" with $Q[] = \{0, 1, 2, 5, 2, 5, 6, 7\}$—no data reordering alone helps as $A[2]$ and $A[5]$ are each accessed by two warps. The hybrid strategy combines the power of the two, having the largest potential. On the aspect of overhead, job swapping incurs the least overhead because unlike the other two strategies, it needs no data movements on memory. In complexity, the hybrid strategy is the most complicated for implementation.

Thread divergence removal relies mainly on job swapping with data reordering as a follow-up remedy for side effects. Between the two ways to realize job swapping, the redirection-based method has lower overhead than the relocation-based method, as by itself, no data movements are needed. However, that benefit is often offset by its side effect on memory references. On the other hand, the relocation-based method, although having no such side effects, are limited in applicability. Generally, if the data to be moved are accessed by threads in more than one warp, relocation-based job swapping is likely to encounter difficulties. (Consider a modified version of the example in Figure 4 (d), where thread 4 originally accesses B[3] rather than B[4].)

Overall, the techniques discussed in this section form a set of options for creating new mappings between threads and data. Next, we discuss what mappings are desirable and how to determine them for the minimization of different types of irregularities.

## 4. Determination of Desirable Data Layouts and Mappings

In this section, we first present some findings and algorithms related to the removal of each individual type of irregularities, and then describe how to treat them when they both exist in a single kernel.

### 4.1 Irregular Memory References

Recall that all three strategies can apply to irregular reference removal. For data reordering, the key is to determine the desirable orders for elements in input arrays; for job swapping, the key is to determine the desirable mappings between threads and jobs; for the hybrid strategy, both data layouts and thread-job mappings are important. We are not aware of any existing solutions to the determination of optimal data layouts or thread-job mappings for irregular reference removal on GPU. In fact, even whether the optimal are feasible to be determined has been an open question.

In this work, by reducing known NP-complete problems, the *3DM* and the *partition problem* [10], we prove that finding optimal data layouts or thread-data mappings is NP-complete for minimizing the number of memory transactions. For lack of space, we elide the proofs, but describe two heuristics-based solutions, respectively for data reordering and job swapping.

***Data Reordering*** For data reordering, we employ data duplication to circumvent the difficulties in finding optimal data layouts. The idea is simple. At a reference, say $A[P[tid]]$, we create a new copy of $A$, denoted as $A'$, such that $A'[i] = A[P[i]]$. Then, we use $A'[tid]$ to replace every appearance of $A[P[tid]]$ in the kernel. With this approach, the number of memory transactions at the reference equals the number of thread warps—the optimal is achieved. The main drawback of this approach is space overhead: When $n$ threads reference the same item in $A$, there would be $n$ copies of the item in $A'$. When there are irregular references to multiple arrays (or multiple references to one array with different reference patterns, e.g., $A[P[tid]]$ versus $A[Q[tid]]$) in the kernel, the approach creates duplications for each of those arrays (or references), hence possibly causing too much space overhead. Section 5 will show how adaptive controls address this problem.

***Job Swapping*** For job swapping, we design a two-step approach. First, consider a case with only one irregular memory reference $A[P[tid]]$. The first step of the approach classifies jobs into $M$ (number of memory segments containing requested items in $A$) categories; category $C_i$ contains only the jobs that reference the $i^{th}$ requested memory segment of array $A$. Then for each category ($C_i$), we put $|W * \lfloor|C_i|/W\rfloor$ of its members evenly into $\lfloor|C_i|/W\rfloor$ buckets ($W$ is warp size). This step ensures that each of those job buckets, when assigned to one warp, needs only one memory transaction at $A[P[tid]]$. The remaining jobs of $C_i$ form a residual set, $R_i$. The second step uses a greedy algorithm to pack the residuals into buckets of size $W$. Let $\Omega = \{R_i | i = 1, 2, \cdots, M\}$. The algorithm works iteratively. In each iteration, it puts the largest residual set in $\Omega$ into an empty bucket, and then fills the bucket with some jobs in the smallest residual sets in $\Omega$. It then removes those used jobs from $\Omega$ and applies the same algorithm again. This process continues until $\Omega$ is empty. This size-based packing helps avoid splitting some residual sets—splits cause jobs accessing the same memory segment to be distributed to different warps, hence incurring extra memory transactions. This job swapping algorithm uses less space than data reordering, but is mainly applicable for kernels having one or multiple references with a single access pattern (e.g., $A[P[tid]]$ and $B[P[tid]]$). For other cases, G-Streamline favors data reordering.

As the previous section shows, the combined use of data reordering and job swapping may create additional opportunities for optimizations. However, the catch is extra complexities for determining the suitable data layouts and job mappings. A systematic exploration is out of the scope of this paper.

### 4.2 Irregular Control Flows

As Section 3 describes, only job swapping is applicable for removing irregular control flows. This section focuses on reference redirection-based job swapping for its broad applicability. The key to its effectiveness is to find a desirable mapping between threads and jobs.

Through reducing the *partition problem* [10], we prove that finding optimal thread-job mappings (in terms of the total number of thread divergences) for the removal of irregular control flows is NP-complete with respect to $K$ ($K$ is the number of condition statements in a kernel; assuming each has two branches). The proof is elided for lack of space.

Designing heuristics-based algorithms for removing irregular control flows is not a main focus of this work. We extend the algorithms proposed in our previous work [22]. In the prior study, we used path-vector–based job regrouping to handle divergences caused by non-loop condition statements. For a kernel with $K$ condition statements, each job has a corresponding $K$-dimensional vector (called *path vector*), with each member equaling the boolean value on a condition statement. The prior work uses loop trip-count (i.e., number of iterations) based sorting to treat thread divergences caused by a loop termination condition. It describes no solutions to the scenarios where both kinds of conditions co-exist. We handle such cases by adding one dimension to the path vector for each loop. The values in those dimensions are categorized loop trip-counts. The categorization is through distance-based clustering [9]. For instance, for a kernel with two condition statements and one loop whose iterations among all threads fall into $L$ clusters (i.e., 0, 100-200, 1000-1300, >10000), the path vectors of all threads would be in three dimensions; the final dimension is for the loop, and can have only $L$ possible values, corresponding to the $L$ clusters. After integrating loops into path vectors, we can simply assign jobs having the same path vector values to threads in the same warps.

### 4.3 Co-Existence of Irregularities

Irregular control flows and irregular memory references co-exist in some kernels. The co-existence may be inherent in the kernel code, or caused by optimizations as already exemplified in Figure 4 (c). As the optimal data layouts or thread-job mappings may differ for the two types of irregularities, the co-existence imposes further challenges to irregularity removal.

G-Streamline circumvents the problem based on the following observation: Even though job swapping affects both control flows and memory references for a thread, data reordering affects only memory references. The corresponding strategy taken by G-Streamline is to first treat irregular control flows using the approach described in the previous sub-section, and then apply data reordering to handle all irregular memory references, including those newly introduced by the treatments to irregular control flows. The handling of irregular memory references does not jeopardize the optimized control flows.

## 5. Adaptive Efficiency Control

Sophisticated techniques for overhead minimization is important for the optimizations described in this paper to work profitably. As dynamic irregularities depend on program inputs and runtime values, transformations for removing them have to happen at run time. These transformations, however, often involve significant overhead. Job swapping, for instance, the most lightweight transformation of the three, requires no data movements, but still involve considerable cost for computing suitable thread-job mappings and the creation of redirection arrays. Without a careful design, the overhead may easily outweigh the optimization benefits.

G-Streamline overcomes the difficulty through a CPU-GPU pipelining scheme, a set of overhead reduction methods, and a suite of runtime adaptive control. These techniques together ensure that the optimizations do not slow down the program in the worst case, and meanwhile, maximize optimization benefits in various scenarios by overlapping transformations with kernel executions, circumventing dependences, and adaptively adjusting transformation parameters. Our description starts with the basic CPU-GPU pipelining—the underlying vehicle supporting the various transformations.

### 5.1 Basic CPU-GPU Pipelining for Overhead Hiding

The basic idea of the CPU-GPU pipelining is to make transformations happen asynchronously on CPU when GPU kernels are running. We first explain how the pipelining works in a setting where the main body of the original program is a loop. Each iteration of the loop invokes a GPU kernel to process one chunk of data; no dependences exist across loop iterations. This is a typical setting in real GPU applications that deal with a large amount of data. The next subsection will explain how the pipelining works in other settings.

Figure 6 shows an example use of the CPU-GPU pipelining. The CPU part of the original program is in normal font in Figure 6 (a). Each iteration of its central loop invokes *gpuKernel* to make the GPU process one chunk of the data. The italic-font lines are inserted code to enable the pipelined thread-data remapping. All functions with the prefix "gs_" are part of the G-Streamline library. Consider that the execution of the $i$th iteration of the loop. At the invocation of "gs_asynRemap ( )", the main CPU thread wakes up an assistant CPU thread. While the assistant thread does thread-data remapping for the chunk of data that is going to be used in iteration $(i+\Delta)$, the main thread moves on to process the $i$th chunk of data. It first checks whether the G-Streamline transformation (started in the $(i-\Delta)$th iteration) for the current iteration is already done. If so (i.e., *cpucpyDone[i]* is true), it invokes the optimized GPU kernel; otherwise, it uses the original kernel. While the GPU executes the kernel, the main CPU thread moves on to "gs_checkRemap $(i+1)$" (pseudo code in the box) to copy the transformed $(i+1)th$ chunk of data from host to GPU. This copying is conditional: The first while loop in "gs_checkRemap ()" ensures that the copying starts only if the transformation completes before the $i$th GPU kernel invocation finishes. The second "while" loop ensures that the main thread moves on normally without waiting for the data copying to finish if the $i$th GPU kernel invocation has completed. These two "while" loops together guarantee that the transformation and

```
pData = & data;
for (i=0; i<N/S; i++) {...
    gs_asynRemap (pData+Δ*S); // remap by assist. CPU thread
    if (cpucpyDone[i])
        gpuKernel_gs_opt <<<... ...>>> (pData, ...);
    else
        gpuKernel_org <<<... ...>>> (pData, ...);
    gs_checkRemap (i+1); ...}
```

```
procedure gs_checkRemap (j) {
    if (j<Δ) return; // no remapping for this iteration
    while ( (!gpuDone[j-1]) AND (!cpuoptDone[j-Δ]) );
    if (cpuoptDone[j-Δ]) {
        gs_dataCpy (j-Δ); // asynchronous copy to GPU
        while ( (!gpuDone[j-1]) AND (!cpucpyDone[j-Δ]) );
    }
}
```

(a) CPU part of an example program with G-Streamline code (italic) inserted.

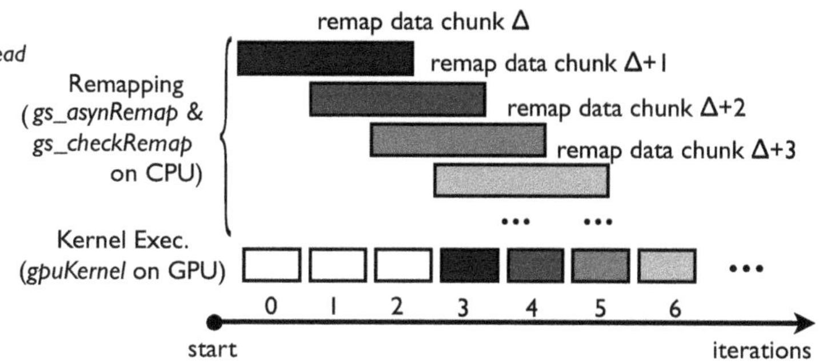


(b) Pipeline when the depth Δ is 3

**Figure 6.** An example illustrating the (simplified) use of CPU-GPU pipelining to hide the overhead in thread-data remapping transformations. The code in the bottom box is part of the G-Streamline library.

associated data copying cause no delay to the program execution even in the worst case.

The status arrays, *gpuDone*, *cpuoptDone*, and *cpucpyDone* in Figure 6, are conceptual. The "cudastreamquery" in CUDA API is actually used for checking the GPU kernel status.

The pipelining scheme trades certain amount of CPU resource for the enhancement of GPU computing efficiency. The usage of the extra CPU resource is not a concern for many GPU applications because during the execution of their GPU kernels, CPUs often remain idle.

## 5.2 Dependence and Kernel Splitting

In some programs, the main loop works on a single set of data iteratively; the arrays to be transformed are both read and modified in each iteration of the central loop. These dependences make the CPU-GPU pipelining difficult to apply because the transformation has to happen on the critical path synchronously after each iteration. Transformation overhead becomes part of the execution time, impairing the applicability of the G-Streamline optimizations.

We introduce a technique called *kernel splitting* to solve the problem. The idea is to split the execution of a GPU kernel into two by duplicating the kernel call and distributing the tasks. Figure 7 shows such an example. In the new program, the invocation of the original kernel *"gpuKernel_org"* is replaced with *gpuKernel_org_sub* and *gpuKernel_opt_sub*. The invocation of the function *gpuKernel_org_sub* behaves the same as the original, but completes only the first $(1-r)$ portion of the data processed by the original kernel (i.e., the tasks conducted by the first $(1-r)$ portion of the original GPU threads), while the invocation of function *gpuKernel_opt_sub* completes the remaining tasks. When GPU is executing *gpuKernel_org_sub*, a CPU assistant thread does G-Streamline transformations for the data to be used in *gpuKernel_opt_sub*. Therefore, with the kernel execution split into two, the CPU-GPU pipelining becomes feasible even in the presence of dependences. The rate $r$ is called *optimization ratio*, the determination of which is discussed in Section 5.4.

In some of these programs, the suitable data layout and mappings do not vary across iterations. In that case, the analysis for finding the appropriate mappings or data layouts is a one-time operation, and can be put outside of the main loop. But the creation of new arrays have to happen after each iteration of the main loop. For programs having no central loops but multiple phases of computation, the pipelining can still be applied through kernel splitting in the similar way as the previous paragraph describes.

```
gpuKernel_org<<<...>>>(pData,...);
        ↓ split
gpuKernel_org_sub<<<...>>>(pData,0, (1-r)*len, ...);
gpuKernel_org_sub<<<...>>>(pData,(1-r)*len+1, len, ...);
```

**Figure 7.** Kernel splitting makes CPU-GPU pipelining remain feasible despite loop-carried dependences.

## 5.3 Approximation and Overlapping

In some cases, the overhead of a full transformation is so large that even the pipelining cannot completely hide the overhead. Approximations are necessary to trade optimization quality for efficiency. The partial transformation mentioned in the previous subsection is one example of such approximations. By only transforming part of the data set that is going to be used in an iteration, the technique reduces transformation time. Even though that technique is described for addressing loop-carried dependences, partial transformation is apparently applicable to all settings regardless of the presence of dependences.

For the elimination of control flow irregularities, we adopt the label-assign-move (LAM) algorithm described in our previous work [22]. The algorithm avoids unnecessary data movements by marking data with a number of class labels and making only necessary switching of data elements such that same classes of data locate adjacently.

An additional technique we use to reduce transformation overhead is to overlap the different parts of a transformation. A transformation usually consists of two steps: producing appropriate data layout or thread-data mappings, copying the produced data to GPU. (For some programs, some data may have to be copied from GPU to host before the transformation.) These steps may all consume considerable time. Our technique treats the to-be-transformed data set as $s$ segments so that the copying of one segment can proceed in parallel with the transformation of another. We call the parameter $s$ the *number of data segments*, determined through the following adaptive control.

### 5.4 Adaptive Control

G-Streamline comes with a multi-level adaptive control that selects the transformation methods and adjusts transformation parameters on the fly.

***Coarse-Grained Adaptation*** The first level of adaptation exists in the CPU-GPU pipelining. As Section 5.1 already shows, a transformation shuts down automatically if it runs too slow, and the main CPU thread moves on to the next iteration regardless of whether the transformation finishes. This level of adaptation guarantees the basic efficiency of the program execution.

The second level of adaptation selects appropriate transformation method to use. Recall that irregular reference removal can benefit from different types of transformations. The implementations of these transformations in G-Streamline show the following properties. Data reordering has the largest space overhead and medium time overhead, but is able to remove all irregular memory references (with data duplication). Job swapping has the smallest overhead in both space and time, but has limited effectiveness and applicability. The strategy in G-Streamline is to use data reordering as the first choice. If its space overhead is intolerable, G-Streamline switches to job swapping. To enable this level of adaptation, multiple copies of the kernel code would need to be created, with each containing the code changes needed for the corresponding transformation. This level of adaptation is optional in the use of G-Streamline.

***Fine-Grained Adaptation*** The third level of adaptation is fine-grained control, which dynamically adjusts the transformation parameters. There are mainly four parameters: the pipeline depth $\Delta$, the optimization ratio $r$, the number of classes in LAM $c$, and the number of data segments $s$.

The pipeline depth $\Delta$ (Section 5.1) determines the time budget for a transformation to finish. In our implementation, we fix it as 1 but allow multiple threads (depending on the number of available CPU cores) to transform for one chunk of data in parallel. This implementation simplifies thread management.

The number of data segments $s$ (Section 5.3) influences the overlapping between transformation and data copying. Its value is 1 by default. In the initial several iterations, if G-Streamline finds that the transformation overhead always exceeds the kernel running time despite what values $r$ takes, it increases this parameter to 5, a value working reasonably well for most benchmarks in our experiments.

The parameters $r$ and $c$ control the amount of work a transformation needs to do. Their determinations are similar. We use $r$ for explanation. We start with the case where no kernel splitting is needed for the target program. A simple way to determine an appropriate value for $r$ is to let its value start with 100%, and decrease by 10% on every failed iteration (i.e., the transformation time exceeds the kernel time). We employ a more sophisticated scheme to accelerate the searching process and meanwhile exert the potential of the transformation to the largest extent. The scheme consists of three stages as follows:

- *Online Profiling*. This stage happens in the first two iterations of the central loop; $r$ is set to a small initial value (10% in our implementation), represented as $r_0$. In the first iteration, the transformation time and the kernel execution time—note, this is the original kernel execution time as no optimizations have been applied yet—are recorded, represented by $T_{tr}$ and $T_{org}$. If the first iteration fails (i.e., $T_{tr} > T_{org}$), no G-Streamline transformations will be applied to all future iterations. Otherwise, in the second iteration ($r_0$ of the data to be used have been optimized), the kernel execution time is recorded, represented by $T_{opt}$. The difference $(T_{org} - T_{opt})$ is the time saved by the optimization, represented by $T_{sav}$.
- *Estimating Transformation Ratio*. The second stage happens at the beginning of the third iteration. Notice that the desirable value of $r$, represented as $r'$, should make the transformation time equal the optimized kernel time—that is, $T'_{tr} = (T_{org} - T'_{sav})$. Assuming that both transformation time and kernel saving time increase proportionally with $r$, we have $T'_{tr} = T_{tr} * r'/r_0$ and $T'_{sav} = T_{sav} * r'/r_0$. Hence, we get $r' = r_0 * T_{org}/(T_{tr} + T_{sav})$.
- *Dynamic Adjustment*. The third stage adjusts $r'$ through the next few iterations in case that the estimated $r'$ is too large or small. A naive policy for the adjustment is (1) to decrease its value by a step, $r_s$, on each failed iteration until reaching a success, and (2) to increase its value on each success until a failure, then decrease it by a step size, and stop adjustment. This simple policy is insufficient, illustrated by the following example. Suppose $r_0 = 10\%$, $r'$ equals 30% at the beginning of this stage, and the third iteration is a success. Note that the kernel execution in this iteration actually is on the data optimized in the second iteration, when the optimization ratio is 10% rather than 30%. Therefore, the success of the third iteration does not mean that the transformation of 30% data takes less time than the optimized kernel with 30% as the optimization ratio. In another word, 30% could be too large so that the fourth iteration (with $r = 30\%$) may fail. The increase of $r$ upon each success in the naive policy is hence inappropriate.

  Figure 8 shows the adjustment policy in G-Streamline. As the right part of the flow chart indicates, $r$ increases its value on two (rather than one) consecutive successes to avoid the problem mentioned in the previous paragraph. An additional condition for the increase is that the value of $r$ has never been decreased. If $r$ has been decreased, two consecutive successes means that the appropriate value of $r$ has been found (further increase can only cause failures, and further decrease produces less optimization benefits), and the adjustment ends. All future iterations use that $r$ value.

In the case that kernel splitting is needed for dependences carried by the central loop, the dynamic adjustment of $r$ is the same as shown in Figure 8 except that the top two boxes on the right are removed. It is due to the fact that the transformed data are used in the current iteration.

In the case that there is no central loop (e.g., *cuda-ec* in Section 7), The kernel tasks are split into three parts, executed by three kernel calls. The first part contains 10% of all. During its execution, the CPU transforms 10% of data. After that, the CPU thread uses the measured kernel time $T_{org}$ and the transformation time $T_{tr}$ to estimate what portion ($\alpha$) of the remaining 90% tasks should run in the second kernel call so that the transformation for the remaining $(1-\alpha)*90\%$ tasks can finish before the finish of the second kernel call. The calculation is $\alpha = T_{tr}/(T_{tr} + T_{org})$. The G-Streamline then optimizes for the remaining $(1 - \alpha) * 90\%$ tasks while the second kernel call is working on the $\alpha * 90\%$ tasks. If the second kernel call still finishes early, the transformation is terminated immediately. Otherwise, the third kernel call uses the optimized data to gain speedups.

The size of a data chunk per central-loop iteration may also be adjusted for runtime adaptation. That size influences the length of a GPU kernel invocation, as well as transformation overhead. However, we find it unnecessary to adjust the chunk size given that the transformation parameters in the adaptive control (e.g., the optimization ratio) can already alter the rate between transformation

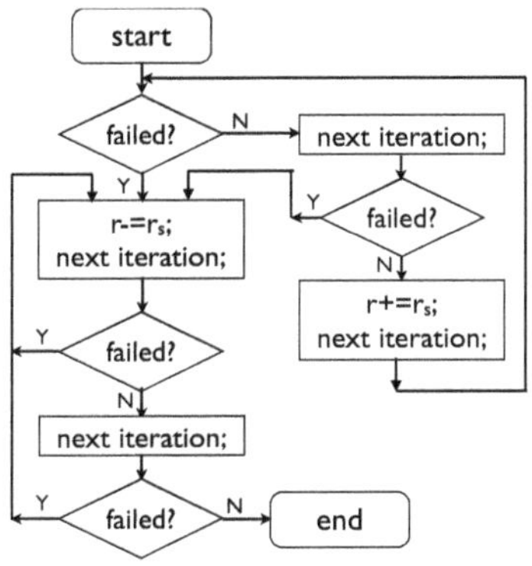


**Figure 8.** Dynamic adjustment for optimization ratio.

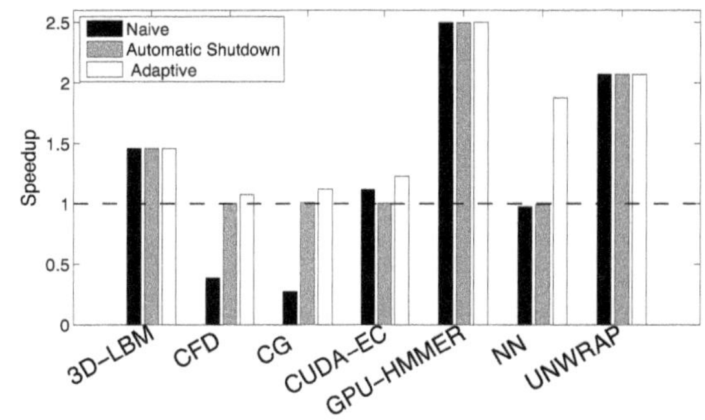


**Figure 9.** Speedup from thread-data remapping.

overhead and kernel length. In our implementation, the chunk size is the default size in the original program.

## 6. Usage and Other Issues

G-Streamline is in form of a library, written in C++ and Pthreads, consisting of functions for various transformations (including the heuristics-based algorithms) described in this paper, along with the functions for enabling the CPU-GPU pipelining and the adaptation schemes. To activate the pipelined transformations, users need to insert several function calls into the CPU code that encloses GPU kernel invocations. Some minor code changes are necessary to GPU kernels, such as the changes to array reference subscripts as shown in Figure 4. Currently, the changes are done manually.

Discussions in this paper have been based on the abstract forms of irregular references ("A[P[tid]]") and condition statements ("if (B[tid])") defined in Section 2. In our experiments, we find that for most applications, "P" and "B" are either some input arrays or results derived by a simple calculation on input arrays. In these cases, their values are easy for G-Streamline to obtain through a simple pre-computation on input arrays before applying the transformations. But in few kernels, the calculations of "P" and "B" are complex. To handle such cases, G-Streamline provides an interface for programmers to provide functions for the attainment of "P" and "B". For efficiency, the function can produce approximated values. The calculation of "P" and "B" is part of the transformation process in G-Streamline, and hence can be hidden by the CPU-GPU pipelining scheme and jeopardizes no basic efficiency of the application.

## 7. Evaluation

We evaluate the effectiveness of G-Streamline on a set of benchmarks shown in Table 1. We select them because they contain some non-trivial dynamic irregularities. The benchmarks come from some real applications [17, 23] and some recently released GPU benchmark collections, including Rodinia [5] and NVIDIA Tesla Bio [19]. One exception is *cg*, a kernel derived from an OpenMP program in the NAS suite [2]. Including it is for a direct comparison with a prior study [11] that has optimized the program intensively.

The seven benchmarks cover a variety of domains, and have different numbers and types of irregularities. The program *3dlbm* contain both diverging branches and irregular memory references. Four of the others have irregular memory references, and the other two contains only thread divergences. Together they make a mixed set for the evaluation of not only the various transformations in G-Streamline but also its adaptation schemes. The original implementation of these programs are in CUDA. Previous documents have shown that they have gone through carefully tuning and outperformed their CPU counterparts substantially (e.g., 10–467x for 3dlbm [23], 20x for cuda-ec [19],9–30x for cfd [5]). The inputs to these programs are shown in Table 1, some of which (e.g., the input to *cfd*) are directly obtained from the authors of the benchmarks as the ones coming with the benchmark suite are too small for experiments and typical practical uses.

Our experiments run on an NVIDIA Tesla 1060 hosted in a quad-core Intel Xeon E5540 machine. The Tesla 1060 includes a single chip with 240 cores, organized in 30 streaming multiprocessors (SM). The machine has CUDA 3.0 installed. We analyze performance through CUDA profiler (v3.0.21), a tool from NVIDIA reporting execution information by reading hardware performance counters in one SM of a GPU.

### 7.1 Results Overview

Figure 9 reports the speedups of the optimized kernels in the seven benchmarks. The baseline is the execution times of the original kernels; bars higher than 1 means speedup, and slowdown otherwise.

Each program has three bars, respectively corresponding to the performance when the transformations are applied with no adaptation control, with first-level control (i.e., automatic shutdown when transformations last too long), and with all adaptions. The first group of bars indicate that the brute-force application of the transformations, although leading to significant speedup to three programs, cause drastic slowdown to two programs. The first-level adaptive control (automatic shutdown) successfully prevents the slowdown, while the other levels of adaptations yield further substantial performance improvement to most programs. (The reason for the first-level adaptation to throttle speedup of *cuda-ec* is shown in Section 7.4.) The benefits of the optimizations are confirmed by the significant reduction of divergences and memory transactions reported by the CUDA profiler, shown in Table 2. Overall, the optimizations yield speedups between 1.07 and 2.5, demonstrating the effectiveness of G-Streamline for exerting GPU power for irregular computations. We acknowledge that compared to the data shown in Figure 2, some of the results are substantially below the full potential. It is mainly due to the dependences across central loops, transformation overhead, and approximation errors. It indicates possible opportunities for further refinement of G-Streamline.

The software rewriting overhead mainly consists of insertion of G-Streamline library calls for data reordering and threads swapping, customized condition computation functions, and the transformed GPU kernels that optimizes data access patterns and control divergence. Table 1 reports the software overhead in terms of the number of lines of inserted code. For most programs, the majority of the inserted code is the duplication of the original code because the new GPU kernels are typically the same as the original except that the thread IDs or array reference IDs are replaced with new IDs. The numbers of lines of newly created code are shown

**Table 1.** Benchmarks and some dynamically determined optimization parameters

sloc: source lines of code; r: optimization ratio; s: num of data segments in one transformation

| Benchmark | Source | Description | Irreg. | Input | sloc | added sloc | | r | s |
|---|---|---|---|---|---|---|---|---|---|
| | | | | | | all | new | | |
| 3dlbm | real app. [23] | partial diff. equation solver | div & mem | 32X32X32 lattice | 1.7k | 200 | 50 | 1 | 1 |
| cfd | Rodinia [5] | grid finite volume solver | mem | 800k mesh | 0.6k | 550 | 200 | 0.37 | 5 |
| cg | NAS (rewritten [11]) | conjugate gradient method | mem | 75k array | 1.2k | 250 | 200 | 0.3 | 5 |
| cuda-ec | Tesla Bio [19] | sequence error correction | div | 1.1M DNA seq. | 2.5k | 900 | 150 | 0.65 | 1 |
| gpu-hmmer | Tesla Bio [19] | protein sequence alignment | div | 0.2M protein seq. | 28k | 350 | 100 | 1 | 1 |
| nn | Rodinia [5] | nearest neighbor cluster | mem | 150M data | 0.3k | 210 | 150 | 0.7 | 1 |
| unwrap | real app. [17] | 3-D image reconstruction | mem | 512x512 images | 1.4k | 100 | 70 | 1 | 1 |

**Table 2.** Numbers of thread divergences and memory transactions on one GPU SM reported by hardware performance counters

opt (div): divergence eliminated; opt (div & mem): memory references and divergences optimized.

| | 3dlbm | | cfd | | cg | | cuda-ec | | gpu-hmmer | | nn | | unwrap | |
|---|---|---|---|---|---|---|---|---|---|---|---|---|---|---|
| | div | mem | div | mem | div | mem | div | mem | div | mem | div | mem | div | mem |
| original | 67k | 103M | 2.2M | 5.2G | 0 | 3.7G | 970k | 580M | 13k | 5.6G | 0 | 7.5M | 8k | 63M |
| opt (div) | 0.5k | 90M | - | - | - | - | 860k | 580M | 0.3k | 1.8G | - | - | - | - |
| opt (div & mem) | 0.5k | 73M | 2.2M | 4.5G | 0 | 3.0G | - | - | - | - | 3 | 2.5M | 8k | 13M |

by the "new" column in the table. We acknowledge that the current design of the G-Streamline interface can be further improved to enable more concise expression. Moreover, compiler transformation may further simplify the code changes.

The different degrees of speedups on the seven benchmarks are due to their distinctive features. These programs fall into three categories based on the presence of central loops and dependences. We next discuss each of the benchmarks in further detail.

### 7.2 Programs with Independent Loops

Each of the four programs, *unwrap, nn, 3dlbm, gpu-hmmer*, has a central loop with different iterations processing different data sets.

***UNWRAP*** The program, *unwrap*, is for reconstructing 3-D models of biological particles from 2-D microscope photos [17]. Each iteration of the central loop invokes a GPU kernel to transform an image from the Cartesian coordinate system to the Polar coordinate system. In doing so, it accesses the data points in a series of concentric circles, from the image center to the outskirt. The reference patterns lead to inefficient memory accesses.

G-Streamline uses data reordering to optimize the memory accesses. Because the appropriate data layout is determined by the image dimension and typically does not change in the loop, its computation is put outside the central loop. The overhead is completely hidden by the 50 initial iterations of the loop. The creation of new data arrays has to happen in every iteration. The corresponding G-Streamline function call is put inside the loop, working in the CPU-GPU pipelining fashion. The array creation overhead is completed hidden by the execution of the GPU kernels.

As Table 2 shows, the transformation reduces the numbers of memory transactions by over 77%. The following table explains the reduction by showing the breakdown of different sizes of memory transactions. (In the GPU, data can be accessed in 32B-, 64B-, or 128B- segments with the same time overhead.) After putting data accessed by the same warp close on memory, the optimization aggregates many small transactions into some large ones, hence reducing the total number of transactions significantly, cutting execution time by half.

| | 32b-ld | 64b-ld | 128b-ld | 32b-st | 64b-st | 128b-st | total |
|---|---|---|---|---|---|---|---|
| org | 57M | 2M | 1M | 0 | 2.5M | 0 | 62.5M |
| opt | 0 | 10M | 0 | 0 | 2.5M | 0 | 12.5M |

***NN*** The nearest neighbor application, *nn*, finds the k-nearest neighbors from an unstructured data set. Each iteration of the central loop reads in a set of records, computes the Euclidean distances from the target latitude and longitude. The master thread evaluates and updates the k nearest neighbors. We optimized the read accesses to the unstructured data set through data reordering. We used both the distance computation kernel and the data transfer from host to device to hide the transformation overhead. As Figure 9 shows, the overhead for optimizing the whole kernel run can't be completely hidden. Using the adaptive scheme, we were able to achieve a speedup of about 1.8 with the automatically selected optimization ratio equaling 0.7.

***3DLBM*** The program, *3dlbm*, is a partial differential equation solver based on the lattice Boltzmann model (LBM) [23]. It contains both divergences and irregular memory references. Thread divergences mainly come from conditional node updates. The memory reference patterns in the kernel depend on the dimensions of the GPU thread blocks. A previous study [22] has showed up to 47% speedup. But it concentrates on the removal of thread divergences and uses ad-hoc transformations to resolve memory issues. In this work, we apply G-Streamline to the program and achieves a similar degree of speedup. The follow-up data reordering transformation successfully cuts both the newly introduced irregular references and the originally existing ones. The number of memory transactions reduces by over 74%. Both analysis and transformations happen asynchronously outside the main loop because the order does not need to change across iterations.

***GPU-HMMER*** The application *gpu-hmmer* is a GPU-based implementation of the HMMER protein sequence analysis suite, which is a suite of programs that uses Hidden Markov Models (HMMs) to describe the profile of a multiple sequence alignment. Thread divergences due to the different lengths of protein sequences impairs the program performance. We remove the divergence by job swapping. We replace the original thread-id with reordered thread-id except that the thread-ids used in read/write accesses of intermediate result arrays remain unchanged because it hurts no correctness of the program and keeps memory accesses regular. As Table 2 shows, the elimination of thread divergences happen to reduce the number of memory transactions as well, indicating that as threads work in a more coordinate way, they fetch data more efficiently than before. We obtain a speedup of 2.5. The thread-data remapping overhead is completely hidden by the kernel executions in the central loop.

### 7.3 Programs with Loop-Carried Dependences

Two programs, *cfd*, and *cg*, belong to this category. The iterations of their central loops work on the same set of data iteratively; the computing results of an earlier iteration influence the data to be read by the later iterations. Kernel splitting and multi-segment data transformation ($s = 5$) are applied to both of them.

***CFD*** The program, *cfd* is an unstructured grid finite volume solver for three-dimensional Euler equations for compressible flow [5]. The inefficient memory references come from the reading of the features of neighboring elements of a node in the unstructured grid of the solver.

The appropriate data layout is loop-invariant and is computed outside the central loop by G-Streamline, while the new array creation has to happen in each iteration. With kernel split, the runtime adaptation of G-Streamline finds that optimization of 37% array elements is appropriate. The optimization yields 7% performance improvement.

***CG*** The program, *cg*, is a Conjugate Gradient benchmark [2]. Lee and others [11] have shown that careful optimizations are necessary when translating *cg* from an OpenMP version to GPU code because of its irregular memory references. They demonstrate that static compiler-based techniques may coalesce some static irregular references in its kernel and achieve substantial performance improvement. But they give no solution to the dynamic irregular references to a vector in its sparse matrix vector multiplication kernel. The vector is read and modified in each iteration, causing loop-carried dependence.

G-Streamline tackles those remaining irregular references by applying data reordering transformation to the vector. The analysis step resides outside of the main loop as the suitable data order does not vary. But the transformation step is in each iteration. G-Streamline decides on 30% data transformation, and produces 12% further performance improvement over the version optimized through the previous technique [11].

### 7.4 Program with No Central Loop

The program, *cuda-ec*, is a parallel error correction tool for short DNA sequence reads. It contains no central loop, but several kernel function calls. We optimize the main kernel *fix_errors1* by removing divergence through job swapping. As Figure 9 shows, the simple application of optimizations without adaptations yields speedup of 1.12. The simple adaptive scheme with automatic shutdown turns off optimizations by default because it cannot tell whether the transformation is beneficial for lack of central loops. G-Streamline, equipped with the complete adaptive control, is able to use the split kernels to estimate optimization ratio (following the scheme described at the end of Section 5.4) such that the transformations can overlap with partial kernel executions. The estimated optimization ratio is 0.65, yielding a speedup of 1.22.

## 8. Related Work

Several previous studies have proposed hardware extensions for reducing the influence of irregular memory references or control flows on GPU program performance. Meng and others [13] introduce dynamic warp subdivision to divide a warp so that diverging threads can execute in an interleaving manner. Tarjan and others [18] propose adaptive slip to allow a subset of threads to continue while other threads in the same warp are waiting for memory. Fung and others [8] try to reduce thread divergences through dynamic warp formation. These hardware approaches have shown promising simulation results. As a pure software solution, our approaches are immediately deployable on current real GPU systems.

In software optimizations, the work closest to this study is our previous study on thread divergence removal [22]. We show that some thread divergences can be removed through runtime optimizations with the support of a CPU-GPU pipeline scheme. This work is enlightened by that study, but differs from it in several major aspects. First, the previous study tackles only thread divergences, while this study shows that it is important to treat thread divergences with irregular memory references at the same time because of their strong connections. We provide a systematic way to tackle both types of irregularities in a holistic manner, including novel techniques stimulated by the distinctive properties of dynamic irregular memory references on GPU. Second, we contribute some in-depth understanding of the inherent properties of irregularity removal, including the NP-completeness of the problems and the approximation algorithms. They substantially enhance current understanding of GPU irregularity removal. Third, even though the previous study has used reference redirection and data relocation for removing thread divergences, our work reveals the full spectrum of transformations that can be constructed from the two basic mechanisms, and uncovers the properties of each type of transformations. Finally, our work develops some novel efficiency-driven adaptations. Together, these innovations advance state of the art of GPU irregularity removal in both theoretical and empirical aspects.

Another work on thread divergences is from Carrillo and others [4]. They use loop splitting and branch splitting in order to alleviate register pressure caused by diverging branches, rather than to reduce thread divergences.

There have been a number of studies on optimizing GPU memory references. The compiler by Yang and others [21] optimizes memory references that are amenable for static transformations. Lee and others [11] show the capability of an openMP-to-CUDA compiler for optimizing memory references during the translation process. Baskaran and others [3] use a polyhedral compiler model to optimize affine memory references in regular loops. Ueng and others [20] show the use of annotations for optimize memory references through shared memory. Ryoo and others [16] demonstrate the potential of certain manual transformations.

All those studies have shown effectiveness, but mostly for references whose access patterns are known at compile time. To the best of our knowledge, this current study is the first that tackles *dynamic* irregular memory references. Its distinctive on-the-fly transformations are complementary to prior static code optimizations.

An orthogonal direction for enhancing GPU program performance is through auto-tuning tools [12, 15]. The combination of dynamic irregularity removal and auto-tuning may offer some special optimization opportunities.

In CPU program optimizations, data relocation and reference redirection have been exploited for improving data locality and hence cache and TLB usage (e.g., [1, 6, 7]). As a massively parallel architecture, GPU display different memory access properties from CPU, triggering the new set of innovations in this paper on both complexity analysis and transformation techniques.

## 9. Conclusion

In this paper, we have described a set of new findings and techniques for the removal of dynamic irregularities in GPU computing. The findings include the interactions between irregular control flows and memory references, the complexity in determining optimal thread-data mappings, a set of approximation algorithms, and the relations among dynamic irregularities, program data, and GPU threads. These findings substantially enhance the current understanding to GPU dynamic irregularities. Meanwhile, we develop a practical framework, G-Streamline. It consists of a set of transformations and adaptive controls for effectively removing dynamic irregularities from GPU applications. G-Streamline works on the fly, requiring no hardware extensions or offline profiling. It treats both irregular memory references and control flows at the same time in a holistic fashion, maximizing the whole-program performance by resolving conflicts among optimizations. Together, the findings and techniques open up many new opportunities for scientific applications involving complex data references or control flows to effectively benefit from massively parallel architectures.

## Acknowledgments

We thank Mary Hall for her help during the preparation of the final version of the paper. The computational complexity analysis in the paper benefits from discussions with Weizhen Mao. We owe the anonymous reviewers our gratitude for their helpful suggestions on the paper. We thank Andrew Corrigan for kindly providing us new input set for *cfd*. This material is based upon work supported by the National Science Foundation under Grant No. 0720499, 0811791 and 0954015, and IBM CAS Fellowship. Any opinions, findings, and conclusions or recommendations expressed in this material are those of the authors and do not necessarily reflect the views of the National Science Foundation or IBM.

## References

[1] A. V. Aho, M. S. Lam, R. Sethi, and J. D. Ullman. *Compilers: Principles, Techniques, and Tools*. Addison Wesley, 2nd edition, August 2006.

[2] D. Bailey, J. Barton, T. Lasinski, and H. Simon. The NAS parallel benchmarks. Technical Report 103863, NASA, July 1993.

[3] M. M. Baskaran, U. Bondhugula, S. Krishnamoorthy, J. Ramanujam, A. Rountev, and P. Sadayappan. A compiler framework for optimization of affine loop nests for GPGPUs. In *ICS*, 2008.

[4] S. Carrillo, J. Siegel, and X. Li. A control-structure splitting optimization for gpgpu. In *CF*, 2009.

[5] S. Che, M. Boyer, J. Meng, D. Tarjan, J. W. Sheaffer, S.-H. Lee, and K. Skadron. Rodinia: A benchmark suite for heterogeneous computing. In *IISWC*, 2009.

[6] T. M. Chilimbi and R. Shaham. Cache-conscious coallocation of hot data streams. In *PLDI*, 2006.

[7] C. Ding and K. Kennedy. Improving effective bandwidth through compiler enhancement of global cache reuse. *JPDC*, 2004.

[8] W. Fung, I. Sham, G. Yuan, and T. Aamodt. Dynamic warp formation and scheduling for efficient gpu control flow. In *MICRO*, 2007.

[9] T. Hastie, R. Tibshirani, and J. Friedman. *The elements of statistical learning*. Springer, 2001.

[10] D. S. Hochbaum. *Approximation Algorithms for NP-Hard Problems*. PWS Publishing Company, 1995.

[11] S. Lee, S. Min, and R. Eigenmann. OpenMP to GPGPU: A compiler framework for automatic translation and optimization. In *PPoPP*, 2009.

[12] Y. Liu, E. Z. Zhang, and X. Shen. A cross-input adaptive framework for gpu programs optimization. In *Proceedings of International Parallel and Distribute Processing Symposium (IPDPS)*, pages 1–10, 2009.

[13] J. Meng, D. Tarjan, and K. Skadron. Dynamic warp subdivision for integrated branch and memory divergence tolerance. In *ISCA*, 2010.

[14] J. Nickolls, I. Buck, M. Garland, and K. Skadron. Scalable parallel programming with CUDA. *ACM Queue*, pages 40–53, Mar./Apr. 2008.

[15] G. Rudy, C. Chen, M. Hall, M. Khan, and J. Chame. Using a programming language interface to describe gpgpu optimization and code generation. 2010.

[16] S. Ryoo, C. I. Rodrigues, S. S. Baghsorkhi, S. S. Stone, D. B. Kirk, and W. W. Hwu. Optimization principles and application performance evaluation of a multithreaded GPU using CUDA. In *PPoPP*, 2008.

[17] G. Tan, Z. Guo, M. Chen, and D. Meng. Single-particle 3d reconstruction from cryo-electron microscopy images on gpu. In *ICS*, 2009.

[18] D. Tarjan, J. Meng, and K. Skadron. Increasing memory miss tolerance for simd cores. In *SC*, 2009.

[19] TeslaBio. NVIDIA Tesla Bio Workbench. http://www.nvidia.com/object/tesla_bio_workbench.html.

[20] S. Ueng, S. Baghsorkhi, M. Lathara, and W. Hwu. Cuda-lite: Reducing gpu programming complexity. In *LCPC*, 2008.

[21] Y. Yang, P. Xiang, J. Kong, and H. Zhou. A gpgpu compiler for memory optimization and parallelism management. In *PLDI*, 2010.

[22] E. Z. Zhang, Y. Jiang, Z. Guo, and X. Shen. Streamlining gpu applications on the fly. In *ICS*, 2010.

[23] Y. Zhao. Lattice boltzmann based pde solver on the gpu. *The Visual Computer*, (5):323–333, 2008.

# Sponge: Portable Stream Programming on Graphics Engines

Amir Hormati, Mehrzad Samadi, Mark Woh, Trevor Mudge, and Scott Mahlke
Advanced Computer Architecture Laboratory
University of Michigan - Ann Arbor, MI
{hormati, mehrzads, mwoh, tnm, mahlke}@umich.edu

## Abstract

*Graphics processing units (GPUs) provide a low cost platform for accelerating high performance computations. The introduction of new programming languages, such as CUDA and OpenCL, makes GPU programming attractive to a wide variety of programmers. However, programming GPUs is still a cumbersome task for two primary reasons: tedious performance optimizations and lack of portability. First, optimizing an algorithm for a specific GPU is a time-consuming task that requires a thorough understanding of both the algorithm and the underlying hardware. Unoptimized CUDA programs typically only achieve a small fraction of the peak GPU performance. Second, GPU code lacks efficient portability as code written for one GPU can be inefficient when executed on another. Moving code from one GPU to another while maintaining the desired performance is a non-trivial task often requiring significant modifications to account for the hardware differences. In this work, we propose Sponge, a compilation framework for GPUs using synchronous data flow streaming languages. Sponge is capable of performing a wide variety of optimizations to generate efficient code for graphics engines. Sponge alleviates the problems associated with current GPU programming methods by providing portability across different generations of GPUs and CPUs, and a better abstraction of the hardware details, such as the memory hierarchy and threading model. Using streaming, we provide a write-once software paradigm and rely on the compiler to automatically create optimized CUDA code for a wide variety of GPU targets. Sponge's compiler optimizations improve the performance of the baseline CUDA implementations by an average of 3.2x.*

***Categories and Subject Descriptors*** D.3.4 [*Programming Languages*]: Processors—Compilers

***General Terms*** Design, Languages, Performance

***Keywords*** Streaming, Compiler, GPU, Optimization, Portability

## 1. Introduction

Support for parallelism in hardware has sharply grown in recent years as a response to performance and power demands of both emerging and traditional high performance application domains. Among the multitude of vastly different solutions offered by hardware companies, graphics processing units (GPUs) have been shown to provide significant performance, power efficiency and cost benefits for general purpose computing in highly parallel computing domains. Recently, heterogeneous systems that combine traditional processors with powerful GPUs have become standard in all systems ranging from servers to cell phones. GPUs achieve their high performance and efficiency by providing a massively parallel architecture with hundreds of in-order cores while exposing parallelism mechanisms and the memory hierarchy to the programmer.



*ASPLOS'11,* March 5–11, 2011, Newport Beach, California, USA.



Recent works have shown that in the optimistic case, speedups of 100-300x [21] and in the pessimistic case, speedups of 2.5x [17] have been achieved between the most recent versions of GPUs compared to the latest processors. Maximizing the utilization of the GPU in heterogeneous systems will be key to achieving high performance and efficiency.

While GPUs provide an inexpensive, highly parallel system for accelerating parallel workloads, the programming complexity posed to application developers is a significant challenge. Developing applications to utilize the massive compute power and memory bandwidth requires a thorough understanding of the algorithm and details of the underlying architecture. Graphics chip manufacturers, such as NVIDIA, have tried to alleviate the complexity problem by introducing user-friendly programming models, such as CUDA [19]. Although CUDA and other similar programming models abstract the underlying GPU architecture by providing a unified processor model, managing the amount of on-chip memory used per thread, the total number of threads per multiprocessor, and the pattern of off-chip memory accesses are examples of problems that developers still need to manage in order to maximize GPU utilization [23]. Often the programmer must perform a tedious cycle of performance tuning to extract the desired performance.

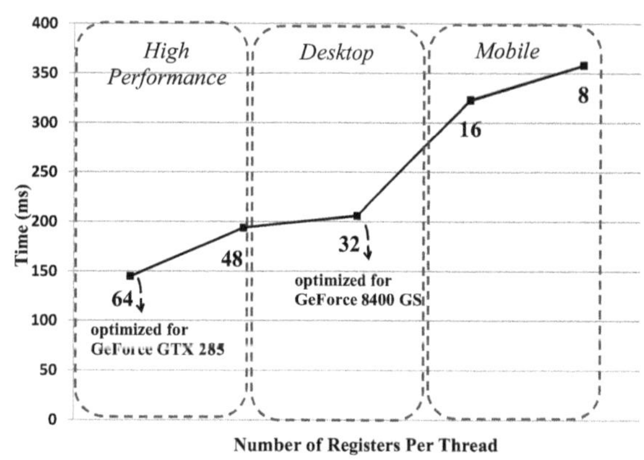


**Figure 1:** *This graph shows the runtime of a kernel optimized for architectures with different number of registers on a GeForce GTX 285 which has the most number of registers. The kernel used in this graph is organized in 128 blocks each with 256 threads.*

Another problem of developing applications in CUDA is the lack of efficient portability between different generations of GPUs and also between the host processors and GPUs in the system. Different NVIDIA GPUs vary in several key micro-architectural parameters such as number of registers, maximum number of active threads, and the size of global memory. These parameters will vary even more when newer high performance cards, such as NVIDIA's Fermi [20], and future resource-constrained mobile GPUs with less resources are released. These differences in hardware lead to a different set of optimization choices for each GPU. As a result, optimization decisions for one generation of GPUs are likely to be poor choices for another generation. An example of this is shown in Figure 1. This figure shows a CUDA kernel that requires 78 registers per thread, running with 128 blocks of 256 threads per block on an NVIDIA GeForce GTX 285. This graph shows how the runtime (lower is better) would change if the benchmark was optimized for GPU architectures with less than 16K registers available on each streaming multiprocessor of the GTX 285. For example, if this kernel is compiled for GeForce 8400 GS, it will use 32 registers per thread since there are 8K registers available for the 256 threads in each block on that architecture. Data elements that do not fit in the smaller register file will be spilled to the slower parts of the memory hierarchy causing performance degradation. In short, CUDA code must be separately customized for each target GPU as the choice of optimizations for peak performance is typically sensitive to the hardware configuration.

One solution to the GPU programming complexity is to adopt a higher level programming abstraction similar to the stream programming model. The streaming model provides an extensive set of compiler optimizations for mapping and scheduling applications to various homogeneous and heterogeneous architectures ([5, 6, 14]). The retargetability of streaming languages, such as StreamIt [26], has made them an excellent choice for parallel system programmers in shared/distributed memory and tiled architectures. Streaming language retargetability and performance benefits on heterogeneous systems are mainly a result of having well-encapsulated constructs that expose parallelism and communication without depending on the topology or granularity of the underlying architecture.

GPUs are important drivers for current and future heterogeneous systems, therefore extending the applicability of streaming languages to GPUs is advantageous for several reasons. First, streaming, which expresses programs at a higher level than CUDA, enables optimizing and porting to different generations of GPUs and between different topologies of CPUs and GPUs. Second, exposed communication in streaming programs help the compiler to efficiently map data transfers onto different memory hierarchies. Finally, streaming applications can be tailored for any number of cores and devices by performing graph restructurings such as horizontal or vertical fusion or fission of actors.

In this work, we introduce *Sponge*, a streaming compiler for the StreamIt language that is capable of automatically producing customized CUDA code for a wide range of GPUs. Sponge consists of stream graph optimizations to optimize the organization of the computation graph and an efficient CUDA code generator to express the parallelism for the target GPU. Producing efficient CUDA code is a multi-variable optimization problem and can be difficult for software programmers due to the unconventional organization and the interaction of computing resources of GPUs. Sponge is equipped with a set of optimizations to handle the memory hierarchy and also to efficiently utilize the processing units.

The Stream-to-CUDA compilation in Sponge consists of four steps. First, Sponge performs graph reorganization and modification on the stream graph and also classifies actors based on their memory traffic. The classification information is used throughout all the phases of the compilation. Second, memory layout optimizations are performed. These optimizations are designed to enable efficient utilization of the memory bandwidth. In this phase, Sponge decides if actors should use the faster but smaller on-chip memories or the slower but larger off-chip memory on the GPU. Also, techniques such as *helper threads* and *bank conflict resolution* in the context of StreamIt are introduced to increase the efficiency of memory accesses. The third compilation phase deals with actor size granularity of each thread. In this step, based on the classification information from step one, Sponge tries to create larger threads by fusing producer/consumer actors in order to reduce communication and kernel call overheads. Finally, software prefetching and loop unrolling are used to exploit unused registers to decrease loop control code overhead and increase memory bandwidth utilization.

In summary, this paper makes the following contributions:

- Extending applicability and portability of synchronous dataflow languages, specifically StreamIt, to GPUs.
- Streaming-specific optimizations for CUDA and generic CUDA optimizations for streaming applications.
- Discussion of the limitations of StreamIt as a GPU programming language.

The rest of the paper is organized as follows. In Section 2, the stream programming model, the input language (StreamIt), and the CUDA programming model are discussed. Portable stream compilation in Sponge and its optimizations are explained in Section 3. Experiments are shown in Section 4. A comparison between two hand-optimized CUDA benchmarks and their StreamIt implementation is done in Section 5. Related works are discussed in Section 6. Finally, Section 7 contains the conclusion.

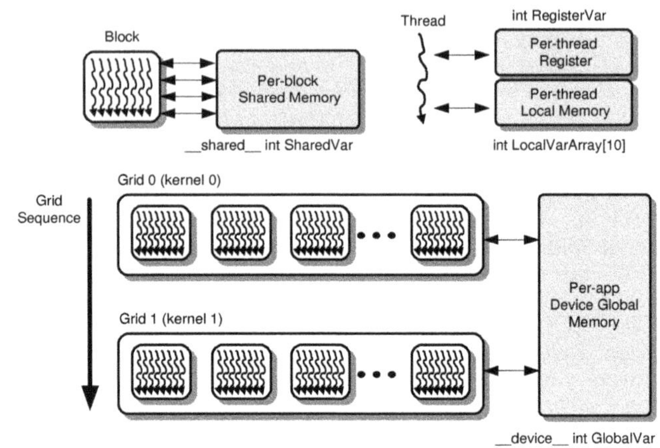


**Figure 2:** *CUDA/GPU Execution Model*

## 2. Background

In this section, the CUDA programming model, GPU architecture, and stream programming model are explained.

### 2.1 CUDA and GPUs

The CUDA programming model is a multi-threaded SIMD model that enables implementation of general purpose programs on heterogeneous GPU/CPU systems. There are two different device types in CUDA: the Host processor and the GPU. A CUDA program consists of a host code segment that contains the sequential sections of the program, which is run on the CPU, and a parallel code segment which is launched from the host onto one or more GPU devices. Data-level parallelism (DLP) and thread-level parallelism (TLP) are handled differently in these systems. DLP is converted into TLP and executed onto the GPU devices, while TLP is handled by executing multiple kernels on different GPU devices launched by the host processor. The threading and memory abstraction of the CUDA model is shown in Figure 2.

The threading abstraction in CUDA consists of three levels of hierarchy. The basic block of work is a single *thread*. A group of threads executing the same code are combined together to form a *thread block* or simply a *block*. Together, these thread blocks combine to form the parallel segments called *grids* where each grid is scheduled onto a GPU at a time. Threads within a thread block are synchronized together through a barrier operation ($\_\_syncthreads()$). However, there is no explicit software or hardware support for synchronization across thread blocks. Synchronization between thread blocks is performed through the global memory of the GPU, and the barriers needed for synchronization are handled by the host processor. Thread blocks communicate by executing separate kernels on the GPU.

The memory abstraction in CUDA consists of multiple levels of hierarchy. The lowest level of memory is *registers*, which are on-chip memories private to a single thread. The next level of memory

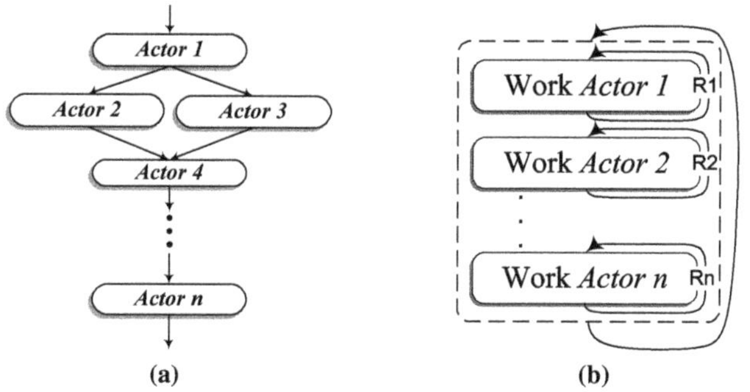


(a) (b)

**Figure 3:** *This figure shows an example stream graph and also the intermediate code template for executing a steady state schedule. $R_i$ is the repetition number for actor i.*

is *shared memory*, which is an on-chip memory shared only by threads within the same thread block. Access latency to both the registers and shared memory is extremely low. The next level of memory is *local memory*, which is an off-chip memory private to a single thread. Local memory is mainly used as spill memory for local arrays. Mapping arrays to shared memory instead of spilling to local memory can provide much better performance. Finally, the last level of memory is *global memory*, which is an off-chip memory that is accessible to all threads in the grid. This memory is used primarily to stream data in and out of the GPU from the host processor. The latency for off-chip memory is 100-150x more than that for on-chip memories. Two other memory levels exist on-chip called the *texture memory* and *constant memory*. Texture memory is accessible through special built-in texture functions and constant memory is accessible to all threads in the grid.

The CUDA programming model is an abstraction layer to access GPUs. NVIDIA GPUs use a single instruction multiple thread (SIMT) model of execution where multiple thread blocks are mapped to streaming multiprocessors (SM). Each SM contains a number of processing elements called Streaming Processors (SP). A thread executes on a single SP. Threads in a block are executed in smaller execution groups of threads called *warps*. All threads in a warp share one program counter and execute the same instructions. If conditional branches within a warp take different paths, called *control path divergence*, the warp will execute each branch path serially, stalling the other paths until all the paths are complete. Such control path divergences severely degrade the performance.

Because off-chip global memory access is very slow, GPUs support *coalesced memory accesses*. Coalescing memory accesses allows one bulk memory request from multiple threads in a half-warp to be sent to global memory instead of multiple separate requests. In order to coalesce memory accesses, three general restrictions apply: each thread in a half-warp must access successive addresses in order of the thread number, the memory accesses can only be 32, 64, or 128-bit, and all the addresses must be aligned to either 64, 128 or 256-byte boundaries. Effective memory bandwidth is an order of magnitude lower using non-coalesced memory accesses which further signifies the importance of memory coalescing for achieving high performance.

In modern GPUs, such as NVIDIA GTX 285, there are 30 SMs each with 8 SPs. Each SM processes warp sizes of 32 threads. The memory sizes for this GPU are: 16K of registers per SM, 16KB divided into 16 banks of shared memory per SM, and 2GB of global memory shared across all threads in the GPU.

## 2.2 Stream Programming Model

With the ubiquity of multi-core systems, the stream programming paradigm has become increasingly important. Exposed communication and an abundance of parallelism are the key features making streaming a flexible and architecture-independent solution for parallel programming. In this paper, we focus on stream programming models that are based on synchronous data flow (SDF) models [15]. In SDF, computation is performed by actors, which are autonomous and isolated computational units. Actors communicate through data-flow buffers (i.e. tapes), often realized as FIFOs. SDF, and its many variations, expose the input and output processing rates of actors, and in turn this affords many optimization opportunities that can lead to efficient schedules (e.g., allocation of actors to cores, and tapes to local memories).

For our purpose, we assume all computation that is performed in an actor is largely embodied in a *work* method. The *work* method runs repeatedly as long as the actor has data to consume on its input port. The amount of data that the work method consumes is called the *pop* rate. Similarly, the amount of data each work invocation produces is called the *push* rate. Some streaming languages (e.g., StreamIt [26]) provide a non-destructive read which does not alter the state of the input buffer. The amount of data that is read in this manner is specified by the *peek* rate. An actor can also have an *init* method that is executed only once for the purpose of initializing the actor before the execution of program starts.

We distinguish between stateful and stateless actors. A stateful actor modifies its local state and maintains a persistent history of its execution. Unlike a stateful actor, which restricts opportunities for parallelism, a stateless actor is data-parallel in that every invocation of the work method does not depend on or mutate the actor's state. The semantics of stateless actors thus allow us to replicate a stateless actor. This opportunity is quite fruitful in scaling the amount of parallelism that an application can exploit, as shown in [5, 6].

We use the StreamIt programming language to implement streaming programs. StreamIt is an architecture-independent streaming language based on SDF. The language allows a programmer to algorithmically describe the computational graph. In StreamIt, actors are known as filters. Filters can be organized hierarchically into *pipelines* (i.e., sequential composition), *split-joins* (i.e., parallel composition), and *feedback loops* (i.e., cyclic composition). StreamIt is a convenient language for describing streaming algorithms, and its accompanying static compilation technology makes it suitable for our work.

A crucial consideration in StreamIt programs is to create a steady state schedule which involves rate-matching of the stream graph. Rate-matching guarantees that, in the steady state, the number of data elements that is produced by an actor is equal to the number of data elements its successors will consume. Rate-matching assigns a static repetition number to each actor. In the implementation of a StreamIt schedule, an actor is enclosed by a *for-loop* that iterates as many times as its repetition number. The steady state schedule is a sequence of appearances of these *for-loops* enclosed in an outer-loop whose main job is to repeat the steady schedule. The template code in Figure 3b shows the inter-

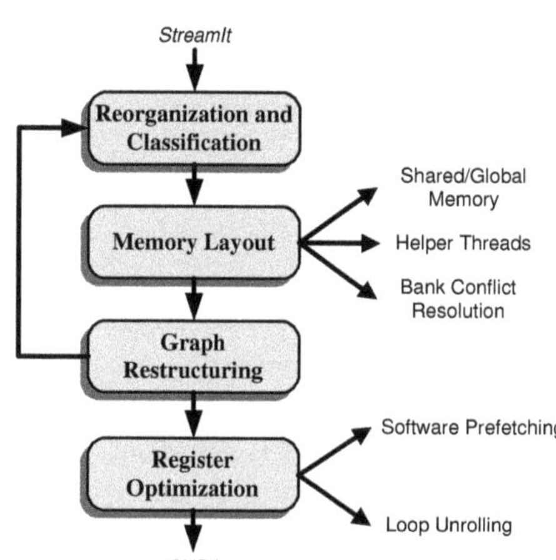


**Figure 4:** *Compilation flow in Sponge.*

$$ActiveWarpsPerSM = \frac{ThreadsPerBlock \times ActiveBlocksPerSM}{THREADS\_PER\_WARP} \quad (1)$$

$$Iterations = \frac{InputBufferSize}{Pop \times ThreadsPerBlock \times Blocks} \quad (2)$$

$$ThreadsPerBlock_{LoT} = \frac{SHARED\_MEMORY\_SIZE}{(Pop + Push)} \quad (3)$$

$$ExecCycles_{LoT} = \frac{CompInsts \times COMP\_INST\_ISSUE\_DELAY}{NUMBER\_SM} \times \frac{ThreadsPerBlock_{LoT} \times Iterations}{ActiveWarpsPerSM} \quad (4)$$

$$ThreadsPerBlock_{HiT} = MAX\_THREAD\_PER\_BLOCK \quad (5)$$

$$MemCycles = (UncoalMemInsts + CoalMemInsts/COAL\_FACTOR) \times MEMORY\_DELAY + MEM\_INST\_ISSUE\_DELAY \quad (6)$$

$$ExecCycles_{HiT} = \frac{MemCycles}{NUMBER\_SM} \times \frac{ThreadsPerBlock_{HiT} \times Iterations}{ActiveWarpsPerSM} \quad (7)$$

| Name | Description | Name | Description |
|---|---|---|---|
| $SHARED\_MEMORY\_SIZE$ | Size of shared memory on GPU | $pop, push$ | push and pop rate of an actor |
| $THREADS\_PER\_WARP$ | Number of threads in each warp | $InputBufferSize$ | Size of input buffer for an actor |
| $NUMBER\_SMs$ | Number of streaming processor on GPU | $ThreadsPerBlock$ | Number of threads in one block |
| $MAX\_THREAD\_PER\_BLOCK$ | Max number of threads allowed per block | $Blocks$ | Number of blocks on the GPU |
| $MEMORY\_DELAY$ | Number of cycles to access global memory | $Iterations$ | Number of iterations to run an actor on the GPU |
| $COAL\_FACTOR$ | Max number of memory accesses that can be coalesced | $ActiveBlocksPerSM$ | Blocks active on one SM |
| $MEM\_INST\_ISSUE\_DELAY$ | Number of cycles to issue a memory instruction | $(Un)CoalMemInsts$ | (Un)Coalesced instructions in one actor |
| $COMP\_INST\_ISSUE\_DELAY$ | Number of cycles to issue a compute instruction | | |

**Figure 5:** *In this Figure, equations for calculating execution cycles of both HiT and LoT actors are shown. Equations 1 and 2 can be used for both HiT and LoT actors. The table summarizes what each variable means.*

mediate code for the steady state schedule of the streaming graph shown in Figure 3a.

## 3. Portable Stream Compilation

Sponge takes StreamIt programs as its input and generates GPU-specific CUDA code. Each actor in the StreamIt graph is converted to a CUDA kernel running with some number of threads and blocks. By performing portable stream compilation, Sponge decides how many threads and blocks to assign to the CUDA kernel generated for each actor. The input buffer size of the first actor, $A_i$, in the graph determines how many times that actor has to run ($R_i$). As a result, $R_i$ is changed to $R_i$ divided by the multiplication of number of threads and blocks assigned to the actor. We call the result *number of iterations* for actor $A_i$.

Portable stream compilation in *Sponge* consists of four main steps as shown in Figure 4. In the first phase, Sponge reads a StreamIt program and performs *Actor Reorganization and Classification* in which simple graph reorganization is done and actors are classified into two categories: *High-Traffic (HiT) and Low-Traffic (LoT)*. The classification information is used throughout all the phases of the compilation flow. The second phase deals with the *Memory Layout and Optimization* of each actor. This step decides if an actor uses shared or global memory, eliminates shared memory bank conflicts and also improves memory performance by introducing *Helper Threads* to better utilize the unused processors and bring the data needed by an actor into shared memory faster. This compilation step is crucial to achieving better performance since memory bandwidth can be a limiting factor on GPUs. The third phase performs *Graph Restructuring* by changing the granularity of the kernels and vertically fusing actors based on classification results. After graph restructuring, the compiler reiterates from the beginning of the compilation flow, treating the post-fused stream graph as the input until no more graph restructuring is possible. Finally, *Register Optimization* tries to utilize unused registers on each SM by employing software prefetching and also by unrolling *for loops* in each kernel.

### 3.1 Actor Reorganization and Classification

As mentioned in Section 2.1, GPUs are built for data-level parallelism and are not suitable for task-level parallelism and global synchronization. Therefore, *splitter-joiner* structures will not perform well on the GPU since each joiner introduces a synchronization point. First, Sponge collapses *splitter-joiners* to one actor in cases that the actors between the *splitter* and *joiner* are stateless and equivalent. This will remove the *splitter* and *joiner* actors and replace the structure with a single actor. In cases where it is not possible to collapse a *splitter-joiner* structure to one actor, Sponge treats the *splitter* and *joiner* as special actors with more than one input and output. Based on the type and weights of the *splitter* and *joiner* actors, Sponge decides to allocate their input and output buffers in shared memory or global memory.

Sponge excludes stateful actors from being executed on the GPU and runs them on the host CPU. This is because only one instance of a stateful actor can be active and data-parallelism is not applicable to these actors. Host to GPU and GPU to host transfers are inserted before and after stateful actors, if necessary.

Next, Sponge classifies actors assigned to the GPU as either High-Traffic (HiT) or Low-Traffic (LoT). HiT actors have a large number of memory accesses. These actors perform better on a GPU if their buffers are mapped to global memory rather than shared memory because mapping the buffers to shared memory will result in having too few threads and under-utilizing the processors and the available memory bandwidth. LoT actors, on the other hand, are mostly computation dominated and if mapped to shared memory will have a reasonable number of threads to utilize the GPU.

In order to determine if an actor is a LoT or HiT, Sponge estimates execution cycles of an actor for both global memory (HiT) and shared memory (LoT) mappings, based on Equations 1-7 in Figure 5. For each actor, Sponge treats that actor as both HiT and LoT and calculates the corresponding execution cycles ($ExecCycles_{LoT}$, $ExecCycles_{HiT}$). The two numbers show if that actor is suitable to be treated as a LoT or HiT actor. If $ExecCycles_{HiT}$ is smaller than $ExecCycles_{LoT}$ for an actor, that actor will perform better if its buffer is mapped to global memory. Otherwise, it will be classified as a LoT actor for which both shared and global memory will be used to help with coalescing of data accesses.

In the equations for LoT actors, number of threads per block ($ThreadsPerBlock$) is determined by the size of shared memory($SHARED\_MEMORY\_SIZE$ [1]) and the number of pushes and pops. Threads per block defines the number of active warps per SM ($ActiveWarpsPerSM$) and the number of iterations based on Equations 1 and 2. Finally, the execution cycle of a LoT actor is estimated depending on the number of compute instructions and the distribution of threads in the GPU (Equation 4).

[1] Variables with all capital characters show GPU-specific parameters

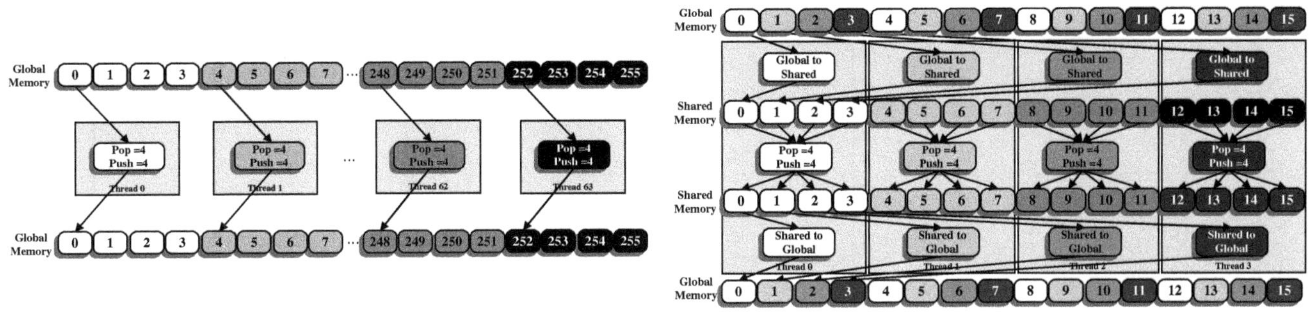


(a) (b)

**Figure 6:** *This figure shows how HiT and LoT threads access their buffers. Part (a) illustrates the memory access pattern for a sample HiT actor with four pops and four pushes. Part (b) shows the access pattern for a LoT actor.*

Execution time of HiT actors is calculated based on their memory access time because these actors are mapped to global memory and have a large number of global memory reads and writes. Equations 5-7 show how execution time estimation is done based on the number of coalesced and uncoalesced memory accesses. Unlike shared memory, the size of global memory does not limit the number of threads. Therefore, the number of threads per block for HiT actors can be equal to the maximum number of threads allowed in each block ($MAX\_THREAD\_PER\_BLOCK$).

In this section, memory layout and optimization techniques used in Sponge are discussed. First, the way shared memory is utilized for LoT actors is explained. Second, helper threads, a technique that Sponge uses to reduce global memory access time of actors, is discussed. Finally, shared bank conflict resolution in Sponge is explained.

#### 3.1.1 Shared/Global Memory

To deal with high-latency memory access issues, Sponge uses the classification information calculated in the previous phase and tries to alleviate the problem by coalescing the buffer accesses or overlapping a large number of uncoalesced buffer accesses to amortize the cost. As discussed earlier, HiT actors will be mapped to global memory and LoT actors will use the shared memory. The kernel generated for these actors will have a large number of threads, each accessing its own buffer sequentially in global memory. The memory accesses will not be coalesced because the accesses of consecutive threads are not consecutive in the memory. Since the number of threads is large, the overhead of memory accesses will be hidden by the execution of many threads. Figure 6a illustrates how a HiT actor with four pops and four pushes accesses global memory. Since the addresses generated by the first pop operations of the threads are not consecutive in the memory, they are not coalesced.

LoT actors, unlike HiT actors, have a higher compute to memory ratio. Therefore, a LoT actor can use shared memory and have a large number of threads. As shown in Figure 6b, threads of a LoT kernel in a block can use coalesced memory accesses to copy their input (output) buffer to (from) shared memory from (to) global memory. To do so, the threads of a block work as a group and bring parts of data that belong to other threads as well as part of their own data. In this way, consecutive threads' accesses to shared memory will be to consecutive locations and will get coalesced. Since all of the data is in shared memory, all threads in a block will have access to it. Figure 7 shows how the CUDA code needs to be changed to utilize shared memory in LoT actors. In the baseline form (Figure 7a) the input and output buffers are allocated in global memory and the work function directly accesses global memory. If shared memory is used, then two *for loops* are added before and after the work function to copy the data in and out of shared memory, as shown in Figure 7b. The addresses for the memory reads and writes in these *for loops* are set based on the $ThreadID$, and the number of pushes and pops. Before and after the two new *for loops*, $L_1$, $L_2$, barriers (*synchthreads*) are necessary because, as mentioned earlier, each thread does not fetch all of its own data and has to wait for other threads in the block to finish their data-fetch phase.

### 3.2 Memory Layout and Optimization

Memory hierarchy in GPUs is significantly different from both conventional shared memory and distributed memory systems. As mentioned in Section 2.1, efficient use of global memory, shared memory and registers on GPUs is crucial to obtain high performance. Coalescing accesses to global memory can greatly reduce memory access overheads, but it will not be possible without careful memory layout. Utilizing shared memory, which is significantly faster than global memory, is also very beneficial. Due to its limited size, shared memory can restrict the number of threads and degrade the performance. In this section, techniques used for memory layout and optimization in Sponge are discussed.

#### 3.2.1 Helper Threads

The first optimization of this phase is to use *helper* threads to fetch data for the $worker$ threads. In cases where there are not enough threads to efficiently utilize all the SMs for LoT kernels or a HiT actor has a fair number of threads when it is treated as a LoT actor (mapped to shared memory), Sponge uses helper threads to reduce the buffer (i.e. memory) accesses of each thread (push and pop rate). Each helper thread aids some worker threads to bring their data to shared memory in a coalesced way.

Figure 7c shows how the CUDA code is modified. Based on the thread IDs, Sponge generates the helper and worker threads. Helper threads are in charge of handling the data accesses and worker threads are in charge of the computation. In order to avoid control flow divergence, the thread assignment is performed such that the helper and worker threads form complete warps. If the number of worker threads are less than the warp size, then the helper threads are placed in the first set of warps and the worker threads form the last warp. This is done by predicating out the work function for the helper threads and the memory access *for loops* for the worker functions. The *if* statement in Figure 7c do this based on $threadID$. This technique works because control flow divergence negatively affects the performance within one warp but not across warps.

Sponge estimates number of instructions that helper threads will add to each thread and also takes into account the parallelism between the helper and worker threads to calculate how beneficial helper thread optimization will be for both LoT and HiT threads. As illustrated in Figure 7c, Sponge counts the time it takes to run $L_1$, $L_2$, and $L_3$ sections and estimates the total execution time based on the equations in Figure 5. If the total execution time using helper threads is reduced, Sponge generates CUDA code using them.

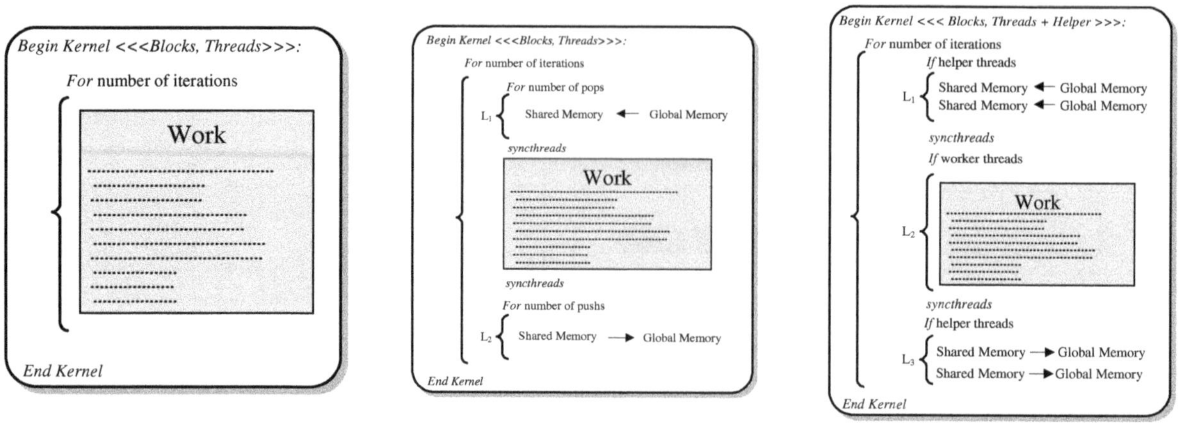


(a) (b) (c)

**Figure 7:** *Part (a) shows the baseline translation for a HiT actor. How shared memory is used in a LoT actor is illustrated in part (b). In part (c) the way Sponge generates CUDA code to divide threads as helpers and workers is shown.*

#### 3.2.2 Bank Conflict Resolution

Shared memory bank conflict is another source of bottleneck in GPU systems. For example, whenever threads of a kernel access their input buffer in shared memory with:

$$data \quad = \quad buffer[baseAddress + s * threadId];$$

threads $threadId$ and $threadId + n$ access the same bank whenever $n$ is a multiple of $m/d$ ($m$ is the number of memory banks) where $d$ is the greatest common divisor of m and $s$. As a consequence, there will be no bank conflicts only if half the warp size is less than or equal to $m/d$. For current NVIDIA devices, this translates to no bank conflict only if d is equal to 1, or in other words, only if $s$ is odd since $m$ is a power of two (16 for GTX 285 [19]). In the StreamIt code, $s$ is the number of pops. To make $s$ odd, if the number of pops is even, Sponge artificially changes the pop rate of an actor by incrementing the pops by one. In this way, an actor with $2k$ pops will use $2k+1$ entries in the memory and the buffers get shifted in the memory. Removing bank conflicts greatly improves the performance of some of the benchmarks. The same technique can be applied for pushes.

### 3.3 Graph Restructuring

In this part, Sponge vertically fuses some actors to improve performance by increasing coalesced memory accesses, removing kernel call overhead, and also increasing instruction overlap. Fusion is not beneficial in all cases because it can increase the memory traffic (push + pop) of a pair of LoT actors and reduce the number of threads (Equation 3). For HiT actors, fusion may increase the memory traffic as a result of register spilling.

The main benefit of fusing HiT actors is replacing uncoalesced memory accesses at the end of the first actor and at the beginning of the second actor with coalesced accesses. The memory accesses become coalesced because the two actors within the fused actor are rate matched. Therefore, the first actor can write to the internal buffer using coalesced memory writes and the second actor can read the same data with coalesced memory reads. Figure 8 illustrates how fusion can lead to coalescing of memory accesses in a simple GPU that has warp size of four and can coalesce two memory accesses into one. In this figure, the memory accesses between actors $A$ (producer with 2 pushes running with 8 threads) and $B$ (consumer with 8 pops running with 2 threads) are shown. $W_{i,j}$ is $j$th push by the $i$th thread of $A$, and $R_{k,m}$ is the $m$th pop of the $k$th thread of $B$. Figure 8a shows how writes and reads are performed between these actors in the case of no fusion. In this case each thread serially writes and reads from global memory which results in all uncoalesced accesses (marked by $U$). If the buffer allocation for $A$ is changed such that its memory accesses can be coalesced (marked by $C$), as shown in Figure 8b, the accesses of threads running $B$ will still be uncoalesced. Figure 8c shows the accesses to the internal buffer between $A$ and $B$ after fusion is performed. The new actor, $(4A)B$, runs with two threads. Since there are 8 pushes and pops between $4A$ and $B$ all the accesses will be coalesced, as shown in Figure 8c.

For the LoT actors, global memory accesses are already coalesced with the help of shared memory. These accesses happen in two *for loops* before and after the work function. Similar to the HiT case, the accesses between the two LoT actors become coalesced. Therefore, the resulting LoT actor does not need to use shared memory anymore. This will result in elimination of a large number of complex address calculations and *for loop* control instructions.

Sponge uses its cost estimation equations to decide if fusing a pair of actors is beneficial or not. For a candidate pair, Sponge calculates the number of cycles for both cases where the resulting actor is HiT or LoT. If in either case the execution time is less than the sum of the original actors' execution times, fusion is performed.

### 3.4 Register Optimization

Registers on GPUs are a precious resource. Efficiently using the registers can greatly improve performance. In this section, two optimizations that Sponge performs to increase register utilization are discussed.

#### 3.4.1 Software Prefetch

To better tolerate long memory access latency, the CUDA threading model allows some warps to make progress while others wait for their memory access results. This mechanism is not effective in some cases where all threads are waiting for their memory access results. This case happens if all threads have very few independent instructions between memory access instructions and the use of the accessed data. Prefetching is a technique that some CUDA programs use to overlap fetching data from global memory for iteration $i+1$ of an actor with compute instructions in iteration $i$ by utilizing the available registers.

Figure 9a shows how software prefetching can be done for LoT actors. Before the main *for loop*, the first batch of data (for iteration 1) is loaded into registers ($L_1$). Once $L_2$ has started, the data is moved from registers into shared memory. At this point, threads have to wait for the shared memory transfers to finish before they

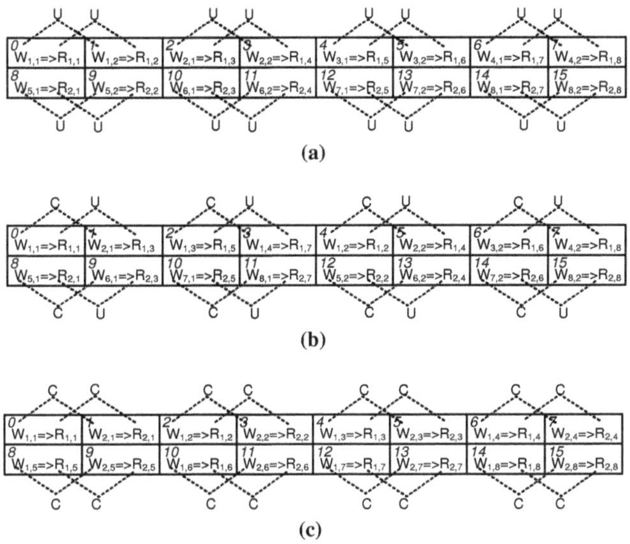

**Figure 8:** *This figure shows the memory accesses between actors A with 2 pushes and 8 threads and B with 8 pops and 2 threads.* $W_{i,j}(R_{i,j})$ *shows* $j$*th memory write (read) performed by* $i$*th thread running actor* $A$ $(B)$*.* $U$ *and* $C$ *denote uncoalesced and coalesced. Part (a) shows the accesses in the base case. Part (b) illustrates the same accesses when the buffer for A is allocated such that its writes are coalesced. Part (c) shows coalesced accesses between these two actors when they are fused as* $(4A)B$ *and executed with two threads. The number on the top left corner of each box shows the memory address of that location.*

can progress because that data is needed for computation after this point. After all threads are done moving the data to shared memory, they pass the barrier synchronization point and begin to load the next batch of data into registers. The key is that the work function does not need the data from these memory accesses and overlapping of compute and memory accesses can happen. Loop $L_4$ has to be wrapped in an *if* statement because the last iteration of the kernel does not need to prefetch any data. This *if* statement does not introduce branch divergence since all the threads take the same path at this point.

One possible downside of this technique is that using additional registers for prefetching can reduce the number of blocks that can run on an $SM$. However, prefetching is beneficial if it significantly reduces the amount of time each thread waits for global memory accesses. Since different classes of NVIDIA GPUs are equipped with different number of registers, Sponge tunes this optimization for each GPU target. If performing prefetching for the whole buffer introduces register spill or reduce the number of concurrent blocks, Sponge tunes the prefetching optimization by applying it to only a fraction of the input buffer.

### 3.4.2 Loop Unrolling

Instruction processing bandwidth on the processing cores of current CUDA graphics engines can negatively affect the performance of an actor. Address calculation and loop control instructions can become important if an actor has small number of computation instructions. In other words, these type of instructions introduce overhead and prevent a kernel from utilizing the peak performance of a GPU. Loop unrolling is one way to reduce the overhead. This optimization can also increase the register utilization by unrolling loops that use registers. The degree of unrolling depends on the number of registers the kernel uses and also the number of registers that are available on the GPU. Since different classes of GPUs are equipped with different number of registers per SM, blindly applying unrolling to the *for-loops* in a kernel may worsen the performance.

An example of the unrolling is shown in Figure 9b. There are five potential *for loops* in a typical LoT actor generated by Sponge, as shown in Figure 9a, 2 for transferring data to and from global memory, 2 for prefetching and 1 for the work function. Depending on the number of registers available on the target GPU and the instruction mix of the kernel, Sponge decides to perform loop unrolling on the *for loops*.

Figure 9b shows how the unrolling is applied to all five *for loops* to both remove the *for loop* overheads and also increase the register utilization. In this example, unrolling factor of two is applied to the *work* function. As shown in Figure 9a, loop $L_1$ is unrolled to $U_1$. Because the work function is unrolled two times, all the corresponding *for loops* now appear twice except $L_4$. Replicating $L_4$ two times will result in having two *if* statements. To remove the conditional branch instruction overhead, these two replicated *for loops* are merged into $U_6$.

### 3.5 A Stream Compilation Example

In this section, a running example, as shown in Figure 10, is used to better illustrate how the optimizations affect the streaming graph. The base graph in Figure 10a has 12 unique actors two of which are in a *splitter-joiner* structure. Each box shows one actor in the program. Each edge in this graph indicates a tape implemented using FIFO queues. The text written inside each box shows how each actor interacts with its input and output tapes. All the actors are stateless except $G$. This actor as well as the source ($A$) and the sink ($H$) actors are mapped to the host processor.

In the classification phase, Sponge will remove the two *splitters* and *joiners* and replace all the copies of $C$ and $E$ with one of each. This is done because GPUs do not support task level parallelism and the *joiner* will introduce synchronization overhead. After this, actors are classified as HiT and LoT based on their memory traffic and computation instructions. LoT actors use shared memory but HiT actors operate on global memory. In the example, actors $D$ and $F$ are identified as HiT actors (shown with a darker color) and $B$, $C$ and $E$ as LoT actors. $[i, j]$ next to each GPU actor shows number of threads ($i$) and number of blocks ($j$) that will run that actor. For the LoT actors, the number of threads depends on the size of shared memory and the memory usage of the actor. For HiT actors, the number of threads is always equal to the maximum number of threads allowed per block because global memory is significantly larger than the actors' memory footprint.

Next, helper threads are used to fetch data from global memory to shared memory more efficiently. After applying this, the number of threads for LoT actors will increase but HiT actors will be running with less threads because they have to use the shared memory. In the example, as shown in Figure 10c, except actor $D$, every actor benefits from using helper threads. If the number of threads for an actor is written as $w + h$, then $w$ shows the number of worker threads and $h$ shows number of helper threads assigned to that actor.

Finally, graph restructuring is performed on the graph and as a result several actors get fused together. Figure 10d shows the result of fusion and then re-applying classification and helper thread optimization. Actor $B$ and $C$ are fused together in a LoT actor and actors $D$, $E$, and $F$ are classified as a HiT actor.

## 4. Experiments

In this section Sponge's optimization techniques are evaluated and compared with two alternative approaches:

1. GPU baseline: All stateless actors of the benchmarks are mapped to the GPU utilizing the maximum number of threads supported ($MAX\_THREAD\_PER\_BLOCK$). In this technique, all of the actors are compiled as HiT actors. Stateful actors as well as source and sink actors are mapped to the host processor.
2. CPU baseline: All the actors are executed sequentially on the CPU.

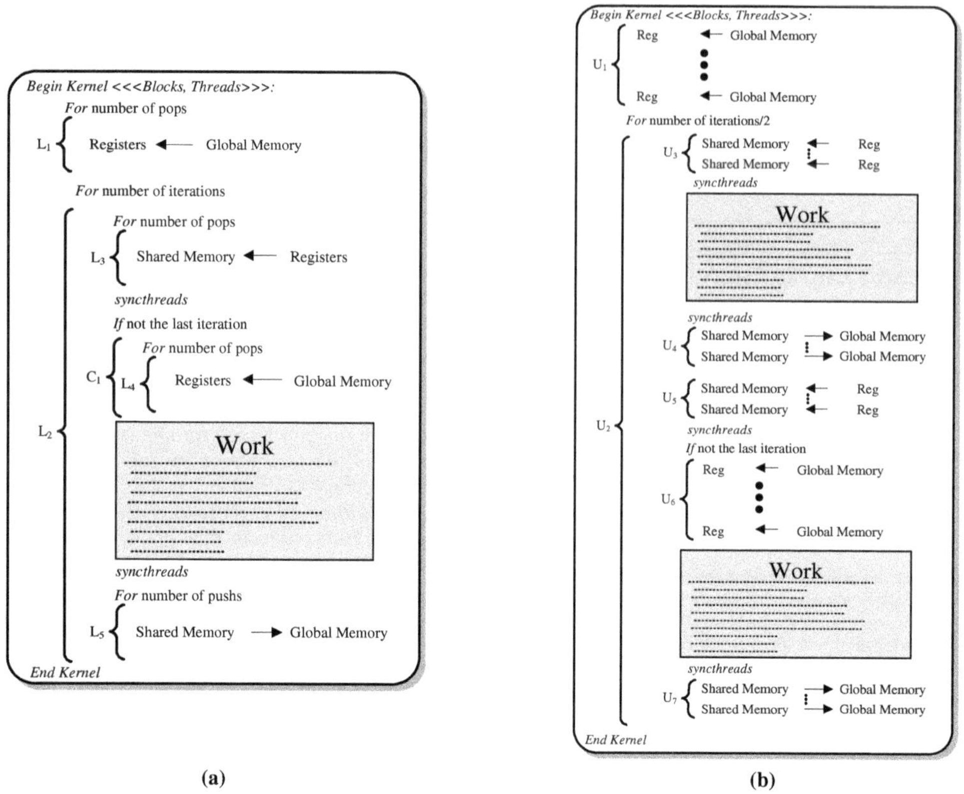


**Figure 9:** *Part (a) shows how prefetching is performed to improve the performance of a kernel. Part (b) depicts the result of unrolling on the kernel in part (a).*

### 4.1 Methodology

A set of benchmarks from the StreamIt suite [26] are used to evaluate Sponge. The benchmarks are compiled and evaluated on a system containing a 3GHz Intel Core 2 Extreme CPU with 6GB of RAM and a GeForce GTX 285 GPU with 2GB DDR3 global memory. Sponge compilation phases are implemented as a compiler backend to the StreamIt compiler. Sponge generates customized CUDA code which is compiled using NVIDIA nvcc 3.1 for execution on the GPU. GCC 4.1 is used to generate the x86 binary for execution on the host processor.

### 4.2 Techniques Performance

In this section, we try to compare the Sponge optimization techniques to the GPU baseline and highlight the effectiveness of each optimization. Figure 11a shows how Sponge-generated CUDA code performs and shows the performance gain of each optimization technique. On average, Sponge improves the performance by 3.2x compared to the GPU baseline.

The first optimization, shared/global memory, which divides actors into two categories LoT and HiT, is one of the most beneficial Sponge techniques. By using shared memory, Sponge is able to coalesce all the memory accesses in LoT actors, therefore performance of benchmarks containing LoT actors will significantly increase. As shown in the Figure 11a, *Matrix Multiply Block* benefits the most because this benchmark has several LoT actors. As a result, most of the actors in *Matrix Multiply Block* have coalesced memory accesses. In some benchmarks, such as *Histogram*, little benefit is seen using this optimization because most actors are HiT actors.

Prefetching and unrolling are two other optimizations illustrated in Figure 11a. These optimizations, collectively, contribute to 3.1% of the total average speedup. Prefetching technique is used only for LoT actors and is useful mostly in applications with many LoT actors such as *Merge sort* and *Bitonic*. Unrolling allows Sponge to utilize unused registers and reduce the number of instructions. This technique can increase the performance of LoT actors that use few registers. *DCT*, *Merge Sort*, *Radix*, and *Bitonic* have such actors and unrolling can increase their performance.

Another effective optimization in Sponge is employing helper threads. As described in the previous sections, helper threads can reduce the execution time of both LoT and HiT actors with two exceptions:

- LoT actors with many threads: In this case, it is not possible to run more threads to help the worker threads. Reducing the number of worker threads would decrease performance.
- HiT actors with few threads: To utilize helper threads, HiT actors would be converted into LoT actors, which have less threads because of the limited shared memory size. Though transferring data to shared memory improves memory performance, too few worker threads can become a bottleneck, underutilizing the SMs and decreasing the overall performance.

As shown in Figure 11a, helper thread optimization effectively increases the performance of *DCT*, *FFT*, *Matrix multiply* and *Merge sort*. For example *DCT* has multiple HiT actors with a large number of worker threads. In this case, coalescing data accesses using shared memory provides enough performance gain that running the actors with less threads will not result in slowdown. On average, helper threads contributes to 16% of the total average speedup compared to the GPU baseline.

Graph restructuring decreases the overhead of kernel launching and uncoalesced memory accesses. As discussed in Section 3.3, there are some cases where fusing two actors may result in degraded performance. Since two actors that are fused must execute together, the number of threads that the resulting actor can run will be less than the number of threads created by running each ac-

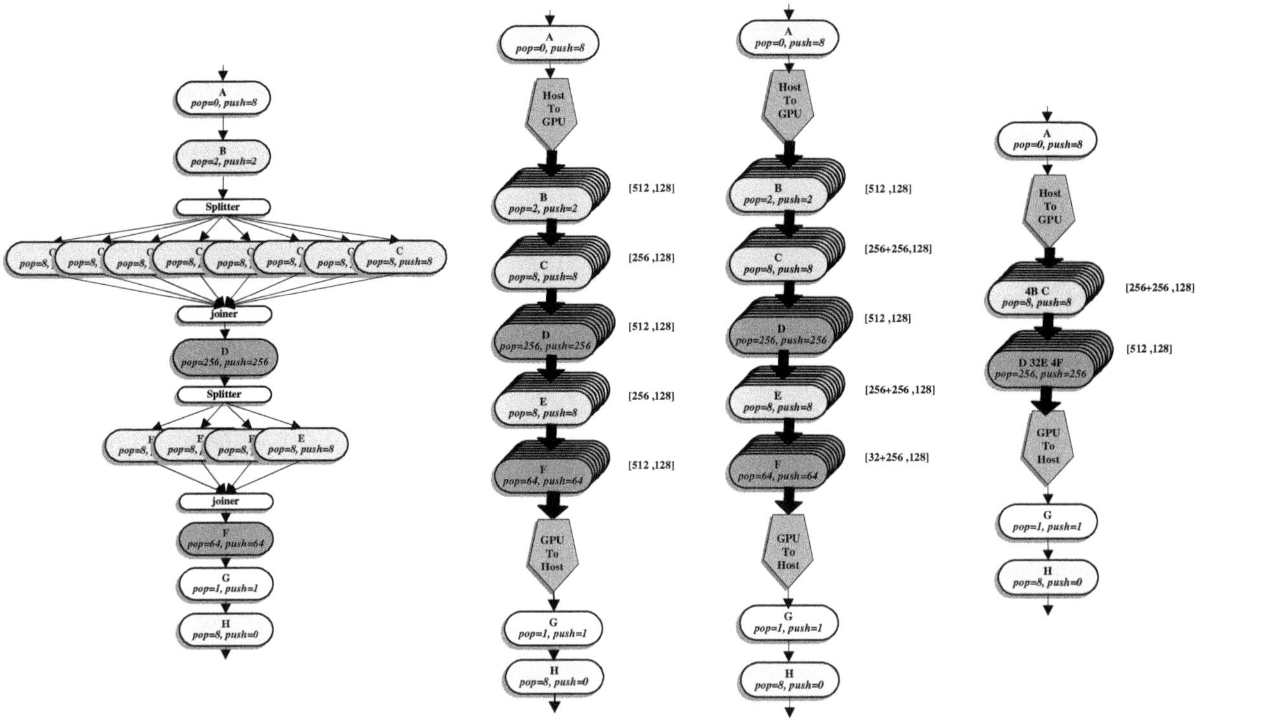


(a) (b) (c) (d)

**Figure 10:** *Part (a) shows a stream graph with 12 unique actors. Part (b) is about how actor classification and graph reorganization affects this graph. In this part, shaded actor are HiT actors. Part (c) illustrates the result of the helper thread optimization. Part (d) depicts the same graph after applying graph restructuring. [i, j] next to each GPU actor shows number of threads (i) and number of blocks (j) that will run that actor. If i is written as $w + h$, $w$ is number of worker threads and $h$ is the number of helper threads.*

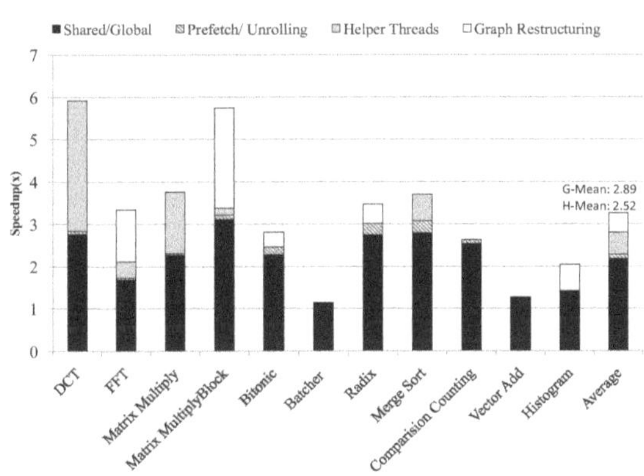


**(a)** *Performance breakdown of Sponge optimizations in comparison to the baseline CUDA code, both running on the GPU.*

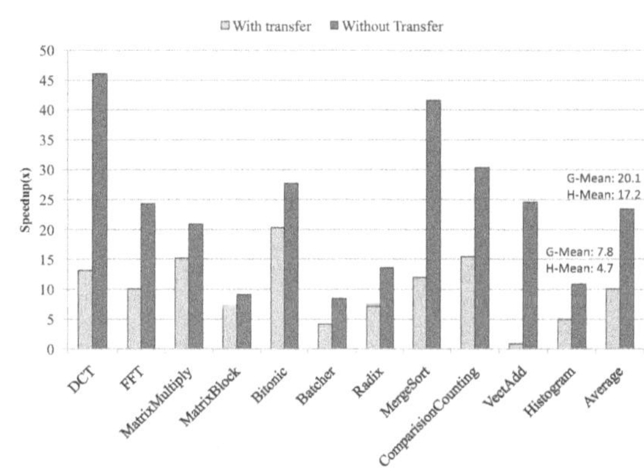


**(b)** *Speedup of Sponge optimized code in comparison to the host CPU with and without data transfer overhead.*

**Figure 11:** *Effectiveness of Sponge optimization techniques on StreamIt benchmarks.*

tor separately. Because the reduction of threads can decrease the performance, Sponge intelligently decides whether or not to use this optimization. Several benchmarks, such as *FFT*, have large pipelines of actors that are all fused together by Sponge. Graph restructuring provides a large portion of the speedup for these types of benchmarks. Since *Batcher* and *Vector Add* have only one actor, fusion cannot increase their performance. In *Merge Sort*, the opportunity for performing fusion is minimal because most of the actors in this benchmark are isolated from each other and do not form a pipeline.

### 4.3 Overall performance

Figure 11b presents the speedup of Sponge's generated CUDA applications against the CPU baseline, both with and without the data transfer time between the GPU and CPU. On average, Sponge achieves about 20x speedup compared to running each benchmark completely on the CPU. The only case that the CPU baseline outperforms Sponge is *Vector Add* including the data transfer overhead. In this special case, the memory to compute ratio in *Vector Add* is very high. Although the GPU can execute the *Vector Add* actor 10x faster than CPU, the overhead of transferring the data

| GTX 285 | | | | | | | | | | | |
|---|---|---|---|---|---|---|---|---|---|---|---|
| | DCT | FFT | MM | MM Block | Bitonic | Batcher | Radix | Merge Sort | Comp Count | Vect Add | Histogram |
| Shared | 66.7 | 66.7 | 62.5 | 80 | 100 | 100 | 100 | 100 | 100 | 100 | 33.3 |
| Prefetch | 0 | 4.2 | 12.5 | 0 | 40.7 | 0 | 0 | 34.8 | 13 | 0 | 0 |
| Unrolling | 50 | 70.8 | 37.5 | 80 | 50.7 | 100 | 100 | 30.4 | 63.2 | 0 | 33.3 |
| Helping Threads | 50 | 16.7 | 25 | 20 | 0.7 | 0 | 0 | 52.1 | 0 | 0 | 0 |
| Tesla C2050 | | | | | | | | | | | |
| Shared | 100 | 100 | 87.5 | 93.3 | 100 | 100 | 100 | 100 | 100 | 100 | 33.3 |
| Prefetch | 0 | 41.7 | 12.5 | 6.7 | 1.5 | 0 | 100 | 0 | 100 | 0 | 66.7 |
| Unrolling | 50 | 33.3 | 50 | 60 | 34.4 | 100 | 0 | 0 | 0 | 0 | 0 |
| Helping Threads | 50 | 0 | 25 | 6.7 | 0.7 | 0 | 0 | 0 | 0 | 0 | 33.3 |

**Table 1:** *This table shows how Sponge optimizes each benchmark differently for two GPU targets. For each benchmark and target, the percentage of actors that are optimized by each optimization is shown.*

between the host and GPU global memory decreases the overall performance.

### 4.4 Portability

Quantifying portability is inherently a hard problem. To show how Sponge solves the portability issue, we show how it optimizes each benchmark differently for two GPUs, Tesla C2050 and GeForce GTX 285. The C2050 is based on the newer NVIDIA architecture (Fermi) which has 48KB of shared memory, 32K registers and 420 streaming processors, providing Sponge with more resources to exploit. Table 1 shows how Sponge makes different decisions based on the target architecture. This table illustrates the percentage of actors in each benchmark optimized using various optimizations in Sponge. As shown in Table 1, Sponge is able to classify more actors as LoT actors and utilize the larger shared memory in C2050. The number of registers also affects how Sponge performs unrolling and prefetching for each target. In general, Sponge adopts its compilation strategy based on the characteristics of the GPU target without any source code modification or programmer involvement.

## 5. Case Study and Future Work

Sponge is designed to reduce the performance gap between automatically generated CUDA programs and hand-optimized ones. In this section two hand-optimized CUDA programs from the NVIDIA SDK are analyzed to highlight the reasons for performance differences between Sponge-generated and hand-optimized CUDA code.

### 5.1 Black-Scholes

The *Black-Scholes* algorithm is a differential equation that can predict how the value of an option changes. This equation reads five parameters from the input data and computes the price for an option call and an option put and writes these two values to the output. In the code generated by Sponge for GTX 285 GPU, there is only one kernel that pops five memory element from the input and calculates the output and pushes two results to the output buffer. This actor is classified as an LoT actor. Therefore, Sponge uses shared memory to coalesce all the buffer accesses in that actor. In the hand-optimized code, only one kernel is launched as well, but each parameter is placed in a different array. The kernel has five input arrays and two output arrays. By using this technique, all threads are able to read data from each input array and write data to each output array consecutively allowing all memory accesses to be coalesced. Coalescing all accesses without using shared memory reduces the number of instructions in the hand-optimized version. As a result, the performance of the hand-written program is 1.3x better than Sponge's generated code.

This input/output buffer re-mapping is not currently done in Sponge because StreamIt does not support actors with multi-inputs and multi-outputs streams. All input and output streams between StreamIt actors are through a single shared buffer between the actors. Future work will try to represent these multiple input/output streams in StreamIt so the compiler can detect such cases and improve memory layout for GPUs.

### 5.2 Histogram

The *histogram* benchmark computes the distribution of pixel intensities within an image. *Histogram* is implemented using a technique called stream reduction, which is common in many GPU applications. Each phase of stream reduction removes some elements of input data, performs computation on them, and sends the results as a new input to the next phase. The *histogram* benchmark has several phases. In the first phase, the input data array is divided into fixed size blocks. In the second phase, a sub-histogram for each block is computed. In the final phase, all the sub-histograms are collated into a single histogram.

A StreamIt graph of stream reduction is shown in Figure 12. The number of actors in these type of benchmarks is data-size dependent, therefore, as the size of the input data grows, the number of phases increases and the overhead of launching the kernels becomes dominant. Sponge can fuse all of these phases together but the final actor would have a large *pop* rate. Since the *pop* rate of this actor is very large, it is not possible to use the limited shared memory to coalesce its memory accesses. In both cases, the large number of kernels and the uncoalesced memory accesses result in degraded performance.

In the hand-optimized CUDA implementation, there is only one kernel for all of the phases of the reduction but the number of threads that do the actual work in each phase is different. As a result, the hand-written CUDA histogram benchmark outperforms Sponge's generate CUDA code by 5x.

We would like to enhance the performance of Sponge in this type of benchmarks by detecting the stream reduction subgraph in the compiler and replacing them with one specialized stream reduction kernel that mimics the behavior of the hand-optimized CUDA.

## 6. Related Work

The most common language GPU programmers use to write CUDA code is "C for CUDA" (C with NVIDIA extensions and certain restrictions). Tuning these C like programs is highly challenging because managing the amount of on-chip memory used per thread, the total number of threads per multiprocessor, and the pattern of off-chip memory accesses are some of the problems that developer need to solve manually to achieve good performance [23]. To alleviate this burden, recent studies has been done to automatically manage these parameters in CUDA programs.

One study, closely related to Sponge, is the optimizing compiler introduced by Udupa et al. [27]. They compile stream programs for GPUs using software pipelining techniques. In the software pipelining approach, different actors from different iterations

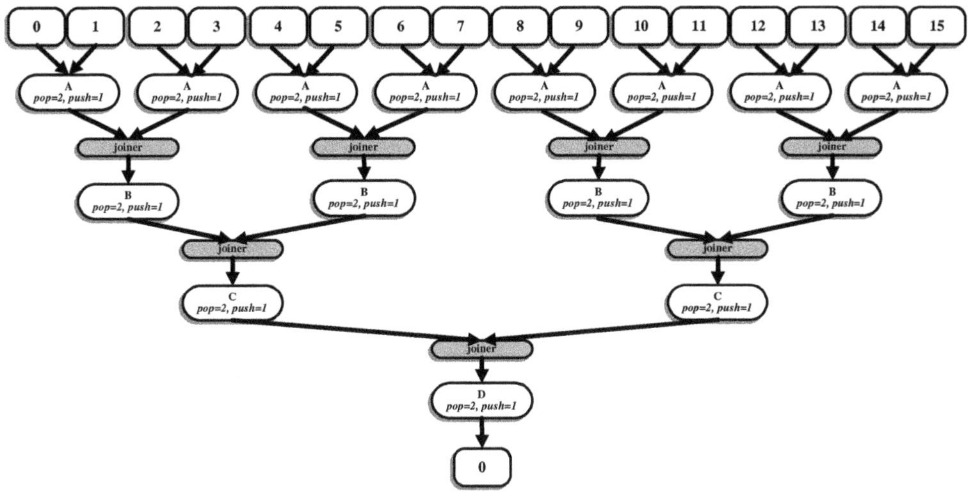


**Figure 12:** *This graph shows the stream graph of a generic stream reduction kernel.*

are simultaneously processed. Their technique, though promising, does not perform well on GPUs because it exploits task-level parallelism and is not able to exploit the massive amount of data-level parallelism power of GPUs. There has been recent work [29] on GPU compilation for memory optimization and parallelism management. The input to this compiler is a naive GPU kernel function and their compiler analyzes the code and generates optimized CUDA code. This work is distinctively different from this work because Sponge is able to exploit the information in the high level stream graph and perform kernel-level optimizations specific to StreamIt, such as graph restructuring, and then apply lower optimizations , such as memory and thread hierarchy management.

CUDA-Lite [30] is another compilation framework that takes naive GPU kernel functions as input and tries to coalesce all memory accesses by using shared memory. Programmers need to provide annotations describing certain properties of data structures and code regions designated for GPU execution. Our work is different because Sponge does not need any annotations. Sponge also uses shared memory to coalesce memory accesses and can maximize the utilization of various resources on GPUs, such as registers. Another difference is that when the size of shared memory limits the number of worker threads, Sponge is able to insert helper threads to accelerate the transferring of data between global and shared memory. hiCUDA [8] is a high level directive based compiler framework for CUDA programming where programmers need to insert directives to define the boundaries of the kernel function into sequential C code. Another work in the area of automatic CUDA generation is [16]. The Authors in this work generate optimized CUDA programs from OpenMP programs. They do not use shared memory in their compiler for coalescing memory accesses. Hong et al. [9] propose an analytical performance model for GPUs that compilers can use to predict the behavior of their generated code. Fung et al. [4] regroup threads into new warps to minimize the number of divergent warps. Chen et al. [2] use communication and computation threads to overlap the data exchange of the boundary nodes between adjacent thread blocks. This is fundamentally different from what Sponge achieves using helper threads by performing parallel prefetching of data.

MCUDA [24] tries to compile CUDA programs for a conventional shared memory architecture. MCUDA can be used to increase the performance of traditional shared memory parallel systems using CUDA optimization techniques. With the stream programming model, it is possible to use architecture specific optimizations for a wide range of architectures. Researchers have already proposed ways to map and optimize synchronous data-flow languages to SIMD engines [12], distributed shared memory systems [14], and also field programmable gate arrays [10].

Performing runtime re-compilation of GPU binaries for adapting code to different targets is another approach that can provide portability across GPUs. OpenCL [13] is one the approaches taken by industry to achieve portability. We believe OpenCL in its current form suffers from the same inefficiencies as CUDA and does not provide an architecture independent solution.

There is a large body of literature that deals with exploiting parallelism in streaming codes for better performance. The most recent and relevant works include compilation of new streaming languages such as StreamIt, Brook [1], Sequoia [3], and Cg [18] to multi-cores or data-parallel architectures. For example, Gordon et al. [6] and [5] perform stream graph refinements to statically determine the best mapping of a StreamIt program to a multi-core CPU. Liao et al. applies classic affine partitioning techniques to exploit the properties of stream operators [28]. There is also a rich history of scheduling and resource allocation techniques developed in Ptolemy that make fundamental contributions to stream-scheduling (e.g., [7, 22]). In a recent work [25], the authors talk about the usefulness of different features of StreamIt to a wide range of streaming applications. Several works, such as [11], propose techniques to dynamically recompile streaming application based on availability of resources in heterogeneous system. Sponge can be a complementary addition to these works as GPUs are becoming a commodity in heterogeneous systems.

## 7. Conclusion

Heterogeneous systems, where sequential work is done on traditional processors and parallelizable work is offloaded to a specialized computing engine, will be ubiquitous in the future. Among the different solutions that can take advantage of this parallelism, GPUs are the most popular solution and have been shown to provide significant performance, power efficiency and cost benefits for general purpose computing in highly-parallel computing domains. GPUs achieve their high performance and efficiency by providing a massively parallel architecture with hundreds of in-order cores and exposing parallelism mechanism and also the memory hierarchy to the programmer. One key to maximizing the performance in these future heterogeneous systems will be to efficiently utilize not only the host processor, but also the GPU.

While GPUs provide a very desirable target platform for accelerating parallel workloads, their programming complexity poses a significant challenge to application developers. Languages, such as CUDA, alleviate the complexity problem to some extent but fail at abstracting the underlying GPU architecture. Therefore, managing the amount of on-chip memory used per thread, the total number of threads per multiprocessor, and the pattern of off-chip memory accesses are problems that developers still need to manage in order to maximize GPU utilization.

In this work, we propose Sponge; a streaming compiler for the StreamIt language that is capable of performing an array of optimizations on stream graphs and generate efficient CUDA code for GPUs. Optimizations in Sponge facilitate a write-once software paradigm where programmers can rely on the compiler to automatically create customized CUDA for a wide variety of GPU targets. The optimizations in Sponge improve the performance compared to naive CUDA implementations by an average of 3.2x. Finally, as a case study, we compare the performance and implementation of two hand-optimized CUDA benchmarks, Black-Scholes and Histogram. For Black-Scholes, Sponge is able to achieve within 30% of the performance of the hand-optimized CUDA code. Future work on Sponge will improve automatic detection of certain memory layout characteristics and stream graph representations that are currently not supported.

## Acknowledgement

Much gratitude goes to the anonymous referees who provided excellent feedback on this work. We also thank Todd Mowry for shepherding this paper. This research was supported by ARM Ltd. and the National Science Foundation under grants CNS-0964478 and CCF-0916689.

## References


[1] I. Buck et al. Brook for GPUs: Stream computing on graphics hardware. *ACM Transactions on Graphics*, 23(3):777–786, Aug. 2004.

[2] J. Chen, Z. Huang, F. Su, J.-K. Peir, J. Ho, and L. Peng. Weak execution ordering - exploiting iterative methods on many-core gpus. In *Proc. of the 2010 IEEE Symposium on Performance Analysis of Systems and Software*, pages 154–163, 2010.

[3] K. Fatahalian, D. R. Horn, T. J. Knight, L. Leem, M. Houston, J. Y. Park, M. Erez, M. Ren, A. Aiken, W. J. Dally, and P. Hanrahan. Sequoia: programming the memory hierarchy. In *Proceedings of the 2006 ACM/IEEE conference on Supercomputing*, page 83, 2006.

[4] W. W. L. Fung, I. Sham, G. Yuan, and T. M. Aamodt. Dynamic warp formation and scheduling for efficient GPU control flow. In *Proc. of the 40th Annual International Symposium on Microarchitecture*, pages 407–420, 2007.

[5] M. I. Gordon, W. Thies, and S. Amarasinghe. Exploiting coarse-grained task, data, and pipeline parallelism in stream programs. In *14th International Conference on Architectural Support for Programming Languages and Operating Systems*, pages 151–162, 2006.

[6] M. I. Gordon, W. Thies, M. Karczmarek, J. Lin, A. S. Meli, A. A. Lamb, C. Leger, J. Wong, H. Hoffmann, D. Maze, and S. Amarasinghe. A stream compiler for communication-exposed architectures. In *Tenth International Conference on Architectural Support for Programming Languages and Operating Systems*, pages 291–303, Oct. 2002.

[7] S. Ha and E. A. Lee. Compile-time scheduling and assignment of data-flow program graphs with data-dependent iteration. *IEEE Transactions on Computers*, 40(11):1225–1238, 1991.

[8] T. Han and T. Abdelrahman. hicuda: High-level gpgpu programming. *IEEE Transactions on Parallel and Distributed Systems*, (99):1–1, 2010.

[9] S. Hong and H. Kim. An analytical model for a gpu architecture with memory-level and thread-level parallelism awareness. In *Proc. of the 36th Annual International Symposium on Computer Architecture*, pages 152–163, 2009.

[10] A. Hormati, M. Kudlur, D. Bacon, S. Mahlke, and R. Rabbah. Optimus: Efficient realization of streaming applications on FPGAs. In *Proc. of the 2008 International Conference on Compilers, Architecture, and Synthesis for Embedded Systems*, pages 41–50, Oct. 2008.

[11] A. H. Hormati, Y. Choi, M. Kudlur, R. Rabbah, T. Mudge, and S. Mahlke. Flextream: Adaptive compilation of streaming applications for heterogeneous architectures. In *Proc. of the 18th International Conference on Parallel Architectures and Compilation Techniques*, pages 214–223, 2009.

[12] A. H. Hormati, Y. Choi, M. Woh, M. Kudlur, T. Mudge, and S. Mahlke. Macross: Macro-simdization of streaming applications. In *18th International Conference on Architectural Support for Programming Languages and Operating Systems*, pages 285–296, 2010.

[13] KHRONOS Group. OpenCL - the open standard for parallel programming of heterogeneous systems, 2010.

[14] M. Kudlur and S. Mahlke. Orchestrating the execution of stream programs on multicore platforms. In *Proc. of the '08 Conference on Programming Language Design and Implementation*, pages 114–124, June 2008.

[15] E. Lee and D. Messerschmitt. Synchronous data flow. *Proceedings of the IEEE*, 75(9):1235–1245, 1987.

[16] S. Lee, S.-J. Min, and R. Eigenmann. Openmp to gpgpu: a compiler framework for automatic translation and optimization. In *Proc. of the 14th ACM SIGPLAN Symposium on Principles and Practice of Parallel Programming*, pages 101–110, 2009.

[17] V. W. Lee, C. Kim, J. Chhugani, M. Deisher, D. Kim, A. D. Nguyen, N. Satish, M. Smelyanskiy, S. Chennupaty, P. Hammarlund, R. Singhal, and P. Dubey. Debunking the 100x GPU vs. CPU myth: an evaluation of throughput computing on CPU and GPU. In *Proc. of the 37th Annual International Symposium on Computer Architecture*, pages 451–460, 2010.

[18] W. Mark, R. Glanville, K. Akeley, and J. Kilgard. Cg: A system for programming graphics hardware in a C-like language. In *Proc. of the* $30^{th}$ *International Conference on Computer Graphics and Interactive Techniques*, pages 893–907, July 2003.

[19] NVIDIA. *CUDA Programming Guide*, June 2007. http://developer.download.nvidia.com/compute/cuda.

[20] NVIDIA. Fermi: Nvidias next generation cuda compute architecture, 2009. http://www.nvidia.com/content/PDF/fermi_white_papers/NVIDIA_Fermi_Compute_Architecture_Whitepaper.pdf.

[21] NVIDIA. Gpus are only up to 14 times faster than cpus says intel, 2010. http://blogs.nvidia.com/ntersect/2010/06/gpus-are-only-up-to-14-times-faster-than-cpus-says-intel.html.

[22] J. L. Pino, S. S. Bhattacharyya, and E. A. Lee. A hierarchical multiprocessor scheduling framework for synchronous dataflow graphs. Technical Report UCB/ERL M95/36, University of California, Berkeley, May 1995.

[23] S. Ryoo, C. I. Rodrigues, S. S. Baghsorkhi, S. S. Stone, D. B. Kirk, and W. mei W. Hwu. Optimization principles and application performance evaluation of a multithreaded gpu using cuda. In *Proc. of the 13th ACM SIGPLAN Symposium on Principles and Practice of Parallel Programming*, pages 73–82, 2008.

[24] J. A. Stratton, S. S. Stone, and W.-M. W. Hwu. Mcuda: An efficient implementation of cuda kernels for multi-core cpus. In *Proc. of the 13th ACM SIGPLAN Symposium on Principles and Practice of Parallel Programming*, pages 16–30, 2008.

[25] W. Thies and S. Amarasinghe. An empirical characterization of stream programs and its implications for language and compiler design. In *Proc. of the 19th International Conference on Parallel Architectures and Compilation Techniques*, page To Appear, 2010.

[26] W. Thies, M. Karczmarek, and S. P. Amarasinghe. StreamIt: A language for streaming applications. In *Proc. of the 2002 International Conference on Compiler Construction*, pages 179–196, 2002.

[27] A. Udupa, R. Govindarajan, and M. J. Thazhuthaveetil. Software pipelined execution of stream programs on gpus. In *Proc. of the 2009 International Symposium on Code Generation and Optimization*, pages 200–209, 2009.

[28] S. wei Liao, Z. Du, G. Wu, and G.-Y. Lueh. Data and computation transformations for brook streaming applications on multiprocessors. *Proc. of the 2006 International Symposium on Code Generation and Optimization*, 0(1):196–207, 2006.

[29] Y. Yang, P. Xiang, J. Kong, and H. Zhou. A gpgpu compiler for memory optimization and parallelism management. In *Proc. of the '10 Conference on Programming Language Design and Implementation*, pages 86–97, 2010.

[30] S. zee Ueng, M. Lathara, S. S. Baghsorkhi, and W. mei W. Hwu. Cuda-lite: Reducing gpu programming complexity. In *Proc. of the 21st Workshop on Languages and Compilers for Parallel Computing*, pages 1–15, 2008.

# Inter-core Prefetching for Multicore Processors Using Migrating Helper Threads

Md Kamruzzaman Steven Swanson Dean M. Tullsen

Computer Science and Engineering
University of California, San Diego
{mkamruzz,swanson,tullsen}@cs.ucsd.edu

## Abstract

Multicore processors have become ubiquitous in today's systems, but exploiting the parallelism they offer remains difficult, especially for legacy application and applications with large serial components. The challenge, then, is to develop techniques that allow multiple cores to work in concert to accelerate a single thread. This paper describes inter-core prefetching, a technique to exploit multiple cores to accelerate a single thread. Inter-core prefetching extends existing work on helper threads for SMT machines to multicore machines.

Inter-core prefetching uses one compute thread and one or more prefetching threads. The prefetching threads execute on cores that would otherwise be idle, prefetching the data that the compute thread will need. The compute thread then migrates between cores, following the path of the prefetch threads, and finds the data already waiting for it. Inter-core prefetching works with existing hardware and existing instruction set architectures. Using a range of state-of-the-art multiprocessors, this paper characterizes the potential benefits of the technique with microbenchmarks and then measures its impact on a range of memory intensive applications. The results show that inter-core prefetching improves performance by an average of 31 to 63%, depending on the architecture, and speeds up some applications by as much as 2.8×. It also demonstrates that inter-core prefetching reduces energy consumption by between 11 and 26% on average.

***Categories and Subject Descriptors*** D.3.4 [*Programming Languages*]: Processors–Optimization

***General Terms*** Languages, Performance

***Keywords*** chip multiprocessors, helper threads, compilers, single-thread performance

## 1. Introduction

Although multi-core processors have become ubiquitous over the past decade, leveraging the parallelism they offer to increase application performance remains challenging. There are several reasons for this, including the prevalence of non-parallelized legacy code, the difficulty of parallel programming, and the inherently serial nature of many programs and algorithms. Even in applications that are amenable to parallelization, the applicability of multicore processors has its bounds: as manufacturers supply an increasing number of cores, more and more applications will discover their scalability limits. Furthermore, Amdahl's law dictates that the more hardware parallelism is available, the more critical sequential performance becomes.

For many applications, then, the only way to get parallel speedup is to exploit non-traditional parallelism – to use multiple cores to accelerate the execution of a single thread. For single-threaded legacy codes, this allows the multicore processor to increase performance without altering the program. Non-traditional parallelism allows programs with limited parallelism to profitably use several cores per thread, increasing the application's scalability.

Previous work [5, 8, 9, 17, 18, 20, 22, 33] has demonstrated the use of "helper threads" which run concurrently in separate contexts of a simultaneous multithreading (SMT) processor and significantly improve single thread performance. Helper thread prefetching has advantages over traditional prefetching mechanisms – it can follow more complex patterns than either hardware prefetchers or in-code software prefetchers, and it does not stop when the main thread stalls, since the prefetch threads and the main thread are not coupled together. However, SMT prefetching has its limitations. The helper thread competes with the main thread for pipeline resources, cache bandwidth, TLB entries, and even cache space. The helper thread cannot target more distant levels of the cache hierarchy without thrashing in the L1 cache. In addition, core parallelism is typically more abundant than thread parallelism – even on a 4-core Nehalem, only 1 SMT thread is available for prefetching. Perhaps most importantly, not all multicores support SMT.

This paper describes and evaluates helper threads that run on separate cores of a multicore and/or multi-socket computer system. Multiple threads running on separate cores can significantly improve overall performance by aggressively prefetching data into the cache of one core while the main thread executes on another core. We call this technique *inter-core prefetching*. When the prefetcher has prefetched a cache's worth of data, it moves on to another core and continues prefetching. Meanwhile, when the main thread arrives at the point where it will access the prefetched data, it migrates to the core that the prefetcher recently vacated. It arrives and finds most of the data it will need is waiting for it, and memory accesses that would have been misses to main memory become cache hits.

Inter-core prefetching can target both distant shared caches and caches private to the core. Inter-core prefetching is especially attractive because it works with currently available hardware and system software. Thus, it would be easy to incorporate in a compiler or runtime system. Previous approaches have required fundamental changes to the microarchitecture or were limited to prefetching into shared caches.



*ASPLOS'11,* March 5–11, 2011, Newport Beach, California, USA.

This paper describes inter-core prefetching and our implementation under Linux. We characterize the potential impact of inter-core prefetching on a range of currently-available multicore processors running focused microbenchmarks and then demonstrate its impact on a wide range of memory-intensive applications. Our results show that inter-core prefetching improves performance by an average of 31 to 63%, depending on the architecture, and speeds up some applications by as much as 2.8×. We also demonstrate that inter-core prefetching reduces energy consumption by between 11 and 26% on average. Finally, we show that because of the separation of resources, inter-core prefetching is more effective than SMT thread prefetching.

The remainder of this paper is organized as follows: Section 2 places inter-core prefetching in context with other work on non-traditional parallelism. Section 3 describes the inter-core prefetching technique in detail. Sections 4 and 5 contain our methodology and results, and Section 6 concludes.

## 2. Related Work

Prefetching is an important technique to speed up memory-intensive applications. There has been significant work on both hardware prefetchers [6, 15] and software controlled prefetchers [2, 7, 25]. The introduction of multithreaded and multicore architectures introduced new opportunities for prefetchers. Multithreaded architectures are a natural target, because threads share the entire cache hierarchy.

Helper thread prefetchers [5, 8, 9, 14, 17, 18, 20–22, 31, 33] accelerate computation by executing prefetch code in another SMT context. Normally, these techniques predict future load addresses by doing some computation in the helper thread and prefetch the corresponding data to the nearest level of shared cache. In many cases, the prefetch code comes from the main thread, allowing those threads to follow arbitrarily complex prefetch patterns.

There are several ways to generate helper threads. The work in [9] uses hand-built helper threads while, Kim and Yeung [18] describe compiler techniques to generate the reduced version statically with the help of profiling. Zhang, et al. [32] and Lu, et al. [21] describe the generation of helper threads in dynamic compilation systems. Collins, et al. [8] generate the helper threads completely in hardware.

Prior research has also targeted prefetching across cores. In Slipstream Processors [14], a reduced version of the program runs ahead of the main program in another core. Multiple specialized hardware pipes transport information (including loaded values) from one to the other. Lu, et al. [21] demonstrate helper thread prefetching on a CMP, but that work is limited to prefetching into a cache that is shared by the main core and the prefetch core. Brown, et al. [3] propose changes to CMP hardware and coherence to enable a thread on one core to effectively prefetch for a thread on a separate core. In contrast to these approaches, inter-core prefetching enables cross-core prefetching into private caches with no new hardware support. Since it requires no special hardware support, inter-core prefetching can work between sockets in a single system. It also works across CMPs from multiple vendors.

Gummaraju, et al. [12] implement a compilation framework that maps a program written for stream processors to general purpose processors. In their system, there are three threads – one for execution, one for data prefetching, and one that manages execution and prefetching. They target SMT threads.

Other research attempts to leverage the hardware parallelism of multicores to accelerate serial execution in other ways. Speculative multithreading [19, 23, 28, 30] uses multiple hardware contexts or cores to execute different parts of the serial execution in parallel and then does runtime verification of correctness. Mitosis [28] additionally uses helper threads to precompute dependent data.

Prescient instruction prefetch [1] is another helper thread-based technique that improves performance by prefetching instructions instead of data.

Other work aggregates cache capacity in multicore/multiprocessor systems to hide memory latency. Cooperative Caching [4] proposes a hardware technique to aggregate private caches. The technique stores cache lines evicted from one private cache to another private cache and ensures maximum utilization of the cache space by keeping a single copy of the same cache line and performing cache-to-cache transfers as needed. Michaud [24] proposes a hardware mechanism to migrate threads and distribute data over the aggregate cache space.

Data Spreading [16] is a software-only mechanism to aggregate the space of multiple private caches. The technique transforms a program to leverage the aggregate cache capacity via compiler-directed migrations. They show that data spreading can provide both performance and power benefits, if the working set fits in the aggregate cache space. However, data spreading does not provide benefit if the working set is too large or the program does not have a repetitive access pattern. Inter-core prefetching removes these two limitations by prefetching data into the next cache. Because of this, inter-core prefetching's performance is much less sensitive to the actual cache size or access pattern.

Using separate threads to access memory and perform computation is similar in spirit to decoupled access/execute architectures [29], but inter-core prefetching accomplishes this without specialized hardware. Decoupled access/execute architectures use a queue to pass data from a memory thread to a compute thread. The queue requires that the two threads be tightly coupled, and that the memory thread correctly compute the result of all branches. As a result, there is rarely enough "slack" between the threads to allow the memory thread to issue memory requests far enough in advance to fully hide their latency. The Explicitly-Decoupled architecture [11] uses the queue only for passing branch outcomes and shares the entire cache hierarchy to get the advantage of prefetching. In our scheme, the private cache of a helper core serves as the "queue", but because inter-core prefetching places no ordering constraints on the accesses, it can completely decouple the threads.

Unlike helper thread prefetching, runahead execution [10, 26] does not require extra hardware contexts or cores. During the long latency load operation, instead of blocking, it assumes a dummy value and switches to the runahead mode to continue execution. When the original load operation is satisfied, it switches back to the normal execution. This improves memory level parallelism but still places all of the burden of prefetching, demand misses, and execution on a single core.

## 3. Inter-core Prefetching

Inter-core prefetching allows a program to use multiple processor cores to accelerate a single thread of execution. The program uses one to perform the computation (i.e., the *main thread*). The other cores run *prefetching threads*, which prefetch data for the main thread. The two types of threads migrate between cores with the prefetching threads leading the way. Thus, when the main thread arrives on a core, much of the data it needs is waiting for it. The result is reduced average memory access time for the main thread and an increase in overall performance. Inter-core prefetching is a software-only technique and requires no special support from the processor's instruction set, the operating system, caches, or coherence.

Inter-core prefetching works by dividing program execution into *chunks*. A chunk often corresponds to a set of loop iterations, but chunk boundaries can occur anywhere in a program's execution. The *chunk size* describes the memory footprint of a chunk. So, a 256 KB chunk might correspond to a set of loop iterations that will

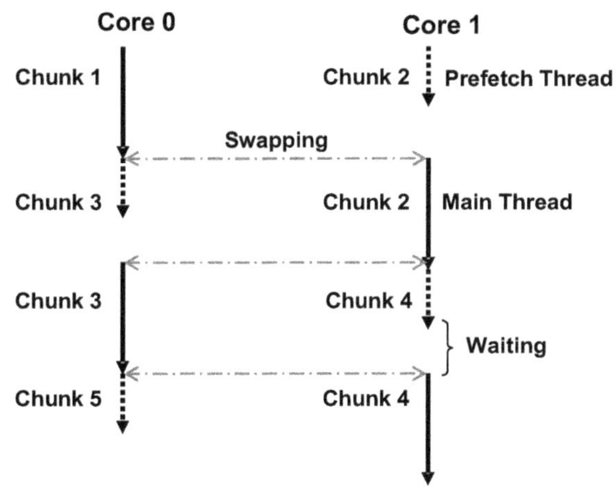


**Figure 1.** Program execution path for inter-core prefetching. The main thread and the prefetch thread swap cores repeatedly, when the main thread reaches a new chunk of data.

access 256 KB of data. For example, if a loop touches 1 MB of data in 100 iterations, then a 256 KB chunk would consist of 25 iterations, a 512 KB chunk would consist of 50 iterations.

Both the main thread and prefetch thread execute one chunk at a time. In the main thread, the chunked code is very similar to the original code, except for the calls to the run-time that implement migration.

The prefetch thread executes a *distilled* [9, 18, 28, 33] version of the main thread, with just enough code to compute addresses and bring the necessary data into the cache. We will use the term prefetch slice, or *p-slice* (terminology borrowed from prior work) to describe the code that the prefetch thread executes to prefetch the data.

Figure 1 illustrates inter-core prefetching with one main thread (solid line) and one prefetcher thread (dotted line) executing on two cores. Execution begins with the main thread executing chunk 1 and the prefetcher executing chunk 2. Once they complete their chunks, they swap cores and the main thread starts on chunk 2 while the prefetcher moves on to chunk 3.

Sometimes, multiple prefetch threads are useful. In a four-core system, three cores would prefetch chunks 2-4 while the main thread executes chunk 1. When the main thread starts executing chunk 2, the prefetch thread for chunk 2 would move on to chunk 5. In this scenario, each prefetcher thread has 3 chunks worth of time to finish prefetching the chunk.

Our implementation of inter-core prefetching comprises three principal components. First, a program analysis algorithm identifies chunk boundaries in the original program. Second, a p-slice generator creates a distilled version of the code for the chunks. Finally, the inter-core prefetching library provides a mechanism to keep the main thread and the prefetcher threads synchronized as they migrate between cores.

Below we describe the key components of inter-core prefetching in detail and present an example that illustrates inter-thread prefetching in action.

### 3.1 Identifying chunks

A chunk is a sequence of executed instructions which access a portion of the application's address space that matches (as closely as possible) the target chunk size. We use two different approaches for partitioning the iteration space into chunks – *aligned chunks* and *unaligned chunks*.

Whenever possible, we use aligned chunks. Aligned chunks force chunk boundaries to align with loop iteration boundaries at some level of the loop nest. For instance, if an inner loop accesses 100 KB and the target chunk size is 256 KB, we will likely start and end a chunk every two iterations of the outer loop.

There are some situations where inner loop iterations follow predictable patterns even though the outer loop does not. In that case, it is easier to add a counter and track inner loop iterations, ignoring the structure of the outer loop – that is an unaligned chunk. Unaligned chunks allow us to swap after a predictable number of inner loop iterations, even if we are not sure how many outer loop iterations will have executed. For example, if we are targeting 1024 inner loop iterations, and the inner loop executes 200, 700, then 300 iterations, the first swap would happen in the middle of the outer loop's 3rd iteration. For some loops, it may not be possible to predict the future addresses at all – pointer chasing code being a prime example. We do not prefetch those loops.

We prefer aligned chunks, even when there is not a precise match between inner loop sizes and the desired chunk size. They introduce less overhead because they allow us to use the existing structure of the code to introduce the thread management primitives. In practice, unaligned chunks are rarely needed.

To identify useful chunks, a profiler selects loops that perform at least 0.5% of the total memory accesses. The profiler also creates a dynamic loop nest tree that spans procedure boundaries, and calculates the average memory footprint of an iteration in each loop. While we will invariably suffer from profile mismatch, the information on the data touched in a single iteration is reliable enough to be useful across multiple inputs.

### 3.2 Distilling code

To build the prefetching thread, we generate p-slices by hand, following the example of much of the original work on helper thread prefetching [9, 22, 33]. Generating aligned chunks is typically simple and the techniques we apply are all implementable in a compiler. Other efforts have used both static [18, 28] and dynamic [32] compilation, as well as specialized hardware [8] to construct p-slices. Those techniques could be applied to inter-core prefetching as well.

For both chunk types (aligned and unaligned), the p-slice contains just the code necessary to compute the prefetch addresses and perform the prefetches. In most cases, the distilled code matches the basic structure of the main thread, but this is not necessary. For instance, if the compiler can determine the range of addresses the code will access, it can easily generate a generic prefetcher to load the data with minimal overhead — unlike SMT prefetchers, the ordering of the accesses within a chunk is unimportant in our scheme.

Our implementation uses normal loads rather than prefetch instructions, because the hardware has the option of ignoring prefetch instructions if there is contention for memory. Using normal loads requires that the prefetcher only issues memory requests to valid addresses. This was not a problem for any of the workloads we examined, but a more aggressive implementation that issued speculative prefetch instructions to potentially invalid addresses could use prefetch instructions to avoid segmentation faults.

Our p-slices include several other optimizations as well: We convert stores into loads to prevent misspeculation and avoid invalidations that could delay the main thread. We use profile information to determine the most likely direction for branches within a loop iteration. For highly biased branches, we remove the unlikely path and the instructions that compute the branch condition.

### 3.3 Thread coordination

For inter-core prefetching to work properly, the main thread and prefetcher threads must work together smoothly. This means that (1) they must take the same path through the program so they execute the same chunks in the same order, (2) the prefetch thread

```
jacobi2D ( ) {
 for(i=1;i<1000;i++)
  for(j=1;j<1000;j++)
   a[i][j]=( b[i][j-1] +
      b[i][j+1]+b[i-1][j]
    + b[i+1][j] )* c
}
```

**Original code**

```
jacobi2D_icp ( ) {
 start_inter_core_pref( )
 for(k=0;k<100;k++) {
  wait_and_swap(k+1)
   for(i=k*10;i<(k+1)*10;i++)
    for(j=1;j<1000;j++)
     a[i][j]=( b[i][j-1]+b[i][j+1]
         + b[i-1][j]+b[i+1][j] )*c
 }
 end_inter_core_pref( )
}
```

**Main thread code**

```
jacobi2D_pslice ( ) {
 while(continue_prefetching){
  t = wait_and_swap(0)
  for(i=t*10;i<(t+1)*10;i++)
   for(j=1;j<1000;j+=8)
    load a[i][j], b[i][j]
 }
}
```

**Prefetch thread code**

**Figure 2.** Inter-core prefetching implementation for the 2D Jacobi kernel. Prefetch thread takes an argument that specifies the chunk it should prefetch. The calls to wait_and_swap() synchronizes the two threads before swapping processors.

must stay far enough of the main thread to make the prefetches useful, and (3) they need to synchronize at swap points to exchange cores.

The first requirement is part of creating valid p-slices: The distiller must ensure that both the prefetcher and the main thread take the same route through the program. To handle the second requirement, we always start a prefetch thread at least a full chunk ahead. The prefetch thread can finish its chunk either earlier or later than the main thread does. The prefetcher usually finishes first, in which case one prefetching thread is sufficient (as in Figure 1) and the main thread will rarely stall. In some cases, the p-slice is slower than the main thread, and the main thread must wait for the prefetcher to finish. When that happens, we start prefetching the next chunk of data in the main thread's core to avoid wasting cycles, but we would prefer to never have to stall the main thread. As an alternative, we could stop the prefetching thread prematurely and allow the main thread to execute without any stall. We experiment with this approach but do not observe any advantage in our experiments. The reason is that if the main thread finishes early, eventually either the main thread or the prefetch thread will have to bring in the missing data for the next chunk to execute. Often the prefetcher (because it has more memory level parallelism and less overhead) will do so faster than the main thread, so it is better to just let it finish.

As a third alternative, very effective when we expect the prefetch threads to consistently be slower, we can use multiple prefetching threads to reduce or eliminate the need for the main thread to stall, and increase the effectiveness of prefetching. This exploits additional parallelism to allow the prefetch threads to stay ahead.

To coordinate thread migration we have implemented a simple user-space migration tool that allows threads to migrate between cores without entering the kernel. This saves significant overhead since normal context switches take about $10\mu s$ on our machines. At each wait and swap point, the distiller inserts a call to a library function in both the main thread and the prefetching thread. The function acts as a barrier across the main thread and the prefetching thread working on the next chunk the main thread will execute, so the threads block until they have both completed their chunk. Then the threads swap cores, and the main thread starts executing on the core with a freshly populated cache while the prefetch thread moves on to start prefetching another chunk.

The tool uses standard Linux APIs – *setcontext*, *getcontext*, *swapcontext*, and pthreads to perform the swap. The library reduces the context switch overhead by a factor of 5. The entire thread management substrate requires only about 25 lines of code, not including comments. We use Linux's scheduler affinity interface to "pin" kernel threads to particular cores, while our thread management system moves logical threads between them.

Figure 2 shows the code for a 2D Jacobi implementation and the corresponding main thread and p-slice code. We use aligned chunking and each chunk is a sequence of the outer loop's iterations. To make the p-slice efficient, we remove all the arithmetic operations, and make it touch each cache line only once by incrementing $j$ by 8 in the inner loop since each cache line holds 8 elements. This transformation speeds up execution by a factor of 2.2× on a Core2Quad machine using four cores.

### 3.4 Impact of cache coherence

Cache coherence concerns do not have a significant impact for SMT based helper thread prefetching because both the helper thread and the main thread share all levels of cache. However, on inter-core prefetching, the underlying coherence protocol has a greater impact when chunks share data. This impacts both the generation of p-slices and the optimal chunk size. We will briefly discuss some of these issues here.

Write sharing is particularly problematic for inter-core prefetching. We do not allow helper threads to write, but if they prefetch data that the main thread writes to, it results in a slow upgrade transaction in the main thread and an invalidation in the helper thread rendering the prefetch useless. Read sharing has less of an impact, particularly when there exists a shared inclusive last level cache (like the L3 cache in Nehalem). In that case, both the main thread and the prefetch thread can get data from the shared cache. However, with an exclusive shared cache (L3 cache in Opteron), the prefetch thread will need to get the data from the other core (via cache-to-cache transfer) rather than from the shared cache. This is not a problem except that on this architecture cache-to-cache transfers are slow – they take 4 to 5 times as long as going to the L3 cache [13]. The Core2Quad, with no global shared cache, has similar issues. Adding additional prefetch threads can potentially hide this extra latency and avoid any impact on the main thread.

The degree of sharing between chunks depends significantly on the chunk size. For instance, if neighboring loop iterations share data, a larger chunk size that covers many iterations will cause less inter-chunk sharing than a smaller chunk size. For the 2D Jacobi case in Figure 2, using one iteration per chunk means that the main thread and prefetching threads share 50% of read data, while using 10 iterations per chunk results in less than 10% shared data.

| System Information | Intel Core2Quad | Intel Nehalem | AMD Opteron |
|---|---|---|---|
| CPU Model | Harpertown | Gainestown | Opteron 2427 |
| No of Sockets×No of Dies×No of cores | 2×2×2 | 1×1×4 | 1×1×6 |
| L1 Cache size | 32KB | 32KB | 64KB |
| L1 hit time | 3 cycles | 4 cycles | 3 cycles |
| L2 Cache size | 6MB (per die) | 256KB private | 512KB private |
| L2 hit time | 15 cycles | 10 cycles | 15 cycles |
| L3 Cache size | None | 8MB shared | 6MB shared |
| L3 hit time | | 38 cycles | 36 cycles |
| Data TLB capacity (Level-1, Level-2) | 16, 256 | 64, 512 | 48, 512 |
| Memory access latency | 300-350 cycles | 200-240 cycles | 230-260 cycles |
| Swapping cost | $2\mu s$ | $1.7\mu s$ | $1.7\mu s$ |

**Table 1.** The three processors have very different memory hierarchies that lead to different optimal points of operation for inter-core prefetching.

| Benchmark name | Suite, Input | Memory footprint | LLC misses / 1000 inst | No of loops icp applied | Chunking technique |
|---|---|---|---|---|---|
| BT | NAS, B | 1200 MB | 19.96 | 20 | Aligned |
| CG | NAS, B | 399 MB | 20.86 | 5 | Aligned |
| LU | NAS, B | 173 MB | 17.42 | 14 | Aligned |
| MG | NAS, B | 437 MB | 11.74 | 6 | Unaligned |
| SP | NAS, B | 314 MB | 19.61 | 35 | Unaligned |
| Applu | Spec2000, Ref | 180 MB | 13.09 | 8 | Aligned |
| Equake | Spec2000, Ref | 49 MB | 28.53 | 4 | Aligned |
| Swim | Spec2000, Ref | 191 MB | 25.16 | 4 | Aligned |
| Lbm | Spec2006, Ref | 409 MB | 19.95 | 1 | Aligned |
| Libquantum | Spec2006, Ref | 64 MB | 24.45 | 6 | Aligned |
| Mcf | Spec2006, Ref | 1700 MB | 47.57 | 6 | Aligned, Unaligned |
| Milc | Spec2006, Ref | 679 MB | 27.34 | 20 | Aligned |
| Svm-rfe | Minebench | 61 MB | 16.97 | 1 | Aligned |

**Table 2.** Our benchmarks, with memory footprint, last level cache misses per 1000 instructions on Opteron, the number of loops where inter-core prefetching is applied, and the chunking technique used.

## 4. Methodology

This section describes the processors and applications we use to experimentally evaluate inter-core prefetching. The next section presents the results of those experiments.

### 4.1 Processors

Inter-core prefetching depends on the details of the processor's memory hierarchy and interconnect. Currently-available processors vary widely in the number of caches they provide on chip, the geometry of those caches, the interconnect between them, and the policies used to manage them. Table 1 summarizes the three processors we use to evaluate inter-core prefetching. On the Core2Quad, we use only one core per die, so that the L2 acts like a private cache.

All of the processors have hardware prefetching enabled. This allows us to evaluate whether inter-core prefetching effectively targets cache misses traditional prefetchers cannot handle.

### 4.2 Applications

To evaluate inter-core prefetching, we use a collection of applications from Spec2000, Spec2006, the NAS benchmark suite, and MineBench [27]. Inter-core prefetching is only of interest for applications that are at least partially memory bound. For applications that are not memory bound, the technique will have little effect. To identify memory bound applications, we used performance counters to count last-level cache misses. If the application incurred more than 10 cache misses per thousand instructions on the Opteron, we included it in our test suite. Table 2 provides details about the workloads and inputs.

The table also lists how many loops we applied inter-core prefetching to and what type of chunks we used. For the NAS benchmarks we used the "W" inputs for profiling. For Spec2000 and Spec2006 we used the train inputs. Svm-rfe does not include multiple inputs, so we profiled on the same input we used to collect performance results.

## 5. Results

We evaluate inter-core prefetching in four stages. First, we use simple microbenchmarks to measure its potential and understand some of its tradeoffs. Then, we evaluate the technique's application-level impact using the workloads described in Section 4. Next, we evaluate inter-core prefetching's effect on power and energy consumption. Finally, we compare inter-core prefetching's performance across cores to a version of the technique that targets SMT contexts, and also with data spreading, another software-only cache optimization.

### 5.1 Microbenchmarks

To establish inter-core prefetching's potential, we use a simple microbenchmark that allows us to study the interplay between the chunk size, the number of prefetching threads, and the ratio of computation to memory access. Our microbenchmark accesses cache lines either sequentially (in virtual address space) or pseudo-randomly – in that case accessing each cache line in a region of

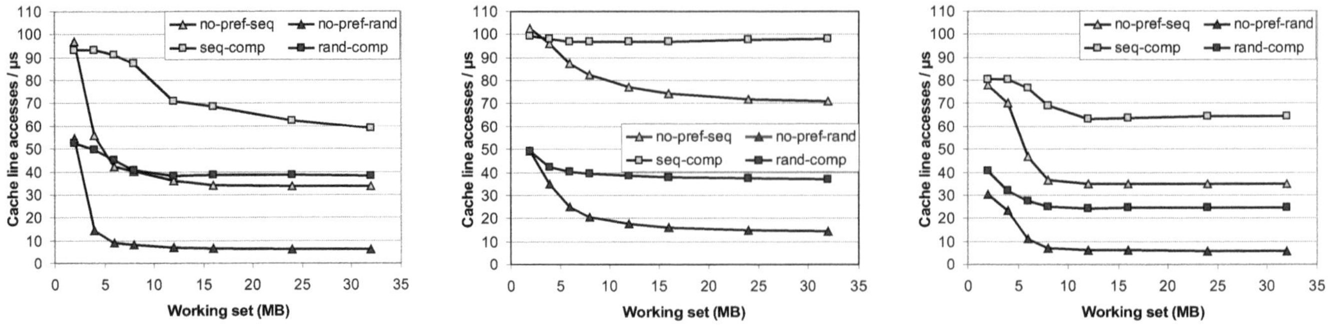


(a) Core2Quad (b) Nehalem (c) Opteron

**Figure 3.** As working set size increases to overflow one processor's cache capacity, inter-core prefetching prevents performance from dropping by using a cache on another processor to stage data.

memory exactly once, but in random order. The order is deterministic, though, allowing the prefetch thread to predict it accurately (this mimics dereferencing an array of pointers, for example). After accessing a cache line, the microbenchmark does a configurable number of arithmetic operations. We consider two cases: The *base* configuration executes four arithmetic operations per cache line access, and the *comp* configuration issues 32 operations. This gives four different microbenchmark configurations: rand-base, rand-comp, seq-base, and seq-comp.

### 5.1.1 The potential of inter-core prefetching

We first use the microbenchmarks to establish the overall potential for inter-core prefetching as the working set size changes. Figure 3 shows the throughput (measured as cache lines accessed per $\mu s$) of seq-comp and rand-comp for the three machines. It compares performance with and without inter-core prefetching over a range of working set sizes. The chunk size is 256 KB, and it uses one prefetch thread (two cores total).

For the microbenchmark without prefetching, throughput is high when the working set fits in local cache, but drops off (sometimes precipitously) when it no longer fits. Inter-core prefetching significantly (and, in one case, completely) mitigates that effect. For working sets that fit within the processor's cache, inter-core prefetching adds a small amount of overhead, reducing performance by between 3 and 4%. As the working set size grows, however, the benefits of inter-core prefetching are potentially large. For instance, for sequential access, throughput improves 1.76×, 1.38× and 1.85× for Core2Quad, Nehalem, and Opteron, respectively. These gains are in addition to the performance that the hardware prefetcher provides. The gains for random accesses are even larger: 6×, 2.5× and 4×, respectively. This is primarily due to the fact that the hardware prefetcher is ineffective for these access patterns.

The performance gains for random accesses are particularly interesting, since inter-core prefetching delivers between 2.5 and 6× improvements in performance using just two threads. It may seem counterintuitive, since the number of cores only doubled relative to running without prefetching. This is an important result – inter-core prefetching is not bound by the limits of traditional parallelism (i.e., linear speedup). Instead, the only limit on speedup it offers is the ratio of memory stall time to compute time in the pipeline. When that ratio is large (i.e., the processor stalls for memory frequently), and the stalls can be removed by a small number of helper cores, we can achieve speedups well above linear. Therefore, inter-core prefetching is more than a fall-back technique to use when thread-level parallelism is not available. For some applications inter-core prefetching will be more effective than conventional parallelism.

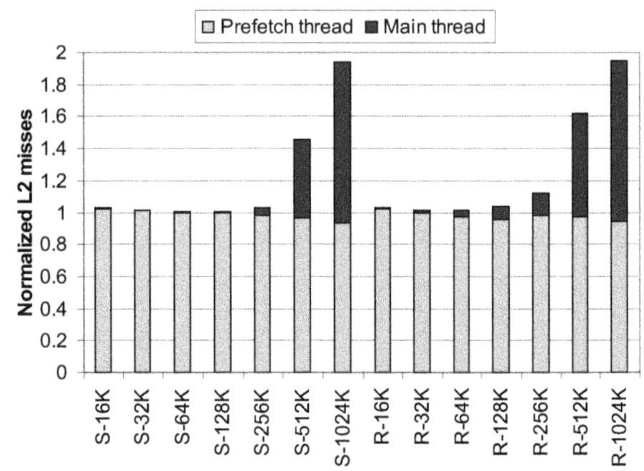


**Figure 4.** Misses incurred by the main thread and prefetch thread for different chunk sizes (R-16K means random access, 16 KB chunk), relative to the number of misses incurred in the baseline (no inter-core prefetching).

Of course, in those cases, a combination of traditional parallelism and inter-core prefetching is likely even better.

Looked at another way, inter-core prefetching achieves large speedups because it adds memory-level parallelism to applications that otherwise lack it. This is not obvious in the 2-core case, because we just move the data accesses from one core to the other. However, not only do the p-slices sometimes remove data dependences between loads that may have been in the code, they also minimize the number of instructions executed between loads and thus maximize the number of loads in the instruction window at one time.

Figure 4 demonstrates that inter-core prefetching moves almost all of the misses from the main thread to the prefetch thread. As long as the chunk fits in the L2 cache (for Opteron in this case), inter-core prefetching neither increases nor decreases L2 cache misses, it just performs them earlier and off the critical path. The speedup comes from the fact that we can access the data more quickly, and with more parallelism, than with a single thread.

In effect, inter-core prefetching partitions the work the application is doing into two, time-intensive parts: Executing non-memory instructions and waiting for cache misses. In this respect, it is similar to a decoupled access/execute [29] approach to computation. If a single thread must handle both tasks, it performs poorly at both: Memory stalls inhibit instruction level parallelism, and dependent

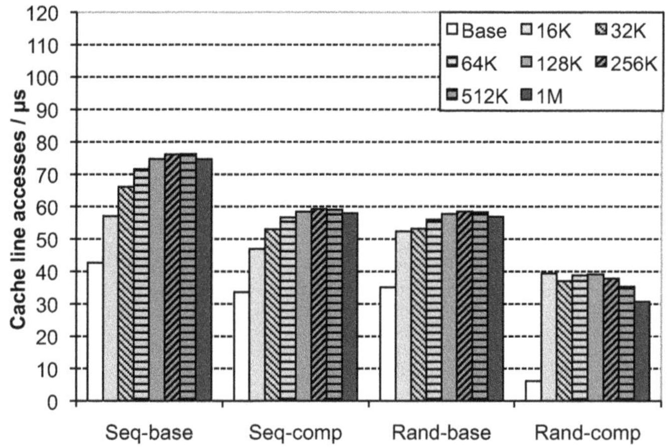


(a) Core2Quad, varying chunk size

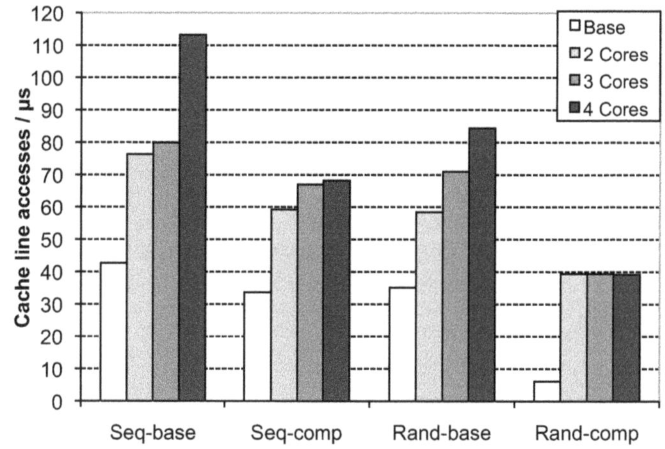


(b) Core2Quad, varying core count

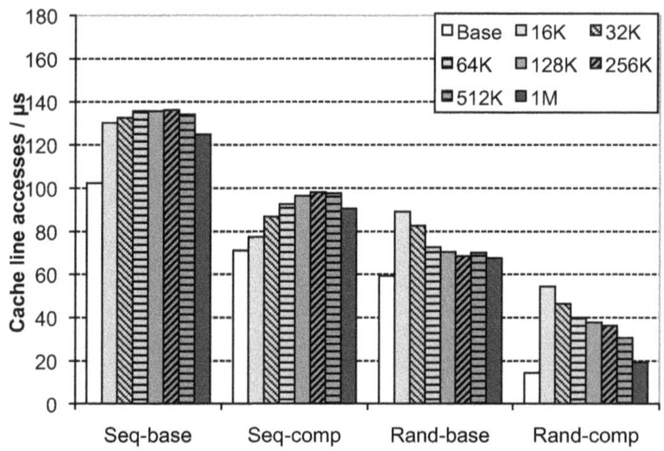


(c) Nehalem, varying chunk size

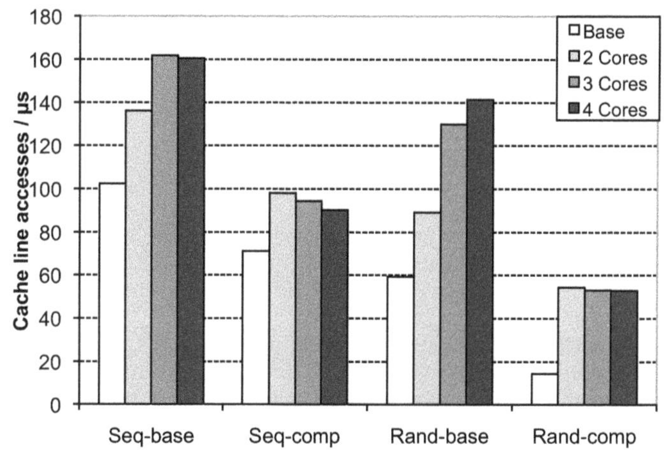


(d) Nehalem, varying core count

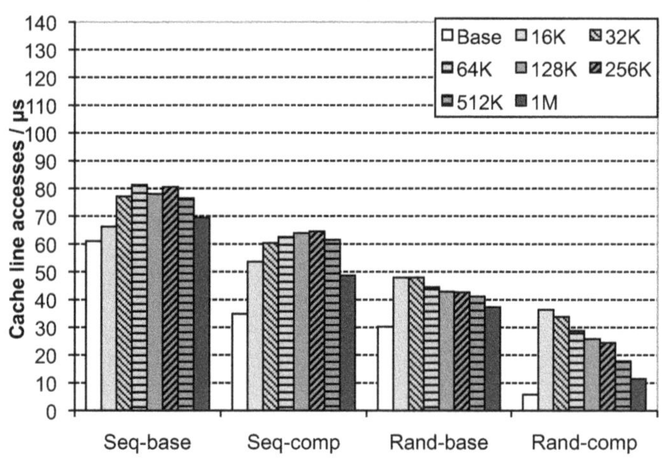


(e) Opteron, varying chunk size

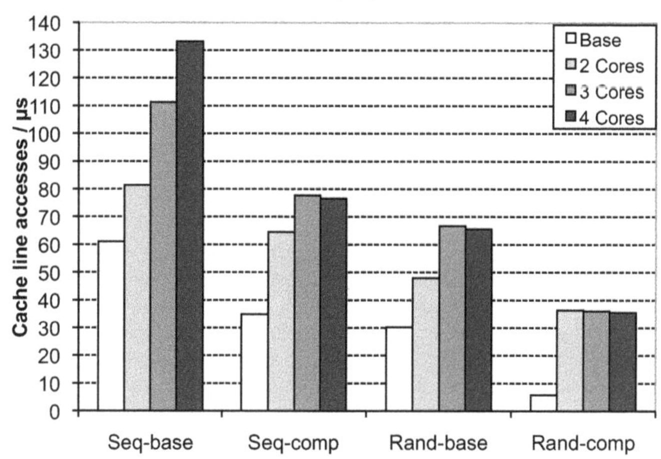


(f) Opteron, varying core count

**Figure 5.** The graphs at left show the impact of chunk size on performance for our microbenchmark. The right hand figures measure the effect of varying the number of prefetching threads. Each pair of figures is for a different processor. Inter-core prefetching is especially effective for random access patterns that the hardware prefetcher cannot handle. For threads with less computation per memory access, more than one prefetching thread is necessary for optimal performance.

// non-memory operations retard memory level parallelism by filling the instruction window. Allocating a core to each task removes these counterproductive interactions and increases the performance of both. Additionally, it separates prefetch accesses and what demand misses the main thread still experiences onto separate cores, potentially increasing total memory bandwidth.

### 5.1.2 Chunk size and the number of prefetch threads

Once the p-slice is generated, two parameters remain to be set – the chunk size and the number of prefetching threads (i.e., the number of cores to use). Changing the chunk size changes the level of the cache hierarchy prefetching will target and how completely we try to fill it, but it also determines how much swapping overhead occurs. For small chunk sizes, the frequent swaps might dominate the gains from prefetching.

Increasing the number of prefetching threads can improve performance if the prefetching threads have difficulty keeping up with the main thread, since using additional cores to prefetch increases the amount of memory level parallelism the system can utilize. However, allocating more cores to prefetching increases power consumption and also means more cores are unavailable to run other threads.

To understand the interplay of chunk size, compute intensity, and number of prefetch threads, we measure throughput for our microbenchmark with a 32 MB working set while varying the chunk size and the number of prefetch threads.

Figure 5 shows the results for our three processors. The figures on the left measure the impact of chunk size, while those on the right measure the effect of total core count. For the Core2Quad, a chunk size of 128 or 256 KB gives the best performance regardless of access pattern, but for other processors sequential accesses favor larger chunks between 64 and 256 KB, while 16 KB chunks perform best for random accesses.

The performance gains are again largest for the random access patterns, where there is limited benefit from hardware prefetching. For 16 KB chunks, inter-core prefetching improves Nehalem throughput by 3.75× and Opteron's performance by 6×.

The right hand graphs in Figure 5 show the impact of using multiple prefetching cores for the optimal chunk size from the left hand graphs. Adding additional prefetchers improves performance almost linearly up to four cores (three prefetchers) for seq-base on the Core2Quad and Opteron machines. Nehelam sees benefits with up to three cores. For seq-comp, conversely, one or two prefetchers give the best results. This is an expected result: When the main thread does little computation for each memory access, it is difficult for a single helper thread to execute as quickly as the main thread. For the random access patterns, results are similar.

It is not surprising that the optimal number of cores varies by memory access pattern and computation/memory ratio. However, the optimal chunk size also varies, especially by access pattern. This implies that the optimal chunk size depends not only on a particular cache size, but also at which level of the memory hierarchy the most misses are occurring, the effectiveness of the prefetcher, and the relative cost of migration/synchronization. For example, with random access, the program runs more slowly. This reduces the relative cost of migration, so smaller chunks are desirable. In fact, the migration overhead is amortized to the point that targeting the L1 cache is the best strategy for Nehalem and Opteron. For sequential access (because it is harder to amortize the swap cost and because the hardware prefetcher is addressing the L1 cache fairly well), the sweet spot seems to be targeting the L2 cache. Less obvious is why the Core2Quad, with its huge L2 cache, tails off at 1 MB chunk size. However, inter-core prefetching allows us to not only pre-fill caches, but also TLB entries. The Core2Quad has 256 TLB entries per core, just enough to hold 1 MB if there are absolutely no conflicts in the TLB. Therefore, the optimal chunk size is just a bit smaller than the maximum space supported by the TLB.

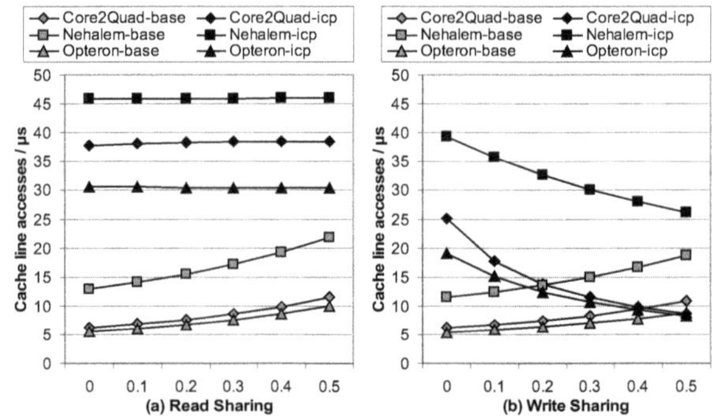


**Figure 6.** Performance improvement for different degree of read/write sharing using inter-core prefetching. Sharing factor of 0.3 means adjacent chunks share 30% of data.

We have also found that prefetching each chunk in reverse is helpful in some cases. By prefetching the same chunk data, but in the opposite order that the main thread will access it, inter-core prefetching can target multiple levels of the cache hierarchy at once – even if a chunk is too big for the L1 cache. In this case, the last data prefetched will be in the L1 when the main thread arrives and tries to access it. In general, though, this technique is more difficult to apply, so we did not include it in our experimental results shown.

### 5.1.3 Inter-chunk sharing

To quantify the effect of inter-chunk data sharing, we modify our microbenchmark by adding a configurable sharing factor. Figure 6 shows the effect of inter-chunk sharing across different machines in the rand-comp case for both read and write sharing. We use 16 KB chunks with one prefetch thread and vary the fraction of shared data from 0 to 50%. As expected, without inter-core prefetching, throughput improves with the sharing because of the increase in locality. With inter-core prefetching, throughput stays the same for read sharing, but degrades rapidly for write sharing. Cache to cache transfer latency is the critical factor for write sharing. Nehalem, having the best cache to cache transfer latency among the three machines, is the most tolerant of write sharing and sees improvement even when the main thread and prefetcher share half their data. Core2Quad, with a private cache design, has expensive cache to cache transfer operations, so inter-core prefetching hurts performance when more than 40% of data is shared.

## 5.2 Application Performance

This section examines the effectiveness of inter-core prefetching on real applications, with the p-slices generated as described in Section 3. Figure 7 displays inter-core prefetching's impact on our benchmark suite. The first three bars represent results for a single chunk size (that gave good performance across the entire benchmark suite) per architecture, varying the number of cores. The last bar gives the result that uses the best chunk size and core count per application (out of the 12 combinations– 2, 3, 4 cores and 128, 256, 512, 1024 KB chunks).

Overall, prefetching improves performance by between 20 and 50% on average without tuning the chunk size or core count for each benchmark. Per-benchmark tuning raises performance gains to between 31 and 63%. A further step would be to tune the parameters on a loop-by-loop basis.

Performance gains are largest for Core2Quad, because it has the largest cache miss penalty. For some applications, the gains are far above the average: Prefetching speeds up LBM by 2.8× (3 cores and 1024 KB chunks) on the Core2Quad and MILC sees

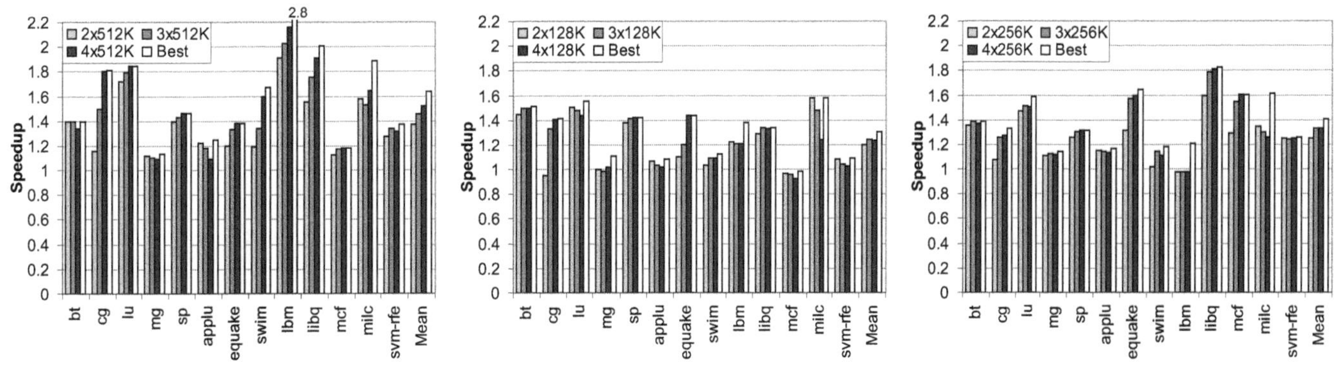


(a) Core2Quad (b) Nehalem (c) Opteron

**Figure 7.** Inter-core prefetching provides good speedups (between 20 and 50% on average) without tuning the chunk size and thread count on a per-application basis. With that level of tuning, performance rises to between 31 and 63% (the "best" bars).

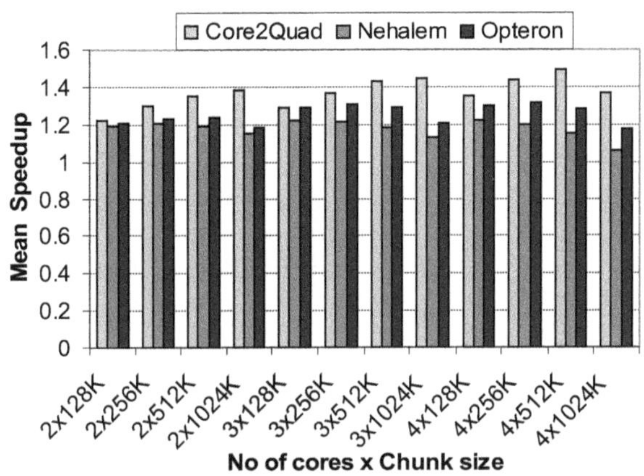


**Figure 8.** Mean speedup across all benchmarks for different combinations of chunk size and number of cores

improvements of nearly 1.6× for Nehalem. Even a complex integer benchmark like MCF gets 1.6× on Opteron. MCF also shows the impact of microarchitectural differences across machines on performance improvements. Unlike Opteron, Nehalem does not see any improvements and Core2Quad sees moderate speedup of 20%. This variation is due to the difference in cache hierarchy, window size, hardware prefetcher implementation, coherence protocol, etc. across these machines. To understand these differences, we measure the percentage of execution time covered by loops selected for inter-core prefetching (measured in the baseline case). Nehalem and Core2Quad spend between 44 and 47% of execution in those loops. Opteron spends 64%, which accounts for the larger overall impact on performance.

The effectiveness of increased prefetching threads varies widely among applications. For some (e.g., CG) additional prefetching threads are useful on all three architectures. For CG running on Nehalem with one prefetch thread, the main thread has to wait for the prefetch thread 89% of the time. With two and three prefetch threads, that number goes down to 25% and 0.4%, respectively. We see similar data for CG on Core2Quad and Opteron. For others (e.g., applu), adding threads hurts performance. If thread count has a strong impact on performance, the trend tends to be consistent across all three processors. The optimal number of cores is a function of the ratio of memory stalls to computation, which tends not to change across architectures.

Figure 8 shows results averaged across all benchmarks, for a wider range of chunk sizes for the three machines. We see again from these results that speedups are somewhat tolerant of chunk size, although there are some poorer choices to be avoided.

### 5.3 Energy Considerations

Inter-core prefetching has two competing effects on application energy consumption. The technique increases performance, which would reduce energy consumption if power remained constant. However, using multiple cores for execution increases power consumption both because multiple cores are active and because the throughput of the main thread increases.

To measure the total impact on energy, we measure total system power and energy with a power meter. The measurement includes everything in the system, including the power supply and its inefficiency, so the results are not directly comparable with simulation studies that focus only on processor power.

Figures 9 and 10 show results for Nehalem and Core2Quad. We were unable to measure results for the Opteron because of system administration issues. Our measurements show that the applications running without prefetching require 282 W (Nehalem) and 381 W (Core2Quad) on average (i.e., total system power increased by 42 W and 87 W while running the application compared to an idle system). Inter-core prefetching with a single prefetcher increases power consumption by 14 W (Nehalem) and 19 W (Core2Quad), and adding another prefetching thread requires an additional 6 W.

In terms of energy, the performance gains that inter-core prefetching delivers more than compensates for the increased power consumption. Per-application energy drops by 11 and 26% on average for the two architectures, and as much as 50% for some applications.

### 5.4 Comparison with SMT Prefetching

Previous work on helper-thread prefetching focused on SMT machines. This section compares that approach with inter-core prefetching.

To provide a reasonable comparison, we use the same chunk and p-slice generation techniques that we use for inter-core prefetching, but we run the p-slice on the second context of one of Nehalem's SMT cores. Since the main thread and prefetching thread will run concurrently on the same core, there is no need for context switches or the associated overhead.

Figure 11(a) compares the performance of applying prefetching across SMT contexts and applying it across cores for Nehalem using our microbenchmark. We see from these results that SMT

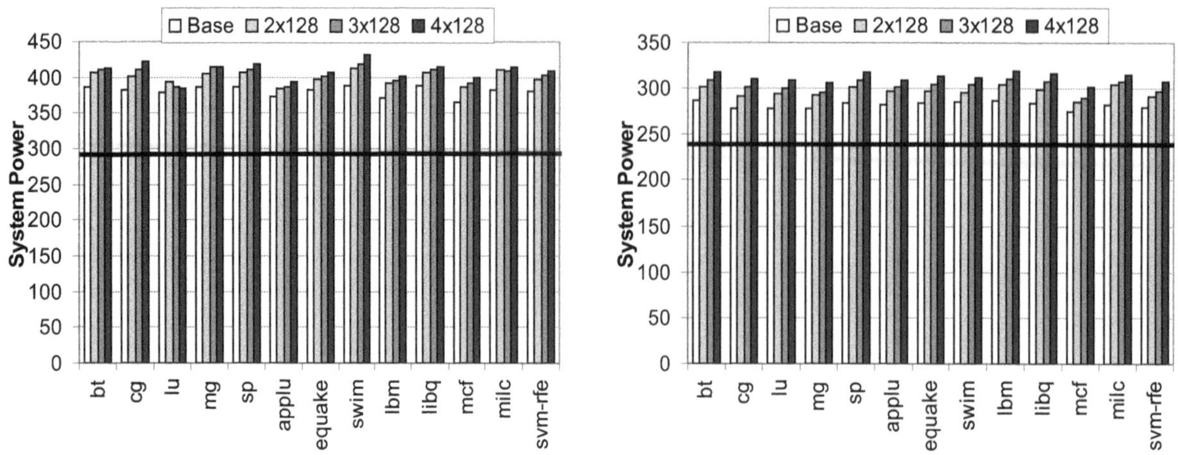


(a) Core2Quad power (b) Nehalem power

**Figure 9.** Inter-core prefetching increases power consumption slightly compared to the non-prefetching version of the application, but the prefetching threads consume much less power than the main thread. The horizontal line denotes idle power on each system.

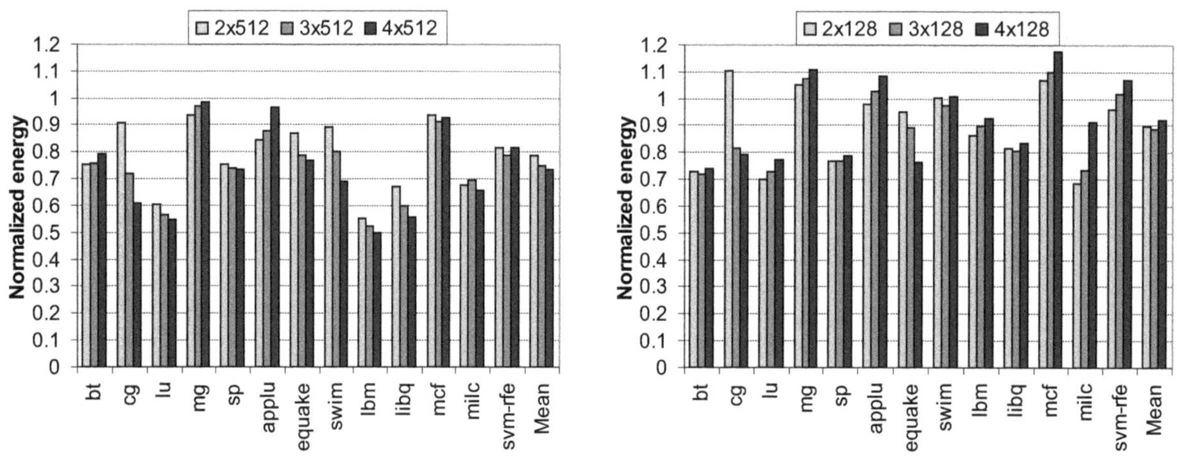


(a) Core2Quad energy (b) Nehalem energy

**Figure 10.** Inter-core prefetching's performance gains counteract the increase in power consumption it causes, resulting in a net reduction in energy of between 11 and 26%. Measurements in the graph are normalized to the application without inter-core prefetching.

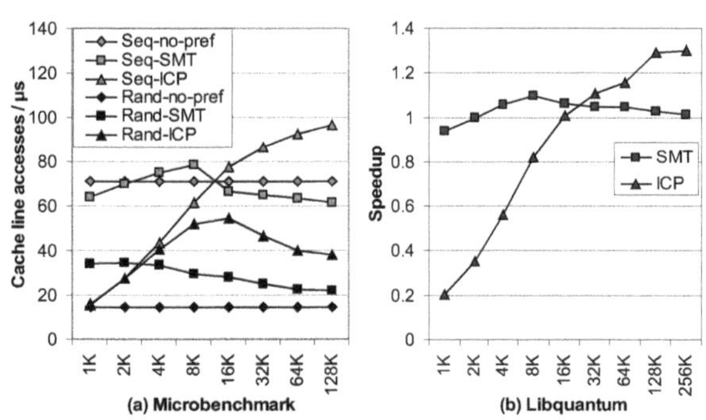


**Figure 11.** Comparing inter-core prefetching and SMT prefetching for different chunk sizes in Nehalem. On SMT, smaller chunk sizes give better performance because migration is not necessary and the prefetcher can target the L1 cache. However, using multiple cores still results in better overall performance.

prefetching favors smaller chunk sizes since they minimize interference between the helper thread and the main thread in the L1 cache. With very small chunks, of course, CMP prefetching is not effective because of the cost of swapping. However, with large chunks inter-core prefetching easily outperforms the best SMT result. Figure 11(b) shows the same comparison for one of our Spec2006 benchmark, *libquantum*. This application has regular memory access pattern, and so it follows the trend of sequential access in Figure 11(a).

Inter-core prefetching, even on architectures where SMT threads are available, benefits from the absence of contention for instruction execution bandwidth, private cache space, TLB entries, cache bandwidth, etc. This lack of contention allows the prefetcher threads to run very far ahead of the main thread and makes it easier to fully cover the latency of cache misses. As a result, inter-core prefetching is vulnerable to neither useless late prefetches nor early prefetches whose data are evicted before the main thread accesses it. This also explains why the hardware prefetcher cannot

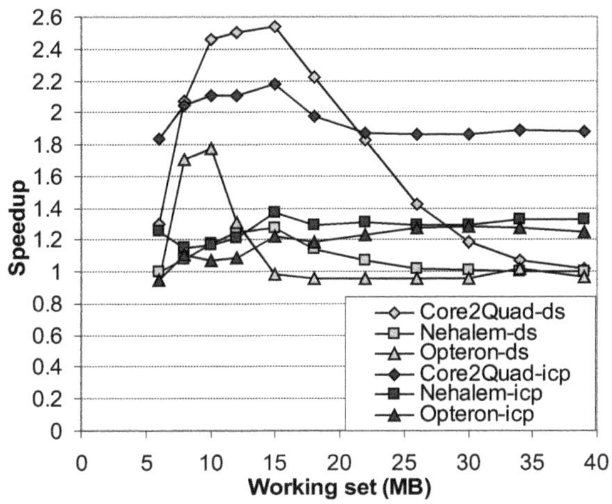


**Figure 12.** Inter-core prefetching and data spreading are complimentary techniques. Data spreading delivers better performance and power savings for small working sets, but for larger working sets, inter-core prefetching is superior. Speedups are relative to a conventional implementation.

completely eliminate the need for inter-core prefetching in case of the fully predictable (e.g. sequential) access pattern. In addition, the hardware prefetcher will not cross page boundaries, while inter-core prefetching ignores them.

### 5.5 Comparison to data spreading

Inter-core prefetching shares some traits with previous work on data spreading [16], which also uses migration to eliminate cache misses. Under that technique a single thread periodically migrates between cores, spreading its working set across several caches. For applications with regular access patterns and working sets that fit in the private caches, data spreading converts main memory accesses into local cache hits. For more irregular access patterns, it converts them into cache-to-cache transfers. The results in [16] show that it can improve performance by up to 70%.

Inter-core prefetching and data spreading are complimentary, but they differ in several ways. First, data spreading is only useful when the working set of the application fits within the aggregated caches. Inter-core prefetching works with working sets of any size. Second, data spreading uses a single thread, and, as a result, does not incur any power overheads: only one core is actively executing at any time. Inter-core prefetching actively utilizes multiple cores. Finally, as datasets grow, data spreading requires more and more cores. In many cases, inter-core prefetching gets full performance with 2 cores, even with very large data sets.

Figure 12 compares inter-core prefetching and data spreading on Jacobi. The figure measures speedup relative to a conventional implementation on the same architecture. The data show that data spreading provides better performance when Jacobi's data set fits within the aggregate cache capacity of the system. Inter-core prefetching offers better performance for larger data sets. The technique also does not require larger private caches. This helps to effectively apply inter-core prefetching in state of the art multicores with moderately sized private L2 caches.

## 6. Conclusion

This paper describes inter-core prefetching, a technique that allows multiple cores to cooperatively execute a single thread. Inter-core prefetching distills key portions of the original program into prefetching threads that run concurrently with the main thread but on a different core. Via lightweight migration, the main thread follows the prefetching threads from core to core and finds prefetched data waiting for it in its caches. Our results show that inter-core prefetching can speed up applications by between 31 and 63%, depending on the architecture, and that it works across several existing multi-core architectures. Our results also show that, although it uses multiple cores, it can reduce energy consumption by up to 50%. Inter-core prefetching demonstrates that it is possible to effectively apply helper thread-based techniques developed for multithreaded processors to multi-core processors, and even overcome several limitations of multithreaded prefetchers.

## Acknowledgments


The authors would like to thank the anonymous reviewers and James Laudon for many useful suggestions. They would also like to thank Sajia Akhter for help with some of the graphics. This work was supported by NSF grants CCF-0702349 and NSF-0643880.


## References


[1] T. M. Aamodt, P. Chow, P. Hammarlund, H. Wang, and J. P. Shen. Hardware support for prescient instruction prefetch. In *Proceedings of the 10th International Symposium on High Performance Computer Architecture*, 2004.

[2] M. Annavaram, J. M. Patel, and E. S. Davidson. Data prefetching by dependence graph precomputation. In *Proceedings of the 28th annual international symposium on Computer architecture*, 2001.

[3] J. A. Brown, H. Wang, G. Chrysos, P. H. Wang, and J. P. Shen. Speculative precomputation on chip multiprocessors. In *In Proceedings of the 6th Workshop on Multithreaded Execution, Architecture, and Compilation*, 2001.

[4] J. Chang and G. S. Sohi. Cooperative caching for chip multiprocessors. In *Proceedings of the 33rd annual International Symposium on Computer Architecture*, June 2006.

[5] R. Chappell, J. Stark, S. Kim, S. Reinhardt, and Y. Patt. Simultaneous subordinate microthreading (ssmt). In *Proceedings of the international symposium on Computer Architecture*, May 1999.

[6] T.-F. Chen and J.-L. Baer. Effective hardware-based data prefetching for high-performance processors. *IEEE Transactions on Computers*, (5), May 1995.

[7] T. M. Chilimbi and M. Hirzel. Dynamic hot data stream prefetching for general-purpose programs. In *Proceedings of the ACM SIGPLAN 2002 Conference on Programming language design and implementation*, 2002.

[8] J. Collins, D. Tullsen, H. Wang, and J. Shen. Dynamic speculative precompuation. In *Proceedings of the International Symposium on Microarchitecture*, December 2001.

[9] J. Collins, H. Wang, D. Tullsen, C. Hughes, Y.-F. Lee, D. Lavery, and J. Shen. Speculative precomputation: Long-range prefetching of delinquent loads. In *Proceedings of the International Symposium on Computer Architecture*, July 2001.

[10] J. Dundas and T. Mudge. Improving data cache performance by pre-executing instructions under a cache miss. In *Proceedings of the 11th international conference on Supercomputing*, 1997.

[11] A. Garg and M. C. Huang. A performance-correctness explicitly-decoupled architecture. In *Proceedings of the 41st annual IEEE/ACM International Symposium on Microarchitecture*, 2008.

[12] J. Gummaraju and M. Rosenblum. Stream programming on general-purpose processors. In *Proceedings of the 38th annual IEEE/ACM International Symposium on Microarchitecture*, 2005.

[13] D. Hackenberg, D. Molka, and W. E. Nagel. Comparing cache architectures and coherence protocols on x86-64 multicore smp systems. In *Proceedings of the 42nd Annual IEEE/ACM International Symposium on Microarchitecture*, 2009.

[14] K. Z. Ibrahim, G. T. Byrd, and E. Rotenberg. Slipstream execution mode for cmp-based multiprocessors. In *Proceedings of the*

*9th International Symposium on High-Performance Computer Architecture*, 2003.

[15] N. P. Jouppi. Improving direct-mapped cache performance by the addition of a small fully-associative cache and prefetch buffers. In *Proceedings of the international symposium on Computer Architecture*, June 1990.

[16] M. Kamruzzaman, S. Swanson, and D. M. Tullsen. Software data spreading: leveraging distributed caches to improve single thread performance. In *Proceedings of the 2010 ACM SIGPLAN conference on Programming language design and implementation*, 2010.

[17] D. Kim, S. Liao, P. Wang, J. Cuvillo, X. Tian, X. Zou, H. Wang, D. Yeung, M. Girkar, and J. Shen. Physical experiment with prefetching helper threads on Intel's hyper-threaded processors. In *International Symposium on Code Generation and Optimization*, March 2004.

[18] D. Kim and D. Yeung. Design and evaluation of compiler algorithm for pre-execution. In *Proceedings of the international conference on Architectural support for programming languages and operating systems*, October 2002.

[19] V. Krishnan and J. Torrellas. A chip-multiprocessor architecture with speculative multithreading". *IEEE Transactions on Computers*, September 1999.

[20] S. Liao, P. Wang, H. Wang, G. Hoflehner, D. Lavery, and J. Shen. Post-pass binary adaptation for software-based speculative precomputation. In *Proceedings of the conference on Programming Language Design and Implementation*, October 2002.

[21] J. Lu, A. Das, W.-C. Hsu, K. Nguyen, and S. G. Abraham. Dynamic helper threaded prefetching on the sun ultrasparc cmp processor. In *Proceedings of the 38th annual IEEE/ACM International Symposium on Microarchitecture*, 2005.

[22] C.-K. Luk. Tolerating memory latency through software-controlled pre-execution in simultaneous multithreading processors. In *Proceedings of the 28th annual international symposium on Computer architecture*, July 2001.

[23] P. Marcuello, A. González, and J. Tubella. Speculative multithreaded processors. In *12th International Conference on Supercomputing*, November 1998.

[24] P. Michaud. Exploiting the cache capacity of a single-chip multi-core processor with execution migration. In *Proceedings of the 10th International Symposium on High Performance Computer Architecture*, February 2004.

[25] T. C. Mowry, M. S. Lam, and A. Gupta. Design and evaluation of a compiler algorithm for prefetching. In *ASPLOS-V: Proceedings of the fifth international conference on Architectural support for programming languages and operating systems*, 1992.

[26] O. Mutlu, J. Stark, C. Wilkerson, and Y. N. Patt. Runahead execution: An alternative to very large instruction windows for out-of-order processors. In *Proceedings of the 9th International Symposium on High-Performance Computer Architecture*, 2003.

[27] J. Pisharath, Y. Liu, W. Liao, A. Choudhary, G. Memik, and J. Parhi. Nu-minebench 2.0. technical report. Technical Report CUCIS-2005-08-01, Center for Ultra-Scale Computing and Information Security, Northwestern University, August 2006. URL http://cucis.ece.northwestern.edu/techreports/pdf/CUCIS-2004-08-001.pdf%.

[28] C. G. Quiñones, C. Madriles, J. Sánchez, P. Marcuello, A. González, and D. M. Tullsen. Mitosis compiler: an infrastructure for speculative threading based on pre-computation slices. In *ACM SIGPLAN Conference on Programming Language Design and Implementation*, June 2005.

[29] J. E. Smith. Decoupled access/execute computer architectures. In *ISCA '82: Proceedings of the 9th annual symposium on Computer Architecture*, 1982.

[30] G. S. Sohi, S. E. Breach, and T. N. Vijaykumar. Multiscalar processors. In *Proceedings of the International Symposium on Computer Architecture*, June 1995.

[31] K. Sundaramoorthy, Z. Purser, and E. Rotenberg. Slipstream processors: improving both performance and fault tolerance. *SIGPLAN Not.*, 35(11), 2000.

[32] W. Zhang, D. Tullsen, and B. Calder. Accelerating and adapting precomputation threads for efficient prefetching. In *Proceedings of the International Symposium on High Performance Computer Architecture*, January 2007.

[33] C. Zilles and G. Sohi. Execution-based prediction using speculative slices. In *Proceedings of the International Symposium on Computer Architecture*, July 2001.

# Improving the Performance of Trace-based Systems by False Loop Filtering


Hiroshige Hayashizaki
IBM Research - Tokyo
1623-14 Shimotsuruma, Yamato,
Kanagawa, Japan 242-8502
hayashiz@jp.ibm.com

Peng Wu
IBM Research - Watson Research Center
P.O. Box 218, Yorktown Heights,
NY, USA 10598
pengwu@us.ibm.com

Hiroshi Inoue
IBM Research - Tokyo
1623-14 Shimotsuruma, Yamato,
Kanagawa, Japan 242-8502
inouehrs@jp.ibm.com

Mauricio J. Serrano
IBM Research - Watson Research Center
P.O. Box 218, Yorktown Heights,
NY, USA 10598
mserrano@us.ibm.com

Toshio Nakatani
IBM Research - Tokyo
1623-14 Shimotsuruma, Yamato,
Kanagawa, Japan 242-8502
nakatani@jp.ibm.com



## Abstract

Trace-based compilation is a promising technique for language compilers and binary translators. It offers the potential to expand the compilation scopes that have traditionally been limited by method boundaries.

Detecting *repeating cyclic execution paths* and capturing the detected repetitions into traces is a key requirement for trace selection algorithms to achieve good optimization and performance with small amounts of code. One important class of repetition detection is *cyclic-path-based* repetition detection, where a cyclic execution path (a path that starts and ends at the same instruction address) is detected as a repeating cyclic execution path.

However, we found many cyclic paths that are not *repeating* cyclic execution paths, which we call *false loops*. A common class of false loops occurs when a method is invoked from multiple call-sites. A cycle is formed between two invocations of the method from different call-sites, but which does not represent loops or recursion. False loops can result in shorter traces and smaller compilation scopes, and degrade the performance.

We propose *false loop filtering*, an approach to reject false loops in the repetition detection step of trace selection, and a technique called *false loop filtering by call-stack-comparison*, which rejects a cyclic path as a false loop if the call stacks at the beginning and the end of the cycle are different.

We applied false loop filtering to our trace-based Java™ JIT compiler that is based on IBM's J9 JVM. We found that false loop filtering achieved an average improvement of 16% and 10% for the DaCapo benchmark when applied to two baseline trace selection algorithms, respectively, with up to 37% improvement for individual benchmarks. In the end, with false loop filtering, our trace-based JIT achieves a performance comparable to that of the method-based J9 JVM/JIT using the corresponding optimization level.



***Categories and Subject Descriptors*** D.3.4 [*Programming Languages*]: Processors—Compilers

***General Terms*** Algorithms, Performance

***Keywords*** Trace-based Compilation, Trace Selection, Repetition Detection




## 1. Introduction

Trace-based compilation has been explored in binary translation systems [1, 7, 8], lightweight JIT for embedded JVMs [12, 20], and more recently in compilers for dynamically typed languages such as JavaScript [4, 13], Lua [17], and Python [6]. In a trace-based compiler, a *trace*, typically defined as a single-entry multiple-exit region formed from executed instructions, is the basic unit for compilation. This is the most distinctive aspect of a trace-based compiler. In this paper, we start with *trace selection*, the process that forms traces out of hot execution paths, and focus on improving the steady-state performance of trace-based compilation systems by improving the trace selection algorithms.

All trace selection algorithms aim to detect *repeating cyclic execution paths* (or *repetitions*) from runtime execution information (*repetition detection*), and capture the detected repetitions into traces, typically by terminating traces when a repetition is detected. By doing so, a trace can capture a large amount of computation in a compact form, which leads to good space efficiency and good optimization.

Repetition detection algorithms used in existing trace selection algorithms fall into the following three categories:

- *Stop-at-backward-branch* repetition detectors [1] consider every backward branch as an indicator of a repeating cyclic execution path, and terminate a trace at every backward branch.
- *Cyclic-path-based* repetition detectors [6, 15, 18] consider an execution sequence as a repeating cyclic execution path when the sequence is *cyclic*, that is, the sequence starts and ends at the same program counter (PC).

```
 1: void f(){
 2:   for(A){
 3:     g();
 4:     B;
 5:     g();
 6:     C;
 7:   }
 8: }
 9: void g(){
10:   P;
11: }
```

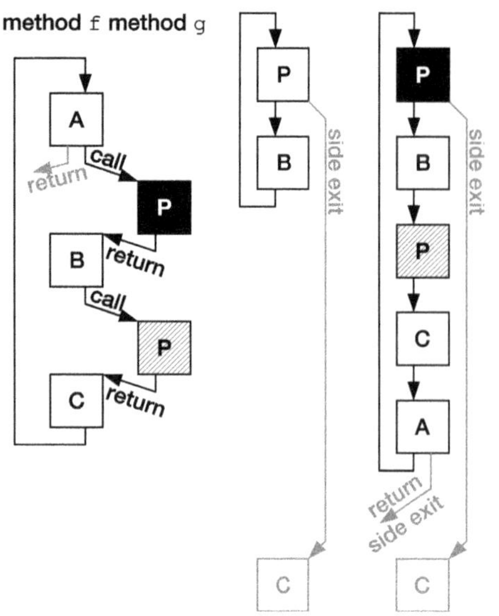


(a) Program 1 (b) CFG of Program 1 (c) Trace 1A (without false loop filtering) (d) Trace 1B (with false loop filtering)

**Figure 1.** False loop and false loop filtering

- Trace selection algorithms with *static-scope-based* repetition detectors [4, 11–13, 17] leverage the information about the program structures such as loops and methods, and construct a trace starting from a loop header and spanning the loop body to capture repeating cyclic execution paths.

While static-scope-based repetition detectors have worked well in recent trace compilers, in this paper, we focus on cyclic-path-based repetition detectors, because they can achieve high performance and are applicable to a wide variety of trace-based systems including binary tracing that static-scope-based repetition detectors may not be suitable for.

### The False Loop Problem

While cyclic-path-based repetition detectors detect cyclic execution paths and capture such paths into traces, they do not always detect *repeating* cyclic execution paths. Consider the example in Figure 1. Suppose a trace starts from instruction P of method g that is called by method f at Line 3. The execution goes as follows:

1. execute P
2. return to method f
3. execute B
4. invoke method g (at Line 5)
5. execute P

At Step 5, a cyclic execution path P-B-P (from Step 1 to Step 5) is detected, and P-B-P is formed into a cyclic trace Trace 1A as shown in Figure 1 (c). The cyclic execution path P-B-P, however, does not capture a real repetitive execution pattern in this example. Consider mapping the execution sequence P-B-P-C-A-P into trace P-B-P. The cycle in the trace is exercised exactly once and the trace is exited when C is executed.

A better trace formation starting from P (Trace 1B) is shown in Figure 1 (d). Trace 1B spans one iteration of a natural loop starting from A, where the instruction sequence P-B-P-C-A-P can be repeated many times in consecutive executions. Not only is Trace 1B a much better target for optimization, it also incurs much lower overhead because trace exit occurs only when the execution finishes iterating the loop.

Intuitively, P-B-P does not represent a real repetitive execution pattern because the cyclic path does not come from a natural loop or a recursion, but rather is the effect of multiple invocations of the same method on one execution path. The rest of the paper refers to a cyclic execution path that does not represent a real repetitive execution pattern as a *false loop*.

Another problem with false loops is that they might prematurely terminate a trace that could have otherwise captured real repetitive execution patterns. This occurs, for example, when a trace selection algorithm terminates a trace when it finds a cyclic path in the middle of a trace, as in the *Rejoined* case discussed in [18]. Consider again the example in Figure 1, and suppose the trace is recorded from A instead. The trace A-P-B-P might be created, because the sequence P-B-P inside the path A-P-B-P is identified as a cyclic path, whereas A-P-B-P-C-A is a better structure.

### False Loop Filtering

In this paper, we propose *false loop filtering* to reject false loops in repetition detectors and to improve the quality of the traces.

Various heuristics can be used to detect false loops. We propose a false loop filtering algorithm, named *call-stack-comparison*. For a cyclic execution path, it rejects the cyclic path as a false loop if the call stacks at the beginning and the end of the cyclic path are different. This rejects the trace shown in Figure 1 (c), which is a major class of false loops. This is one of the best performing algorithms among those being tested, and the most direct and exact solution to the false loop problem.

Using call stacks to detect false loops is based on the following insights. Although there is only one instruction address for P in Figure 1, there are two instances of P on the trace: P called from Line 3 (shown in a black box) and P called from Line 5 (shown in a slashed box). When the call stacks of two dynamic instructions are different, the execution paths following the two dynamic instructions would diverge after some method returns (that lead to the differing callers on the call stacks). Therefore it is a strong indicator that forming a trace out of such a cycle is unlikely to capture a long repetitive execution sequence. Distinguishing the two instances of P from different calling contexts results in the superior trace shown in Figure 1 (d).

We also show an approximation algorithm that achieves almost the same performance (at risk of a small number of false loops), and algorithms that can be applied to systems where less information on executed instructions is available such as binary tracing systems.

We evaluated false loop filtering on a trace-based just-in-time compiler for Java (*trace JIT*) that is built on top of IBM's J9 JVM [14]. The trace JIT supports the basic functions of the original J9 JVM including GC, threading, exceptions, monitor events, and JNI, as well as basic optimizations from the original method-based JIT in J9. Details of the trace JIT are described in [16].

On the DaCapo benchmark [5, 9], we demonstrated that false loop filtering achieved an average speedup factor of 1.16x and 1.10x, respectively, when applied to our two linear trace selection algorithms, with a reasonable increase of code size and compilation time. With our best performing trace selection configuration with false loop filtering, the trace JIT achieved a performance comparable to the method JIT at the corresponding optimization levels.

### Contribution and Organization

The paper makes the following contributions:

1. We describe the false loop problem in existing trace selection algorithms and propose the concept of false loop filtering. To

the best of our knowledge, this paper is the first one that explicitly addresses the false loop problem in trace selection.

2. We propose a false loop filtering algorithm which we named *call-stack-comparison*, and showed the impact of false loops and false loop filtering in a real trace-based compiler.

The rest of the paper is organized as follows. Section 2 gives an overview of trace-based systems and repetition detection. We propose false loop filtering and describe false loop filtering algorithms in Section 3. Section 4 describes our implementation of the trace-based system for Java. Evaluations of false loop filtering and the trace JIT are in Section 5. Section 6 discusses the related work and we conclude in Section 7.

## 2. Background

### 2.1 Trace-based Compilation

In a trace-based system, the basic unit for compilation and execution is a trace as opposed to the method of traditional method-based compilers. At the heart of any trace-based system lies *trace selection*, the mechanisms that form traces out of executed instructions.

The next-executing-tail (NET) selection used in Dynamo [2] pioneered many early concepts of trace selection that are still in use today. Dynamo interprets the instruction stream until a taken branch is encountered. The execution transfers to compiled code if the branch target corresponds to the start of a compiled trace. Otherwise, a counter is maintained for the target of each backward branch and trace exiting branch, and the counter of the branch target is incremented every time the branch is executed. When the counter value of a branch target exceeds a threshold, a trace is recorded from the branch target until one of these conditions is encountered: (a) a backward branch is taken, (b) a branch whose target address is the head of another trace is found, or (c) a maximum trace length is exceeded.

There have been many advances in trace selection algorithms since Dynamo. In general, a trace selection algorithm involves these three steps.

**Trace-head selection** identifies a set of program counter (PC) addresses that are the likely starting points of hot regions (*potential* trace-heads). A potential trace-head can be the target of a backward branch or a trace exiting branch (*exit-head*). The system monitors the execution frequency of each potential trace-head. A potential trace-head becomes a trace-head if its execution frequency reaches a predefined threshold, and trace recording is started.

**Trace recording** forms a trace by recording every instruction[1] that follows the execution of a newly selected trace-head until a trace termination condition is met. The recorded instructions are stored in the *trace recording buffer*, and everytime an instruction is executed, the instruction is put into the buffer and trace termination conditions are checked.

Trace termination conditions generally fall into the four categories:

1. when a repeating cyclic execution sequence is detected in the trace recording buffer
2. when the recorded trace exceeds the maximum length
3. when there is an unusual or unsupported instruction sequence such as exception handling
4. when other heuristics apply, such as a rule terminating a trace at the head of another trace (*stop-at-existing-head*)

**Trace grouping** combines multiple individually recorded traces into one trace (group) for compilation [4, 11, 12, 17]. Trace grouping requires multiple recording and sometimes recompilation. Grouped traces often have a complex topology that allows split paths, such as trees or general graph. Some trace selection algorithms do not involve trace grouping.

Once a trace or a trace group is formed and compiled, the generated code is stored in the *trace cache*. A compiled trace is dispatched either from the interpreter or at the exit point of another trace. Trace dispatch often involves looking up a trace based on the original PC of the next instruction. This overhead is unique to trace-based systems, but can be reduced by several techniques such as trace linking [2] for trace exits with very few targets. When the execution exits from a trace, there is a *trace transition*. For example, the execution may return to the interpreter or jump directly to the next compiled trace.

### 2.2 Repetition Detection in Trace Selection

Every trace selection algorithm uses heuristics to detect repeating cyclic execution paths (or *repetitions*) during trace recording. We refer to such mechanisms as *repetition detection*. Repetition detection is a critical element of trace selection for these reasons.

**Time and space efficiency.** Since traces are formed from runtime executions, capturing repeating cyclic execution paths into a compact form is key to the time and space efficiency of a trace selection algorithm.

**Trace quality.** Repeating cyclic execution paths typically represent a large amount of computation. Capturing such execution patterns into one trace reduces the runtime overhead due to trace exits, and improves code quality by exposing a larger compilation scope to the compiler.

There are three approaches to repetition detection in existing trace selection algorithms: stop-at-backward-branch, cyclic-path-based, and static-scope-based repetition detection.

#### 2.2.1 Stop-at-backward-branch Repetition Detector

The NET selection [2] uses backward branches as an indicator of a repeating cyclic execution pattern, where a trace is terminated at a backward branch (*stop-at-backward-branch*) during trace recording.

Stop-at-backward-branch has good time and space-efficiency, but it tends to terminate traces before repeating cyclic execution paths are detected [15]. In many cases, it does not form traces that are cyclic. This repetition detector has been largely superseded by the cyclic-path-based repetition detector.

#### 2.2.2 Cyclic-path-based Repetition Detector

A *cyclic path* refers to an execution path that starts and ends at the same PC. A *cyclic-path-based repetition detector* uses cyclic paths detected at trace recording as the indicator of a repeating cyclic execution pattern.

A cyclic-path-based repetition detector was first proposed for the last-execution-iteration (LEI) selection method [15] and subsequently used in PyPy [6] and by Merrill et al. [18]. When a PC appears twice in the trace recording buffer, the LEI selection creates a trace corresponding to the path between the repeating PCs.

The main benefit of cyclic-path-based repetition detection is its simplicity and flexibility. It can be applied to a wide variety of trace selection algorithms, tracing systems and target workloads. The main drawback is the accuracy of the repetition detection. This is because not every cyclic path represents a true repeating cyclic

[1] The unit for trace recording and trace selection can be an instruction, a (taken) branch, or a basic block. In this paper, our description uses an instruction as the unit, but can be naturally applied to other units.

execution pattern, as shown in Section 1. When a repetition detector terminates a trace due to a falsely detected repeating pattern, it hurts the selection algorithm's ability to form long traces.

#### 2.2.3 Static-scope-based Repetition Detector

A *static-scope-based* repetition detector leverages the information about the static scopes and program structures (such as loops and methods), and constructs a trace starting from a loop header and spanning the loop body to capture repeating cyclic execution paths. The traces resemble loop structures in the source program. This is based on the observation that loops are the primary sources of repeating cyclic execution paths.

HotpathVM [12] was the first to use a static-scope-based repetition detector. The system forms traces in a tree topology, where the root is a loop header and the branches are different recorded execution paths that start from the loop and end when the execution (1) returns to the loop header, (2) leaves the owning method of the loop header (*stop-when-leaving-method*), or (3) the number of backedges in the tree exceeds the limit. Traces formed in this way resemble the control-flow representation of a loop region that includes only hot execution paths and inlined methods called by the loop. SPUR [4] and TraceMonkey [13] also use trace tree formation but with some variations, such as (4) ending a trace when leaving the loop scope (*stop-when-leaving-loop*) or (5) when the stack depth of the inlined calls exceeds a threshold.

Unlike stop-at-backward-branch or cyclic-path-based repetition detectors, static-scope-based repetition detectors do not suffer from false loop problems. A false loop like the one shown in Figure 1 always contains a method return from the owing method of the starting point of the false loop. Therefore, such false loops are filtered out implicitly by the stop-when-leaving-owning-method or the stop-when-leaving-loop conditions.

A static-scope-based repetition detector typically requires the selection algorithm to form only traces starting from loop headers. For this reason, they are most suitable to forming trace trees, where paths along the side-branches of a loop can be incorporated into a trace tree that is rooted at a loop header. Such trace trees are close to traditional program representations and are typically good for compiler optimizations and implementations.

The main limitation of a static-scope-based repetition detector is its applicability. When a static-scope-based repetition detector is used, the traces always start from a loop header and must fit within the maximum trace size. For workloads that are not particularly loop intensive, trace trees representing loops may only capture a small fraction of the dynamic execution paths. Therefore, they are not applicable to systems forming traces that do not start from non-loop headers or that do not align with static program structures. Static-scope-based repetition detectors also require knowledge of the loops and the methods of the target programs, and thus they are hard to apply to systems where such information is not available, such as binary tracing systems. For these reasons, a static-scope-based repetition detector is not a replacement for a cycle-based repetition detector in many systems.

## 3. False Loop Filtering

We propose *false loop filtering* to improve the accuracy of cyclic-path-based repetition detectors by rejecting the false loops described in Section 1.

We first formalize a repetition detector and false loop filtering. We define a *repetition detector* as a component that, for a given instruction sequence $insts[0, ..., n]$ (typically given by the trace recording buffer) and an integer $0 \leq s < n$, determines whether the instruction subsequence $insts[s, ..., n]$ is a repeating cyclic execution sequence. Typically the repetition detector is used in the trace recording step of the trace selection algorithm, and the input sequence for a repetition detector is a trace recording buffer. The trace selection algorithm uses the result of a repetition detector to determine whether or not to terminate a trace. For example, when the repetition detector returns **true** for some $s$, the recording is terminated and a trace is formed.

The parameter $s$ indicates the starting point of a repeating cyclic execution sequence inside the instruction sequence. We use this formalization to support both a repeating cyclic execution sequence starting from the head of a trace ($s = 0$) and the middle of a trace ($s > 0$). The parameter $s$ is given by the trace selection algorithm that uses a repetition detector, for example by enumerating all possible values of $s$ or by using a fixed value $s = 0$.

A cyclic-path-based repetition detector without false loop filtering checks whether the address of the first and the last instructions of the subsequence are the same, as shown in Algorithm 1. If that is the case, the repetition detector considers the sequence as a repeating cyclic execution path (though it can be a false loop).

**Algorithm 1** Cyclic-path-based Repetition Detector without False Loop Filtering

**Input:** $insts[0, ..., n]$: a sequence of dynamic instructions
**Input:** $s$: the candidate for the starting point of a repeating cyclic execution sequence ($0 \leq s < n$)
**Output:** **true** if the subsequence $insts[s, ..., n]$ is a repeating cyclic execution sequence, or **false** otherwise

1: **if** $insts[n].address \neq insts[s].address$ **then**
2:     **return false** // Not a cyclic path
3: **else**
4:     **return true** // Cyclic path
5: **end if**

Algorithm 2 describes a repetition detector with false loop filtering. In addition to checking the instruction address at Line 1, it further applies false loop filtering, as shown in Line 5 in Algorithm 2, to reject false loops.

**Algorithm 2** *isRepetitionDetected*($insts[s, ...n]$): Cyclic-path-based Repetition Detector with False Loop Filtering

**Input:** $insts[0, ..., n]$: a sequence of dynamic instructions
**Input:** $s$: the candidate for the starting point of a repeating cyclic execution sequence ($0 \leq s < n$)
**Output:** **true** if the subsequence $insts[s, ..., n]$ is a loop, or **false** otherwise

1: **if** $insts[n].address \neq insts[s].address$ **then**
2:     **return false** // Not a cyclic path
3: **else**
4:     apply false loop filtering
5:     **if** $insts[s, ..., n]$ is a false loop **then**
6:         **return false** // False loop
7:     **else**
8:         **return true** // True repeating cyclic execution sequence
9:     **end if**
10: **end if**

### 3.1 Design Considerations for False Loop Filtering

In this section, we cover the basic aspects of false loop filtering. False loop filtering can be used with trace selection algorithms in a wide variety of systems, so different false loop filtering algorithms can be used depending on the system requirements.

First, the false loop filtering algorithm depends on the type of information that is available for each instruction $insts[i]$. For example,

- ***insts[i].address***: The address of the instruction.

- ***insts*$[i]$*.isBackwardBranch***: Whether or not the instruction is a backward intra-procedural branch. This is available in most systems including binary code, but is unavailable in a few systems.
- ***insts*$[i]$*.isMethodInvoke***: Whether or not the instruction is a method invocation.
- ***insts*$[i]$*.isMethodReturn***: Whether or not the instruction is a method return.
- ***insts*$[i]$*.callStack***: The call stack (that is, the stack of return addresses) at the instruction. This can be obtained via a stack walk, or reconstructed from *insts*$[0,..,n]$*.isMethodInvoke*, *insts*$[0,..,n]$*.isMethodReturn*, and *insts*$[0,..,n]$*.address*, as shown in Section 3.2.2.
- ***insts*$[i]$*.method***: the method to which the instruction belongs.

Second, the false loop filtering algorithm depends on the trace selection algorithm being used. For example, some trace selection algorithms always start traces from loop headers, while others can create traces starting from arbitrary program points.

Third, the precision of false loop filtering algorithms affects the performance and code size.

- **Accepting false loops as true repetitions** has a large negative impact on the performance (though it probably leads to smaller code), because the false loops terminate traces prematurely and are suboptimal for compiler optimizations. In this case, a true repeating cyclic execution path is split into multiple traces, and trace exits occur at every iteration.
- **Missing true repetitions** (that is, considering true repeating cyclic execution paths as a non-loop sequence or a false loop) has a relatively small negative impact in the performance. Even when true repeating cyclic execution paths are missed, trace recording continues and a longer trace may be created in most trace selection algorithms (unless the trace recording is aborted), and thus trace exits are not so frequent compared to accepting false loops. This, however, leads to larger amounts of code.

### 3.2 False Loop Filtering Algorithms

We propose a false loop filtering algorithm, *call-stack-comparison*, designed for systems where all of the information described in Section 3.1 is available:

**#1: Call-stack-comparison** considers a cyclic execution sequence as a repeating cyclic execution path if the top $k$ elements of the call stacks at the first and last instructions are the same, in addition to the instruction addresses. The number $k$ is set so that this algorithm can support both natural loops and recursive calls. We describe this in more detail in Section 3.2.1.

We think this is a direct and accurate way to detect false loops such as the one shown in Figure 1. This call-stack-comparison algorithm is also one of the best false loop filtering algorithms among the false loop filtering algorithms we tested. The call-stack-comparison algorithm achieved the best steady-state performance among all of them, and the generated binary code size was the smallest among the algorithms with the best steady-state performance. Therefore, we use this as the default false loop filtering algorithm.

We can design simpler approximation algorithms with similar performance and small number of false loops. Here is one example of such approximation algorithms:

**#2:** The **one-backward-branch-in-head-method** algorithm considers a cyclic execution path as a repeating cyclic execution path if it contains at least one backward branch in the path and the backward branch belongs to the same method as the first instruction of the path. This is based on the intuition that a repeating cyclic execution path in a loop contains at least one backward branch in the path. Formally, the algorithm considers *insts*$[s,...n]$ as a repeating cyclic execution path if *insts*$[s]$*.address* = *insts*$[n]$*.address* and, for some $t$ such that $s \leq t < n$, *insts*$[t]$*.isBackwardBranch* is **true** and *insts*$[t]$*.method* = *insts*$[s]$*.method.*

This algorithm requires a separate mechanism to detect recursive method calls, and cannot filter out some false loops. However, this worked well when applied to our trace selection algorithm and the benchmark we used, as shown in the evaluations.

This algorithm does not require call stack information, and thus the implementation can be simpler than the call-stack-comparison algorithm.

These two algorithms require information related to methods and call stacks. In some systems such as binary tracing in some architectures, such information might be not directly available. In such systems, one approach is to obtain the information about methods by approximation or heuristics. For example, when the instruction set architecture has explicit call and/or return instructions such as IA-32, or when we can assume a standard binary application interface (that is, a standard calling convention) and typical code patterns for method invocation and return, then we might be able to infer method calls and returns. This approximation is safe, because the approximation only affects the precision of false loop filtering, and does not affect the correctness of program execution itself.

Another approach is to use false loop filtering algorithms that do not use information about methods. We present two false loop filtering algorithms below that do not require such information. We can use these algorithms, at the cost of performance or code size.

**#3: Repeated-twice** considers an instruction sequence as a repeating cyclic execution path if the sequence is executed twice consecutively. Formally, the algorithm consider *insts*$[s,...(n+s)/2]$ as a repeating cyclic execution path if, for all $i$ such that $s \leq i \leq (n+s)/2$, *insts*$[i]$*.address* = *insts*$[i+(n-s)/2]$*.address.*

This algorithm requires only the instruction address information and thus is applicable broadly. It incurs no false loops, because detected repeating paths can be repeated at least twice. However, it tends to create longer traces and results in larger amounts of code, as shown in the evaluations.

**#4: End-with-backward-branch** considers an instruction sequence as a repeating cyclic execution path if the sequence goes back to the head at a backward branch. In other words, this checks repeating cyclic execution path only at backward branches. Formally, the algorithm considers *insts*$[s,...n]$ as a repeating cyclic execution path if *insts*$[s]$*.address* = *insts*$[n]$*.address* and *insts*$[n-1]$*.isBackwardBranch* is **true**.

This is intuitive, but we show this also leads to larger code size in the evaluations. It can also accept false loops, and it also misses repeating cyclic execution paths not starting from backward branch targets.

#### 3.2.1 Call-stack-comparison False Loop Filtering

We show the call-stack-comparison false loop filtering algorithm in Algorithm 3. Our algorithm first compares the addresses of the instruction at the end (*insts*$[n]$) and possible start instruction of a repeating cyclic execution path (*insts*$[s]$) at Line 1. If they are the same, the algorithm compares the top $k$ elements of the call stacks of both instructions (Line 10). If the call stacks are the same,

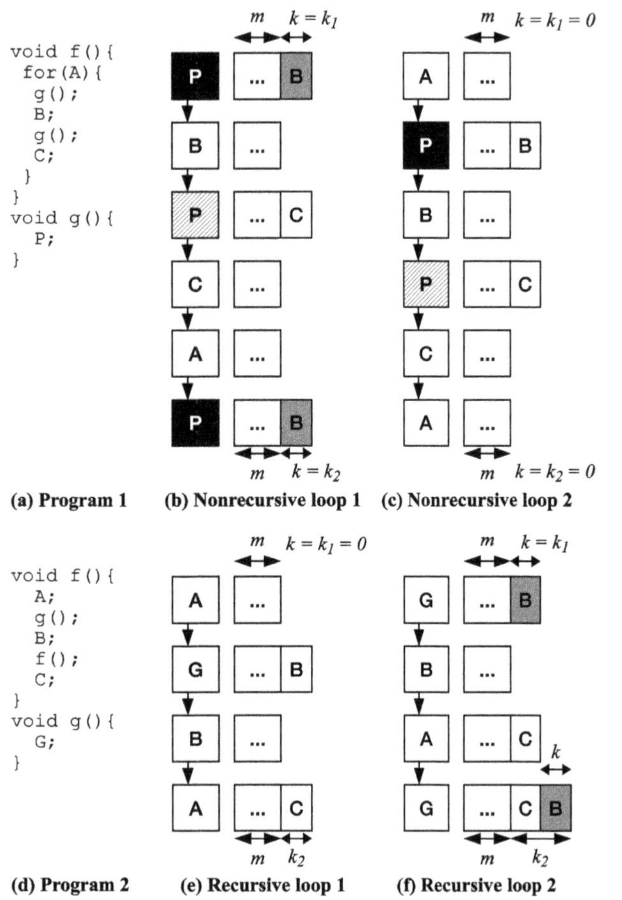


**Figure 2.** Examples of call stack comparison

our algorithm considers it as a repeating cyclic execution path, or otherwise rejects it as a false loop.

---

**Algorithm 3** Cyclic-path-based Repetition Detector with False Loop Filtering by call-stack-comparison

---

**Input:** *insts*$[0, ..., n]$: a sequence of dynamic instructions
**Input:** $s$: the candidate for the starting point of a repeating cyclic execution sequence ($0 \leq s < n$)
**Output:** **true** if the sequence is a repeating cyclic execution sequence, or **false** otherwise

1: **if** *insts*$[n]$.*address* $\neq$ *insts*$[s]$.*address* **then**
2:     **return false**
3: **else**
4:     // false loop filtering begins
5:     // *insts*$[i]$.*callStack* is the call stack at *insts*$[i]$.
6:     $m = \min_{s \leq i \leq n}$ *insts*$[i]$.*callStack.depth*
7:     $k_1 =$ *insts*$[s]$.*callStack.depth* $- m$
8:     $k_2 =$ *insts*$[n]$.*callStack.depth* $- m$
9:     $k = \min(k_1, k_2)$
10:     **if** the top $k$ elements of call stacks *insts*$[s]$.*callStack* and *insts*$[n]$.*callStack* are the same **then**
11:         **return true**
12:     **else**
13:         **return false** // false loop
14:     **end if**
15: **end if**

---

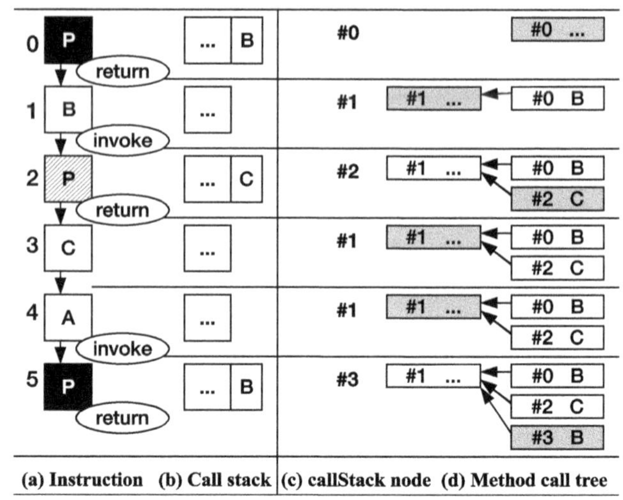


**Figure 3.** Call stack building

By comparing only the top $k$ elements and calculating $k$ as shown in Lines 6-9, our algorithm can detect repeating cyclic execution paths in non-recursive loops and recursive method calls. For non-recursive loops, our partial call stack comparison is the same as comparing the entire call stacks. For recursive loops, call stack elements added by recursive calls are not compared and thus recursive loops can be detected as true loops.

Figure 2 shows examples of call stack comparisons, with the values of $k, k_1, k_2$ and $m$. Examples of non-recursive loops are shown in Figures 2 (a), (b), and (c) (for the same program as in Figure 1), and examples of recursive calls are shown in Figures 2 (d), (e), and (f). Figures 2 (b), (c), (e), and (f) show execution paths on the left and the call stacks for each instruction on the right (the rightmost element is the top element in the stack).

The top $k$ call stack elements being compared are shown in grey boxes. Call stack elements added due to recursive calls (for example, the `C`s in Figures 2 (e) and (f)) are not compared.

In fact the call stacks are longer in actual execution (there are call stack elements corresponding to the callers of method `f`), but only the relevant parts are shown in Figure 2, and the irrelevant parts are shown as boxes with "`...`". The irrelevant parts are always excluded from the top $k$ elements compared.

Each element of a call stack contains a return address. For example, the top element `B` of the call stack "`...-B`" in the first row of Figure 2 (b) means that control will return to `B` after the next method return.

### 3.2.2 Incremental Call Stack Generation

Call stack information (*insts*$[i]$.*callStack*) can be obtained by doing a stack walk when recording each instruction *insts*$[i]$. It can also be incrementally reconstructed using these two types of information for each instruction *insts*$[i]$.

1. the instruction address (*insts*$[i]$.*address*) and
2. the instruction type, that is, whether the instruction is a method invocation, method return, or other (*insts*$[i]$.*isMethodInvoke* or *insts*$[i]$.*isMethodReturn*).

We do not need to start our call stack generation from a known stack state, but rather can infer it as we encounter new instructions.

Figure 3 (a) shows the instruction sequence `P-B-P-C-A-P` for the sample code shown in Figure 1, starting with the first instruction in Row 0. Figure 3 (b) shows call stacks for each instruction that we are going to reconstruct.

We do not initially know the call stack state at the first instruction P. We will later find it is "...-B", because the control returns to B at the return instruction from P to B. This method return implies that the caller of $P$ was actually $B$, so we can update the call stack information. There is still no information on the callers of $B$.

We can determine the call stack at Row 2 by pushing C onto the call stack at Row 1, because we know the instruction at Row 1 (B) is a method invocation and C is the return address (C is the next instruction of B). Similarly, we can calculate the call stack at Row 3 by simply popping one element from the call stack at Row 2, because we know the instruction at Row 2 (P) is a method return.

Formally, Algorithm 4 shows the algorithm to incrementally build the call stacks from a given sequence of instructions.

**Algorithm 4** Call Stack Building

**Input:** *insts*$[0, ..., n]$: a sequence of instructions, where *address*, *isMethodInvoke*, and *isMethodReturn* information is available.
**Output:** *tree*: a call stack tree
**Output:** *insts*$[0, ..., n]$*.callStack*: *insts*$[i]$*.callStack* points to a node in *tree* that represents the call stack at *insts*$[i]$

```
1: tree ← a call stack tree with only one node
2: p ← the root node of tree
3: for i = 0 to n − 1 do
4:    insts[i].callStack ← p
5:    if insts[i].isMethodReturn then
6:       if p.parent does not exist then
7:          p.address ← insts[i + 1].address
8:          create a new parent node newp
9:          p.parent ← newp
10:      end if
11:      p ← p.parent
12:   else if insts[i].isMethodInvoke then
13:      create a new child node newc
14:      newc.address ← address of the next instruction of insts[i]
15:      // insts[i].address + 4 in a 32-bit fixed length instruction
16:      newc.parent ← p
17:      p ← newc
18:   else
19:      // do nothing
20:   end if
21: end for
22: insts[n].callStack ← p
```

For efficiency, we represent call stacks by nodes in a method call tree. We define the *method call tree* as a directed tree where each node has an ID (left field) and a return address value (right field), as shown in Figure 3 (d). Edges are drawn from child to parent (that is, callee to caller), and the root node is always "..." to represent an irrelevant part of the call stack. A node represents a call stack, which means that the path from the root node to that node corresponds to a call stack. For example, Node #2 represents the call stack "...-C".

First, we create an initial call stack tree *tree* in Lines 1-2, as shown in Row 0 in Figure 3. The $p$ indicates the node that corresponding to the current call stack. Then, for each instruction $i$, we update *tree* and $p$ and set *insts*$[i]$*.callStack* (Lines 3-21), according to the instruction addresses and instruction types. In other words, at method invocation we move $p$ to a child node corresponding to the callee method (corresponding to pushing a new element to the call stack), and at method return we move $p$ to a parent node (popping an element from the call stack). If needed, a new node is created. For each $i$, the call stack tree (at Line 4) is shown in Figure 3 (d) Row $i$, where $p$ is indicated by the grey node, and *insts*$[i]$*.callStack* is shown in Figure 3 (c) Row $i$.

The time and space complexity of this call stack building algorithm is $O(n)$, and it is independent of the maximum depth of the call stack. Also, this algorithm collects only the necessary portion of the call stacks. This can be faster and space-efficient than recording all of the call stack elements at every instruction.

### 3.3 False Loop Filtering for Trace Trees

In the evaluation in Section 5, we will evaluate false loop filtering algorithms by using them with linear trace selection algorithms. However, false loop filtering can also be applied to the trace trees when a cyclic-path-based repetition detector is used.

Figure 4 shows an example of the false loop problem in trace tree formation. Here we collect the execution paths starting from each trace head and terminated when a repeating cyclic execution path is detected (using a cyclic-path-based repetition detector), and merge those paths into one tree-shaped trace. We do not use the stop-when-leaving-owning-method or the stop-when-leaving-loop conditions.

Program 3 shown in Figure 4 (a) contains interprocedural nested loops. The inner loop is executed more frequently than the outer loop, so P in method g, the loop head of the inner loop, is selected as the trace head. In cyclic-path-based repetition detectors, the sequences P-Q-P (a true iteration of the loop in method g), P-B-P, and P-C-A-P (these two are false loops) are considered as cyclic execution sequences, and Trace 3A is formed by merging them, as shown in Figure 4 (c). However, if we can exclude false loops, the sequences P-Q-P, P-B-P-C-A-P, P-B-P-Q-P-C-A-P, P-B-P-Q-P-Q-P-C-A-P, ... are detected as repeating cyclic execution sequence, and Trace 3B is formed, as shown in Figure 4 (d). The three sequences P-B-P-C-A-P, P-B-P-Q-P-C-A-P, and P-B-P-Q-P-Q-P-C-A-P are true iterations of the loop in method f, with zero, one, and two iterations of the inner loop are unrolled and inlined, respectively. Trace 3B is longer and more suitable for optimization than Trace 3A.

## 4. Implementation

We prototyped a trace-driven system based on IBM's J9 JVM. The original J9 interpreter was modified to send control-flow events such as branches and method invocations to the trace selection engine that forms traces out of the executed Java bytecode. Once a trace has been recorded, it is added to a compilation queue shared by all of the Java threads, which is compiled by a compilation thread. To compile the traces, we extended the original method-based JIT in J9 to take traces as the basic unit for compilation [16].

Once a trace is compiled, the binary code is placed in a global trace cache. Dispatches to compiled code are initially done by the interpreter that checks if the next bytecode to be executed corresponds to the head of a compiled trace. When the execution exits from a trace, a runtime helper is invoked to link the traces if a compiled trace is available at the exit target.

The rest of the section discusses a few implementation details of the system.

### 4.1 Interpreter event monitoring

The trace selection engine is driven by these control-flow events generated by the interpreter.

- **method invocation**: when executing an invoke bytecode.
- **method enter**: when entering a Java method.
- **method return**: when executing a return bytecode or returning from a JNI method.

```
void f(){
  for(A){
    g();
    B;
    g();
    C;
  }
}
void g(){
  for(P)
    Q;
}
```

(a) Program 3

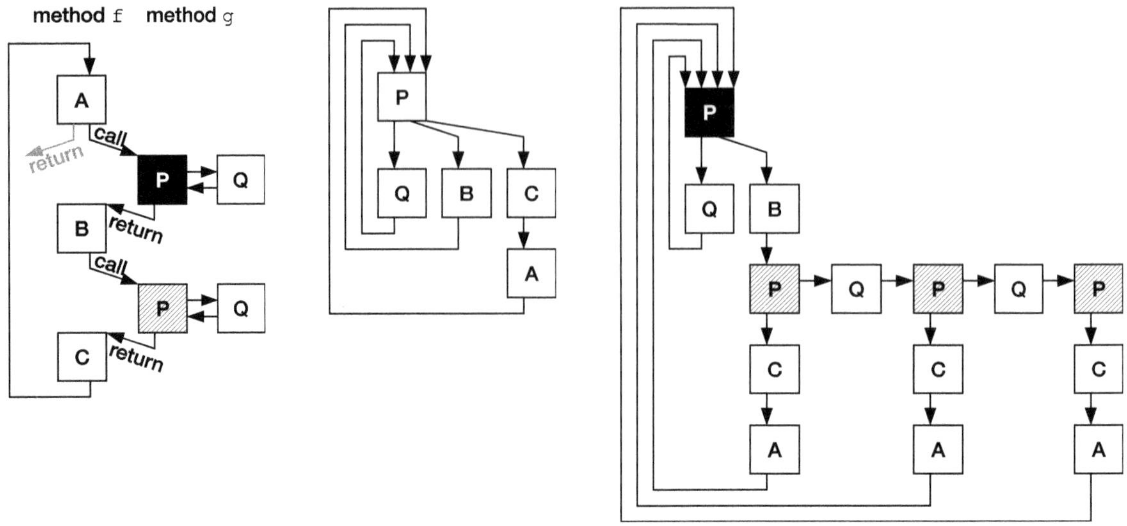


(b) CFG of Program 3 (c) Trace 3A (without false loop filtering) (d) Trace 3B (with false loop filtering)

**Figure 4.** False loop filtering for trace tree selection

- **branch**: when executing a branch bytecode (such as `goto`, `ifeq`, or `tableswitch`).
- **exception throw**: when an exception occurs or the interpreter executes an `athrow` bytecode.
- **exception catch**: when an exception is caught by a catch block.
- **trace exit**: when returning from a compiled trace to the interpreter (i.e., via unlinked trace exits).

For each monitored event, the interpreter invokes a call-back function to the trace selection engine with the event information and its context, such as the current and next PCs, the caller/callee methods, and the receiver object class.

### 4.2 Trace Selection

The trace selection engine is implemented as a runtime library driven by the control-flow events described in Section 4.1. The selection engine maintains a counter to track the execution frequency for each target PC of a backward branch (at branch events) or a trace exit (at trace exit events). Currently our trace selection engine only creates linear traces.

When the counter of the current PC exceeds a predefined threshold, the selection engine switches to trace recording mode and records subsequent interpreter events until a termination condition is met. Since the interpreter monitors every control-flow bytecode, a trace of bytecodes (basic blocks) can be constructed out of the sequence of recorded control-flow events.

The trace selection engine can be configured to use the various subsets of trace termination conditions defined here:

1. When the repetition detector detects a repeating cyclic execution sequence
   1a. that cycles back to the head of the buffer (the repetition detector returns **true** for $s = 0$), or
   1b. that cycles back to the middle of the buffer (the repetition detector returns **true** for $s > 0$).
2. When the recorded events exceed the maximum length.
3. When there is an unusual or unsupported instruction sequence such as
   3a. an exception-throw event,
   3b. certain JNI invocation event[2],
   3c. returning to JNI event, or
   3d. an unexpected event sequence.
4. When the last basic block is the head of another existing trace (i.e., *stop-at-existing-trace-heads*).

Conditions (1a) and (1b) use a repetition detector. Whether or not to use false loop filtering in repetition detectors is another configurable parameter of the trace selection engine. Condition (4), stop-at-existing-trace-head, is a heuristic used in NET, LEI, and [18] for space efficiency.

### 4.3 Trace JIT

To compile the traces selected by the trace runtime, we implemented our trace JIT compiler by enhancing the existing (method-based) JIT compiler in the IBM's J9 JVM. Our trace JIT compiler assumes the mixed execution of the interpreter and the trace JIT. It does not support mixed execution of the method-based JIT and the trace JIT.

The trace JIT is implemented from the same code base as the method JIT and the interpreter. It supports the basic functions of the method JIT including exception handling, GC, synchronization, and JNI calls. Compilation is done by a separate dedicated thread, similar to the method JIT.

Our trace JIT guarantees that the JVM states, such as the Java stack and the program counter value, are compatible with the interpreter at the trace exit points. We do not maintain the JVM states in the middle of the trace to improve the performance. If a stop-the-world garbage collection begins while a Java thread is executing a compiled trace, we reconstruct the Java stack before the garbage collector walks the stack frames of this Java thread. We prepare the

[2] We allow a small set of JNI methods in the Java standard library to be included in traces. Invocation and return events for these JNI methods do not terminate a trace [16].

| Benchmark | Description |
|---|---|
| antlr | A parser generator and translator generator |
| bloat | A bytecode-level optimizer and analyzer for Java |
| chart | A graph plotting toolkit and pdf renderer |
| eclipse | An integrated development environment |
| fop | An output-independent print formatter |
| hsqldb | An SQL relational database engine written in Java |
| jython | A python interpreter written in Java |
| luindex | A text indexing tool |
| lusearch | A text search tool |
| pmd | A source code analyzer for Java |
| xalan | An XSLT processor |

**Table 1.** Description of the `DaCapo` benchmark.

special metadata for this reconstruction at the JIT compilation time. If an exception occurs during the execution of compiled trace, we update the JVM states and fall back to the interpreter to handle the exception.

Our trace compiler applies optimizations that are almost equivalent to the "warm" optimization level in the existing IBM's Java JIT compiler. These optimizations include common subexpression elimination, dead store elimination, dead code elimination, value propagation, and global register allocation. Currently we only support one optimization level and we do not support recompilation.

Our trace JIT also supports trace linking optimizations to reduce the overhead in the trace runtime. The execution jumps directly from a trace exit to the entry point of the next trace without going back to the interpreter if, for example, the trace exit has only one candidate for the next program counter value.

# 5. Evaluation

## 5.1 Benchmarks and Setup

We used the DaCapo benchmark suite [5, 9] with the default data size (`-s default`) to evaluate false loop filtering. Table 1 gives a brief description of the benchmarks. We executed 10 iterations of the long `eclipse` benchmark, and 25 iterations for the other benchmarks.

The trace selection engine uses these default parameters. The trace-head selection threshold is 500, which was determined based on the thresholds used by the original method JIT for method compilation. The maximum trace length is 128 basic blocks, which was determined based on an experimental evaluation. Using these default parameters , the coverage of traces (the ratio of dynamic basic blocks executed in the compiled binary code of traces) was more than 98.9% at steady-state for the DaCapo benchmarks. The trace JIT used its highest optimization level, which is equivalent to the warm-level optimization in the original method JIT.

To study the impact of the false loop filtering, we defined two baseline trace selection algorithms without false loop filtering, *BASE* and *BASE+*.

- **BASE** uses termination conditions (1)-(4) (defined in Section 4.2) to model a LEI-like selection, and uses the repetition detector without false loop filtering (Algorithm 1).
- **BASE+** uses termination conditions (1)-(3) and and uses the repetition detector without false loop filtering (Algorithm 1). Condition (4), stop-at-existing-trace-head, is removed to allow the creation of longer traces.

We then define two variations of the baseline selection algorithms with the false loop filtering by using call-stack-comparison:

| | BASE | BASE w/FLF | BASE+ | BASE+ w/FLF |
|---|---|---|---|---|
| Condition (1) | Yes | Yes | Yes | Yes |
| False loop filtering | No | Yes | No | Yes |
| Condition (2) | Yes | Yes | Yes | Yes |
| Condition (3) | Yes | Yes | Yes | Yes |
| Condition (4) | Yes | Yes | No | No |

**Table 2.** Summary of trace selection algorithms

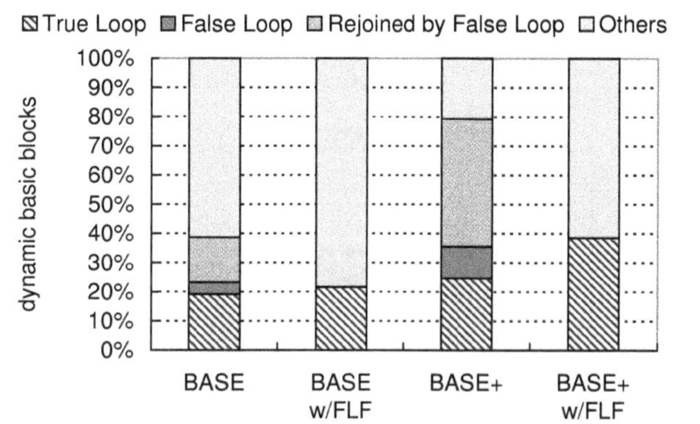


**Figure 5.** Average distribution of true-loops and false-loop-related traces in `DaCapo`.

- **BASE w/FLF** uses termination conditions (1)-(4) and uses the repetition detector with the false loop filtering by call stack comparison (Algorithm 3).
- **BASE+ w/FLF** uses termination conditions (1)-(3) and uses the repetition detector with the false loop filtering by call stack comparison (Algorithm 3). This is the default trace selection algorithm for our trace JIT.

We summarized the four trace selection algorithms in Table 2.

We also compared the trace JIT with the following configurations for the method JIT.

- **method (warm)** uses the method JIT with warm-level optimizations.
- **method (full)** uses the method JIT with default (full) optimization levels and upgrade compilation.

All performance data was gathered on a 4.0-GHz IBM® POWER6® blade center with 4 cores (8 threads) running on IBM AIX® 6.1. We averaged 16 runs to gather the performance data.

We also collected detailed statistics for the trace JIT (Figures 5 and 13) by executing 16 instrumented runs (only for the trace JIT). In these runs, the trace JIT generates JITed code with statistics collection code.

## 5.2 Quantify False Loops and FLF

Figure 5 shows the ratios of the numbers of dynamic basic blocks executed in each of the following types of traces, averaged over the `DaCapo` benchmarks:

- **True loop:** A trace is terminated because it forms a cycle and the cycle is a true repeating cyclic execution path (after the false loop filtering by call-stack-comparison). In other words, a trace is terminated by the condition (1a) and the detected repetition is a true repeating cyclic execution path.

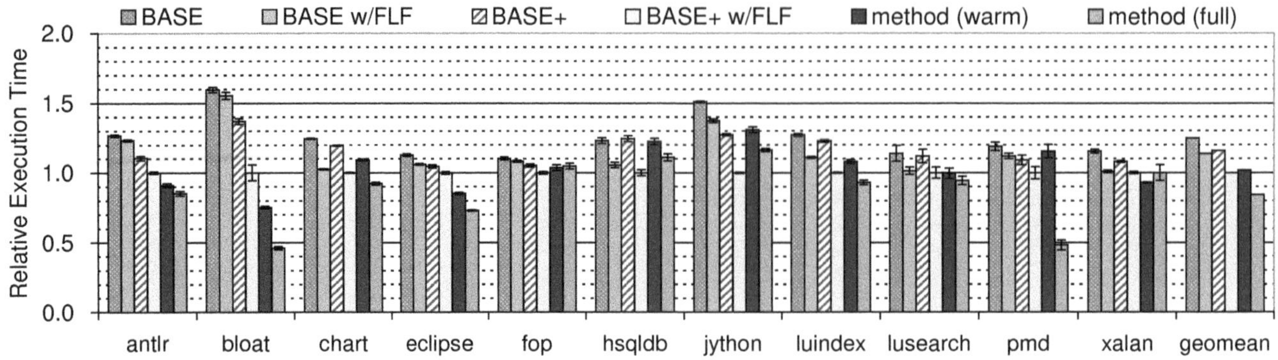


**Figure 6.** Relative steady-state execution time (normalized to **BASE+ w/FLF**)

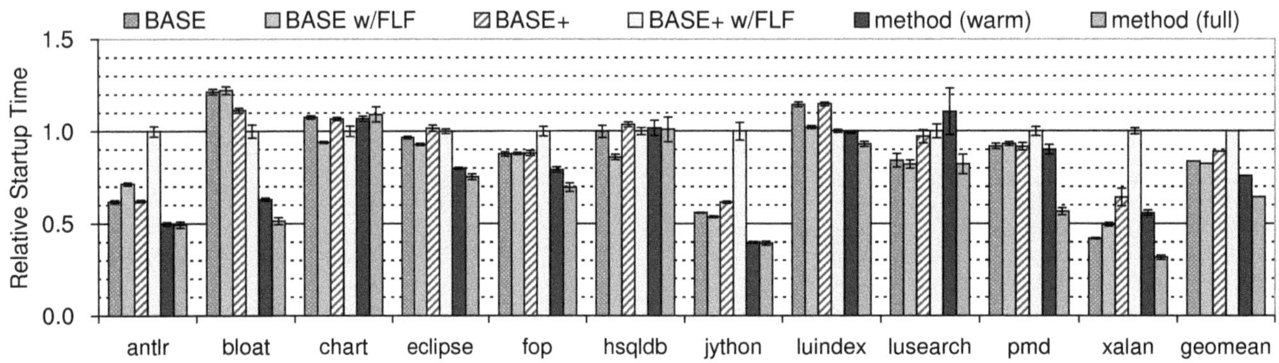


**Figure 7.** Relative startup time (normalized to **BASE+ w/FLF**)

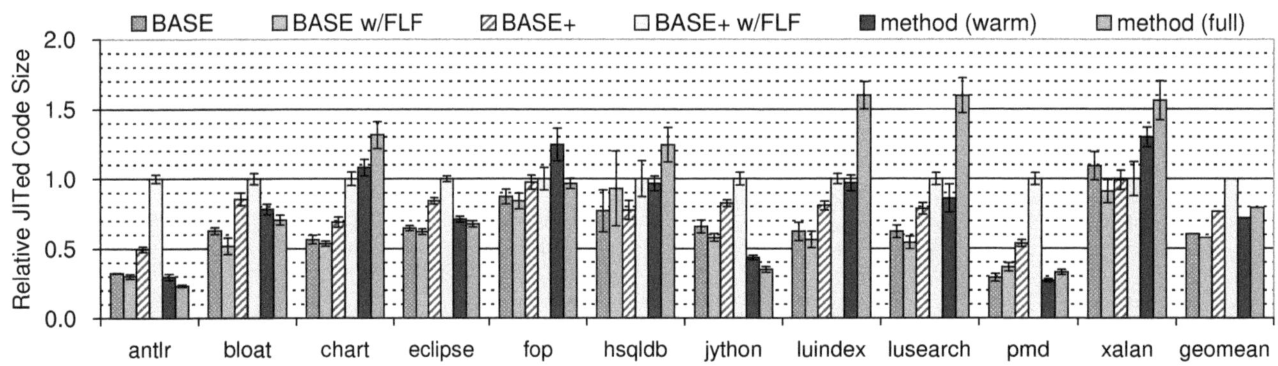


**Figure 8.** Relative compiled code size (normalized to **BASE+ w/FLF**)

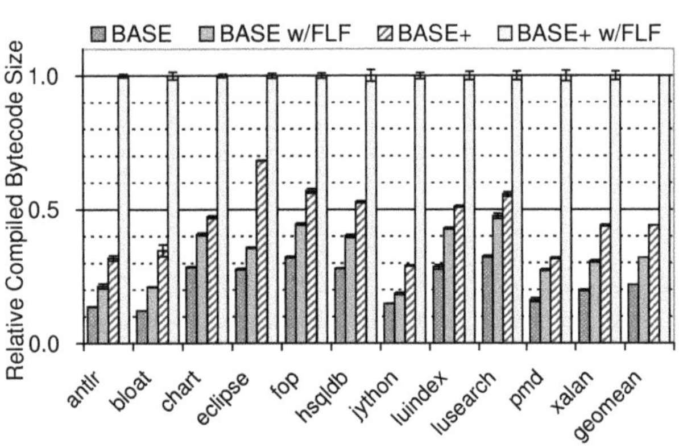


**Figure 9.** Relative number of bytecodes compiled (normalized to **BASE+ w/FLF**)

- **False loop:** A trace is terminated because it forms a cycle, but is a false loop. In other words, a trace is terminated by the condition (1a) and the detected repetition is a false loop.
- **Rejoined by false loop:** A trace is terminated because a false loop cycle is formed in the middle of the trace recording buffer. In other words, a trace is terminated by the condition (1b) and the detected repetition is a false loop.
- **Others:** A trace is ended by other termination conditions.

Figure 5 quantifies the extent of the false loop problem in the DaCapo benchmarks using our baseline selection algorithms: 55% (for *BASE+*) and 19% (for *BASE*) of the dynamic basic blocks are executed on traces terminated by false loops or rejoined by false loops. *BASE* suffers much less from false loops than *BASE+* because *stop-at-existing-trace-head* often terminates a trace before a false loop cycle can be formed.

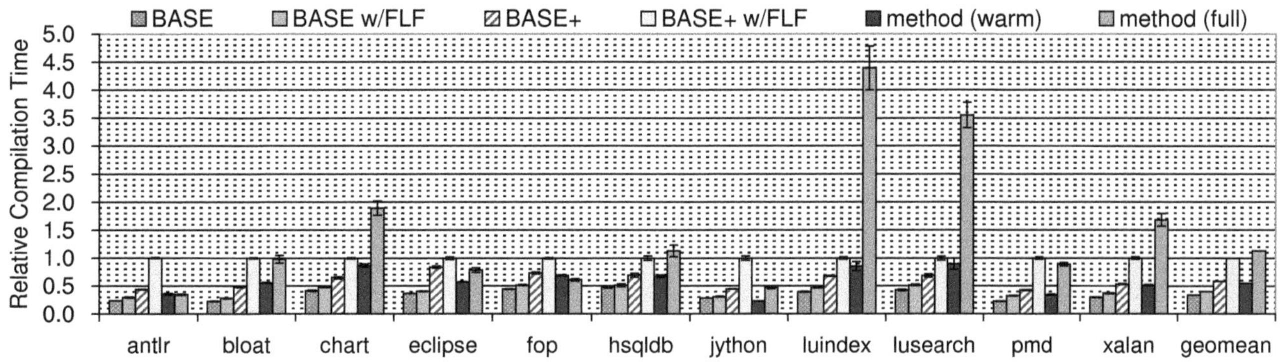


**Figure 10.** Relative compilation time (normalized to **BASE+ w/FLF**)

Most false loops are caused by multiple invocations of the same method in one execution path. This pattern is quite common in object-oriented programs, which often makes frequent calls to small methods such as accessor methods.

Figure 5 also shows one positive effect of false loops filtering: the ratio of true loop traces has increased from 19% to 22% (for *BASE*) and from 25% to 38% (for *BASE+*).

### 5.3 Impact of FLF on the Trace JIT

We next evaluate the impact of the false loop filtering on key measurable aspects of the trace-driven system: steady-state performance, start-up performance, compiled code size, and compilation time.

Figure 6 shows the steady-state execution time of the trace JIT and the method JIT normalized to that of BASE+ w/FLF. In Figure 6 and the following figures, the error bars show the sample standard deviations. The steady-state performance is measured as the average execution time of each of the last 5 iterations, to avoid fluctuation due to garbage collection events. On average, false loop filtering improved the steady-state performance by 16% for *BASE+* and 10% for *BASE*. The benefit is much smaller for *BASE* because, as shown in Figure 5, fewer traces are terminated by false-loop related termination conditions due to the use of another termination condition, stop-at-existing-head. At the same time, for *BASE+*, the improvements from false loop filtering are quite significant for some benchmarks, such as 37% for `bloat`, 27% for `jython`, and 24% for `hsqldb`.

For systems with a larger trace runtime overhead, we expect the impact from false loop filtering on the runtime component to be more significant. For example, if we disable a runtime overhead optimization (fast trace look-up using shadow arrays [16]), the steady-state performance improvement from false loop filtering was 64% and 32% for *BASE+* and *BASE*, respectively, which are much larger than the results shown in Figure 6.

In steady-state execution, the execution time of the false loop filtering algorithm itself was negligible (typically less than 0.1%), because trace recording occurs rarely in steady state.

Figure 7 shows the start-up execution time, which is the execution time of the first iteration of each benchmark. False loop filtering increases the start-up time by an average of 12% for *BASE+* and decreases it slightly for *BASE*. This is because in our system the start-up performance is dominated by how soon a trace is compiled. While longer traces are in general preferable for better code quality, they can be detrimental to start-up performance due to the longer compilation time.

Figure 9 shows the total number of bytecodes being compiled. False loop filtering almost doubles the cumulative bytecode size for *BASE+*. This leads to an increase in compilation time (by 71%) and the compiled code size (by 31%) for *BASE+*, as show in Figure 10 and Figure 8, respectively.

Ways to reduce code size expansion and compilation times are also an important aspect of trace compilation and will be future work.

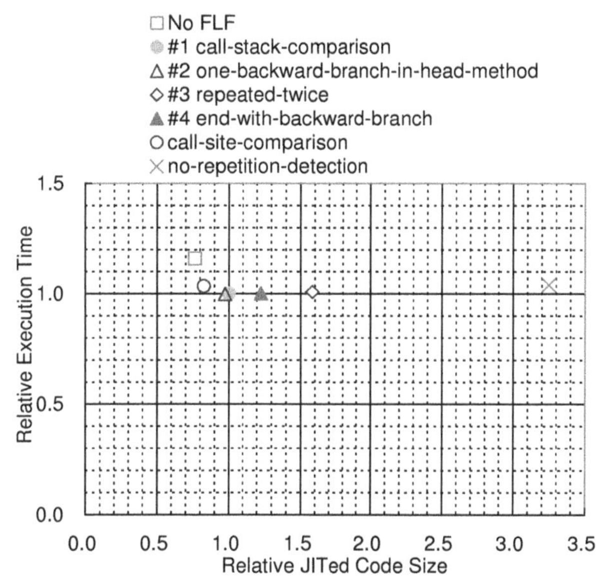


**Figure 11.** Relative execution time and compiled code size when various false loop filtering algorithms are applied to *BASE+*, normalized to the call-stack-comparison.

### 5.4 Comparison of False Loop Filtering Algorithms

Figure 11 shows the relative steady-state execution times and relative compiled code sizes for the other variations of false loop filtering algorithms described in Section 3.2, relative to *call-stack-comparison*. All schemes are applied to *BASE+*.

Two algorithms, *call-stack-comparison* and *one-backward-branch-in-head-method*, achieve the best performance and the minimum code size among those with equivalent performance. *One-backward-branch-in-head-method* is slightly more conservative in detecting false loops than *call-stack-comparison*, where 4% of its traces are either false loops or rejoined by false loops. But these false loops have little effect on the performance and the the compiled code size.

Two other algorithms, *repeated-twice* and *end-with-backward-branch*, also achieved the best performance, but with a much larger amounts of code. These algorithms are overly aggressive in their

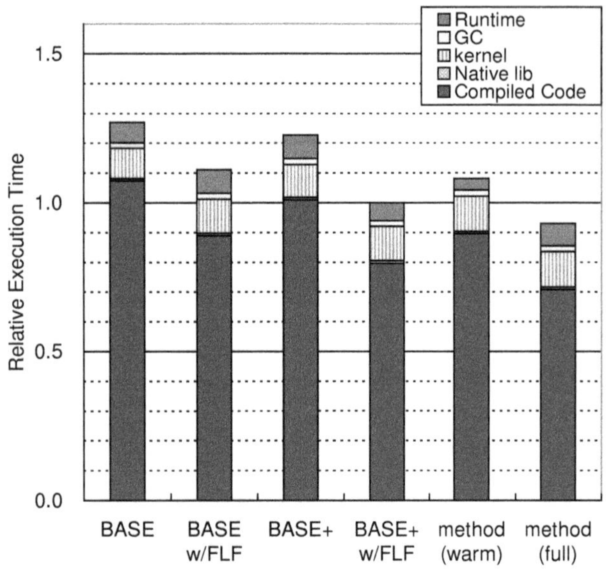


(a) `luindex`

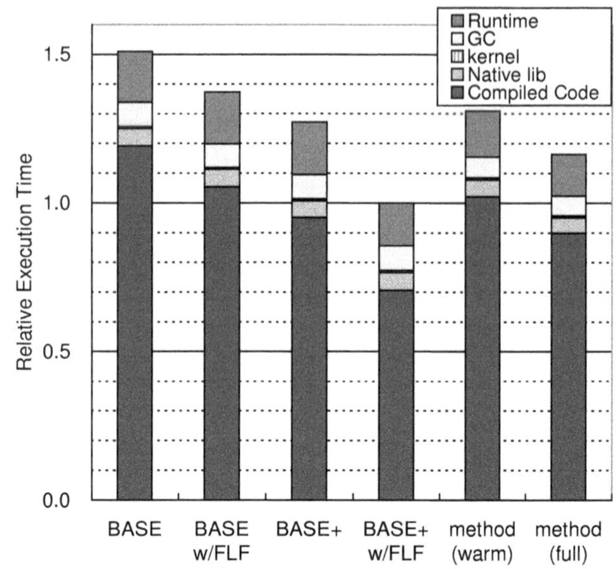


(b) `jython`

**Figure 12.** Relative steady-state execution time breakdown (normalized to **BASE+ w/FLF**)

false loop detection in the sense that certain true loop cycles (e.g., ones that start from non loop-headers) may be detected as false loops, leading to longer traces. The value of these algorithms is that they require less information for the executed instructions than the first two. For example, *end-with-backward-branch* requires *isBackwardBranch* and *address*, and *repeated-twice* requires only the *address*. Therefore, they may be used for binary trace-based systems where precise information on executed instructions, such as the owning methods or call stack information, is not available.

We added two additional configurations, *call-site-comparison* and *no-repetition-detection*, which are inferior to the other algorithms but are evaluated to demonstrate the inefficiency of simpler heuristics.

Call-site-comparison compares the callers of the first and the last instruction on a cyclic path and detects a false loop if the callers are not the same. This scheme can be viewed as a restricted form of call-stack-comparison (#1) where only the top of the call stacks are compared. Call-site-comparison is 3% slower than call-stack-comparison and fails to detect a significant portion of false loops. For example, with call-site-comparison, 29% of dynamic basic blocks are still executed from traces related to false loops. This indicates that comparing only the call sites is not sufficient and a deeper call stack needs to be inspected.

When traces are not terminated in any repeating cyclic paths (*no-repetition-detection*), the code size is more than 3x larger than *call-stack-comparison*. This demonstrates the importance of repetition detection to achieve good space-efficiency in trace formation.

### 5.5 Why False Loop Filtering Improves Performance?

To understand the performance benefit of false loop filtering, we profiled the steady-state execution of `luindex` and `jython` in our trace system and divide the time spent into components.

- **Compiled code** represents the execution time of compiled (JITed) traces.
- **Runtime** represents the execution time of the interpreter, helper functions called from compiled code, and trace execution overhead.

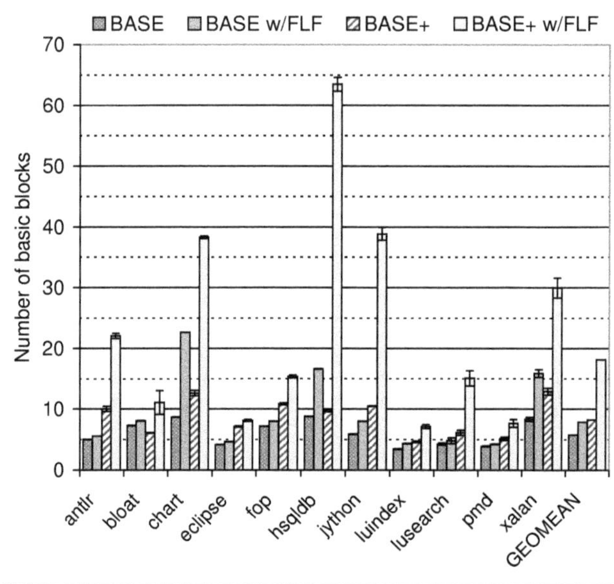


**Figure 13.** Average dynamic trace length in BBs

- **Native library**, **GC**, and **OS Kernel** represent the execution time of native parts of the Java class libraries, garbage collection, and OS kernel, respectively.

As shown in Figure 12, the steady-state performance improvements from false loop filtering come mostly from the compiled code component.

To further understand these improvements, we measured several metrics of trace execution in the instrumented runs. We found that improvements in the *dynamic trace lengths*, defined as the average number of consecutive basic blocks executed between entering and exiting from a trace in a program, is a good indicator of relative performance among different selection algorithms. Figure 13 shows average dynamic trace lengths of the four selection al-

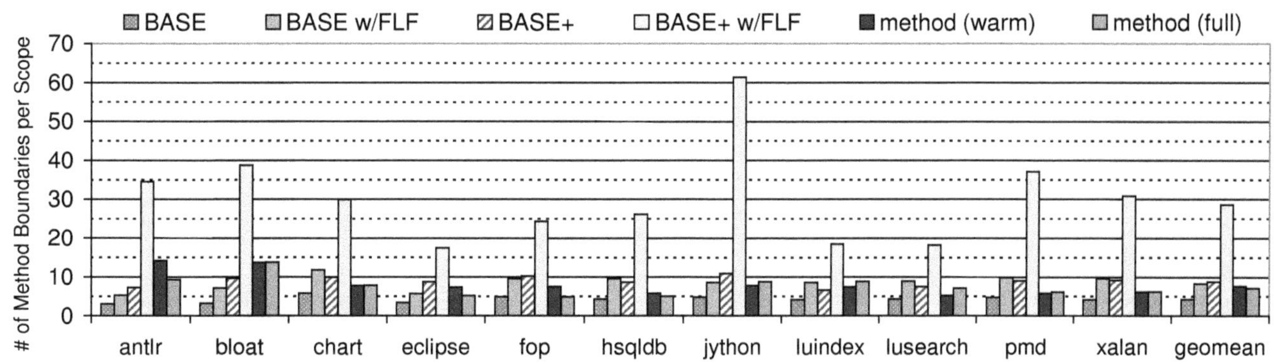


**Figure 14.** Average number of method boundaries per compilation scope

gorithms, where longer dynamic trace lengths often correspond to shorter running time in Figure 6.

A longer dynamic trace length means fewer trace exits and less runtime overhead. However, Figure 12 shows only a slight reduction in trace runtime overhead (part of Runtime) by false loop filtering despite a significant reduction in the number of dynamic trace exits (the inverse of the dynamic trace length). This is because our system has aggressively optimized the runtime overhead due to trace exits [16] using techniques such as trace linking, fast trace look-up using shadow arrays, and inlining of trace look-up sequence into compiled code. As a result, the trace runtime overhead at steady-state is quite small.

Another indicator is the number of method boundaries (both method invocations and method returns) crossed in one compilation scope. In the trace JIT, a trace can naturally span multiple methods (since we do not terminate traces at method invocations or method returns). In the method JIT, method boundaries are included in a compilation scope by method inlining.

The direct effect of crossing method boundaries in a compilation scope is the elimination of method invocation and return overhead. The indirect but more significant benefit is the expansion of compilation scope that facilitates more effective optimizations.

Figure 14 shows the average number of method boundaries per compilation scope. We counted a method invocation or a method return as one method boundary crossing. For example, when a method is entered and returned in a compilation scope (for example, a method is inlined once in the method-based JIT), the number of method boundaries in the compilation scope is two. Figure 14 shows that our trace JIT (BASE+ w/FLF) crosses many more method boundaries than the method JIT. The improved code quality in the current trace JIT most likely comes from this effect.

## 6. Related Work

Dynamo is the most influential trace-based compilation system [1, 2, 10]. Traces are formed out of binaries and collected using a native binary interpreter. The system optimizes traces for better code layout and for partial redundancy elimination [19]. Dynamo introduced the next-executing-tail (NET) policy for trace selection. The NET policy achieves much lower profiling overhead than exhaustive path profiling schemes such as the one presented by Ball and Larus [3] with the same prediction quality and faster convergence. The NET policy terminates traces at every backward branch. That is, it uses a stop-at-backward-branch repetition detector.

Hiniker, Hazelwood and Smith [15] introduced the last-executing-iteration (LEI) policy as an improvement over the NET policy. The LEI policy uses a cyclic-path-based repetition detector, instead of a stop-at-backward-branch repetition detector. Merrill and Hazelwood [18] focused on evaluating the potential of using traces for better code layout for a Java virtual machine using the LEI policy.

PyPy tracing JIT [6] applies trace compilation to Python. Pypy's tracing JIT traces a language interpreter executing a user program, and aims to capture the repeating cyclic execution paths in the user program, not those in the language interpreter. This is done by, for example, considering an execution path as a repetition if the program counter in the language interpreter *and* the program counter in the user program are the same at the beginning and the end of the execution path. The program counter in the user program is given as a hint by the implementers of the interpreter. This is also a cyclic-path-based repetition detector, where the program counter used by the repetition detector is that in the user program, rather than that in the direct target program.

Static-scope-based repetition detectors are used in trace compilers that support tree-shaped traces, such as HotpathVM [11, 12] for Java, TraceMonkey [13] for JavaScript, LuaJIT [17] for Lua, and SPUR [4] for CIL (and JavaScript converted to CIL). They utilize loop structures and methods of programs, and start trace recording of a root trace from a loop header. The trace recording is terminated or aborted when the execution leaves the method scope (HotpathVM) or loop scope (TraceMonkey, LuaJIT, and SPUR) which the loop header belongs to.

## 7. Conclusion

In this paper, we identified the problem of false loops in existing trace selection algorithms, which was not explicitly addressed in previous literature. We quantified the impact of false loops on trace selection algorithms using cyclic-path-based repetition detection. Depending on the trace selection algorithms being used, we showed that on average 55% and 19% of dynamic basic blocks are executed on traces affected by false loops (for BASE+ and BASE selection, respectively). We suggest false loop filtering is an important aspect in trace selection algorithm design.

We proposed the concept of false loop filtering and explored the design space of false loop filtering heuristics. We proposed a technique called false loop filtering by call-stack-comparison as well as several alternatives to satisfy other systems with different requirements. False loop filtering increased the dynamic trace length and method boundary crossings per trace, which produced better code and fewer trace exits.

We showed that our false loop filtering algorithm improved the steady-state performance of our trace-based Java system significantly (by 16% and 10% on average when applied to BASE+ and BASE, respectively) with acceptable code size and compilation time increases (by 31% and 71%, respectively). We also observed that improvements are much larger on systems with more trace runtime overhead (64% and 32% improvement on average when applied to BASE+ and BASE, respectively, when a runtime overhead optimization is disabled).

False loop filtering has a significant positive impact on the performance and its concept is useful for designing trace selection algorithms that maximize steady-state performance.

## Trademarks

IBM, the IBM logo, ibm.com, POWER6 and AIX are trademarks of International Business Machines Corp., registered in many jurisdictions worldwide. Other product and service names might be trademarks of IBM or other companies. A current list of IBM trademarks is available on the Web at "Copyright and trademark information" at www.ibm.com/legal/copytrade.shtml.

Java and all Java-based trademarks and logos are trademarks or registered trademarks of Oracle and/or its affiliates.

## References


[1] V. Bala, E. Duesterwald, and S. Banerjia. Transparent dynamic optimization: The design and implementation of Dynamo. Technical Report HPL-1999-78, HP Laboratories, 1999.

[2] V. Bala, E. Duesterwald, and S. Banerjia. Dynamo: a transparent dynamic optimization system. In *Proceedings of the ACM SIGPLAN 2000 Conference on Programming Language Design and Implementation*, PLDI '00, pages 1–12, New York, NY, USA, June 2000. ACM.

[3] T. Ball and J. R. Larus. Efficient path profiling. In *Proceedings of the 29th Annual ACM/IEEE International Symposium on Microarchitecture*, MICRO 29, pages 46–57, Washington, DC, USA, 1996. IEEE Computer Society.

[4] M. Bebenita, F. Brandner, M. Fahndrich, F. Logozzo, W. Schulte, N. Tillmann, and H. Venter. SPUR: a trace-based JIT compiler for CIL. In *Proceedings of the ACM International Conference on Object-Oriented Programming, Systems, Languages, and Applications*, OOPSLA '10, pages 708–725, New York, NY, USA, 2010. ACM.

[5] S. M. Blackburn, R. Garner, C. Hoffmann, A. M. Khang, K. S. McKinley, R. Bentzur, A. Diwan, D. Feinberg, D. Frampton, S. Z. Guyer, M. Hirzel, A. Hosking, M. Jump, H. Lee, J. E. B. Moss, B. Moss, A. Phansalkar, D. Stefanović, T. VanDrunen, D. von Dincklage, and B. Wiedermann. The DaCapo benchmarks: Java benchmarking development and analysis. In *Proceedings of the 21st Annual ACM SIGPLAN Conference on Object-Oriented Programming, Systems, Languages, and Applications*, OOPSLA '06, pages 169–190, New York, NY, USA, Oct. 2006. ACM.

[6] C. F. Bolz, A. Cuni, M. Fijalkowski, and A. Rigo. Tracing the meta-level: PyPy's tracing JIT compiler. In *Proceedings of the 4th Workshop on the Implementation, Compilation, Optimization of Object-Oriented Languages and Programming Systems*, ICOOOLPS '09, pages 18–25, New York, NY, USA, 2009. ACM.

[7] D. Bruening and S. Amarasinghe. Maintaining consistency and bounding capacity of software code caches. In *Proceedings of the International Symposium on Code Generation and Optimization*, CGO '05, pages 74–85, Washington, DC, USA, Mar. 2005. IEEE Computer Society.

[8] D. Bruening, T. Garnett, and S. Amarasinghe. An infrastructure for adaptive dynamic optimization. In *Proceedings of the International Symposium on Code Generation and Optimization*, CGO '03, pages 265–275, Washington, DC, USA, Mar. 2003. IEEE Computer Society.

[9] DaCapo. The DaCapo benchmark suite. `http://dacapobench.org/`.

[10] E. Duesterwald and V. Bala. Software profiling for hot path prediction: less is more. In *Proceedings of the 9th International Conference on Architectural Support for Programming Languages and Operating Systems*, ASPLOS-IX, pages 202–211, New York, NY, USA, Oct. 2000. ACM.

[11] A. Gal and M. Franz. Incremental dynamic code generation with trace trees. Technical report, University of California Irvine, November 2006.

[12] A. Gal, C. W. Probst, and M. Franz. HotpathVM: an effective JIT compiler for resource-constrained devices. In *Proceedings of the 2nd International Conference on Virtual Execution Environments*, VEE '06, pages 144–153, New York, NY, USA, June 2006. ACM.

[13] A. Gal, B. Eich, M. Shaver, D. Anderson, D. Mandelin, M. R. Haghighat, B. Kaplan, G. Hoare, B. Zbarsky, J. Orendorff, J. Ruderman, E. W. Smith, R. Reitmaier, M. Bebenita, M. Chang, and M. Franz. Trace-based just-in-time type specialization for dynamic languages. In *Proceedings of the 2009 ACM SIGPLAN conference on Programming Language Design and Implementation*, PLDI '09, pages 465–478, New York, NY, USA, 2009. ACM.

[14] N. Grcevski, A. Kielstra, K. Stoodley, M. Stoodley, and V. Sundaresan. Java just-in-time compiler and virtual machine improvements for server and middleware applications. In *Proceedings of the 3rd conference on Virtual Machine Research And Technology Symposium - Volume 3*, pages 12–12, Berkeley, CA, USA, June 2004. USENIX Association.

[15] D. Hiniker, K. Hazelwood, and M. D. Smith. Improving region selection in dynamic optimization systems. In *Proceedings of the 38th Annual IEEE/ACM International Symposium on Microarchitecture*, MICRO 38, pages 141–154, Washington, DC, USA, Dec. 2005. IEEE Computer Society.

[16] H. Inoue, H. Hayashizaki, P. Wu, and T. Nakatani. A trace-based Java JIT compiler retrofitted from a method-based compiler. In *Proceedings of the International Symposium on Code Generation and Optimization (to be published)*, CGO '11, Apr. 2011.

[17] LuaJIT. LuaJIT design notes in lua-l mailing list. `http://lua-users.org/lists/lua-l/2008-02/msg00051.html`, `http://lua-users.org/lists/lua-l/2009-11/msg00089.html`, `http://lua-users.org/lists/lua-l/2008-06/msg00228.html`.

[18] D. Merrill and K. Hazelwood. Trace fragment selection within method-based JVMs. In *Proceedings of the 4th ACM SIGPLAN/SIGOPS International Conference on Virtual Execution Environments*, VEE '08, pages 41–50, New York, NY, USA, June 2008. ACM.

[19] K. Pettis and R. C. Hansen. Profile guided code positioning. In *Proceedings of the ACM SIGPLAN 1990 conference on Programming Language Design and Implementation*, PLDI '90, pages 16–27, New York, NY, USA, June 1990. ACM.

[20] M. Zaleski, A. D. Brown, and K. Stoodley. YETI: a graduallY extensible trace interpreter. In *Proceedings of the 3rd International Conference on Virtual Execution Environments*, VEE '07, pages 83–93, New York, NY, USA, 2007. ACM.

# Author Index

www.ingramcontent.com/pod-product-compliance
Ingram Content Group UK Ltd.
Pitfield, Milton Keynes, MK11 3LW, UK
UKHW051511290926
15471UKWH00008B/1553

9 781450 302661